Norway v England
... Newsclips

By Frederick Delaware

Published by Felix Kruger at Felix Associates Press Group, Cobham, Surrey KT11 3DB, England.

Email: f.associates@mail.co.uk

Preface

There's an old British saying: 'Today's newspapers are tomorrow's fish and chip paper'. Probably an adage used the world over. Many of the stories and articles in the press are, however, frequently invaluable sources of information. Expert opinion ... with a great amount of research behind them. Written by leading figures. The subject matter always embraces politics, religion, finance, morality (or a lack of it), football and sexual misdemeanour. Some stories, on the other hand, are way off the mark and often written by reporters with an axe to grind.

In our case this book compares newsclips mostly from the Norwegian and English press over the last twenty five years or so. Norway is to most people a mountainous, sparsely populated country with oil - and well off the beaten track. The last time the Norwegians faced great danger was when Hitler invaded the country in 1940. It didn't stop thousands of Norwegian girls sleeping with the German soldiers though. Later, when the tide turned, the resulting offspring were called the "German whore children" who were, not infrequently, thoroughly abused. Small countries are usually very homogenous in thought and deed, especially when the populace is of the same race. As is the case with Norway. In 2011 there came on the scene one Anders Behring Breivik – the next worst thing to Adolf Hitler in deed ... but not in thought. For although he blew up government offices in Oslo on 22 July 2011 and proceeded to drive unhindered to Utøya Island and shoot dead 69 youths at a Labour Party seminary, his political thinking and related ideas were generally well received by the majority of Norwegians. For his abiding passion in life was to hate Muslims and in parallel to love Slobodan Milošević, Radovan Karadžić and Ratko Mladić, who advocated the ethnic cleansing of Muslims from the Serb populated areas of Bosnia in the former Yugoslavia. In Anders Breivik's case he reasoned that the Norwegian political establishment's ruling Labour Party had to be punished for letting too many Muslim immigrants in to Norway. He decided to kill the next generation of Labour Party leaders at their annual Summer get-together: the kids on Utøya island. But what Commander Breivik (as he liked to be known) did not understand was that the establishment he so despised were closer to him in thought than he realised.

Readers will find that what the Norwegian newspapers wrote on Muslims in the decade before Anders Breivik came to prominence would never be entertained by the British Press. You can't call your English 'victim' the 'Muslim man' nineteen times in one article, as the Bergens Tidende newspaper did on 24 May 1995. Indeed, the Metropolitan Police told the author that any British newspaper would be prosecuted if they printed likewise. There were not too many Muslims in Norway in the 1990's to protest. This is changing now, so the Norwegian establishment and their xenophobic mouthpiece, the Norwegian Press, are more wary now of causing offence. The Norway Shockers books that must be read in conjunction with this newsclips edition will altogether demonstrate why far-right quasi-racist journalists dominated the Norwegian Press and certainly encouraged Anders Breivik to think and eventually act as he did. He was undoubtedly egged on by the frequently virulent Muslim-hating Norwegian Press whose owners were often no better than their Serb colleagues in 1990's Yugoslavia.

The Norwegian government for the years 1995 to 2011 supported their Press when sued on the more hateful articles highlighted in this book. Until the very week of Breivik's day of action. After that it all changed, or so it seemed. These mainstream hypocrites were taught a self-inflicted lesson. Norway learnt the hard way.

As Friedrich Nietzsche once said: "The State does not lend towards the truth, but only toward useful truth – more precisely, whatever is useful to the State, be it truth, half-truth or lies".

Frederick Delaware November 2020

Norway Newsclips

Another raw slice of Norwegian life

SOME RAIN MUST FALL: MY STRUGGLE BOOK 5
by Karl Ove Knausgård, trans Don Bartlett
(Harvill Secker, £17.99)

ANDREW NEATHER

Unflinching revelations: Karl Ove Knausgård

"THE 14 years I lived in Bergen, from 1988 to 2002, are long gone, no traces of them are left other than as incidents a few people might remember," confesses Karl Ove Knausgård. "There is surprisingly little." Yet this material nevertheless sustains him for more than 650 pages of this, volume five of the sprawling autobiography of the world's most-talked-about memoirist.

Knausgård has become an international phenomenon since the translation of volume one of Min Kamp (My Struggle), A Death in the Family, in 2012 (it appeared in his native Norway in 2009). His flat, hyperrealist style, documenting the mundanities and frustrations of his life in real-time detail; the unflinching honesty of this often hard-to-like man; stylistic tics such as flashbacks lasting hundreds of pages: all these have both enthralled and enraged readers. And the latest instalment is similarly both indulgent and utterly compelling.

Here there are no flashbacks: like volume three, Boyhood Island, Some Rain Must Fall is a relatively straight narrative, if rendered in the finest-grained of detail. Volume four, documenting his teenage years, left off with the 20-year-old Knausgård more insecure, gauche and sexually frustrated than ever. His subsequent years here, at Bergen University's Writing Academy, are, naturally, a disaster.

We get plenty of signature confessional: his masturbation, his sexual indiscretions, his professional jealousy, his wild drunken excesses, all revealed with tortured self-loathing. His fear of his domineering father, the central emotional drama of A Death in the Family, is painfully clear once more.

And – for most of the time – he can't really write. There is almost a grim humour to his account: "I deleted it. Two pages, six months' work." Even reading good writers is an ambivalent experience for him, "enjoyment and jealousy, happiness and despair, in equal portions".

He is sustained by his burning writerly ambition and his love of women. Starting with his mother, women are good for Knausgård: as he says of his delightfully nice girlfriend, Gunvor: "When I was with her it was as though something was being drawn out of me. The darkness became lighter, the crippled straighter."

But not enough to straighten him out for long: days after getting together with the girl who becomes his first wife, Tonje ("I ached with happiness"), he is slashing his own face with broken glass in a frustrated rage.

So how much is fiction and how much autobiography? There is clearly no way he can remember the hundreds of conversations recounted here, his drunken impressions of a particular street 20 years ago. He confesses that he burnt his diaries from the period.

Does it matter? For all the reconstruction, he manages to encapsulate the essence of lasting moments in a way that rings true. He recounts catching a huge fish in a fjord: "Inside my head I had the image of it rising through the water. It was as though it came from another era than ours, up and up it came from the depths of time... The rain beating down on the dead fish and coursing down its scales and perfectly white belly."

And his constant, all-encompassing effort to grasp his own past renders regular if random flashes of insight: "With the darkness outside the windows like an ocean and the rooms sparsely illuminated I saw them as I had done when I was a small boy." And then his struggle continues once more. Ultimately it is the detail of Knausgård's outpouring that makes us realise, paradoxically, how unrecoverable and unknowable our past lives are.

London Evening Standard 18 February 2016

This book review is Norway in a nutshell: sex, drink, excess and regret. And it starts so early.

The Times and The Sunday Times Compact Disc Edition

SOURCE: Sunday Times DATE: 07 May 1995 PAGE: 9/3
Gloom with a view;Norway
Roland White

High taxes, cold weather, grim plays, expensive beer. No wonder the Norwegians can't stand the sight of Pamela Anderson, says Roland White.

The man at Oslo airport examined my passport, smiled, and asked: ``Business or pleasure?'' This was a bit of a surprise because the Norwegians have never gone in for pleasure in a big way. They are surely the world's least excitable race. If Walt Disney had been Norwegian, there would have been a dwarf called Gloomy. As my plane had descended over Oslo, there were spectacular views of the fjords. ``Gosh, what spectacular views of the fjords,'' I said to my neighbour, obviously flying home from London. ``Yes,'' he said, unimpressed. ``I am a chemical engineer.'' And we lapsed back into solemn silence.

It is in this spirit that feminists have been tearing down pictures of Pamela Anderson over the past week. Anderson, the sun-kissed star of Baywatch, features in 5,000 posters advertising bikinis for Hennes. Leaving aside the fact that there can't be too much demand for bikinis in Norway, where temperatures can plunge to -24C, the protestors complained that Anderson represented ``an impossible and unhealthy ideal''. This from the country that invented the blonde.

The leader of the protest, Bente Bjoerdal, complained: ``Much of Pamela Anderson's beauty has been created on the operating table and with the help of silicone breast implants.''

Feminist groups in other countries have largely grown out of defacing advertising posters, having found more sophisticated ways of highlighting women's issues. But Norway carries on. Why? Because Anderson she represents pleasure of a type that Norwegians cannot stomach. She is bikini-wrapped frivolity, whereas the Norwegians are not just a serious nation, they verge on the morose. Here is the evidence.

Skiing was invented in Norway. There are few sports that are more enjoyable than skiing. Mountains, fresh air, hurtling down slopes with abandon. Very nice, except that it was not this type of skiing that Norway invented. Norwegians prefer cross-country skiing, at which they regularly thrash all comers. It is a demanding sport which often involves tiring slogs uphill. It's not all hard work, though. Sometimes you get to ski on level ground, for miles and miles, in a straight line. An early Norwegian hero was Fridtjof Nansen, who crossed Greenland on skis. Not content with cross-country skiing, Norway also invented telemark skiing, a complicated technique involving bending the knees so far that they almost touch the snow. It was left to the loucher nations of Britain, Germany and Austria to invent alpine skiing as we know it.

Following last year's Winter Olympic games in Lillehammer, central Norway, the country was hoping to attract more tourists. This will be an uphill struggle as long as beer is still Pounds 3.50 a bottle, as it was when I last visited. Every night, in the small mountain village where I stayed, dinner was over by 7pm so that the staff would not be trapped by snow. So we headed for the bar, where a hefty German organist performed nightly. He played the same songs every evening and when he reached Que Sera Sera a party of Swedes would begin to waltz. I made an excuse and left.

Beer is so expensive because it is heavily taxed to encourage sobriety. But the reason Norwegians want to drink in the first place is to forget that they pay the world's highest income taxes. The 1992 rate of 65% is listed in The Guinness Book Of Records, but that figure has since fallen to 54%. The law even allowed the government to take more than 100% from particularly lavish earners by dipping into capital. In 1974, shipping magnate Hilmer Reksten paid 491% of his annual income. Wouldn't you be depressed?

Ah yes, depression. This is the country that has turned depression into a culture. What is Norway's best-known work of art? Perhaps a celebration of its striking countryside, its dramatic history? No, it is The Scream by Edvard Munch, which pictures a woman in utter despair. This is a familiar theme. The heroine of A Doll's House, by Norway's best-known playwright, Henrik Ibsen, is a woman who is depressed by her marriage. Just like Hedda Gabler, another Ibsen heroine. Ibsen himself was subject to fits of depression, so he wasn't one for light entertainment.

But then, few Norwegian entertainers are. A-Ha had the light touch when they got to No 1 in 1986 with The Sun Always Shines On TV, but the only other well-known Norwegian pop singer is Jahn Teigen, the 1978 Eurovision entry who gave the world the phrase ``Norway, null points''. According to William Hill, the odds on Norway winning this year's contest on Saturday with their entry, Eurovis, are 20-1.

Three years ago, Norway made a brief foray into the world of the West End musical with a rock opera called Which Witch. Were we grateful? Not much. ``They should have stuck to herring boats,'' said one critic. ``Three mind-numbing hours,'' said another. The criticism was so harsh that it nearly caused a diplomatic incident, and Which Witch closed with losses of Pounds 2m after a run of 10 weeks.

Norway has always had a high regard for Britain, which played a significant role in liberating the country from Nazi occupation. So failure in London was a severe disappointment. Which was a pity, because Norwegians are always so nice, so accommodating. Or are they?

A colleague spent two years living on the outskirts of Oslo as a child and recalls this period with a shudder. ``People pushed notes through our door saying: `Go home, British pigs.' And they drew pigs in the snow outside. As if this was not enough, it was so boring. We went to bed at about 7pm because there wasn't anything else to do.''

Tony Samstag, a foreign correspondent based in Oslo, paints a similar picture. ``There isn't much to do in this country,'' he says. ``That's probably why they started pulling down the posters. There was a similar incident in 1993 with Anna Nicole Smith again on a Hennes poster but this time the authorities got involved because they said it was a traffic hazard she was in her underwear. Apart from that, feminists were last in the news for trying to close down strip joints. It is all real 1970s stuff.''

It could be this lack of entertainment that has made British football so popular in Norway. Local papers are packed not only with reports from our Premier League but the results of Bolton, Sunderland, Barnsley and other less glamorous sides from the Endsleigh League first division. Fans organise trips to England to watch their favourite team, then the reserves, then the youth team, then a tour of the club shop and back home to Trondheim.

In this climate it is no wonder that Anderson proved too much: high taxes, expensive beer, gloomy plays, cold weather, not much daylight, and Norway's environment minister was once bad-tempered enough to refer to John Selwyn Gummer, his British counterpart, as a drittsekk, which loosely translated means a ``bag of dung''. Perhaps things aren't so bad there, after all?

Sunday Times 7th May 1995

This very expansive 1995 Sunday Times exposé of Norway is spot on: the Norwegians hated it.

SOURCE: Sunday Times DATE: 11 June 1995 PAGE: 1/21
Norway finds it's fun out in the cold
Tony Samstag, Oslo

WHEN Norway won the Eurovision Song Contest this year, television switchboards in neighbouring Scandinavian countries were jammed with protests that such an accolade should be bestowed on a nation of whale-killers who had turned their backs on European Community membership.

To Norwegians, triumph in an area where they had been an international joke was a sweet vindication of their present mood. They have persuaded themselves that singing alone on the international stage pays dividends.

It was the same story six months ago, when Norway voted for the second time since 1972 to reject EC membership, provoking embarrassment and anger among their European friends. The only congratulations came from Vladimir Zhirinovsky and Jean-Marie Le Pen, the extreme nationalist leaders from Russia and France, who recognised Norwegians' xenophobia and distrust of foreigners.

Those traits were spelled out candidly by Aase Kleveland, Norway's culture minister. ``Nations which are central to the European cultural tradition and political ideas are regarded by Norwegians as barbarians who wish to destroy Norwegian culture,'' Kleveland declared.

Soon Eurosceptics within the EC began to wonder aloud whether the Norwegians were not uniquely blessed as members of an exclusive extra-European club with Iceland, Liechtenstein and Switzerland. Within weeks of the referendum, the booming Norwegian economy was being written up as proof that eschewing the hegemony of Brussels was good for one's fiscal health.

``The gloom which should have set in after Norway's `No' has just not materialised,'' said Stein Bruun, a financial analyst. Only last month the government said Norway's foreign debt was expected to disappear this month and its $1billion fiscal deficit would become a $1.6billion surplus next year.

One result has been the revival of plans for an investment fund to stockpile wealth for future generations. The fund, set up in 1990 under the management of Norges Bank, the state central bank, stagnated as revenues continued to be diverted to finance budget deficits. To some, the latest move is tacit recognition that Norway has saved nothing from its North Sea treasure for 20 years.

The good news about the economy had been preceded by a warning from the Norges Bank on the dangers of relying too much on the offshore oil industry, which accounts for more than a third of the country's export earnings. A 30% oil price fall would cut annual revenues by about $6billion and destroy more than 10,000 jobs a year, it warned.

Another omen has left Norway, always described as one of the world's richest countries, quivering. Even in boom times, economic indicators consistently show that when the cost of living is considered, the average Norwegian enjoys living standards rather lower than those of the average Spaniard or Italian.

Privately, politicians and businessmen concede that Norway's exclusion from the EC aggravates this economic vulnerability. Immediately after the referendum the government tried to convince Brussels that Norway was entitled to a sort of favoured nation status in effect, continuing its role as member-in-waiting with the right to sit in on various EC deliberations.

This ended in national embarrassment after one exasperated EC minister blurted out on television: ``When are these Norwegians going to realise that they have said `No' and `No' means `No'?''

This has not deterred a new wave of xenophobia. Last year the Centre party emerged from the lunatic fringe to become the country's second strongest political force.

This year it is the turn of the Progress party to boost its support by using the run-up to the local elections to concentrate on immigrants.

Small in number, the mainly refugee minorities are blamed for everything from the inadequacies of the school system to the smell of garlic on the trams. Carl Hagen, the party's leader, told a recent conference: ``Immigration of people from Asia and Africa with strange cultures, different lifestyles and different norms of social behaviour create new conditions for conflict and the basis for jealousy among population groups because of preferential treatment.''

It is a song that will win few votes for Norway among its European neighbours

Sunday Times 11th June 1995

Another Sunday Times article from 1995 deals with Norwegian xenophobia.

CHIEF OF POLICE EXPOSED ONLINE

Oppland Arbeiderblad - 20 September 2011

[An image of the front page of the JohanMartinWelhaven.com website was placed here]

LIBEL: This website is the first hit for Johan Martin Welhaven on Google. The man behind the website is English. Welhaven has been in contact with UK police to have the threat assessed.

A standalone website has been set up in the name of Johan Martin Welhaven, exposing the new Chief of Police as an Islamophobe and laying some of the responsibility for 22 July at his door.

Morten Høitomt
Published 20.09.2011 03:00 Updated 20.09.2011 17:37

Last Friday Welhaven was appointed Chief of Police for Vestoppland in southern Norway.

On the website that bears his name, Welhaven tops a list of people accused of Islamophobia and harassment of Muslims. It's an English-language website and the domain is also registered to a man in the United Kingdom.

The home page begins: "Hatred for Islam permeates all levels of society in Norway. Mass murderer Anders Behring Breivik is the extreme manifestation of this bigotry. But the Norwegian establishment bears a heavy burden of responsibility: they openly participated in the Muslim-bashing year in, year out."

"Manipulators"

This is followed by the names and photographs of 19 persons who the originator of the site believes "had a defining role in the Islamophobic abuse".

The website's owner describes these people as "Protecting and nourishing perversion; clever manipulators from this isolated corner of Europe".

Client relationship

It is not clear on the website why the originator is focusing on Welhaven. The accusations of Islamophobia and manipulation are not elaborated on. However, Johan Martin Welhaven himself knows the reason. "The Englishman behind the website has had a client relationship with the Norwegian Bureau for the Investigation of Police Affairs, of which I am still Deputy Director. He bears a grudge against me and a number of others because of the case he was involved in," Welhaven told Oppland Arbeiderblad. He goes on to explain that the man in question has been writing on the website for several years, but the Islamophobe slant is new. Previously, the web pages had a different content.

Contacted the police

Although he is now trying to ignore the Englishman, Welhaven admits that the matter has taken its toll.

"I've taken a number of steps in terms of assessing my safety. Among other things I've been in contact with the UK authorities, as well as speaking to people in Norway with expertise in the field," he says. Have you reported the situation? "No. There are legal steps that can be taken, which might deal with material of this nature on the web in the short term, but it could still pop up again in a different form at a later stage. So although I perceive it as harassment, I've decided that I can live with it so far, in any case. I haven't been bothered by it beyond the knowledge that the website actually exists."

The dark side of the web

Johan Martin Welhaven is a lawyer by training, but finds it difficult to protect himself against the smear campaign. **"This case, and others that are worse, are a reminder that the Internet has a seriously dark side. It is somewhere people can easily torment and harass others completely unchecked,** "he states.

ONLINE HARASSMENT

Oppland Arbeiderblad - 21 September 2011

People will never be able to totally protect themselves from online bullying. Published 21.09.2011 06:01 Updated 21.09.2011 06:01

The Editor writes: “For many years the new Chief of Police for Vestoppland, Johan Martin Welhaven, has been exposed to an online smear campaign and harassment by an Englishman. He is accused of being an Islamophobe and held partly responsible for the terror attacks in Oslo and on the island of Utøya on 22 July. It goes without saying that the claims are completely unfounded, but are linked to a client relationship the outgoing Deputy Director of the Norwegian Bureau for the Investigation of Police Affairs had with the Englishman a number of years ago.

Nevertheless, protecting himself against such statements is extremely challenging for Welhaven. When someone who is a lawyer and employed by the police chooses NOT to go down the legal route to have a website like this taken down, it says a lot about just how difficult it is to fight the dark side of the web.

Anyone can procure any domain at all – it’s a free for all: first come, first served. In Welhaven’s case, the person concerned has bought up his entire name as a domain. This means that searches for the name “Johan Martin Welhaven” on Google, the world’s largest search engine, will always show this page at the top of the list of hits. It is not difficult to imagine how this technique could be abused by people wanting to use the web to harass, spread false information about, or harm another person.

Digital bullying is a key topic in Norwegian schools this year. Since the campaign was launched in the autumn, a number of local schools have organised targeted activities to increase knowledge of and change attitudes to unwanted activity online. At Raufoss, the whole school took part in an anti-bullying procession to show that bullying will not be tolerated. However, pupils and teachers are making no secret of the fact that this is a problem that will never go away. In recent years, online bullying in particular has become increasingly prominent.

Ever younger children and young people have access to the web. Many also have their own computers that they use on a more or less daily basis without any adult supervision whatsoever. This makes it very easy to take a wrong step. Neither are young people making any secret of the fact that it is easy to publish opinions of other people in anger that absolutely do not belong in the public domain. They also believe that many young people do not understand the scope of a statement or an image published online.

Although netiquette and data safety have come to the fore in the last few years, there is no reason not to have full focus on this going forward. People will never be able to totally protect themselves from online bullying.

Preventive work with children and young people is therefore absolutely vital. To an even greater degree than the adults of today, they will need to understand both the benefits and drawbacks of the opportunities the web offers.

Here's a translation of a revenge article on a U.K Solicitor written by a provincial newspaper in Norway - upset that one of its local police chiefs got a taste of his own medicine. They call it ‘harassment’ – others call it ‘justified comment’.

MINARET MYTHS

New Statesman - 1 August 2011

False claims about Muslims are fuelling Islamophobia in Europe, says Andreas Malm

There is nothing particularly Norwegian about Anders Behring Breivik's manifesto, 2083: a European Declaration of Independence. It is a bulky précis of all the standard tropes in Islamophobic ideology that have evolved in Europe over the past decade. Its plagiarism — the enormous excerpts from authors such as Melanie Phillips, Roger Scruton, Daniel Pipes, Bruce Bawer, Robert Spencer, Bat Ye'or, Mark Steyn, Ayaan Hirsi Ali and, above all, the Norwegian blogger Fjordman — show how standardised right-wing thought has become. It also points to a disconcerting conclusion: these events could have happened anywhere in Europe.

Breivik's concerns about "Islamisation" are typical of those expressed by European tabloids and politicians. He has familiar worries about Muslims establishing no-go areas in cities, sharia courts, swimming pools with Muslim- only sessions, the contradiction between Islam and freedom of speech, the all- Muslim duty to perform jihad and the anti-Semitic inclinations of Muslim communities. And he wants to draw a line. "The veil should be banned in all public institutions, thus also contributing to breaking the traditional subjugation of women," he writes in 2083. "Companies and public buildings should not be forced to build prayer rooms for Muslims. Enact laws to eliminate the abuse of family reunification laws."

What strikes the reader of Breivik's work is its terrible normality. At least the first 6o pages, up to the initial musings on military tactics, could be found in your average European book-shop, or in articles written by well-regarded politicians and intellectuals. Despite this, the denial of the Nordic media has not ceased. Norwegian and Swedish readers are now being told that Breivik has merely copied the "Unabomber" (the loner Ted Kaczynski, who sent a series of mail bombs in the US between 1978 and 1995). Does anyone in the Nordic countries even remember the Unabomber? How far are we willing to go to avoid looking in the mirror?

While much of what Breivik has to say is the staple of mainstream right-of- centre discourse, some of it is distinctly fascist. But this is a coherent and successful brand of fascism whose core tenet is the belief in "Eurabia". The thesis of Eurabia is that Muslim countries, using the oil embargo of the early 1970s to blackmail the European Community, forced our treacherous politicians to hand over power. Ever since, it claims, we have been ruled by a secret Muslim conspiracy intent on transforming Europe into a colony— Eurabia —where we, the native Europeans, are subjugated. The Egyptian-born British writer Bat Ye'or is the author of the Eurabia doctrine, but the far-right Sweden Democrats and the Danish People's Party echo her ideas.

Neither the denial of global warming nor the virulent anti-feminism is an invention of Breivik's. And his hatred of Marxism, real and imaginary — the strand of thought that eventually led him to Utøya — places him in an almost century-long tradition.

Yet didn't Breivik leave all other Islamophobes far behind him when he contemplated murder? We hear, even from experts on the Nordic extreme right, that violence and terrorism are inherent to neo-Nazi groups, but alien to well- dressed Islamophobic populists. Once more, the disclaimers are almost as revelatory as the 22 July atrocity. In recognising the non-violent, parliamentary, well-mannered nature of modern European Islamophobia, we have — even if disagreeing with it— failed to trace its roots and keep track of its development.

The world of Islamophobic ideas is permeated with military imagery and language. Muslims are conquerors, colonisers, occupiers. Mosques and minarets are their victory monuments. The history of Islam is a long series of onslaughts on Christian civilisation, which defended itself at

Poitiers in the 8th century and Vienna in the 16th and now has to rise to the occasion again; we are the descendants of Charlemagne. Our nations are being betrayed, a war is being fought against us — and the time has come to fight back. From the Danish commentator Lars Hedegaard to the Italian Lega Nord, from the Swedish politician Jimmie Akesson to the German politician Thilo Sarrazin, this is the mantra. Breivik's originality is merely in acting it out.

Serbian brothers

At the end of 2083, Breivik answers a series of questions he imagines a reporter would want to ask him. "What tipped the scales for you? What single event made you decide you wanted to continue planning and moving on with the assault?" Answer: "For me, personally, it was my government's involvement in the attacks on Serbia [Nato bombings in 1999] several years back. It was completely unacceptable how the US and western European regimes bombed our Serbian brothers. All they wanted was to drive Islam out by deporting the Albanian Muslims back to Albania."

Breivik's obsession with the Serbs' struggle against Muslim intruders, his praise for the Serbian politician Radovan Karadzic as an "honourable crusader" and a "war hero", his vision of Arkan's paramilitary brigade as a model for his "resistance" are all symptomatic. The ideas of today's Islamophobic right were put into practice in the Balkans in the 1990s, in the most recent genocide on European soil. There is a straight line running from Srebrenica to Utøya. The military leader Ratko Mladic burned with the same fire as Anders Behring Breivik. The only difference is that Breivik targeted the "traitors" rather than the "conquerors".

Andreas Malm is a journalist and the author of books in Swedish on European Islamophobia

This particular Swedish journalist, Andreas Malm, is 100% correct in his analysis of the collective Norwegian perversion that expressed itself in the persona of Norway's mass-murderer Anders Behring Breivik.

Breivik ready for girlfriend visits after court win

RAY COLLINS/THE SUN; JONATHAN NACKSTRAND/AFP/GETTY

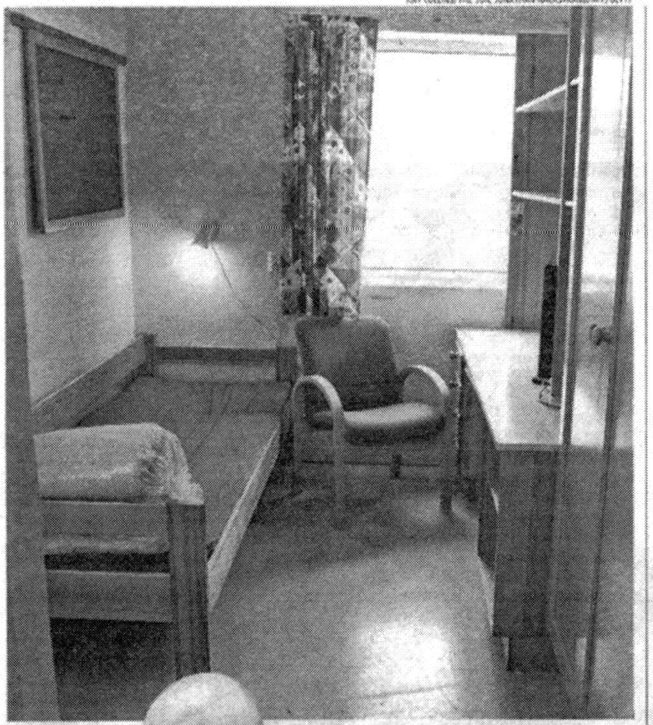

Norway

David Charter Berlin

The mass murderer Anders Behring Breivik could be allowed visits from a female admirer after a court ruled that his human rights had been violated by being kept in isolation.

The self-declared Nazi, 37, claimed that his health was suffering from being locked up alone without seeing even guards for at least 22 hours every day.

Breivik planted a bomb in Oslo that killed eight people and then shot dead 69 people attending a Labour party youth camp on the island of Utoya near the Norwegian capital in July 2011.

His lawyers welcomed the ruling and called for his isolation to be eased.

That could mean that he is allowed visits from a Swedish woman who calls herself his girlfriend but who has been refused permission to meet him. The woman, known only as Victoria, has exchanged hundreds of letters with him and is believed to be the woman he speaks to when he is allowed to use the phone. She encountered Breivik before the massacre while playing computer games online and said last year that she was in love with him.

The only person other than prison staff or doctors known to have entered the same cell as Breivik since he was convicted in 2012 was his terminally ill mother, who came to say her farewells in 2013. Prison and legal professionals who visit remain behind a glass panel.

Breivik complained that his captivity amounted to inhuman, degrading treatment or punishment in breach of the European Convention on Human Rights. When he brought the case in March he complained that cold coffee and microwaved meals were "worse than waterboarding".

Helen Andenaes Sekulic said in her written ruling: "The prohibition of inhuman and degrading treatment represents a fundamental value in a democratic society. This applies no matter what — also in the treatment of terrorists and killers."

The judge ruled that the Norwegian state had broken the convention because Breivik spent 22 to 23 hours a day alone in his cell.

She said that there had been no attempt to ease the security "even though Breivik has behaved in an exemplary manner during his time in prison".

His isolation was an inhuman treatment in the meaning of the European convention, she ruled, but the Norwegian state did not violate Breivik's right to a private and family life — which may yet frustrate any request to meet his girlfriend.

Oystein Storrvik, a lawyer for Breivik, said after the verdict: "He must first and foremost be allowed to be in contact with other people." He declined to describe Breivik's reaction to the ruling.

Marius Emberland, one of the two lawyers representing Norway, said that they would consider an appeal: "We are surprised by the verdict."

Björn Ihler, a survivor of the shootings, said on Twitter that the verdict was a sign that Norway had a working court system, respecting human rights even under extreme conditions. "We have to take the ruling seriously," he said.

Anders Behring Breivik, who killed 77 people, has been subject to inhuman isolation in his jail cell, a judge ruled

The Times 21 April 2016

Nicer prisons in Norway!

Mystery buyer sets art auction record

By **Eleanor Harding** and **Daniel Bates**

FOR more than a century it has been one of the best known, and most imitated, images in art.

Now The Scream has changed hands for an astonishing £74million – making it the most expensive artwork ever sold at auction.

The pastel drawing, one of four versions of the piece by artist Edvard Munch, went to an anonymous buyer at Sotheby's in New York on Wednesday after a bidding war lasting only 12 minutes.

The final sale price was one-and-a-half times the estimate, and £8million more than the previous record-holder, Picasso's Nude, Green Leaves And Bust, sold in 2010.

Sotheby's said it went for so much because it 'transcends art history and reaches a global consciousness' and had become the 'visual embodiment of modern anxiety and existential dread'.

When Munch painted The Scream in 1895 he was an alcoholic, heartbroken, penniless and in fear that he was going to fall prey to the mental illness that affected much of his family.

This version is the most sought after of the four because it is the only one with a poem about the work by the artist in the frame.

The bids started at £6million. After more than ten minutes it was down to a contest between two anonymous phone bidders. With the buyer's premium, the total price was £74,035,374, or $119.9million. There was a moment of comic tension as the price rose when the auctioneer responded to a brief delay in proceedings with the words: 'For $99million, I have all the time in the world!'

Yesterday some experts speculated that it may have been bought by Chelsea FC owner Roman Abramovich, whose girlfriend Dasha Zhukova is a patron of the arts, or the Metropolitan Museum of Art in New York.

Microsoft founder Bill Gates denied he was the buyer, but others pointed to the Qatari royal family, which last year privately purchased Cezanne's The Card Players for £160million, a record for any painting.

This version of The Scream, originally bought by collector Arthur von Franquet in 1895, was sold in 1937 to Norwegian businessman Thomas Olsen, a patron of Munch. It has remained in his family ever since.

It is the most colourful of the versions and the only one in which one of the two figures in the background turns to look outward on to the cityscape.

The three other Screams – two paintings and one pastel drawing, all held in galleries in Norway – have never been auctioned but are thought to be of similar value to the version sold in New York.

Both painted versions have been stolen, one in 1994 and one in 2004, but were later recovered by police.

COMMENTARY
by A. N. Wilson

£74m for this silly cartoon – it just makes you want to... SCREAM!

THE auctioneer who sold The Scream by Edvard Munch for £74million said: 'It is worth every penny.' He would, wouldn't he, given the vast commission he must have made off it?

As a salesman, Tobias Meyer deserves the highest praise, but we do not all have to agree with his judgment of the painting.

Just *why* is The Scream worth so much money? Mr Meyer explains that it is, wait for it, 'one of the great icons of the art world'. The word icon must be one of the most over-used clichés of our time.

Of course, having persuaded a rich buyer to part with enough money to buy a fully-equipped small hospital, or 20 primary schools, Mr Meyer is hardly likely to see this grotesque expenditure as a fantastic waste of money. What he sees as this great icon, the rest of us can see as something which just happens to be a very famous picture.

The Scream, of which Munch produced a number of versions in the 1890s, became popular in the 1960s. Andy Warhol – who was in many ways a much more interesting artist than Munch – made copies of it.

He saw its simple, cartoon-like outlines as saying something which the drug-crazed, dippy 1960s were desperate to hear. Something that was blindingly obvious and could be translated as 'This is doing my head in, Man'.

The skinny writhing figure in the foreground of the picture is neither male nor female, and is simply emoting before our eyes. The quality of the brushwork in the painted versions is crude and lumpy. This too appealed to the young ravers of the 1960s who had come to love American expressionism, and the works of Jackson Pollock who 'expressed' his anxiety about life by hurling pots of paint at giant canvases.

These in many ways clever but in other ways simple-minded American leaders of fashion found something in Munch which 'spoke' to them.

MUNCH had lived in Norway during the troubled 1890s. It was a generation which had seen the collapse of religion, and the growth, among intellectuals, of the idea that life was empty, pointless and horrible.

Such thoughts were expressed bleakly and brilliantly, in previous decades, in the novels of the great Russian writer Dostoevsky – who stated that if God did not exist to impose some form of moral order on society, then was not any kind of outlandish behaviour permitted?

It was to be found in the wild music of the German composer Richard Wagner who depicted the collapse of religion and moral order in his operas; it was to be heard in the mad screams of the philosopher Friedrich Nietzsche, who pronounced God to be dead shortly before he was himself confined to a straitjacket and the ministrations of mental nurses.

These were three great geniuses who definitely captured something about the bleak spirit of those times – times which would culminate in the struggles of the European superpowers and the outbreak of the First World War which marred, some would say destroyed, Europe for ever.

Hindsight is a wonderful thing. Those who lived in the 20th century were able to look back at Munch and find in his feeble picture The Scream a prophecy of what was to come.

Coming to the picture with deep serious thoughts, these admirers mistook it for a deep, serious picture. But it isn't. It is a rather silly, badly executed cartoon.

Awestruck admirers of Munch note that he and a friend were walking down this stretch of road near Oslo when, against a flaming sunset, he was suddenly overcome by horror and anxiety about the pointlessness of life. If, as some believe, the town of Ekburg is in the background, this is where poor Munch's mad sister was incarcerated in a lunatic asylum.

These facts might be sad, but they do not make his picture into great art. The three versions, all of the same subject, which are lovingly treasured in Oslo galleries, are among the proudest exhibits in the Norwegian national collections.

BUT there are very many better Scandinavian artists, all more skilful with paint brushes or pastel chalks than Munch, and many of them easily affordable by you and me!

Did the buyer – rumoured to be a billionaire member of the Qatari royal family – really want one of the 'icons' of modern art because he was so obsessively fond of drawings and paintings? Or did he actually want it because it was so expensive?

If you could buy a Munch for £74, rather than £74million, in your local auction house, do you think the buyer would have had the smallest interest in it? Of course not. The motive for buying this picture was to show off.

It was to prove to himself and perhaps to posterity that he was a big swanky fellow who could afford to spend on one measly pastel drawing an amount of money that could have built countless schools or a small hospital.

I am enough of an aesthete (or snob if you prefer the word) to believe that such an expenditure would not have been a 'waste' of money if he had bought one of the great masterpieces of the Italian Renaissance such as the works of Leonardo da Vinci or Titian.

The fact that he has been mug enough to spend it on Munch shows that he is a philistine, and the fact that he has chosen to spend it on a painting rather than a good cause makes me see red.

With such purchases happening in our midst while the European economy founders and the Third World teeters always on the brink of famine, it is not just ridiculous, it is ugly.

In fact, it's enough to make you want to scream.

"Munch had lived in Norway during the troubled 1890's. It was a generation which had seen the collapse of religion, and the growth, among intellectuals, of the idea that life was empty, pointless and horrible." **Daily Mail** 4 May 2012

Nordic au pairs invade in hot pursuit of love

by Jasper Gerard

THEY are over here and hunting. Scandinavian au pairs — pursued by wayward husbands and viewed with suspicion by wives — are coming to Britain in record numbers, with many seeking to marry Englishmen.

Since Sweden and Finland joined the EC at the begining of the year, their au pairs can stay here to work. Many do, seduced by the apparent excitement of London and "gentlemanly" Britons.

The Norwegians are just as keen. Their church in Rotherhithe, in London's Docklands, has become the unlikely venue for Anglo-Nordic dating. On Sundays, au pairs from around the capital gather for dinner there.

Fortified by boiled lamb and potatoes, they await the arrival of young Englishmen and the party begins.

"I don't quite know why but they seem to like Scandanavian girls," said Elin Andersen, a former pastry chef who is employed full time by the Norwegian Church to counsel distressed au pairs. "Perhaps it is because they are more modern in their thinking.

"A lot of English boys come here and they are really quite popular. They seem very caring and know how to charm Norwegian girls."

Even living in suburban Croydon, Anne Linn Johansen, 19, enjoys English life. "There are a couple of other Norwegian girls living nearby," she said. "We go to a club called the Blue Orchid — it's the wildest place in Croydon."

Just how wild does Croydon get? "When you come from a village with 1,000 inhabitants, even Croydon seems exciting," replies Miss Johansen, who is considering staying to attend a British university.

"If I find Mr Perfect — such as an English farmer — I think I could live here forever."

The Swedes — identifiable by their shorts and sandals in even the coldest weather — are just as enthusiastic. There are 25,000 of them in Britain.

The number applying to come here rose by more than 30 per cent last year. "There is nothing in Sweden," said Mari Rönn, a 19-year-old athlete. "It is great just to soak-up the atmosphere here."

Her enthusiasm has not been blunted by a series of disasters since arriving in London a month ago to work

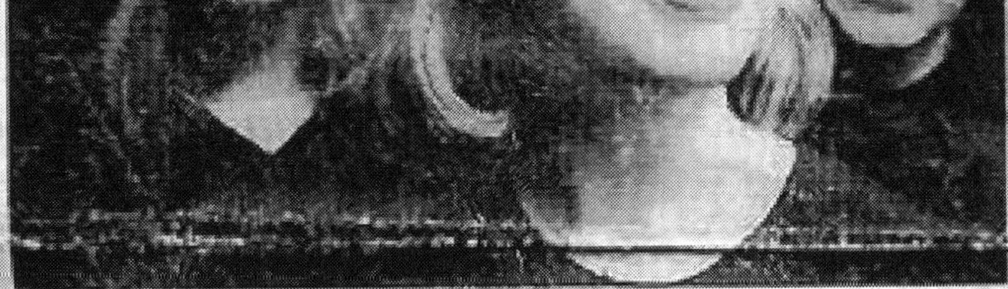

Wild one: Anne Linn Johansen (centre) and friends

Brit pack: Annelie Nynas (left) meets up with fellow Swede Karin Pettersson *Photograph: Madeleine Waller*

as an au pair. She has lived in six places, complaining that she was expected to work all day, cooking, cleaning and looking after children — for £40 a week.

She is now camping out at a youth hostel exclusively for Swedes in the West End. It, too, has become a mecca for young Englishmen brimming with excess testosterone.

"Scandinavian men can be rather hard and they don't talk much," said Erica Jensen, 22. "Englishmen tend to be darker but they are also more sensitive than Latins. I love their accents and their manners. In fact, I think it would be great to marry one."

While working as an au pair, Annelie Nynas, 22, decided to apply to Cambridge University to read economics.

"I love the clubs and the pubs here," she said. "The family I work for are wonderful — they have a gardener and a cleaner and a lovely child. I am free to go out and have fun. The only problem is that I am forever getting lost."

Another Swede at the hostel, Anna Andersson, 21, came to Britain in the hope of following Abba to pop stardom. "I saw an advert in a British music paper for a female singer so we decided to turn up in person as we thought that would impress the band." She is now handing out leaflets at stations.

Romance is unlikely. "Scandinavian men drink too much and only show their emotions after dark," she said.

"But at least they are good-looking. Englishmen wear terrible clothes and look badly fed."

The Sunday Telegraph 29 October 1995

Too true. The girls actively look for sex ... so long as they fancy you.

Page 54 Daily Mail, Saturday, April 19, 2003

SUDDEN and violent death overtook the people of Northumberland in 793. They had guessed it was coming, for fiery dragons had been seen in the night skies. Real ones followed, carved on the prows of the lean Viking longboats that came ashore at Lindisfarne.

Warriors emerged, stormed the abbey, massacred priests, monks and nuns even at the altar, carried off golden ornaments and fired the building. This was the first raid on England by the Vikings — a loose term used then, and now, for Norwegians, Swedes and Danes.

A reign of terror and devastation had begun that would soon encompass England, Scotland, Ireland and large swathes of North-West Europe for more than a century.

The names of the Viking warlords were resonant with barbarism and slaughter: Ragnar Hairy Breeks, Ivar the Boneless, Erik Bloodaxe, Thorfinn the Skullsplitter. More onslaughts followed, and during the 9th century, Christian civilisation seemed to be tottering.

by Lawrence James

Bewildered and fearful congregations prayed: 'Oh Lord, deliver us from the fury of the Northmen.' Moralists claimed that the Viking raiders had been sent by God to scourge a sinful world.

Now a tranquil Europe wishes to banish Viking predators from the history books. It was reported this week that European history has been tidied up and sanitised over the past decade in the hope that the new, bland version will foster harmony between people who were once at loggerheads.

Researcher Dr Yasemin Soysal, of the European Sociological Association, has examined school textbooks and discovered that, in contrast to those of 30 years ago, they describe Vikings as traders and farmers, as opposed to fierce raiders, and ignore the fact that Europe was born of bloody conflict.

A contrived and false past is being created in which there are no winners or losers and, most importantly, no heroes or villains. Europe's history of conflict is being repackaged as a fairy story.

This means Thorfinn the Skullsplitter, his companions-in-arms and their exploits are banished.

Viking literature has to be sidelined, for the finest of it is hardly censorious when describing the deeds of seafarers in search of plunder, and warriors on the battlefield.

Political correctness has blinded the pen-pushers of education to the obvious. The values and behaviour of people in the Dark Ages were profoundly different from our own.

However hard we try, we cannot imagine ourselves in that time, or penetrate its consciousness. Its inhabitants thought and reacted differently, and would never have recognised, let alone understood, the assumptions of those who now sit in judgment on them.

The Viking cult of the warrior may be inexplicable, even abhorrent to us, but it was at the centre of the Scandinavian world. It exalted courage in battle, which we still admire — a warrior's grave in Sweden has the proud boast: 'He did not flee, but fought on while he could hold weapons.'

But the cult of the warrior also elevated killing for its own sake. Doing so efficiently and swiftly was an art that was learned from childhood by the sons of noblemen. These were the future elite fighting men, small bodies that were, quite literally, the spearhead of the predatory bands.

THE APPRENTICE warrior learned how to twist and turn wearing a heavy mail shirt and iron helmet (you can see one at the Yorvik centre in York), handle a sword, spear and axe and protect his body with his shield.

The sword was the specialist weapon of the Viking warrior. Its blade was well tempered, its hilt richly decorated. Such weapons were treasured, having passed down through the generations. They sometimes acquired mystical qualities and were given such names as Brainbiter.

Mastery of swordplay was part of the warrior's preparation for hand-to-hand combat in which eye and muscle were vital. It was arduous work, equivalent to SAS training, and required the same stamina and strength.

The deft warrior aimed his strokes at the thigh or arm to disable his adversary and then struck the lethal blow against his skull. Enormous physical force was needed: skeletons of men who died in battle reveal blows that smashed through helmets and skulls to the brain.

To fight in this way, the Viking warrior had to 'psych' himself up to a war frenzy. He became 'berserk', that is, literally, bear-like in his blood lust and strength. On the eve of one battle, a body of fighters became as 'mad as dogs or wolves and bit their shields and were strong as bears'.

Another band was described in a poem as 'Wolfcoats ... who bear blood-stained swords to battle; they redden spears when they come to the slaughter'. These warriors would have worn wolf skins, imagining that they could absorb the ferocity of the beast.

The Viking war machine spread shock and awe. The raiders had surprise on their side, for they were consummate sailors who could launch their amphibious assaults wherever they wished.

The Vikings were brilliant shipwrights and navigators, and their longboats, lovingly described by one poet as 'wave stallions' were capable of long voyages.

RAVENS were painted on the sails of the longboats. Vikings joked that these carrion eaters were their brothers-in-arms, following the raiding parties into battle to feast on the flesh of the dead.

The Vikings left their homelands in Scandinavia because they were facing an economic crisis: overpopulation and underproduction of food. These hard facts triggered the raids, together with the knowledge that the petty states of Britain and Ireland were incapable of defending themselves.

The raiding bands targeted monasteries and churches where they knew there were gold, silver and jewelled reliquaries, torched buildings and seized livestock from villagers, killing animals they could not carry off.

In one raid on the monastery at Iona, a defiant priest was 'cut in pieces with severed limbs' and his unsated assailant hacked at his entrails.

Priests, men, women and children were cut down randomly. Women were raped. When they were taken, prisoners were eventually sold into slavery, sometimes to Arab merchants.

No wonder that a warrior boasted of how 'great numbers of English flee before our swords'. Forewarned of a raid, the men and women of Fife 'dragged themselves off to the woods and wastes with weeping and wailing'. They would return to famine, for the Vikings would have smashed their farm implements and either burned or plundered granaries.

The Vikings could be undisciplined and fought between themselves over their spoils. Rivals defeated in such feuds suffered a traditional, hideous death.

Torf-Einar, the one-eyed earl of Orkney, ordered his warriors to cut the outline of an eagle on a prisoner's back, slice the ribs from the backbone and then pull out the man's lungs as an offering to the god, Odin, in thanks for victory.

These ritualised deaths were meted out, too, on Anglo-Saxon leaders as, gradually, the predator raiders were followed by immigrants hungry for land.

Most colonised northern and eastern England and the original settlers are now recalled by the names of towns and villages. Kettlethorpe in Yorkshire began its existence as Ketil's hamlet.

A masterful piece on the reality of the heathen Viking invaders.

Daily Mail April 19th 2003

Færre aborter i 1994

I 1994 ble det i alt utført 14 533 svangerskapsavbrudd i Norge. Dette er en nedgang på 376 sammenliknet med 1993.

Dagens lov om svangerskapsavbrudd trådte i kraft 1. januar 1979, og i årene fra 1979 til 1994 har antall provoserte aborter variert mellom 13 531 (1982) og 16 208 (1989). Tallet på svangerskapsavbrudd har de siste fem år vist nedgang sammenliknet med 1989. Vi må tilbake til 1984 for å finne et lavere antall utførte aborter enn i 1994. Antall svangerskapsavbrudd i prosent av levendefødte var 24 i 1994. Sør- og Vestlandet har færrest abortinngrep pr. 1 000 kvinner i fruktbar alder.

I Ukens statistikk nr. 40 vil det komme flere opplysninger om statistikken.

Ny statistikk

Svangerskapsavbrudd, 1994.
Statistikken utgis årlig i Ukens statistikk.
Mer informasjon: Finn Gjertsen, tlf. 22 86 45 44.

A 1994 Norwegian language abortion statistics report: 17 years later Anders Breivik expressed his fury at the huge numbers of Norwegian children killed by abortion – "... more than I have ever killed" he said.

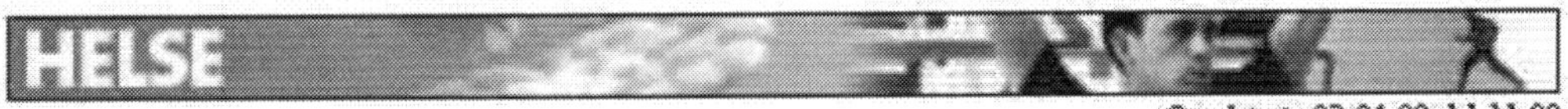

Oppdatert 23.04.02, kl 11:08

Aborter i 2001

Norge:13867

Oslo totalt: 2367

LES OGSÅ
- Stadig færre Oslokvinner tar abort - 23.04.02

Aborter blant tenåringer i Norge:2448 (18,8 pr. 1000)

Aborter blant tenåringer i Oslo: 258 (23,7 pr. 1000)

Tall for bydelene i Oslo
GrünerløkkaSofienberg: 213
Sagene-Torshov: 171
Gamle Oslo: 168
Søndre Nordstrand: 163
Uranienborg: 156
St.Hanshaugen: 149
Furuset: 128
Bygdøy-Frogner: 111
Helsfyr-Sinsen: 103
Stovner: 99
Bjerke: 85
Grorud: 79
Røa: 66
Ullern: 64
Sogn: 58
Grefsen: 57
Vinderen: 56
Ekeberg-Bekkelaget: 54
Manglerud: 48
Østensjø: 46
Nordstrand: 45
Bøler: 44
Hellerud: 43
Lambertseter: 39
Romsås: 35
Uoppgitt bydel: 87

(Kilde: Statistisk sentralbyrå)

Abortion figures for 2001 in Norway.

HELSE

Oppdatert 23.04.02, kl 11:08

Stadig færre Oslokvinner tar abort

Ikke siden midt på 90-tallet har det vært færre aborter. I fjor avbrøt 2367 Oslo-kvinner svangerskapet. 258 av dem var tenåringer.

LINE KASPERSEN

LES OGSÅ

- 1 av 3 sexdebuterer i fylla - 23.04.02
- - Mer sex på timeplanen, takk! - 23.04.02
- Aborter i 2001 - 23.04.02

Tidligere toppet Oslo abortstatistikken, men nå har Nordland, Troms og Finnmark gått forbi, viser ferske tall fra Statistisk sentralbyrå.

I fjor tok 2367 Oslo-kvinner abort, mot 2640 i 2000 og 2661 i 1999. Også blant de yngste er tendensen klar: 258 tenåringer tok abort i fjor. I 2000 var tallet 284, året før 304.

-Gledelig utvikling, sier Lisbet Nortvedt ved Klinikk for seksuell opplysning (KSO). Hun tror at nedgangen har en sammenheng med bedre tilgjengelighet til både p-piller og andre typer prevensjonsmidler. Men hun tviler på at den reseptfrie angrepillen Norlevo har så mye å si i denne sammenheng.

-Litt har den nok å si, men ikke mye. At man nå får kjøpt angrekur direkte på apoteket, betyr ikke stort annet enn at kvinner kjøper det der fremfor via andre kanaler - for eksempel gjennom oss. Få bruker angrepillen ofte, sier Nortvedt.

Tall fra Farmastat AS viser at det ble omsatt 14792 døgndoser av angrepillen Norlevo i Oslo i fjor. I første kvartal i år ble det kjøpt 4373 doser, mot 2857 i samme periode i fjor.

Prosjektet "Jeg har et valg" er et av flere opplegg som har hatt som mål å forhindre uønsket graviditet. Hittil er prosjektet prøvd ut på to skoler på Romsås og Sagene-Torshov, og nå står evalueringen for tur. Bak står Statens institutt for folkehelse og helsestasjonene i de to bydelene.

-Undervisningen formidler kunnskaper om sex og prevensjon, man får selvtillitstrening og samtaler om sosialt press, blant annet i kjæresteforhold, sier Ingri Myklestad, som er ansvarlig for prosjektet hos Folkehelsa.

Evalueringen kan føre til at undervisningsprogrammet, som drives av lærere i samarbeid med helsepersonell, videreføres til flere skoler i byen.

-Jeg har inntrykk av at elevene likte opplegget. Tilbakemeldingene til oss var at det var interessant og spennende, sier Myklestad.

Karin Yrvin, kvinnepolitisk leder i Oslo Arbeiderparti, mener at det er en klar sammenheng mellom abortforebyggende tiltak som "Jeg har et valg" og færre aborter.

-Det er bedre å satse på å forebygge uønsket graviditet fremfor å gi råd når man først er blitt gravid. Men prosjektene bør bygges ut til å bli en mer permanent del av skoleundervisningen, sier Yrvin.

Abortion figures for 2001 in Norway.

Oppdatert 23.04.02, kl 11:08

1 av 3 sexdebuterer i fylla

Oslo-ungdom debuterer seksuelt når de gjennomsnittlig er 16,6 år.

- Vel halvparten bruker ikke prevensjon under første samleie.

- 1 av 3 norske ungdommer debuterer i fylla.

LES OGSÅ

- Stadig færre Oslokvinner tar abort - 23.04.02

- 1,4 prosent av alle 14/17-åringer i Oslo har solgt sex.

- Norske tenåringsjenter føder flere barn enn sine skandinaviske medsøstre. Årlig får 12 av 1000 jenter under 20 år barn.

- 1 av 3 jenter i videregående skole sier de har vært utsatt for uønskede seksuelle handlinger.

- 36 prosent av ungdom mellom 15 og 18 år sier de har fått den viktigste informasjonen om seksualitet fra venner. 41 prosent har fått den fra helsepersonell.

Abortion figures for 2001 in Norway.

HELSE

Oppdatert 23.04.02, kl 11:08

- Mer sex på timeplanen, takk!

Fint at aborttallene er på retur, synes Ine Schick og Miriam Halvorsen fra Oslo. Men de tror mange unge bruker angrepillen som prevensjonsmiddel.

Seksualopplysningen i skolen er elendig, mener de to tenåringsjentene på 17 og 18 år.

-Det holder ikke med en pinlig skoletime med en nervøs helsesøster i 6. klasse og ett besøk på Klinikk for seksuell opplysning (KSO) i 10. klasse. Ungdom vet altfor lite om sex, prevensjon og kjønnssykdommer. Dette temaet må inn i den ordinære undervisningen, sier Ine Schick.

Hun og venninnen Miriam Halvorsen tror at de fleste på deres alder har fått det meste av sine kunnskaper om sex og samliv gjennom TV, eldre søsken og venner - og ved å lese informative bøker.

Skolen må skjerpe seg. *Seksualopplysningen i Oslo-skolen er altfor dårlig, mener Ine Schick (t.v) og Miriam Halvorsen.*

FOTO: Paal Audestad

LES OGSÅ

- Stadig færre Oslokvinner tar abort - 23.04.02

-Du er nødt til å ta initiativet selv, og det er litt dumt. Vi har mange bekjente som oppsøker "Det gule huset" (KSO) for å få gratis konsultasjon, gode råd og hjelp til å velge prevensjon. Det er et kjempefint tilbud, noe skolene burde lære mer av. For det er jo ikke alle som tør å snakke like åpent om slike ting, mener Miriam.

I dag kan man få den såkalte angrepillen reseptfritt på apoteket. Men "nødpillen" brukes ofte av ungdom som droppet kondomet kvelden før, fordi den ene eller den andre ville ha sex uten, tror Ine og Miriam.

-På en måte er det fint at man kan sikre seg, iallfall nesten, mot uønsket graviditet bare ved å kjøpe en pillekur. Men egentlig synes jeg det blir litt for lettvint. Og angrepillen hjelper jo absolutt ingen ting mot kjønnssykdommer!

Norwegian girls explain their addiction to sex ... and an abortion on a whim.

Nordmenn har mest tilfeldig sex

National Norwegian newspaper Dagbladet discusses herpes and sexual pleasure in 2002.

Dagbladet.no
med MAGASINET

Kvinner kan vaksineres mot kjønnssykdommer

I tillegg til vaksine mot livmorhalskreft og kjønnsvorter, er en ny vaksine mot herpes under utvikling. Men vaksinen virker bare på kvinner.

LINN KATHRINE YTTERVIK

Fredag 29. november 2002 6:56, oppdatert 7:30

Dagbladet skrev i forrige uke om en nyutviklet vaksine som kan gi kvinner full beskyttelse mot livmorhalskreft. Vaksinen som er utarbeidet av en stor gruppe forskere fra universiteter i USA, er testet på 2000 kvinner og synes å være hundre prosent effektiv. Livmorhalskreft skyldes i hovedsak viruset humant papilloma virus (HPV). Et annet virus i samme familie forårsaker kjønnsvorter, dermed er vaksinen også effektiv mot dette. **Interessant**
I tillegg til vaksinen mot livmorhalskreft og kjønnsvorter, er en vaksine mot herpes på kjønnsorganer under utvikling. Vaksinen er foreløpig på et tidlig stadium. Over 10000 mennesker har blitt testet i blant annet Australia, USA, Storbritannia og Canada. Det er legemiddelfirmaet GlaxoSmithKlane som står bak forskningen på den nye vaksinen. Forskningssjef der, Lorna Knapstad, opplyser at vaksinen viser seg å ha beskyttende effekt mot herpes for 73 prosent av alle kvinnene som er testet. Hvorfor den bare har effekt på kvinner kan forskningen foreløpig ikke svare på. Vi skal nå i gang med å teste vaksinen randomisert på 7550 amerikanske kvinner mellom 18 og 30 år. I tillegg skal vi ha en like stor undersøkelse fordelt på Europa og USA hvor vi håper at Norge kan delta til neste år, forklarer Knapstad.

Smitte Rundt 20- 25 prosent av seksuelt aktive nordmenn har herpes. De fleste vet det ikke selv. Seksjonsoverlege ved generisk poliklinikk ved Haukeland sykehus, Turid Thune, sier at personer som har herpes like godt kan smitte andre, selv om de ikke har utbrudd selv.

- En herpesvaksine ville ha mye å si, spesielt for utlandet hvor det er et enda større problem enn i Norge. Det viser seg at hiv smitter lettere dersom du allerede har herpes. Derfor ville en vaksine ha mye å si for land med stor hivsmittefare, forklarer hun. Det er flest kvinner som har kjønnssykdommer, og når de først er smittet er de verst rammet. Ved å utvikle vaksiner som hjelper kvinner, hjelper vi også menn, sier hun. **Håp** Professor i hud- og kjønnssykdommer ved Olafiaklinikken i Oslo, Harald Moi, skal i dag i møte med forskningssjef Lorna Knapstad, for å vurdere om vaksinen skal testes ut på norske kvinner. Det er mange som har nedsatt livskvalitet på grunn av herpes, så det ville være bra med en vaksine mot sykdommen. Men dette er en vaksine som måtte gis til ungdom før de blir seksuelt aktive dersom den skulle ha en effekt. Det er mange hensyn å ta i forhold til bivirkninger, sier han.

Han mener den nye forskningen kan gi håp i utviklingen av hivvaksine og behandling av kreft.

Aftenposten

Sex toys replace Tupperware

Times have changed and Norwegian women seem fully liberated - how else to explain the success of the 'Condomery' (Kondomeriet), a "girl"-run business that has expanded operations to include home parties.

The Condomery is now fully run by women, which they feel might give them an edge in the male-dominated sex industry - since they have a better sense of how to keep a presentation of merchandise on the tasteful side of the slippery line towards vulgarity. The Condomery stocks more than an inventive range of male contraceptives, also offering oils, creams, sexy underwear and a range of toys and aids for men and women.

The concept has steadily grown in popularity in Norway, and as the average browser becomes more comfortable with the store's range, the girls behind the business have taken their shop on the road and into private homes.

The new home party is really just the evolution of the classic Tupperware evening.

"Many of us have had home demos of everything from make-up to plastic bowls. The principle is the same, but the products our consultants bring home to you are maybe a bit more exciting?" says Therese Warner, who heads the company's home party project.

Warner says that the atmosphere at these get-togethers is often giddy as a variety of toys, lubricants, and other fun items are passed around for the participants to examine.

Warner explains that they have used their 13 years of experience in the business to train consultants to make their presentations serious and educational, while at the same time positive and entertaining.

"Our 65 consultants have long waiting lists, with women of all ages who want to shop for sex toys in their living rooms," Warner said.

Since the service started in August this year turnover has increased by a factor of ten, and Warner expects to have 200 consultants ready to visit homes across the country in 2003.

Aftenposten English Web Desk
Jonathan Tisdall

Norway's leading daily Aftenposten, in its English language section in 2002, celebrates the fact of Norwegian women's fascination for sex toys.

Monday 23rd December 2002

Shock, sorrow and soul-searching follow ex-minister's death

Norwegian politicians and business leaders were among those still trying to come to grips Monday with the apparent suicide of former cabinet minister Tore Toenne over the weekend. One blamed the media, while others were re-examining their own roles in the controversy that swirled around Toenne this autumn.

Jens Ulltveit-Moe blamed newspaper Dagbladet for Toenne's apparent suicide.

PHOTO: CORNELIUS POPPE / SCANPIX

Industrial magnate Kjell Inge Roekke, who had made payments to Toenne that later landed him in trouble, broke his silence late Sunday by releasing a brief statement. Roekke and his industrial concern Aker Kvaerner, of which Toenne was a director, called Toenne's death "an incomprehensible tragedy" that left them "in deep sorrow." They offered sympathy and condolences to Toenne's widow, his two grown sons and his friends. Toenne's lawyer at the Oslo law firm BA-HR, which also has Roekke as a client, said he couldn't understand why Norway's white-collar crime unit (Okokrim) had opted to indict Toenne on fraud charges.Lawyer Olav Braaten, who has played a key role in the controversy around Toenne, claimed Toenne's acceptance of payments from Roekke after also having accepted state compensation during the same time period "may have broken some rules, but was unintentional." The payments were made through BA-HR and led to a conflict within the firm after their appropriateness was questioned.

The head of Norway's main employers' group (NHO), who was a friend of Toenne, claimed newspaper Dagbladet's coverage of the controversy drove Toenne to take his own life. Jens Ulltveit-Moe told newspaper Dagens Naeringsliv that Dagbladet's stories over the past few weeks amounted to "overkill," a position shared by NHO's former arch-rival, Yngve Haagensen, who recently retired as head of Norway's trade union federation (LO).

Haagensen noted that the media in Norway withholds the identity of people charged with murder, rape and most other crimes, while Toenne found himself splashed over the front pages.

Others, however, noted that Toenne clearly found his personal problems insurmountable. He was also a man surrounded with a vast network of resourceful, powerful and affluent friends, but that didn't seem to help.

"I've asked myself whether I could have done more (to help him)," said Labour Party leader Jens Stoltenberg, who, as prime minister, named Toenne to his cabinet.

That's something many others clearly were asking themselves as the country's holiday week got underway. ***Aftenposten English Web Desk Nina Berglund***

Former Norwegian cabinet minister commits suicide in 2002.

Aftenposten
NEWS FROM NORWAY
Monday 23rd December 2002

Law firm caught up in Toenne tragedy

BA-HR has ranked as one of Oslo's most powerful and prestigious law firms. Now Norway's white-collar crime unit has fined one its lawyers, others are directly involved in the controversy around the late Tore Toenne and businessman Kjell Inge Roekke, and the firm itself is grappling with serious internal conflict.

It's been a rough autumn for BA-HR. First one of its lawyers was linked to another scandal involving the now-defunct Finance Credit. Then the firm was ripped apart by a conflict between its managing director, its senior partner and ultimately its board, which in turn was tied to questionable payments the firm handled from Roekke to Toenne.

Toenne got word Friday that he was under indictment on fraud charges tied to the payments. He later disappeared and was found dead Saturday, in what police have ruled an apparent suicide.

Norway's white-collar crime unit (Okokrim), which indicted Toenne, also charged BA-HR lawyer Oyvind Eriksen with violating accounting rules. Eriksen allegedly submitted unspecified bills to Aker RGI Holding AS, controlled by Roekke and one of the firm's major clients.

Okokrim claimed the bills didn't adequately describe services rendered, which included consulting services delivered by Toenne in connection with Aker RGI's takeover of Kvaerner.

BA-HR, it's claimed, actually was billing Aker RGI on behalf of Toenne, not itself, even though that wasn't made clear. BA-HR later passed on NOK 1.5 million (about USD 200,000) it received from Roekke's Aker RGI to Toenne.

That payment sparked more trouble, because Toenne performed the consulting services while still receiving state severance pay after his government service ended. BA-HR's managing director questioned whether it was appropriate, and was later suspended amidst charges she was disloyal to the firm.

Eriksen of BA-HR has agreed to pay a fine of NOK 50,000 in connection with Okokrim's charges, and said he was sorry he hadn't properly specified the bill.

BA-HR's involvement in the Toenne case has raised questions about the firm, which counts the son of former prime minister Gro Harlem Brundtland among its partners.

Aftenposten English Web Desk
Nina Berglund

Norwegian law firm embroiled in suicide controversy of former cabinet minister.

Aftenposten
NEWS FROM NORWAY
Thursday 2nd January 2003

'Coincidence' that New Year's speeches both addressed bullying

Prime Minister Kjell Magne Bondevik said he had no idea King Harald would also take up the issue of bullying in his traditional New Year's speech to Norwegians. Both the king and the premier implored Norwegians to be nicer to one another.

King Harald opted to stand in his office while giving this year's traditional New Year's speech.

PHOTO: SCANPIX/ERLEND AAS

Prime Minister Kjell Magne Bondevik gave his speech while sitting behind his desk.

PHOTO: SCANPIX

"No, we didn't talk about our New Year's speeches beforehand," Bondevik told wire service NTB. "I wasn't aware he would focus on bullying until my speech was nearly finished." The king always makes his annual televised address on New Year's Eve in Norway, while the prime minister delivers his traditional speech on the evening of January 1.

King Harald used nearly his entire annual speech to decry the rising incidences of bullying both in the schools, in the workplace and among all age groups.

The somewhat unusual speech, delivered standing instead of sitting behind a desk, also urged Norwegians to treat each other with more respect. King Harald has seen the popularity of the monarchy itself fall off in recent years, while his son and daughter and their new controversial spouses also have been criticized and made fun of.

The prime minister, meanwhile, also urged Norwegians to stop bullying one another. Bondevik himself was the target of ridicule this year by television comedians, and also has had to tolerate intense political pressure as he tries to keep his coalition government intact.

Bondevik touched on several other issues in his speech, from the threat of war against Iraq to health care.

He also announced that Norway will launch new Peace Corps initiatives aimed at attracting both young volunteers and retirees to foreign aid work.

The prime minister's New Year's speech was nonetheless branded as "tame," and criticized for lacking any concrete measures.

"I had expected that he (Bondevik) would put forward more actual proposals," said Anders Folkestad, head of one of Norway's main educational organizations (UHO). "There are so many shortcomings in the public sector now."

Aslam Ashan of the Labour Party also was criticial. He said Bondevik's promises to tackle the bullying problem can't be realized as long as the local townships financing Norway's schools continue to suffer budget cutbacks.

"When there's not even enough resources in the communities to operate the schools in a proper way, I can't understand where the money will come from to finance an anti-bullying campaign," Ashand told wire service NTB.

Aftenposten English Web Desk
Nina Berglund

Norwegian King speaks out on bullying and depression.

btno
Forbruker

Nordmenn gjør det i fylla

Ikke uventet er nordmenn europamestere i å drikke seg fulle før en «one night stand». Mer overraskende er det, kanskje, at 76 prosent av italienere avstår fra alkohol før sex med ny partner.

NORGE «VERSTING»: Mer enn hver tredje nordmann var «litt» eller «skikkelig» full første gangen de hadde sex med en ny partner siste år, ifølge en undersøkelse. Det er en langt større andel enn i andre europeiske land.

ILLUSTRASJONSFOTO: IDA VON HANNO BAST

LENE SKOGSTRØM

Europeere oppfører seg nokså forskjellig før de hopper til køys med en ny «date». En ny undersøkelse basert på tall fra seksualvaneundersøkelser i fem europeiske land viser at inntak av alkohol før sex varierer sterkt.

Fullest i Norge

Andelen som hevdet at de var «skikkelig fulle» første gangen de hadde sex med en ny partner siste år, var desidert høyest i Norge. En av ti nordmenn svarte det, mot null i Italia og en knapp prosent i Sveits. Samlet svarte mer enn hver tredje nordmann at de hadde vært «litt» eller «skikkelig» fulle.

Men hvorfor drikker så mange nordmenn seg fulle før de har sex med en ny partner, mens italienere unngår kombinasjonen fyll og sex?

- Det har med drikkekultur å gjøre, mener Bente Træen, som er en av forskerne bak studien. I Italia og andre middelhavsland nytes alkohol som et dagligdags fenomen, men det er ikke sosialt akseptert å bli full. Å være voksen i disse landene betyr å kunne kontrollere sitt alkoholinntak.

«Blir voksen ...»

Machismo-rollen, som ofte er fremtredende blant menn i de latinske landene, gjør det viktig for menn å ta kontroll over sin drikking og seksualitet istedenfor å bli kontrollert av den. Å bruke kondom kan tolkes inn i macho-rollen som et tegn på at mannen har kontroll. Norske tenåringer ser derimot både det å drikke og bli full som et tegn på å bli voksen.

I alle de fem landene var alkoholbruk før samleie vanligst hvis man følte lite overfor partneren, og hvis de to hadde møtt hverandre samme dag. Andelen som sa de hadde drukket, men ikke var beruset er ganske lik mellom landene.

Sammenheng mellom alkoholbruk og kondombruk fant forskerne i tre av landene - Tyskland, Italia og Norge. Men med motsatt fortegn: Lettere drikking før sex henger sammen med økt kondombruk i Italia, mens det å drikke eller være beruset minsker sannsynligheten for å bruke kondom i Norge og Tyskland.

Liten kondombruk

Norge er for øvrig en versting også når det gjelder kondombruk: bare 38 prosent av nordmennene som hadde sex med ny partner brukte kondom, mot 72 prosent av grekerne. Forskerne forklarer dette med at kondombruk er en mer integrert del av livet til italienere og grekere enn til tyskere og nordmenn, blant annet fordi hiv er mer utbredt i disse landene.

- Vi skal være forsiktige med å se på alkohol og fyll som en direkte årsak til at folk har risikosex uten kondom. Det er ikke alkoholen som gjør at man «glemmer seg bort», det er mer slik at man aldri hadde tenkt på å bruke kondom i det hele tatt.

De bruker alkoholen som unnskyldning i ettertid for å gjenopprette troen på seg selv som kontrollerte og opplyste mennesker, mener Træen.

Publisert: 20. jan, 2003,06:00
Oppdatert: 21. jan, 17:33

Bergens Tidende newspaper gets in on the ‘sex is everything’ act.

Aftenposten
NEWS FROM NORWAY

New sex survey planned

Researchers are about to put Norwegian sex habits under the magnifying glass again. The latest study will also attempt to widen knowledge by better mapping self-image and homosexuality.

RELATED ARTICLES
Norwegians top list over 'one-night stands' - 26.11.02

This year's survey - the Norwegian Institute of Public Health examines Norwegian sex life every five years - will include a question on what people feel their sexual orientation is, and if they have ever had sex with a member of the same gender.

Researchers believe that the current number given by homosexual organizations – 5 percent homosexual population - is too high. Besides these new questions, the survey as a whole wants to know more than how, who, and how often.

"This is the first time that we try to discover the connection between self-image and sexual behavior in such a large survey in Norway," said Bente Traeen, head of the sexual habits investigation for the NIPH. "It is important to determine such connections if we are to hinder unwanted pregnancy, transmission of HIV and venereal disease in segments of the population," Traeen said.

The researchers believe that self-image and condom use are connected, with self-assured people more likely to insist on their use. The overconfident won't see any need to use condoms, they predict.Norwegians recently topped a survey of 22 countries around the world for number of one-night stands. A new European study fills in the picture even more, with Norwegians most likely to be drunk en route to their one-night stand. By contrast, no Italians felt the need to tank up before first-time sex with a partner.

"In Italy and other Mediterranean countries alcohol is a daily phenomenon, but it is not socially acceptable to be drunk. Norwegian teens on the other hand, associate drinking and being drunk with becoming an adult," Traeen said. A correlation between alcohol consumption and condom use was found in three countries - Germany, Italy and Norway. Again, the results were quite different. In Italy, some drinking before sex led to increased condom use, farther north, in Germany and Norway, boozing it up meant condoms were forgotten.

Traeen said that it was not necessarily the alcohol causing the forgetfulness, but rather drinking was often used as an excuse for loss of self-control for those who had no intention of using condoms anyway.

Aftenposten's Norwegian reporter
Lene Skogstrøm
Aftenposten English Web Desk
Jonathan Tisdall
Monday 20 January 2003

Sex-obsessed Norway?

En dildo uten begjær

Aftenposten
NEWS FROM NORWAY

Aftenposten newspaper in 2002 discuss the benefits of girls using a dildo

Signalrøde dildoer får ingen i 10A ved Høyenhall skole til å rødme. 16 åringer våger både å snakke og spørre om sex.

Sex og holdninger. En formiddag på Klinikk for seksuell opplysning avslutter et tverrfaglig prosjekt om seksualitet og holdninger for tiende klasse. For helt utlært i faget er de ikke ennå. Skjønt sex fremkaller ikke mer fnis og knis enn andre tema. I takt med seksualiseringen av alle produkter som skal selges til ungdom, så har ungdom selv fått et mer avslappet forhold til sex.

-De kan ganske mye, og de er mye tryggere enn før, sier klasseforstander Elisabeth Lillehagen. -Det er typisk at de kan mye om sitt eget kjønn og sex, men mindre om det motsatte kjønn. Det er i denne alderen de ofte går inn i langvarige parforhold, og da er det viktig at de vet hvordan de skal beskytte seg både

SCAN+ **Aftenposten** Lillehammer Turist

Friday 11 April 2003 NEWS FROM NORWAY Updated: 12 Mar, 11:43 (GMT+1)

Queen tells girls to fight sex pressure

Norway's Queen Sonja has thrown her support behind groups fighting widespread sexualization in today's society, and particularly how it results in sex pressure on ever-younger girls.

Queen Sonja attended the Anti-incest Support Center's (SMI) congress on sexuality and sexual assault on Tuesday, and clearly had strong feelings about the topic. "It is frightening that young girls, as young as 10-12, are influenced by the sexualized society they live in. Young girls must say no and define their own limits," Queen Sonja said.

The two-day congress will discuss both sexual assault on children, as well as the trickier issue of pervasive sexuality in all aspects of society, particularly the commercial sphere - examining sex as a tool in the advertising, media, fashion and music industries.

Queen Sonja has spent recent years supporting anti-incest groups and wants to help children be children during their early years, and shield them from things like kid's T-shirts flashing glittery messages like "Sexbabe" and "Fuck me I'm good".

"This is not about sexual candor, it is about sex sells. Pop stars and models bank on their body, image and sex. Young girls are influenced and would like to identify themselves with such role models. This is and will be wrong and society needs a counterweight to this development," said Miss Munchausen B. Grande of Save the Children's youth group PRESS.

Aftenposten's Norwegian reporter Wenche Fuglehaug
Aftenposten English Web Desk Jonathan Tisdall

Norwegian Queen on 'sex pressure'.

SCAN+

Aftenposten

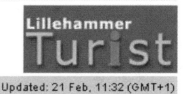

Lillehammer Turist

Friday 11 April 2003 NEWS FROM NORWAY Updated: 21 Feb, 11:32 (GMT+1)

Bosses prefer strip clubs

More and more Norwegian firms are dropping their traditional restaurant visits when entertaining employees or having company functions. The new trend in corporate entertainment is stripping, reports the Newspapers' News Agency (ANB).

"Our operation has had marked visits from business clients, and it is not just the male-dominated companies that book with us," said Atle Maaoe, manager of the Dreams Go Go bar and strip club in Trondheim.

According to Maaoe, stripping is well on its way to respectability in Norway. One Oslo strip club has gone so far as to specialize in major events for corporate gatherings.

Several Norwegian strip clubs rent out their artists to companies that want partial to full nudity at private shows at firm offices. Maaoe told the ANB that this is another type of corporate entertainment on the rise.

"Clients are companies in every category, which are also made up of men and women. Therefore we have to hire a staff of male strippers as well," Maaoe said.

Aftenposten English Web Desk
Jonathan Tisdall

Afternpoften 11 April 2003

Aftenposten on the attraction of strip clubs for Norwegian bosses.

SCAN+
Aftenposten
NEWS FROM NORWAY
Lillehammer Turist

First to choose chemical castration

For the first time in Norway two sex offenders have chosen to undergo chemical castration. The option has been a success in Denmark where 25 Danes have taken the hormone treatment and none have become repeat offenders.

According to Norwegian law the course of treatment - the drug Androcur - must be voluntary and cannot be part of punitive action. The hormone treatment reduces the production, concentration and effect of testosterone. If the drug is no longer taken the sexual drive returns to normal after a few months. "The treatment is based on voluntary participation from inmates convicted of crimes such as rape, incest, assaulting minors or exposing themselves," said Jim Aage Nøttestad, chief psychologist at the Brøset security division in South Trøndelag.

The Ministry of Justice and Police and the Directorate for Health and Social Services have given Brøset the assignment of establishing Norway's first hormone treatment program for those convicted of grave sexual crimes.

Convicts will receive a combined program of drugs and conversational therapy to help them understand why they carry out their attacks.

"This is an offer for people whose sexuality is not normal. It could apply to from five to 15 people a year," said Anne-Grete Kvanvig from Health and Social Services.

SCAN+
Aftenposten
NEWS FROM NORWAY
Lillehammer Turist

Litt mindre skråsikkerhet, takk

- Jeg hadde gjerne sett litt mer ydmykhet, sier generalsekretær Per Edgar Kokkvold i Norsk Presseforbund og tar plass i mindretallets rekker. Blant pressefolkene, i det minste.

PER EGIL HEGGE

Nå begrenser Bill Clinton og George W. Bush' jevnaldrende norske pressegeneral ikke sitt ønske til massemediene. Det er disse ekspertene også.

- De kunne da være litt mindre skråsikre? Det var en lettelse å høre Henrik Thune fra NUPI en kveld, hvor han gang på gang svarte at dette var det ikke mulig å svare på, eller han sa rett ut at han visste ikke.

De andre er så sikre. Det var de i 1991 også: Det var galt å gå til krig mot Saddam Hussein for å få ham ut av Kuwait. Det var galt å stanse folkemordet i Kosovo og Bosnia. Det var galt, og dessuten ville det aldri gå, å bombe Taliban ut av Afghanistan. Det var helt sikkert, og de var helt sikre.

- Men krigsmotstanderne kan jo ha rett denne gangen?

- Det kan de. Poenget er at vi vet ikke. Men det er vel ikke så overraskende at det er vanskeligere å drive Saddam Hussein ut av Bagdad enn å feie ham ut av Kuwait. Vel, de kaller seg krigsmotstandere. Problemet er at de konsekvent er motstandere av en type krig, nemlig når Vesten er involvert. Det kom ikke et pip fra dem da det avskyelige argentinske militærdiktaturet gikk til invasjon på Falklandsøyene, bare da britene gikk til aksjon for å drive dem ut. Ikke sa de stort om folkemordet i Bosnia eller Kosovo heller. Men da NATO grep inn og hindret Milosevic i å fullføre sitt folkemord - på muslimer, for øvrig - da protesterte de. Dette er en form for omvendt rasisme, og den er like motbydelig som den regelrette rasismen.

- Men pressen skal jo være kritisk, skal den ikke det?

- Vi skal ha en kritisk presse. Men det betyr ikke at vi utelukkende skal ha en USA-kritisk presse.

- Du vil ha førstesidebilder hvor folkemassene på to personer som står langs Iraks landeveier med nystrøkne amerikanske flagg som de har hatt liggende i skuffen siden 1991?

- Jeg sa nei takk til å være oppmann i en diskusjon mellom VG og Dagbladet om hvem som hadde blamert seg mest. Den førstesiden i VG - Kokkvold snakker om forrige ukes søndagsblemme hos naboen - blir jo stående. Og hvorfor i all verden kunne ikke VGs sjefredaktør da innrømme hva alle skjønner, nemlig at her ble det skivebom? Men nei da.

Beleilig influensa

Rett skal være rett, også for Kokkvold (i motsetning til alle oss andre i yrket) har det tatt litt tid før han begynte å innrømme feil. Men etter hvert har rørosingens lune sindighet presset seg opp gjennom arrogansens skurer som fjellyng på den karrige vidda. Og når verden går ham imot - og ofte når den slett ikke gjør det - drar han med hustruen på utflukt til det fjerne Karlstad, hvor han vet om et par storartede restauranter. Eller han dyrker sin hobby: Britisk politikk fra 1880-tallet til, nå ja, til i dag, sånn omtrent.

Spør ham om når han sist leste en britisk politikerbiografi, og han lyser opp fordi det viser seg at han var så svineheldig å ha en liten influensa nylig.

- Så da fikk jeg lest litt om Campbell Bannerman og Bonar Law og Lord Curzon og Stanley Baldwin.

- Nyttig kunnskap, sikkert?

- Ja. Hvis du leser biografier om politikere rundt 1900, og deres dagbøker, får du et gyldig og varig innblikk i hvordan politisk strid foregår. Det er et råd jeg fikk av Paul Johnson, som var redaktør i The New Statesman, og som siden er havnet på høyrefløyen.

- Disse britiske politikerbiografiene samler du på? - Nei. Det jeg samler på, er karikaturer fra Vanity Fair.

For yngre lesere skal det opplyses at Kokkvold snakker om det virkelige Vanity Fair, det som ifølge ham utkom i årene 1869-1913, ikke disse glorete moderne greiene med lett påkledte damer og rockeartister som innbyr til hoftefest.

- I en liten sidegate til Tottenham Court Road er det to bokhandlere som selger disse karikaturene. Der har jeg nok lagt igjen en del av min beskjedne formue.

- Det er du som holder dem gående?

- Vi er blitt riktig gode venner.

Så oppslukt er Kokkvold av alt som engelsk er, at man hører Røros-dialektens musikalske kadenser når han begynner å snakke om England og britisk politikk. Og når den siste nattevakt engang slukker hans anglofile lys, vil det mørkne rundt den siste norske pressemann som uten vanskelighet kan plassere Sir Henry Campbell Bannerman i kongerekken. (For ordens skyld, han var regjeringssjef fra 1905 til 1908).

Men bortsett fra at ingen kan vite hvilken kunnskap som kan komme til nytte, for journalister som for andre, så skal ingen beskylde generalsekretær Kokkvold for å neglisjere stoff som det mer umiddelbart kan bli bruk for.

- Jeg har hørt folk dosere på Journalisthøgskolen at det er en fordel for journalister ikke å kunne noe, ikke å vite noe, eller for mye, om det de skal fortelle om. For da stiller de med blanke ark, på samme nivå som leseren, og er ubundet av stoffet. Det skal visst finnes redaktører også som mener det. De er heldigvis på vei ut. For det ser man jo gang på gang: Hver gang en avis eller et annet massemedium har fremført noe som statsmakten eller andre maktinstanser ikke har likt, så har de gjort det på grunnlag av kunnskap, med den trygghet som kunnskap gir. Men journalister er blitt flinkere på ett punkt: De er blitt dyktigere til å skrive en ingress, altså en innledning, slik det skal gjøres. Det de er blitt mye dårligere til, det er å bruke vårt viktigste redskap, ordet. Jeg blir jo selv intervjuet i blant. Og det er altfor mange som ikke har respekt for ordenes valør, for det at du velger akkurat det ordet og ikke et annet. Når jeg kritiserer noe, får jeg noen ganger spørsmålet: Kan vi si at du raser? Da skriker jeg NEI NEI jeg RASER ikke! Det er for mange som har bestemt seg på forhånd hva slags sak de skal lage.

Dessuten har jo radio og TV en annen norm. De bruker lang tid på å finne ut hva du mener, og så tenker de seg om og så sier de at nei, da er det ikke interessant.

- Du har kanskje et program for journalistikk også, for hva det skal være?

- Vi skal stå på siden av makten, og vi skal kunne si at de har makten, men vi har ordet i vår makt. Og så pleier jeg å ty til en formulering av Olof Lagercrantz, den svenske forfatteren og journalisten, som sa at «journalistikk er fornuftens rastløse søken blant millioner av fakta». Det er jo det. Vi skal informere, avdekke og målbære holdninger. Jeg tror vi er blitt flinkere til å informere, flinkere til å avdekke også. Men vi er blitt dårligere til å ta standpunkt. Og standpunkter er en viktig del av den offentlige samtale. Partipressen er en saga blott, og jeg gråter ikke over det. Men utvikler det seg dit at vi ikke lenger ser forskjell på Aftenposten og Dagsavisen, er det en svekkelse.

Tilbake til ordet
Nå har det gått flere avsnitt uten at Kokkvold har nevnt en eneste engelskmann, så her kommer neste:

- Da C.P. Scott, den legendariske redaktøren i The Manchester Guardian, ble begravet, var det titusener av mennesker som fulgte hans båre. Hvor mange er det som følger norske redaktører til graven? Hehe.

- Det er vel ingen sammenstimling rundt liket av generalsekretærer heller. Hvor fælt var det å holde opp med å skrive?

- Jeg fortsatte jo litt, helt til i fjor, med en ukentlig spalte i Dagsavisen. Da mente jeg det var på tide å gi seg. Jeg kommer vel til å fortsette å skrive litt. Det er svært tilfredsstillende å skrive og kanskje synes at du får til noe, og så treffer du folk på gaten, helt vanlige folk som ikke har noe å tjene på at de skryter av deg, og som sier at dette var noe de hadde utbytte av. Jeg tror vi må tilbake til ordet. Og det må holdes ved like. Du vet jo hvor tregt det går når du skal ta fatt etter en lengre ferie.

- Så er det SKUP-utdeling for gravende og undersøkende journalistikk snart. Det er blitt noen bulker i SKUP-pokalene, er det ikke det?

- Det er jo et tankekors at ett av de journalistiske prosjekter som ville ha ligget på juryens bord under andre og mindre tragiske omstendigheter, er Tønne-saken. Dagbladet har vel hatt anstendighet nok til ikke å sende den inn som kandidat. Nå kommer i stedet Brurås-utvalget rapport om massemedienes håndtering av Tore Tønnes økonomiske forhold i mai. Det er en utredning som jeg tok initiativet til. Jeg mente at vi trengte en kritisk gjennomgåelse av den saken. Og jeg ble forbannet da jeg fikk høre at det bare var et PR-stunt, et brannslukningsforsøk. Det er helt naturlig at man foretar en granskning av medienes metoder. Og jeg mener at hver journalist må tvinges, tvinges,til å skjønne hva det koster å være i medienes søkelys. Ubehaget, frykten for at noe ufordelaktig blir kjent, den ligger i oss fra det norske bygdesamfunnet.

Så er det en ting til: Vi lever jo i revisjonismens tidsalder, det som blir satt høyt, det blir tatt ned igjen. Vi glemmer jo at beslutninger som var naturlige og fornuftige i sin samtid, ser annerledes ut i dag. Vi får stadig høre at det var merkelig at vi ikke nevnte at statsminister Gro Harlem Brundtland mistet sin sønn fordi han begikk selvmord, og at det ville ha vært annerledes i dag. Antagelig ville det ha blitt åpent omtalt i dag. Men vi skal huske at den eneste avisen som nevnte det, var Annonse

Søndag-Søndag. Og jeg går ikke med på at det var fordi man i akkurat den redaksjonen hadde høyere presseetiske kriterier enn andre steder.

Kokkvold skal på kontoret. Og så skal han hjem med Drøbak-bussen. Hvis han nå bare kunne få seg en aldri så liten forkjølelse til, så ble det nok tid til en britisk politikerbiografi i stabilt og ydmykt sideleie.

Litt mer stabilt enn ydmykt, kanskje.

Norway's head of the Press Complaints Commission, Per Edgar Kokkvold, in 2003. What a hypocrite.

SCAN+ Aftenposten NEWS FROM NORWAY Lillehammer Turist

Annual graduation debauchery looms

The notorious Norwegian tradition of celebrating the end of compulsory education with weeks of unrestrained dissipation before final exams is around the corner - and this year's crop vow ever wilder behavior, newspaper Dagsavisen reports.

Russ from Bergen making it clear that they defend their right to party.

The "russ" - final year students who traditionally wear red or blue overalls depending on their line of study - compete with each other in extreme drunken debauchery, with certain tasks earning them the right to add knots to dangle from their caps.

Some of the new tasks up for this year's knot-earning ritual are having sex with at least 17 partners, picking up a tender teen, getting a vagrant drunk and vomiting on the person next to you.

In Oslo's Manglerud district, the russ are ready.

"We are going to get as many knots as possible," Stine Hazeland told Dagsavisen.

"It's a sign of how crazy you have been. But I don't think I'll be able to earn more than 20 knots," Helene Fryys said.

According to a recent nationwide survey, half of this year's crop of russ rate earning cap knots an important part of the celebratory ritual. In Manglerud, they are determined but not fanatical.

"Sleeping with 17 people during the russ celebrations is a bit low - but I bet someone will do it," Fryys said.

Many of the male segment are convinced they will run naked through downtown Oslo, where schoolchildren of all ages parade every year to mark Norway's national day on May 17th.

Social anthropologist Allan Sande wrote his doctoral thesis on the russ phenomenon, and calls the tradition a transition ritual marking the passage to adulthood.

"It illustrates the passage from childhood to adulthood and one breaks rules to become an adult. They come to grips with taboos like sex and intoxication," Sande said. He isn't shocked by the latest wrinkles in the knot stakes.

"It is a form of ritualized play, very organized and regulated. The recognition of the one with most knots, the elite russ, reflects our career society - the knots can be compared to a résumé," Sande said.

While seven out of ten russ agree that the three-week party is a non-stop booze-fest, the traditional emphasis on earning recognition for swift and heavy drinking is gradually being replaced by an emphasis on sex.

Ethnologist Anne-Sofie Hjemdahl also sees this as a mirror of today's society.

"It is connected to the greater sexualization of society. Running naked down Karl Johan (Oslo's central, royal boulevard) would have been much more provocative 30 years ago. The taboos that the russ challenge are always changing," Hjemdahl said.

More babies have unmarried parents

Norwegian couples have long had a penchant for living together without being married. Now, for the first time, the majority of babies born in Norway are also being born out of wedlock.

Paal Nupen and Ragnhild Hvidsten don't see any pressing need to get married. They've lived together for four years and have two children, Tora, 2 and Fanny, five months.

PHOTO: TOR ERIK H MATHIESEN

"I've never been preoccupied with the symbolic ritual," Paal Nupen of Bergen told newspaper Aftenposten. He and Ragnhild Hvidsten are typical examples of the thousands of Norwegians who share a household and are raising a family without bothering to get married. A new study shows that just over half of all the babies born in Norway last year had unmarried parents. Even though Scandinavians in general have a long tradition of living together, the numbers show a marked societal change in the past 30 years.

In the 1970s, only 10 percent of all Norwegian babies were born out of wedlock. Last year, the figure had grown to 50.7 percent of the roughly 55,000 babies born in the country. The number of women opting to have children on their own also has grown significantly. In 2002, 9 percent of the babies born in Norway had single mothers, double the number 30 years ago. "The amount of children born out of wedlock has never been bigger, since birth statistics started being kept several centuries ago," said Lars Oestby, a researcher with the state Central Bureau of Statistics.

North versus south
In some areas of Norway, the percentage is even higher. In Nord-Troendelag, for example, 58 percent of all babies were born to unmarried parents. In the county of Nordland, the figure was 55 percent.

More traditional lifestyles were found in southern Norway. In Vest-Agder, which is also known for its religious sects, 25 percent of babies born in the country had unmarried parents. Only Iceland, Sweden and Estonia registered more births among unmarried mothers.Frode Thuen, a lifestyles researcher at the Hemil Center in Bergen, said marriage no longer marks the beginning of a life together for two people. "Now it's used more as a confirmation that two people want to live together, after testing out their relationship over time," he said.

Thuen also noted that couples who have children without being married remain three times as likely to break up than married couples are. Aasa Rytter Evensen, a local expert on lifestyles, said it was "unfortunate" that so many Norwegians have children without being married. "It's worrisome that people who choose to have children together don't dare to commit themselves more in relation to each other," she said. "The children risk growing up with less stability."

Aftenposten's Norwegian reporter
Haakon EH Eliassen
Aftenposten English Web Desk
Nina Berglund

More Horror Stories Emerge from Childrens Institution

More than 20 former residents of childrens' institutions in Oslo claim they were beaten, kicked and raped when living as juvenile wards of the state during the 1950s. They're demanding compensation for ruined lives.

Truls Braathen says there was rampant child abuse at this children's home in Oslo 50 years ago. He was a victim himself.

PHOTO: JAN TOMAS ESPEDAL

Their stories are the latest to emerge, following similar revelations from former residents of childrens' institutions around Bergen. Township officials recently agreed to compensate victims of child abuse and psychic terror with up to NOK 725,000 (about USD 100,000).

Now Oslo officials face similar claims. Truls Braathen, now 53, says he was placed in a juvenile institution (barnehjem) in Oslo's St Hanshaugen district at the age of two.

Five years of physical and psychic abuse followed. Braathen says staff members routinely beat and kicked children, often for minor infractions. He says he remembers staff binding his genitals for wetting the bed, while another time he was dangled from a second-floor balcony.

When he was seven, he says he was moved to another childrens' institution in Oslo and then the abuse got worse. He claims he and several other boys were repeatedly raped by a staff member who was supposed to take them on summer outings.

Braathen said he was always afraid to talk about the abuse, and knows of several other boys who committed suicide later in life, unable to cope with the psychological problems that resulted from years of abuse.

Braathen has written to city council leader Erling Lae revealing the abuse, while a national association is claiming NOK 500,000 on his behalf. Many of the former staff workers at the institutions are now deceased.

Orphanage scandal continues to grow

The now-grown-up residents of Norwegian orphanages, who have charged they were physically and sexually abused for years, are now also urging a full investigation of state-run boarding schools where they were placed later. The abuse continued there, they claim.

State and county officials have been trying for months to come to grips with the sudden torrent of charges that started being reported in earnest last year. Several investigations are underway into conditions at orphanages in the 1950s and 1960s.

Scores of former residents have gone public after Truls Braathen, now age 53, came forward with his story. "I can remember that I endured so many beatings," he said at a conference for victims of orphanage abuse this week. "I was thrown in a cellar, in dark rooms, and was forced to eat food that had been dipped in soapy water."

He told newspaper Dagsavisen that children in the city-run orphanage in Oslo where he grew up were also often forced to eat their own vomit and had their fingers squashed in doorframes.

Bjoerg Johansen (left), Jarl Eik and Arne Refstad are all former residents of Norwegian orphanages now seeking compensation for years of abuse. PHOTO: PAAL AUDESTAD

Newspaper Aftenposten reported that calls are also being made for investigations into the boarding schools where childrens' home residents were later placed. "These were isolated institutions where children lived and got instruction," says Ola Oedegaard, secretary general of the agency trying to further residents rights (Stiftelsen Rettferd for Taperne). "Here, the abuse was often worse."

He said his group has now registered more than 700 complaints from former residents of childrens' homes. Norway ran 59 boarding schools at one point, most of them in Oslo and Akershus. Oedegaard, who also was tormented at children's homes, said those run by Christian organizations were "the worst." He has said that much of the abuse was carried out "in God's name."

Aftenposten English Web Desk
Nina Berglund

Aftenposten
NEWS FROM NORWAY

Saturday 27 September 2003 | Updated: 25 Sep, 14:16 (GMT+1)

AFTENPOSTEN
English frontpage
Norwegian frontpage

NEWS
Local
Sports
Business
Press release

FEATURES
Webcams in Norway
Most-read stories
Readers respond

PICTURE SERIES

Arctic adventure

More photos from Norway

100 latest stories

WEBCAMS

See Norway live. See our webcams.

Most visited

Norway world leader in casual sex

Seven out of ten Norwegians have had a random sex partner and the country is a world leader in one-night stands. At the same time they are among the least sexually satisfied citizens in the world, according to the latest findings in the Durex Global Sex Survey for 2003.

Interviews of 150,000 people from 34 nations form the basis of the study released this week. The statistics provide a fascinating look into the different private habits around the world, and insight into what makes Norwegians warm all over.

In terms of sheer numbers, Norway was about average with 124 sex sessions a year, well behind winners Hungary with an active 152. Satisfaction was worse for Norwegians, with only 62 percent saying they were content with their sex life, placing them as low as 29th on the list.

Neighbor Denmark was even unhappier, ranking 30th in contentment. Swedes were even gloomier, only slightly more content but with a low average of 102 times a year.

What Norwegians are enthusiastic about is casual sex, with only Icelanders and Vietnamese more likely to collect one-night stands.

Other findings in the condom maker's study: 11 percent of Norwegians have paid for sex, 42 percent have had telephone or Internet sex, 10 percent have faked orgasms and 12 percent have had homosexual sex.

Norwegians lust after movie stars George Clooney, Vin Diesel and Halle Berry, and think that doctors and nurses represent the sexiest professions.

Aftenposten's Norwegian reporter
Line Kaspersen
Aftenposten English Web Desk
Jonathan Tisdall

Saturday 27 September 2003

Norway world leader in casual sex: And very proud of it too!

Aftenposten

Friday 03 October 2003 NEWS FROM NORWAY Updated: 30 Sep, 12:49 (GMT+1)

Norwegians least religious in Europe

A new study suggests that one in 10 Norwegians say they're not religious at all, while most say they're only moderately so. That makes Norwegians the least religious in Europe.

The survey, financed by the European Commission, asked respondents to rank how religious they were on a scale from zero to 10.

Only 9 percent of Norwegians questioned ranked themselves with an "8" or higher, reports newspaper *Vaart Land*.

None of the other 15 countries participating in the survey scored so low.

Norwegians also ranked low in church attendance. In Poland, on the other hand, half the population attends church services at least one a week, according to survey results. Greece, Ireland and Portugal also were on the other end of the scale from Norway.

Professor Harald Hegstad at the University of Oslo said Norwegians are "spiritually lazy." Earlier studies have suggested that while the vast majority of Norwegians are members of the state church because they're automatically born into it, only around 4 percent regularly attend church services.

"We have a sort of ritualized Christianity here that doesn't demand much of people," he said.

Aftenposten English Web Desk
Nina Berglund/NTB

Friday 3 October 2003

Aftenposten
NEWS FROM NORWAY

16 July 2003

Sex hot line calls worry operators

The telephone line to the Oslo Red Cross' sexual information service has been ringing off the hook lately, and the calls are alarming Red Cross workers. Some of the callers are as young as eight, and they're asking detailed and shocking questions.

"There's been a huge increase in specific questions about sex," says Tone Rustad Fagerhaug of the Red Cross. Youngsters are asking about oral sex, anal sex and group sex, and wondering whether it's normal.

"The children have either heard about people who have had such sex, they've read about it or maybe just heard the terms," Fagerhaug said. She thinks they call the Red Cross because they don't dare talk with anyone else.

The majority of callers are young girls, she said, adding that she thinks sexual pressure is greater than ever before.

"I think many are just curious, but some are also scared," Fagerhaug said. "It's disturbing that so many children and youngsters are thinking about these things.

"I think they're being forced into the adult world too early."

She says her staff is careful with its answers and mostly asks where they've heard of such things. "It's a tough balancing act between informing them and registering all this," she said.

Nina Olsen, a nurse in the public health department, said the department's web site also handles questions on sexuality. She blames the media, the Internet and music videos for introducing so many youngsters to sex so early.

"But I doubt they're really doing everything they're talking about," Olsen told newspaper Aftenposten Aften. "I think even the young set some limits."

Aftenposten
NEWS FROM NORWAY

23 October 2003

Norwegian women demand good sex

Norwegian women are the most optimistic in Europe, and among the most demanding when it comes to sex. A vast majority think a good man is far more important than their jobs, their friends or even children.

The conclusions appear in the latest issue of magazine "Elle," which sponsored a survey of 52,000 female readers aged 24-35 in 35 countries around the world.

Included in the survey, which was conducted by Sociovision of Paris, where "Elle" is based, were responses from 500 Norwegian women.

Fully 65 percent said they were optimistic about Norway's future, while 90 percent said they also were optimistic over the outlook for women and their own situation over the next two years. That's 10 to 20 percentage points higher than the response among other European women on average.

Some 91 percent of the Norwegian women questioned said they need to be sexually satisfied, compared to 75 percent of their European counterparts. A solid majority (84 percent) said fidelity in a relationship was important, while 75 percent said sex before marriage was absolutely necessary.

Norway leads world statistics in couples who live together without being married, while more babies now are born out of wedlock than within the confines of marriage.

The results contrast with those from Swedish women, of which a majority said the most important thing in their lives was to feel independent.

Aftenposten

NEWS FROM NORWAY

29th December 2003

Imams anger Bondevik

Norway's Prime Minister Kjell Magne Bondevik admits to being strongly provoked after a close look at Oslo imam Sohail Ahmed's criticism of Norwegian society as having a lack of fundamental values.

Bondevik told state broadcaster NRK that Ahmed's speech, which was broadcast on NRK's evening news, painted a biased view of Norwegian society.

Imam Ahmed, leader of the Idarah mosque in Oslo, emphasized the breakup of families, depression, psychological problems among children and HIV as manifestations of the lack of values in Norwegian society.

Bondevik appealed to Muslim communities to stop letting prejudice damage immigrant integration. "The power of the imams in immigrant communities is great which makes their message extremely important," said Bondevik to NRK.

"If we are going to achieve positive integration it is important that they learn more about the values on which our society is built. Perhaps then we can contribute something to each other instead of heading for a powerful confrontation, which this could easily lead to," said Bondevik.

Aftenposten English Web Desk
Jonathan Tisdall/NTB

Imams, when pointing out the obvious in 2003: that rampant promiscuity is not good for society, upset the Norwegian Prime Minister. Muslims eh! Who needs them?

Aftenposten
Saturday 13 March 2004 NEWS FROM NORWAY Updated: 12 Mar, 16:39 (GMT+1)

Suicide rate drops, but still 'too high'

Nearly 500 Norwegians committed suicide in 2002, with 362 men and 132 women opting to take their own lives. That's down 10 percent from the year before, but officials worry it's still too high.

Einfrid Halvorsen, secretary general of the organization Mental Health, told news bureau NTB Friday that the number of suicides remains nearly double that of traffic fatalities. "The number is at any rate quite high," she said.

Professor Lars Mehlum, who leads a suicide research and prevention unit at the University of Oslo, is nonetheless encouraged by the decline in suicides. The most recent statistics are the lowest since 1979.

"It confirms a trend we've seen for a few years now," he said. "The decline comes after a long period in the 1970s and 1980s when we saw an increase every year."

Suicide remains a delicate subject in Norway, and they're generally not reported in local media. When they are, it's nearly always written that the victim simply was "found dead" or that the death was "a personal tragedy." It's almost never written that the victim was believed to have committed suicide.

When former Prime Minister Gro Harlem Brundtland's own son committed suicide in the early 1990s, none of the major newspaper or broadcast channels reported it. Only years later, when the suicide proved to have political consequences and Brundtland's husband wrote about it himself, did the incident start to be publicly discussed.

There have been efforts to increase openness around suicides, with varying success. Halvorsen said she thinks suicide prevention efforts and better psychiatric health offers have contributed to the decline.

Norway's suicide statistics rank in the middle compared to other European countries'. Mehlum said several other countries, especially those in the former Eastern Europe, have higher rates, while other countries have lower rates.

Aftenposten English Web Desk
Nina Berglund/NTB

Aftenposten

NEWS FROM NORWAY

Saturday October 22 2005

First published: 20 Apr 2004, 10:56

AFTENPOSTEN
English frontpage
Norwegian frontpage

NEWS
Latest 100 stories
Press release

FEATURES
Only in Norway
Picture series
Norway's Centennial
The Royals
Webcams in Norway
Readers respond

PICTURE SERIES

Norway's 'Structure of the Century'

100 latest stories

WEBCAMS

See Norway live. See our webcams.

Most visited
- Tromsø: torget
- Oslo: Aker Brygge
- Honningsvåg havn
- Oslo havn - Vippetangen
- Oslo: Tryvann
- Tolga
- Bodø: småbåthavna
- Oslo: Frognerseteren
- Ny Hellesund

Graduating 'russ' in new porno shock

A group of Norway's hard-partying graduates known as the *russ* have now managed to shock even their own organizers: 26 girls from two Oslo high schools agreed to take part in a porno film to finance the bus that's an integral part of their spring party season. Two of the girls are even performing sex scenes n the film.

Officials at the two schools, along with fellow graduates who form the *russ'* governing board, are incredulous and shocked after being told about the girls' porno film participation by a reporter from newspaper VG.

"This sounds really sick," said Aleksander Diesen, who's been functioning as president of the *russ* in Oslo and Akershus.

Diesen doesn't deny that it's expensive to acquire and operate a so-called "russ-bus," which are painted red or blue, equipped with sofas and powerful stereo systems, and serve as "party-mobiles" for the graduating students throughout the spring. There's also no denying that the *russ* are known for flaunting rules associated with good behaviour.

For years, graduating Norwegian students like these from long ago have ridden around in brightly colored cars and buses to celebrate the end of school and party with abandon. This year's "porno bus" deal takes the *russ'* debauchery to a new level.

PHOTO: SCANPIX

RELATED STORIES:
- 'Russ' banned from royal visit - 29.03.2004
- Picture Story: 'Russ bus' ablaze -
- Graduating 'russ' went wild in Oslo -
- Safe sex for reveling teens -
- Annual graduation debauchery looms -

▸ Partying students get mornings 'off' -

But Diesen and the principals of the two schools involved (neither of which was identified) are bashing the porno film project. "This is terrible, one of the most hair-raising incidents I've run into," one of the principals told VG. "Let there be no doubt that we'll take this up with those involved."

The film will reportedly feature the Norwegian porno actor Thomas Rocco Hansen, and shooting will take place within and around the girls' bus. The girls also have agreed to be interviewed about their sexual habits and fantasies. For that, Rocco and another sponsor will pay the girls NOK 20,000 (about USD 3,000).

"We're in an economic squeeze and I'm doing this for my friends," said one of the girls, age 18, who also has agreed to perform a sex scene in the film. "I felt one of us had to do the scene, because then we'll get even more money for the bus."

She said their bus cost NOK 130,000. They've also needed to pay NOK 25,000 for repairs to it, NOK 50,000 for its stereo system, NOK 20,000 for its driver, nearly NOK 10,000 for the bus' interior improvements and another NOK 10,000 for fuel.

In addition come expenses for their *russ* clothing (featuring red or blue overalls with accessories), party passes, food and drink during the hectic party season.

One of the 26 girls involved called the porno film deal "pure business" to offset the worrisome costs of being *russ,* and then admitted it was was "a bit cool" to be known as "the porno bus." But, she said, "we are a bit afraid of what our parents will think."

Aftenposten English Web Desk
Nina Berglund

ANNONSE

Aftenposten

Saturday October 22 2005 NEWS FROM NORWAY First published: 18 Jun 2004, 14:03

Norway's 'Structure of the Century'

See Norway live.See our webcams.

Sex merit badge on offer

Young Norwegians can earn a merit badge in sex this summer. The pin, modeled on a popular summer swimming merit badge, is an offer from Swedish-Norwegian sex education group RFSU, also the main producer and importer of condoms to Norway, newspaper VG reports.

The badge, which displays sperm cells swimming in waves, can be won by correctly answering 10 out of 13 questions about sex.

"You need a license to drive a car and you should have a sex certificate that shows you don't take health risks. This is done seriously and with humor and the goal of course is to get more people using condoms," said RFSU manager Tone-Berit Lintho.

The summer is also high season for sex and sexually transmitted diseases and the RFSU specializes in attention-getting campaigns to promote safe sex.

A recent survey of this year's 'russ' - the reveling high school graduates who go wild for three weeks of debauchery before final exams - revealed the teenagers have a lot to learn.

* While 75 percent of Norwegian youngsters are positive towards condom use, only 1 in 5 actually used them when last having sex.

* Fully 90 percent of Norwegian boys believe 'no' means 'maybe'.

* Three out of four youths put the condom on incorrectly and many bite open the package, creating the danger of condom puncture.

Contraction of venereal diseases and HIV reached a new high last year, and an average of 45 Norwegians a day contracted chlamydia.

Aftenposten English Web Desk
Jonathan Tisdall

Aftenposten
NEWS FROM NORWAY

Saturday October 22 2005

First published: 20 Sep 2005, 10:54

Psychiatric problems plague one of four Norwegians

Norway seems to be offering living proof that money can't buy happiness. The country often is referred to as among the world's wealthiest, and the best place to live, but a new study indicates that 25 percent of the adult population falls mentally ill every year.

The study, conducted by the Psychiatric Institute at the University of Oslo, is based on data collected by health authorities in eastern Norway.

Norwegian Prime Minister Kjell Magne Bondevik has been among those seeking psychiatric help, after being diagnosed with a "depressive reaction" during his first term in the late 1990s. He and other government officials have been calling for more openness and funding for mental health programs.
PHOTO: JON HAUGE

The amount of people seeking psychiatric treatment amounts to 25 percent of all adult Norwegians. Another 450,000 Norwegians are believed to suffer psychiatric problems, but don't bother visiting a doctor.

Anxiety and depression are the most common ailments, reported Norwegian Broadcasting (NRK) on Tuesday morning.

"The health authorities and the population itself is having great difficulty comprehending the enormous amount of psychiatric problems, and the enormous need for treatment that exists," Professor Per Høglend, who led the study, told NRK.

The study results come just days after newspaper *Dagens Næringsliv* ran a front-page story hailing Norway as "the richest country of all time" based on its foreign trade surplus and balance of payments. Norway's oil wealth continues to fuel its economy, but it's clear that not everyone is enjoying the results.

On the same day, newspaper *Dagsavisen* ran a front-page story noting how local crisis telephone lines were ringing off the hook with people seeking help. "We can't manage to answer more than 50 percent of the calls," said Mette Kammen of Mental Helse.

Paradox

It's clearly a paradox, and the question is why so many Norwegians are so unhappy. There's always the old clichés about Norway's long, dark winters, but one expert suggests the threshold for identifying someone with a problem as "depressed" has been lowered, and that people are more willing to seek professional counselling.

She also cited a reluctance by many Norwegians to openly discuss relatively common problems such as grief, divorce or the loss of a job with friends or family. A high percentage of Norwegians live alone, and loneliness is a problem in itself.

"There are lots of lonely people around the country, without a social network," said Kammen. "Many just need someone to talk to."

Aftenposten English Web Desk
Nina Berglund/NTB

AFTENPOSTEN
English frontpage
Norwegian frontpage

NEWS
Latest 100 stories
Press release

FEATURES
Only in Norway
Picture series
Norway's Centennial
The Royals
Webcams in Norway
Readers respond

PICTURE SERIES

Norway's 'Structure of the Century'

100 latest stories

WEBCAMS

See Norway live. See our webcams.

Most visited
- Tromsø: torget
- Oslo: Aker Brygge
- Honningsvåg havn
- Oslo havn - Vippetangen
- Oslo: Tryvann
- Tolga
- Bodø: småbåthavna
- Oslo: Frognerseteren
- Ny Hellesund
- Beitostølen

TO THE CAMERAS

SEARCH
News in english:
Search for | Search
How to search

INFO
About the newsdesk
Contact us
Advertising info
Rate calculator
Advertising contacts

IN NORWEGIAN
Innenriks (local)
Utenriks (world)
Økonomi (business)
Sport (sports)
Subscribe
Weather
TV-guide
Streetmap

Now there's a surprise!
(It should of course say: 'One in four Norwegians' in the heading).

ANNONSE

Aftenposten

NEWS FROM NORWAY

Saturday October 22 2005

First published: 28 Sep 2005, 12:50

AFTENPOSTEN
English frontpage
Norwegian frontpage

NEWS
Latest 100 stories
Press release

FEATURES
Only in Norway
Picture series
Norway's Centennial
The Royals
Webcams in Norway
Readers respond

PICTURE SERIES

Norway's 'Structure of the Century'

100 latest stories

Girls on drugs

Nearly 3000 girls between the ages of 15 to 19 were prescribed antidepressants last year and experts warn of an increased risk of suicide.

RELATED STORIES:
- Pills cause more traffic deaths than alcohol - 01.04.2004
- Drugs-related deaths soar in Norway -

The Norwegian Medicines Agency (SLV) warns that antidepressant drugs are considered to pose a heightened risk for suicide attempts after a recent European study by the EMEA (European Agency for the Evaluation of Medicinal Products).

A new survey from the Norwegian Institute of Public Health revealed that the use of such medication is now widespread in Norway. Over two percent of girls aged 15-19 take antidepressants and a total of 116,240 women and 56,553 men were prescribed such drugs in 2004, newspaper *Vårt Land* reports.

The use of such pill increases with age, with 4.4 percent of women in the 20-29 age bracket taking such drugs in 2004 and fully 13.3 percent of women aged 60-69 took antidepressants last year.

The SLV noted that patients who wish to stop taking such medication should contact their physician first, as use of antidepressants should be gradually phased out.

(Aftenposten English Web Desk/NTB)

SHOWDOWN IN PARIS

Uefa red card for 'stupid' official caught in shirt row

By Nick Szczepanik

WHEN referees' assistants make the news, it is usually for the wrong reasons, as Ole Hermann Borgan will have cause to reflect when he sits down to watch the Champions League final this evening.

Borgan should have been running the line in the Stade de France but was replaced by Uefa last night after a photograph of him wearing a Barcelona shirt appeared in his local newspaper in Norway.

Borgan, 41, a sales manager from Drammen, 25 miles southwest of Oslo, said that he had been "stupid" to allow the photograph to be published and protested that he had no loyalty to the Catalan club, but to no avail. Arild Sundet, Borgan's compatriot, will fly to Paris this morning to take his place.

According to Per Jan Brekke, the Sports Editor of *Drammens Tidende*, the plan had been for Borgan to wear Arsenal and Barcelona shirts for a photo shoot. Although it was discovered that no Arsenal jersey was available, the shot of the official sporting the blue-and-maroon top of their opponents still found its way into yesterday's edition of the paper.

"It was both insensitive and stupid of me," Borgan said. "I didn't think the situation and consequences through when I was asked to put on the shirt. The newspaper asked if I had both uniforms, Barcelona and Arsenal. I said, 'No, I don't. I only have the Barcelona one'. I didn't think any more about it until I started getting phone calls early this morning. I don't have either Barcelona or Arsenal as a favourite team."

Arsène Wenger, the Arsenal manager, and Frank Rijkaard, the head coach of Barcelona, had played down the significance of the photograph, but Uefa, perhaps extra-sensitive in view of recent allegations about corruption involving referees in Italy, felt that it had no choice but to replace Borgan. What is more surprising is that such an experienced official agreed to the photo shoot.

The all-Norwegian team of Terje Hauge, the referee, Borgan and Steinar Holvik, who were due to officiate tonight, had worked together on many occasions, including at the 2004 European Championship finals in Portugal.

MARC ASPLAND

Wenger: - Beklagelig flause

Out of line: Borgan, the Norwegian assistant referee, left, looks on at a meeting of officials before he lost his place for the final after pictures of him in a Barcelona shirt were published in his local newspaper, above

Borgan's gaffe was embarrassing for his colleagues and his national association. "It was not very smart of him to pose with one of the teams' shirts ahead of the final," Hauge said. "It was a stupid thing to do, but I can assure you that he did it in pure joy at being chosen to take part in this event. It does not mean he is a Barça fan."

Rune Pedersen, Norway's head of refereeing, was nonplussed. "There is an unwritten rule that officials must not do anything which will cast doubt on their impartiality," he said.

Borgan is not, however, a stranger to controversy. He was assisting Hauge at Stamford Bridge this season when the officials attracted the ire of José Mourinho, the Chelsea manager, after Barcelona's 2-1 victory in the first leg of the Champions League tie during which Asier Del Horno, the Chelsea defender, was sent off.

THE TIMES 17 May 2006

Aftenposten
NEWS FROM NORWAY
Friday January 12 2007
First published: 09 Jan 2007, 12:47

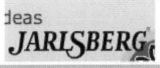

Young women opt for abortion

More than half of ethnic Norwegian women under age 25 choose abortion if they get pregnant, according to a new study. The professor behind the study calls the statistic "surprising" and "worrisome."

This group of student advocates understands why young women often opt for abortion if they get pregnant.

PHOTO: JON-ARE BERG-JACOBSEN

A woman's right to choose abortion is deeply engrained in Norwegian society, but it's only most common among young women and women with little education, says Professor Anne Eskild of Akershus University Hospital.

Eskild's study marked the first time that researchers tracked the incidence of abortions and births among ethnic Norwegian women. Results showed major differences between those who chose to abort and those who chose to give birth.

More than half of pregnant women under 25 chose abortion, a rate double that for pregnant women over 40. The abortion rate for women under age 20 was nine times higher than that for women over 40.

Only 2.9 percent of women with a university education chose abortion, according to the study.

"It's very surprising that it's more common for women under 25 to have an abortion than it is to carry out their pregnancy," Eskild told newspaper *Aftenposten*. She was responsible for the study that been published in the medical journal *Acta Obstetricia et Gynecologica Scandinavica*.

She questioned whether Norway's generous maternity benefits may in fact be to blame, since the benefits are based on a woman's income at the time she gives birth. Many women under age 25 are still students, and don't qualify for the benefits available later in life.

Others cite economic concerns, dreams for the future, career and self-realization as reasons why young women opt against having children.

Aftenposten's reporter
Anne Hafstad

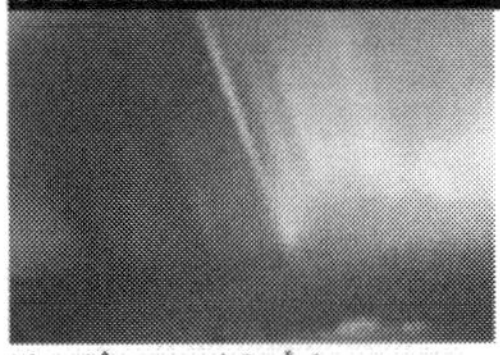

Northern Lights over Oslo

ANNONSE ▼

Aftenposten

NEWS FROM NORWAY

JARLSBERG

Friday February 23 2007

First published: 05 Feb 2007, 10:55

AFTENPOSTEN
English frontpage
Norwegian frontpage

NEWS
Latest 100 stories
Press release

FEATURES
Only in Norway
Picture series
Norway's Centennial
The Royals
Webcams in Norway
Readers respond

PICTURE SERIES

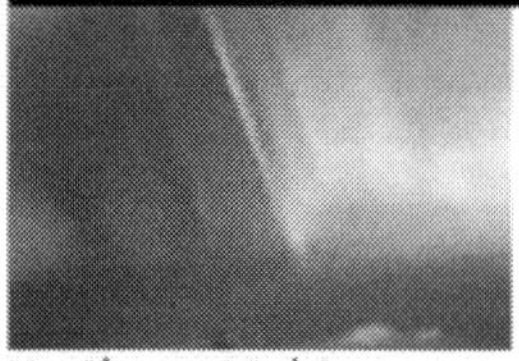

Northern Lights over Oslo

100 latest stories

WEBCAMS

See Norway live. See our webcams.

Most visited

- Oslo: Frognerseteren
- Oslo havn - Vippetangen
- Kristiansand: festningen
- Oslo: Aker Brygge
- Oslo: Youngstorget
- Oslo havn
- Tromsø: torget
- Molde
- Oslo: Bjørvika
- Ålesund: Fjellstua

Soaring suicide rate

Over a recent ten year period the number of young girls who have attempted suicide in Norway has risen nearly 30 percent.

RELATED STORIES:

- Low blood pressure linked to depression - 24.01.2007
- Psychiatric problems plague one of four Norwegians - 20.09.2005
- Healthy, wealthy and sad - 03.02.2005

This trend was uncovered by a study, Young in Norway, carried out by Norwegian Social Research (NOVA) studied the time period 1992-2002 and concluded that psychological problems are growing worse.

"I can say with my hand on my heart that this was a surprise. I would not have believed there were so many suffering," Professor Lars Wichstrøm of the Norwegian University of Science and Technology (NTNU) told newspaper *Dagsavisen*.

He believes the increase in suicide attempts among girls can be linked to increased substance abuse, particularly alcohol, conflicts while under the influence and serious arguments with parents.

Heidi-Wibeke Bakkland of Young Mental Health sees alternative explanations, such as prestige at school and among friends as concerns that can wear down a young person mentally.

"You must have the right clothes, a lot of friends and top grades. You should be something. I think the young need to have more information about mental health," Bakkland said.

Research in several European countries indicates that Norway is not alone in witnessing an increase in the young committing suicide attempts.

NOVA also found a marked increase in the number of youth with depressive symptoms, especially boys. Twice as many boys were depressed in 2002 compared to 1992.

Substance abuse, weight problems, and dissatisfaction with appearance can be contributing factors, Wichstrøm believes.

(Aftenposten English Web Desk/NTB)

Aftenposten
NEWS FROM NORWAY

JARLSBERG

Saturday April 28 2007

First published: 25 Apr 2007, 11:35

Winter's last hurrah

Women to blame

Every other Norwegian man believes that flirtatious women have themselves to blame if they are raped.

The shock results appear in a report compiled by Amnesty in cooperation with Reform - resource center for men.

Nearly half of men surveyed felt that open flirtation was an invitation to sexual assault.

PHOTO: JOHNNY SYVERSEN

RELATED STORIES:
- Sex threats abound - 26.04.2007

One in five men surveyed said that a woman known to have several partners is fully or partly responsible if sexually assaulted, and 28 percent believed that a woman who dresses sexily is wholly or partly responsible for a sexual assault.

"I think the results of this study are frightening. I am the father of a teenage girl. It is disturbing to see that Norwegian men believe she is responsible if she should be assaulted after flirting with a man," John Peder Egenæs, secretary general of Amnesty International Norway told newspaper VG.

Fully 48 percent of those surveyed believe that women are fully or partly responsible for a sexual assault if they openly flirt before the attack.

"It is unacceptable to blame women who have been exposed to sexual assault and violence. This confirms that female-hostile attitudes are alive and well," said victim's legal counsel Trine Rjukan.

Prime Minister Jens Stoltenberg said he was disappointed over Norwegian men's attitude towards women and found the study's results frightening.

"I had hoped and believed that we had come further than that in terms of men's view of violence against women," Stoltenberg said.

(Aftenposten English Web Desk/NTB)

Aftenposten
NEWS FROM NORWAY
Friday 10 January 2003

Coach denies sexual harassment charges

The coach of soccer club Aalesund conceded Friday that sex was among topics discussed in a meeting he had with the agent mother of soccer players John Arne and Bjoern Helge Riise. But he denies her charge, made on national TV Thursday night, that he sexually harassed her.

Berit Riise used a live TV2 program to level serious charges against soccer club Aalesund and its coach, Ivar Morten Normark.

PHOTO: ARNFINN MAUREN

"This has been completely taken out of context," coach Ivar Morten Normark told newspaper VG Friday. He claims he was only joking when he tried to tell Berit Riise what Norway's soccer community thought of her.

"I told her how my acquaintances view her, and that it wasn't always positive," Normark said.

He claimed there are always two questions soccer players and officials get when they say they're from Aalesund: "Do you know Berit Riise, and how many times have you had sex with her?"

Riise claims Normark sexually harassed her during the conversation, which took place during the summer of 2001, and that she's had problems ever since. Riise is perhaps Norway's ultimate "soccer mom." She's worked as agent for her sons John Arne, who now plays professionally for Liverpool, and Bjoern Helge, who has been having a troublesome transfer to soccer club Cardiff.

Her charges came out of the blue during a televised debate on Bjoern Arne's move, shocking both those on the TV2 show and viewers as well.

Bjoern Arne has played for Aalesund's B team, which Riise claims has caused trouble by demanding money when Bjoern Arne tried to transfer first to Manchester City and then to Cardiff. A debate on the topic with Aalesund chairman Arne Aambakk took an abrupt turn when Riise started yelling at him during the broadcast and demanded he "tell the truth." She then leveled her sexual harassment charges. Club management said they'd hold a meeting Friday to discuss Riise's charges.

Aftenposten English Web Desk
Nina Berglund

Aftenposten

NEWS FROM NORWAY

Drapstrusler mot Berit Riise

Berit Riise har mottatt drapstrusler etter at hun gikk ut i debattprogrammet Tabloid og beskyldte Aalesund-trener Normark for sextrakassering.

På FK Aalesunds hjemmesider på internett er det framsatt så alvorlige trusler mot Berit Riise at politiet er koblet inn i saken. Politiet ser også alvorlig på drapstruslene og har satt ut vakt ved familiens Riises hus i Ålesund.

- Jeg tar disse truslene veldig alvorlig, sier en rystet og nedbrutt Berit Riise til NTB.

Hun bestemte seg også for å koble kjendisadvokat Tor Erling Staff på saken fredag formiddag, men det skjedde ikke før injurieadvokat Per Danielsen gikk ut og mente at den typen injurier det her er snakk om kan straffes med fengsel inntil to år.

Etter påstanden om at hun kunne risikere så lang fengselsstraff dersom FK Aalesund går til sak mot henne følte Berit Riise behov for juridisk bistand.

Hun skal i møte med Staff senere fredag for å gjennomgå hele saken.

FK Aalesunds ledelse satt også i møte fredag for å bestemme seg for hva klubben skal gjøre i etterkant av de saftige beskyldningene om sextrakassering Berit Riise kom med under torsdagens TV-program og som var rettet mot trener Ivar Morten Normark.

(NTB) 10/01/03

Aftenposten
NEWS FROM NORWAY

- Kan aldri forhindre utbrudd på direkten

Generalsekretær i Norsk Presseforbund Per Edgar Kokkvold mener at beskyldninger og utbrudd er en risiko man må leve med så lenge man har direktesendinger i fjernsyn.

- Det er alltid en risiko med direktesendinger. Alt er avhengig av hvilke personer som deltar, hva som er tema og hvilken temperatur det er i programmet, sier Per Edgar Kokkvold i Norsk Presseforbund i NTB. Men han ønsker ikke en begrensning av hva man kan si i direktesendte program.

- Ytringsfriheten har sin pris, sier han.

Kokkvold mener også at TV2 handlet helt riktig da Berit Riise helt overraskende på direkten beskyldte Aalesund-trender Ivar Morten Nordmark seksuell trakassering av henne. Debatten dreide seg egentlig om hennes sønn Bjørn Helge Riises fotballfremtid.

- Programleder Pål T. Jørgensen maktet å snu debatten over på det opprinnelige tema før det hele utartet, sier Kokkvold.

Han ønsker ikke å kommentere Riise-saken direkte, men påpeker at man alltid bør være forsiktig med å komme med beskyldninger av en slik følelsesmessig art som det fremkom i programmet.

(NTB) 10/01/03

Berit Riise, mother of Liverpool footballer Jon Arne Riise, put herself about apparently. In the end she made peace with the Aalesund football coach.

- Sex-påstandene kan gi to års fengsel

Av ELISABETH BREIEN ELLINGSEN

(VG Nett) Advokat og injurieekspert Per Danielsen mener Berit Riise har opptrådt ulovlig uansett om påstandene om sex-sjikane er sanne eller usanne. Strafferammen er inntil 2 års fengsel.

PROBLEMER: Advokat Per Danielsen mener at Berit Riise er ille ute hvis Ivar Morten Normark bestemmer seg for å gå til sak.

Foto: Espen Sjølingstad Hoen

Advokat Per Danielsen arbeider mye med saker som omfatter injurier i media. Han hoppet i stolen da han hørte Berit Riises påstander om sex-trakassering i «Tabloid» torsdag kveld.

- Hun har klart opptrådt ulovlig. Et klarere eksempel på bokstavelig sagt et «slag under beltestedet» er vanskelig å finne, sier Danielsen til VG Nett.

Private forhold

- Det er utilbørlig uansett om det er sant eller ikke, og det rammes av en spesiell bestemmelse i injurielovgivningen. Det er fremsatt beskyldninger om private forhold på TV. Uansett hvem som har rett om hva som skjedde her, så skal ikke slike beskyldninger fremsettes for åpen scene, sier Danielsen.

Han sier at overtredelse kan straffes med inntil to års fengsel, og det kan kreves oppreisning for tort og svie i tillegg.

- Hun vet hva hun har sagt og forsterker det etterpå i intervju med VG. Noe som gjør det verre, sier injurieeksperten.

- Riise har et stort problem hvis Ivar Morten Normark bestemmer seg for å gå til sak, mener Per Danielsen.

Ledelsen i Aalesund FK vil vurderere i ettermiddag om de skal gå til sak mot Berit Riise. Aalesund-leder Arne Aambakk sier til VG Nett at de venter på en unnskyldning fra Berit Riise. Les mer her.

TV 2 uten skyld

Advokat Per Danielsen mener at TV 2 ikke kan lastes for at beskyldningene gikk direkte ut i norske hjem.

- TV 2 har ikke noe juridisk ansvar for det som skjer på direkten. Det finnes et unntak i loven som gjelder nettopp direktesendinger på TV. Programleder Pål T. Jørgensen opptrådte korrekt, sier Danielsen.

Pål T. Jørgensen sier til VG Nett at uttalelsene kom som lynet, og at han stanset debatten da Normarks navn ble nevnt. Les mer her.

(VG NETT 10.01.03 kl. 11:38)

Norwegian Ex – Prime Minister, Mrs Brundtland's Sadness

[redacted]. "Some people in Norway think that we can stand alone up here," she chides. "They are stuck in their ways, suspicious of the outside world and scared of change. They don't think ahead. That really will not do."

The Prime Minister's private life has been less happy than her public one. Two years ago, her eldest son committed suicide, and a diplomat daughter had to return home recently from Copenhagen after a nervous breakdown. Her husband, Arne, is an unexciting political scientist who ditched his own conservative allegiance for the sake of his wife's career. "In the Brundtland household," goes one lugubrious Norwegian joke, "you laugh next week."

Despite her doughty feminism, she admits that the balance between family and public life has evaded her: even in a country where the Foreign Minister's campaign photograph shows him at home, ironing his own shirt for the next day. "There simply isn't time to be a mother, a wife and a politician," says Mrs Brundtland briskly. "I like being a politician best."

(LONDON) EVENING STANDARD 12/3/99 John Ronson

Who wants to be a Norwegian?

IN NORWAY, they are currently encouraging couples to copulate, right this instant, so the country can get itself on the map as the land that bore the first baby of the new millennium.

Erotic movies are being shown free of charge in cinemas, and one can attend a hotel afterwards, gratis, for up to three hours.

One has to remember that Norway has always been at a news disadvantage as a result of it's crazy seasonal affectations — statisticians agree that news events are far more likely to occur during daylight hours. So one cannot reproach them for attempting to capitalise on one of the few activities that benefit from darkness.

Nonetheless, it sounds to me like a terrible idea. Perhaps the Norwegians are better at these things than I am, but this sort of intense pressure — the clock ticking, the whole world watching — would be tantamount to utter mortification in my downstairs region.

I believe that God chooses the most suitable country for us to be born in. I really do. My temperament is entirely unsuited for the cultural tenor of Iraq, for instance. I'd get into terrible trouble walking around Baghdad saying: "But it all just seems so mad!" This is why I am delighted to live in a country that neither puts you to death for having sex nor tries to talk you into having lots of it, right this second. I think we've got the balance just right.

London Evening Standard - 12th March 1999

Page 32 Daily Mail, Monday, October 4, 2004

Visit Norway, where you can kill a seal for £110. They'll lend you the gun

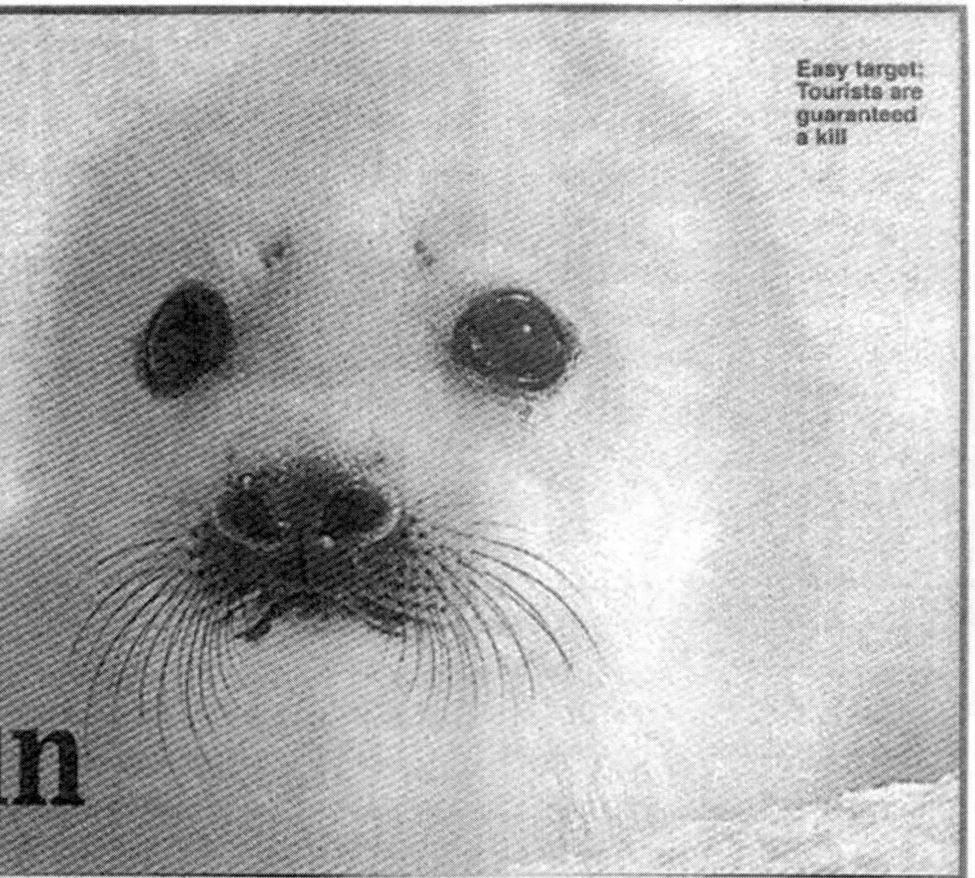

Easy target: Tourists are guaranteed a kill

By Allan Hall

BRITISH holidaymakers are being offered the chance to kill seals in Norway.

Amateur hunters will be able to borrow high-powered rifles and join culling expeditions.

On a £110 day-long hunt they will be guaranteed at least one seal-kill, or two if they choose the four-day £650 package.

Wildlife and animal rights groups last night condemned the trips as 'organised sadism' but the Norwegian government is in favour.

Fisheries Minister Svein Ludvigsen said the tourists would be helping to 'restore the balance' between fish and seals along his country's coast.

A drastic fall in fish and shellfish stocks is being blamed on growing seal populations, though wildlife groups blame other predators.

Paul Watson, founder of the Sea Shepherd group, said: 'Killing a baby seal is about the easiest thing you can do if you're inclined to be sadistic.

'You certainly can't say there is any sport in it – the animal is totally defenceless.'

Amateurs will be invited to join professional culls in January, with one company, NorSafari, advertising the one-day and four-day trips on the Internet.

Its Norway-based website shows hunters posing with their kill.

It also offers trips that include accommodation, food and help with cutting up and preserving carcasses.

The company could not be contacted yesterday but newspaper reports say there have been inquiries from the UK, Germany and France – three nations with strong hunting traditions.

Kjetil Kristofferson, boss of Polar Events, said his tourists will be given rifles to hunt their prey. 'Seals have been hunted in Norway for many years and it's part of the culture,' he added.

'We want people who are interested in hunting, not people who just come to shoot the animal. The tradition here is that we hunt the seal to eat it. It's food.'

Animal rights activists and conservation groups fear that baby seals will become the easy targets of tourists and say there is a danger of over-hunting.

But fisheries minister Ludvigsen says there are too many seals and hunting them is the same as hunting moose.

a.hall@dailymail.co.uk

Daily Mail October 4th 2004

DAILY EXPRESS

The World's Greatest Newspaper

TUESDAY JUNE 7, 2005 40p

SNORE NO MORE

TOP-CLASS HEALTH ADVICE STARTS ON PAGE 30

Who got the Best of it?

GEORGE HAS THE SCARS AND HIS LOVER HAS AN ARM IN A SLING

SEE PAGE 5

WIFE WHO CRIED 'RAPE' IS JAILED

She lied to cover up a one-night stand, putting the man she accused through hell

A MOTHER of two was jailed for 12 months yesterday for crying rape to cover up a sordid one-night stand with a stranger.

Merete Underwood, 32, claimed she had been kidnapped, sexually abused and raped by at least two men, prompting a police investigation costing at least £20,000.

She told detectives about her "terrifying ordeal," drew up an E-fit and finally identified one of her "attackers".

The man was arrested, held in a cell for 24 hours and endured 15 months of hell before the Norwegian born blonde confessed she made up the whole story.

Underwood showed no remorse yesterday as she was jailed after she admitted perverting the course of justice at London's Middlesex Guildhall

By **Sarah White** and **John Twomey**

Crown Court. Last night her husband Toby choked back tears as he condemned his errant wife and told how he has been left to bring up the two-year-old son she had by another man.

Mr Underwood said: "This is just one part of what has been a horrible situation. She has put so many people through so much and now I'm left bringing up her son on my own.

"I've already had to spend £30,000 in court costs fighting for custody while she has got legal aid despite moving away and abandoning her son.

"She hasn't even visited him since last November. I'm not even his biological father, I'm just another one of her

TURN TO PAGE 7, COLUMN 1

WEDDING DAY: Bride Merete Underwood, who went on to have a secret night of shame with a stranger

Daily Express 7 June 2005

This is a story which made the British press big time in 2005: a Norwegian woman living in London went to prison for lying about her rape claim against an Englishman. It was her cunning 'butter wouldn't melt' attitude that was so shocking in this episode. And there are many others like her.

Mother is jailed for a year after lying to hide her shame with a stranger

The wife who cried rape over her one-night stand

By **Stephen Wright**
and **Fiona MacRae**

A CHEATING wife was jailed for 12 months yesterday after crying rape to cover up a one-night stand with a stranger.

Merete Underwood, 32, left her husband and two-year-old son in a pub to seduce another man in a nearby wine bar.

The Norwegian blonde spent the night in a hotel with him before telling her husband she had been kidnapped and raped.

Underwood then wasted thousands of pounds of taxpayers' money and hundreds of police hours by giving a statement about her 'ordeal' and helping draw up an e-fit image of one of her 'attackers'.

The 34-year-old interior designer she spent the night with then faced 15 months with the finger of suspicion pointing at him and has been left traumatised.

Even when she was charged with perverting the course of justice, Underwood continued to lie. It was only as the jury was about to be sworn in to try her that she confessed.

Underwood – who is being divorced by her husband Toby – wept as the judge said her belated plea and previous good character could not save her from jail.

'Rape is an extremely serious offence and quite rightly any allegation of rape is dealt with very seriously by police,' Recorder
with very seriously by police,' Recorder
Andrew McCooey told her.

'I have heard from the prosecution the impact this had on this innocent man, not

Merete is ok but she crays and want to get home to you but we are not finish with her here.

Part of Underwood's text to her husband

to mention the many thousands of pounds that has been wasted, all brought about by your pack of lies.'

Underwood, of Kingston, South-West London, had taken her son to meet her husband for a drink after he finished work on the evening of February 25 last year.

A few drinks in one pub were followed by several more in another, in Paddington, West London.

'Then at about 9.30pm she went to the bathroom,' Joanne Hacking, prosecuting, told Middlesex Guildhall Crown Court, West London. 'A few minutes later her husband, curious as to why she had not returned, asked bar staff to check the toilets. There was no sign of her there and no sign of her outside.'

Although worried, Mr Underwood took the view that his priority was their son's welfare and took him home.

'He eventually went to bed, woke up at 5am and realised his wife was still not home,' said Miss Hacking. 'He was astounded by this and very worried.'

Later that day he reported his wife's disappearance to the police.

Not long afterwards he received a text message from her mobile saying: 'Merete is ok but she cries and wants to get home to you but we are not finished with her here. Good f***.'

Mr Underwood was 'obviously desperately concerned' but very soon after that received a phone call from his boss to say his wife had been found outside their office and had been taken to a police station.

She claimed she had left the pub for some fresh air when a stranger approached, grabbed her by the hair, forced her into a car and drove her to a hotel where two men took turns to rape her. She said she was held captive for 12 hours.

Miss Hacking said the defendant gave a full description of one of the so-called rapists and later 'identified' the interior designer.

The court heard significant police resources were wasted by her deceit. Besides the officers involved in the investigation, forensic laboratory facilities were tied up and CCTV footage had to be examined.

Miss Hacking said the 'unfortunate victim' did everything he could to convince police he was innocent.

He explained he had been with a group of friends in the wine bar when Underwood walked up to him, began chatting, kissed him on the mouth and held his hand. Later they left the wine bar and went to his hotel where they shared a can of beer and had sex. They had sex again the following morning.

Then they left his room and went to a post office where surveillance cameras captured Underwood 'laughing and smiling and entirely at ease' with her lover.

'The impact of the allegations on this man were to leave him terribly traumatised,' said Miss Hacking.

'He had never had any problems with the police before and as a result of all this he became very nervous and insecure. He has been left always wondering whether people know of the allegations made against him.

'He still feels ashamed and is very worried that his reputation has been tarnished.'

Told that Underwood was now 'full of remorse', the judge retorted: 'Words come cheap. The fact is she kept the finger of suspicion and accusation pointing for 15 months at an innocent man.

'As far as I can see her sorrow is directed at her plight, not the victim.'

Perverting the course of justice carries a maximum sentence of life imprisonment. But the culprits in most serious cases are jailed for between one and two years.

Underwood will serve a maximum of six months behind bars but could be out a few weeks earlier if considered eligible for electronic tagging.

Merete Underwood on her wedding day: She wept in the dock as she was sentenced

'You didn't have the decency to put this man out of his misery'

Toby Underwood: Divorce

Marrying her was a big mistake

THE husband of Merete Underwood told yesterday how another man got her pregnant within months of their marriage.

Toby Underwood, 34, a procurement manager for an engineering company, described her as 'vindictive and deceitful'.

He said drink would make her uncontrollable and she would bring lovers back to the matrimonial home while he was there.

He met Merete in Norway in February 2001 while he was working there. Within a week they were engaged and they married five months later. But

The husband

just weeks after their honeymoon in Bali she became pregnant.

Mr Underwood now looks after the result of that pregnancy, three-year-old James, the child he at first thought was his own and whom he says she has now abandoned.

'When I first met Merete I liked all the things that were eventually her downfall. She's a fantastic party girl, great for having a good time, but she's not able to separate those things from day-to-day life.

'She's a binge drinker and has never worked. I paid for everything and gave her a better life than she ever could have imagined.'

Referring to her rape allegations, Mr Underwood said: 'This incident is just one little bit of a horrible, horrible situation. She has put so many people through so much.'

Asked about the man falsely accused, he said: 'Nobody deserves to be put through what he has been put through. He has had a year of hell. I can't really put it into words.'

Daily Mail 7 June 2005

SUE CARROLL

Crying rape sullies name of all women

METROPOLITAN Police Commissioner Sir Ian Blair has this week ordered a review of the way his officers investigate rape claims. He's curious, as well he might be, that only one rape complaint in 18 results in a conviction.

AWFUL LIES: Merete

Since there are now 12,000 cases reported a year, it doesn't take a genius to work out that our streets must either be packed with menacing sexual predators walking free, or many of these men are the innocent victims of false allegations.

The question is this:

Now that it's easier – quite rightly – to report a genuine rape, is it also easier by the same token to allege a totally fictitious one?

The answer – looking at Merete Underwood, jailed this week for crying rape – has to be yes.

If ever there was an instance of police accepting blithely that when a woman claims to have been violated by a man she must be telling the truth, it's the case of Mrs Underwood.

The rather sordid and depressing reality about this mother of two is that, tired of bickering with her husband and young son, she slipped out of a pub where they were drinking, via the loo, to find herself a little adventure. It came in the form of a young man in a wine bar who, suffice to say, found the attractive, accommodating blonde more than willing to come with him to his hotel.

Alarm bells rang only when, waking up in a strange bed and probably hungover, Merete realised she had some uncomfortable truths to face.

Her husband, fearing for her safety, had alerted the police. And so began the spinning of a lie which escalated into a police investigation costing £20,000.

Let's not even consider how many hours of their time was taken up as she embellished the story of her "ordeal" and helped to draw up an e-fit image of her so-called "attacker" who, she alleged, had grabbed her by the hair, forced her into a car and, with an accomplice, raped her.

Wholly believable of course.

The "ladette" culture has brought about a massive sea change. Young girls out of their heads on cheap booze have made the life of sexual predators alarmingly easy. And yes, convictions against them are hard to stand up when all the victim has to offer in the way of detail is a memory blurred by vodka or Rohypnol.

Merete, on the other hand, was able to supply a meticulous portrait of her alleged assailant. The man in question, a 34-year-old interior designer, has spent the past 15 months in purdah waiting to stand trial.

He is, apparently, traumatised, nervous and insecure. Small wonder. Having never had any dealings with the police he found himself suddenly accused of a crime almost as heinous as murder and facing a sentence which, at worst, could mean life.

Even now, no doubt, the words "no smoke without fire" still haunt him. The law can't legislate against rumour and speculation as Stephen McLaughlin, falsely accused of rape by an ex-girlfriend, would doubtless testify if he were here to tell the story. He killed himself 18 months after she admitted fabricating the case against him.

This week, by coincidence, I received a letter from a decorator who, in 1999, was accused of rape by the woman whose house he was painting.

The case was dropped because of lack of evidence but his name remains on police files. "I still suffer nightmares, depression, and have trouble comprehending what happened to my life," he wrote.

It's against this background that Sir Ian Blair is said to be considering making it easier for police to convict alleged rapists.

One suggestion is that less evidence will be required. What a terrifying precedent when women like Merete are able to take their fiction into a courtroom and near as dammit destroy an innocent man's life.

There can't be a bloke in Britain who doesn't feel contempt for her.

But women, too, have every right to be furious. Her lies damn us all.

Daily Mirror 8 June 2005

Mirror.co.uk
THE BEST NEWSPAPER ON THE WEB

8 June 2005

CRY RAPE WIFE DID IT BEFORE

One-night stand liar exposed..by her mother

By Greig Box

THE wife jailed after she cried rape had falsely accused a man before, her mother said yesterday.

Jane Nordhaug said she was shocked by the 12-month sentence handed out on Monday to Merette Underwood, below.

Underwood, 32, who is Norwegian, invented the rape story to cover up a one-night stand and fool husband Toby.

Mum Jane said: "There has been a lot of trouble with many boys in the past. It is not the first time she has cried rape. It happened here about 10 years ago."

Mrs Nordhaug, speaking from Fauske in Norway, said police found no firm evidence.

She added: "They dropped the investigation. All the problems with her different boyfriends have led to psychological problems for my daughter.

"I talked to her last Saturday and she did not mention it was this serious. But I knew there was some kind of trouble."

She now wants Underwood transferred to a Norwegian prison.

Mrs Nordhaug said: "It is so expensive to fly to England, so I don't know if I can afford to see her.

"I am not mad or angry with her. I just feel sorry for her."

Underwood was sentenced in London for lying to police over a sex session with an interior designer she met in a bar.She had left husband Toby and her two-year-old son in another pub.

Meanwhile, builder Kevin Blakey, 36, who has been living with Underwood in Sussex, plans to wait for her release - then take her to Norway "away from all this".

Mirror.co.uk
THE BEST NEWSPAPER ON THE WEB

9 June 2005

By Stephen Moyes

JAILED..BUT IS HE CRY RAPE WIFE'S 3RD VICTIM

DOUBTS OVER HER CLAIMS

A MAN was jailed for two years after being accused of raping Merete Underwood, the woman sentenced for lying about another sex attack.

She received a 12-month prison term this week after lying to police over a sex session with an interior designer she met in a bar in London.

She had invented the rape story to cover-up a one-night stand to fool her husband Toby.

Now doubt has been raised over the conviction of a man who Merete, 32, claimed raped her in Norway in 1992. On that occasion the Norwegian, then 18, said she was grabbed off a pavement in Fauske and bundled into a car and attacked.

After her claims a 24-year-old man came forward to tell police he had met her after getting out of his car to relieve himself. He said they chatted and she willingly had sex with him, although they were strangers. But he was not believed and jailed for two years.

His appeal was rejected and was ordered to pay £7,000 compensation.

It has also emerged in 1997, Kai-Magne Hansen, a 39-year-old foreman, was accused of raping Merete in the street after a disco in Fauske.

He recalled: "She was very drunk and came over and tried to sit on my lap. I asked her to get off. That was the only time I spoke to her."

But after she picked him out at an identity parade he was charged with rape and held in a cell for two weeks before being released without charge.

She later tried and failed to claim £20,000 in compensation from him.

Last night it was reported she plans to appeal against her jail term for perverting the course of justice.

MY CRY-RAPE EX IS SO EVIL

'She was out every night drinking and picking up men. She said she'd been raped before and she'd had a brain tumour'

LIAR: Merete Underwood is now in prison

THE first husband of rape liar Merete Underwood told yesterday how her boozing and cheating tore his life apart too.

EXCLUSIVE from ROBERT STANSFIELD in Stavanger, Norway

Frank Ogreid said she went out nightly to meet men in bars, sometimes dumping their baby son in a pushchair outside.

He blasted: "Merete is pure evil and has ruined my life. She might be locked away for her evil crimes, but every night I sit alone as our son sleeps. Hers is a prison sentence, mine is for life."

Underwood, 32, now serving 12 months for perverting justice, even lied that she had a brain tumour to cover up her flings.

Her chequered past also includes a bid to drown herself in a bath and rape claims in 1992 and 1997, the first of which saw a man jailed for two years.

Frank, 36, of Stavanger, southern Norway, was so concerned about her mental state that he even had her put in a mental hospital for six months.

They met in a local bar in 1995 and within a year she was pregnant with Michael, now eight.

Although he begged her to have an abortion as he felt she was not ready for motherhood, she insisted she was, and cleaned up her act.

But three months after their son was born she was back on booze. Shipping manager Frank said: "She was desperate to have a child and well-behaved when she was pregnant. "But after the birth being able to drink again sent her into a spiral of destruction.

"She was out every night, drinking and picking up men while I was left to look after Michael.

"She wouldn't come home at night and made up crazy excuses, such as all the taxis refused to take her because she had cancer, which she didn't."

Even when Michael was with her she did not stop. Frank said: "Friends would tell me they saw her in bars drinking while our son was left in a pushchair outside.

"I worked hard but any money I made she wasted on men and alcohol." After walking out on him in 1999, she began fighting for custody of Michael. But she gave up to spend more time with a new lover. Her ex revealed: "She had visiting rights but didn't turn up half the time as she was too hung over. When she did take Michael out, she just left him in bars."

This week Middlesex Guildhall crown court heard Underwood, of Kingston, Surrey, falsely accused a stranger of rape after a one-night stand. She picked him up in a bar after leaving second husband Toby Underwood, 34, and son James, two, in another.

Frank blames her behaviour on her troubled history. As well as the two rape claims in the 90s and the suicide bid, she hardly knew her father. "She told me she'd been raped in 1992 and someone was jailed," he said. "I believe it happened as it made her funny in the head. She tried to kill herself.

"She became desperate for attention. In 1997 she lied about being raped again and said she had a brain tumour.

"None of it was true, so me and my mum put her in a mental hospital but it didn't help.

"She only met her dad once. I think she's searching for a man to take his place. And boy, has she been through a lot of them."

Frank added: "Michael visited her last year has had little contact since. He asks, 'When's Mummy coming home?' Now I have to tell him what she's done.

"He misses her terribly. The truth will hit him badly when he realises she's deserted him once and for all."

b.stansfield@mirror.co.uk

TORMENT: Her ex-husband Frank

Picture: IAN VOGLER

Daily Mirror 10 June 2005

Jailed . . . Underwood

Fifth fella accuses cry rape woman

From MARTIN PHILLIPS
in Stavanger, Norway

A FIFTH man yesterday told how he was falsely accused by "cry rape" wife Merete Underwood.

The 34-year-old oilman, who asked not to be identified, bedded the blonde hours after she picked him up in a bar in Stavanger, Norway, in 1999.

She left his house before he woke next day – and soon afterwards cops knocked at his door.

He said: "They questioned me then let me go. They said they knew all about her. They knew she'd made claims before."

Underwood, 32, of Kingston, Surrey, is serving a year in jail for perverting the course of justice. She left her husband and young son in a pub to pick up a stranger.

She claimed she had been kidnapped, sparking a huge police probe – but this week admitted in court she had lied.

Underwood has cried rape at least **SIX** times, The Sun has discovered. But she pleaded from jail yesterday: "I don't belong here. I want to go home."

The Sun 10 June 2005

SLEEPING WITH THE ENEMY

Spat at, abused, shunned by neighbours. Their crime? Being the offspring of Norwegian women and occupying Nazi soldiers. Sixty years on, Julia Stuart meets the war children who are fighting back

Photographs by Tom Craig

As a child growing up in Norway, Tove Laila Strand learnt to take the pain of being whacked with a wooden clothes hanger. It was the names her mother and stepfather called her during the assaults that hurt her more. "Hit me all you want, but please don't call me a German child," she would beg. For children born of a Norwegian mother and a soldier from the occupying German forces, this was a particularly vindictive insult. Today, sitting in a café in Oslo, the 61-year-old grandmother's eyes fill with tears as she recounts eight years of abuse, which included being repeatedly raped by her stepfather. "It wasn't that strange," she says. "I was, after all, the child of the enemy."

Some weeks ago, Laila Strand was spat at while shopping in Oslo. That too made her cry. No doubt she had been recognised from her recent television appearances as one of an estimated 10,000 to 12,000 "war children" born in Norway. Such was the level of abuse meted out to them after the war that, last December, Norway's parliament finally agreed to formally apologise and award them compensation. If Laila Strand and other claimants consider the amount to be insufficient, they will take their case to the European Court of Human Rights.

Norway declared itself neutral at the start of the Second World War, but was invaded by Germany in April 1940. The following June, the country's government, king and crown prince fled to London to continue their fight against Hitler, and the remaining troops capitulated. A Nazi government was formed under the auspices of the leader of the Norwegian National Socialist Party, Vidkun Quisling, whose name became a byword for traitor.

That December, Wilhelm Rediess, the chief of the SS and German police in Norway, wrote to SS leader Heinrich Himmler about the increasing number of relationships between Norwegian women and occupying troops. "Individual cases are already arising... of Norwegian women, made pregnant by Germans, seeking the aid of the German Reich, above all on the ground that they are despised and boycotted by the Norwegian population because their pregnancy was caused by a German", he wrote. It was a matter of particular interest to Himmler. In 1935, concerned about the falling birth rates among Aryans in Germany, he set up the Lebensborn (Spring of Life) association to care for unmarried, racially valuable pregnant mothers. The mothers, who otherwise may have had an abortion, checked into specially set up secretive maternity homes, where they received free, high-quality nursing and medical care. Some Lebensborn mothers had their children adopted, and the Lebensborn placed them with staunchly Nazi families.

As the vast majority of women in Norway were Nordic – the purest Aryans in Nazi terms – the fraternising mothers could not have been more racially valuable. In his letter, Rediess noted that only a small proportion of the German fathers wanted to marry the pregnant women and bring them back to the German Reich. There was another potential problem. If they failed to do anything for Norwegian mothers, they could increase the number of opponents to Germany's occupation. To add to the "stock of racially valuable blood in our racial community", Rediess suggested establishing German-controlled maternity homes.

In March 1941 – six years after the scheme had been set up in Germany – the Lebensborn arrived in Norway, the first of such ventures outside Germany. Hotels and villas were requisitioned and around 10 centres were established. As well as paying all the costs for the birth, the association gave the mothers substantial child support, and money for clothes and a pram or cot.

Most mothers took their children home, some took them to Germany to live with the father's family. Around 200 children were adopted by families in Germany and 100-odd were taken in by Norwegian couples.

It was the most successful Lebensborn outside Germany (there would eventually be two such homes in Austria and one each in Belgium, Holland, France, Luxembourg and Denmark). By the end of the War, 8,000 children had been registered. Many more were born outside the scheme by women who refused to reveal, or could not prove, the identity of the father, making the estimated number of war children in Norway as high as 12,000. It is believed that around 10 per cent of all Norwegian women between 15 and 30 had a German boyfriend during the war.

There have been claims that the homes operated as "stud farms". However, Kare Olsen, an historian at Norway's National Archives and author of *Children of War, The Norwegian War Children and Their Mothers*, dismisses this idea. "Having read through hundreds of files in the Lebensborn archive, I am convinced that nearly all the women had their children as a result of a 'normal' relationship," he says. "The soldiers were encouraged to be polite and behave well towards the Norwegians, who were considered to belong to the same race as them. It was largely a peaceful occupation. Many of the soldiers came from cultivated parts of Germany to the farming areas of Norway and were seen as exciting strangers."

One woman who found herself captivated was Agnes Moller Jensen, now 79, who met her German lover, Toni Mensch, in a coffee shop in Larvik, where she still lives. She was 20 and he was 24. "I just liked him, as you would anyone," she says. Many of her friends also had a German boyfriend. "People didn't like it so we hid by taking trips to the woods. People didn't dare say anything at the time. That started in 1945 [although the war ended in that year, many of the occupying soldiers were unable to leave Norway until 1947]." The couple had a child, Bjorn Toni, but didn't marry as Moller Jensen would have lost her Norwegian citizenship. The pair kept in touch until Mensch's death last year. ▶

19

The Norwegian government in exile in London, who had heard of these liaisons, warned of the consequences through BBC broadcasts. One stated that: "Women who do not reject contact with Germans, will have to pay a dreadful price for the rest of their lives." Another declared the women imbeciles.

When the war ended, many Norwegians needed no further encouragement and took it upon themselves to cut off the hair of many of the "German whores". Though the women hadn't broken any law, several thousand were arrested and many interned. A large number lost their jobs, some just for having been seen talking to a German. "The reaction against these women was far stronger than those who collaborated economically," says Olsen.

While this was echoed across Europe, what appears to be unique to Norway was the rabid hatred also shown to the resulting children. Immediately after the war, letters and articles started appearing in the Norwegian press condemning them. In July 1945, one writer in *Morgenbladet* feared the boys would "bear the germ of some of those typical masculine German characteristics of which the world has now seen more than enough". Many insisted that the children would grow up to become a "fifth column", and there were loud calls for them and their mothers to be sent to Germany. In August 1945, the Norwegian government brought in a new law stating that any women who had married a German soldier would lose her citizenship and be sent to Germany. Several thousand were duly sent packing.

Perhaps the cruellest claim was that many of the children were mentally retarded. Else Vogt Thingstad, a doctor who took part in a meeting on European war children in Zurich after the war, wrote an article in *Arbeiderbladet* in December 1945 claiming that many of the "German women" were retarded "... and that we therefore expected their children to a large extent to have hereditary weaknesses". One doctor said these children had as much chance of growing into normal citizens as cellar rats had of becoming house pets.

Twenty-seven children in Godthaab, the Lebensborn home just outside Oslo, were considered to be mentally retarded. Seventeen of them – including Paul Hansen (see below) – were sent to Emma Hjorth, the state asylum nearby. The rest to other institutions. Many spent their lives there, a situation believed to have been repeated in other parts of Norway. In 1990, one of the doctors at Emma Hjorth said: "If the children had got the possibility of a new start and a normal life in 1945, they probably would have grown up normally."

At one stage, Norway's Children of War Committee, set up by the Ministry of Social Affairs after the War to decide what should be done with these children, offered all 8,000 to representatives from Australia, who had approached Norway looking for new immigrants. The idea was abandoned.

In the end, around 3,000 children grew up with their single mothers, and between 2,500 and 3,000 were raised by their mothers and stepfathers. Around the same number were adopted. About 100 lived with their fathers in Germany, and several hundred grew up in orphanages or other institutions in Norway. Many mothers tried to conceal their children's heritage, by giving them their own surname or that of their stepfather.

But for some, there was no escape. "If the mother was a 'German whore' then the child was the same, and you were free to do whatever you wanted with them. Nobody cared," says Tor Brandacher, spokesman for the War Child Organisation Lebensborn. "Everybody hated them, everybody beat them, everybody sexually abused them, everyone urinated on them. Every perversion known to man was performed on them," he claims. "One boy was raped by nine men, who then urinated on him to clean him up. Another woman told me that when she was four, and in a foster home, she would be hung up inside a barn and when the farmer needed oral sex he just opened the door and helped himself."

In a children's home in Trysil, youngsters were force-fed until they vomited, and were made to eat the vomit, says Brandacher. A war child himself, he started researching the subject in 1987 when adoption laws changed to allow people to know the identities of their biological parents. Elsewhere, he says, people came to the homes at night, paid staff half a ham and a bottle of alcohol, and were let in the back door to abuse the children. One group of men branded a girl's forehead with a swastika. It has also been claimed that 10 of the war children were subjected to official experiments with LSD. Four or five are said to have died as

a result. At least six are believed to have committed suicide – the most recent, a former academic at Oslo University, died last November.

Agnes Moller Jensen's son, Bjorn Toni, drank himself to death at the age of 37. "They called him terrible things in school and all the time he was growing up," she says. "It built up inside and he tried to forget it by drinking. I can't describe the pain of losing him. But I don't regret what I did. There was nothing wrong with my son. There was something wrong with the people." Nearly 60 years after the war, Moller Jensen – known locally as the Mother Teresa of Larvik for her work with homeless people – is still discriminated against. Like all women who had a relationship with the enemy, if her Norwegian husband dies, the state will not pay her his war pension.

For some, the torment is still to come. After the War, 30 children found living in a home in Germany were secretly sent by the Norwegian authorities to Sweden. Their names were changed and they were adopted by couples who were told that their parents were resistance fighters or that they were Jewish orphans. "One woman, a war child, suffered great psychological trauma when she found out the truth," says Lars Borgersrud, who is working on a research project funded by the Norwegian

Tove Laila Strand – 'My German family were angels'

Tove Laila Strand was born in Honefoss, 60km from Oslo, in 1941. Her parents met in a laundry. Her father was sent to the Russian border and was killed in 1942. Her mother stopped caring for her and was convicted for neglect. Laila Strand spent several months in the Lebensborn home in Godthaab, near Oslo. Then, at the age of three, the association sent her to her paternal grandparents in Germany. "They were angels," she says.

In 1948, aged seven, the Norwegian government forced her to return to Norway. Her mother beat her when she spoke German and her stepfather physically, mentally and sexually abused her. Her mother's sister threatened to chop off her head if she visited.

Laila Strand left home at 15, by which time she was vomiting blood. She married at 20 and had two children. She is now divorced, for which, in part, she blames the legacy of the sexual abuse. She stopped working in an office 20 years ago because of continuing stomach problems. She is in regular touch with her father's two siblings. "When I go to my aunt's place it really feels like home," she says.

Karl Otto Zinken – 'I will never work again'

Karl Otto Zinken was born in Bergen in 1941, the result, he believes, of a one-night stand. When he was a year old, he was sent to the nearby Stalheim Lebensborn home, and returned to his mother when the War ended. She couldn't cope with having a Lebensborn child so sent him to a state children's home. "I sat in a room with six doctors and was told that I was mentally retarded, that I shouldn't have kids and that I was the scum of the earth. Two guys who worked in social services performed oral sex on me, claiming it was therapy. I was about five." After two years, he was sent to a special school where he was bullied.

Zinken spent 12 years in the merchant navy. In 1996 he had a breakdown and lost his job as a salesman. His marriage collapsed and he spent a year in a psychiatric hospital with manic depression. He has been in and out of hospital eight times since.

His mother died in the late 1980s. His father, "a nice man" whom he traced and met in 1997, died a year ago.

"I have no good feelings towards Norwegians," he says, "I feel empty. I will never work again."

Facing the future, clockwise from left: Paul Hansen outside his former Lebensborn home; Gerd Fleischer, a war children seeking compensation; Agnes Moller Jensen; Solvi Kuhrig Henningsen; and pictures from the Norwegian National Archive of a Lebensborn

government. "The majority probably don't know even today. I know their true identity, but it's not my task as a historian to inform them as it will create a huge change in their lives." Some mothers fled with their children to Sweden after the War to escape harassment. One such woman was the mother of Frida Lyngstad, of Abba, whose father was a German soldier.

Brandacher believes the "whore children" were treated so badly because of the nation's guilt over the occupation. "Around 250,000 men volunteered to work for Nazi Germany. Norway was the biggest collaborative state that has ever existed in Europe," he says. "There was full employment and a building boom like none other in Norwegian history. The resistance in Norway was a joke. After the war people needed somebody to hate to get rid of all the shame they felt."

After appeals for redress failed, in 1999 seven war children started legal proceedings against the state claiming that it had violated the European Convention on Human Rights, seeking between £50,000 to £200,000 each. They have since been joined by a further 115. "The stigmatisation, the shame, the oppression was so absolute it took us 50 years to come forward," says one, Gerd Fleischer.

Prime minister, Kjell Magne Bondevik, apologised to the war children in his New Year's speech in 2000. Last December, Norway's Supreme Court determined that the case fell under the statute of limitations. On the same day, the country's parliament unanimously voted, however, to pay compensation and to formally apologise. The details are still to be decided by the government.

Finn Kristian Marthinsen, a member of the Justice Committee that recommended to parliament that the war children be compensated, said: "Norwegian society has to say that we are sorry. It was wrong because these children did nothing criminal. It is a black spot on the history of Norway."

Randi Hagen Spydevold, lawyer for 122 claimants, says she will wait to see the government's proposals before deciding whether to take their case to Strasbourg. "This is an embarrassment for Norway. It seems that parliament has been shamed into action," she says.

Gerd Fleischer, whose Norwegian stepfather, a former member of the resistance, was particularly violent to her, believes the state felt compelled to act because of embarrassing international press coverage. "There has not been much public pressure inside Norway about this. The press has written about it, but very silently. It started coming out in the foreign media and then the Norwegian embassies starting reporting back.

"Norwegian society is not an inclusive one. The same discrimination exists today. It has only changed focus. Before it was the Sami, the German children and the gypsies. Now it's the dark ones. But officially racism doesn't exist in Norway. We don't do those bad things here," says Fleischer.

While most in Norway support parliament's decision, in some cases, the hatred lingers. When Laila Strand appeared on television, a neighbour, whom she considered a very good friend, ignored her. When asked what was wrong, the woman sneered: "I don't say hello to whore children and my tax money will certainly not go to paying your compensation." Kristian Marthinsen has been accused of being a traitor. "There are still people who call me or write saying that I'm not a supporter of Norway because I'm giving the children of the enemy a kind of reward," says the MP.

For a number of war children, finding their German relatives has finally given them a sense of identity and a unique source of comfort. Solvi Kuhrig Henningsen, 59, still lives in Sandefjord where she grew up and keeps her past quiet as she still feels hostility. She was mistreated by her stepfather, her mother turned to drink and her neighbour refused to allow her to play with her daughter.

In 1995, encouraged by her husband and children, she traced eight relatives in Germany. "At last Otto's daughter has found us," was her delighted aunt's reply. Kuhrig Henningsen, whose face still carries the pain of her childhood, says: "I became a new person when I met them because not only did they look like me, they loved me." ■

Paul Hansen – 'I never felt loved by anyone'

Paul Hansen was born in 1942. When his mother, who worked in the barracks kitchen in Drammen, told her father that she was pregnant by a Luftwaffe pilot he threatened her with an axe. Hensen was born in a Lebensborn home in Hurdals Verk. His parents split up and he was sent to a Lebensborn orphanage in Godthaab. His mother hated him. "I was the reason she had been kicked out of the family."

When he was three, he was moved to the Emma Hjorth asylum. "The first thing I heard was people screaming. They ate and relieved themselves in the same place – on the floor, on the tables. I was scared to death. People were sitting in chains."

Deemed retarded, he went from one institution to another, most of them for the mentally ill. In 1964 he got a job as a steel worker. That year, he met his mother, who lived in East Germany with her husband. She still hated him. He found out his father had died in 1952.

Hansen is now a cleaner at Oslo University. "The worst thing about all this is that I missed my education. I still can't read or write very well. And I never felt loved by anyone."

Reidun Myking – 'I have been destroyed'

Reidun Myking was born in 1943, two days after her father was killed at sea. At six months, she was sent to Godthaab, as her mother was too ill to look after her. When the War ended, it was claimed that she was retarded and, at the age of seven, she was sent to the Emma Hjorth asylum where she remembers being put into a straitjacket at night. From there she was sent to succession of institutions, many for the mentally ill.

Myking joined society at about the age of 30. She's worked in an old people's home and for 10 years as a cleaner at Emma Hjorth. She has been hospitalised for short periods for psychosis.

She and Paul Hansen (left) who was with her in a number of institutions, were married for five years from 1975. They didn't have children.

Her mother, who didn't know where she was, was traced Myking just before she turned 40. The pair kept in touch until her death in 1991. "I feel the way I have been treated has totally destroyed my life," says Myking. "I've been on medication for 37 years and I think it's slowed my brain."

THE INDEPENDENT ON SUNDAY 2 February 2003 21

The Independent February 2nd 2003

This Independent on Sunday story from 2003 illustrates Norwegian hypocrisy at its worst: Norwegian girls fell in love very easily with the invading German soldiers in World War II. After the war, when the full horror of the Nazi assault on humanity became apparent the children of these love unions were vilely abused both physically and mentally by 'upright' Norwegian citizens. These illegitimate children were labelled 'the German whore children'. Eventually they received an official government apology.

'Wipe Israel off map'
Iranian president spreads alarm
↘ Page 16

Norway finally forgives women who slept with Hitler's soldiers

By Kate Connolly
in Berlin

NORWEGIAN women who slept with German soldiers during the Second World War and have been denied a special pension ever since as punishment are finally to be forgiven.

Known as "tysketöser", German whores, they have until now been excluded from the war pension paid to all who remained true to "good national principles" during the occupation.

Now, however, Norway's government has quietly reversed its policy of discrimination against the women and will start paying the money to the few dozen still left.

"Very few are still alive and most went to their graves as shamed Norwegians," said Eva Simonsen of the University of Oslo. "But the important thing here is the principle. These women are no longer to be punished for the love stories of their youth that took place 60 years or more ago." In fact, the Nazis who occupied Norway actively encouraged affairs between local women and German soldiers, part of an SS plan to enrich the Aryan gene pool. But when the occupiers fled and the puppet regime of Vidkun Quisling fell, the "tysketöser" were denounced as traitors.

Around 14,000 women who had relationships with the enemy were arrested at the end of the war and 5,000 were sent to labour camps.

Even today the estimated 12,000 children they gave birth to are seen by many older Norwegians as a danger to society. After the war they were separated from their mothers, placed in homes where they suffered sexual and physical abuse and often classed as mentally deficient. The then authorities justified their treatment by arguing that the offspring of the German-Norwegian couples were a potential fifth column.

The most prominent "tyskerunge," or "German brat", is Anni-Frid Lyngstad, the brunette singer from the 1970s Scandinavian super group, Abba. Her mother, Synni, had an affair with a German soldier and was forced to flee with her to Sweden when they were ostracised in their village in northern Norway. Synni died in the late 1940s and her daughter did not meet her German father, Alfred Haase, until she was in her 30s.

Those of the women's children who finally received compensation payments of £2,000 this summer have cautiously welcomed the belated acknowledgment of their mothers.

"I was silent about my suffering for 50 years, like the other children only coming forward to tell my story in the late 1990s," said Gerd Fleischer, the daughter of a Norwegian mother and German father. "But my mother's silence lasted until the grave".

The payments are calculated on the basis of average income during a working life. Those still eligible will not receive backdated payments.

Around 160 "war children," led by an Oslo lawyer, Randi Spydevold, are fighting for more compensation at the European Court of Human Rights.

Harriet von Nickel, 63, another plaintiff in the case, said: "When I was nine or 10, drunken villagers branded by forehead with a swastika. I rubbed sandpaper on my skin to get rid of it."

Abba singer Anni-Frid Lyngstad was one of the many German-Norwegian children, top

Father: Alfred Haase

Mother: Synni Lyngstad

The Daily Telegraph October 27th 2005

THE Sun

GAMECARD INSIDE £10,000 MILK GAME SEE PAGE 13

Monday, April 27, 1998 28p DEDICATED TO THE PEOPLE OF BRITAIN

I'VE BEDDED 227 GIRLS

Brit conman seduces lonely Norway lasses

EXCLUSIVE

From **KATHRYN LISTER** in Bergen

A CASANOVA conman told yesterday how he has bedded 227 girls — and tricked them out of a fortune.

Boastful rat David Coombs, 34, had sex with a host of lonely beauties in Norway before fleecing them of £100,000-worth of cash and jewellery.

Now police in the Scandinavian country have put out a nationwide alert to women about the penniless painter and decorator from Southampton. They have plastered his photo across Norway's top newspaper under the headline: "Impossible to get rid of." One duped victim also put up wanted posters.

Coombs has been kicked out of Norway four times as cops had 63 complaints from tricked lovers. But he sneaks back. He is also wanted in Finland.

Coombs woos targets by pretending to be a dashing pilot, then cons them into funding his high life.

The Sun tracked him down to Rick's Café in Bergen, Norway.

The conman said: "Norwegian women are easy, and with charm and good sex they open their handbags. I know I'm a bad boy but I love women and they love me."

Coombs, who holds on to conquests' business cards so he can keep a tally, breaks no laws with his cheating.

But one victim, Kari Masterson, 29, warned: "If you meet him, run home, lock the door and phone the police."

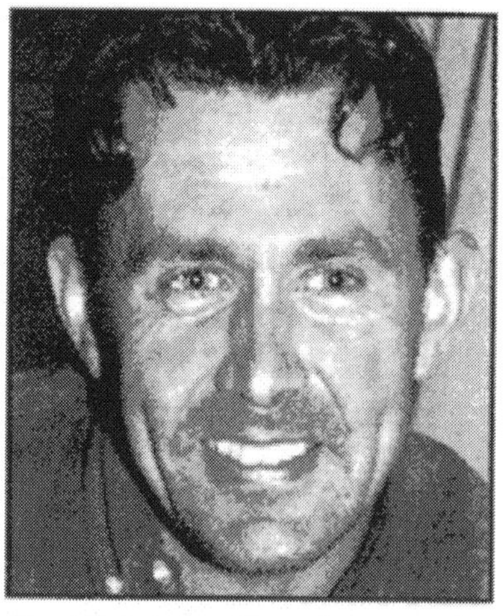

Sex trickster . . Coombs yesterday

NORWAY TO TREAT A LADY

Girls here are stupid so it's easy to bonk 'em...then con 'em

RAT DAVID COOMBS

By KATHRYN LISTER in Bergen, Norway

Borghild . . . Coombs 'borrowed' her £13,000 car

COCKY conman David Coombs claims Norwegian girls are easy to dupe because they are bimbos.

He told The Sun: "They are fairly stupid – and the police here aren't too bright either.

"That's why I've managed to get away with it for so long."

Cheat Coombs, 34, also believes the girls are "easy prey" for sex because Norwegian fellas are hopeless lovers.

And he boasted: "I've never had a single complaint about my performance between the sheets. I'm very well-endowed, keep myself in good shape and never suffer from brewer's droop."

Coombs – who has loved and left 227 Norwegian women, including a string of blonde beauties – added: "I know I'm a bit of a cad but I adore sex and women, and have an in-built desire to flirt with them.

"The most I've slept with in one night is three, one after the other. And I've also had a threesome with two sisters."

His oldest victim was a 31-year-old hairdresser and his youngest a student aged 18 whom he swindled out of her grant.

Coombs, a former painter and decorator from Southampton, is not ashamed to talk about his "favourite" cons.

And he is well aware Norwegian authorities cannot throw him in jail because he never actually breaks the Scandinavian country's deception laws. He said: "Over here it's not illegal to borrow money and possessions if you give a person a guarantee that you will pay them back.

"I give them the guarantee – but I never pay them back."

EXCLUSIVE

Cheat has even conned parents

Police in his main hunting ground of Bergen have managed to expel him from Norway four times. But Coombs, who has even swindled his mum and dad back in Britain, always manages to slip back.

He bragged: "When I was booted out for the third time in 1993, two officers accompanied me to London on the plane to make sure I got there.

"I jumped off, bought a ticket on a return flight and was back in Bergen before they were."

He added: "Since my last expulsion in 1995 they have relaxed the immigration laws, which has made it easier for me to keep coming back."

The conman first went to Norway nine years ago. He met a Norwegian girl in Britain and flew to Scandinavia to marry her, but dumped her eight days before the wedding.

He set up with another blonde but walked out on her when she was six months pregnant with their son. He has only seen the lad, now eight, twice. And he does not pay any maintenance. These days the oily-haired creep seeks most of his targets in Bergen's cafés and bars.

Revealing his technique for snaring another sucker, he said:

"Usually I start by going into a bar and looking around for an attractive woman to make eye contact with. If I'm in a hotel I buy them a drink but I always put it on their room bill when they're not looking.

"I prefer smartly-dressed slim blondes aged between 20 and 38. I can't stand ugly, overweight women in tight-fitting clothes.

"After an initial bit of flirting with my eyes, I walk over and bowl them over with one of my famous chat up lines.

"The ones that work the best are either 'You have a beautiful smile and should use it more often' or 'Hi, I'm not chatting you up but I'd love to sit and talk to you.'

"I usually score the first night and if it doesn't happen after two dates then I move on to the next woman. I'm not waiting around for weeks just to s*** a woman."

He added: "If I met the right girl I'd like to settle down and start a family but for the moment I'm having too much fun. I'd like to see my son but I'm denied access to him because his mother hates my guts."

Without batting an eyelid, Coombs moved on to describe how he fleeces his victims.

He said: "My favourite con is getting a woman to agree to a date but then convincing her I've left my suit somewhere.

"It never ceases to amaze me how many hand over their money or credit cards so I can buy some new clothes.

'Cops are fed up to back teeth'

"I always shop at Armani or Hugo Boss. I've had a whole new wardrobe out of them.

"The police are fed up to the back teeth with me but I'm too sharp for them. I always stay one step ahead of everyone."

He said he totted up his tally of conquests while "languishing in a police cell one night."

And he added: "I have a fantastic memory and keep the business cards of most with marks out of ten for their performance written on the back."

Coombs's heartbroken victims queued up to condemn him last night. His most recent, Borghild Oksland, 34, wept as she said:

"He was very charming and told me he worked as a helicopter pilot and had gone to a public school in England.

"He said his parents were extremely wealthy and he had several well-known showbiz friends.

"I met him at a friend's party and he swept me off my feet.

"He went to get some money out of a cash machine but told me he had punched in the wrong numbers and his card had been swallowed. He was very convincing and clung to me like a leech.

"The next day he persuaded me to lend him my Escort car. He called several times to say he was returning it, but never showed up."

Beautiful Borghild added: "I realised my terrible mistake and stuck 'Wanted' posters with his photo on lampposts around town."

Coombs was arrested in the sporty white Escort, worth £13,000, last Thursday.

But he was released hours later after telling police he had merely borrowed it. And Borghild got the car back.

Conned computer consultant Kari Masterson, 29, said: "I lent him money which he promised to pay back. But his promises are empty, like his affections.

"I want to warn other women to keep well away from him."

Bergen's police chief Jan Johnsen branded Coombs a "menace to women." He said: "He has broken the hearts of women all over Norway and has more chat-up lines than there are cases against him.

"Usually he tells them he is a helicopter pilot and he flits like a fly from one to another.

"He always promises the women he will pay them or return whatever he has borrowed, but it never happens.

'We want to kick him out for good'

"I currently have 63 complaints about him on file but the true figure must be at least double that. Most women are too embarrassed or ashamed to come forward or leave police their name."

The police chief added: "We just want to kick him out of the country and keep him out."

Back in Britain, Coombs's parents learned not to trust him after he took them for several rides. He owes them around £1,000 in loans and unpaid bills.

Coombs once sold his dad Barry's car to another man while he was out. Barry, 63, a retired boat skipper of Hythe, Hants, said: "I had to go and get it back from the bloke."

He added: "David is a smooth talker who could sell anything to anybody. But I would never leave him alone in my house – I don't trust him enough. When he lived with me he tapped into my bank account to get money."

Coombs's mum Barbara, who split up with Barry 16 years ago, said: "David would spend a night in a hotel when he was in England and in the morning just walk out without paying.

"Then, because he'd left my address with them they'd ask me to pay the bill. Other times he would run up a taxi fare of around £80 and then get out without paying. The drivers always turned up at our door.

"He once took back a pair of shoes I'd bought him as a present and exchanged them for a more expensive pair – using my money, of course."

Coombs's older brother Michael, 37 – a dad-of-three who has been happily married for 16 years – refuses to speak to him.

Barbara, 62, who also lives in Hythe, said Coombs calls her up to eight times a day and always has a dramatic story to tell.

But she added: "He believes all his lies – he lives the part. I'm afraid he has been nasty and not a very good son. Wherever he goes he causes havoc. I do get a bit cross with him."

● **HAVE YOU** been had by the cad? Tell us if smarmy David Coombs left you in the lurch by calling **0171 782 4105**. We'll phone straight back.

Your turn to pay, sweetheart . . . trickster Coombs on a restaurant date with Kjersi Feste, one of the Norwegian beauties he loved and left

SLICK? HE'S MORE LIKE AN OIL SLICK

By KATHRYN LISTER

Night to forget . . Kathryn meets rat

I SPENT an evening with David Coombs in a hotel bar — and at the end was only too glad to get away from the oily little conman.

Even more so when I realised next morning that he had charged every round to MY bill, plus phone calls, postcards and stamps.

I had imagined Coombs to be a tall, dark Casanova — but mistook him for a porter when he arrived in his ill-matching brown shirt and trousers. I shook his sweaty hand and noted the greasy hair, the shaving nicks dotting his face and his yellowing teeth.

As he ordered drinks he began boring me with boasts about his sex life and the size of his manhood. His eyes swept the bar looking for prey before spotting a blonde Norwegian girl wearing a short skirt and sitting alone.

"Nice pair of legs," he said. "Bet it would only take me a few minutes to pull her."

Finally he puffed out his chest, winked and said: "So come on Kathryn, how about it?"

His face stiffened as I burst into giggles. Sorry David, you just didn't do it for me.

The Sun April 27th 1998

The Sun newspaper do a front page story on Brit seducer David Coombs' exploits with the 'lonely' ladies of Norway in 1998. 'Lonely' is a euphemism for freely available Norwegian girls whom mass-murderer Anders Breivik in 2012 labelled as promiscuous sluts on the make. Easy Living.

THE CASE OF THE PROTESTING JEW

Let us take a look at the case of a Norwegian citizen, a Jew, whose unborn child was, behind his back, aborted by his Norwegian non-Jewish partner. Our Jewish friend took his case to the European Commission of Human Rights under Application Number 17004/90 by R.H against Norway. The Commission, on the 19th May 1992 decided that the prospective father had no rights to stop the atrocity.

The Facts

The applicant is a Norwegian citizen, born in 1962. He resides at Bærum, Norway. Before the Commission he is represented by Mr. Gustav Høgtun, a lawyer practising is Oslo.

The particular facts of the case as submitted by the applicant.

In 1986 the applicant lived together with a young Norwegian woman. They were not married. In June 1986 she became pregnant, the applicant being the father. In early August they went to Israel and planted three trees as a symbol of their wish to have the child. The mother, however, changed her mind and together with the applicant she consulted a clinic in order to obtain information about a possible abortion.

As the mother was determined to go through with the abortion and as the foetus was now more than 12 weeks old she was called to appear before a board of two doctors on 1 September 1986 and state her reasons. It does not appear that any medical reasons were submitted in support of an abortion but rather social indications seem to have been the reasons for the request. The request was granted on the same day and the abortion was carried out on the 5 September 1986, when the foetus was 14 weeks and 1 day old. The actual abortion followed a routine procedure according to which the mother received medicine whereby "birth" was provoked. The foetus would in such circumstances "suffocate" and appear in the same manner as during normal birth. The applicant was not consulted or heard before the abortion was carried out. Subsequently the applicant requested the hospital to hand over to him the remains of the foetus in order to inter them in accordance with his Jewish faith. However, his request remained unanswered.

Prior to these events, on 31 August 1986, the applicant had applied for an injunction (begjæring om midlertidig forføyning) in order to prevent the mother from terminating the pregnancy. The application was rejected by the City Court on 6 September, by the High Court on 17 September and by the Appeals Committee of the Supreme Court on 23 October 1986.

On 10 March 1987 the applicant instituted proceedings in the City Court of Oslo (Oslo Byrett) against the State represented by the Ministry of Social Affairs claming vindication and damages inter alia on the ground that the abortion allegedly had been carried out contrary to Articles 2, 3, 8 and 9 of the Convention in respect of himself and the foetus. By judgment of 14 June 1988, which was rendered following hearings held from 26 to 31 May 1988, the City Court dismissed some of the applicant's claims and for the remainder found in favour of the State. The Court did not find that any Convention rights had been violated.

The applicant appealed against the judgment to the High Court of Eidsivating (Eidsivating Lagmannsrett). The Court was composed of three professional and four lay judges, one of whom was Director of Finances (økonomichef) at the hospital where the abortion had been carried out. Hearings were held from 30 October to 3 November 1989. The Court heard five experts, three witnesses and the representatives of the parties. Before the High Court the applicant claimed inter alia as follows:

1) That he was entitled to receive information concerning the foetus,

2) That he was entitled to receive information as to whether a danger to the mother's life or health was invoked as a reason for the abortion,

3) That he was entitled to be heard on the question whether or not to terminate the pregnancy,

4) That the abortion was illegal as being inhuman treatment in respect of the foetus,

5) That he was entitled to receive the remains of the foetus after the abortion in order to inter them in accordance with his religion,

6) That he was entitled to have the foetus interred after the abortion,

7) That the state was not entitled to allow the abortion since the mother did not fulfil the requirements under Norwegian law for terminating the pregnancy after 14 weeks and 1 day.

By judgment of 17 November 1989 the High Court rejected the applicant's claims. In respect of the Convention the High Court stated inter alia:

(translation)

"The question arises whether the Norwegian Act on Termination of Pregnancy violates Article 2 of the Convention when it allows board approved abortion on social indications in the 15th week of the pregnancy. The High Court refers as a starting point to the Supreme Court judgment in the Børre Knutsen Case.... The Supreme Court left the question open whether Article 2 of the convention protects the unborn life at all and started in this connection:

'In any case the provision must be regarded as not imposing any far-reaching restrictions on the legislator's right to set the conditions for abortion. The Norwegian Act, under which the woman herself makes the final decision whether or not to terminate her pregnancy, provided the operation can be made before the end of the twelfth week of pregnancy, is similar to the legislation of a number of other countries belonging to the same culture and which also have acceded to the European Human Rights Convention. This is hardly immaterial to the consideration of a matter of international law.

' This view on the protection of the foetus under the Convention was expressed by the Supreme Court after considering the Commission's decisions in the case of X.v. the United Kingdom (no. 8416/79, Dec 13.5.80, D.R 19 p 244) and the case of Brüggemann & Scheuten v. Germany (Comm. Report 12.7.77.)

Thus the High Court finds that a possible protection of the foetus under Article 2 must be decided on the basis of the balance of interests to the extent that the protection is adapted to the degree of biological maturity of the foetus at every stage of its development on the one hand and the considerations which likewise speak in favour of allowing the woman to terminate a pregnancy on the other. The Supreme Court found that an abortion based solely on the woman's choice within the first 2 weeks of pregnancy was not in violation of Article 2. Having regard thereto the High Court does not find that a system, which protects a foetus in requiring a board to establish that the pregnancy birth or care for the child might place the woman in a difficult situation of life, would be in violation of Article 2 either

(The applicant) has submitted that the rights of the foetus were particularly strongly protected under Article 8 of the Convention due to the agreement he had with the mother not to terminate the pregnancy.

This provision protects the individual's right to family life.

The prospective father's arguments were all dismissed by the High Court in Norway who concluded that the European Convention on Human Rights was not violated. The applicant asked for leave to appeal against the judgment to the Supreme Court (høyesterett). In addition to the issues considered by the High Court the applicant also complained of the fact that the Director of Finances at the hospital where the abortion was carried out has participated as a lay judge. On 22 May 1990 the Appeals Committee of the Supreme Court refused leave to appeal.

FURTHER ARGUEMENTS BY PROSPECTIVE FATHER

Under Article 2 of the Convention the applicant complains that the termination of the pregnancy involving a 14 week old foetus was unnecessary in order to protect the mother's life or health.

Furthermore, he had entered into an agreement with the mother not to deprive the unborn child of its life and he had expressly undertaken to care for the child after its birth. He had vigorously protested against the abortion from the time it was contemplated by the mother.

Under the circumstances which existed in this case, the applicant maintains that the lack of protection of the unborn child under Norwegian law is unsatisfactory and constitutes a violation of Article 2 of the Convention.

The applicant further submits that he had an agreement with the mother to the effect that an abortion would not be carried out and he had made clear his willingness to assume sole responsibility for that child after the birth. Under these circumstances, he complains that Article 6 has been violated as he had no right to 1) object to the proposed abortion; 2) apply to the Court in order to prevent or postpone the abortion; 5) demand that the abortion board consist of impartial individuals and 6) request possession of the unborn child's remains.

Under this provision the applicant also complains that one of the lay judges in the High Court was an employee at the hospital where the abortion was carried out, and that therefore his case was not heard by an impartial tribunal.

Under Article 8 of the Convention the applicant submits that he and the mother were living together as a family although they were not married and that he had insisted, and the mother had agreed, that no abortion would take place.Under these circumstances, so the applicant alleges, Article 8 of Convention must ensure that a father to a 14 week old foetus has a minimum of rights regarding his unborn child where the health of the mother is not endangered. In this case, a foetus of this age should be considered to be part of his family.

In respect of Article 9 of Convention the applicant submits that the unborn child meant something particular to him and that, at least at the beginning, the mother shared and accepted this view. The planting of three trees in Israel, one for each of the parents and one for the unborn child, illustrates this. The taking of the foetus's life in the absence of a medical necessity was obviously not in accordance with that concept nor was the denial of his request to be given the child's remains in order in inter them.

Such a step would not have implied a lack of respect for the wishes of the mother. There is no evidence that the mother was asked about her wishes regarding this matter by the doctors or any other persons employed by the hospital. Therefore, the applicant finds that he was unnecessarily denied a manifestation of his conscience and religion which for him was extremely important and vital to his health and well-being.

In order to prevent the termination of the pregnancy, the applicant sought the services of an attorney to intervene on his behalf. However, the board would not listen to any argument from the applicant. Furthermore, the applicant's attorney filed a complaint with the ordinary courts but these complaints were not admitted. No other effective remedy exists in Norway. The applicant considers this to be a violation of Article 13 of the Convention.

Finally, the applicant submits that his actions were based on the conviction that the life of an unborn child should be protected and it should not be deprived of life for non-medical reasons. His relationship with the mother rested on that condition which was also accepted by the mother. Furthermore, the pregnancy and birth of the child in question was planned. It was the result of an agreement between two free, independent and equal persons, mature and under no pressure whatsoever.

Well, our Jewish friend's arguments were all dismissed by the European Commission. This particular Norwegian lady, in terminating the life of her own child, had committed an abomination. This case will send shivers down the spines of all prospective fathers everywhere.

The question they will constantly be asking themselves is **'Will she abort, won't she abort?'**

This is the heart-breaking story of a Jewish man's desperate, but futile, efforts to prevent his Norwegian girlfriend aborting their child. How often does this happen one wonders?

The Muslim man

2 NYHETER BERGENS TIDENDE - ONSDAG 24. MAI 1995

Vergeløs mot 13 års forfølgelse

OSLO: I mer enn 13 år har bergenseren Heidi Schøne (31) blitt drapstruet og trakassert fordi hun ikke ville bli hustru til en muslimsk mann som er bosatt i England. Familie, venner og kolleger får stadig skriftlige «rapporter» om Heidis liv. Den muslimske juristen har også benyttet privatdetektiv for å oppspore Heidi Schøne.

FORFULGT I 13 AR. Heidi Schøne fra Bergen har blitt trakassert, forfulgt, drapstruet og ærekrenket av en muslim i England i 13 år. Muslimen er besatt av tanken på å gifte seg med henne. Bergenskvinnen og mannen Runar regner med at de må leve med terroren i lang tid ennå.

De færreste kan forestille seg hvilke belastninger Heidi Schøne og hennes nærmeste har gjennomlevd siden tidlig på 80-tallet.

For noen uker siden fant en av Bergens Tidendes frilans-fotografer et brev i postkassen, sendt fra Watford i England. På konvolutten stod der ikke navn, bare adresse. Innholdet, under tittelen «Rapport om Heidi Schøne», var rått og dypt ærekrenkende. Bergens Tidende kontaktet Schøne som i dag bor sammen med sin ektemann utenfor Drammen, og fortalte henne om brevet.

— Hvordan skal dette ende, hvor mange skal få disse brevene? kom det sårt fra Heidi første gang avisen kontaktet henne.

Pose med brev

Bergens Tidende møtte i går Heidi Schøne og ektemannen Runar i Oslo. Under armen bar hun en pose med brev fra den muslimske mannen, alle like grovt ærekrenkende. De siste 13 årene har vært en enorm påkjenning. Hemmelige adresser har ikke hjulpet.

Det hele startet for 14 år siden, da Heidi Schøne var au pair England. På en båttur fra Frankrike til England møtte hun og en venninne muslimen.

— Han var grei og understreket sin muslimske tro, og skulle han gifte seg måtte det være med en muslimsk jente. Jeg følte meg på trygg grunn. I England møtte vi ham flere ganger som gode venner. Etter ni måneder flyttet jeg hjem igjen til Bergen, sier hun.

«Stygg og dum»

Da forandret den gode vennen lynne. Muslimens ønske var at Heidi skulle bli hans livsledsager.

– Han oppsøkte meg flere ganger i Bergen uten å være invitert. Han ønsket å gifte seg med meg, og sa at jeg var stygg og dum og at han var den eneste som ville elske meg når jeg ble 50 år gammel. Det ble gnisninger mellom oss. Siden har han kommet med drapstrusler og trakassert meg. Han har også truet med å drepe familien min, sier Heidi. I 1990 ble den 35 år gamle muslimen arrestert i Bergen. Men politiet kom ingen vei. Terroren fortsatte.

Muslimen snakker ikke norsk, men den siste «rapporten» er skrevet på norsk og sendt fra Watford der han bor. I 1990 fant politiet materiale som viste at muslimen hadde samarbeidet med en nordmann for å etterforske Heidi Schøne og finne hennes hemmelige adresser som det ble en del av etter hvert.

Hun tapte hver gang.

Sendes til naboer

Nå har hun gitt opp hemmelige adresser. Hennes nye naboer er gjennom «rapporter» fra muslimen gjort kjent med hele livet hennes, slik muslimen beskriver det.

– Hvordan skal man kunne forklare dette fornuftig. Ikke har vi flørtet eller vært kjærester. Han lever seg jo helt inn i dette, kommer det oppgitt fra bergenskvinnen.

I seks år har hun bodd utenfor Drammen. For halvannet år siden giftet hun seg med Runar Schøne. Da trappet muslimen opp virksomheten. Det er ikke få «rapporter» som er sendt Bergen og Drammen i løpet av disse årene.

Hennes mann har også fått brev, sendt personlig til ham.

– Denne muslimske mannen sendte som avtalt «rapporter» om Heidi som jeg skulle ha bestilt. Det var bare tull. Han gjorde alt han kunne for å sverte Heidi, sier Runar Schøne. Han er forståelig nok forbannet på den muslimske mannen.

– Ikke redd

Redselen for muslimen har avtatt med årene. Nå er ikke Heidi redd lenger. Redselen er redselen byttet ut med sinne og fortvilelse. Og det er belastende at familie, venner kolleger og ukjente naboer får «rapporter».

– Men inntil for noen år siden var jeg vettskremt, kunne noen ganger ha gjemt meg under sengen, svarer Heidi.

– Han har ingen grenser. Når han har ringt på dører og ingen åpnet, har han svart med å risse inn ord i dørene, legger hun til. Ordene Heidi gjengir egner seg ikke på trykk. Hun vet at det vil gå lang tid før terroren stanser.

«Erotisk paranoia»

Personer som opptrer slik muslimen gjør mot Heidi Schøne er ikke noe nytt fenomen. I følge psykiater Kjell Noreik, som er medlem av Rettsmedisinsk kommisjon er dette personer som ikke har tålt motgangen ved å bli avvist. Diagnosen erotisk paranoia har psykriater Nils Retterstøl skrevet mye om og denne muslimen går inn i dette mønsteret. Kjell Noreik setter ingen diagnose på muslimen men sier at erotisk paranoia er erotiske vrangforestillinger. Han sier at slike personer bygger opp forestillinger om et annet individ som de bli avvist av.

— Dette er et problem, men ikke så forferdelig stort. Det er imidlertid uhyre plagsomt for de som utsettes for dette. Det kan pågå i årevis og det stanser ikke ved tilsnakk. Enkelte går også til voldeligheter.

Sammen med mannen har hun engasjert advokat Tom Skau i Oslo, ved siden av å ha anmeldt muslimen.

– Heidi Schøne har vært utsatt for årelang terror av en sinnssyk person som hun tidligere i livet har vært venn med, og ikke noe annet. Hun opplever dette meget vanskelig. Jeg har sett brevene og vil følge opp anmeldelsen. Men det er problematisk så lenge han er i England og ikke i Norge, sier advokat Tom Skau til Bergens Tidende.

TEKST: HAAKON B. SCHRODER
FOTO: HÅVARD BJELLAND BT

Vergeløs mot 13 års forfølgelse, Bergens Tidende - 24th May 1995

This Bergens Tidende story from Norway in May 1995 involved a London Solicitor, a Muslim, who we are told was a "sex-terrorist"! He fought back. The Met Police told him that if a British newspaper had printed the word 'Muslim' nineteen times, as did Bergens Tidende, they would be prosecuted. The Norwegian Press carried on with this story until 2011 – when mass-murderer Anders Breivik took over as Public enemy no.1. Breivik, of course, hated Muslims: we suspect that in reading about this London Solicitor for over a decade he hated Muslims even more. The irony was that on 22 July 2011 he blew up the offices of Verdens Gang newspaper who themselves did a 'sex-terror' story on the Solicitor in May 1995. Google 'Norway Shockers' for the full story. The girl in question, Heidi Schøne, was a registered mental patient with a long history of sexualised behaviour. A fantasist. The story unfolds in the following pages with English translations

When the Solicitor sent hundreds of faxes via a commercial facilitator all over Norway with his take the Norwegian woman's own sexual history the Norwegian Courts gave him two criminal convictions for 'harassment' - in 2001 and 2003. Free speech? Not a bit of it when it comes to teaching the Norwegians a well-deserved lesson. A conflict of laws.

English Translation

13 Years of Harassment.

A Bergen lady, Heidi Schøne (pictured) has been harassed and threatened with her life over a period of thirteen years by a man who she accidentally met when she was an au pair in England. Her secret addresses haven't helped against the English lawyer, whose attitude is similar to one suffering from erotic paranoia.On page 2 the headline is Defenceless against 13 years of pursuit.

OSLO:-

For more than thirteen years the Bergen lady Heidi Schøne (31) has been threatened with her life and harassed because she didn't want to be the wife of a Muslim man who lives in England. Family, friends and colleagues often received written reports about Heidi's life. The Muslim lawyer has also used a private detective to trace her. People will find it hard to imagine the pressure Heidi and her immediate family have been under since the early 1980s. A few weeks ago, a Bergen freelance photographer received a letter from Watford in England, although the letter did not have any sender's name and address. The title of the letter was 'Report on Heidi Schøne' which was defamatory and humiliating. The freelance photographer contacted Bergens Tidende who in turn contacted Heidi Schøne and her husband who lived outside Drammen and they told her about the letter. Heidi answered the phone crying "Where shall this end? How many people will have got this letter?"

Bag with letters Yesterday, Bergens Tidende met Heidi Schøne and her husband Runar in Oslo. Under her arm she carried a bag with letters from the Muslim man; all the letters were very rude and insulting. The last 13 years have been very traumatic. Secret addresses haven't helped. All of this started 14 years ago when Heidi Schøne was an au pair in England. On a boat trip from France to England with a girlfriend, she met a friendly Muslim man. He was very nice and he told her about his Muslim beliefs and that if he got married the girl must be Muslim as well. "I felt quite safe", she said. "In England we met him several times just as good friends. After nine months I moved back to Bergen".

Ugly and Stupid

Then he changed. The Muslim man wanted Heidi to be his wife. "He visited me several times in Bergen without being invited. He said he wished he could marry me; and said I was ugly and stupid and that he would be the only one who would love me when I was 50 years old. Arguments between us followed. Since then he has made threats on my life and has harassed me. He has also threatened to kill my family", said Heidi. In 1990 the 35 year old Muslim man was arrested in Bergen but the police didn't take the matter any further. The harassments carried on. The Muslim man didn't speak Norwegian but the aforementioned report is written in Norwegian and sent from Watford where he is living. In 1990 the police found material which indicated that the Muslim man had liaised with a Norwegian man with the purpose of following Heidi Schøne and finding her secret address, one of several secret addresses which followed for Heidi and she lost out every time

Sent to the neighbours

Now she has given up with secret addresses. Her new neighbours have got the reports explaining to them what her old life was like as the Muslim man saw it. "How can one make sense of it? We haven't been lovers or had feelings for each other. He fantasises about it", the Bergen woman said painfully. For six years she has lived outside Drammen. Six months ago she got married to Runar Schøne. Then the Muslim chap worked even harder on the matter. Numerous 'reports' were sent to Bergen and Drammen recently.

Her husband also got a letter sent personally to him-

"The Muslim man sent the report about Heidi to me as if I had requested it myself. The report was totally false. He did all he could to blacken Heidi's name", said Runar Schøne. He is sick and tired of the Muslim man.

Not afraid

The fear of the Muslim man has receded as the years have gone by. Heidi is not afraid anymore. The fear has changed to frustration and anger. Family, friends, colleagues and neighbours feel overwhelmed by these reports.

"Just a few years ago, I was very frightened and kept hiding under the bed", said Heidi.

"He has no limits. When he knocks on the door and finds no-one in, he writes obscene words on the door", she adds. The words Heidi refers to are unprintable. She knows that it will take a long time before the terror will stop. With her husband she has hired a lawyer called Tomm Skaug in Oslo and she has also reported the Muslim man to the police.

Heidi Schøne has been terrorised for several years by an insane man who she had earlier been friendly with but with whom there was no serious relationship. This situation is very difficult for her.

"I have seen the letters and I will follow the case. But it will be difficult so long as he is living in England and not in Norway", said the lawyer Tomm Skaug to Bergens Tidende.

EROTIC PARANOIA

A person who acts like this Muslim man against Heidi Schøne is not a new phenomenon in the view of the psychiatrist Kjell Noreik, a member of the medico legal group of psychiatrists. These people don't like to take no for an answer. The diagnosis is called erotic paranoia. One psychiatrist, Nils Rettersdøl has been writing much about Muslim behavioural patterns. Kjell Noreik doesn't place this diagnosis on the Muslim man but says that erotic paranoia is erotic delusions. He says that a person with this condition builds up a fantasy in relation to the other individual even though the former is rejected. Now this is a problem but not too serious a one. But it is very painful for the victims of this behaviour. This behaviour can carry on for years and doesn't stop even if the perpetrator is admonished. Some will also become violent.

Story: Haakon B. Schrøder

GP-LØVLAND I 15 LAND

● SIDE 49

NORGES STØRSTE AVIS 50 ÅR 1945 - 1995

VG

Nr. 138 Fredag 26. mai 1995 Uke 21 Kr. 8,00

Heidi (31) fortvilet:

-13 års SEX-terror

■■ I 13 år har Heidi Schøne fra Drammen blitt sextrakassert og terrorisert av en mann hun traff på ferie da hun var 18 år.

■■ Mannen startet med telefon- og brevterror. Da han ble avvist, fortsatte han med terrorisering av hennes venner, fysisk oppmøte og drapstrusler.

■■ – Jeg har tigget, grått og truet for at han skulle la meg være i fred, men det har ikke hjulpet, sier fortvilte Heidi. ● SIDE 10–11

Foto: JANNE MØLLER-HANSEN

7 052960 808472

Gull-Hoen ANGREP inntrenger

● SIDE 39

NORGE — GHANA 3 — 2

JEG VIL DØ FOR DRILLO

Tomåls-skårer Jan Åge Fjørtoft ● SPORTEN

- Aftenposten-LEDELSEN BESTILTE mikrofonene

– mener servicesjefen som monterte dem ● SIDE 6–7

FORFULGT

TERRORISERT: *Heidi Schøne (31) har levd i 13 år med terroren fra den halvt arabiske engelskmannen hun traff under en tur til Paris. – Han oppsøkte meg uansett hvor jeg flyttet. Han sa at jeg og familien min skulle drepes.*

»En gang gjorde han obskøne ting mens jeg måtte se på. Det rare var at jeg etter hvert begynte å tro på ham«

Heidi Schøne (31)

– Grovt trakasserende

BERGEN (VG) Personlig ville jeg ha reagert til dels sterkt på å bli utsatt for noe slikt, sier lensmannsbetjent Gunnar Fossum ved Nedre Eiker lensmannskontor.

Han har mottatt anmeldelsen fra familien Schøne, og har gjort de første forberedelser til etterforskning: Televerket har koblet inn telefon-terror-søker på familien Schønes telefonnummer.

Intimiteter

Blant dokumentene Fossum sitter på, er et omfattende skriv med angivelig faktiske intime personlige opplysninger om Heidi Schøne. Disse har han oversatt til godt norsk før han sendte dem til Heidis ektemann, og til naboer og familie og venner.

– Det var da dette skjedde i vinter at vi bestemte oss for å gå til **advokat og politiet, sier ektemannen Runar Schøne.**

– Jeg har sett hvor forferdelig nervøs Heidi blir når dette nå kommer opp igjen. Han må ha fått et mentalt grep på henne. Det er utrolig at hun klarer seg så bra etter så mange år med terror, sier Runar.

– Selv har jeg mottatt en telefon fra engelskmannen. Han bare skrek på engelsk, trolig banneord.

English Translation

Verdens Gang 26th May 1995

THIRTEEN YEARS OF SEX TERROR

For thirteen years, Heidi Schøne, from Drammen has been sexually harassed and terrorised by a man she met on a holiday when she was eighteen years old. The man started off with telephone and letter harassment. When he was rejected, he continued with terrorising her friends, showing up in person at her door, and death threats.

"I have begged, cried and threatened to make him leave me alone, but it has not helped", says the frustrated Heidi. As an eighteen year old she gave her address to a slightly peculiar, obtrusive Englishman. In this way began thirteen years of fear and sex terror for Heidi.

When the half Arab, Muslim man was rejected by her later on, he started with obscene phone calls, death threats, threatening letters, showing up in person at her door and harassing her friends for years and years.

Psychiatrists think that the behaviour of the Englishman possesses all the symptoms of erotic paranoia: the sick person is convinced that another person is in love with him or her. Moving to a secret address and getting a secret telephone number didn't help. Suddenly a postcard dropped into the letterbox saying "Freddie's back" - taken from the horror film with the main character with the name Freddie Kruger. "He found me again! Me and my family were threatened with our lives and he came to my door many times. At one door he wrote 'Fuck you' with a knife".

"It didn't help moving to a secret address and getting a secret telephone number". Heidi Schøne was born and raised in Bergen, and stayed for a while in England as an au pair with a family. She and her friend had a trip to Paris.

LIKED HIM

On the ferry she became aware of a person watching her from a distance. "When we came to the train, he sat down with the same group of young people that I was with. He was a Muslim, five to six years older than us and proved to have strong opinions about life, among other things. We thought that he was somehow a bit peculiar, but completely harmless".

"I liked him. We had a cup of tea together with him and later on we had some contact, but purely as friends. He would marry a Muslim girl, he said".

HELL

But sometime after Heidi had returned to Bergen, the harassment started. At the time she had a boyfriend in Bergen, but she still was followed by the Englishman. "I let him in the beginning. He was very manipulating. He had bombarded me with telephone calls and letters telling me that I was stupid, and that nobody but him wanted me. At one point he did obscene things while I had to watch. The funny thing was that I started to believe him bit by bit."

ASHAMED

"It was all so unreal and I felt ashamed. I was more and more frightened, and isolated myself. For long periods of time I didn't go out. I lay down under the bed when the doorbell rang. I just couldn't open the door.". "Those I spoke to said that it would probably stop. He was probably just a bit too eager, a persistent sort of guy".

She involved just a few people in the case and thought for a very long time that it would stop; "The ones I spoke to, said that it would probably stop. He was probably just a bit too eager. Nobody took it seriously".

PRIVATE DETECTIVE

But the Englishman had hired a private detective, and managed to trace her time after time. In strange ways he also managed to collect sensitive information about persons close to Heidi. He sent this to her, and she was able to show it to the police. But the years went by, and when Heidi was about to marry her boyfriend, Runar Schøne, an unpleasant and obscene letter was sent to her from the Englishman indicating that he knew her sexually. "When I think about it now, about how I was manipulated, I just get so angry. I didn't understand it but after a while when I realised he had to be sick I gained my self-respect back. I have begged, cried and threatened him to leave me alone, but it has not helped", says Heidi.

THREW AWAY

Three years ago she threw away all the material she had received from the Englishman. She wanted to burn him out of her life, but in vain.

"The last half year I have received 30 to 40 consignments of letters, postcards and books. Books about AIDS or abortion. As if I have AIDS? I have also received him on tape".

"When I think about it today, how I was manipulated, I just get so angry". And on this tape she has made him admit things. This and the latest consignment of letters she will hand over to her lawyer, Tomm Skaug, who will try to stop the Englishman.

EXTREME

Psychiatrists think that the threatening and lovesick Englishman who has bugged Heidi Schøne for 13 years might suffer from erotic paranoia.

"I don't know this particular case, and do believe that if this can be called erotic paranoia, this is an extreme case", says the Professor in Psychiatry Nils Rettersdøl.

MISCONCEPTION

Erotic paranoia is a disease of the mind in which a person has a misconception that another person is in love with him or her. "To wish or imagine that someone is in love with you is truly a normal phenomena, but the sick person is totally convinced that this is how it actually is, and won't be talked out of it". In German psychiatry the suffering is called erotic self-seduction, other people call it "old maids psychosis".

MOST OFTEN WOMEN

It most often strikes woman and mostly women in their menopause. Among the known cases of this is a woman who has this relationship towards a male person who has authority and is exposed, for example the local priest. The person who is suffering from this, has no idea of it. The sick person can plan a wedding and won't be talked out of it.

EXPERT:

Erotic paranoia is hard to heal. "It just stops after a couple of years", says Professor in psychiatry, Nils Rettersdøl.

"However, persons with erotic paranoia are seldom directly mean - it can of course be unpleasant and absolutely unwanted that a woman rises up in the congregation and proclaims her imagined relationship with the priest, or another official authority.

But direct unfriendliness like in this case is not normal. The very case described here must be in some extreme form, in that case. It is hard to heal erotic paranoia; most often it just stops after some years by itself. But seldom have the sick the insight and the understanding that it is wrong and imagined", says Rettersdøl.

Just below a full page photograph of Heidi and her husband, sombrely looking at my letters to her with the Aids and Abortion Christian booklets on the kitchen table before them, ran the caption:

TERRORIZED:

Heidi Schøne (31) has for 13 years lived under terror of the half-Arab Englishman she met on a trip to Paris - "He sought me out regardless of where I moved to. He said that I and my family would be killed". "On one occasion, he did obscene things which I had to watch. The strange thing was that I gradually began to believe him" Heidi Schøne (31).

-ooOoo- Below this photo, another sub-story:-

SEVEREHARASSMENT

BERGEN (VG) "Personally, I would have reacted rather strongly to being subjected to this sort of thing", says police constable Gunnar Fossum of Nedre Eiker police office. He received the report from the Schøne family and made the preliminary preparations for investigation. The Telecommunications Administration ('Televerket') connected up the nuisance callers search system to the Schøne family's telephone number.

INTIMATE REFERENCES

Among the documents held by Fossum is a lot of written material containing apparently factual intimate personal particulars concerning Heidi Schøne. He translated these into good Norwegian before he sent them to Heidi's husband and to neighbours, family and friends.

"It was when this happened last winter that we decided to go to a lawyer and to the police", husband Runar Schøne says.

"I have seen how terribly nervous Heidi becomes, now that this is happening again. He must have got a hold of her mentally. It is unbelievable how well she manages after so many years of being terrorized", Runar says. "I myself have had a telephone call from the Englishman. He just screamed in English what were probably swear words".

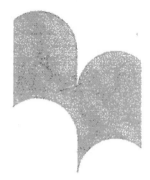

DT·BB *Helgeværet*

Drammens Tidende · Buskeruds Blad

NR. 119 LØRDAG 27. MAI 1995 – UKE 21 LØSSALG KR. 10,00

Trakassert og forfulgt i 13 år

En sinnslidende mann har terrorisert Heidi Schøne (31) fra Nedre Eiker i 13 år. Mannen har sendt Heidi over 400 perverse brev, truet henne på livet og drevet telefonterror.

I 13 år har en sinnslidende mann drevet telefonterror og forfølgelse av Heidi Schøne (31) fra Nedre Eiker. Mannen har sendt Heidi over 400 perverse brev, og truet både Heidi og hennes familie på livet. Mannen er blitt besatt av Heidi, og har i alle disse årene fulgt hennes minste bevegelse. En lang periode hadde han en privatetterforsker som fotfulgte henne, og en rekke ganger har mannen dukket opp hjemme hos Heidi og drevet seksuell trakassering.

Heidi har politianmeldt mannen flere ganger, men det er lite politiet kan gjøre så lenge han ikke angriper noen fysisk.

Side 4

Terrorisert i 13 år

I 13 år er Heidi Schøne (31) fra Nedre Eiker blitt terrorisert og forfulgt av en sinnslidende mann som har truet med å drepe både henne og familien hennes.

Ingunn Røren
Nils J. Maudal (foto)

I 13 år har Heidi Schøne (31) fra Nedre Eiker blitt trakassert av en sinnslidende mann som har sendt henne over 400 perverse brev og sendt krenkende «rapporter» om Heidi til familie, venner og naboer.

Etter 13 års helvete går Heidi ut med sin historie for å sette søkelys på et problem hun vet at langt flere enn henne sliter med. Hun blir forfulgt av en sinnslidende mann som er besatt av henne, og føler seg maktesløs. Hun har flere ganger anmeldt mannen til politiet, men det er lite de kan gjøre så lenge han ikke angriper noen fysisk.

Ga adressen

Marerittet begynte da Heidi var 18 år gammel og ga adressen sin til en halvt tysk, halvt arabisk mann bosatt i England som hun møtte mens hun var au pair. Det ble starten på årelang sjikane for Heidi og hennes familie. I 13 år har mannen drevet telefonterror hjemme hos Heidi, og sendt henne over 400 brev - alle med perverst innhold. Hun har også fått tilsendt bøker om AIDS og aborter, samt kassetter om seg selv.

– Det verste er imidlertid alle «rapportene» han har sendt om meg til naboer, familie, venner og kollegaer, der han kommer med en rekke grove, ærekrenkende og falske opplysninger om meg, sier Heidi.

Hun har flyttet fem ganger på disse årene, og hatt flere hemmelige adresser. Hver gang har engelskmannen, som jobber som jurist, klart å oppspore Heidi, blant annet ved å true hennes tidligere naboer på livet til de oppgir hvor hun befinner seg.

– Det er en enorm påkjenning når du får vite at også dine nye naboer har fått disse «rapportene» før du selv har rukket å bli kjent med dem, sier Heidi.

Drar til Norge

Heidi og mannen Runar har siden januar bodd i et nybygd hus på Solbergmoen. Også der har alle naboene fått tilsendt krenkende «rapporter» der det påstås at Heidi lever et svært utsvevende liv og er et moralsk ødelagt menneske.

– Selv om mannen er bosatt i England har han fløyet til Norge en åtte - ni ganger på disse årene og kommet på døren min. Den første gangen slapp jeg ham inn fordi jeg trodde han kom som en venn, men allerede neste gang han dukket opp var jeg blitt redd ham fordi han forhørte seg om hvor jeg var hvis han ringte og jeg ikke var hjemme, sier Heidi.

De neste gangene han dukket opp hjemme hos henne har Heidi smelt døren i ansiktet på ham, men da har han gått løs på døren hennes med kniv og risset inn obskøne meldinger. Han har også gått løs på naboenes dører, og skrevet «I'm gonna get you» på vinduene.

– Jeg veksler mellom å være livredd for mannen og fly forbannet på ham. Jeg har grått, tigget og rast når han har ringt meg for å få ham til å slutte å plage meg, men det nytter ikke. Når han setter i gang med telefonterroren sin ringer han med rundt en times mellomrom hele døgnet rundt, sier Heidi.

Heidi angrer bittert på at hun ga mannen navnet sitt og adressen for 13 år siden.

– Jeg var ung og dum, og hadde et helt annet inntrykk av mannen enn det jeg har i dag. Jeg la merke til at han fulgte etter meg på ferjen mellom England og Frankrike, men tenkte ikke noe spesielt over det. Vi kom i kontakt, tok en kopp te og så hverandre en fire-fem ganger i løpet av de ti månedene jeg bodde i England. Noe forhold har vi aldri hatt, sier Heidi.

Det hun ikke kunne vite var at den hyggelige mannen skulle bli helt besatt av henne og bruke de neste årene til å følge Heidis minste bevegelse. En periode hadde han en privatetterforsker som fotfulgte henne. Heidi selv, hennes familie og hennes venner er alle blitt truet på livet av mannen, som også har truet med at Heidis ni år gamle sønn skulle utryddes. I 1988 fikk Heidi tilsendt begravelseskort på seg selv fra mannen, som truet med at «hennes dager var omme».

I 1990 tok mannen med seg en bekjent til Bergen der Heidi var på besøk for å ta henne. Heidi fikk varslet politiet, som pågrep mannen og holdt ham i varetekt i to dager.

– Politiet hadde for lite på ham, og måtte løslate ham. Det eneste de kunne gjøre var å følge ham på flyet, og terroren fortsatte, sier Heidi, som føler seg maktesløs overfor mannens metoder. Etter at hun giftet seg med Runar for noen år siden ble det verre enn noensinne. Rett etter bryllupet fikk hun et brev der mannen skrev at han gjerne skulle vært til stede på bryllupsnatten. Bare de siste månedene har hun fått over 40 brev og utallige telefoner. Alle med den samme beskjeden: at Heidi lever et moralsk forkastelig liv, at engelskmannen hater henne og at han skal ta henne. Ordlyden i brevene egner seg ikke på trykk, men de er svært grove og perverse.

Når mannen ringer, hyler og skriker han i røret og slenger ut banneord. Heidi har båndopptak av en slik samtale, og har levert både mesteparten av brevene, rapportene og kassettene til sin advokat, som nå vurderer om de skal saksøke mannen for ærekrenkelser, personforfølgelse og redusert livskvalitet.

Det siste brevet kom for rundt en uke siden.

– Før gråt jeg når jeg fikk slike brev, nå lurer jeg bare på når det skal ta slutt, sier Heidi. Nylig fikk hun vite at mannen er anmeldt for lignende forhold i England, der han skal ha trakassert en yngre kvinne. For ikke lenge siden fikk han en dom på at han ikke kan nærme seg denne kvinnen, og Heidi håper å få noe lignende på ham her. Heidi vet at mannens mor har forsøkt å få ham tvangsinnlagt, men mannen er tydeligvis et av de vanskelige psykiatriske tilfellene som er for syke til å fengsles, men for friske til å legges inn til behandling.

– Retsapparatet må da kunne beskytte vanlige mennesker mot sinnslidende personer, sier Heidi, som er sliten etter årelang trakassering.

Engelskmannen har i 13 år drevet telefonterror mot Heidi og hennes familie, og har sendt henne over 400 perverse brev, kassetter og bøker om AIDS. Her er et par av brevene bare fra de siste månedene.

Drammens Tidende - 27th May 1995

English Translation

DRAMMENS TIDENDE 27TH May 1995

BADGERED AND HUNTED FOR THIRTEEN YEARS

For thirteen years an insane man has been making obscene telephone calls and has been stalking Heidi Schøne (31) from Nedre Eiker. This man has sent Heidi more than 400 obscene letters and threatened the lives of both Heidi and her family.

The man is obsessed with Heidi and has followed her movements for many years. For a long period he had a private investigator following her, and he has also several times shown up at Heidi's home and harassed her sexually.

Heidi reported him to the police many times but the police can't do much as long as he does not attack anybody physically.

TERRORISED FOR 13 YEARS

For thirteen years, Heidi Schøne from Nedre Eiker has been terrorised and chased by an insane man who has threatened to kill both her and her family.

After thirteen years of hell Heidi is now telling her story to cast light on the problem she knows that far more people than herself are struggling with; she is being chased by an insane man who is obsessed with her, and she feels powerless. She has on several occasions reported the man to the police, but their response is limited unless he attacks someone physically.

GAVE HER ADDRESS

The nightmare started when she was eighteen years old and gave her address to a half-German, half-Arab man living in England, who she met when she was an au pair. This was to become the start of years of derision for Heidi and her family. For thirteen years the man has been making obscene phone calls to Heidi and sent her more than 400 letters - all of them with perverse contents. She has also been sent books about AIDS and abortion and audio cassettes about herself.

"The worst part though are the 'reports' about me that he has sent my neighbours, family, friends and colleagues in which he is making a number of coarse and false statements about me", says Heidi. She has moved 5 times during all these years and has had several secret addresses. Each time, the Englishman, who works as a lawyer, managed to find Heidi, by means of threatening the lives of the neighbours until they tell him where she is.

"It is an enormous strain on you when you discover that your neighbours have received these 'reports' before you have got to know them yourself", says Heidi.

GOES TO NORWAY

Heidi and her husband, Runar, have since January lived in a new house at Solbergmoen. All of her neighbours have received scandalous 'reports' which claim that Heidi lives a very wild life, and is a morally destroyed human being.

"Even though the man lives in England, he has flown to Norway eight or nine times during these years and has come to my door. The first time I let him in, because I thought he came as a friend, but the next time he came I was already becoming afraid of him, because he had wanted to know where I was if he called and I was not at home", says Heidi.

The next time when he showed up, she slammed the door in his face; he has attacked her door with a knife and scratched obscene words on the door. He has also vandalised the neighbours' doors and written 'I am going to get you' on the windows.

"I changed between being terrified by the man and being totally irritated with him. I have begged, cried and raved when he has called to make him stop bothering me, but it doesn't help. When he started making frightening telephone calls, he calls on hourly intervals the whole night through", Heidi says.

Heidi deeply regrets that she gave her name and address to the man thirteen years ago.

"I was young and stupid and had then a completely different impression of the man than what I have today. I noticed that he followed me on the ferry between England and France, but I didn't give it much thought. We got in touch, had a cup of tea and met four or five times during the ten months I lived in England. We had never had any kind of relationship", says Heidi.

What she couldn't know was the 'nice man' would become completely obsessed with her and spend the next few years following her smallest moves. For a while he had a private detective follow her. Heidi, her family, and her friends have all been threatened by this man, who has also threatened to kill her 9 year old son. In 1988 Heidi was sent funeral cards by the man who told her 'her days were numbered'.

In 1990 the man brought a friend to Bergen, where Heidi was staying, in order to get her. Heidi managed to alert the police who apprehended him and kept him in custody for two days.

"The police didn't have enough on him to charge him and had to release him. The only thing they could do was take him to the plane, and the terror continued", says Heidi, who felt powerless in the face of the methods of this man. After marrying Runar a couple of years ago, the harassment became worse than ever. Immediately after the wedding, she received a letter in which the man wrote that he would have loved to have been there at the wedding night. Only in the last month, she has had more than 40 letters and countless numbers of telephone calls, all with the same message, that she is living a morally depraved life, that the Englishman hates her and is going to get her. The words in the letter are not suitable to print but they are very mean and perverse.

When the man calls, he yells and screams into the receiver and throws curses. Heidi recorded one of these calls and has delivered most of the letters, reports and the cassettes to her lawyer, who is now considering suing the man for defamation, stalking and reduced quality of life.

The last letter arrived about a month ago.

"Early on I cried when I received these kind of letters, now I just wonder when it will end", says Heidi.

Recently she found out that the man is known to the police for a similar case in England, where he is said to have harassed a younger woman. Not long ago he received a restraining order saying that he was not allowed to come near this woman and Heidi is hoping to get something similar done for her. Heidi knows that the man's mother has tried to commit him to a mental hospital, but the man is obviously one of those most difficult psychiatric cases where the person is too sick to be imprisoned, but too well to be committed to an institution.

"The judicial system has to be able to protect normal human beings against insane people", says Heidi, who is exhausted after years of harassment.

Story by Ingunn Røren (LINK)

Englishman's Comments:-

Although in Drammens Tidende there is not one reference to my being Muslim, they credit me with being "half-German, half-Arab". This is an accurate label but one must remember that Germany invaded Norway in World War Two and the word 'Arab' is often synonymous with the word 'Muslim'. The reference to "half-German, half-Arab" was used in this context as a derogatory term. The contents of this article are nauseating for the wholesale perversion of the truth. I never made a single obscene phone call, let alone continuously over a thirteen year period. Come on you wankers of the press; your desperation is pathetic! As if it was not possible to record one single obscene phone call in thirteen years. Besides which, Heidi had no phone at all from 1988 to 1993. When the newspaper said Heidi recorded one of my calls, no evidence ever subsequently came out on this aspect.

As far as all my "perverse, unprintable letters and cards" are concerned, I would love the press to have printed them in full. Then all will be able to see what total bollocks their claims were.

All these attacks against me in the newspaper articles were complete fabrications by Heidi and I now had the task of trying to counter those gross defamations and terrible lies. None of the newspapers had named me. But why not? Any guesses? One thing that did occur to me was that when Heidi spoke to the press, surely she would have had no idea that I myself would have got hold of the press reports as, of course, she was not to know I was instructing a lawyer at the same time in Bergen and it was he who alerted me to the newspaper articles. Thus from Heidi's point of view she would assume that no-one would have known any better from the stories she was telling, making them, therefore, versions of fact instead of what they really were, total fiction.

Z

VG NETT
Forsiden

7/7/98

Blir ikke kvitt sex-gal engelskmann
Av ALEXANDER NORDBY

I 16 år har en sex-gal engelskmann terrorisert Heidi Schøne med brev, telefoner og trusler.

BLIR PLAGET: Engelskmannen har hittil i år sendt 300 brev til Heidi Schøne. Foto: VG

Engelskmannen er fullstendig besatt av den norske kvinnen, og siden 1982 har han bombardert Heidi Schøne med telefonterror, drapstrusler, brevterror, fysisk oppmøte på døren hennes og trakkasering av hennes venner.

Mannen har også sendt hundrevis av brev til helt tilfeldige mennesker i Norge med alvorlige sex-anklager og intime påstander om den norske kvinnen.

Jeg har tigget, grått og truet for at han skulle la meg være i fred, sa Heidi Schøne til VG snakket med henne for tre år siden.

Fortsatt har Schøne og hennes familie hemmelig adresse og telefonnummer. Posten blir sortert av det lokale lensmannskontoret, som hittil i år har mottatt over 300 brev fra den 40 år gamle engelskmannen.

Påtrengende

Som 18-åring reiste Heidi Schøne til England for å jobbe som au pair. På en togtur kom hun i snakk med en halvt arabisk mann. Mannen oppførte seg rart og var påtrengende, men hun likte ham og snakket vennskapelig med ham. Helvetet startet da hun var kommet tilbake til Norge.

Mens hun oppholdt seg i Bergen, dukket engelskmannen plutselig opp. Til å begynne med slapp hun ham inn, men etter hvert ble han svært plagsom. Han ringte i et sett, sendte henne utallige brev, og ved en anledning måtte hun se på mens han gjorde obskøne ting.

Etter å ha blitt avvist risset han inn «fuck you» på døren med en kniv. Hun skaffet seg hemmelig adresse, men likevel dukket det opp et postkort med teksten «Freddy is back» - hentet fra en skrekkfilm med en hovedperson ved navn Freddy.

Saken er tidligere blitt etterforsket av politiet i Bergen. For tre år siden anmeldte Schøne på ny forholdet til politiet i Drammen.

- Det blir opp til statsadvokaten å vurdere om det skal sendes en henstilling til engelske myndigheter, sier politiinspektør Dag Einar Lyngås.

VG NETT

Forsiden

07/07/98

Erotisk paranoia

Psykiatere mener at den truende og elskovssyke engelsmannen kan lide av ekstrem erotisk paranoia.

Lidelsen er en vrangforestilling der en person er overbevist om at et annet menneske må være forelsket i vedkommende.

Erotisk paranoia rammer oftest kvinner, og særlig kvinner i overgangsalderen. Ofte går lidelsen over av seg selv etter noen år.

Personer med erotisk paranoia er sjelden slemme, som i tilfellet med engelskmannen.

(VG 07.07.98 kl. 06:41)

English Translation

Impossible to shake off sex-crazed Englishman

By **Alexander Nordby**

For 16 years a sex-crazed Englishman has terrorised Heidi Schøne with his letters, telephone calls and threats.

The Englishman is completely obsessed with the Norwegian woman, and since 1982 he has bombarded Heidi Schøne with terrorising phone calls, death threats, intimidating letters, and by turning up on her doorstep and harassing her friends.

The man has also sent to random individuals in Norway hundreds of letters containing serious sexual allegations and intimate claims about the Norwegian woman.

"I have begged, cried and threatened him to get him to leave me alone," said Heidi Schøne when VG spoke with her three years ago.

Ms Schøne and her family still have a secret address and an unlisted telephone number. Her post is sorted by the local police force, who so far this year have received more than 300 letters from the 40-year-old Englishman.

Forces himself on people

When Heidi Schøne was 18, she travelled to England to work as an au pair. While on a train, she met a man who was half Arabic. The man behaved strangely and was pushy, but she liked him and spoke to him in a friendly manner. Her life of hell began when she returned to Norway.

While she was staying in Bergen, the Englishman suddenly appeared on her doorstep. To begin with she let him in, but he gradually became extremely bothersome. He called her incessantly, sent her countless letters, and on one occasion he forced her to watch while he did obscene things.

After he had been rejected, he carved the words "fuck you" on a door with a knife. She moved to a secret address, but a postcard nevertheless appeared containing the words "Freddy's back" - taken from a horror film where the main character is called Freddy.

The case was previously investigated by the police force in Bergen. Three years ago, Ms Schøne reported the matter to the police in Drammen.

"It will be up to the public prosecutor to decide whether a request will be sent to the English authorities," says Dag Einar Lyngås, assistant chief of police.

Caption: HARASSED: The Englishman has sent 300 letters to Heidi Schøne so far this year.

Photo: VG

Erotic paranoia

Psychiatrists believe the threatening and lovesick Englishman may suffer from a case of extreme erotic paranoia.

This condition is a delusional disorder in which the individual is convinced that another person is in love with him or her.

Erotic paranoia most frequently affects women, particularly menopausal women. The disorder generally passes by itself after a few years.

People who suffer from erotic paranoia seldom act in an ill-willed manner, as is the case with the Englishman.

DT·BB
Drammens Tidende · Buskeruds Blad
NR. 159 · TIRSDAG 14. JULI 1998 · UKE 29 · LØSSAL

Tirsdagsværet

ELVEFE 98 Drammen

Forfulgt av gal mann i 16 år

ARKIVFOTO

I 16 år har en sinnslidende engelskmann plaget og forfulgt Heidi Schøne (bildet) fra Solbergelva. Flere ganger har hun flyttet og skaffet seg hemmelig adresse og telefonnummer, men mannen sporer henne opp. Bare i år har han sendt over 300 brev, og ringt en rekke ganger.

Sex-trakassert i 16 år

I 16 år er Heidi Schøne fra Solbergelva blitt trakassert og forfulgt av en sinnslidende engelskmann. Bare det siste året har mannen sendt Heidi over 300 brev og ringt en rekke ganger.

Ingunn Røren

Den muslimske mannen har vært besatt av Heidi Schøne (34) siden hun var 18 år gammel. Hans årelange trakassering av Heidi og hennes familie har vært en enorm belastning. DT-BB omtalte saken første gang for tre år siden. Fortsatt trakasseres familien Schøne av den samme mannen.

Vil være i fred

– Vi ønsker bare å få være i fred. Denne mannen er svært syk, og hans utallige brev og telefoner er en enorm påkjenning, sier Heidis mann, Runar Schøne.

I årevis har familien Schøne levd med en rekke hemmelige telefonnumre og hemmelige adresser. Hver gang klarer mannen å oppspore dem etter en stund, og da fortsetter terroren inntil familien får gjemt seg på nytt.

«Rapporter»

I løpet av de 16 årene har mannen sendt ut en rekke «rapporter» til Heidis familie, venner, naboer, kolleger og en rekke ukjente mennesker. Rapportene er grovt ærekrenkende, og opplysningene som står der har ikke rot i virkeligheten. Nå har nok en gang en rekke drammensere fått «rapporter» om Heidi i postkassen. Rapportene er utformet som om de er svar på en forespørsel fra Drammens Tidende, VG og Bergens Tidende, men ingen av avisene har på noen måte bedt om å få en slik rapport.

«Ekstrem ondskap»

- Jeg aner ikke hvem Heidi Schøne er, og skjønte ingenting da jeg åpnet konvolutten og fant bilder av Heidi Schøne og hennes mann samt en skittkasting jeg aldri har sett maken til. Det må være forferdelig for familien Schøne å bli utsatt for noe slikt. Hele brevet gir uttrykk for en ekstrem ondskap, sier Per Lieblein fra Konnerud som mottok brevet mandag.

Trakasseringen er anmeldt til politiet. Nedre Eiker lensmannskontor har etterforsket saken i tre år.

Utleveres ikke

- Problemet er at forholdene

ARKIVFOTO

I årevis har Heidi Schøne og hennes familie levd med en rekke hemmelige telefonnumre og hemmelige adresser. Men en psykisk syk engelskmann har gang etter gang sporet opp adressen og sender trakasserende brev.

mannen er siktet for ikke holder til å få ham utlevert fra England. Han har imidlertid fått klar beskjed om at han vil bli pågrepet hvis han kommer til Norge, sier lensmannsbetjent Toril Sorte Kjennås ved Nedre Eiker lensmannskontor.

Sortert post

For å skåne Heidi og hennes familie blir all post som kommer til dem sortert på lensmannskontoret. Hittil i år har Sorte Kjennås og hennes kolleger tatt hånd om over 300 brev mannen har sendt til Heidi. Familien har hemmelig telefonnummer, og hos Telenor er nummeret merket med beskjed fra politiet om at det er konfidensielt og ikke skal gis ut under noen omstendighet. Familiens adresse er hemmelig, og er sperret for utlevering fra Folkeregisteret.

Trusler

- På tross av dette har mannen likevel klart å spore oss opp et par ganger, og da setter telefonterroren i gang igjen. Mannen bruker all sin tid på å finne Heidi, og utgir seg for å være forskjellige personer for å få tak i nummeret vårt, sier Runar Schøne. Mannen har tidligere truet naboer av familien på livet for å få vite hvor de har flyttet.

Drakk te sammen

Heidi Schøne møtte den muslimske mannen da hun som 18-åring var au pair i England. Hun så på mannen som en venn, og drakk te med ham et par ganger. De har aldri hatt noe kjærlighetsforhold, men i 16 år har engelskmannen vært besatt av tanken på å gifte seg med Heidi. En lang periode hadde han en privatdetektiv som fulgte alle Heidis bevegelser. Trakasseringen økte i omfang da Heidi for ni år siden giftet seg.

Psykiatere mener at engelskmannen lider av et ekstremt tilfelle av erotisk paranoia.

English Translation

Drammens Tidende 14/07/1998

SEXUALLY HARASSED FOR 16 YEARS

For 16 years Heidi Schøne from Solbergelva has been pestered and followed by a mentally ill Englishman. In only the last year the man has sent more than 300 letters to Heidi and made numerous phone calls

The Muslim man has been obsessed by Heidi Schøne (34) since she was 18 years old. His long time pestering of Heidi and her family has been a huge strain. DT-BB first covered this case three years ago. Still, the family is being badgered by the same man. Want to be left alone

"All we want is to be left alone. This man is very ill and his countless letters and phone calls put an enormous strain on us all" says Heidi's husband Runar Schøne. For years the Schønes have been living with a string of secret phone numbers and addresses, but each time the man manages to find them and the terror continues until they manage to hide themselves away again.

"Reports"

In the course of the 16 years this man has sent out many "reports" to Heidi's family, friends, neighbours, colleagues and a number of strangers. These reports are grossly defamatory and the information listed has no basis in reality. Once again, many people from Drammen have received "reports" about Heidi in their mail box. The reports are modelled like answers for questionnaires from Drammens Tidende, VG and Bergens Tidende, but none of the newspapers mentioned have ever asked for such a report.

Extreme evil

"I do not know who Heidi Schøne is and I didn't understand anything when I opened the envelope containing pictures of Heidi Schøne and her husband together with revelations of filth, I have never seen the likes of. It must be awful for the Schøne family to be exposed to something like that. The entire letter reeks of extreme evil" says Per Leiblein from Konnerud who received a letter on Monday.

The harassment has been reported to the police. Nedre Eiker Constabulary has been investigating this case for three years.

No extradition

The problem is that the circumstances this man is being charged for are not enough to have him extradited from England. He has on the other hand been clearly told that he will be arrested if he comes to Norway, says local policewoman Torill Sorte Kjennås at Nedre Eiker Constabulary.

Screening Mail

To protect Heidi and her family, all their mail is screened at the Constabulary. So far this year Sorte Kjennås and her colleagues have dealt with more than 300 letters from the man. The family has got a secret phone number, and Telenor have been notified by the police that the number is confidential and is not to be given out to anyone, no matter what the circumstances. The family's address is secret and is barred from disclosure by the National Registration Office (Folkeregistret).

Threats

"In spite of all this the man has nevertheless managed to trace us down a couple of times, and when he does, the phone terror starts again. The man spends all his time tracking Heidi and passes himself off as different persons in order to get hold of our number," says Runar Schøne. The man has previously threatened neighbours of the family with lethal force to know where they have moved.

Drank tea together

Heidi Schøne met the Muslim man when at the age of 18 she was in England as an au pair. She regarded the man as a friend and drank tea with him on a couple of occasions. They have never had any relationship, but for 16 years the Englishman has been obsessed by the idea of marrying Heidi. For a long period he hired a private investigator to follow Heidi's every move. The harassment increased nine years ago when Heidi got married.

Psychiatrists believe the Englishman suffers from an extreme case of erotic paranoia. (Under Heidi's photo):-

For years Heidi Schøne and her family have lived with a number of secret phone numbers and secret addresses. But a mentally ill Englishman has time and time again traced their address and is sending harassing letters.

Drammens Tidende
Nettutgaven dt.no

26 August 2000

Kom for å kreve penger - ble bøtelagt

Engelskmannen kom til Drammen for å kreve nesten 400 000 kroner i oppreisning fra en Nedre Eiker-kvinne og Drammens Tidende, men ble møtt med en bot på 10 000 kroner. Han fikk boten for å ha krenket den 38 år gamle kvinnens privatliv i en årrekke. Sammen med boten ble han presentert for et ilagt forbud mot å kontakte kvinnen på noen som helst måte. Politiinspektør Dag Einar Lyngås har sendt begjæringen om besøksforbud til byretten for godkjenning. Engelskmannen vedtok ikke forelegget, og ble umiddelbart stevnet for hovedforhandling i byretten 9. oktober.
Han kom egentlig til Norge og Drammen for å kreve penger fra Drammens Tidende og kvinnen. For tre år siden sto kvinnen fram i Drammens Tidende med historien om hvordan hun i 16 år var blitt forfulgt av mannen hun traff mens hun var au pair i England. Mannen saksøkte i etterhånd både avisen, redaktør Hans Arne Odde, journalisten som skrev saken og Nedre Eiker-kvinnen. Han krever 50 000 kroner i oppreisning fra henne, mens kravet mot avis og journalist er på totalt 330 000 kroner. Da det ble klart at han kom til Norge i forbindelse med søksmålet, benyttet politiet anledningen. Etter det Drammens Tidende forstår, ville politiet neppe krevd mannen utlevert til Norge.
Den 38 år gamle kvinnen anmeldte engelskmannen for flere år siden. I en årrekke skal han ha ringt henne og sendt utallige brev. Andre personer, offentlige institusjoner og private firmaer mottok også brev og telefaxer, som ble sporet tilbake til mannen. Innholdet i brevene og faxene var svært ufordelaktige opplysninger om kvinnen.
På spørsmål fra Drammens Tidende, svarer mannens advokat, Stig Lunde, at han ikke har noen kommentarer til boten og besøksforbudet.

English Translation

Drammens Tidende 26/08/2000

Came to demand money - was fined

The Englishman came to Drammen in order to demand nearly 400 000 kroner in compensation from a Nedre-Eiker woman and Drammens Tidende, but was met with a fine of 10 000 kroner. He got the fine for having violated the 38 year old woman's private life over a number of years. Together with the fine, he was banned from contacting the woman in any way whatsoever.

Police Inspector Dag Einar Lyngås sent to the county court for approval the application for a ban on visits. The Englishman did not accept the fine and was immediately summonsed for the main hearing in the county court on 9 October.

Actually, he came to Norway and Drammen in order to demand money from Drammens Tidende and the woman. Three years ago, the woman appeared in Drammens Tidende with the story of how, at the age of 16, she had been pursued by the man she met while she was an au-pair in England. The man sued successively both the newspaper, editor Hans Arne Odde, the journalist who wrote up the case and the Nedre-Eiker woman. He is demanding 50 000 kroner compensation from her, while the claim against newspaper and journalist totals 330 000 kroner.

When it became clear that he had come to Norway in connection with the lawsuit, the police took advantage of the opportunity. According to the understanding of Drammens Tidende, the police would hardly have demanded extradition of the man to Norway.

The 38 year old woman reported the Englishman several years ago. For a number of years, it is reported, he telephoned her and sent innumerable letters. Other people, public institutions and private firms also received letters and faxes, which were traced back to the man. The contents of the letters and faxes were information greatly to the discredit of the woman.

In reply to questions from Drammens Tidende, the man's lawyer, Stig Lunde, says that he does not have any comments to make on the fine and the ban on visiting.

Drammens Tidende

Fredag 16. november 2001 – Uke 46 * * – Nr. 266 – Løssalg kr. 10.00 – dt.no

MED RADIO- OG TV-MAGASIN

DRAMMENS TIDENDE · BUSKERUDS BLAD

Bot for grov sexterror

Plaget kvinne i 16 år - må betale 10 000

43-åringen som har sex-terrorisert en kvinne fra Nedre Eiker med utallige telefonoppringer og brev og postkort gjennom 16 år, slipper fengselsstraff. 10 000 kroner i bot synes retten er en passende straff. At mannen er bosatt i England er grunnen til at han slipper fengsel. Retten legger ikke skjul på at denne straffen er svært mild. Forholdene som mannen er dømt for, har en strafferamme på inntil seks måneders fengsel.

Side 3

10 000 i bot for 16 års sexterror

Slapp fengsel fordi han bor i England

43-åringen som ble dømt for å ha terrorisert en kvinne fra Nedre Eiker med utallige telefonoppringer og rundt 200 brev og postkort gjennom 16 år, slipper fengselsstraff. 10 000 kroner i bot synes retten er en passende straff.

Av Lars Arntzen
lars.arntzen@dt.no

Den 43 år gamle engelskmannen ble idømt en bot på 10 000 kroner allerede i fjor høst, men denne nektet han å betale.

Dermed endte saken i herredsretten, hvor han tapte på samtlige punkter. At mannen er bosatt i England, er faktisk grunnen til at han slipper fengselsstraff. Aktor, politiinspektør Dag Einar Lyngås, valgte å legge ned påstand om bot istedenfor fengsel fordi en utleveringssak fra England ville bli for kostbar.

Mild straff

Retten legger imidlertid ikke skjul på at denne straffen er svært mild. Forholdene som mannen er dømt for, har en strafferamme på inntil seks måneders fengsel, og retten mener at straffen normalt ville ligget opp mot denne maksimumsstraffen.

Advokat Vegard Aaløkken har representert kvinnen i rettssaken, og han har rådet sin klient til ikke å uttale seg til media. Men han bekrefter at kvinnen er glad for at mannen ble dømt i herredsretten.

- Hun er først og fremst glad for å bli trodd av retten, sier Aaløkken til Drammens Tidende.

- Hvordan reagerer hun på at mannen ikke ble idømt fengselsstraff?

- Normalt ville det vært naturlig med en strengere reaksjon, men hun er vel enig i rettens merknader. Det viktigste for henne er at mannen ble dømt.

Rapport om livsførsel

Telefonsamtalene, brevene og postkortene til kvinnen skal ha båret preg av til dels svært grov sjikane. En del av brevene og postkortene, hvor kvinnen omtales i nedlatende ordelag, skal også ha blitt sendt til andre privatpersoner og offentlige og private bedrifter. Temaene i brevene har stort sett dreid seg om hennes seksualliv, aborter, selvmordsforsøk og rusmisbruket til partneren.

Ifølge kvinnen skal også mannen ha distribuert en «rapport» om henne til naboer, venner og slektninger. Notatet innledes med «Vi kan nå avlegge rapport angående Deres livsførsel», og var hans versjon av hennes livshistorie. I retten forklarte kvinnen at det var svært vanskelig for henne at så mange personer i nærmiljøet mottok «rapporten» fra 43-åringen. At deler av innholdet var sant, gjorde det hele bare enda vanskeligere for henne.

Engelskmannen og Nedre Eiker-kvinnen møttes første gang for over 20 år siden da hun var au-pair i Storbritannia. I begynnelsen skal kontakten ha båret preg av vennlighet, og mannen ble beskrevet som sjarmerende og veltalende. Kvinnen valgte etter hvert å betro ham sine personlige problemer, og på den måten fikk han innsyn i livet hennes. I løpet av årenes løp gjorde kvinnen en rekke forsøk på å hindre tiltalte fra å ta kontakt. Hun skaffet seg blant annet hemmelig adresse og telefonnummer, men ingenting hjalp. Via privatdetektiv klarte 43-åringen å spore henne opp igjen.

«Truslene ble provosert fram»

43-åringen nekter fortsatt straffskyld for telefonsamtalene og brevene til Nedre Eiker-kvinnen. Advokaten hans mener alt er fremprovosert av kvinnen selv.

I retten ba advokat Harald Bjelke Wibye derfor om at klienten måtte frifinnes. Responsen på provokasjonene er etter hans syn ikke grunn god nok for å idømme engelskmannen straff.

I 1990 anmeldte kvinnen mannen for voldtekt. Senere har hun også gått ut i avisene og fortalt om hans oppførsel. Retten avviser imidlertid at dette er provokasjoner som kan frita 43-åringen fra straff.

I dommen skriver retten at voldtektsanmeldelsen ble foretatt fordi hun mente det var foregått et overgrep og ikke for å provosere tiltalte. Når det gjelder avisskriveriene, kom disse i stand etter initiativ fra journalister, og tiltaltes navn er ikke nevnt i artiklene.

Advokat Bjelke Wibye er ikke fornøyd med dommen, men han vil foreløpig ikke si noe om en eventuell anke. Dommen er i ferd med å bli oversatt, slik at også engelskmannen kan lese den. Deretter skal de vurdere hva som skjer videre i denne saken, men sannsynligvis går det mot en anke.

- Min klient føler seg uskyldig dømt. Han mener at kvinnens opplysninger er feilaktige og grovt injurierende. Blant annet faller voldtektsanmeldelsen på sin egen urimelighet, hevder advokaten.

Uansett er det ikke siste gang Bjelke Wibyes klient og Nedre Eiker-kvinnen har møtt hverandre i retten. Allerede i januar møtes de igjen. Da er det en privat straffesak som mannen har reist mot henne, som skal behandles.

English Translation

Pestered woman for 16 years - must pay 10,000 kroner

A 43 year old man who sex-terrorized a woman from Nedre Eiker with countless phone calls and letters and postcards over 16 years escapes imprisonment. The Court considers a 10,000 kroner fine is an appropriate punishment. The fact that the man is resident in England is the reason why he is escaping imprisonment. The Court makes no secret of the fact that this punishment is extremely lenient. The charges on which the man has been convicted carry a maximum penalty of up to six months imprisonment.

10,000 fine for 16 years of sex terror

Escaped imprisonment because he lives in England.

A 43 year old convicted of terrorising a woman from Nedre Eiker with countless phone calls and around 200 letters and postcards over 16 years escapes imprisonment. The Court considers a 10,000 kroner fine is an appropriate punishment.

The 43 year old Englishman was fined 10,000 kroner last autumn but refused to pay this.

That concluded the action in the County Court, in which he lost in all respects. The fact that the man is resident in England is the real reason why he is escaping imprisonment. The prosecutor, police inspector Dag Einar Lyngås, opted to ask for a fine instead of imprisonment because extradition from England would be too expensive

Lenient punishment

However, the Court is making no secret of the fact that this punishment is extremely lenient. The charges on which the man has been convicted carry a maximum penalty of up to six months imprisonment, and the Court is of the view that the punishment would normally have been approaching this maximum penalty.

Lawyer Vegard Aaløkken represented the woman in the case, and he has advised his client not to speak to the media. But he confirmed that the woman is pleased that the man has been convicted in the County Court.

"She is first and foremost pleased to have been believed by the Court," Aaløkken told Drammens Tidende. Asked about her reaction to the man not having been sentenced to imprisonment, he replied:

"A stronger reaction would normally have been natural, but she is in full agreement with the Court's remarks. The most important thing for her is that the man has been convicted."

Report on life

The telephone calls, the letters and the postcards to the woman are said to have been marked by in part extremely serious malice. Some of the letters and the postcards, in which the woman is referred to in condescending terms, are also said to have been sent to other private individuals and public and private businesses. The subject matter of the letters was on the whole concerned with her sex life, abortions, suicide attempts and partner's drug abuse.

According to the woman, the man also distributed a 'report' about her to neighbours, friends and relatives. The note began "We can now submit a report about your life" and was his version of her life story.

In Court, the woman explained that it was extremely difficult for her that so many people in her immediate circle had received "the report" from the 43 year old. The fact that some of the content was true only made the whole thing even more difficult for her.

The Englishman and the woman from Nedre Eiker first met over 20 years ago when she was an au pair in Britain. Initially, the contact is said to have been marked by friendliness, and the man was described as charming and eloquent. The woman chose to confide her personal problems in him gradually, and this was how he gained an insight into her life. Over the years, the woman made a number of attempts to prevent the defendant from making contact. Among other things, she obtained a secret address and telephone number, but to no avail. The 43 year old managed to trace her again through a private detective.

"The threats were provoked"

The 43 year old continues to deny culpability for the telephone calls and the letters to the Nedre Eiker woman. His lawyer is of the opinion that everything was provoked by the woman herself.

In Court, lawyer Harald Bjelke Wibye therefore asked for his client to be acquitted. In his view, the response to the provocations is not a good enough reason to convict the Englishman.

In 1990, the woman reported the man for rape. Later, she also appeared in the newspapers and gave an account of his behaviour. The Court nevertheless refused to accept that these are provocations which could exempt the 43 year old from punishment.

In its sentence, the Court states that the rape report was made because in her opinion an assault had taken place and not in order to provoke the defendant. As far as the items in the papers are concerned, these were arranged on the initiative of journalists, and the name of the defendant was not mentioned in the articles.

Lawyer Bjelke Wibye is not satisfied with the sentence, but will for the time being not say anything about a possible appeal. The sentence is in the process of being translated so that the Englishman can read it as well. They will then assess what happens next in this case, but in all likelihood there will be an appeal.

"My client feels he has been wrongfully convicted. He believes the woman's statements are wrong and grossly defamatory. Among other things, the rape report is down to her own unreasonableness", the lawyer said.

In any case, this is not the last time Bjelke Wibye's client and the Nedre Eiker woman have met one another in Court. They are to meet again as early as in January. Then, it is a private criminal case the man has brought against her that is to be dealt with.

ENGELSKMANNENS SVAR TIL DRAMMENS TIDENDES OVERSKRIFT:

"BOT FOR GROV SEXTERROR" 16. NOVEMBER 2001, AV LARS ARNTZEN

Ifølge hans rett til å svare, sier engelskmannen ovennevnte artikkel viser til som følger:

1) Engelskmannen var ikke til stede under rettsmøtet den 30. oktober 2001 fordi han ikke hadde tid til å forberede seg i saken. Den vesentligste grunnen var at hans advokat ikke fikk politiets "bevismateriale" før dagen før rettsmøtet; dessuten var en hel del av dette ikke bevist og kunne derfor ikke godtas av retten.

2) Ingen journalister var til stede under rettsmøtet. Ovennevnte artikkel i Drammens Tidende gir et tvers igjennom villedende inntrykk av rettsmøtet.

3) Faktum er at politiet i Drammen var villig til å gjøre opp saken ved at engelskmannen betalte boten på kr. 5.000, noe vedkommende nektet av prinsippmessige grunner.

4) Bevisene som felte engelskmannen bestod kun av "rapporter" til den norske offentligheten som ga hans side av historien til kriminelt injurierende avisartikler fra 1995, som inkluderte provoserende og helt falske påstander fra den norske kvinnens side - både nå og tidligere en psykiatrisk pasient. Det har aldri vært noen såkalte "16 år med sexterror", medmindre man da regner med den sexterror norske menn drev overfor denne kvinnen.

5) "Rapportene" ble sendt over et tidsrom av tre år, 1995 til 1998, og det var da egentlig kjernen i politiets påtale.

6) Hvorfor svarte engelskmannen på denne måten? Opprinnelig var det bare en håndfull "rapporter" om kvinnens livshistorie som ble sent p.g.a. ekstrem provokasjon fra den norske kvinnens side (falsk påstand overfor politiet om voldteksforsøk), fulgt av flere "rapporter" etter ekstrem provokasjon fra Verdens Gang, Bergens Tidende og Drammens Tidende i 1995 og 1998. Disse avisene viste mange fotografier av kvinnen og navnga henne. Den norske kvinnen hadde gitt frivillig avkall på hennes rett til å forbli anonym. Imidlertid trodde ikke de tre avisene at engelskmannen ville finne ut noe om de tre artiklene da han var bosatt i England. Men han fikk omgående greie på det fordi han allerede i desember 1994 hadde bedt en norsk jurist om å undersøke kvinnen og hennes forsøk på å villede retten.

7) Politianklagen 30. oktober 2001 gjaldt bare et ansvarsforhold, nemlig det å sende ut detaljer om kvinnens livshistorie; en anklage som ikke kan forsvares fordi den norske kvinnen var allerede navngitt i "rapportene".

8) Imidlertid navnga ikke de norske avisene ham når de rettet skytset mot ham, en forsvarsløs utlending, idet de mente at hvis han mot formodning skulle få greie på artiklene, så ville han stå overfor den nesten umulige opgaven å finne en nordmann som kjente ham igjen fra artiklene før han kunne anlegge krininal- eller sivilsak om injurier. Noe som ville medføre enorme personlige, økonomiske omkostninger.

9) Før hun var 18 år hadde den norske kvinnen hatt to aborter med samme nordmann. Hun hevdet så at hun ble gjort gravid av en annen elsker senere, nå med tvillinger, men aborterte etter at hun oppdaget hans utroskap. Hun forsøkte å begå selvmord. Senere gikk hun til sengs med den utro mannen igjen, samt med en

annen nordmann, i et forsøk på å bli gravid med den ene eller begge. Den utro mannen brukte nå heroinsprøyte idet han tidligere hadde sittet i militærfengsel. Hun lyktes i bli gravid med heroinbrukeren, og fødte en sønn. Faren støtte henne fra seg igjen, og hun forsøkte å begå selvmord igjen, som sa at det eneste hun hadde felles med faren var "god sex". De hadde knapt bodd sammen. Kvinnen ble så innlagt på en psykiatrisk klinikk, og giftet seg i 1993 med en mann som hevdet at han "talte i tunger". Ekteskapet brøt sammen, og hun ble skilt i 2001.

10) I hele tidsrommet 1982-1990 bad den norske kvinnen engelskmannen om hjelp med å løse de problemene hun hadde med menn, men fortsatte med katastrofale forbindelser, til engelskmannens store fortvilelse, som selvsagt følte seg tvunget til å si henne "noen sannhetsord".

11) Drammens Tidende antyder at engelskmannen svek kvinnens betroelser om hennes promiskuøse privatliv og personlige problemer. Engelskmannen mente at kvinnen, gjennom sin troløshet overfor ham, hadde forsaket enhver rett til fortrolighet.

12) I 1995 oppdaget engelskmannen at kvinnen hadde klaget til politiet i Bergen i 1986 at engelskmannen hadde forsøkt å voldta henne i april 1985. Hun ventet i 20 måneder før hun kom med denne (falske) anklagen; en klage hun fremsatte bare to uker etter at engelskmannen hadde varslet hennes familie om hennes utrygge seksuelle vaner og selvmordstendenser. Klagen var som hevn for at engelskmannen fortalte hennes familie om hennes fortid, idet familien hadde vært helt uvitende om den sexterror norske borgere hadde utøvet mot henne.

13) Under rettsmøtet i Drammen den 30. oktober 2001, innrømmet den norske kvinnen at hun også hadde anklaget en butikkeier i Bergen for voldtekt i 1980-årene. Politiet kom aldri med anklagepåstand. I 1980-årene hevdet den norske kvinnen også at greske menn hadde forsøkt å voldta henne og truet henne med kniv. I 1995 hevdet hun overfor Drammens Tidende at engelskmannen hadde forsøkt å voldta henne. I 1998 forandret hun mening.

Da engelskmannen bad politiet i Drammen om å undersøke hennes påstand om voldtektsforsøk, hevdet kvinnen nå at det dreiet som reell voldtekt. Politiet har aldri kommet med anklagepåstand. Ikke desto mindre, disse falske påstandene mot engelskmannen, som tok sikte på å ødelegge ham og ihvertfall få han arrestert og forhørt, var tilstrekkelig provokasjon for engelskmannen til å offentligjøre kvinnens tidligere historie for å understreke de problemene han hadde hatt å stri med på grunn av en syk kvinne. Til å begynne med var det bare hennes naboer som ble informert.

14) Drammens befolkning må også meddeles at kvinnen fortalte Drammens Tidende i 1995 at i 1988 hadde engelskmannen etter sigende truet med å myrde hennes 2 år gamle sønn. Ingunn Røren offentliggjorde denn påstanden som et faktum, uten noe som helst understøttende bevismateriale! Senere undersøkelser avslørte at kvinnen fortalte politiet at den påståtte mordtruselen ble gjort av engelskmannen i et brev som ble "gitt til politiet i Bergen". Politiet i Bergen fortalte politiet i Drammen at de ikke hadde et slikt brev. Påstanden er selvfølgelig falsk og tar sikte på å skape store vansker for engelskmannen, eller kanskje til og med ødelegge ham fullstendig.

Slik ondaktig påstand må da være provokasjon stor nok til at engelskmannen kan gjøre den norske befolkning kjent med sannheten til pikens fortid, og dermed bakgrunnen til den kvinnen som har fremsatt slike påstander mot ham i både lokalaviser og landsdekkende aviser. Engelskmannen hadde ingen annen måte å svare på.

15) Dessuten har den norske kvinnen innrømmet overfor politiet i Drammen at selv etter at hun kom med disse påstandene mot engelskmannen, om voldtektsforsøk og trusel om å myrde en 2-åring, så fortsatte hun likevel å be om engelskmannens hjelp i 1988 til å holde styr på den ubehagelige oppførselen til barnets far. Ingen normal kvinne ber en som hevdes å ha begått voldtekt og truet med å drepe et barn om hjelp. Faktum er at barnets far overfalt henne i 1990, og han ble anmeldt til politiet.

16) I august 1990 gjenopptok den norske kvinnen et hyggelig forhold til engelskmannen i den grad at hun til og med sendte ham postkort og brev og kristelig litteratur.

17) Engelskmannen tror at kvinnen er en sinnsyk som langt fra å være "et uskyldig offer" slik det hevdes av den xenofobiske pressen, tvertimot er en kaldt beregnende løgner som tar lite eller intet hensyn til vanlig standard for sivilisert oppførsel.

18) Den tidligere journalisten i Drammens Tidende, Ingunn Røren, har beviselig begått mened overfor Pressens Faglige Utvalg; fakta som for tiden behandles av Drammen Byrett.

19) I England trykker avisene ofrenes navn hvis de sitter inne med riktige fakta. Den omfattende tåkeleggingen som gjøres av det norske etablissement er en permanent skamplett på dets omdømme.

English Translation

The "Englishman's" Response to Drammens Tidende headline "Fine for Serious Sex Terror" of 16th November 2001 by Lars Arntzen

In accordance with his right to reply the Englishman referred to in the above articles states as follows:-

1. The Englishman did not attend the Court hearing on 30th October 2001 as he had no time to prepare for the case, particularly as his lawyer only received the police "evidence" the day before the hearing, a lot of which was in fact not proven and inadmissible to the Court.

2. No journalists attended the hearing. The above Drammens Tidende article is a complete misrepresentation of the Court proceedings.

3. The fact is that the Drammen police were prepared to settle the matter if the Englishman paid a 5,000 Kroner fine, which he refused on grounds of principle.

4. The evidence which convicted the Englishman consisted merely of 'reports' to the Norwegian public giving his side of the story to criminally libellous newspaper stories from 1995 which included provocative and wholly false allegations from the Norwegian woman - presently and in the past a psychiatric patient. There has never been any so called "16 years of Sex Terror", unless one counts the sex terror inflicted by Norwegian men on this woman.

5. The 'reports' were sent for a three year period, 1995 to 1998 and that in essence was the reason for the police prosecution.

6. Why did the Englishman respond in this manner? Only a handful of 'reports' on the woman's life history were initially sent due to extreme provocation by the Norwegian woman (a false allegation to the police of attempted rape), followed by more 'reports' after extreme provocation by Verdens Gang, Bergens Tidende and Drammens Tidende in 1995 and 1998, which newspapers showed many photographs of the woman and named her. The Norwegian woman had voluntarily waived her right to anonymity. However, the three newspapers did not think the Englishman would find out about the articles as he was of course living in England. But he did immediately find out as he had earlier, in December 1994, asked a Norwegian lawyer to investigate the woman for her attempts to pervert the course of justice.

7. The police charge of 30th October 2001 was for a strict liability offence, i.e. sending out details of the woman's life history, for which there is no defence available as the Norwegian woman was named in "the reports".

8. However, the Norwegian newspapers in targeting a defenceless foreigner did not name him, meaning that in the unlikely event that he did find out about the articles, he would have to face the almost impossible task of finding a Norwegian who recognised him from the articles in order to enable him to sue for criminal and civil libel and at enormous personal, financial and emotional cost.

9. By the time she was 18, the Norwegian woman had had two abortions to the same Norwegian man. She then claimed she got pregnant later to another lover carrying twins, but miscarried after discovering his infidelity. She then attempted suicide. Later she resumed sleeping with the unfaithful man and at the same time with yet another Norwegian man, trying to get pregnant to both, or either. The unfaithful man was injecting heroin having been in military prison previously. She succeeded in getting pregnant to the I.V. heroin user and a son was born. The father again rejected the girl and a further suicide attempt followed by the girl who said all she had in common with the father was "good sex". They had rarely lived together. The woman then entered a psychiatric clinic and in 1994 married a man who claimed to "speak in tongues". Her marriage failed and she was divorced in 2001.

10. Throughout the period 1982-1990 the Norwegian woman was asking the Englishman for help in solving her problems with men, but repeatedly kept on with disastrous liaisons, much to the exasperation of the Englishman, who naturally was forced to tell her some "home truths".

11. Drammens Tidende intimated that the Englishman betrayed the woman's confidences about her promiscuous private life and personal problems. The Englishman decided that by the woman's treachery towards him, she has waived her right to these confidences being kept.

12. In 1995, the Englishman discovered that in December 1986 the woman had complained to the Bergen police that the Englishman had attempted to rape her in April 1985. There was a delay of 20 months in making this (false) allegation, which complaint was made a mere two weeks after the Englishman had warned her family of her unsafe sexual practices and suicidal tendencies. The complaint was in revenge for the Englishman's revelations of her past to her own family who had been ignorant of the sex terror inflicted on her by Norwegian citizens.

13. At the Drammen Court hearing on 30th October 2001, the Norwegian woman admitted also that she made an allegation against a Bergen shopkeeper in the 1980s of rape. The police did not bring charges. In the 1980s, the Norwegian woman also claimed Greek men had tried to rape her at knifepoint. In 1995, she alleged to Drammens Tidende that the Englishman had attempted to rape her. In 1998, she changed her story. At the request of the Englishman of the Drammen police to investigate the allegation of attempted rape, the woman now claimed it was actual rape. The police have never brought charges. Notwithstanding this, these false allegations against the Englishman, designed to ruin him and at the very least get him arrested and questioned, were sufficient provocation for the Englishman to release the woman's past history to the public to highlight the problems he had been facing from a sick woman. Initially, only her neighbours were told.

14. The Drammen public must also be made aware that the woman told Drammens Tidende in 1995 that the Englishman had in 1988 allegedly threatened to murder her 2 year old son. Without any corroborative evidence Ingunn Røren printed this allegation as 'a fact'. Later enquiries revealed that the woman told police that the alleged murder threat was made by the Englishman in a letter which was "given to the Bergen police". The Bergen police told the Drammen police they had no such letter. Of course, the allegation is false and designed to cause much trouble to the Englishman, if not to ruin him.

Such a malicious allegation is surely provocation enough for the Englishman to be able to acquaint the Norwegian public with the truth of the girl's past so they knew the background of a woman making such allegations against him, via her national and local press. The Englishman had no other means to reply.

15. Besides which the Norwegian woman has admitted to the Drammen police that even after making allegations of attempted rape and threats to murder a 2 year old against the Englishman, she still proceeded in 1988 to request the Englishman's help in restraining the abusive father of her child. No woman in her right mind asks an alleged rapist and alleged potential child killer over to help her. The fact is that the father of her child assaulted her in 1990 and he was reported to the police.

16. In 1990, August, the Norwegian woman resumed a cosy friendship with the Englishman even sending him postcards and letters and Christian literature.

17. The Englishman believes the woman is a lunatic who far from being the "innocent victim" as portrayed by her xenophobic press, is a calculating, scheming opportunistic liar with little regard for normal standards of civilised behaviour.

18. The former Drammens Tidende journalist Ingunn Røren in on record as having given perjured evidence to the Norwegian Press Complaints Commission; facts presently with the Drammen City Court.

19. In England, Newspapers print the name of their victims if they've got their facts right. The extensive cover-up by the Norwegian establishment is a permanent stain on its reputation.

I telephoned the newspaper on 10th April 2002 as once they had seen my website they e-mailed my ISP to ask me to make contact:

Answer: Aftenposten

F. Yes, good afternoon. Have you got a journalist called Reidun Samuelsen?

Answer: Yes.......I'll try for you.

RS. Samuelsen

F. Oh hi there, you're Miss Samuelsen?

RS. Mrs. Samuelsen, yes.

F. Oh Mrs; Oh. Ok. Hi there um ....I understand you're doing a story on Heidi Schøne or want to.

RS. Yes that's right.

F. Well I'm the chap that's taking her to court.

RS. OK.

F. And I'm just wondering what your angle's going to be this time.

RS. I haven't written about this before.....Actually I haven't decided yet.....I'm in a phase where I'm collecting material...

F. There have already been some big stories on this in 1995....

RS. Yes, I know...

[And I related related briefly a little bit about Heidi's psychiatric past].

RS. For me the story here is not her past it's why are you writing [on the internet] about this?

F. Because the newspapers wrote about me.

RS. Is that how it all started?

F. Yes....she's made some pretty awful allegations against me...

RS. In public or...

F. Well to the police....and in public.....in the newspapers. She says I've threatened to kill her son....a terrible lie....kill her neighbours....She doesn't get on with her stepmother....you know the story on her stepmother because you've seen the website haven't you?

RS. I have seen the website, yes.

F. Have you been in touch with her?

RS. I've talked to her briefly but I'm gonna talk to her again, yes.

F. The thing is you see, she's supposed to be mentally ill....I mean she had her psychiatrist in court [and she talks about] how I rung her up asking what underwear she's wearing,[that] I've written to her saying that if she doesn't get pregnant then her breasts will fall off.....[that] I've written 400 obscene letters to her that she's thrown away....[that] I wrote a letter to her threatening to kill her son.....

RS. I...I'm not familiar with all of that stuff. What I've been seeing is the website. For us this is more of a - how can I say - an example of the use of the internet.

F. Well it's the abortion images isn't it....the pictures of the abortions that er....there's been a lot of complaints I understand...I mean have you seen the pictures?

RS. Yeah.

F. The thing is.....one of the main things about why I've been so upset is because your newspapers called me "the Muslim man". Bergens Tidende called me "the Muslim man" 18 times.

RS. I can't answer for what other newspapers have been writing about....the thing that I would like to ask you is why are you putting all these stories about Heidi into the public [domain]?

F. I'm putting it into the public because nobody....you see when the newspapers started this story off they are supposed to ring me for my side of the story OK....I know that from the PFU - and no one did - no one rang me.

RS. Now you are calling me so that's a good thing.

F. Huh?

RS. And now you are calling me so then I don't have to call you afterwards. That's a good thing.

F. I'm supposed to have my side of the story printed.

RS. Yes so please tell me why you are doing it.

F. Well, so that people know my side of the story. People don't know she's mentally ill you see....and I've taken her to court....and we're still in a legal process so....

RS. But you actually lost the last court case didn't you?

F. Well, I've appealed. The only reason I've lost is because I think it's more of a political decision.

RS. I see....[and later] For me I'm not very interested in - what can I say - printing the details here because it will be your word up against hers and... the important thing for me is that you chose to put it out in public by the internet and I guess you must see that this will affect her life....

F. My life has been affected too because of the rubbish that has been printed....I do not write letters threatening to kill two year children....I did not write 400 obscene letters to her....but the point is this - it's never going to go away is it? This story will never go away because it's basically something your newspapers should've apologized for once they knew that my story was true on Heidi....

RS. From my point of view that's not the most important thing here because I can know many bad things about a friend, a neighbour but the moment I put it out in public that's another [thing]....

F. But she put out in public - in the newspaper - that I've threatened to kill her son. Is that not...?

RS. Did they put your name in print or something?

F. No they didn't put my name....the main thing is that I'm Muslim....they don't care about my name. They care that I'm Muslim. You've seen the [newspaper] articles on the website ....You people in general do not like Muslims. I know that because I've spoken to enough Norwegians, OK. And the main thrust of the [May 1995 Bergens Tidende] article....they don't care what my name is....they know and want to attack me as a Muslim.

RS. I didn't know that you were a Muslim....[Obviously she hadn't in fact looked at my website for very long because the three 1995 newspaper articles were up there in Norwegian together with the English translations]....Nobody told me that and it doesn't matter for me....

[And later]:

F. You've got so many dishonest people up there [in Norway] and I've exposed them because I tape all my phone calls - I'm taping this phone call with you now just in case you....

RS. That's something you should have told me before we started.

F. Well, I don't do that, otherwise....I tape all my phone calls with the police, journalists....

RS. OK, I think I've got your side of the picture now and I don't think I need to talk to you anymore. OK.

F. OK but I'm warning you if you print anything bad then there'll be pretty tough consequences for you.

RS. So are you threatening me?

F. With a law suit, yeah. With a law suit. See, you've already changed your attitude so I can tell how sorry you feel for Heidi and your people over there but as I said, we'll get a photograph of you and put it up there [on the internet as I had already done for several of my other Norwegian adversaries] and....

RS. This is actually a threat.

F. Well it's not....putting a photograph of you [I was not allowed to finish]....

RS. It's a threat OK. I'm not talking to you anymore.

F. Well I'll talk to your boss then.

RS. Bye-bye.[And she put the phone down].

Mrs Reidun J. Samuelsen on 10th April 2002

Aftenposten 15 April 2002

Started after an au pair job 20 years ago

British Muslim terrorises Norwegian woman on the Internet

For 17 years an Englishman has terrorised a woman from the Drammen area. Now he has begun to use the Internet. "He has taken many years of my life," she says.

By Reidun J. Samuelsen

Intimate details. The women first became acquainted with the Brit when she was an au pair in England around 20 years ago. Although they have never had a boyfriend-girlfriend relationship, he nevertheless urged her to convert to Islam in order to marry him during a visit he made to Norway three years later. She refused, and that was when it all started. Since then he has threatened her directly and spread erroneous information about her over the telephone and by means of letters. "He has made this his goal in life. He regards me as a despicable and worthless person. Yet at the same time he is obsessed with me," she says. The Englishman has sent out e-mails in which recipients are urged to read the web pages he has created. In addition, he has faxed the same message to people who live near the 38-year-old woman. His intention has been to get as many people as possible to visit the web pages where the woman is described in strong terms.

She is accused of being mentally unstable and of having lived a wild life. The Englishman lists her previous relationships, regularly citing intimate details. Everything is richly illustrated with photographs of the 38-year-old. He also makes a point of the fact that the woman is alleged to have had an abortion. The title of the e-mail that has been issued is "Censured" Pictures of Aborted Foetuses. "It's been terrible, and my self-confidence has taken a beating. At times I have feared for my life," says the woman. The long period of harassment has taken its toll on the woman.

New report to the police

According to the Englishman, the woman has made incorrect allegations against him, both to the police and to the media. He says he has posted the information about her on the internet so that people can hear his side of the story. In January of this year he was convicted of defamatory behaviour towards the woman, for which he was fined NOK 10,000. It was in the wake of this case that he began in earnest to use the internet to spread his campaign of harassment, which resulted in the 38-year-old reporting him to the police once again. Police officer Torill Sorte of Nedre Eiker Police Force, who was a witness in the case in January, has also reported the Englishman.

"We hope to bring a new case against him," says Ms Sorte.

She has been profiled on the web pages with her full name and address, and has been accused of making false statements in court.

"Actions of this nature require a reaction," says Torill Sorte. She is interested in receiving copies of e-mails and faxes that the man has spread.

Error!

Aftenposten
NEWS FROM NORWAY 15/04/02

Slik kan nettsjikane stanses

Et nytt EU-direktiv gjør det nå mulig å få stengt Internett-sider som inneholder sjikane.

REIDUN J. SAMUELSEN

Operatøren ansvarlig. - Et nytt direktiv, det såkalte e-handelsdirektivet, pålegger operatørene å ta større ansvar for nettsidene de er vertskap for, sier professor Jon Bing ved Institutt for rettsinformatikk, Universitetet i Oslo.

Dersom operatøren blir kjent med at innholdet kan være rettsstridig, blir man automatisk ansvarlig for det som står der. De nye bestemmelsene skal ha vært innført i lovs form i alle europeiske land innen februar. Etter at Aftenposten tok kontakt med operatøren Skymarket, der nettsiden mot Drammen-kvinnen lå, ble siden stengt etter få timer.

-Problemet er selvfølgelig at en som vil bruke Internett til å spre sjikane kan hoppe til en ny operatør som ikke er kjent med innholdet på sidene hans. Han kan også finne frem til operatører som ligger i land som ikke følger e-handelsdirektivet, sier Jon Bing.

Professoren mener folk selv kan gjøre en innsats for å stanse nettsider, ved å spore opp operatøren og tipse om at et nettsted kan være rettsstridig. Dette er en langt enklere prosess enn å gå via domstolene.

-Det er vanskelig å få stengt sider i utlandet gjennom en kjennelse, sier Bing.

Politiadvokat Erik Moestue i politiets datakrimsenter, Økokrim, sier at norske myndigheter ikke har mulighet til å gi pålegg i andre land.

Justisminister Odd Einar Dørum mener feltet krever oppmerksomhet. Regjeringen har gitt Datakrimutvalget, som ble nedsatt i januar, i oppdrag å undersøke om norsk straffelovs geografiske virkeområde er hensiktsmessig avgrenset når det gjelder ulovlig materiale på nettet. Utvalget skal dessuten vurdere om politiet har tilstrekkelig adgang til å kreve at slikt materiale fjernes.

Aftenposten - 15th April 2002

Aftenposten 15 April 2002

Internet harassment can be stopped in the following way

A new EU directive makes it possible to shut down web pages containing defamatory statements.

By Reidun J. Samuelsen

The host is liable. "A new directive, the so-called E-business Directive, orders web hosting providers to take greater responsibility for the web pages they host," says professor Jon Bing at the Norwegian Research Centre for Computers and Law at the University of Oslo. If the web hosting provider is aware that the content may be illegal, he is automatically responsible for what may be found there. The new provisions are to be enacted in all European countries by February. When Aftenposten contacted Skymarket, the web hosting provider that hosts the web site containing information about the woman from Drammen, the site was closed in a matter of hours."The problem is of course that anyone wishing to use the internet to spread harassment can shift to another web hosting provider who is not familiar with the content on his pages. He may also find web hosting providers in countries who do not comply with the E-business Directive," says Jon Bing.

The professor is of the opinion that people themselves can make an effort to stop web pages by tracing the web hosting provider and inform him that a web site may be illegal. This is a far simpler process than going through the courts.

"It is difficult to shut down web sites overseas by means of a court ruling," says professor Bing. Erik Moestue, a police lawyer at the computer crime centre in Økokrim, the Norwegian National Authority for Investigation and Prosecution of Economic and Environmental Crime, says that the Norwegian authorities have no opportunity to grant orders in other countries.

Odd Einar Dørum, the Norwegian minister of justice, feels that this area requires attention. The government has commissioned the Computer Crimes Committee, which was appointed in January, to investigate whether the Norwegian Criminal Law's geographical scope is appropriately delimited as regards illegal material on the internet. The committee shall also consider whether the police have sufficient opportunity to demand that such material be removed from web sites.

Drammens Tidende
Nettutgaven dt.no
26/10/03

Saksøker pågrepet i retten

Sjikane på nettet. Engelskmannen nøyer seg ikke lenger med å trakassere kvinnen direkte. På denne nettsiden kan hele verden lese de sjikanøse beskyldningene mot kvinnen.

Engelskmannen som i snart 20 år har trakassert en Nedre Eiker-kvinne, saksøkte henne for ærekrenkelser. I retten ble han pågrepet, siktet for grov sjikane på Internett.

45-åringen, som ble kjent med Nedre Eiker-kvinnen da hun i sin ungdom var au pair i England har forfulgt og trakassert henne i 18 år. Høsten 2001 ble han idømt en bot på 10 000 kroner, men betalte ikke.
Engelskmannen saksøkte i stedet kvinnen for ærekrenkelse, fordi hun fortalte sin historie i mediene. Sist uke var sivilsaken oppe i lagmannsretten, men før engelskmannen rakk å forlate Tinghuset i Drammen ble han pågrepet. Bakgrunnen for pågripelsen var nye, alvorlige tilfelle av trakassering, blant annet beskyldninger lagt ut på Internett.

Cashet ut bøtene. 45-åringen ble fremstilt for varetektsfengsling, og kom med full tilståelse. Det åpnet for pådømmelse i forhørsretten. Mannen fremsto som en angrende synder, og uttalte at han forsto at han hadde utsatt kvinnen for mye vondt.
Tingrettsdommer Erik Stillum mente passende straff var åtte måneders betinget fengsel, på følgende vilkår: All informasjon om Nedre Eiker-kvinnen som er lagt ut på Internett skal slettes, nettsiden der sjikanen ligger skal fjernes og innholdet skal ikke republiseres i noen form. Videre får ikke 45-åringen lov å på noen måte ta kontakt med kvinnen, ei heller på noen måte formidle opplysninger om henne til tredjepersoner (f. eks. aviser). I tillegg fikk mannen en bot på 10 000 kroner.
Engelskmannen godtok dommen på stedet, og velvillig gikk han i minibanken sammen med politiet og cashet ut både den nye og gamle boten, altså 20 000 kroner tilsammen. Deretter forlot han landet frivillig.
- En fornuftig dom, og en god løsning på hele saken, mente advokat Svein Duesund, som ble oppnevnt som mannens forsvarer i forhørsretten.

Vurderer omgjøring. Fredag gikk Drammens Tidende inn på nettsiden, som på ingen måte er slettet. Det sjikanøse innholdet ligger der fortsatt. Engelskmannen har bare byttet ut Nedre Eiker-kvinnens egentlige navn med et fiktivt navn, og sladdet øynene hennes på bilder som er lagt ut. Politiadvokat Ingunn Hodne i Søndre Buskerud politidistrikt har også registrert at nettsiden er operativ.
- Vi vurderer å sende dommen til omgjøring. Han har allerede brutt vilkårene, sier Hodne. Politiadvokaten hadde et lite håp om at mannen skulle gi seg nå, siden angeren han ga uttrykk for i retten var nye toner. Begjæres dommen omgjort, vil Hodne påstå ubetinget fengsel. Mannen stevnes da for hovedforhandling via engelsk politi, og pålegges å møte i retten. Gjør han ikke det, kan det utstedes uteblivelsesdom. Ifølge Hodne vil det bli en vurdering om hvorvidt han skal begjæres utlevert til Norge for hovedforhandling her i landet, eller om saken skal oversendes til England for pådømmelse der.
- Hvis vilkårene er brutt, kan saken bringes inn for omgjøring. Men jeg kan ikke fastlå at vilkårene er brutt, sier advokat Svein Duesund.

Herborg Bergaplass

Drammens Tidende 26 October 2003

Plaintiff arrested in court By Herborg Bergaplass

An Englishman who had persecuted a woman from Nedre Eiker for more than 20 years sued her for libel. While in court, he was arrested and charged with severe persecution on the internet. The 45-year-old man, who made the acquaintance of the woman from Nedre Eiker when she was a young au pair in England, has harassed and persecuted her for 18 years. In the autumn of 2001, he was sentenced to pay a fine of NOK 10,000, which he did not pay. Instead the Englishman sued the woman for libel, because she had told her story to the media. Last week the civil case was heard in the Court of Appeal, but before the Englishman had time to leave the courthouse in Drammen he was arrested. The background for his arrest was new, severe instances of persecution, including allegations posted on the internet. Withdrew cash to pay fines. The 45-year-old was remanded in custody, where he made a full confession, which opened for sentencing in the court of examination and summary jurisdiction. The man appeared as a repentant sinner, and stated that he understood that he had subjected the woman to a lot of pain. Erik Stillum, the municipal court judge, felt that a suitable punishment would be eight months' conditional imprisonment, under the following terms: All information about the woman from Nedre Eiker that has been posted on the internet is to be deleted, the web page where the persecution appears shall be removed and the content shall not be republished in any form. Furthermore, the 45-year-old is not permitted to have any form of contact with the woman, nor shall he in any way communicate information about her to third parties (e.g. newspapers). In addition, the man was sentenced to pay a fine of NOK 10,000.The Englishman accepted the verdict on the spot, and willingly went to a cashpoint machine together with the police and withdrew funds to pay both the new and the old fine, i.e. NOK 20,000 in total, after which he left the country of his own accord. "A reasonable verdict, and a good solution to the whole case," said Svein Duesland, who was appointed defending counsel for the man in the court of examination and summary jurisdiction. Alteration of terms under consideration. On Friday, the staff of Drammens Tidende accessed the web site, which in no way has been deleted. The harassing content is still there. The Englishman has merely changed the to a fictitious name the real name of the woman from Nedre Eiker, and covered up her eyes on the pictures posted on the internet. Ingunn Hodne, the police lawyer in Søndre Buskerud Police Force, has also noted that the web site is still operative. "We will consider applying for an alteration of the terms of the judgment. He is already in breach of the terms," says Ms Hodne. The police lawyer had hoped that the man would give up now, since the regret he showed in court represented a change of tone. If a petition is lodged to have the judgment altered, Ms Hodne will claim that he be sentenced to unconditional imprisonment. The man will then be summoned to a main hearing via the British police, and will be ordered to appear in court. If he fails to do so, a judgment by default may be delivered. According to Ms Hodne, it will be decided whether a request will be issued for his extradition from the UK to attend the main proceedings in Norway, or whether the case will be transferred to England for sentencing there. "If he is in breach of the terms of the judgment, the case can be brought before the court for alteration. However, I cannot ascertain whether the terms have been breached," says advocate Svein Duesland.

VG   VG LIVE   TV-GUIDE   SØK   ≡

NYHETER | kategorier ∨   LOGG INN

Blir ikke kvitt sex-gal engelskmann

I 16 år har en sex-gal engelskmann terrorisert Heidi Schøne med brev, telefoner og trusler.

Oppdatert 25. februar 2003

Engelskmannen er fullstendig besatt av den norske kvinnen, og siden 1982 har han bombardert Heidi Schøne med telefonterror, drapstrusler, brevterror, fysisk oppmøte på døren hennes og trakkasering av hennes venner.

Mannen har også sendt hundrevis av brev til helt tilfeldige mennesker i Norge med alvorlige sex-anklager og intime påstander om den norske kvinnen.

- Jeg har tigget, grått og truet for at han skulle la meg være i fred, sa Heidi Schøne til VG snakket med henne for tre år siden.

Fortsatt har Schøne og hennes familie hemmelig adresse og telefonnummer. Posten blir sortert av det lokale lensmannskontoret, som hittil i år har mottatt over 300 brev fra den 40 år gamle engelskmannen.

Påtrengende

Som 18-åring reiste Heidi Schøne til England for å jobbe som au pair. På en togtur kom hun i snakk med en halvt arabisk mann. Mannen oppførte seg rart og var påtrengende, men hun likte ham og snakket vennskapelig med ham. Helvetet startet da hun var kommet tilbake til Norge.

Mens hun oppholdt seg i Bergen, dukket engelskmannen plutselig opp. Til å begynne med slapp hun ham inn, men etter hvert ble han svært plagsom. Han ringte i et sett, sendte henne utallige brev, og ved en anledning måtte hun se på mens han gjorde obskøne ting.

Etter å ha blitt avvist risset han inn «fuck you» på døren med en kniv. Hun skaffet seg hemmelig adresse, men likevel dukket det opp et postkort med teksten «Freddy is back» - hentet fra en skrekkfilm med en hovedperson ved navn Freddy.

Saken er tidligere blitt etterforsket av politiet i Bergen. For tre år siden anmeldte Schøne på ny forholdet til politiet i Drammen.

- Det blir opp til statsadvokaten å vurdere om det skal sendes en henstilling til engelske myndigheter, sier politiinspektør Dag Einar Lyngås.

Erotisk paranoia

Psykiatere mener at den truende og elskovssyke engelsmannen kan lide av ekstrem erotisk paranoia.

Oppdatert 25. februar 2003

Lidelsen er en vrangforestilling der en person er overbevist om at et annet menneske må være forelsket i vedkommende.

Erotisk paranoia rammer oftest kvinner, og særlig kvinner i overgangsalderen. Ofte går lidelsen over av seg selv etter noen år.

Personer med erotisk paranoia er sjelden slemme, som i tilfellet med engelskmannen.

Drammens Tidende
Nettutgaven dt.no

Forkastet ærekrenkelse-anke

Lagmannsretten forkastet anken fra engelskmannen (45) som i årevis har trakassert en Nedre Eiker-kvinne, og som saksøkte henne for ærekrenkelser.
Engelskmannen er to ganger dømt for trakassering av kvinnen. 45-åringen har sendt henne hundrevis av brev, ringt henne utallige ganger, og sendt "rapporter" med diverse beskyldninger om henne til flere aviser og andre instanser i Norge. Nedre Eiker-kvinnen traff mannen da hun for over 20 år siden var au pair i England. Forholdet tok slutt, og trakasseringen begynte.
Etter at kvinnen fortalte sin historie i Drammens Tidende og andre norske aviser, svarte mannen med å saksøke henne for ærekrenkelser og krevde 50 000 kroner i oppreisning. Han vant ikke fram i tingretten, og ble dømt til å betale saksomkostninger. 45-åringen anket til Borgarting lagmannsrett, og i oktober møttes partene i tinghuset i Drammen.
- Min klient er godt fornøyd med at tingrettens dom er stadfestet, og at mannen er dømt til å betale saksomkostninger, sier kvinnens prosessfullmektig, advokat Vegard Aaløkken.

Pågrepet i retten. Innen 14 dager fra dommen er forkynt, må engelskmannen betale saksomkostninger på tilsammen 105 000 kroner.
Han ble forøvrig pågrepet av politiet straks forhandlingene i lagmannsretten var over, siktet for nye tilfelle av grov trakassering, denne gang på Internett. 45-åringen ble fremstilt for varetektsfengsling, og fremsto i fengslingsmøte som en angrende synder. Han erkjente sjikanen mot kvinnen, og det endte med pådømmelse der og da. Dommeren mente åtte måneders betinget fengsel var passelig, med vilkår at all informasjon om kvinnen på Internett skulle slettes.

Brøt vilkårene. Alt han gjorde var å gi kvinnen et fiktivt navn på nettsiden. Det holder ikke for politiet.
Politiadvokat Ingunn Hodne ved Søndre Buskerud politidistrikt kommer etter alt å dømme til å begjære dommen omgjort. Hodne opplyser til Drammens Tidende at hun ikke har rukket å vurdere saken ennå, men kommer til å gjøre det om kort tid.

Herborg Bergaplass
herborg.bergaplass@dt.no

Drammens Tidende 18 November 2003

Libel appeal dismissed

By Herborg Bergaplass

The court of appeal has dismissed an appeal by a 45-year-old Englishman who for years has harassed a woman from Nedre Eiker, and who had sued her for libel.

The Englishman has twice been convicted of harassing the woman. The 45-year-old has sent her hundreds of letters, telephoned her countless times, and sent "reports" containing various allegations about her to several newspapers and other entities in Norway. The woman from Nedre Eiker met the man when she was an au pair in England over 20 years ago. When their relationship ended, the harassment began. And when the woman told her story to Drammens Tidende and other Norwegian newspapers, the man responded by suing her for libel and demanding NOK 50,000 in compensation for non-pecuniary damages. He lost the case in the municipal court, and was ordered to pay costs. The 45-year-old appealed to Borgarting Court of Appeal, and in October the parties met in the courthouse in Drammen.

"My client is pleased that the verdict delivered by the municipal court has been upheld, and that the man has been ordered to pay court costs," says the woman's lawyer, advocate Vegard Aaløkken.

Arrested in court. No later than 14 days after service of the verdict, the Englishman is required to pay court costs totalling NOK 105,000. He was arrested by the police immediately after the proceedings in the court of appeal were concluded and he was charged with new cases of severe persecution, this time on the internet. The 45-year-old was brought before the court for a remand hearing, and appeared to be a repentant sinner. He pleaded guilty to harassing the woman, and was sentenced there and then. The judge felt that eight months' conditional imprisonment was appropriate, on condition that all information posted on the internet about the woman be deleted.

Terms breached. All he did was to give the woman a fictitious name on the web site, which is not enough for the police.

Ingunn Hodne, police lawyer at Søndre Buskerud Police Force, will apparently file for an alteration of terms. Ms Hodne says to Drammens Tidende that she has not had time to consider the case yet, but will do so shortly.

Sexjages av gal brite

I 23 år har Heidi Schøne (41) vært sextrakassert av mannen hun traff da hun var 18. Nå bruker han nettet som terrorvåpen.

NETTSJIKANE: På dette nettstedet driver briten sjikane av Heidi Schøne (innfelt). Tross at han i 2003 ble dømt til å fjerne nettsidene, ligger de fremdeles på nett.

SPERRET: Flere norske nettsteder, blant dem Aftenposten og Dagbladet, har de siste dagene sperret sine servere for britens IP-adresse. Her faksimile av innlegg han hadde på VG Nett.

Faksimile: DB.no

MORTEN ØVERBYE

Tirsdag 20.12.2005, 10:08

(Dagbladet.no) I går sperret Aftenposten.no sine nettsider for den halvt arabiske, muslimske briten; etter at han hadde oversvømmet deres blogger med innlegg. Også flere andre norske nettaviser har blitt nedrent av innlegg fra mannen.

- Han har fått tatt alt for mange år av mitt liv. Det er det som er så tragisk. Han har forfulgt meg i 23 år. Han hadde forfulgt en annen norsk jente også, midt oppe i alt dette, sier Schøne til Dagbladet.no.

For henne startet marerittet da hun som 18 år gammel aupair møtte en halvt arabisk brite på en båtreise mellom Frankrike og England. Hun var på tur med en venninne, da hun la merke til en fem-seks år eldre mann som kikket på henne.

- Jeg synes det var litt ubehagelig, så jeg stakk av. Men da vi stod i køen for å gå ombord, var han der igjen og prikket meg i skulderen. Vi gikk langt innover for å sette oss. Men jammen kom han ikke etter og satte han seg der også.

Den merkelige mannen var påtrengende, men likevel hyggelig selskap for de to venninnene under turen.

Etter turen holdt de kontakten.

- Vi var aldri kjærester. Men jeg lot ham jo komme på besøk noen ganger etterhvert. Jeg synes synd på ham så han fikk lov til å feire nyttårsaften med oss, sier Schøne.

Under tiden i Storbritannia, ble han stadig mer pågående.

- Jeg var bare 18 år den gangen. Jeg visste ikke hva jeg har gjort ham. Det eneste jeg hadde gjort, var at jeg ikke ville gifte meg med fyren. Jeg ville ikke bli muslim.

Terrorisert

Hun ville ikke ha mer kontakt med ham da hun senere flyttet hjem til Norge. Da dukket han opp. Han var veldig manipulerende. Om jeg ikke slapp ham inn, laget han helvete og banket på døren til naboene. Han bombarderte meg hele tiden med telefoner og brev. Der fortalte han hvor dum og stygg jeg var, sier Schøne.

Terroriseringen varte helt frem til 1992. Da ble mannen tvangsinnlagt på psykiatrisk sykehus i Storbritannia. En norsk polititjenestemann som etterforsket saken, forklarte senere at det var hans mor som fikk ham tvangsinnlagt.

Da han kom ut igjen to år senere, fortsatte det - verre enn noen gang.

Han begynte å sende andre mennesker brev om Schøne. Alt oversatt til flytende norsk. Hundretalls brev ble sendt til alle fra Den nationale scene i Bergen, til det lokale lensmannskontoret, naboer, venner og kjente. Alle brevene med intime påstander om kvinnen. Gikk til sak, fikk bot

Da hun gikk ut i avisene med historien, kom han til Norge for å saksøke henne.

Istedet ble han selv dømt.

november 2001 fikk han bot på 10.000 kroner. Herredsretten bemerket at straffen var svært mild. Men fordi han var bosatt i England, valgte retten å gi ham bot. Han betalte ikke.

I februar 2002 ble Heidi Schøne frifunnet i sivilsaken i Drammen tingrett, men engelskmannen anket til lagmannsretten.

I november 2003 tapte han det sivile søksmålet i også lagmannsretten. Da hadde han i mellomtiden - i oktober samme år - blitt arrestert og på ny bøtelagt. I herredsretten fremstod han som en angrende synder. Etter full tilståelse fikk briten åtte måneders betinget fengsel og nok en bot på 10.000 kroner.

I tillegg lovte han å ta ned nettsidene der han spredte sjikanen.

Briten godtok dommen på stedet, fulgte med politiet til en minibank der han tok ut 20.000 kroner og satte seg deretter på flyet til England. Deretter fortsatte han som før. Anker til Haag

Da han tapte det sivile søksmålet også i lagmannsretten, anket han til Høyesterett - som i mars 2004 avviste saken. På sine nettsider sier briten nå at han vil anke saken helt til menneskerettsdomstolen i Haag.

Samtidig fortsetter han sjikanen på internett.

- Det som er verst - ikke bare for meg, men for alle som opplever det - er hvor lite samfunnet reagerer på det. Det er sykt hvordan han bare kan fortsette, sier Schøne.

- I andre land er det mye strengere lover. Hadde dette vært i England, hadde han fått en skikkelig smell. Her får han slippe med bot gang etter gang, sier hun.

PS! Også en politikvinne som ledet etterforskningen av briten, blir nå sjikanert med navn på hans nettsider.

English Translation

Sexually pursued by mad Briton

For 23 years, Heidi Schøne (41) has been sexually harassed by the man she met when she was 18. Now he is using the Net as a weapon of terror.

MORTEN ØVERBYE

(Dagbladet.no) Yesterday Aftenposten.no closed its Internet pages to the half-Arab, Muslim Briton, after he had swamped their blogs with contributions. Several other Norwegian online newspapers have also been overrun by contributions from the man.

He has succeeded in taking too many years of my life. That is what is so tragic. He has pursued me for 23 years. He had pursued another Norwegian girl as well, right in the middle of all this, Schøne told Dagbladet.no.

For her the nightmare began when as an 18 year old au pair she met a half-Arab Briton on a boat trip between France and England . She was travelling with a girlfriend when she noticed a five-six years older man looking at her.

I felt a little uncomfortable, so I moved away. But when we were queueing to embark, he was there again and tapped me on the shoulder. We went a long way in to sit down. But of course he followed and sat down there as well.

The strange man was persistent but all the same pleasant company for the two girlfriends during the trip.

After the trip, they stayed in contact.

We were never going out. But I did let him visit occasionally as time went by. I felt sorry for him so he was allowed to celebrate New Year's Eve with us, says Schøne.

During the time in the UK , he became increasingly persistent. I was only 18 at the time. I did not know what I had done to him. The only thing I had done was that I did not want to marry the guy. I did not want to become a Muslim.

Terrorized

She did not want to have any further contact with him when she later moved back to Norway . He then turned up there.

He was extremely manipulative. If I didn't let him in, he created hell and pounded on the neighbours' doors. He bombarded me with telephone calls and letters the whole time. In these he told me how stupid and nasty I was, says Schøne.

The terrorizing continued right up to 1992. The man was then committed to a psychiatric hospital in the UK. A Norwegian police official who investigated the case explained later that it was his mother who had him committed.

When he came out again two years later, it carried on worse than ever.

He began to send other people letters about Schøne. All translated into fluent Norwegian. Hundreds of letters were sent to everybody from Den Nationale Scene in Bergen to the local bailiff's office, neighbours, friends and acquaintances, all the letters containing intimate statements about the woman.

Took legal action, was fined

When she went to the newspapers with the story, he came to Norway to bring a legal action against her.

Instead he himself was punished.

In November 2001, he was fined NOK 10,000. The District Court observed that the punishment was very mild. But the court chose to fine him because he was resident in England. He never paid.

In October 2003, he lost the civil action in the Court of Appeal, where he himself was arrested and fined again. He then appeared as a repentant sinner. After a full confession in the magistrate's court, the Briton was given a suspended eight month sentence and again fined NOK 10,000.

In addition, he promised to remove the Internet pages where he was conducting the persecution.

The Briton accepted the judgement on the spot, accompanied the police to a cash dispenser where he withdrew NOK 20,000 and then boarded the plane to England. Then he carried on as before.

Appealing to The Hague

When he lost the civil action in the Court of Appeal as well, he appealed to the Supreme Court which dismissed the case in March 2004. On his Internet pages, the Briton says that he wants to appeal the case all the way to the court of human rights in The Hague .

At the same time he is continuing the persecution on the Internet.

The worst thing not just for me but for everybody who is living through it □ is how little society reacts to it. It is crazy how he can simply continue, says Schøne.

In other countries, there are much stricter laws. If it had been in England , he would have been punished properly. Here he is allowed to get off with a fine time after time,□ she says.

PS! A policewoman who conducted the investigation into the Briton is now being persecuted by name on his Internet pages.

CLOSED: Several Norwegian Internet sites, including Aftenposten and Dagbladet, have in recent days closed their servers to the Briton's IP address. This is a facsimile of contributions he posted on VG Nett. Facsimile: DB.no

Øks. Drepe. Kamp. Spionasje. Krig.

Dette er ordene hun søkte etter i e-postene SIDE 4, 5 OG 6

Dagbladet

Onsdag 21. desember 2005 Nr. ??? Uke ??. 137. årgang. Løssalg kr 10,00

Monica Kristensen Solås

Foto: Torbjørn Kønning

Maria Mena

Foto: Elisabeth Sperre Aines

- Har aldri hatt det SÅ BRA

SIDE 32 OG 33

Jaget av SEX-GAL mann i 23 år

SIDE 10 OG 11

«Han har holdt sitt løfte om å ødelegge livet mitt.»

HEIDI SCHØNE (41)

Foto: Privat

Oslo - Haugsund BILLIGST via London

SIDE 12 OG 13

REISE-SIDER

SIDE 24-27

TIPSTELEFON 22 20 00 00 SMS OG MMS TIL 1937 (merk sendingen med tips) MAIL/DIGITALFOTO TIL 1000tipset@dagbladet.no

Dagbladet 21 December 2005

English Translation

Pursued by SEX-MAD man for 23 years

PAGES 10 AND 11

"He has kept his promise to ruin my life." HEIDI SCHØNE (41)

SEXUALLY harassed for 23 years

23 years ago, Heidi Schøne (41) met a half-Arab Briton on a boat trip between France and England . Since then her life has been a nightmare.

Words: Morten Øverbye

morten@dagbladet.no

Anders Holth Johansen

ahj@dagbladet.no

In recent days, the Briton has swamped online newspapers' blogs with malicious contributions to such an extent that the major Norwegian online newspapers have been forced to block the man's access. But threats and accusations are nothing new for Heidi Schøne. She has lived with them for the last 23 years.

"It has been a nightmare, but now I am not so scared any more. Now I am more angry at society which did not take the signs seriously early enough," says Schøne.

The threats and the harassment have been a strain for her whole family. Today she is divorced and has two children.

"I had a small child he thought should die. In other countries, he would have been punished severely for that kind of threat," says Schøne.

Several letters a day

The sexual harassment has continued regularly for the last 23 years.

"New letters with "Fuck You!" written on them in red were constantly coming through the letter box. The number of letters varied with his mood. I could receive three or four letter a day," says Schøne.

In the end, the post office agreed to sort out the letters from the man. But the mad Briton could not be stopped. He got others to send letters for him and to phone. Friends and colleagues also received letters and faxes containing intimate statements.

"At times he sought me out frequently. Suddenly he could be there outside my window," says Heidi Schøne.

The nightmare began when as an 18 year old au pair she met the half-Arab Briton on a boat trip between France and England . She was travelling with a girlfriend when she noticed the five-six years older man looking at her.

The strange man was persistent but all the same pleasant company for the two girlfriends during the trip. After the trip, they stayed in contact.

"We were never going out. But I did let him visit occasionally as time went by. I felt sorry for him so he was allowed to celebrate New Year's Eve with us," says Schøne.

During the time in the UK , he became increasingly persistent.

"I was only 18 at the time. I did not know what I had done to him. The only thing I had done was that I did not want to marry the guy. I did not want to become a Muslim."

She did not want to have any further contact with him when she later moved back to Norway . Then he turned up.

"He was extremely manipulative. If I didn't let him in, he created hell and pounded on the neighbours' doors. He bombarded me with telephone calls and letters the whole time. In these he told me how stupid and nasty I was," says Schøne. The terrorizing continued right up to 1992. His mother then arranged for him to be committed to a psychiatric hospital in the United Kingdom . When he came out again two years later, it carried on – worse than ever.

He began to send other people letters about Heidi Schøne. All translated into fluent Norwegian. Hundreds of letters were sent to everybody from Den Nationale Scene in Bergen to the local bailiff's office, neighbours, friends and acquaintances, all the letters containing intimate statements about the woman.

"He wants people to dislike me, and he can be very good at persuading people," says Schøne.

Captions: INTERNET HARASSMENT: On this web site, the Briton carries on harassment of Heidi Schøne (inset). In spite of the fact that he was ordered to remove the web pages in 2003, they are still on the Internet. NIGHTMARE: Since Heidi Schøne (41) met the Briton 23 years ago, he has been obsessed with her and has sent hundreds of letters with intimate statements about the woman, both to her and to those around her. "He wants people to dislike me, and he can be very good at persuading people."

Heidi Schøne (41), persecuted.

Took legal action In 1999, the Briton took action against Heidi Schøne for libel because she had been interviewed about the situation. That ended with the man himself having to pay NOK 10,000 for invasion of privacy. In its judgement of 14 November 2003 , Borgarting Court of Appeal stated that "Overall, the case appears to be a misuse of the legal system". The Court thought that there was overwhelming documentary evidence of sexual harassment and ordered the Briton to pay NOK 104,585 in costs.

Insulting web page

The man has a web page which is intended to reveal " Norway 's exotic, erotic and extremely psychotic mentality". The web page contains a series of gross lies about Heidi Schøne's intimate life. The man has been ordered to delete all information about Heidi Schøne from his web pages. He has not done so. "I am not afraid of him any more. But I don't understand why we in Norway do not take this more seriously. This is about human life after all," says Schøne.

Investigator was also harassed Police inspector Torill Sorte of Nedre Romerike police district was the investigator in the case against the Briton. Then she herself was harassed.

"It finally ended with me having to ask to be taken off the case, because I myself wanted to report the man," says Sorte. "There were faxes and e-mails which said I was mad and that I am a liar. It was quiet for a while but he has started again in recent weeks," says Sorte.

The man has today been ordered to stay away from the police inspector.

Emails Received In Response From Norway

msn Hotmail®

norway_2003@hotmail.com — Printed: 20 December 2005 14:20:13

From : Grise Spiser <youareapigoinkoink@operamail.com>
Sent : 20 December 2005 12:48:04
To : norway_2003@hotmail.com
Subject : Nice website

Wow, I just browsed your website and I must say you strike me as the most filthy, pigeating muslim maniac I have ever encountered.

When you eat pigs, do you lick the pigs asshole clean before digging in?

I have one advice for you, take out your willy, that is your mangled penis, and showe it into a pigs ass, maybe you'll get some weird looking kids. I seriously doubt that anything other than a pig would take your seamen.

Best regards and good luck on dying pigfucker!

By the way, you really do a great job in showing of muslims as crazy, even better than Osama!

OINK OINK fucker ;)

Burn in hell!

--

Surf the Web in a faster, safer and easier way:
Download Opera 8 at http://www.opera.com

Powered by Outblaze

msn Hotmail®

norway_2003@hotmail.com — Printed: 20 December 2005 13:50:08

From : Jule G Roten <getawayrobbie49@hotmail.com>
Sent : 20 December 2005 10:28:14
To : <norway_2003@hotmail.com>
Subject : Sick devil.

Sick devil, go fuck Allah the Camel.

msn® Hotmail®

norway_2003@hotmail.com | Printed: 20 December 2005 13:52:56

From : Madeleine B[redacted]s <mrs.sainsbury@gmail.com>
Sent : 20 December 2005 10:44:54
To : norway_2003@hotmail.com
Subject : heidi

hey you. i amfrom bergen in norway and i have read all your stories and the norwegian side. i dont really know what to belive but yours seems more likely. i dunno. in norway you are made out to be a sexed up maniac who was a freak from the first meeting. wel i dunno but today it si all over the net in norway about you and how thay had to block you from lots op norwagian intrenet sightscoz u were disturbed. well i dunno but i hope it all gets sorted out and i think.. im not sure but i think i support you

from
Madeleine Sainsbury

msn® Hotmail®

norway_2003@hotmail.com | Printed: 21 December 2005 12:13:09

From : Torbjørn [redacted]bekk <tor_bekk@hotmail.com>
Sent : 20 December 2005 16:28:15
To : norway_2003@hotmail.com
Subject : Hehe

Very funny site :D
Keep up the good work.

msn Hotmail

norway_2003@hotmail.com Printed: 20 December 2005 13:51:11

From : Johnnysgonna Getyousucka <skrsks@hotmail.com>
Sent : 20 December 2005 10:41:42
To : norway_2003@hotmail.com
Subject : You're gonna get what you deserve!

You are gonna get what you deserve if you dont take down your website you sick fuck! People will find you sooner or later, mark my words you loser! You got one week... You sick fuckin muslim fucker! Leave the Norwegian girl alone and take down the website, otherwise we'll come and pay you a visit!

- Stalkers

MSN Hotmail http://www.hotmail.com Med markedets beste SPAM-filter. Gratis!

msn Hotmail

norway_2003@hotmail.com Printed: 20 December 2005 14:28:54

From : Marcus G <svenskmarcus@hotmail.com>
Sent : 20 December 2005 11:21:55
To : norway_2003@hotmail.com
Subject : Going to get you

we have put an 10.000 Euro reward on your head...we going to get you man, we going to clear the world from an idiot like you..:)

Burn in hell..

ps. going to FUCK your mother...she like WHITE man...

MSN Messenger http://messenger.msn.no Den korteste veien mellom deg og dine venner

msn Hotmail

norway_2003@hotmail.com Printed: 21 December 2005 12:25:17

From : Tom Bano <tombano@hotmail.com>
Sent : 21 December 2005 10:23:49
To : norway_2003@hotmail.com
Subject : Clearly..

After visiting your website, I 'can now understand why Your mother had you "put away" for a while.
Clearly the best option.

Regards,
Tom Bano

Last ned MSN Messenger gratis http://messenger.msn.no/ - Den raskeste veien mellom deg og dine venner

msn Hotmail

norway_2003@hotmail.com Printed: 21 December 2005 12:37:51

From : Student14 <student14@itetpost.no>
Sent : 20 December 2005 11:53:07
To : <norway_2003@hotmail.com>
Subject : You are fucking cracy

I would like to give a big laugh to you. Most stupid cracy fuck, have u gotten ur head examined lately. I would like to point out to you that beeing stupid knows no color. I was once a muslim. But when I realised that Mohammed counldnt be anything else than a confused peadophile. I knew that a true God would never speak to such a looney. So you think that killing a featus that has not gained consciouness is more wrong than reaping children. It is more and more clearly that you are insane. The only humane thing to do is to place a gun to your head and pull the trigger. But I supose it wouldnt do to much damage, hence the damage is clearly well done. I heard that your mother got you into hospital, bad muslim taking orders from a woman. May I recomend a rope around your neck since you are never comming to paradise. Better to end your misory right?

msn Hotmail®

norway_2003@hotmail.com Printed: 20 December 2005 14:24:59

From : Geir Abrahamsen <party-chief@hotmail.com>
Sent : 20 December 2005 11:43:31
To : norway_2003@hotmail.com
Subject : Bastard list

Hey
Cant see you on top of the bastard list where you should have been
Of cause kristian people hate muslims with a person like you around
Get som help they have doctores for persons like you

regards
one of many kristian norwegian merried a cataloic, whitch you in war with inside UK

MSN Hotmail. http://www.hotmail.com Gjør det lett å holde kontakten i ferien. Send postkortene med e-post.

msn Hotmail®

norway_2003@hotmail.com Printed: 20 December 2005 14:23:04

From : eetfuk <eetfuk@www3.powertech.no>
Sent : 20 December 2005 11:51:05
To : norway_2003@hotmail.com
Subject : Please Read this as it is urgent

People agrees with me. Your website about the norwegians are extremely misinterpreted, we hope you remove the norwegianuncovered site and kill yourself, because the world would be a better place without you, stupid fuck.

msn Hotmail

norway_2003@hotmail.com Printed: 20 December 2005 14:27:35

From : Sylvi Strandman <sylvi_m_strandman@hotmail.com>
Sent : 20 December 2005 11:18:07
To : norway_2003@hotmail.com
Subject : You'r site

You are a very disturbed guy. You only write lies about Norway and the girl you have terrorized for many years. And last but not least you only have lies on you'r site. And you don't mention that you have been in a mental institution. so you see you are the disturbed one not everybody else.

SMS

MSN Hotmail http://www.hotmail.com Med markedets beste SPAM-filter. Gratis!

Home | **My MSN** | **Hotmail** | **Shopping** | **Money** | **People & Groups** **Sign Out** Web Search: Go

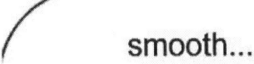

msn Hotmail **Today** | **Mail** | **Calendar** | **Contacts**

norway_2003@hotmail.com

Reply | Reply All | Forward | Delete | Junk | Put in Folder | Print View | Save Address

From : Ole Dahl <choppa@online.no> Inbox
Sent : 20 December 2005 13:26:25
To : <norway_2003@hotmail.com>
Subject : GET THE CRAP BEAT OUT OF YOU SOON, BOY????

YOU ARE THE SICKEST FUCKER I EVER LET MY EYES ON!!!! COME TO NORWAY, AND I W I L L SHOW Y O U WHAT A R E A L MAN WILL DO TO Y O U!!!!! YOU ARE A LITTLE MAN WITH NO BALLS AND A BIG DANGEROUS MOUTH!!!! TOO DANGEROUS FOR YOUR HEALTH!!!! MAYBE YOU LIKE A VISIT??? STAY OF HEIDI'S BACK! YOU SHOULD HAVE BEEN LOBOTOMIZED!!!!
SICK SICK FUCK!

O. Dahl

msn Hotmail®

norway_2003@hotmail.com Printed: 20 December 2005 14:12:47

From : Mattis Henriksen <st.odin@hotmail.com>
Sent : 20 December 2005 10:08:09
To : norway_2003@hotmail.com
Subject : In god we trust.......

May allah put you back behind bars where you belong!!! Fucking creep!!

Express yourself instantly with MSN Messenger! Download today it's FREE! http://messenger.msn.click-url.com/go/onm00200471ave/direct/01/

msn Hotmail®

norway_2003@hotmail.com Printed: 21 December 2005 12:14:27

From : Christian Ingebrigtsen <cingebri@hotmail.com>
Sent : 20 December 2005 19:07:41
To : norway_2003@hotmail.com
Subject : Really great work!

I have to laugh....what a pathetic little muslim bastard you are. You're obviously insane....just like most of your kind.

I can understand your fascination and envy of Norway and our women. However, you can never in your entire lifetime have such a great life as we have. The world isn't made that way.

I strongly advice you to immediately shut down wour website, at least all references to norwegian persons. We don't like it when you and your people publish such crap.

MSN Search http://search.msn.no/ Raskere. Rett på sak. Mer presist.

msn Hotmail®

norway_2003@hotmail.com — Printed: 21 December 2005 12:15:07

From : Lars Rune NÃ¸stdal <larsnostdal@gmail.com>
Sent : 20 December 2005 19:14:41
To : norway_2003@hotmail.com
Subject : diediediediediediediediediediediediediediediediediediediediediediediediediediediediediediediedie

ï»¿

diediediediediediediediediediediediediediediediediediediediediediediediediediediediediediediedie

..yes, i hope you die.. ..asshole..

(i've blocked your email - so i will not recieve any response from you)

msn Hotmail®

norway_2003@hotmail.com — Printed: 21 December 2005 12:17:11

From : americum <americum@gmail.com>
Sent : 21 December 2005 02:43:49
To : norway_2003@hotmail.com
Subject : hello, whats this i smell? donkeypoop or monkeypiss? one million dollars for the first wanker who reads this!

are you by any chance a catholic priest? and did you daddy touch your penis and/or dropped you on the head when you were born? or maybe your parents suffered for BSS (baby shaking syndrome) eitherway you are one fucked up dude.

did someone touch your bum bum in the mental ward? oh hell, all norway knows you are crazy as fuck man. but i think you are funny, very sad but funny. i give you, lets say... 10 years and i bet that you have killed yourself or atleast gotten another hobby than harrasing women you cant get, haha such a wanker.

what triggered your funny behaviour? are you sick or just a horny helpless looser? tried prozac combined with viagra? oh wait, im sure someone tried that combo in the mental ward when they made love love to your bum bum. do you call your penis king kong?

happy christmas motherfucker. oh wait, i bet you are inbreed! your dad is your son is you mum is your sister is your uncler is your bum bum.

ps. I EAT FOETUSES FOR BREAKFEAST.

AND ITS MR.AMERICUM.

msn Hotmail®

norway_2003@hotmail.com Printed: 21 December 2005 12:11:29

From : Yeah Baby <pointless911@hotmail.com>
Sent : 21 December 2005 11:06:39
To : norway_2003@hotmail.com
Subject : Farid!

You most be the sickes fuck ever! Muslims are root to all evil and you are the living proof of it.

MSN Messenger http://messenger.msn.no Den enkleste og raskeste måten å holde kontakten på

Fortsetter trakassering av politikvinne

Av Roy Hansen, 11.01.06

Engelskmannen [redacted] fortsetter trakasseringen av norske kvinner. Etter å ha sjikanert Heidi Schøne fra Solbergelva i en årrekke, går han nå løs på politiførstebetjent Torill Sorte ved Nedre Eiker lensmannskontor.

Politiførstebetjent Torill Sorte ved Nedre Eiker lensmannskontor har den siste tiden blitt utsatt for sjikane gjennom DTs nettsider.

Gjennom en rekke «innlegg» på Drammens Tidendes nettsider den siste tiden har engelskmannen fortsatt sin hets mot politiførstebetjent Torill Sorte ved Nedre Eiker lensmannskontor. Dette skjer blant annet ved at han legger ut link til en internettside han er dømt til å fjerne fra nettet så sent som 17. oktober 2003. Nå lover DTs nettansvarlig, Lars Lager Espevalen at de skal overvåke sidene sine bedre for å slette uønskede innlegg så fort som mulig.

- Mannen har plaget Heidi Schøne og familien hennes siden 1982, og det har vist seg å være meget vanskelig å stoppe ham, sier Torill Sorte. I 2003 var hun etterforskningsleder i saken som endte opp med en dom på to år betinget fengsel og en bot for grov sjikane i Eiker, Modum og Sigdal Tingrett. Siden den gang har den muslimske mannen også lagt politietterforskeren for hat.

Sendte fakser
En rekke offentlige instanser, aviser og media, samt private virksomheter har mottatt fakser fra mannen om hennes engasjement i saken, og det er lite flatterende det han skriver om henne. – Jeg takler dette og vet at jeg ikke har gjort noe galt i sakens anledning. Selv ikke en intern granskning har avdekket noe galt, sier Sorte.

Hun tar likevel sjikanen gjennom DTs nettsider alvorlig fordi de er lett tilgjengelige og på grunn av det faktum at mannen er dømt til å fjerne sidene fra nettet. Dessuten er sjikane et økende problem i samfunnet, der Nedre Eiker ikke er noe unntak.

Vanskelige saker
- Sjikanesaker er vanskelige saker fordi det skal mye til for at vi kan reise en tiltale. Som regel skjer sjikanen ved samlivsbrudd, og selv om vi kan ilegge bøter hjelper det sjeldent, sier hun. Nedre Eiker lensmannskontor behandler i snitt 25 – 30 slike saker i året, men få er så graverende som saken mot engelskmannen.

- Det er flere former for sjikane, og dersom det for eksempel er en forsmådd ektemann som sender tekstmeldinger til sin eks, stopper det sjeldent selv om det ilegges bøter. Er det derimot snakk om ærekrenkelser og plagsom atferd som involverer flere personer er det litt lettere å få idømt en reaksjon, sier Torill Sorte.

Tar opp saken
Hun vil nå ta sjikanesaken mot seg selv opp med ledelsen for Søndre Buskerud Politidistrikt. I fjor sommer hadde engelskmannen sendt telefaks til politidirektoratet, og denne ble videresendt gjennom tjenestevei til henne for kommentar. Selv om hun sier at det ikke plager henne personlig, vil Torill Sorte at denne saken ikke skal få utvikle seg. Det er også etter det vi kjenner til tatt et initiativ overfor justisdepartementet om å få endret lovgivningen på dette området.

- Mannen er tydelig mentalt ustabil og må bruke utrolig mye tid og krefter, for ikke å snakke om penger, på å sjikanere Heidi Schøne og undertegnede, i tillegg til noen andre kvinner vi kjenner til. Dessverre er lovene slik at vi ikke kan begjære ham utlevert for videre straffeforfølgelse, sier Sorte.

(Publisert i Eiker Bladet 11.01.06)

Published in Eiker Bladet 11.01.06

English Translation

Continuing the harassment of policewoman

By Roy Hansen, 11.01.06

Briton [.......................] is continuing his harassment of Norwegian women. After having harassed Heidi Schøne from Solbergelva for years, he is now attacking police inspector Torill Sorte at Nedre Eiker police station. The Briton has continued his smear-campaign against police inspector Torill Sorte at Nedre Eiker police station through a series of "contributions" made recently to Drammens Tidende's Internet pages. This takes the form of among other things him posting links to an Internet page he was ordered to remove from the Internet as recently as 17 October 2003 . DT's Internet head Lars Lager Espevalen is now promising that they will monitor their pages more closely in order to delete undesirable contributions as soon as possible. "The man has plagued Heidi Schøne and her family since 1982, and it has proved very difficult to stop him," says Torill Sorte. In 2003, she led the investigation in the case which ended in a two year suspended sentence and a fine for severe harassment in Eiker, Modum and Sigdal district court. Since then, the Muslim man has also made the police investigator the object of his hatred.

Sent faxes A number of public bodies, newspapers and media organizations as well as private businesses have received faxes from the man about her involvement in the case, and what he writes about her is not very flattering. "I deal with it and know that I did not do anything wrong in the matter. Not even an internal inquiry revealed anything wrong," says Sorte.

She nevertheless takes the harassment through DT's Internet pages seriously because they are easily accessible and owing to the fact that the man was ordered to remove the pages from the Internet. Harassment is moreover a growing problem in society, and Nedre Eiker is no exception.

Difficult cases

"Harassment cases are difficult cases because it takes a lot for us to be able to bring a prosecution. As a rule, the harassment occurs when relationships break down and, even though we can impose fines, this rarely helps," she says. Nedre Eiker police station handles 25-30 such cases a year on average, but few are as serious as the case against the Briton. "There are several forms of harassment, and if, for example, it is a spurned husband who is sending text messages to his ex, it rarely stops even though fines are imposed. On the other hand, if it is a question of defamation and annoying behaviour which involves a number of people, it is a little easier to get a sanction imposed," says Torill Sorte. Raising the issue She now wants to raise the issue of harassment against herself with the administration of Southern Buskerud Police District. Last summer, the Briton sent a fax to the police directorate, and this was forwarded to her through official channels for comment. Even though she says that it is not bothering her personally, Torill Sorte does not want this matter to be allowed to develop. We also understand that an initiative has been put before the justice department aimed at having the legislation in this area changed. The man is obviously mentally unstable and must be putting an incredible amount of time and energy, not to mention money, into harassing Heidi Schøne and the undersigned, in addition to some other women we know about. Unfortunately, the laws are such that we cannot apply for him to be extradited for further criminal prosecution," says Sorte.

Engelskmann sjikanerer politikvinne

En engelskmann sjikanerer ei politikvinne via diskusjonsfora i flere norske nettaviser.

Av Morten W Røkeberg og Maria Kommandantvold . Publisert 13.06.2006 17:23

Politiførstebetjent Torill Sorte ved Nedre Eiker lensmannskontor anmelder nå en engelskmann som i flere år har trakassert henne.

Mannen har det siste halvåret skrevet krenkende innlegg på diskusjonsfora i flere norske nettaviser, med henvisning til sine egne hjemmesider.

Sorte håper at hun ved å anmelde ham, kan få mannen domfelt.

NRK Buskerud

English Translation

Englishman harasses policewoman

Chief Inspector Torill Sorte at Nedre Eiker district police office.

Photo: Maria Kommandantvold/NRK

An Englishman harasses a policewoman via the discussion fora in several Norwegian Internet newspapers.

By Morten W. Røkeberg and Maria Kommandantvold.

Published 13.06.2006 17:23

Chief Inspector Torill Sorte at Nedre Eiker district police office is now lodging an official complaint against an Englishman who has harassed her for several years.

Over the last half a year the man has written defamatory articles in the discussion fora in several Norwegian Internet newspapers, with references to his own homepages.

Sorte hopes that by lodging an official complaint against him, she can have him punished.

"Will not accept being harassed"

"This has, in fact, been going on for several years, while the harassment via Norwegian Internet newspapers has taken place since before the New Year. I do not believe that one should accept being harassed by other people without doing something about it."

"Do you believe it will help by lodging an official complaint against him?"

"I don't think so, but he will have a legal case brought against him at any rate, and hopefully he will receive a suitable punishment," says Sorte.

Found guilty of persecution

The man has previously been found guilty in this country of having persecuted another woman in the district. This woman got to know him in England in the 1980's. She took out a case against him and he was found guilty. Torill Sorte was the head of the investigation team in that case and she subsequently became a victim of his persecution. Initially through him telephoning to friends and acquaintances and sending letters but, since December last year, also persecution on the Internet.

"He accuses me of having written falsely in the case for which he was sentenced. He maintains that I am dishonest and corrupt," says Sorte.

Yesterday statements from this man were displayed on the Drammens Tidende discussion forum for a couple of hours, with reference to his Internet page on which he harasses several people in Norway . Sorte says that it is difficult to stop him because he constantly finds new ways round things.

Blocked Internet page

"We have blocked the Internet page but he constantly finds new ways of putting it out, so it is difficult to maintain control over such a page."

What can the police do?

"We can initiate an official complaint and take action in relation to it. The problem is that he does not live in this country and that makes things more complicated."

What do you known about him?

"I know a great deal about him. I know that he does not live here in this country and I know him through the investigation into the other matter."

What does this do to you?

"I have had many approaches from people who feel that this is awful, something that I really appreciate. Even though I am in the police, it has an affect on me that there are constantly unjustified assertions about me on the Internet," says Torill Sorte.

Give a friend a tip-off

To (e-mail) From (e-mail) Comment:

Send tip-off

Sjikanerer politikvinne dt.no

En engelskmann bruker nettaviser til å sjikanere en politikvinne fra Nedre Eiker. Erik Modal

Politiførstebetjent Torill Sorte ved Nedre Eiker lensmannskontor anmelder nå en engelskmann som i flere år har trakassert henne. En av nettavisene engelskmannen hyppig bruker, er dt.no.

Mannen har det siste halvåret skrevet krenkende innlegg på diskusjonsfora i flere norske nettaviser, med henvisning til sine egne hjemmesider, melder NRK Buskerud.

Sorte håper at hun ved å anmelde ham, kan få mannen domfelt.

English Translation

An Englishman uses online newspapers to harass a police woman from Nedre Eiker.

Erik Modal

Police Chief Torill Sorte at the Nedre Eiker County Sheriff's Office is now reporting an Englishman who has been harassing her for several years. One of the online newspapers the Englishman frequently uses is dt.no.

In the last six months, the man has written abusive posts on discussion forums in several Norwegian online newspapers, citing his own websites, reports NRK Buskerud.

Sorte hopes that by reporting him, she can get the man prosecuted. Been going on for several years The case has been going on for several years. Harassment through Norwegian online newspapers has been ongoing for the past six months.

The man has previously been convicted in this country of harassing another woman in the district. This woman got to know him in England in the 1980s.

She sued him and he was given a penalty. Torill Sorte was the lead investigator in this case, and since then she has been the victim of his harassment. "He accuses me of having written incorrectly in the case in which he was convicted. He then thinks that I am dishonest and corrupt," Sorte told NRK.

Hard to stop He uses discussion boards to distribute advertisements for the site. One of the newspapers that is frequently used is Drammens Tidendes online edition dt.no.

Sorte says it's hard to stop him because he finds new detours all the time.

"We have blocked the website, but he is constantly finding new ways to publish it, so it is difficult to have control over such a site," she told the channel.

The problem with ending the harassment is that the man does not live in Norway. It makes the work of stopping the man more difficult.

Editor Lars Lager Espevalen in dt.no says the Englishman has abused the debate function on dt.no and other online newspapers for a long time. - We have implemented measures that have made the man's activities more difficult. This has been important to us, because named individuals have been offended. We are constantly working on quality assurance of this part of dt.no. Already during the summer, we are implementing new measures to prevent abuse of the debate function

LIBEL: This website is the first hit for Johan Martin Welhaven on Google. The man behind the website is English. Welhaven has been in contact with UK police to have the threat assessed. A standalone website has been set up in the name of Johan Martin Welhaven, exposing the new Chief of Police as an Islamophobe and laying some of the responsibility for 22 July at his door.

Morten Høitomt

Published 20.09.2011 03:00 Updated 20.09.2011 17:37

Last Friday Welhaven was appointed Chief of Police for Vestoppland in southern Norway. On the website that bears his name, Welhaven tops a list of people accused of Islamophobia and harassment of Muslims. It's an English-language website and the domain is also registered to a man in the United Kingdom. The home page begins: "Hatred for Islam permeates all levels of society in Norway. Mass murderer Anders Behring Breivik is the extreme manifestation of this bigotry. But the Norwegian establishment bears a heavy burden of responsibility: they openly participated in the Muslim-bashing year in, year out."

"Manipulators"

This is followed by the names and photographs of 19 persons who the originator of the site believes "had a defining role in the Islamophobic abuse".

The website's owner describes these people as "Protecting and nourishing perversion; clever manipulators from this isolated corner of Europe".

Client relationship

It is not clear on the website why the originator is focusing on Welhaven. The accusations of Islamophobia and manipulation are not elaborated on. However, Johan Martin Welhaven himself knows the reason. "The Englishman behind the website has had a client relationship with the Norwegian Bureau for the Investigation of Police Affairs, of which I am still Deputy Director. He bears a grudge against me and a number of others because of the case he was involved in," Welhaven told Oppland Arbeiderblad. He goes on to explain that the man in question has been writing on the website for several years, but the Islamophobe slant is new. Previously, the web pages had a different content. Contacted the police

Although he is now trying to ignore the Englishman, Welhaven admits that the matter has taken its toll. "I've taken a number of steps in terms of assessing my safety. Among other things I've been in contact with the UK authorities, as well as speaking to people in Norway with expertise in the field," he says. Have you reported the situation? "No. There are legal steps that can be taken, which might deal with material of this nature on the web in the short term, but it could still pop up again in a different form at a later stage. So although I perceive it as harassment, I've decided that I can live with it so far, in any case. I haven't been bothered by it beyond the knowledge that the website actually exists." The dark side of the web Johan Martin Welhaven is a lawyer by training, but finds it difficult to protect himself against the smear campaign. "This case, and others that are worse, are a reminder that the Internet has a seriously dark side. It is somewhere people can easily torment and harass others completely unchecked," he states.

Online harassment

People will never be able to totally protect themselves from online bullying. Published 21.09.2011 06:01 Updated 21.09.2011 06:01

The Editor writes: "For many years the new Chief of Police for Vestoppland, Johan Martin Welhaven, has been exposed to an online smear campaign and harassment by an Englishman. He is accused of being an Islamophobe and held partly responsible for the terror attacks in Oslo and on the island of Utøya on 22 July. It goes without saying that the claims are completely unfounded, but are linked to a client relationship the outgoing Deputy Director of the Norwegian Bureau for the Investigation of Police Affairs had with the Englishman a number of years ago.

Nevertheless, protecting himself against such statements is extremely challenging for Welhaven. When someone who is a lawyer and employed by the police chooses NOT to go down the legal route to have a website like this taken down, it says a lot about just how difficult it is to fight the dark side of the web.

Anyone can procure any domain at all – it's a free for all: first come, first served. In Welhaven's case, the person concerned has bought up his entire name as a domain. This means that searches for the name "Johan Martin Welhaven" on Google, the world's largest search engine, will always show this page at the top of the list of hits. It is not difficult to imagine how this technique could be abused by people wanting to use the web to harass, spread false information about, or harm another person.

Digital bullying is a key topic in Norwegian schools this year. Since the campaign was launched in the autumn, a number of local schools have organised targeted activities to increase knowledge of and change attitudes to unwanted activity online. At Raufoss, the whole school took part in an anti-bullying procession to show that bullying will not be tolerated. However, pupils and teachers are making no secret of the fact that this is a problem that will never go away. In recent years, online bullying in particular has become increasingly prominent.

Ever younger children and young people have access to the web. Many also have their own computers that they use on a more or less daily basis without any adult supervision whatsoever. This makes it very easy to take a wrong step. Neither are young people making any secret of the fact that it is easy to publish opinions of other people in anger that absolutely do not belong in the public domain. They also believe that many young people do not understand the scope of a statement or an image published online.

Although netiquette and data safety have come to the fore in the last few years, there is no reason not to have full focus on this going forward. People will never be able to totally protect themselves from online bullying.

Preventive work with children and young people is therefore absolutely vital. To an even greater degree than the adults of today, they will need to understand both the benefits and drawbacks of the opportunities the web offers.

Heidi Schøne: Drammens Tidende, Bergens Tidende, Verdens Gang, Aftenposten og Dagbladet. Uttalelsen nedenfor om Heidi Schøne ble styrt som "mer eller mindre korrekt" av dommer Anders Stilloff ved Drammen tingrett i februar 2002:

Vi kan nå avlegge rapport angående Deres forespørsel. Heidi Schøne ble født 20 August 1963 og bor nå sammen med sin ektemann Runar Schøne.

I 1981 drog Heidi Schøne til England fra Bergen som au pair og oppholdt seg i St Albans i Hertfordshire. Hun dro fra Norge for å komme seg etter den andre aborten . Begge abortene (kunstig fremkalt) ble tatt etter anmodning fra den vordende far, som bare er kjent under navnet Petter. Fr Schøne hadde håpet at kjaeresten hennes, Petter, fortsatt ville vaere glad i henne hvis hun tok abortene. Imidlertid ble det slutt på forholdet og etter det man har fortstått, hadde fr.Schøne samleie med to forskjelltige menn på stranden mens hun var på sommerferie på Rodos i 1982.

I 1983 traff Heidi Schøne en herre ved navn hr. Gudmund Johannessen pa Naustv. 32, 5088 Mjølkeråen Bergen som innen 1984 hadde han gjort henne gravid og hun ventet tvillinger . Heidi Schøne aborterte tvillingene da hun fant ut at hr. Johannessen lå med hennes beste venninne. Sommeren 1984 forsøkte Heidi Schøne å begå selvmord ved å ta en overdose. Senere delte hun leilighet med en 17 år gammel forhenvaerende prostituert, Iren.

I 1985 ventet Heidi Schøne igjen barn med hr. Johannessen og 1 April 1986 fikk de en sønn. På den tiden da de hadde seksuell omgang, injiserte hr. Johannessen heroin og han hadde også samleie med andre jenter, noe fr.Schøne var fullt klar over. Begge to ble faktisk testet for Aids to ganger etter at sønnen ble født, med negativt resultat.

Vi har fått vite at hr. Johannessen ble fengslet for straffbare handlinger han begikk mens han var i haeren - han satt i varetekt i seks måneder i 1980 -årene

I 1988 ble Heidi Schøne igjen vraket av hr Johannessen og hun forsøkte å begå selvmord ved å ta en overdose. Heidi Schøne reiste deretter fra Bergen for å bo hos sin søster, i Drammen, men ble like etterpå innlagt på B.S.S Psykiatrisk klinikk i Lier hvor hun ble vaerende i to måneder.

Mor til Heidi Schøne ble skilt da Heidi Schøne var i begynnelsen av tenårene og døde dessverre da hun var 16 år gammel, etter det man forstår av årsaker forbundet med alkohol - og stoffmisbruk. En kort tid før dette hadde Heidi Schøne far forsøkt å sende henne på barnehjem for vanskelige barn, men dette ble det ikke noe av.

Etter vår mening har Heidi Schøne rykte på seg for å lyve og har etter det vi forstår hatt flere seksuelle partnere før hun ble gift våren 1994.

Tidlig på 1980-tallet (date ukjent) meldte fr.Schøne fra til politiet om et påstått voldtektsforsøk begått av en butikkinnehaver i Bergen og i Desember 1986 meldte hun fra om et annet voldtektsforsøk som man senere fant ut var oppspinn for å miskreditere mannen det gjaldt som hadde avslørt hennes opptreden ovenfor hennes foreldre og også hr.Johannessen's foreldre. Senere i 1990 slo hr. Johannessen fr.Schøne halvt fordervet og hun meldte ham til politiet.

I 1993 giftet hr. Johannessen seg med og de har ett barn. Fr. Nina Engeberg og Gudmund Johannessen pa Rollandslia 233, 5095 Ulset, Bergen.

Heidi Schøne har påstått at hun fikk drevet ut onde ånder under en eksorsisme i 1988 av hennes kristne naboer i Solbergelva, Asbjørn og Heidi-Anita Skjortnes. Heidi-Anita Skjortnes forlot senere sin mann Asbjorn for an annen mann som hun traff nar hun begynte a jobbe pa en i Drammen. Hun brunker na Heidi-Anita Dahlen-Nilsen.

Etter hennes såkalte eksorsisme traff og giftet Heidi Schøne seg med hr. Runar Schøne en kristen mann som hevder at han kan tale i tunger og som avviser helt og holdent mennesker av en annen tro enn hans egen litt merkelige type av evangelistisk kristendom. Ekteparet hr. Schøne fikk en liten gutt i 1996, Heidi Schøne første "legitime" barn etter seks unnfangelser.

Det har også kommet for dagen at Heidi Schøne hadde i 1985 et seksuellt forhold til en hr. Bjørn-Morten som faktisk trodde han var far til [sonn XX]. Denne viste det seg var egentlig sønn av Hr. Gudmund Johannessen. Hr. Bjørn-Morten utsatte seg uten vitende for risikoen over å bli HIV-smittet som et resultat av Fr.Schøne gjenopptagelse av hennes seksuelle forhold til Hr. G. Johannessen som er sprøytenarkoman.

Heidi Schøne venter for tiden på tiltale i norsk rettsal for å prøve og forhindre lovens gang i sammenheng med påstandene som ble trykt i de ovennevnte aviser i 1995 og 1998. Det er antatt at Heidi Schøne lider av en psykiatrisk lidelse kjent som Munchausen Syndrom, en forferdelig sykdom som innebaerer at pasienten lyver kompulsivt, noe som ikke har blitt kurert til tross for Heidi Schøne antatte konversjon til kristendom.

English Translation

Heidi Schone (Overaa): Verdens Gang, Bergens Tidende and Drammens Tidende

We now report as follows on the subject of enquiry, Ms. Heidi Overaa, born 20th August 1963, now living with her husband Runar Schøne at Sollikroken 7, 3058 Sobergmoen.

In 1981 Ms. Overaa went to England as an au pair from Bergen and stayed in St. Albans, Hertfordshire. She left Norway to recuperate from her second abortion. Both abortions were at the request of the prospective father, only known as Peter. Ms. Overaa had hoped to retain the affections of her boyfriend, Peter, by having the abortions. This relationship however ended and it is understood that Ms. Overaa whilst on holiday in Rhodes in the summer of 1982 had sex with two different men on the beach.

In 1983 Ms. Overaa met a gentleman called Gudmund Johannessen from Åsane, Bergen who by 1984 had got Ms. Overaa pregnant with twins. Ms. Overaa miscarried the twins when she discovered that Mr. Johannessen was sleeping with her best friend. Ms. Overaa then attempted suicide in the summer of 1984 by taking an overdose. She later took as a flatmate a 17 year old ex-prostitute, Iren.

In 1985 Ms. Overaa again got pregnant to Mr. Johannessen and on 1st April 1986 they had a son, Daniel Sebastian Overaa. At the time of their sexual relations, Mr. Johannessen was injecting heroin and also sleeping with other girls, facts Ms. Overaa was fully aware of. Indeed both had two Aids tests, each of which proved negative, after the birth of their son.

We have ascertained that Mr. Johannessen went to prison for offences committed whilst in the Norwegian Army and for which the sentence was one of six months custody, during the 1980's.

In 1988 Ms. Overaa was again rejected by Mr. Johannessen and attempted suicide by taking an overdose. Ms. Overaa then left Bergen to stay with her sister, Elisabeth, in Drammen, but was soon admitted to the B.S.S Psychiatric Clinic in Lier where she remained for two months.

Ms. Overaa's mother divorced in Heidi's early teens and unfortunately died when Heidi was 16 years old, it is understood from causes related to drink and drug abuse. Shortly before this Ms. Overaa's father had sought to put her in a home for delinquent children but this move did not materialise.

We believe Ms. Overaa has a reputation for lying and also is understood to have had numerous different sexual partners until her marriage in the spring of 1994.

Ms. Overaa on an unknown date in the early 1980s reported to the police an alleged attempted rape by a Bergen shopkeeper and in December 1986 reported another man for attempted rape which it has been ascertained was a fabrication made in order to discredit the gentleman concerned who had exposed Ms. Overaa's behaviour to her parents and Mr. Johannessen's parents. Mr. Johannessen later in 1990 beat up Ms. Overaa who reported the matter to the police.

In 1993 Mr. Johannessen married Nina Engeberg and they have one child.

Heidi has claimed that she was exorcised from possession of demons in 1988 by her Christian neighbours in Solbergelva, Asbjorn and Heidi-Anita Skjortnes. Heidi-Anita Skjortnes later left her husband Asbjorn for another man whom she met when she started work in a Drammen department store. She now goes by the name of Heidi-Anita Dahlen-Nilsen. After her so-called exorcism, Heidi Overaa met and married Runar Schøne, a Christian man who claims to speak in tongues and who rejects utterly all people of faiths other than his own peculiar brand of evangelical Christianity. The Schønes had a baby boy in 1996, Heidi's first legitimate child in six conceptions.

It has also emerged that Heidi Overaa in 1985 was having full sexual relations with one Bjorn-Morten, who in fact thought he was the father of Daniel Overaa but Daniel subsequently turned out to be the son of Gudmund Johannessen. Bjorn-Morten unwittingly exposed himself to the risk of H.I.V infection as a result of Ms. Overaa's resumption of sexual relations with Mr. Johannessen, the intravenous drug user.

Heidi Schøne is presently awaiting prosecution in the Norwegian Courts accused of attempting to pervert the course of justice in connection with allegations that were printed in the above-mentioned newspapers in 1995 and 1998. It is believed Mrs. Schøne is suffering from the psychiatric illness known as Munchausen's Syndrome, a terrible affliction which involves the patient in serial lying, which has not been cured in spite of Mrs. Schøne's supposed conversion to Christianity.

A general hatred of Muslims?

THE TIMES **OSLO NOTEBOOK** by Tony Samstag 27 DEC 1990

Norwegians' charity to foreigners ends at home

Aslam Ashan, aged 48, is a graphic artist who came to Norway 20 years ago from his native Pakistan, settling in a suburb of the capital. Recently he had what must have seemed a good idea: a Christmas party for those residents of Oslo, particularly the elderly, who would otherwise be alone. Mr Ashan and his friends, mainly Muslims, reasoned that their willingness to work during the Christian holiday was, as he put it, "an exploitable resource".

According to what statistics you read, up to half the population of Oslo may be living alone, ironic in a society crippled by religious fundamentalism where the sanctity of family life is cited as justification for a depressing shortage of social amenities.

The local council was happy to put up about £3,000 for the party. But weeks passed and not one Norwegian had accepted the invitation. So Mr Ashan went on a national religious radio programme to repeat his offer. This time the lonely responded in force, from all over the country: not, however, with even one grateful acceptance, but with scores of abusive telephone calls. A consensus emerged that the bloody foreigners, not content with taking their jobs, social benefits, women and so on, were now trying to steal Christmas from the Norwegians as well. This seasonal tale from the folk who claim to have invented Father Christmas illustrates the Dag Hammarskjöld Syndrome: the tendency of small, provincial countries to wax idealistic over exotic, impoverished peoples, while abhorring the stranger in their midst.

Norway is justly proud that it gives 1.11 per cent of its gross national product to development aid, one of the highest percentages in the world. At the same time, few foreigners actually living in Norway, perhaps 4 per cent of the population, will be surprised by the natives' response to Mr Ashan's generous impulse.

There is an elegant variation on the Hammarskjöld Syndrome — the Brundtland Effect: a preoccupation with wide-ranging threats to the environment while allowing one's own immediate habitat to be plundered and despoiled. This phenomenon is named after Gro Harlem Brundtland, the prime minister. She is well known as chairman of the United Nations World Commission on Environment and Development. Her exhortations about sustainable development and the like have earned her many international awards. At home, however, she and her ministers have consistently demonstrated a talent for evading sensitive conservation issues.

This year's crop of scandals includes the continuing illegal slaughter of Scandinavia's last wolves by Norwegian farmers and the proposed siting of an Olympic skating hall at a protected wetland.

The Times - 27th December 1990

The Norwegian Press assault on the Muslim London Solicitor was no aberration. It was a common trait to denigrate Muslims and by association Islam as the following collection of stories will illustrate.

William Nygaard, Norwegian publisher and translator of Salman Rushdie's book, 'The Satanic Verses' pictured above on British television in October 2000.

On the programme William Nygaard proclaimed that it was his moral duty to publish 'The Satanic Verses'. The former British Foreign Secretary, Lord Howe, on the same programme described 'The Satanic Verses' as being "utterly perverse and offensive to Muslims".

For a strict definition of the "Satanic Verses" refer to The Concise Encyclopaedia of Islam (Third Edition) by Cyril Glassé

Salman Rushdie was born Muslim but ended up hating Islam with a passion. His hatred extended to a foul assault on the character of the Prophet Muhammad in his book 'The Satanic Verses' which included associated diminishment of the Prophet's mission and the Quran by playing up and emphasising a myth of the Prophet condoning the worship of three pagan female divinities: anathema to Islam and God's actual instruction. Unfortunately, the Ayatollah Khomeni, to stir things up issued a ruling condemning Salman Rushdie to death. The resulting publicity caused a deal of Muslim upset. Prince Charles condemned Rushdie, whose Norwegian translator was shot.

Mail Online

How Charles and Martin Amis had a dinner party row over Salman Rushdie's fatwa: Prince of Wales refused to back author over The Satanic Verses because he thought book was offensive to Muslims

- **Author Martin Amis made the revelations in an article in Vanity Fair magazine**
- **He says he had a dinner-party row with Charles over the Satanic Verses**
- **Charles said he wouldn't support someone who 'insults someone else's deepest convictions'**
- **Rushdie's fatwa issued for 'insulting' Prophet Mohammed and Koran in 1989**

By DANIEL BATES
PUBLISHED: 17:10, 14 April 2014 | **UPDATED:** 19:12, 14 April 2014

Prince Charles refused to support Sir Salman Rushdie during his fatwa over The Satanic Verses because he thought the book was offensive to Muslims.

In an article for **Vanity Fair** magazine, Martin Amis claimed that the Prince's views caused a row at a dinner party after Rushdie was issued with the death sentence by Islamic clerics in 1989.

Amis claims that Charles told him that he would not offer support 'if someone insults someone else's deepest convictions'.

Civil conversation: The Prince of Wales talks to Padma Lakshmi, the then-girlfriend of author Sir Salman Rushdie (right) at the British Library in 2001 - 11 years after Rushdie was issued with the death sentence by Islamic clerics

What he really thought: But behind the scenes, Prince Charles refused to support Sir Salman (right) during his fatwa over The Satanic Verses because he thought the book was offensive to Muslims

Amis remonstrated with him but all Charles did was 'take it on board', even though Rushdie is a British-Indian citizen.

Rushdie's fatwa was issued by Iran's Ayatollah Ruhollah Khomeini over the publication of The Satanic Verses, which supposedly insulted the Prophet Mohammed and The Koran.

The fatwa, or 'spiritual opinion', followed a wave of book burnings in Britain and rioting across the Muslim world which lead to the deaths of 60 people and hundreds being injured.

Rushdie was put under round-the-clock security at the expense of the British taxpayer when a £1.2million bounty was put on his head.

Deepest convictions: Martin Amis (pictured with Rushdie in 2010) said Charles told him that he would not offer support 'if someone insults someone else's deepest convictions'

Strong stance: The Vanity Fair article says novelist Stephen King (left) refused to let stores in America sell his books if they refused to carry The Satanic Verses. Charles' lack of support for Rushdie comes at a time when he is under the spotlight for his supposed willingness to meddle in the affairs of others

In the Vanity Fair article Rushdie's friends and literary colleagues such as Ian McEwan tell the inside story of the controversy, but Amis' comments about Charles are the most frank.

Amis says: 'I had an argument with Prince Charles at a small dinner party.

'He said - very typically, it seems to me - 'I'm sorry, but if someone insults someone else's deepest convictions, well then,' blah blah blah...

'And I said that a novel doesn't set out to insult anyone: 'It sets out to give pleasure to its readers,' I told him.

'A novel is an essentially playful undertaking, and this is an exceedingly playful novel.'

'The Prince took it on board, but I'd suppose the next night at a different party he would have said the same thing.'

Angry: Rushdie's fatwa was issued by Iran's Ayatollah Ruhollah Khomeini over the publication of The Satanic Verses, which supposedly insulted the Prophet Mohammed and The Koran

Charles' lack of support for Rushdie comes at a time when he is under the spotlight for his supposed willingness to meddle in the affairs of others.

Some £250,000 of taxpayers' money has been spent on legal fees trying to stop publication of letters he sent to politicians that will supposedly show he was trying to influence policy, a breach of Royal protocol.

The Vanity Fair article says that, in contrast to Charles, novelist Stephen King refused to let stores in America sell his books if they refused to carry The Satanic Verses.

He called the head of one US bookstore chain and said: 'You don't sell The Satanic Verses, you don't sell Stephen King.

'You can't let intimidation stop books. It's as basic as that. Books are life itself.'

During the Fatwa Rushdie lived in permanent terror and at one point thought his ex-wife Clarissa Luard and their son Zafar, who was nine at the time, had been killed by assassins or kidnapped.

'Spiritual opinion': The fatwa, or 'spiritual opinion', followed a wave of book burnings in Britain and fierce demonstrations across the Muslim world (such as this in Pakistan) which lead to the deaths of 60 people and hundreds being injured

Round-the-clock guard: Rushdie was put under round-the-clock security at the expense of the British taxpayer when a £1.2million bounty was put on his head

In 1998 Iran's reformist president relaxed the fatwa and said it had no intention of tracking Rushdie down and killing him.

Technically it still stands but is unlikely to be enforced.

In recent years Rushdie, 66, has been more known for his relationships than his books.

He has has two children from his four marriages - his other son is called Milan - but has been linked with many other women including Indian model Riya Sen.

Daily Mail 15 April 2014

During these years, one of Rushdie's translators was murdered, and two other translators of Rushdie's work suffered knife attacks.

Was it not monstrous, then, that the Prince of Wales refused to speak up for Rushdie, a wronged British citizen?

At the time of the fatwa, I might have been inclined to think this. But the passage of the years confirms the wisdom of Prince Charles's position.

For a start, let us consider what we mean by freedom of thought or expression.

In many ways, we have less freedom of expression than when I was a young person. Forty years ago, you could be as abusive as you liked about gay people, black people or anyone who was 'different'. Such remarks would have been in poor taste, but they were very much more common.

Today, many of the gags that would have been the stock in trade of stand-up comedians in working men's clubs are utterly unacceptable, if not illegal.

Some of this censorship may seem po-faced but, as we have become a more multicultural society, inevitably we have had to become more sensitive to what might cause offence: in any civilised society, minorities deserve protection from abuse.

The Islamic world was, at the time, in a more volatile state than it had been for decades

The point is that Rushdie knew when he included one short passage about the Prophet Muhammad in The Satanic Verses that he would grossly offend not only 'extremist' opinion, but ordinary Muslim sensibilities.

Anyone who read his book before it was published would have advised strongly that this short passage should be excised. He must have known that, in the Islamic world, the book would cause uproar if it contained these pages.

The Islamic world was, at the time, in a more volatile state than it had been for decades. Relatively recently, the British journalist Auberon Waugh had made a scurrilous joke about Muslims in one of his articles. It was intended to amuse a British audience at home.

The result was that a British Council building in Rawalpindi in Pakistan was burned to the ground. Rushdie therefore knew that, if he published his novel with the offending paragraphs, it would not only cause offence to Muslims, but could endanger lives all over the planet.

Freedom of speech, as its most earnest advocates would agree, does not include the right to shout 'FIRE!' in a crowded cinema. It does not include the right to publish pornography that is harmful to children.

The fatwa issued by Iran's Supreme Leader Ayatollah Ali Khomeini sparked uproar and fear across the globe

The novel was superb, but Rushdie knew the outrage he would cause with his words

It does not permit the disclosure of military secrets that would damage the security of the State. It does not permit you to write or say things that would inspire others to go out and torch a synagogue.

Freedom of speech in a volatile world has to be tempered by good manners and by tolerance towards those whose opinions you despise. But Rushdie was never concerned with good manners.

Certainly, he began as a good writer. He wrote one superb novel — Midnight's Children — about Indian independence.

It deservedly won the Booker Prize and I still recollect my thrill when I first read it, overblown as much of its writing is.

He went on to write the excellent Haroun And The Sea Of Stories. But, like many writers, Rushdie is a man of quite colossal vanity. He refuses to see that most of his books since Midnight's Children have been laughably bad and that The Satanic Verses, the book that caused all the fuss, is actually unreadable.

I doubt whether any of the literati who so loudly defended it had managed to read more than 40 of its pages.

For the sake of publishing this unreadable drivel in its entirety, Rushdie was prepared to unleash mayhem and anarchy on the whole world. Don't be under any illusions: it was vanity, pure and simple, that made Rushdie refuse to trim his novel.

In effect, he was saying: 'I know many people will find my book offensive, but I am still going to publish. I know that publication might lead to acts of violence — I am still going to publish. I know that people might get killed — I am still going to publish.'

In our divided world, we do not need people fanning the flames of ignorance and hatred

At huge cost, most of it borne by the taxpayer (though, to be fair, the novelist contributed to it, in part) Rushdie required round-the-clock police protection.

He went into hiding, where he could continue to have girlfriends, dinner parties with smart pals and everything he wanted to eat and drink, all paid for by the publishers.

He whined about it all, however, and felt he was being punished. The reality is that he did not suffer nearly as much as the people on whom he inflicted such damage.

The translators who were stabbed or killed paid a far higher price. He emerged from hiding, a little balder and plumper, several million pounds richer (since the bad book had become a multi-million best-seller). And then, Tony Blair made him a Knight of the Realm!

Rushdie's translators were not the only ones who suffered. So, too, did his fellow Muslims in his native India.

Indian Muslims, decent, moderate citizens, felt and still feel under threat from the Far-Right Hindu nationalist party, who feel justified in their anti-Muslim prejudice as a result of incidents like the fatwa against Rushdie.

The lives of British Muslims were also smeared by Rushdie and his conceited friends, who like to depict anyone who follows a religion as some kind of fundamentalist fool.

In our divided world, we do not need people fanning the flames of ignorance and hatred.

There is an immense arrogance in the secular-minded, rich literati of the London and New York dinner-party set, in the way they despise anyone who does not share their shallow values.

Who has done more good in the world: Prince Charles, with his brave attempt to build bridges between the different faith communities?

Or the dinner-party sophisticates like Rushdie who are so conceited, so sure of their own rightness, that they are prepared to do and say things that will lead to other people being killed, rather than curb their smug instincts to jeer at religion?

Daily Mail 16 April 2014.

VG LIVE TV-GUIDE SØK

NYHETER | kategorier LOGG INN

Blir ikke kvitt sex-gal engelskmann

I 16 år har en sex-gal engelskmann terrorisert Heidi Schøne med brev, telefoner og trusler.

Oppdatert 25. februar 2003

Engelskmannen er fullstendig besatt av den norske kvinnen, og siden 1982 har han bombardert Heidi Schøne med telefonterror, drapstrusler, brevterror, fysisk oppmøte på døren hennes og trakkasering av hennes venner.

Mannen har også sendt hundrevis av brev til helt tilfeldige mennesker i Norge med alvorlige sex-anklager og intime påstander om den norske kvinnen.

- Jeg har tigget, grått og truet for at han skulle la meg være i fred, sa Heidi Schøne til VG snakket med henne for tre år siden.

Fortsatt har Schøne og hennes familie hemmelig adresse og telefonnummer. Posten blir sortert av det lokale lensmannskontoret, som hittil i år har mottatt over 300 brev fra den 40 år gamle engelskmannen.

Påtrengende

Som 18-åring reiste Heidi Schøne til England for å jobbe som au pair. På en togtur kom hun i snakk med en halvt arabisk mann. Mannen oppførte seg rart og var påtrengende, men hun likte ham og snakket vennskapelig med ham. Helvetet startet da hun var kommet tilbake til Norge.

Mens hun oppholdt seg i Bergen, dukket engelskmannen plutselig opp. Til å begynne med slapp hun ham inn, men etter hvert ble han svært plagsom. Han ringte i et sett, sendte henne utallige brev, og ved en anledning måtte hun se på mens han gjorde obskøne ting.

Etter å ha blitt avvist risset han inn «fuck you» på døren med en kniv. Hun skaffet seg hemmelig adresse, men likevel dukket det opp et postkort med teksten «Freddy is back» - hentet fra en skrekkfilm med en hovedperson ved navn Freddy.

Saken er tidligere blitt etterforsket av politiet i Bergen. For tre år siden anmeldte Schøne på ny forholdet til politiet i Drammen.

- Det blir opp til statsadvokaten å vurdere om det skal sendes en henstilling til engelske myndigheter, sier politiinspektør Dag Einar Lyngås.

Erotisk paranoia

Psykiatere mener at den truende og elskovssyke engelsmannen kan lide av ekstrem erotisk paranoia.

Oppdatert 25. februar 2003

Lidelsen er en vrangforestilling der en person er overbevist om at et annet menneske må være forelsket i vedkommende.

Erotisk paranoia rammer oftest kvinner, og særlig kvinner i overgangsalderen. Ofte går lidelsen over av seg selv etter noen år.

Personer med erotisk paranoia er sjelden slemme, som i tilfellet med engelskmannen.

Verdens Gang (VG), Norway's biggest tabloid, in 2003 again attributes the mental illness of 'erotic paranoia' or Old Maid's syndrome to the Muslim London Solicitor: he allegedly imagined the Norwegian girl loved him. Total bullshit as the evidence showed.

Blir ikke kvitt sex-gal engelskmann

Oppdatert 25. februar 2003

Aftenposten

NEWS FROM NORWAY

Years Anniversar JARLSBERG

Saturday August 19 2006

First published: 06 Feb 2002, 15:03

AFTENPOSTEN
English frontpage
Norwegian frontpage

NEWS
Latest 100 stories
Press release

FEATURES
Only in Norway
Picture series
Norway's Centennial
The Royals
Webcams in Norway
Readers respond

PICTURE SERIES

Summer on the Oslo Fjord

100 latest stories

WEBCAMS

See Norway live. See our webcams.

Minister rebukes sex-obsessed imams

Minister of Local Government and Regional Development Erna Solberg is shaken by the condescending attitude by Islamic religious leaders in Norway and what she feels is their labeling of Norwegian women as 'whores'. Minister Solberg is most worried about the potential damage the imams may cause by spreading their attitudes in immigrant communities, the newspaper Bergens Tidende reports.

Solberg believes that Muslim leaders impart an image of Norwegian women as more than generally promiscuous and unfaithful.

"I have been personally met with imams and it strikes me that several of them live and work here without learning to know Norwegian society. They come here and barely learn how to speak Norwegian. This has to be a serious problem for Muslim communities," said Solberg.

Solberg believes that the attitudes held by imams give immigrant boys a mistaken view of Norwegian girls.

It damages Norwegian immigrant youth, because by their behavior they strengthen prejudices against Norwegian society," Solberg said.

At a Conservative Party conference in Bergen Tuesday Solberg announced that problems concerning integration have a central spot on the agenda. Solberg said the government would see that a far more effective and demanding Norwegian language education program would be put in place. So far such education has been offered, now it will become mandatory.

Aftenposten English Web Desk
Jonathan Tisdall/NTB

Classic Norwegian paranoia and hypocrisy. The Muslim imams in Norway were only voicing what everyone the world over thought anyway. See the next couple of Aftenposten reports. Erna Solberg later became the Prime Minister of Norway whereupon she was more conciliatory towards the Muslims in her midst.

Aftenposten

NEWS FROM NORWAY

Saturday August 19 2006

First published: 26 Nov 2002, 11:17

Summer on the Oslo Fjord

Norwegians top list over 'one-night stands'

Young, sex-happy Norwegians are the quickest to hop in bed with casual conquests, according to a new survey. Perhaps they're only bragging, but 72 percent of those questioned said they've had "one-night stands." Next in line were the South Africans, with 70 percent claiming one-night stands. The survey was conducted by condom maker Durex over its web site, with 50,000 men and women in 22 countries taking part.

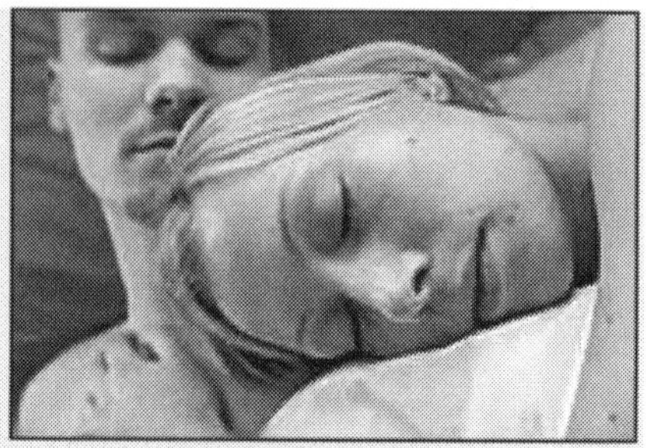

Norwegians often fall for one-night stands, according to the Durex study.

PHOTO: BAST, IDA VON HANNO

The Norwegians also scored highest among those reporting sex on the first date. A full 32 percent of the 2,500 questioned claimed that first dates often ended with more than a kiss.

The French, however, lived up to their reputation as the world's most amorous. The average French man and woman, according to the survey, has sex 167 times a year.

That compares to 152 times a year for the Danes and 144 times a year for the Norwegians. The average among all 22 countries taking part in the survey was 139 times a year.

Only half of all Norwegians said they used condoms during their "one-night stands," even though half of all Norwegians believe HIV and AIDS are major problems.

"This means that both we and the health authorities still have a lot of work to do, in encouraging people to have safe sex," said Arianne Gravdal of SSL Healthcare, which owns Durex. The survey, she said, shows that Norwegians are willing to take a big risk to have sex.

Kjell-Olav Svendsen, a doctor and lecturer at the University of Oslo, said he finds the survey results disturbing.

"It's worrisome that so many fail to use a condom during casual sex," he said.

Aftenposten English Web Desk

Email this article   Print this article

Aftenposten

NEWS FROM NORWAY

Saturday 27 September 2003 — Updated: 25 Sep, 14:16 (GMT+1)

AFTENPOSTEN
English frontpage
Norwegian frontpage

NEWS
Local
Sports
Business
Press release

FEATURES
Webcams in Norway
Most-read stories
Readers respond

PICTURE SERIES

Arctic adventure

More photos from Norway

100 latest stories

WEBCAMS

See Norway live. See our webcams.

Most visited

Norway world leader in casual sex

Seven out of ten Norwegians have had a random sex partner and the country is a world leader in one-night stands. At the same time they are among the least sexually satisfied citizens in the world, according to the latest findings in the Durex Global Sex Survey for 2003.

Interviews of 150,000 people from 34 nations form the basis of the study released this week. The statistics provide a fascinating look into the different private habits around the world, and insight into what makes Norwegians warm all over.

In terms of sheer numbers, Norway was about average with 124 sex sessions a year, well behind winners Hungary with an active 152. Satisfaction was worse for Norwegians, with only 62 percent saying they were content with their sex life, placing them as low as 29th on the list.

Neighbor Denmark was even unhappier, ranking 30th in contentment. Swedes were even gloomier, only slightly more content but with a low average of 102 times a year.

What Norwegians are enthusiastic about is casual sex, with only Icelanders and Vietnamese more likely to collect one-night stands.

Other findings in the condom maker's study: 11 percent of Norwegians have paid for sex, 42 percent have had telephone or Internet sex, 10 percent have faked orgasms and 12 percent have had homosexual sex.

Norwegians lust after movie stars George Clooney, Vin Diesel and Halle Berry, and think that doctors and nurses represent the sexiest professions.

Aftenposten's Norwegian reporter
Line Kaspersen
Aftenposten English Web Desk
Jonathan Tisdall

Norwegian jailed for Web racism

April 23, 2002 Posted: 11:46 AM EDT (1546 GMT)

OSLO, Norway --A Norwegian extremist has been jailed for posting racist and anti-Semitic propaganda via a server based in the United States.

It is the first time anyone in Norway has been jailed for racist Web postings and campaigners say there could be repercussions beyond Norway's borders.

Tore Tvedt, 59, was sentenced to 75 days in jail with 45 days suspended and two years probation after being convicted on anti-racism charges.

Tvedt, founder of the Vigrid far-right group, was arrested after the Anti-Racism Centre in Oslo found possibly illegal material on the group's Web site.

The Asker and Baerum District Court said that in sentencing Tvedt it had put special weight on his efforts to draw children and young people into anti-Semitic and racist beliefs.

Anti-Racism Centre spokesman Henrik Lunde told The Associated Press: "This is historic because it is the first time someone in Norway has been sentenced to prison and has to serve jail time for making racist statements."

He said the conviction was also important because Tvedt was held responsible for the contents of his home page, even though it was posted on a server that was based in the United States and out of Norway's jurisdiction.

"He (Tvedt) was convicted for many reasons, which was possible because he stood up and clearly identified himself as the responsible publisher of the material," Lunde added.

On its Internet site, Vigrid professes a doctrine that mixes neo-Nazism, racial hatred and religion, claiming to worship Odin and other ancient Norse gods.

Tvedt's lawyer, Vidar Lind Iversen, said he would appeal.

 Find this article at: http://www.cnn.com/2002/WORLD/europe/04/23/norway.web/index.html
See also: http://www.vnunet.com/News/1131186

The dark side of Norwegian popular xenophobia and Islamophobia begins to emerge. It leads straight on to Anders Breivik. The Danes and Swedes followed suit to some extent.

Aftenposten

NEWS FROM NORWAY

Tuesday 17 December 2002

Supreme Court acquits neo-Nazi charged with racist remarks

A Norwegian neo-Nazi who unleashed a stream of Nazi rhetoric during a demonstration two years ago did not violate a key law meant to fight racism. Norway's Supreme Court ruled Tuesday that the neo-Nazi's claims are protected by other laws guaranteeing freedom of expression.

Terje Sjoelie made his claims during a march celebrating German Nazi Rudolph Hess in Askim in 2000.

PHOTO: HANS O. TORGERSEN

Terje Sjoelie, former leader of the white supremacist group called "Boot Boys," had been convicted of violating Norway's so-called "anti-racism paragraph" when he launched an anti-Jewish and anti-immigrant tirade. The right-wing extremist had claimed during a public demonstration that, roughly translated, "every day, our people are being plundered and destroyed by Jews who suck our land empty of wealth and replace it with immoral and un-Norwegian thoughts." He also claimed that "immigrants rob, rape and kill Norwegians every day." A lower court ruled that his claims violated Norway's anti-racism law. It calls for fines or a jail term of up to two years for those who make claims that spread hate or make threats against others on the basis of religion, race, skin color or national or ethnic background. The Supreme Court disagreed. A majority of 11 high court judges determined that Sjoelie's remarks weren't punishable. They noted that the remarks didn't contain any concrete threats. The head of Norway's Anti-Racism Center, Nadeem Butt, was shocked by the decision. She equated it to an attack on the rights of minorities in Norway."The majority didn't even consider how offensive the claim was for Norwegian Jews," she said, regretting that since neo-Nazi groups are legal, the court rules their propaganda is, too.She claimed the court decision "has moved the barriers" for how offensive people can be against ethnic groups in Norway.

Aftenposten English Web Desk

Nina Berglund

SCAN+
Aftenposten
Lillehammer Turist
Tuesday 27 May 2003 NEWS FROM NORWAY Updated: 27 May, 16:46 (GMT+1)

AL-QAIDA STOPS NORWEGIAN GARAGE

Employees at an Oslo building firm were so shocked and outraged by the Al-Qaida threats against Norway that they have refused to carry out assignments for Muslims. One customer, born and raised in Norway, has had his plans to build a garage derailed, newspaper VG reports.

You are probably a Muslim and after the recent Muslim terror threats none of my employees want to work for Muslims," read the letter sent by company head Olav Oeye.

The letter arrived the day after the terror threats, and while the 27-year-old Muslim was waiting for Oeye's firm to deliver a price after surveying the plot for the garage.

"I had an offer from Grimstad Garages. In the offer they gave the names of three contractors who I could call to build the foundation. Olav Oeye Inc. said they could come Saturday at 11 am," the man told VG.

"I could hardly believe what I was reading. I am just as Norwegian as others, even if I have brown skin and have another religion. I have never had my feelings hurt so badly before," the ex-customer said. He will now charge Olav Oeye Inc. with religious discrimination and promises legal action.

"The garage will get built anyway but now it has become an important matter of principle for me to pursue this. My Norwegian friends are the most shocked," the Norwegian-Pakistani said.

Olav Oeye remains unrepentant, and is not swayed by the argument that the 27-year-old is born and raised in Norway.

"After reading the papers and listening to the radio it wasn't amusing thinking about working for Muslims. WE have it a few times before and there are always problems with the bill. No, why should I (regret) it? I am retired and have five or six employed who do what I want," Oeye said.

Lawyer Abid Q. Raja said he had never heard such a clear case of religious harassment and, according to VG, nearly began to laugh when he heard the contents of the letter.

"This must be the most unprofessional firm in Norway. But it also indicates that there are very many who have similar opinions in Norway but are not brave enough to say so," Raja said, and said the letter clearly violates the law.

The National Association of the Building Industry also expressed shock and said they would consider reactions if Oeye Inc. was a member, but did not believe they had the jurisdiction to exclude the company.

"This is so odd that our ethical rules don't cover it. It is irrelevant if a prospective client is a Muslim or not, regardless of threats to Norway. This is completely unreasonable. It is just not on," said Association director Odd Trender to VG.

Aftenposten
NEWS FROM NORWAY

Thursday 05 November 2003

BISHOP CRITICAL OF MINISTER'S ADVICE TO ISLAM

Oslo's bishop, Gunnar Staalsett has warned Minister of Local Government and Regional Development Erna Solberg of the dangers of criticizing Islam after she told Norway's Muslims that they should modernize their religion. Staalsett fears that the statement will create a warped view of Islam.

Cabinet Minister Erna Solberg

"There is naturally a need for reform in all religious communities, but an initiative from the government sounds a special note," Staalsett told Norwegian Broadcasting (NRK). Staalsett is concerned that the minister's remarks can cause provide a mistaken image of Islam as a whole.

"One should be very careful about portraying a religion from its worst sides," Staalsett said.

Aftenposten English Web Desk
Jonathan Tisdall

Aftenposten
NEWS FROM NORWAY

8th November 2003

FACING MECCA FRIGHTENS PIOUS VILLAGERS

Residents of Bykle, population 864, are reportedly deeply troubled that their new church, currently under construction, faces Islam's holy city of Mecca. Fear of the anti-Christ runs through the town, newspaper Faedrelandsvennen reports.

The old church in Bykle lay east-west with its entrance from the west. The new church points southeast. Hallvard Gjerden, 64, of the Norwegian Lutheran Mission (NLM) was one of the first to make a connection.

"The church is facing directly towards Mecca - to the millimeter. I've checked," Gjerden told the newspaper.

"People fear that the Muslims will seize the church and use it as a mosque. You don't dare write this, but the mosques are the church's greatest enemy. The Muslims want to conquer the earth and kill Christians," Gjerden said.

The head of the building commission for Bykle church, Tor Mosdoel, was only amused by Gjerden's theories.

"This is just something people have made up," said Mosdoel, who has no fear of Muslims whatsoever. "The church had to have a northern entrance because the building site gave us no choice," he said.

Aftenposten English Web Desk
Jonathan Tisdall

Aftenposten
NEWS FROM NORWAY

Saturday July 24 2004

First published: 14 Jul 2004, 11:56

Anti-Muslim remarks rock the boat

Populist Norwegian politician Carl I Hagen has a long track record of provocation in Norway. His latest frontal attack on Muslims at a Christian gathering this week may set a new record for the degree of reaction he's getting.

Rival politicians are blasting remarks made by Progress Party boss Hagen that compared Muslims to Hitler, poked fun at Mohammed and raised fears that Muslims are trying to take over the world.

Progress Party boss Carl I Hagen is making waves with his remarks about Muslims.

PHOTO: DAG GRUNDSETH

RELATED STORIES:
- Students reject proposal to ban hijab - 02.07.2004
- State chides ex-pat Norwegians in Spain - 30.06.2004
- More voters shun Prime Minister's party - 28.06.2004
- Socialist parties gain in polls - 14.06.2004
- Female politicians impress most - 10.06.2004
- Politicians back off on fighter jet threat - 08.06.2004
- Churches should not become mosques - 05.05.2004
- Krekar wins damages - 21.04.2004
- Krekar can't pay court claim -
- Krekar gets bill after Hagen trial -

Local theologists say they're shocked, a university professor claimed Hagen went way too far this time, and at least one anti-discrimination organization is threatening to sue him.

Hagen's outbursts came during a speech he made at a Christian festival in Bergen on Tuesday.

"The Islamic fundamentalists, along the same lines as Hitler, made it clear a long time ago that their long-term plan is to 'Islamify' the world," Hagen claimed. "They're well underway, they've come far in Africa and are on their way into Europe, and then we have to fight it."

Hagen also talked about children being used as suicide bombers. "We Christians are very concerned about children, 'Let the children come to me,' said Jesus," Hagen declared. "I can't see Mohammed saying the same."

That remark spurred laughter and applause from his Christian audience, perhaps encouring Hagen to add: "If he (Mohammed) did say such a thing, it must have been: 'Let the small children come to me, so that I can exploit them in my effort to make the world Islamic."

Angry response
While Hagen found himself preaching to the choir at the Christian festival of the organization *Levende Ord,* (Living Word), other politicians were furious.

Afshan Rafiq, a member of Parliament from the Conservatives, blasted Hagen for "stygmatizing an entire religion." He was backed by Erna Solberg, head of the Conservatives, who said Hagen's remarks further distance the two parties from each other even though they're both on the right of Norway's political spectrum.

Solberg said there now was even less probablity that her party and Hagen's could cooperate to form a non-socialist government in Norway. An official from the Christian Democrats also said Hagen "crossed the line when he didn't only attack fundamentalists, but also the prophet Mohammed."

'Shocked'
Solberg's reaction likely comes as a relief to Jens Vidar Bjørkedal, Norway's only Muslim sheriff. He told newspaper VG he was shaken by Hagen's remarks. "I hope he never gets into the government," Bjørkedal told VG. "I'm shocked that a leading politician can say such things."

Some commentators said it likely will be up to Progress Party deputy Siv Jensen "to clean up" after Hagen's latest provocation. Hagen, they say, enjoys stirring up trouble, only to let party colleagues smooth ruffled feathers afterwards.

Aftenposten English Web Desk
Nina Berglund

LATEST NEWS
Local:
- 'Circus Ari' takes over island
- Sheriff carries woman three kilometres
- Police find a surprise at small farm
- Officials set to close 40 refugee centers
- Train wreck embarrasses Turkish government
- Robbery suspect also tied to post heist
- Coldest summer in 11 years
- 'Shame' blamed in daughter's murder

Business:
- Young buyers fuel housing boom
- Telenor reports big jump in profits
- Røkke sells Florida property

Sports:
- Soccer enthusiasts descend on Oslo
- Arvesen finally pleased in Tour de France

World:

Aftenposten
NEWS FROM NORWAY
Monday April 25 2005
First published: 22 Apr 2005, 13:38

Norwegian preacher kindles religious strife

Celebrity Pentecostal preacher Runar Søgaard is under protection by Swedish police after receiving death threats. A high-profile sermon where Sögaard called the prophet Mohammed "a confused pedophile" has triggered fears of religious war.

Runar Søgaard has always managed to combine Pentecostalism and celebrity.

PHOTO: BERIT ROALD / SCANPIX

Søgaard, 37, enjoys celebrity status in Sweden after his marriage to recording star and Eurovision song contest winner Carola, even though they are now divorced.

"Even if I see Runar while he has major police protection I will shoot him to death," a radical Islamist told Swedish newspaper Expressen.

Persons connected to the Kurdish group Ansar al-Islam claim to have received a fatwa, a decree from a Muslim religious leader, to kill Søgaard.

Muslim organizations have called Søgaard's sermon, which is on sale on CD at the Stockholm Karisma Center's web site, a hateful attack on Islam and fear the type of violent conflict that scarred the Netherlands after filmmaker Theo van Gogh was killed by an Islamic extremist for a controversial film.

Carola Häggkvist Søgaard, an adored singer in Sweden, assured her Norwegian husband celebrity status.

PHOTO: UGLUM, MORTEN

Islam expert Jan Hjärpe at the University of Lund told Expressen that such an assassination is a real risk, and he wondered if conflict was the motive for the sermon.

"It was a statement from an odd man in an odd sect but the effect is stronger antagonism between different groups. It becomes a pure religious polemic and is extremely unpleasant," Hjärpe told the newspaper.

Hjärpe saw the incident as a type of beginning of a religious war in Sweden. "It (Sögaard's sermon) has power and influence. It seems to have been Runar's intention to provoke and promote antagonism," Hjärpe said.

Søgaard said he fears for his life and understands that he has angered the wrong people. He received police protection after questioning by Swedish police.

Imam Hassan Moussa, head of Sweden's imam council, demanded that Christian communities repudiate Søgaard's remarks, and promised that Sweden would avoid the ugly scenes experienced in Holland.

Aftenposten English Web Desk
Jonathan Tisdall

Aftenposten
Saturday May 06 2006 NEWS FROM NORWAY First published: 05 May 2006, 11:54

DRUNK NORWEGIAN TOURISTS NEARLY LYNCHED IN EGYPT

Two Norwegians, part of a group of intoxicated Scandinavian tourists on holiday in Egypt, were nearly lynched at there sort town of Hurghada this week, after their antics deeply offended the local population.

This was the mermaid statue in Hurghada that figured into the Scandinavian tourists' offensive behaviour.

Residents of Hurghada generally tolerate tourists, but the group of Scandinavians went too far.

The two Norwegians and three Swedes ended up being arrested by local police, who protected them from an angry mob.

The troubled started after the five Scandinavian tourists got drunk, dressed themselves up like Muslim pilgrims and started dancing around the statue of a mermaid located in a town square, and pretending she symbolized Allah.

The Scandinavians apparently were trying to parody Muslim pilgrimages to Mecca. When they started stripping off their clothes, the local Egyptians had had enough and went on the attack.

A local policeman told Swedish newspaper ***Aftonbladet*** that his colleagues had to step in to protect the tourists from angry local residents. "If they hadn't been arrested, they probably would have been lynched," an Islamic expert told ***Aftonbladet.***

The tourists were initially held on charges of indecent conduct, since some of the men exposed themselves. The charges were later raised to blasphemy, which can be punished severely.

Norway's foreign ministry was pulled into the case, but an official at the Norwegian Embassy in Cairo said he hoped to be able to get the Norwegians released and sent home.

He said the embassy had been in contact with Egyptian authorities. An official at the Norwegians' tour company, Apollo, could confirm on Friday that the men, all aged 35-40, had been released and were free to leave Egypt.

Hurghada is a popular tourist destination for Scandinavians, and the local population generally tolerates the partying and scanty clothing so foreign to their own culture.

Aftenposten
NEWS FROM NORWAY

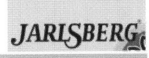

Tuesday November 13 2007

First published: 09 Nov 2007, 12:01

AFTENPOSTEN
English frontpage
Norwegian frontpage

NEWS
Latest 100 stories
Press release

FEATURES
Only in Norway
Picture series
Norway's Centennial
The Royals
Webcams in Norway
Readers respond

PICTURE SERIES

Summer house fit for a king

100 latest stories

WEBCAMS

See Norway live. See our webcams.

Most visited
- Tromsø: torget
- Bergen
- Molde
- Oslo: Frognerseteren
- Arendal
- Ålesund: Fjellstua
- Stavanger
- Oslo: Youngstorget
- Longyearbyen
- Oslo havn - Vippetangen

TO THE CAMERAS

SEARCH
News in english:
Search for | Search
How to search

INFO
About the newsdesk
Contact us
Advertising info
Rate calculator

Memoir insults Muslims

The autobiography of outspoken Progress Party politician Carl I. Hagen "Ærlig talt" - Speaking Honestly - has offended Norwegian Muslims.

PHOTO: AFTENPOSTEN

RELATED STORIES:
- Few escape insults - 01.11.2007

A passage where the controversial Hagen calls the prophet Mohammed a warlord, man of violence and abuser of women has, unsurprisingly, caused offense.

"That the Islamic council is disappointed and angry and furious is as expected. I had more or less counted on this to happen when I wrote that," Hagen told newspaper *Vårt Land*.

Norway's Islamic Council asked Norwegian Muslims to refrain from reacting to Hagen's book.

Hagen's remarks come in connection with the massive trouble linked to the publication of caricatures of the prophet Mohammed.

Hagen writes that the government's handling of the matter led to freedom of speech "taking a back seat to respect for the warlord, man of violence and woman abuser Mohammed, who murdered and accepted rape as a method of conquest".

"If one puts religious feelings high, one cannot remain indifferent to such talk," said Islamic Council Norway leader Senaid Kobilica to Vårt Land.

The council is now working on a statement taking exception to Hagen's remarks and asking Norwegian Muslims not to react in an unsuitable way.

Hagen's memoirs has also received attention for the denigrating comments rained over most of Norway's leading politicians.

Aftenposten.no 9th November 2007

Aftenposten

Saturday January 19 2008 NEWS FROM NORWAY First published: 14 Jan 2008, 15:46

AFTENPOSTEN
English frontpage
Norwegian frontpage

NEWS
Latest 100 stories
Press release

FEATURES
Only in Norway
Picture series
Norway's Centennial
The Royals
Webcams in Norway
Readers respond

PICTURE SERIES

Norway's 'most important' buildings

100 latest stories

WEBCAMS

See Norway live.See our webcams.

Most visited
- Molde
- Tromsø: torget
- Bergen
- Oslo: Frognerseteren
- Kristiansand: festningen
- Stavanger
- Oslo: Herbern Aker Brygge
- Oslo: Youngstorget
- Ålesund: Fjellstua
- Oslo havn

TO THE CAMERAS

SEARCH
News in english:
Search for | Search
How to search

INFO
About the newsdesk
Contact us
Advertising info
Rate calculator
Advertising contacts

IN NORWEGIAN
Innenriks (local)
Utenriks (world)
Økonomi (business)
Sport (sports)
Subscribe
Weather
TV-guide
Streetmap

Oslo mosque boosts security

The World Islamic Mission's mosque in Oslo has boosted security measures after somone left a pig's head and a Nazi flag inside the mosque's entrance during Friday prayer services.

Someone tried to offend and/or threaten the World Islamic Mission's mosque in Oslo.
PHOTO: ARASH A NEJAD

"It's clear that someone has done this to provoke us," the chairman of World Islamic Mission, Jehangir Bahadur, told newspaper *Aften* on Monday.

He called the act "offensive" and "a clear threat" against the mosque. "Pork is strictly forbidden in Islam, and that makes the incident very serious," he said.

Bahadur said the mosque has also received racist e-mail that it hadn't been taking very seriously, but that's changed now. World Islamic Officials reported the unwelcome delivery of the pig's head and Nazi flag, which occurred just before Christmas, to Oslo police.

Tom Gulliksen of the Grønland Police Station, nearest the mosque, said a police investigation was suspended for lack of evidence, but it will be taken up again if new leads emerge. A surveillance camera picked up an image of the person making the delivery, but it was too grainy to reveal any identity.

Both the flag and the pig's head were sent to the police crime lab. Since Nazi items were involved, Norway's criminal intelligence unit PST was notified as well.

"I think that the person who did this is either unbalanced, or was mounting a PR stunt," Gulliksen said.

Aftenposten's reporterk
Ida Giske

Aftenposten English Web Desk
Nina Berglund

Email this article Print this article

MOST TIPPED	MOST READ
Hangover hits rich man hard	Hangover hits rich man hard
Cave man causes trouble for nursing home	Cave man causes trouble for nursing home
Elderly not getting the care they need	Huge grotto found under Norwegian glacier
Pickpockets rampage Oslo	Storm warnings for the west
Huge grotto found under Norwegian glacier	Royal couple asked to drop official trip to Chile
Storm warnings for the west	Elderly not getting the care they need
Cars are not welcome	

Aftenposten.no 14th January 2008

16 | **WORLD NEWS**

FRIDAY, NOVEMBER 4, 2005 | THE DAILY TELEGRAPH

BRING ON THE CONCUBINES
Japanese prince rejects calls for an empress **Page 20**

Muslims march over cartoons of the Prophet

By Kate Connolly in Berlin

A DANISH experiment in testing "the limits of freedom of speech" has backfired – or succeeded spectacularly – after newspaper cartoons of the Prophet Mohammed provoked an outcry.

Thousands of Muslims have taken to the streets in protest at the caricatures, the newspaper that published them has received death threats and two of its cartoonists have been forced into hiding.

Jyllands-Posten, Denmark's leading daily, defied Islam's ban on images of the Prophet by printing cartoons by 12 different artists.

In one he is depicted as a sabre-wielding terrorist accompanied by women in burqas, in another his turban appears to be a bomb and in a third he is portrayed as a schoolboy by a blackboard.

The ambassadors of 11 Muslim countries called on Anders Fogh Rasmussen, the prime minister, to take "necessary steps" against the "defamation of Islam".

But Mr Rasmussen, the head of a centre-Right minority coalition dependent for its survival on support from an anti-foreigner party, called the cartoons a "necessary provocation" and refused to act.

"I will never accept that respect for a religious stance leads to the curtailment of criticism, humour and satire in the press," he said.

The Danish debate over how to integrate Muslims has raged for years, with nursery school menus and women-only opening hours for swimming pools particular battlegrounds. But the cartoons satirising the Prophet have injected a dangerous new element into the controversy.

"This is a pubescent demonstration of freedom of expression that consciously and totally without reason has trampled over the feelings of many people," said Uffe Ellemann Jensen, a former foreign minister and member of Mr Rasmussen's party.

Carsten Juste, the editor of *Jyllands-Posten*, spurned demands that he apologise, saying he "would not dream" of saying sorry.

"To demand that we take religious feelings into consideration is irreconcilable with western democracy and freedom of expression," he said. "This doesn't mean that we want to insult any Muslims."

Juste commissioned the cartoons after learning of the difficulties a children's writer, Kare Bluitgen, had in finding an illustrator for his book on the Koran and the Prophet's life. Bluitgen said all the artists he approached feared the wrath of Muslims if they drew images of Mohammed.

Many cited the murder of the Dutch filmmaker Theo Van Gogh by an Islamist as a reason for refusal.

Juste said he wanted to counter growing "self censorship" and see how many cartoonists would be "bold enough" to draw the Prophet.

One artist, Franz Füchsel, said he intended no offence. "But I live in 2005, not 905 and I use my quill in the way that Danish law allows me."

Ayaan Hirsi Ali, the Dutch MP famous for her criticism of Islam and author of the screenplay for Mr Van Gogh's film *Submission*, supported the paper. "It's necessary to taunt Muslims on their relationship with Mohammed," she said.

"Otherwise we will never have the dialogue we need to establish with Muslims on the most central question: 'Do you really feel that every Muslim in 2005 should follow the way of life the Prophet had 1,400 years ago, as the Koran dictates?'"

kate.connolly@telegraph.co.uk

The Daily Telegraph, Friday November 4th 2005

THE TIMES TUESDAY JANUARY 31 2006

TIMES WORLD NEWS
timesonline.co.uk/world

JAPAN
Extortion, murder, theft: a nation in the grip of geriatric crimewave
PAGE 31

WEST BANK
Hamas begs world not to cut off aid lifeline as money starts to run out
PAGE 34

Denmark faces international boycott over Muslim cartoons

By Anthony Browne

DENMARK faced the full fury of the Muslim world yesterday as a long-simmering row over newspaper cartoons depicting the Prophet Muhammad finally erupted.

There were street demonstrations and flag-burnings in the Middle East. Libya joined Saudi Arabia in withdrawing its ambassador from Copenhagen. Islamic governments and organisations, including the Muslim Council of Britain, issued denunciations and a boycott of Danish goods took hold across the Muslim world.

The Danish Government warned its citizens about travelling to Algeria, Egypt, Jordan, Lebanon, Pakistan, Saudi Arabia and Syria, and withdrew aid workers from the Gaza Strip.

Last night EU foreign ministers issued a statement in support of Denmark, and the European Commission threatened to report any government backing the boycott to the World Trade Organisation.

The fury echoed the outcry that followed the publication in 1988 of the Salman Rushdie novel *The Satanic Verses*. The trigger for the latest clash of cultures was the publication by the Danish newspaper *Jyllands-Posten* on September 30 of 12 cartoons of Muhammad. A biographer of the prophet had complained that no one would dare to illustrate his book, and the newspaper challenged cartoonists to draw pictures of the prophet in a self-declared battle for freedom of speech.

One submission showed Muhammad wearing a bomb-shaped turban; in another he tells dead suicide bombers that he has run out of virgins with which to reward them. Any portrayal of Muhammad is blasphemous in Islam, lest it encourages idolatry.

In October ambassadors from ten Muslim countries complained to Anders Fogh Rasmussen, the Danish Prime Minister, who refused to interfere with the press's freedom.

But the issue began to boil this month after the cartoons appeared in Magazinet, a Christian newspaper in Norway, and on the website of the Norwegian newspaper Dagbladet.

Imams denounced Denmark from their pulpits, the Arab press inflamed pent-up Muslim anger at the West and last Friday the Saudi Government recalled its ambassador, but still Mr Rasmussen refused to apologise. He condemned attempts to "demonise people because of religious beliefs", but argued: "The Government can in no way influence the media."

PATRICK BAZ / AFP / GETTY IMAGES

Protests against the cartoons have spread across the Muslim world, including Gaza City, where an activist stamped this footprint on a makeshift Danish flag

By yesterday governments across the Arab world were responding to public outrage. Libya closed its embassy in Denmark and the Egyptian parliament demanded that its Government follow suit. The Kuwaiti and Jordanian governments called for explanations from their Danish ambassadors. President Lahoud of Lebanon condemned the cartoons, saying his country "cannot accept any insult to any religion". The Justice Minister of the United Arab Emirates said: "This is cultural terrorism, not freedom of expression." In Gaza, gunmen briefly occupied the EU office in Gaza and warned Danes and Norwegians to stay away. Palestinians in the West Bank burnt Danish flags. The Islamic groups Hamas and Hezbollah and the Egyptian Muslim Brotherhood demanded an apology.

Supermarkets in Algeria, Bahrain, Jordan, Kuwait, Morocco, Qatar, Tunisia, the United Arab Emirates and Yemen all removed Danish produce from their shelves. Arla Foods, a Danish company with annual sales of about $430 million in the Middle East, said that the boycott was almost total and suspended production in Saudi Arabia.

The Muslim Council of Britain, whose leaders are to meet the Danish ambassador tomorrow, deplored the newspapers' refusal to apologise for printing "sacrilegious cartoons vilifying the Prophet Muhammad".

Bill Clinton, the former US President, added his voice, telling a conference in Qatar that he feared anti-Semitism would be replaced with anti-Islamic prejudice. He condemned "these totally outrageous cartoons against Islam".

Per Stig Moeller, Denmark's Foreign Minister, insisted in Brussels last night: "We condemn blasphemy. We want respect for religions. But we cannot intervene. We have sent explanations but, as we have said before, freedom of expression is a matter for the courts, not for the Government."

A spokesman for Peter Mandelson, the EU Trade Commissioner, said that if the Saudi Government had encouraged the boycott of Danish goods, Mr Mandelson would take the matter to the WTO.

Carsten Juste, editor-in-chief of *Jyllands-Posten*, said that the drawings "were not in violation of Danish law but have offended many Muslims, which we would like to apologise for". However, a spokesman for the newspaper said: "We do not apologize for printing the cartoons, it was our right to do so. We stand by our decision to print them."

www.timesonline.co.uk
Lastest news
www.dagbladet.no/kultur/2006/01/18/454375.html

FROM NEWSPAPER CHALLENGE TO DIPLOMATIC INCIDENT

September 30, 2005 Danish newspaper *Jyllands-Posten* publishes 12 cartoons of the Prophet Muhammad

October 20 Ambassadors of ten Muslim countries complain to Danish Prime Minister. *Jyllands-Posten* reports that illustrators have received death threats

November 14 Jamaat-e-Islami, a Pakistan-based group, protests in Islamabad

January 10, 2006 Cartoons reprinted by *Magazinet*, a Norwegian newspaper

January 26 Saudi Arabia recalls its ambassador and initiates boycott of Danish goods

January 27 Thousands denounce the cartoons during Friday prayers in Iraq

January 28 Danish company Arla places adverts in Middle Eastern newspapers to try to stop boycott of its produce

January 29 *Jyllands-Posten* prints a statement in Arabic saying the drawings were published in line with freedom of expression and not a campaign against Islam. Palestinians burn Danish flags and Libya announces it will close its embassy in Denmark

January 30 EU says it will take World Trade Organisation action if boycott persists. Several Islamic groups, including Hamas and the Egyptian Muslim Brotherhood, call for worldwide boycott of Danish products. Masked gunmen in storm EU office in Gaza

ISLAMIC CONFLICT

- **1988** Ayatollah Khomeini issues fatwa against Salman Rushdie after publication of *The Satanic Verses*
- **2001** The author Khalid Duran faces mass condemnation from Muslims for his book which sought to explain Islam to Jews, culminating in alleged death threats for his apostasy
- **2002** Fatwa issued against the Nigerian journalist Isioma Daniel after she suggested that Muhammad might approve of the Miss World contest
- **2004** Extremist kills the Dutch director Theo van Gogh after he made Submission, a ten-minute film about the abuse of Muslim women featuring Koranic verses written on female bodies
- **2005** Swedish museum is forced to remove a painting depicting a couple making love while covered in verses from the Koran

The Times, Tuesday, January 31st 2006

FEB 2006 | MUHARRAM 1427 | NO.365

Q-NEWS

Something Rotten in the State of Denmark

The uproar caused by the Danish broadsheet *Jyllands-Posten*'s publication of a number of caricatures of the Prophet Muhammad has put Denmark firmly on the map, but it's the kind of attention the country would have been perfectly happy without. With Muslim ambassadors being recalled from Copenhagen, Danish embassies burning in Beirut and Damascus, angry protests from London to Lahore and a consumer boycott across the Middle East, the case has now escalated to a point where it's gone from being another far from atypical event in an increasingly xenophobic little country - better known for its bacon, beer and the Little Mermaid - to an international crisis with Denmark now being referred to as the "frontline in the cultural battle between Islam and the West". So how did it come to this? Danish Muslim commentator Omar Shah traces the roots of the controversy.

For most Muslims in Denmark, accustomed to an increasingly hostile climate, in which both the press and politicians have quite a liberal view of "freedom of expression" (at least when it comes to Islam), the drawings were just another in a long series of provocations and had it not been for a foolhardy decision by the Danish Prime Minister it might have stayed that way.

In September 2005, Kaare Bluitgen, a leading Danish critic of Islam announced in Jyllands-Posten that he had written a "children's" book about the Prophet Muhammad but could not find any artist to illustrate the book out of fear of the violent Islamists. Though widely perceived by Muslims as being a publicity stunt to get attention, Jyllands-Posten, perhaps deeply touched by Bluitgen's predicament and the "great threat to Danish freedom of expression", invited 12 artists to submit drawings of the prophet in order to demonstrate to "fanatics" that the freedom of expression in Denmark is absolute and far above irrational, archaic sensitivities.

The author of the book - which was released at the end of January - describes it as a historical account based on the Quran, Sunnah and the famous Seerah by Ibn Ishaq, written for a young Danish audience. In a recent interview, he explained that he wanted to show the "human side" of the Prophet, and that one of the incidents described in the book "entirely from Muslim sources" is the one "where the Prophet fell in love with his daughter in law [the wife of Zaid], got her divorced from her husband and conveniently received a revelation allowing him to marry his adopted sons wife." He went on to explain that Muslims are immensely proud of the Prophet "being a real man who could get any woman he wanted."

In view of this, it's hardly surprising that several artists (one would hope out of decency rather than fear) had reservations about illustrating his book.

Had Jyllands-Posten been a tabloid - Denmark's equivalent of The Sun perhaps - the stunt might have been understandable, but Jyllands-Posten is the broadsheet with one of the largest circulations in Denmark. Although its right wing sympathies are no secret, as it often functions as a mouthpiece for various reactionary personalities, the latest incident marked a new low point. The drawings caused an uproar, particularly due to the derogatory nature of the caricatures informed be a combination of old orientalist stereotypes and modern Islamophobic imagery. One drawing depicted the Prophet with a bomb in his turban, while another depicted him as a fierce looking man with a dagger in his hand and four niqab-clad women behind him.

As expected (and intended) the reactions from the Muslim community were heated, complete with demonstrations, fierce condemnations and even a bomb threat from a 17 year old boy. All the while the newspaper could gloat at its role as "protector of Danish values" and publish new editorials and commentaries lecturing Muslims about freedom of expression. Several politicians also banged on the drum of how the Muslim community supposedly did not understand sacrosanct Danish values and how this could pose a threat to the stability of Denmark.

The fact that a leading "quality" newspaper had so clearly violated the sensitivities of the Muslims citizens of Denmark seemed irrelevant. The Muslim reaction was widely misreported in the press, as anger over the flaunting of the Muslim prohibition against drawing the Prophet, rather than anger over the shameless and derogatory way in which he had been depicted.

A number of ambassadors from Muslim countries (with the

Egyptian and the Turkish representatives at the forefront), concerned by this public ridicule of the Prophet and vilification of the Muslim community, asked Prime Minister Anders Fogh Rasmussen for a meeting and called upon him to distance himself from the actions of the newspaper. The Prime Minister however publicly humiliated them by not only refusing to meet them, but also lecturing them (again) on freedom of speech in Denmark and on the independence of the Danish press. Following this arrogant refusal to even acknowledge that Muslim feelings had been hurt, the diplomats and a number of Danish Muslims organizations decided to seek support abroad, a course of action which was to prove to be even more controversial than the original drawings themselves.

All the world's a stage

The case was raised both at the Arab league and the Organisation of the Islamic Conference and calls were issued for Denmark to apologize. These reactions were widely derided in the Danish press. That that such backward countries could have the audacity to criticize Denmark was simply unheard of. This strong belief in the infallibility of the Danish model and the perception of it being a beacon of liberal light in a dark world has incidentally been one of the main obstacles to meaningful dialogue in Denmark.

Following the international attention a rumour arose (originated by the same newspaper that published the drawings) that the Jamaat-i-Islami of Pakistan had issued a bounty on the head of the drawers invoking fresh memories of the Rushdie case, and the artists subsequently got police protection, which led to further protests about how Danish freedom was being threatened.

In addition to the diplomats, a number of local Muslim organizations had also tried to engage the government, but were met with similar responses. Thus shunned by the government and ridiculed by the press, a delegation of Danish Muslims (of primarily Palestinian origin) associated with the largest Ikhwan congregations in Denmark went on a tour of the Middle East to raise awareness of the issue, and visited officials and scholars in countries such as Lebanon and Egypt. This coupled with the OIC and Arab League's stance on the case led to it being widely reported in the Arabic press.

The level of reactions from abroad and the potential dent in Denmark's "nice image" has taken Danish politicians by surprise, and veteran politicians have criticized the current government for jeopardizing Denmark's long term projects in the Middle East such as a "democratization initiative" in Yemen, Jordan and Egypt. This was also the position of a number of former Danish diplomats who delivered a petition to the Prime Minister.

Furious about the negative attention, a campaign has been launched by right-wing MP's (from the Danish Peoples Party) accusing the delegation of treason and of deliberately misinforming the Middle Eastern press to blow the case out of proportion in order to harm Denmark's international interests. Rather than being lauded for making use of their "freedom of expression" a number of newspapers have jumped on this bandwagon. Additionally leading Danish "terror experts" have accused the delegation's reckless behaviour of increasing the terror threat against Denmark, which has already participated militarily in both Iraq and Afghanistan with widespread public support. However while other "crusader nations" might have attacked Muslims no other country has overtly endorsed such ridicule of the Prophet Muhammad.

In early January the regional prosecutor stated that it did not find any reason to take legal action against the newspaper over the drawings, a decision which has now been appealed to the High Court, while the group of Muslims accused of treason have launched a libel case against the Danish People's Party. In the Middle East the boycott of Danish products is spreading day by day and "militant" groups have started issuing threats against Danish interests. As of going to press the situation has become so critical that the Danish papers hardly write about anything else, and The Danish Chamber of Commerce as well as opposition politicians have started putting pressure on the Government and the paper to apologize once and for all. It seems that condemnation from governments across the Muslim world and the potential loss of hundreds of millions of pounds worth of agricultural exports, especially the Gulf countries, have somewhat modified at least some Danes' views of freedom of speech, and helped them find a tolerance and concern that local Muslim protests could not.

On the 30th of January Jyllands-Posten after intense pressure from several Danish politicians and industrialists (especially Arla with annual sales of dairy products to the Gulf exceeding £300 million) finally issued an "apology", stating that while the caricatures were not illegal under Danish law and the paper was not sorry for publishing them, they were sorry for any offence caused. A position diametrically opposed to their own stated aim in publicizing the drawings in the first place, and a position it took four months to arrive at.

Hath not a Muslim eyes

To a reader unfamiliar with the climate in Denmark the whole situation may seem grotesque and shocking: why would a broadsheet want to engage in such senseless provocation in the first place and why would the Danish government take such a foolish and arrogant stance without even acknowledging Muslim sensitivities?

The answer lies partially in domestic politics and partially in the "cultural battle" which has been taken place in Denmark for the last half a decade, a battle with a stated aim to "revive Danish values" and to stop the encroaching Islamism and "Islamisation" of society.

It is hard to perceive how a minority comprising 4% of the population could Islamise society but in Denmark Muslims are already vilified and deemed too sensitive and demanding. Any concessions to Muslim sensitivities are seen as accommodating fanaticism and "harming integration".

It is also worth noting that Venstre, the party leading the current government, is heavily dependant on Dansk Folkeparti (Danish Peoples Party) a rabidly anti-Muslim and anti-immigration party which holds 14% of the seats in Parliament, for its mandate. Several of its members have been accused of racism for making statements not dissimilar to those which have currently seen the BNP's Nick Griffin in court. In the UK, such statements would have meant the end of any serious political career, but not in Denmark.

Had Jyllands-Posten been a tabloid - Denmark's equivalent of *The Sun* perhaps - the stunt might have been understandable, but Jyllands-Posten is the broadsheet with one of the largest circulations in Denmark. Although its right wing sympathies are no secret, as it often functions as a mouthpiece for various reactionary personalities, the latest incident marked a new low point.

While politicians increasingly pay lip service to Christianity as part of the Danish heritage (much to the chagrin of many who like one left wing commentator detest the new "I am not Muslim, hence I am Christian" attitude), the only thing which is religiously guarded is secular democracy - ridiculing democracy is considered a grave sin while ridiculing religion is not. Secular fundamentalism has been elevated to the status of religion in a way perhaps surpassing even France. Unfortunately for the Muslim immigrants the result is one and the same, whether its criticism for not adhering to Denmark's "Christian values" or Denmark's "secular values".

With this increased polarization, the boundaries for what is acceptable to say have been steadily moved and expanded to a point where some statements bring chilly memories from Germany in the 1930s. In addition to the general aversion against "demanding Muslims" a further problem when it comes to a case such as the drawings is that Danes despite their immense pride in Denmark have very few tangible symbols they hold sacred. Religion is freely made fun of and not even the queen or the flag is held in the esteem leading to an inability to relate to the hurt and anger Muslims feel.

This manifested itself clearly in the Danish reaction to the Van Gogh murder case which saw Denmark gripped by hysteria, the case making headlines in Danish newspapers for several weeks, and being discussed almost as had it happened in Denmark. Sadly, most Danes were oblivious to what Van Gogh had in fact done, only horrified by the fact that a man was killed. The perception of right and wrong in the case was summed up when Ayan Hirsi Ali - Van Gogh's collaborator on the film which led to the murder - was later given the "freedom prize" by the Danish Prime Minister Anders Fogh Rasmussen. When vilification and ridicule of Islam is deemed to be synonymous with freedom, the reaction to the drawings is not very surprising. Again and again "freedom of expression" is hailed as a universal right, with no one seemingly worried that this is used as a freedom to offend. Sadly this grandiose attitude is not expanded to include people who are considered "Islamists" as the Danish spokesman for Hizb-ut Tahrir realised when he received a suspended sentence of two months in prison for a leaflet found on the HT website referring to Jews as "a slanderous people".

To be or not to be, that is the question

In a country where referring to Jews as slanderous gets you an, albeit suspended, prison sentence, but referring to Muslims on the other hand as a "cancer that should be operated away", terrorists and people who consider it their "right to rape Danish girls based on the Koran" (as expressed by several Danish MPs) is apparently not racism, one could perhaps excuse the Muslim youth for being a little more than disillusioned.

The attitude of the establishment reinforced by the cultural battle has not done much for community relations, on the contrary if anything it has made immigrants more insular and created a staunchly anti-Danish "immigrant" subculture especially amongst the second generation. Any British politicians worried about lack of social cohesion or the "failure of the British model" should visit Denmark. When asked to describe their affiliation many Muslims would say "Denmark is where I was born" instead of saying "I am Danish". A not so insignificant minority would stumble on the word Danish. The term for immigrant, "perker" (Danish racist slang for a brown person") is in fact used as a badge of honour. There is also a very strong multiethnic unified immigrant subculture even across religious lines and there are not many countries in which an Albanian, an Iraqi and a Cuban would largely define themselves as belonging to the same group. In Denmark, Danish means a white ethnic group, not a citizenship

The stigmatization of Muslims has also fuelled not only a marked increase in the practice of Islam but also the rise in a what I would term secular Islamism, where adherence to a political aspect of Islam is promoted without strict adherence to the religion. Over the last decade immigrants have increasingly started to define them as Muslims (as this is what society calls them) and Islam has become a strong identity marker even where it does necessarily lead to a deeper practice of the religion.

There is something definitely rotten in the state of Denmark where the stage has been set for a tragic play where the roles of the Muslim antagonists and secular Danish protagonists have been firmly defined in advance, with the majority of Muslims still playing the role of extras. The plot is laid out, but it is now up to the Danish establishment to decide whether to follow the script punctually, deliver a good stage-show complete with a disastrous ending, or whether there is courage to depart from the script, redefine the roles, include the extras and achieve a happy ending before curtain call. As for now the very likely economic consequences of a stunt gone far too wrong might be viewed as poetic justice and will hopefully make future events of the same type less likely.

Omar Sayyid Shah is of Danish-Afghan origin, born in Denmark and now residing in the United Kingdom. He has participated extensively in the Danish debate on immigration and religion through political commentaries in leading Danish broadsheets, and has contributed to two books on the subject: Islam, Christianity and modernity *(2004) and* With other eyes *(2003), both published in Danish.*

Q News, February 2006 issue

THE TIMES WEDNESDAY FEBRUARY 1 2006

LETTERS TO THE EDITOR

1 PENNINGTON STREET, LONDON E98 ITA ■ FAX: 020-7782 5046 ■ E-MAIL: letters@thetimes.co.uk

A free society must respect all its religions

From the New York President of the World Jewish Congress

Sir, Although freedom of religion and freedom of speech are both fundamental rights, they sometimes come into conflict which each other, as is the case with the caricatures recently published in the Danish newspaper *Jyllands-Posten* depicting the Prophet Muhammad (report, Jan 31). This has provoked an uproar among Muslims, not just in Denmark, but across the Islamic world, as it is widely understood that Islam forbids the depicting of Muhammad.

The issue at stake here is not "self-censorship", which Flemming Rose, the newspaper's culture editor, claims has befallen Europe since the murder of the Dutch film-maker Theo van Gogh. It is whether respect for other religious beliefs, traditions and practices really applies to everybody, including Muslims.

We prefer the word "respect" to "tolerance" because to be "tolerated" is not a positive notion, and in addition "respect" is not a one-way concept; it is mutual. If the cartoons in question were deliberately made and published to provoke Muslims and to stir up public opinion in Denmark, as Mr Rose seems to suggest, something has gone wrong. What the cartoons managed to do was to offend all Muslims instead of focusing on those fanatics that actually merit criticism.

Sometimes, provocations are necessary to wake people up. Over the past 30 years, the World Jewish Congress has been no stranger to that. But religious customs, practices, beliefs, should be respected by followers of other religions and non-believers alike, because this is a prerequisite for being respected oneself.

Mutual respect and understanding between members of different religions is the key to ending hatred and to creating a better world. We consider desecration of any holy book an insult to ourselves. Desecration of the Koran, the Torah or the Bible, or any religious site, should be offensive to all of us.

To consciously provoke and offend the fairly small Muslim minority in Denmark was wrong. Yes, immigrants must integrate in their host societies, be they Muslims, Jews or Christians, while retaining their own identities, beliefs, customs and faiths. Parallel societies can easily become a breeding ground for fanatics, zealots and, ultimately, terrorists. Immigration sometimes fails because immigrants do not make enough effort. But sometimes it is made harder because of an intolerant and harsh host country.

It is the job of governments and lawmakers to make sure that immigrants are not treated as newly conquered, but with respect. Those who make an effort to integrate should be welcomed with open arms, and allowed to make more than just financial contributions to their new countries' tax coffers.

Over the past 2,000 years and until the creation of the state of Israel, Jews have always been a small minority in every country they have settled in. Our ancestors have suffered from pogroms, anti-Semitism and, finally, the Holocaust.

Lies about Jews, the Jewish faith and traditions have never disappeared. In fact, they are staging a comeback, especially in Western democracies which we thought had become immune to anti-Semitism after the horrors of the Holocaust.

Nonetheless, Jewish intellectuals and politicians have always been at the forefront of the fight for human rights, democracy and free speech. But there are limits to the latter that should be respected, and publishing materials considered offensive by a small religious minority is going too far. It is as wrong as the discrimination against Christian or Jewish populations that takes place in some Islamic countries. Democracies are tested on how they treat their minorities.

Over the decades since the publication of the Second Vatican Council declaration *Nostra Aetate*, the Catholic Church and the Jewish community have been engaged in dialogue with each other. Christians, Jews and Muslims are all children of Abraham, and we should learn what we have in common.

EDGAR M. BRONFMAN
New York

From the New York President of the World Jewish Congress

The Times, Wednesday February 1st 2006

MINARET MYTHS

New Statesman - 1 August 2011

False claims about Muslims are fuelling Islamophobia in Europe, says Andreas Malm

There is nothing particularly Norwegian about Anders Behring Breivik's manifesto, 2083: a European Declaration of Independence. It is a bulky précis of all the standard tropes in Islamophobic ideology that have evolved in Europe over the past decade. Its plagiarism — the enormous excerpts from authors such as Melanie Phillips, Roger Scruton, Daniel Pipes, Bruce Bawer, Robert Spencer, Bat Ye'or, Mark Steyn, Ayaan Hirsi Ali and, above all, the Norwegian blogger Fjordman — show how standardised right-wing thought has become. It also points to a disconcerting conclusion: these events could have happened anywhere in Europe.

Breivik's concerns about "Islamisation" are typical of those expressed by European tabloids and politicians. He has familiar worries about Muslims establishing no-go areas in cities, sharia courts, swimming pools with Muslim- only sessions, the contradiction between Islam and freedom of speech, the all- Muslim duty to perform jihad and the anti-Semitic inclinations of Muslim communities. And he wants to draw a line. "The veil should be banned in all public institutions, thus also contributing to breaking the traditional subjugation of women," he writes in 2083. "Companies and public buildings should not be forced to build prayer rooms for Muslims. Enact laws to eliminate the abuse of family reunification laws."

What strikes the reader of Breivik's work is its terrible normality. At least the first 6o pages, up to the initial musings on military tactics, could be found in your average European book-shop, or in articles written by well-regarded politicians and intellectuals. Despite this, the denial of the Nordic media has not ceased. Norwegian and Swedish readers are now being told that Breivik has merely copied the "Unabomber" (the loner Ted Kaczynski, who sent a series of mail bombs in the US between 1978 and 1995). Does anyone in the Nordic countries even remember the Unabomber? How far are we willing to go to avoid looking in the mirror?

While much of what Breivik has to say is the staple of mainstream right-of- centre discourse, some of it is distinctly fascist. But this is a coherent and successful brand of fascism whose core tenet is the belief in "Eurabia". The thesis of Eurabia is that Muslim countries, using the oil embargo of the early 1970s to blackmail the European Community, forced our treacherous politicians to hand over power. Ever since, it claims, we have been ruled by a secret Muslim conspiracy intent on transforming Europe into a colony— Eurabia —where we, the native Europeans, are subjugated. The Egyptian-born British writer Bat Ye'or is the author of the Eurabia doctrine, but the far-right Sweden Democrats and the Danish People's Party echo her ideas.

Neither the denial of global warming nor the virulent anti-feminism is an invention of Breivik's. And his hatred of Marxism, real and imaginary — the strand of thought that eventually led him to Utøya — places him in an almost century-long tradition.

Yet didn't Breivik leave all other Islamophobes far behind him when he contemplated murder? We hear, even from experts on the Nordic extreme right, that violence and terrorism are inherent to neo-Nazi groups, but alien to well- dressed Islamophobic populists. Once more, the disclaimers are almost as revelatory as the 22 July atrocity. In recognising the non-violent, parliamentary, well-mannered nature of modern European Islamophobia, we have — even if disagreeing with it— failed to trace its roots and keep track of its development.

The world of Islamophobic ideas is permeated with military imagery and language. Muslims are conquerors, colonisers, occupiers. Mosques and minarets are their victory monuments. The history of Islam is a long series of onslaughts on Christian civilisation, which defended itself at

Poitiers in the 8th century and Vienna in the 16th and now has to rise to the occasion again; we are the descendants of Charlemagne. Our nations are being betrayed, a war is being fought against us — and the time has come to fight back. From the Danish commentator Lars Hedegaard to the Italian Lega Nord, from the Swedish politician Jimmie Akesson to the German politician Thilo Sarrazin, this is the mantra. Breivik's originality is merely in acting it out.

Serbian brothers

At the end of 2083, Breivik answers a series of questions he imagines a reporter would want to ask him. "What tipped the scales for you? What single event made you decide you wanted to continue planning and moving on with the assault?" Answer: "For me, personally, it was my government's involvement in the attacks on Serbia [Nato bombings in 1999] several years back. It was completely unacceptable how the US and western European regimes bombed our Serbian brothers. All they wanted was to drive Islam out by deporting the Albanian Muslims back to Albania."

Breivik's obsession with the Serbs' struggle against Muslim intruders, his praise for the Serbian politician Radovan Karadzic as an "honourable crusader" and a "war hero", his vision of Arkan's paramilitary brigade as a model for his "resistance" are all symptomatic. The ideas of today's Islamophobic right were put into practice in the Balkans in the 1990s, in the most recent genocide on European soil. There is a straight line running from Srebrenica to Utøya. The military leader Ratko Mladic burned with the same fire as Anders Behring Breivik. The only difference is that Breivik targeted the "traitors" rather than the "conquerors".

Andreas Malm is a journalist and the author of books in Swedish on European Islamophobia
New Statesman, 1 August 2011

Cartoonist shrugs at Islamic death threat: 'It's good to know how much one is worth'

▶ **Swedish companies in Middle East lie low**

▶ **22 ambassadors called in by Prime Minister**

David Charter Europe Correspondent

Swedish companies lowered their profile in the Middle East yesterday amid fears that a newspaper cartoon depicting the Prophet Muhammad with the body of a dog could spark bloody reprisals.

Ericsson, the telecoms giant, removed the Swedish flag from offices in several countries including Iraq after a statement purporting to be from al-Qaeda put a $100,000 (£50,000) bounty on the head of the cartoonist, Lars Vilks.

The statement, in the name of Abu Omar al-Baghdadi, head of al-Qaeda in Iraq, offered a 50 per cent bonus if Mr Vilks was "slaughtered like a lamb" by having his throat cut. It also placed $50,000 on the life of Ulf Johansson, editor-in-chief of *Nerikes Allehanda*, the local newspaper that printed the cartoon last month.

Muslim leaders in Sweden condemned the threats and Fredrik Reinfeldt, the Prime Minister, has sought to calm tensions over the cartoon at a meeting with ambassadors from 22 Islamic countries. The row recalls the controversy over 12 cartoons lampooning Islam published in a Danish newspaper in 2005 that provoked violent demonstrations, including attacks on Danish embassies.

Islam forbids as idolatry any depiction of Muhammad, and Sweden, which has about 350,000 Muslims among a population of 9.1 million, has been consumed by a fierce debate over freedom of expression after the publication in the newspaper based in the western town of Örebro.

Mr Vilks, who lives in an isolated area of Sweden, has been given police protection. He said: "I suppose you could say I was an easy target. But I am not paranoid. I think I possess a healthy rationality; I know that there are some risks involved but one should not exaggerate them either."

But he added: "We must not give in. I'm starting to grow old. I could die at any time — it's not a catastrophe."

The internet threat stated: "We know how to force you to apologise. If you do not, expect us to strike the businesses of firms like Ericsson, Scania, Volvo, Ikea and Electrolux."

Åse Lindskog, a spokeswoman for Ericsson, said that staff had been told to keep a low profile in Muslim countries and to take extra care in deciding where to go or park their cars.

Helena Benouda, head of the Muslim Council of Sweden, denounced the threats. "We do not think like this. It is criminal to call to kill somebody. It is really unnecessary and it is ugly, especially in the month of Ramadan."

Egypt, Iran and Pakistan have lodged formal protests with the Swedish Government and religious leaders in Afghanistan and Jordan have condemned the cartoon.

Mr Reinfeldt yesterday used a TV interview to appeal for calm. "We shall deny all who call for the use of violence and keep at bay the extremists' attempts to worsen the issue," he said.

He said that the Government had been watching developments closely, including monitoring media reports in the Muslim world and talking to Muslim representatives in Sweden and abroad. The Swedish Foreign Ministry has also advised its nationals to exercise caution in the Middle East.

Mr Vilks arrived back in Sweden from Germany yesterday and made light of the assassination call. "I suppose that this makes my art project a bit more serious. It is also good to know how much one is worth," he said. Mr Johansson said that he had already received a number of threats via e-mail and telephone. He added: "I have received various types of threats but none have been so explicit. This is a direct death sentence."

The Swedish Ambassador to Saudi Arabia, Jan Thesleff, met Ekmeleddin Ihsanoglu, head of the Organisation for the Islamic Conference (OIC), last week in Jeddah and offered his "deepest apologies for the controversy created by the publishing of the hurtful depiction", according to a statement from the 57-nation group.

The Swedish Foreign Ministry, however, immediately denied that the Ambassador had made any apology, saying that he had only expressed regret. A spokeswoman said: "The Ambassador repeated his regret at the controversy created by the publication, but not for the publication itself."

A leading Swedish daily newspaper, *Dagens Nyheter*, yesterday republished the cartoon in an act of solidarity with the local paper that first printed it.

Thorbjörn Larsson, the editor, said in an opinion piece: "We live in a country where freedom of expression is not dictated by fundamentalists, nor by governments. To me, publishing it was the obvious thing to do."

The daily newspaper *Svenska Dagbladet* urged Swedes to defend their right to free speech in the face of religious fanaticism. It said: "Freedom of expression is not a privilege for the media companies and journalists but a guarantee that citizens can have different impressions, numerous sources of information and inspiration, as well as the possibility of drawing their own conclusions."

Lars Vilks said he was getting old, so death would not be a "catastrophe"

"I suppose that this makes my art project a bit more serious
Lars Vilks

Repeat performance?

- The decision by *Jyllands-Posten*, a Danish newspaper, to publish 12 cartoons of the Prophet Muhammad in September 2005 caused international Muslim anger on a level not seen since the release of Salman Rushdie's book *The Satanic Verses*. The publication was prompted by writer Kåre Bluitgen, who claimed that artists were too scared of Islamic reprisals to provide illustrations for his book about the life of Muhammad.
- The printed cartoons included one depicting Muhammad greeting suicide bombers in heaven, saying: "Stop. Stop. We have run out of virgins!" — some Muslims believe that male suicide bombers are rewarded with 72 virgins. Another cartoon, however, depicted a Danish boy called Muhammad writing in Arabic on a blackboard the words: "*Jyllands-Posten*'s journalists are a bunch of reactionary provocateurs."
- At least two Muslim countries recalled their ambassadors to Denmark. The resulting protests lasted six months and led to the deaths of dozens of people.
- *Jyllands-Posten* apologised in January last year, but to show solidarity with the newspaper a Norwegian paper, a Canadian magazine and two French publications reprinted the cartoons.

Source: Times archives, Agencies

The Times, September 17th 2007

Vergeløs mot 13 års forfølgelse

OSLO: I mer enn 13 år har bergenseren Heidi Schøne (31) blitt drapstruet og trakassert fordi hun ikke ville bli hustru til en muslimsk mann som er bosatt i England. Familie, venner og kolleger får stadig skriftlige «rapporter» om Heidis liv. Den muslimske juristen har også benyttet privatdetektiv for å oppspore Heidi Schøne.

FORFULGT I 13 ÅR. Heidi Schøne fra Bergen har blitt trakassert, forfulgt, drapstruet og ærekrenket av en muslim i England i 13 år. Muslimen er besatt av tanken på å gifte seg med henne. Bergenskvinnen og mannen Runar regner med at de må leve med terroren i lang tid ennå.

De færreste kan forestille seg hvilke belastninger Heidi Schøne og hennes nærmeste har gjennomlevd siden tidlig på 80-tallet.

For noen uker siden fant en av Bergens Tidendes frilans-fotografer et brev i postkassen, sendt fra Watford i England. På konvolutten stod der ikke navn, bare adresse. Innholdet, under tittelen «Rapport om Heidi Schøne», var rått og dypt ærekrenkende. Bergens Tidende kontaktet Schøne som i dag bor sammen med sin ektemann utenfor Drammen, og fortalte henne om brevet.

— Hvordan skal dette ende, hvor mange skal få disse brevene? kom det sårt fra Heidi første gang avisen kontaktet henne.

Pose med brev

Bergens Tidende møtte i går Heidi Schøne og ektemannen Runar i Oslo. Under armen bar hun en pose med brev fra den muslimske mannen, alle like grovt ærekrenkende. De siste 13 årene har vært en enorm påkjenning. Hemmelige adresser har ikke hjulpet.

Det hele startet for 14 år siden, da Heidi Schøne var au pair England. På en båttur fra Frankrike til England møtte hun og en venninne muslimen.

— Han var grei og understreket sin muslimske tro, og skulle han gifte seg måtte det være med en muslimsk jente. Jeg følte meg på trygg grunn. I England møtte vi ham flere ganger som gode venner. Etter ni måneder flyttet jeg hjem igjen til Bergen, sier hun.

«Stygg og dum»

Da forandret den gode vennen lynne. Muslimens ønske var at Heidi skulle bli hans livsledsager.

– Han oppsøkte meg flere ganger i Bergen uten å være invitert. Han ønsket å gifte seg med meg, og sa at jeg var stygg og dum og at han var den eneste som ville elske meg når jeg ble 50 år gammel. Det ble gnisninger mellom oss. Siden har han kommet med drapstrusler og trakassert meg. Han har også truet med å drepe familien min, sier Heidi. I 1990 ble den 35 år gamle muslimen arrestert i Bergen. Men politiet kom ingen vei. Terroren fortsatte.

Muslimen snakker ikke norsk, men den siste «rapporten» er skrevet på norsk og sendt fra Watford der han bor. I 1990 fant politiet materiale som viste at muslimen hadde samarbeidet med en nordmann for å etterforske Heidi Schøne og finne hennes hemmelige adresser som det ble en del av etter hvert.

Hun tapte hver gang.

Sendes til naboer

Nå har hun gitt opp hemmelige adresser. Hennes nye naboer er gjennom «rapporter» fra muslimen gjort kjent med hele livet hennes, slik muslimen beskriver det.

– Hvordan skal man kunne forklare dette fornuftig. Ikke har vi flørtet eller vært kjærester. Han lever seg jo helt inn i dette, kommer det oppgitt fra bergenskvinnen.

I seks år har hun bodd utenfor Drammen. For halvannet år siden giftet hun seg med Runar Schøne. Da trappet muslimen opp virksomheten. Det er ikke få «rapporter» som er sendt Bergen og Drammen i løpet av disse årene.

Hennes mann har også fått brev, sendt personlig til ham.

– Denne muslimske mannen sendte som avtalt «rapporter» om Heidi som jeg skulle ha bestilt. Det var bare tull. Han gjorde alt han kunne for å sverte Heidi, sier Runar Schøne. Han er forståelig nok forbannet på den muslimske mannen.

– Ikke redd

Redselen for muslimen har avtatt med årene. Nå er ikke Heidi redd lenger. Redselen er redselen byttet ut med sinne og fortvilelse. Og det er belastende at familie, venner kolleger og ukjente naboer får «rapporter».

– Men inntil for noen år siden var jeg vettskremt, kunne noen ganger ha gjemt meg under sengen, svarer Heidi.

– Han har ingen grenser. Når han har ringt på dører og ingen åpnet, har han svart med å risse inn ord i dørene, legger hun til. Ordene Heidi gjengir egner seg ikke på trykk. Hun vet at det vil gå lang tid før terroren stanser.

«Erotisk paranoia»

Personer som opptrer slik muslimen gjør mot Heidi Schøne er ikke noe nytt fenomen. I følge psykiater Kjell Noreik, som er medlem av Rettsmedisinsk kommisjon er dette personer som ikke har tålt motgangen ved å bli avvist. Diagnosen erotisk paranoia har psykiater Nils Retterstøl skrevet mye om og denne muslimen går inn i dette mønsteret. Kjell Noreik setter ingen diagnose på muslimen men sier at erotisk paranoia er erotiske vrangforestillinger. Han sier at slike personer bygger opp forestillinger om et annet individ som de bli avvist av.

— Dette er et problem, men ikke så forferdelig stort. Det er imidlertid uhyre plagsomt for de som utsettes for dette. Det kan pågå i årevis og det stanser ikke ved tilsnakk. Enkelte går også til voldeligheter.

Sammen med mannen har hun engasjert advokat Tom Skau i Oslo, ved siden av å ha anmeldt muslimen.

– Heidi Schøne har vært utsatt for årelang terror av en sinnssyk person som hun tidligere i livet har vært venn med, og ikke noe annet. Hun opplever dette meget vanskelig. Jeg har sett brevene og vil følge opp anmeldelsen. Men det er problematisk så lenge han er i England og ikke i Norge, sier advokat Tom Skau til Bergens Tidende.

TEKST: HAAKON B. SCHRØDER
FOTO: HÅVARD BJELLAND

Bergens Tidende - 24th May 1995

Bergens Tidende newspaper take registered mental patient Heidi Schøne's word for it on the alleged sex-terrror. They print the epithet 'Muslim' 19 times in their story to describe the London Solicitor's background; he who fell out with his former girlfriend, Heidi Schøne ... who admitted to having had 21 sexual partners by age 21, as well as two abortions to the same Norwegian man whilst still at school, two suicide attempts over another Norwegian lover and had accused three men of attempting to, or actually, raping her. The drama carried on until 2011, when Anders Breivik came to world prominence. See below, with English translations.

Bergens Tidende 24th May 1995

English Translation

13 Years of Harassment

A Bergen lady, Heidi Schøne (pictured) has been harassed and threatened with her life over a period of thirteen years by a man who she accidentally met when she was an au pair in England. Her secret addresses haven't helped against the English lawyer, whose attitude is similar to one suffering from erotic paranoia.

On page 2 the headline is Defenceless against 13 years of pursuit.

OSLO:-

For more than thirteen years the Bergen lady Heidi Schøne (31) has been threatened with her life and harassed because she didn't want to be the wife of a Muslim man who lives in England. Family, friends and colleagues often received written reports about Heidi's life. The Muslim lawyer has also used a private detective to trace her. People will find it hard to imagine the pressure Heidi and her immediate family have been under since the early 1980s.

A few weeks ago, a Bergen freelance photographer received a letter from Watford in England, although the letter did not have any sender's name and address. The title of the letter was 'Report on Heidi Schøne' which was defamatory and humiliating. The freelance photographer contacted Bergens Tidende who in turn contacted Heidi Schøne and her husband who lived outside Drammen and they told her about the letter.

Heidi answered the phone crying "Where shall this end? How many people will have got this letter?"

Bag with letters

Yesterday, Bergens Tidende met Heidi Schøne and her husband Runar in Oslo. Under her arm she carried a bag with letters from the Muslim man; all the letters were very rude and insulting. The last 13 years have been very traumatic. Secret addresses haven't helped. All of this started 14 years ago when Heidi Schøne was an au pair in England. On a boat trip from France to England with a girlfriend, she met a friendly Muslim man. He was very nice and he told her about his Muslim beliefs and that if he got married the girl must be Muslim as well. "I felt quite safe", she said. "In England we met him several times just as good friends. After nine months I moved back to Bergen".

Ugly and Stupid

Then he changed. The Muslim man wanted Heidi to be his wife. "He visited me several times in Bergen without being invited. He said he wished he could marry me; and said I was ugly and stupid and that he would be the only one who would love me when I was 50 years old. Arguments between us followed. Since then he has made threats on my life and has harassed me. He has also threatened to kill my family", said Heidi. In 1990 the 35 year old Muslim man was arrested in Bergen but the police didn't take the matter any further. The harassments carried on. The Muslim man didn't speak Norwegian but the aforementioned report is written in Norwegian and sent from Watford where he is living. In 1990 the police found material which indicated that the Muslim man had liaised with a Norwegian man with the purpose of following Heidi Schøne and finding her secret address, one of several secret addresses which followed for Heidi and she lost out every time.

Sent to the neighbours

Now she has given up with secret addresses. Her new neighbours have got the reports explaining to them what her old life was like as the Muslim man saw it. "How can one make sense of it? We haven't been lovers or had feelings for each other. He fantasises about it", the Bergen woman said painfully.

For six years she has lived outside Drammen. Six months ago she got married to Runar Schøne. Then the Muslim chap worked even harder on the matter. Numerous 'reports' were sent to Bergen and Drammen recently.

Her husband also got a letter sent personally to him-

"The Muslim man sent the report about Heidi to me as if I had requested it myself. The report was totally false. He did all he could to blacken Heidi's name", said Runar Schøne. He is sick and tired of the Muslim man.

Not afraid

The fear of the Muslim man has receded as the years have gone by. Heidi is not afraid anymore. The fear has changed to frustration and anger. Family, friends, colleagues and neighbours feel overwhelmed by these reports.

"Just a few years ago, I was very frightened and kept hiding under the bed", said Heidi.

"He has no limits. When he knocks on the door and finds no-one in, he writes obscene words on the door", she adds. The words Heidi refers to are unprintable. She knows that it will take a long time before the terror will stop. With her husband she has hired a lawyer called Tomm Skaug in Oslo and she has also reported the Muslim man to the police.

Heidi Schøne has been terrorised for several years by an insane man who she had earlier been friendly with but with whom there was no serious relationship. This situation is very difficult for her.

"I have seen the letters and I will follow the case. But it will be difficult so long as he is living in England and not in Norway", said the lawyer Tomm Skaug to Bergens Tidende.

EROTIC PARANOIA

A person who acts like this Muslim man against Heidi Schøne is not a new phenomenon in the view of the psychiatrist Kjell Noreik, a member of the medico legal group of psychiatrists. These people don't like to take no for an answer. The diagnosis is called erotic paranoia. One psychiatrist, Nils Rettersdøl has been writing much about Muslim behavioural patterns. Kjell Noreik doesn't place this diagnosis on the Muslim man but says that erotic paranoia is erotic delusions. He says that a person with this condition builds up a fantasy in relation to the other individual even though the former is rejected. Now this is a problem but not too serious a one. But it is very painful for the victims of this behaviour. This behaviour can carry on for years and doesn't stop even if the perpetrator is admonished. Some will also become violent.

Story: Haakon B. Schrøder

Photo: Havard Bjelland

10 Fredag 26. mai 1995 VG

FORFULGT

TERRORISERT: *Heidi Schøne (31) har levd i 13 år med terroren fra den halvt arabiske engelskmannen hun traff under en tur til Paris. – Han oppsøkte meg uansett hvor jeg flyttet. Han sa at jeg og familien min skulle drepes.*

En gang gjorde han obskøne ting mens jeg måtte se på. Det rare var at jeg etter hvert begynte å tro på ham

Heidi Schøne (31)

– Grovt trakasserende

BERGEN (VG) Personlig ville jeg ha reagert til dels sterkt på å bli utsatt for noe slikt, sier lensmannsbetjent Gunnar Fossum ved Nedre Eiker lensmannskontor.

Han har mottatt anmeldelsen fra familien Schøne, og har gjort de første forberedelser til etterforskning: Televerket har koblet inn telefon-terror-søker på familien Schønes telefonnummer.

Intimiteter

Blant dokumentene Fossum sitter på, er et omfattende skriv med angivelig faktiske intime personlige opplysninger om Heidi Schøne. Disse har han oversatt til godt norsk før han sendte dem til Heidis ektemann, og til naboer og familie og venner.

– Det var da dette skjedde i vinter at vi bestemte oss for å gå til advokat og politiet, sier ektemannen Runar Schøne.

– Jeg har sett hvor forferdelig nerves Heidi blir når dette nå kommer opp igjen. Han må ha fått et mentalt grep på henne. Det er utrolig at hun klarer seg så bra etter så mange år med terror, sier Runar.

– Selv har jeg mottatt en telefon fra engelskmannen. Han bare skrek på engelsk, trolig banneord.

VG Fredag 26. mai 1995

I 13 ÅR

Av HARALD VIKØYR og JANNE MØLLER HANSEN (foto)

BERGEN/DRAMMEN (VG) Som 18-åring ga hun adressen sin til en litt rar, påtrengende engelskmann. Slik startet 13 års skrekktilværelse og sex-terror for Heidi Schøne (31).

Heidi (31) terrorisert med slibrige telefoner og brev

Da den halvt arabiske, muslimske mannen senere ble avvist av henne, startet han telefonterror, drapstrusler, brevterror, fysisk oppmøte på døren hennes og trakassering av hennes venner – i år etter år.

Psykiatere mener at engelskmannens oppførsel kan minne om lidelsen erotisk paranoia: Den syke er hellig overbevist om at en annen person er vilt forelsket i seg.

– Det nyttet ikke at jeg flyttet til hemmelig adresse og fikk hemmelig telefon. Plutselig kom det et kort i posten med teksten «Freddy is back» – hentet fra skrekkfilmen med en hovedperson med navn Freddy. Han hadde funnet meg – igjen! Jeg og familien min ble truet på livet, og han kom på døren min mange ganger. På en dør skrev han inn «fuck you» med kniv.

> *Det nyttet ikke at jeg flyttet til hemmelig adresse og fikk hemmelig telefon.*

Heidi Schøne er født og oppvokst i Bergen, og oppholdt seg en tid i England som au pair i en familie. Hun og en venninne dro en tur til Paris.

– Likte ham

– På båten ble jeg oppmerksom på en person som fulgte meg på avstand. Da vi kom på toget, satte han seg i den gjengen ungdommer hvor jeg satt. Han var muslim, fem-seks år eldre enn oss, og tilkjennega sterke meninger om blant annet kjærlighet. Vi syntes nok han var rar, men helt ufarlig.

– Jeg likte ham. Vi tok en kopp te med ham, og senere hadde vi en viss kontakt, men bare rent vennskapelig, han skulle gifte seg muslimsk, sa han.

Helvete

Men en tid etter at Heidi hadde vendt hjem, begynte helvetet. Hun hadde da en kjæreste i Bergen, men ble likevel oppsøkt av engelskmannen:

> *Jeg slapp ham inn i starten. Han var manipulerende.*

– Jeg slapp ham inn i starten. Han var veldig manipulerende. Han hadde bombardert meg med telefoner og brev som fortalte hvor dum jeg var, at jeg ville bli stygg og at ingen andre enn han ville ha meg. En gang gjorde han obskøne ting mens jeg måtte se på. Det rare var at jeg etter hvert begynte å tro på ham.

Skamfull

– Det var så uvirkelig, og jeg følte meg skamfull. Jeg ble mer og mer redd, og isolerte meg. I lange perioder gikk jeg ikke ut. Jeg la meg under sengen hvis det ringte på døren. Klarte ikke å åpne.

> *De jeg snakket med, sa det ville sikkert gå over. Det var vel bare en litt ivrig beiler, liksom.*

Hun involverte svært få i saken, og mente i det lengste at det ville gå over:

– De jeg snakket med, sa det ville sikkert gå over. Det var vel bare en litt ivrig beiler, liksom. Ingen ville ta det alvorlig.

Privatdetektiv

Men engelskmannen hadde åpenbart engasjert privatdetektiv, og klarte å oppspore henne gang etter gang. Han klarte også på underlig vis å få tak i sensitiv informasjon om personer som sto Heidi nær. Dette sendte han til henne, og hun kan legge det frem før politiet.

Men årene gikk, og da Heidi skulle gifte seg med sin mann, Runar Schøne, kom det et ubehagelig obskønt postkort fra engelskmannen – som indikerte at han kjente henne seksuelt.

– Når jeg tenker på det i dag, hvordan jeg ble manipulert, så blir jeg bare så sint. Jeg forsto jo etter hvert at han måtte være syk, og jeg fikk tilbake min egen verdighet. Jeg har tigget, grått og truet ham til å la meg være i fred, men det har ikke hjulpet, sier Heidi.

Kastet

For tre år siden kastet hun alt materiale hun hadde fått fra engelskmannen. Hun ville brenne ham ut av livet sitt. Men forgjeves.

– Det siste halvåret har jeg samlet 30–40 forsendelser med brev, kort og hele bøker. Bøker om AIDS – eller abort. Som om jeg har AIDS? Jeg har også sørget for å ta ham opp på lydbånd.

> *Når jeg tenker på det i dag, hvordan jeg ble manipulert, så blir jeg bare så sint.*

Og på dette lydbåndet har hun fått ham til å gjøre innrømmelser. Dette og de siste brevforsendelsene vil hun overlate sin advokat, Tomm Skaug, som vil forsøke å stanse engelskmannen ad rettslig vei.

– Ekstremt

BERGEN (VG) Psykiatere mener at den truende og elskovssyke engelskmannen som har plaget Heidi Schøne i 13 år, kan lide av erotisk paranoia.

– Jeg kjenner ikke dette tilfellet, og tror nok at hvis dette kan kalles erotisk paranoia, er det et ekstremt tilfelle, sier professor i psykiatri, Nils Retterstøl.

Vrangforestilling

Erotisk paranoia er en lidelse som består i en vrangforestilling – den syke tror at en annen person er forelsket i seg.

– Å ønske eller forestille seg at noen er forelsket i seg, er i sannhet et normalt fenomen, men den syke er hellig overbevist om det forholder seg slik, og lar seg ikke snakke fra det.

I tysk psykiatri kalles lidelsen erotisk selvhenføring, andre kaller den «Old maid psychosis» – gamle kvinners psykose.

Oftest kvinner

– Den rammer oftest kvinner, og oftest kvinner i overgangsalderen. Blant de kjente tilfellene er kvinner som får et slikt forhold til en mannsperson som har rang og er eksponert – for eksempel sognepresten. Den som er utsatt for dette, har ikke peiling. Den syke kan planlegge bryllup, og lar seg altså ikke snakke til rette.

EKSPERT: *Erotisk paranoia lar seg vanskelig helbrede. Det går bare over etter noen år, sier professor i psykiatri, Nils Retterstøl.*

Likevel er personer med erotisk paranoia sjelden direkte slemme.

– Det kan selvsagt være ubehagelig og sterkt uønsket at en kvinne reiser seg i forsamlingen og forkynner sitt innbilte forhold til presten – eller andre øvrighetspersoner. Men direkte uvennlighet som i dette tilfelle er ikke vanlig. Det tilfellet som er beskrevet her, må være i en ekstrem form, i så fall.

– Det er vanskelig å helbrede erotisk paranoia, som oftest går det over av seg selv etter noen år. Men sjelden har den syke i ettertid innsikt og forstått at det var galt og innbilt, sier Retterstøl.

VG - 26th May 1995

Verdens Gang 26th May 1995

English Translation

THIRTEEN YEARS OF SEX TERROR

For thirteen years, Heidi Schøne, from Drammen has been sexually harassed and terrorised by a man she met on a holiday when she was eighteen years old.

The man started off with telephone and letter harassment. When he was rejected, he continued with terrorising her friends, showing up in person at her door, and death threats.

"I have begged, cried and threatened to make him leave me alone, but it has not helped", says the frustrated Heidi.

As an eighteen year old she gave her address to a slightly peculiar, obtrusive Englishman. In this way began thirteen years of fear and sex terror for Heidi.

When the half Arab, Muslim man was rejected by her later on, he started with obscene phone calls, death threats, threatening letters, showing up in person at her door and harassing her friends for years and years.

Psychiatrists think that the behaviour of the Englishman possesses all the symptoms of erotic paranoia: the sick person is convinced that another person is in love with him or her.

Moving to a secret address and getting a secret telephone number didn't help. Suddenly a postcard dropped into the letterbox saying "Freddie's back" - taken from the horror film with the main character with the name Freddie Kruger. "He found me again! Me and my family were threatened with our lives and he came to my door many times. At one door he wrote 'Fuck you' with a knife".

"It didn't help moving to a secret address and getting a secret telephone number".

Heidi Schøne was born and raised in Bergen, and stayed for a while in England as an au pair with a family. She and her friend had a trip to Paris.

LIKED HIM

On the ferry she became aware of a person watching her from a distance. "When we came to the train, he sat down with the same group of young people that I was with. He was a Muslim, five to six years older than us and proved to have strong opinions about life, among other things. We thought that he was somehow a bit peculiar, but completely harmless".

"I liked him. We had a cup of tea together with him and later on we had some contact, but purely as friends. He would marry a Muslim girl, he said".

HELL

But sometime after Heidi had returned to Bergen, the harassment started. At the time she had a boyfriend in Bergen, but she still was followed by the Englishman.

"I let him in the beginning. He was very manipulating. He had bombarded me with telephone calls and letters telling me that I was stupid, and that nobody but him wanted me. At one point he did obscene things while I had to watch. The funny thing was that I started to believe him bit by bit."

ASHAMED

"It was all so unreal and I felt ashamed. I was more and more frightened, and isolated myself. For long periods of time I didn't go out. I lay down under the bed when the doorbell rang. I just couldn't open the door.".

"Those I spoke to said that it would probably stop. He was probably just a bit too eager, a persistent sort of guy".

She involved just a few people in the case and thought for a very long time that it would stop; "The ones I spoke to, said that it would probably stop. He was probably just a bit too eager. Nobody took it seriously".

PRIVATE DETECTIVE

But the Englishman had hired a private detective, and managed to trace her time after time. In strange ways he also managed to collect sensitive information about persons close to Heidi. He sent this to her, and she was able to show it to the police.

But the years went by, and when Heidi was about to marry her boyfriend, Runar Schøne, an unpleasant and obscene letter was sent to her from the Englishman indicating that he knew her sexually. "When I think about it now, about how I was manipulated, I just get so angry. I didn't understand it but after a while when I realised he had to be sick I gained my self-respect back. I have begged, cried and threatened him to leave me alone, but it has not helped", says Heidi.

THREW AWAY

Three years ago she threw away all the material she had received from the Englishman. She wanted to burn him out of her life, but in vain.

"The last half year I have received 30 to 40 consignments of letters, postcards and books. Books about AIDS or abortion. As if I have AIDS? I have also received him on tape".

"When I think about it today, how I was manipulated, I just get so angry".

And on this tape she has made him admit things. This and the latest consignment of letters she will hand over to her lawyer, Tomm Skaug, who will try to stop the Englishman.

EXTREME

Psychiatrists think that the threatening and lovesick Englishman who has bugged Heidi Schøne for 13 years might suffer from erotic paranoia.

"I don't know this particular case, and do believe that if this can be called erotic paranoia, this is an extreme case", says the Professor in Psychiatry Nils Rettersdøl.

MISCONCEPTION

Erotic paranoia is a disease of the mind in which a person has a misconception that another person is in love with him or her. "To wish or imagine that someone is in love with you is truly a normal phenomena, but the sick person is totally convinced that this is how it actually is, and won't be talked out of it".

In German psychiatry the suffering is called erotic self-seduction, other people call it "old maids psychosis".

MOST OFTEN WOMEN

It most often strikes woman and mostly women in their menopause. Among the known cases of this is a woman who has this relationship towards a male person who has authority and is exposed, for example the local priest. The person who is suffering from this, has no idea of it. The sick person can plan a wedding and won't be talked out of it.

EXPERT:

Erotic paranoia is hard to heal. "It just stops after a couple of years", says Professor in psychiatry, Nils Rettersdøl.

"However, persons with erotic paranoia are seldom directly mean - it can of course be unpleasant and absolutely unwanted that a woman rises up in the congregation and proclaims her imagined relationship with the priest, or another official authority.

But direct unfriendliness like in this case is not normal. The very case described here must be in some extreme form, in that case. It is hard to heal erotic paranoia; most often it just stops after some years by itself. But seldom have the sick the insight and the understanding that it is wrong and imagined", says Rettersdøl.

Just below a full page photograph of Heidi and her husband, sombrely looking at my letters to her with the Aids and Abortion Christian booklets on the kitchen table before them, ran the caption:

TERRORIZED:

Heidi Schøne (31) has for 13 years lived under terror of the half-Arab Englishman she met on a trip to Paris - "He sought me out regardless of where I moved to. He said that I and my family would be killed".

"On one occasion, he did obscene things which I had to watch. The strange thing was that I gradually began to believe him" Heidi Schøne (31).

Below this photo, another sub-story:-

SEVERE HARASSMENT

BERGEN (VG) "Personally, I would have reacted rather strongly to being subjected to this sort of thing", says police constable Gunnar Fossum of Nedre Eiker police office.

He received the report from the Schøne family and made the preliminary preparations for investigation. The Telecommunications Administration ('Televerket') connected up the nuisance callers search system to the Schøne family's telephone number.

INTIMATE REFERENCES

Among the documents held by Fossum is a lot of written material containing apparently factual intimate personal particulars concerning Heidi Schøne. He translated these into good Norwegian before he sent them to Heidi's husband and to neighbours, family and friends.

"It was when this happened last winter that we decided to go to a lawyer and to the police", husband Runar Schøne says.

"I have seen how terribly nervous Heidi becomes, now that this is happening again. He must have got a hold of her mentally. It is unbelievable how well she manages after so many years of being terrorized", Runar says.

"I myself have had a telephone call from the Englishman. He just screamed in English what were probably swear words".

Terrorisert i 13 år

I 13 år er Heidi Schøne (31) fra Nedre Eiker blitt terrorisert og forfulgt av en sinnslidende mann som har truet med å drepe både henne og familien hennes.

Ingunn Røren
Nils J. Maudal (foto)

Etter 13 års helvete går Heidi ut med sin historie for å sette søkelys på et problem hun vet at langt flere enn henne sliter med. Hun blir forfulgt av en sinnslidende mann som er besatt av henne, og føler seg makteslos. Hun har flere ganger anmeldt mannen til politiet, men det er lite de kan gjøre så lenge han ikke angriper noen fysisk.

Ga adressen

Marerittet begynte da Heidi var 18 år gammel og ga adressen sin til en halvt tysk, halvt arabisk mann bosatt i England som hun møtte mens hun var au pair. Det ble starten på årelang sjikane for Heidi og hennes familie. I 13 år har mannen drevet telefonterror hjemme hos Heidi, og sendt henne over 400 brev - alle med perverst innhold. Hun har også fått tilsendt bøker om AIDS og aborter, samt kassetter om seg selv.

–Det verste er imidlertid alle «rapportene» han har sendt om meg til naboer, familie, venner og kollegaer, der han kommer med en rekke grove, ærekrenkende og falske opplysninger om meg, sier Heidi.

Hun har flyttet fem ganger på disse årene, og hatt flere hemmelige adresser. Hver gang har engelskmannen, som jobber som jurist, klart å oppspore Heidi, blant annet ved å true hennes tidligere naboer på livet til de oppgir hvor hun befinner seg.

–Det er en enorm påkjenning når du får vite at også dine nye naboer har fått disse «rapportene» før du selv har rukket å bli kjent med dem, sier Heidi.

I 13 år har Heidi Schøne (31) fra Nedre Eiker blitt trakassert av en sinnslidende mann som har sendt henne over 400 perverse brev og sendt krenkende «rapporter» om Heidi til familie, venner og naboer.

Drar til Norge

Heidi og mannen Runar har siden januar bodd i et nybygd hus på Solbergmoen. Også der har alle naboene fått tilsendt krenkende «rapporter» der det påstås at Heidi lever et svært utsvevende liv og er et moralsk ødelagt menneske.

–Selv om mannen er bosatt i England har han fløyet til Norge en åtte - ni ganger på disse årene og kommet på døren min. Den første gangen slapp jeg ham inn fordi jeg trodde han kom som en venn, men allerede neste gang han dukket opp var jeg blitt redd ham fordi han forhørte seg om hvor jeg var hvis han ringte og jeg ikke var hjemme, sier Heidi.

De neste gangene han dukket opp hjemme hos henne har Heidi smelt døren i ansiktet på ham, men da har han gått løs på døren hennes med kniv og risset inn obskøne meldinger. Han har også gått løs på naboenes dører, og skrevet «I'm gonna get you» på vinduene.

–Jeg veksler mellom å være livredd for mannen og fly forbannet på ham. Jeg har grått, tigget og rast når han har ringt meg for å få ham til å slutte å plage meg, men det nytter ikke. Når han setter i gang med telefonterroren sin ringer han med rundt en times mellomrom hele døgnet rundt, sier Heidi.

Heidi angrer bittert på at hun ga mannen navnet sitt og adressen for 13 år siden.

–Jeg var ung og dum, og hadde et helt annet inntrykk av mannen enn det jeg har i dag. Jeg la merke til at han fulgte etter meg på ferjen mellom England og Frankrike, men tenkte ikke noe spesielt over det. Vi kom i kontakt, tok en kopp te og så hverandre en fire-fem ganger i løpet av de ti månedene jeg bodde i England. Noe forhold har vi aldri hatt, sier Heidi.

Det hun ikke kunne vite var at den hyggelige mannen skulle bli helt besatt av henne og bruke de neste årene til å følge Heidis minste bevegelse. En periode hadde han en privatetterforsker som fotfulgte henne. Heidi selv, hennes familie og hennes venner er alle blitt truet på livet av mannen, som også har truet med at Heidis ni år gamle sønn skulle utryddes. I 1988 fikk Heidi tilsendt begravelseskort på seg selv fra mannen, som truet med at «hennes dager var omme».

I 1990 tok mannen med seg en bekjent til Bergen der Heidi var på besøk for å ta henne. Heidi fikk varslet politiet, som pågrep mannen og holdt ham i varetekt i to dager.

–Politiet hadde for lite på ham, og måtte løslate ham. Det eneste de kunne gjøre var å følge ham på flyet, og terroren fortsatte, sier Heidi, som føler seg makteslos overfor mannens metoder. Etter at hun giftet seg med Runar for noen år siden ble det verre enn noensinne. Rett etter bryllupet fikk hun et brev der mannen skrev at han gjerne skulle vært til stede på bryllupsnatten. Bare de siste månedene har hun fått over 40 brev og utallige telefoner. Alle med den samme beskjeden: at Heidi lever et moralsk forkastelig liv, at engelskmannen hater henne og at han skal ta henne. Ordlyden i brevene egner seg ikke på trykk, men de er svært grove og perverse.

Når mannen ringer, hyler og skriker han i røret og slenger ut banneord. Heidi har båndopptak av en slik samtale, og har levert både mesteparten av brevene, rapportene og kassettene til sin advokat, som nå vurderer om de skal saksøke mannen for ærekrenkelser, personforfølgelse og redusert livskvalitet.

Det siste brevet kom for rundt en uke siden.

–Før gråt jeg når jeg fikk slike brev, nå lurer jeg bare på når det skal ta slutt, sier Heidi. Nylig fikk hun vite at mannen er anmeldt for lignende forhold i England, der han skal ha trakassert en yngre kvinne. For ikke lenge siden fikk han en dom på at han ikke kan nærme seg denne kvinnen, og Heidi håper å få noe lignende på ham her. Heidi vet at mannens mor har forsøkt å få ham tvangsinnlagt, men mannen er tydeligvis et av de vanskelige psykiatriske tilfellene som er for syke til å fengsles, men for friske til å legges inn til behandling.

–Rettsapparatet må da kunne beskytte vanlige mennesker mot sinnslidende personer, sier Heidi, som er sliten etter årelang trakassering.

Engelskmannen har i 13 år drevet telefonterror mot Heidi og hennes familie, og har sendt henne over 400 perverse brev, kassetter og bøker om AIDS. Her er et par av brevene bare fra de siste månedene.

Drammens Tidende 14/07/1998

English Translation

SEXUALLY HARASSED FOR 16 YEAR

For 16 years Heidi Schøne from Solbergelva has been pestered and followed by a mentally ill Englishman. In only the last year the man has sent more than 300 letters to Heidi and made numerous phone calls

The Muslim man has been obsessed by Heidi Schøne (34) since she was 18 years old. His long time pestering of Heidi and her family has been a huge strain. DT-BB first covered this case three years ago. Still, the family is being badgered by the same man.

Want to be left alone

"All we want is to be left alone. This man is very ill and his countless letters and phone calls put an enormous strain on us all" says Heidi's husband Runar Schøne. For years the Schønes have been living with a string of secret phone numbers and addresses, but each time the man manages to find them and the terror continues until they manage to hide themselves away again.

"Reports"

In the course of the 16 years this man has sent out many "reports" to Heidi's family, friends, neighbours, colleagues and a number of strangers. These reports are grossly defamatory and the information listed has no basis in reality. Once again, many people from Drammen have received "reports" about Heidi in their mail box. The reports are modelled like answers for questionnaires from Drammens Tidende, VG and Bergens Tidende, but none of the newspapers mentioned have ever asked for such a report.

Extreme evil

"I do not know who Heidi Schøne is and I didn't understand anything when I opened the envelope containing pictures of Heidi Schøne and her husband together with revelations of filth, I have never seen the likes of. It must be awful for the Schøne family to be exposed to something like that. The entire letter reeks of extreme evil" says Per Leiblein from Konnerud who received a letter on Monday.

The harassment has been reported to the police. Nedre Eiker Constabulary has been investigating this case for three years.

No extradition

The problem is that the circumstances this man is being charged for are not enough to have him extradited from England. He has on the other hand been clearly told that he will be arrested if he comes to Norway, says local policewoman Torill Sorte Kjennås at Nedre Eiker Constabulary.

Screening Mail

To protect Heidi and her family, all their mail is screened at the Constabulary. So far this year Sorte Kjennås and her colleagues have dealt with more than 300 letters from the man. The family has got a secret phone number, and Telenor have been notified by the police that the number is confidential and is not to be given out to anyone, no matter what the circumstances. The family's address is secret and is barred from disclosure by the National Registration Office (Folkeregistret).

Threats

"In spite of all this the man has nevertheless managed to trace us down a couple of times, and when he does, the phone terror starts again. The man spends all his time tracking Heidi and passes himself off as different persons in order to get hold of our number," says Runar Schøne. The man has previously threatened neighbours of the family with lethal force to know where they have moved.

Drank tea together

Heidi Schøne met the Muslim man when at the age of 18 she was in England as an au pair. She regarded the man as a friend and drank tea with him on a couple of occasions. They have never had any relationship, but for 16 years the Englishman has been obsessed by the idea of marrying Heidi. For a long period he hired a private investigator to follow Heidi's every move. The harassment increased nine years ago when Heidi got married.

Psychiatrists believe the Englishman suffers from an extreme case of erotic paranoia.

(Under Heidi's photo):-

For years Heidi Schøne and her family have lived with a number of secret phone numbers and secret addresses. But a mentally ill Englishman has time and time again traced their address and is sending harassing letters.

Drammens Tidende - 27th May 1995

VG NETT
Forsiden

7/7/98

Blir ikke kvitt sex-gal engelskmann
Av ALEXANDER NORDBY

I 16 år har en sex-gal engelskmann terrorisert Heidi Schøne med brev, telefoner og trusler.

BLIR PLAGET: Engelskmannen har hittil i år sendt 300 brev til Heidi Schøne. Foto: VG

Engelskmannen er fullstendig besatt av den norske kvinnen, og siden 1982 har han bombardert Heidi Schøne med telefonterror, drapstrusler, brevterror, fysisk oppmøte på døren hennes og trakkasering av hennes venner.

Mannen har også sendt hundrevis av brev til helt tilfeldige mennesker i Norge med alvorlige sex-anklager og intime påstander om den norske kvinnen.

Jeg har tigget, grått og truet for at han skulle la meg være i fred, sa Heidi Schøne til VG snakket med henne for tre år siden.

Fortsatt har Schøne og hennes familie hemmelig adresse og telefonnummer. Posten blir sortert av det lokale lensmannskontoret, som hittil i år har mottatt over 300 brev fra den 40 år gamle engelskmannen.

Påtrengende

Som 18-åring reiste Heidi Schøne til England for å jobbe som au pair. På en togtur kom hun i snakk med en halvt arabisk mann. Mannen oppførte seg rart og var påtrengende, men hun likte ham og snakket vennskapelig med ham. Helvetet startet da hun var kommet tilbake til Norge.

Mens hun oppholdt seg i Bergen, dukket engelskmannen plutselig opp. Til å begynne med slapp hun ham inn, men etter hvert ble han svært plagsom. Han ringte i et sett, sendte henne utallige brev, og ved en anledning måtte hun se på mens han gjorde obskøne ting.

Etter å ha blitt avvist risset han inn «fuck you» på døren med en kniv. Hun skaffet seg hemmelig adresse, men likevel dukket det opp et postkort med teksten «Freddy is back» - hentet fra en skrekkfilm med en hovedperson ved navn Freddy.

Saken er tidligere blitt etterforsket av politiet i Bergen. For tre år siden anmeldte Schøne på ny forholdet til politiet i Drammen.

- Det blir opp til statsadvokaten å vurdere om det skal sendes en henstilling til engelske myndigheter, sier politiinspektør Dag Einar Lyngås.

VG NETT
Forsiden

07/07/98

Erotisk paranoia

Psykiatere mener at den truende og elskovssyke engelsmannen kan lide av ekstrem erotisk paranoia.

Lidelsen er en vrangforestilling der en person er overbevist om at et annet menneske må være forelsket i vedkommende.

Erotisk paranoia rammer oftest kvinner, og særlig kvinner i overgangsalderen. Ofte går lidelsen over av seg selv etter noen år.

Personer med erotisk paranoia er sjelden slemme, som i tilfellet med engelskmannen.

(VG 07.07.98 kl. 06:41)

Drammens Tidende 14/07/1998

English Translation

SEXUALLY HARASSED FOR 16 YEARS

For 16 years Heidi Schøne from Solbergelva has been pestered and followed by a mentally ill Englishman. In only the last year the man has sent more than 300 letters to Heidi and made numerous phone calls

The Muslim man has been obsessed by Heidi Schøne (34) since she was 18 years old. His long time pestering of Heidi and her family has been a huge strain. DT-BB first covered this case three years ago. Still, the family is being badgered by the same man.

Want to be left alone

"All we want is to be left alone. This man is very ill and his countless letters and phone calls put an enormous strain on us all" says Heidi's husband Runar Schøne. For years the Schønes have been living with a string of secret phone numbers and addresses, but each time the man manages to find them and the terror continues until they manage to hide themselves away again.

"Reports"

In the course of the 16 years this man has sent out many "reports" to Heidi's family, friends, neighbours, colleagues and a number of strangers. These reports are grossly defamatory and the information listed has no basis in reality. Once again, many people from Drammen have received "reports" about Heidi in their mail box. The reports are modelled like answers for questionnaires from Drammens Tidende, VG and Bergens Tidende, but none of the newspapers mentioned have ever asked for such a report.

Extreme evil

"I do not know who Heidi Schøne is and I didn't understand anything when I opened the envelope containing pictures of Heidi Schøne and her husband together with revelations of filth, I have never seen the likes of. It must be awful for the Schøne family to be exposed to something like that. The entire letter reeks of extreme evil" says Per Leiblein from Konnerud who received a letter on Monday.

The harassment has been reported to the police. Nedre Eiker Constabulary has been investigating this case for three years.

No extradition

The problem is that the circumstances this man is being charged for are not enough to have him extradited from England. He has on the other hand been clearly told that he will be arrested if he comes to Norway, says local policewoman Torill Sorte Kjennås at Nedre Eiker Constabulary.

Screening Mail

To protect Heidi and her family, all their mail is screened at the Constabulary. So far this year Sorte Kjennås and her colleagues have dealt with more than 300 letters from the man. The family has got a secret phone number, and Telenor have been notified by the police that the number is confidential and is not to be given out to anyone, no matter what the circumstances. The family's address is secret and is barred from disclosure by the National Registration Office (Folkeregistret).

Threats

"In spite of all this the man has nevertheless managed to trace us down a couple of times, and when he does, the phone terror starts again. The man spends all his time tracking Heidi and passes himself off as different persons in order to get hold of our number," says Runar Schøne. The man has previously threatened neighbours of the family with lethal force to know where they have moved.

Drank tea together

Heidi Schøne met the Muslim man when at the age of 18 she was in England as an au pair. She regarded the man as a friend and drank tea with him on a couple of occasions. They have never had any relationship, but for 16 years the Englishman has been obsessed by the idea of marrying Heidi. For a long period he hired a private investigator to follow Heidi's every move. The harassment increased nine years ago when Heidi got married.

Psychiatrists believe the Englishman suffers from an extreme case of erotic paranoia.

(Under Heidi's photo):-

For years Heidi Schøne and her family have lived with a number of secret phone numbers and secret addresses. But a mentally ill Englishman has time and time again traced their address and is sending harassing letters.

Verdens Gang - 7th July 1998

DT·BB
Drammens Tidende · Buskeruds Blad

NR. 159 · TIRSDAG 14. JULI 1998 · UKE 29 · LØSSALG KR. 10,00

Forfulgt av gal mann i 16 år

ARKIVFOTO

I 16 år har en sinnslidende engelskmann plaget og forfulgt Heidi Schøne (bildet) fra Solbergelva. Flere ganger har hun flyttet og skaffet seg hemmelig adresse og telefonnummer, men mannen sporer henne opp. Bare i år har han sendt over 300 brev, og ringt en rekke ganger.

Sex-trakassert i 16 år

I 16 år er Heidi Schøne fra Solbergelva blitt trakassert og forfulgt av en sinnslidende engelskmann. Bare det siste året har mannen sendt Heidi over 300 brev og ringt en rekke ganger.

Ingunn Røren

Den muslimske mannen har vært besatt av Heidi Schøne (34) siden hun var 18 år gammel. Hans årelange trakassering av Heidi og hennes familie har vært en enorm belastning. DT-BB omtalte saken første gang for tre år siden. Fortsatt trakasseres familien Schøne av den samme mannen.

Vil være i fred

–Vi ønsker bare å få være i fred. Denne mannen er svært syk, og hans utallige brev og telefoner er en enorm påkjenning, sier Heidis mann, Runar Schøne.

I årevis har familien Schøne levd med en rekke hemmelige telefonnumre og hemmelige adresser. Hver gang klarer mannen å oppspore dem etter en stund, og da fortsetter terroren inntil familien får gjemt seg på nytt.

«Rapporter»

I løpet av de 16 årene har mannen sendt ut en rekke «rapporter» til Heidis familie, venner, naboer, kolleger og en rekke ukjente mennesker. Rapportene er grovt ærekrenkende, og opplysningene som står der har ikke rot i virkeligheten. Nå har nok en gang en rekke drammensere fått «rapporter» om Heidi i postkassen. Rapportene er utformet som om de er svar på en forespørsel fra Drammens Tidende, VG og Bergens Tidende, men ingen av avisene har på noen måte bedt om å få en slik rapport.

ARKIVFOTO

I årevis har Heidi Schøne og hennes familie levd med en rekke hemmelige telefonnumre og hemmelige adresser. Men en psykisk syk engelskmann har gang etter gang sporet opp adressen og sender trakasserende brev

«Ekstrem ondskap»

-Jeg aner ikke hvem Heidi Schøne er, og skjønte ingenting da jeg åpnet konvolutten og fant bilder av Heidi Schøne og hennes mann samt en skittkasting jeg aldri har sett maken til. Det må være forferdelig for familien Schøne å bli utsatt for noe slikt. Hele brevet gir uttrykk for en ekstrem ondskap, sier Per Lieblein fra Konnerud som mottok brevet mandag.

Trakasseringen er anmeldt til politiet. Nedre Eiker lensmannskontor har etterforsket saken i tre år.

Utleveres ikke

-Problemet er at forholdene mannen er siktet for ikke holder til å få ham utlevert fra England. Han har imidlertid fått klar beskjed om at han vil bli pågrepet hvis han kommer til Norge, sier lensmannsbetjent Toril Sorte Kjennås ved Nedre Eiker lensmannskontor.

Sortert post

For å skåne Heidi og hennes familie blir all post som kommer til dem sortert på lensmannskontoret. Hittil i år har Sorte Kjennås og hennes kolleger tatt hånd om over 300 brev mannen har sendt til Heidi. Familien har hemmelig telefonnummer, og hos Telenor er nummeret merket med beskjed fra politiet om at det er konfidensielt og ikke skal gis ut under noen omstendighet. Familiens adresse er hemmelig, og er sperret for utlevering fra Folkeregisteret.

Trusler

-På tross av dette har mannen likevel klart å spore oss opp et par ganger, og da setter telefonterroren i gang igjen. Mannen bruker all sin tid på å finne Heidi, og utgir seg for å være forskjellige personer for å få tak i nummeret vårt, sier Runar Schøne. Mannen har tidligere truet naboer av familien på livet for å få vite hvor de har flyttet.

Drakk te sammen

Heidi Schøne møtte den muslimske mannen da hun som 18-åring var au pair i England. Hun så på mannen som en venn, og drakk te med ham et par ganger. De har aldri hatt noe kjærlighetsforhold, men i 16 år har engelskmannen vært besatt av tanken på å gifte seg med Heidi. En lang periode hadde han en privatdetektiv som fulgte alle Heidis bevegelser. Trakasseringen økte i omfang da Heidi for ni år siden giftet seg.

Psykiatere mener at engelskmannen lider av et ekstremt tilfelle av erotisk paranoia.

Drammens Tidende 14/07/1998

English Translation

SEXUALLY HARASSED FOR 16 YEARS

For 16 years Heidi Schøne from Solbergelva has been pestered and followed by a mentally ill Englishman. In only the last year the man has sent more than 300 letters to Heidi and made numerous phone calls

The Muslim man has been obsessed by Heidi Schøne (34) since she was 18 years old. His long time pestering of Heidi and her family has been a huge strain. DT-BB first covered this case three years ago. Still, the family is being badgered by the same man.

Want to be left alone

"All we want is to be left alone. This man is very ill and his countless letters and phone calls put an enormous strain on us all" says Heidi's husband Runar Schøne. For years the Schønes have been living with a string of secret phone numbers and addresses, but each time the man manages to find them and the terror continues until they manage to hide themselves away again.

"Reports"

In the course of the 16 years this man has sent out many "reports" to Heidi's family, friends, neighbours, colleagues and a number of strangers. These reports are grossly defamatory and the information listed has no basis in reality. Once again, many people from Drammen have received "reports" about Heidi in their mail box. The reports are modelled like answers for questionnaires from Drammens Tidende, VG and Bergens Tidende, but none of the newspapers mentioned have ever asked for such a report.

Extreme evil

"I do not know who Heidi Schøne is and I didn't understand anything when I opened the envelope containing pictures of Heidi Schøne and her husband together with revelations of filth, I have never seen the likes of. It must be awful for the Schøne family to be exposed to something like that. The entire letter reeks of extreme evil" says Per Leiblein from Konnerud who received a letter on Monday.

The harassment has been reported to the police. Nedre Eiker Constabulary has been investigating this case for three years.

No extradition

The problem is that the circumstances this man is being charged for are not enough to have him extradited from England. He has on the other hand been clearly told that he will be arrested if he comes to Norway, says local policewoman Torill Sorte Kjennås at Nedre Eiker Constabulary.

Screening Mail

To protect Heidi and her family, all their mail is screened at the Constabulary. So far this year Sorte Kjennås and her colleagues have dealt with more than 300 letters from the man. The family has got a secret phone number, and Telenor have been notified by the police that the number is confidential and is not to be given out to anyone, no matter what the circumstances. The family's address is secret and is barred from disclosure by the National Registration Office (Folkeregistret).

Threats

"In spite of all this the man has nevertheless managed to trace us down a couple of times, and when he does, the phone terror starts again. The man spends all his time tracking Heidi and passes himself off as different persons in order to get hold of our number," says Runar Schøne. The man has previously threatened neighbours of the family with lethal force to know where they have moved.

Drank tea together

Heidi Schøne met the Muslim man when at the age of 18 she was in England as an au pair. She regarded the man as a friend and drank tea with him on a couple of occasions. They have never had any relationship, but for 16 years the Englishman has been obsessed by the idea of marrying Heidi. For a long period he hired a private investigator to follow Heidi's every move. The harassment increased nine years ago when Heidi got married.

Psychiatrists believe the Englishman suffers from an extreme case of erotic paranoia.

(Under Heidi's photo):-

For years Heidi Schøne and her family have lived with a number of secret phone numbers and secret addresses. But a mentally ill Englishman has time and time again traced their address and is sending harassing letters.

Drammens Tidende - 14th July 1998

5 - 10 - 1998

Håper statsadvokaten kan stoppe marerittet

I 16 år har Heidi Schøne levd i et sammenhengende mareritt. Nå håper hun at statsadvokaten skal få satt en stopper for mannen som har forfulgt henne siden hun var 18 år gammel.

Ingunn Røren

Heidi Schøne (35) fra Solbergelva har blitt forfulgt og trakassert av en engelskmann i 16 år.
- Han har i løpet av disse årene sendt ut hundrevis av brev, både om meg og til meg. I tillegg har han ringt døgnet rundt i perioder, sier Heidi Schøne.
Saken har siden 1995 vært under etterforskning ved Nedre Eiker lensmannskontor etter at Heidi Schøne anmeldte engelskmannen for personforfølgelse og trakassering. Saken er ferdig etterforsket, og er videresendt til statsadvokaten.
- Problemet er at lovverket er altfor svakt når man blir utsatt for den type trakassering som jeg har måttet leve med de siste 16 årene. Jeg er forferdelig sliten av dette, og håper nå at politiet og statsadvokaten får satt en stopper for trakasseringen, sier Heidi Schøne.
Ifølge norsk lov regnes trakassering vanligvis som en forseelse og ikke en forbrytelse. Norge har ingen utleveringsavtale med England for personer som er siktet for forseelser og ikke forbrytelser.
- Denne saken er imidlertid spesiell, fordi trakasseringen har pågått over svært mange år og har et stort omfang, sier lensmannsbetjent Torill Sorte Kjennås ved Nedre Eiker lensmannskontor.
Det er dette statsadvokaten nå skal ta stilling til.
Heidi Schøne møtte engelskmannen da hun som 18-åring var au-pair i England. Hun drakk te med mannen et par ganger, og ga ham adressen sin i Norge da hun skulle hjem.
- Jeg ante ikke da at mannen var blitt fullstendig besatt av meg, og at han skulle plage meg de neste 16 årene. Siden 1982 har han sendt meg i gjennomsnitt et brev hver eneste dag, og ringt utallige ganger. Jeg har tryglet, bedt og grått, men han lar oss ikke være i fred, sier Heidi Schøne. I tillegg til brevene som har blitt sendt til Heidi Schøne, har mannen sendt ut dypt krenkende «rapporter» om Heidi Schøne til hennes naboer, kolleger, venner og familie. Familien Schønee har flyttet flere ganger og hatt flere hemmelige telefonnumre, men mannen har klart å oppspore familien hver gang.
- Dette er en enorm belastning for meg og resten av familien, sier Heidi Schøne, som er gift og har to barn.
Utallige ganger har hun måttet forklare vilt fremmede mennesker hvorfor de har fått tilsendt rapporter om henne.
- Naboene her i Solbergelva har vært veldig fine og støttet oss, men det er selvfølgelig en belastning for oss at alle som befinner seg i nærheten av oss blir plaget med brev og telefoner fra mannen, sier Runar Schønee, Heidi Schønes mann.
Den siste tiden har lensmannskontoret i Nedre Eiker stanset alle brev som er sendt fra mannen til Heidi Schøne.
- Vi har tatt hånd om over 400 brev, sier lensmannsbetjent Torill Sorte Kjennås.
- Det har vært en befrielse å slippe å få disse brevene i postkassen. Jeg vet jo at han fortsatt sender brev til meg, men det er fint at politiet sorterer posten vår, sier Heidi Schøne.
De siste månedene har mannen på nytt sendt ut en rekke brev om Heidi Schøne til en rekke enkeltpersoner, offentlige institusjoner og firmaer i Drammens-distriktet. Brevene har et grovt sjikanøst innhold, og inneholder en rekke usannheter om Heidi Schøne og hennes familie. De nyeste brevene er utformet som om de er svar på en forespørsel fra Drammens Tidende, men DT-BB har aldri sendt ut noen slik forespørsel om Heidi Schøne.
- Jeg er sliten, sint og fortvilet over situasjonen. Brevene han sender til alle og enhver har gjort at jeg har isolert meg stadig mer. Nå håper jeg inderlig at statsadvokaten finner en løsning slik at mannen kan bli dømt. Mest av alt ønsker jeg at retten skal gi ham forbud mot å nærme seg meg eller kontakte meg. Da kunne vi kanskje endelig få fred, og slippe å leve med hemmelig adresse og telefonnummer, og være redde hver gang telefonen ringer, sier Heidi Schøne.

Drammens Tidende 5th October 1998

English Translation

Hopes the public prosecutor can stop her nightmare

For 16 years Heidi Schøne has lived a continuous nightmare. She now hopes that the public prosecutor will be able to stop the man who has persecuted her since she was 18 years old.

By Ingunn Røren

Heidi Schøne, 35, from Solbergelva has been persecuted and harassed by an Englishman for 16 years. "During the course of these years he has sent out hundreds of letters, both about me and to me. In addition, he has telephoned me at all hours of the day for some periods," says Heidi Schøne. Since 1995 the case has been under investigation by the district sheriff's office in Nedre Eiker after Heidi reported the Englishman to the police for victimisation and harassment. The case has been fully investigated, and has now been sent to the public prosecutor's office. "The problem is that the legislation is far too weak in cases where one is subjected to the type of harassment that I've had to live with for the last 16 years. I'm terribly tired of this, and hope now that the police and the public prosecutor will be able to stop this persecution," says Heidi Schøne. Under Norwegian law, harassment is generally considered to be a misdemeanour and not a criminal offence. Norway has no extradition treaty with England for individuals who are charged with misdemeanours and not criminal offences.

"This case is special, however, since the harassment has continued for very many years and to such a great extent," says Toril Sorte Kjennås, police officer at the district sheriff's office in Nedre Eiker. The decision now rests with the public prosecutor.

Heidi Schøne first met the Englishman when she was 18 and an au pair in England. She drank tea with the Englishman a couple of times, and gave him her address in Norway when she left England to return home."I didn't know then that the man had become completely obsessed with me, and that he would bother me for the next 16 years. Since 1982 he has sent me an average of one letter every single day, and called on countless occasions. I have begged, pleaded and cried, but he just won't leave us alone," says Heidi. In addition to the letters he has sent Heidi, the man has sent highly offensive "reports" about Heidi to her neighbours, colleagues, friends and family. The Schøne family have moved several times and have had several unlisted telephone numbers, but the man has managed to trace the family each time. "This puts an enormous strain on me and on the rest of my family," says Heidi, who is married and has two children. On countless occasions she has had to explain to complete strangers why they have received reports about her. "Our neighbours here in Solbergelva have been great and have supported us, but it naturally puts a strain on us when everyone around us is pestered with letters and telephone calls from the man," says Runar Schøne, Heidi's husband. Recently the district sheriff's office in Nedre Eiker has begun to intercept letters that the man sends sent to Heidi. "We have taken charge of more than 400 letters," says police officer Toril Sorte Kjennås. "It's been a relief not to have these letters in my letter box. Of course, I know he's still sending me letters, but it's good that the police sort through our mail," says Heidi. In recent months the man has once again sent several letters about Heidi to a number of individuals, public institutions and companies in the Drammen area. The letters have a grossly defamatory content, and contain a number of untruths about Heidi and her family. The most recent letters have been formulated so that they look like they are answers to an enquiry from Drammens Tidende, but DT-BB has never sent out such an enquiry about Heidi Schøne. "I am tired, angry and desperate about the situation. The letters he sends to everyone have made me isolate myself more and more. I sincerely hope that the public prosecutor can find a solution so that the man can be sentenced. More than anything else I want the court to ban him from approaching me or contacting me. Perhaps then we'll finally be able to get some peace, and will not have to have a secret address and unlisted telephone number, and be frightened every time the telephone rings," says Heidi.

Drammens Tidende - 5th October 1998

8 - 12 - 1998

Trakassert og forfulgt - saken stilles i bero

Beslutningen er tatt: Politiet trapper ned innsatsen for å få tak i engelskmannen som i 16 år skal ha trakassert og forfulgt Heidi Schøne (35) fra Solbergelva.

Morten Wold

- Det er klart vi er skuffet, sier hennes ektemann Runar Schøne til DT-BB.
Politifullmektig Dag Einar Lyngås ved Drammen politikammer kan bare beklage at politiet ikke ser seg i stand til fortsatt å bruke ressurser på å få fatt i engelskmannen som siden 1982 skal ha trakassert, forfulgt og spredt usannheter om Heidi Schøne i form av brev og telefoner til både slekt, venner, arbeidsgivere og avisredaksjoner i Norge.

Familien skuffet
- Saken stilles i bero og vil ligge til observasjon på bestemte tidspunkter, sier Lyngås til DT-BB.
Han understreker at saken ikke er henlagt, men at politiet vil følge med i utviklingen og se om trakasseringen fortsetter.
Runar Schøne sier man finner beslutningen skuffende og at dette innebærer at familien må fortsette å leve nærmest i «eksil».
- Vi har hemmelig adresse og telefonnummer, som vi har måttet skifte flere ganger. Vi har ikke gjort noe galt, men straffes gjennom mannens virksomhet med forringelse i livskvalitet, mens han går fri og får ture fram som han vil, sier Schøne.
Marerittet for Heidi Schøne startet i 1982 da hun traff engelskmannen mens hun arbeidet som au-pair i England. Han skal ha blitt fullstendig besatt av henne og skal siden den gang ha sendt henne brev omtrent hver eneste dag og sporet opp hennes adresse og telefonnummer - selv om hun har flyttet og skaffet seg hemmelig telefonnummer flere ganger.

Posten sorteres
Så ille har det vært at lensmannskontoret i Nedre Eiker nå sorterer posten hennes for å stoppe det som ser ut som brev fra mannen. Mer enn 400 brev er stanset og oppbevares på lensmannskontoret - for å skjerme Heidi Schøne og hennes familie. Saken har vært under etterforskning siden 1995 og ble for en tid tilbake oversendt statsadvokaten. Heidi Schøne håpet at det skulle resultere i at mannen ble dømt.
Påtalemyndigheten har imidlertid problemer med å gripe saken an og vil ha vanskeligheter med å oppnå varetektsfengsling siden mannen er siktet etter straffelovens paragraf 390 A, som har en strafferamme på inntil seks måneders fengsel. For å bli satt i varetekt må det være snakk om forbrytelser med over seks måneders strafferamme og det må foreligge fare for gjentakelse.
- Fare for gjentakelse er det i høyeste grad her, men forøvrig oppfylles ikke vilkårene, sier Dag Einar Lyngås til DT-BB.
Det betyr at politiet nå vil forholde seg noenlunde passivt, men pågripe mannen dersom man gjøres oppmerksom på om han tar seg til Norge

Drammens Tidende 8th December 1998

English Translation

Harassed and persecuted - case put on hold

A decision has been taken: The police are to step down their efforts to apprehend an Englishman who over a period of 16 years is alleged to have harassed and persecuted Heidi Schøne (35) from Solbergelva.

By Morten Wold

"Of course we're disappointed," says Runar Schøne, Ms Schøne's husband, to DT-BB. Dag Einar Lyngås, police superintendant at Drammen Police Force, can only apologise that the police find they are unable to continue to employ the resources necessary to apprehend the Englishman. Since 1982 he has harassed, persecuted and spread untruths about Heidi Schøne in the form of letters and telephone calls to her relations, friends, employers, and to newspapers in Norway.

A disappointed family

"The case will be put on hold and will be under periodical observation," says Mr Lyngås to DT-BB.

He stresses that the case has not been closed, but that the police will follow developments to see whether the harassment continues.

Runar Schøne says the police decision is disappointing and that this means the family will have to continue living in a virtual "exile".

"We have a secret address and an unlisted telephone number, which we have had to change several times. We haven't done anything wrong, but are being punished with a poorer quality of life as a result of this man's activities, while he goes free and can do whatever he wants," says Mr Schøne.

Heidi Schøne's nightmare began in 1982, when she met the Englishman while working as an au pair in England. He allegedly became obsessed with her and has since then sent her letters almost every day and managed to trace her address and telephone number - even though she has moved and obtained an unlisted telephone number several times.

Post sorted

Things became so bad that the district police force in Nedre Eiker now sort her post in order to stop any letters that may be from the man. More than 400 letters have been stopped and stored by the district police force - to shield Heidi Schøne and her family.

The case has been under investigation since 1995 and was sent to the public prosecutor some time ago. Heidi Schøne hoped then that this would lead to the man's conviction.

The public prosecuting authority has encountered problems in dealing with this matter, however, and will have difficulty in remanding the man in custody since he has been charged pursuant to section 390A of the Norwegian General Civil Penal Code, which carries a maximum sentence of six months' imprisonment. In order to be held on remand, a minimum sentence of more than six months is required plus the danger of repetition of the offence.

"There is most certainly a danger of repetition here, but at present the conditions have not met," says Dag Einar Lyngås to DT-BB.

This means that the police will now remain relatively passive, but will arrest the man if it is brought to their attention that he is coming to Norway.

26 August 2000

Kom for å kreve penger - ble bøtelagt

Engelskmannen kom til Drammen for å kreve nesten 400 000 kroner i oppreisning fra en Nedre Eiker-kvinne og Drammens Tidende, men ble møtt med en bot på 10 000 kroner. Han fikk boten for å ha krenket den 38 år gamle kvinnens privatliv i en årrekke. Sammen med boten ble han presentert for et ilagt forbud mot å kontakte kvinnen på noen som helst måte. Politiinspektør Dag Einar Lyngås har sendt begjæringen om besøksforbud til byretten for godkjenning. Engelskmannen vedtok ikke forelegget, og ble umiddelbart stevnet for hovedforhandling i byretten 9. oktober.

Han kom egentlig til Norge og Drammen for å kreve penger fra Drammens Tidende og kvinnen. For tre år siden sto kvinnen fram i Drammens Tidende med historien om hvordan hun i 16 år var blitt forfulgt av mannen hun traff mens hun var au pair i England. Mannen saksøkte i etterhånd både avisen, redaktør Hans Arne Odde, journalisten som skrev saken og Nedre Eiker-kvinnen. Han krever 50 000 kroner i oppreisning fra henne, mens kravet mot avis og journalist er på totalt 330 000 kroner. Da det ble klart at han kom til Norge i forbindelse med søksmålet, benyttet politiet anledningen. Etter det Drammens Tidende forstår, ville politiet neppe krevd mannen utlevert til Norge.

Den 38 år gamle kvinnen anmeldte engelskmannen for flere år siden. I en årrekke skal han ha ringt henne og sendt utallige brev. Andre personer, offentlige institusjoner og private firmaer mottok også brev og telefaxer, som ble sporet tilbake til mannen. Innholdet i brevene og faxene var svært ufordelaktige opplysninger om kvinnen.

På spørsmål fra Drammens Tidende, svarer mannens advokat, Stig Lunde, at han ikke har noen kommentarer til boten og besøksforbudet.

Drammens Tidende 26/08/2000

English Translation

Came to demand money - was fined

The Englishman came to Drammen in order to demand nearly 400 000 kroner in compensation from a Nedre-Eiker woman and Drammens Tidende, but was met with a fine of 10 000 kroner. He got the fine for having violated the 38 year old woman's private life over a number of years. Together with the fine, he was banned from contacting the woman in any way whatsoever.

Police Inspector Dag Einar Lyngås sent to the county court for approval the application for a ban on visits. The Englishman did not accept the fine and was immediately summonsed for the main hearing in the county court on 9 October.

Actually, he came to Norway and Drammen in order to demand money from Drammens Tidende and the woman. Three years ago, the woman appeared in Drammens Tidende with the story of how, at the age of 16, she had been pursued by the man she met while she was an au-pair in England. The man sued successively both the newspaper, Error! editor Hans Arne Odde, the journalist who wrote up the case and the Nedre-Eiker woman. He is demanding 50 000 kroner compensation from her, while the claim against newspaper and journalist totals 330 000 kroner.

When it became clear that he had come to Norway in connection with the lawsuit, the police took advantage of the opportunity. According to the understanding of Drammens Tidende, the police would hardly have demanded extradition of the man to Norway.

The 38 year old woman reported the Englishman several years ago. For a number of years, it is reported, he telephoned her and sent innumerable letters. Other people, public institutions and private firms also received letters and faxes, which were traced back to the man. The contents of the letters and faxes were information greatly to the discredit of the woman.

In reply to questions from Drammens Tidende, the man's lawyer, Stig Lunde, says that he does not have any comments to make on the fine and the ban on visiting

Drammens Tidende

Fredag 16. november 2001 – Uke 46 * * – Nr. 266 – Løssalg kr. 10.00 – dt.no

DRAMMENS TIDENDE · BUSKERUDS BLAD

MED RADIO- OG TV-MAGASIN

Bot for grov sexterror

Plaget kvinne i 16 år - må betale 10 000

43-åringen som har sex-terrorisert en kvinne fra Nedre Eiker med utallige telefonoppringer og brev og postkort gjennom 16 år, slipper fengselsstraff. 10 000 kroner i bot synes retten er en passende straff. At mannen er bosatt i England er grunnen til at han slipper fengsel. Retten legger ikke skjul på at denne straffen er svært mild. Forholdene som mannen er dømt for, har en strafferamme på inntil seks måneders fengsel.

Side 3

10 000 i bot for 16 års sexterror

Slapp fengsel fordi han bor i England

43-åringen som ble dømt for å ha terrorisert en kvinne fra Nedre Eiker med utallige telefonoppringer og rundt 200 brev og postkort gjennom 16 år, slipper fengselsstraff. 10 000 kroner i bot synes retten er en passende straff.

Av Lars Arntzen
lars.arntzen@dt.no

Den 43 år gamle engelskmannen ble idømt en bot på 10 000 kroner allerede i fjor høst, men denne nektet han å betale.

Dermed endte saken i herredsretten, hvor han tapte på samtlige punkter. At mannen er bosatt i England, er faktisk grunnen til at han slipper fengselsstraff. Aktor, politiinspektør Dag Einar Lyngås, valgte å legge ned påstand om bot istedenfor fengsel fordi en utleveringssak fra England ville bli for kostbar.

Mild straff

Retten legger imidlertid ikke skjul på at denne straffen er svært mild. Forholdene som mannen er dømt for, har en strafferamme på inntil seks måneders fengsel, og retten mener at straffen normalt ville ligget opp mot denne maksimumsstraffen.

Advokat Vegard Aaløkken har representert kvinnen i rettssaken, og han har rådet sin klient til ikke å uttale seg til media. Men han bekrefter at kvinnen er glad for at mannen ble dømt i herredsretten.

- Hun er først og fremst glad for å bli trodd av retten, sier Aaløkken til Drammens Tidende.

- Hvordan reagerer hun på at mannen ikke ble idømt fengselsstraff?

- Normalt ville det vært naturlig med en strengere reaksjon, men hun er vel enig i rettens merknader. Det viktigste for henne er at mannen ble dømt.

Rapport om livsførsel

Telefonsamtalene, brevene og postkortene til kvinnen skal ha båret preg av til dels svært grov sjikane. En del av brevene og postkortene, hvor kvinnen omtales i nedlatende ordelag, skal også ha blitt sendt til andre privatpersoner og offentlige og private bedrifter. Temaene i brevene har stort sett dreid seg om hennes seksualliv, aborter, selvmordsforsøk og rusmisbruket til partneren.

Ifølge kvinnen skal også mannen ha distribuert en «rapport» om henne til naboer, venner og slektninger. Notatet innledes med «Vi kan nå avlegge rapport angående Deres livsførsel», og var hans versjon av hennes livshistorie. I retten forklarte kvinnen at det var svært vanskelig for henne at så mange personer i nærmiljøet mottok «rapporten» fra 43-åringen. At deler av innholdet var sant, gjorde det hele bare enda vanskeligere for henne.

Engelskmannen og Nedre Eiker-kvinnen møttes første gang for over 20 år siden da hun var au-pair i Storbritannia. I begynnelsen skal kontakten ha båret preg av vennlighet, og mannen ble beskrevet som sjarmerende og veltalende. Kvinnen valgte etter hvert å betro ham sine personlige problemer, og på den måten fikk han innsyn i livet hennes. I løpet av årenes løp gjorde kvinnen en rekke forsøk på å hindre tiltalte fra å ta kontakt. Hun skaffet seg blant annet hemmelig adresse og telefonnummer, men ingenting hjalp. Via privatdetektiv klarte 43-åringen å spore henne opp igjen.

«Truslene ble provosert fram»

43-åringen nekter fortsatt straffskyld for telefonsamtalene og brevene til Nedre Eiker-kvinnen. Advokaten hans mener alt er fremprovosert av kvinnen selv.

I retten ba advokat Harald Bjelke Wibye derfor om at klienten måtte frifinnes. Responsen på provokasjonene er etter hans syn ikke grunn god nok for å idømme engelskmannen straff.

I 1990 anmeldte kvinnen mannen for voldtekt. Senere har hun også gått ut i avisene og fortalt om hans oppførsel. Retten avviser imidlertid at dette er provokasjoner som kan frita 43-åringen fra straff.

I dommen skriver retten at voldtektsanmeldelsen ble foretatt fordi hun mente det var foregått et overgrep og ikke for å provosere tiltalte. Når det gjelder avisskriveriene, kom disse i stand etter initiativ fra journalister, og tiltaltes navn er ikke nevnt i artiklene.

Advokat Bjelke Wibye er ikke fornøyd med dommen, men han vil foreløpig ikke si noe om en eventuell anke. Dommen er i ferd med å bli oversatt, slik at også engelskmannen kan lese den. Deretter skal de vurdere hva som skjer videre i denne saken, men sannsynligvis går det mot en anke.

- Min klient føler seg uskyldig dømt. Han mener at kvinnens opplysninger er feilaktige og grovt injurierende. Blant annet faller voldtektsanmeldelsen på sin egen urimelighet, hevder advokaten.

Uansett er det ikke siste gang Bjelke Wibyes klient og Nedre Eiker-kvinnen har møtt hverandre i retten. Allerede i januar møtes de igjen. Da er det en privat straffesak som mannen har reist mot henne, som skal behandles.

English Translation

Fine for serious sex terror

Pestered woman for 16 years - must pay 10,000 kroner

A 43 year old man who sex-terrorized a woman from Nedre Eiker with countless phone calls and letters and postcards over 16 years escapes imprisonment. The Court considers a 10,000 kroner fine is an appropriate punishment. The fact that the man is resident in England is the reason why he is escaping imprisonment. The Court makes no secret of the fact that this punishment is extremely lenient. The charges on which the man has been convicted carry a maximum penalty of up to six months imprisonment.

10,000 fine for 16 years of sex terror

Escaped imprisonment because he lives in England.

A 43 year old convicted of terrorising a woman from Nedre Eiker with countless phone calls and around 200 letters and postcards over 16 years escapes imprisonment. The Court considers a 10,000 kroner fine is an appropriate punishment.

The 43 year old Englishman was fined 10,000 kroner last autumn but refused to pay this.

That concluded the action in the County Court, in which he lost in all respects. The fact that the man is resident in England is the real reason why he is escaping imprisonment. The prosecutor, police inspector Dag Einar Lyngås, opted to ask for a fine instead of imprisonment because extradition from England would be too expensive

Lenient punishment

However, the Court is making no secret of the fact that this punishment is extremely lenient. The charges on which the man has been convicted carry a maximum penalty of up to six months imprisonment, and the Court is of the view that the punishment would normally have been approaching this maximum penalty.

Lawyer Vegard Aaløkken represented the woman in the case, and he has advised his client not to speak to the media. But he confirmed that the woman is pleased that the man has been convicted in the County Court.

"She is first and foremost pleased to have been believed by the Court," Aaløkken told Drammens Tidende. Asked about her reaction to the man not having been sentenced to imprisonment, he replied:

"A stronger reaction would normally have been natural, but she is in full agreement with the Court's remarks. The most important thing for her is that the man has been convicted."

Report on life

The telephone calls, the letters and the postcards to the woman are said to have been marked by in part extremely serious malice. Some of the letters and the postcards, in which the woman is referred to in condescending terms, are also said to have been sent to other private individuals and public and private businesses. The subject matter of the letters was on the whole concerned with her sex life, abortions, suicide attempts and partner's drug abuse.

According to the woman, the man also distributed a 'report' about her to neighbours, friends and relatives. The note began "We can now submit a report about your life" and was his version of her life story.

In Court, the woman explained that it was extremely difficult for her that so many people in her immediate circle had received "the report" from the 43 year old. The fact that some of the content was true only made the whole thing even more difficult for her.

The Englishman and the woman from Nedre Eiker first met over 20 years ago when she was an au pair in Britain. Initially, the contact is said to have been marked by friendliness, and the man was described as charming and eloquent. The woman chose to confide her personal problems in him gradually, and this was how he gained an insight into her life. Over the years, the woman made a number of attempts to prevent the defendant from making contact. Among other things, she obtained a secret address and telephone number, but to no avail. The 43 year old managed to trace her again through a private detective.

"The threats were provoked"

The 43 year old continues to deny culpability for the telephone calls and the letters to the Nedre Eiker woman. His lawyer is of the opinion that everything was provoked by the woman herself.

In Court, lawyer Harald Bjelke Wibye therefore asked for his client to be acquitted. In his view, the response to the provocations is not a good enough reason to convict the Englishman.

In 1990, the woman reported the man for rape. Later, she also appeared in the newspapers and gave an account of his behaviour. The Court nevertheless refused to accept that these are provocations which could exempt the 43 year old from punishment.

In its sentence, the Court states that the rape report was made because in her opinion an assault had taken place and not in order to provoke the defendant. As far as the items in the papers are concerned, these were arranged on the initiative of journalists, and the name of the defendant was not mentioned in the articles.

Lawyer Bjelke Wibye is not satisfied with the sentence, but will for the time being not say anything about a possible appeal. The sentence is in the process of being translated so that the Englishman can read it as well. They will then assess what happens next in this case, but in all likelihood there will be an appeal.

"My client feels he has been wrongfully convicted. He believes the woman's statements are wrong and grossly defamatory. Among other things, the rape report is down to her own unreasonableness", the lawyer said.

In any case, this is not the last time Bjelke Wibye's client and the Nedre Eiker woman have met one another in Court. They are to meet again as early as in January. Then, it is a private criminal case the man has brought against her that is to be dealt with.

ENGELSKMANNENS SVAR TIL DRAMMENS TIDENDES OVERSKRIFT:

ENGELSKMANNENS SVAR TIL DRAMMENS TIDENDES OVERSKRIFT: "BOT FOR GROV SEXTERROR" 16. NOVEMBER 2001, AV LARS ARNTZEN

Ifølge hans rett til å svare, sier engelskmannen ovennevnte artikkel viser til som følger:

1) Engelskmannen var ikke til stede under rettsmøtet den 30. oktober 2001 fordi han ikke hadde tid til å forberede seg i saken. Den vesentligste grunnen var at hans advokat ikke fikk politiets "bevismateriale" før dagen før rettsmøtet; dessuten var en hel del av dette ikke bevist og kunne derfor ikke godtas av retten.

2) Ingen journalister var til stede under rettsmøtet. Ovennevnte artikkel i Drammens Tidende gir et tvers igjennom villedende inntrykk av rettsmøtet.

3) Faktum er at politiet i Drammen var villig til å gjøre opp saken ved at engelskmannen betalte boten på kr. 5.000, noe vedkommende nektet av prinsippmessige grunner.

4) Bevisene som felte engelskmannen bestod kun av "rapporter" til den norske offentligheten som ga hans side av historien til kriminelt injurierende avisartikler fra 1995, som inkluderte provoserende og helt falske påstander fra den norske kvinnens side - både nå og tidligere en psykiatrisk pasient. Det har aldri vært noen såkalte "16 år med sexterror", medmindre man da regner med den sexterror norske menn drev overfor denne kvinnen.

5) "Rapportene" ble sendt over et tidsrom av tre år, 1995 til 1998, og det var da egentlig kjernen i politiets påtale.

6) Hvorfor svarte engelskmannen på denne måten? Opprinnelig var det bare en håndfull "rapporter" om kvinnens livshistorie som ble sent p.g.a. ekstrem provokasjon fra den norske kvinnens side (falsk påstand overfor politiet om voldteksforsøk), fulgt av flere "rapporter" etter ekstrem provokasjon fra Verdens Gang, Bergens Tidende og Drammens Tidende i 1995 og 1998. Disse avisene viste mange fotografier av kvinnen og navnga henne. Den norske kvinnen hadde gitt frivillig avkall på hennes rett til å forbli anonym. Imidlertid trodde ikke de tre avisene at engelskmannen ville finne ut noe om de tre artiklene da han var bosatt i England. Men han fikk omgående greie på det fordi han allerede i desember 1994 hadde bedt en norsk jurist om å undersøke kvinnen og hennes forsøk på å villede retten.

7) Politianklagen 30. oktober 2001 gjaldt bare et ansvarsforhold, nemlig det å sende ut detaljer om kvinnens livshistorie; en anklage som ikke kan forsvares fordi den norske kvinnen var allerede navngitt i "rapportene".

8) Imidlertid navnga ikke de norske avisene ham når de rettet skytset mot ham, en forsvarsløs utlending, idet de mente at hvis han mot formodning skulle få greie på artiklene, så ville han stå overfor den nesten umulige opgaven å finne en nordmann som kjente ham igjen fra artiklene før han kunne anlegge krininal- eller sivilsak om injurier. Noe som ville medføre enorme personlige, økonomiske omkostninger.

9) Før hun var 18 år hadde den norske kvinnen hatt to aborter med samme nordmann. Hun hevdet så at hun ble gjort gravid av en annen elsker senere, nå med tvillinger, men aborterte etter at hun oppdaget hans utroskap. Hun forsøkte å begå selvmord. Senere gikk hun til sengs med den utro mannen igjen, samt med en annen nordmann, i et forsøk på å bli gravid med den ene eller begge. Den utro mannen brukte nå heroinsprøyte idet han tidligere hadde sittet i militærfengsel. Hun lyktes i bli gravid med heroinbrukeren, og fødte en sønn. Faren støtte henne fra seg igjen, og hun forsøkte å begå selvmord igjen, som sa at det eneste hun hadde felles med faren var "god sex". De hadde knapt bodd sammen.

Kvinnen ble så innlagt på en psykiatrisk klinikk, og giftet seg i 1993 med en mann som hevdet at han "talte i tunger". Ekteskapet brøt sammen, og hun ble skilt i 2001.

10) I hele tidsrommet 1982-1990 bad den norske kvinnen engelskmannen om hjelp med å løse de problemene hun hadde med menn, men fortsatte med katastrofale forbindelser, til engelskmannens store fortvilelse, som selvsagt følte seg tvunget til å si henne "noen sannhetsord".

11) Drammens Tidende antyder at engelskmannen svek kvinnens betroelser om hennes promiskuøse privatliv og personlige problemer. Engelskmannen mente at kvinnen, gjennom sin troløshet overfor ham, hadde forsaket enhver rett til fortrolighet.

12) I 1995 oppdaget engelskmannen at kvinnen hadde klaget til politiet i Bergen i 1986 at engelskmannen hadde forsøkt å voldta henne i april 1985. Hun ventet i 20 måneder før hun kom med denne (falske) anklagen; en klage hun fremsatte bare to uker etter at engelskmannen hadde varslet hennes familie om hennes utrygge seksuelle vaner og selvmordstendenser. Klagen var som hevn for at engelskmannen fortalte hennes familie om hennes fortid, idet familien hadde vært helt uvitende om den sexterror norske borgere hadde utøvet mot henne.

13) Under rettsmøtet i Drammen den 30. oktober 2001, innrømmet den norske kvinnen at hun også hadde anklaget en butikkeier i Bergen for voldtekt i 1980-årene. Politiet kom aldri med anklagepåstand. I 1980-årene hevdet den norske kvinnen også at greske menn hadde forsøkt å voldta henne og truet henne med kniv. I 1995 hevdet hun overfor Drammens Tidende at engelskmannen hadde forsøkt å voldta henne. I 1998 forandret hun mening. Da engelskmannen bad politiet i Drammen om å undersøke hennes påstand om voldtektsforsøk, hevdet kvinnen nå at det dreiet som reell voldtekt. Politiet har aldri kommet med anklagepåstand. Ikke desto mindre, disse falske påstandene mot engelskmannen, som tok sikte på å ødelegge ham og ihvertfall få han arrestert og forhørt, var tilstrekkelig provokasjon for engelskmannen til å offentligjøre kvinnens tidligere historie for å understreke de problemene han hadde hatt å stri med på grunn av en syk kvinne. Til å begynne med var det bare hennes naboer som ble informert.

14) Drammens befolkning må også meddeles at kvinnen fortalte Drammens Tidende i 1995 at i 1988 hadde engelskmannen etter sigende truet med å myrde hennes 2 år gamle sønn. Ingunn Røren offentliggjorde denn påstanden som et faktum, uten noe som helst understøttende bevismateriale! Senere undersøkelser avslørte at kvinnen fortalte politiet at den påståtte mordtruselen ble gjort av engelskmannen i et brev som ble "gitt til politiet i Bergen". Politiet i Bergen fortalte politiet i Drammen at de ikke hadde et slikt brev. Påstanden er selvfølgelig falsk og tar sikte på å skape store vansker for engelskmannen, eller kanskje til og med ødelegge ham fullstendig. Slik ondaktig påstand må da være provokasjon stor nok til at engelskmannen kan gjøre den norske befolkning kjent med sannheten til pikens fortid, og dermed bakgrunnen til den kvinnen som har fremsatt slike påstander mot ham i både lokalaviser og landsdekkende aviser. Engelskmannen hadde ingen annen måte å svare på.

15) Dessuten har den norske kvinnen innrømmet overfor politiet i Drammen at selv etter at hun kom med disse påstandene mot engelskmannen, om voldtektsforsøk og trusel om å myrde en 2-åring, så fortsatte hun likevel å be om engelskmannens hjelp i 1988 til å holde styr på den ubehagelige oppførselen til barnets far. Ingen normal kvinne ber en som hevdes å ha begått voldtekt og truet med å drepe et barn om hjelp. Faktum er at barnets far overfalt henne i 1990, og han ble anmeldt til politiet.

16) I august 1990 gjenopptok den norske kvinnen et hyggelig forhold til engelskmannen i den grad at hun til og med sendte ham postkort og brev og kristelig litteratur.

17) Engelskmannen tror at kvinnen er en sinnsyk som langt fra å være "et uskyldig

offer" slik det hevdes av den xenofobiske pressen, tvertimot er en kaldt beregnende løgner som tar lite eller intet hensyn til vanlig standard for sivilisert oppførsel.

18) Den tidligere journalisten i Drammens Tidende, Ingunn Røren, har beviselig begått mened overfor Pressens Faglige Utvalg; fakta som for tiden behandles av Drammen Byrett.

19) I England trykker avisene ofrenes navn hvis de sitter inne med riktige fakta. Den omfattende tåkeleggingen som gjøres av det norske etablissement er en permanent skamplett på dets omdømme.

The "Englishman's" Response to Drammens Tidende headline "Fine for Serious Sex Terror" of 16th November 2001 by Lars Arntzen

In accordance with his right to reply the Englishman referred to in the above articles states as follows:-

1. The Englishman did not attend the Court hearing on 30th October 2001 as he had no time to prepare for the case, particularly as his lawyer only received the police "evidence" the day before the hearing, a lot of which was in fact not proven and inadmissible to the Court.

2. No journalists attended the hearing. The above Drammens Tidende article is a complete misrepresentation of the Court proceedings.

3. The fact is that the Drammen police were prepared to settle the matter if the Englishman paid a 5,000 Kroner fine, which he refused on grounds of principle.

4. The evidence which convicted the Englishman consisted merely of 'reports' to the Norwegian public giving his side of the story to criminally libellous newspaper stories from 1995 which included provocative and wholly false allegations from the Norwegian woman - presently and in the past a psychiatric patient. There has never been any so called "16 years of Sex Terror", unless one counts the sex terror inflicted by Norwegian men on this woman.

5. The 'reports' were sent for a three year period, 1995 to 1998 and that in essence was the reason for the police prosecution.

6. Why did the Englishman respond in this manner? Only a handful of 'reports' on the woman's life history were initially sent due to extreme provocation by the Norwegian woman (a false allegation to the police of attempted rape), followed by more 'reports' after extreme provocation by Verdens Gang, Bergens Tidende and Drammens Tidende in 1995 and 1998, which newspapers showed many photographs of the woman and named her. The Norwegian woman had voluntarily waived her right to anonymity. However, the three newspapers did not think the Englishman would find out about the articles as he was of course living in England. But he did immediately find out as he had earlier, in December 1994, asked a Norwegian lawyer to investigate the woman for her attempts to pervert the course of justice.

7. The police charge of 30th October 2001 was for a strict liability offence, i.e. sending out details of the woman's life history, for which there is no defence available as the Norwegian woman was named in "the reports".

8. However, the Norwegian newspapers in targeting a defenceless foreigner did not name him, meaning that in the unlikely event that he did find out about the articles, he would have to face the almost impossible task of finding a Norwegian who recognised him from the articles in order to enable him to sue for criminal and civil libel and at enormous personal, financial and emotional cost.

9. By the time she was 18, the Norwegian woman had had two abortions to the same Norwegian man. She then claimed she got pregnant later to another lover carrying twins, but miscarried after discovering his infidelity. She then attempted suicide. Later she

resumed sleeping with the unfaithful man and at the same time with yet another Norwegian man, trying to get pregnant to both, or either. The unfaithful man was injecting heroin having been in military prison previously. She succeeded in getting pregnant to the I.V. heroin user and a son was born. The father again rejected the girl and a further suicide attempt followed by the girl who said all she had in common with the father was "good sex". They had rarely lived together. The woman then entered a psychiatric clinic and in 1994 married a man who claimed to "speak in tongues". Her marriage failed and she was divorced in 2001.

10. Throughout the period 1982-1990 the Norwegian woman was asking the Englishman for help in solving her problems with men, but repeatedly kept on with disastrous liaisons, much to the exasperation of the Englishman, who naturally was forced to tell her some "home truths".

11. Drammens Tidende intimated that the Englishman betrayed the woman's confidences about her promiscuous private life and personal problems. The Englishman decided that by the woman's treachery towards him, she has waived her right to these confidences being kept.

12. In 1995, the Englishman discovered that in December 1986 the woman had complained to the Bergen police that the Englishman had attempted to rape her in April 1985. There was a delay of 20 months in making this (false) allegation, which complaint was made a mere two weeks after the Englishman had warned her family of her unsafe sexual practices and suicidal tendencies. The complaint was in revenge for the Englishman's revelations of her past to her own family who had been ignorant of the sex terror inflicted on her by Norwegian citizens.

13. At the Drammen Court hearing on 30th October 2001, the Norwegian woman admitted also that she made an allegation against a Bergen shopkeeper in the 1980s of rape. The police did not bring charges. In the 1980s, the Norwegian woman also claimed Greek men had tried to rape her at knifepoint. In 1995, she alleged to Drammens Tidende that the Englishman had attempted to rape her. In 1998, she changed her story. At the request of the Englishman of the Drammen police to investigate the allegation of attempted rape, the woman now claimed it was actual rape. The police have never brought charges. Notwithstanding this, these false allegations against the Englishman, designed to ruin him and at the very least get him arrested and questioned, were sufficient provocation for the Englishman to release the woman's past history to the public to highlight the problems he had been facing from a sick woman. Initially, only her neighbours were told.

14. The Drammen public must also be made aware that the woman told Drammens Tidende in 1995 that the Englishman had in 1988 allegedly threatened to murder her 2 year old son. Without any corroborative evidence Ingunn Røren printed this allegation as 'a fact'. Later enquiries revealed that the woman told police that the alleged murder threat was made by the Englishman in a letter which was "given to the Bergen police". The Bergen police told the Drammen police they had no such letter. Of course, the allegation is false and designed to cause much trouble to the Englishman, if not to ruin him.

Such a malicious allegation is surely provocation enough for the Englishman to be able to acquaint the Norwegian public with the truth of the girl's past so they knew the background of a woman making such allegations against him, via her national and local press. The Englishman had no other means to reply.

15. Besides which the Norwegian woman has admitted to the Drammen police that even after making allegations of attempted rape and threats to murder a 2 year old against the Englishman, she still proceeded in 1988 to request the Englishman's help in restraining the abusive father of her child. No woman in her right mind asks an alleged rapist and alleged potential child killer over to help her. The fact is that the father of her child assaulted her in 1990 and he was reported to the police.

16. In 1990, August, the Norwegian woman resumed a cosy friendship with the Englishman even sending him postcards and letters and Christian literature.

17. The Englishman believes the woman is a lunatic who far from being the "innocent victim" as portrayed by her xenophobic press, is a calculating, scheming opportunistic liar with little regard for normal standards of civilised behaviour.

18. The former Drammens Tidende journalist Ingunn Røren in on record as having given perjured evidence to the Norwegian Press Complaints Commission; facts presently with the Drammen City Court.

19. In England, Newspapers print the name of their victims if they've got their facts right. The extensive cover-up by the Norwegian establishment is a permanent stain on its reputation.

CONVERSATION BETWEEN PLAINTIFF AND JOURNALIST MRS REIDUN J. SAMUELSEN ON 10TH APRIL 2002.

I telephoned the newspaper on 10th April 2002 as once they had seen my website they e-mailed my ISP to ask me to make contact:

Answer: Aftenposten
F. Yes, good afternoon. Have you got a journalist called Reidun Samuelsen?
Answer: Yes.......I'll try for you.
RS. Samuelsen
F. Oh hi there, you're Miss Samuelsen?
RS. Mrs. Samuelsen, yes.
F. Oh Mrs; Oh. Ok. Hi there um ....I understand you're doing a story on Heidi Schøne or want to.
RS. Yes that's right.
F. Well I'm the chap that's taking her to court.
RS. OK.
F. And I'm just wondering what your angle's going to be this time.
RS. I haven't written about this before.....Actually I haven't decided yet.....I'm in a phase where I'm collecting material...
F. There have already been some big stories on this in 1995....
RS. Yes, I know...
[And I related related briefly a little bit about Heidi's psychiatric past].
RS. For me the story here is not her past it's why are you writing [on the internet] about this?
F. Because the newspapers wrote about me.
RS. Is that how it all started?
F. Yes....she's made some pretty awful allegations against me...
RS. In public or...
F. Well to the police....and in public.....in the newspapers. She says I've threatened to kill her son....a terrible lie....kill her neighbours....She doesn't get on with her stepmother....you know the story on her stepmother because you've seen the website haven't you?
RS. I have seen the website, yes.
F. Have you been in touch with her?
RS. I've talked to her briefly but I'm gonna talk to her again, yes.
F. The thing is you see, she's supposed to be mentally ill....I mean she had her psychiatrist in court [and she talks about] how I rung her up asking what underwear she's wearing,[that] I've written to her saying that if she doesn't get pregnant then her breasts will fall off.....[that] I've written 400 obscene letters to her that she's thrown away....[that] I wrote a letter to her threatening to kill her son.....
RS. I...I'm not familiar with all of that stuff. What I've been seeing is the website. For us this is more of a - how can I say - an example of the use of the internet.
F. Well it's the abortion images isn't it....the pictures of the abortions that er....there's been a lot of complaints I understand...I mean have you seen the pictures?
RS. Yeah.
F. The thing is.....one of the main things about why I've been so upset is because your newspapers called me "the Muslim man". Bergens Tidende called me "the Muslim man" 18 times.
RS. I can't answer for what other newspapers have been writing about....the thing that I would like to ask you is why are you putting all these stories about Heidi into the public [domain]?
F. I'm putting it into the public because nobody....you see when the newspapers started this story off they are supposed to ring me for my side of the story OK....I know that from the PFU - and no one did - no one rang me.
RS. Now you are calling me so that's a good thing.

F. Huh?
RS. And now you are calling me so then I don't have to call you afterwards. That's a good thing.
F. I'm supposed to have my side of the story printed.
RS. Yes so please tell me why you are doing it.
F. Well, so that people know my side of the story. People don't know she's mentally ill you see....and I've taken her to court....and we're still in a legal process so....
RS. But you actually lost the last court case didn't you?
F. Well, I've appealed. The only reason I've lost is because I think it's more of a political decision.
RS. I see....[and later] For me I'm not very interested in - what can I say - printing the details here because it will be your word up against hers and... the important thing for me is that you chose to put it out in public by the internet and I guess you must see that this will affect her life....
F. My life has been affected too because of the rubbish that has been printed....I do not write letters threatening to kill two year children....I did not write 400 obscene letters to her....but the point is this - it's never going to go away is it? This story will never go away because it's basically something your newspapers should've apologized for once they knew that my story was true on Heidi....
RS. From my point of view that's not the most important thing here because I can know many bad things about a friend, a neighbour but the moment I put it out in public that's another [thing]....
F. But she put out in public - in the newspaper - that I've threatened to kill her son. Is that not...?
RS. Did they put your name in print or something?
F. No they didn't put my name....the main thing is that I'm Muslim....they don't care about my name. They care that I'm Muslim. You've seen the [newspaper] articles on the website ....You people in general do not like Muslims. I know that because I've spoken to enough Norwegians, OK. And the main thrust of the [May 1995 Bergens Tidende] article....they don't care what my name is....they know and want to attack me as a Muslim.
RS. I didn't know that you were a Muslim....[Obviously she hadn't in fact looked at my website for very long because the three 1995 newspaper articles were up there in Norwegian together with the English translations]....Nobody told me that and it doesn't matter for me....
[And later]:
F. You've got so many dishonest people up there [in Norway] and I've exposed them because I tape all my phone calls - I'm taping this phone call with you now just in case you....
RS. That's something you should have told me before we started.
F. Well, I don't do that, otherwise....I tape all my phone calls with the police, journalists....
RS. OK, I think I've got your side of the picture now and I don't think I need to talk to you anymore. OK.
F. OK but I'm warning you if you print anything bad then there'll be pretty tough consequences for you.
RS. So are you threatening me?
F. With a law suit, yeah. With a law suit. See, you've already changed your attitude so I can tell how sorry you feel for Heidi and your people over there but as I said, we'll get a photograph of you and put it up there [on the internet as I had already done for several of my other Norwegian adversaries] and....
RS. This is actually a threat.
F. Well it's not....putting a photograph of you [I was not allowed to finish]....
RS. It's a threat OK. I'm not talking to you anymore.
F. Well I'll talk to your boss then.
RS. Bye-bye.[And she put the phone down].

Aftenposten
NEWS FROM NORWAY
15th April 2002

Startet etter au pair-opphold for 20 år siden
Britisk muslim sjikanerer norsk kvinne på nettet

I 17 år har engelskmannen sjikanert kvinnen fra Drammens-området. Nå har han tatt Internett i bruk. - Han har tatt mange år av mitt liv, sier hun.

REIDUN J. SAMUELSEN

LES OGSÅ
Intime detaljer. Kvinnen ble kjent med briten da hun var au pair i England for rundt 20 år siden.

Det har aldri vært noe kjæreste-forhold mellom dem, men han oppfordret henne likevel å konvertere til islam for å gifte seg med ham under et besøk i Norge tre år senere. Hun avslo, og det var da det begynte. Siden har han truet henne direkte og spredt uriktig informasjon om henne via telefon og post.

-Han har gjort dette til sin livsgjerning. Han ser på meg som et usselt menneske som ikke er verdt noe. Samtidig er han besatt av meg, sier hun.

Engelskmannen har sendt ut e-poster der mottagerne oppfordres til å lese nettsidene han har laget. I tillegg har han faxet den samme meldingen til folk i den 38 år gamle kvinnens nærområde. Hensikten har vært å få så mange som mulig til gå inn på nettsidene der hun beskrives i grove ordelag.

Hun anklages for å være psykisk ustabil og for å ha levd et utsvevende liv. Engelskmannen lister opp hennes tidligere forhold, og smører tykt på med intime detaljer. Alt er rikt illustrert med bilder av 38-åringen. Han gjør også et poeng ut av at kvinnen skal ha fått utført selvbestemt abort.

"Sensurerte" bilder av aborterte fostre, er overskriften på e-posten som er sendt ut.

-Det har vært forferdelig, og det har gått på selvtilliten løs. Tidvis har jeg vært redd for livet mitt, sier kvinnen.

Den langvarige sjikanen har tatt på.

Ny anmeldelse
Ifølge engelskmannen har kvinnen rettet uriktige beskyldninger mot ham, både til politiet og til media. Han sier han har lagt informasjon om henne ut på Internett for at folk skal få høre hans del av historien.

I januar i år ble han dømt for ærekrenkelser mot kvinnen. Straffen ble en bot på 10000 kroner. Det var i etterkant av denne saken han for alvor tok Internett i bruk for å spre sjikanen. Det førte til en ny anmeldelse fra 38-åringen. Også lensmannsførstebetjent Torill Sorte ved Nedre Eiker, som vitnet i saken i januar, anmelder nå engelskmannen.

-Vi håper å få kjørt en ny sak mot ham, sier Sorte.

Hun blir hengt ut på nettsidene med fullt navn og adresse, og beskyldt for å ha avgitt falsk forklaring i rettssaken.

-Slike handlinger skal få konsekvenser, sier Torill Sorte. Hun er interessert i å få tilsendt e-poster og faxer han har spredt.

Aftenposten 15 April 2002

Started after an au pair job 20 years ago **British Muslim terrorises Norwegian woman on the Internet**

For 17 years an Englishman has terrorised a woman from the Drammen area. Now he has begun to use the Internet. "He has taken many years of my life," she says.

By Reidun J. Samuelsen

Intimate details. The women first became acquainted with the Brit when she was an au pair in England around 20 years ago.

Although they have never had a boyfriend-girlfriend relationship, he nevertheless urged her to convert to Islam in order to marry him during a visit he made to Norway three years later. She refused, and that was when it all started. Since then he has threatened her directly and spread erroneous information about her over the telephone and by means of letters.

"He has made this his goal in life. He regards me as a despicable and worthless person. Yet at the same time he is obsessed with me," she says.

The Englishman has sent out e-mails in which recipients are urged to read the web pages he has created. In addition, he has faxed the same message to people who live near the 38-year-old woman. His intention has been to get as many people as possible to visit the web pages where the woman is described in strong terms.

She is accused of being mentally unstable and of having lived a wild life. The Englishman lists her previous relationships, regularly citing intimate details. Everything is richly illustrated with photographs of the 38-year-old. He also makes a point of the fact that the woman is alleged to have had an abortion.

The title of the e-mail that has been issued is "Censured" Pictures of Aborted Foetuses.

"It's been terrible, and my self-confidence has taken a beating. At times I have feared for my life," says the woman.

The long period of harassment has taken its toll on the woman.

New report to the police
According to the Englishman, the woman has made incorrect allegations against him, both to the police and to the media. He says he has posted the information about her on the internet so that people can hear his side of the story.

In January of this year he was convicted of defamatory behaviour towards the woman, for which he was fined NOK 10,000. It was in the wake of this case that he began in earnest to use the internet to spread his campaign of harassment, which resulted in the 38-year-old reporting him to the police once again. Police officer Torill Sorte of Nedre Eiker Police Force, who was a witness in the case in January, has also reported the Englishman.

"We hope to bring a new case against him," says Ms Sorte.

She has been profiled on the web pages with her full name and address, and has been accused of making false statements in court.

"Actions of this nature require a reaction," says Torill Sorte. She is interested in receiving copies of e-mails and faxes that the man has spread.

Aftenposten
NEWS FROM NORWAY 15/04/02

Slik kan nettsjikane stanses

Et nytt EU-direktiv gjør det nå mulig å få stengt Internett-sider som inneholder sjikane.

REIDUN J. SAMUELSEN

Operatøren ansvarlig. - Et nytt direktiv, det såkalte e-handelsdirektivet, pålegger operatørene å ta større ansvar for nettsidene de er vertskap for, sier professor Jon Bing ved Institutt for rettsinformatikk, Universitetet i Oslo.

Dersom operatøren blir kjent med at innholdet kan være rettsstridig, blir man automatisk ansvarlig for det som står der. De nye bestemmelsene skal ha vært innført i lovs form i alle europeiske land innen februar. Etter at Aftenposten tok kontakt med operatøren Skymarket, der nettsiden mot Drammen-kvinnen lå, ble siden stengt etter få timer.

-Problemet er selvfølgelig at en som vil bruke Internett til å spre sjikane kan hoppe til en ny operatør som ikke er kjent med innholdet på sidene hans. Han kan også finne frem til operatører som ligger i land som ikke følger e-handelsdirektivet, sier Jon Bing.

Professoren mener folk selv kan gjøre en innsats for å stanse nettsider, ved å spore opp operatøren og tipse om at et nettsted kan være rettsstridig. Dette er en langt enklere prosess enn å gå via domstolene.

-Det er vanskelig å få stengt sider i utlandet gjennom en kjennelse, sier Bing.

Politiadvokat Erik Moestue i politiets datakrimsenter, Økokrim, sier at norske myndigheter ikke har mulighet til å gi pålegg i andre land.

Justisminister Odd Einar Dørum mener feltet krever oppmerksomhet. Regjeringen har gitt Datakrimutvalget, som ble nedsatt i januar, i oppdrag å undersøke om norsk straffelovs geografiske virkeområde er hensiktsmessig avgrenset når det gjelder ulovlig materiale på nettet. Utvalget skal dessuten vurdere om politiet har tilstrekkelig adgang til å kreve at slikt materiale fjernes.

Aftenposten 15 April 2002

English Translation

Internet harassment can be stopped in the following way

A new EU directive makes it possible to shut down web pages containing defamatory statements.

By Reidun J. Samuelsen

The host is liable. "A new directive, the so-called E-business Directive, orders web hosting providers to take greater responsibility for the web pages they host," says professor Jon Bing at the Norwegian Research Centre for Computers and Law at the University of Oslo.

If the web hosting provider is aware that the content may be illegal, he is automatically responsible for what may be found there. The new provisions are to be enacted in all European countries by February. When Aftenposten contacted Skymarket, the web hosting provider that hosts the web site containing information about the woman from Drammen, the site was closed in a matter of hours.

"The problem is of course that anyone wishing to use the internet to spread harassment can shift to another web hosting provider who is not familiar with the content on his pages. He may also find web hosting providers in countries who do not comply with the E-business Directive," says Jon Bing.

The professor is of the opinion that people themselves can make an effort to stop web pages by tracing the web hosting provider and inform him that a web site may be illegal. This is a far simpler process than going through the courts.

"It is difficult to shut down web sites overseas by means of a court ruling," says professor Bing.

Erik Moestue, a police lawyer at the computer crime centre in Økokrim, the Norwegian National Authority for Investigation and Prosecution of Economic and Environmental Crime, says that the Norwegian authorities have no opportunity to grant orders in other countries.

Odd Einar Dørum, the Norwegian minister of justice, feels that this area requires attention. The government has commissioned the Computer Crimes Committee, which was appointed in January, to investigate whether the Norwegian Criminal Law's geographical scope is appropriately delimited as regards illegal material on the internet. The committee shall also consider whether the police have sufficient opportunity to demand that such material be removed from web sites.

Drammens Tidende
Nettutgaven dt.no
26/10/03

Saksøker pågrepet i retten

Sjikane på nettet. Engelskmannen nøyer seg ikke lenger med å trakassere kvinnen direkte. På denne nettsiden kan hele verden lese de sjikanøse beskyldningene mot kvinnen.

Engelskmannen som i snart 20 år har trakassert en Nedre Eiker-kvinne, saksøkte henne for ærekrenkelser. I retten ble han pågrepet, siktet for grov sjikane på Internett.

45-åringen, som ble kjent med Nedre Eiker-kvinnen da hun i sin ungdom var au pair i England har forfulgt og trakassert henne i 18 år. Høsten 2001 ble han idømt en bot på 10 000 kroner, men betalte ikke.
Engelskmannen saksøkte i stedet kvinnen for ærekrenkelse, fordi hun fortalte sin historie i mediene. Sist uke var sivilsaken oppe i lagmannsretten, men før engelskmannen rakk å forlate Tinghuset i Drammen ble han pågrepet. Bakgrunnen for pågripelsen var nye, alvorlige tilfelle av trakassering, blant annet beskyldninger lagt ut på Internett.

Cashet ut bøtene. 45-åringen ble fremstilt for varetektsfengsling, og kom med full tilståelse. Det åpnet for pådømmelse i forhørsretten. Mannen fremsto som en angrende synder, og uttalte at han forsto at han hadde utsatt kvinnen for mye vondt.
Tingrettsdommer Erik Stillum mente passende straff var åtte måneders betinget fengsel, på følgende vilkår: All informasjon om Nedre Eiker-kvinnen som er lagt ut på Internett skal slettes, nettsiden der sjikanen ligger skal fjernes og innholdet skal ikke republiseres i noen form. Videre får ikke 45-åringen lov å på noen måte ta kontakt med kvinnen, ei heller på noen måte formidle opplysninger om henne til tredjepersoner (f. eks. aviser). I tillegg fikk mannen en bot på 10 000 kroner.
Engelskmannen godtok dommen på stedet, og velvillig gikk han i minibanken sammen med politiet og cashet ut både den nye og gamle boten, altså 20 000 kroner tilsammen. Deretter forlot han landet frivillig.
- En fornuftig dom, og en god løsning på hele saken, mente advokat Svein Duesund, som ble oppnevnt som mannens forsvarer i forhørsretten.

Vurderer omgjøring. Fredag gikk Drammens Tidende inn på nettsiden, som på ingen måte er slettet. Det sjikanøse innholdet ligger der fortsatt. Engelskmannen har bare byttet ut Nedre Eiker-kvinnens egentlige navn med et fiktivt navn, og sladdet øynene hennes på bilder som er lagt ut. Politiadvokat Ingunn Hodne i Søndre Buskerud politidistrikt har også registrert at nettsiden er operativ.
- Vi vurderer å sende dommen til omgjøring. Han har allerede brutt vilkårene, sier Hodne. Politiadvokaten hadde et lite håp om at mannen skulle gi seg nå, siden angeren han ga uttrykk for i retten var nye toner. Begjæres dommen omgjort, vil Hodne påstå ubetinget fengsel. Mannen stevnes da for hovedforhandling via engelsk politi, og pålegges å møte i retten. Gjør han ikke det, kan det utstedes uteblivelsesdom. Ifølge Hodne vil det bli en vurdering om hvorvidt han skal begjæres utlevert til Norge for hovedforhandling her i landet, eller om saken skal oversendes til England for pådømmelse der.
- Hvis vilkårene er brutt, kan saken bringes inn for omgjøring. Men jeg kan ikke fastlå at vilkårene er brutt, sier advokat Svein Duesund.

Herborg Bergaplass

Drammens Tidende 26 October 2003

English Translation

Plaintiff arrested in court

By Herborg Bergaplass

An Englishman who had persecuted a woman from Nedre Eiker for more than 20 years sued her for libel. While in court, he was arrested and charged with severe persecution on the internet. The 45-year-old man, who made the acquaintance of the woman from Nedre Eiker when she was a young au pair in England, has harassed and persecuted her for 18 years. In the autumn of 2001, he was sentenced to pay a fine of NOK 10,000, which he did not pay. Instead the Englishman sued the woman for libel, because she had told her story to the media. Last week the civil case was heard in the Court of Appeal, but before the Englishman had time to leave the courthouse in Drammen he was arrested. The background for his arrest was new, severe instances of persecution, including allegations posted on the internet. Withdrew cash to pay fines. The 45-year-old was remanded in custody, where he made a full confession, which opened for sentencing in the court of examination and summary jurisdiction. The man appeared as a repentant sinner, and stated that he understood that he had subjected the woman to a lot of pain. Erik Stillum, the municipal court judge, felt that a suitable punishment would be eight months' conditional imprisonment, under the following terms: All information about the woman from Nedre Eiker that has been posted on the internet is to be deleted, the web page where the persecution appears shall be removed and the content shall not be republished in any form. Furthermore, the 45-year-old is not permitted to have any form of contact with the woman, nor shall he in any way communicate information about her to third parties (e.g. newspapers). In addition, the man was sentenced to pay a fine of NOK 10,000. The Englishman accepted the verdict on the spot, and willingly went to a cashpoint machine together with the police and withdrew funds to pay both the new and the old fine, i.e. NOK 20,000 in total, after which he left the country of his own accord. "A reasonable verdict, and a good solution to the whole case," said Svein Duesland, who was appointed defending counsel for the man in the court of examination and summary jurisdiction. Alteration of terms under consideration. On Friday, the staff of Drammens Tidende accessed the web site, which in no way has been deleted. The harassing content is still there. The Englishman has merely changed the to a fictitious name the real name of the woman from Nedre Eiker, and covered up her eyes on the pictures posted on the internet. Ingunn Hodne, the police lawyer in Søndre Buskerud Police Force, has also noted that the web site is still operative. "We will consider applying for an alteration of the terms of the judgment. He is already in breach of the terms," says Ms Hodne. The police lawyer had hoped that the man would give up now, since the regret he showed in court represented a change of tone. If a petition is lodged to have the judgment altered, Ms Hodne will claim that he be sentenced to unconditional imprisonment. The man will then be summoned to a main hearing via the British police, and will be ordered to appear in court. If he fails to do so, a judgment by default may be delivered. According to Ms Hodne, it will be decided whether a request will be issued for his extradition from the UK to attend the main proceedings in Norway, or whether the case will be transferred to England for sentencing there. "If he is in breach of the terms of the judgment, the case can be brought before the court for alteration. However, I cannot ascertain whether the terms have been breached," says advocate Svein Duesland.

Forkastet ærekrenkelse-anke

Lagmannsretten forkastet anken fra engelskmannen (45) som i årevis har trakassert en Nedre Eiker-kvinne, og som saksøkte henne for ærekrenkelser.
Engelskmannen er to ganger dømt for trakassering av kvinnen. 45-åringen har sendt henne hundrevis av brev, ringt henne utallige ganger, og sendt "rapporter" med diverse beskyldninger om henne til flere aviser og andre instanser i Norge. Nedre Eiker-kvinnen traff mannen da hun for over 20 år siden var au pair i England. Forholdet tok slutt, og trakasseringen begynte.
Etter at kvinnen fortalte sin historie i Drammens Tidende og andre norske aviser, svarte mannen med å saksøke henne for ærekrenkelser og krevde 50 000 kroner i oppreisning. Han vant ikke fram i tingretten, og ble dømt til å betale saksomkostninger. 45-åringen anket til Borgarting lagmannsrett, og i oktober møttes partene i tinghuset i Drammen.
- Min klient er godt fornøyd med at tingrettens dom er stadfestet, og at mannen er dømt til å betale saksomkostninger, sier kvinnens prosessfullmektig, advokat Vegard Aaløkken.

Pågrepet i retten. Innen 14 dager fra dommen er forkynt, må engelskmannen betale saksomkostninger på tilsammen 105 000 kroner.
Han ble forøvrig pågrepet av politiet straks forhandlingene i lagmannsretten var over, siktet for nye tilfelle av grov trakassering, denne gang på Internett. 45-åringen ble fremstilt for varetektsfengsling, og fremsto i fengslingsmøte som en angrende synder. Han erkjente sjikanen mot kvinnen, og det endte med pådømmelse der og da. Dommeren mente åtte måneders betinget fengsel var passelig, med vilkår at all informasjon om kvinnen på Internett skulle slettes.

Brøt vilkårene. Alt han gjorde var å gi kvinnen et fiktivt navn på nettsiden. Det holder ikke for politiet.
Politiadvokat Ingunn Hodne ved Søndre Buskerud politidistrikt kommer etter alt å dømme til å begjære dommen omgjort. Hodne opplyser til Drammens Tidende at hun ikke har rukket å vurdere saken ennå, men kommer til å gjøre det om kort tid.

Herborg Bergaplass
herborg.bergaplass@dt.no

Drammens Tidende 18 November 2003

English Translation

Libel appeal dismissed

By Herborg Bergaplass

The court of appeal has dismissed an appeal by a 45-year-old Englishman who for years has harassed a woman from Nedre Eiker, and who had sued her for libel.

The Englishman has twice been convicted of harassing the woman. The 45-year-old has sent her hundreds of letters, telephoned her countless times, and sent "reports" containing various allegations about her to several newspapers and other entities in Norway. The woman from Nedre Eiker met the man when she was an au pair in England over 20 years ago. When their relationship ended, the harassment began. And when the woman told her story to Drammens Tidende and other Norwegian newspapers, the man responded by suing her for libel and demanding NOK 50,000 in compensation for non-pecuniary damages. He lost the case in the municipal court, and was ordered to pay costs. The 45-year-old appealed to Borgarting Court of Appeal, and in October the parties met in the courthouse in Drammen.

"My client is pleased that the verdict delivered by the municipal court has been upheld, and that the man has been ordered to pay court costs," says the woman's lawyer, advocate Vegard Aaløkken.

Arrested in court. No later than 14 days after service of the verdict, the Englishman is required to pay court costs totalling NOK 105,000. He was arrested by the police immediately after the proceedings in the court of appeal were concluded and he was charged with new cases of severe persecution, this time on the internet. The 45-year-old was brought before the court for a remand hearing, and appeared to be a repentant sinner. He pleaded guilty to harassing the woman, and was sentenced there and then. The judge felt that eight months' conditional imprisonment was appropriate, on condition that all information posted on the internet about the woman be deleted.

Terms breached. All he did was to give the woman a fictitious name on the web site, which is not enough for the police.

Ingunn Hodne, police lawyer at Søndre Buskerud Police Force, will apparently file for an alteration of terms. Ms Hodne says to Drammens Tidende that she has not had time to consider the case yet, but will do so shortly.

Sexjages av gal brite

I 23 år har Heidi Schøne (41) vært sextrakassert av mannen hun traff da hun var 18. Nå bruker han nettet som terrorvåpen.

NETTSJIKANE: På dette nettstedet driver briten sjikane av Heidi Schøne (innfelt). Tross at han i 2003 ble dømt til å fjerne nettsidene, ligger de fremdeles på nett.

SPERRET: Flere norske nettsteder, blant dem Aftenposten og Dagbladet, har de siste dagene sperret sine servere for britens IP-adresse. Her faksimile av innlegg han hadde på VG Nett.

Faksimile: DB.no

MORTEN ØVERBYE

Tirsdag 20.12.2005, 10:08

(Dagbladet.no) I går sperret Aftenposten.no sine nettsider for den halvt arabiske, muslimske briten; etter at han hadde oversvømmet deres blogger med innlegg. Også flere andre norske nettaviser har blitt nedrent av innlegg fra mannen.

- Han har fått tatt alt for mange år av mitt liv. Det er det som er så tragisk. Han har forfulgt meg i 23 år. Han hadde forfulgt en annen norsk jente også, midt oppe i alt dette, sier Schøne til Dagbladet.no. For henne startet marerittet da hun som 18 år gammel aupair møtte en halvt arabisk brite på en båtreise mellom Frankrike og England. Hun var på tur med en venninne, da hun la merke til en fem-seks år eldre mann som kikket på henne.

- Jeg synes det var litt ubehagelig, så jeg stakk av. Men da vi stod i køen for å gå ombord, var han der igjen og prikket meg i skulderen. Vi gikk langt innover for å sette oss. Men jammen kom han ikke etter og satte han seg der også. Den merkelige mannen var påtrengende, men likevel hyggelig selskap for de to venninnene under turen.

Etter turen holdt de kontakten.

- Vi var aldri kjærester. Men jeg lot ham jo komme på besøk noen ganger etterhvert. Jeg synes synd på ham så han fikk lov til å feire nyttårsaften med oss, sier Schøne.

Under tiden i Storbritannia, ble han stadig mer pågående.

- Jeg var bare 18 år den gangen. Jeg visste ikke hva jeg har gjort ham. Det eneste jeg hadde gjort, var at jeg ikke ville gifte meg med fyren. Jeg ville ikke bli muslim.

Terrorisert

Hun ville ikke ha mer kontakt med ham da hun senere flyttet hjem til Norge. Da dukket han opp.

- Han var veldig manipulerende. Om jeg ikke slapp ham inn, laget han helvete og banket på døren til naboene. Han bombarderte meg hele tiden med telefoner og brev. Der fortalte han hvor dum og stygg jeg var, sier Schøne.

Terroriseringen varte helt frem til 1992. Da ble mannen tvangsinnlagt på psykiatrisk sykehus i Storbritannia. En norsk polititjenestemann som etterforsket saken, forklarte senere at det var hans mor som fikk ham tvangsinnlagt.

Da han kom ut igjen to år senere, fortsatte det - verre enn noen gang.

Han begynte å sende andre mennesker brev om Schøne. Alt oversatt til flytende norsk. Hundretalls brev ble sendt til alle fra Den nationale scene i Bergen, til det lokale lensmannskontoret, naboer, venner og kjente. Alle brevene med intime påstander om kvinnen.

Gikk til sak, fikk bot

Da hun gikk ut i avisene med historien, kom han til Norge for å saksøke henne.

Istedet ble han selv dømt.

I november 2001 fikk han bot på 10.000 kroner. Herredsretten bemerket at straffen var svært mild. Men fordi han var bosatt i England, valgte retten å gi ham bot. Han betalte ikke.

I februar 2002 ble Heidi Schøne frifunnet i sivilsaken i Drammen tingrett, men engelskmannen anket til lagmannsretten.

I november 2003 tapte han det sivile søksmålet i også lagmannsretten. Da hadde han i mellomtiden - i oktober samme år - blitt arrestert og på ny bøtelagt. I herredsretten fremstod han som en angrende synder. Etter full tilståelse fikk briten åtte måneders betinget fengsel og nok en bot på 10.000 kroner.

I tillegg lovte han å ta ned nettsidene der han spredte sjikanen.

Briten godtok dommen på stedet, fulgte med politiet til en minibank der han tok ut 20.000 kroner og satte seg deretter på flyet til England. Deretter fortsatte han som før.

Anker til Haag

Da han tapte det sivile søksmålet også i lagmannsretten, anket han til Høyesterett - som i mars 2004 avviste saken. På sine nettsider sier briten nå at han vil anke saken helt til menneskerettsdomstolen i Haag.

Samtidig fortsetter han sjikanen på internett.

- Det som er verst - ikke bare for meg, men for alle som opplever det - er hvor lite samfunnet reagerer på det. Det er sykt hvordan han bare kan fortsette, sier Schøne.

- I andre land er det mye strengere lover. Hadde dette vært i England, hadde han fått en skikkelig smell. Her får han slippe med bot gang etter gang, sier hun.

PS! Også en politikvinne som ledet etterforskningen av briten, blir nå sjikanert med navn på hans nettsider.

Dagbladet.no Home news

English Translation

Sexually pursued by mad Briton

For 23 years, Heidi Schøne (41) has been sexually harassed by the man she met when she was 18. Now he is using the Net as a weapon of terror.

MORTEN ØVERBYE

Tuesday 20.12.2005, 10:08updated 10:30

(Dagbladet.no) Yesterday Aftenposten.no closed its Internet pages to the half-Arab, Muslim Briton, after he had swamped their blogs with contributions. Several other Norwegian online newspapers have also been overrun by contributions from the man.

He has succeeded in taking too many years of my life. That is what is so tragic. He has pursued me for 23 years. He had pursued another Norwegian girl as well, right in the middle of all this, Schøne told Dagbladet.no.

For her the nightmare began when as an 18 year old au pair she met a half-Arab Briton on a boat trip between France and England. She was travelling with a girlfriend when she noticed a five-six years older man looking at her.

I felt a little uncomfortable, so I moved away. But when we were queueing to embark, he was there again and tapped me on the shoulder. We went a long way in to sit down. But of course he followed and sat down there as well.

The strange man was persistent but all the same pleasant company for the two girlfriends during the trip.

After the trip, they stayed in contact.

We were never going out. But I did let him visit occasionally as time went by. I felt sorry for him so he was allowed to celebrate New Year's Eve with us, says Schøne.

During the time in the UK , he became increasingly persistent.

I was only 18 at the time. I did not know what I had done to him. The only thing I had done was that I did not want to marry the guy. I did not want to become a Muslim.

Terrorized

She did not want to have any further contact with him when she later moved back to Norway . He then turned up there.

He was extremely manipulative. If I didn't let him in, he created hell and pounded on the neighbours' doors. He bombarded me with telephone calls and letters the whole time. In these he told me how stupid and nasty I was, says Schøne.

The terrorizing continued right up to 1992. The man was then committed to a psychiatric hospital in the UK. A Norwegian police official who investigated the case explained later that it was his mother who had him committed.

When he came out again two years later, it carried on worse than ever.

He began to send other people letters about Schøne. All translated into fluent Norwegian. Hundreds of letters were sent to everybody from Den Nationale Scene in Bergen to the local bailiff's office, neighbours, friends and acquaintances, all the letters containing intimate statements about the woman.

Took legal action, was fined

When she went to the newspapers with the story, he came to Norway to bring a legal action against her.

Instead he himself was punished.

In November 2001, he was fined NOK 10,000. The District Court observed that the punishment was very mild. But the court chose to fine him because he was resident in England. He never paid.

In October 2003, he lost the civil action in the Court of Appeal, where he himself was arrested and fined again. He then appeared as a repentant sinner. After a full confession in the magistrate's court, the Briton was given a suspended eight month sentence and again fined NOK 10,000.

In addition, he promised to remove the Internet pages where he was conducting the persecution.

The Briton accepted the judgement on the spot, accompanied the police to a cash dispenser where he withdrew NOK 20,000 and then boarded the plane to England. Then he carried on as before.

Appealing to The Hague

When he lost the civil action in the Court of Appeal as well, he appealed to the Supreme Court which dismissed the case in March 2004. On his Internet pages, the Briton says that he wants to appeal the case all the way to the court of human rights in The Hague.

At the same time he is continuing the persecution on the Internet.

The worst thing not just for me but for everybody who is living through it – is how little society reacts to it. It is crazy how he can simply continue, says Schøne.

In other countries, there are much stricter laws. If it had been in England, he would have been punished properly. Here he is allowed to get off with a fine time after time, she says.

PS! A policewoman who conducted the investigation into the Briton is now being persecuted by name on his Internet pages.

Øks. Drepe. Kamp. Spionasje. Krig.

Dette er ordene hun søkte etter i e-postene

SIDE 4, 5 OG 6

Monica Kristensen Solås

Foto: Torbjørn Rønning

Dagbladet

Onsdag 21. desember 2005 Nr. ??? Uke ??. 137. årgang. Løssalg kr 10,00

Maria Mena

Foto: Elisabeth Sperre Alnes

- Har aldri hatt det SÅ BRA

SIDE 32 OG 33

Oslo - Haugsund **BILLIGST via London**

SIDE 12 OG 13

REISE-SIDER

SIDE 24-27

Jaget av SEX-GAL mann i 23 år

SIDE 10 OG 11

«Han har holdt sitt løfte om å ødelegge livet mitt.»

HEIDI SCHØNE (41)

Foto: Privat

TIPSTELEFON 22 20 00 00 SMS OG MMS TIL 1937 (merk sendingen med tips) MAIL/DIGITALFOTO TIL 1000tipset@dagbladet.no

Dagbladet 21 December 2005

Pursued by SEX-MAD man for 23 years

PAGES 10 AND 11

"He has kept his promise to ruin my life." HEIDI SCHØNE (41)

SEXUALLY harassed for 23 years

23 years ago, Heidi Schøne (41) met a half-Arab Briton on a boat trip between France and England . Since then her life has been a nightmare.

Words: Morten Øverbye

morten@dagbladet.no

Anders Holth Johansen

ahj@dagbladet.no

In recent days, the Briton has swamped online newspapers' blogs with malicious contributions to such an extent that the major Norwegian online newspapers have been forced to block the man's access. But threats and accusations are nothing new for Heidi Schøne. She has lived with them for the last 23 years.

"It has been a nightmare, but now I am not so scared any more. Now I am more angry at society which did not take the signs seriously early enough," says Schøne.

The threats and the harassment have been a strain for her whole family. Today she is divorced and has two children.

"I had a small child he thought should die. In other countries, he would have been punished severely for that kind of threat," says Schøne.

Several letters a day

The sexual harassment has continued regularly for the last 23 years.

"New letters with "Fuck You!" written on them in red were constantly coming through the letter box. The number of letters varied with his mood. I could receive three or four letter a day," says Schøne.

In the end, the post office agreed to sort out the letters from the man. But the mad Briton could not be stopped. He got others to send letters for him and to phone. Friends and colleagues also received letters and faxes containing intimate statements.

"At times he sought me out frequently. Suddenly he could be there outside my window," says Heidi Schøne.

The nightmare began when as an 18 year old au pair she met the half-Arab Briton on a boat trip between France and England . She was travelling with a girlfriend when she noticed the five-six years older man looking at her.

The strange man was persistent but all the same pleasant company for the two girlfriends during the trip. After the trip, they stayed in contact.

"We were never going out. But I did let him visit occasionally as time went by. I felt sorry for him so he was allowed to celebrate New Year's Eve with us," says Schøne.

During the time in the UK , he became increasingly persistent.

"I was only 18 at the time. I did not know what I had done to him. The only thing I had done was that I did not want to marry the guy. I did not want to become a Muslim."

Committed

She did not want to have any further contact with him when she later moved back to Norway . Then he turned up.

"He was extremely manipulative. If I didn't let him in, he created hell and pounded on the neighbours' doors. He bombarded me with telephone calls and letters the whole time. In these he told me how stupid and nasty I was," says Schøne.

The terrorizing continued right up to 1992. His mother then arranged for him to be committed to a psychiatric hospital in the United Kingdom . When he came out again two years later, it carried on – worse than ever.

He began to send other people letters about Heidi Schøne. All translated into fluent Norwegian. Hundreds of letters were sent to everybody from Den Nationale Scene in Bergen to the local bailiff's office, neighbours, friends and acquaintances, all the letters containing intimate statements about the woman.

"He wants people to dislike me, and he can be very good at persuading people," says Schøne.

Took legal action

In 1999, the Briton took action against Heidi Schøne for libel because she had been interviewed about the situation. That ended with the man himself having to pay NOK 10,000 for invasion of privacy.

In its judgement of 14 November 2003 , Borgarting Court of Appeal stated that "Overall, the case appears to be a misuse of the legal system". The Court thought that there was overwhelming documentary evidence of sexual harassment and ordered the Briton to pay NOK 104,585 in costs.

Insulting web page

The man has a web page which is intended to reveal " Norway 's exotic, erotic and extremely psychotic mentality". The web page contains a series of gross lies about Heidi Schøne's intimate life.

The man has been ordered to delete all information about Heidi Schøne from his web pages. He has not done so.

"I am not afraid of him any more. But I don't understand why we in Norway do not take this more seriously. This is about human life after all," says Schøne.

Captions:

INTERNET HARASSMENT: On this web site, the Briton carries on harassment of Heidi Schøne (inset). In spite of the fact that he was ordered to remove the web pages in 2003, they are still on the Internet.

NIGHTMARE: Since Heidi Schøne (41) met the Briton 23 years ago, he has been obsessed with her and has sent hundreds of letters with intimate statements about the woman, both to her and to those around her.

"He wants people to dislike me, and he can be very good at persuading people."

Heidi Schøne (41), persecuted.

Investigator was also harassed

Police inspector Torill Sorte of Nedre Romerike police district was the investigator in the case against the Briton. Then she herself was harassed.

"It finally ended with me having to ask to be taken off the case, because I myself wanted to report the man," says Sorte.

"There were faxes and e-mails which said I was mad and that I am a liar. It was quiet for a while but he has started again in recent weeks," says Sorte.

The man has today been ordered to stay away from the police inspector.

Fortsetter trakassering av politikvinne

Av Roy Hansen, 11.01.06

Engelskmannen [redacted] fortsetter trakasseringen av norske kvinner. Etter å ha sjikanert Heidi Schøne fra Solbergelva i en årrekke, går han nå løs på politiførstebetjent Torill Sorte ved Nedre Eiker lensmannskontor.

Politiførstebetjent Torill Sorte ved Nedre Eiker lensmannskontor har den siste tiden blitt utsatt for sjikane gjennom DTs nettsider.

Gjennom en rekke «innlegg» på Drammens Tidendes nettsider den siste tiden har engelskmannen fortsatt sin hets mot politiførstebetjent Torill Sorte ved Nedre Eiker lensmannskontor. Dette skjer blant annet ved at han legger ut link til en internettside han er dømt til å fjerne fra nettet så sent som 17. oktober 2003. Nå lover DTs nettansvarlig, Lars Lager Espevalen at de skal overvåke sidene sine bedre for å slette uønskede innlegg så fort som mulig.

- Mannen har plaget Heidi Schøne og familien hennes siden 1982, og det har vist seg å være meget vanskelig å stoppe ham, sier Torill Sorte. I 2003 var hun etterforskningsleder i saken som endte opp med en dom på to år betinget fengsel og en bot for grov sjikane i Eiker, Modum og Sigdal Tingrett. Siden den gang har den muslimske mannen også lagt politietterforskeren for hat.

Sendte fakser
En rekke offentlige instanser, aviser og media, samt private virksomheter har mottatt fakser fra mannen om hennes engasjement i saken, og det er lite flatterende det han skriver om henne. – Jeg takler dette og vet at jeg ikke har gjort noe galt i sakens anledning. Selv ikke en intern granskning har avdekket noe galt, sier Sorte.

Hun tar likevel sjikanen gjennom DTs nettsider alvorlig fordi de er lett tilgjengelige og på grunn av det faktum at mannen er dømt til å fjerne sidene fra nettet. Dessuten er sjikane et økende problem i samfunnet, der Nedre Eiker ikke er noe unntak.

Vanskelige saker
- Sjikanesaker er vanskelige saker fordi det skal mye til for at vi kan reise en tiltale. Som regel skjer sjikanen ved samlivsbrudd, og selv om vi kan ilegge bøter hjelper det sjeldent, sier hun. Nedre Eiker lensmannskontor behandler i snitt 25 – 30 slike saker i året, men få er så graverende som saken mot engelskmannen.

- Det er flere former for sjikane, og dersom det for eksempel er en forsmådd ektemann som sender tekstmeldinger til sin eks, stopper det sjeldent selv om det ilegges bøter. Er det derimot snakk om ærekrenkelser og plagsom atferd som involverer flere personer er det litt lettere å få idømt en reaksjon, sier Torill Sorte.

Tar opp saken
Hun vil nå ta sjikanesaken mot seg selv opp med ledelsen for Søndre Buskerud Politidistrikt. I fjor sommer hadde engelskmannen sendt telefaks til politidirektoratet, og denne ble videresendt gjennom tjenestevei til henne for kommentar. Selv om hun sier at det ikke plager henne personlig, vil Torill Sorte at denne saken ikke skal få utvikle seg. Det er også etter det vi kjenner til tatt et initiativ overfor justisdepartementet om å få endret lovgivningen på dette området.

- Mannen er tydelig mentalt ustabil og må bruke utrolig mye tid og krefter, for ikke å snakke om penger, på å sjikanere Heidi Schøne og undertegnede, i tillegg til noen andre kvinner vi kjenner til. Dessverre er lovene slik at vi ikke kan begjære ham utlevert for videre straffeforfølgelse, sier Sorte.

(Publisert i Eiker Bladet 11.01.06)

Continuing the harassment of policewoman

By Roy Hansen, 11.01.06

Briton [........................] is continuing his harassment of Norwegian women. After having harassed Heidi Schøne from Solbergelva for years, he is now attacking police inspector Torill Sorte at Nedre Eiker police station.

The Briton has continued his smear-campaign against police inspector Torill Sorte at Nedre Eiker police station through a series of "contributions" made recently to Drammens Tidende's Internet pages. This takes the form of among other things him posting links to an Internet page he was ordered to remove from the Internet as recently as 17 October 2003 . DT's Internet head Lars Lager Espevalen is now promising that they will monitor their pages more closely in order to delete undesirable contributions as soon as possible.

"The man has plagued Heidi Schøne and her family since 1982, and it has proved very difficult to stop him," says Torill Sorte. In 2003, she led the investigation in the case which ended in a two year suspended sentence and a fine for severe harassment in Eiker, Modum and Sigdal district court. Since then, the Muslim man has also made the police investigator the object of his hatred.

Sent faxes

A number of public bodies, newspapers and media organizations as well as private businesses have received faxes from the man about her involvement in the case, and what he writes about her is not very flattering. "I deal with it and know that I did not do anything wrong in the matter. Not even an internal inquiry revealed anything wrong," says Sorte.

She nevertheless takes the harassment through DT's Internet pages seriously because they are easily accessible and owing to the fact that the man was ordered to remove the pages from the Internet. Harassment is moreover a growing problem in society, and Nedre Eiker is no exception.

Difficult cases

"Harassment cases are difficult cases because it takes a lot for us to be able to bring a prosecution. As a rule, the harassment occurs when relationships break down and, even though we can impose fines, this rarely helps," she says. Nedre Eiker police station handles 25-30 such cases a year on average, but few are as serious as the case against the Briton.

"There are several forms of harassment, and if, for example, it is a spurned husband who is sending text messages to his ex, it rarely stops even though fines are imposed. On the other hand, if it is a question of defamation and annoying behaviour which involves a number of people, it is a little easier to get a sanction imposed," says Torill Sorte.

Raising the issue

She now wants to raise the issue of harassment against herself with the administration of Southern Buskerud Police District. Last summer, the Briton sent a fax to the police directorate, and this was forwarded to her through official channels for comment. Even though she says that it is not bothering her personally, Torill Sorte does not want this matter to be allowed to develop. We also understand that an initiative has been put before the justice department aimed at having the legislation in this area changed.

"The man is obviously mentally unstable and must be putting an incredible amount of time and energy, not to mention money, into harassing Heidi Schøne and the undersigned, in addition to some other women we know about. Unfortunately, the laws are such that we cannot apply for him to be extradited for further criminal prosecution," says Sorte.

Engelskmann sjikanerer politikvinne

En engelskmann sjikanerer ei politikvinne via diskusjonsfora i flere norske nettaviser.

Av Morten W Røkeberg og Maria Kommandantvold . Publisert 13.06.2006 17:23

Politiførstebetjent Torill Sorte ved Nedre Eiker lensmannskontor anmelder nå en engelskmann som i flere år har trakassert henne.

Mannen har det siste halvåret skrevet krenkende innlegg på diskusjonsfora i flere norske nettaviser, med henvisning til sine egne hjemmesider.

Sorte håper at hun ved å anmelde ham, kan få mannen domfelt.

Chief Inspector Torill Sorte at Nedre Eiker district police office.

Photo: Maria Kommandantvold/NRK

An Englishman harasses a policewoman via the discussion fora in several Norwegian Internet newspapers.

By Morten W. Røkeberg and Maria Kommandantvold.

Published 13.06.2006 17:23

Chief Inspector Torill Sorte at Nedre Eiker district police office is now lodging an official complaint against an Englishman who has harassed her for several years.

Over the last half a year the man has written defamatory articles in the discussion fora in several Norwegian Internet newspapers, with references to his own homepages.

Sorte hopes that by lodging an official complaint against him, she can have him punished.

"Will not accept being harassed"

"This has, in fact, been going on for several years, while the harassment via Norwegian Internet newspapers has taken place since before the New Year. I do not believe that one should accept being harassed by other people without doing something about it."

"Do you believe it will help by lodging an official complaint against him?"

"I don't think so, but he will have a legal case brought against him at any rate, and hopefully he will receive a suitable punishment," says Sorte.

Found guilty of persecution

The man has previously been found guilty in this country of having persecuted another woman in the district. This woman got to know him in England in the 1980's. She took out a case against him and he was found guilty. Torill Sorte was the head of the investigation team in that case and she subsequently became a victim of his persecution. Initially through him telephoning to friends and acquaintances and sending letters but, since December last year, also persecution on the Internet.

"He accuses me of having written falsely in the case for which he was sentenced. He maintains that I am dishonest and corrupt," says Sorte.

Yesterday statements from this man were displayed on the Drammens Tidende discussion forum for a couple of hours, with reference to his Internet page on which he harasses several people in Norway . Sorte says that it is difficult to stop him because he constantly finds new ways round things.

Blocked Internet page

"We have blocked the Internet page but he constantly finds new ways of putting it out, so it is difficult to maintain control over such a page."

What can the police do?

"We can initiate an official complaint and take action in relation to it. The problem is that he does not live in this country and that makes things more complicated."

What do you known about him?

"I know a great deal about him. I know that he does not live here in this country and I know him through the investigation into the other matter."

What does this do to you?

"I have had many approaches from people who feel that this is awful, something that I really appreciate. Even though I am in the police, it has an affect on me that there are constantly unjustified assertions about me on the Internet," says Torill Sorte.

Error!

Sjikanerer politikvinne dt.no

En engelskmann bruker nettaviser til å sjikanere en politikvinne fra Nedre Eiker. Erik Modal

Politiførstebetjent Torill Sorte ved Nedre Eiker lensmannskontor anmelder nå en engelskmann som i flere år har trakassert henne. En av nettavisene engelskmannen hyppig bruker, er dt.no.

Mannen har det siste halvåret skrevet krenkende innlegg på diskusjonsfora i flere norske nettaviser, med henvisning til sine egne hjemmesider, melder NRK Buskerud.

Sorte håper at hun ved å anmelde ham, kan få mannen domfelt.

Politiførstebetjent Torill Sorte ved Nedre Eiker lensmannskontor anmelder nå en engelskmann som i flere år har trakassert henne. En av nettavisene engelskmannen hyppig bruker, er dt.no. Mannen har det siste halvåret skrevet krenkende innlegg på diskusjonsfora i flere norske nettaviser, med henvisning til sine egne hjemmesider, melder NRK Buskerud.Sorte håper at hun ved å anmelde ham, kan få mannen domfelt.

Pågått over flere år

Saken har pågått i flere år. Sjikaneringen gjennom norske nettaviser har pågått det seneste halvåret. Mannen er tidligere domfelt her i landet for å ha trakassert en annen kvinne i distriktet. Denne kvinnen ble kjent med ham i England på 1980-tallet. Hun gikk til sak mot ham, og han fikk en straff. Torill Sorte var etterforskningsleder i denne saken, og etter det har hun vært offer for hans trakasseringer.

- Han beskylder meg for å ha skrevet uriktig i den saken som han ble dømt i. Han mener da at jeg er uærlig og korrupt, sier Sorte til NRK.

Vanskelig å stoppe

Han bruker diskusjonsfora til å spre reklame for nettstedet. En av avisene som blir hyppig brukt, er Drammens Tidendes nettutgave dt.no. Sorte sier det er vanskelig å stanse ham fordi han finner nye omveier hele tiden. - Vi har sperret internettsiden, men han finner stadig nye måter å legge den ut på, så det er vanskelig å ha kontroll på en slik side, sier hun til kanalen. Problemet med å få slutt på trakasseringen, er at mannen ikke bor i Norge. Det gjør arbeidet med å stanse mannen vanskeligere.

dt.no gjør noe

Redaktør Lars Lager Espevalen i dt.no sier engelskmannen har misbrukt debattfunksjonen på dt.no og andre nettaviser i lengre tid. - Vi har iverksatt tiltak som har gjort mannens aktiviteter vanskeligere. Dette har vært viktig for oss, fordi navngitte enkeltmennesker er blitt krenket. Vi arbeider kontinuerlig med kvalitetssikring av denne delen av dt.no. Allerede i løpet av sommeren iverksettern

Bardot fined yet again for inciting racial hatred of Muslims

Brigitte Bardot: 'France is in a period of decadence'

BRIDGET BARDOT, the 1960s "sex kitten" French film star, was convicted yesterday of inciting racial hatred and ordered to pay £3,300 for her fourth such offence since 1997.

Last year, 69-year-old Bardot published a book called *A Cry in the Silence*, an outspoken attack on gays, immigrants and the jobless which shocked France. In it, she laments the "Islamisation of France" and the "underground and dangerous infiltration of Islam".

The court in Paris yesterday said: "Mme Bardot presents

BY THIERRY LEVEQUE
in Paris

Muslims as barbaric and cruel invaders, responsible for terrorist acts and eager to dominate the French to the extent of wanting to exterminate them."

France's five million-strong Muslim community is the largest in Europe. Bardot, an ardent animal rights campaigner, who was not present yesterday, denied the charges tearfully in court last month, saying her book did not target Islam or people from North Africa. She said France was in a period of decadence and said she opposed inter-racial marriage. "I was born in 1934, at that time inter-racial marriage wasn't approved of," she said.

"There are many new languages in the new Europe. Mediocrity is taking over from beauty and splendour. There are many people who are filthy, badly dressed and badly shaven."

In her book, she also attacks homosexuals as "fairground freaks", condemns the presence of women in government and denounces the "scandal of unemployment benefit". The court said she had presented Muslims as "invaders, barbaric and cruel, responsible for terrorist acts, wishing to subdue the French people to the point of extermination".

Two anti-racism groups launched legal proceedings against the former star, who turned her back on cinema after 46 films to concentrate on animal welfare. The fine is to be paid to them.

The court awarded a symbolic one euro in damages to France's anti-racism movement MRAP and to the League for Human Rights. It also sentenced the head of Bardot's publishing house, Le Rocher, to a similar £3,300 fine and ordered both to pay for advertisements in two newspapers announcing their conviction.

Bardot, in her heyday the epitome of French sexual allure, was fined £1,800 in January 1998 for inciting racial hatred in comments about civilian massacres in Algeria. Four months earlier, she was fined for saying that France was being overrun by sheep-slaughtering Muslims. *(Reuters)*

The Independent 11th June 2004

Anders Breivik's Unfinished War

What many non-Muslims fail to understand is that Islam accepts all the prophets and messengers of God that came before the Prophet Muhammad. The Prophet adored Abraham, Moses and Jesus Christ but added to their teachings when administering to the pagan Arabs. It was the irrational Christian hatred for another messenger in Muhammad that has so disrupted the equilibrium of World order since the advent of Islam - which simply means 'surrender to God'. The Crusaders embedded this vice for 200 years and it still resonates the world over: the Muslims are not like us.

Christians cannot stand the fact that the Jews do not recognise Jesus Christ as a man sent by God. But when the Christians are themselves asked about the Prophet Muhammad they do as the Jews do to them: they say Muhammad is an imposter. The Reverend Isaac Taylor in Brighton, England in 1903 wanted Christianity to accept and combine with Islam. He realised that this was a natural progression. Few others did, save perhaps Queen Victoria with the advice of her trusted man-servant Abdul Karim - and today her relative, Prince Charles: a personal friend of the late Sheikh Dr Sir Zaki Badawi, former senior imam at the Central London Mosque, Regent's Park and Principal of the Muslim College, who was an advisor to one particular British Prime Minister and several other politicians.

Today it is Norway who combine their pagan Viking heritage with their quasi-Christian Crusader mentality that is the root of so much enmity.

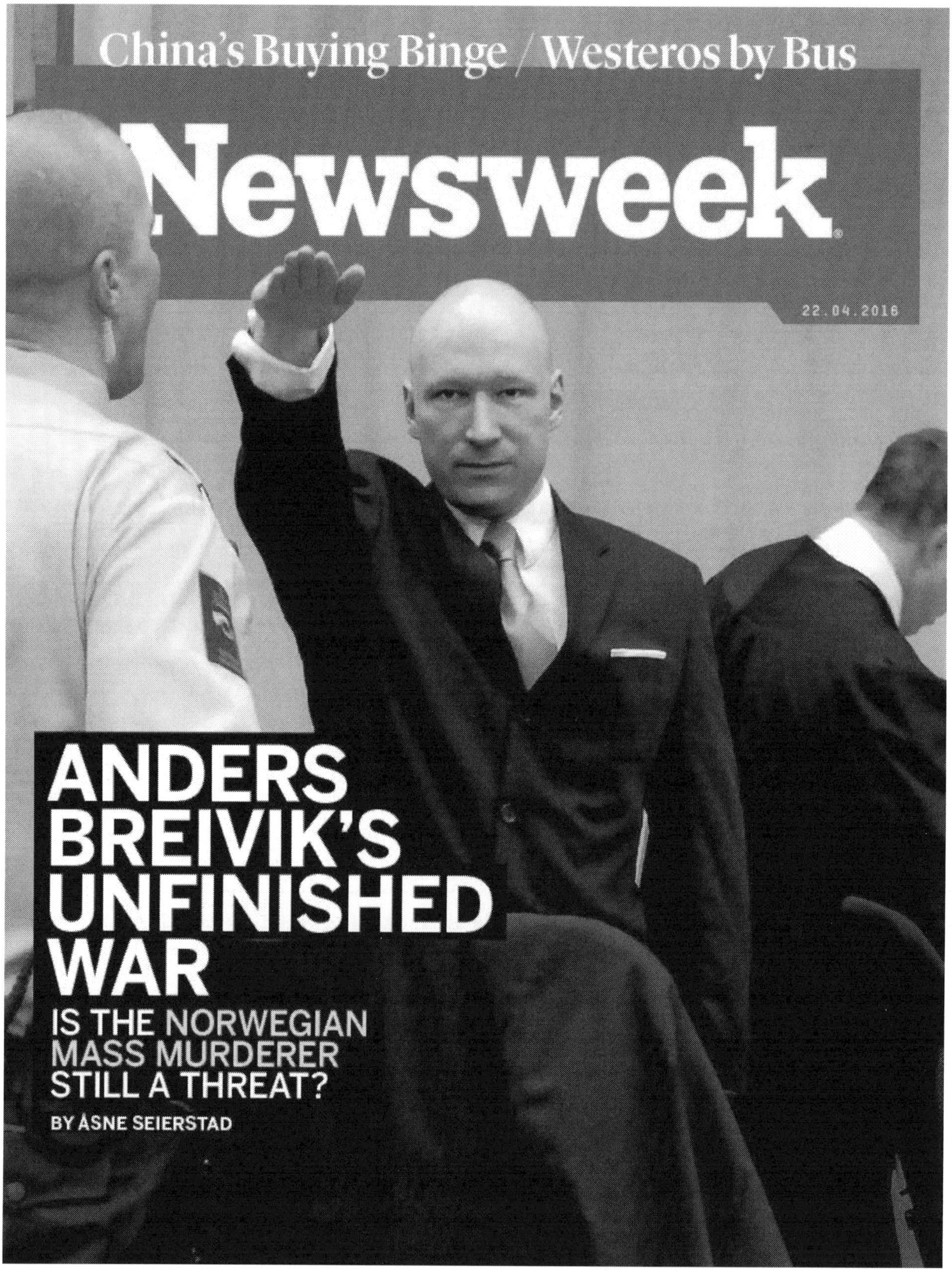
China's Buying Binge / Westeros by Bus
Newsweek
22.04.2016
ANDERS BREIVIK'S UNFINISHED WAR
IS THE NORWEGIAN MASS MURDERER STILL A THREAT?
BY ÅSNE SEIERSTAD

There now follows a Newsweek discussion of Anders Breivik, his motivations and his attitude towards the main obstacle in his life: Islam and its several million adherents.

PRESENT DANGER

IS ANDERS BREIVIK STILL A THREAT TO EUROPE? BY ASNE SEIERSTAD

NEWSWEEK 39 04/22/2016

AS ANDERS BEHRING BREIVIK ENTERED THE GYM TURNED COURT ROOM IN SKIEN PRISON, THE JAIL IN SOUTHERN NORWAY THAT HAS HELD HIM SINCE AUGUST 2013, A SMILE CROSSED HIS LIPS.

He waited eagerly for one of the four guards who stood next to him to unlock his handcuffs. He looked around to see who was in the gym: two dozen journalists and some prison officials. And then he looked in the direction of the journalists and raised his right arm in a Nazi salute. Breivik kept it there for nine long seconds. One of his two lawyers already had her back to the man who murdered 77 Norwegians on July 22, 2011. The second turned away as soon as he saw Breivik's arm go up.

Breivik's gaze was focused not on the people in the courtroom last month; he was looking at the cameras. Instantly, pictures and live footage of his Nazi salute were transmitted to news agencies around the world and shared online. Like his media-savvy brethren in the Islamic State militant group (ISIS), the 37-year-old Norwegian extremist, who wants to establish a party called the Nordic State, has long known that he needs to shock to get the world's attention. "I was wondering how many people I needed to kill to be read," he said after he had committed his acts of violence in 2011. He had calculated that he had to kill a dozen people to be noticed. He ended up killing many more; 33 of his victims were under 18.

Breivik later described his massacre as his "book launch." In a way, he was right: No one had been interested in reading his polemics before he placed a bomb outside the prime minister's office in downtown Oslo and later that day shot teenagers at a Labor Party youth camp on the island of Utøya, an hour's drive from the capital. Only then did thousands of people read, discuss and comment on his 1,500-page manifesto.

Breivik has not forgotten the power that comes from sparking outrage. This appearance in court in mid-March was not an appeal against his conviction; Breivik was suing the Norwegian state, claiming it was violating his human rights by holding him in isolation and preventing him from freely communicating with the outside world. The Norwegian authorities argue that he remains a threat and that solitary confinement is necessary to prevent him from inspiring or directing right-wing extremists eager to commit their own atrocities.

Even far from Norway, Breivik's supporters found comfort in seeing him perform the Nazi salute. "He is a hero of his people, and I cannot wait for his liberation from captivity at the hands of swine," says one supporter, Andrew Auernheimer, an American extremist who now lives in the breakaway republic of Abkhazia, in Georgia. "We all love and support him unconditionally. His lawsuit and Roman salute have only increased sympathy and appreciation for him."

Breivik's court appearance posed a fresh challenge to the Norwegian state. To uphold the country's democratic values, the authorities had to allow him to appear in court, knowing full well that the proceedings would be televised and that he would likely use the occasion to reach out to potential followers. Adele Matheson Mestad, a lawyer for the Norwegian state, told the court Breivik's ideology is especially dangerous right now because the large numbers of refugees entering Europe have given rise to an increase in right-wing activity on the continent. Were he able to communicate freely, Mestad said, Breivik could encourage sympathizers to commit acts of violence.

The court hearings were agonizing for survivors, for the families of the dead, for most Norwegians—and they raised an unsettling question: In an era of copycat extremist attacks and social media wannabes, would this court appearance make Breivik a greater threat?

'OUR ELITES ARE TRAITORS'

EUROPE IS becoming increasingly familiar with attacks by extremists, but Breivik's actions made him the deadliest lone wolf attacker in the continent's history. On the afternoon of July 22, 2011, he detonated a bomb outside the prime

+
LONE WOLF: Breivik is suing, claiming that keeping him in isolation violates his rights; authorities insist it is necessary because he is determined to recruit prisoners to his cause.

HANDS UP: Over 100,000 people rallied in downtown Oslo on the day Breivik made his first court appearance after being arrested for the massacre of 77 people.

minister's office in Oslo, killing eight people. Two hours later, wearing a police uniform he had made, he took a ferry to Utøya, site of the youth camp run by Norway's then-ruling Labor Party. There, he shot dead 69 people before police arrived on the island and arrested him.

Deeply troubled as a child, Breivik joined Norway's right-wing Progress Party at the age of 18 and then steadily moved further to the right. He began to read and engage with a range of white supremacist, neo-Nazi and anti-jihadi websites. These different sources of hate influenced his manifesto, an often contradictory mixture of ideas he cut and pasted from the internet, interspersed with some of his own thoughts. The general gist: Europe is being invaded by Muslims, and governments are doing nothing to stop this catastrophe; our elites are traitors who deceive us; if we don't react now, Europe will end up as an Islamic caliphate.

Breivik tried to make contact with right-wing ideologues online, but he struggled to find a sympathetic audience, so he started buying weapons and ammunition and rented a farm so he could buy hundreds of kilograms of fertilizer and other ingredients for a bomb. From the farm, in the dense forests by Sweden's border, he planned his attack on these so-called traitors, the political elites and their children. He wanted to spark a broad war in Europe that would end with the Christians finally defeating the Muslims. At that point, he anticipated all Muslims would be able to choose between deportation, converting to Christianity and changing their names, or death. All mosques would be demolished or used for other purposes; all Muslim artworks destroyed; and the use of Arabic, Farsi, Urdu and Somali would be banned.

During his trial, the court deliberated over whether Breivik

"I WAS WONDERING HOW MANY PEOPLE I NEEDED TO KILL TO BE READ."

SLOW RESPONSE TEAM: Before landing on Utøya, police stood on the shore opposite the island, some 600 yards away, listening to the gunshots as Breivik stalked and gunned down his victims.

was mentally ill and in need of treatment or whether he was a cold-blooded, rational mass killer. Some of the psychiatrists who evaluated Breivik diagnosed him as having narcissistic and antisocial personality disorder. (An earlier group of doctors said he suffered from schizophrenia.) In August 2012, the court sided with the second group and ruled that because he was not psychotic and had understood what he was doing, he was legally accountable for his actions. The judge in the case gave Breivik the maximum penalty for committing an act of terrorism—21 years, with a possible extension until the end of his life. As long as he is considered a danger to society, he can be kept in prison.

Almost as soon as Breivik's name became known after his arrest, extremists began lionizing him. His so-called manifesto, "2083 — A European Declaration of Independence," was seen as valuable reading material. Right-wing blogs and social media accounts frequently praised him. One of the best-known blogs in this small, dark corner of the internet, The Commander Breivik Report, dutifully recorded all news relating to the shooter and archived his letters, court transcripts and psychiatric reports.

Breivik was particularly popular in Russia. "Glory to Anders Breivik" was chanted in the nationalist movement's annual Russian March in central Moscow. Pictures of Breivik and his statements were shared extensively on the right-wing forums of VKontakte, Russia's largest social-networking website. Breivik was "a holy man" whose acts "lit up" the darkness, his fans wrote.

Less than a year after Breivik's attack, copycats emerged. In August 2012, Czech police arrested Vojtěch Mlýnek, who was planning a Breivik-style attack. In online posts and emails, he had used Breivik's name as a pseudonym. Three months later, Polish police arrested an admirer of Breivik who had planned to blow up Polish government buildings. In the U.K., four people inspired by Breivik were arrested between January 2013 and June 2015 on suspicion of planning or carrying out extremist attacks.

The admirers were not confined to Europe. On December 14, 2012, American Adam Lanza, 20, opened fire at the Sandy Hook Elementary School in Newtown, Connecticut. Lanza shot and killed 26 people, 20 of them young children, before he shot himself. Sources told CBS News that investigators had found evidence that

Lanza was "obsessed" with Breivik and wanted to top the Norwegian's toll.

But as the months and years passed, his acclaim faded. The last post on The Commander Breivik Report is from January 2015. Cut off from their hero, Breivik's fans began discussing other nationalist issues. Some shut down their blogs. Some sites were left without any updates.

The decline in adulation for Breivik online and in the material world was partly a result of the passage of time and partly a result of his increasingly limited ability to correspond with sympathizers. When he was first detained, he received hundreds of letters every month. Most were from right-wing extremists. A large number were from women who said they were in love with him. Several were from boys and girls who saw Breivik as their new hero.

For the first 12 months, prison officials let all the letters through. Then they realized Breivik was building a cult around himself. They asked the Norwegian Ministry of Justice to provide new guidelines on how to interpret laws, and starting in August 2012, prison officials began to censor Breivik's incoming and outgoing letters to prevent him from inspiring or directing any more crimes. He wrote to three leaders of the Aryan Brotherhood, a white supremacist prison gang in the U.S.; the letters never left the censor's desk. A letter from Nikolai Korolev, a Russian nationalist convicted in 2008 of killing 14 market traders, mainly Central-Asians, in a 2006 bombing attack in Moscow, never reached Breivik.

Breivik decided to contest the terms of his imprisonment. For two years, he and his lawyer appealed unsuccessfully to prison authorities to end his isolation. They got nowhere. In February 2015, his lawyer announced Breivik was preparing to file a lawsuit against the state for violating his human rights. He wanted visits and phone calls. He wanted internet access and a PlayStation 3. He wanted to influence the world.

THE LINE WENT DEAD

FREDDY LIE still wakes up at night hearing that scream. His daughter's scream. The one he heard on July 22, 2011.

He was driving in the rain when 16-year-old Elisabeth called from the youth camp on Utøya. She just howled into the phone. It was a kind of scream he had never heard before. What was happening? Was she being raped? There, at the summer camp? And then the line went dead. When he called back it went straight to voicemail. Breivik had shot Elisabeth in the head, a bullet in her left temple. It went through her brain and out the right side of her head into the phone. Only when it hit the pink back cover of the phone did the bullet stop. Elisabeth fell sideways, and Breivik shot her twice more. When she was found, her long, blond hair was colored red by blood; her fingers had stiffened in the grip around the pink phone.

"HE IS A HERO OF HIS PEOPLE, AND I CANNOT WAIT FOR HIS LIBERATION FROM CAPTIVITY AT THE HANDS OF SWINE."

"We just marked what should have been her 21st birthday," Lie said, standing outside the gym in Skien during a break in the court proceedings. "Last week. At her grave." He said he had to see Breivik's legal challenge himself, rather than reading about it in the papers or seeing it on TV. (A handful of other parents of Breivik's victims followed the trial on direct video link from Oslo District Court, but most stayed away.) "We've been through hell," Lie said as the hearings were about to resume.

Lie and a small group of parents of the dead considered suing the state for failing to protect their kids at the summer camp, for taking too long to understand that an act of mass murder was unfolding. That July afternoon, police forces were standing on the mainland, some 600 yards across the water from the island, able to hear the sound of gunshots ringing out from the island. Sixty minutes elapsed between the time the police were notified of the shooting and the time an officer stepped foot on the island. The reaction time was too slow, some parents of Breivik's victims say; it allowed him to continue shooting people on the island and in the waters of the lake as they tried to swim to safety for more than an hour before special forces apprehended him.

CULTURE WAR: Breivik targeted the summer camp on the island because he wanted to punish the children of Norway's elite, who he believes are traitors.

Officers followed the sound of gunfire to a clearing in the woods; Breivik, despite still having ammunition left, then surrendered. The police found him standing between some bushes and ordered him to raise his hands. He quietly put down his rifle. One of the officers noticed a wire that appeared to emerge from his bulging vest and run down his body. Thinking Breivik could be wearing explosives, the officers ordered him onto his knees and then told him to lie flat on his stomach. An officer then jumped on him and handcuffed him.

"It's not you lot I'm after," Breivik said, turning his head as an officer bound his legs with plastic cuffs. "I see you as my brothers." The wire turned out to be Breivik's iPod headphones. He had planned to listen to music during the attack but ended up doing without it, saying later that he needed to hear what was happening around him.

Lawyers whom Lie and the other parents approached declined to represent them, saying there was no chance they could win the case against the state. After a couple of years, they are about to give up. They don't have the strength to pursue a suit; mourning is hard work. They grieve. They are sleepless. Some feel they are going mad. So no one sued the state until he did: the killer

'LOW INTENSIVE TORTURE'

"I AM the general secretary of the party the Nordic State," Breivik told Judge Helen Andenaes Sekulic on the opening day of the court proceedings in March. (She is expected to issue her decision on the case in late April or early May.) While in prison, he had "converted" to national socialism, he told her. "The only important right for me is the right to have national socialist friends and a national socialist spouse—everything

+
SPLENDID ISOLATION: Because Breivik is kept away from the other prisoners, he has three cells, a shower and a storage room, plus a TV, a typewriter, a treadmill, a stationary bike, an elliptical trainer, a DVD player and a PlayStation.

else is meaningless." He asked for the right to advertise for a wife who shares his political views, and he said he also needed to "build relations with" people with the same values.

Breivik claimed that his isolation violates the European Convention on Human Rights, specifically Article 3, which states, "No one shall be subjected to torture or to inhuman or degrading treatment or punishment." His suit also argues that the Norwegian state has breached Article 8, which protects a person's "right to respect for his private and family life, his home and his correspondence," according to the suit.

Breivik lives in three separate cells of 8 square meters each. He also has a shower and a storage room. One of the three rooms has a bed, a chair with a padded seat, a footrest, a TV, books, a DVD player and a PlayStation. In the second room, he has a table and a typewriter. The third is his mini-gym; it contains a treadmill, a spinning bicycle and an elliptical trainer.

"It's a farce," Lie, the still-grieving father, said of Breivik's complaints. "After this trial, I think the state can tighten the nuts a bit more."

Breivik's lawyer, Øystein Storrvik, told the court his client has been impaired by the isolation. Breivik said in court that his brain had become so damaged that he had even started to enjoy a dating reality series called *Paradise Hotel*. He called the prison regime "low intensive torture" and complained about plastic cutlery, paper cups and coffee that was sometimes cold. "For people from Oslo West," the affluent part of the city where Breivik lived, the food he was given was "worse than waterboarding." Sometimes he even got the same dish two days in a row. And sometimes, when he called the guards to let him out of his training cell and into another room (the rooms are not contiguous), he had to wait for a full 20 minutes.

To many people, those complaints are absurd, even sickening. But there is a large body of scientific evidence to suggest that solitary confinement is an extreme form of punishment that can cause serious psychological and emotional damage. The prison authorities acknowledge that and say they would like to allow Breivik more contact with other prisoners, but they say his attempts to spread his ideology make it dangerous for them to change the rules. They are also concerned that other prisoners might harm Breivik, or that he might try to harm them.

In the lawsuit, Breivik requested a change in the prison's policy on visits, letters and phone calls. Storrvik described that policy like this: "Those who want to see Breivik are not allowed to, and those who are allowed to, Breivik does not want to see."

Breivik does not want to see his family, rel-

atives or old friends, whom he called "meaningless" visitors. Just before his mother died, in 2013, he told prison authorities that he might not want to see her again because she wasn't as proud of him as she should be. When his father, who had not seen him for 20 years, wanted to visit him, Breivik agreed but only on the condition that the elderly man would become a member of the Nordic State and declare allegiance to national socialism. His father declined. For a while, he was in regular telephone contact with one of his female fans, but he eventually stopped talking to her because he did not find the conversations politically stimulating.

About 4,000 letters—to and from Breivik—have passed through the prison's censorship department during the past four years. The prison has censored 600 of them, mostly those written by Breivik, and has kept only a few dozen of the many letters sent to him. The monitoring of the mail, expensive and laborious as it is, needed to continue, the state's lawyers argued. "The plaintiff has not shown any sign of remorse," Marius Emberland, the lawyer in charge of the state's case, said in court. "Breivik is a very dangerous man."

NARCISSISTIC AND REVOLUTIONARY WISHES

SO WHAT does this dangerous man believe? What viral, threatening ideas does he nurture in his pampered isolation? The answer is in that Nazi salute. Breivik has slightly altered his political message. In 2011, he wanted to rid Europe of all Muslims; now his belief system appears to have shifted to a more extreme form of neo-Nazism, with a focus on maintaining what he sees as the purity of the Nordic, or Aryan, race.

HE WANTED TO SPARK A BROAD WAR IN EUROPE THAT WOULD END WITH THE CHRISTIANS FINALLY DEFEATING THE MUSLIMS.

HER LONG, BLOND HAIR WAS COLORED RED BY BLOOD; HER FINGERS HAD STIFFENED IN THE GRIP AROUND THE PINK PHONE.

"He's an opportunist," says Tore Bjørgo, director at the Center for Research on Extremism at the University of Oslo. "The leading ideologues on the anti-jihadist scene rejected him. They found his murders horrendous. Now he rejects them in return and clings to those who gave him support—the most extreme neo-Nazis in Eastern Europe and Russia."

I have spent a few years studying Breivik and his crimes for my book *One of Us: The Story of Anders Breivik and the Massacre in Norway*. That's how I came to be in contact with him. The first letter he wrote to me began: "Dear Åsne, I have been following your career with great interest since 2003. I respect and admire you for your mentality, competence and intelligence."

The letter continued, flattering me, trying to manipulate me into serving his purposes. He made me an offer in the letter. He wanted us to write the book together. "I have enough insight to realise that 'The Breivik Diaries' [a still-unpublished manuscript he is not permitted to send to anyone] will be boycotted by the established publishing houses, and therefore want to offer you the chance of selling the book as a package within your project, that is, you top and/or tail your book with a quick hack job by me." He ended his letter: "With narcissistic and revolutionary wishes, Anders Behring Breivik."

I declined the offer but continued to ask him questions in my attempt to understand what had made him a mass murderer and political terrorist at the age of 32. In his manifesto, and during the 2012 trial, Breivik's main enemy was multiculturalism, a system he called cultural Marxism. He claimed in court that he had committed his attack to save Norway's Christian culture.

Since then, his hatred of people of different racial or ethnic backgrounds, and of mainstream political thought, seems to have lost none of its intensity. The last letter I received from him came on November 13, 2015. He said that this was the fifth version of the letter and that the previous four had been stopped by the censors. He wrote, "It was neither a Christian, nor a contra-jihadist who acted on 7/22" but rather "one of the most fanatical National Socialists in Northern Europe." He said he had converted to Odinism, a racist pagan movement, and prayed to the same God as the Vikings did in the 10th century.

Breivik's main preoccupation in the letter was with how to preserve what he calls "the Nordic genes." One of his ideas was that the state should establish a fertility clinic where Nordic embryos would be for sale. The clinic would hire surrogate mothers to deliver "100% pure" Nordic babies for adoption. He ended the letter by saying that "saving the racially distinctive character of the Aryans" was the most important issue on the agenda for the Nordic State.

But here's where Breivik may bump up against a painful reality: His so-called Nordic State exists only in his mind and in his writings. "This trial hasn't really made an impact," Alexander Verkhovsky tells me by phone from Moscow. He is the director of Sova Center, a Moscow-based think tank that conducts research on nationalism and xenophobia in Russia. Since Breivik committed his crimes in 2011, other issues have competed for the attention of Russia's far-right activists. Ukraine has been a focal point, as has the influx of refugees from the Middle East, North Africa and Central Asia. "He is an old story now and hasn't been able to keep the support up here in Russia. He almost disappeared from the scene," Verkhovsky says, referring to the social media and blogosphere of the extreme right wing.

Even the pictures of his Nazi salute hardly got a nod from many of his old fans. "It's warm and cozy, where he is, not a Russian gulag," one person wrote on a nationalist page. Another made fun of Breivik's request for a PlayStation 3. On the website Pravye Novosti (Right-Wing News), a commentator wrote that Breivik acted too early. "He hurried, did not wait for the Arab immigrants. Today nobody would have convicted him. Jackass."

+
BROADSIDE BROADCAST: While in prison, Breivik has converted to national socialism, and he insists that he has the right to communicate with like-minded individuals inside and outside his prison walls.

LASTING MEMORIES: Families of Breivik's victims are determined to not let the world forget their loss, while his admirers across Europe are trying to keep his cause alive.

But some supporters remain loyal and were delighted to see their old idol on television again. Some still call him a "hero of the white race" and address him as "Commander Breivik" or "Beauty." Auernheimer, the American living in Georgia, says, "I network with thousands of nationalists. My crew has 30 core people working daily. Breivik came up recently. Not a bad word was said. We all love and support him unconditionally."

Roman Dedushkin is one of Breivik's Russian fans. "My stance towards Breivik in the last five years has only become more positive," he says. "This is because of his active stance whilst being in prison, as well as the fact that I have thoroughly studied his texts, translated into Russian. He is most definitely an authoritative figure, and I think that the numbers of those who support and sympathize with him will only grow."

Wishful thinking, perhaps. But many involved in the Breivik case warn that if he, a lone attacker, can cause so much damage in three hours, so could a copycat killer. "Our greatest fear is not that he will be let out. He won't. It is that he will be able to spread his message. It is a message that kills," says Lisbeth Røyneland, the leader of a support group for the victims of July 22. She lost her 18-year-old daughter, Synne, in the attack. Synne had tried to swim away when Breivik started shooting but then turned back. She was found behind a stone, with three bullet holes in her forehead. The forensic experts at first thought she had been about to drown because of severe damage to her lungs. Then they realized that the damage was the result of extreme hyperventilation from her desperate, rapid panting as she died.

"I can never forgive him," Røyneland says. "I lie awake at night and think of her fear, her last seconds, alone behind that stone. But I trust the Norwegian rule of law. I support his right to put his case forward. It is important for us that he is treated like any other prisoner. Not better. Not worse."

UK Newsclips

In turning to some classic British newsclips one can see just how excellent so many of the stories and the morals behind them are. Unlike the Norwegian Press, the British Press are far more professional. For all their faults the British Press have a good measure of integrity. They always try to get in touch with a subject before doing a story: the Norwegian Press do not. The UK Press are far more circumspect than the Norwegian Press when it comes to having a go at Muslims. They try to check their facts.

The Daily Mail are favourites for moralising, frequently with complete justification: they call a tart a tart; they call a moron a moron. They call abortion an abomination. They address teenage promiscuity without picking on the Muslims or traditional Christians for over-moralising. They accept many women are strumpet liars when it comes to accusations of rape. But they give their victims a chance to reply. Peter Hitchens of the Mail is very good. His book entitled 'The Abolition of Britain' was spot on regarding the later betrayal of old-fashioned values and attitudes that made Britain so reasonable a place to live in. But do the reprobates in Parliament listen? Not much.

Why today's young girls are just so FEEBLE

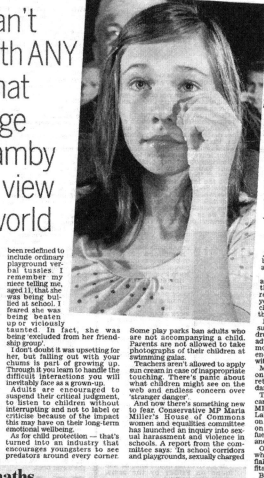

They can't cope with ANY ideas that challenge their namby pamby view of the world

by Claire Fox

SOME of the girls were sobbing and hugging each other, while others shrieked. The majority appeared at the very least shell-shocked.

It was distress on a scale appropriate for some horrible disaster. Thankfully, however, I wasn't in a war zone or at the scene of a pile-up — but in a school hall filled with A-level students.

What had provoked such hysteria? I'd dared express an opinion that went against their accepted way of thinking.

'Generation Snowflake' is the term for these teens, one that's now used frequently in the U.S. and becoming more common here. It describes a fragile, thin-skinned younger generation that can't cope with conflicting views, let alone criticism.

Being faced by a roomful of weepy teenagers certainly isn't the only example of such behaviour I could cite, but it's the most dramatic I have experienced.

It happened when I was taking part in a debate at a North London school as director of the Institute of Ideas early last year.

The subject under discussion was footballer Ched Evans — who was then a convicted rapist and had just been released from prison (he's since had his conviction quashed and is awaiting a retrial). His team, Sheffield United, had taken him back, and we were debating whether the subsequent furore was social justice or mob rule.

I knew many wouldn't agree with my stance, which was that Evans had completed his sentence and should be able to return to his profession. But during the final Q&A all hell broke loose. I dared suggest (as eminent feminists have before me) that rape wasn't necessarily the worst thing a woman could experience.

I expected robust discussion — not for them all to dissolve into outraged gasps of, 'You can't say that!'

THEIR reaction shocked me. I take no pleasure in making teenagers cry, but it also brought home the contrast to previous generations of young people, who would have relished the chance to argue back.

It illustrated this generation's almost belligerent sense of entitlement. They assume their emotional suffering takes precedence. Express a view they disagree with and you must immediately recant and apologise.

But as I argue in my new book — I Find That Offensive! — Generation Snowflake believe it's their right to be protected from anything they might find unpalatable.

This mindset is particularly rife in universities. The examples are beyond parody: a National Union of Students conference banning clapping as it might trigger trauma ('please use jazz hands', delegates were told); the Edinburgh University student threatened with expulsion from a meeting after raising her hand in disagreement.

Last year, students at the University of East Anglia banned a Mexican restaurant from giving out sombreros because of racist stereotyping.

In March, Cambridge University banned an 'Around The World in 80 Days' themed party over fears wearing ethnic costumes might cause offence.

Students demand that universities are 'safe spaces', free from opinions that will make them feel uncomfortable. There has been a rise in 'No platforming' — barring someone with controversial views from speaking at an event at all.

Faced with such thin-skinned students, no wonder Oxford University has introduced 'trigger warnings' about 'potentially distressing subject matter' in law lectures on cases involving sexual violence.

Never mind that a future in criminal law will mean dealing with all the unpleasant aspects of human experience.

The list goes on. And on.

It makes me sad that these teens and 20-somethings have become so fearful that they believe a dissenting opinion can pose such a serious threat. But can we really be surprised when it's us who have taught them to think this way? We tell children their wellbeing is paramount, but we are also guilty of mollycoddling them. There's a constant emphasis on their vulnerability, which is proving toxic.

Children are more restricted than ever when it comes to taking physical risks — one of the ways previous generations built resilience. Thanks to health and safety mania, leapfrog, marbles and conkers are now considered unsafe.

In March, a Leeds primary school banned games of tag as children had been getting upset and having clothes torn. There's a campaign to stop tackling in school rugby, and to assess the safety of other contact sports such as hockey.

We drill children about healthy eating, so they grow up fearing sugary drinks and told that too much salt and fat will kill them. We weigh and measure them at primary school and then wonder why they become obsessed with their bodies.

Meanwhile, the old motto 'Sticks and stones...' is now forgotten, as we teach children that words can indeed hurt them. Bullying has been redefined to include ordinary playground verbal tussles. I remember my niece telling me, aged 11, that she was being bullied at school. I feared she was being beaten up or viciously taunted. In fact, she was being 'excluded from her friendship group'.

I don't doubt it was upsetting for her, but falling out with your chums is part of growing up. Through it you learn to handle the difficult interactions you will inevitably face as a grown-up.

Adults are encouraged to suspend their critical judgment, to listen to children without interrupting and not to label or criticise because of the impact this may have on their long-term emotional wellbeing.

As for child protection — that's turned into an industry that encourages youngsters to see predators around every corner. Some play parks ban adults who are not accompanying a child. Parents are not allowed to take photographs of their children at swimming galas.

Teachers aren't allowed to apply sun cream in case of inappropriate touching. There's panic about what children might see on the web and endless concern over 'stranger danger'.

And now there's something new to fear. Conservative MP Maria Miller's House of Commons women and equalities committee has launched an inquiry into sexual harassment and violence in schools. A report from the committee says: 'In school corridors and playgrounds, sexually charged behaviour drives young people's physical interactions.' But a look at the 'evidence' suggests an expansive definition of what constitutes sexual harassment.

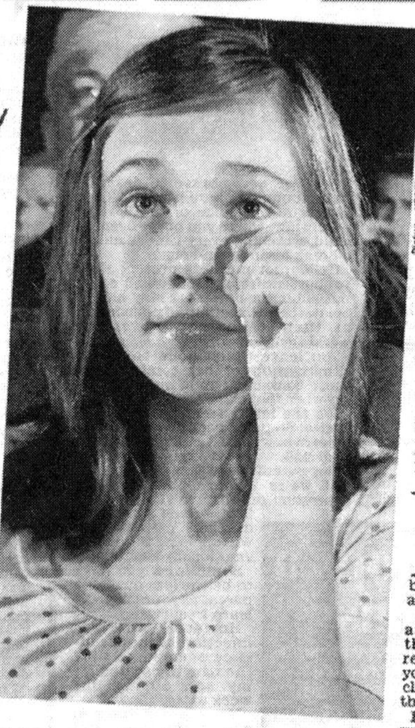

Picture: UPPERCUT IMAGES, posed by model

Is giving a compliment based on looks really 'unsafe' behaviour? If a boy pings a girl's bra it may be unpleasant and annoying, but is it really assault?

An ever-widening definition of abuse can incite a culture of fear and complaint: encouraging teachers and girls to name and shame could mean labelling sexually awkward teenage boys as sex pests.

There is a danger of adults losing a sense of proportion. When I was five, we played a game where we girls wore our cardigans as capes and ran away squealing from the boys chasing us with frogs from the local pond.

NO DOUBT today that would be dubbed a sinister sex game, and the boys certainly wouldn't be allowed near the pond.

I am particularly concerned we are teaching girls to see themselves as victims. Recent research showing that fewer young people are going to nightclubs is revealing. It's not because they can't afford it.

Rather, women cite reasons such as the fear of encountering drunken men who may try to take advantage of them. How sad that modern women are frightened enough to associate a night out with sexual assault.

Many say they prefer to socialise on the internet. Not only is this retreat from the public sphere damaging — it's not safe either.

The Reclaim The Internet campaign, launched last month by MPs including Maria Miller and Labour's Yvette Cooper, focuses on the impact sexist trolling has on young women — yet it only fuels stereotypes of them as weak and fragile.

Of course, it's not just women who embody Generation Snowflake and not every young person fits the criteria.

But there is a strand of self-absorption and fragility running through this generation; all too ready to cry 'victim' at the first hint of a situation they don't like.

We need a younger generation that's prepared to grow a backbone, go out into the world, take risks and make difficult decisions. Otherwise the future doesn't bode well for any of us.

■CLAIRE FOX is Director or the Institute of Ideas. Her new book 'I Find That Offensive!' was published by Biteback in May.

Why today's young girls are just so FEEBLE
Daily mail, 9th June 2016

Daily Mail, Friday, December 2, 2011

Daily Mail, Friday, December 2, 2011

JAN MOIR

jan.moir@dailymail.co.uk

Since when did women's lib mean dressing like a porn star?

AT 6am last Saturday, I was at Paddington station in London, catching an early train on a cold winter morning. In front of me on the concourse were three young women, all wearing Ugg boots and tiny shorts.

Members of a school hockey team, I half-thought, before spending a few happy moments jogging off down memory lane. Remembering the frozen winter hockey pitches of my youth — then snapping back to reality and looking at them again.

Dalek voice; something doesn't compute. Why weren't the girls wearing track pants to keep warm? Why were their legs so brown in that odd, inside-of-a-teapot way? And can you really play hockey with so much lacquered and basted duck breast, so much up-and-at-'em cleavage on display?

Of course, sports practice was the last thing on these girls' minds. They were refugees from the night before, clubbers wending their weary way home after a night of having fun in the big city.

The high-heeled shoes stuffed into bags, the inky landslides of mascara, the flimsy tops, the shivering and miserable faces all told their own story. And, as my mother would say, not so much as a liberty bodice between them.

Yet every weekend, in towns up and down this country, thousands of young women dress up — or should that be dress down — just like this. They go out to pubs and clubs in skimpy outfits that would put a porn star to shame.

They wear micro bras and hot pants. They teeter about on freezing city streets in plunge-front, backless, sideless, blink-and-you'll-miss-'em outfits.

They make hookers seem like prom queens. They look as though they should be dancing on podiums in sex clubs, not having a laugh and a crafty glass of chardonnay with their mates after a hard week's work.

And as the Christmas season blasts off for another year, their highly sexualised appearance and check-me-out mob mentality will be absolutely everywhere.

This week, a report in the Daily Mail highlighted this peculiarly British tarty-party charter, where girls strut their stuff in streetwalker chic.

On our pages, fun-seeking women in four cities were photographed clattering along in their heels, with all their goods on display like the Christmas windows in Harrods. Let us be blunt — they looked just a little bit too slutty for comfort.

Joanne from Newcastle, who featured in the article, was probably an extreme case. The 23-year-old wore a Playboy skirt, slung low enough to reveal a thong and a buttock tattoo that read 'Couldn't give a f***'. A tattoo on her arm read 'Raw Sex'.

To be honest, I found Joanne a bit cheering. She may not be the kind of girl many young men would want to take home to meet mother. But if her blunt tats are anything to go by, at least she knows what she wants out of life. It's not much, but it's *hers*. A mission statement, in ink and kink.

ELSEWHERE, the girls all said they dressed in a deliberately provocative fashion to attract male attention. OK, fair enough for women to enjoy their sexual power. It is properly liberating, if used in a responsible and mature way. But what was also clear was that many of the women were also self-conscious, self-critical and used the sex plumage as a means of boosting their own self-esteem.

The sisters weren't doing it for themselves, despite the popular feminist mantra. They did it because their friends did it. They did it because men liked it. And the more provocative their outfit and the greater the reaction it elicited from the opposite sex, the more of a success it was deemed to be.

Is this really what empowerment is supposed to be?

I find it sad that so many young women seem to find validation in the mild sexual assault represented by a grasp of their bottom, or to allow themselves to be defined by a spark of lust in a stranger's eye.

The joke is that dressing like a porn star is seen as a manifestation of modern, sexual liberation — but it is hardly liberating if you dress like that to conform, to be like the other girls, just to please the boys.

It is becoming increasingly clear that the harsh and brutal aesthetics of pornography have gone mainstream, seeping into chainstores, infiltrating pop music and dictating to innocent girls what is deemed cool to wear. Advertising, particularly for luxury goods such as handbags and perfume, reeks of sex.

Mainstream rap artists continue to make videos that show half-naked women as cheap commodities with nary a cheep of complaint from anyone. To look sexually available, verging on the gagging for it, has become acceptable.

Rihanna and Christina Aguilera in their pants, simulating S&M on The X Factor, have a direct correlation to small-town girls going to discos in nothing more than a scrap of tissue and a thong, hoping for a 'shout-out' from the beered-up guys in the corner.

Instead of applauding their liberation, we should be asking why there's a generation of girls who place such a cheap value on themselves. Is it related to self-esteem? Class? The rise of a new narcissism? Or a mixture of all three.

I'm not sure anyone knows, least of all the girls. But this Christmas, I wish they'd at least put a coat on. Otherwise they'll catch their deaths.

Since when did women's lib mean dressing like a porn star?
Daily Mail, 2nd December 2011

How teenage girls lost their innocence

More than a quarter lose virginity below age of consent

By **Sophie Borland**
Health Reporter

MORE than a quarter of young women today lost their virginity when they were below the legal age of consent, NHS figures reveal.

Some 27 per cent of 16 to 24 year-olds admit they were 15 or under when they had sex for the first time.

One in eight of this age group have already had sex with at least ten different partners.

MPs and campaigners yesterday blamed the 'pornification of society' for encouraging young girls to dress themselves up as sex objects before they have even reached puberty.

The figures detail for the first time how young girls are increasingly losing their virginity before they reach 16.

They reveal how by comparison, just 4 per cent of women now aged 55 to 64 first had sex when they were under-age. This rises to 10 per cent of 45 to 54 year-olds, and 14 per cent of 35 to 44 year-olds.

Critics say the rise in promiscuity over the generations is linked to increased sex

'Pornification of society'

education in schools that has 'broken down the natural inhibitions of children with regard to sexual conduct'.

The figures also show that more than a fifth of sexually active women aged 16 to 24 have taken the morning-after pill at least once in the past year. Almost 60 per cent admitted they did not always use contraception.

By comparison 22 per cent of men aged 16 to 24 lost their virginity when they were 15 or under. Some 41 per cent said they used a condom every time, although only 5.4 per cent said they had caught a sexually transmitted infection.

Diane Abbott, shadow health minister, said: 'Too many young girls are absorbing from the popular culture around them that they only have value as sex objects. Inevitably they act this notion out.

'The rising numbers of girls having under-age sex is alarming. It is not a cost-free phenomenon. It poses public health policy challenges and social challenges. The underlying cause must be the pornification of British culture and the increasing sexualisation of pre-adolescent girls.'

Norman Wells, director of the Family Education Trust said: 'Over recent years we have witnessed the systematic removal of every restraint which in previous generations served as a disincentive to underage sexual activity.

'Sex education in many schools has had the effect of breaking down the natural inhibitions of children with regard to sexual conduct, and the age of consent is rarely enforced, so young people no longer have any fear of legal proceedings.

'On top of that, the ready availability of contraception means that a girl's fear of pregnancy is no longer considered a good enough reason for rejecting her boyfriend's advances, and confidentiality policies mean that a girl need not worry about what her parents would think about her being sexually active, obtaining contraception, being treated for a sexually transmitted infection or even having an abortion, because they don't have to be told.'

The figures have come from a survey of the sexual behaviours of 8,420 men and women aged 16 to 69, carried out by the NHS this year for the first time.

They also reveal that one in seven women aged 16 to 24 who had lost their virginity had caught a sexually transmitted infection at least once. Only four in ten said they always used contraception when having sex.

Across all age groups, the statistics show that 14 per cent of women lost their virginity before the age of 16 compared with 20 per cent of men.

The average age for losing virginity was 17, although for those aged 16 to 24 it was 16.

Although Britain's teenage pregnancy rates have recently started to fall, they still remain among the highest in Europe. In 2009, there were 38,259 pregnancies in girls under 18 compared with 41,361 in 2008, a decline of 7.5 per cent. Every year around 3,700 girls under 16 have an abortion.

There is concern that society is becoming increasingly 'sexualised'. Last year the final of ITV's the X Factor final attracted more than 4,000 complaints following raunchy performances by singers Christina Aguilera and Rihanna.

SEX EDUCATION THROUGH THE GENERATIONS

Percentage who lost virginity before 16

27% — **16 to 24-year-olds:** This age group was taught sex education at primary and secondary school. Lessons could often be explicit. In some schools, five-year-olds were told to label the body parts of pictures of naked men and women.

18% — **25 to 34-year-olds:** They learnt about puberty, sex, contraception and AIDs in primary schools. Some were also shown how to put condoms on models, as emphasis moved on to safe sex.

14% — **35 to 44-year-olds:** Sex education was taught outside biology classes, though mainly confined to secondary schools. Pupils had lessons about contraception.

10% — **45 to 54-year-olds:** Subject was largely confined to biology classes in secondaries, where pupils were taught in clinical detail about human reproduction.

4% — **55 to 64-year-olds:** Pupils learnt about reproduction in animals and pollination in plants. Basic details about human reproduction in biology lessons.

■ NOW: A lesson in a modern school

■ THEN: A classroom of the 1950s

How teenage girls lost their innocence
Daily Mail, 16th December 2011

Punish women for abortions: Trump

Backlash as even pro-life campaigners condemn him

From **Daniel Bates**
in New York

ABORTION should be illegal and women who have one should be punished, Donald Trump declared last night.

The Republican presidential candidate said the procedure must be outlawed – even if it meant the return of backstreet abortion clinics.

Mr Trump said he was pro-life and he wanted to emulate the policies of former president Ronald Reagan.

The comments shocked many in the US and brought sharp condemnation from the tycoon's presidential rivals. Mr Trump has been criticised for his sexist comments and has already called women pigs and joked about a TV reporter being on her period during a presidential debate.

In a heated appearance on the US TV network MSNBC, host Chris Matthews asked him: 'You're about to be chief executive of the United States. Do you believe in punishment for abortion, yes or no?'. Mr Trump said: 'The answer is, there has to be some form of punishment'.

When asked 'Ten days? Ten years?', he replied 'I don't know. It's a very complicated position'.

Asked how an abortion ban would work, Mr Trump said: 'You go back to a position like they had where they would perhaps go to illegal places. But you have to ban it'.

His comments drew a rebuke from Hillary Clinton who tweeted: 'Just when you thought it couldn't get worse. Horrific and telling'. Her rival for the Democratic nomination Bernie Sanders tweeted: 'Your Republican frontrunner, ladies and gentlemen. Shameful'

Even anti-abortion groups came out against Mr Trump. One leading campaigner Jeanne Mancini said: 'No pro-lifer would ever want to punish a woman who has chosen abortion. This is against the very nature of what we are about.'

'Doctors would be responsible'

Within hours Mr Trump tried to reverse course – but the damage was already done. He said: 'The doctor or any other person performing this illegal act upon a woman would be held legally responsible, not the woman.'

The furore followed a girl of 15 being pepper sprayed in the face and apparently sexually assaulted as she protested at a Trump rally.

A video of the chaotic incident showed the girl screaming at a man in the crowd: 'You ****ing touched my chest'. Around 30 seconds later another man from the crowd sprayed her face at close range.

Trump: Declared he was pro-life

The attack in Wisconsin is the latest disturbing incident in Mr Trump's campaign.

Critics of the billionaire, who is leading the polls among Republicans, say brawls and violence at his rallies are a direct consequence of his inflammatory rhetoric.

Protesters squared off against his supporters at the Holiday Inn in Janesville. Wisconsin hosts the next big primary vote next Tuesday.

The girl was named only as Alex. Her attacker was identified as Dan Crandall. He denies groping her.

On the video a man in the crowd can be heard calling her a 'communist n***** lover' before another sprays leans over to pepper spray her. The victim was taken to hospital for checks.

Mr Trump has said that he will not support the Republican presidential candidate if it is not him. The state primaries will be followed by the party convention in July when the Republicans will name their candidate.

Punish women for abortions: Trump
Daily Mail 31 March 2016

'FGM felt like a car was running over my body'

Egypt has one of the world's highest rates of female genital mutilation. In the first of a series, **Martin Bentham** reports from the city of Assiut on the victims who are fighting to demolish the myths that perpetuate this barbaric practice

I WAS circumcised when I was 10 and I have never forgiven my parents. I can't forget that day," says 27-year-old Egyptian graduate Amna Mohamed. "I suffered severe bleeding. We need to stop FGM. It has never been in our religion so why are we continuing with it? We need to eliminate it."

Ms Mohamed's story is far from rare in Egypt. The country has the unenviable reputation as one of the worst for inflicting female genital mutilation – figures from the UN children's organisation Unicef have shown a rate above 90 per cent among those aged 15 or over.

Religion plays a part, although Ms Mohamed, who campaigns against FGM as a community volunteer in the Upper Egypt city of Assiut, insists that this motivation is similarly misconceived. "FGM is against Islam which has prohibited it since very old years, but it continues because of tradition. There are many negative consequences: women can't enjoy sexual intercourse and it can lead to divorce. It also causes pain and psychological damage. Girls suffer trauma. They find someone holding them and cutting an important part of their body. The genital part of a girl should not be cut: it is exactly the same as a man, he would not be enjoying it and it would be violating his rights. It is the same for girls."

Another misconception, she explains, is that FGM – or circumcision as it is often labelled – can control a girl's sexual desire and prevent promiscuity and pre-marital intercourse

"Think of prostitutes. There are many prostitutes who have been circumcised. So how you behave doesn't have anything to do with whether you are circumcised – it is about how you bring up your daughter. FGM is haram, it is forbidden."

Apart from the notion that mutilation makes a girl "polite", rather than "badly behaved", further false claims prevalent in Egypt include a belief that cutting improves fertility. Others think FGM aids growth or is needed to stop a girl's genitals looking male.

Ms Mohamed's determination is clear and shared by others in Assiut who work with her on a project funded by British donations to the "Girls' Fund" of the charity Plan UK. It uses "community development associations" to promote girls' rights and includes the elimination of FGM among its objectives.

Methods include "awareness-raising sessions" to which doctors and religious leaders are invited to set out the facts about the harm caused by cutting and other traditions such as early marriage.

Volunteers also conduct home visits to families where parents or grandparents support cutting to lobby against the practice. Overall, 6,500 people – including girls, boys, teachers, social workers and clerics – are due to receive training on equality and children's rights over the next three years.

Progress remains mixed, however, as the experiences of girls participating in the scheme show. Many have been cut in recent years, despite Egypt's government passing a law to ban FGM in 2008. Doctors, rather than the untrained "midwives" who traditionally carried out the procedure, are often responsible.

Mervat, 14, is among those cut since mutilation became illegal. She gives a disturbing account, which illustrates some of the continuing problems.

"I was circumcised when I was nine," she says. "I was at home and the midwife arrived. I knew who she was so I rushed to hide. I was crying. My father said it would be okay, that it was not hard, then he pulled me into a room with the midwife.

"I bit him and ran back to my room. Then my father and mother came and held me down so the midwife could circumcise me. I was bleeding heavily, crying and shivering. It was like a car running over my body. I made a vow that I will never circumcise my daughters." She says her friends are divided over FGM, with some still in favour, and adds: "I try to convince them by telling

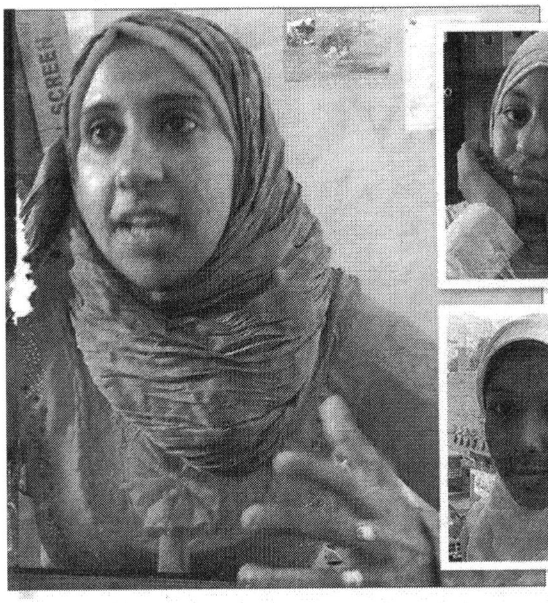

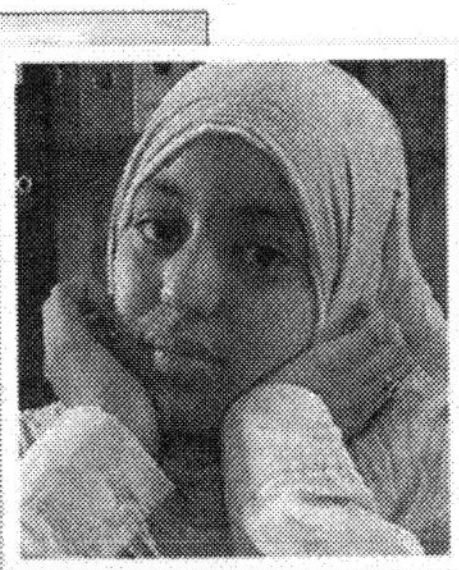

Changing attitudes: graduate Amna Mohamed, who campaigns against FGM as a community volunteer in Assiut, and left, Hala, 14. Below left, Mervat, also 14, and, inset right, Shaimaa, 12, who has escaped FGM

'I suffered, but my cousin died. My uncle took her to Cairo to be circumcised but she bled to death'
Hala, 14

them about my aunt, who is in her twenties and has not been circumcised. She is successful, in good health and enjoys life. I pray to God that FGM will come to an end."

Hala, 14, was also cut at nine, a common age for FGM to take place in Egypt, and campaigns against it because of what she has learned about its impact. She says her cousin died, aged five, after being cut. "I tell my classmates and friends not to get circumcised because FGM is harmful. I bled a lot. I was taken by surprise. I was told I was going to the dentist. When I went in the doctor asked me to lie down. She gave me an injection but I could feel everything. I was full of pain. It was like death. When I asked my mother she said I had been circumcised and that all girls get circumcised." She adds: "I suffered, but my cousin died. My uncle took her to Cairo to be circumcised but she bled to death. She was five and she died because of FGM. My goal is to share information about what happened because I don't want any girl to suffer as I did and she did."

MONA, 13, was circumcised two years ago and, after attending the educational sessions run by Plan UK, is seeking to persuade her parents not to cut her younger sister. She has yet to succeed. "My mother told me that she was going to circumcise me so that when I got married I would be able to give birth," she says.

"At the time I accepted it because I didn't know what it was. I started to bleed and was in hospital for four days. My mother has said she won't circumcise my sister, who is five, but my father keeps saying it is a must."

Their graphic stories demonstrate how the noble intent of Egypt's FGM law has still to convert to reality. Meanwhile, work to alter attitudes among other Egyptians, both male and female, continues.

One tactic is to use education sessions to contrast the successful lives of women who have not been mutilated with the negative experiences of others whose sex lives and marriages have suffered from the physical and psychological consequences of FGM. The teams funded by Plan UK also counter the threat to girls at risk of imminent mutilation by identifying the family "decision-maker" and the reason that they still favour FGM. A visit to the home follows with a doctor or religious leader often invited to challenge any misconceptions which the parent or grandparent holds.

Despite such efforts, false beliefs remain rife, even among some girls who have escaped FGM. Shaimaa, 12, thinks, for example, that mutilation is safe if performed by a doctor, rather than a midwife, and adds that many of her friends still view FGM as necessary to avoid infertility. She says: "After my sister bled my mother said she would never circumcise me or my other sisters. My father insisted and all my aunts kept pushing my mother too, but she has said no. I am happy. I don't want to get circumcised."

Such confusion and division abounds and will take years to address but Amna Mohamed is positive about the future. She is convinced that facts about the harm done by cutting are registering with parents.

"Most mothers don't want their girls to repeat their experiences. I also tell them that if you have FGM you don't have happy sexual relations and there's a risk of divorce. Parents are afraid of that. They are listening to our arguments and realising the truth about FGM."

@martinbentham

■ *Anyone wishing to support work against FGM can find out more at plan-uk.org/girlsfund or by calling 0300 777 9779.*

'FMG felt like a car was running over my body'
Evening Standard, 14th April 2016

Peter Hitchens

When hanging is humane

I AM always amazed by the 'humanitarians' who oppose the death penalty because it is cruel.

The same people claim to be in favour of rehabilitation and against harsh punishment.

Do they have any idea what it's like to be in prison without any hope of release?

Soham murderer Ian Huntley will eventually manage to kill himself, or another inmate may kill him in some savage manner.

When this happens, it will be another triumph for liberal cruelty which is, in fact, a cowardly unwillingness to act with resolve.

It seems obvious to me that it would have been far more humane, as well as far more just, if Huntley had been swiftly hanged.

DEATH WISH: Ian 'untley

peter.hitchens@mailonsunday.co.uk http://hitchensblog.mailonsund

When hanging is humane
The Mail on Sunday 10th September 2006

Death penalty

From Dr M. P. Cardew

Sir, While sympathising with the Marquess of Milford Haven in his anger at the thought of releasing the murderer of Lord Mountbatten after 15 years (letter, November 9), I feel impelled to point out the hypocrisy of many present-day attitudes to crime and punishment.

The public recoils from the death penalty mainly because of the archaic and inhumane method used right up to its abolition; but the same public appears not to mind a jot if prisoners are kept without hope of release. Some of these prisoners are violent and dangerous men, posing a constant threat to those whose job it is to keep them confined.

If really wicked and dangerous men are to be imprisoned for the rest of their natural lives, most of the constraints on their behaviour will have been removed. They might as well kill their fellow inmates and prison officers, for they will know that they are already serving the maximum sentence. If there is to be no hope, far better to reintroduce the death penalty. A man with no hope is better dead, and the prison officers' wives will sleep more easily.

Yours faithfully,
M. P. CARDEW
(Part-time medical officer,
Parkhurst Prison),
Rookley Manor,
Rookley, Isle of Wight.
November 11.

Death Penalty
Letter to The Times November 11th 1994

Daily Mail, Wednesday, December 5, 2007

Girl Power? In this excoriating attack, FAY WELDON accuses the Spice Girls of killing feminism, subverting morality and — with the sheer cynicism of their reunion tour —

Page 23

Shameless Spice: From top left, Mel C, Mel B, Emma Bunton and Victoria Beckham, with Geri Halliwell in that dress

Daily Mail, Wednesday, December 5, 2007

FORGIVE me for being blunt, but if a generation of our young womanhood has taken to binge drinking, Saturday night sluttishness and 'happy-slappings', I blame the Spice Girls. There are one or two other factors, I dare say, such as the cult of consumerism, the decline of religion, easy credit, alco-pops, morning-after pills and the rest: but, if we're going to look for scapegoats, Posh, Ginger, Sporty, Baby and Scary are, surely, obvious candidates.

Though some will no doubt disagree, and argue that the Spice Girls are simply a slice of bubblegum pop history, I believe the aspirations and attitudes of these five women go hand-in-hand with the decline of our culture over the past decade.

Think back to those brilliant, suggestive, addictive pop songs of ten years back, when they swept across the nation's playgrounds: 'Well it's a Saturday night. You know the feeling is right. Don't you know we'll get so high.' Yeah! Grope, vomit, whoops: aren't we having fun?

A decade on, the message has seeped deep into the culture, with the results plain for all to see on every High Street on, yes, any Saturday night.

At first blush, of course, it was hard not to be seduced by those five perfectly-branded young women. They were brash and sassy, and seemed to be driven by an unstoppable energy and a spirit of independence that defied the male race.

Looking back, alarm bells should have been ringing loud and clear. But, then, hindsight is a wonderful thing. What we thought was the ultimate triumph of feminism was, in fact, its death knell.

Girl Power was a sham, and its five proponents nothing more than desperate wannabes, not much better than today's reality TV stars, desperate for a quick fix of fame.

Now they're on tour again, soaring above the world in their specially chartered Boeing 747, along with their crèches and their entourage. But this time around the image they project is obviously and entirely contrived, with all that youthful zest replaced by weary cynicism.

The difference between those five breezily-sexual, energetic, bouncy girls singing about Girl Power ten years back and the five sugar-coated, air-brushed, painfully-thin, desperate mums-on-tour is clear to see.

Seeing them strutting about the stage in weird Bacofoil-style corsets — like trussed-up festive turkeys — in Canada this week, I found myself wishing this reunion had never taken place. I was embarrassed for them.

I also feel embarrassed for myself. And for feminism and for Britain, whose flag has become far too synonymous with Spice Girl glory ever since Geri wore that dress nearly a decade ago.

I'm embarrassed for them because, despite the fact that they already have so much, they are still desperately clinging on by their brittle, lacquered acrylic nails to the fame which they so craved when they were young, and the hunger for which, it seems, has still not sated them. All the riches and fame in the world wouldn't be enough to feed that hunger.

Somehow, they make rather a pathetic spectacle, these Spice Women (no longer Spice Girls) clinging to youth, celebrity, a tiny bum, and the fading memory of a fabulous and fortuitous meeting with the then zeitgeist, when they sang about friends and love — and all the little girls (and the big ones, too) sang along.

It all seemed so empowering at the time: the idea that girls should take charge of their own sexuality. But did anyone stop to think what would happen next? Now, with the dubious privilege of hindsight, we have the answer.

For a start, we are now living in the Age of Easy Couplings. What chance did formal sex education have when faced with the catchy lyrics — written by men, of course — that told young girls to indulge in such things as 'weekend love' and encouraged 'playing games'? What it did of course was to separate love from sex.

THE Spice Girls killed romance. Their singable, suggestive lyrics took away the innocence of the playground — or at least what was left of it. And it's never coming back. They turned difficult love into temporary sex, and reduced female aspiration to a series of consumer choices. They turned little girls into paedophile bait, and in doing so they helped destroy our concept of childhood.

And why am I embarrassed for myself? Because I admit I once rather liked the Spice Girls. Five seemingly enthusiastic, hard-working young women given names that sounded as if they had been plucked from a range of lipsticks by their Pygmalion manager, Simon Fuller.

The Spice Girls didn't, honestly, have much talent of their own, except for Mel C with her lovely voice and her songwriting skills. And she's the one who has aged best, looks most human, is still most likeable.

The others, as time goes on, seem to have dieted and airbrushed themselves into what they think men want: fearful of turning back into the naturally pretty, unpretentious young girls they originally were before the pop industry cast its greedy eye on them.

With the Spice Girls came the 'Because I'm worth it' culture. Implicit in this was the idea that all men were idiots — crass bumbling fools: an idea reinforced and exploited by ad agencies trying to sell, for example, cars to women. 'Dump the boyfriend, the car's more fun' ran the slogans.

But however much one laments the damage they caused, at least the Spice Girls had their moment — their desperately longed-for appointment with destiny. I don't think that will happen this time round.

Ten years on, those bouncy, slightly unkempt girls are wives and mothers. In readiness for their money-spinning world tour, they have been hammered into a kind of robotic perfection, every curve calculated and every move choreographed.

But every smile seems false; every gesture of togetherness suspect. Look long and hard and it seems as if at any moment the lacquer is about to crack and peel.

WITH their tumbling hair, spiced-up smiles and carved cheekbones, the girls who once raged about Girl Power now seem desperate for male approval. They may brandish the whips and tight leather costumes of the S&M dungeon on stage, but the act just comes across as risible.

Victoria, the bad-tempered one who won't smile, can't smile, pouts her mouth and squeezes her tiny frame into bondage gear. But in the end, it's just embarrassing.

The attempt at eroticism doesn't work. For all the lighting tricks and clever camera angles (or, indeed, perhaps because of them), it remains as sexy as second-rate soft porn.

Each to their own, I suppose; except they've got five children between them. Sexy strip-teases, I ask you! Of the five of them, two are married (one of those for the second time and not to the father of her baby), one is a single mother, and two have long-term partners.

According to the rumour mill, chicken-pox has struck on the tour. It must be dreadful in that 747.

Well, what did the feminists think would happen? That these girls wouldn't have messy relationships and have to drag their kids round the world so they could go to work? At the end of the day, a working mother's a working mother.

In the cotton mills 150 years ago, toddlers crawled about the dusty factory floors. Now it's on the aircraft floor, up and down the aisle. What's the difference?

Not a lot, except these working mothers have a lot more money and wouldn't starve if they put their feet up and stayed at home for the rest of their lives.

I'm saddened for the feminist movement because Posh, Ginger, Sporty, Baby and Scary were once meant to be Girl Power role models — independent, sexy, high achievers. And now look at them.

There's a feminist country-and-western song by Deanna Carter, 'Did I shave my legs for this?', in which a young wife heads for the door, tired of her couch-potato husband.

Similarly, faced with what has become of the Spice Girls, I am inclined to say 'Did I take off my wedding ring for this?' — which I did, back in the Seventies, out of fellow feeling for the way any woman over 30 was made to feel inferior if she didn't have one.

All those old gestures seem pointless in retrospect. The inheritance has been squandered.

So I'm embarrassed for the feminists, clinging on to the dream of a proud, equal, serious society, where justice ruled and lasses didn't throw away their hard-won equality in the pubs and clubs, puking up their resentments on the shoes of paramedics trying to help them out of the gutter.

Those little girls who first listened to the Spice Girls ten years ago are the ones who are now running up vast credit card bills on designer shopping they can't afford.

They are the ones who are anorexic or bulimic (just like Geri was). They are the ones who are fuelling a rise in sexual diseases the like of which we haven't seen for generations.

And I'm embarrassed for the nation because, thanks to Geri's famous Union Jack dress, worn back in the heady days of Blair's New Cool Britannia, and worn once again on stage this week, the Spice Girls remain 'our' representatives. Just like them, we're clinging to one-time glory, to the time when British Airways really was the world's favourite airline, England could beat Croatia at football, and the Spice Girls were the biggest pop group on the planet.

But I'm afraid the world will yawn and sneer at this attempt to resurrect past glories.

■ *FAY WELDON'S new novel, The Spa Decameron, published by Quercus, £14.99.*

Girl Power? The Spice Girls
Daily Mail December 5th 2007

Daily Mail

MONDAY, DECEMBER 31, 2007 www.dailymail.co.uk 45p

Record spate of unwanted pregnancies feared after reckless teenage drinking

NEW YEAR BINGERS' ABORTION LEGACY

By Colin Fernandez and Steve Doughty

DRUNKEN one-night stands over New Year will bring a record number of abortions among teenagers.

A lethal mix of binge drinking and unprotected casual sex will also mean a sharp increase in sexually-transmitted diseases.

The warning from the Marie Stopes International organisation, which carries out around one in three UK abortions, comes as Ministers admit their £138million drive to reduce teenage pregnancies is failing.

A target of halving the rate by 2010 now looks well out of reach.

There are fears that some girls see a termination as just another form of contraception.

Abortion in Britain has already reached record levels, with more than 200,000 each year. Nearly one in five are on girls under 18.

Labour's liberal licensing laws, which made alcohol widely available into the early hours, are further fuelling casual sex.

The Marie Stopes group said it carried out 6,000 abortions last February, the peak month for young women who become pregnant over Christmas and New Year. The figure was 13 per cent up on 2006, and a similar increase is expected this year.

Spokesman Steve Kerridge said: 'When alcohol is involved

Turn to Page 4

Abortion legacy

Continued From Page One

inhibitions come down. It's not just unplanned pregnancies but rampant rates of sexually transmitted infections. It's very difficult to get that message out there.

'Many women tell us that they have used a condom, but mistakes happen, particularly when alcohol is involved.'

Leading doctors said the organisation was right. Professor Ian Gilmore, president of the Royal College of Physicians, said: 'Binge drinking is a matter for both sexes but sadly it is the women that end up holding the baby – or having the abortion.

'Binge drinking in young women is one of the biggest health risks. But the worst dangers are not long-term liver disease but accidents and sexual accidents including unwanted pregnancy, rape and sexually transmitted diseases.

'We need to get the message through that getting drunk isn't cool and it makes young women extremely vulnerable.'

Victoria Gillick, a campaigner with the Life anti-abortion group said: 'What's happening here is a massacre of the innocents. As a pregnancy counsellor you find a lot of people coming for pregnancy tests in late January and February.

'It's clearly Christmas spirits and alcohol taking away inhibitions.'

The Marie Stopes group has launched a £15 'festive family planning' pack at its clinics containing a morning-after pill, two condoms, two 'spikeys' – luminous plastic lids to stop drinks being spiked – and a sexual health guide.

The fresh admission of difficulties with the Government's Teenage Pregnancy Strategy came in a Health Department document which said 'progress needs to accelerate'.

The original aim was to halve the rate of under-18 pregnancies between 1998 and 2010.

But the cut has so far been only 11.4 per cent – and critics say even that is misleading because 1998 was a year with an unusually high rate of teen pregnancies. The number of youngsters becoming pregnant has actually risen, despite the fall in the rate, because there are now more teenage girls.

Ministers have promised to review the policy and have called for greater efforts by parents to prevent their daughters becoming pregnant.

But there has as yet been no change to the main tactic of trying to teach teenagers that sex can lead to pregnancy and disease and to persuade them to use contraception.

Critics say the Government's approach simply encourages teenagers to engage freely in sex.

Jim Dobbin, Labour MP for Heywood and Middleton, said: 'For there to be a perceived increase in abortion at this time of year, it has to be drink or drug related.

'But it's not just drink. The government's sexual education programme isn't working and hasn't been working for a long time. I think it backfires by encouraging youngsters to take part in sexual activity, rather than discourage them.

'We need more restraint'

'There really needs to be a move back to instil in youngsters a feeling of restraint, and to think before they have sex. They need to respect their boyfriends and girlfriends and try to encourage them not to have sex outside marriage.'

The number of abortions has risen steadily every year since it was legalised in 1968. Just 23,641 abortions were carried out in that year.

In 2006, the most recent year for which figures are available, there were 201,173, up from 194,353 the previous year.

Girls under 19 were the age group most likely to have an abortion – with 35 under-19s out of every 1,000 having an abortion.

c.fernandez@dailymail.co.uk

New year Bingers' abortion legacy
Daily Mail Monday, 31st December 2007

As the abortion pill becomes readily available and contraceptives are handed out to school pupils...

UNDER government plans to help women deal with unwanted pregnancies, the 'abortion pill' is set to become more widely available. Meanwhile, Superdrug is planning to provide sex counsellors for teenagers in its branches, and Ministers have given the go-ahead for schools to supply contraception. But what will be the long-term cost of these worrying measures? Gill Penn believes she knows. Now 46, she lost her virginity at 14 and slept with more than a dozen boys while she was underage, which she now believes had a disastrous effect on her life.

If anyone says girls at 14 are emotionally ready for sex they're wrong. I'm 46 and still coming to terms with the consequences

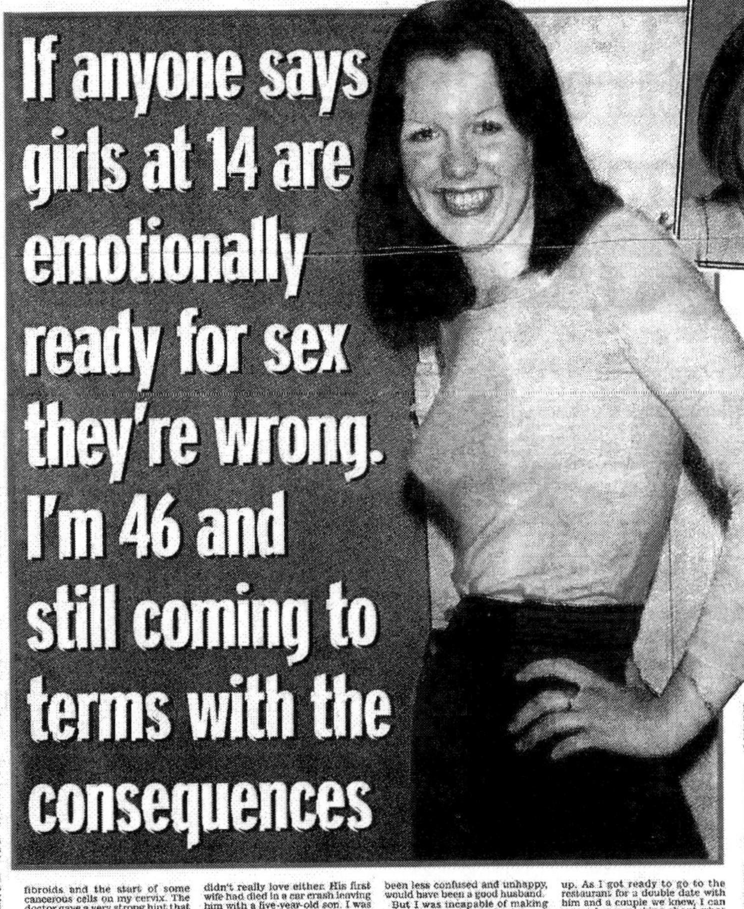

Regrets: Gill as she is today, above, and as a teenager, left

Interview by **Becky Morris**

AT 14, I used to go pony-riding at weekends, helping all day in the stables for an hour's free riding lesson. I loved climbing trees and bird-watching, and my keenest desire was to be a marine biologist. But one Saturday afternoon I learned far more about biology than any child of that age should.

I'd been out playing with a schoolfriend near our home in Orpington, Kent, when we bumped into two boys a year or so older. One of them had the run of his family house because both parents were out at work.

'Did we want to go back with them and listen to some records?'

'Why not,' I thought.

Once inside the house, the older of the two boys asked me to go upstairs with him. I had no idea why, but I was egged on by my schoolfriend.

'Would you like to lie down on the bed with me?' he asked.

I was honestly so naive that my reply was: 'Why?' I was soon to find out.

I lost my virginity with that boy, and although I can still picture him clearly, I can't even remember his name.

We weren't in love. In fact, we hardly knew each other. We met only a few times, always for sex in the afternoon. There was no question of us going out on dates because my parents, who had no idea what was going on, would not have dreamed of letting me go to the cinema or a disco with a boy.

I was the middle child of a family of five, my parents were old-fashioned working-class people. Dad was a builder, Mum was a housewife, and all they wanted for their children was for us to marry happily and settle down nearby.

They were very strict, expecting us to go to church twice on Sundays, once in the morning while Mum cooked lunch, and back again for Evensong.

But for all my moral upbringing, I still gave away my virginity without a second thought. The truth is I was just too naive to know any better.

Looking back, I was little more than a child — though at 5ft 7in and wearing a 34B bra, I looked much older. With long dark hair and a trim, sporty figure, I found, to my amazement, that I was the centre of male attention wherever I went.

Boys would stop and talk to me in the park, at church youth club and even on the way home from school. It was then that I really could have benefited from some wise words from my mother, or perhaps even teachers.

But in our house — and at my girls' grammar school — such things were, quite simply, never mentioned.

On my first encounter with the boy who took my virginity, I did no more than lie on the bed with him. We kissed and cuddled, which I liked. Then, he struggled to put his hand up my shirt, which I didn't like. I managed to fight him off and after a while we went back downstairs and rejoined the other couple.

ON MY way home I was shocked and astonished to hear that my friend had actually had sex with her boyfriend — and was showing off about it. All I had been told by way of sex education led me to expect her to be pregnant and, for good measure, to be struck down by lightning and disappear into the bowels of hell.

To my confusion, there were, for her, seemingly no repercussions, which made me think perhaps, in some way, it was acceptable after all.

The next time the four of us got together, I ended up having sex with my so-called 'boyfriend'.

It was a strange, worrying experience. I liked the cuddling, the affection, and the fact that he found me attractive. But the actual sex I found weird, uncomfortable and shameful.

And no, we didn't use contraception. I am sure we could have got some condoms, but I was too shy to mention it and he clearly didn't think it was his responsibility. We met up a few more times for sex, but the relationship, such as it was, soon fizzled out.

We had so little in common and the sex was something I did to please him. I'd have got more pleasure out of climbing trees with him, and it would have meant as much to me. Luckily, I didn't fall pregnant.

It was at around that time that I had started to suffer from very painful, heavy periods. My mother took me to the doctor and I was prescribed some pills which the chemist gave to me in a medicine bottle.

HE TOLD me to take one a day for 21 days and then have seven days with no medication before starting a new 21-day course. I was a smart enough girl, and it wasn't long before I said to my GP: 'This is the contraceptive Pill, isn't it?'

I knew that it could also be used to regulate periods. His reply was astonishing. 'I was wondering how long it would take you to work that out. Now we can stop taking them out of the packets.'

So I was not even 15 and on the Pill. I knew my mother would be horrified that I was taking advantage of the fact that I could not get pregnant. But, nonetheless, I did exactly that, rationalising to myself that, because I was on the Pill, there would be no consequences and I was not doing any harm to myself by having sex.

I had a string of short-term boyfriends, all for a couple of weeks or months, which my parents knew nothing about.

We'd have sex at friends' houses and at teenage parties, in the upstairs bedrooms. It meant almost nothing to me. I did it purely because I'd come to expect that this was what boys would want, that it would guarantee me their attention and make me feel wanted.

But the actual act gave me little pleasure. It was simply 'what you did'. And I wasn't alone. This was the Seventies, when the morals of the country were changing rapidly due to the arrival of the Pill and permissive society.

My parents believed that we should wait until we married to have sex. Many of my schoolfriends, however, thought very differently, and our boyfriends were only too happy to take advantage of this.

I can remember feeling that my first sexual experience should have meant something and realising, in a state of some dismay, that it hadn't. But, meaningless as it was, the physical and emotional aftermath of my early experimentation was all too significant.

At 32, I had to have a hysterectomy because I had severe endometriosis, fibroids and the start of some cancerous cells on my cervix. The doctor gave a very strong hint that early sexual activity could have been the cause of my problems.

At the time, I was unhappily married with one daughter and not keen to have more children. But today, I look back and think that if things had been different, I would have liked to have had a loving relationship with my husband, and a big family.

But my early sexual experiences not only destroyed my fertility, they prevented me from finding happiness in any relationship with a man.

In fact, I feel that the psychological impact has been even more damaging. I'd lost all self-confidence and self-esteem by being treated purely as a sex object from such a young age. I lost sight of what I wanted from a relationship and felt that my role was simply to give a man pleasure through sex.

I first married, at 17, to a man who didn't love me, and who I didn't really love either. His first wife had died in a car crash leaving him with a five-year-old son. I was attractive, in fact working part-time as a model, so I was both a trophy wife and someone who would look after his child.

I was so used to doing what men said that I was completely submissive, and that, I believe, brought out the bully in him. Within a year he was hitting me.

MY MOTHER insisted I come home and get divorced. But I went on to have two more very similar marriages. In each, I didn't have the confidence to be myself and was subservient to my husbands, which brought out the worst in them.

I'm particularly regretful about my second marriage, to the father of my daughter, now 30. He was, essentially, a good man and, if I had been less confused and unhappy, would have been a good husband.

But I was incapable of making any man a friend and, after 14 years together, communication broke down utterly and we split up.

My third husband was abusive, a heavy drinker and used to put me down at any opportunity. And so, three years ago, I left him and vowed to sort myself out once and for all. I started counselling, got myself a job and moved house from Sevenoaks to Cheddar, Somerset, for a fresh start.

I'm still attractive and still have that certain something which made men so desire me as a teenager. But now things are different. I'm not interested in disguising my true feelings to please men and get their attention.

I was single for a long time until a friend introduced me eight months ago to John, a 45-year-old training consultant.

I can remember our first meeting clearly. I'd been told about him and that my friends were keen to fix us up. As I got ready to go to the restaurant for a double date with him and a couple we knew, I can remember panicking about what to wear, as I always have over the years.

But then a sort of calmness descended and I realised that the best thing to do would be to wear whatever I liked and felt comfortable in. And so I did.

As soon as I saw him, I thought to myself: 'Oh you're lovely.' As I walked across to shake hands I could see exactly the same thought written across his face.

To be honest, it was the first time I had ever really felt that about a man. Before, I always let him choose me and played a passive role in the courtship.

John asked me if we could meet again and I said: 'Thank you, I would like that very much.' He's since said that my directness and honesty almost took him aback, but that he found it very attractive.

Today, we are living together and plan to get married. But it still never fails to amaze me when I see John loading the washing machine or doing the ironing. He treats me as an equal and expects to do his share of the work in the relationship.

And he is so supportive of my achievements, both at work, at Royal Mail, where I have been promoted rapidly, and in my private life, where I do a lot of fund-raising and voluntary work for Riding for the Disabled.

I can remember people saying about their husbands, 'He is my best friend' and wondering what they meant.

Today, with John, I understand. And what's more, I am truly relaxed and comfortable with our sex life, for the first time.

I just think it is a terrible shame that it has taken me so long to discover the joy of being in a good relationship. I think that my life could have been so different if I had not ruined my childhood with casual sexual encounters.

PERHAPS I would have married happily long ago and had lots of children. Instead, I suffered a series of unhappy relationships and my daughter comes from a broken home.

Even today, I am haunted by the experiences of my teenage years and, looking back, find it very sad indeed. Equally, I am horrified that the Government is even considering handing out contraceptives at schools.

My daughter is now at university. Throughout her early teens I said to her so often: 'Never have sex with someone unless you really love them.'

It is one of my proudest achievements that I was able to give her the confidence to say no and wait until she was ready. This meant so much to me, because I am convinced that no child of 13, 14 or 15 is emotionally ready to have sex, even if they appear to be more than ready physically.

If contraception is available in schools, the message is that underage sex is acceptable and that the only thing that matters is not getting pregnant or catching a disease.

In fact, our children need to be guided to have the confidence to wait until they are in love and truly ready to make love. And I know from bitter experience that no child of 14 is ready for that.

Teenage Sex - paying the price.
Daily Mail July 8th 2002

July 8th 2002.

Daily Mail

COMMENT

Tragic cost of the sexual revolution

NOT content, it seems, with this country having the highest teenage abortion rate in the EU, the Government appears determined to push up the rate still further with its plan to offer faster and easier terminations.

So-called abortion pills, currently obtainable only in hospital wards and special day units, are also to be made available to all from family planning centres.

Given this seemingly relentless, almost fanatical, determination to promote abortion, the Royal College of Obstetricians and Gynaecologists' chilling estimate that one in three British women is likely to have a termination before the age of 45 comes as no surprise.

Let us be honest. Abortion is today available in this country on demand, making a mockery of the supposedly strict grounds – concerning the welfare or condition of mother-to-be and expected child – on which it was first allowed when it was legalised by Parliament 35 years ago.

But, of course, since those days Britain has undergone a total moral and sexual revolution, where anything goes.

We now have a Government that thinks nothing of handing out free birth control pills in schools, including to girls under 16, whose bodies have not stopped growing and who could be storing up terrible problems for the future.

Yet only last March a study by researchers at Nottingham University suggested – surprise, surprise – that giving contraceptives to this age group *raises* the number of underage pregnancies rather than lowers it.

What a devastating condemnation of three decades of value-free, non-judgmental sex education and unlimited contraception: a combination that has fostered the kind of morally incontinent behaviour exhibited by young Britons holidaying on the Greek island of Rhodes, on which this paper reported last Saturday.

What a stunning indictment it is of those who trumpeted this liberal approach as the way to curb underage pregnancy and abortion.

But most tragic of all, what a cost in emotionally scarred lives.

Tragic Cost of the Sexual Revolution.
Daily Mail July 8th 2002.

Daily Mail

MONDAY, JULY 8, 2002 40p

First it was the morning-after pill, then contraceptives in the classroom. And now...

ABORTION PILL FOR TEENAGERS

By **Beezy Marsh** Medical Reporter

AN abortion pill which will open the floodgates to thousands of terminations is to be handed out to girls and women.

Furious campaigners warned last night that easy access to the drug will lead to a huge increase in teenage pregnancies and abortions.

The controversial move comes only days after ministers announced that contraceptive pills and condoms will be given to schoolchildren.

The abortion pill – known as RU486 – requires no surgery and makes terminations easier and faster.

It is taken in the first nine weeks of pregnancy and effectively causes a miscarriage.

At the moment access is restricted, but under the shake-up teenagers and women will be able to obtain the drugs easily from NHS family planning clinics and GPs.

However, campaigners said making it easier for girls to gain contraceptives and abortion will only worsen Britain's appalling teenage pregnancy rate. It is already one of the highest in Europe.

Promiscuity will increase and result in even more terminations, especially among the young, they warn.

There are also fears that some teenagers resorting to the abortion pill could lose the ability to have children in later life.

And the spread of sexually transmitted infections could also worsen. Numbers have already doubled among the young in the last five years.

Josephine Quintavalle, of the Pro-Life Alliance, said: 'This move is irresponsible and short-term.

'We have a government which is obsessed by offering abortion without thinking about the

Turn to Page 4, Col. 1

Cat got your tongue, Charles?

TV presenter Cat Deeley cheekily sticks out her tongue at Prince Charles in Hyde Park

SEE PAGE 3

Women warned over abortion pill dangers

Continued from Page One

consequences. These are not drugs for children – there is the potential for danger particularly in the developing body.

'The idea of younger girls using this is just unbelievable.'

Nuala Scarisbrick, trustee of the charity LIFE, said: 'The Government is clearly going to be targeting this at young people – they say it is quick and easy for women.

'Women, and particularly young women, are being betrayed.

'They are being handed out pills and condoms in school which encourage them to experiment and get sexual diseases and now they are being told not to worry, because there is an easy abortion option for them. It is an appalling deceit.'

Conservative Party deputy leader Michael Ancram condemned the move as 'socially damaging' and 'morally questionable'.

'Personally I am against it because I think that anything that makes abortion easier and simpler, in the end is harmful to people,' he added.

Abortions among the under-16s have risen relentlessly during the past decade, from 3,510 in 1992 to 4,382 in 2000.

But, despite warnings that this will worsen, it will be easier for them to obtain a so-called medical abortion using the pill. The change means many patients will no longer have to go to hospital or pay around £300 for a surgical termination at a private clinic.

Patients will still have to obtain certification from two doctors before they can go ahead with the procedure, which involves taking two different drugs over two days.

The costs to the NHS will be lower as there will be no need for anaesthetists, operating theatre staff or surgeon.

Miss Quintavalle added: 'You save a lot of money not using anaesthetics. It is quicker, easier and cheaper – I would put cheaper in very big capitals.

'This is being touted as an easy method, well it may not be easy either physically or emotionally.

'The woman is very much involved.

'She sees what is happening and may find it very hard to come to terms with what she has done as she may see the foetus.'

The controversy surrounds plans outlined in a Department of Health document, Implementing the Sexual Health Strategy.

The Government is committed to cut the rate of conceptions among under-18s by 15 per cent by 2004 and to halve it by 2010.

More than 8,000 girls under 16 become pregnant every year. Including the under-18s pushes the figure up to around 41,000.

A Department of Health spokesman said: 'The strategy pointed out that younger people tend to go for advice later in their pregnancy. If they are going to have a termination they need to do so as soon as they can.

'This could be useful for young people, but it is not targeted at them. It is not excluding them either, because it would not be right to exclude anyone on grounds of age.'

Officials said widening access to the abortion pill aimed to slash waiting lists for operations.

Patients can wait five or six weeks for a surgical termination, increasing their anguish.

The Department was unable to provide statistics on the cost of surgical and medical abortions last night.

The spokesman added: 'This is not about cost cutting. Using the medical abortion just means people do not have to have surgery.'

The British Pregnancy Advisory Service has already allowed more than 1,000 women to undergo an abortion using the pill at home, after being monitored by doctors in a clinic.

Ian Jones, chief executive, said: 'Our experience is this is a safe and effective method. Some women find it not very painful, and others find it very painful, but they prefer this to surgery.'

So-called 'bedroom abortions' have proved popular with those who want a quick solution without surgery, in the relative privacy and comfort of their own home.

There is a trained nurse available over the phone if needed.

Just under 20 per cent of the 188,000 women undergoing NHS abortions every year use the abortion pill early in their pregnancy. First they take the drug, mifepristone, which blocks the hormone needed to make a fertilised egg cling to the womb lining. This cuts off the foetus from the blood and nourishment needed for life.

A second drug called misopristol is used 48 hours later. But it has been at the centre of health fears over womb rupture when used on women with more advanced pregnancies.

Another drug which may be used, called gemeprost, has known side-effects including nausea, vomiting, rashes and severe womb pain during contractions.

Womb and urinary infections have also been reported.

Comment – Page TEN
How under-age sex wrecked my life – Pages 26-27

'They are, of course, more effective if you take them <u>instead</u> of intercourse.'

HOW IT WORKS

Women up to nine weeks pregnant can use the abortion pill method after two doctors have certified that they can do so.

PILL 1 RU486, also known as mifepristone, is taken orally first in hospital or a clinic. Woman is monitored for an hour for side effects and sent home. Drug forces the foetus to detach from the womb lining by altering hormone levels within the body. Woman may feel period pain sensations at this time.

PILL 2 *Misopristol is inserted by doctors 48 hours later, to force the foetus to be expelled. Contractions, which may be extremely painful, or milder like period pain, are followed by an enforced "miscarriage" which may take up to six to eight hours. Doctors then check the woman to ensure the process has completed properly. Surgery may follow if it has not.*

'Not about cost cutting'

So who else allows it, and when?

THE RU486 pill has been available for more than a decade but not all countries have accepted it.

Countries which have accepted RU486:

France

RU486 has been available since 1988 under the brand name Mifegyne for use for up to nine weeks after conception.

It is restricted and prescribed only by approved doctors and health care practitioners.

Women must sign a letter of consent to say they have been completely informed of the risks associated with the procedure.

They take the pill at home but must have a follow-up visit eight to 12 days afterwards.

One third of the 170,000 French women who terminate pregnancies each year choose this method.

Surgical abortions can be performed up to 12 weeks after conception but cannot be used as early as the abortion pill.

Smokers over the age of 35 and women with cardiovascular problems are advised not to use the pill after it was found there was a heightened risk of heart complications in some women. There was fierce opposition from pro-life and Christian campaigners when it was launched and they are still fighting to have it banned.

Germany

RU486 has been available since 1999. Once prescribed by a doctor it cannot be supplied by pharmacists, but only by the drug company which holds the manufacturing and distribution rights.

This rule is aimed at ensuring it is used only for legal abortions but pro-life campaigners in the country have labelled it 'the pill of death'.

In the first half of 2001, nearly 1,800 terminations were carried out using the drug, less than three per cent of the total.

Studies have shown that there is little 'negative attitude' towards terminations using the drug among women, counselling centres and doctors.

Patients have to undergo a session of counselling to satisfy doctors that they have thoroughly considered their decision.

They are then sent home for another week before a second counselling session. The counsellor then decides whether or not to issue a certificate permitting an abortion to be carried out.

At no point is the counsellor allowed to indicate any approval for a decision against continuing with the pregnancy.

United States

THE abortion pill mifepristone, the name by which RU486 is known in America, was approved for use across all states in September 2000.

The decision was based on extensive U.S. studies and on the pill's 12-year usage in some European countries.

The Federal Drug Administration – one of the most cautious regulatory agencies in the world – concluded that serious side-effects were extremely rare.

However, approval was controversial and the anti-abortion lobby launched a campaign to stop it.

Earlier this year, leading medical schools began offering students special courses on the abortion pill and also on the morning-after contraceptive which can be dispensed in some states by chemists without a prescription. Acceptance of mifepristone has been slow, largely because anti-abortion activists threaten and picket doctors known to offer it.

It is estimated that more than 90 per cent of mifepristone prescriptions are written by abortion clinics.

Two months ago, the distributors of the pill wrote to all doctors saying that six women who took mifepristone in the U.S. and Canada had become ill. Two of them died, although no direct link had been established with the drug.

Countries which do not accept RU486:

Australia

IT IS not available, despite a survey of women who took part in trials in 1997 expressing a high level of satisfaction with it.

A survey of 41 patients said they believed it offered them a more active role in a termination compared to surgical means – although, paradoxically, they also felt less involved.

The health ministry was opposed to its introduction and drug companies said they were not prepared to take it on in the years leading up to 2001.

Then opposition Democrats tried to force its acceptance through the Senate but failed to win changes to the law. Many women protested that Australia, once seen as a progressive nation, was failing them.

Italy

SINCE the introduction of a morning-after pill two years ago there have been calls from doctors for the abortion pill to be legalised.

Late last year the health ministry relented and allowed a hospital in Turin to apply to buy a limited amount of RU486 from other EU countries so its effects could be monitored but these results have not yet been made public.

The strongest opponents of RU486 is the Roman Catholic Church, which when the morning-after pill was legalised, condemned the then Italian government and urged doctors to take a 'deep long look at their moral conscience' before they prescribed it.

Of RU486 the Church has said: 'Anything that makes abortion easier is to be condemned.'

Abortion Pill for Teenagers
Daily Mail July 8th 2002.

Daily Mail, Monday, November 18, 2002 V1 Page 19

Rush to give morning-after pills to girls as young as 11

Picture posed by models

By **Beezy Marsh**
Medical Reporter

THOUSANDS of young girls are being offered the morning-after pill as councils rush to take up a Government scheme to bring contraception into schools.

Pupils as young as 11 have already received the emergency contraception from school nurses, it emerged yesterday.

Organisers of a pilot scheme in Oxfordshire, which started giving out the pill to children five years ago, say councils around the country are clamouring to follow their lead.

The rush has dismayed family campaigners who warn making contraception freely available without parents' consent will not stem the tide of unwanted teenage pregnancies and the spread of sexual diseases.

There is also concern that the powerful dose of hormones in the pill, which prevents an embryo implanting in the womb, may have health effects which are not yet known.

Ministers have backed the school clinics as part of a drive to cut teenage pregnancies by half by 2010.

Nearly 500 girls at 16 schools in Oxfordshire have already been given the morning-after pill, called Levonelle-2, since 1997. Of these, two-thirds were under the age of 16.

Dr Liz Greenhall, director of family planning in Oxfordshire, said other areas were hoping to follow suit.

In the South London borough of Wandsworth, governors at Chestnut Grove School in Balham will allow the morning-after pill to be handed out to children in the New Year. If the trial is a success it will be expanded across the borough.

Dr Greenhall said: 'Since the Government's endorsement of this service there has been a lot of interest across the country.'

She said girls under 16 were encouraged to talk to their parents if they were sexually active, but parental consent was not needed to dispense contraception. Pupil confidentiality is respected and most clinics are 'teacher-free' zones.

But Dr Greenhall also told the Daily Mail that the service had not had a major effect on reducing teen pregnancy rates or sexually transmitted infections (STIs).

'In terms of pregnancy and STIs I don't think we would be able to say, yes, we have made a huge impact,' she said. 'This is a more long-term effort, trying to say to young people that health professionals are approachable.'

Latest figures show the pregnancy rate among under-18s in the UK is Europe's highest, while rates of the sexual diseases chlamydia and gonorrhea are soaring.

Labour MP Jim Dobbin, of the parliamentary Pro-Life Group, said: 'The Government should look carefully at making the pill available to young girls, especially when the policy does not appear to be working.'

Nuala Scarisbrick, of the charity LIFE, said: 'These schemes are condoning under-age sex, which is illegal. Who will be responsible if a girl takes the pill and becomes ill?'

The Department of Health said research showed that youth contraceptive services increased use of contraception without increasing sexual activity.

b.marsh@dailymail.co.uk

11 year old schoolgirls receive the morning after pill
Daily Mail Monday November 18th 2002.

I don't mind, I don't have to go to school, says mother-to-be

This girl is 12 and pregnant by a boy of 15 whose name she cannot recall

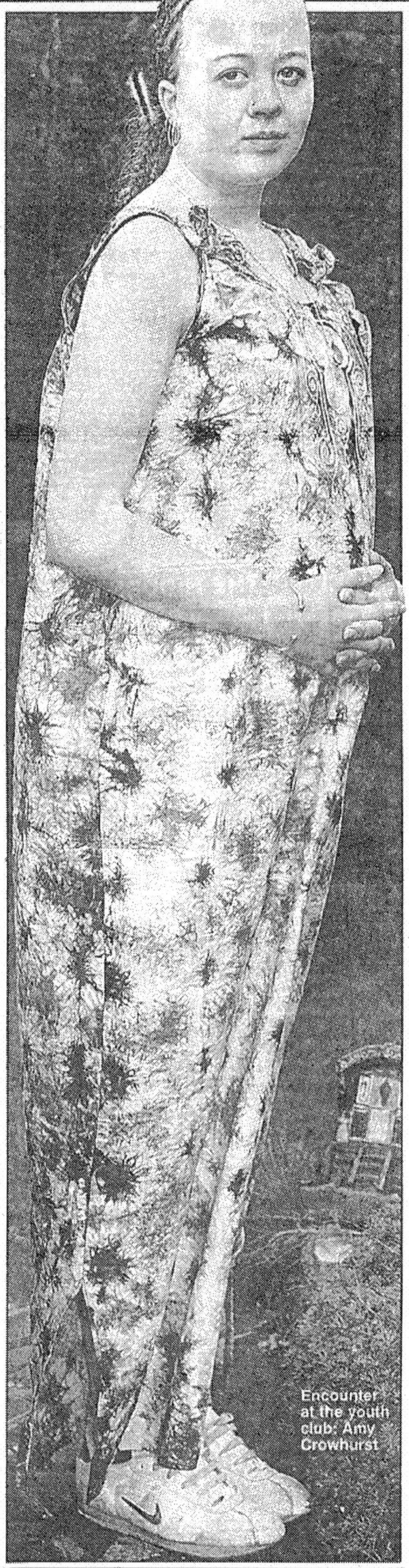

Encounter at the youth club: Amy Crowhurst

By **Kate Sherry** and **Richard Price**

AMY Crowhurst is four months pregnant. She is also just 12 years old.

Her child was conceived in a one-night stand at the local youth club with a 15-year-old boy. She does not know his surname or where he lives.

'I know I was stupid to get pregnant but I'm not that bothered really,' she admitted yesterday. 'Of course I wish it had never happened but it's too late now.'

Amy, one of Britain's youngest recorded mothers-to-be, spoke to the Daily Mail after we were invited into the family home in Crawley, West Sussex.

This consists of two council houses knocked into one – to accommodate the still growing family of Amy's 42-year-old mother Rose.

She has given birth to nine children by two different fathers. The children's ages range from 21 years to just four months old.

Three years ago Amy's father walked out on the family and set up home with another woman. Since then her mother has had a number of relationships.

The most recent of these resulted in the birth of Amy's youngest sibling, a boy called Momodou whose father has since returned to his wife and children in the Gambia.

Speaking with her mother's approval Amy – who smokes, and has had her nose, ears and belly button pierced – said: 'I don't really mind because I don't like school anyway and now I don't have to go any more.

'I don't need to go to ante-natal classes because nobody knows more than my mum about bringing up children.'

Two weeks ago a doctor confirmed that Amy was pregnant. At first she had been reluctant to tell her mother, but suspicions were aroused when Amy began putting on weight and fainted.

She had confided in her mother that she was missing periods.

'But I put that down to smoking,' said Mrs Crowhurst, who knew her daughter was already a regular smoker. 'When she kept putting on weight I went out and bought a home pregnancy kit, which was when we found out the truth.'

The child's teenage father does not know about the pregnancy. Amy's mother knows only that he is 'a Jamaican boy from London' who visited Crawley for a night out.

Amy claims to have had sex with the boy only once. The result of that meeting has been the end of Amy's childhood.

She can no longer play sport or even go to school with her friends. After missing several weeks of school her own personal tutor visited her at home for the first time yesterday.

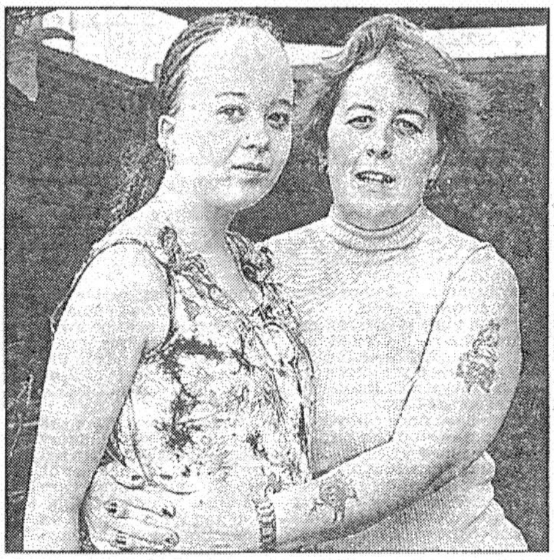

Growing family: Amy and her mother Rose yesterday

Mrs Crowhurst said she had been surprised by her daughter's pregnancy because 'she knows all about condoms and that'.

She added: 'I don't think she realises the magnitude of what she has done yet.

'She thinks it's all exciting being pregnant and having a baby, but she is throwing half her life away. She's really just a girl herself. She is still a giggly little 12-year-old at heart. But she's mature for her age and I'm sure she'll be a good mum.'

'She's throwing half her life away'

The family lives on £185-a-week benefits, as Mrs Crowhurst has given up her job as a dinner lady to care for her clan.

Amy's father, Peter Crowhurst, a 47-year-old maintenance engineer, was unavailable for comment yesterday but is said to have 'reluctantly' accepted his daughter's intention to go through with the pregnancy.

He is understood to be 'deeply concerned' that Amy, who wears his wedding ring on a chain around her neck, is racing towards motherhood when she is still so young.

Amy said: 'I am worried about the actual birth because I'm so small and I know it's quite painful.

'But I know I can cope. I've had lots of practice with my brothers and sisters. I know all about feeding, bathing and changing.'

She rejected talk of an abortion after seeing a scan of her unborn child. Nevertheless, claims of maturity pale into insignificance when the 12-year-old reveals that her only craving during pregnancy is for sweets.

Social services have visited the family. 'But they said everything was fine and they haven't made any arrangements to come back,' said Mrs Crowhurst.

A spokesman for West Sussex social services said: 'We produce an individually tailored package of care and support for the child and family.

'This is arranged in close consultation with them, with colleagues in the education department and with the health service.'

Britain's youngest mother is believed to be a girl of 11, who fell pregnant when she was just ten. The world's youngest recorded mother was an eight-year-old from Arkansas in the U.S., who had twins in 1994.

k.sherry@dailymail.co.uk

Pregnant 12 year old rejects talk of abortion after seeing scan of unborn child
Daily Mail Friday November 15th 2002.

Sun CAMPAIGN

BAN THE BUTCHER

Fury as abortion doc who nearly killed a patient is allowed to carry on doing ops

By JACQUI THORNTON Health Editor and DIANA BLAMIRES

THE SUN today launches a campaign to ban the surgeon who horrifically butchered a woman patient — after loony health chiefs let him CARRY ON operating.

In a botched abortion, consultant gynaecologist Andrew Gbinigie ruptured the woman's womb and removed an ovary, a Fallopian tube and part of her bowel.

The General Medical Council yesterday found him guilty of serious professional misconduct – but, incredibly, decided **NOT** to strike him off.

Gbinigie, 47, can continue doing abortions subject to set conditions.

But we are warning all women – do not let this man operate on **YOU**.

Our campaign received wide support yesterday. Peter Walsh of the charity Action for Victims of Medical Accidents said: "The public will be asking, 'What does a doctor have to do in order to be struck off?'

"The case will cause further damage to public confidence in the way doctors are regulated."

Joyce Robins, of Patient Concern, said: "I back you absolutely. Such mistakes wreck lives.

"I would like to see a national register of people who have had cases proven against them so you could see who was operating on you."

Mum Bronwyn Whitehouse, 47, who suffered two years of hell following a bungled hysterectomy by Nigerian-born Gbinigie in 1996, said: "I am really disgusted by this decision. He has got away with it. I wouldn't let him operate on me again."

Medical negligence solicitors Alexanders Harris described the abortion case as "shocking" and said the patient could win £100,000 in civil damages.

The Royal College of Obstetricians and Gynaecologists would not comment on the GMC decision but a spokesman described the case as "deeply disturbing".

Abused

The abortion patient, Miss A, was 20 weeks pregnant when Gbinigie operated at the private Calthorpe clinic in Birmingham in November 2000. She nearly died of her injuries.

Gbinigie, from Barnt Green, Birmingham, will now be allowed to do abortions on women up to 12 weeks pregnant unsupervised. He will be allowed to operate beyond 12 weeks after being retrained. Any operations must be at hospitals with intensive care facilities and with other surgeons at hand. His work will be subject to random checks.

The GMC's Professional Conduct Committee said Gbinigie abused his position as a doctor, had been dishonest and was not clinically competent to carry out the operation.

He would not be removed from the medical register because he had not repeatedly botched operations.

But the committee heard a patient had to be taken to hospital when Gbinigie failed to fully remove a foetus **AFTER** the Miss A incident.

Calthorpe Clinic manager Tracey Allsopp said: "We immediately reported the doctor."

● **HAVE YOU** been a victim of bungling Gbinigie? Contact Jacqui Thornton today on 0207 782 4083.

Don't let this man near you
DO not let this man operate on you — he is butcher doctor Andrew Gbinigie.
Remember his face and make sure he does NOT carry out an abortion, hysterectomy or any other surgery on you.

Botched Abortion - Killed one and nearly the other
The Sun 21st March 2003

Peter Hitchens

Why the new Gestapo says it's all right to kill babies

THE British State has just helped a child kill her baby in the womb, and kept the act secret from the girl's own mother.

The law says this is all right. The grand people who decide what is best for us from their remote offices and their comfortable suburbs think it is all right.

I think it is revolting and frightening, though my opinions – like yours – count for little in a nation governed by an arrogant elite.

Most of the things that are wrong with our diseased, debauched society are wrapped up in this story.

Fourteen-year-old Michelle Smith is yet another victim of the immoral propaganda pumped into the minds of the young, who are told by schools, TV and the rock music industry that chastity is a joke and 'Virgin' is a brand name.

Her unborn baby is yet another victim of our culture of death, in which we sacrifice the priceless lives of others for our convenience. The sex education fanatics use taxpayers' money to maintain their relentless campaign against traditional morality, even though the results are the exact opposite of their official purpose.

And the Government, while it wails about under-age pregnancy, single mothers and sexual diseases, continues to pursue the very policy which has greatly worsened all these problems. Why? Why weaken the morals that kept us safe from these things? Why weaken the families whose strength once kept 14-year-old girls away from such perils?

Because the married family gets in the way of two mighty forces in our society. One is the 'parental state', which believes it is so good that it wants to be all-powerful.

The other is the greed of business which doesn't want mothers staying home running happy households when they could be hunched in offices or factories, making profits.

NEITHER of them wants private life, where people form their own opinions and tastes. They want a population that thinks what it is told, buys what it is told, laughs at the same jokes, wears the same clothes, votes for the same party. Even now, a law is grinding through Parliament which will take away the last remaining traces of privacy in the home.

The horrible Children Bill gives a blank cheque to any future government to set up a vast database tracking every child, allowing endless interference in what parents do by the linked organisations of the State.

Incidentally, a Labour MP is likely to move an amendment to this Bill banning smacking, which will give the authorities endless power to persecute parents with false allegations, as they now harass teachers.

The excuse for this new domestic Gestapo will be 'child abuse'. But abuse of children is 33 times more common in the kinds of non-family – unmarried mother, serial boyfriends – the Government seems so anxious to create and subsidise than it is in old-fashioned married households.

If they really wanted to reduce abuse, they would promote and strengthen marriage.

If they really wanted to reduce unwanted pregnancy, abortion and disease, they would back abstinence.

But they don't. Are they stupid, or lying?

I WONDER if we shall still have a Navy when, in October 2005, we mark the bicentenary of Nelson's victory at Trafalgar. Does it matter? Yes it does.

A Navy allows the nation that possesses it to act independently of others. Without that, it is not a nation, as current events show.

Pathetic, yes, but Maxine is not evil

HATE FIGURE: Maxine Carr has served her time and should now be allowed to live in peace

LEAVE Maxine Carr alone. The foam-flecked rage against her is irrational, unjust and barbaric.

Carr is undoubtedly dim but she is not evil.

As a conservative commentator who hates crime, believes in the death penalty for murder and severe punishment for wrongdoers, it is my duty to say this.

Carr has served her time under law.

She ought to be able to live undisturbed in any place she chooses. The fake rage against her is like the savagery of burglars and muggers who attack sex offenders in prison because they love to have someone to whom they can feel superior.

Yes, Ian Huntley should have been hanged.

Campaign all you like for the just return of capital punishment. But don't take out your frustrations on this pathetic woman.

THE new list of unmentionable words, issued by the politically correct authorities to the wretched judges who now run our injustice system, warns against the use of the expression 'common sense'. Now that's a surprise. Not long now before it's actually illegal.

WOULDN'T a serious government now be making detailed plans to reduce our national dependence on oil? Do we really want our future decided in Iraq, Saudi Arabia or Russia? But all this lot can come up with are forests of silly, useless windmills.

IF WE still had gallons, we would know just how costly petrol is. If we still had the old money, and pounds and ounces, we would know how much the EU had increased the price of food. The destruction of these landmarks looks more and more intentional. If we brought them back, we'd find out how much we had been diddled.

Gender benders who are perverting human nature

THE miserable story of David Reimer – the boy brought up as a girl, who rebelled passionately against this when he found out and who has just killed himself – is surely a warning to all those who think that male and female roles are just a matter of conditioning.

The vast attempt to change human nature now under way will have an equally unhappy end on a much larger scale.

By the way, how is it that the very people who say that male or female behaviour is learned are the same ones who insist that homosexuals are unalterably born that way?

MANIPULATED: David Reimer

WHY would it be irresponsible to get out of Iraq now? It was certainly irresponsible to go there in the first place on this absurd, unplanned adventure, and every week we stay there strengthens the fanatics, the mullahs and the men of violence. Can we seriously pretend peace and order in Iraq depend on our presence?

peter.hitchens@mailonsunday.co.uk

Why the new Gestapo says it's all right to kill babies
The Mail on Sunday May 16th 2004

Binge-drinking ladettes follow the men into oblivion

Daily Mail Reporter

YOUNG women are not only drinking as much as men. They are increasingly matching them in their drunken behaviour, a survey reveals.

Among women aged 16 to 24, nearly six in ten admit they have got so drunk at least once that they had no clear memory of the occasion.

One in five says she has lost keys or valuables while under the influence while one in seven has had a fight.

The figures are revealed in a survey of 1,000 women aged 16 to 34 for the magazine Company.

It found that 42 per cent had been on binges so heavy they had no recollection of the night before – with the figure rising to 57 per cent among under-24s.

A third admitted to having unprotected sex while drunk, with a similar number having at least once woken up with no idea how they had got home from their night out.

One in ten had lost consciousness through drink. Around half had walked home alone because they were too drunk to realise the risk.

Although many young women may laugh off these laddish binges the next day at the office, they are putting themselves at risk of health problems, assault and rape, says the magazine, whose survey was timed to coincide with the start of the Christmas party season.

While most young women are aware of the perils from spiked drinks or date-rape drugs, alcohol can often prove just as dangerous.

As well as leaving themselves at risk of attack, they are also more likely to be in accidents or injure themselves as a result of being drunk, it adds.

The survey adds to the evidence that women are matching men's drinking and the behaviour associated with it. This is particularly true among young women, possibly because they are more likely to be single and have more spare time.

Long term drink-related health dangers could include osteoporosis, sexual dysfunction including infertility, shrinking breasts, anaemia and other ailments.

Simple precautions could help women avoid some of the dangers, said Company editor Sam Baker.

'Young women should be able to go out and enjoy themselves and a drink whenever they like,' she said. Fortunately, it is easy to prevent contributing to these alarming statistics.

'These days, it isn't only your outfit that should be carefully planned.

'With a few simple preparations – carrying cab numbers for example, or alternating water and wine – anyone can have a fantastic night out knowing they'll be safe and healthy at the end of it.'

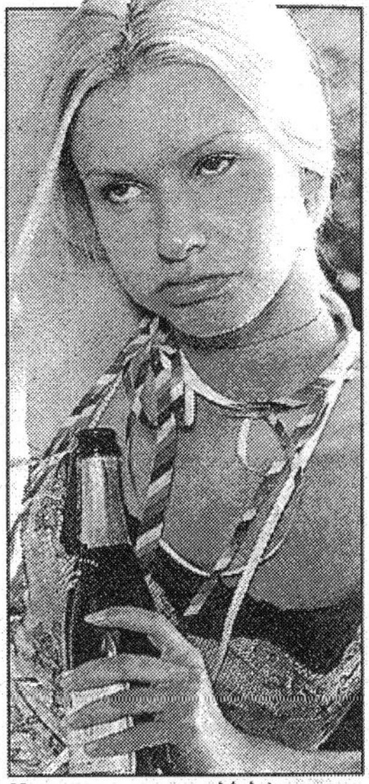

More young women drink to excess

Daily Mail, Wednesday, February 5, 2003

Ladette drinking culture 'can harm baby before birth'

By **Beezy Marsh**
Health Correspondent

THE growing trend for hard drinking among young women is putting unborn babies at risk of crippling disorders, experts warned yesterday.

Doctors fear hundreds of babies born in Britain every year suffer physical disabilities, brain damage and behavioural problems because of their mothers' love of alcohol.

The 'ladette' culture of binge-drinking and hard partying is feared to be increasing the dangers to unborn children.

The percentage of women regularly drinking above recommended levels has almost doubled, from 29 per cent in 1988 to 52 per cent in 2000.

Some women may not realise they are pregnant and continue

'Sober up on a Sunday'

to consume large quantities of alcohol in the crucial early weeks.

Others choose to carry on drinking during pregnancy, despite the dangers.

An investigation by BBC2's Newsnight revealed the growing threat from foetal alcohol syndrome (FAS).

It causes low birth weight, short stature, flattened features, brain, heart and kidney abnormalities, deafness and brain damage leading to poor hand-eye co-ordination and behavioural difficulties.

Britain is one of the few developed countries where pregnant women are officially advised they can drink.

Government guidance is that mothers-to-be can have up to four units of alcohol a week.

For those women who are not pregnant, 'safe' levels are 21 units a week, with a unit being a glass of wine, half a pint of beer or a measure of spirits.

However, alcohol abuse experts warn that women may choose to consume many of their units in weekend binges and may unwittingly expose their unborn child to harm as a result.

Moira Plant, a specialist in foetal alcohol syndrome from the Alcohol and Health Research Centre at the University of West England in Bristol, said: 'It appears that heavy drinking bouts – binge drinking – is the key to the severity of the damage caused to the baby.

'We drink in a northern European pattern – binge drinking. We drink heavily on a Friday and Saturday night and sober up on Sunday to go back to work on Monday. That kind of pattern can cause harm to the baby.'

No official figures exist on the number of babies born with foetal alcohol syndrome and related disorders.

But the National Organisation on Foetal Alcohol Syndrome estimates at least 26 babies are born every week showing signs of alcohol damage.

That means that in Britain alone, more than 1,300 children a year could be harmed by alcohol while still in the womb.

'We have to take seriously the possibility that we have a growing number of children born with alcohol-related damage that is not being identified – which means that, as they get older, the care they need is not there,' said Dr Plant.

She called for the Health Service to take the issue of preg-

'The care they need is not there'

nant women drinking more seriously to identify which babies were at risk.

'We will always ask women how much they smoke and very intimate questions about their sexual behaviour, diet and even finances,' she said.

'However, we often don't ask about drinking. Sometimes people in antenatal clinics say women's drinking is a very personal thing.'

The survey by Newsnight found that getting a diagnosis of FAS in order to help a vulnerable child get the correct care was fraught with difficulties.

Of 81 members of the Foetal Alcohol Syndrome Trust who responded to the Newsnight straw poll, a quarter said it took more than a year to get a diagnosis.

One in eight took more than three years.

b.marsh@dailymail.co.uk

Party hard: DJ Sara Cox, right, and TV presenter Sarah Cawood

Ladette Drinking culture 'can harm baby before birth'
Daily Mail Wednesday, February 5, 2003

One in five who falls pregnant opts for abortion

MORE than one in five pregnancies ended in abortion last year, official records showed last night.

This figure rose to nearly one in three in London.

According to the Office for National Statistics, 32.5 per cent of women in the capital who conceived in 2001 opted for a termination.

In the East of England, the region with the lowest proportion of abortions, 19.1 per cent of women decided not to have the baby.

There was a small drop in the number of pregnancies among 15 to 17-year-olds, from 45 conceptions per 1,000 to 43.8 in 2001. Of these pregnancies, 44 per cent were aborted.

The figures were greeted with dismay by pro-life campaigners.

Rachel Heath, of the UK's leading anti-abortion charity Life, said: 'Unfortunately, we are not surprised by these numbers.

'We live in a society where most British universities will give a student money to fund an abortion but will not make free child care available if she wants her baby,' she added.

'In a so-called civilised society women should not have to choose between their education or the life of their babies.'

Tony Kerridge, of the Marie Stopes family planning agency, said a desire to protect career prospects was one possible reason for many terminations. He called on the Government to offer sex education to children aged ten or 11, saying: 'Sex education in this country leaves a lot to be desired.

'There's a whole generation out there who are not properly informed of their contraceptive choices.'

But he insisted women had a right to terminate pregnancies and said they were not so 'irresponsible' as to use abortion as a contraceptive.

FOUR out of ten babies were born outside marriage last year as the number of illegitimate children continues to rise.

A decade ago, under one in three were born to unmarried parents.

Last year, two-thirds of illegitimate babies were registered by parents living together. One in three had parents living apart or was only registered by one, said the Office for National Statistics The under-25s had the highest number of unmarried births.

The steady rise in illegitimate births since the late 1970s has prompted alarm.

Hugh McKinney, of the National Family Campaign, urged the Government to encourage more couples to tie the knot before having children.

He said Ministers had refused to help young couples 'accept the responsibilities and commitment of bringing up children.'

One in five who falls pregnant opts for abortion
Daily Mail 13th December 2002

In Britain, one in five pregnancies ends in abortion

■ Thousands of women regret decision, says charity ■ Sexual disease among young doubles in a decade

By Sarah Womack
Social Affairs Correspondent

MORE than one in five pregnancies in Britain ends in abortion while the number of childless women over 40 "increases substantially", according to new figures.

For the general population, parenthood has largely become a matter of choice as opposed to chance, says the Office for National Statistics.

Its report said 36 per cent of all pregnancies in women under 20 were terminated, a figure that has continued to rise despite the widespread availability of contraception and the "morning after" pill.

Among women of all ages, 23 per cent of pregnancies were terminated in 2000.

The report suggested that many women wanted to delay their families until they were married or financially secure.

But often the delay was detrimental and – despite the huge rise in the number of multiple births over the past 10 years as a result of fertility treatment – the birth rate is at an all-time low.

Patrick Cusworth, a research spokesman at Life, Britain's largest anti-abortion charity, said: "The abortion statistic is devastating.

"It's tragically ironic that while 600 babies a day are aborted, only 300 a year are placed for adoption despite growing requests from would-be parents who cannot have children naturally.

"There is no question that we now have abortion on demand in this country. The law supposedly places certain obligations on the part of doctors [to sanction them], but there is very little debate with regard to the fact that many of these requirements [for abortion to take place] have just become boxes that need to be ticked.

"We have dealt with thousands of women who have regretted their decision to have an abortion."

Tony Kerridge, of Marie Stopes International UK, a pro-choice family planning agency, said: "I don't think there is any real evidence that women are using abortion as a method of contraception.

"Some women come to our centres who have had repeat terminations but we always discuss contraception with them. The vast majority of pregnancies are the result of unprompted and unplanned sex acts, maybe where contraception was not available."

He refuted suggestions that the abortion law needed to be tightened. "The legal requirement is that you need to seek the permission of two doctors. We think it is patronising and paternalistic to expect women to justify their decision. Individuals should be allowed to make choices about their health."

> ‘There is no question that we now have abortion on demand’

A spokesman for the FPA, formerly the Family Planning Association, said: "Half of all pregnancies in Britain are unplanned and we would like to see a reduction in that and more information and advice on contraception available.

"Abortion is an essential part of fertility control."

But she did not agree that women who sought an abortion should be warned of the dangers of leaving motherhood too late.

"If the time is wrong for you to have a child, you cannot go ahead [and have the child] on the proviso that you may not have another opportunity."

The ONS report also showed that sexually transmitted diseases among teenagers had doubled in the past decade.

New episodes of sexually transmitted infections (STIs) among people under 20 in England, Wales and Northern Ireland rose from 669,291 to 1,332,910 between 1991-2001.

Rates of chlamydia in female adolescents have more than doubled since 1991. More than a third of women with the infection are under 20.

The report's authors, the Health Protection Agency, said the data underestimated the true prevalence of chlamydial infection, which does not present symptoms in up to 90 per cent of infected females and can lead to infertility if left untreated.

The FPA said there had been a dramatic rise in public awareness of chlamydia and other STIs.

Its spokesman said: "Young people are more aware, they are coming forward more and testing more, so you are actually getting more diagnoses.

"At the same time, it is worrying that young people don't think that STIs are a real risk for them, and it also shows that condoms are not being used consistently."

He called for mandatory programmes to be introduced in all schools to provide advice and information on sexual health.

Figures on diet and nutrition showed that one in five boys and 27 per cent of girls were overweight.

Paul Burstow, the health spokesman for the Liberal Democrats, said the figures were "shocking" and revealed "a public health timebomb". He added: "The safe sex message is just not getting through to today's teenagers.

"These young people should be given the information and the support they need to discuss sex and relationships and to understand the dangers they face.

"It is not enough to just treat the symptoms of obesity, the causes must also be tackled."

In Britain, 1 In 5 Pregnancies Ends In Abortion
Daily Telegraph March 31st 2004

Lisa faced an appalling choice: should she have the baby of the man who raped her? Her decision took courage and caused great pain – but it has led to a unique kind of love

Picture: DAVID CRUICKSHANKS

Facing up to the future: Lisa with Callum as a baby, above, and as she is today

by **Natasha Courtenay-Smith**

EVERY morning, three-year-old Callum Askew throws his arms around his mother's neck and tells her he loves her. Such unbounded affection would warm the heart of any woman, but for Lisa, her son's words are particularly poignant because for the first six months of his life, she doubted she would ever love him.

For Lisa's son was conceived in the most harrowing of circumstances. At 16, she was brutally raped and, six weeks later, found out to her horror that she was pregnant.

Not only did she have to deal with the emotional fall-out of the rape (which was her first and only sexual experience), she also had to decide whether to keep the baby, knowing her son would always remind her of the man who had violated her. Against the advice of friends and family, Lisa chose to have the baby and, understandably, her life since has been fraught with difficulties.

At her lowest ebb, Lisa longed to miscarry and contemplated suicide. By her own admission, she felt 'repulsed' when she first set eyes on her newborn son, and psychiatrists considered that she posed such a danger to Callum that she wasn't allowed to be left alone with him.

It is a testament to her courage, and determination to make the best of the situation for the sake of her child, that she has put some of the trauma behind her and is finally able to give Callum the unconditional love he shows her.

There can be no doubt that Lisa is still haunted by the memory of her ordeal. Once an ambitious and popular girl, she is now shy and introverted. She rarely socialises and has yet to trust another man or enjoy a physical relationship.

And she lives in dread of the day when she must tell Callum the truth. As she says: 'What sort of effect will it have on him to discover his father is a rapist?'

It is certainly not a situation Lisa could have imagined when she celebrated her 16th birthday surrounded by family and friends five days before the attack.

Then, she was more interested in schoolwork than boys, and was determined to do well in her exams so she could go to university and train to be a midwife.

At the time of the rape she was living with her mother, a care worker, and two sisters and brother in the family home in Ipswich.

Like most teenage girls, Lisa also dreamed of a fairytale wedding to the man of her dreams and children of her own.

But her hopes were shattered when, on October 8, 1999, she bumped into Robert Hubert, an acquaintance of her older brother, on the way home from school.

'I had no reason to fear Robert, who was 19 at the time, as he was a familiar face,' says Lisa. 'I was also very naive when it came to boys and hadn't even had my first kiss.'

Less than an hour after they met, Hubert had raped Lisa and left her half naked, covered in mud and shaking with fear on the ground of a nearby playing field.

It is a memory which makes her voice tremble and her eyes fill with tears.

ROBERT and I started chatting and walked out into the playing fields, where we sat on a log. It was getting dark and I was thinking about heading home, when suddenly, he leaned forward and kissed me.

'I was so shocked, I pulled away and fell to the ground. Next thing I knew, he was on top of me, forcing himself on to me. Then he raped me.

'I froze. I couldn't scream, speak or move, I was so terrified. I don't remember how long it lasted, but when he finished, he looked me straight in the eye and said: "Don't tell your mother."

'Then he walked away and left me, curled up in a ball on the mud, sobbing. Somehow, I pulled on my clothes and got the bus home.

'My Mum knew something terrible had happened. I was crying so much I could hardly speak, but I managed to say I'd met up with Robert Hubert.

'She took one look at the state of me and said: "Did he rape you?" I nodded and begged to have a bath, but she said I couldn't until she'd phoned the police. I curled up, sobbing under my duvet while we waited for the police to arrive.'

That night, Lisa was taken to a special police centre that deals with the victims of sexual attacks.

'I was examined and interviewed,' she says. 'I asked the police if I could be pregnant, but they gave me the morning-after pill and told me not to worry.

AFTERWARDS, I was finally allowed to have a bath. I sat there with tears running down my cheeks, scrubbing and scrubbing at my skin until it was red raw, desperate to wash the feeling of Robert, and the rape, off my skin, but I couldn't.

'Over the following few weeks, I bathed at least six times a day — I felt so dirty. My whole body ached and my legs were covered in angry black bruises.'

Robert Hubert was arrested and charged with rape on November 25, 1999. He initially pleaded not guilty.

Lisa, meanwhile, was convinced she was pregnant despite taking the morning-after pill. She says: 'That thought scared me more than the memory of the rape. What would I do if I was carrying a rapist's child?'

Her worst fears were realised when two weeks after Hubert's arrest, she went to a family planning clinic accompanied by her older sister, to be tested for sexually transmitted diseases. Lisa also asked the nurse to do a pregnancy test.

'Afterwards, the nurse sat down next to me and put her hand on my arm. She had a troubled look on her face and I knew the test was positive.

'I could hardly breathe. My instant thought was that I couldn't have the baby and I begged the nurse to get it out of me.'

Lisa was advised to go home and think about what she wanted to do. Her mother advised her to opt for a termination, painful though she knew it would be, because she felt having a baby in such circumstances could have devastating consequences on her young daughter's life.

'Abortion had been my first thought as well. But once I'd had a bit of time to think about it, I wasn't so sure,' says Lisa.

'I knew I'd find an abortion distressing and also felt as though it was my baby, too, not just Robert's, and I didn't just want to destroy it.

'Mum and I sat talking for hours. She told me that having a baby so young would further devastate my life — I'd be a single mum with no job and be unable to continue my education.

'She asked if it was fair to bring a child into the world when it had been conceived in such horrific circumstances. But the baby, my child, was as much a victim as I was and I thought it deserved a chance of happiness.' Lisa's mother, desperate to see her daughter's life back on track, then suggested the baby should be put up for adoption.

'I considered it, but didn't think I could live my life knowing a child of mine was out there being raised by someone else,' says Lisa.

'If I was going to have the baby, there was no question of me not being responsible for its wellbeing.

'I can't remember the moment I decided to go ahead with the pregnancy. It was more of a gradual realisation that I couldn't bear to get rid of the baby.'

But it was never going to be easy.

'My friends slowly turned against me as they couldn't understand why I wasn't having an abortion. Everyone except my family abandoned me.

'I had panic attacks, in which I'd be overcome by a feeling of suffocation and felt too afraid even to leave the house. I felt so alone and afraid I contemplated suicide — it felt like the only way to resolve the situation.

'Eventually my GP put me on antidepressants, but they didn't help. I couldn't enjoy the pregnancy or feel any love towards the child growing inside me. Even seeing the baby on the screen at my first scan filled me with horror.

'There were many times when, anxious I wasn't developing feelings of love for it, I wondered why on earth I hadn't taken my Mum's advice and had an abortion.

'I began to ask myself what on earth I was doing bringing a rapist's child into the world — a child that would only serve as a constant reminder of my ordeal.

'I wished I could change my mind, but I'd left it too late. I dreaded that the baby would be a boy who looked like Robert, or even worse, behaved like him.

'At night, I sobbed into my pillow and prayed that I'd have a little girl who looked like me.'

On June 30, Lisa gave birth to a boy. The labour, which lasted eight hours, was made worse by the fact she was also suffering from pre-eclampsia. But both her mother and grandmother were there to support her.

'I heard the words "It's a boy" and my blood ran cold. The nurse held him up for me to see, but I turned away from him and told her to take him out of the room. I couldn't even look at him. All I felt was numbness.

'I saw him properly for the first time the following day, when my mother placed him in my arms. But all I could see in my son tiny's face was Robert, pinning me to the ground.'

THE psychiatrist advised doctors that, because of the way she'd rejected Callum, Lisa was a danger to her baby. In order to take him home, her mother had to agree not to leave Lisa alone with him.

'I knew that because I'd taken the decision to have Callum, I had to try to form a bond with him,' says Lisa. 'At first, I found it impossible. I didn't like touching him, I didn't like the feel of his skin, because it was Robert's skin.

Lisa couldn't breastfeed because she was on antidepressants but didn't want to anyway, and doesn't think that it would have helped their bonding. 'I didn't find his tiny hands enchanting, because they might grow into the same hands that had held me to the ground while I was raped,' she says.

'When Callum reached out to me, I pushed him away. Every time I looked at him, I was reminded of how my confidence had been destroyed and my dreams shattered by his father.

'I was also terrified of facing Robert and giving evidence at the upcoming trial, and Callum reminded me of the ordeal I still had to go through.

'Mum did most of the caring for Callum, although she made me help feed and bath him to encourage bonding. Gradually, I started to feel fonder of Callum, although I still didn't love him.

'After a few months, I was no longer considered a danger and my mum began to leave me alone with him.

'Then, on my 17th birthday, three weeks before the hearing, Robert changed his plea to guilty. It was the best birthday present I could have hoped for because it meant I wouldn't have to stand up in court and relive my ordeal. I was elated.'

Lisa went to court to see Hubert sentenced to three and a half years in prison in October 2000. 'I felt like a huge weight had been lifted from my shoulders and I could start living again.

'That night, I told my mum I would take over all the care of Callum. I wanted to be a proper mother and hoped that with Robert in jail, I could start loving my baby.

'I even started sharing a bed with Callum in the hope that we'd develop a bond. But the feelings I expected to wash over me didn't come and I still felt empty inside.

love him.

'It wasn't until Callum was 11 months old and learning to walk that everything changed. He looked so thrilled as he took his first, wobbly steps across the room that my heart filled with pride.

'He stumbled, but before he could fall, I'd thrown my arms around him and caught him. In that moment, all my maternal instincts kicked in.

'Suddenly, I loved my son and, for the first time since his birth, I felt like a proper mother.'

FOR now, Lisa's focus is on the future. Robert Hubert was released from jail after serving 21 months, but Lisa and her mother have moved to a quiet cul-de-sac on the other side of Ipswich in order to reduce their chances of bumping into him.

When Callum is at school full-time, Lisa hopes to return to college and train to be a primary school teacher.

'The rape has changed me — it took away all my confidence,' she says. 'I've had counselling, which helped, but I'm very shy and rarely socialise. I can't even contemplate the idea of a boyfriend.

'I hope that one day, I'll be able to form a caring sexual relationship, but I feel it won't be for many years to come.'

More pressing on Lisa's mind is telling her son the truth about his father, something she dreads, but which is becoming an issue already.

When Callum asks after his father, all Lisa is able to do is mumble: 'You don't have a daddy, darling.'

Lisa, now 20, says that, most importantly, she no longer thinks about Robert every time she looks at her son.

'Callum may have Robert's eyes and hair, but when I look at him all I see is my beautiful little boy. It has been difficult, but Callum has also brought incredible joy into my life. I've had to accept the past because, without it, he wouldn't be here.'

Lisa faced an appalling choice: should she have the baby of the man who raped her?
Daily Mail Friday January 30, 2004

Experienced users face as much risk as first-timers, says study

Ecstasy? You may as well play Russian roulette warn doctors

The victim: Lorna Spinks, 19, who died in May 2001 after taking two Ecstasy tablets in a Cambridge nightclub

By **Jenny Hope**
Medical Correspondent

THE RISING toll of Ecstasy deaths yesterday brought a warning from doctors that young people are playing 'Russian roulette' with the drug.

They said Ecstasy can kill even those who have taken it many times before.

And they pointed to research showing that increasing numbers of users are taking it in dangerous cocktails with other drugs.

Ecstasy deaths had risen because supplies had become more easily available while users had become increasingly complacent about the dangers, addiction researcher Dr Fabrizio Schifano said.

'Our research shows it is possible to die after taking small amounts of Ecstasy, even when the drug has been used before – it is very unpredictable,' he added. 'But most people are taking it in combination with other drugs, which has an even greater risk.'

'Impossible to predict'

The research is the most comprehensive analysis of deaths caused by Ecstasy to be carried out.

Data collected for the National Programme on Substance Abuse Deaths showed there were 81 Ecstasy-related deaths in England and Wales between 1997 and 2000.

A report on the study in the British Medical Journal shows most victims were employed white men in their late 20s, with 66 of the victims being male, 71 white and 37 employed.

Fifty victims died from a cocktail of drugs which included Ecstasy.

Six died from poisoning by Ecstasy, also known as MDMA, and the rest died from causes such as cardiac failure, trauma or drowning.

Dr Schifano, of the National Programme on Substance Abuse Deaths at the European Centre for Addiction Studies at St George's Hospital Medical School in London, said young drug users may be lulled into a false sense of security if they have previously taken drugs with no ill effects.

'This doesn't mean they won't have a problem the next time. Heroin breeds tolerance but "uppers" such as cocaine and Ecstasy can trigger reverse tolerance where suddenly a user has a bad effect from even a small dose.'

Tablets of Ecstasy are getting stronger – up to five times the strength of pills available four years ago – and users are confronted with 180 different versions of the drug.

Dr Schifano, a consultant psychiatrist, said for the first time a death has been reported involving a compound called PMA (paramethoxyamphetamine), which is similar to Ecstasy but far more toxic.

He warned that young people had no idea of the potentially fatal effects of taking combinations of drugs.

'Young people don't take drugs singly anymore, as they mostly did in the 1970s and 1980s. They may take two or three different drugs on the same night with alcohol – and on more than one occasion.

'We may have some idea what one drug will do, but it's impossible to predict how they will react together. In drug-taking, one and one sometimes equals five.'

Professor Hamid Ghodse, who set up the national programme to monitor drug-related deaths through coroners' reports, said: 'The inexorable upward trend in Ecstasy-related deaths is very striking.

'We are particularly concerned about the youth of those who die and about the very blase attitudes towards the risk of drug-taking.'

Apart from the immediate health hazards of drug-taking, including overdose, chemical overload and heart attacks, research suggests they may cause long-term damage. Ecstasy use triggers memory problems and attention deficits.

In 2001 the parents of Ecstasy victim Lorna Spinks, 19, released a picture of her shortly after her death in the hope of shocking other users into rejecting the drug.

j.hope@dailymail.co.uk

Police alarm at rise of the Christmas drug-drivers

DISTURBING evidence emerged yesterday of the scale of drug-driving on our roads.

A snapshot survey of motorists over Christmas found that two thirds of those tested had taken an illegal substance before setting out.

The survey was carried out by the Lothian and Borders force.

Those tested had been driving erratically. Despite passing an alcohol test, they were considered to be behaving in a way that suggested they had taken drugs.

Of 28 drivers checked, 17 had drugs present in their bloodstreams. Road safety campaigners said the figure proved the drug-driving menace needed to be addressed.

At present, there is no standard roadside test for drugs.

The variety of drugs available mean it is very hard to find a test to cover them all.

Police therefore have to use their judgment along with a series of 'impairment' tests to see if it is worth taking someone back to the station for a blood test.

The Royal Society for the Prevention of Accidents said research was needed to determine how many accidents were caused by those under the influence of drugs.

Ecstasy? You may as well play Russian roulette warn doctors
Daily Mail - Friday, January 10, 2003

Daily Mail, Friday, February 14, 2003 Page 21

Is this Britain's most honest policeman?

Chief Constable who said drug dealers should be shot

By **Ben Taylor**
Crime Correspondent

ONE of the country's top policemen yesterday called for drug dealers to be shot.

Terry Grange, chief constable of Dyfed-Powys in West Wales, said he would be quite happy to see all pushers lined up against a wall.

'What I would like to say to them is, "If you would be so kind as to stand up against that wall for a minute",' he said.

'Then I'd be shouting, "Load, aim, fire". Personally, I'd shoot.'

Mr Grange, a former soldier who has a reputation for tough talking, made the comments while launching a campaign to rid shops of drugs-related paraphernalia.

It followed reports that heroin was being sold to children as young as 12 in Llanelli, which is in his force's area.

Mr Grange fears that some shops are selling items that could be used for drug use.

'Retailers should not sell anything that makes drugs look clever or cool,' he told the Llanelli Star, the local newspaper behind the campaign.

'Spiral of drugs, theft and prison'

'They should have a sense of responsibility about what they sell to kids and what they say to kids. We all should.

'We had a bloke in Brecon that we arrested last year. He was sticking needles in his neck – now that means everything else is failing. He was still selling drugs to other people.

'These people have got themselves in a position where they need drugs. Somehow or another they are going to have to get the nerve up to get themselves out of that position.

'At the end of the day, the only person in that position is them. If they don't then they just follow the spiral of ever more drugs, thieving and prison.

'To any young person who is finding themselves involved in drugs I would urge them to go to school, get an education and join the police.'

But Mr Grange, 53, who has three children, admitted that he has a certain amount of sympathy for young people involved in drugs. 'It's when you can see what drugs can do to people. Yes, I can have sympathy, but not enough to make me think anything other than that they themselves have got themselves into the state.

'I think, "We should help you to get out of it, but you've got to do it". Telling me that you've got to steal because you take drugs doesn't wash with me.

'Nobody has to steal unless they are starving and how many are actually starving in West Wales?'

There are an estimated 8,750 drug addicts within the Gwent, South Wales and Dyfed-Powys police force areas, as well as 32,000 'recreational' drug users. Mr Grange, who served for seven years as a paratrooper before joining the police, also spoke passionately about his belief that drug addicts should be forced to seek treatment for their addiction in prison, instead of being given a drug treatment order.

'I think the best place to get good treatment for drug addiction in Wales is in prison,' he added. 'The only way you are going to get that is a minimum 12-month sentence.'

Peter Stoker, of the National Drugs Prevention Alliance, said: 'We should use the strongest sanctions available to deal with drug dealers. The death penalty is not something that is available in the UK. There is no doubt, however, that some dealers are using a proactive marketing approach to get young people hooked.

'This is causing an unravelling of society in the UK.'

Norman Brennan, director of the Victims of Crime Trust, said: 'While I do not necessarily support Mr Grange's stance, I do understand his frustration and concerns. Drug dealers peddle in death sentences themselves. Their trade causes the death of many young children.

'I only wish that other chief constables could show the same vigour in tackling the problem.'

b.taylor@dailymail.co.uk

Dealers operate openly on some of Britain's streets

'What I would like to say to them is: 'If you would be so kind as to stand up against that wall for a minute.' Then I'd be shouting, 'Load, aim, fire.' Personally I'd shoot'

Terry Grange, chief constable of Dyfed-Powys Police

Britain's most honest Policeman
Daily Mail - Friday, February 14 2003

GOOD HEALTH Daily Mail, Tuesday, March 11, 2003

So what IS smoking doing to your body?

OF the UK's 13 million smokers, 70 per cent say they can't kick the habit. Here, with the help of Dr Dawn Milner, chairman of tomorrow's No Smoking Day campaign, ANGELA EPSTEIN takes you on a journey through a smoker's body to show why it's so important to quit.

SMOKER'S COUNTDOWN TO A HEALTHIER LIFE

Time stopped	Benefits
20 minutes	Blood pressure and pulse returning to normal. Circulation improving, especially to hands and feet.
8 hours	Oxygen level in blood rises to normal level. Chances of heart attack start to fall.
24 hours	Carbon monoxide leaves body. Lungs start to clear out mucus and debris.
48 hours	Nicotine no longer found in body. Sense of taste and smell improve.
72 hours	Breathing becomes easier. Energy levels rise.
2-12 weeks	Circulation improves throughout body. Walking and exercising become easier.
3-9 months	Breathing problems, coughing, shortness of breath and wheezing improve. Lung efficiency increased 5-10%.
5 years	Risk of heart attack falls to about half that of smoker.
10 years	Risk of lung cancer falls to around half that of smoker. Risk of heart attack falls to about same as someone who has never smoked.

NHS Smoking Helpline: 0800 169 0169

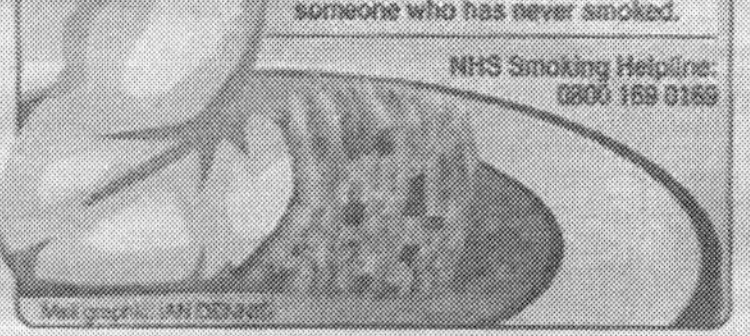

Mail graphic: IAN DENNIS

BRAIN

WHEN you light up, smoke inhaled through the lungs travels via their tiny air sacs to the bloodstream and is then transported to the body's vital organs, including the brain and nervous system.

The chemicals in smoke cause the lining of the arteries to become porous, which allows cholesterol, white cells and blood clots to stick to them. Clogging arteries which supply blood to the brain leaves smokers at risk of a stroke.

EYES

SMOKING can lead to defective vision and even blindness. A condition called age-related macular degeneration (AMD) is the largest cause of blindness to people in the UK and is most common among smokers.

Smoking damages the eyes because it reduces the levels of plasma antioxidant, a substance in the bloodstream which protects retinal cells.

Smoking also causes the protective layer between the retina and blood vessels to wear away, resulting in poor circulation, irritation and scarring. Some scientists now also believe smoking could contribute to the incidence of cataracts.

NOSE

MANY smokers complain that their habit affects their sense of smell. This is because smoking irritates the delicate membranes of the respiratory tract, including those inside the nose.

Another problem for smokers is that in a bid to get rid of noxious smoke fumes, the nose secretes more mucus than normal. This causes the nasal cells to swell, restricting breathing and possibly leading to chronic sinusitis.

MOUTH

USE of tobacco is connected to 90 per cent of oral cancers, including lip, tongue and palate.

Many of the chemicals found in tobacco smoke are carcinogenic, and therefore when the tissues of the mouth are bathed in toxic substances, this can lead to oral cancer.

Smoking also increases the risk of periodontal disease which affects the teeth and gums. Smokers tend to develop hard layers of plaque on the teeth called calculus (tartar).

If not removed, it remains below the gum line, destroying tissue and causing gums to pull away from the teeth. This, in turn, creates deep pockets between the teeth and gums which allow in bacteria to destroy tissue and supporting bone.

Eventually, teeth loosen and fall out. As smoking affects blood supply round the body, smokers bleed less easily so there will be no warning signs such as bleeding gums.

SKIN

ACCORDING to research, smoking is at least as damaging to the skin as the sun. Every inhalation creates thousands of wrinkle-forming free radicals which attack collagen, cell membranes and the skin's fatty layer.

It is also thought that smoking impairs blood flow and lowers levels of vitamin A, which is vital for healthy skin growth, so producing a dull, dry complexion.

Smoking can also lead to crow's feet as smokers unconsciously squint to avoid the smoke's irritating and drying effects on their eyes.

THROAT

MANY smokers develop a hoarse speaking voice caused by smoke drawing down over the larynx.

The toxic content of smoke damages the delicate membranes of the larynx, making the smoker prone to laryngitis and in more severe cases, cancer of the larynx.

Smokers who suffer chronic nasal congestion may also have a nasal drip which leaks down the throat and leads to pharyngitis, laryngitis and bronchitis.

LUNGS

MOST people are aware of the connection between lung cancer and smoking. Around 90 per cent of people who develop the disease are or were smokers. Lungs are so vulnerable to damage because the tar that forms from burning tobacco settles in them, damaging the surfaces and clogging the cilia — tiny hairs that protect the lungs from dirt and infection.

However, smoking can cause many other serious lung diseases. These include chronic bronchitis, which is caused when the air passages produce too much mucus.

As the lungs become more damaged, the body cannot rid itself of the mucus which becomes infected. Eventually, the air passages are blocked causing permanent breathing difficulties.

Emphysema is a lung disease which can follow on from chronic bronchitis and is caused by damage to the air sacs of the lungs.

This reduces the lungs' ability to exchange the oxygen we breathe in with the carbon dioxide we breathe out and can be fatal.

STOMACH

SMOKING is harmful to all parts of the digestive system. Chronic cigarette smoke may increase the amount of acid secreted by the stomach causing peptic ulcers — lesions in the lining of the stomach.

Smoking is also linked to Crohn's disease, an inflammation deep in the lining of the intestine.

Doctors believe this may be because smoking could lower the intestine's defences against infection.

Many smokers complain of heartburn, and this may be because smoking lessens the strength of a valve at the lower end of the oesophagus or gullet, which would normally stop stomach acid flowing back up the food pipe.

HEART

TOBACCO smoke produces carbon monoxide, a highly poisonous gas which combines with haemoglobin in the blood and makes breathing difficult.

This reduces the body's ability to carry oxygen, putting the heart under strain.

Smokers also have a higher risk of hardening and narrowing of the arteries, which can cause a wide range of cardiovascular problems.

BONES

FEMALE smokers face an increased risk of developing osteoporosis, a condition that reduces bone substance and results in fragile bones that are liable to fracture.

This is because smoking makes the ovaries less effective at producing the hormone oestrogen which is vital for maintaining a healthy bone mass.

Uncover six common smoking myths at www.femail.co.uk/health

So what IS Smoking doing to your body?
Daily Mail - Tuesday, March 11 2003

DAILY Mirror

Wednesday July 3 2002

20p

NEWSPAPER OF THE YEAR

RAPED

ACQUITTED OF RAPE: Snooker ace Quinten Hann yesterday

NO, NOT HER. HIM. BY A SYSTEM THAT LETS 'MISS S' TROT BACK TO ANONYMITY WHILE HIS NAME IS TARNISHED FOR EVER

ACCUSER: Miss S leaves court before yesterday's verdict. She cannot be identified

SHOOKER STAR CLEARED: SEE PAGES 6 & 7

PAGE 6 DAILY MIRROR, Wednesday, July 3, 2002 ★ ★ DAILY MIRROR, Wednesday, July 3, 2002 PAGE 7

The REAL rape victim

NOT GUILTY: Hann leaves the Old Bailey yesterday

By ADRIAN SHAW

SNOOKER star Quinten Hann was labelled the real victim yesterday after he was cleared of raping a drunken student.

The flamboyant Australian was accused of attacking the girl even though she allowed him to strip her, willingly straddled his naked body, kissed him goodbye after the claimed assault and gave him her phone number.

But while Hann has faced public humiliation his "spiteful and lying" accuser, who was not in court to hear the verdict, is protected by legal anonymity.

His solicitor Ugo Palazzo said after the hearing: "A celebrity like Quinton is often exposed to a greater risk of false allegation than ordinary members of the public and the consequences are far more damaging.

"The evidence did not support the complainant's account and the decision to pursue the case should have been reviewed.

"That Quinten did not benefit from the anonymity afforded the complainant means, sadly, that in this case the victim was, and remains, Quinten Hann."

Hann – who said he stopped sex after about 20 seconds – had insisted: "As much as a woman can go after a man, she went after me. She was very willing."

He sighed with relief as he was unanimously cleared by a jury after a six-day hearing. Unusually, trial judge Timothy Pontius said he "personally agreed" with the verdict.

Leaving the Old Bailey with his mother Mandy, who had clapped in joy, the 25-year-old star said: "I'm very relieved. Now I can get on with my life. I'd like to thank everyone for their support."

The 21-year-old student, known as Miss S, met Hann and businessman Darren James in a London nightclub while on a booze-fuelled night with her friend Miss E.

During the evening she downed alcopops, Smirnoff Ice, lager, Reef, a vodka based chaser called Aftershock, champagne and Sex on the Beach vodka cocktails.

Later the foursome went back to Hann's apartment at the Savoy Hotel where James and Miss E retired to the bedroom.

Meanwhile, Miss S allowed Hann – ranked 14 in the world – to kiss and cuddle her before letting him take off her clothes and straddling him naked.

She said she repeatedly called out "no" when he wanted sex claiming she was pinned to the floor and raped. She also said she screamed loudly.

But Miss E told the jury she heard nothing, and said: "There was nothing that gave me cause for concern."

SNOOKER ACE CLEARED OF ATTACK ON DRUNK MISS S

WHAT SHE DOWNED Champagne, lager, Reef, vodka-based Sex on the Beach and Aftershock and Smirnoff Ice

THE STUDENT: She let Hann strip her then straddled his naked body

After the alleged attack, the jury heard, Miss S kissed Hann, arranged to meet him for lunch and programmed her phone number into his mobile.

She said goodbye to Miss E, who said she seemed normal, took a cab home and told a friend: "I think I've been raped."

Four hours later, police raided Hann's apartment where he was in bed with another woman. He told them: "I've got nothing to be ashamed of."

Miss S later told police she wanted to drop the case. But then she changed her mind.

Giving evidence, the tearful student was accused by defence QC Sir Ivan Lawrence of feeling guilty because she had sex while having a steady boyfriend.

Sir Ivan said: "You have invented this to explain to your boyfriend what an innocent little girl you are, haven't you?"

He added that Miss S was a "spiteful, lying young lady".

But Miss S said: "I remember constantly saying I didn't want to do this. I kept saying 'no' to him. I got the impression that it was almost expected of me.

"But the whole time this was happening he wasn't listening to me. It was almost like he was in a trance." Miss S added that Hann allegedly told her: "I hope you're pregnant because you'll have my child."

Asked why she gave him her phone number and agreed to meet for lunch, she said: "I'd have done anything to get out of that hotel room."

But Hann said Miss S was

> **"She was a spiteful, lying young lady"**

"very willing" to have sex. He said he started having intercourse twice and stopped both times when she said "no".

He said: "Both times she told me it was because she had a boyfriend and felt she didn't want to be with me because of him.

"I didn't try to seduce her. As much as a woman can go after a man, she went after me." The prosecution said it would have taken "a superhuman effort" by him to halt intercourse. But Hann replied: "I did stop. It is possible."

He added: "It started fine and it ended fine. I don't know why she's lying or why she's done this. I've thought about this for months. I thought at the start it was to make money but now I don't know."

Hann – who was on legal aid despite earning a claimed £75,000 a year – agreed it was "not smart" to have unprotected sex with a woman on the first night.

He said: "I've spent the last 12 years of my life trying not to get women pregnant."

During the trial former Tory MP Sir Ivan roused controversy by saying that a man can believe a woman is consenting to sex even if she repeatedly says she does not want it.

He said: "Even the most hardened feminists must accept that a man confronted with a naked woman, could be forgiven for believing her refusal doesn't mean no.

"Sometimes, in the heat of passion when a woman says no she doesn't necessarily mean no.

"You can say 'no' a thousand times but if you show by your actions that you don't mean it, it doesn't necessarily mean that consent is withdrawn."

Sir Ivan was even more outspoken in remarks to Judge Pontius in the absence of the jury which can only now be reported.

In a failed attempt to have the case thrown out at the end of prosecution evidence, he said: "Sometimes a woman says 'no' to make it more exciting to the man."

He said a man could find sex more arousing if he was doing something he was not supposed to do.

After Sir Ivan asked whether judges were aware of this, Judge Pontius said tartly: "We're not all impotent geriatrics."

Last night legal insiders were astonished that Judge Pontius took the unusual step of telling the jury in open court that he agreed with their verdict.

One barrister said: "It has happened before, but it is far from the norm.

"Once a verdict is given, the judge normally accepts it without question."

The Lord Chancellor's Department said: "It is a matter of personal choice for judges."

a.shaw@mirror.co.uk

THE CLAIMS THAT WERE THROWN OUT

SEX attack allegations have been thrown out in a number of high-profile cases:

FEB 2001: PC Shaun Taylor, 28, was cleared of raping a 37-year-old accountant after a 90-minute romp on his sofa. The woman claimed she woke to find the officer on top of her as she lay in a drunken stupor after an 11-hour bender. He was acquitted after a five-day trial at Maidstone crown court.

NOV 2000: Singer Mick Hucknall was quizzed by police for six hours following a similar allegation by a dancer. But less than 24 hours later, Surrey Police closed their investigation without charging him.

NOV 2000: Cambridge University student Nicholas Tuoy, 24, was cleared of raping a woman. The 28-year-old "victim" admitted being drunk at a party where she alleged the rugby blue forced himself on her.

OCT 2000: Pop star Paul Weller was arrested by police over an allegation he had raped a woman four years before. The then 42-year-old father-of-four was never charged with any crime.

JULY 2000: A jury took just 45 minutes to acquit 18-year-old Ashley Pittman of raping a female student after a boozy night out during their first week at Aberystwyth University.

Ashley spent two nights in a police cell and endured three trials before being given his freedom.

FEB 2000: Pharmacist Martin Garfoot, 46, a father of two, sued colleague, Lynn Walker, 33, for libel after she alleged he raped her after work. A jury in Newcastle awarded £400,000 in damages.

FEB 1999: Stuart Nicol, a 30-year-old oil worker, was hounded out of his home town, Alness in Scotland, after babysitter Wendy McClung, 18, told police he had raped her. Eight months later she admitted she had made the whole story up.

JUN 1997: Dutch footballer Patrick Kluivert, 25, was arrested in Scotland over an alleged gang-rape but charges were dropped after two years.

FEB 1996: Stephen McLaughlin, a 23-year-old airport worker, was accused of rape by a former girlfriend. She later admitted that she had concocted the story and was prosecuted. But 18 months later, convinced that his innocence would always be called into question, he drove to a forest in Ayrshire and gassed himself in his car.

FEB 1996: Soccer ace Paul Gascoigne, 35, was interviewed by police over a sex attack claim but the matter was dropped.

MAR 1995: Craig Charles, 38, star of TV comedy Red Dwarf, was accused of being involved in the gang rape of a stripper. He was cleared by a jury in 90 minutes.

OCT 1994: David Warren quit his university course because of the pressure following a rape accusation. The judge ordered the jury at Winchester Crown Court to acquit him.

OCT 1993: Austen Donnellan, a 21-year-old King's College student was cleared of rape by an Old Bailey jury. Donnellan had sex with a girl so drunk she could barely walk and lay "like a rag doll". The case led to a review of whether men accused of rape should be named before being found guilty.

Daily Mirror - July 3rd 2002

NEVER A RAPE

Relief . . . Hann yesterday

By SARA NATHAN

RAPE claims against snooker ace Quinten Hann should NEVER have reached court, MPs said last night.

They blasted prosecutors after the star was cleared at the Old Bailey.

And campaigners said the case was an **INSULT** to real sex attack victims.

A 21-year-old student falsely accused Hann, 25, of raping her at his flat in The Savoy Hotel, London.

But a unanimous jury of seven men and five women threw out the allegations.

Tory MP Julie Kirkbride said: "It seems incredible

Continued on Page Five

Snooker case 'insult to real victims'

STUDENT

The girl, her ID protected, claimed the snooker star ignored her pleas to stop

CLEARED *Delighted Quinten Hann seen after the verdict yesterday. He told the court the girl was a liar*

£150,000 TRIAL BILL

By MARTIN WALLACE

THE trial is believed to have cost the taxpayer at least £150,000 — not including police time.

But as the hearing ended, Judge Pontius questioned why £75,000-a-year Quinten Hann got legal aid for the case.

The judge said the charge did not warrant Hann having to use a top QC like defence counsel Sir Ivan Lawrence.

Sir Ivan said he would have preferred private funding, adding: "Legal aid fees are hardly worth getting out of bed for."

Hann was staying in a £2,000-a-week flat at the time he met the girl.

But Sir Ivan said Hann had not won a championship in 12 months — partly because of the stress of the rape claim.

The Aussie star was awarded £5,000 to cover his travelling expenses to Britain for the trial.

NEVER A RAPE

Continued from Page One

from what we know that the police and Crown Prosecution Service felt it worth bringing to court.

"Given Mr Hann has been found not guilty, it is a massive waste of public money and a terrible ordeal for him."

Ann Widdecombe, a former Tory Home Office minister, said after Aussie Hann was cleared: "We all recognise the distress a woman goes through when she suffers sexual assault or rape.

"But we do not recognise the distress caused to a man who is subject to a false allegation.

"If there is any question the complainant has committed perjury, the full rigour of the law should be applied."

George McAuley, head of the UK Men's Movement pressure group, said: "Women who make false claims hugely damage genuine rape victims by undermining their credibility."

He added: "These cases are a complete stitch up.

"Celebrities are particularly at risk because a lot of women throw themselves at them. Spite and

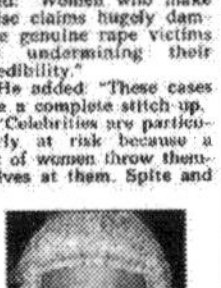

Agreed . . . Judge Pontius

malice then raise their ugly heads." The blonde South African student – who was not in court for the verdict – alleged Hann raped her after she and a pal were introduced to him at a club last October.

The snooker player – ranked 14th in the world and dubbed the Wizard of Oz – took her to his £2,000-a-week rented flat in Central London.

The girl, drunk on champagne and a vodka-based cocktail called Sex on the Beach, was said to have sat astride the obviously aroused star when they were both naked in his lounge.

She claimed he then forced himself upon her although she said she did not want to have sex.

The court heard she left in the early hours without complaining to Hann or her female friend who was in the adjoining bedroom with the star's friend, Darren James.

Defence barrister Sir Ivan Lawrence, QC, described the student as "a strange, lying, spiteful young lady".

And he asked the court to consider that "in the heat of passion, when a woman says 'no,' she does not necessarily mean 'no'."

Judge Timothy Pontius told the jury after it cleared Hann: "The verdict you reached is one with which I agree."

And Hann, who consistently denied rape, said as he prepared to fly home to Melbourne: "I'm relieved it's over. I can get on with life now."

3G

BY
SHARON HENDRY
SUN WOMAN EDITOR

This time No didn't mean No. She has let us all down

SAYS Sun WOMAN EDITOR

THE real message that came out of the Quinten Hann rape trial yesterday was that when a girl says No she doesn't necessarily mean No.

This case clearly supports that contentious sentiment.

But no two rape cases are the same – and there are countless circumstances in which No does and always should mean No.

The student who accused the snooker star has done much to devalue this vital maxim. She has also given more credence to those who argue that men accused of rape should not have their identities revealed unless or until they are found guilty.

Yesterday's jury verdict was a unanimous not guilty.

It was no surprise given the evidence and meant that hours of police time had been wasted along with at least £150,000 of taxpayers' money.

So I'd like to ask: How the hell did the case get to court in the first place? Let's look at the details . . .

FACT: Hann said the girl asked him to stop – because she was feeling guilty about a boyfriend – after "a small amount of penetration".

Desperate

FACT: He admits he was desperate to persuade her otherwise and his smooth talk resulted in another 15 seconds of sex before she said No again.

FACT: She gave Hann her phone number before leaving his flat and did not mention the so-called rape to a pal who went there with her.

Sound dodgy to you? It doesn't take a genius to work out that Hann was not at fault.

So why was the Crown Prosecution Service so keen to pursue the case?

Let's get this straight. Going to a hotel for a one-for-the-road drink with someone you've met in a nightclub is not a crime – particularly if you are sensible enough to keep your best friend in tow. Most of us have been there.

But the water began to cloud as soon as this girl entered the flat Hann was renting from the hotel. Surely she wasn't expecting private snooker lessons?

While her best mate headed for the bedroom with another bloke, she got intimate in the lounge.

The message is clear. If you don't want sex with a stranger, steer clear of his hotel room.

Fondling

After all, if you're not intending to get intimate, what's wrong with the downstairs bar?

It is also **NOT** the best time to say No after kissing, fondling and sitting astride a naked man.

Reiterating it after 15 seconds of sex is no good either. In this case I am convinced it could just as easily have been interpreted as a teasing Yes.

Being deep in the throes of passion is simply not the best time to have a Bridget Jones-style indecision dilemma.

Moving on to the identity issue, Hann is just the latest of a long line of men cleared of rape who have argued the case for anonymity.

They say their reputations are permanently blighted by the accusation, whatever the jury's verdict.

Law student Edward Watt recently announced he is to sue a fellow scholar who accused him of rape.

He was cleared in March last year after a trial in which the 22-year-old girl claimed he attacked her in halls of residence at Aberdeen University.

Care assistant Julie Renouf, 34, of Redruth, Cornwall, was jailed for six months in January for falsely crying rape.

She admitted she had sex in a layby with a man she met over the internet, then accused him of rape because she was ashamed at having betrayed her husband.

Boots pharmacist Martin Garfoot, 49, won £400,000 damages after colleague Lynn Walker falsely accused him of raping her in a staff tea room. Her allegations were thrown out of a Newcastle court two years ago.

Mr Justice Hooper ruled that Mrs Walker, then 44, did not have the right to anonymity after Garfoot's barrister argued: "She should not be able to walk away and hide in her tent after she has been found to be an out-and-out liar."

Celebrities other than Hann have also been caught in the unforgiving glare of accusation.

Last year pop stars Paul Weller and Mick Hucknall were both named over allegations of rape that were later dropped.

Former Jam frontman Weller called for a change in the law to give the accused the same anonymity as the victim.

Risk

Yesterday Hann's solicitor Ugo Palazzo took a similar line. He said celebrities are often "exposed to a greater risk of allegation than ordinary members of the public". And he added: "The fact that Quinten did not benefit from the anonymity afforded to the complainant meant sadly in this case the victim was, and remains, Quinten Hann."

Neatly put – but there is a problem. If revealing victims' identities became common practice the number of women reporting genuine rapes would be greatly reduced.

They are the majority. They are the ones who say No and mean No.

But their fate is being put at risk by a tiny minority of reckless females like the one who accused Quinten Hann.

CLUB *The Roadhouse nightclub, where Hann and girl met*

HOTEL *Savoy, where Hann took the girl to flat he rented*

The Sun - July 3rd 2002.

Snooker star cleared of rape 'is real victim'

Anonymous: the student who kissed her 'attacker' goodbye before going to the police

By Sue Clough
Courts Correspondent

AN AUSTRALIAN snooker player cleared yesterday of raping a student was the true victim in the case, his solicitor said.

An Old Bailey jury took just two hours to acquit Quinten Hann of raping the 21-year-old woman at an apartment next to the Savoy hotel in London. The judge said he agreed with the verdict.

The woman, from a wealthy Johannesburg family, admitted that she willingly accompanied Hann, 25, to the £2,000-a-week flat in central London. She raised no objection when he removed all the clothing from the lower part of her body.

She even sat astride his naked body, but said she did not want intercourse because of guilt about her boyfriend.

Hann, known as the Wizard from Oz, embraced his mother, Mandy, as he left court. He said: "It has been tough. It has been a long nine months. I can get on with my life now."

His mother said: "It was the right verdict."

The Hann family solicitor, Ugo Palazzo, said: "A celebrity like Quinten is often exposed to a greater risk of false allegation than ordinary members of the public and the consequences are far more damaging regardless of final outcome."

His character had been unfairly damaged, particularly abroad, where the media were not subject to the same reporting restrictions.

Mr Palazzo said the prosecution had a "special duty of care" to be sure before instigating and continuing court proceedings. "The evidence did not support the complainant's account and a decision to pursue the case should have been reviewed thoroughly before the case came to trial as the evidence began to unravel.

"In the absence of independent corroboration or indeed in the light of contradictory evidence, the prosecution should continuously test the complainant's version of events and be prepared to stop the proceedings if in any doubt about the authenticity of the claims being made.

"The fact that Quinten did not benefit from the anonymity afforded the complainant meant sadly that in this case the victim was and remains Quinten Hann."

> 'In the heat of passion when the woman says no, she may not mean no'

His accuser was not in court to hear the verdict or the comment by Judge Timothy Pontius to the jury of seven men and five women that it was "one with which I personally agree – although my personal view is neither here nor there".

The woman and a friend had accepted an invitation to drink champagne and cocktails with two friends of Hann's after meeting them in a West End club last October. When the snooker player joined them, he danced with the student and they kissed.

The woman claimed that Hann later ignored her protests and raped her on the floor of the flat where he was staying. Hann maintained that she made all the running and was a willing partner until she began to feel guilty about her boyfriend. He added that he stopped twice during sex when asked to.

Having failed to persuade her to stay the night, he said, he had gone to bed with another girlfriend. They were asleep together when police came to arrest him.

Hann said that before leaving him, the student had put her number into his mobile, accepted an invitation to lunch and kissed him.

Sir Ivan Lawrence, QC, defending, called the student "a strange, lying, spiteful young lady". He said that "in the heat of passion when the woman says no, she does not necessarily mean no".

At the end of the case, the judge raised concerns about the decision to grant legal aid to the snooker player, who was said to earn £75,000 a year.

Sir Ivan said: "Apparently anyone charged with a criminal offence in this country can get legal aid. They may have to pay back the costs later."

He added that he and his daughter, Rachel, his junior counsel, would rather have been privately paid because "legal aid fees have been so depressed it hardly makes it worth getting out of bed".

Although ranked 14th in the world, Hann's earnings were hit because he had lost sponsorship because of the charge, added Sir Ivan.

Pictures: PHOTONEWS SERVICE, PA

Free man: Quinten Hann leaves the Old Bailey after being acquitted

Law of consent 'loophole' may be tightened

By Philip Johnston
Home Affairs Editor

THE acquittal of Quinten Hann was the latest in a long line of unsuccessful prosecutions for so-called "date rape".

Fewer than one in 10 allegations of rape ends in a conviction compared to one in three in 1977. Where a trial takes place, only 60 per cent result in a guilty verdict, largely because the jury refuses to convict when the woman willingly accompanied the alleged attacker home.

The South African student who claimed that she had been raped had sat astride a naked Hann as they talked about his business interests. She had also given him her telephone number and made a date for lunch after the alleged attack.

However, she also told the court that she was drunk after an evening at a club with the snooker player and his friends.

Ministers are so concerned at the failure rate that they are considering changing the law to set a lower consent test.

The prosecution would have to show a victim had not given her "voluntary and genuine agreement" to sexual intercourse, possibly because she was incapacitated through drink.

The prosecution would still need to prove that the victim did not consent to sex if the defence said she did but the law would list examples of where consent was not present, including where a person was asleep or too affected by alcohol or drugs to consent.

The Government has decided against a new, lesser, offence of date rape. Juries will continue to be invited to convict for a crime that has a maximum sentence of life imprisonment.

Some judicial figures believe that, if the Crown Prosecution Service wants to secure convictions in such cases, then the law should differentiate between sexual intercourse without consent with someone known to the victim and a violent attack by a hooded, armed stranger.

Jonathan Davies, a criminal barrister who sits as a Crown Court recorder, said this year that acquittals were commonplace in rape trials because women were being encouraged to make allegations that would never convince a jury.

The Daily Telegraph - July 3rd 2002

Why I, a real rape victim, say Miss S should be named

I'm the victim says snooker star cleared of student's rape

From yesterday's Mail

THE VICTIM of a brutal rape has joined the growing calls for a change in the law that protects women who make malicious accusations, after false allegations against snooker star Quinten Hann were thrown out of court this week.
CAROLINE FAIRFAX SCOTT, who courageously tells her remarkable story here, is adamant that the woman who falsely claimed Mr Hann had raped her should be named and shamed.
Shadow Home Secretary Oliver Letwin is now considering submitting a Private Member's Bill calling for change. It is likely to propose that rape case defendants should remain anonymous until conviction.

Fighting for justice: Caroline Fairfax Scott

In this brave and remarkable article, a rape victim waives her anonymity to speak out

THE NIGHT I genuinely thought I was about to die is burned for ever on my memory. And in the months that followed my ordeal, I sometimes wished I had died. On a Sunday evening three years ago, I was dragged from my car outside my flat in Bristol and forced into a squalid garage by a man wielding a knife.

He beat me, stabbed me severely, raped me and subjected me to a series of sexual assaults and indignities so brutal and disgusting that I could not begin to describe them here and still can hardly bear to discuss them with my doctor.

Although I am now recovering — thanks to the love of my family and sons — my life will never be the same. My relationship with my partner was destroyed, I have been unable to return to work as a doctor's receptionist and find it difficult to live alone. Even now I can hardly walk down a dark street by myself.

So I never dreamed I would find myself feeling sorry for a young man accused of such a foul crime. But I pity Quinten Hann, the Australian professional snooker player cleared of raping a student who had falsely accused him of assaulting her after a drunken night out.

This was only the latest in a series of so-called date rape cases that have done grave damage to those who are struggling to force the courts and the Government to take rape seriously.

Drunken coupling with a stranger is not most people's idea of a romantic end to an evening. As recounted in court, it was obviously a squalid sexual encounter, and no one emerges well from the occasion.

But judge and jury clearly believed that the young lady had lied when she claimed to have been forced into these unseemly antics. They decided that she had, in fact, consented to her part in the unpleasant performance in Mr Hann's hotel bedroom.

Indeed, Judge Timothy Pontius took the very unusual step of telling the jury that he agreed with their verdict.

Even so, amazingly, the young lady remains safely protected by a cloak of anonymity (I shall have to continue to refer to her as Miss S) while the reputation of the innocent Mr Hann, who is a celebrity with a public image to protect, is tarnished for ever. Professional sportsmen and women make a good part of their incomes from endorsements and sponsorships. How many manufacturers of family-friendly products will now want to pay for Mr Hann's blessing?

At best he has been revealed as the sort of chap who picks up drunken girls in night clubs and takes them back to his hotel to try his luck.

At worst, lads in saloon bars across the nation will be nudging each other tonight and chuckling, quite unfairly, of course, that good old Quinten was 'lucky to get away with it'.

The truth is that mud sticks. But the wicked girl who made the false accusations — and who, immediately after the alleged rape, programmed her name and number into Mr Hann's mobile phone, arranged to have lunch with him, kissed him good night and called him from her cab — can never be named.

She has walked free.

If she is not mentally unstable then it would appear she is deeply malicious, for she has done great harm.

And it is grossly unfair that she will be protected from the righteous anger and contempt of those around her.

But it is not just Mr Hann's reputation that worries me, or even that of Miss S.

This foolish girl has done grave damage to the cause of women such as me who have genuinely been raped, often with the savage brutality I endured.

My assailant was eventually caught. But because, up until the week before the trial, he claimed to be not guilty, I spent the best part of the year after my ordeal constantly reliving my attack.

I feared I would have to go into the witness box and face a cruel and prolonged grilling about the most intimate aspects of what had been done to me.

AS IT happened, the man finally decided to plead guilty, no doubt in an attempt to gain a lighter sentence, so I was spared that further strain. He was sentenced to 12 years in prison.

For all this suffering, the compensation offered by the Criminal Injuries Compensation Authority was £7,500 — less than I could have expected for a broken arm.

That is why I have waived my right to anonymity, in order to fight for better terms.

However, I passionately believe that the cloak of anonymity, designed to be thrown over rape victims who face the fearful prospect of appearing in court to prove the allegations, should be lifted in vexatious date rape cases — if the accusations have been deemed false.

It may sound vindictive, but I would like to see Miss S named and shamed. Her name and picture should be in every newspaper as a warning to other women not to bring this fearful charge for frivolous reasons.

FOR MR Hann has become a victim of ridiculous political correctness, which means all allegations of rape are treated with equal seriousness and that the woman's name must be protected come what may.

Yet this was an obviously ridiculous case which should never have come to court. Miss S should surely pay some penalty for her obnoxious behaviour.

Exposure, I believe, would be an utterly appropriate form of punishment.

Quite simply, to accuse an innocent man of rape is one of the most appalling things you can do, for society has increasingly come to accept that to be a rapist is about as low as you can sink. The stigma is overwhelming and will not fade with time.

Yet the absolute right to anonymity offered to any women who claims, however dishonestly, to have been raped, can only encourage the twisted and the malicious to bring false charges — perhaps to ruin the reputation of a former lover, perhaps to protect their own reputation after a drunken night out.

And what I would like to say to little Miss S, safe behind her shield of anonymity, is this.

By your self-indulgent and dishonest accusations you have trivialised the suffering that I, and so many like me, have gone through. You have made it more difficult for our cries to be taken seriously.

You should be named and shamed.

THE INNOCENT MEN WHOSE LIVES WERE LEFT IN TATTERS

A STRING of high-profile rape cases have ended with the accused man being cleared — and his name besmirched for ever as a result of being named.

■ AUSTEN DONNELLAN: In October 1993, the student was accused by a fellow student at King's College, London, of date rape. A jury cleared Donnellan, 21, after hearing that the girl was so drunk that she could hardly walk. Donnellan went on to complete his history degree.

■ ANDREW BOND: Rape charges against the 25-year-old were dropped in February this year after CCTV footage was discovered which showed his accuser fabricating evidence against him. Mr Bond, of Liverpool, had given up his university place to defend himself and had the charges hanging over him for six months before they were finally dropped. He is still receiving counselling, but hopes to start university this year.

■ NICHOLAS BUOY: The 25-year-old student was cleared in November 2000 of raping a 28-year-old teacher after they both got drunk at a housewarming party. He later qualified as a PE teacher but said his future had been 'blighted'.

■ ASHLEY PITTMAN: A computer sciences student, he had to leave his course in July 2000 and turn down a job to defend himself against a rape allegation made by a fellow student at The University of Wales in Aberystwyth. The girl made the claim two years after the alleged incident, after she started having problems with a boyfriend. A jury took just 41 minutes to clear Mr Pittman, 24, who later returned to his studies.

■ ROY McGREGOR: The police officer was cleared of rape in January 2000 after a jury decided his accuser, a 23-year-old who got into bed with him, had made up the allegation. The 30-year-old was suspended from his job for the duration of the case.

■ OLIVER THOMPSON: In July 1996, the 35-year-old builder's labourer was awarded £5,000 compensation by a judge after being put through a rape trial on the strength of a false allegation.

■ STEPHEN McLAUGHLIN: He was accused of rape by a former girlfriend in February 1996. She later admitted that she had made up the story and was prosecuted. But 18 months later, having never recovered from the shock of the accusation, the 23-year-old airport worker drove into a forest and gassed himself to death.

Daily Mail - July 4th 2002.

THE TIMES WEDNESDAY JULY 3 2002 SL

Snooker star cleared of rape claims he is the victim

PHOTONEWS

Mr Hann leaves the Old Bailey yesterday after the nine-day trial. Ugo Palazzo, his solicitor, said: "The victim was, and remains, Quinten Hann"

By Michael Horsnell

THE Australian snooker player Quinten Hann was cleared by an Old Bailey jury yesterday of raping a student on the floor of his London apartment.

Mr Hann, 25, known as The Wizard from Oz, said: "It's been tough. I am just very relieved. It's been a long nine months. I can get on with my life now."

He left in a taxi with his mother, Mandy, and supporters who included Mark Shay, an official of the Australian High Commission. His alleged victim, a 21-year-old South African who has since completed her degree course at London University, was not in court.

Mr Hann has earnings from snooker this year of £75,300, but his sponsorship was stopped after he was charged with rape. Ugo Palazzo, his solicitor, said: "From the moment he was arrested, his character was unfairly damaged, particularly abroad where the media are not subjected to the same reporting restrictions as in England.

"The fact that Quinten did not benefit from the anonymity afforded the complainant meant, sadly, that in this case the victim was and remains Quinten Hann."

MPs called for a change in the "unfair" law relating to anonymity in rape cases. Ann Widdecombe, the former Shadow Home Secretary, said: "The judge should have discretion at the end of an unsuccessful rape prosecution to name the complainant if he deems the complaint was without foundation. We all recognise the distress a woman goes through when she suffers sexual assault or rape, but we do not recognise the distress caused to a man who is subject to a false allegation. If there is any question at all in this particular case that the complainant has committed perjury, then the full rigour of the law should be applied."

Roger Gale, Conservative MP for North Thanet, said: "There is, in my view, an unfair imbalance between the quite proper protection that is given to the complainant in rape cases and the lack of protection given to the accused.

"If the system is to be fair to both parties, then the accused should be given the same protection as his accuser, and remain anonymous until conviction. In this case today, Mr Hann has been rightly acquitted, but the fact remains that a lot of people will still wrongly believe him to be a rapist." Both MPs said that the issue would be addressed when the next Criminal Justice Bill comes before Parliament.

The world No 14-ranked player had denied raping the student, to whom he had been introduced at a nightclub, at the £2,000-a-week flat he was borrowing from a friend in the Savoy Apartments in Central London last October.

After meeting him in the Covent Garden club the student had walked to the apartment arm-in-arm with Mr Hann and made no objection to his advances, allowing him to remove her clothes and sitting astride him naked, but claimed he ignored her pleas to stop because she felt guilty about her infidelity to her boyfriend. She agreed that she left the flat 90 minutes later, giving him a peck on the cheek, tapping her name and number into his mobile telephone and agreeing to see him for lunch later that day. On her way home in a taxi she had taken part in a telephone conversation lasting more than four minutes with Mr Hann.

> 'If the system is to be fair, the accused should be given the same protection as his accuser'

The case hinged on a plea to the jury by Sir Ivan Lawrence, QC, his defence counsel, to consider that when a woman says "no" to sex in the heat of passion, she may mean "yes".

Sir Ivan said: "What is a man to think when a naked woman is sitting on his ... laughing, talking about all kinds of things, and she says 'no'? Does it mean 'no'? Can he be forgiven for thinking it doesn't mean 'no'? You can say 'no' a thousand times but if you show by your actions that you don't mean it, it does not necessarily mean consent is withdrawn."

Judge Timothy Pontius told the jury that he agreed with their verdict "although my personal view is neither here nor there". He awarded Mr Hann, from Wagga Wagga, £5,000 for his travel expenses.

The Times - July 3rd 2002.

PETER McKAY

Proof that rape law is a farce

WHEN the snooker player Quinten Hann, 25, was acquitted last week of raping a young woman, there was a great hue and cry.

Why should his accuser's identity be protected when it appeared that she — described in court as 'a strange, lying, spiteful young lady' — had told a pack of lies?

Yesterday, the 22-year-old woman involved told her story in a Sunday newspaper under the assumed name of Suzannah Stapleton.

She said two other women — Freya Brown, 22, an Australian, and Janine Thorpe, 25, from Manchester — had come forward to say they'd been assaulted by Mr Hann, but their evidence was disallowed.

'Surely it isn't coincidence that he has been accused of sexual assault three times?' said Miss Stapleton.

The claims by the other two women have not been tested in court. Miss Stapleton's have, and were found wanting. Small wonder. She had let Mr Hann strip her. She had straddled his naked body.

After the alleged 'rape', she kissed him goodbye and gave him her telephone number.

It's an insult to women who have been raped to put this kind of behaviour in the same category. Roping in two other women who say they were assaulted by Mr Hann doesn't make it any better.

We have never spent as much as we do now on education. Young people have more freedom than at any other time in our history. Why do they involve all of us — via the courts — in trying to make sense of the stupid decisions they make?

Classic rape is violent sexual assault by a stranger and it merits heavy punishment. What Miss Stapleton suffered was involuntary intercourse with a man she had sexually aroused.

Some women make no distinction, of course. Rape is rape, they say. 'No' means 'No', no matter how much pre-intercourse sexual activity has gone on.

What they want is all the advantages of the permissive society but — the moment they've decided they don't want to go any further — the full protection of the rape laws.

AS A result, we get messy, inconclusive cases in which guilt and innocence count for less than the individual performances of the complainant, defendant and lawyers.

Who will put a stop to these grisly charades? The Government will do nothing which might be portrayed as limiting the rights of women.

Indeed, such changes as have been made in recent times — including the right of women alleging rape not to identify themselves — are all in the other direction.

Most lawyers working in this area know that many cases they handle are farcical, but we can't expect them to do or say anything that might limit their right to earn high fees from prosecuting or defending the clowns who have got themselves involved in faux rape cases.

Politicians — especially male politicians — won't speak out against frivolous rape cases, either, because their words will be wilfully misinterpreted by the professional feminists.

The situation has got worse because few mothers — and more importantly in the case of girls, fathers — now advise their daughters how to handle themselves viz the opposite sex. It's considered sexist.

Even if they did, the advice would more than likely fall on stony ground. From pre-pubescence, girls are drenched in talk about sex via magazines, TV and films.

There should be no let-up in the prosecution of real rapists, but maybe it's time to tell the fools who muck about with each other that if they want to go to court to prove that 'No' meant 'No', they'll have to pay for it themselves.

FILMSTAR Julia Roberts was married on her 50-acre ranch in New Mexico last week. The last detail intrigued me the most. Can you have a 50-acre ranch?
It reminded me of the story of the Irishman who met a friend at JFK Airport in New York for the first time in 30 years and said he was a big name in Texan cattle circles. He'd devised his own cattle brand featuring a host of Irish emblems such as a pint of stout, a shillelagh, a shamrock and a harp.
Impressed, the friend asked how many head of cattle he had.
Fifty was the reply.
Fifty thousand? inquired the friend. No, just 50.
That doesn't seem many, said his friend.
The Irish cattle baron said: 'I know, but the fact is very few of them seem to survive the branding.'

Little house on the prairie: Julia Roberts

A perk for Blair

THOSE who become MPs — or Prime Ministers — aren't special, priestly beings, fashioned by God to be immune from the temptations of hypocrisy.

The most successful adhere to the norms when it comes to saying one thing and doing another. They are usually no more hypocritical than the average voter they represent.

Most of us, if pressed, say we long to be led by honest politicians who are in it for neither power nor money. The truth is leaders are made in the image of the led — and that's how we like it.

This explains yesterday's poll saying that 57 per cent of those questioned about the Prime Minister's 'more equal than others' arrangements for his children's education think Mr Blair is 'acting properly'.

And 45 per cent think the Blairs 'manipulated' the education system to help their children, while 52 per cent believe 'politicians should be free to send their children to private schools if they can afford it'.

In other words, we take exception to their hypocrisy only when we begin to see them as failures. By failing to govern well, Mr Blair is in danger of losing his licence to be a hypocrite.

A galaxy of godfathers

SHE MAY have neglected to arrange a proper father, but Elizabeth Hurley chose no fewer than six godfathers for Damian — and they were all celebrities: her ex-boyfriend Hugh Grant, multi-millionaires Henry Dent-Brocklehurst and Teddy Forstmann, Sir Elton John and partner David Furnish, and comedian Dennis Leary.
Posh and Becks were at the christening, as was model Elle Macpherson and actress Patsy Kensit. Curiously, there were no godmothers.
It's usual to include someone nice and normal on such occasions, but maybe Miss Hurley doesn't know anyone who fits this description any more. She lives in Celebrityland where the natives kiss each other all the time, hold each other's hands and say, 'Darling, you are wonderful!', while ogling and winking at the cameras.
Makes you sick, doesn't it?

Crime pays

BURGLAR Brendan Fearon, who has 32 convictions, is given legal aid of £5,000 to prepare a damages case against Tony Martin, the farmer who wounded him with shotgun pellets during a break-in.
Since he'd been conducting a crime at the time — for which he was sentenced to three years — Fearon was at first refused Legal Aid. But his appeal was upheld by a Legal Services Commission committee, made of independent solicitors and barristers.
Imagine how difficult it must have been for these legal luminaries to decide on the issue. It's like setting up a committee of vampires to consider the possibility of visiting a hostel for orphaned virgins.

Mind games take the thrill out of romance

THE LATEST absurdity to haul itself, winking and giggling, over our horizon from America is The Love Contract.

This piece of nonsense is devised by Dr Robert Epstein, editor of Psychology Today, who says it could be 'a real alternative to dating'. Radio 4's Today programme is conducting experiments with volunteer couples over six months.

Dr Epstein says the natural methods of falling in love are untrustworthy. 'Many people fall head over heels in love, then discover ten years later they've completely different ideals and principles and no longer want to be together. The Love Contract means you find out right away.'

How will the couples tell if they're in love?

'A host of experts on love, sex and relationships will give their opinions . There'll be brain scans and blood tests. We can use physiological measures to detect whether we are, in fact, in love at the end of six months.'

Is nothing sacred? Human love is practically all that redeems us in the sorry daily struggle of life. Surely its random nature must be retained. Who says we have to have the same ideals and principles?

Dr Epstein is a divorcé who's been single for a year. He's on the lookout for a new partner, as well as publicity for his magazine and ideas.

Surely it would have been more useful if he'd simply recorded for posterity his own attempts to find love instead of giving the Today show's resident donkeys, James Naughtie and Ed Stourton, something to hee-haw about over the next six months as their volunteer couples jump through Epstein's hoops.

WORKING in small groups, the SAS is said to have killed scores of Al Qaeda fighters in Afghanistan, we are told, while the Americans are in hot water for bombing a wedding party, allegedly killing 40 guests.
The bombing attacks that destroyed the Taliban regime helped Americans to get over the September 11 atrocities, but might it not have been better to make war against the perceived perpetrators in SAS fashion?

Proof that Rape Law is a farce.
Daily Mail - July 8th 2002

Daily Mail, Wednesday, July 24, 2002

A Home Office survey claims 1 in 20 women has been raped

The student who falsely alleged that she'd been raped by snooker star Quinten Hann

Lies, damned lies and rape 'statistics'

Melanie Phillips

MARK TWAIN famously observed that there are three kinds of untruth: lies, damned lies and statistics. Now we should add a fourth category of whopper: the Home Office research study.

According to one such specimen published this week, no fewer than one in every 20 women aged between 16 and 59 in England and Wales has been raped, and one in ten has experienced some form of 'sexual victimisation'.

Most of these assaults, said the study, had been committed not by strangers but by 'intimates' — partners, former partners or acquaintances.

If true, this would indeed be an appalling state of affairs. Such huge numbers suffering serious sexual assault would mean that women were living in the shadow of an intolerable level of violence by men.

After all, rape is one of the most serious crimes on the statute book because of the damage it does to a woman, both physical and psychological.

If the researchers were correct, one would therefore expect to hear an enormous amount of female distress and rage being expressed against these male 'intimates'. We would all of us know women friends or relatives who had been raped or sexually assaulted.

But we are not hearing this. We are instead shocked and amazed by these figures. The reason for our incomprehension is simple. What the researchers are telling us is not true.

Indeed, this study is a load of manipulative, malevolent rubbish which must call the credibility of the Home Office research department seriously into question.

The devil here is in the definition. To most people, rape means sexual penetration against the victim's consent, which implies of necessity an act of violence or the threat of violence.

The Home Office researchers have muddied this concept. Instead of the legal definition of rape as 'penile penetration', the study defines it merely as 'forced to have sexual intercourse against your will'.

But the definition of 'forced against your will' is highly subjective. It can so easily translate into 'if you didn't want to', which can become meaningless. Although the study claims the word 'forced' implies an assault, it does nothing of the kind.

A woman might feel forced to have sex against her will, for example, if her lover tells her that otherwise he will leave her for another woman.

Or she might be an unwilling participant because he is drunk, hasn't had a bath for a week or she doesn't love him.

THE crucial point is that in such circumstances she is participating in sex even though she could choose not to do so. She is therefore not the victim of violence.

By any fair-minded or common-sense definition, this is not rape. Yet the Home Office researchers appear to have included this kind of experience in their definition.

This already highly questionable exercise then becomes positively surreal.

For, believe it or not, many of the 'raped' women in the survey themselves don't think what has happened to them is rape.

The study actually admits that, of the women who the researchers said had been raped, fewer than two-thirds themselves described what had happened to them as rape.

And fewer than three-quarters of those who the researchers said had experienced sexual victimisation thought of this as a crime. The reason for the discrepancy is perfectly obvious to anyone who is not busy playing sexual politics. These events were simply not rapes or sexual assaults, and the women concerned knew this perfectly well.

That is because most of these incidents happened within sexual relationships with 'intimates', and the women involved appeared to accept what most people would think — that the issue of consent between lovers can be highly ambiguous.

Yet what these women themselves made of their experiences seems to be of no consequence to these Whitehall researchers who, of course, know better than the victims what has happened to them (so much for Home Office rhetoric about putting the victim first).

They therefore drum up one self-serving reason after another to explain why sexual experiences which the women didn't think were rape were indeed rape.

Thus, they suggest that the women might not want to admit they have been raped because this is degrading and stigmatising; or they may not want to acknowledge that someone they like or love is a rapist.

The idea that they knew perfectly well that the person they liked or loved was not a rapist does not occur to these researchers. The women are simply wrong.

This astonishing display of contempt arises because nothing as inconvenient as a few facts can get in the way of the assumption behind this study: that women are being raped, and men are getting away with it.

The ideological bias that is clearly driving this research is underlined by a crucial omission. The study says that most sexual violence is committed by partners.

But — highly significantly — it omits to make a distinction between partners and spouses. It therefore does not tell us whether women suffer as much sexual assault from husbands as from boyfriends or cohabitants.

YET all the available research suggests that the risk of sexual violence is negligible within marriage, and is hugely increased among cohabitants or more casual sexual partners. Marriage is actually the best physical protection against sexual violence.

But this study states instead that home life is not safe. Here we get to the nasty core of this whole misleading exercise. For the underlying purpose is to demonise men and write them out of the domestic script altogether.

It is this agenda of marriage-busting, man-hating feminism which has now got the Home Office well and truly in its clutches. Ever since New Labour came to power, it has been spouting a torrent of distorted information about domestic violence.

It has been exaggerating its incidence, omitting a vast amount of international evidence that women are equally aggressive as men and — again — refusing to acknowledge the key fact that most domestic violence takes place between cohabiting and other unmarried couples.

The fact is that sexual mores have dramatically changed. Women now initiate casual sex; they carry condoms in their bags and drink, smoke, swear and often parody the worst caricature of macho culture.

As a result, the rules of the mating game have totally altered. The room for ambiguous signals has hugely expanded. That's why the courts are reluctant to convict men accused of rape.

But Whitehall's feminists cannot allow a little thing like injustice to interrupt their agenda. So the Government is now hellbent on rigging the justice system itself to get men convicted of rape, by hook or by crook.

To justify this, men have to be shown as perpetrating an intolerable level of violence upon women.

The result of this lie is not only to commit a calumny upon the male sex. It will also trivialise real rape when it occurs, make it harder to convict the guilty and betray the true needs of women to be protected against violence.

m.phillips@dailymail.co.uk

Daily Mail - July 24 2002

Hamilton accuser guilty of telling rape lies for cash

By Sam Lister

A TRAINEE teacher and mother of four is facing a jail sentence after being convicted at the Old Bailey yesterday of falsely accusing the former MP Neil Hamilton and his wife, Christine, of rape.

Nadine Milroy-Sloan, 29, was convicted of two counts of perverting the course of justice at the end of a six-week trial into the sex allegations, which she was found to have concocted to make money.

Mr and Mrs Hamilton were arrested after Milroy-Sloan complained to police in May 2001 that they and Barry Lehaney, an arthritic pensioner, had subjected her to a serious sexual assault at a flat in Ilford, Essex.

Milroy-Sloan, who had a criminal record, later admitted that she had never met the Hamiltons. The couple were having dinner with friends at a West London restaurant on the night in question.

Barry Lehaney: "I was totally innocent"

Speaking from her Cheshire home after the verdict yesterday, Mrs Hamilton said that a large number of questions remained unanswered as to how such a "grotesque charade" could ever have been taken seriously by the police.

"I'm relieved," she said. "We have known we were right from the outset and that what she said about us was a pack of lies. The whole thing has just been a grotesque charade, but I'm delighted at last, over two years after she made the original allegations, justice has been done.

"I don't have any feelings about Miss Milroy-Sloan. I have never met her. I don't know whether and in what combination she is mad, bad and dangerous to know. She's certainly a bit of all three."

The Hamiltons said that they had not decided whether to pursue further legal action, adding that it was outrageous that the £1.5 million cost of the trial and police investigation was being met by the taxpayer.

Mr Hamilton called on the Government to change the law so that those accused of rape were given the same anonymity as victims. He said that yesterday's verdict drew a line under the ordeal for him and his wife but that action needed to be taken so the same thing could not happen to others.

Financial schemer: Nadine Milroy-Sloan arriving at court yesterday. She was told to expect a custodial sentence

Judge Simon Smith granted Milroy-Sloan conditional bail to appear at Middlesex Guildhall Crown Court on June 13, but said that she could expect a substantial custodial sentence. Milroy-Sloan hugged her third husband as she was released from the dock.

The judge, who adjourned sentence for psychiatric reports, told her that bail was on condition that she stayed at her home and did not contact any media organisations or prosecution witnesses.

'She was a Machiavellian liar driven by sheer greed and a bent for sexual fantasy'

During the trial, the jury was told that Milroy-Sloan, of Grimsby, had gone to see the publicist Max Clifford with a story about the Hamiltons being involved in a vice ring and tax scam. Mr Clifford told her that she could expect up to £100,000 if she could substantiate the claims. A week later she reported the rape allegations to police, giving a tearful account of a sexual encounter at Mr Lehaney's Ilford flat with three men and a woman.

The jury agreed with the prosecution that Milroy-Sloan was a Machiavellian liar driven by "sheer greed" and a bent for sexual fantasy. It had been told that Milroy-Sloan had discovered an outlet for her voracious sexuality on the internet, where she corresponded regularly with men.

Mr Lehaney, 62, was also arrested after Milroy-Sloan made her allegations, but was not charged. He said yesterday: "I was totally innocent from beginning to end. This woman has turned me into a virtual recluse."

Internet sex trawl led to plot that ensnared the innocent

By Daniel McGrory

A 19-STONE arthritic pensioner's trawl through internet chat rooms led to some of Britain's top figures being ensnared in a plot involving allegations of group sex and rape.

Efforts by Barry Lehaney, 62, to entice a young mother into a sexual liaison would draw in not only Neil Hamilton, his wife, Christine, but also Mohamed Al Fayed and the publicist Max Clifford.

The trial demonstrated how easy it is for sexual predators using the internet to assume the identities of well-known personalities.

This saga of sexual duplicity and greed began two years ago in a backroom of Mr Lehaney's flat in Essex where on the internet he posed as a bisexual female aristocrat.

Mr Lehaney was hoping to entice women to reveal their lesbian fantasies. He used the name of Lady Joan Hamilton and was delighted when an attractive 29-year-old blonde began e-mailing him and sending topless photographs of herself.

What he did not realise was that the woman, Nadine Milroy-Sloan, had her own plan to make money.

The impoverished mother of four, embittered after her marriage failure and a string of unsuccessful affairs, was convinced that Lady Joan was Christine Hamilton.

In trial, Orlando Pownall, QC for the prosecution called Milroy-Sloan "naive and cunning in equal measure".

Milroy-Sloan became more explicit in her e-mails.

Mr Lehaney told her that Lady Joan and her husband, Sir James, attended high society sex parties involving lawyers, politicians, barristers and senior policemen. At these gatherings they boasted of being entertained by prostitutes.

The Hamiltons outside the police station after their arrest

Mr Lehaney then introduced himself into the liaison, claiming to be the Hamiltons' chauffeur, saying that the couple wanted to meet her for sex games.

What followed was months of anguish for the real Hamiltons, who were photographed on the steps of an East London police station when they were held over rape the allegations. Christine Hamilton was so traumatised by the ordeal that police had to call a doctor after she collapsed.

In a statement read to the court Mrs Hamilton said she was "deeply frightened" and "terrified" by the allegations, which she described as preposterous.

The couple strenuously denied the charges, and said that they had never met any of the people in question.

During the trial, Mr Lehaney told the jury of his delight in May 2001 when Milroy-Sloan telephoned and suggested a meeting. He did not know that by then Milroy-Sloan had been to see Max Clifford about her supposed relationship.

The court was told that during this meeting Mr Clifford telephoned Mohamed Al Fayed. The owner of Harrods was interested in any scandal involving his old adversaries, the Hamiltons. Milroy-Sloan was told that the Harrods owner wanted to have lunch with her, and Mr Clifford said that a Sunday newspaper was desperate for her story.

All she needed to do was provide the damning proof.

However, her ambitions crumbled when she met Mr Lehaney and saw his flat in Ilford. Aware that he had been caught out, Mr Lehaney decided to ply Milroy-Sloan with drink, hoping that he might still have sex with her.

Milroy-Sloan changed her plan and asked to stay the night. The pair argued and she offered to perform a sex act so that she could stay. She wanted a DNA sample as supposed proof that she had been raped.

Mr Lehaney told the jury that she would not accept that the aristocratic couple did not exist.

In May 2001 she told her uncle that she had been raped and the police were called in.

She described how Neil and Christine Hamilton and a man she called Andrew had turned up at Mr Lehaney's flat. She said that she was drugged and raped by Mr Lehaney, while the Hamiltons sexually assaulted her and that she was held captive until the next morning.

A police doctor who examined her said that his "medical findings were entirely consistent with her being raped", the court was told.

Milroy-Sloan had fixed up a deal to sell her story to a tabloid newspaper once the Hamiltons had been arrested in August 2001. She said that she had been paid £50,000 by a Sunday newspaper to reveal her identity after making the allegations.

What she had not anticipated was that the Hamiltons had an alibi. The other flaw in her story was that she said that Mr Lehaney had knelt in front of her during the attack, which he could not have done because of his arthritis.

In March, days before her trial, she changed her story. In court, she apologised to the Hamiltons and said she had made an "honest mistake".

The Times Saturday May 17 2003

Hamiltons' rape accuser faces a prison sentence

By Michael Paterson

THE woman who lied to police that she had been raped by Neil and Christine Hamilton was yesterday found guilty of perverting the course of justice.

Nadine Milroy-Sloan, 29, was warned that she faced a substantial jail sentence after she was convicted by a jury at the Old Bailey.

She complained to police in May 2001 about an attack by Mr Hamilton, 54, the former Conservative minister, and his wife, 53, in a flat in Ilford, Essex. She said she had been lured there by Barry Lehaney, 62, who she said had told her he was the couple's chauffeur.

But Milroy-Sloan, who had a criminal record, had never met the couple and invented the story to make money.

Two days before the date of the fictitious attack, Milroy-Sloan offered the publicist Max Clifford a story about the Hamiltons being involved in a vice ring and a tax scam.

Nadine Milroy-Sloane: lied

The jury heard that Mr Clifford told Milroy-Sloan she could expect about £100,000 from the media if she could prove her claims.

Orlando Pownall, QC, prosecuting, said she then set out to "get the evidence" and arranged to see Mr Lehaney, with whom she had been exchanging explicit emails.

Milroy-Sloan told Lehaney "she wanted to bring girls to his flat and asked him to arrange a meeting with Neil and Christine Hamilton for the purpose of a sexual encounter".

In court, Milroy-Sloan denied making false rape allegations against the Hamiltons and Mr Lehaney. She told the court she "apologised" if she had made an "honest mistake".

Judge Simon Smith granted Milroy-Sloan, from Grimsby, conditional bail until June 13, warning her she faced "a substantial period of custody".

Mr Hamilton added afterwards: "For a woman to accuse another woman of such horrible crimes; it is quite appalling."

Mrs Hamilton said: "The whole thing has just been a grotesque charade."

The Daily Telegraph Saturday May 17 2003

KIRSTY WIGGLESWORTH / PA

Milroy-Sloan arrives at Middlesex Guildhall Crown Court for sentencing yesterday

Hamiltons' rape accuser jailed for three years

By Steve Bird

THE trainee teacher and mother of four who falsely accused the former Tory MP Neil Hamilton and his wife, Christine, of rape was jailed for three years yesterday.

Judge Simon Smith said that Nadine Milroy-Sloan, 29, had hatched a lurid plot aimed at making her rich and famous. She wept as she was led to the cells. She had falsely claimed the Hamiltons and Barry Lehaney, an arthritic pensioner, had taken part in a sex attack on her at a flat in Ilford, Essex. She was convicted of two counts of perverting the course of justice after a six-week trial last month.

The allegations caused acute embarrassment for the Hamiltons who were arrested, despite having a cast iron alibi, and held for five hours at a police station in August 2001.

Looking pale and drawn, Milroy-Sloan, from Grimsby, dressed in a grey trouser suit, bowed her head as the judge passed sentence. Sitting at Middlesex Guildhall Crown Court in Central London, Judge Smith said: "You have mentioned your feelings at the thought of being sent to prison. But you must have realised that the sentences for rape, of which you were accusing these people, fall somewhere between five and ten years.

"For innocent people, two of them whom you had never even met, that must have been a cynical attempt to make money and by dragging in the Hamiltons, whose names had been very much in the public eye at the time, whom the jury found you knew perfectly well weren't there."

Referring to her visit to Max Clifford, the publicist, and her intention to sell her "story", Judge Smith continued: "It's becoming all too easy for people to sell false allegations against well-known people or about well-known people to the press, and the courts have got to deal firmly with it."

He added that he felt her earlier apology to the the Hamiltons appeared "reluctant".

The Hamiltons, who were not in court, said they were "pleased and relieved" with a sentence that sent out the right signal to those prepared to make money out of lies.

The Times Saturday June 14 2003

Hamilton rape accuser faces jail for perverting justice

Milroy-Sloan, left, made false rape allegations against Christine Hamilton and her husband, Neil

BY MATTHEW BEARD

A WOMAN who falsely claimed she had been raped by the former Tory MP Neil Hamilton and his wife was facing a lengthy jail sentence last night.

Nadine Milroy-Sloan, 29, was convicted of two charges of perverting the course of justice. A jury found her guilty of fabricating the story in pursuit of money and celebrity friends.

Judge Simon Smith, sitting at the Old Bailey, bailed Milroy-Sloan pending psychiatric reports but warned her that when she returned on 13 June she might be sentenced to "a substantial period of custody".

The jury was told Milroy-Sloan invented the attack after meeting Barry Lehaney, who posed as the Hamiltons' chauffeur, in his flat in Ilford, east London. She had already approached the publicist Max Clifford with her story and was paid £50,000 by the *News of the World* to reveal her identity.

Shortly before the trial began in March, she dropped the allegations against the Hamiltons, explaining it was a case of mistaken identity.

Yesterday the Hamiltons said they were relieved but criticised police for arresting them in August 2001 – 10 weeks after the allegations were made – without any evidence or and for failing to establish that they had a firm alibi.

The couple, whose ordeal was filmed as part of a documentary by Louis Theroux, refused to discuss whether they were considering further legal action against the police. Christine Hamilton said after the verdict: "We've known right from the outset that what she said about us was a pack of lies. It's cost the taxpayer a fortune. The police have brought the prosecution, so the taxpayer pays for that. She's been on legal aid, so the taxpayer pays for that. The whole thing has just been a grotesque charade."

Her husband added: "At the time it was terribly traumatic, and everybody saw live television coverage, particularly of the way it affected Christine."

Milroy-Sloan, from Grimsby, was described in court as a "sex-obsessed" divorcée who wanted to make celebrity friends. Posing as "Sexybabe" in an internet sex-chatroom, she made contact with someone posing as a bisexual woman aristocrat, who turned out to be Mr Lehaney, a 19-stone asthmatic living in an east London bedsit.

Milroy-Sloan became convinced she was in contact with Christine Hamilton. When Mr Lehaney posed as the Hamiltons' chauffeur and suggested a meeting to take part in a sex party involving the couple she accepted. Two days before the meeting Milroy-Sloan visited Mr Clifford, who estimated the story would sell for £100,000.

Although she realised she had been duped by Mr Lehaney, she spent the night with him and committed a sexual act to obtain a semen sample, which she hoped would bolster the rape allegations.

Mr Lehaney said later: "It's been a nightmare for me. She deserves a long sentence." Prosecuting counsel Orlando Pownall QC said Milroy-Sloan was a "cunning but naive" fantasist who had "damaged the credibility of every rape victim who comes forward".

The Independent Saturday May 17 2003

Sex fantasist who accused Hamiltons is given three years

By Sue Clough
Courts Correspondent

A SEX-OBSESSED fantasist who falsely claimed that she was raped by Neil and Christine Hamilton in an attempt to make money by selling her story wept yesterday as she was jailed for three years.

Afterwards, the former MP branded Nadine Milroy-Sloan "a gold-digging little slut who has now been properly punished. Let this be a lesson to all the others of her ilk not to follow her example".

He called for the same anonymity for those accused of rape as is given to victims.

"I think the sentence is just because she committed not just a crime against the Hamiltons by falsely accusing us, but against all genuine victims of rape and sexual assault," he said. Mrs Hamilton said: "I am pleased it is a strong sentence but I am not pleased in a vindictive sense. She deliberately set out to tell lies about us and to cash in on it."

The Hamiltons did not attend the trial and were not in court yesterday to hear Martin Heslop, QC, in mitigation for Milroy-Sloan, accuse them of courting publicity.

He said that while not seeking "to underestimate the difficulties that may have been created for them", the Hamiltons had, a month before their arrest, "flatly refused" to tell police where they were at the time of the alleged rape.

Mr Heslop said that, in order to minimise publicity surrounding the case, the police specially opened the little used police station in Barkingside, Essex, but the couple chose to arrive with "the press and a TV crew in tow". They declined a discreet exit through the back of the building and "chose to give a press conference on the steps of the police station".

Ten days after their arrest, "Mrs Hamilton sold her own story to the press and got no less than £35,000 from the interviews she gave", Mr Heslop said.

Milroy-Sloan, a 29-year-old mother of four, had gone to police alleging that she had been raped and sexually assaulted by the Hamiltons, another man and by Barry Lehaney in his flat in Ilford, Essex.

But days before, soon after she arrived in London from her home in Grimsby, she had gone to see Max Clifford, the publicist, who said she could make up to £100,000 if she could prove her claims that the Hamiltons were involved with prostitutes and in a tax fraud. Although Milroy-Sloan accepted during her trial that the Hamiltons were not at the flat and apologised, Judge Simon Smith, passing sentence at Middlesex Crown Court, told her: "I cannot help saying it came across to me as reluctant.

"It is becoming all too easy for people to sell allegations about well-known people to the press, and the courts have to deal firmly with it."

Orlando Pownall, QC, prosecuting, said Milroy-Sloan met Mr Lehaney, 62, through the internet and exchanged sexually explicit e-mails with him and "Sir James and Lady Joan Hamilton", a fictitious couple he had invented. In 2001 Milroy-Sloan, who had convinced herself that "Sir James and Lady Joan" were the former MP and his wife, came to London intent on making money.

She met Mr Lehaney, spent the night at his flat and then went to the police with her claims. She was convicted of two charges of attempting to pervert the course of justice.

Picture: PA & ENTERPRISE NEWS

Neil and Christine Hamilton, who welcomed the sentence as a 'lesson to all others of her ilk'

Nadine Milroy-Sloan arriving at court yesterday

The Daily Telegraph Saturday June 14 2003

Hamiltons scalp the silver fox of Fleet Street

Max Clifford, scandalmonger to the tabloid press, pays a heavy price in cash and credibility for libelling his arch antagonists. Neil Tweedie reports

Nadine Milroy-Sloan was jailed over her fantasy rape claims

THERE are more than a few scalps – both political and celebrity – dangling from the belt of Mr Max Clifford, purveyor of sexual scandal to Her Majesty's Press (Tabloid Division).

Who could forget his portrayal of David Mellor cavorting in that Chelsea strip with the "actress" Antonia De Sancha or Air Chief Marshal Sir Peter Harding spiralling down in flames after being caught in the crosshairs of "Lady" Bienvenida Buck?

But yesterday was not so good for the maker and breaker of B, C and Z list showbusiness careers, for it was Mr Clifford's scalp – silver-grey and bouffant – doing the dangling, in luxuriant locks from the belts of his arch antagonists: Neil and Christine Hamilton.

Mr Clifford is a considerably poorer man today after settling in court with the couple over allegations that they were involved in the serious sexual assault of a woman calling herself Nadine Milroy-Sloan during an orgy at a flat in London in May 2001.

His mistake – a rare one for a man who has so artfully manipulated Fleet Street – was to give credence to Milroy-Sloan's allegation during interviews with the media, including one on GMTV. The problem was that her tale, related at length in various tabloids, was utter fantasy.

The price for her was a three-year prison sentence for perverting the course of justice. For Mr Clifford, the penalty was counted only in sterling and credibility.

During a brief hearing at the High Court in London, the solicitor for the Hamiltons read out an apology from Mr Clifford, the result of tortuous negotiations carried out at great expense.

It said: "The defendant [Mr Clifford] now accepts and wishes to publicly make clear that there was no truth whatsoever in the allegations made by Nadine Milroy-Sloan and the defendant wishes to entirely withdraw, without any qualification, all his remarks and comments which could be taken to mean otherwise.

"The defendant acknowledges that his remarks could be interpreted in a way that

A gleeful Christine and Neil Hamilton outside court yesterday

> ‘It's a full and abject apology. As for the figure: all I can say is that the £100,000 reported is a wild underestimate’

is both highly offensive to Neil and Christine Hamilton and damaging to their reputations. The defendant has therefore agreed to pay damages to compensate for the harm and to pay all their costs of the proceedings."

It was a high point for the Hamiltons, who have so often felt the sharp end of the sword of justice. They could hardly contain their glee as they spoke in Court 13, a famous libel venue, after the hearing.

Mr Hamilton, 56, the former Tory MP for Tatton, who was forced to declare bankruptcy after his disastrous libel action against Mohammed Fayed, said the damages were significantly more than £100,000. He added: "I can't tell you how much because there is a confidential agreement. But it is the end of a three-and-a-half-year struggle and the sum will pay off our lawyers and go towards reducing our substantial debts.

"We are very happy with the outcome and have achieved everything we wanted. We have a had a full retraction of the original allegations and acceptance by Mr Clifford that he should not have said what he did. It is an abject and full apology. As for the figure: all I can say is that the £100,000 reported is a wild underestimate. It was a very large sum of money with lots of noughts on the end."

Howard Pinkerfield, for the Hamiltons, told Mr Justice Eady that Mr Clifford had defamed them on no fewer than 25 occasions.

Mr Clifford was notable by his absence yesterday, but Mr Hamilton said his long-time adversary's non-appearance had in no way lessened the pleasure of the moment.

"Mr Clifford is an acquired taste which I have no wish to acquire," he said.

Following his disgrace in court and the ruin of his political career, Mr Hamilton has rebuilt his finances with a career as a minor celebrity.

Along with his wife, he has become a staple of the after-dinner circuit and low-budget television shows – including a recently-filmed one in which their London flat received a makeover courtesy of two designers called Justin and Colin.

The couple's recovery can be seen in their purchase of a small manor house near Malmesbury, Wilts.

Contacted yesterday, Mr Clifford was in bullish mood, claiming the defeat, his first in the libel courts, had not distracted him from his tennis.

How had he done?

"I won 7-5, 6-4, 6-4 on the tennis court and not in the High Court. This is small blip on a very, very sunny horizon."

He added: "I'm much happier being Max Clifford than being Neil or Christine Hamilton. I couldn't imagine anything worse."

Mr Clifford said his £2 million house had not been bought with money in "brown paper envelopes" – nor had his home in Spain. He denied making any money out of deals between Nadine Milroy-Sloan and the tabloids.

"Did I represent Nadine Milroy-Sloan? No."

Mr Clifford said he had settled only because of one remark during the GMTV interview which might have been misconstrued.

"I have lost this on what I could have meant rather than what I did mean," he said.

Following their victory, Mr and Mrs Hamilton departed for their next engagement, an after-dinner speech at Barnsley Football Club.

Max Clifford said his defeat was 'a blip on a sunny horizon'

The Daily Telegraph Thursday, February 3, 2005

Mother imprisoned for false rape claim against her ex-lover

THE INDEPENDENT
★ Friday 15 August 2003

BY JASON BENNETTO
Crime Correspondent

AN INNOCENT man spent two months in prison after his former lover staged her own abduction and falsely accused him of raping her.

Alison Welfare, 26, who has four children, was found by a cleaner on the floor of a McDonald's lavatory, semi-naked, bound and gagged, with her clothes torn and covered in paint. She told police that Christopher Wheeler, 38, a former boyfriend, had abducted her from a street in south-east London and held her at knifepoint before raping her. She claimed the attack followed sustained harassment.

Blackfriars Crown Court was told yesterday that Mr Wheeler spent eight weeks at High Down prison in Surrey before police discovered his accuser had made up the story.

Sentencing Welfare to 12 months in jail, the judge, Nicholas Valios QC, described it as a "worrying case".

He told her: "You embroiled a wholly innocent man in very serious allegations of rape, threats to kill and kidnap, and you spun a web of lies and deceit in order to bring about the arrest and, indeed, remand in custody of that innocent man for a period of two months. False allegations of this nature must be deterred. People who make these false allegations not only do great harm to those subjected to genuine sexual attacks, but to the criminal justice system itself."

Jennifer Knight, for the prosecution, said Welfare and Mr Wheeler, who are both deaf and from Orpington, Kent, met in February last year. Welfare first went to police in August 2002 and complained that Mr Wheeler had harassed her and sent her threatening mail.

Ten days after first going to the police, on 31 August, Welfare went to McDonald's in Peckham, south-east London, to set up the bogus rape attack.

Ms Knight told the court: "She was found in one of the cubicles half-naked with her clothes torn. She had been bound, gagged and her clothes torn and covered from head to toe with white paint ... She was dazed and distressed and taken to hospital."

Welfare told police she had been forced to stop by another car flashing its lights while she was driving in Orpington High Street and she had been shoved into a vehicle by two men. "She said a plastic bag had been pushed over her head and [she was] threatened with a knife," said Ms Knight.

Earlier that day she said she had received menacing text messages. But it turned out she had sent them to her phone from an internet café.

On 6 September Mr Wheeler was arrested and charged with rape, conspiracy to kidnap, making threats to kill and harassment. He was remanded in custody for two months and his case sent to the Old Bailey.

But police checked surveillance cameras and discovered that Welfare had gone into McDonald's on her own. Mr Wheeler was then released as Welfare was no longer a credible witness. She later admitted making up the allegations and pleaded guilty to perverting the course of justice. She has no previous convictions.

Jocelyn Gibbs, for the defence, said Welfare had become pregnant by another man while in a relationship with Mr Wheeler and made the allegations "out of fear" that Mr Wheeler would take her baby.

Welfare was jailed yesterday for a year for perverting justice — *Ed Willcox/Central News*

Mother Imprisoned for false rape claim
The Independent Friday 15 August 2003

Daily Mail, Friday, March 12, 2004

Bailed at midnight: Paul Dickov, Frank Sinclair and Keith Gillespie

Football stars in rape case freed to fly home

From **Christian Gysin** and **Tom Kelly** in Cartagena

THREE Leicester City footballers facing rape charges in Spain were freed to fly home early today.

Within hours of being bailed by a judge, nearly £200,000 was raised to let the players leave the jail where they had spent more than a week.

The ruling came just after midnight Spanish time, following a 14-hour hearing.

Hurried efforts to raise the cash meant that Paul Dickov, Frank Sinclair and Keith Gillespie were spared a last night behind bars in the overcrowded Sangonera prison, near Murcia.

The bail figure includes around £30,000 from Leicester City and a similar figure from the three players which would act as compensation for their alleged victims if they are found guilty.

Their lawyer, Ana Ruiperez, said the trio could return to England while Spanish authorities continue to investigate allegations that they raped three African-born German women at a five-star hotel in La Manga.

Earlier the players had faced their accusers as part of a 'careo' – a legal device which sees alleged victims and defendants standing next to each other in court.

Luis Ruiperez, a member of the legal team defending the players, said: 'The first careo took place shortly after 6pm. The first player and the first woman who accused him stood just six feet apart.

'They both read from their statements and were then able to ask questions of each other. The judge also questioned them looking for inconsistencies in any account.'

Lawyers for Dickov, 31, Sinclair, 32, and Gillespie, 29, had argued that they should be allowed home while they await any trial.

Leicester City chief executive Tim Davies said early today: 'The players are delighted that they are able to return to England after what has been a very traumatic time for them.'

The three tourists making the accusations of rape – two Kenyans and one from Malawi – claim the footballers followed them to a room in the Hyatt Regency Hotel in the La Manga resort and attacked them.

It is alleged that club captain Dickov raped one of the women as she was pinned against a wall by Gillespie while a third, unnamed, player watched and cheered.

'They were after men'

Yesterday it was claimed that one of the women went to bed with another player four hours before the alleged attack.

Ville Lehtinen, who used to play for Sheffield United, said she took him to her hotel room for sex after he met her and two friends.

The 25-year-old said that immediately afterwards the woman got dressed, put on her make-up and returned to the hotel bar where she was later photographed with her leg wrapped around Sinclair.

Speaking from his home in Bodo, northern Norway, Mr Lehtinen said: 'They were after men that night and it was clear it was going to end in bed. She gave an ice-cold performance and knew what she was doing.'

He added: 'When the Leicester players walked in, I told the women they were a Premiership team and they were very well known.

'They said, "Why don't you ask the boys over?" I said they were probably married. They replied, "What the hell? What does marriage mean? It doesn't mean anything".'

Mr Lehtinen said the women soon made eye contact with the players.

He dismissed the idea they were prostitutes, but added: 'I doubt they are totally innocent.'

Football stars in rape case freed to fly home
Daily Mail Friday March 12, 2004

EXCLUSIVE: NIGHTMARE OF INNOCENT ANDY

Rape lie strumpet wrecked my life.. I'll never trust any girl again

By CAROLINE BARRETT

A BOUNCER falsely accused of rape after a drunken one-night stand said: "I'll never trust a woman again."

Respectable Andrew Grindle, 22, is a nervous wreck after being branded a sex beast by lying 19-year-old Clare Newson.

The distraught doorman told The People how he...

- **SUFFERED** a barrage of verbal abuse and threats of violence.
- **FACED** the humiliation of arrest and a grilling by police.
- **WAS FORCED** to change his job.
- **HID** in his home for seven months and barely spoke to his parents until the truth emerged in court.
- **CHANGED** from being life and soul of the party to a withdrawn, argumentative grump.

Andrew, speaking after Newson was given six months' detention for attempting to pervert justice, said: "I've been to hell and back.

"I'm not the person I used to be - I'm absolutely crushed.

"She destroyed me and my family and it'll be a long time before I regain my confidence and get my life back on track.

"It will be ages before I trust a woman again.

"I haven't slept with anyone since it happened and I doubt I will for a long, long time."

Hurt

Andrew, who lives with his parents and three brothers in the village of Chacombe, near Banbury, Oxfordshire, has decided to speak out to raise awareness of the devastating consequences of a false rape allegation.

He said: "For seven months my life was practically none existent. I had to leave my job. I hardly left the house and I was unable to have a civil conversation even with my parents. One woman's catalogue of lies has caused me so much hurt and misery.

"I felt ashamed to walk down my own road, the place where I had grown up. But I'd done nothing wrong.

"People were shouting 'rapist' at me in the street. It was just terrible."

Andrew's nightmare began last August when he bumped into Clare in the Exchange nightclub in Banbury.

The pair had known each other for a year after being introduced by a mutual friend but never had a romance.

Andrew said: "We were both leaving at the same time and she just looked over and said hello. I was about to walk off and she said 'Don't go, don't go'.

"She suggested we shared a taxi home. But when were in the taxi she leaned forward and started to kiss me. I kissed her back and it seemed to be getting quite passionate.

"When we got near her house she said she wanted to sleep with me. She was drunk, but she seemed OK and she could handle herself. She kept telling me she was single.

"We walked down the road from her house and had sex down an alleyway. It didn't last that long, but it was mutual. I wasn't expecting us to have sex, but I'm a young lad and she seemed up for it.

"Afterwards I walked her back to her house and she asked me where I was working the next night and did I want to meet up with her.

"I used my mobile to order a taxi outside her house. She said she would see me next day and I left thinking we were on good terms." But several days later Clare's boyfriend visited Andrew's house at 10pm with a pal and accused him of attacking his girlfriend.

Andrew said: "I denied it straight away and told them to ring the police. I knew I was innocent and had nothing to worry about."

But three weeks later, Andrew was arrested by police on suspicion of rape and released on bail.

Andrew said: "I couldn't believe it. I felt doomed, I felt dirty, I was panic-stricken. Telling my parents was the hardest thing I've ever had to do. Like me they just couldn't believe it."

Andrew returned to his job but news of his arrest spread quickly and his life became a misery.

"People were shouting rapist at me as they walked past," recalled Andrew. "I'd always been proud of the fact that my job involved looking out for women and making sure they were safe during their nights out.

"But suddenly I was accused of being one of the people I tried to protect them from. I felt so ashamed, but I hadn't done anything wrong. My employers were great and they agreed to give me two months off.

Miserable

"But I couldn't sleep properly and I became really grumpy. I would wake up in the middle of the night in a cold sweat worried about going to prison.

"I went from being the life and soul of the party to being thoroughly miserable." But just days after his arrest, police told Andrew that Clare had been arrested for attempting to pervert justice.

A taxi driver who had picked Andrew up from Clare's house had seen her pull him back to kiss him before he got in the car.

It contradicted her claims she had run down the street after Andrew had ripped her clothes.

Andrew said: "Of course I was relieved but then things started getting worse again. Clare kept changing her plea from guilty to not guilty." Andrew had to wait seven months before the case was heard at Oxford Crown Court and Clare finally admitted she had lied to pacify her boyfriend after telling him about the sexual encounter.

But for Andrew and his family the damage is done. His mum, who asked not to be named, said tearfully: "He used to be very happy-go-lucky. Now he is grumpy and argumentative and aggressive.

"He's so clingy now too. I joke that I've been waiting 22 years for my son to be affectionate, but I didn't want it to be in these circumstances and as a result of such a horrendous lie."

Andrew added: "My outlook on life and dating has completely changed.

"I'd not had many lovers before this happened. But now I'm even more worried about getting involved.

"What I did that night is no different from what millions of blokes and girls my age are doing.

"I will definitely make sure I get to know a girl a lot better before I embark on a sexual relationship."

caroline.barrett@people.co.uk

GUILTY: Clare Newson lied about being raped

RAPE LIAR CAGED

- Sex-shame girl accused innocent lad
- He suffered death threats and arrest

INNOCENT: Andrew has been devastated by the false accusation Pictures: INS

Rape Lie Strumpet - **The People** April 4th 2004

Soccer players' rape charges dropped

By **Christian Gysin**

THE Leicester City footballers accused of raping three German tourists at a luxury hotel in Spain were cleared of the charges yesterday.

The move came 72 hours after forensic tests on clothing and the women's personal belongings failed to link them to the players.

It also follows a newspaper investigation which claimed the women were prostitutes.

Last night the club said lawyers for Paul Dickov, Frank Sinclair and Keith Gillespie had successfully applied for them to be cleared of charges of 'sexual aggression with penetration' – the equivalent of rape under Spanish law.

Luis Ruiperez, the players' Spanish lawyer said: 'This is probably the most important piece of news they have ever received.'

'They have been through hell. These women are despicable. Not only have they brought shame on themselves but have called into question the testimonies of all those women who are genuine victims of sexual assault.'

No further action will be taken against a fourth player, Jamie Scowcroft, 29, who was accused of breaking into a hotel room and then failing to assist the women.

It was unclear last night whether the women's lawyers would appeal against the decision, which was made at a court hearing in Cartagena – 15 miles from the hotel in La Manga, Southern Spain, where the assaults were alleged to have taken place.

However, legal observers in Spain said they thought an appeal was unlikely.

'The decision has been taken to shelve the case,' said one of Spanish judge, Jacinto Areste's staff. The way could now be open for the players to sue the women for damages for making false claims.

Last night striker Dickov, 31, described the move as 'great, fantastic news'.

'My wife has been through a terrible ordeal that I would never wish upon anyone and her support has never wavered,' he said.

The player thanked his club, manager Micky Adams and team-mates who all helped him 'keep his head above water'.

Gillespie, 29, said: 'I am delighted that we have been totally vindicated. Hopefully, our lives can now get back to normal.'

It was claimed that Dickov, Gillespie and 32-year-old Sinclair assaulted the women – all originally from Africa but living in Cologne, Germany – during a training trip to the five-star Hyatt Regency Hotel complex in March.

The players spent five days in prison before being released on £200,000 bail.

The legal move now also puts other Leicester players in the clear. Matt Elliott, Lilian Nalis, Nikos Dabizas and Danny Coyne had been on bail over claims they broke into the women's room.

Soccer players rape charges dropped
Daily Mail May 21st 2004

DAILY EXPRESS
The World's Greatest Newspaper
TUESDAY JUNE 7, 2005 40p

SNORE NO MORE
TOP-CLASS HEALTH ADVICE STARTS ON PAGE 30

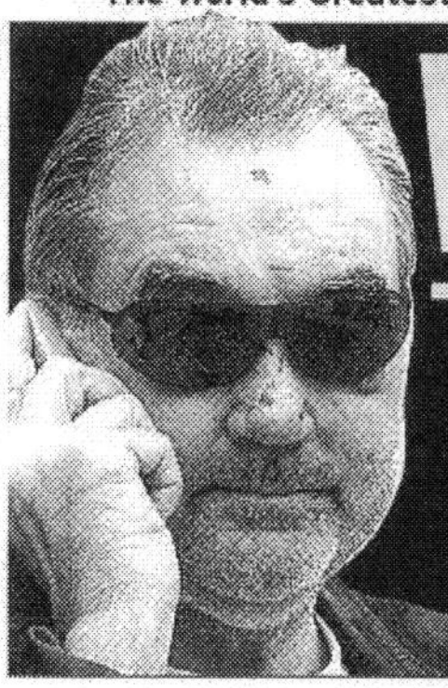

Who got the Best of it?

GEORGE HAS THE SCARS AND HIS LOVER HAS AN ARM IN A SLING

SEE PAGE 5

WIFE WHO CRIED 'RAPE' IS JAILED

She lied to cover up a one-night stand, putting the man she accused through hell

By **Sarah White** and **John Twomey**

A MOTHER of two was jailed for 12 months yesterday for crying rape to cover up a sordid one-night stand with a stranger.

Merete Underwood, 32, claimed she had been kidnapped, sexually abused and raped by at least two men, prompting a police investigation costing at least £20,000.

She told detectives about her "terrifying ordeal," drew up an E-fit and finally identified one of her "attackers".

The man was arrested, held in a cell for 24 hours and endured 15 months of hell before the Norwegian-born blonde confessed she made up the whole story.

Underwood showed no remorse yesterday as she was jailed after she admitted perverting the course of justice at London's Middlesex Guildhall Crown Court. Last night her husband Toby choked back tears as he condemned his errant wife and told how he has been left to bring up the two-year-old son she had by another man.

Mr Underwood said: "This is just one part of what has been a horrible situation. She has put so many people through so much and now I'm left bringing up her son on my own.

"I've already had to spend £30,000 in court costs fighting for custody while she has got legal aid despite moving away and abandoning her son.

"She hasn't even visited him since last November. I'm not even his biological father, I'm just another one of her

TURN TO PAGE 7, COLUMN 1

WEDDING DAY: Bride Merete Underwood, who went on to have a secret night of shame with a stranger

Love cheat's rape lie

Pictures: STEVE BELL

ON HONEYMOON: Merete in Bali and, right, in a more recent picture. Above: Her husband Toby after the court case yesterday

FROM PAGE ONE

men." The court heard how the man she seduced then accused of rape had been "terribly traumatised" by the false allegations and he felt his reputation had been devastated.

Far from being abducted, Underwood had simply deserted her husband and her little boy in a west London pub because she was bored.

In a nearby wine bar, she met the 34-year-old interior designer, seduced him and later had sex in a hotel.

Underwood, who also has an eight-year-old son by another man, was so ashamed of herself that she cried rape in a bid to keep her night of shame a dark secret.

But police saw through her story and even found CCTV footage of her laughing and joking with the man she claimed had attacked her only hours before.

Judge Andrew McCooey told Underwood: "You have shown no remorse in any meaningful way. If you had any contrition or sorrow you would have done all you could to clear this man's name.

"You were only concerned for yourself. There is the impact this had on the innocent man, not to mention the waste of public money running to thousands of pounds.

"This was a pack of lies and you did not have the decency and honesty to admit it and put this man out of his misery."

The saga of sex, binge-drinking and false allegations of rape began in February last year when Underwood turned up unexpectedly at her husband's office with her two-year-old son.

Her husband, who is a procurement manager for an engineering firm, said: "She came up as a surprise. She'd been sending me messages saying how much she loved me and brought her son up to meet me.

"We arranged to meet my boss and had a couple of drinks. I thought it was nice of my wife to want to do that.

"My boss left and I said I wanted to go home because it was February and the temperature was minus six and her son was young and I thought he needed to go home. I tried for nearly two hours to get her to leave the first pub we were in, then we started having an argument and she agreed to go home."

Underwood later went into another pub to use the lavatory. After 10 minutes of waiting outside, Mr Underwood decided to take the little boy home.

When she did not return the next day he contacted the police,

Mr Underwood, who lives in Kingston, Surrey, later received a text message which read: "Merete is OK but cries and wants to go home. But we are not finished with her."

He said: "I thought that was it. She has come up against exactly that sort of thing I'd warned her about, she's going to end up in some body-bag somewhere."

Underwood later told police she had been raped and indecently assaulted by two men in a flat in London's Bayswater.

HOME: Where the Underwoods lived in upmarket Kingston

Officers took detailed statements and drove her around the area looking for any of the "suspects". She later identified the man she had spent the night with and he was arrested. After 24 hours in a cell at Paddington Green police station, he was released pending further inquiries.

Mr Underwood met his wife in Norway in February 2001. Five months later they married and enjoyed a honeymoon in Bali.

"In hindsight, this was a big mistake," he said. "She was a fantastic party girl and great for having a good time.

"When she goes out drinking she goes off with people and is completely unreasonable. She's a different person. I tried to get her help with her binge drinking by making her seek medical help and a counsellor."

Mr Underwood said he would have done anything for his now estranged wife.

"All she had to do was flutter her eyes and I would have supported her," he said. "I loved her and would have done anything for her."

Daily Express, Tuesday June 7th 2005

Mother is jailed for a year after lying to hide her shame with a stranger

The wife who cried rape over her one-night stand

By **Stephen Wright** and **Fiona MacRae**

A CHEATING wife was jailed for 12 months yesterday after crying rape to cover up a one-night stand with a stranger.

Merete Underwood, 32, left her husband and two-year-old son in a pub to seduce another man in a nearby wine bar.

The Norwegian blonde spent the night in a hotel with him before telling her husband she had been kidnapped and raped.

Underwood then wasted thousands of pounds of taxpayers' money and hundreds of police hours by giving a statement about her 'ordeal' and helping draw up an e-fit image of one of her 'attackers'.

The 34-year-old interior designer she spent the night with then faced 15 months with the finger of suspicion pointing at him and has been left traumatised.

Even when she was charged with perverting the course of justice, Underwood continued to lie. It was only as the jury was about to be sworn in to try her that she confessed.

Underwood – who is being divorced by her husband Toby – wept as the judge said her belated plea and previous good character could not save her from jail.

'Rape is an extremely serious offence and quite rightly any allegation of rape is dealt with very seriously by police,' Recorder
with very seriously by police,' Recorder
Andrew McCooey told her.

'I have heard from the prosecution the impact this had on this innocent man, not

Merete is ok but she crays and want to get home to you but we are not finish with her here.

Part of Underwood's text to her husband

to mention the many thousands of pounds that has been wasted, all brought about by your pack of lies.'

Underwood, of Kingston, South-West London, had taken her son to meet her husband for a drink after he finished work on the evening of February 25 last year.

A few drinks in one pub were followed by several more in another, in Paddington, West London.

'Then at about 9.30pm she went to the bathroom,' Joanne Hacking, prosecuting, told Middlesex Guildhall Crown Court, West London. 'A few minutes later her husband, curious as to why she had not returned, asked bar staff to check the toilets. There was no sign of her there and no sign of her outside.'

Although worried, Mr Underwood took the view that his priority was their son's welfare and took him home.

'He eventually went to bed, woke up at 5am and realised his wife was still not home,' said Miss Hacking. 'He was astounded by this and very worried.'

Later that day he reported his wife's disappearance to the police.

Not long afterwards he received a text message from her mobile saying: 'Merete is ok but she cries and wants to get home to you but we are not finished with her here. Good f***.'

Mr Underwood was 'obviously desperately concerned' but very soon after that received a phone call from his boss to say his wife had been found outside their office and had been taken to a police station.

She claimed she had left the pub for some fresh air when a stranger approached, grabbed her by the hair, forced her into a car and drove her to a hotel where two men took turns to rape her. She said she was held captive for 12 hours.

Miss Hacking said the defendant gave a full description of one of the so-called rapists and later 'identified' the interior designer.

The court heard significant police resources were wasted by her deceit. Besides the officers involved in the investigation, forensic laboratory facilities were tied up and CCTV footage had to be examined.

Miss Hacking said the 'unfortunate victim' did everything he could to convince police he was innocent.

He explained he had been with a group of friends in the wine bar when Underwood walked up to him, began chatting, kissed him on the mouth and held his hand.

Later they left the wine bar and went to his hotel where they shared a can of beer and had sex. They had sex again the following morning.

Then they left his room and went to a post office where surveillance cameras captured Underwood 'laughing and smiling and entirely at ease' with her lover.

'The impact of the allegations on this man were to leave him terribly traumatised,' said Miss Hacking.

'He had never had any problems with the police before and as a result of all this he became very nervous and insecure. He has been left always wondering whether people know of the allegations made against him.

'He still feels ashamed and is very worried that his reputation has been tarnished.'

Told that Underwood was now 'full of remorse', the judge retorted: 'Words come cheap. The fact is she kept the finger of suspicion and accusation pointing for 15 months at an innocent man.

'As far as I can see her sorrow is directed at her plight, not the victim.'

Perverting the course of justice carries a maximum sentence of life imprisonment. But the culprits in most serious cases are jailed for between one and two years.

Underwood will serve a maximum of six months behind bars but could be out a few weeks earlier if considered eligible for electronic tagging.

Merete Underwood on her wedding day: She wept in the dock as she was sentenced

'You didn't have the decency to put this man out of his misery'

Toby Underwood: Divorce

Marrying her was a big mistake

The husband

THE husband of Merete Underwood told yesterday how another man got her pregnant within months of their marriage.

Toby Underwood, 34, a procurement manager for an engineering company, described her as 'vindictive and deceitful'.

He said drink would make her uncontrollable and she would bring lovers back to the matrimonial home while he was there.

He met Merete in Norway in February 2001 while he was working there. Within a week they were engaged and they married five months later. But just weeks after their honeymoon in Bali she became pregnant.

Mr Underwood now looks after the result of that pregnancy, three-year-old James, the child he at first thought was his own and whom he says she has now abandoned.

'When I first met Merete I liked all the things that were eventually her downfall. She's a fantastic party girl, great for having a good time, but she's not able to separate those things from day-to-day life.

'She's a binge drinker and has never worked. I paid for everything and gave her a better life than she ever could have imagined.'

Referring to her rape allegations, Mr Underwood said: 'This incident is just one little bit of a horrible, horrible situation. She has put so many people through so much.'

Asked about the man falsely accused, he said: 'Nobody deserves to be put through what he has been put through. He has had a year of hell. I can't really put it into words.'

Daily Mail Tuesday June 7th 2005

SUE CARROLL

Crying rape sullies name of all women

METROPOLITAN Police Commissioner Sir Ian Blair has this week ordered a review of the way his officers investigate rape claims. He's curious, as well he might be, that only one rape complaint in 18 results in a conviction.

Since there are now 12,000 cases reported a year, it doesn't take a genius to work out that our streets must either be packed with menacing sexual predators walking free, or many of these men are the innocent victims of false allegations.

AWFUL LIES: Merete

The question is this:

Now that it's easier – quite rightly – to report a genuine rape, is it also easier by the same token to allege a totally fictitious one?

The answer – looking at Merete Underwood, jailed this week for crying rape – has to be yes.

If ever there was an instance of police accepting blithely that when a woman claims to have been violated by a man she must be telling the truth, it's the case of Mrs Underwood.

The rather sordid and depressing reality about this mother of two is that, tired of bickering with her husband and young son, she slipped out of a pub where they were drinking, via the loo, to find herself a little adventure. It came in the form of a young man in a wine bar who, suffice to say, found the attractive, accommodating blonde more than willing to come with him to his hotel.

Alarm bells rang only when, waking up in a strange bed and probably hungover, Merete realised she had some uncomfortable truths to face.

Her husband, fearing for her safety, had alerted the police. And so began the spinning of a lie which escalated into a police investigation costing £20,000.

Let's not even consider how many hours of their time was taken up as she embellished the story of her "ordeal" and helped to draw up an e-fit image of her so-called "attacker" who, she alleged, had grabbed her by the hair, forced her into a car and, with an accomplice, raped her.

Wholly believable of course.

The "ladette" culture has brought about a massive sea change. Young girls out of their heads on cheap booze have made the life of sexual predators alarmingly easy. And yes, convictions against them are hard to stand up when all the victim has to offer in the way of detail is a memory blurred by vodka or Rohypnol.

Merete, on the other hand, was able to supply a meticulous portrait of her alleged assailant. The man in question, a 34-year-old interior designer, has spent the past 15 months in purdah waiting to stand trial.

He is, apparently, traumatised, nervous and insecure. Small wonder. Having never had any dealings with the police he found himself suddenly accused of a crime almost as heinous as murder and facing a sentence which, at worst, could mean life.

Even now, no doubt, the words "no smoke without fire" still haunt him. The law can't legislate against rumour and speculation as Stephen McLaughlin, falsely accused of rape by an ex-girlfriend, would doubtless testify if he were here to tell the story. He killed himself 18 months after she admitted fabricating the case against him.

This week, by coincidence, I received a letter from a decorator who, in 1999, was accused of rape by the woman whose house he was painting.

The case was dropped because of lack of evidence but his name remains on police files. "I still suffer nightmares, depression, and have trouble comprehending what happened to my life," he wrote.

It's against this background that Sir Ian Blair is said to be considering making it easier for police to convict alleged rapists.

One suggestion is that less evidence will be required. What a terrifying precedent when women like Merete are able to take their fiction into a courtroom and near as dammit destroy an innocent man's life.

There can't be a bloke in Britain who doesn't feel contempt for her.

But women, too, have every right to be furious. Her lies damn us all.

Daily Mirror, Wednesday, June 8th, 2005

Mirror.co.uk
THE BEST NEWSPAPER ON THE WEB

8 June 2005

CRY RAPE WIFE DID IT BEFORE
One-night stand liar exposed..by her mother

By Greig Box

THE wife jailed after she cried rape had falsely accused a man before, her mother said yesterday.

Jane Nordhaug said she was shocked by the 12-month sentence handed out on Monday to Merette Underwood, below.

Underwood, 32, who is Norwegian, invented the rape story to cover up a one-night stand and fool husband Toby.

Mum Jane said: "There has been a lot of trouble with many boys in the past. It is not the first time she has cried rape. It happened here about 10 years ago."

Mrs Nordhaug, speaking from Fauske in Norway, said police found no firm evidence.

She added: "They dropped the investigation. All the problems with her different boyfriends have led to psychological problems for my daughter.

"I talked to her last Saturday and she did not mention it was this serious. But I knew there was some kind of trouble."

She now wants Underwood transferred to a Norwegian prison.

Mrs Nordhaug said: "It is so expensive to fly to England, so I don't know if I can afford to see her.

"I am not mad or angry with her. I just feel sorry for her."

Underwood was sentenced in London for lying to police over a sex session with an interior designer she met in a bar.

She had left husband Toby and her two-year-old son in another pub.

Meanwhile, builder Kevin Blakey, 36, who has been living with Underwood in Sussex, plans to wait for her release - then take her to Norway "away from all this".

Mirror.co.uk
THE BEST NEWSPAPER ON THE WEB

9 June 2005

JAILED..BUT IS HE CRY RAPE WIFE'S 3RD VICTIM DOUBTS OVER HER CLAIMS

By Stephen Moyes

A MAN was jailed for two years after being accused of raping Merete Underwood, the woman sentenced for lying about another sex attack.

She received a 12-month prison term this week after lying to police over a sex session with an interior designer she met in a bar in London.

She had invented the rape story to cover-up a one-night stand to fool her husband Toby.

Now doubt has been raised over the conviction of a man who Merete, 32, claimed raped her in Norway in 1992. On that occasion the Norwegian, then 18, said she was grabbed off a pavement in Fauske and bundled into a car and attacked.

After her claims a 24-year-old man came forward to tell police he had met her after getting out of his car to relieve himself. He said they chatted and she willingly had sex with him, although they were strangers. But he was not believed and jailed for two years. His appeal was rejected and was ordered to pay £7,000 compensation.

It has also emerged in 1997, Kai-Magne Hansen, a 39-year-old foreman, was accused of raping Merete in the street after a disco in Fauske.

He recalled: "She was very drunk and came over and tried to sit on my lap. I asked her to get off. That was the only time I spoke to her."

But after she picked him out at an identity parade he was charged with rape and held in a cell for two weeks before being released without charge.

She later tried and failed to claim £20,000 in compensation from him.

Last night it was reported she plans to appeal against her jail term for perverting the course of justice.

DAILY MIRROR, Friday, June 10, 2005 PAGE 29

MY CRY-RAPE EX IS SO EVIL

'She was out every night drinking and picking up men. She said she'd been raped before and she'd had a brain tumour'

LIAR: Merete Underwood is now in prison

THE first husband of rape liar Merete Underwood told yesterday how her boozing and cheating tore his life apart too.

EXCLUSIVE from ROBERT STANSFIELD in Stavanger, Norway

Frank Ogreid said she went out nightly to meet men in bars, sometimes dumping their baby son in a pushchair outside.

He blasted: "Merete is pure evil and has ruined my life. She might be locked away for her evil crimes, but every night I sit alone as our son sleeps. Hers is a prison sentence, mine is for life."

Underwood, 32, now serving 12 months for perverting justice, even lied that she had a brain tumour to cover up her flings.

Her chequered past also includes a bid to drown herself in a bath and rape claims in 1992 and 1997, the first of which saw a man jailed for two years.

Frank, 36, of Stavanger, southern Norway, was so concerned about her mental state that he even had her put in a mental hospital for six months.

They met in a local bar in 1995 and within a year she was pregnant with Michael, now eight.

Although he begged her to have an abortion as he felt she was not ready for motherhood, she insisted she was, and cleaned up her act.

But three months after their son was born she was back on booze. Shipping manager Frank said: "She was desperate to have a child and well-behaved when she was pregnant. "But after the birth being able to drink again sent her into a spiral of destruction.

"She was out every night, drinking and picking up men while I was left to look after Michael.

"She wouldn't come home at night and made up crazy excuses, such as all the taxis refused to take her because she had cancer, which she didn't."

Even when Michael was with her she did not stop. Frank said: "Friends would tell me they saw her in bars drinking while our son was left in a pushchair outside.

"I worked hard but any money I made she wasted on men and alcohol." After walking out on him in 1998, she began fighting for custody of Michael. But she gave up to spend more time with a new lover. Her ex revealed: "She had visiting rights but didn't turn up half the time as she was too hung over. When she did take Michael out, she just left him in bars."

This week Middlesex Guildhall crown court heard Underwood, of Kingston, Surrey, falsely accused a stranger of rape after a one-night stand. She picked him up in a bar after leaving second husband Toby Underwood, 34, and son James, two, in another.

Frank blames her behaviour on her troubled history. As well as the two rape claims in the 90s and the suicide bid, she hardly knew her father. "She told me she'd been raped in 1992 and someone was jailed," he said. "I believe it happened as it made her funny in the head. She tried to kill herself.

"She became desperate for attention. In 1997 she lied about being raped again and said she had a brain tumour.

"None of it was true, so me and my mum put her in a mental hospital but it didn't help.

"She only met her dad once. I think she's searching for a man to take his place. And boy, has she been through a lot of them."

Frank added: "Michael visited her last year has had little contact since. He asks, 'When's Mummy coming home?' Now I have to tell him what she's done.

"He misses her terribly. The truth will hit him badly when he realises she's deserted him once and for all."

b.stansfield@mirror.co.uk

TORMENT: Her ex-husband Frank

Daily Mirror, Friday, 10th June 2005

Jailed . . . Underwood

Fifth fella accuses cry rape woman

From MARTIN PHILLIPS
in Stavanger, Norway

A FIFTH man yesterday told how he was falsely accused by "cry rape" wife Merete Underwood.

The 34-year-old oilman, who asked not to be identified, bedded the blonde hours after she picked him up in a bar in Stavanger, Norway, in 1999.

She left his house before he woke next day – and soon afterwards cops knocked at his door.

He said: "They questioned me then let me go. They said they knew all about her. They knew she'd made claims before."

Underwood, 32, of Kingston, Surrey, is serving a year in jail for perverting the course of justice. She left her husband and young son in a pub to pick up a stranger.

She claimed she had been kidnapped, sparking a huge police probe – but this week admitted in court she had lied.

Underwood has cried rape at least **SIX** times, The Sun has discovered. But she pleaded from jail yesterday: "I don't belong here. I want to go home."

The Sun, Friday, June 10th, 2005

Outraged peer unmasks 'serial fantasist' in speech to House of Lords

Named, woman whose false rape claim sent a dad to jail for 3 years

By Sam Greenhill

A WOMAN who cried rape and sent an innocent man to jail was yesterday named and shamed in Parliament.

Shannon Taylor, described as a 'serial liar', was unmasked by a peer said to be outraged by the case.

Lord Campbell-Savours used parliamentary privilege to name her and lambast the 'shabby' police investigation that put father of two Warren Blackwell behind bars for more than three years.

Miss Taylor is said to have made at least seven other fake sex attack claims in the past, including one against her father.

Legal experts praised his decision to expose her to prevent other men falling victim.

Mr Blackwell, 36, was cleared at the Appeal Court last month after Miss Taylor's background was exposed by a Criminal Cases Review Commission investigation.

Although his name was blackened, anonymity laws meant his accuser's was protected, and she became known only as 'Miss A'.

Even the appeal judges wanted to name her to warn the public – but were powerless to do so.

The Daily Mail led calls for her identity to be revealed. Yesterday, Lord Campbell-Savours stood up and publicly did so.

He asked fellow peers: 'Is not the inevitable consequence of the workings of the law, as currently framed, that we will carry on imprisoning innocent people like Warren Blackwell, who was falsely accused by a serial and repeated liar, Shannon Taylor, with a history of false accusations and multiple identities?

'As a result of her accusations, he spent three-and-a-half years in prison following a shabby and inadequate police investigation, and was only exonerated when the Criminal Cases Review Commission inquiry cleared him and exposed her history.'

'Fantastic': The Blackwells

'rom the Daily Mail, September 13

The Labour peer added: 'Shouldn't mature accusers who perjure themselves in rape trials be named and prosecuted for perjury?'

Miss Taylor's own daughter backed the decision to disclose her name, saying: 'She is a danger and the public needs to be warned.'

Mr Blackwell's ordeal began when his accuser, now 38, claimed she had been seized with a knife outside a village club early on New Year's Day 1999, taken to an alley and indecently assaulted.

'This woman needs to be stopped'

She picked him out of an identity parade and a jury found him guilty, even though there was no forensic evidence and he had no previous convictions. His wife Tanya never doubted his innocence.

Eventually, the case was investigated by the Criminal Cases Review Commission which found Miss Taylor had fabricated at least seven other allegations of sexual and physical assault. She frequently changed her name and police forces did not realise they were dealing with the same woman.

Her own mother has described her as 'a persistent liar, very manipulative and a bully' who frequently claimed to have been beaten, sexually attacked and raped – all of which were untrue.

She has a history of mental illness and self-harm.

The original investigation by Northamptonshire Police was exposed as shoddy, with Mr Blackwell's lawyers claiming that normal safeguards and procedures were completely ignored. He plans to sue.

Yesterday, a friend of Lord Campbell-Savours, 63 explained why he decided to speak out.

He said: 'He named her because he was outraged. He doesn't think it's got anything to do with the issue of rape, he thinks it's an issue of perjury.

'This woman made up the story and told lies and he can't see why a person who has perjured themselves should be protected, irrespective of the type of offence.

'Sometimes people have to stick their heads above the parapet in cases where the law is clearly an ass and needs to be reformed.'

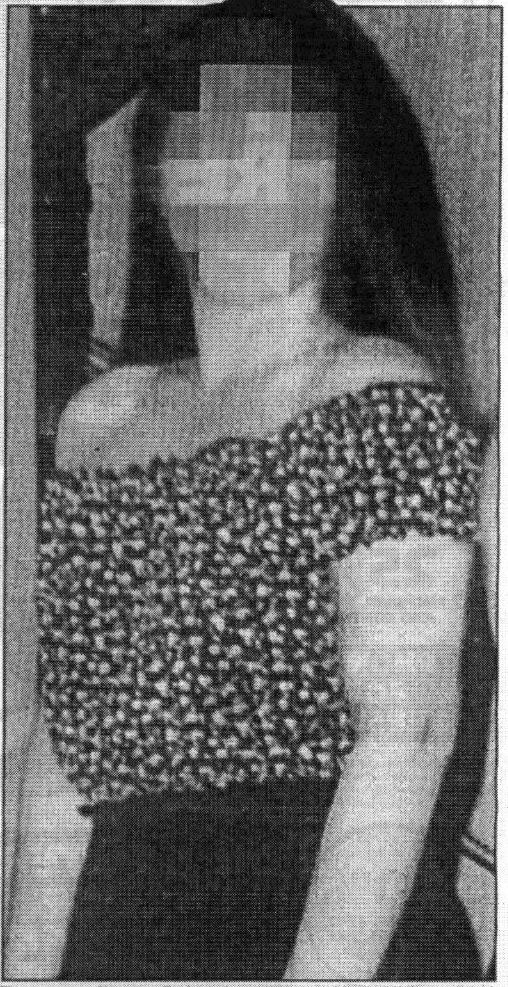

The accuser: Shannon Taylor's face still cannot be publicly revealed

Mr Blackwell, from Woodford Halse, Northamptonshire, said: 'It's absolutely fantastic. I didn't think anybody would have the guts to name her.

'This woman needs to be stopped. The fact is, she remains free to carry on crying rape and up till now has been enjoying the full protection of the law. Now I hope she will go on to be prosecuted.'

But she is unlikely to face charges for perjury or perverting justice.

Northamptonshire Police say there is 'insufficient evidence', and Crown Prosecution sources have cited her mental illness as a barrier.

But Mr Blackwell's barrister Anne Johnson said yesterday: 'There is a clear public interest in her being prosecuted for perjury or the very least wasting police time.

'It's fantastic that somebody of authority has finally come out and named this woman.'

At Mr Blackwell's appeal last month, Mr Justice Tugendhat admitted similar cases could follow, adding that Parliament had not seemed to have considered this possibility when framing the law.

In the 1970s, the Daily Mail campaigned for women in sex cases to be granted automatic anonymity, to protect genuine victims of crime.

Callers to Miss Taylor's most recent address yesterday were told by her boyfriend that she no longer lived there.

Comment – Page 14

s.greenhill@dailymail.co.uk

Rape liar named
Daily Mail October 20th 2006

After six years in jail for double rape, man is cleared

Sir Igor: Warned over false claims

By **Christian Gysin** and **Ben Clerkin**

A MAN who spent almost seven years in prison for rape was freed yesterday after a judge ruled the conviction was unsafe.

David Carrington-Jones was convicted on the evidence of a woman who had a history of making false allegations, the court heard.

Quashing the 64-year-old lorry driver's conviction, Sir Igor Judge warned that women who cry rape undermine those who make genuine complaints.

He said: 'Rape is a repulsive crime. It requires substantial punishment.

'On the other hand, just because rape is a repulsive crime, a false allegation can have very dreadful consequences, obviously and immediately, for the innocent man who has not perpetrated the crime.

'But also – and this is not to be overlooked – because every occasion of a proved false allegation has an insidious effect on confidence in the truth of genuine complaints of rape.'

Three judges in London's Court of Appeal yesterday ruled that Mr Carrington-Jones's convictions were 'demonstrably unsafe'.

They said he had been at the centre of a 'profoundly troublesome case' when found guilty of two counts of rape and sexual assault against a pair of teenage sisters in December 2000.

It was later found that one of his accusers had also made complaints of rape against her brother, fiancee, stepfather and even a customer at her work.

She admitted to police she made up the allegations against her stepfather because she 'did not like him'.

But the jury did not know this, and Mr Carrington-Jones was sentenced to a ten-year jail term at Lewes Crown Court.

He was later refused parole hearings because he refused to admit his guilt.

He was finally released on August 13 this year, having served six years and nine months of his sentence.

Sir Igor Judge, sitting with Mr Justice Pitchford and Sir Richard Curtis, said that his principal accuser 'had a proved tendency to make false allegations that she was a victim of sexual crime'.

> **5.7%**
> **of reported rape cases result in a conviction**

Mr Carrington-Jones, of Burgess Hill, West Sussex, had his case referred to the Court of Appeal after an inquiry by the Criminal Cases Review Commission, the independent body which investigates possible miscarriages of justice.

After the case, Mr Carrington-Jones thanked his legal team – who could now seek compensation on his behalf – and the Commission.

He added: 'I am very relieved that this ordeal is now over for me, but my heart goes out to other men and women who have been put inside because of false allegations they just can't challenge.' He said he had remained 'true to himself' by refusing to say he was guilty.

'The consequence was that five years later – in December 2005 – I was refused parole,' he added. 'And the same thing happened again in December 2006.'

By this time Sussex police had found Mr Carrington-Jones was just one of many men against whom his accuser had made 'demonstrably false allegations'.

He had always denied any offence against either of the two women – sisters who can be referred to only as KJ and LJ for legal reasons.

After admitting making a false allegation against her stepfather, KJ, who is now 23, received a caution for wasting police time.

Last June, she made a complaint of rape against a former boyfriend — before later admitting this was also false.

Sir Igor said: 'A moment's glance at the facts would demonstrate this new material would severely undermine any confidence that any jury could have had in KJ's evidence.

'The credibility of this witness is damaged beyond repair.'

Sir Igor added that the other supposed victim, LJ, 'only made the allegations she made after she was aware of allegations made by KJ'.

He said: 'In our judgment the evidence that we now have would have had a direct impact, not only on the jury's judgment of the allegations made by KJ, but also those made by LJ.'

The court also heard that the original allegations against Mr Carrington-Jones had emerged 'out of the blue'.

Daily Mail Wednesday 17th October 2007

THE TIMES Wednesday April 25 2007 — News | 15

Girl's rape lie destroyed taxi driver's life

▶ Drunk teenager exploited kindness

▶ Accused lost job, home and his name

Russell Jenkins

An Asian taxi driver told yesterday how his life had been ruined by false allegations that he had raped a white teenage girl in his vehicle.

Aftab Ahmed, 44, of Allerton, Bradford, lost his home, livelihood, reputation and found his family relationships and marriage under strain in the 14 months it took for the lies of his 17-year-old accuser to be exposed in court.

The teenager, who cannot be identified for legal reasons, was sentenced at Bradford Magistrates' Court to a four-month detention and training order after admitting perverting the course of justice.

It emerged that, far from assaulting his fare, the taxi driver had gone out of his way to ensure that the extremely drunk and disorientated girl got home safely and had somebody to look after her.

District Judge David Thomas told her: "You repaid that kindness by alleging that he had raped you. The consequences were disastrous for Mr Ahmed, who was arrested in front of his family."

The blonde girl made the claim against the taxi driver in January last year after a night of drinking in Bradford with her sister and friends.

Mr Ahmed, who has a degree in political science and once worked as a police officer in Kashmir, told how a group of girls negotiated a £13 fare to take the drunken girl home to Baildon, north of the city. He gave her sister his registration and name before driving off. The trip, which should have taken 15 minutes, took three quarters of an hour because she vomited over the seats six times and Mr Ahmed was forced to stop repeatedly.

Unable to find her home address, he had to knock on doors and ask for directions. At one stage, he stopped a bus to ask the driver. He also phoned the girl's sister to tell her that she was in a poor state of health, that he was worried about leaving her at home alone and said that he would leave her in the care of neighbours.

Mr Ahmed insisted that he had done his best to look after her but once home she dialled 999 and told police she had been raped. Several hours after he returned to work Mr Ahmed was arrested.

Duncan Wilcock, for the prosecution, said that the girl took officers to a remote spot on Baildon Moor where she claimed that the rape had taken place.

The court was told that the girl had initially made the allegation because she had felt a pain in her groin area and had assumed that she had been raped. As soon as she sobered up, she realised her mistake but continued with the pretence.

Mr Wilcock said: "Mr Ahmed was arrested the same evening in front of his family and endured a degrading, full medical examination, and denied the allegations during interview. He was released on police bail but had his taxi licence revoked."

After six weeks police were satisfied that the allegations against Mr Ahmed were false but it was not until last month that the accuser admitted she had been keeping up a lie.

Mr Wilcock said: "These allegations have had a profound effect on Mr Ahmed and his family. He is no longer prepared to work as a taxi driver in the evenings for fear of other allegations against him. His wife is taking tablets for depression and it has affected his position within the community."

Edward Renvoize, for the defence, told the court that his client had made the allegations not out of malice, but naivety and immaturity. She was deeply remorseful.

But the judge told her: "Sorry does not put matters right."

Aftab Ahmed: went out of his way to make sure the drunken girl, right, got home safely

After the hearing Mr Ahmed said he had been forced to sell the semi-detached home he shares with his wife, Amber, 32, and twin 11-year-old daughters because he could not afford the mortgage. He has been ostracised by former friends, relatives and fellow Muslims.

"During the ordeal I had my taxi badge taken away, which meant I could not work. We fell into arrears with the mortgage and the house is now sold because we cannot afford to live here any longer," he said. "When my twin girls asked me where I had been when I returned from the police station I had to tell them I had been on a long fare. I hated lying to my children and have finally been able to explain what really has gone on.

"The accusations have destroyed my family. It has impacted on myself, my wife and my children. To be accused of rape is the most serious crime in my religion of Islam. It is seen as worse than murder, because we are told to honour women and that they are sacrosanct.

"Four months is not long enough for what that girl has put me through. Her lies have destroyed my life and I feel I will never recover from what has happened to me and my family. The whole thing has been hell."

The Times Wednesday April 25th 2007

THE TIMES FRIDAY OCTOBER 20 2006

Anonymous accusers who ruin lives

By David Brown

WITH just one in twenty cases of rape leading to a conviction there have been growing demands for changes to the law to make it easier bring prosecutions.

However, there have also been growing numbers of cases where men have had their rape convictions overturned and prosecutions of women who have made up allegations.

Last month a teenager was jailed after four men were held in police cells for 36 hours after she accused them of rape. Cinzia Sannino, then 17, only admitted her lies when police showed her footage on a mobile telephone of her performing naked lap-dancing for the men after returning home with them from a Cardiff club.

The case led a spokesman for the False Allegations Support Organisation to comment: "Too many people jump on the bandwagon, aware that they can get compensation for false allegations."

Two weeks later a woman who falsely cried rape against her former husband was also convicted of perverting the course of justice.

Sally Henderson, 40, a mother of two, described by the prosecution as a "wicked liar", claimed that Richard Cooke, 39, had repeatedly raped her during their year-long marriage.

However, police discovered that her claims were almost identical to false allegations she had made five years earlier against a previous boyfriend, Gloucester Crown Court heard.

Lifting an order preventing her identification, Recorder David Lane, QC, said: "The public has a right to know the identity of a person who makes such allegations and who seeks to use the system of justice for her own, unscrupulous ends."

A month earlier an obsessed stalker who accused her psychiatrist of rape was convicted of harassment, threats to kill and perverting justice.

Maria Marchese, 45, rummaged through Jan Falkowski's dustbin for a used condom to clinch DNA evidence. The case against the consultant, of Limehouse, East London, was dropped — but his relationship with his fiancée collapsed.

There have been growing calls for men accused of rape to be granted anonymity until they are convicted.

The Liberal Democrats voted last month to grant anonymity to anyone accused of rape until conviction.

Anonymous accusers who ruin lives
The Times October 20th 2006

Mercy for woman who cried rape eight times

By Luke Salkeld

A WOMAN who made eight separate false claims of rape or sexual assault has been spared jail.

Gemma Gregory, 28, accused seven different men over a six-year period.

Former boyfriends were subjected to police questioning and DNA testing to clear their names.

Her fantasy stories also wasted huge amounts of police time.

As long ago as 2002, she admitted in a statement to police that she was 'seeking attention' from them. But it was not until last year, after recording several hundred calls either from her or about her, that they took action.

She was given a one-year jail term suspended for two years at Plymouth Crown Court for perverting the course of justice. Judge Francis Gilbert said she must receive mental treatment.

Her latest offence was in May when she rang police to say she had been raped at her home. She stuck to her story in a video interview three days later despite being warned she would be prosecuted if it was another lie.

A 34-year-old man was interviewed by police and for the next five months Gregory regularly contacted officers to ask how the case was progressing.

Yesterday, the victim spoke of his ordeal.

'We were going out for five to six months. I ended the relationship with her, but she got back in touch with me a couple of months later.

'We met up at a pub and saw each other for about two or three nights after that. I stayed at her flat one of those nights and we had sex just the once.'

He continued: 'She then left a message on my phone saying come round tonight but I was doing other things.

'The next thing I knew the police rang me up and asked me to come to see them. I was not arrested but attended the police station voluntarily. It wasn't very nice to be accused of rape.

'The police told me they thought the accusation against me was a load of rubbish.

'But I didn't know about the previous incidents. I had heard rumours but nothing more than that.'

Plymouth Crown Court heard that Gregory suffers from a personality disorder as well as other disorders.

Detective Constable Paul Weymouth, of Plymouth CID, said yesterday: 'We conducted a thorough rape inquiry.

'Because of previous allegations she had made it was strenuously explained to her about the implications of making a false claim.

'She was medically examined and video-interviewed. Forensic evidence was taken from her. She rang us every two or three days to keep it going and claimed that her ex-boyfriend had made silent calls.

'She wanted him put in prison. She kept this going for a long time.' He said that some of the earlier 'suspects' had been arrested and had intimate samples taken as part of the inquiries.

'It causes serious anguish'

The judge warned Gregory that if she did not comply with the terms of his order over the next two years, she would be jailed. 'False allegations of rape not only cause a great deal of wasted police time but also serious anguish to the person against who the complaint is made,' he said.

At a previous hearing he had told her: 'There are two possible outcomes – a lengthy period of imprisonment or treatment at an institution which will help you in the long run.'

It is understood that Gregory was not prosecuted earlier because of her apparent mental health problems and previous efforts to admit her difficulties.

A spokesman for Devon and Cornwall Police said: 'These types of allegations are of a particularly sensitive nature.

'We have to treat each case individually and on its own merits and investigate any such claims thoroughly.

'It was not thought appropriate to take action at an earlier stage.'

Daily Mail Wednesday 14th November 2007

Rushing to court is not the answer to life's mistakes and misfortunes

DAVID AARONOVITCH

What a monumental waste of time and cash. I would have given in, rather than go through this prolonged daftness

Why can't people see the bleeding obvious? On Wednesday, after an entire year of legal nonsense – which has, I dare say, enriched only their lawyers – two sets of professionals have secured a judgment in their footling case: an adjudication that favours neither and yet that both have hailed as a triumph.

The case was well reported because Sarah Butterfield, the artist, is the other half of the agreeably intelligent front-bench Conservative, David Willetts. The Butterfield-Willettses send their son to the same school as a Charlotte and Simon Hood, who, upon attending an exhibition of Ms Butterfield's work, told the artist that they would simply adore it if she (and David) were to go and stay at their holiday home in France, what with its pool and its acre of grounds. She did, painted 10 pictures there and then, as she was about to leave, was requested by the Hoods (she said) to leave two paintings behind by way of payment. "When I left," Ms Butterfield told Brentford Crown Court, "I knelt before the paintings and felt absolutely gutted."

Mrs Hood had a slightly different story, in which Ms Butterfield had laid on her need for a holiday "with a trowel", at which payment by picture had been suggested. "We may be generous," explained Mrs Hood, "but we don't let casual acquaintances have a week's holiday in our house for nothing." Which makes you wonder what she thinks the word "generous" means. In any case, the Hoods received an invoice for £2,700 plus VAT per picture. Since French valuers estimated the paintings at £200 for the pair, the Hoods refused and the matter took a year to resolve. The judge ruled that one picture should go to the Hoods and one to the Butterfield-Willettses. It was this that both sides declared themselves satisfied with.

What a monumental waste of time and cash. Were I on either side of this row I would have given in, rather than go through this prolonged daftness. Adults simply should have been able to sort this out between them. It argues a kind of wilful egoism that they didn't. But at least the litigiousness of the people involved harmed no one but themselves and sits in the great, tragic tradition of Dickens's Richard Carstone who, in *Bleak House*, becomes addicted to seeking non-existent remedy through legal action.

Others who go to court may have little alternative. Many of those who sue the NHS do so for want of any other form of redress, according to the report by the Public Accounts Committee, published yesterday. Its chairman, Edward Leigh, commented that, upon complaint, "patients suffer delay and an almost systematic lack of compassion. Often they are effectively cornered into pursuing litigation, and in more than six out of 10 smaller-value cases, the legal costs outweigh the compensation paid". In April the National Audit Office estimated a possible bill for medical negligence claims amounting to £4.4bn.

Certainly the family of a man in south Wales who had the wrong kidney removed look like having an overwhelming case for compensation. Another court, trying the two surgeons for manslaughter, heard this week that a woman student had tried to warn one that he was about to remove the wrong organ. If the court accepts this account, then it will be a real warning about the dangers of medical arrogance.

But what is one to make of the possibly landmark case of the woman from the North Country? This anonymous complainant is hiring lawyers to bring a case for medical negligence against the NHS, following an abortion operation a few years ago. But not because the procedure went wrong, or because she hadn't given consent to a termination. No, Ms X wants to sue because, she says, she wasn't warned about the potential psychological side-effects of undergoing an abortion, and she feels she should have been.

Could Ms X have a point? For years after the 1967 Act allowed abortion under certain circumstances, many women complained bitterly that doctors would try to dissuade them from having the operation, and that pressure was brought to bear for them to go to term and then keep their unwanted babies, or to have them adopted. So is it possible that, in reaction to these complaints, the medical establishment has declined to offer advice that might sound as though it was aimed at discouraging abortion? And has there, as a consequence, been negligence?

According to the woman, at the time of the abortion she felt she was doing something wrong. But it wasn't until the birth of a son three years later that she began to feel intensely guilty about the termination. According to BBC Online it was then, she said, that, she "realised what (she'd) lost… I just felt near a nervous breakdown then, so I had to go to my GP to ask for help… since then we've been working through things like guilt and forgiveness. It helps a bit, but I won't ever be the same."

So what should the NHS have done? Ms X, as it happens, had worked in the health service. She says that, from her own experience, she would expect any patient to be warned of the possible side-effects – including psychological ones – of a particular procedure. But she was not so warned, thus her consent was not informed. Her aim in suing, she says, is to "make the NHS aware of the approach they have on the wards, just to let them know what women are going through, how serious it is, and I think they need to do something about it".

Hardly surprisingly, the zealots of the anti-abortion movement have adopted Ms X as yet another of their icons, and are parading her around town. "She is a courageous woman," Nuala Scarisbrick of Life said. "She has been devastated by an abortion carried out in her local hospital… Had she known what the risks were, she would not have gone ahead with the operation. Perhaps we are seeing the start of a big fight-back by women against male-dominated abortionism."

She hopes. But given the antics of her allies in the anti-abortion movement, both here and in America, it is hard to accept that Ms Scarisbrick gives a rosary bead for the psychological wellbeing of women. Not when there are foetuses to protect. Meanwhile, equally predictably (though better-intentioned, in my view), the medical establishment has been at pains to stress that psychological complications following abortion are rare and that far more problems arise from the birth of unwanted children.

But I wonder whether there isn't another issue here, which is about Ms X's lack of adultness. She says that she didn't feel right in the period of her termination, but she coped. It was only when she brought a baby to term and saw it in her arms that she began to feel guilty. What's so wrong with that? Why shouldn't she feel sad about it? Why not cry about it? And why would it be anybody's job to protect her against this feeling? Unlike having the wrong kidney taken out, it's what life is like. And, as one friend said to me yesterday, sadness is an achievement of sorts. Ms X should drop the case now, before litigation enters her soul.

David.Aaronovitch@btinternet.com

Abortion Regret - suing for Psychological Side Effects.
The Independent - 14th June 2002.

ABORTION: THE

A NEW study reveals that it can take at least five years to get over the trauma of an abortion, because women who have them simply cannot come to terms with what they have done. They are also more anxious and depressed than those who have had a miscarriage.
VICTORIA CARPENTER and HELEN RENSHAW spoke to three women, of different ages, who had abortions as teenagers — and discovered the disturbing legacy of ending a pregnancy.

LINDA PORTER-ROBINSON, 47, is a housewife from Borehamwood, Herts. She lives with her three children, aged 21, 11 and 10, and her husband, Norman, a sales manager. Linda had an abortion when she was 19.

WHEN I was 19, I discovered I was pregnant and initially, I was thrilled. I'd met my fiancé three years earlier, when I was 16, and we were very much in love, becoming engaged when I turned 18. I had no doubts. We often talked of our future, our wedding plans and children.

After our engagement we became intimate, and I was taking contraceptive pills, but one month, I forgot to take one or two. I suspected I was pregnant, but it was 1977 and, in those days, you couldn't buy a home-testing kit.

So I took a urine sample to my local chemist. When it came back positive, I could barely wait to tell my fiancé. But instead of wrapping his arms around me joyfully as I had envisioned, his reaction was cold, shocked anger.

He told me he didn't want me to have the baby or be tied into fatherhood while we were so young. He withdrew, and began going out alone, returning later and later at night. Within two weeks, he ended our relationship.

I was devastated, terrified — and not yet in my 20s. At first I didn't know what to do. I came home to tell my mother my fiance had left me.

I received sympathy, until I added that I was pregnant. Shockingly, she coldly told me I could only live at home if I had an abortion.

I was stunned — my parents weren't overly religious or strict. But the shame of being an unmarried mother was still a huge stigma.

I have often looked back and wondered if I could have refused, but at the time I felt I had no choice.

I had no home, no money, and a baby on the way. I've spent my life feeling bitter and angry at what she made me do. I've never forgiven her.

The next day, I went for what was meant to be pre-termination counselling, but in reality, it was nothing more than a transaction.

I sat silently in a cold, bland office, where the doctor turned to me once, briefly, and asked if I wanted to keep the baby. Under my mother's baleful stare, I said 'no'.

The following week, I went back for the procedure. I have never felt more alone. After a general anaesthetic was administered, I went into theatre. Upon waking, I was given a sandwich before I was abruptly sent home.

I suffered abdominal cramps for a few days afterwards, but it was the emotional pain which lingered.

I felt a wrenching sense of loss and guilt, so I began drinking heavily. I simply wanted to forget it.

I sank into a lethargic depression, which has resurfaced on and off throughout the 20 years since.

As months passed, however, I began to tell myself that perhaps the abortion had been the right thing.

I had always dreamed of working as an actress, and began to get work on TV shows like The Professionals and Minder and in the film Quadrophenia.

I soon began a new relationship, and told my new boyfriend about the abortion almost straight away. His reaction of understanding and acceptance helped me to trust again.

But the after-effects were far from over. We married when I was 25, and I immediately began trying to get pregnant. For the 18 gruelling months that followed, each time my period arrived, I became quite hysterical.

I couldn't bear to be around babies, because I didn't have one. I knew the physical side-effects of the abortion could have affected my fertility.

Thankfully, I finally became pregnant — and my daughter arrived on March 4, 1984.

I was utterly elated. But I also became unreasonably possessive.

I'd feel guilty about the baby I'd lost, and block out the thought by focusing on my daughter — but then my love became suffocating.

Sadly, my marriage began to break down and we divorced when our daughter was eight.

Just a few weeks later, I met my new husband, Douglas. I had another beautiful baby girl a year later, and a son 12 months on.

Holding my tiny boy in my arms with my two girls around me, I felt the demons recede, and thought I had healed and moved on.

But at 42, I became pregnant once again and suffered a miscarriage at 14 weeks. I was instantly pulled back to my teenage abortion. I was convinced I was being punished for killing my baby as a teenager.

Cruelly, I underwent the same procedure to 'abort' my lifeless child that I'd undergone all those years ago.

It was sheer emotional agony. All the pain and guilt returned as vividly as if I was back 20 years ago. The miscarriage forced me to confront the feelings of loss and pain I'd buried.

The love and support of Douglas has helped me come to terms with those feelings. An abortion is a bereavement — it doesn't 'go away', you learn to live with it.

FULL-TIME mother Anna Weaver, 39, lives in Gloucester with her two children and businessman husband.

AT 16, I had the world at my feet. Academically successful and popular, I was the girl my teachers tipped to succeed in life. But that confident, optimistic girl was lost for ever — for at 16, I had the abortion that has blighted my life.

My boyfriend and I were childhood sweethearts, but waited three years to make love. When we did, it was in a forest clearing with the sun streaming through the trees.

It was perfect — except for one mistake. I'd started taking the Pill, but hadn't waited for it to take effect.

When my period didn't arrive, I panicked. All I could picture was the disappointment on my dad's face, so from the moment my pregnancy was confirmed, I was convinced that a secret abortion was my only option.

I'd always had a stormy relationship with my mum, and my dad was old-fashioned, so I felt there was no way I could tell them. I didn't see it as a baby but as a problem that must be swept under the carpet.

A GP put me in touch with the Pregnancy Advisory Service, which booked me for a consultation in London. Getting there involved concocting a lie, but the consultation itself was easy.

I'd expected to have to fight for my termination, but, after a brief discussion with the doctor, I had my appointment. It seemed far too easy.

I had the procedure — paid for by my boyfriend — at 12 weeks. I was very scared, but felt I was being punished for being a silly, dirty little girl.

Afterwards, I woke up writhing in agony. There was a dreadful burning, pinching pain in my abdomen, but no one paid me much attention.

And on top of the pain, I was hit by a vast and unexpected sense of loss.

Instead of feeling relief, as I'd imagined, my shame had been replaced by a deep guilt. There was no one for me to turn to. I went home and did my homework.

My pretence of normality didn't last long. I remained in dreadful pain and bled very heavily. After a week, I'd developed flu-like symptoms and my sister took me to hospital — it was to be the first of 12 visits to A&E.

The following two years passed in a haze of pain, guilt and worse.

An infection in my womb and fallopian tubes — caused because 'by-products' of the abortion had been left behind — flared up repeatedly.

I was admitted to hospital eight times and subjected to intravenous medicines, catheters and painful examinations. At one point, I was taking 24 tablets a day. I felt I was being punished for my terrible sin.

Meanwhile, my parents discovered the truth because of my hospital visits.

They were absolutely devastated at first and horrified their little girl had got herself pregnant, but came round

PRICE WE PAID

A new report says it takes at least five years to recover emotionally from a termination. Here three women reveal they may NEVER get over theirs . . .

when they saw how I was suffering.

My boyfriend wasn't much help — he was far too immature to deal with such grown-up problems.

Then, one day when I was 20, I collapsed at work in total agony — I'd suffered a ruptured ectopic pregnancy and was rushed to hospital for life-saving surgery.

I was told that the infection had blocked my Fallopian tubes, making it extremely unlikely I'd ever conceive naturally.

It made sense — having murdered one baby, why should I ever be blessed with another?

After that, my self-esteem hit rock bottom. I hated myself.

What saved me was meeting my husband, at 23. He saw the person I really was and we fell madly in love.

Telling him about my infertility was incredibly hard. But when I did, he said he wanted me, whatever.

We married when I was 25 and — miraculously — I fell pregnant naturally two years later. My husband was ecstatic.

I should have been overjoyed, too. But deep down, I was convinced my pregnancy was just a cruel trick. In my mind, I didn't deserve a baby and just waited for the miscarriage.

When my son was born, he was perfect — too perfect. Convinced this was some kind of cruel punishment for taking a life, I waited for him to die.

I developed bizarre rituals to protect my son's life, taking seven steps across the room to his cot, and checking him every seven minutes precisely.

After eight months, my strange behaviour had become obvious to everyone and I began seven years of mental health treatment. I was given medication and counselling that focused on my abortion. Slowly, I recovered and had another baby — this time a daughter. I loved her just as much, but fortunately didn't suffer the same torments.

My darling boy survived and is now 11. But I still fear he'll be taken from me and my over-protective behaviour stifles him.

My husband's loyalty has been miraculous, but my behaviour has taken a toll on our marriage, and we're going through marriage counselling.

Twenty-three years later, the mental scars still blight my life.

JENNY TYRELL-CHARLES, 20, is a PA and model from Leicester. Jenny had an abortion as a 13-year-old.

THE father was my best friend's brother. He was 21 and I had an enormous crush on him. When I used to flirt and giggle at him, he'd laugh and say: 'You'll have to wait until you're 16, Jenny.' But he kissed me on my 13th birthday, and then we began to see each other in secret.

Within the first month, we began sleeping together. One evening a condom split, and even though I took the morning-after pill, within a few weeks I had missed my period and was suffering morning sickness.

I burst into tears when the pregnancy test came out positive.

'You'd better get rid of it' was my boyfriend's flat response when I told him. Looking back, I wish I had confided in my mother, but I was too afraid. I don't know why — she wasn't strict or religious and when I did tell her, she was incredibly supportive.

We were about to go on holiday to the Caribbean for two weeks. I persuaded her that I didn't want to go. She reluctantly agreed to let me stay with her friends instead.

My boyfriend's family then became involved. They also urged me to go through with an abortion quickly.

The family planning clinic referred me to Leicester Royal Infirmary.

The consultant talked me through the procedure and explained that the possible side-effects could include infection, infertility and even the very small risk of death. I was then asked to sign a disclaimer.

Although I was offered pre-counselling, I turned it down. I was convinced I wouldn't need it at all. I didn't realise how much an abortion can affect you afterwards. I'd also heard that pre-counsellors can try to talk you out of having an abortion.

I was alone when I went into hospital the following week. I really wished my mum was there. I was given a pessary a short while before being taken into theatre to have the baby removed by a suction procedure. I had an injection in my hand. I woke up and it was all over.

THE PAIN was phenomenal, worse than I could ever have imagined. It felt as though something had been violently ripped out of me. As I lay in terrible pain, feeling frightened and guilty, my boyfriend arrived and asked if I was alright. The agonising cramping in my abdomen meant I could scarcely speak, and I'm sure I couldn't have found the words to describe how I felt anyway.

He took me to the house where I had been staying while my mum was away. Despite being warned that I should be accompanied for 24 hours, he dropped me there and I have never seen him since.

I told my mother's friends I was ill and shut myself in my room. I bled heavily for nearly two weeks, and was in so much pain I was unable to get out of bed. A heavy depression set in. I felt black and lethargic, and couldn't leave my bed or dress for weeks.

I would just sob and sob and sob, then punch the pillows, trying to get my anger and pain out. After the first few weeks, I tried to get my life back to normal, but for the next six months or a year, I would often find myself crying, and realise I was still upset about what had happened.

It took me two years before I found the courage to tell my mum. She was deeply hurt that I hadn't turned to her, but as I told her what I'd been through, we couldn't stop crying.

It was the hardest decision I have ever faced, and I feel angry that it was something I had to go through while I was still a child myself. It has changed me. I'm not a naturally sentimental person, and I don't think that as a 13-year-old I could have handled being a single mother, but the experience has left emotional scars. It cut my childhood short. I'm more defensive now.

I was heartbroken after the abortion and I'm afraid of feeling that emotional pain again. Even now, seven years on, there are times when I find myself thinking about the baby and wondering: 'What if?'

At 20, I have a good job, a strong relationship with my boyfriend of four years and I'm buying my first house. But no matter what you achieve, an abortion stays with you forever.

Now, I worry about my chances of having a baby in the future. My boyfriend wants them, and I really hope I still can, too.

Linda Porter-Robinson: 'I was devastated, terrified, and not yet in my 20s.'

ABORTION: THE PRICE WE PAID

Daily Mail - December 13th 2005

Swiss vote to relax strict laws on abortion

BY MARCEL MICHELSON
in Zurich

SWITZERLAND VOTED overwhelmingly yesterday to relax its strict abortion laws in a referendum that will bring legislation into line with domestic practice and the rules of most European countries.

A 72 per cent majority favoured a proposal passed by Swiss lawmakers in March last year to allow abortion in the first 12 weeks of a pregnancy. Eighty-two per cent rejected a proposal by an anti-abortion coalition for a complete ban.

"This result shows the maturity of voters," said Martine Desplands-Dondenaz, a member of the pro-reform campaign. "They have opted to respect personal choice."

Under Swiss law, terminations are allowed only if the woman's health is in danger, but since 1988 there has been no condemnation of any woman or doctor for having or carrying out an abortion. The government reckons that up to 13,000 abortions a year are performed.

The anti-abortion lobby used the country's constitutional provision to force a referendum by gathering more than triple the 50,000 signatures needed.

Despite the liberal interpretation of the present law, dating from 1942, women seeking abortions in some smaller rural cantons still sometimes have to find a doctor in another canton.

The federal government will now propose the formal legislative change. But no deadline has been set. *(Reuters)*

The Daily Telegraph - Monday 3rd June 2002.

International news

Low-birth Russia curbs abortions

Women denounce law reducing reasons for legal terminations

Nick Paton Walsh
in Moscow

Russia has quietly clamped down on the conditions under which women can have abortions, a sign of the slow increase of the church's influence and growing fears over falling birth rates.

Abortions are common in Russia, with some estimates suggesting there are 4.5m a year — four times the number in the US, and approximately one for every 35 people in the country. The ease with which Russian women can get an abortion — adverts offering the service are displayed on the metro — has led to an estimated 13 abortions for every 10 live births.

But the government recently reduced from 13 to four the reasons women can present for a legal abortion on the state after 12 weeks of pregnancy. Previously, women who were not married, too poor, unemployed, had too small a flat, or three children already, could get an abortion.

Now the option is there only if women have been raped, are in jail, or have a disabled husband. The option also exists if either partner is judged unfit to be a parent.

Abortions after 22 weeks remain, as before, only permissible if the mother's health is at risk. The majority of abortions happen in the first 12 weeks and are unaffected by the change in legislation.

The new law has also been interpreted as a sign that the Orthodox church's long-standing, large constituency, which was suppressed during Soviet times, is slowly finding a more public voice in state morality and legislation.

The law is also a response to the proliferation of "underground" private abortions and the reproductive health issues this has raised. Officially only 2m abortions happen each year.

Women's rights campaigners have denounced the move as an attempt to curb women's right to choose, whereas critics of abortion have hailed it as the first Russian recognition of the rights of the unborn child. It becomes law in the coming months when officially implemented by the health ministry.

Figures released last week showed that the 144.5 million strong population is falling at a rate of about a million a year, caused by a falling birth rate and low life expectancy. Campaigners have argued that commonplace abortions are just compounding Russia's demographic crisis.

In 1955, Stalin's ban on abortions was repealed allowing the procedure to take root in society, and in the early 1990s a law "on the protection of citizens' health" was passed outlining the initial 13 conditions.

"It was a liberal government and an extremely liberal law," said Alexander Chuyev, an independent MP, Christian and anti-abortion campaigner. "I'm sure it contradicted the interests of the state and its citizens."

He said the birth rate was very low and that "millions of [unsafe] abortions" were "increasing the ranks of women who can never have children".

He also blamed the state for only providing £1.50 a week in child support, thereby "forcing" women to terminate pregnancies.

Anti-abortion MPs, whom Mr Chuyev classifies as "left-wing or patriotic", are trying to reintroduce the old Soviet notion of the Mother Heroine — a woman flooded with state benefits as a reward for her massive brood.

Some groups already offer women finance to try to persuade them to choose birth over abortion.

Natasha Bukharova, 19, is unemployed, and now lives in a flat with her four-year-old son after the charity Life gave her financial support. Her partner left her a year after they decided to marry and have a child.

"Practically all my girlfriends had an abortion," she said. "I think choice is good. Why have a baby if you can't give him normal conditions, food or even education?

"But all of us, if we dared have an abortion, are very afraid. You never know what kind of doctor you will come across."

She said one of her friends had her womb removed after an abortion led to a serious infection.

She added that information about contraception was passed by word of mouth between her friends.

guardian.co.uk/russia

Russia. The Guardian - Wednesday September 24, 2003

THE INDEPENDENT ON SUNDAY
11 DECEMBER 2005

The sexual revolution sweeps across China

HIV, divorce and abortion rates soar as the new generation rejects repression and creates its own permissive society

A model displays lingerie at the sex toy fair in Guangzhou AFP

By David Elmer
IN BEIJING

When logging online became possible in China in 1995, the authorities cannot have imagined that a decade later millions of people would crash an internet provider in their efforts to access a website where they could listen to a 27-year-old female blogger having sex.

But that is what happened when the publicity-hungry Muzi Mei released a 25-minute recording of an encounter with her latest lover. The former sex columnist, who shot to fame in 2003 after she started publishing graphic accounts of her many one-night stands on her blog, symbolises the sexual revolution in China. Political freedom may be unattainable, but the bedroom is the one place the government cannot monitor and young people are taking advantage. Not only are they having more sex than their parents ever did, they are doing it far earlier.

A survey by Li Yinhe, China's only female sexologist, shows that 70 per cent of Beijingers have had premarital sex, compared with 15.5 per cent in 1989. In the major cities, the average age at which people in the 14-to-20 age group first have sex is 17, as opposed to 24 for those aged between 31 and 40.

The new permissiveness means that being faithful to one's partner is no longer obligatory; a March 2005 survey revealed that a third of young people in urban areas believe extra-marital affairs should be tolerated.

Professor Li, who teaches at the Chinese Academy of Social Sciences, has spent 10 years researching the sex lives of the Chinese, and she believes China will "catch up" with the West in terms of sexual practices within 20 years.

But judging by the 50,000 people who flocked to last month's Sex and Culture festival in Guangzhou city in southern Guangdong Province to browse the latest in sex toys – 70 per cent of the world's total are made in the province – it may be sooner than that.

> **'PEOPLE USED TO** BE FIRED FOR AFFAIRS AND PUNISHED FOR LIVING IN SIN'

It is a far cry from the days of the Cultural Revolution, when sex was branded as "decadent". Then, women were banned from wearing skirts and dresses, and the authorities were far more concerned about controlling what people got up to in their spare time.

"There used to be a whole layer of government involved in snooping into people's lives," Professor Li said. "People were fired for having affairs and punished for living with their boyfriends or girlfriends."

Some sociologists believe the policy introduced in 1979 restricting urban couples to having just one child was the spark for the sexual permissiveness. Professor Pan Suiming, of the Renmin University of China, said: "The one-child policy shattered the Confucian belief that reproduction is the only purpose of sex."

But the internet has really fuelled the sexual revolution in China. With more than 100 million internet users and sex education in its infancy, young people turn to the internet for everything from information about sex to pornography, which is illegal in China. In the absence of a pub culture, they also use it to meet partners. Some surveys claim 30 per cent of all one-night stands in China are arranged on the web.

Unsurprisingly, this newfound sexual freedom has a negative side. The number of young single women having abortions has soared: 65 per cent of women terminating pregnancies in 2004 were single, compared to 25 per cent in 1999. Rates of HIV infections are growing quickest amongst the 15-to-24 age group, and the number of couples getting divorced in 2004 was 1.6 million, a 21 per cent rise on 2003. But now the genie is out of the bottle, it seems there is no turning back.

China. The Independent Sunday - 11 December 2005

TIMES WORLD NEWS
THE TIMES TUESDAY JANUARY 10 2006
timesonline.co.uk/world

AMERICA
Broadway Phantom emerges from his lair to outrun Cats
PAGE 33

ITALY
Judge fears freedom could mean death for man who shot the Pope
PAGE 34

The ten million baby girls lost to the ultrasound generation

From Dan McDougall
in Delhi

DAVID KATZENSTEIN / CORBIS

Girls in India are often seen as a burden. There are now only 927 born for every 1,000 boys, largely because of prenatal scans that lead to gender-based abortions

RENDERED illegible by layers of grime, most shop signs in Delhi serve little obvious purpose. But on a filthy side street in the Greater Kailash district, there is an obvious exception. A bright green neon sign above a busy textile workshop advertises a "fertility clinic" — a thoroughly misleading description.

Inside, on a PVC sofa, sits Gurpreet Kaur, 26, who admits she has already had two abortions after illegal antenatal tests showed that she was expecting girls. Today she is awaiting her third scan in as many years, having earlier gone to a Sikh temple to pray for a boy.

This clinic is not one of the illegal abortion clinics so common in Delhi's backstreets, but it certainly feeds their business.

Since the advent of ultrasound equipment, hundreds of so-called fertility clinics have opened. Ostensibly they offer scanning services for expectant mothers; in reality most offer nothing more than gender identification. And for many, that represents the first heartbreaking step towards abortion.

A 1994 law bans the use of technology to determine the sex of unborn children, along with the termination of pregnancies on the basis of gender, but these clinics offer a seemingly legitimate façade for a multibillion-pound racket to which the police — for a price — usually turn a blind eye.

Gender determination is big business. Male offspring are typically regarded as a blessing — future breadwinners who will look after parents in old age — but many parents still see girls as a financial burden, and the consequences are chilling.

According to a study published yesterday in *The Lancet*, more than ten million female foetuses may have been aborted in India in the past twenty years after gender checks.

Shirish Sheth, of the Breach Candy hospital in Bombay, a co-author of the *Lancet* report, said: "To have a daughter is socially and emotionally accepted if there is a son, but a daughter's arrival is often unwelcome if the couple already have a daughter.

"Daughters are regarded as a liability. Because she will eventually belong to the family of her future husband, expenditure on her will benefit others. In some communities where the custom of dowry prevails, the cost of her dowry could be phenomenal."

She added: "We conservatively estimate that prenatal sex determination and selective abortion accounts for 500,000 missing girls yearly. If this practice has been common for most of the past two decades since access to ultrasound became widespread, then a figure of ten million missing female births would not be unreasonable."

Population censuses in India show that the number of girls has fallen steadily. In 1981 there were 962 girls for every 1,000 boys up to the age of 6. In 2001 there were only 927.

Gurpreet Kaur, whose husband is a computer programmer, says it is her in-laws, not her husband, who are pressuring her to have a boy. "If I don't produce one I have failed in their eyes. They tell me they need a boy, a breadwinner, to secure the future of the family."

The owner of the Greater Kailash clinic, who refused to be identified, said that selective pregnancies were common not just among poorer Indians, but in wealthy families too. "We don't perform abortions. We carry out scans. It is then up the family what they do," she told *The Times*. "A normal ultrasound costs about 200 rupees [£3] but when you want to disclose the sex of the child, it varies from 800 to 1,200. We get hundreds of customers every week. Many can barely afford to pay for the scans but they see them as an investment."

She added: "Every doctor in India will admit that sex-selective abortions are being performed with a recklessness that is bound to have an effect on the population. Urban areas are much worse than the rural ones. In the rural area people often wait but the urbanites — modern Indians — want to check out on the sex of the child as soon as they can."

Neelam Gupta, senior programme officer at the Indian Council of Child Welfare, believes the present law, which imposes very tough restrictions on abortion, is useless, and that technology has created a population time bomb. "The discovery of the ultrasound technique and its cheap availability has proved to be the nemesis of the female foetus in India."

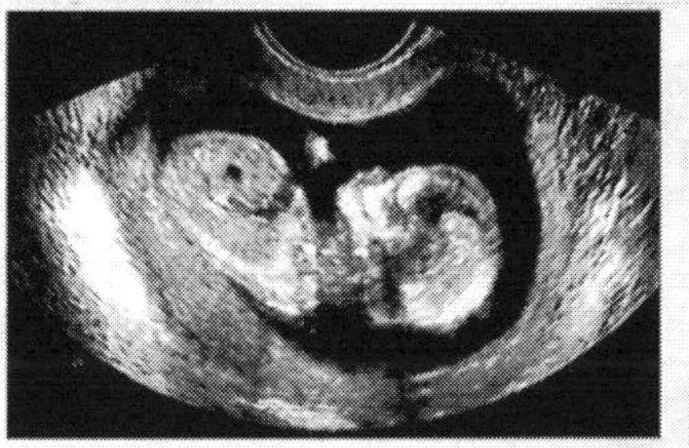

FROM BATS TO BABIES

- Ultrasound was discovered in 1794 when Lazzaro Spallanzani demonstrated how bats used high-frequency sound waves for navigation
- The first patents for underwater iceberg-detecting devices were filed after the *Titanic* sank. Submarines navigated using ultrasound in the First World War
- Ultrasound was first used medically in the late 1930s in America, to alleviate pain
- In 1953 the Swedish cardiologist Inge Edler and the physicist Carl Hellmuth Hertz used it to investigate the motion of the heart
- In 1957 Professor Akf Sjovall visited doctors in Glasgow to study ulstrasound techniques with a view to using them in early pregnancy
- A handheld ultrasound device for monitoring the foetus is now available online for around £150

INDIA'S GENDER GAP

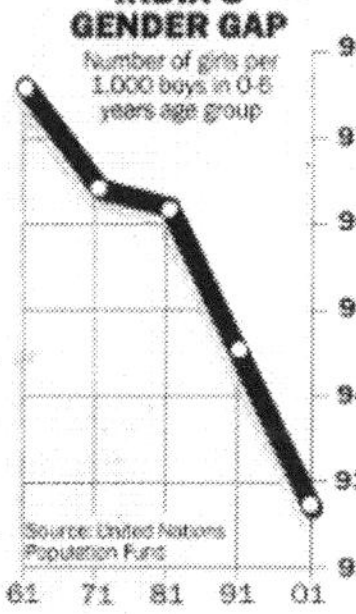

CHINA: In the early 1980s, the ratio of boys to girls was 108.5 to 100, rising to 111 boys in 1990, and is close to 120 today

PAKISTAN: 1,500 babies abandoned every year, 80 per cent of them female

SOUTH KOREA: Up to 30,000 female foetuses are aborted annually, producing a ratio of 110 boys born for every 100 girls

NEPAL: Ratio of last-born children reported to be 146 boys for every 100 girls

India. The Times - January 10th 2006

Babies' bodies found in abandoned well

▶ Grim find raises fears of female infanticide

▶ Managers at local clinic being questioned

Jeremy Page Delhi

The remains of dozens of foetuses and newborn babies have been found in an abandoned well in India, apparently aborted or discarded after birth because they were female.

Police are investigating whether a clinic in the state of Orissa identified the infants' sex before birth, which is illegal yet widespread in India, and then disposed of them at their parents' request.

A 12-year-old boy raised the alarm after finding the remains of seven baby girls stuffed into bloody polythene bags in a disused well near the Krishna clinic in the district of Nayagarh on July 14. Police told *The Times* yesterday that they had found the skulls and body parts of 23 more infants over the weekend. Some reports now put the body count at as high as 37.

The find is the latest illustration of how widespread female foeticide and infanticide remain in India, despite repeated government attempts to eradicate the practices. Many Indian families still regard a daughter as a financial burden because tradition dictates that when she is married they must pay her husband's family a large dowry. Sons are also preferred because they are considered stronger workers and because daughters traditionally look after their in-laws in old age, rather than their own parents.

The Government outlawed ultrasound gender tests for unborn babies in 1994, but prosecutions are rare and many families bribe doctors to get past the ban and then choose to abort if the child is a girl.

Estimates of the number of girls aborted annually vary widely. Last year an international team of researchers claimed that over the past two decades half a million female foetuses had been aborted each year in India, which has a population of 1.1 billion. The Indian Medical Association believes that the figure could be ten times higher.

The result is an increasingly severe gender imbalance, with 927 women for every 1,000 men, according to the 2001 census — down from 945 women per 1,000 men a decade earlier. That compares with a global average of 1,050 women for every 1,000 men.

The imbalance in Nayagarh, a poor rural area, is even more extreme, with an estimated 901 females for every 1,000 males — the worst ratio in all of Orissa's 30 districts.

Yogesh Bahadur Khurania, a local police official, said that investigators had yet to establish the precise number and genders of the corpses found in the well.

But he confirmed that Sabita Sahu, the Krishna clinic's owner, and Shyam Sahu, its manager, had been detained for questioning.

Tapasi Praharaj, a women's rights activist, said that the Krishna clinic was one of 11 unlicensed clinics allegedly involved in an illegal abortion racket with local police and health officials. "They're all in this nexus and they should all be punished," she said, calling for the health minister of Orissa to resign.

"The Government is totally careless and doesn't take any action. What we really need is for attitudes to change at every level of society."

While female infanticide is still largely a rural problem, some studies show that female foeticide is most prevalent among the urban middle classes, which have ready access to ultrasound technology.

Last month police arrested a man posing as a doctor in a wealthy suburb of Delhi, the Indian capital, after remains of aborted babies were found in a septic tank at his clinic.

In February police found the remains of at least 14 infants buried in the backyard of a hospital in the central state of Madhya Pradesh.

Last year police recovered 25 foetuses from a well in the northern state of Punjab.

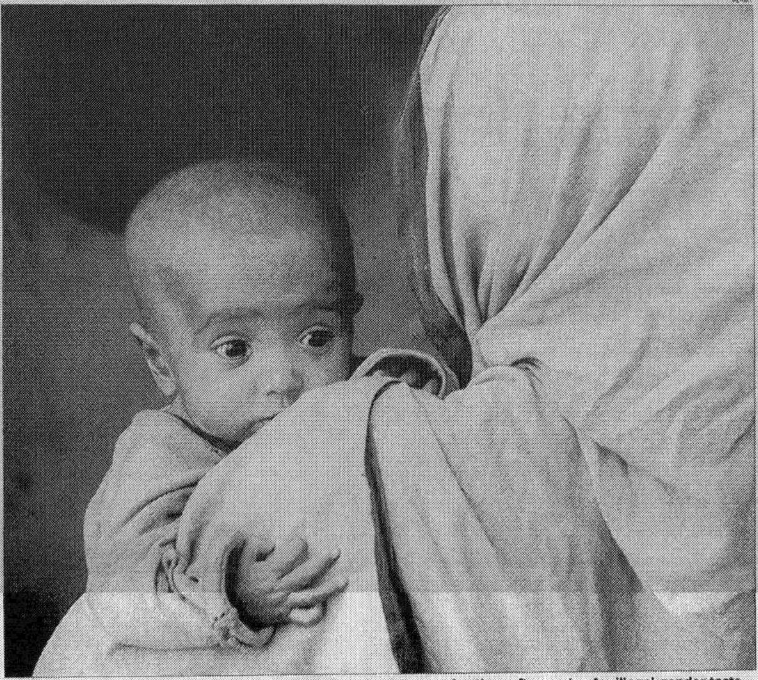

Many families still regard a daughter as a liability, and some choose abortions after paying for illegal gender tests

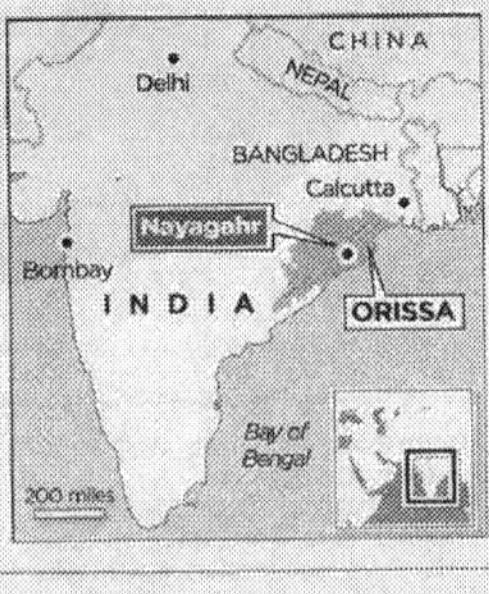

Gender gap

- India's gender deficit has increased more than tenfold since the 1901 census, when the country had 3.2 million fewer women than men; a century later the gap had grown to 35 million
- Among the 0-6 age group, the number of girls per 1,000 boys plummeted from 1,010 in 1941 to 927 in 2001; 80 per cent of Indian districts underwent an increase in the gender imbalance between the 1991 and 2001 censuses. Only Pondicherry, Lakshadweep and Kerala improved
- The disparity is larger and increasing at a faster rate in urban areas than rural ones
- In 14 of India's richest districts, around Haryana and Punjab, there are fewer than 800 girls per 1,000 boys
- Despite a law banning foetal sex determination being passed in 1994, it was 12 years before there was a conviction. In 2006 a doctor was fined 5,000 rupees (£60) and imprisoned for two years
- In Salem, Tamil Nadu, researchers found a mobile ultrasound scanning unit being advertised with the slogan: "Pay 500 rupees and save 50,000 rupees later". Girls often require a large dowry to get married

Sources: Unicef; UN Population Fund; Oxfam; overpopulation.org

India, The Times - July 24th 2007

International news

Protest at 'abortion' doctor's trial for murder

Jeevan Vasagar in Nairobi

The head of Kenya's medical association has urged doctors to protest at the murder trial of a gynaecologist accused of carrying out abortions.

When John Nyamu goes on trial next week it will provoke a split in his profession between colleagues who regard him as a martyr and other doctors who back the prosecution.

Stephen Ochiel, chairman of the Kenya Medical Association, has criticised the decision to charge Dr Nyamu with murder — which carries the death penalty in Kenya — rather than procuring abortion, which is punishable with a jail term. He called on colleagues to attend a rally at Nairobi high court, dressed in white medical coats and wearing stethoscopes.

They have also been asked to contribute to a defence fund for the gynaecologist, who was arrested in June after the discovery of 15 foetuses dumped in refuse bags.

Dr Ochiel said: "There's a penal code on abortion. That would have been the right charge, not murder.

"Murder brings a death sentence, if found guilty, and the trial could take years in our court system ... we are destroying Dr Nyamu. Even if he is found not guilty after three years we will have destroyed him as a person."

Dr Ochiel said the law on abortion, which is banned even in cases of rape or incest, is driving women to "back street" clinics. "Women are coming to us after attempting to procure abortions. When they present themselves to us they are too sick, and they die.

"Far too many women are dying from this cause and society needs to examine itself."

Dr Nyamu, who ran two reproductive health clinics in the Kenyan capital, was arrested along with two nurses in June. The three have been charged with murdering two foetuses, a boy and girl.

Reflecting the split over the issue in Kenyan society, Dr Ochiel has come under attack from two leading gynaecologists, who urged him to withdraw the letters and apologise to the association's membership.

Stephen Karanja and Jean Kagia, who are members of an anti-abortion movement, said in a statement: "If [doctors are] alleged to have committed a crime they must, like any other Kenyan, be vigorously prosecuted. The position taken by Dr Ochiel is unacceptable ... it will disgrace the profession and bring it to disrepute."

The discovery of the dumped foetuses triggered a national debate in Kenya, where an estimated 20,000 women are admitted to hospital each year to be treated for complications following "back street" abortions. A study by a US charity, Ipas, indicated that 2,600 Kenyan women die each year because of post-abortion complications.

Last year Kenyan women MPs called for abortion to be legalised, saying the major reason that women resorted to terminations was because men were not required to pay for the upkeep of children fathered outside wedlock.

For many women, the MPs said, abortion was the only means of preventing their existing children sinking further into poverty.

Public opinion in Kenya is broadly anti-abortion. A requiem mass held for the 15 foetuses drew a crowd of thousands this summer, and the letters pages of newspapers have been filled with condemnation of the alleged abortionists, as well as the mothers of the foetuses.

The head of Kenya's Catholic church, Archbishop Ndingi Mwana a'Nzeki, has vowed to mobilise the faithful to "vote out politicians who support abortion". But newspaper editorials have called for a debate on legalisation, and a former attorney general, Charles Njonjo, has called for the ban to be lifted.

In Africa only Tunisia, Cape Verde and South Africa provide abortions on request, during the first trimester of pregnancy.

guardian.co.uk/kenya

Kenya. The Guardian, Wednesday November 3rd 2004

Catholic Portugal set to decide on future of abortion

By Barry Hatton
in Lisbon

Portugal was deciding in a national referendum yesterday whether to discard its strict abortion law and adopt a more liberal policy that would bring the country into line with most other European nations.

The centre-left Socialist government wants to grant women the right to opt for abortion during the first 10 weeks of pregnancy.

Portugal, where more than 90 percent of people say they are Catholic, has one of the most restrictive abortion laws in the EU. Its legislation places it in a minority in the bloc with Poland, Ireland and Malta.

The procedure is allowed only in cases of rape, foetal malformation or if a mother's health is in danger, and only in the first 12 weeks of pregnancy.

In the 23 other EU nations, abortion is permitted within much broader limits. Women can ask for abortions up to the 24th week of pregnancy in Britain and up to the 12th week in Germany, France and Italy.

The Portuguese government has portrayed the ballot as a measure of the country's willingness to adopt more modern attitudes.

Its effort to change the law, though, has run into emphatic opposition from the influential Roman Catholic Church, which wants to keep the restrictions in place.

The single question on the ballot asks voters if they want to allow abortion up to the 10th week. Voters at more than 12,000 polling stations are to tick a box under "yes" or "no."

The National Election Commission said the turnout might be too low to make it binding. By 4pm, only 31 per cent of the eligible voters had cast ballots.

A 1998 referendum on the same issue was nullified after it fell short of the required participation.

Anticipating a repeat of that ballot, Prime Minister Jose Socrates has said that, if the turnout is too low to make the ballot binding but the "yes" camp collects most of the votes cast, he will use his party's majority in Parliament to push through legislation allowing abortion.

If the turnout is too low, the PM will use his majority to push through legislation

Manuel Antonio, 58, voting with his wife in central Lisbon, said: "I've come to vote because I don't want the outcome to be that of the other referendum where nothing was decided. What's at stake is women's ability to decide. The current law does not fit with Europe."

Another voter at the same station, Ismael Luzia, 22, said he was voting against the change. "For me, there is nothing more important than saying 'yes' to life," he said.

Maria Candida Duarte, 72, voting at a Lisbon polling station in the Alvalade neighbourhood, said she was voting to keep the strict policies in place. "It's urgent to maintain our position. A child has a right to life – from conception," she said.

Carlos Sousa, 56, condemned the existing legislation: "It's a bad law, not adjusted to our society. Ultimately, the choice is about the intimate resolve of a person."

Recent opinion polls have indicated that a majority of Portugal's 8.9 million voters intend to approve the change. Maria Georgina Gomes da Silva, 52, said she was casting a ballot in favour of change. "I'm voting today because I am a woman and I'm with the cause" for a more liberal policy.

Mr Socrates, who has long campaigned for abortion rights, has called the current law "backward" and "a national disgrace".

He says women seeking to terminate their pregnancies simply travel to EU countries where it is legal, especially private clinics across the border in Spain, or resort to shady, back-street clinics at home.

He cites figures compiled by abortion rights groups – and disputed by their opponents – that around 10,000 women are taken to hospital every year with complications arising from botched back-street abortions. AP

A pregnant woman at a mass for the campaign against abortion ARMANDO FRANCA/AP

Portugal. The Independent 12th February 2007

INTERNATIONAL NEWS

Vatican stands by bishop sacked in Argentine abortion row

BY JUSTIN STARES
in Buenos Aires

ARGENTINA'S RELATIONS with the Vatican grew increasingly strained this weekend after the government sacked a bishop in a row over the country's ban on abortion.

Bishop Antonio Baseotto, who is bishop to Argentina's armed forces, was fired for saying that Ginés González Garcia, the Argentine health minister, should be "thrown into the sea with a millstone around his neck" for seeking to decriminalise abortion.

The bishop was alluding to Jesus's words in the Gospels: "And whosoever shall offend one of [these] little ones that believe in me, it is better for him that a millstone were hanged about his neck, and he were cast into the sea."

For most Argentines, however, his comments brought back unwelcome memories of "death flights" by the military government between 1976 and 1983, when political opponents and misfits were drugged, handcuffed and thrown into the River Plate.

Rafael Bielsa, the minister of foreign affairs and worship, said that the reference was "unacceptable", but Joaquin Navarro Valls, the Pope's spokesman, countered that the bishop's sacking was a "violation of religious freedom".

Rome retaliated immediately by reconfirming Bishop Baseotto in his role. Although in theory he is free to preach, he has been effectively stripped of his staff position as government undersecretary and monthly salary of £800. He cancelled his military Mass last week and no Easter address to troops has been confirmed.

The minister, Mr Garcia, had argued that decriminalising abortion would help save the lives of thousands of pregnant women who seek backstreet terminations each year. For the Church, however, Mr Garcia's comments amounted to "apologism for the crime of homicide".

Officials on both sides of the abortion dispute now fear that relations with the Vatican, which were already rocky, will deteriorate further. Rival factions have already been squabbling during the power vacuum caused by the Pope's illness.

The Catholic Church and the Argentine government fell out over the government's proposal to ratify a UN treaty on women's rights, which the Church believed would open the door to abortion.

There has also been criticism of the government's welfare efforts and an unseemly battle over a "blasphemous" state-funded art exhibition, which included an exhibit of birds defecating on religious icons.

Public opinion, however, could lie with the government. According to one survey published last week, six out of 10 people living in Buenos Aires favour the decriminalisation of abortion, and anti-church graffiti has started to appear on the streets of the capital. Parallels have been drawn with the confrontation between the Church and President Juan Peron in the 1950s, a duel which led to the burning of churches and helped to bring down Peron's first government.

He challenged the Church's authority openly with reforms that included demands for legalising divorce and prostitution.

In 1955, Pope Pius XII excommunicated Peron and threatened his followers with similar punishment. Argentina's Catholics sided with the Church, prompting Peron to resign and go into exile.

In this tussle, however, public opinion of Bishop Baseotto has been dented by reports that he made anti-Jewish comments in the 1980s. The Argentine Church has not commented on the allegations, which claim that the bishop said that Jews were prepared to make money from selling drugs and pornography. Buenos Aires is home to one of the largest diaspora communities of Jewish people outside the United States.

Catholics in Argentine have been left to wait for the next move from the Vatican.

Management of the crisis in Rome has been complicated by the Pope's incapacity, and rumours that Cardinal Angelo Sodano, the Vatican's 77-year-old secretary of state, could retire after Easter. Cardinal Sodano has been one of the key players in the Baseotto affair. "We hope that this is just an isolated incident and not an example of deteriorating relations between the Vatican and Argentina," said Father Jorge Oesterheld, a spokesman for the Argentine conference of bishops.

"We are now waiting for the next response from the Vatican, which I understand will come on Monday or Tuesday."

Bishop Antonio Baseotto, left, and Ginés García, the health minister

Argentina. The Sunday Telegraph, March 27th 2005

The Mail
ON SUNDAY

The liberals and lawyers who are destroying justice

SOMETHING has gone wrong with the law of the land. Each day brings new examples of police or courts proving useless in the face of blatant wrongdoing. Each week sees the authorities moving to punish those they would once have protected, from householders defending their property to citizens expressing unfashionable views in public.

These things follow the abolition of common sense. Also to blame is the defeatism of senior policemen and Crown prosecutors, faced with courts where skilled and cynical lawyers strangle justice in a web of petty technicalities.

The case of the 12-year-old girl apparently having a sexual relationship with a 22-year-old man surely ought to be clear-cut enough. Yet the girl's distraught mother and father have watched in despair while the police have failed to prosecute in spite of strong circumstantial evidence.

Here are parents trying to be responsible, as Mr Blair is urging all parents to be on pain of losing child benefit. The reaction of the authorities is to do nothing, for the insane reason that a girl barely out of primary school must initiate the complaint.

Equally simple is the affair of the callous hit-and-run driver who is not being taken to court although there are several willing witnesses. Here the police cannot be bothered to proceed, supposedly because nobody was actually maimed or killed and the damage was minor. As it happens, the victim will suffer for the rest of her life and a public-spirited witness has been heavily penalised by his insurance company because he used his car to block the offender's escape.

Just as disturbing is the way an elderly preacher was convicted and fined – at vast expense to the taxpayer. It is now illegal to disapprove of homosexuality in public, in case such behaviour upsets a passing homosexual. It also seems to be quite legal for homosexuals to harass, abuse and assault frail pensioners, if those pensioners have the wrong opinions.

Clearly, a revolution has swept through the police and courts. It has succeeded thanks to a cynical alliance between the legal profession and politically correct elite liberals. The lawyers benefit from tangled rules which lengthen trials and give them extra employment and fees. Perhaps the money helps silence their consciences as the guilty in their thousands return to the streets to spread misery and fear – but not to the streets where the lawyers live.

The liberals, who dislike common sense because it is conservative, rejoice to see the old rules of right and wrong first blurred and then abolished. They support the sexual revolution which is destroying family life. They think criminals need treatment, not punishment, and that many of them deserve sympathy for their plight. They believe proper policing is repression.

For nearly four decades this dismal coalition of greed and folly has been gnawing through what used to be a fine criminal justice system. Only now can we see the scale of the damage this has done.

If the Government is still serious about being tough on crime, and if the Home Secretary is really concerned about the lawlessness and despair which besiege the poor and threaten all of us, then they must defy the lawyers and the liberals by restoring common sense as the core and foundation of our law.

The liberals and lawyers who are destroying justice - Abandoning the old rules of right and wrong.
The Mail on Sunday - May 5th 2002.

Keep your beliefs to yourself – or you'll be next

By **PETER HITCHENS**

FREE speech is in danger in modern Britain. The opinions of millions are being quietly criminalised.

An English court has punished a man for his views. The cowards and bullies who physically attacked a frail and elderly man for those views were not punished. His offence was to have annoyed them. Apparently the law of England now thinks his assailants acted within their rights.

The court which condemned Harry Hammond knew that he had fallen to the ground after a young woman seized his placard and tried to pull it from him. They knew that his opponents were younger and stronger than him, and greatly outnumbered him. They knew that he had been pelted with clods of earth, one striking him on the head, and had a bottle of water tipped over him in an act of public humiliation.

Technically, the sloppy wording of the (Tory) 1986 Public Order Act could be said to support this prosecution if you stretch its meaning to breaking point. But was this law, portrayed as a new weapon against louts and troublemakers, really intended to prevent an elderly evangelist proclaiming the message of the Bible?

Mr Hammond's placard contained no swearwords or obscenities. It named no individual. It did not call for the killing of homosexuals or for violence against them, ideas from which the devout and gentle Mr Hammond recoils.

Yet the Crown Prosecutor laid into Mr Hammond as if he were a serious malefactor. Unable to restrain or punish thieves and louts, it is strange how our courts love to humble the respectable when they get them into the dock. He said the offending placard was 'insulting to people and people's intelligence. It was insulting to gay people and gay people's friends and he knew that'. And a magistrate pronounced that the sign 'clearly insulted members of the crowd who had gathered round him'. Guilty, she said, and fined him £300 and £395 in costs. And in a rather creepy footnote, she ordered the sign to be destroyed. I do hope they did not burn it.

This case is a severe warning to the politically incorrect that their words will no longer be judged by what they say. They will be judged by what their opponents believe them to have said and by how strongly their opponents disapprove.

Thanks to this prosecution, the sexual morality of tens of millions is now a criminal offence if uttered in a public place. The cunning key word in this affair is 'insulting'. Once an idea can be called 'offensive' then it is on the way to becoming a criminal offence.

Just in case you think this is all a silly incident in a seaside town involving a daft old codger, be warned. Eccentrics and so-called 'extremists' are the first to feel these things, just as canaries were the first to notice poison gas in coal mines.

And eccentric is what Mr Hammond is, magnificent in his refusal to swim in the mainstream. He is not crazy, just unconventional, unworldly and rather brave. Every society needs such people. We should be grateful to the good-humoured landlady who rather touchingly looks after him. He is a lonely but engaging man, knowledgeable, well mannered, precise in his speech and thoughtful.

He sees the current fashion for approving of homosexuality as a sign of this country's departure from Christian morals. He also knows that what he says is likely to provoke dissent because he thinks homosexuals are especially unwilling to listen to criticism of what they do.

BY CONTRAST his opponents now seem to be in the mainstream. One of those who gave evidence against him was Sean Tapper, 32, a homosexual who, while he claims to have been offended by the sign, took absolutely no part in the attacks on Mr Hammond. Like the magistrate, he seems to think that any trouble which happened was Mr Hammond's fault for holding up his sign. He thinks the old man should have gone home when the trouble started.

Mr Hammond with his Bible stands for an older Britain. Cool, articulate, charming Mr Tapper for the new one. If this were really the multicultural, tolerant society we are told it is, they could co-exist happily. But the supposedly relaxed and open new Britain turns out to be far more intolerant than the old one. Back in the repressed Fifties, homosexuals were only prosecuted for what they did, not for what they thought or said.

peter.hitchens@mailonsunday.co.uk

Keep your beliefs to yourself - or you'll be next.
The Mail on Sunday - May 5th 2002.

We're far too stressed for love, says one in three women

By **Lech Mintowt-Czyz**

Katherine Bolton: 'We're like ships passing in the night'

THE pressures of modern life have left women too stressed to make love, a survey has found.

One in three said they had no energy while one in five claimed they had simply lost interest.

Half said they had sleepless nights worrying about managing both home and work and 40 per cent claimed to have experienced eating problems.

The struggle to achieve equality for women in the work place had backfired, the survey found.

Two-thirds felt a woman's life was less stressful 50 years ago and 90 per cent believed the increased opportunities available to women had put them under extra pressure.

Good Housekeeping magazine interviewed 1,000 women between 30 and 55.

Editor in chief Lindsay Nicholson said the findings were a wake-up call to women trying to do too much.

'Many, perhaps even the majority of women in Britain today, live in a permanent state of shattered nerves and chronic fatigue,' she said.

'The effect on their health, their marriages and on how they raise their children makes uncomfortable reading.

'It cannot be either wise or morally right for a civilised, rich western country to turn a blind eye to these appalling levels of stress and to allow so many of its citizens to feel like drudges.

'The women in our survey told us that despite enjoying greater freedom than their mothers or grandmothers, they envied those earlier generations. It's hardly progress.' The survey found more than 95 per cent had endured physical symptoms from panic attacks to migraines.

One in five said they felt they had lived more than half their lives under stress.

One in 20 described it as a permanent state.

A third of those surveyed blamed themselves, saying the stress was of their own making.

Management consultant Katherine Bolton, 40, is one of those who admitted stress had affected her love life with her husband Tony, a 45-year-old police officer.

'I just want to go to sleep'

'Tony and I are the archetypal ships passing in the night,' she said.

'Quite often I'm so tired that all I want to do is cuddle up and go to sleep.

'It seems neither I nor my friends have any room for spontaneity in our lives now, whether it's due to work or children.

'I always say there are never enough hours in the day but I am not convinced my male counterparts are under so much pressure.

'They seem to think I have a support network at home but actually I am part of that support system.'

Two days ago Britain was carpeted by the European Union for failing to enforce the right of workers to limit their working time to 48 hours a week.

Lindsay Nicholson said women needed to have more realistic ambitions at work and home. She also called for a dramatic cultural reassessment of work in relation to domestic life.

'More women must give up the unachievable standards of perfection lodged in their heads and men must take more responsibility in the home,' she added.

'Most importantly, the workplace must change to reflect the fact that both women and men have domestic responsibilities.

'We need a sea change in society as a whole so that we stop thinking of a business model stuck in the Fifties and start thinking about work in a way that genuinely reflects life today.'

l.mintowt-czyz@dailymail.co.uk

We're far too stressed for love, says one in three women Ladies - the conflict between home and work. Daily Mail - Wednesday 1st May 2002.

The region where most of the births are illegitimate

By **Nick Craven**

FOR the first time since records began, the majority of babies in an entire region is now born out of wedlock, disturbing official statistics show.

The figures, a stark illustration of the breakdown of family values, show that in the North-East of England more illegitimate children are born than those within a marriage.

And while the North-East holds the record with a figure of 50.5 per cent, many other regions are not far behind.

In the country as a whole, while the birth rate is falling generally, the percentage of children born out of wedlock is rising. It went from 38.8 per cent in 1999 to 39.5 per cent in 2000.

The report, from the Office of National Statistics, is based on figures collated from birth certificate entries.

The underlying trend becomes clear with a glance at the 1995 snapshot, when the proportion of children whose parents were unmarried was 33.9 per cent across the UK and 41.5 per cent in the North-East.

It compares with a national average across England now of 39.1 per cent – up from 28.3 per cent a decade ago.

The Key Population and Vital Statistics report shows 679,029 children were born alive in the UK in 2000, of whom 347,941 were male and 331,088 female. The previous year, the number of live births was more than 20,000 higher – a fall in the birth rate which has been under way for some years.

'No incentive to marry'

The figures were a depressing confirmation for family campaigners that the institution of marriage was not only dying, but 'rapidly approaching extinction'.

Dr Adrian Rogers, of the pressure group Family Focus, said: 'The figures are disturbing, if not surprising. We know that the future for children whose parents do not marry is very significantly worse than for those whose parents are married.

'The children are more likely to fail to marry themselves. It will also affect their educational advancement and job prospects.

'Society no longer sets the store by marriage in the way that it did and the incentives to get married are not there, either in terms of tax breaks or enhanced respect in society.

'The institution of marriage is not just dying, it is becoming extinct, and quite rapidly.'

A spokesman for the Church of England said it preferred children to be born within marriage, but added that in many cases where this didn't happen, the parents were living together and married later.

'There is a lot of anecdotal evidence to suggest that many people do get married after a child is born,' he added. 'It is not the ideal, but it does happen.'

Happy to be single

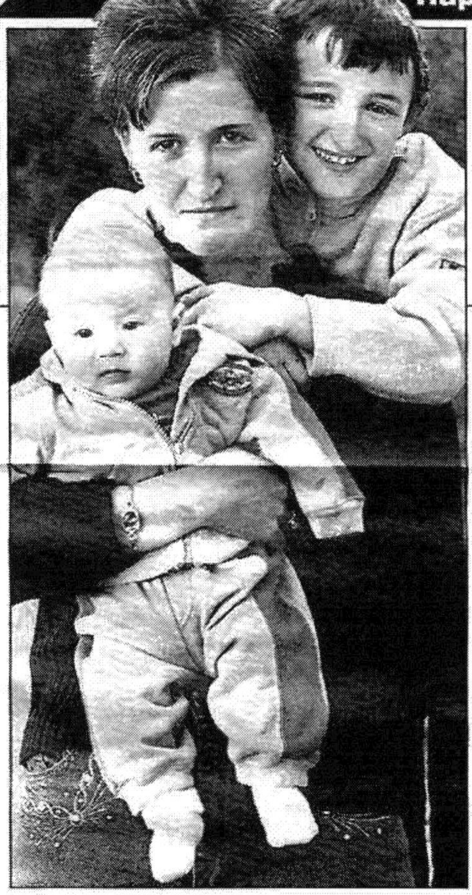

Two sons, two fathers: Amanda Fenwick with Ryan and Joel

The starkest pictures of the disappearance of traditional family life are reflected in some of the country's most deprived towns, such as Corby in Northamptonshire.

The percentage of children born out of wedlock in the former steel town was a staggering 63.5 per cent, of which a third of mothers are not living with the child's partner.

The lowest rate was in Fleet, Hampshire, where just 19.3 per cent were born to unmarried parents. Of those, 83.5 per cent were registered with the father and mother giving the same address.

The region with the lowest number of births outside marriage was the South-East, with 34.1 per cent. The average for Wales was 47.2 per cent, Scotland, 42.6 per cent, and Northern Ireland, 31.8 per cent.

Other surveys have already shown how the number of births outside marriage vary across Europe – ranging from just 4 per cent in Greece to 55 per cent in Sweden.

Dean Mahoney, of the National Family and Parenting Institute, said: 'It is not totally surprising because because families have been heading this way.

'Over the past ten to 15 years people have been getting married much later and women have been delaying having their first child.

'There are many more family types than there used to be and the family unit is vastly different to what it used to be in Britain.

'Of course, there are less social pressures and stigmas for parents who want a child without getting married.

'Marriage is still overwhelmingly popular in this country and for most people is the norm if they have children.

'However, the number of people who are choosing to delay marriage or not to get married at all is increasing year by year.

n.craven@dailymail.co.uk

The region where most of the births are illegitimate disturbing statistics on illegitimacy.
Daily Mail - Wednesday 1st May 2002.

Weddings below 250,000 for first time since 1897

Marriage slump that would not amuse Victoria

Till death us do part: A Victorian bride and groom

By **Steve Doughty**
Social Affairs Correspondent

THE popularity of marriage has sunk to an historic low.

Fewer couples exchanged wedding vows in 2001 than at any time since the Victorian era, figures show.

In 1897, as Queen Victoria celebrated her diamond jubilee, 249,145 marriages took place.

In 2001, the latest year available for statistics, the situation had barely changed, with 249,227 ceremonies held, the first time since that the number had dipped below 250,000.

The big difference is in the proportion of those choosing to say 'I will'.

In Victorian times the population of England and Wales was a mere 31million. Now, it is 52million.

The 2001 marriage rate represented a seven per cent drop on the previous year, when there were 267,961 weddings.

Although numbers in 2000 had been slightly up on the previous year, the latest figures show marriage has been steadily declining for 30 years. Marriages have dropped to the current level from an early 1970s peak of 426,241. The high water mark for weddings came in the war year 1940, when nearly a million married in 470,549 ceremonies.

HOW LIFE HAS CHANGED

	1897	2001
Marriages	249,145	249,227
Population	31m	52m
Divorces	503	143,800
Births	921,683	594,600
Births outside marriage	4%	40%

Figures for England and Wales

DECLINE OF MARRIAGES

1897	249,145
1940	470,549
1972	426,241
1981	352,000
1991	306,800
1996	279,000
1999	263,500
2000	267,961
2001	249,227

The new low marks the collapse of a society in which almost all parents were married, divorce was rare, and most women in their twenties had children.

Fast-falling marriage rates have gone alongside rapidly declining births, soaring divorce, and the spread of cohabitation and single parenthood.

Critics link the decline of marriage to increasing civil disorder, rising crime and lives blighted by joblessness, crime and serial relationships. They blame successive governments for neglecting the institution of marriage and sweeping away its legal and financial props.

Although pensions can be a minefield for couples who are not married, there have been some changes in tax laws which mean there are fewer financial benefits in being married compared with simply living with someone.

The current Labour government has ended the last tax break for marriage, the Married Couples Tax Allowance.

Ministers take the line that marriage is merely a lifestyle choice, with all other forms of domestic arrangement equally good as a basis for raising children.

Statistics, however, indicate that in almost every area of life children of married parents do better than those whose parents are not married.

Only 26 of every 1,000 unmarried men tied the knot in 2001, and fewer than 24 of every 1,000 unmarried women. Men marry for the first time on average at the age of 30 and eight months and women at the age of 28 years and four months.

'Legal and financial props'

One in five women now reaches the age of 40 without having children.

The average number of children each woman gave birth to has dropped to 1.64.

In 2001, the percentage of weddings which were a first marriage for both bride and groom rose by two points on the previous year to 60 per cent. Eighteen per cent of all weddings were remarriages.

s.doughty@dailymail.co.uk

Marriage Slump
Daily Mail - March 21st 2003

Safe-sex policy 'spreads disease among young'

BY LORRAINE FRASER
Medical Correspondent

THE GOVERNMENT'S policy on sex education has been blamed for a "galloping" rise in sexually transmitted diseases among young people that threatens in turn to cause increasing rates of infertility and cancer.

A leaked Parliamentary report labels the level of sexually transmitted infections among teenagers and young adults a "crisis". Critics claim that the report proves that the Government's approach to sex education is a failure.

Nuala Scarisbrick, a trustee of the charity Life, said that the Government's concentration on a "safe-sex" rather than "no-sex" message – designed to cut teenage pregnancy rates – had deprived millions of people of the information they need to protect their health.

"Now we are seeing the results: more teenage pregnancies, many ending in abortion, and more sexually transmitted disease. Some of these infections are incurable, others can lead to infertility and there is a proven link between early sex and cervical cancer. But they just don't tell young people about this."

According to the most recent figures, the number of people suffering from STDs declined in the 1980s and early 1990s but has risen sharply since 1995. One in 10 women under the age of 25 is now infected with chlamydia, which is linked with cervical cancer as well as infertility. The figures for 2001 show that more than 22,500 people contracted gonorrhoea, with men aged 20 to 24 and girls aged 16 to 19 most likely to become infected. Rates of syphilis have also increased, with young women most at risk.

The report by the Commons select committee on health is expected to blame the increase in STDs among women on the "ladette" culture of female drinking and one-night stands.

The report, due to be published next month, follows a furore over a programme in the South-West that encourages teachers to discuss details of oral sex and homosexual activity with pupils.

Safe Sex
Sunday Telegraph - February 23rd 2003

Just say No

THE crisis in sexual health is terrifying. According to a Commons Committee, Aids infections have shot up by 203 per cent in less than ten years. Syphilis is up 500 per cent. Infertility-causing chlamydia is up 108 per cent and gonorrhoea 86 per cent.

When Britain has the highest rate of teenage pregnancies in Europe, there could hardly be a more damning indictment of New Labour's value-free, studiously non-judgmental approach to sex education.

A 'good grope' guide for pupils aged 14... lessons in how to put on a condom... under-16s encouraged to experiment with oral sex... such reckless episodes flourish in a country where Ministers back the free availability of contraceptives, including the morning-after pill, for young people – even girls under the age of consent – despite the obvious dangers.

Tragically, the Government seems to find it difficult to call for restraint and abstinence. Doesn't it know the promotion of such supposedly outmoded values in America has cut teenage pregnancies by 20 per cent?

Or is it so wrapped up in its self-satisfied 'liberalism' that it prefers to look the other way, while so many children succumb to disease and despair?

Soaring rates of sexual infection
Daily Mail Thursday 12 June 2003

THE TIMES

MONDAY APRIL 5 2004 4M SL

Free pills and condoms 'boost promiscuity'

Venereal disease increase shows failure of sex education policy

By Alexandra Frean
Social Affairs Correspondent

GOVERNMENT attempts to reduce high-risk sexual behaviour among teenagers have had exactly the opposite effect, according to an authoritative new study.

Expanding contraceptive services and providing the morning-after pill free to teenagers have encouraged sexual behaviour rather than reducing it, according to economists at Nottingham University.

In a study which throws into question the Government's entire teenage sexual health strategy, they discovered that sexual activity and sexually transmitted diseases have risen fastest in those areas where the Government's policy has been most actively pursued.

Critics said that the findings exploded the official line that the best way to tackle rising teenage pregnancy and sexually transmitted infections (STIs) was by making contraception more easily available. Robert Whelan, of the independent think-tank Civitas, said: "The method which the Government's teenage pregnancy strategy relies upon is almost guaranteed to produce these results. They have always promoted condom use, but have never contemplated the possibility of teaching young people abstinence."

By making the morning-after pill free to teenagers, the Government had masked real levels of sexual activity among teenagers, he said. Because the pill causes early abortions, some conceptions are never counted in the teenage pregnancy figures. "The morning-after pill may cut pregnancies, but it won't do anything to decrease STIs. That is why the STI rate is now a much more reliable indicator of sexual activity among young people."

But proponents of widespread family planning for young people rejected the findings. Anne Weyman, chief executive of the Family Planning Association, said: "The evidence is that in areas other than London, teenage pregnancy rates have fallen by between 8 and 15 per cent since 1998.

"The awareness of sexually transmitted infections is quite low among young people. In the last few years, increased screening has been introduced, particularly aimed at young women, and of course, if you start looking for more infections you will find them."

She believed that the teenage pregnancy strategy could be improved. "One area where it needs to be greatly strengthened is the provision of sex education to young people," she said. "We want to see young people delaying having sex until they are able to make responsible decisions. I don't think this research helps to achieve any of those aims."

The Government has welcomed falling teenage pregnancy levels. But last month figures showed that after three years of decline, the number of teenagers becoming pregnant increased by 2.2 per cent to 41,868 in 2001-02.

The new study, to be presented today at the Royal Economic Society's annual conference in Swansea, is based on data collected by 95 health authorities in England between 1998 and 2001. They covered a wide range of indicators of teenage sexual activity and contraception, including teenage pregnancy rates, reported cases of STIs and the number of local family planning sessions. It also took into account factors such as family background, parental employment rates and educational qualifications.

The results show that the areas with the biggest increases in family planning sessions since the introduction of the teenage pregnancy strategy in 1999 have seen greater increases in STI rates than others. A doubling of the clinics in an area led, on average, to a 6 per cent increase in STI rates.

The study also found that the availability of more clinic sessions did not lead to bigger reductions in teenage pregnancy. In some areas, increased clinics were linked with higher pregnancy rates for under-18s.

David Paton, the author of the study, said: "When you introduce policies that seem obvious, it is important to factor in the possibility that the policies may actually cause people to change how they behave. In this case, it appears that some measures aimed at reducing teenage pregnancy rates induced changes in teenage behaviour that were large enough not only to negate the intended impact on conceptions, but to have an adverse impact on another important area of sexual health — sexually transmitted infections."

The Government had

MONDAY APRIL 5 2004 4M SL

THE SEX LOTTERY
UP TO 25 SEXUALLY TRANSMITTED INFECTIONS COULD BE YOURS!
CHLAMYDIA
GONORRHOEA
SYPHILIS
HIV
GENITAL HERPES
If you have sex without using a condom, you're gambling on catching one of 25 sexually transmitted infections (STIs). 8 of these don't always have symptoms and 4 are incurable. And the chances of picking something up are surprisingly high - 1 in 9 people has had an STI. So to make sure you play it safe, use a condom.
DON'T PLAY THE SEX LOTTERY. USE A CONDOM.
NHS
Worried you've picked up something? Visit www.playingsafely.co.uk or call, free and confidentially, 0800 567 123.

A poster promoting condom use. Sexually transmitted infections rose fastest where such campaigns were most intense

outcome of random decisions. His findings suggested that adolescents thought rationally about the decision to become sexually active.

So, when the cost of birth control goes down, its use goes having sex and not using birth control and for adolescents who were previously not having sex.

This interpretation is underlined by Professor Paton's data on the morning-after pill. A reduction in teenage pregnancy rates, but STI rates had risen.

"Teenage sexual behaviour appears to be little different to other fields in at least one important respect: incentives matter to teenagers too," he said.

the number of cases of STIs are rising among younger poeple, and we are not complacent about this. But individuals as well as government have a responsibility to tackle this problem."

Free pills and condoms "boost promiscuity"
The Times April 5th 2004

THE TIMES

No. 68139 ■ WEDNESDAY JULY 28 2004 ■ www.timesonline.co.uk ■ 50p

THE FIRST LADY

Teresa Heinz Kerry speaks out

DEMOCRATIC CONVENTION PAGE 27

IS THIS THE BEGINNING OF THE END FOR SVEN? SPORT

Safe-sex message is lost as disease soars

By Nigel Hawkes
Health Editor

BRITAIN is facing an epidemic of sexually transmitted diseases as the safe-sex message fades and treatment clinics are forced to turn more people away.

More people than ever are now contracting infections through sex, figures released by the Health Protection Agency yesterday show.

Cases of chlamydia rose by 9 per cent between 2002 and 2003, while syphilis showed a 28 per cent increase, the HPA figures show. Taken together, all sexually transmitted infections (STIs) rose by 4 per cent.

The true incidence of chlamydia is probably far higher because, in the majority of cases, it has no symptoms. But it can cause inflammatory disease of the pelvis, ectopic pregnancy and infertility.

Experts believe that 10 per cent of people aged 16 to 24 may be carriers of the disease, unaware of its dangers.

Yesterday sexual medicine specialists blamed high-risk sexual behaviour, especially among the young, ignorance about the risks and the failure to invest more in genito-urinary medicine (GUM) clinics, for the looming crisis.

Dr Angela Robinson, president of the British Association of Sexual Health and HIV, said: "Prompt access to GUM services for patients is essential if the number of new infections is to be reduced."

Nick Partridge, chief executive of the Terrence Higgins Trust, said: "It's no surprise that the figures are continuing to rise, given the excessive waiting times at many sexual health clinics.

"The NHS has failed to prioritise sexual health and HIV, and these figures are an indictment of their inaction."

James Johnson, chairman of the British Medical Association, said: "With a 9 per cent rise of chlamydia cases, thousands of women could become infertile. It is a scandal that the service we offer patients today is worse than 90 years ago.

"During the First World War a free, rapid and totally confidential service was set up to treat sexually transmitted infections. Nearly a century later patients who turn up at GUM clinics can wait up to six weeks for an appointment. What use is that?"

MAIN POINTS

- Cases of chlamydia up by 9 per cent in a year to 90,000
- Syphilis cases rise by 28 per cent
- Overall, sexually transmitted infections rise by 4 per cent
- Chlamydia rates have increased by 140 per cent in six years
- 708,083 people had an STI diagnosed in 2003

Catherine Phillips, 25, a novelist who had a diagnosis of chlamydia four years ago, said that the Government was failing to inform young people of the dangers posed by STIs.

"In terms of the standards of sex education, it just has not progressed," she said. "Kids are having sex younger and younger. Instead of burying our heads in the sand we need to be telling people what they can do to themselves if they have unprotected sex."

Today Sir Liam Donaldson, the Chief Medical Officer, is expected to condemn the "unacceptably long waits" for treatment in his annual report. He will also give warning that infections are being missed when patients visit clinics.

Yesterday's figures show that the largest increases were in diagnoses of syphilis, once a disease that had almost disappeared from Britain. It remains uncommon, with just 1,575 diagnoses in GUM clinics in 2003, but this was more than ten times the figure of 136 recorded in 1995.

Chlamydia is the most commonly diagnosed, with nearly 90,000 cases in 2003, 40,000 in men and 50,000 in women. Eight years ago only a third as many cases were being seen.

The HPA figures do not

Continued on page 5, col 1

Catherine Phillips, who developed chlamydia, says the real dangers of sexually transmitted diseases are not made clear

Hidden disease that left sufferer

As new figures show that sexual infections are increasing, two women talk about the impact on their lives.
Sam Lister and **James Doughty** report

CASE 1

THREE months before her 21st birthday, Catherine Phillips found her life in turmoil after hospital tests for a nagging pain around her pelvis showed that she was infected with chlamydia.

Mrs Phillips, a novelist, spoke yesterday of having broken down in tears as she and her fiancé were told by doctors that she was carrying an infectious disease that would probably prevent her from having children. Mrs Phillips said that a whole range of emotions had taken over when she received the diagnosis. "I wished with all my heart that Robin was the only man I had ever slept with," she said. She had thought, that day, that if only that had been the case, "we could be looking forward to having a family of our own. Instead, I was looking at a much bleaker future — possibly alone and certainly childless.

"It was just the most devastating news you could imagine,"

> 'I was looking at a much bleaker future — possibly alone and certainly childless'

she said. "I had been carrying this infection for maybe two years and had never known. I didn't want children straight away, but suddenly to look forward and see your life without kids was just devastating."

Speaking from her home in Bristol yesterday, Mrs Phillips, now 25, said it came as no surprise that rates of sexually transmitted infections were continuing to increase, as the latest figures from the Health Protection Agency show.

She said that the surge in cases of chlamydia — which rose by more than 9 per cent last year — reflected the lack of education for young people about the perils of STIs. "I had hardly even heard of chlamydia; at school the message was all about avoiding getting pregnant, with the odd picture of warts and other visible infections. I never knew you could catch things you wouldn't even be aware of."

Mrs Phillips discovered she had chlamydia — known as the silent infection — only after complaining to her GP for almost two years about a pain around her pelvis. The doctor initially dismissed it as a muscle strain, before putting her on tablets to counter a possible hormone imbalance.

"I just had enough," she said. "I had been put on all sorts of pills but nothing was working. Eventually I decided to go and see a gynaecologist, and only then did I find out what the real cause of the problem was."

She described lying in her hospital bed, terrified, as she awaited the results of an internal examination. Her fiancé, Robin, had also been asked to attended the clinic, which she had taken as the most ominous of signs.

"I had been told, after an earlier examination, that I might have pelvic inflammatory disease caused by infection with chlamydia. I had been warned that if this was the cause, the long-term result could be infertility. Robin and I were so worried that we had taken out a bank loan of £2,500 to pay for private treatment as soon as possible."

Yet despite warnings that she would be unable to conceive, Mrs Phillips became pregnant three years ago. Her son Callum is now aged 2.

"Initially they thought it was a cyst, caused by operations I was having to prepare for fertility treatment. But then it became apparent I was pregnant. It was just the most wonderful news.

"At one awful point in time I had thought my life was over before I was even 21. So I would like to warn any young woman who might be feeling pressurised into sex before she is ready to think twice before risking her future fertility.

"Never be afraid to put yourself, and your health, first. I wish I had."

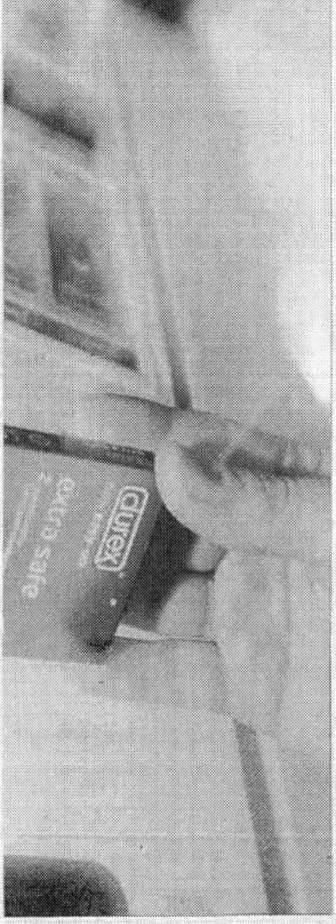

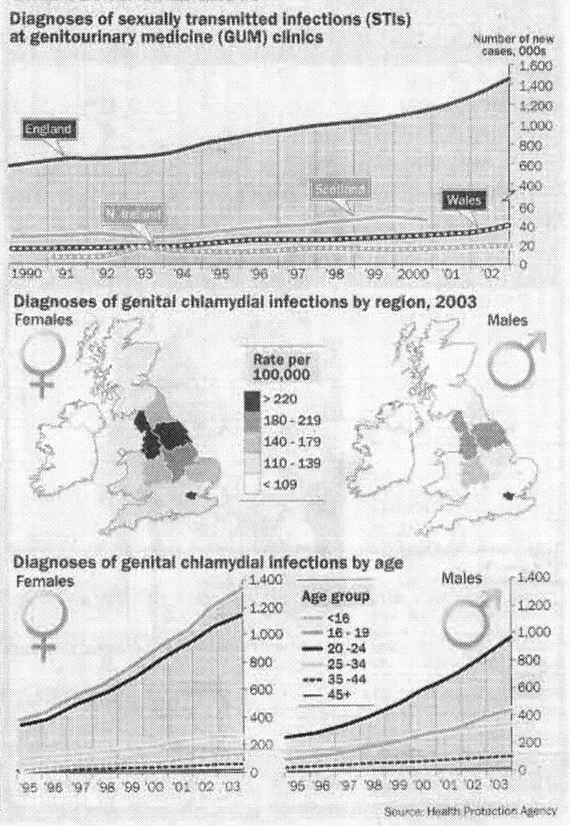

Source: Health Protection Agency

The shock of testing positive

CASE 2

RACHEL ROSS had no idea that she was HIV-positive until she took a compulsory test in order to emigrate to America. The 30-year-old psychologist from Surrey was about to marry her long-term partner and set up a new life across the Atlantic.

What she found out was to change her life for ever. "The result was totally unexpected," she said. "The doctor told me that the good news was I didn't have syphilis, but the bad news was I was HIV-positive."

Ms Ross said that her first reaction was one of devastation and disbelief. She immediately arranged a second test. "The result filled me with terror and denial, so I took a second test. It was positive, again.

"I had unprotected sex just three or four times. That's all it took. HIV wasn't something you expected to find in the Home Counties. I was sexually active during the 'Don't Die of Ignorance' Aids campaign of the 1980s. The focus was very much upon gay sex and I naively believed that I was immune from sexual infections. I believed then that they were restricted to drug users, gay people and distant countries."

Ms Ross, now 35, regularly attends Chelsea and Westminster Hospital, where she receives drugs to control her illness. She added: "Since I started on my current drug programme I have not experienced any side-effects or complications."

Ms Ross has refused to be stigmatised or "fall into victimhood" and is passionately open with friends and family about her HIV status. She has turned her back on the lucrative career that she was so dedicated to before being diagnosed.

She married her partner but they have since separated, although the split was not connected with her illness, she said. Now she helps others who have contracted the virus to overcome depression and rebuild their lives.

And Ms Ross is optimistic about her future. "I intend to live until old age," she said.

The names in this article have been changed.

Quick access to treatment is key to defeating this epidemic

DR THOMAS STUTTAFORD
MEDICAL BRIEFING

WHEN I started working in a VD clinic more than 30 years ago, the doors were open at 8.30am and closed at 8pm.

Nobody was ever sent away to come back on another day. By the time I left the NHS eight years ago the clinic closed earlier but was still open into the evening. Even then we managed to see every patient on the day they came to consult us.

It is a sign of the changing performance of the NHS and of the pattern of sexually transmitted diseases that in some London areas patients now have to wait for two weeks to see a doctor in a genitourinary medical clinic. In other parts of the country this can take two months.

The secret of running a good unit and a good service is that the consultation must be confidential and non-judgmental.

But if patients have no easy access, they will become accustomed to their symptoms and may not re-attend. Many are young and testosterone-rich, so that the consequences of any action are often only thought about afterwards.

During this time they may infect other people and it becomes difficult to trace casual contacts. If untreated they too will spread the disease.

Having an immediate service is therefore essential if the Department of Health is to control the current outbreak of sexually transmitted infections (STIs). In the 1970s syphilis was common but nowhere near as prevalent as during and just after the Second World War. Even before HIV blunted the desire for casual sex in the 1980s, the incidence of syphilis was declining fast.

Most STIs became less prevalent as sexual activity declined in response to the advertising campaign about the dangers of HIV. Methods of treating HIV, along with a misplaced contempt of its lethal effects, have now caused some return to the sexual mores prevalent in the Sixties and Seventies.

Overseas travel has also played a part. In one survey 35 per cent of men and 62 per cent of women who developed syphilis in Britain caught it in the Caribbean.

How should sexual health be tackled?
Send your e-mails to **debate@thetimes.co.uk**

facing a life without children

SCIENCE PHOTO LIBRARY

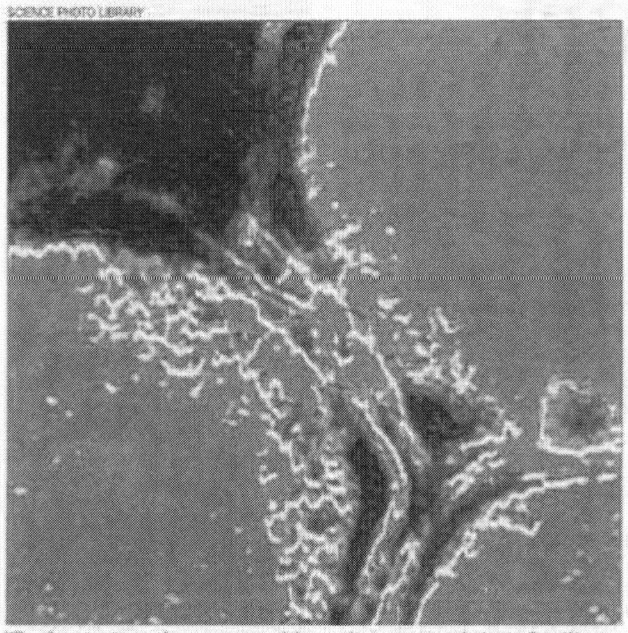

The bacterium that causes chlamydia can result in infertility

Infections soar

Continued from page 1
include HIV infections, which have also been rising. The gloom is offset by reductions in gonorrhoea and herpes but experts cautioned against reading too much into this.

Sir William Stewart, chairman of the HPA, said: "These are all preventable infections and it is a cause of considerable concern that we are still seeing increases in new diagnoses of STIs across the UK, and unsafe sex is undoubtedly a main contributor to this.

"This is the time of year when many young people go on holiday. These figures are a timely reminder of how important it is for people to take responsibility for their own, and their partners', sexual health and to use a condom."

Peter Greenhouse, a consultant gynaecologist and head of sexual health services at Bristol Royal Infirmary, said that, while the issue was now a political priority, realities on the ground had not changed.

They now turned away 500 people a week compared with 400 last year and struggled to recruit staff because of a historical pay gap with GPs.

In addition he said that the present generation of teenagers had not been brought up with the Aids message. "They are not quite as aware, they're not quite as scared as teenagers were in the past," he said.

Anne Weyman, Chief Executive of the fpa (formerly the Family Planning Association) said: "Just last week the Government missed a vital opportunity to improve the situation by failing to include sexual health as one of the measurable targets in the new NHS Planning and Priorities Framework.

"Without such a target, sexual health will fail to get the priority it so urgently needs at local level."

Melanie Johnson, the Public Health Minister, took comfort from the fact that the rate of increase in STIs had slowed. "However, there is no room for complacency and a great deal of work to do," she said.

"We are increasing capacity in sexual health services. We have already invested £26 million to reduce waiting times and improve access to GUM clinics with further funding available to modernise buildings and develop services."

Leading article, page 16

MOST COMMON INFECTIONS

■ Chlamydia, pictured, is caused by a bacterium, it can be carried by both sexes without symptoms. It can cause inflammation of the urethra in men, and in women of the womb and urethra, leading to chronic infection and in some cases, infertility.

■ Syphilis was almost eliminated in the UK by antibiotics, but has made a comeback. If untreated it passes through three stages, ending in GPI — general paralysis of the insane. It is caused by a spirochaete, a bacterial organism. London and Manchester are the main centres of the new outbreak.

■ Gonorrhoea is the second-commonest STI, and tends to be concentrated in groups such as homosexual men and black ethnic populations. It can block the Fallopian tubes and cause sterility in women.

■ Genital warts are small, flat, flesh-coloured bumps or tiny, cauliflower-like bumps that grow on the genital areas of both sexes. They may be too small to see. Caused by the human papilloma virus, they may lead to cancer of the cervix in women or cancer of the penis in men.

■ Genital herpes is caused by the herpes simplex virus and is extremely common. In many people it causes no symptoms but in others it produces sores around the genital areas. It can linger for years, causing regular flare-ups in some people.

SEX AND SENSIBILITIES

The rise in STDs reflects a sad failure to speak the truth

As the chairman of the British Medical Association noted yesterday, the latest figures on sexually transmitted diseases (STDs) in Britain make very depressing reading. With the exception of those on Aids, they concern a set of clinical problems so straightforward that in scientific terms they had been solved by the end of the First World War. Yet the obstacles to prevention have proved so intractable that, despite sustained investment in specialised clinics and education, the overall incidence of these diseases is still increasing. In the case of chlamydia and syphilis the rate of increase threatens an epidemic.

What distinguishes these infections from others — and often renders them immune to both common sense and science — is, of course, sex. In the five generations since soldiers returning from the European fronts in 1918 were offered quick, free and effective treatment for prevalent STDs, the West has thrown itself into a prolongued revolution in sexual practice and assumptions, one of which now holds that feverish teenage coupling is a rite of passage too instinctual and inevitable to be worth challenging. The onset of the Aids epidemic in the late 1980s temporarily dented the appeal of promis cuity and slowed the advance of other STDs, but an explosion in foreign travel since 1997, thanks largely to low-cost airlines, has hastened it again. As a result nearly three quarters of a million Britons had STDs diagnosed last year.

The increase of 4 per cent over 2002 is not catastrophic, although the surprising 9 per cent rise in chlamydia is disturbing; some of this increase may stem from heightened awareness of the risks of STDs and a greater number of people seeking check-ups. If so, this may help to forestall a more serious increase in future years, but it does not disguise a fundamental weakness in the sex education offered by most schools, which the Sex Education Forum described at the weekend as "too little, too late and too biological". Nor does it alter the terms of the broader debate on sex and promiscuity, in which parents, teachers and public health officials continue to censor themselves unnecessarily about the central importance of personal responsibility.

Abstinence may not seem to be an option for many in the crucial 16-24 age range, which accounts for much of the overall spread of STDs and has proved stubbornly resistant to pleas for more consistent use of condoms. But neither should it be deemed freakish; as a species we are uniquely capable of self-control should we wish to use it. More generally, inculcating respect for sex, and the stable relationships that ideally form its context, is not reactionary.

It has been observed that some social conventions are as contagious as sexually transmitted diseases. Indeed. It is hard to overstate the peer pressure on teenagers and young adults of both sexes to "perform" when the lights go down and alcohol begins to flow, especially when those constraints that a home-town setting may have imposed are discarded on the beaches of Ibiza or Devon. This is why the message that freedom brings with it responsibilities should be a constant refrain in schools, where mandatory sex education is currently so narrowly defined that it is often squeezed into a single science class. That definition must be broadened. Sex is not merely more than biology. It is the centre of a complex web of issues that schools alone cannot be expected to "teach". Unfashionable as it may be to invoke the uncertain powers of today's parents, they are the first line of defence against the behaviour that spreads STDs.

Such diseases will not go away. Clinics should offer walk-in treatment. Most are today too overwhelmed to do so, but they need not be if potential clients have more than sex on their minds.

The Times, Wednesday July 28th 2004

EXTREMISTS SEND IN POISON PEN LETTERS BEFORE COMMONS BID TO RELAX LAW

Activists target female MPs with 'baby-killer' hate mail

By Isabel Oakeshott
Political Correspondent

FEMALE MPs are being targeted with hate mail by anti-abortion extremists.

Labour politicians have received anonymous letters branding them "baby killers" prior to a new debate over abortion laws.

Campaigners are targeting them at random in an effort to deter them from voting for any relaxation in legislation.

Today one Labour backbencher told how she had received a string of malicious letters. Jane Griffiths, MP for Reading East, claimed she had received the "flood of hate mail" despite the fact that she had never spoken out on the issue.

She said: "They were very unpleasant letters, which look as if they were scribbled off very quickly. One called me a baby killer and another described me as a prostitute.

"It is widely assumed that all female Labour MPs think women should have easy access to abortions so we get these letters. It is very nasty."

One group has revealed plans for a radical campaign. The UK Life League, which insists it is not behind the anonymous letters, is preparing to use hard-hitting tactics to discourage MPs from voting for changes in the autumn.

The Evening Standard has learned that a string of backbenchers will compete to table Private Member's Bills on the issue when they return.

The UK Life League is vowing to "stigmatise" pro-choice politicians. Activists will meet in London this week to decide tactics but are already working on mass mailshots, "naming and shaming" MPs who have a record of backing the right to decide on a pregnancy.

Activist Jim Dowson said: "We are trying to put a price on being pro-abortion. We are stepping it up and we are getting more professional at it." The debate was reignited after the Evening Standard published extraordinary pictures of foetuses in the womb.

The ultrasound images showed them moving and sucking their thumbs. The pictures prompted calls for a reduction in the time limit for abortions, which stands at 24 weeks — an age at which premature babies can now survive.

However, anti-abortion campaigners are deeply suspicious of such a move — fearing it will be accompanied by measures to make very early abortions easier. Many MPs believe women still find it too difficult to obtain terminations in the early stages of pregnancy and they want abortions to be more widely available.

The UK Life League claims to have 13,000 members in England. It recently sent 3,800 highly inflammatory letters to people on the Isle of Wight, where there are plans to open a new abortion clinic. The activists hope similar tactics will intimidate MPs.

Abuse: Jane Griffiths, who has never spoken on abortion, received malicious letters

The law...

WOMEN are entitled to have abortions until the 24th week of pregnancy.

After that, terminations can only be performed for serious medical reasons — for example, if the woman's life is in danger or there is compelling evidence the baby will be born handicapped.

Today's laws date back to 1967, when abortion became legal up to 28 weeks. In 1990 the law was revised. Babies can now survive outside the womb at even less than 24 weeks. This has led to calls for further restrictions.

Tony Blair has made it clear that any change in the law should be initiated by backbenchers, and several MPs want to table Private Member's Bills.

Photos that sparked a debate

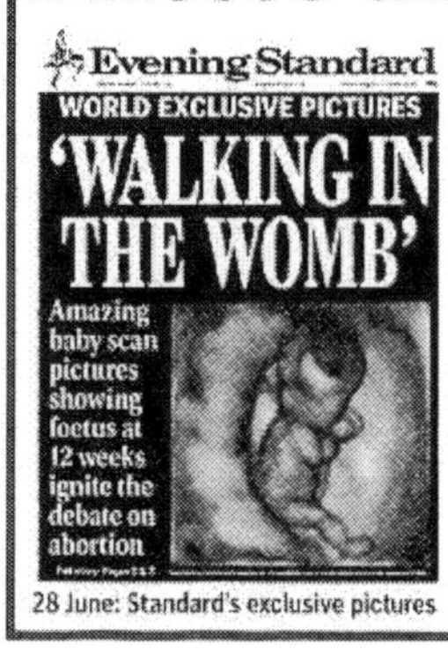
Evening Standard
WORLD EXCLUSIVE PICTURES
'WALKING IN THE WOMB'
Amazing baby scan pictures showing foetus at 12 weeks ignite the debate on abortion

28 June: Standard's exclusive pictures

AMAZING pictures in the Evening Standard showing a baby "walking" in the womb reignited the ethical debate over abortion law.

The photographs revealed a foetus clearly moving its developing limbs only 12 weeks after conception.

Other images showed 15-week foetuses sucking their thumbs and yawning, and one opening its eyes at 18 weeks.

The pictures, taken during ultrasound scanning, revealed that the foetus is physically developed at an extremely early stage, and that the unborn child has a far more complex life than previously thought. All of the images — taken by Professor Stuart Campbell, former head of obstetrics at King's College Hospital in London — were of foetuses well within the legal time limit for abortions.

They caused a sensation and raised new ethical questions over terminations.

The images were seized upon by some as evidence that foetuses should be regarded as human beings rather than "blobs of jelly".

The pictures also encouraged some of those who previously thought the current legislation on abortion was satisfactory to reassess their views.

Evening Standard, Wednesday 18th August 2004

Daily Mail

FRIDAY, AUGUST 20, 2004 www.dailymail.co.uk 40p

A-LEVELS: HOW DID YOUR SCHOOL DO?

SEE PAGES 8 - 9 and 64 - 66

Unwanted pregnancies soar for women in their early twenties

IS ABORTION THE NEW PILL?

By **Beezy Marsh**
Health Correspondent

YOUNG women are increasingly using abortion as a form of birth control, alarming official figures suggested yesterday.

Despite easy access to contraception and the morning-after pill, the trend for terminations among those in their 20s is rising inexorably.

There are fears that a generation now sees an unwanted pregnancy as a minor setback which is easily remedied. That can mean women being rushed into abortion rather than taking the time to consider having a baby adopted.

Unprotected sex and promiscuity have already been blamed for increases in sexually-transmitted diseases among women in their early 20s.

The latest figures from the Office for National Statistics show terminations are highest among that 20 to 24 age group – and rising year on year.

There was a three per cent increase in the first quarter of last year, compared with the same period in 2002. Some 13,000 abortions were carried out in that age group in those three months alone.

If that trend is eventually shown to have continued through the year, more than 52,000 pregnancies among women in their early twenties will have been terminated in 2003. The figure has increased steadily since Labour came to power in 1997.

Over all age groups there were 185,400 abortions in 2002, the last year for which full figures are available. The vast majority were carried out before 12 weeks – meaning they were for 'social' reasons.

Two doctors must judge the risk to the woman's physical or mental health of

Turn to Page 6, Col. 5

Alarm at abortion increase

Continued from Page One

continuing the pregnancy outweighs the dangers of termination. In reality, this means women who do not want a baby are able to easily terminate it up to 24 weeks.

Abortion advice charities said last night that some women in their early twenties were ending pregnancies in order to climb the career ladder.

The Family Planning Association said those in the 20 to 24 age group were more likely to have terminations because they were concentrating on their careers or had just finished university.

A spokesman said: 'The average age for women having a baby is now 29, so younger women will tend to make more of a choice to end the pregnancy, particularly if they have just left university or are building a career.

'What we do find is that abortion figures tend to go up and down, so while it may be higher now, it may well go down again.'

Association chief executive Anne Weyman said the figures highlighted the need for improvement in NHS contraceptive services, which were essential to prevent unplanned pregnancy.

She said: 'They are in dire need of greater investment to both improve access and provide much-needed training for health professionals.'

Jack Scarisbrick, of the campaigning charity LIFE, said: 'The figures are depressing evidence that the Government's approach to sexual health is not working.

'Generations of teenagers are being told it is OK to have sex and they are exposing themselves not only to unwanted pregnancies, but to sexual diseases such as chlamydia which can ruin their chances of having a family later in life.

'The figures suggest women in their twenties are seeing abortion as a safe and easy option, when in fact there is a risk of post-abortion trauma.

'It is extremely callous. Women are being treated as if they are on a conveyor belt and babies' lives are being lost.' The latest abortion figures also show there has been no decline in the number of terminations among teenagers,

'Extremely callous'

despite Government campaigns to prevent teenage pregnancies.

The rise in abortions comes despite easy access to the morning-after pill, which went on sale over the counter in chemists' shops in 2001.

Critics warned at the time that the development would encourage promiscuity.

The pill, which contains a dose of hormones six times as high as the regular contraceptive pill and prevents an embryo from implanting in the womb, is intended to be used only in an 'emergency', when a condom has failed, for example.

Government figures show the use of it has soared. Around 20 per cent of 16 and 17-year-olds say they have used it, and three per cent say they have used it more than once.

Some ten per cent of women over 20 used the morning-after pill, compared with 5 per cent of women over 30. Only 2 per cent of married women used it.

Experts have stressed repeatedly that women who have unprotected sex put themselves at risk of sexually transmitted diseases.

Doctors are particularly worried about chlamydia, described as a 'silent' infection because victims may show no symptoms.

One in ten women aged 16 to 25 has the disease – cases rose from 30,877 a year to 64,000 between 1995 and 2000.

Chlamydia can trigger pelvic inflammatory disease, which may make women infertile or more susceptible to an ectopic pregnancy, which can lead to fertility problems.

The 2002 abortion total includes 2,966 – 1.6 per cent – carried out after 20 weeks.

Earlier this year revolutionary 3D scans showed that foetuses are capable of 'walking' in the womb at just 12 weeks, and suck their thumb and yawn by 14 and 15 weeks.

The images prompted calls for a review of the current law, which allows termination for 'social' reasons up to 24 weeks of pregnancy – when a baby is fully formed.

Under the Abortion Act, a foetus can legally be terminated right up to the end of a pregnancy if doctors believe there is a substantial risk that the baby will have a serious physical or mental disability.

This is called Ground E, but it has become increasingly controversial as it allows an abortion well after the point at which a baby, if born prematurely, could survive.

b.marsh@dailymail.co.uk

Daily Mail, Friday August 20th 2004

One liberal broadcaster describes her startling change of heart over one of the most emotionally charged issues of our times

I'd always been pro-abortion ... until the day I became a mother

Soul-searching: The birth of baby Patrick caused Miranda to re-examine her beliefs on abortion

Picture: DAVID WOOLFALL/First magazine

by Miranda Sawyer

WHEN I discovered I was pregnant in February 2005, after several weeks of heavy drinking and flying to and from the U.S. for work, I was 38 and in a settled relationship. And, despite my non-ideal lifestyle, our baby was planned. So far, so straightforward.

What was unplanned, for me, were all the questions that resulted. Was I having a boy or a girl? Would we like the same music? Would we like each other? But I also found myself pondering other, trickier, dilemmas. I spent quite some time thinking about the precise point that our baby came into existence.

Was he there before I did the pregnancy test? Clearly something was or the test couldn't have come up positive. But what was it? A person? A potential person? Life? What was life, exactly?

Skip forward two years — during which I gave birth to a son, Patrick — and I am making a TV documentary about abortion rights in the U.S., trying to answer the questions about whether it is ever morally right to kill.

The anti-abortion Pro-Lifers say it is wrong to take innocent life (though they often support the death penalty). They say it's irrelevant whether the pregnant woman loves or doesn't love her baby, whether she wants it or not: it's alive, so she shouldn't kill it.

And they believe that it should make no difference that the life inside her has only just embarked on its journey to full personhood. It's made from a human sperm and egg, it's living, so it is morally wrong to kill it.

The Pro-Choicers say it's up to the woman to decide if she wants a pregnancy to continue to its full term.

I have always been firmly in the Pro-Choice camp because, like most women, I've spent nearly all of my sexually active life trying not to get pregnant. Throughout my 20s and the better part of my 30s, I did everything that was required for me not to have a child (other than not having sex).

I wasn't always safe, but I was lucky enough not to end up in a situation where I was pregnant and didn't want to be. I've never had an abortion, though I am mighty glad that legal abortion exists.

When I got pregnant, it felt weird. My mind kept returning to the pregnancy test. If my reaction to those fateful double lines had been horror instead of hooray — and, to be honest, it wasn't unalloyed joy that I felt when I saw them: I was scared, too — then I would have had little hesitation in having an abortion. But it was that very fact that was confusing me.

I was calling the life inside me a baby, because I wanted it. Yet if I hadn't, as would perhaps have been the case ten years earlier, I would have thought of it as just a group of cells it was OK to kill. It was the same entity. It was merely my response to it that determined whether it would live or die. That seemed irrational to me. Maybe even immoral.

But I couldn't be an anti-abortionist! I'm not religious. I have ethics: I'm humanist, liberal, anti-establishment. And I'm a feminist. I certainly don't want to shackle women to their wombs. A civilised society should allow us to have children if and when we desire them.

What would we do if he was a Down's baby?

As I was an older mother-to-be, much fuss was made about Down's Syndrome and other possible disabilities. I thought about those questions, too. If a test showed that our baby had Down's, and we decided we didn't like that, would he become a thing again, a non-baby that we could get rid of as we wished?

We decided not to have the test. We were having a wanted child, whoever he turned out to be.

When I went for the 12-week scan, I was given a picture of our baby, in profile. He seemed to be waving, but that's just the way the limbs move, isn't it? The way they fall when the photo is taken. At about 18 weeks into my pregnancy, I felt a kick. It's a strange sensation, like an internal giggle.

Traditionally, this is called the quickening and is the point at which the life inside you is named as a baby.

But I could still have aborted this quick, kicking thing, legally. In the UK you can terminate up until 24 weeks, though the cases of such late abortions are extremely rare, and it's almost always for medical reasons.

It was a 1990 amendment to the UK's 1967 Abortion Act that reduced the abortion limit from 28 weeks to 24; this was due partly to the viability argument, which holds that if a baby/foetus/whatever you want to call it can survive outside the womb at 23 weeks, then abortion shouldn't really be allowed past that point.

Recently, in the U.S., a child named Amillia Taylor survived after being born at just under 22 weeks into her mother's pregnancy. Science is moving viability closer and closer to conception. So it seems to me to be a loose argument. Why should abortion be moral only at times when science says it is? Either abortion is right, or it isn't.

In the U.S., law has restricted the right to a termination

After my son, Patrick, was born, I looked at his 12-week scan picture again. He had the same profile. He has it now. He was himself in there. But if I believed that, how could I morally continue to support abortion?

My questions weren't being answered in the UK, where abortion isn't really talked about. So I decided to go to America, where abortion is a hot, divisive and political topic.

In the U.S., legislation initiated by pro-lifers has brought in more and more restrictions on a woman's right to a legal termination, which was established by the 1973 landmark Supreme Court case of Roe v Wade.

Since then, Republican Presidents such as Reagan and Bushes Sr and Jr have installed pro-choice judges into the Supreme Court: the last time Roe v Wade was challenged, in 1992, it was upheld only by a 5-4 majority.

The pro-choice supporters feel under threat. And in the deep South of the U.S., they are. Most people there are pro-life. Their politicians are the same and thus there are very few abortion facilities around. In Mississippi, a vast state of more than 48,000 square miles, with almost three million inhabitants, there is only one abortion clinic. One! Despite my dilemmas, I could feel my feminist hackles rise.

The clinic, I discovered, has pro-life protesters campaigning outside it every day. They shout, they plead, they put up placards, they hand out leaflets. They include Roy McMillan. I hung out with Roy outside the clinic as he confronted young, mostly black, women coming in for terminations and tried to persuade them to turn back.

It wasn't a comfortable morning. 'Shame on you, coming in here with a cross around your neck!' Roy shouted at one poor girl. 'Are you going to nail your baby to the cross?' I couldn't understand some of his logic. Say I was pregnant. If Roy believes that abortion is murder, and I, having listened to his arguments, nevertheless decide to have an abortion, then surely I should be arrested and tried as a murderer? Or at least tried for paying someone else to commit the murder for me.

But Roy pulled back from this, saying that it's the abortion doctors who should be prosecuted. 'They are,' he declared, 'the pushers of abortion. Women are the victims.' Like we're abortion addicts.

As I travelled through the Deep South, I read arguments for and against abortion. Moral philosophy, political discourse, rants. If I'm honest, it seemed that everyone — philosopher, politician, crank — just takes a stance, and then justifies it.

Some thinkers argue that abortion is OK, and infanticide is fine, too, because foetuses and little children aren't fully human: they can't look after themselves and they have no concept of death.

This made me think of my son, Patrick, back home, with his dad. I missed them both.

In Louisiana, I found that one pro-life argument — that life begins at conception — had been taken to extremes. Unborn embryos in Louisiana have the same legal status as children. So they can never be destroyed, as it would be legally the same as killing a child.

As my mind boggled, I realised that this has huge implications for things such as IVF. If you freeze your IVF embryos, you can never destroy the ones you don't use. You have to keep them frozen for ever, and make provisions for them in your will.

I met a New Orleans couple whose second baby came from an embryo that was rescued during Hurricane Katrina. During the hurricane, the fertility clinic flooded and the electricity was cut off; this meant that thousands of frozen embryos had to be rescued, by armed National Guard, because they could not be allowed to die.

Meanwhile, of course, actual living people were being left to perish in the Superdome, or being shot for looting shops for food. Who says that Americans don't get irony? Perhaps only the young and the old are confident enough to see things in black and white. Hit your late 30s and everything's greyer. Either that, or you just get lazy: you believe whatever suits you at the time.

One of the oddest people I met on my travels was Norma McCorvey.

I have to agree that life begins at conception

Initially, she was given the pseudonym Jane Roe to keep her anonymity in the landmark 1973 case of Roe v Wade, which established the right to abortion in the U.S. Norma won her right to a legal termination, though it was too late for her: she had the baby and it was adopted.

Once a poster girl for the Pro-Choice movement, Norma is now — and I couldn't quite believe this — anti-abortion. A lonely woman, she turned to the Church a few years ago, converted to Catholicism and rejected abortion. Now she's the jewel in the Pro-Life crown.

Unlike Norma, I don't want to be the kind of person who changes her beliefs according to her circumstances: like people changing from Labour to Conservative as they become richer.

And I don't want to tell other people — other women — what to do. But when you see women's abortion rights whittled away, as they have been in the U.S., you can't help but get angry.

On the other hand, when you've experienced pregnancy and birth, and the fantastic beauty of the resulting child, it's hard not to question what a termination does, or is.

My trip did eventually end with me coming to terms with my two opposing beliefs.

Maybe it's as spurious as all the other arguments I heard, but it was when a moral philosopher pointed out to me that being alive is one thing, but being a human is something else, that something clicked.

In the end, I have to agree that life begins at conception.

So yes, abortion is ending that life. But perhaps the fact of life isn't what is important. It's whether that life has grown enough to take on human characteristics, to start becoming a person.

In its early stages, the foetus clearly hasn't, so I have no problems with early abortions. In fact, I think they should be given on demand, as they are in France, rather than the UK system which forces women to get two different doctors' signatures in order to get an abortion. It's in everyone's best interest for a termination to be performed as soon after the pregnancy starts as possible.

But once an embryo has developed enough to feel pain, or begin a personality, then it has moved from cell-life into the first stages of being a human. Then, for me, ending that life is wrong.

■ *TRAVELS With My Camera: A Matter Of Life And Death is on More 4 at 10.30pm tonight.*

Daily Mail, Wednesday April 11th 2007

The abortion backlash

More doctors are refusing terminations on ethical grounds

By **Jenny Hope**
Medical Correspondent

THE NHS abortion service is heading for a crisis because increasing numbers of doctors refuse to carry out terminations, it was claimed yesterday.

There has been a big rise in young medics with 'conscientious objections' to abortion.

The increase has been revealed by the Royal College of Obstetricians and Gynaecologists.

It says there is evidence of a 'slow but growing problem' of young doctors opting out of abortion training on moral grounds.

Some senior doctors have blamed declining interest on the lack of 'glamour' involved in the work.

This has been dubbed 'dinner party syndrome' where doctors don't want to admit to their friends that they do abortions.

In addition, changes to training schedules and reductions in working hours mean trainee doctors are opting out of a branch of specialist work that may not enhance their career prospects.

RCOG spokesman Kate Guthrie, who is head of abortion services in Hull, said: 'You get no thanks for performing abortions, you get spat on. Who admits to friends at a dinner party that they are an abortionist? It is not a sexy area – it is a bog standard area of women's care.

'There is an increasing number of young doctors who are not participating in the training. The college and the Department of Health are really worried.'

She said abortion care must become part of core training in a new curriculum being introduced in August, although it should not be compulsory.

The college was not able to produce any figures to back up its claims, however.

But the situation has prompted abortion groups to call for a change in the law which would allow nurses to carry out early surgical and medical abortions – procedures which are technically simple.

Last night a spokesman for Marie Stopes, Britain's biggest private provider of abortions, said this would dramatically increase provision.

Spokesman Tony Kerridge said: 'Ninety per cent of terminations take place before 12 weeks when they are simple, low-tech procedures.

'It's not glamorous work for doctors which may partly explain the increasing difficulty in recruitment over the last five or six years, and younger people no longer understand or recall the time when abortion was illegal.

'Our research published in The Lancet shows nurses and paramedics in Vietnam and South Africa do the work extremely successfully, but they are not allowed to here. This must change.'

Marie Stopes currently carries out one in three British abortions, with two-thirds funded by NHS contracts. Mr Kerridge said surveys show one in five GPs oppose abortion but most do not let it stand in the way of caring for their patients.

Julia Millington of the ProLife Alliance, agreed that doctors are turning away from the work on moral grounds.

She said: 'We have been hearing for some time now that young doctors, in particular, do not want to work in this field. Those choosing to go into medicine presumably do so because they want to cure sickness and disease not end the lives of innocent human beings.

'Public and Parliamentary opinion on the abortion issue has shifted in recent years and this is further evidence that the law must be reviewed.'

But the British Pregnancy Advisory Service said it was not aware of any documented rise in conscientious objections where a doctor refuses to work in abortion or IVF services on the grounds of moral conviction.

Chief executive Ann Furedi said 'The current crop of medical students have not themselves seen women dying slowly and painfully after self-induced and unsafe abortion in the UK – but if they went to the many countries overseas where abortion is still illegal or only available to rich people, they would see this.

'Abortion is an absolutely essential, life-saving part of medical care – it may not be the most glamorous medical speciality on the face of it, compared to stem cell research or neurosurgery – but it is seen as heroic work by the women that it helps.'

Dr Kate Paterson, a consultant obstetrician working in abortion care, said: 'There are an awful lot of doctors already working helping women to get pregnant in the NHS and in the private IVF sector.

'There are a hell of a lot less who want to help women when they are pregnant and can't cope.

'There is a desperate need for this kind of work and women can be in really extreme situations.'

A Department of Health spokesman said 'We are aware that a minority of doctors choose to opt out from performing abortions, as they are legally entitled to do.

'However, this is not preventing women from accessing abortion services. The statistics show that the number of abortions being performed remains stable year on year and that more abortions are being performed earlier.'

She said the Department of Health would be discussing the issue of training with the college.

j.hope@dailymail.co.uk

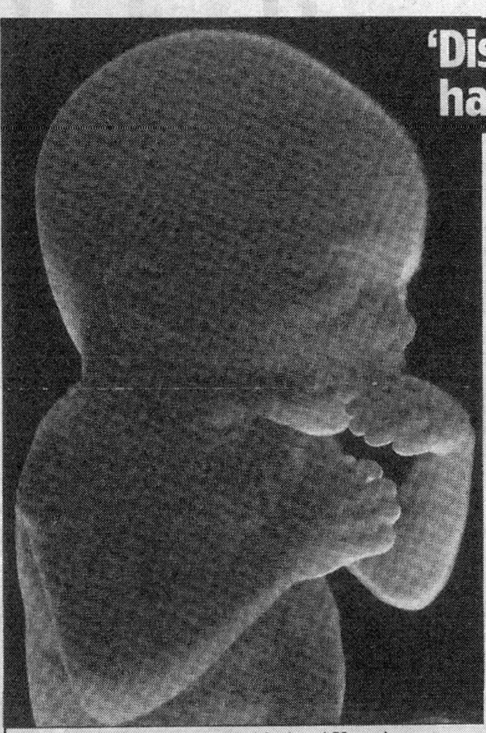

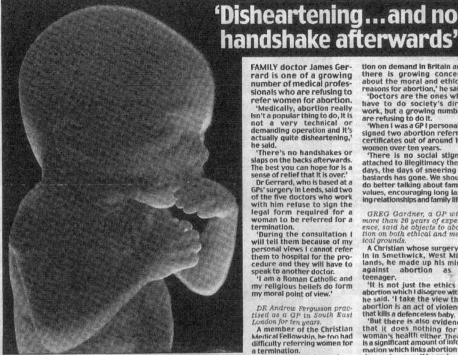

Sucking its thumb in the womb: A foetus at 20 weeks

'Disheartening...and no handshake afterwards'

FAMILY doctor James Gerrard is one of a growing number of medical professionals who are refusing to refer women for abortion.

'Medically, abortion really isn't a popular thing to do, it is not a very technical or demanding operation and it's actually quite disheartening,' he said.

'There's no handshakes or slaps on the backs afterwards. The best you can hope for is a sense of relief that it is over.'

Dr Gerrard, who is based at a GPs' surgery in Leeds, said two of the five doctors who work with him refuse to sign the legal form required for a woman to be referred for a termination.

'During the consultation I will tell them because of my personal views I cannot refer them to hospital for the procedure and they will have to speak to another doctor.

'I am a Roman Catholic and my religious beliefs do form my moral point of view.'

DR Andrew Fergusson practised as a GP in South East London for ten years.

A member of the Christian Medical Fellowship, he too had difficulty referring women for a termination.

'We effectively have abortion on demand in Britain and there is growing concern about the moral and ethical reasons for abortion,' he said.

'Doctors are the ones who have to do society's dirty work, but a growing number are refusing to do it.

'When I was a GP I personally signed two abortion referral certificates out of around 100 women over ten years.

'There is no social stigma attached to illegitimacy these days, the days of sneering at bastards has gone. We should do better talking about family values, encouraging long lasting relationships and family life.'

GREG Gardner, a GP with more than 20 years of experience, said he objects to abortion on both ethical and medical grounds.

A Christian whose surgery is in in Smethwick, West Midlands, he made up his mind against abortion as a teenager.

'It is not just the ethics of abortion which I disagree with,' he said. 'I take the view that abortion is an act of violence that kills a defenceless baby.

'But there is also evidence that it does nothing for a woman's health either. There is a significant amount of information which links abortion to depression or self harm.'

OUR DUTY IS TO SAVE LIVES
GOOD HEALTH – PAGE 57

Daily Mail, Tuesday April 17th 2007

Daily Mail, Tuesday, April 17, 2007 v1 Page 57

GoodHealth

I quit as a GP rather than refer women for abortions. Our duty is to SAVE lives

INCREASING numbers of doctors are refusing to carry out abortions, forcing the NHS to pay private hospitals for the procedures. Here, Dr Robert Hardie, a former GP, explains why he resigned rather than refer women for terminations.

GoodHealth VIEWPOINT

by Dr ROBERT HARDIE

NO GP should go against their conscience. So says the General Medical Council. If only the Department of Health understood this ethical stance, the droves of young doctors now refusing to perform abortions would not have to worry about losing their jobs for sticking to their principles.

That is effectively what happened to me, when I refused to sign the new General Practitioner's contract in 2004. It basically forced me to offer what is called a 'full family planning service' to any patient who asked for it. In practice, this meant I would be expected to refer women for a termination.

In my 25 years as a GP, first in Swanage, Dorset, and then in Melksham, Wiltshire, I have always tried to be guided by my conscience, which tells me that the taking of life, however small, is simply wrong.

This was against everything I — as a human being and as a doctor — believe in. My freedom to follow my conscience was at stake, so I quit. It was my only option, I had no choice. Principally, it is because I am a Catholic and believe in the sanctity of human life. This is not dogmatic belief. I was not born a Catholic but converted to the Roman Catholic Church in 1976, after the birth of my son Tim.

My wife Clare was a Catholic, and I was a committed Anglican, so it seemed a natural step at the time. But even before I converted I'd always believed that you just don't kill people. It is a doctor's role to protect life — it's what we're trained to do, which is why so many of us dislike the ideas of Living Wills and Euthanasia.

Before becoming a GP, I'd worked as a general surgeon. That was easy. There were no great dilemmas — if a bit needed chopping off, off it went. But abortions are entirely different and as I scoured the writings of medical ethicists, they only convinced me further of the sanctity of life.

My other prime concern was, of course, the patient. The legacy of abortion can be powerful. We're only just beginning to learn through research that, as well as the physical problems such as infertility, those who have had terminations may even suffer long-term psychiatric problems.

In my career, I have seen many young women who have suffered as a result of a decision to have an abortion. Sadness is easy to disguise at first, but their true suffering, which can take years to emerge, may manifest itself as unsuspected physical illness.

Doctors have a duty to these women for all their lives, not just one moment in time. Yet now, if a woman asks for a termination, her doctor must accede to her request.

I was also deeply concerned about what the GP contract meant for practitioners' independence. In my first practice, which was a large one, I was able to hand over any patients with concerns about abortion, or contraception, for that matter, to my colleagues. It was just a question of saying, sorry, wrong GP for that, and passing them on. I certainly didn't want to, and still don't, impose my beliefs on anyone else.

My partners didn't mind; with my surgical background, I trained as a general surgeon, I performed minor ops such as varicose veins and hernias for their patients. It was all pretty easy going.

But when I moved up to Melksham, Wiltshire, and started my own one-man practice, it became slightly more complicated. I made it plain to all my patients both in person and in the literature in my surgery that if that kind of treatment was what they wanted, they should seek help elsewhere.

UNFORTUNATELY, it became time for me to agree the new GP contract in 2004. Not only would I have been financially penalised for not offering the complete family planning package, which includes providing referrals for termination. But had I signed up, I would also have had to offer the referrals I so object to.

Faced with this, I quit as a GP and returned to surgery, operating at a local hospital removing skin cancers from faces and hands.

The Department of Health has effectively taken away the right for GPs to make our own medical decisions. It's all about ticking boxes, rather than treating individual patients. Doctors are increasingly being bullied by the health authorities, and their ability to work in an ethical fashion is being undermined.

Our society becomes more anti-life all the time. Terminations are on the rise, the abortion pill can be bought at the chemist, and euthanasia is creeping in through the back door, too.

If we GPs are not to be allowed to follow our consciences and protect life, who will?

Interview: VICTORIA LAMBERT

Daily Mail, Tuesday April 17th 2007

Half of late abortions are for women who didn't notice they were pregnant

Rosemary Bennett
Social Affairs Correspondent

Most women who have had late abortions say that they had not known they were pregnant for up to three months.

An extensive study of women who had abortions between 13 and 24 weeks found that half did not know they were pregnant for at least two months, and a further quarter only discovered their pregnancy at three months or later. Two in five said that their periods had continued.

The findings, published today by the University of Southampton and the University of Kent, will reignite the row over whether the limit for abortions should be reduced from 24 weeks to 22 or even 20 weeks.

The campaign to reduce the limit is fuelled by medical advances, which mean that babies born at 22 weeks can survive.

About 11 per cent of the 191,000 abortions carried out each year come in the second trimester. Ministers say they are not convinced by arguments to reduce the time limit and believe that there is no consensus among doctors.

The research, involving 883 women, found that while ignorance of their pregnancy was the primary reason for women seeking late abortions, other factors often conspired to push back the termination further.

About a third admitted that they had delayed for more than two weeks before carrying out a pregnancy test.

Once they were certain, half of the women took more than a week to decide what to do — often because of concerns about the procedure and disagreements with partners.

Another delay came when the women saw their doctor. Almost two thirds said that a significant period elapsed between their requesting an abortion and having it, even though medical guidelines emphasise the need for urgency at this stage.

Two in five waited for two weeks, and nearly a quarter waited three weeks. The main reason for delay was confusion among GPs over where late abortions could be carried out.

Investment in services has been heavily concentrated in early "chemical" abortions for women up to nine weeks pregnant, which are available widely in hospitals and clinics.

Late abortion services have almost all been contracted out, partly because many hospital doctors are unwilling to carry out the procedure. There are only about a dozen clinics specialising in late abortions.

Anne Furedi, of the British Pregnancy Advisory Service, said: "We see women who did not know enough about their own bodies to recognise the early symptoms of pregnancy, especially if they have irregular or continuing periods and continue to use contraception. We know that many family doctors are not up to date with modern abortion techniques and give women unclear advice."

Court ruling, page 43

SCIENCE PHOTO LIBRARY

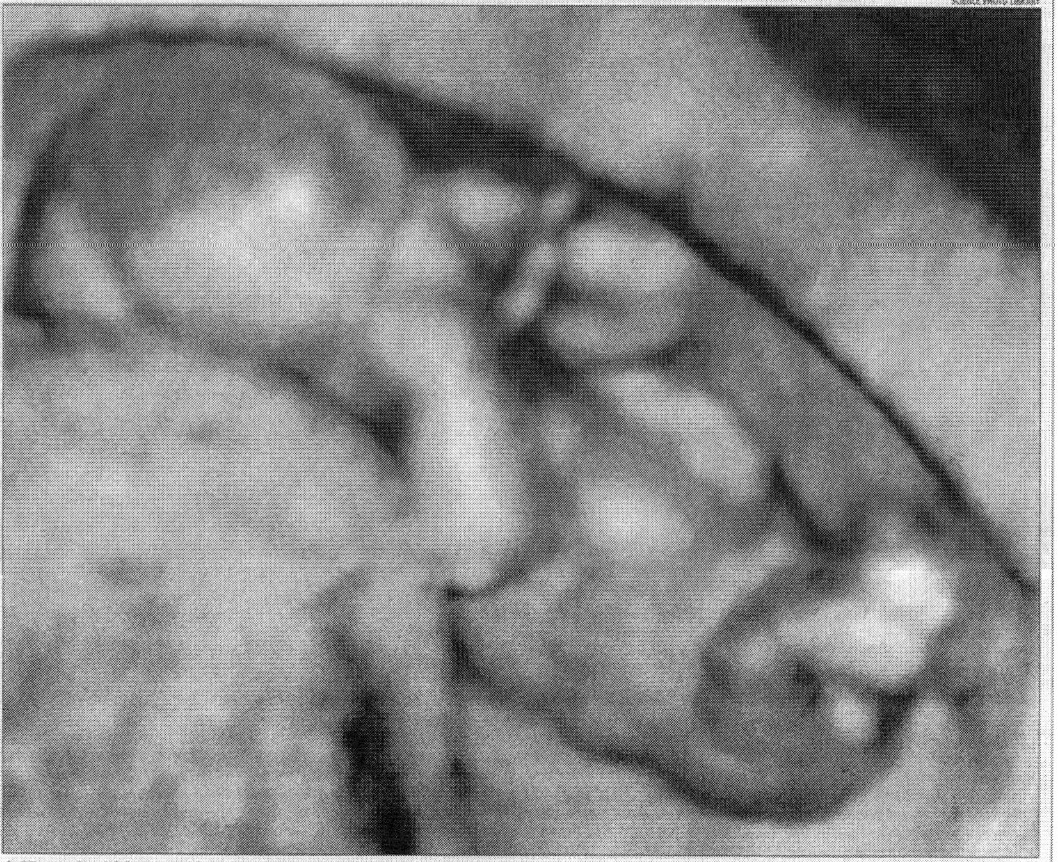

A 13-week-old foetus. Abortion is permitted up to 24 weeks, although medical advances allow babies born at 22 weeks to live

The figures

- 191,000 British women had abortions in 2005
- 89 per cent of the total were carried out before 13 weeks gestation, and 67 per cent before 10 weeks
- 32 per cent had had at least one previous abortion
- 84 per cent of abortions are funded by the NHS
- 52 per cent are performed under NHS contract in independent clinics, such as those run by Marie Stopes and the British Pregnancy Advisory Service

Source: Department of Health

'I put sudden weight gain down to comfort eating'

Jenny Gibb had no idea she was more than three months' pregnant until her ex-boyfriend persuaded her to take a test (Rosemary Bennett writes).

An advertising executive from Hampshire, she had longed for a child when she married but had been unable to conceive. When the marriage broke up she give up on the idea of starting a family.

"At the time I was 33, very lonely and miserable. I'd just ended a short relationship, there had been a death in my family and I was trying to sell my home. I knew I was putting on weight but put it down to comfort eating," she said.

Although she went to see her GP, he wasted time by referring her to the local hospital, an appointment nine days away. Then the hospital said that it could not help her as it did not offer a late abortion service. A consultant told her that the British Pregnancy Advisory Service might be able to help.

Ms Gibb contacted the organisation and had to travel to Brighton for her appointments. She was almost 18 weeks pregnant by the time she had the termination.

The Times, Thursday April 19th 2007

GAZETTE In Practice 31.05.07

RETIREMENT SCHEME
The Law Society's retirement benefits scheme unit linked section personal plan was 8089.9 on 24 May 2007.

EXPENSE OF TIME
Notional salaries for partners are £41,450 for London and £31,500 elsewhere.

INTEREST RATE
The base interest rate changed to 5.5% on 10 May 2007. The Law Society's interest rate is 9.5%.

Media law

By Amber Melville-Brown, David Price Solicitors and Advocates, London

The right not to be offended

***Veronica Connolly v Director of Public Prosecutions* [2007] EWHC 237 (Admin)**

The High Court has held that the rights of pharmacists not to receive grossly offensive material through the post outweighed the right of a Catholic protestor against the 'morning-after pill'.

Veronica Connolly was convicted in the magistrates' court of an offence under the Malicious Communications Act 1988, which provides that any person who sends to another person an article that conveys a message which is indecent or grossly offensive is guilty of an offence if his purpose or one of his purposes in sending it is to cause distress or anxiety to the recipient.

She had sent photographs of aborted foetuses to a number of chemists to express her view about abortion, including via the morning-after pill. One of the pharmacies complained, leading to her arrest, charge and conviction. She appealed to the Crown Court and then to the High Court by way of case stated. According to Lord Justice Dyson, who heard the appeal, she had to show that the decision that the photographs were indecent and grossly offensive 'was one which no court acquainted with the ordinary use of language could have reached'.

Ms Connolly argued that given current standards were so low, the material could not be regarded as indecent or grossly offensive, and that where the communication of complaint was part of a lawful protest, conviction under the Act would constitute an infringement of her rights to freedom of expression (and religious expression) guaranteed by article 10 (and 9) of the European Convention on Human Rights.

The High Court found, as a matter of fact, that she had sent 'close-up colour photographs of dead 21-week-old foetuses', that she did so with the purpose of causing distress or anxiety and that recipients of the material were actually offended by it: 'They are shocking and disturbing. That is why Mrs Connolly sent them to the pharmacists.' According to Lord Justice Dyson: 'It is impossible to say that no reasonable tribunal could have concluded that these images were grossly offensive.' However, the court had to consider her competing article 10 (and 9) rights.

The court found that her article 10 rights were engaged: 'The sending of the photographs was an exercise of the right to freedom of expression... Since it related to political issues, it was an expression of the kind that is regarded as particularly entitled to protection by article 10.' It then considered whether the interference with that right was prescribed by law, necessary in a democratic society, and was to further the legitimate aim of the rights of others.

The court accepted the Director of Public Prosecutions' submission that the right not to receive such material, when it was sent for the purpose prescribed in the Act, was a 'right of others' within the meaning of article 10(2), although the right to be protected would depend both on the offensiveness of the material and the party requiring protection. For example, a doctor used to seeing such things might be 'less likely to find the photographs grossly offensive than the pharmacist's employees'.

Undertaking a final balancing exercise between the relevant engaged rights, the court found that Mrs Connolly's right to express her views about abortion did not justify the distress and anxiety that she intended to cause.

The recipients were not targeted because they could influence a public debate on abortion. The most she could hope to do was to persuade the recipient shops not to sell the morning-after pill. Even if she managed to achieve that limited result, it would not be likely to contribute greatly to any public debate about abortion. Accordingly, the offence had been made out and was not mitigated by the exercise of her free speech or indeed freedom of thought under guaranteed by article 9.

Photograph: Alamy

Post: fine balance between rights of the sender and recipient

The right to offend

***Vereinigung Bildender Kunstler v Austria* ECHR 25 January 2007, Application number 68354/01**

While Ms Connolly was convicted in the UK for having offended others, an art exhibition in Austria did not offend to such an extent as to outweigh the artist's and exhibitor's right to freedom of expression.

In 1998, an association of artists put on a public exhibition entitled 'the century of artistic freedom', which included 'Apocalypse', a painting by Austrian artist Otto Muhl, which so offended one incensed exhibition goer that he defaced it with red paint shortly before the exhibition closed. Mr Meischberger, a member of the National Assembly (*Nationalratsabgeordneter*) was equally incensed, given that he featured in it, being shown gripping the ejaculating penis of Jorg Haider while at the same time being touched by two other politicians and ejaculating on Mother Teresa.

He sought an injunction against

Media law

any further exhibition of the work, claiming it 'debased him and his political activities, and made statements as to his allegedly loose sexual life'. The Vienna Commercial Court rejected the claim on the grounds, as summarised by the European Court of Human Rights (ECtHR) majority judgment, that it 'resembled a comic strip' and 'obviously did not represent reality'. It also featured representatives of the claimant's political party, the FPO, which had strongly criticised Mr Muhl's work and could consequently be considered 'a kind of counter attack'.

On appeal, the Vienna Court of Appeal granted an injunction prohibiting any further exhibition of the work; his image was substantially deformed by wholly imaginary elements without it being evident that it was aimed at satire or exaggeration. The painting did not fall within the scope of article 10 and merely constituted a debasement of the claimant's political standing. The Supreme Court rejected an appeal and the matter proceeded to the ECtHR.

The majority here accepted that the painting did portray Mr Meischberger in a somewhat outrageous manner, but it 'amounted to a caricature of the persons concerned using satirical elements'. It did not concern his private life but his public standing as a politician and, accordingly, he had to 'display a wider tolerance in respect of criticism'. Further, the court did not find unreasonable the first instance finding that the portrayal could be understood to constitute some sort of counter-attack against the FPO. It held that 'satire is a form of artistic expression and social commentary and, by its inherent features of exaggeration and distortion of reality, naturally aims to provoke and agitate. Accordingly, any interference with an artist's right to such expression must be examined with particular care'. And so it did. The injunction was 'disproportionate to the aim it pursued and therefore not necessary in a democratic society'. There had been a violation of article 10.

The court was finely divided in this case, finding in the applicant's favour by a majority of four to three. The huge divergence of opinion may not be surprising given the subject-matter, which Judge Loucaides described as 'a senseless, disgusting combination of lewd images whose only effect is to debase, insult and ridicule each and every person portrayed'.

The majority decision of the court reiterated that freedom of expression 'constitutes one of the essential foundations of a democratic society, indeed one of the basic conditions for its progress and for the self-fulfilment of the individual'. It is applicable 'not only to "information" or "ideas" that are favourably received or regarded as inoffensive or as a matter of indifference, but also to those that offend, shock or disturb'.

These cases show that the courts have to undertake a fact-specific assessment of the various rights at play when considering matters of this nature. While these two decisions might seem to run counter to each other, it is this personalised analysis of the individual facts and rights at play that should result in cases which affect individuals but also societies as a whole, that the right to offend or not to be offended are in the majority of cases fairly balanced and justice is ultimately done.

Law Society's Gazette May 31st 2007

Page 20 XA Daily Mail, Wednesday, June 20, 2007

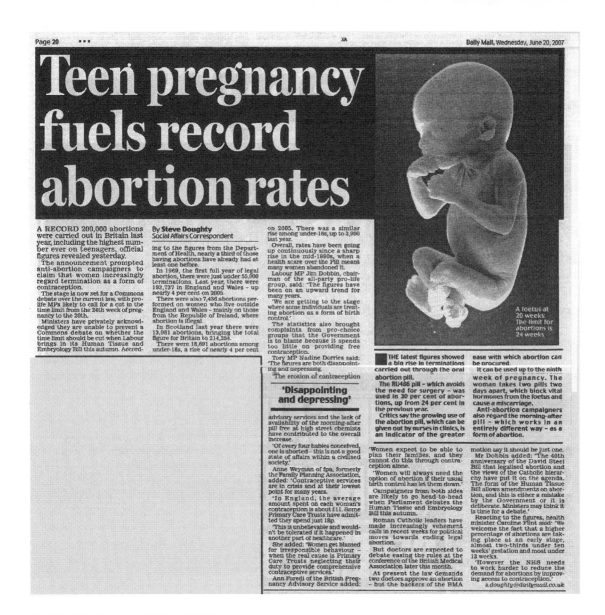

Teen pregnancy fuels record abortion rates

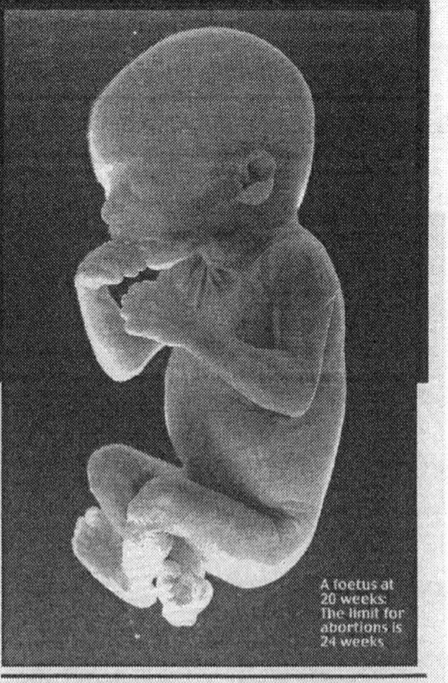

A foetus at 20 weeks: The limit for abortions is 24 weeks

By **Steve Doughty**
Social Affairs Correspondent

A RECORD 200,000 abortions were carried out in Britain last year, including the highest number ever on teenagers, official figures revealed yesterday.

The announcement prompted anti-abortion campaigners to claim that women increasingly regard termination as a form of contraception.

The stage is now set for a Commons debate over the current law, with pro-life MPs likely to call for a cut in the time limit from the 24th week of pregnancy to the 20th.

Ministers have privately acknowledged they are unable to prevent a Commons debate on whether the time limit should be cut when Labour brings in its Human Tissue and Embryology Bill this autumn. According to the figures from the Department of Health, nearly a third of those having abortions have already had at least one before.

In 1969, the first full year of legal abortion, there were just under 55,000 terminations. Last year, there were 193,737 in England and Wales – up nearly 4 per cent on 2005.

There were also 7,436 abortions performed on women who live outside England and Wales – mainly on those from the Republic of Ireland, where abortion is illegal.

In Scotland last year there were 13,081 abortions, bringing the total figure for Britain to 214,254.

There were 18,691 abortions among under-18s, a rise of nearly 4 per cent on 2005. There was a similar rise among under-16s, up to 3,990 last year.

Overall, rates have been going up continuously since a sharp rise in the mid-1990s, when a health scare over the Pill meant many women abandoned it.

Labour MP Jim Dobbin, chairman of the all-party pro-life group, said: 'The figures have been on an upward trend for many years.

'We are getting to the stage where some individuals are treating abortion as a form of birth control.'

The statistics also brought complaints from pro-choice groups that the Government is to blame because it spends too little on providing free contraception.

Tory MP Nadine Dorries said: 'The figures are both disappointing and depressing.

'The erosion of contraception advisory services and the lack of availability of the morning-after pill free at high street chemists have contributed to the overall increase.

'Disappointing and depressing'

'Of every four babies conceived, one is aborted – this is not a good state of affairs within a civilised society.'

Anne Weyman of fpa, formerly the Family Planning Association, added: 'Contraceptive services are in crisis and at their lowest point for many years.

'In England, the average amount spent on each woman's contraception is about £11. Some Primary Care Trusts have admitted they spend just 18p.

'This is unbelievable and wouldn't be tolerated if it happened in another part of healthcare.'

She added: 'Women get blamed for irresponsible behaviour – when the real cause is Primary Care Trusts neglecting their duty to provide comprehensive contraceptive services.'

Ann Furedi of the British Pregnancy Advisory Service added: 'Women expect to be able to plan their families, and they cannot do this through contraception alone.

'Women will always need the option of abortion if their usual birth control has let them down.'

Campaigners from both sides are likely to go head-to-head when Parliament debates the Human Tissue and Embryology Bill this autumn.

Roman Catholic leaders have made increasingly vehement calls in recent weeks for political moves towards ending legal abortion.

But doctors are expected to debate easing the rules at the conference of the British Medical Association later this month.

At present the law demands two doctors approve an abortion – but the backers of the BMA motion say it should be just one.

Mr Dobbin added: 'The 40th anniversary of the David Steel Bill that legalised abortion and the views of the Catholic hierarchy have put it on the agenda. The form of the Human Tissue Bill allows amendments on abortion, and this is either a mistake by the Government or it is deliberate. Ministers may think it is time for a debate.'

Reacting to the figures, health minister Caroline Flint said: 'We welcome the fact that a higher percentage of abortions are taking place at an early stage, almost two-thirds under ten weeks' gestation and most under 13 weeks.

'However the NHS needs to work harder to reduce the demand for abortions by improving access to contraception.'

s.doughty@dailymail.co.uk

THE latest figures showed a big rise in terminations carried out through the oral abortion pill.

The RU486 pill – which avoids the need for surgery – was used in 30 per cent of abortions, up from 24 per cent in the previous year.

Critics say the growing use of the abortion pill, which can be given out by nurses in clinics, is an indicator of the greater ease with which abortion can be procured.

It can be used up to the ninth week of pregnancy. The woman takes two pills two days apart, which block vital hormones from the foetus and cause a miscarriage.

Anti-abortion campaigners also regard the morning-after pill – which works in an entirely different way – as a form of abortion.

Daily Mail June 20th 2007

Restraint in sexual practice is a common theme with the British Press as readers will discover for themselves. In Norway restraint is regarded as an abnormality of mind or puritanical fanaticism. But even Anders Breivik blamed the 'moral sickness' of Norwegian female promiscuity on the annual abortion cull of his beloved Aryan Norwegians. The point is these clots of blood will, if left alone, go on to be living human beings. Abortion regret is rampant. Children-to-be ... that barren women long to have and pay vast sums for fertility treatment to try to remedy. This segment finishes off with British Press commentary on religion, homosexuality which for many is still a perversion. And Anders Breivik, a man whose beliefs, but not actions, received widespread support in Norway. His hatred for Muslims was mirrored in the former Yugoslavia by his Serb heroes: and to this day the vitriolic diatribe against Muslims continues in Norway.

THE TIMES

Monday October 15 2007 timesonline.co.uk No 69142 3GM 70p

Male infertility alert over hidden bacteria

▶ Chlamydia shown to pose risk for both sexes

▶ 10 per cent of young Britons carry infection

Mark Henderson Science Editor
Washington

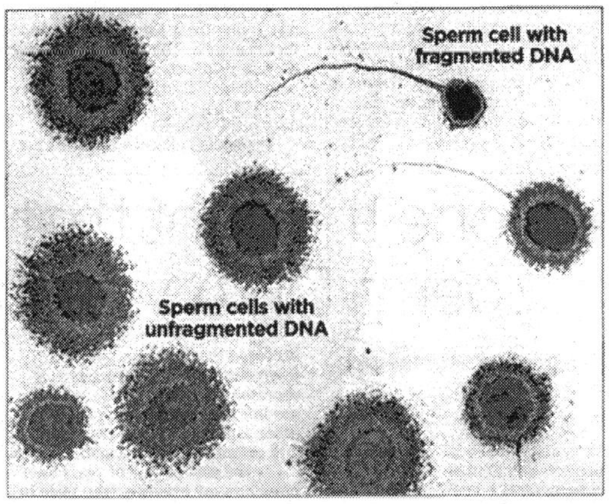

Chlamydia, the sexually transmitted infection (STI) carried by one in ten sexually-active young British adults can make men infertile by damaging the quality of their sperm, new research has shown.

While the condition, which usually passes undetected, has long been known to threaten female fertility, scientists from Spain and Mexico have now established that it presents similar risks for men.

Men with chlamydia have three times the normal number of sperm with genetic damage that can impair their ability to father children, the study found.

Antibiotic treatment can reverse the effect, and preliminary results indicate that it may dramatically enhance pregnancy rates when couples are trying for a baby. But the discovery suggests that the prevalence of the disease may be contributing to infertility across an entire generation of young adults.

Britain's national screening programme has found that 10.2 per cent of both men and women aged 18 to 25 carry the bacteria, and studies have found infection rates as high as 5 per cent among older groups with a lower risk.

The findings indicate that untreated chlamydia infections should not just concern women, who have long been warned that the condition can make them infertile, but has direct consequences for men.

This will create fresh pressure for chlamydia screening to be more effectively targeted at young men, who rarely seek testing and treatment unless they develop symptoms, which are often absent or quickly fade.

Doctors have already warned that the rise in the number of chlamydia cases in Britain may rob thousands of young women of the chance to have children. Figures from the Health Protection Agency reveal that cases of chlamydia have increased by more than 200 per cent in England in the past decade.

Chlamydia is easily treated with antibiotics, typically a week's course of doxycycline or a single dose of azithromycin, but testing is necessary first.

Allan Pacey, senior lecturer in andrology at the University of Sheffield and secretary of the British Fertility Society, said that the emerging understanding of how chlamydia affects male fertility should change the way that society approaches the condition.

"We might think of chlamydia as a disease that damages female fertility, but we need to think again," he said. "It does damage female fertility, but it appears to damage male fertility, too.

"Previously, it was thought that the most worrying thing about chlamydia infections in men was as a conduit for the infection of women. The thing that drives most men to sexual health clinics is symptoms, and chlamydia is often symptom-free. Chlamydia is getting out of control. We have got to encourage men as well as women to go for screening."

In the study, a team led by José Luis Fernández, of the Juan Canalejo University Hospital in La Coruña, examined sperm samples taken from 193 men seeking fertility treatment with their partners in Monterey, Mexico.

Of these, 143 were infected with

Continued on page 2, column 3

Brown told to stand up to EU treaty 'bullies'

Gordon Brown was urged to fight back against "bullying tactics" by European nations determined to water down British sovereignty in the EU treaty. Late changes may make it harder for Britain to preserve the red lines intended to defend national control of justice and police systems. **News, page 4**

Thai flood kills Briton

A British woman who was the sole survivor of a flash flood in Thailand that killed eight people last night described how she saw her fiancé washed to his death after saving her life. **News, page 3**

Stop using fresh milk

Civil servants have proposed that Britons stop using fresh milk in favour of the long-life alternative in an attempt to reduce the greenhouse gas emissions caused by refrigeration. **News, page 15**

Britain's top quality newspaper

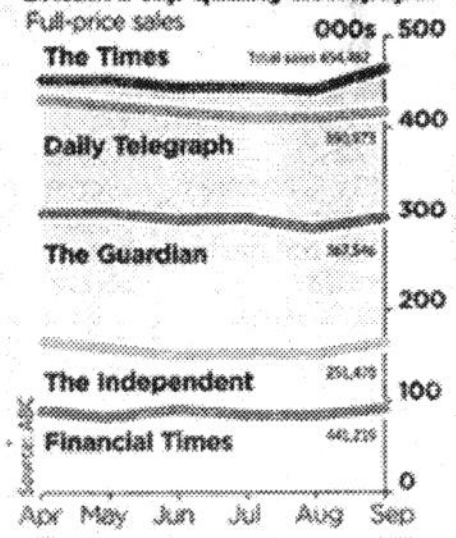

Full-rate sales of *The Times* were ahead of *The Daily Telegraph* for the 35th consecutive month, according to the latest figures from the Audit Bureau of Circulation.
Total circulations: The Times 654,482, The Daily Telegraph 890,973, The Guardian 367,546, The Independent 251,470, Financial Times 441,219

Male fertility alert over hidden bacteria carried by 1 in 10 young Britons

Continued from page 1

both chlamydia and mycoplasma, another common sexually transmitted bacterium, while 50 were uninfected and served as healthy controls.

Dr Fernández, who will present his findings today at the American Society for Reproductive Medicine conference in Washington, then examined the men's sperm for a form of genetic damage called DNA fragmentation. This can cause sperm to die, as well as hindering their ability to fertilise eggs and embryonic development.

An average of 35 per cent of the infected men's sperm was damaged, a proportion 3.2 times higher than in the healthy controls.

"We found there was a three-fold increase in the fragmentation of DNA in sperm cells compared with controls, and this could have a potential role in subfertility," Dr Fernández said.

In the infected group, both partners were treated with antibiotics. During the early stages of treatment, just 12.5 per cent of the couples conceived but, when therapy was complete, 85.7 per cent had achieved a pregnancy.

Successful treatment of the male partners is more likely to have been responsible for this effect.

Chlamydia causes female infertility as a result of chronic infection, which causes damage to the Fallopian tubes, and once this has occurred it is not usually reversed by treatment.

Men, however, produce new sperm so quickly and in such abundance that removing the infection will rapidly improve sperm quality. After treatment, the infected men produced many fewer genetically damaged sperm.

"After four months of treatment, there was a significant decrease in DNA damage that could improve pregnancy rates in these couples," Dr Fernández said. "It seems related to an improved pregnancy rate. It's a very dramatic difference, but this is a small number of couples, so the results are only preliminary."

The findings suggest that infertility patients of both sexes should be routinely screened for chlamydia, as already happens in most British clinics.

Dr Pacey said: "I would advise couples trying for a baby to be screened for chlamydia. The difficulty is that a positive diagnosis carries implications of infidelity, but of course as it can be asymptomatic the infection could have been there for many years."

Chlamydia's effects on female infertility are well-established. If left untreated, up to 40 per cent of women will develop pelvic inflammatory disease, which can cause tubal scarring that leads to infertility and an increased risk of ectopic pregnancy.

In men, chlamydia can lead to swelling of the testicles or epididymis, and either can cause sterility if not treated. However, both conditions are generally treated before they cause long-term damage as they are painful.

Leading article, page 20

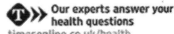

Most common sexually transmitted infection

- Chlamydia is caused by the bacterium *Chlamydia trachomatis*
- It is the most common sexually transmitted infection in Britain, with 109,958 confirmed diagnoses in 2005, and the incidence is increasing
- The true figure is thought to be much higher as the condition often has no symptoms, and can pass undetected for years
- Symptoms can include discharge from the vagina or penis or pain on urination, but it often has no symptoms at all
- A study of male Army recruits found that one in ten had chlamydia, but 88 per cent of these had had no symptoms

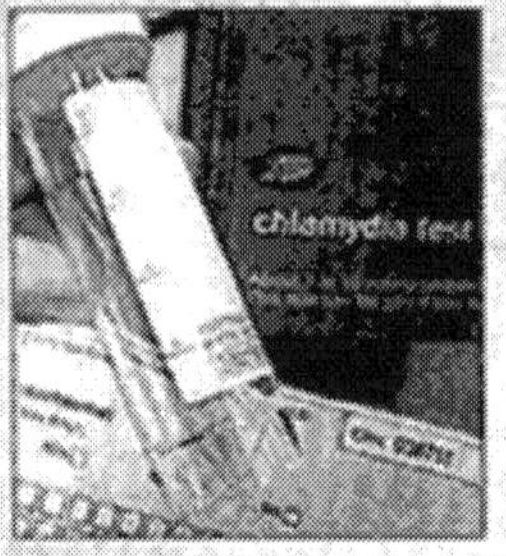

- Left untreated, it will cause pelvic inflammatory disease in up to 40 per cent of women. This can cause scarring to the Fallopian tubes, leading to infertility or a raised risk of ectopic pregnancy
- In men, it can cause epididymitis or orchitis — swelling of the epididymis at the top of the testicle, or of the testicle itself. This is painful, and can cause scarring and infertility if untreated
- Chlamydia can be detected by a simple urine test; swabs are no longer necessary. Postal kits, above left, are available from Boots at £25, and a national free screening programme exists for under-25s

Source: Health Protection Agency, Times database

Comment

Chlamydia's Young Toll

Complacency over safe sex has led to a worrying rise in cases

One in ten sexually active young British adults carries chlamydia, which can cause serious damage to fertility. And as infection rates rise steeply, doctors have stepped up warnings on the dangers of this disease. The awareness campaign has focused on women, as chlamydia was thought to affect them particularly. But new research now shows that the risk to men is equally worrying: men with chlamydia have three times the normal number of sperm with genetic damage. The findings coincide with recent indications that infection rates are rising fast for a range of other sexually transmitted infections (STIs) and that young people, who are most at risk, have become complacent about public health warnings.

Convincing young people to be responsible in their sexual behaviour is hard enough; it is particularly difficult to make men aware of the dangers to themselves of chlamydia, as there are often no symptoms and many are unaware that they are carrying the bacteria. Nevertheless, Britain's national screening programme has found that 10.2 per cent of those aged 18-25 are infected, and even among older groups less at risk the rate is running at 5 per cent. Male reluctance to be tested is particularly unfortunate, as chlamydia is easily treated with antibiotics. Typically, a week's course of doxycycline or a single dose of azithromycin is sufficient. If untreated, however, the disease can produce real harm: sperm suffers a form of genetic damage called DNA fragmentation, which can cause it to die as well as hindering its ability to fertilise eggs and normal embryonic development. Tests in America have found that more than one in three infected men have damaged sperm, although this recovers after treatment. For women, the consequences are more obvious: chronic infection will cause damage to the Fallopian tubes that is not normally reversible.

Any infection, however, also increases the risk of catching other STIs, some of which are far more serious. Syphilis and gonorrhoea, diseases that caused panic a few centuries ago, are on the rise again after falling sharply in the 1980s, when the warnings on Aids produced generally more responsible sexual behaviour. Between 1997 and 2006, syphilis increased by 1,607 per cent, gonorrhoea by 46 per cent, chlamydia by 166 per cent and herpes by 36 per cent. The number of cases of gonorrhoea, at 19,000 a year, is still below the peak rate of 80,000 in 1975. But the rise is similar to the other worrying trend, which appears to be born of complacency: the rise in HIV infection.

The Conservative Government's dramatic public awareness campaign to promote safe sex amid fears of an Aids epidemic in the 1980s was one of the most successful of all public health campaigns. HIV-deniers ridiculed the stark warnings, saying that the relatively small incidence of Aids showed there was never a danger; more responsible commentators applauded a campaign that may have prevented the kind of social catastrophe now seen in southern Africa and elsewhere. The message needs repeating. It need not be so apocalyptic: Aids can now be contained, if not cured. But it is still important to warn people about the dangers, physical, social and moral, of irresponsible sexual behaviour. The message needs constant updating, both for the naive young and for complacent adults, and no taboo should curb communication. The choice is clear: spread the message or allow infection to spread.

The Times October 15th 2007

£0.80
Wednesday 24.10.07
Published
in London and
Manchester
guardian.co.uk
the guardian

Too many abortions: Lord Steel

Sponsor of 1967 Act calls for greater sexual responsibility

Lucy Ward and Riazat Butt

Lord Steel, architect of the 1967 Abortion Act, says today that abortion is being used as a form of contraception in Britain and admits he never anticipated "anything like" the current number of terminations when leading the campaign for reform.

The Liberal Democrat peer, whose bill legalising abortion in certain circumstances marks its 40th anniversary on Saturday, says an "irresponsible" mood has emerged in which women feel they can turn to abortion "if things go wrong".

"Everybody can agree that there are too many abortions," he says in an interview in today's Guardian, calling for better sex education and access to contraceptive advice and a debate over sexual morality to help bring the numbers down.

There were almost 194,000 terminations in England and Wales last year, rising to over 200,000 when women coming from Northern Ireland and the Irish republic are included. That was almost 4% up on the previous year, with abortions among teenagers the fastest rising group.

The figures were described yesterday by Catholic church leaders as "a source of distress and profound anguish for us all", in the run-up to likely attempts by both pro- and anti-abortion campaigners to reform the current law this autumn.

Lord Steel, who endured threats of violence and sacks of hate mail when pushing through his private member's bill as a young MP 40 years ago, makes clear he has "no regrets" over the landmark legislation, and does not regard restricting access to abortion as the answer to the rising number of terminations.

He says he is not yet persuaded that the upper legal time limit should be cut from its present 24 weeks – a limit endorsed by the BMA and other medical bodies – and believes there is a strong case that the requirement for two doctors' signatures in order to have an abortion should be dropped in the first 13 weeks of pregnancy in order to limit delays and distress.

He conceded yesterday that the Archbishop of Canterbury, Dr Rowan Williams, "had a point" in warning in an article in last Sunday's Observer that abortion is now being treated as too easy to obtain.

Lord Steel said: "I accept that there is a mood now which is that if things go wrong you can get an abortion, and it is irresponsible, really. I think people should be a bit more responsible in their activities, and in particular in the use of contraception."

He says a lack of research into the reasons women choose to have an abortion is hampering efforts to tackle the problem of rising numbers. But, asked whether abortion is being used in some cases as a form of contraception, he said: "I am afraid it is."

He added: "At the moment we are all operating in the dark. But I think there is a view that particularly those who present for repeated abortions are treating it as 'long stop' [back-up] contraception." Parliament never intended the law to be used in that way, said Lord Steel, who brought his legislation in an effort to save the lives of pregnant women dying at the hands of back street abortionists or by suicide.

He wants improved sex education in schools covering both sexual ethics and the use of contraception.

But he said the Catholic church's opposition to contraception "is absolutely contributing to the use of abortion as contraception".

Lord Steel's comments, in which he effectively qualifies the gains brought by his legislation, provoked surprise and frustration from women's health campaigners. Ann Furedi, chief executive of BPAS, the UK charity providing abortion and contraceptive care, said: "There are many positive reasons why abortion numbers can increase – because women are more easily able to access the services they need, because more abortion care is funded by the NHS, and because more women now believe abortion is an acceptable option

9»

Continued on page 2 »

There are too many abortions, says Lord Steel

« continued from page 1

if they are faced with an unintended pregnancy.

"If you are opposed to abortion in principle, these changes will be unwelcome, but if you believe that women should be able to make decisions about their reproductive future, then these are positive changes.

"Of course its better to prevent an unwanted pregnancy than to end one in abortion. I've never met a woman in a BPAS abortion clinic who didn't want to not be there. No woman aspires to have an abortion.

"But abortion is not in itself the problem. The problem is the unwanted pregnancy and abortion can be the solution to that for many women. There's no right or wrong number; we need as many abortions as are necessary to solve the problem pregnancies that women face."

She added: "We see parenthood completely differently now – it is not something you drift into because a condom slipped any more. We spend a lot of time worrying about parenting. Women today feel much more strongly about being able to plan when and whether to become a mother."

Lord Steel's comments come as the debate over abortion in Britain reaches its highest pitch in years.

Public health minister Dawn Primarolo is expected today to tell a Commons science and technology committee inquiry into scientific developments affecting abortion that she sees no evidence of the need to reduce the 24-week limit.

That view is shared by medical leaders, including the BMA, the Royal College of Obstetricians and Gynaecologists, and the Royal College of Nursing.

The MPs' committee will also examine the question of whether women should still need to obtain two doctors' signatures to secure an abortion in the first three months of pregnancy.

Polling released yesterday by the pro-choice group Abortion Rights suggests a slight majority – 52% – of the public support liberalisation of the law to require the permission of only one doctor or none.

The NOP poll also showed 83% of the public believe it is a woman's right to decide to have an abortion, with only 13% saying they thought a woman should not have this right.

Changes to restrict or liberalise access to abortion could come via amendments to the human tissue and embryology bill, which is due to come before parliament within weeks.

In an open letter to the British public, cardinals from the Catholic church sidestepped the issue of the law, saying the abortion rate could fall dramatically if enough hearts and minds were changed.

The letter outlined several ways that institutions and individuals could effect a drop in numbers, including offering more sympathetic counselling for pregnant young women, dismantling the "conveyor belt" that could take a young woman through to having an abortion without a thorough exploration of alternatives and providing more and better facilities for young women who choose to have their babies.

The letter, signed by Cardinal Cormac Murphy O'Connor and Cardinal Keith O'Brien, said: "The 1967 Act was intended to solve the problem of illegal abortion, on the basis that it was a major cause of death in pregnant women. Yet our countries now perform nearly 200,000 abortions every year.

"Whatever our religious creed or political conviction, abortion on this scale can only be a source of distress and profound anguish for us all. There is nothing to stop our society from acting now to foster a new understanding and approach to relationships, responsibility and mutual support."

Society, cover story »

The Guardian Wednesday 24th October 2007

Aids fear as Bush blocks sex lessons

US undermines global declaration

by Gaby Hinsliff
Chief Political Correspondent

PRESIDENT George W. Bush is blocking an international drive to provide teenage sex education because of his belief in chastity before marriage. Health experts say this could fatally undermine the battle against Aids.

Bush has poured millions of dollars into 'true love waits'-style programmes in America, which teach that abstinence out of wedlock is the best way to avoid underage pregnancy.

Now he has triggered a row with British and other European Union governments by refusing to sign a United Nations declaration on children's rights – designed to set funding priorities across the Third World – unless pledges on sexual health services are scrapped.

Experts argue that inflicting such views on Aids-stricken nations could have a catastrophic impact on millions of young people, threatening funding for life-saving drives to encourage condom use and safe abortions.

Clare Short's Department for International Development insists there should be no retreat on contraception – setting the stage for a clash at this week's UN summit on children's rights.

'All the evidence shows that women who have access to good reproductive health services have fewer children, grow up healthier and, in turn, are more likely to go to school,' said Hilary Benn, Minister for International Development, who will attend the summit.

The Bush delegation objects to pledges to guarantee 'reproductive and mental health services' for under-18s and 'protect the right of adolescents to sex education and avoiding unwanted/early pregnancies'.

Backed by the Vatican, it is understood to have been pushing for guarantees that UN-funded sex education programmes will include commitments to preach chastity outside marriage.

That would stop Third World teachers discussing contraception honestly, campaigners say, with fatal consequences. Every minute, five people under 25 are infected with HIV worldwide, while 10 teenage girls undergo an unsafe abortion.

President Bush objects on moral grounds to wider sex education.

'I think it's just a scandal,' said Françoise Girard, senior programme officer for the International Women's Health Coalition. 'In today's world with HIV/Aids and sex abuse scandals, it is really unconscionable that the US should be objecting to a discussion of a full range of topics.

'This weakens the political will and also affects the budgets and the plans of UN agencies. If it goes to a vote, the US will lose. But the US is a big funder, and the worry is that they will follow that with a refusal to fund UN agencies involved in this work.'

A similar impasse over the morning-after pill at a UN summit on women's health two years ago – triggered by the Vatican – prompted Short to accuse the Catholic Church of being 'morally destructive' and in an 'unholy alliance with reactionary forces'. Talks to broker a deal resume tomorrow, but the Bush administration, supported by the Vatican and Islamic countries, is sticking to its guns.

ABCEFHPRST 9 770029 771427 18

★★★ No 10,986

President Bush: Chastity before Marriage Campaign.
The Observer - Sunday 5th May 2002

26 4M **The Times** **FRIDAY OCTOBER 31 2003** WORLD NEWS

God helped me to quit drinking, says Bush

From Tim Reid
in Washington

PRESIDENT Bush publicly asserted for the first time yesterday that it was his discovery of God that ended his days of heavy drinking and wild behaviour.

Offering an unusually candid assessment of how religion had delivered him from his wayward youth and early adulthood, Mr Bush told an audience at a Christian youth centre in Dallas, Texas: "You've got to understand that sometimes, and a lot of times, the best way to help the addict, a person who is stuck on drugs and alcohol, is to change their heart. See, if you change their heart, then they change their behaviour. I know."

Mr Bush, a born-again evangelical Christian, rediscovered God 17 years ago when he gave up drinking the morning after his 40th birthday, a move triggered by a colossal hangover and a desire to help his marriage.

His faith in the power of God now permeates the White House and underscores all his policies, making his presidency the most overtly religious of modern times.

Mr Bush has often spoken of how important religion is in his life, but yesterday was the first time that he linked his discovery of God so directly to his decision to give up drinking and mend his boorish ways.

Much has been written about Mr Bush's days as a heavy drinker, but his reference to "drugs and alcohol" intrigued some political observers. It is unlikely Mr Bush was making a subtle admission that he also took drugs in the past, but questions of cocaine use dogged his presidential campaign in 1999.

Mr Bush was finally forced to say in August 1999 that he had not used illegal drugs at any time during the past 25 years.

The stories of his wild days as a Yale student, which continued into his married life and early business and political career, are manifold.

He admitted driving over the alcohol limit in 1976, when he was 30. His irreverence and sometime boorishness even continued through his father's presidency and into his own.

In May 1991 his father played host to the Queen at a White House state banquet. When his mother introduced him to the monarch he told her that he was the black sheep of the Bush family, and then asked her: "Who's yours?" She told him it was none of his business.

Since the September 11 terrorist attacks, however, Mr Bush has imbued his domestic and foreign policy with an understated but evangelical zeal.

One of the cornerstones of his domestic programme, which formed part of his visit to Texas yesterday, is his "faith-based initiative".

This gives churches and religious groups the chance to run federal welfare programmes, a bid to cut federal costs while promoting religion at a grass-roots level.

Although every US president has invoked God and asked for divine guidance, no recent White House has appeared so rooted in a president's belief in God, or the conviction that faith is an answer to society's problems and combating terror.

Although repeatedly emphasising that Islam is a "religion of peace", Mr Bush told the American public that in Saddam Hussein the nation was "encountering evil".

Marking his decision to invade Iraq reflected Mr Bush's division of the world into the forces of good and evil. "If anyone can be at peace," he said shortly before the invasion, "I am at peace about this."

At the White House very few staffers drink or smoke. Non-attendance at Bible class is frowned upon. As soon as he rises every day, Mr Bush reads a daily devotional written by Oswald Chambers, a First World War Scottish preacher.

"There is a fatalistic element in Mr Bush's faith," wrote David Frum, a former White House speechwriter in his autobiography of the President. "You do your best and accept everything is in God's hands."

But Mr Bush has been at pains to distance himself from comments made by Lieutenant-General William Boykin, an evangelical Christian recently appointed as the Pentagon's chief intelligence officer. In addition to portraying the war on terrorism as a clash with Satan and a religious conflict, General Boykin told church audiences in recent months that: "George Bush was not elected by a majority of voters in the United States, he was appointed by God."

Mr Bush made clear on Tuesday that General Boykin's views did not reflect his own.

Evangelical Christians and the religious Right are Mr Bush's strongest supporters. Turning them out next year to vote in the presidential election is one of the top priorities of Karl Rove, Mr Bush's political strategist.

The cornerstone of Republican success in presidential elections now lies in the South. Since the late 1960s the Republicans have wrested control of the South from the Democrats — a political revolution that was key to the victories of Ronald Reagan and of President Bush's father as well as his own. One of the voting blocs that has handed the Republicans this new-found dominance in the South is formed by conservative Christians.

CHARLES DHARAPAK / AP

True confession: Mr Bush told a Christian youth centre in Dallas of his battle with drink

God helped me to quit drinking, says Bush
The Times Friday October 31, 2003

Daily Express

WEDNESDAY SEPTEMBER 14 1994 WEATHER: CHILLY 32p ★★★

Explosion of lone mothers

Threat to family life as figures triple in decade

By PATRICK HENNESSY
Chief Political Correspondent

A STERN warning of the social problems posed by the rising tide of single mothers was given by the Government yesterday.

Social Security Minister Alistair Burt also sounded the alarm on the growing number of divorces — and parents who have children without getting married.

New statistics out yesterday showed that for the first time almost one in five households with children is headed by a single parent.

Divorced

Other figures revealed the number of single lone parents rose by nearly three times in a decade, from 150,000 in 1981 to 430,000 in 1991. The number of divorced or separated lone parents increased over the same period from 500,000 to 670,000.

In total, there are now around 1.3 million single people bringing up more than two million children.

Mr Burt said: "Clearly there are serious social and personal problems arising from the disruption of family life. We cannot ignore them.

"The fastest growing group is the single never-married lone mothers. About a third of lone parents on income support started out as teenage lone parents. The ideal of the

Page 2 Column 7

Warning over lone mothers

From Page One

traditional family is under pressure from the reality of family life today."

Last year £6.6 billion was spent on single parents in state benefits.

This figure has more than doubled in real terms since 1979.

Mr Burt, in a speech to the Royal Society for the Prevention of Cruelty to Children in Glasgow, insisted: "Although two-parent families are still the norm there have been tremendous changes over recent years.

"Change need not always be bad but recent changes have made the family a less stable environment, a less secure place to raise a child.

"Stability is important in a child's life and stability is provided by the strength of the parent's relationship.

Harmed

"Research shows that instability is bad for children and that their development can be harmed by the break-up of their parents' relationship."

Mr Burt said the fact that more than one in three marriages ended in divorce represented a "huge toll of human suffering".

He added: "The decline of marriage as an institution and the increase in cohabitation are to be regretted if this results in more separations and more relationships breaking up."

The Government should not be society's "moral arbiter" but it "does have a role where there is an impact on others, particularly children".

Sometimes this meant intervention as in the case of the CSA.

The figures came from the Social Security Department's latest statistical bulletin.

Diana Maddock, Lib Dem spokeswoman on the family, said: "Mr Burt should be careful over using emotive language."

Explosion of lone mothers / Minister warns against illegitimacy
Daily Express - Wednesday September 14th 1994.

THE SUN, Saturday, March 30, 2002 15

'TREAT HER LIKE A TORY'

LIAR NAOMI SHOULD FACE PERJURY RAP SAYS TEBBIT

Court win . . . but judge said model Naomi told lies in the dock

By JOHN KAY, Chief Reporter

TORY big gun Lord Tebbit last night urged police to consider prosecuting lying supermodel Naomi Campbell for perjury.

The former Conservative Party chairman hit out after a judge branded 31-year-old Naomi a liar when he awarded her a paltry £3,500 in a privacy fight.

Lord Tebbit said that two top Tories – ex-Cabinet Minister Jonathan Aitken and best-selling author Lord Archer – had been jailed for perjury. And he told The Sun: "I want to be satisfied that there are not two standards of justice – one for politicians and one for models.

Blast . . . Lord Tebbit

"Is Miss Campbell to be prosecuted for perjury? Or are such prosecutions brought only against leading Conservative Party members?"

Aitken got 18 months in 1999 after admitting perjury in a libel case.

Last year Lord Archer was given four years for deceiving a libel jury over an action which won him £500,000.

Earlier this week Naomi won her High Court battle against The Mirror on a technicality.

But judge Sir Michael Morland said in his ruling that she had told "deliberate lies" during her witness box testimony.

Lord Tebbit, 71 yesterday, said in an interview with The Sun: "Prosecutions for perjury are comparatively rare.

Decision

"It is odd that two leading Conservatives have been prosecuted in recent times – Mr Aitken and Lord Archer.

Jailed . . . Lord Archer

"This lady Miss Campbell has been referred to by the judge as having lied in front of him.

"In other words, it is the judge who has accused her of perjury and I await to see whether the Crown Prosecution Service are going to move on it.

"I want to be satisfied that there are not two standards of justice – one for politicians and one for models.

"It would certainly be unjust if that was the case and I await to hear whether there will be a prosecution.

"If there is not a prosecution, I will be intrigued to find out what considerations were taken into account in reaching that decision."

Scotland Yard chiefs will have to decide whether to press charges against Naomi for perjury.

The key question to be considered will be whether she "knowingly" lied in court – or simply made an incorrect statement.

Jailed . . . Tory Aitken

Liar Naomi Campbell - prosecution for perjury??
The Sun - Saturday March 30th 2002.

Model's regret over judge who called her liar

Reaction

By Hugh Davies
Entertainment Correspondent

NAOMI Campbell appeared to admit last night in Los Angeles that she had committed perjury at the High Court after a judge said that he had considered her evidence in the privacy case with caution.

Told that Mr Justice Morland ruled he was "satisfied that she lied on oath" at one point, she replied, "I do apologise to the judge for that." The supermodel said the reason she gave evidence was "because that's privacy, and I didn't want to bring a focus on it".

The judge said the lie was about her rushed admission to hospital in Gran Canaria. He also "had doubts" about the accuracy of her descriptions of assaults on an assistant and her dealings with Matthew Freud, the publicist.

Miss Campbell used an ITV interview to insist she was no longer "using drugs" although she refused to say for how long she had been free of narcotics. "I care to keep that private."

She was staying in America, she said, because it was where she felt safe to go to a recovery meeting if ever she felt "vulnerable".

Miss Campbell said that *The Mirror* story and picture had made her feel "raped". She said: "I felt that if I can't take care of this problem I can't make myself better." But the court case was probably "something I'd never do again".

The model said she had hardly slept for a month. "It was hard. I didn't expect it to be the way it's blown up like this. I just wanted to go and fight for something I thought was very important to me, having the privacy to take care of myself and to better my life, to change the way I was and become the way I am now."

The Narcotics Anonymous story was "very damaging" because if she had felt strong enough "to come out" and talk about it "I would have done so".

Miss Campbell, 31, said: "Recovery is something that takes time. You feel that you're getting better in the right direction. I wasn't hiding. But first of all an addict had to admit to themselves that they have a problem before they can admit it to anybody else. That is the first step."

Piers Morgan, editor of *The Mirror*, which is having to pay Miss Campbell £3,500 in damages plus possibly £70,000 in legal costs, hardly blinked at the judgment. "I only wish the judge had put an order on us never to mention Naomi Campbell again."

He said: "I'm bored with the whole damned thing. If I never run another story about Naomi Campbell it will be too soon. I think she's a washed-up old has-been."

Noting that she was in Los Angeles, he said: "So much for her point of principle. From what I understand she couldn't even be bothered to turn up for the result."

Mr Morgan pounced on the fact that the judge said he was "satisfied" she had lied in the witness box under oath.

"As she cracks open the champagne, she might consider this: a knock on the door from the police on a perjury charge that could get her seven years in the slammer, and maybe that's what she really deserves in coming here – lying through her back teeth and winning some ludicrous pyrrhic victory."

He insisted that the outcome was "a complete joke"

Piers Morgan: damages

'I just wanted to go and fight for something I thought was very important to me'

as the damages were "derisory." He said all she had won was "a small technical point of law in relation to confidence which we will be disputing".

He said: "This is a case that should never have been brought. It is quite clear that the judge thought we had every right to say she was a drug addict. We had every right to tell the public that she was having treatment. The only thing we couldn't do – and this was what the whole case came down to – was say she was going to Narcotics Anonymous."

Naomi Campbell - Lied on oath

The Daily Telegraph - Thursday March 28th 2002

Naomi Campbell ruling welcomed

Media lawyers this week welcomed the Court of Appeal's ruling overturning Naomi Campbell's privacy claim against the *Mirror* newspaper.

Earlier this year, the supermodel was awarded £3,500 damages after the newspaper printed photographs of her leaving a Narcotics Anonymous meeting in Los Angeles and details of her treatment. The judge ruled that although the *Mirror* was entitled to publish the fact that she was a drug addict, disclosing details of her treatment was an invasion of privacy.

In overturning the case, the court said the details of her treatment formed a legitimate part of the story, which was justified in order to show that Ms Campbell had been deceiving the public when she had previously said she had not taken drugs.

The Mirror's solicitor, Kevin Bays, a partner at London firm Davenport Lyons, said the ruling was a 'major triumph' for freedom of speech.

'Cases of this type must each be looked at on their own merits, but in this case the *Mirror* had not stepped over the line,' he said. 'This means that the media can now get on with their job without fear of a string of claims.'

Media expert Mark Stephens, a partner at Finers Stephens Innocent in London, said: 'The judge has recognised the media's role as watchdog: this judgment effectively says that if a public figure is going to lie, or if spin-doctors put misinformation into the public domain, it is incumbent on the media to reveal the truth.'

Ms Campbell was represented by leading media firm Schillings, which was unavailable for comment.

Victoria MacCallum

Model Naomi finally defeated in Court - her lies must be exposed

Law Society Gazette - 17th October 2002

FREE KICK

The merits of naming an unfaithful footballer

From the Presidency to the Premiership there is a rule that governs scandals. It can be thought of as Nixon's law. The cover up brings more trouble than the crime.

After two lovers of a Premier league football player told the *Sunday People* their story, the soccer star sought to prevent publication by taking legal action to protect his privacy. He hoped, in this way, to prevent his wife hearing about the trysts. This morning he will wake up to find his name and the details of his affairs made known to a much larger number than if he had let the *Sunday People* proceed. His wife now knows that, not content with deceiving her with his extra marital liaisons, he spent hundreds of thousands of pounds of their money preventing her from discovering this deceit and has potentially exposed her to much unwanted media coverage. He has, in other words, scored a spectacular own goal.

The story is tawdry and sad. Some have, therefore, questioned Lord Woolf's important judgment that publication was in the public interest. They object to the judge's argument that although the interests of the public and the public interest are not exactly the same thing, they are very closely related. They disagree, also, with his view that even a Premiership football player who has no pretensions to any larger social role lays himself open to close media scrutiny because of his fame. Yet Lord Woolf is right and his critics are mistaken.

The critics assume that anyone has the right to keep their behaviour secret and that any infringement of this right needs to be justified carefully. In a free society it is far better to look at things in the opposite way. There is a right to free expression and it should only be curtailed in very special circumstances. Seen like this, it is clear why Lord Woolf was correct.

The football star and his lawyers were attempting to prevent his two lovers from publishing their own stories, which is certainly within their rights. They were also arguing that a judge should decide that an ignorant public did not know what was in its own interest and needs to be protected from certain types of information. In reality, they wanted to use the courts to prevent the player from suffering the consequences of his actions. It was important that they should not succeed and right that they did not.

The usefulness and taste of newspaper stories varies wildly. This court case has been fought over facts that many will regard as tacky or tedious. However, the information that might best hold the powerful to account and illuminate the truth about society is varied and unpredictable. "Publish and be damned" the Duke of Wellington once said. Newspapers must remain free to do both.

Naming of adulterous footballer

The Times - Saturday March 30th 2002.

Law reports

CONFIDENTIAL INFORMATION

Publication of details of celebrity's private life without consent – publication justifiable in public interest – newspaper exempt from data protection obligations

Campbell v Mirror Group Newspapers plc: CA (Lord Phillips of Worth Matravers Master of the Rolls, Lords Justice Chadwick and Keene): 14 October 2002

The claimant was an internationally famous fashion model who had courted publicity, had volunteered information to the media about her private life and had averred publicly and untruthfully that she did not take drugs. A newspaper published articles which disclosed her drug addiction, the fact that she was receiving therapy with Narcotics Anonymous, gave details of its meetings, which she was attending and showed photographs of her in a street as she was leaving a meeting. The claimant claimed damages against the newspaper publisher for breach of confidentiality and compensation under section 13 of the Data Protection Act 1998. The judge gave judgment for the claimant. The publisher appealed.

Desmond Browne QC, Richard Spearman QC and Mark Warby QC (instructed by Davenport Lyons) for the publisher; Andrew Caldecott QC and Antony White QC (instructed by Schilling & Lom & Partners) for the claimant.

Held, allowing the appeal, that the detail and photographs were a legitimate part of the journalistic package designed to demonstrate that the claimant had deceived the public and publication was justified in the public interest; that hard copy which reproduced personal data previously processed by means of equipment operating automatically formed part of the processing and fell within the scope of the Data Protection Act 1998; that the newspaper was entitled, after publication, to invoke section 32 to exempt it from its obligations under the Act where it reasonably believed that publication was in the public interest and that compliance was incompatible with the special purpose of journalism; and that, in the circumstances, the conditions of exemption were satisfied and the Act was not infringed. (WLR)

Campbell: privacy bid

Naomi finally defeated

Law Society Gazette - October 2002

PRIVACY: breach of confidence victory against *Daily Mirror*

Lawyers back Lords ruling in Naomi Campbell case

Supermodel Naomi Campbell's victory last week in her House of Lords breach of confidence case against the *Daily Mirror* was broadly welcomed by lawyers this week.

Timothy Pinto, a media and entertainment lawyer at City firm Taylor Wessing, said: 'This is a further step in the trend of English courts to protect a person's personality. The Campbell judgment gives full recognition that English law can protect a person's privacy from disclosure of private information by the press.

'But the court must always balance the right of privacy against the right of freedom of expression. So if, for example, a person has misled the public, the press will usually be entitled to set the record straight.'

Sarah Webb, a partner at national firm Russell Jones & Walker, said: 'This is good news all round. For claimants it gives clarity now that the Law Lords have recognised the laws of privacy... it is good news that there is a line over which newspapers shouldn't go.'

Amber Melville-Brown, a consultant with London-based David Price Solicitors and Advocates and the

Photograph: PA

Campbell: warning to media

Gazette's media correspondent, said: 'The court has fired a warning shot across the bows of the media that invasive journalism, prying into people's private lives and dishing up details to the public, is not acceptable. And that is whether the subjects are celebrities or not.'

Alasdair Pepper, a partner with Peter Carter-Ruck & Partners, said: 'I think the judgment is good and right because everyone is entitled to the right to privacy, particularly for matters relating to their medical affairs, and I don't think it matters who it might be.'

Jeremy Fleming

Lawyers back Lords ruling in Naomi case

Law Society Gazette 13th May 2004

VOICE OF THE Mirror

voice@mirror.co.uk

The law's a wonderful equaliser..

AN expectant world awakes this morning with one question on its lips: Garry WHO?

For months we have been tantalised by the name of the footballer with two mistresses.

He was so desperate to stop the public finding out who he was that he went to court to get a gagging order.

But the Sunday People fought the case to the Court of Appeal for the sake of press freedom and won. At midnight the name of Mr A could finally be revealed.

And what a damp squib it turned out to be.

Football fans may have heard of Garry Flitcroft, but he is hardly a household name. At least, he wasn't until today.

Because of his ridiculous fight to stop people finding out he had been cheating on his wife with two women, everyone has now heard of him.

And will think of him as the double adulterer who wanted to keep his name secret.

When will the lesson be learned that the worst thing someone can do if they want to keep something quiet is to run to the courts?

The result is the opposite, as Naomi Campbell discovered to her cost when she took on The Mirror.

The judgment in the Flitcroft case is another blow for press freedom. Wrongdoers will continue to be exposed — and named.

'Wrongdoer named and shamed'

The Mirror - Saturday March 30th 2002.

Media law

By Amber Melville-Brown, Finers Stephens Innocent, London

Power of the press: complaints commission has been called a 'dog with a bark but no bite'

What's new pussycat?

The Queen on the application of Anna Ford and the Press Complaints Commission

While the press has been described as the watchdog of society, performing a vital role as a bloodhound in investigative journalism, the Press Complaints Commission (PCC) has suffered under the ignominious description of being a dog with a bark but no bite. In the view of the newsreader, Anna Ford, the press's own watchdog has now been demoted to a 'pussycat'.

In what is reported to be the first case of its kind, Ms Ford sought judicial review of the PCC's rejection of her complaint that her privacy had been invaded. The matter arose over the publication in the *Daily Mail* and *OK!* magazine of photographs of Ms Ford while on holiday with her partner and children. The pictures were taken at the quiet end of a public beach by the use of long-lens photography. On 31 July 2001, her application for judicial review was rejected by the court.

The PCC is the press's self regulatory body, the ostensible aim of which is to 'ensure that British newspapers and magazines follow the letter and spirit of an ethical code of practice dealing with issues such as inaccuracy, privacy, misrepresentation and harassment.' It is chaired by Lord Wakeham and consists of 15 other members, six of whom are editors of various publications. Their role is to enforce the code to which members voluntarily agree to abide, with a view to maintaining the 'highest professional and ethical standards.' The relevant publication is required to carry, with due prominence, any PCC adjudication which criticises the publication under the code.

Clause 3 relating to privacy, reads: 'Everyone is entitled to respect for his or her private and family life, home, health and correspondence. A publication will be expected to justify intrusions into any individual's private life without consent. The use of long-lens photography to take pictures of people in private places without their consent is unacceptable. Note – Private places are public or private property where there is a reasonable expectation of privacy.'

Despite representations that Ms Ford had believed the beach outside the hotel to be private, that she had chosen this holiday destination deliberately for its seclusion, and that she therefore had a reasonable expectation of privacy, the PCC said that it 'could not conclude that a publicly accessible Majorcan beach was a place where the complainants could have a reasonable expectation of privacy.'

Mr Justice Silber made it clear at the beginning of his (draft) judgment that the court's function in relation to Ms Ford's application was not to conduct an appeal of the facts of the PCC's determination, nor to determine whether the use of long-lens photography in this case had infringed Ms Ford's privacy, nor that the publications had behaved wrongfully or unjustly by publishing the photographs. Rather, it was to 'rule on whether [Ms Ford] had an arguable case to pursue her complaint by invoking the administrative court's limited but defined supervisory jurisdiction over the commission in relation to the determination.'

The court considered whether and to what extent, in view of recent cases decided after the incorporation of the Human Rights Act 1998 (HRA), the courts should scrutinise any determination of the PCC. It concluded that public bodies 'can, in appropriate cases, enjoy a discretionary area of judgment' and that in this case, the court should not interfere in the PCC's decision but should defer to the views of the body.

Although the minutiae of the High Court judgment has not received as much publicity as the question of Ms Ford's privacy and the use of long-lens photography, the decision is not a mere sideshow to the PCC determination. In Mr Justice Silber's judgment, 'the commission does have a realistic margin of discretion in their judgment in the way in which they determine complaints... In consequence, the courts will be deferential to and not be keen to interfere with decisions of the commission...'

He continued: 'The commission is a body whose membership and expertise makes it much better equipped than the courts to resolve the difficult exercise of balancing the conflicting rights of Ms Ford and Mr Scott [her then partner] to privacy and of the newspapers to publish', suggesting that the PCC is better placed to hear such applications than the court, despite a long list of cases before and after the incorporation of the HRA, which illustrates the court's willingness and competence to address these issues.

Ruling on the privacy of individuals is not a matter from which the courts shirk. It is being considered in the high-profile case of Michael Douglas and Catherine Zeta Jones and *Hello!* magazine. And actress Amanda Holden recently went straight to the courts to obtain an injunction on the grounds that her rights under the HRA had been breached, rather than invoke the PCC code over the alleged invasion of her privacy by the publication of long-lens photographs. The model Naomi Campbell has also taken legal action rather than go to the PCC over the publication of photographs to which she did not consent.

So consider this. Will two different levels of privacy be generated through the consideration of these issues in the courts and in the PCC? Will the decisions of the PCC, being the press's own self-regulatory body, give the impression that it is not impartial, with more to gain than the courts in leaning away from individual privacy and towards freedom of expression?

While this may appear a good thing for the press in the short term, if the 'pussycat' PCC is not seen to be protecting the rights of individuals who complain to it, it may find itself defending further calls for an end to self-regulation and the cat may be put out for more than the night.

Britain's Press Complaints Commission - "A Dog with a Bark but no Bite"

Law Society Gazette - 9th August 2001

Call to review Net defamation law

The Law Commission has called for a full review of the law of defamation over fears that it puts Internet service providers (ISPs) under pressure to remove potentially defamatory material without considering whether there is actually a problem.

The commission's preliminary investigation into the issue, carried out at the request of the Lord Chancellor, said that if a further study finds there is a need for reform, potential changes include exempting ISPs from liability for defamatory material on Web sites they host, and extending section 1 of the Defamation Act 1996 to widen the 'innocent dissemination' defence.

Law Commissioner Professor Hugh Beale QC said some ISPs receive more than 100 defamation complaints a year – including solicitors' letters from companies objecting to Web sites set up by disgruntled customers – and that because of the law, ISPs often remove the sites without considering whether the information is in the public interest, or true.

'There is a possible conflict between the pressure to remove material, even if true, and the emphasis placed on freedom of expression by the European Convention on Human Rights,' he said.

The commission also said there was no need to reform the law of contempt to deal with the possibility that jurors might find out about a defendant's previous convictions on the Internet, saying it already contains 'sufficient safeguards'.

This puts the commission at odds with Justin Walford, in-house barrister at Express Newspapers, who last week told a conference that contempt of court laws need to be reformed to deal with the danger of the Internet influencing jurors.

'The real problem is not publications or broadcasts, but the unfettered access many jurors have to the Internet, and the vast array of official and unofficial sites and e-mails they can view,' he said, speaking at last week's Law for Journalists conference, organised by the Newspaper Society and *UK Press Gazette*.

He suggested more research be carried out inside the jury room to find out what is prejudicial.

Also at the conference, Alastair Brett, head of legal at Times Newspapers, expressed concern about libel cases which remain live for years because material remains in newspapers' on-line archives and are regarded as new publications when downloaded.

The Law Commission has recommended a review of how the definition of a 'publication' in defamation law interacts with the limitation period applied to archive material.

Neil Rose and Victoria MacCallum

99/49 19 December 2002

Call to review Net defamation law

Law Society Gazette - 19th December 2002

Media law

By Amber Melville-Brown, Schillings, London

America or Australia? that is the question

***Joseph Gutnick v Dow Jones & Company* (2002) December**

This case, heard before Australia's highest court, regarding an Australian claimant and a US publisher, is of greater interest to libel lawyers in the UK than one might imagine, given that it relates to that insidious, omnipresent phenomenon, the Internet.

Whether or not this decision is a disaster for publishers, as some commentators have said, it is an important case in that it restates the general principles of publication and confirms they apply to the Internet as to any other form of communication of a defamatory statement.

This long-standing principle provides that publication takes place not where the libel is created, but where it is read. An easy-to-grasp example is of a defamatory letter. This does no harm when penned and popped into the post, but the poison begins its damage when the letter is opened and read by a third party. In this case, Dow Jones sought to argue that the normal principles were not appropriate to the Internet, that publication should take place where the article first became available and that this rule should be applied globally.

The case arose out of the publication in *Barron's Online* – an edition of the US magazine, published on Dow Jones' subscription Internet news site, www.WSJ.com – of an article which Joseph Gutnick complained was defamatory of him. Mr Gutnick lives in the Australian state of Victoria, and while conducting business outside the country, including in the US, he had his headquarters in Victoria and conducted much of his social life there. He agreed to limit his damages to those flowing from the publications in Australia alone.

The principal issue of where the material of complaint was published, would affect which laws were to be applied and the jurisdiction in which the proceedings should be brought. Given the differences in the laws of defamation around the world, including between the US and Australia, this was likely to have had a significant impact on the standards applied, the defences run and on the eventual outcome of the case.

While the claimant argued that publication took place in Australia, where the information was downloaded from the Internet, the defendant argued that publication occurred at the Internet servers maintained by it, in the US state of New Jersey.

It is not hard to understand the vehemence of Dow Jones' argument that publication took place in the US. There, freedom of speech carries much weight. Publishers have in their armoury the public figure defence, the actual malice standard, the single publication rule and a reverse burden of proof.

Dow Jones argued that practical considerations meant that the claimant's proposition that Internet publication takes place where the libels are downloaded, put publishers in an almost impossible position. They would have to be aware of the libel laws of any country in the world from which an article could be downloaded; there are 'no boundaries which a publisher could effectively draw to prevent anyone, anywhere, downloading the information it put on its Web server'.

However, despite the defendant's protestations, Chief Justice Gleeson, and Justices McHugh, Gummow and Hayne saw little difference here than at the advent of other methods of mass communication. In a joint judgment, they ruled that 'the problem of widely disseminated communications is much older than the Internet and the world-wide Web. The law has had to grapple with such cases ever since newspapers and magazines came to be distributed to large numbers of people over wide geographic areas.'

In his judgment, Mr Justice Callinan also said the defendant's proposed approach was open perhaps not to abuse, but to unwelcome practices at the expense of claimants: 'Publishers would be free to manipulate the uploading and location of data so as to insulate themselves from liability in Australia or elsewhere; for example, by using a Web server in "defamation free jurisdictions" or, one in which the defamation laws are tilted decidedly towards defendants. Why would publishers, owing duties to their shareholders to maximise profits, do otherwise?'

Despite various practical concerns raised by Dow Jones, including uncertainty for the publishers and a potential multiplicity of claims, the High Court judges, variously, disposed of them. A claim for substantial damages would only be made if the claimant has a reputation in the place where the publication is made; claimants are unlikely to sue in a jurisdiction in which they will be unable to enforce the judgment against the assets of the defendant; the suggestion that a publisher would have to consider the laws of every country 'from Afghanistan to Zimbabwe' was unreal; 'in all except the most unusual of cases, identifying the person about whom the material is to be published will readily identify the defamation law to which that person may resort.'

In considering the fundamental principle 'whether the development of the Internet calls for a radical shift in the law of defamation', Mr Justice Callinan held that arguments about the ubiquity of the Internet seemed to include, on the defendant's part, 'more than a suggestion that any attempt to control, regulate, or even inhibit its operation, no matter the irresponsibility or malevolence of a user, would be futile, and that no jurisdiction should trouble to do so'. This argument found little favour with him. Neither did the submission that by having the matter dealt with under the laws of Australia rather than those of the US – which 'leans heavily, some might say far too heavily, in favour of defendants' – the defendant would be deprived of the Constitutional protection available in the US. He restated the principals of Australian law which, rightly in his opinion, place 'real value on reputation and views with scepticism claims that it unduly inhibits freedom of discourse'.

Damage occurs 'at the place (or the places) where the defamation is comprehended'. The court was not to be shaken from that view or from the view, acknowledged by the defendant, that to succeed it had to show that these long established principles of publication should be departed from for the Internet. In the court's view, the defendant had not done so and the appeal was dismissed.

When the Internet first thrust its way into society, it was feared and misunderstood, on the one hand, and seen as a modern Messiah by others. In his judgment, Mr Justice Kirby quoted from our own Lord Bingham of Cornhill (writing in Collins's *The Law of Defamation and the Internet*) saying the Internet will require 'almost every concept and rule in the field... to be reconsidered in the light of this unique medium of instant worldwide communication'. While acknowledging that the appeal in *Gutnick* 'enlivens such a reconsideration', and that this fundamental role of publication had been reconsidered, Mr Justice Kirby nevertheless agreed with his fellow judges that following the logical conclusion of the existing law, the appeal failed, although that did 'not represent a wholly satisfactory outcome', and that 'intuition suggests that the remarkable features of the Internet – make it more than simply another medium of human communication'.

Concluding his judgment, Mr Justice Kirby appeared to suggest that consideration of the various issues, technological, legal and practical that this matter raises might be more appropriate for national legislative attention and international discussion, suggesting a glimmer of hope for those championing the cause, that perhaps the fight to change the law in this regard is not over yet. Mr Justice Kirby said: 'Where large changes to settled law are involved, in an area as sensitive as the law of defamation, it should cause no surprise when the courts decline the invitation to solve problems that others, in a much better position to devise solutions, have neglected to repair.'

Internet defamation again

Law Society Gazette - 23rd January 2003

26

LEGAL UPDATE

Media law

By Amber Melville-Brown, Schillings, London

Sorry seems to be the hardest word

***John Cleese v Peter Clark, Associated Newspapers Limited* (2003) LTL 11 February**

In the recent case of John Cleese against the *Evening Standard*, the experienced libel judge Mr Justice Eady gave some useful guidance and practical suggestions in relation to the procedure of offer of amends. He explained that he did so 'in the hope that [his suggestions] may be of assistance to other parties, who wish to achieve a fair result for their respective clients while avoiding some of the delays and expense traditionally associated with this form of litigation.'

While I was not involved personally in the case, the claimant was advised by my partner Martin Cruddace, so I declare that interest here.

The claimant took offence at an article concerning a US sitcom, which while not well received by UK critics had nonetheless resulted in glowing reviews for Mr Cleese in relation to his small role.

Mr Cleese claimed the *Evening Standard* article suggested that the American nation had turned on him, that he had faced humiliation as a result and that, according to the article, this was deserved because of his arrogance and presumption. He alleged that there were numerous falsities within the article and that the newspaper had totally disregarded his positive reviews of which they would certainly have been aware. Within a couple of weeks, the newspaper acknowledged that the article 'was not entirely fair' and later went on to make an offer of amends.

Under section 2 of the Defamation Act 1996, defendants may accept that they have 'got it wrong' and attempt to extricate themselves from litigation at an early stage by making an offer to apologise, pay a sum of damages and the costs of the claimant. If the claimant accepts, the terms can be agreed or decided by the court. If the claimant refuses, the defendant can rely on the offer as a defence at any subsequent trial.

Photograph: PA

Cleese: alleged numerous falsities in a newspaper article

In the best of all possible worlds, the parties would reach an amicable agreement on damages, costs and the apology. But we do not live in the best of all possible worlds and there can be disagreement, in which case the court can be asked to decide on the damages and the costs. But not the terms or prominence of the apology. That is entirely within the discretion of the newspaper. But the judge can compensate the claimant with a greater award of damages, if he accepts that any apology published was disproportionate.

In this case, the defendant published a unilateral apology, given the disagreement between the parties as to its terms and prominence. The claimant maintained that the offer package was insufficient in light of the damage done and while he had accepted the newspaper's offer to make amends, he asked that the level of damages and costs be decided by the court.

The article was held clearly to suggest 'that a long, slow decline in [Mr Cleese's] talents and professionalism has finally ended with a bump'. The judge noted that 'by the offer of amends, it has clearly been recognised that this is simply not true.' In light of the 'manifestly vitriolic' article, the offer made by the defendant was considered insufficient by the court.

Mr Justice Eady was reminded by counsel of talks that had taken place between him and counsel in the previous case of *Fernandes v Associated Newspapers Limited* (unreported) and 'off-the-cuff suggestions as to the appropriate course of action' in offer to make amends cases. He decided to adopt them in his judgment in *Cleese*, 'for what they are worth', to assist parties in the future.

'It was in the contemplation of Parliament,' he said, 'and those who formulated the relevant rules, that once an offer has been validly accepted discussions should take place, on an informal basis, so as to avoid as far as possible any need to attend before the court.'

Libel is often considered a bit of a gamble. And a gambling metaphor, which triggers mental pictures of exhausted men with rolled-up sleeves, whisky bottle on the table in a dark and smoky room, did creep into the practical suggestions made by the judge:

- A sensible course of action would be for a meeting to take place round the table, if practicable, without going straight to the court for directions as though a contested hearing were inevitable. This should signify a spirit of compromise on both sides.
- The parties should set about identifying and resolving the issues still outstanding. The parties – and their lawyers where they are represented – have an obligation to identify the issues promptly and with frankness.
- They should engage in a frank exchange of views, placing their cards face-up on the table. There is no point making the other team guess at what one is after.
- They should keep no cards up their sleeves, as is a tendency when dealing with these matters through correspondence, nor obfuscate or posture, as is a tendency to do in lawyers' letters. Clearly a proponent of the school of plain English, Mr Justice Eady remarked that 'there can be no form of human communication more stilted than letters between litigation solicitors of the type with which we are all too familiar, where endless points are scored of the we-are-surprised-to-note variety.'
- Where delay in bringing the negotiations to fruition is attributable to the complainant, this will reduce the level of compensation. Any delay attributable to the defendant will increase the award.

These proposals appear sensible and appropriate, but they will require a certain openness of mind on the part of both parties and their legal advisers. Cynics might argue that this may not come easily where the parties have such different agendas. A claimant might accept the offer to mitigate the damage to his reputation and to ensure some form of compensation at an early stage; a defendant might make the offer in an attempt to save the cost of a full libel trial.

But if both parties are prepared to play the game, they may find that they both come out winners.

Sorry seems to be the hardest Word

Media law

By Amber Melville-Brown, David Price Solicitors & Advocates, London

Pride and privilege

***George Galloway MP v Telegraph Group Ltd* [2004] EWHC 2786 (QB), Mr Justice Eady, 2 December 2004**

Mr Justice Eady's decision to award £150,000 libel damages to George Galloway MP, and to strike out the newspaper's defence of privilege, has caused as much alarm in some media arenas as that caused by the broadcast in 1938 of the Orson Welles radio show 'War of the Worlds', with cries that the end of the world is nigh reverberating around newsrooms.

That may be overstating it somewhat. But while some consider that the judgment is a characteristically thorough analysis of the law and a straightforward application of the *Reynolds* defence, some commentators have expressed fears that the judge's application of the qualified privilege defence – developed in *Reynolds v Times Newspapers Ltd* [1999] ICHRL 148, and welcomed with open arms in media circles at its birth as making our 'Draconian' UK libel laws much fairer – was too severe, inconsistent with the current European jurisprudence, and that the damages award was too high.

In early 2003, *The Daily Telegraph* published a series of articles that set out in full various documents which had been found by a *Telegraph* journalist in the badly damaged offices of the Iraqi Foreign Ministry after the fall of Baghdad. The newspaper added editorial comment. The claimant, a Labour party member and a strenuous anti-war campaigner, argued that the documents were fake and issued proceedings for libel. In finding in favour of the claimant, the judge held that the articles meant that:

- Galloway had been in the pay of Saddam Hussein, secretly receiving sums in the region of £375,000 a year;
- He had diverted monies from the oil-for-food programme, depriving Iraqi people, whose interests he claimed to represent, of food and medicine;
- He probably used the Mariam Appeal – named after an Iraqi girl whom he had taken to a Scottish hospital for cancer treatment – as a front for personal enrichment; and
- What he had done was tantamount to treason.

There were disputes as to meaning, but suffice to say that the defendant newspaper did not seek to justify what in essence were serious allegations. Instead, it claimed that it was entitled to rely on *Reynolds* privilege (it also ran a defence of fair comment in respect of the editorials). In essence, the defence is concerned with protecting responsible journalism where a publisher is under a duty to convey particular information, in the way that it is conveyed, to the world. As summarised by Mr Justice Eady, the defence claimed that the public interest was such that 'the public had a right to know the content of the documents... even if it was defamatory of the claimant and irrespective of whether the factual content was true or not'.

The defence also argued that recent European jurisprudence impacted in its favour on the right of the press to free speech. Referring to the recent European Court of Human Rights (ECHR) judgment in *Selisto v Finland*, ECHR (Application No 56767/000), the newspaper sought to persuade the court that its reports amounted to no more than reportage. This was described by Lord Justice Simon Brown in *Al-Fagih v HH Saudi Research and Marketing (UK) Ltd* [2002] EMLR 13, as 'a convenient word to describe the neutral reporting of attributed allegations rather than their adoption by the newspaper', where any dispute between parties should be reported 'fully, fairly and disinterestedly'.

Reportage entitles the publisher to depart from the repetition rule and to report alleged facts said by others or within documents without having to prove them, provided that the publisher does not go beyond the allegations, embellish them, add allegations of his own and/or draw inferences from them.

Photograph: Rex Features

Galloway: raises privilege alert

In *Selisto*, the defendant had been fined for publishing defamatory allegations about an unnamed surgeon who had been cleared of implication in the death of a patient, where its articles had included quotes from pre-trial statements provided to the prosecution. The ECHR found that the fines imposed on the defendant under Finnish defamation law had breached its article 10 rights and that 'in the court's opinion, no general duty to verify... statements contained in such documents can be imposed on reporters and other members of the media, who must be free to report on events based on information gathered from official sources. If this were not the case, the efficacy of article 10 of the convention would to a large degree be lost'. Not surprisingly, *The Daily Telegraph* argued that this ruling assisted it in its defence, and that any finding against it would be unsustainable in the European court.

But Mr Justice Eady did not agree. First, he did not consider that *The Daily Telegraph* reports were reportage. Hardly reporting them in a neutral way, he found that 'they did not merely adopt the allegations. They embraced them with relish and fervour. They then went on to embellish them...'

He did not consider that the documents on which the defendant relied were of a sufficient status, unlike in *Selisto*, to justify reliance on them and unverified publication. 'It is perhaps ironic,' he said, 'that *The Daily Telegraph* should pray in aid the documents' status at the same time as decrying Saddam's intelligence service as being one of the most sinister and feared organisations in the world.'

While he confirmed that he would have regard to European decisions, the judge found that he would have to take the current UK law as convention-compliant and he did not take the view that it was necessary 'for individual judges in every case that comes along to apply and interpret the convention afresh'.

The judge continued: 'I can do no better than apply the principles in *Reynolds* to the (very special) facts of the present case.' Accordingly, he went on to consider in turn each of the ten of Lord Nicholls' criteria. For example, he did not ignore the urgency for a newspaper to maintain its 'scoop' and accepted that news can be a 'perishable commodity'. But he did not consider that this justified a speedy publication without verification, as the story in this case 'would be of interest at any time'. And as regards to the tone of the articles, he found it 'dramatic and condemnatory'.

Having applied the ten-point test to the facts, he applied the classic common law test of 'whether in all the circumstances "the duty-interest test of the right to know test" has been satisfied so that qualified privilege attaches', as per the Master of the Rolls Lord Phillips in *Loutchansky*. Was *The Daily Telegraph* under a social or moral duty to communicate what it chose to publish about and concerning the Iraqi documents?

He found that the reporting had not been neutral; there was no duty to publish the information in the way that the newspaper had done; *The Telegraph* had not met the requisite standard of responsible journalism and, accordingly, the *Reynolds* privilege defence had not been made out.

Whether one agrees with the judgment or considers that the various tests have been too harshly applied, the short lesson is that five years on from *Reynolds*, those publishing in the UK must still remind themselves daily of the principles of responsible journalism against which they will be measured in the UK courts.

Law Society Gazette 10th February 2005

6 news.telegraph.co.uk ***

News

David and Goliath battle is a story of modern times

By Joshua Rozenberg
Legal Editor

AS THE European Court of Human Rights said yesterday, the inequality of arms between the McLibel Two and McDonald's could not have been greater.

At the time the fast-food company took the two campaigners to court over a leaflet called *What's Wrong with McDonald's?*, the judges added, "its economic power outstripped that of many small countries".

While McDonald's enjoyed worldwide sales of approximately £15billion in 1995, Helen Steel was a "part-time bar worker earning a maximum of £65 a week" and David Morris was an "unwaged single parent".

Long extracts from the leaflet were printed in yesterday's ruling, thus ensuring that it will remain available – and quotable – for as long as there are law reports. Some idea of its flavour is given by a cartoon, showing a burger with a cow's head sticking out of one side and a man's head sticking out of the other. The cow says: "If the slaughterhouse doesn't get you ..." and the man adds "...the junk food will!".

The High Court judge found that it was untrue of the leaflet to claim that McDonald's was to blame for starvation in the Third World or destruction of the rainforest.

However, Mr Justice Bell said it was true that McDonald's exploited children by using them as more susceptible subjects of advertising and true, overall, to say the company was "culpably responsible for cruel practices in the rearing and slaughter of some of the animals which are used to produce their food".

The Court of Appeal added that there was justification for the claim that "if one eats enough McDonald's food, one's diet may well become high in fat, etc, with the very real risk of heart disease".

In their application to Strasbourg, Miss Steel and Mr Morris claimed that the lack of legal aid had deprived them of their right to a fair hearing under Article 6 of the Human Rights Convention.

Finding in their favour, the court said the "disparity between the respective levels of legal assistance enjoyed by the applicants and McDonald's was of such a degree that it could not have failed, in this exceptionally demanding case, to have given rise to unfairness, despite the best efforts of the judges at first instance and on appeal".

Sporadic help by volunteer lawyers and judicial latitude was no substitute for competent representation by an experienced libel lawyer. There was also a breach of their right to freedom of expression under Article 10.

Helen Steel and Dave Morris

The Government had argued that campaigners should not receive as much protection as journalists. But the court said that even small and informal campaign groups must be able to carry on their activities effectively.

IAN JONES

...outside a McDonald's in London after their victory in the European Court of Human Rights

'McDonald's took a sledgehammer to crack a nut, and cracked themselves'

There was a "strong public interest in enabling such groups and individuals outside the mainstream to contribute to the public debate". It rejected claims that public corporations should not be allowed to defend their reputations. However, there had to be "procedural fairness and equality of arms".

When McDonald's launched its libel action, Miss Steel and Mr Morris had to choose between withdrawing the leaflet and proving, without legal aid, the truth of its allegations. "Given the enormity and complexity of that undertaking, the court does not consider that the correct balance was struck" between the need to protect the applicants' rights to freedom of expression and the need to protect McDonald's rights and reputation", the judges said.

After receiving the court's ruling by e-mail, the two campaigners held a news conference outside the branch of McDonald's at Charing Cross in central London where their battle started 20 years ago.

Mr Morris said: "We are elated. It is a total victory. The Government will have to change the law."

Mark Stephens, the solicitor who represented the McLibel Two at the Human Rights Court, said his clients had been vindicated.

"McDonald's took a sledgehammer to crack a nut – and cracked themselves," he said.

The fast-food company declined to comment on the judgment, saying it was not involved in the action the campaigners had brought against the Government.

Editorial Comment: Page 25

The Daily Telegraph Wednesday February 16 2005

The principle of free speech matters more than a doubtful ruling on taste

"THIS CASE is about the censorship of political speech," declared Lord Justice Laws, opening his judgment on the appeal by the Prolife Alliance against the refusal by the television companies to transmit its election broadcast in its original form.

If only more judges were bold enough to proclaim their verdicts with such a ringing declaration of principle. Against the strength of the principle of free speech, the judges rightly found weak the arguments of the BBC for not showing the anti-abortion broadcast complete with its disturbing footage of dismembered foetuses. Against the clarity of the right to freedom of expression, the BBC's talk of its legal duty to protect viewers from "material that offends against good taste and decency" seemed woolly and subjective and, worse than that, patronising.

The Independent strongly supports a woman's right to choose on abortion. We believe the Prolife Alliance is profoundly mistaken in its absolutism. When those unbalanced beliefs are translated into law, common sense tends to temper them with reality, as in Ireland, which voted in this month's referendum to allow abortions to continue if the mother is suicidal. In practice, therefore, the argument is always one of where to draw the line.

However, we also support – to the last – the Prolife Alliance's right to put its argument. There can be no doubt that it was entitled to a broadcast – only in Wales – on the basis of the number of candidates it fielded. Nor should there be any doubt that, as Lord Justice Simon Brown said in his supporting judgment, "the prohibition of abortion is a legitimate political programme".

The broadcasters all pretend to believe in free speech, too, in which case the argument turns on taste and decency. But the test for censorship must be set high. Many people would find the images the Prolife Alliance wanted to use deeply disturbing, as Lord Justice Laws did when he saw them. They may find them difficult to explain to children who might be watching. But they are real pictures of the consequences of real abortions that happen all the time in this country. Britons ought to be able to look at the sad truth of the often difficult decisions that we make as individuals and as a society.

We are confident that, if the broadcast were shown with its original images – instead of the voiceover-only version that was eventually transmitted – the British public would remain unpersuaded of the case for banning abortion. However, our confidence in the ability of the British to maintain a balanced view of a difficult issue is irrelevant to the principle of free speech.

That principle is not at stake, however, in another controversy this week that seemed to touch on similar questions. Creationists may share with some anti-abortionists a faith-based absolutism. But when it comes to teaching in state schools that the world was created in six days, the distinction that needs to be drawn is not one between free speech and censorship, but between fact and opinion. So long as creationism is taught in religious education classes as an explanation that some people believe literally, some figuratively and some not at all, the right of freedom of expression is satisfied.

It would be dangerous, however, if it were taught in science lessons as an alternative theory to that of evolution. That is a negation of the scientific method, because it is a matter not of evidence but belief. Although Emmanuel College, the school raised in Prime Minister's Questions, has gone close to this line, it does not seem to have gone over it.

In both cases – the campaigns against abortion and the teaching of evolution – the best defence of truth is free and fair debate. That creationists feel they need to indoctrinate children is a measure of the weakness of their arguments. Let them, and the Prolifers, make their case out in the open.

Abortion and the principles of free speech.

The Independent, 15th March 2002.

ProLife Alliance broadcast battle lost

BY JOSHUA ROZENBERG
LEGAL EDITOR

THE ProLife Alliance has lost a High Court claim that it was entitled to show pictures of aborted foetuses in a party election broadcast.

Refusing the alliance permission to apply for judicial review, Mr Justice Scott Baker said there was no duty to allow someone from a political party "to broadcast any images he likes, however offensive they may be".

"The BBC is not preventing the election broadcast," said the judge. "It is saying it cannot condone these images of an offensive nature."

Lawyers for the group, which campaigns "for absolute respect for innocent human life from fertilisation until natural death", had accused the BBC and the independent television authorities of unlawfully blocking the broadcast.

David Anderson, QC, appearing for ProLife, asked for permission to appeal. He said the case raised fundamental legal issues, including whether or not the public in general had "a right not to be offended".

Permission was refused, but Bruno Quintavalle, ProLife's spokesman, said the Court of Appeal itself would now be asked to hear the case.

"It seems the more terrible the abuses authorised by Parliament the less right one has to depict the reality," he said.

The BBC decided that the broadcast would not comply with its guidelines. The Independent Television Commission also said it would be against its programme code.

ProLife's complaint was that the subject of abortion "barely figured on the political landscape" and mainstream political parties had decided it was not in their interests to address it because it was so emotive.

To put the issue on the political agenda it was necessary to let people know what was involved in this commonly-performed operation.

ProLife Alliance broadcast battle lost (but not for long)

The Daily Telegraph, 25 May 2001

TV firms were wrong to block 'shocking' images of abortion, says Court of Appeal

BY DAVID LISTER
Media and Culture Editor

THE BBC, ITV and Channel 4 may be obliged to show party political broadcasts containing "shocking" images of abortion because of a ruling by the Court of Appeal yesterday.

The ruling means images including the bloodied and dismembered limbs of an unborn baby can be shown under the aegis of a party political broadcast by the Prolife Alliance.

The decision by the Court of Appeal, which overturned an earlier *High Court judgment* by saying refusal to show part of the broadcast was illegal, caused deep concern at the TV companies. The BBC's chief political adviser, Anne Sloman, warned: "This means that viewers may be subjected to material *that will cause widespread* and gross offence."

Lord Justice Laws said in his judgment yesterday that he had seen the party political broadcasts that were rejected by the TV companies. He described one of them, saying: "It shows the products of a suction abortion: tiny limbs, bloodied and dismembered, a separated head, their human shape and form plainly recognisable."

He added: "The pictures are real footage of real cases. They are *not a reconstruction, nor in* any way fictitious. Nor are they in any way sensationalised.

"They are, I think, certainly disturbing to any person of ordinary sensibilities. But if we are to take political free speech seriously, those characteristics *cannot* begin *to justify the* censorship that was done in this case," he said.

The BBC, which fought the case on behalf of all terrestrial broadcasters, decided the intended broadcast would not comply with its producers' guidelines. The Independent Television Commission said the broadcast would be against its programme code because pictures were used to depict the consequences of abortion.

The BBC said it would be seeking leave to appeal to the House of Lords because the decision seemed to undermine the *obligation not to broadcast* material that could cause offence.

A spokesman said: "The broadcasters have been entrusted by Parliament with the obligation not to broadcast material that offends against good taste or decency or is likely to be offensive to public feeling.

"This obligation has effectively been overridden by the Court of Appeal for the purposes of party election broadcasts save in the most exceptional of circumstances. This means that viewers may be subjected to material that will cause widespread and gross offence."

But Lord Justice Laws, who described the ban on images of abortion operations as an act of censorship, said in the judgment: "I have well in mind that the broadcasters do not at all accept that their decision should be so categorised.

"*Maybe the feathers of* their liberal credentials are ruffled at the word's overtones; maybe there is an implicit plea for the comfort of a euphemism.

"However, in my judgment this court must, and I hope the broadcasters will, recognise unblinking that censorship is exactly what this case is about."

Leading article,
Review, page 3

ProLife Victory.

The Independent, 15th March 2002.

Patrons of the Association:
The Right Hon. Lord RAWLINSON OF EWELL, P.C., Q.C.
The Most Hon. the Marquess of READING Sir Hugh ROSSI

The Association of Lawyers for the Defence of the Unborn

35 WEST STREET, CONGLETON, CHESHIRE, CW12 1JN

Chairman: R. M. HAIG, LL.B., 35 Parkway, Wilmslow, Cheshire, SK9 1LS
Vice Chairman: Senator C. G. P. LAKEMAN, B.A., Dip. Dt. Fr. (Paris – XI), 47 Esplanade, St. Helier, Jersey, JE1 0BD
Hon. Treasurer: T. G. A. BOWLES, M.A. (Cantab.), 40 Bedford Street, London, WC2E 9EN

Spring 2003 **News and Comment** **Number 97**

Triple Whammy

May 2003 was a gloomy month, and not only overhead, but in the courts. Three cases stood out :-

1. *R. (Pro-Life Alliance) v. BBC*, House of Lords, Lords Nicholls, Hoffman, Millett, Scott and Walker.

On 15th May 2003 the House of Lords by a majority ruled on the BBC's appeal against an earlier ruling by Laws L.J. that its refusal to transmit a 2001 General Election broadcast by the Pro-Life Alliance containing images of abortion infringed the European Convention on Human Rights. Allowing the appeal, the Law Lords held that restrictions on the transmission of offensive material applied to election broadcasts and that the BBC could not be faulted.

Comment

The offensive material in question consisted of images of aborted foetuses. These images made it clear :

(a) that the foetuses were very human, and

(b) that they were very dead – deliberately killed as they had been with the full approval or at least connivance of the English Law, which is what the Alliance, by bringing the images before the public's eye, was seeking by lawful and peaceful means to change.

Of course the images were offensive. Images of the Jewish holocaust and other such images are by their very nature offensive and are rightly broadcast and re-broadcast time and again in the hope that men will not forget. This bitterly-disappointing decision of a majority of the Law Lords, so it seems to us, flies not only in the face of that right to freedom of expression supposedly enshrined in the Convention, but also, by hobbling the attempts of the Alliance to bring home to the electorate precisely what is happening in the clinics, in the face of ordinary notions of fair play.

House of Lords- ProLife defeat

May 2003

Friday, September 5, 2003 THE DAILY TELEGRAPH

Pro-Life activists acquitted

Two anti-abortion campaigners accused of insulting passers-by by displaying a poster of an aborted foetus were cleared yesterday of all charges.

Fiona Pinto, 23, an Oxford University graduate from Potters Bar, Herts, and Joseph Biddulph, 52, from Pontypridd, now plan to sue Gwent Police for false imprisonment. They were arrested in Newport in April during a Welsh Assembly election campaign.

Pinto, described during the two-day hearing at Abergavenny magistrates' court as the "darling of the ProLife Alliance", and Biddulph denied displaying a sign with the intention of insulting people.

Alternative charges of disorderly behaviour were withdrawn yesterday after legal argument.

Aborted foetus posters OK

The Daily Telegraph Friday 5th September 2003

National

Women who delay babies until late 30s get health warning

Mothers advised to stick to 20-35 childbearing age

People have become blasé, warns consultant

James Meikle
Health correspondent

Women who delay having children until their late thirties are "defying nature and risking heartbreak" as well as building up public health problems for the future, senior doctors say today. Those who want families and room to manoeuvre in their life and career choice should not wait that long before trying to have a baby.

Doctors and healthcare planners should urge women to achieve "biologically optimal childbearing" between the ages of 20 and 35, say the authors of an editorial in the British Medical Journal.

Susan Bewley, consultant obstetrician at Guy's and St Thomas' NHS Foundation

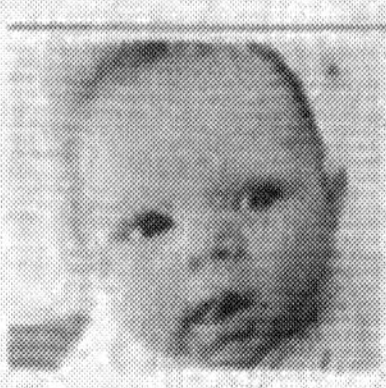

'More than one in seven women now conceive over the age of 35, and more than one in 40 conceive over 40. Many turn to IVF'

Trust, London, and colleagues, are urging doctors and health agencies to do more to tackle the "epidemic" of middle-aged pregnancy. Pregnancies in women older than 35 have increased markedly in western countries and with that has come more age-related fertility problems for women, especially for the over 40s. Delay also affects partners, as semen counts drop gradually every year, and children of older men have an increased risk of schizophrenia and genetic disorders.

More than one in seven women in England and Wales now conceive over the age of 35, and more than one in 40 conceive over 40. Increasing numbers are turning to IVF, but seven in 10 women fail to achieve a pregnancy that ends in a live birth in their first cycle of treatment and 90% of the over-40s fail to do so.

Although most pregnancies in the over-35s still have successful outcomes, obstetricians and gynaecologists have been witnesses to tragedies too, say the three doctors, two of whom are women.

"The pain of infertility, miscarriage, smaller families than desired, or damage to pregnancy, mothers and children is very private, particularly when women blame themselves for choices without being fully aware of the consequences.

"It is ironic that as society becomes more risk-averse and pregnant women more anxious than in the past, a major preventable cause of this ill-health and depression is unacknowledged.

"Public health agencies target teenagers but ignore the epidemic of pregnancy in middle age.

"Women want to 'have it all' but biology is unchanged ... Their delays may reflect disincentives to earlier pregnancy or maybe an underlying resistance to childbearing as, despite the advantages brought about by feminism and equal opportunities legislation, women still bear full domestic burdens as well as work and financial responsibilities."

Reasons for difficulties lay not with women but "with a distorted and uninformed view from society, employers and health planners".

The other authors of the editorial are Melanie Davies, consultant obstetrician at Elizabeth Garrett Anderson and University College hospitals, London, who is president-elect of the Medical Women's Federation, and Peter Braude, head of the women's health department at Guy's, King's and St Thomas' medical school, London, and chairman of the scientific advisory committee of the Royal College of Obstetricians and Gynaecologists.

Dr Bewley, chair of the ethics committee of the college, said: "I think people have become slightly blasé." The biological window for the best age to have a baby "has not moved despite the fact celebrities are having their babies older and Cherie Blair has her baby older".

Patients "used to think they were old at 30, then 35, and now it is 40, but their bodies are exactly the same as 20 or 30 years ago. I think people know the health hazards but it sort of drifts past them".

Women doctors were as bad or even worse than others interested in a career, Dr Bewley said. "I look at my own consultants' body, and largely men have children when their wives are in their 20s and early 30s, and largely women have children in their 30s and 40s."

The Guardian Friday September 16 2005

T2 reportage

As the Republic of Ireland goes to the polls in a bid to tighten the abortion laws, **Carol Midgley** hears the harrowing stories of women whose only option is to travel to England for the operation

A desperate decision

Bernadette rose early this morning, long before her teenage sons were awake, and made the two-hour journey to Dublin in a fog of nausea caused partly by nervousness and partly by the new life growing inside her.

At Dublin airport she boarded the 6.55am Ryanair flight to Stansted, touching down at 8am to find a minicab driver holding her name aloft on a card. A £35 taxi ride later and she is in the waiting room of a Marie Stopes clinic in Essex, where her pregnancy will soon be aborted. Later today she will fly back to Dublin, drive home and try to carry on as if nothing has happened. She is 40 years old.

Bernadette is feeling a "cement mixer" of emotions today — sadness, fear, guilt, shame — but most of all she is angry. Angry that at a time of crisis in her life when she most wants to be in familiar surroundings, she has been forced to deceive her family and friends and travel in secret to a foreign country for an operation that she believes is best for her and for her children. She has also had to pay almost £1,000 for something that women in Britain could access with ease on the NHS.

Abortion is illegal in the Republic of Ireland unless the mother's life is in grave danger, which means that every year some 7,000 women make the unhappy journey across the Irish Sea to have terminations in the UK. Today Bertie Ahern's Fianna Fail-led Government will ask the electorate to vote in its second referendum on abortion in ten years. A "yes" vote will outlaw abortions for women whom doctors believe may commit suicide if the pregnancy continues and permit them only for women whose physical health is threatened. This will, in effect, reverse a Supreme Court ruling of 1992, in which a 14-year-old girl who had been raped by a friend of her parents and was suicidal was allowed to have an abortion.

The Bill has thrown much of Ireland into confusion, a deliberate tactic by some campaigners, it is claimed. Walk down a street in Dublin and a poster on one side screams: "Babies will die — vote no." On the opposite side another says: "Babies will die — vote yes." Many people mistakenly believe that by voting yes they are voting to allow abortions. In fact, the Bill would introduce prison sentences of up to 12 years for anyone aiding or procuring an illegal abortion.

The pro-choice and pro-life lobbies have been campaigning in force. As Bernadette was walking down the street last week a pro-life protester thrust a leaflet into her face that denounced all women who seek terminations as murderers. She was en route to a pre-counselling session about her own termination.

But she is lucky in one respect. At least her husband is by her side today at the Buckhurst Hill clinic, in Essex, and fully supports her decision. Many married women dare not tell their husbands that they are having an abortion, such is the stigma, and nurse the secret all their lives.

JOHN EVANS/IRISH PICTURE LIBRARY

An Irish ferry in the 1950s. These days many women use cut-price flights to come to Britain for abortions

Bernadette fell pregnant when her intra-uterine device (coil) was removed because it was making her unwell. Her boys, 15 and 17, will soon sit exams that will shape their futures, and she thinks it unfair to bring a newborn baby into the home and disrupt their lives. Nor can the couple cope with the idea of starting again from scratch; they were hoping to take early retirement and enjoy each other's company in later life.

But that doesn't stop Bernadette breaking down in tears as she explains her decision. "Having an abortion is traumatic enough, but all this — the secrecy, the travelling — just makes it a hundred times worse. I've lied to my sons and to my mother, who hates abortion. Everyone thinks that we've gone shopping in London."

'Things are a lot more liberal in England. There was nothing but kindness'

She rubs her stomach, which she thinks is already showing signs, despite her being only eight weeks pregnant, and is concealed beneath a woolly jumper. Bernadette's friends have seen her wearing a lot of baggy clothes lately. "If I'd been able to have this done in Ireland, I could have done it ten days ago and wouldn't be so big," she says. She had seen an advert for Marie Stopes in a copy of *Marie Claire* magazine.

"I keep thinking that I'm killing something, but I just can't have this baby, and the fact that I've had to go through all this because of my country's backward laws makes me furious. I'm Catholic, but I believe that any woman has the right to do what she wants with her own body. The worst thing for me is that I've had kids and I know what I'm giving up. I would rather be doing this in complete ignorance."

As recently as a decade ago most Irish women seeking terminations travelled to Liverpool on the ferry — the "abortion boat" — staying in cheap B&Bs and telling their families they were visiting friends. But the burgeoning market in low-cost airfares means hundreds now fly into London every week and do not even stay the night, in order to save money.

Despite the popular image of these women as, in the main, teenagers who sneak behind their parents' backs and make the harrowing journey to Britain alone, the reality is that most Irish women who seek abortions in Britain are in their twenties and thirties, many of them married with four or five children already.

Younger people would find it almost impossible to find £1,000 without help, and most teenage girls end up having the babies. "Away-day abortions", as one graphics designer who had a termination last year says, are a middle-class option. Only those with well-paid jobs and credible excuses to spend time away can countenance them.

Clinics also say that attitudes have softened recently and that few women come alone. At the clinic this morning six Irish women await operations. Two are with their mothers, four with their partners. The youngest is 23, the eldest 40. This is about average. Last week there were ten Irish clients in one day, including a young doctor.

Some women are politicised about the abortion referendum, others have no interest and just want to forget all about it. There is little interaction as the women sit pensively in the lounge with their bags and rucksacks waiting for their name to be called.

Faith Rees, the nurse in charge at Buckhurst Hill, says young girls still come with shocking stories. "In some cases doctors have told them that they are not pregnant when they are, or pretended the pregnancy was less advanced than it really was so that by the time she came to seek an abortion, it was too late", she says. "Most people don't bother seeing their GP at all."

Recently a girl from the Irish Republic turned up here for an abortion. A few weeks earlier her GP had told her that she had plenty of time as the pregnancy was at a primary stage. She arrived believing that she was 14 weeks advanced; an examination showed that she was nearly 28 weeks, four weeks past the legal limit. The clinic could only counsel her about adoption and fostering options. She returned home tearfully to face her parents. She was 17.

Last month a newborn baby was found strangled in the toilet of a hotel room in Nice on the Côte d'Azur. The 21-year-old Irish mother had travelled to France from Dublin 24 hours earlier with her boyfriend because, French police say, she didn't want anyone at home to know about the pregnancy. The death is the subject of a police investigation.

The story was covered widely in the French media but received little attention in Ireland.

Denise Darrell-Lambert, of the British Pregnancy Advisory Service in Liverpool, says: "We see a lot of Irish girls in Liverpool but not as many as we used to because low-cost airlines are now as cheap as the ferry. Many go to our Richmond clinic, near Heathrow. Nationally in 2001 we saw 2,400 Irish women but that figure could be higher because some don't give Irish addresses."

Most women arrive at under nine weeks pregnant but some

come much later, when operations carry more risk. It also rules out the RU486 "abortion pill", a non-surgical alternative, that must be taken at around seven or eight weeks. "It takes time for them to save up the money and organise their lives," adds Darrell-Lambert. "Money is a big factor." Once back in Ireland, some dare not see their GPs for post-operation check-ups; they simply cross their fingers and hope for the best.

Orla, 24, from Co Clare, had her abortion in the North of England last month. She paid £120 for a flight to Liverpool and money for the operation, about £450, was provided by her 30-year-old boyfriend.

Orla, a bank worker, told her family that she was going to Manchester for a pop concert and stayed with a friend from university. Now back at home, she recalls the experience as being slightly surreal. "I couldn't believe how nice everyone was to me at the clinic," she says. "You know things are a lot more liberal over in England, but I still expected the odd word of disapproval. There was nothing but kindness." She had got pregnant on a "drunken night" when the couple neglected to use a condom. "It was my own fault. Stupid, stupid girl," she says, angrily. The trip to the UK was "horrendous" but she found the abortion itself far less traumatic than the aftermath.

"When it was over I felt great relief, but having to go home and put on a brave face when inside I still felt so emotional was hideous. I told only my boyfriend and one other friend, and it was a nightmare going back to work and being cheery around my parents when something so enormous had happened in my life. But Dad is anti-abortion and I couldn't risk them knowing so I just had to grit my teeth."

In the centre of Dublin an unimposing building carries a plaque bearing the name Marie Stopes. But this clinic cannot offer abortions. It is independent and must call itself "Reproductive Choices" to comply with the law. It can offer only pregnancy examinations, counselling and advice on fostering, adoption or how to fix abortions in the UK. Staff can give out phone numbers but must not make the calls themselves. Still, it is a lifeline for thousands of bewildered pregnant women who have nowhere else to turn. (Not so long ago women would get phone numbers from graffiti scrawled on the back of public lavatory doors.)

Deidre Jones runs the clinic, which sees about 20 women a day. They range in age from 13 to 50. Jones says a yes vote would seriously endanger women's health. "Many women have no idea how advanced their pregnancy is when they come here. Recently we had a girl who was hoping to get an abortion at 35 weeks. A lot of these pregnancies are alcohol related, but the very poor girls can't afford an abortion. They tend to have the baby."

For most women, going in secret and telling lies to their families adds hugely to the trauma. "But the Government would rather them get the deed done elsewhere," says Jones.

At the Essex clinic, there are three options for surgical abortion — with local anaesthetic, during which the cervix is numbed, conscious sedation, in which the patient is drowsy but not unconscious, and under general anaesthetic. The abortion pill is impractical for most Irish women since it requires three trips to the clinic.

PAUL McERLANE/REUTERS

Referendum posters in Dublin

Proposed Protection of Human Life in Pregnancy Act 2002.

- Defines abortion as taking place after the embryo has implanted in the womb.
- States that if a doctor conducts a procedure in an approved place to prevent real risk to a woman's life other than by suicide, it will not be regarded as abortion.
- Restates the right to information on abortions and the right to travel to obtain them.
- Prison sentences of up to 12 years for anyone aiding or procuring an illegal abortion.

Bernadette's operation is drawing closer. She has opted for conscious sedation. With a consultation it costs £435. The couple's flights were £365, plus there are the taxi fares.

Often it is not possible to obtain cut-price flights as they must be booked far in advance, so women end up forking out for day-return business fares. Bernadette is a housewife and has not needed to juggle time off work. Money isn't a problem as her husband has a good job. But, she says: "Can you imagine what it would be like for a young girl? Impossible. This is horrendous enough for me, and I'm an adult."

She looks at her husband. "We've been so stressed since we found out I was pregnant that we've been biting each other's head off. I've had morning sickness, which I've had to try and hide, but my eldest isn't stupid. He senses something's wrong. My hormones have been all over the place."

She has not told her GP as "he knows absolutely everybody where I live". When she gets home she will pretend to him that she has stomach cramps and hope that he gives her some antibiotics in case she has picked up an infection.

Bernadette's husband looks at her sadly. "It has been terrible for us, because every time you switch on the TV news at the moment they're going on about abortion and the referendum. That's all we need."

Will they be voting? "Yes we will! And it will be a 'no'. Most people, though, don't even understand what it's about."

Pro-lifers argue that a yes vote would clarify the law and protect the unborn from the moment of implantation in the womb, though many hardliners will vote no as they don't think it goes far enough; they would like an embryo protected from the moment of conception.

Pro-choice campaigners are appalled that suicide is being disregarded as a ground for abortion and will criminalise women who are so desperate that they will attempt to perform it on themselves.

The probability is that few people will vote today. The Government fears that it may be the lowest recorded turnout for a referendum. Whatever happens, it will have no effect on the droves of unhappy people who come to Britain each year seeking abortions. Or on the bleak joke that Ireland's biggest export is pregnant women.

The names in this article have been changed.

Contribute to the Debate via comment@thetimes.co.uk

Death weekend.

The Times, 6th March 2002

Cost of loving

Peking: Tianjin in northern China is imposing a "sin tax" on unmarried couples living together, the Xinhua agency said. The couples can be fined up to 1,000 yuan (£80) under a new code in the city. *(Reuter)*

China's "sin tax"

LIZ Hurley and Jordan – two of the most beautiful and desirable women in the world – are both pregnant. They should be enjoying the happiest and most fulfilling time in their lives. But incredibly BOTH stars have been let down

EXCLUSIVE

by the men they expected would want to share their joy.

They have suffered the trauma of rejection and now face life as single mums. The same question will be on the lips of women everywhere – WHY? **RACHAEL BLETCHLY** and **JAMES DESBOROUGH** reveal just why these two beautiful stars have been left alone and heartbroken...

Liz ditched her baby's tycoon dad after he told her to have abortion

LIZ Hurley's playboy lover wanted her to have an ABORTION when she told him she was pregnant.

Stunned Liz, 36, hoped multi-millionaire Steve Bing would share her joy that she was expecting his child.

But now one of her closest friends has revealed that the 37-year-old American movie mogul told Liz he did not want her to have the baby.

Thrilled

Now their 18-month relationship has hit the rocks and Liz has moved back to Britain to give birth – supported by her old flame Hugh Grant.

Her friends and family have dubbed the tycoon "Bing Laden" over his behaviour.

Close friend William Cash – who dined with Liz this week – said: "You'd have thought that most men would be ecstatic, as well as flattered, at the prospect of fathering a baby, married or not, to one of the most beautiful and famous women in the world.

LIZ'S AGONY

But apparently Bing does not agree. A friend in LA tells me that he did not share Elizabeth's elation when she discovered she was pregnant.

"Indeed the friend went so far as to add that in fact Bing made it clear to Elizabeth that he did not want her to have the baby.

"Since she dropped her bombshell, their relationship has all but fallen off the tracks.

"On top of this, he has spoken to her only occasionally on the phone, and has hardly seen her."

Liz confirmed last week that she is three months pregnant.

Speaking outside her home in Chelsea, West London, the radiant-looking star said she was "overwhelmed" with excitement.

But she tellingly refused to discuss her relationship with Bing. Liz told friends she plans to raise the child as a single mother.

But ex-love Hugh Grant is already proving a tower of strength and even went to hospital with her for her first scan.

Cash said: "For the past six weeks, Elizabeth has effectively been single again with Hugh Grant standing by her and acting like the true English gent he is.

"He is there for her, just as she has always been for him."

Playboy Bing – set to inherit a £400 million fortune from his father – has been linked to a string of stars including Uma Thurman and Sharon Stone.

He began dating Liz in October 2000. They split up briefly but got back together again in March.

Marry

Bing wooed Liz with expensive gifts like a sapphire and diamond ring and Rolex watch.

Liz rented a house close to him in LA's plush Bel Air district.

Cash revealed: "During the 18 months they were together, they were pretty much inseparable. Friends had said they wouldn't be surprised if she and Bing were to marry.

"But when somebody gets pregnant, it's only then that you really find out what the person's true colours are."

● Clare Morrisroe: See Page 21

Liz Hurley - Abortion request.

Call to protect children from body piercing

By Sam Lister and Patrick Barkham

BODY piercings below the neck, once the preserve of fetishists and freak shows, should be outlawed for those under the age of 16, public health experts said yesterday.

The surge in the popularity of body piercings has made the Chartered Institute for Environmental Health call for tougher hygiene and licensing controls to reduce the risk of blood-related diseases such as hepatitis and HIV, and simpler infections.

Among the recommendations is a minimum age of consent for piercings below the neck, a craze among teenagers influenced by celebrities such as Britney Spears and Victoria Beckham. A spokesman for the institute said that belly button piercings were an area of particular concern.

"More and more people are getting piercings, and there are big public health issues," he said. "Often kids under 16 are not in a position to be allowing these things to happen to their bodies.

"Areas like the belly button are very sensitive and not designed for such interference. [People] do not consider the serious health implications, and the most basic hygiene requirements frequently are not followed."

The spokesman said that because the body piercing profession was unregulated it was impossible to collate the increasing incidents of infection, but a growing number of GPs were reporting cases of young people contracting infections from piercings. The cost to the NHS has been estimated at £1.5 million a year.

A recent health survey in Rochdale, Greater Manchester, found that 95 per cent of local GPs had treated complications arising from body piercing. While ear piercings generally heal in four to six weeks, navel and deep genital piercings can take up to six months to heal and so are more likely to get infected. Navel piercings are also more prone to infection because tight-fitting clothes prevent the circulation of air and allow moisture to build up.

Other areas of concern include the growth in oral piercings — a fad taken up by Princess Anne's daughter Zara Phillips, who was spotted wearing a tongue stud — and multiple piercings through ear cartilage. Dentists have reported chipped teeth, excessive bleeding, nerve damage and speech impediments in people with pierced tongues.

Anyone in Britain can set up a body piercing parlour without any form of training. Controls derive only from the Tattooing of Minors Act, 1969, the Health and Safety at Work Act, 1974 and local legislation.

Launching its campaign at its annual conference in Harrogate yesterday, the institute said that it was time to follow the lead of countries such as America, where body piercing is subject to federal legislation and a national licensing scheme.

Ian Foulkes, director of technical policy, said that acupuncturists and electrolysists had well-organised self-regulation with national member organisations to oversee them, but this was not true of piercers.

Three years ago the Royal College of Nursing was bombarded with calls from delegates to its annual conference for action to curb the number of botched piercings.

The Dangers of Body Piercing

The Times - Tuesday 10th September 2002

EXCLUSIVE: Nicole Appleton reveals the story that will shock the music industry

The pressure that forced me to abort Robbie's baby

By **Katie Nicholl**
SHOWBUSINESS REPORTER

Read Nicole's full haunting story only in Night & Day magazine

NICOLE APPLETON today reveals the full harrowing story of how she was forced to abort a baby fathered by Robbie Williams that she desperately wanted to keep.

Nicole, part of the girl group All Saints and now a successful solo artist, claims she was pressured to have a 'quickie' abortion for the sake of the band.

Her account, which appears in today's Night & Day magazine, is a devastating indictment of the music industry and the cynical way it manipulates the lives of its vulnerable young stars.

Nicole, 28, who was four months pregnant, describes the abortion as 'the worst day of my life' and reveals it left her feeling suicidal.

Shockingly, the operation – at a private clinic in New York – was not complete and tissue was left behind in her womb. Weeks later she was still in terrible pain but flew with All Saints to Brunei – against doctors' orders – to perform a private concert to celebrate the birthday of the Sultan's daughter.

When she returned to the UK she was told by doctors that she had been given the wrong type of operation and there was a risk she might never be able to conceive.

'I was horrified, violated by what I felt was the power of an industry that leads a woman to sacrifice her child to keep a band together,' she says. 'My life had been in the hands of a doctor who had taken less care of it than he would a stray dog's.'

Nicole lost two stones in weight and bled continually – but says she received little sympathy or support. 'No one mentioned it,' she says. 'It was as if nothing had happened.' She adds: 'What mattered was our success and ability to make money. I felt powerless.'

Nicole's revelations are made in an explosive new book, Together, co-written with sister Natalie, which is being serialised today and next week in The Mail on Sunday and the Daily Mail.

In a painfully honest account, Nicole says Robbie Williams had been 'really happy' to hear she was pregnant in March 1998. If the baby was a girl, they planned to call her Grace and Williams wrote a song called Grace which appeared on one of his albums.

Says Nicole: 'Rob put his hands on my belly and said, "This baby is saving my life". It was an answer for him, a reason for his life.' Neither has ever revealed they were expecting a child together. Nicole believes the abortion contributed to their break-up and says she does not know if the former Take That star has forgiven her.

All Saints, who were signed to London Records, were a pop phenomenon of the Nineties – their debut album sold 10 million copies.

When Nicole and her bandmate Melanie Blatt, who was also pregnant, broke the news to the other girls and their manager John Benson, Nicole recalls that Shaznay Lewis, the fourth member of All Saints, was furious. 'I thought she was going to hit me,' Nicole claims.

One of the most telling episodes in the book involves a telephone call to Nicole's family home. Nicole says her mother told her: 'The record company telephoned. They told me you are making a big mistake and that Rob is bad news.

'They want me to help you change your mind, help you think about the repercussions on you and Natalie.'

BABY BLUES: Nicole with Robbie Williams, father of the child she aborted

In April 1998 Nicole was called in to a meeting with her record company in New York. She says: 'They wanted to talk to me about my pregnancy, and the meeting ended with the record company asking me: Did I want them to organise an abortion for me?

'They said that, if so, they could organise it for the very next day, and that it would be quick and easy – I would be out of the clinic the same day.

'I was speechless. Even the record company had an interest in my private life. After the weeks of pressure I had been under, I was so battered. I felt weak. The fight went out of me and I just gave in.'

Robbie Williams - his child aborted against his wishes.

The Mail on Sunday - September 22nd 2002

Number living alone doubles in 30 years

BY MATTHEW BEARD

ONE IN three Britons lives alone, double the number 30 years ago, according to a government survey.

Since 1971, the proportion of one-person households has risen from 17 per cent to 32 per cent, according to the *General Household Survey* published yesterday, which paints a bleak picture of family life. In the 25 to 44 age group, 12 per cent live alone, compared to half of those aged 75 or over.

Average household size has fallen in three decades from 2.9 to 2.3 people, increasing pressure on housing and causing psychological problems.

During the same period, the proportion of single-parent families has tripled to 26 per cent, according to the survey of 19,000 adults by the Office for National Statistics. Figures for last year showed 23 per cent of families were raised by lone mothers, while the number of families with dependent children raised by a single father reached an unprecedented 3 per cent. In 2000, 9 per cent of men and women were co-habiting ,while 54 per cent of men and 51 per cent of the female population were married.

The survey, conducted between April last year and March 2001, showed that, in the past three years, modern technology has become increasingly common in British households. The number of homes with satellite, cable or digital access to television has increased from 29 per cent in 1998 to 40 per cent last year. In the same period, the number of homes with a CD player rose from 69 per cent to 77 per cent. Personal computers were a feature of 45 per cent of homes.

In 58 per cent of households there was at least one mobile phone owner, while 4 per cent had a mobile phone and no fixed telephone.

The *General Household Survey 2000* can be read in full at www. statistics.gov.uk/lib

Leading article, Review, page 3

Number living alone doubles.

The Independent, 12th December 2001.

8 Financial Mail on Sunday December 10, 2000

LAWYERS' WATCHDOG FAILED TO ACT DESPITE WARNING OVER SOLICITOR WHO FLED TO INDIA

Law Society ignored tip-off on £9m fraud

By Simon Fluendy

A SOLICITOR wanted for questioning about frauds totalling £9 million was under suspicion six months before he fled to India. But the Law Society, which was warned he might be acting dishonestly, failed to act.

Dixit Shah, believed to have left Britain in September, is at the centre of police inquiries into the disappearance of £6 million from a dozen small firms of solicitors and £3 million missing from the pension fund of a Birmingham engineering firm.

The Law Society's regulatory body admitted it was tipped off about Shah, but said it was snowed under by thousands of complaints and did not have the resources to investigate.

Shah bought up the firms of solicitors specialising in conveyancing and became involved in the pension fund of lockmaker C. W. Cheney through his interest in a firm of accountants and solicitors.

The Law Society was warned by one of the firms of solicitors, but the regulatory body for lawyers intervened only after Shah had left Britain, closing the offices and sending in teams of solicitors to seize control.

With Shah in hiding, they are turning their inquiries to the lawyers who sold their practices to him and have seen their businesses destroyed.

The Law Society's Office for the Supervision of Solicitors (OSS) has a team of up to six investigating the disappearance of money from special accounts for clients buying new homes.

The society said: 'Yes, we received a tip-off about Shah, but we already had concerns. We get 3,000 tip-offs a year, mostly from solicitors, but sometimes from the Legal Services Commission, in charge of administering Legal Aid, some from police, some from banks and building societies.

'We would have to quadruple our staff to investigate every one and the tip we received in February, even with our own concerns, was not specific enough to act on.'

Shah, thought to be in Bombay, has said he plans to return to Britain voluntarily to explain what happened. But an OSS source said: 'An innocent solicitor would be on the first plane home.'

West Midlands Police wants to question Shah about the money missing from C. W. Cheney's pension fund.

Shah owned Morgan Matisse & Co, the firm of solicitors that signed off the company's accounts last April.

The concerns raised by lawyers about Shah last February did not touch on illegal access to client accounts.

One solicitor said: 'We saw some very strange invoices and hire-purchase agreements that did not appear to be backed by equipment, or the equipment appeared to be of a much lower value than stated on the agreements.

'It was a sign of dishonesty. We reported this to the Law Society, the Inland Revenue and Customs & Excise.'

The OSS's concerns are also thought not to have included interference with client accounts and came from former police officers working for the OSS who 'pick up rumours and rumbles', according to a source in the department.

The alleged fraud will almost certainly lead to a rise in the £100-a-year levy that lawyers pay to a central compensation fund.

If the pension funds cannot be recovered, most of the shortfall will have to be made good by the Government.

Missing: Dixit Shah is at the centre of fraud allegations

Crooked Solicitor

Financial Mail on Sunday December 10th 2000

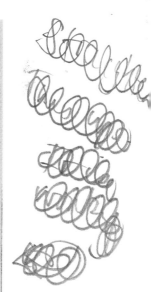

Pre-nuptial deals gain validity after wife loses £1.6m claim

BY ROBERT VERKAIK
Legal Affairs Correspondent

THE LEGAL validity of pre-nuptial agreements has received an important boost after a former model lost a £1.6m claim for compensation against her wealthy husband.

Setting out new tests for agreements between the super-rich, a High Court judge upheld a contract signed the day before the couple's wedding limiting the wife's claim to £120,000.

The court heard that Mr and Mrs K, from west London, married after Mrs K, 28, became pregnant. Mr K, a chartered surveyor with assets estimated to be worth £100m, agreed to the marriage after the bride's father put pressure on him not to have a child out of wedlock.

The father proposed a pre-nuptial agreement that restricted any financial claim upon the husband to £120,000 plus £600,000 in trust to provide a home for his former wife and son. The wife's family insisted on an £82,000 wedding while the husband wanted a quiet ceremony. Shortly afterwards, the couple spent £30,000 on a three-week Christmas holiday in the Caymans.

The marriage broke up after 14 months and the wife, who had her own assets worth £1m, claimed £1.6m compensation, plus £57,000 a year for herself.

Rodger Hayward Smith QC, a deputy High Court judge, rejected Mrs K's claim because she had freely entered into the agreed terms of the pre-nuptial contract. He said none of the husband's wealth came from his wife, nor did she contribute in any way to its accretion.

Lawyers said the case, details of which have just been published, was important because the court laid down tests for enforcing pre-marital agreements. Under laws in this country pre-nuptial contracts have no binding force on a court.

Judge Hayward Smith ruled that where both parties were legally advised independently, where the important facts were known and no duress was evident, the court should hold the couple to the contract's terms.

Pre-nuptial deals-further progress

The Independent 14th April 2003

Daily Mail, Wednesday, November 13, 2002 Page 21

Court recognises millionaire's pre-nuptial agreement in landmark divorce case

'Shotgun' cash deal backed by a judge

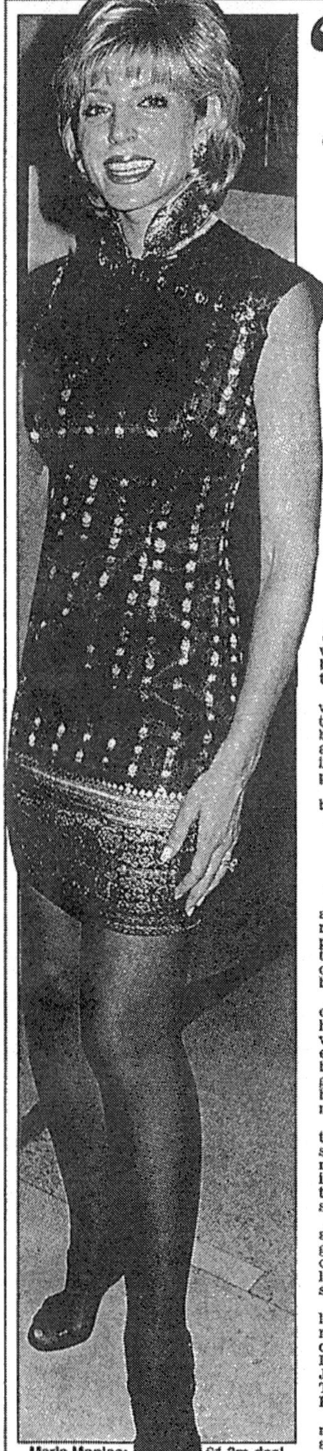

Marla Maples: £1.3m deal

By **Steve Doughty**
Social Affairs Correspondent

A DIVORCED couple must divide a multi-million-pound fortune according to the terms of their pre-nuptial agreement, the High Court ruled yesterday.

Lawyers said the landmark decision was likely to encourage more brides and grooms to shield themselves from the financial consequences of a break-up before they marry.

It also means judges are more likely to accept the terms of pre-nuptial agreements in divorce cases.

The case involved a model and her property developer husband from London, known only as the Ks.

The couple had drawn up a pre-nuptial agreement as part of a 'shotgun wedding' which was pressed on the groom by the bride's parents after their daughter became pregnant.

The 26-year-old bride, whose wealth amounted to a £1million trust fund from her father, became pregnant two months after meeting the groom, who is in his 30s and whose fortune was put at about £150million.

Backed by her parents, the bride said she would have an

'Increased weight'

abortion unless the father married her. Her father suggested a pre-nuptial agreement to protect the groom from the possible loss of his fortune if the marriage broke down.

Under its terms, in the event of divorce the bride would get a house for herself and the baby which would be reclaimed by her ex-husband after the child became an adult. She would also get a lump sum of £100,000, rising by 10 per cent for each year the marriage lasted.

The wedding, staged a day after the pre-nuptial agreement was signed, included lavish entertainment and cost £82,000 - not including the flowers. But within ten months, the woman had started divorce proceedings.

Under British law, pre-nuptial agreements may be taken as guidance by a divorce court but cannot bind judges, who regularly set them aside if they consider the deal is unfair.

But in the U.S. they are regularly used and have become a major element of celebrity weddings including those of Michael Douglas and Catherine Zeta Jones, Jane Fonda and Ted Turner, and Andre Agassi and Brooke Shields.

Donald Trump had two agreements - once with first wife Ivana and then with Marla Maples, who received just £1.3million of the tycoon's huge fortune when they divorced.

Last week, the wedding of society journalist William Cash and jewellery heiress Ilaria Bulgari was said to have been postponed because Bulgari family lawyers insisted on a pre-nuptial agreement.

Mr Cash was said to have been prepared to waive any right to a share of his bride-to-be's fortune but was unwilling to give up any claim to custody of any children of the marriage.

In the case of the Ks, the judge accepted the basic terms and the wife was allowed the lump sum - which had reached £120,000 by the time the divorce was settled - and a house worth £1.2million.

He also awarded the woman £15,000 a year in maintenance on top of the £15,000 a year the husband intended to spend on his child's schooling. The Lord Chancellor, Lord Irvine, considered giving pre-nuptial deals legal force in the late 1990s.

But when the Government dropped its troubled no-fault divorce reforms, the idea was abandoned.

Divorce expert Mark Harper, of the legal firm Withers, said: 'There have been cases in which judges are tending to place increased weight on pre-nuptial agreements. Increasingly, judges will take greater account of them unless the end result is grossly unfair.'

Pre-nuptial agreements - High Court Sanction

Daily Mail - Wednesday November 13th 2002.

Tying the knot around pre-nuptials

District Judge Ivor Weintroub on how the courts currently view pre-nuptial agreements and what legal changes we may see in the future

That's a pre-nuptial backhand if ever I saw one!

Rod is rich and extremely keen on tennis. His service has improved so much that he now wishes to get married to Beth, a regular playing partner, a local girl who is now three months pregnant by him. Your client Rod's father, even richer, is concerned advantage might be taken. He has heard about pre-nuptial agreements and seeks your advice.

In *K v K (Ancillary Relief: Pre-nuptial Agreement)* [2003] 1 FLR 120, Roger Hayward Smith QC, sitting as a High Court judge, considered such an agreement that Mr K sought to uphold, and Mrs K sought to ignore. The couple separated after 14 months of marriage. Mrs K, when married, was pregnant by Mr K. Mrs K benefited from a trust fund of £1 million, but Mr K declared assets of £25 million. The driving force behind the marriage was the wife's family, the husband wanting a long engagement, but the marriage proceeded on the conclusion of the agreement the day before the wedding. The agreement provided that if the marriage dissolved within five years, the wife would receive a lump sum of £100,000 compounded by 10% per annum for each year the marriage continued, and the husband was to make reasonable financial provision for any children.

Mr Justice Wilson had said in *S v S (Divorce: Staying Proceeding)* [1977] 1 WLR 100: 'I am aware of a growing belief that in a despatch of a claim for ancillary relief in this jurisdiction, no significant weight will be afforded to a pre-nuptial agreement, whatever the circumstances. I would like to sound a cautionary note in that respect... there will come a case... where the circumstances surrounding the pre-nuptial agreement and the provisions therein contained might, when viewed in the context of the other circumstances of the case, prove influential or even crucial.'

Mr Justice Connell in *M v M (Pre-nuptial Agreement)* [2002] 1 FLR 654, thought the agreement in that case significantly crucial, concluding it could be considered a circumstance of the case, or conduct that the court would find inequitable to disregard.

Mr Hayward Smith's conclusion in *K v K* was that it would be both. He posed himself a number of questions in deciding whether the wife should be bound, or by which he should be influenced in his decision concerning the agreement, under section 25(1) and (2) of the Matrimonial Causes Act 1973 – page 131 B. The questions he posed, and answers he reached, follow. However, each case must turn on its own circumstances.

- Did the wife understand the agreement? Yes.
- Was she properly advised as to the terms? Yes.
- Did the husband put her under any pressure to sign it? No.
- Was there sufficient disclosure of assets? No.
- Did the wife press for values of assets? No.
- Was either party put under pressure to sign from others – for example, pressure from Mrs K's family to enter the agreement to secure marriage? Yes, but at the actual time of signature he concluded she was no longer under pressure to do so.
- Was the agreement willingly signed? Yes.
- Did the husband exploit a dominant financial position? No.
- Was the agreement entered into in the knowledge that there would be a child? Yes.
- Have any unforeseen circumstances arisen that would make it unjust to bind the parties? No.
- Is there sufficient clarity in the terms? Yes.
- Does the agreement preclude an order for periodical payments for the wife? No.
- Would injustice be done by holding the parties to terms? No.

He held the wife to the capital terms of the agreement. Concerning periodical payments for the wife the court was not prepared to prevent the claim, as it was not excluded. Even so the judge took the view that, if that were wrong – because the wife had to make the important and enormous contribution of bringing up the child – it would be unjust to exclude her claim even though the marriage was of short duration.

He also provided additional capital on reversionary trusts to Mr K to suitably house the child, his welfare being the court's first consideration, during the time the child would be living there, but only incidentally to house the wife. The reasoning was that otherwise the fund would benefit the wife, and go beyond the agreed lump sum provision.

The court was not referred to *N v N (Jurisdiction: Pre-nuptial Agreement)* [1999] 2 FLR 745, where Mr Justice Wall held that it was contrary to public policy to seek to enforce a pre-nuptial agreement. The agreement sought to oust the jurisdiction of the court, and entering into an agreement before marriage undermined the concept of marriage. The case sought to uphold agreements providing for Orthodox Jewish couples, in the event of dissolution of their marriage, referring financial disputes to the Court of the Chief Rabbi in London for determination, thus also ensuring the wife would receive the benefit of a religious divorce (Get), without which she would not be able to enter into another religious marriage.

The particular difficulties highlighted by that case have now been relieved substantially by the Divorce (Religious Marriages) Act 2002, supported by the rule change contained in The Family Proceedings (Amendment) Rules 2003 SI No. 184, both of which have been in force since 24 February 2003.

The Law Society has published its proposals for reform of ancillary relief proceedings (May 2003). Lord Justice Thorpe, in the foreword, welcomes its publication on behalf of the president's ancillary relief advisory group, saying it 'makes a significant and lasting contribution to public debate on an area of law reform that affects many families.'

The report recognises that 'if the law was changed to provide that pre-marital contracts should be binding on a court when looking at financial provision on divorce this could, in certain cases, lead to significant unfairness'. It recommends that pre-marital contracts should continue to be one of the factors to be taken into account when looking at the financial provision between the parties. The reservation is that such agreements have not, since 1995, been considered by the Court of Appeal.

District Judge Ivor Weintroub sits at Bournemouth County Court

Pre-nuptial agreement guidelines

Law Society Gazette 31 July 2003

COMMENT

Bride and gloom

The only realistic choice for any wealthy client who wants to protect their financial position is to not get married, writes Damian Baron

Am I alone in thinking that the recent series of cases culminating with the Court of Appeal's decision in *Charman* has taken the law of ancillary relief too far when it comes to business and/or wealthy clients?

Pre-*White*, solicitors could confidently advise that the courts were reluctant to make any decision which materially affected either spouse's business so as not to kill the goose that laid the golden egg. Over recent years and since *White*, the courts are increasingly willing to view the value of the business as just another asset to go into the pot for division, whether the other party worked in the business or even had any part in it at all.

Not only do we have the yardstick of equality in respect of capital and pension, we now have an emerging series of cases in the higher courts where the future earning capacity of the higher earner is viewed, once again, as just another matrimonial asset to be divided. However, what does not seem to be a consideration is that only one party actually has to go out to work to generate this income. Can this be right in principle?

I firmly believe that the general perception of what is going on in these cases is one of the factors leading to an increase in a number of enquiries about pre-nuptial agreements. While we usually advise our clients that having a pre-nuptial agreement is better than nothing, we do, of course, have to further advise that the court can, and in all probability will, tear them up in any ensuing divorce proceedings.

My point is that the perception of the person in the street is that the law is becoming increasingly unfair and that he or she will be penalised if they are hard working and successful in the event that their marriage or civil partnership breaks down, even if the breakdown may be the fault of the other party.

So, just as we will usually advise some of our clients not to sign any pre-nuptial agreements, are we now at the point where we have to start advising our wealthy or potentially wealthy clients not to marry?

A couple of years ago, two clients in their late 20s sought my advice. They were about to have transferred to them their parents' business. Its value was about £7 million. They were both engaged to be married and wanted to know what the position would be if they did get married and, perhaps after a few years and a couple of children, it all went wrong. I advised accordingly as to the likely orders that maybe made by the court. Perhaps not surprisingly, both clients are still single.

I further recently advised a very wealthy individual who was considering marriage to a much younger partner. The client sought advice as to how they could, within reason, protect their financial position should the marriage fail. My advice, and that of counsel, was simple: if the individual wished to achieve any certain level of protection, don't get married.

We have now reached a point where the law is discouraging marriage in some cases, not only those involving significant wealth. Are we confident that this is a good thing? Should the law not now allow intelligent human beings with quality legal advice to agree the regulation of financial provision in the event of a break-up?

One final thought. Bearing in mind the huge discretion under section 25 of the Matrimonial Causes Act 1973 that judges have always had to make, for example, proper allowance for the indirect contributions of the economically weaker spouse or partner, was the 'reasonable needs' approach such a bad thing?

Damian Baron is head of family law at Napthens in Preston

Bride and gloom - beware the wealthy client.

The Law Society's Gazette 19th July 2007

Avarice, cruelty and what this tawdry case tells us about the injustice of modern divorce

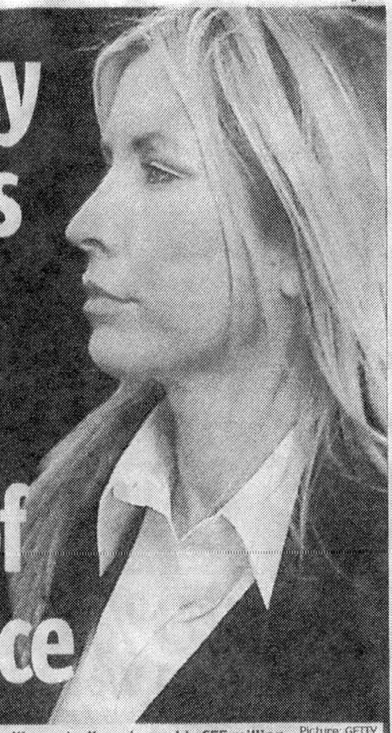

Undeserving? Heather Mills will reputedly get roughly £55 million Picture: GETTY

by Amanda Platell

WHAT an utterly unedifying spectacle the divorce of Paul McCartney and Heather Mills has turned out to be. Treachery, greed, drug-taking, violence — the allegations have been endless.

Few now could doubt that here was a marriage as short as it was miserable, ending in a lingering acrimony that no amount of PR spin or brave smiles outside the courtroom can disguise.

Now, as the final scenes are played out in the High Court and the couple reportedly edge towards a deal, it is tempting to dismiss this nightmare as belonging to a world apart from ours, a world of private jets and public histrionics.

But the truth is that this carnival of bile, this showbiz showdown, demonstrates everything that is wrong with the divorce laws of Britain today.

Let's step back and take stock of the settlement that Heather is said to be seeking. The sums differ wildly, according to which of the warring camps you believe. But the most reliable estimate thus far is that the former Ms Mills is in line for roughly £55 million, made up of a £20 million lump sum, plus £2.5 million a year for the next 14 years, until their daughter Bea turns 18.

By any reckoning, that's an astronomical return on a marriage that lasted just four short and unhappy years.

Heather denies she ever set out to be a gold-digger, yet the result is that she will emerge from that courtroom with a fortune far, far beyond anything she could have hoped to earn independently.

And for her to suggest that it is in any way an equitable return on the emotional investment and sacrifices she made in motherhood and marriage is farcical.

Granted, if she and Macca had been married for 40 years, she would have a far more persuasive case for sympathy. But four years? That's not a marriage, it's an overgrown fling.

Nonetheless, the law is on Heather's side. Because common sense, it seems, counts for nothing in the divorce courts today, still less a modicum of decency and fair play. The result is that marriage itself has been cheapened.

For if this bitter case has served one purpose, it has been to send a powerful message that divorce is a bonanza for women, however badly they behave, and especially if they choose to give up work the moment they marry.

Whether she intended it or not, Heather has become an icon for the Great Female Gold-Digger's Movement, and one who will have lasting consequences.

We saw a precursor to this case with the landmark judgment in 2005 when the £85,000-a-year PR executive Melissa Miller took £5 million of her husband's earnings after less than three years of a childless marriage.

HOW can it be right, in our age of equal opportunities, that a divorced man is forced to work into perpetuity to compensate an ex-wife — even successful, professional, skilled women who are more than capable of supporting themselves independently?

The same is true, incidentally, of those increasingly common cases where a high-earning woman separates from a husband she has been supporting financially.

Whatever the sexes concerned, it is manifestly unfair that when two adults are capable of working, only one should continue to shoulder the main financial burden in the event of a separation — all the more so when that burden is so unnecessary.

Yesterday a High Court judge decided that serial divorcee Susan Sangster will walk away from her fourth marriage without a penny from her last husband because they had both signed a pre-nuptial agreement and both were independently wealthy. But how had Ms Sangster amassed her personal £18 million fortune? Yes, through her three previous divorces.

Heather Mills will certainly be independently wealthy as well, after her divorce. Just look at the list of demands that the Mills camp has presented as justification for the massive payout it is seeking. We are led to believe Heather needs two homes, one in Britain and another in the U.S., 24-hour security and two full-time nannies, household staff, a secretary and personal trainer — all to be paid for by her ex-husband.

Now, of course, children must be properly provided for financially. But this isn't a checklist of necessity, it's a shopping basket of greed and indulgence from a woman who, until she got her talons into Macca, was living a comfortable but by no means luxurious life in the mews flat she shared with a tennis tournament organiser.

Ah, say Heather's team, but the fall-out from her acrimonious divorce is such that she is now virtually unemployable. I rather doubt that. Even if she is obliged to sign a gagging clause as part of the deal, her future bankability will owe far more to her brief marriage to a Beatle than to her own rather limited talents.

Indeed, without it she'd be earning a pittance. How much do you imagine Heather Mills — landmine campaigner and former glamour model — would be earning now, aged 40, if she hadn't shot to fame thanks to her marriage? She'd be lucky if she netted £50,000 a year. So how can it be right that she should walk away with £50 million?

But perhaps even more damagingly, this case also teaches us that in today's divorce courts, women who engage in cruelty and smear tactics — egged on by their lawyers — can be sure that it will increase their eventual payouts.

By all accounts, Paul is no saint, but the lengths Ms Mills' so-called friends have gone to vilify him have been breathtaking.

He may well be mean with his money (who can blame him for that, given the way things turned out?), but a wife-beater, an alcoholic, a druggie? Three decades of marriage to Linda would suggest differently, despite the rocky patches that they supposedly encountered.

So, why smear his character through carefully placed leaks? Why propagate such hateful stories? Because, as any divorcing dad knows to his cost, they serve to threaten the one thing in life they hold most dear — access to the children.

For a vengeful and unscrupulous wife, allegations of cruelty and abuse are the ultimate weapon in her armoury. Never mind that 'abuse' is a term now so loose in law it can mean anything from being a wife-beater to a husband who shouts at the dog.

A wife doesn't have to prove her allegations for them to be taken seriously in the eyes of the divorce courts. A judge must rightly consider the safety of the children first. Proof is difficult to ascertain.

THE result? All too often a father, damned by his wife's allegations, knows that it is better to be the victim of an unjust financial settlement than to be denied access to his children.

Some might call that justice. I'd call it blackmail.

For little Bea, of course, it may already be too late. With a vilified mother and a humiliated father, no amount of luxury homes or holidays will compensate for the fall-out from her parents' very public cruelty to each other.

Who are the winners here? Paul's entourage of lawyers, supposedly the most expensive ever assembled for a divorce case in Britain, will walk away with millions. And this circus will doubtless be a nice little earner for Heather's hangers-on, the personal trainer and the make-up artist.

But as for the main protagonists, Heather will get her blood-money, yes, but in the process she has become one of the most vilified women in Britain. The once-great Beatle is now living proof that there's no fool like an old and rich fool. Lasting damage has been inflicted on all the children caught up in the crossfire — not just Bea, but Paul's three grown-up offspring, too.

No, whatever the eventual deal, there are no winners here.

But the real legacy of the Mills v. McCartney case is this: it has demonstrated, in all-too painful detail, exactly what's wrong with divorce in this country. It is no longer about justice; it is an opportunity for avarice, a theatre for character assassination and a gladiatorial contest in which everyone loses — except the lawyers.

Paul McCartney and the avarice of Heather Mills

Daily Mail, February 14th 2008

Alarming conclusion of the world's biggest smoking and drinking study

One glass of wine a day 'raises breast cancer risk'

By **Jenny Hope**
Medical Correspondent

DRINKING a single glass of wine a day increases a woman's risk of getting breast cancer by six per cent, according to shocking figures.

They show that every year thousands of British women could be saved from the trauma of the disease by giving up drinking.

A huge Cancer Research UK study reveals that heavy alcohol consumption is particularly dangerous, with women drinking more than a bottle of wine a day at 40 to 50 per cent higher risk of the disease.

Rising levels of drinking by women have already contributed to more cases of breast cancer in recent years – and the toll could go higher if the trend continues upwards.

The study estimates around one in 20 British breast cancer cases – around 2,000 in total – each year can be blamed on drinking.

Its results, which come at a time when young women are drinking more than ever, could lead to revised guidance from the Department of Health which currently recommends women drink no more than the equivalent of two to three small glasses of wine a day.

Professor Valerie Beral, of Cancer Research UK's Cancer Epidemiology Unit at the Radcliffe Infirmary, Oxford, said: 'This research tells us there is a definite link between alcohol and breast cancer and the evidence suggests that the more a woman drinks the greater her risk.'

She said drinking had contributed to rising numbers of breast cancer cases, although other factors such as the trend for women to remain childless or have smaller numbers of children and not breastfeed has probably had a bigger effect.

'But women are drinking more now than they used to and if this pattern continues it is bound to have an impact on the rates of breast cancer in the future,' she warned.

The research, the world's largest study of drinking and smoking, concludes that smoking does not cause breast cancer.

But Sir Richard Doll, a co-author of the study and the scientist who first revealed the link between smoking and lung cancer, said women should not think of smoking as a 'safer' option because it actually causes 15 types of cancer.

He said: 'A woman is more likely to die of lung cancer because it is notoriously difficult to treat.'

Previous research on the level of breast cancer risk to women who drink and smoke has produced conflicting results, mainly because it has been difficult to disentangle the influence of each of the two factors.

But the sheer size of the new study, to be published in the British Journal of Cancer, has allowed the researchers to make the most accurate estimates yet of the risks.

Data from more than 50 studies involving 150,000 women worldwide – including 23,000 non-drinkers – was analysed.

It shows there is a six per cent rise in risk for every alcoholic drink consumed on a daily basis by British women. The risk remains the same regardless of other factors such as a family history of disease.

The risk rises for each glass of wine to between 40 and 50 per cent when drinking seven to eight glasses or units a day.

This means by the age of 80, 8.8 women out of every 100 who don't drink will have developed breast cancer compared with 10.1 women out of every 100 having two drinks a day.

Professor Beral said it was unclear how drinking alcohol promotes breast cancer but it may work by raising levels of the hormone oestrogen in the body.

'If every woman stopped drinking, then there would be 2,000 fewer breast cancer cases a year in the UK,' she said. This represents a fall of five per cent in the total of 40,000 cases – around 13,000 British women are killed by the disease each year.

She said a woman's age might affect her attitude towards drinking because breast cancer is a more important cause of death before 60 than heart disease. Younger women are worried about breast cancer – even though it is more common in later life – but 'here is something they can do about it', she said.

Professor Doll pointed out older women benefit from modest drinking because heart disease cases soar after the menopause.

'There is a 20 per cent reduction in heart disease for one drink a day which has to balanced against a six per cent increase in breast cancer.

'Huge amounts of alcohol are bad for you but we don't want to dissuade people from having one or two drinks a day if they enjoy it because of a small risk of breast cancer when there are similar risks from all sorts of things in this world.'

j.hope@dailymail.co.uk

Risky pleasure: Scientists have directly linked alcohol to breast cancer

The guidelines

HEALTH Department guidelines suggest men can have between three and four units of alcohol a day and women between two and three without a significant health risk.

A unit is half a pint of beer, one measure of spirits or one small glass of wine.

The 1995 guidelines came out of a Government report showing alcohol in moderation protects men over 40, and women after the menopause, from heart disease and strokes.

Recent research suggests occasional drinking may stave off Alzheimer's and also reduce bone loss in women after the menopause.

Wine is thought to have more benefits than other drinks. Heart attack survivors having two or more glasses of wine a day reduce their risk of having another attack by more than 50 per cent compared with non-drinkers.

Red wine is also said to boost levels of 'good' cholesterol in the blood and enriches it with compounds that cut the chances of a heart attack.

Alcohol link to breast cancer

Daily Mail - Wednesday November 13th 2002.

THE INDEPENDENT
Friday 30 November 2001 ★★★

Former supermodel claims she was raped by royalty

BY JOHN LICHFIELD
in Paris

A FRENCH magistrate is investigating allegations by the retired Dutch supermodel Karen Mulder that she was raped by a member of a European royal family, other famous people and leading figures in the French modelling industry.

Ms Mulder, 33, first made the allegations during the recording of a French television programme before a studio audience last month. Her claims were regarded as so devastating, and so potentially libellous, that the interview was cut from the show.

However, Ms Mulder had made almost exactly the same accusations in a statement to French police several days earlier. The public prosecutor's office in Paris confirmed yesterday that it was taking her allegations seriously enough to start a criminal investigation for "rape by persons unknown".

Her allegations will be investigated by an examining magistrate, Jean-Pierre Gaury. Sources in the public prosecutor's office said he would be looking at physical and other evidence which appeared to corroborate at least part of Ms Mulder's story.

Ms Mulder, born in the Netherlands in 1968, was for many years among the 10 best-paid models in the world. She retired a year ago and is currently being treated in a private psychiatric clinic in Paris.

The former supermodel was invited to record an interview on 31 October for a show on France 2 television, called *Tout le Monde en Parle* (*Everyone is Talking About It*). The intention was to revisit allegations made by a BBC documentary two years ago that young models were often sexually exploited by leading figures in the modelling industry. To the astonishment of the show's presenters and the studio, Ms Mulder dissolved into tears and said she had been persistently raped from her childhood up until last April.

She alleged that she had been "hypnotised" and raped by modelling agency executives and a series of well-known men, including a member of a continental royal family.

The interview was cut from the show and the studio audience was sworn to secrecy. Nevertheless, accounts of what happened have been circulating on the internet and by e-mail for the past four weeks.

An e-mail account by a person claiming to have witnessed the television show says Ms Mulder claimed to have been raped by an "incalculable number of famous people in France and abroad".

Yesterday the newspaper *Le Parisien* reported that Ms Mulder had previously approached French police and made a formal statement containing very similar allegations to those made on the show. The public prosecutor's office confirmed yesterday that it had ordered an investigation against "X" (or persons unknown) for rape.

"Considering the celebrity of the complainant, but also taking account of evidence which she has provided which could form the basis of proofs, we have decided to appoint an examining magistrate to investigate the case," a judicial source told *Le Parisien*.

The source said the information to be examined included "physical evidence".

The newspaper said the judge would now be seeking a medical report on Ms Mulder, who was said to be in a state of "acute distress".

Friends of the model told *Le Parisien* that her psychiatric problems might be connected to her difficulties in adjusting to her retirement a year ago.

But Ms Mulder's friends also pointed out that the former supermodel had been known as a level-headed person, who had always been prepared to lend her celebrity to help charitable causes.

Her modelling career was launched at the age of 17 when she won a competition organised by the French modelling agency Elite. She later worked for Yves Saint-Laurent, Chanel, Valentino and Versace. She stopped appearing on the catwalk in 1997 and retired from modelling last year, saying she wanted a new career as a film actor or singer.

Karen Mulder alleges that she was repeatedly raped from her childhood until earlier this year

Karen Mulder - "One more not so clever girl"

The Independent, 30th November 2001

KAREN MULDER

SUPERMODEL IN 'SUICIDE BID' DRAMA

Supermodel Karen Mulder, who a year ago suffered a highly publicised breakdown and spent several months in a psychiatric clinic, was last week at the centre of a confusing "suicide bid" story.

First, press reports across the world claimed that the 34-year-old Dutch-born beauty had taken a near-fatal overdose of sleeping pills in her luxury Paris apartment and been rushed to the American Hospital in a coma. After having her stomach pumped, doctors pronounced that she would survive.

According to the reports, Karen had been saved by the quick thinking of a former boyfriend, French playboy and property developer Jean-Yves Le Fur. He had known that Karen had been feeling depressed and, when she did not answer the phone, he smashed through the front door to find her unconscious. Had emergency services arrived just one hour later, it was claimed, it would probably have been too late.

Shortly after the overdose story made headline news, however, Karen's father Ben Mulder told the Dutch press that it was "nonsense". Instead, he said, his daughter was suffering from hallucinations and overfatigue and had checked herself back into the French psychiatric clinic from which she had been discharged earlier this year. "Karen went to her psychiatrist last Saturday and he convinced her that she should have herself committed again," he told the Dutch daily *De Telegraaf*. "And that's what she has done. I'm sure now that she'll have a peaceful and quiet Christmas. She's been admitted into one of the best clinics in France and I hope that Karen will now take the time to fully recover."

Then, last Thursday, a third version of events emerged. Karen's former boyfriend Jean-Yves Le Fur, the man who had supposedly discovered the supermodel lying unconscious in her apartment, apparently denied that she had taken an overdose or that she had been rushed to hospital. While he refused to make a statement on the matter, sources close to him supplied some further information. They said Le Fur had gone to Karen's apartment on the day in question to pick her up and take her to a lunch appointment. Two paparazzi were waiting outside the building and a row ensued. Le Fur apparently hit one of them and the photographer then took "revenge" by putting out the story about Karen's attempted suicide.

Since retiring from modelling, Karen has been enjoying some success as a pop singer and Le Fur's sources indicated that rather than being in hospital in Paris, she was elsewhere in France writing songs for her first album. Meanwhile, they said, Karen herself would not talk about what had happened and wanted the whole matter to die down.

By the end of last week, mystery still surrounded exactly what had gone on. However, the furore brought fresh expressions of concern from Karen's friends about how she is adapting to life away from the modelling limelight.

A decade ago, she was one of the world's best-paid supermodels, appearing at glamorous parties on the arm of Prince Albert of Monaco or racing driver Eddie Irvine. However, she hit rock bottom last year when she recorded an interview with a French TV chat show in which she made untruthful claims – which she later withdrew – that she had been raped by former members of her model agency and been forced to sleep with various men, including Prince Albert, to advance her career.

Her claims were so wild that the producers felt they could not transmit the interview and destroyed the tape. Fearful about her paranoid state, they contacted her family and she was taken to the psychiatric clinic.

Karen's father Ben blamed the incident on drugs and the end of her career. "I'm convinced her sad breakdown is a result of her using cocaine," he said in an interview last year. "But she's also exhausted. For ten years she'd been flying all over the world and worked very hard. Physically and mentally she is burned out. And then her career was suddenly over."

Karen, meanwhile, later denied drugs had triggered her breakdown, but admitted she'd suffered from depression. "It was so bad that I couldn't get up," she said.

However, after several months of treatment at the psychiatric clinic, she checked herself out and declared that she was "moving back towards the light". She revealed she had written to Prince Albert to apologise for her untrue allegations and she lined up a role in a small French film. Karen then found immediate success as a pop singer when she released a version of Gloria Gaynor's hit *I Am What I Am*, which made the top ten in France.

However, friends last week expressed concern that there might not be anyone close by to pull her up again should Karen plunge back into depression. As one French magazine recently pointed out: "Karen Mulder has no love, no man and no children." H

REPORT: LESLEY HUSSELL

Psychiatric patient Karen Mulder writes to Prince Albert to withdraw her allegation of rape. Karen Mulder - Supermodel in 'Suicide Bid' Drama

Hello Magazine - December 24th 2002.

THE TIMES THURSDAY AUGUST 22 2002

Mad or malingering? It is hard to tell them apart

Dr Thomas Stuttaford
Medical Briefing

THERE are few medical problems more difficult to differentiate between than conversion and dissociative disorders, and malingering.

The conversion and dissociative disorders are those that my grandfather and his contemporaries would have described as hysteria and my father and his colleagues in the First World War would have known as shell-shock. Conversely malingering is the intentional production of the signs of a physical and mental disorder so as to deceive others and thereby achieve gain — money, insurance, sexual or emotional support, or the avoidance of something unpleasant — even the retribution of the courts.

In conversion disorders, publicised by Sigmund Freud, there is the sudden onset of physical symptoms that have no pathological basis but are merely a subconsciously assumed medical problem. Although subconscious, these symptoms, like those intentionally displayed by malingerers, are likely to result in benefit to the patient. The patient may, for instance, have a sudden inability to walk, to talk, to see or to hear. Malingerers may have autonomic abnormalities such as inexplicable vomiting, dribbling or drooling.

Conversion disorders are more common in women than men, they occur suddenly during times of severe stress and may disappear as quickly as they came, or they may, as those who treated shell-shock know, last for years.

The important difference between conversion disorders and malingering is that the former are beyond the patient's control because their origins are subconscious. The secondary gain for patients with conversion dissociative disorders is that their subconscious has, by assuming a sick role and the symptoms that in their opinion are associate with it, the ability to pour balm on their disturbed psyche. They have sought to avoid the horrors that circumstances, their foolishness, violence or villainy — in particular sexual misbehaviour — has precipitated. The symptoms they have subconsciously assumed thereby ease their anxiety.

Conversion and dissociate symptoms have to be differentiated from malingering. Sorting out the two is extremely difficult and, as one of the standard textbooks suggests, may be almost impossible. The expert in deciding between the two diagnoses is helped not only by specialist neurological and forensic psychiatric opinions but by a series of tests to exclude physical causes.

Careful consideration of the past history of the patient is all important. Malingerers often have a past history of anti-social personality disorder (the condition known to most people as psychopathy). Dissociative disorders are more common in women, malingering is more common in men.

To diagnose malingering doctors must be able to point to an obvious recognisable goal that this will achieve for the patient. They must thereby achieve obvious legal, financial or other material or emotional advantages. So common is the association between anti-social personality disorders and malingering that there should be evidence of this before the diagnosis is made.

Malingerers usually give a history of events that does not accord with the facts as known to others. Refusal to co-operate with any evaluation always tends to favour the diagnosis of malingering rather than conversion of dissociative disorder. Those with the latter would apparently like to help, whereas malingerers seek to mislead.

Those who refuse to speak but have normal neurological function of their lips, tongues palate and vocal cord, and cough normally, are unlikely to have a physical cause for their disability.

The law on insanity was defined in 1843 after a man named McNaghten. For insanity to be an acceptable defence it must be shown that the criminal at the time the act was performed did not know that what he or she was doing was wrong, and did not know the consequences and nature of his, or her, actions.

Any change in the mental state after the crime was committed does not allow excuse on the grounds of insanity. Conversely if it can be shown that an accused has no memory of the incident, this may be accepted as the reason why he, or she cannot have a fair trial.

Psycopathy - the anti-social personality disorder.

The Times - August 22 2002.

THE SUNDAY TIMES · 28 FEBRUARY 1993 2·3

Return of the family

THE FAMILY has not been fashionable for at least a generation. The British intelligentsia have long derided it as at best a hindrance to progressive lifestyles, at worst a form of bourgeois repression. The insidious influence of the prevailing intellectual consensus encouraged a social climate and policies which undermined the nuclear family and produced a popular culture which went out of its way to disparage it (when did you last see a British television series lauding traditional family values?). Now the nation is having to deal with the consequences of this *trahison des clercs* in the form of soaring crime, increasing squalor, widespread welfare dependency, the spread of the yob culture and crumbling communities. And, suddenly, the family is back in fashion.

It is becoming increasingly clear to all but the most blinkered of social scientists that the disintegration of the nuclear family is the principal source of so much social unrest and misery. The creation of an urban underclass, on the margins of society but doing great damage to itself and the rest of us, is directly linked to the rapid rise in illegitimacy. In the worst "sink" estates the illegitimacy rate is approaching 60%, which is close to the levels of the American ghetto (but in Britain the underclass is largely white, not black or brown). What is not widely understood is that this is a new phenomenon: 15 years ago the rate was considerably less. Of course illegitimacy has increased among all social groups: but the biggest increase has been overwhelmingly among the poorer, the unskilled, the unemployed. As a result, they have gone from being merely poor to becoming an underclass.

The past two decades have witnessed the growth of whole communities in which the dominant family structure is the single-parent mother on welfare, whose male offspring are already immersed in a criminal culture by the time they are teenagers and whose daughters are destined to follow in the family tradition of unmarried teenage mothers. It is not just a question of a few families without fathers; it is a matter of whole communities with barely a single worthwhile male role-model. No wonder the youths of the underclass are uncontrollable by the time (sometimes before) they are teenagers. Illegitimacy produces an underclass for a compelling practical reason which has nothing to do with morality or the sanctity of marriage: for communities to function successfully they need families with fathers. In communities without fathers, the overwhelming evidence is that youngsters begin by running wild and end up running foul of the law.

When Charles Murray, an American political scientist, first pointed this out in a seminal study in The Sunday Times Magazine just over three years ago he was widely attacked at the time by fashionable opinion, and even by Margaret Thatcher, who stupidly refused even to acknowledge that a British underclass existed. The usual suspect commentators rushed to condemn him for casting a slur on single-parent families. But single parenthood comes in many guises — widows, middle-aged divorcees, unmarried teenage mums — and lumping them all together is no guide to social analysis. Dr Murray had identified the growth of a particular form of single parenthood — illegitimacy — and the disastrous social consequences that followed when it was the prevalent birth status in a community. There are signs that his lesson is finally dawning in some surprising quarters.

Two left-wing academics recently published a pamphlet, Families without Fatherhood, blaming the decline of the nuclear family for creating an underclass which threatened the stability and cohesion of society. Last week one of the great gurus of socialism, Professor A H Halsey, publicly repudiated a generation of social policy by saying this to The Guardian: "We're talking about a situation where the man never *arrives*, never mind *leaves*. There is a growing proportion of children born into single-parent families where the father has never participated as a father . . . and from the missing father flows the missing community ethic." Only a few days before, Tony Blair, a leading light of the intelligent tendency in the Labour party, chose to emphasise the individual responsibility of criminals and the moral vacuum behind teenage lawlessness. There are the beginnings of the national consensus The Sunday Times called for last week to produce the policies needed to stop the rot.

There is another important reason why the family should take centre stage. Just over a decade ago Thomas Sowell, a black American professor, explained how family structure, rather than racial discrimination, was the best guide to the relative performance of various ethnic groups. The stronger the family unit, the better the economic progress. Orientals were doing best of all in modern America because they had the strongest nuclear families; then came Asians, who also enjoyed tightly knit family structures. Whites were only third in the pecking order because illegitimacy, divorce and the huge growth of single-parent families had undermined the ability of white youngsters to compete; followed by Hispanics, whose family structure was even weaker. Last of all came blacks, where the nuclear family had become the exception rather than the rule. Indeed, even within the black community, family structure explained differential performance: those of West Indian or Ethiopian or even Haitian origin were doing better than American blacks because their family structures remained more intact.

Nobody took any notice of this analysis in Britain, and even in America it was controversial because it showed that racial discrimination alone could no longer explain the plight of the American black condition. But the British experience has confirmed Professor Sowell's analysis: British Asian children, with their strong sense of family, now regularly outperform white children at school, for among whites of all classes the nuclear family is in retreat; British blacks, with a weaker family structure than Asians, do considerably less well; and among the white underclass, the nuclear family has become as rare as it is in a black American ghetto.

The time has come to put the nuclear family at the centre of social policy. It needs to be preserved and nurtured; too many existing policies and attitudes only serve to undermine it. The bad news from America is that once an underclass is allowed to take root it becomes almost impossible to erase it. But at the very least it must surely be within the wit of public policy to stop the rot spreading further and even to rescue some from the despair of underclass life. In the United States there are imaginative ideas being floated to empower the poorest to have more control over their lives, to wean people off welfare dependency and to discourage the spread of single-parent welfare mothers. The problems are daunting, but at least the debate is under way. In Britain it has barely begun; it is time it did, if social despair and unrest are not to engulf more and more of our communities.

Return of the family

The Sunday Times, 28 February 1993

THE SUNDAY TIMES - JULY 1, 2001

Anti-abortionists adopt US extremist tactics

Guy Dennis

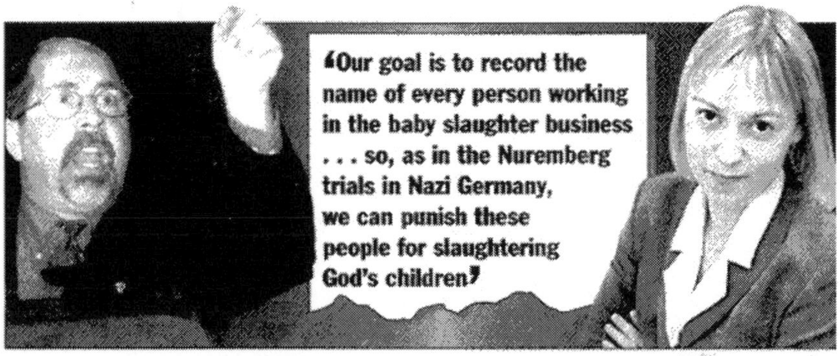

‘Our goal is to record the name of every person working in the baby slaughter business . . . so, as in the Nuremberg trials in Nazi Germany, we can punish these people for slaughtering God's children’

Radical protest: Mahoney has visited Britain while the Nuremberg Files list the names of medical staff such as Kilday

MEDICAL staff in family planning clinics throughout Britain are being targeted by American anti-abortion extremists whose website has been linked to the deaths of several doctors.

At least eight American doctors listed as "baby butchers" on the notorious Nuremberg Files website have been murdered. Their names are now scored through and labelled "fatalities". There is no suggestion that those running the website caused the murders, but there are suspicions that the killers might have obtained information from it.

Last week the site added its first British target, Hawys Kilday, the chief executive of the Brook Advisory Centre in Edinburgh. She had first been targeted by the UK Life League (UKLL), a British anti-abortionist group, which put her details on its website.

The Nuremberg Files publisher, Neil Horsley, said last week that his group would target staff involved in abortions throughout Britain. He said it would publish the details of all "abortionists" identified by the UKLL.

It has now emerged that the UKLL, which has offices in London, Liverpool and Cumbernauld in Scotland, is targeting staff at a Glasgow clinic, gathering intelligence on doctors and other personnel. The Sandyford Clinic in the city centre is a family planning clinic which also refers women for abortions.

An undercover reporter posing as an anti-abortion campaigner joined the UKLL and was asked by one of its national leaders to find out the names and addresses of staff and any information she could get on council and health officials involved in funding the clinic. She was told the personal details would be posted on the group's website.

The founder of the UKLL, Jim Dowson, told the reporter that if he was provided with the names of consultants, nurses, health workers or anyone involved in allocating funding to the clinic, he could trace their telephone numbers, addresses and even car numberplates.

Dowson — whose comments were tape-recorded — said the idea was to "hassle" these people and let others know that they were involved in "butchering children". He said the names, pictures and addresses would be added to the UKLL website so that others could find out who was responsible for the "murder of innocent children".

"I've followed people through the car park of Tesco, telling them they are baby killers. Once their neighbours and friends find out and they're exposed, they stop, just like that," he said.

Information gathered by the UKLL will be used by Horsley, a 57-year-old computer consultant, who is expanding the Nuremberg Files to form an "international pulpit" of abortionists. He said that British names could appear on the website within days.

"We'll take information from anyone we can trust and I certainly do trust them [the UKLL]," he said. "They have earned their spurs in resisting legalised abortion."

Kilday last week became the first non-American to be posted on the Nuremberg Files. She had previously won a legal battle to have her name removed from UKLL's website, which has a link to the Nuremberg Files.

However, Dowson, who is subject to the legal order won by Kilday, denied that he was co-operating with Horsley or other extreme US anti-abortion campaigners such as the Rev Pat Mahoney, the director of the US-based Christian Defence Coalition who visited Britain last month.

Dowson's website says: "It is absolutely deplorable that eight abortion industry doctors have been killed in the United States. Strange how the 55 pro-life activists killed over there never seem to get a mention in the press."

When asked about the reporter's findings, Dowson refused to condemn harassment or violence against people who work in abortion clinics.

"A human being is at its most vulnerable in the womb," he said. "These people think nothing of violating that, tearing that baby out limb from limb, and murdering it in its own home. Putting their address on things and making that available to the public gives some idea of the outrage and disgusting attack on decency that violating the home really is.

"As long as they're killing babies, we'll come up with ingenious methods to make life as uncomfortable for them, within the law, as possible."

Ann Furedi, the director of communications for the British Pregnancy Advisory Service, Britain's biggest provider of abortions, whose name is already listed on the UKLL website, said: "I think it's despicable for them to be posting doctors' and other health workers' names on a website encouraging anti-choice activists to take violent action against them, if that is what they are doing."

She dismissed claims that listing personal details was not an incitement to violence. "What is the point of them providing the address of an individual unless there is an implication that others should do something with that," Furedi said.

However, she said she did not find the prospect of her own name appearing on the Nuremberg Files website intimidating, saying that there had been no support to date in Britain for violent protest against abortion.

3G NEWS 1·5

Loud and clear: many of America's abortion protest tactics are crossing the Atlantic

Anti-abortionists adopt US extremist tactics

The Sunday Times, 1 July 2001

Militants inflame abortion law battle on Channel Island

By Russell Jenkins

THE leaflets, bearing the image of an 11-week-old foetus in the womb, carry the words "Is this a choice? Or a child?" They will be dropping through the letterboxes of the people of Guernsey during the coming weeks, the latest salvo in a fiercely contested battle over abortion, which remains illegal on the Channel Island.

The tactic is a direct import from the slick American Right to Life campaign, and for many island women will be a harrowing, and largely unwelcome, reminder of a dilemma they themselves have faced. About 100 women a year make the secretive trip, often disguised as a shopping expedition, to an abortion clinic on the mainland to terminate a pregnancy.

With the exception of the Republic of Ireland, the independently governed Bailiwick of Guernsey, which takes in Sark, Alderney and Herm, is the last place in the British Isles where abortion remains a criminal offence.

Thirty years after the mainland wrestled with and resolved the problem, Guernsey is debating abortion law reform, stirring deeper passions than anything since the German occupation more than half a century ago. In May, proposed changes to the law will be put to the island's 55 elected representatives. Before them will be a Board of Health working party report recommending adoption of the mainland model. The abortion

Is this
a Choice?
Or a Child?

Part of the leaflet to be distributed by 'pro-lifers'

law reformers want to go further and adopt the full "women's right to choose" available in France.

Islander is ranged against islander in a debate that has grown personal, heated and virulent. A meeting on the subject was described in the local paper as "like a Nuremberg-style rally in support of a charter for good-time girls".

The so-called pro-lifers believe the "women's right to choose" lobby is in thrall to international feminism. Words such as "murder" and "slaughter" have filled newspaper letters columns.

Jenny Moore, 51, co-founder of the Guernsey Abortion Law Reform Group, believes the wealth brought to the island by offshore banking has cushioned women from many harsh realities of life. They had grown complacent.

However, they were shocked into political activism when the States of Deliberation, the Guernsey Parliament, refused to ratify clauses in the UN Convention on Human Rights on the equality of the sexes, putting Guernsey below Egypt and Bangladesh in its treatment of women.

At the centre of the Channel Islands Right to Life campaign is Cynthia Kennedy, a veteran of the American Right to Life movement who arrived on Guernsey two years ago from Grand Rapids, Michigan. Demonised by her enemies, she is a charming and determined woman with an unshakeable belief that abortion is the same as murder.

She dismisses as "preposterous" suggestions that she was dispatched from America to keep Guernsey an abortion-free zone.

Islanders say that the eleventh commandment on Guernsey is "Thou shalt not rock the boat". Mrs Kennedy, 46, has done just that. Worse, she is a newcomer.

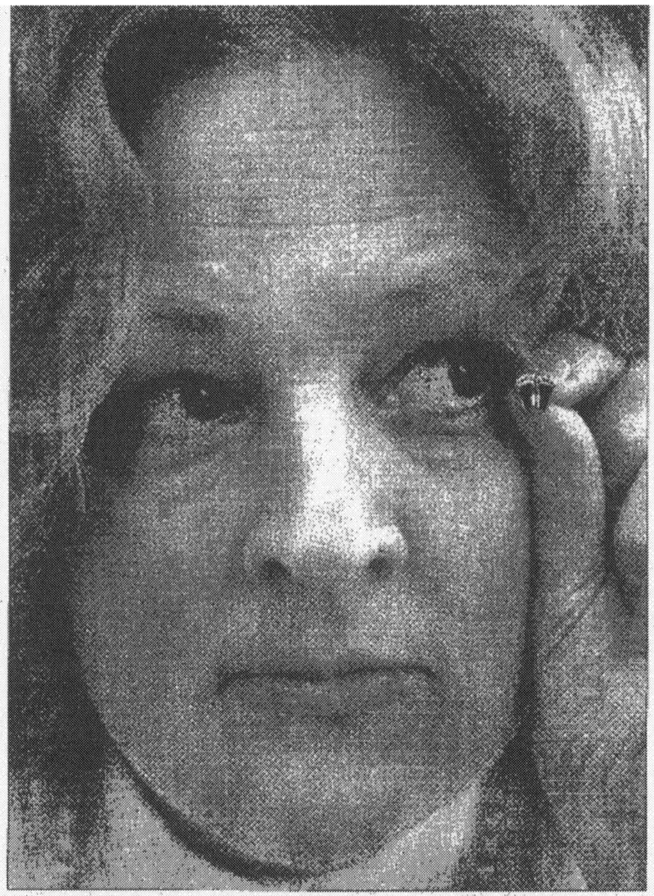

Cynthia Kennedy, the Right to Life campaigner from America, holds her lapel badge which shows two feet the size of those on a ten-week-old foetus

According to Mrs Kennedy, her allies are the Guernsey people who are naturally "pro-life", law-abiding and innately conservative. They observe Sunday closing and live in dread of receiving a speeding ticket.

"Isn't it wonderful that Guernsey still has more enlightened laws than the rest of Europe?" she said. "We have always affirmed life in Western culture. Only now, in the last 30 years, have we had this tremendous push by one segment of society — women — who have taken on the right to kill the unborn child."

The island's parliament is under pressure to reform a law that has fallen into disuse. "We have always said we are 20 years behind England," Mrs Moore said. "Now it is finally time to come up to date."

Militants inflame abortion law battle

The Times, 22 January 1996

Cardinal: Rights laws can halt abortions

By Robert Verkaik
Legal Affairs Correspondent

THE LEADER of the Roman Catholic church in England and Wales has made a direct appeal to the legal profession to use new European legislation to stop women having abortions.

Cardinal Cormac Murphy-O'Connor, the Archbishop of Westminster, urged lawyers to bring "right-of-life" cases under the Human Rights Act 1998 and the European Charter of Fundamental Rights. Writing in the official barristers' magazine, *Counsel*, he said there had been a "grave erosion of the right to life through laws on abortion and embryo research". He said the Human Rights Act meant that the Government and the courts will have to reconsider these laws.

Cardinal Murphy-O'Connor stated: "Lawyers concerned to promote and defend a genuine human rights culture will have opportunities through case law to explore and defend the foundational right to life."

The European Charter, he said, provided the opportunity for protecting human embryos, and medical advances demonstrated the injustice of "denying the unborn child the right to life from conception".

He called for a return to 19th-century common law, when abortion was illegal. He asked lawyers to follow the lead of Lord Denning, one of the most respected judges of the past century, who had urged the judiciary to respect life from the time of conception.

The cardinal added: "Many people would recognise a foetus as having the same moral status as a newborn infant."

Last month, he provoked a storm of protest when he called on voters to consider withholding support from candidates in the general election

Cardinal Murphy-O'Connor: Appealed to barristers

who support a woman's right to have an abortion.

Women's sexual health groups reacted angrily after he said voting against pro-abortion candidates was for the "common good". At the launch of a document entitled *Vote for the Common Good*, the Archbishop said abortion should be top of the list of questions a constituent should ask.

He said: "Clearly, what we would be saying to people is that a candidate's attitude on abortion should have quite considerable sway, but it shouldn't be the only matter. We've made the importance of human life clear, and we would feel quite strongly about it."

Last month, a man cited the Human Rights Act in an attempt to stop his former girlfriend having an abortion. Although the pregnancy was terminated, the case raised questions about the role of prospective fathers in decisions to carry out abortions.

Leading article, Review, page 3

Cardinal: Rights laws can halt abortions

The Independent, 9 April 2001

Women in the dock

SENIOR barristers are said to be extorting sex from vulnerable women trainees, Barbara Hewson of the Association of Women Barristers insists female law students are forced into sexual relationships in return for being given junior posts.

Ms Hewson is talking about clever, high-flying graduates but conjures up an image of a bunch of pathetic, desperate, manipulated women.

I'm not convinced by her sordid scenario. However, if it contains an ounce of truth these women are tarts by choice not coercion.

They are training for influential careers. Ultimately, they will need to advise the vulnerable, support the defenceless and depend on their own wisdom and judgment. If they can't defend even their own bodies then I suggest they are in the wrong job. I certainly would not want to be represented in court by such a stupid woman.

Bartering sex in return for favours is as unpleasant as selling it for cash. In fact, it's like the old joke about the millionaire who says to the beautiful society hostess: 'Would you sleep with me for £1 million?'

She flutters her eyelashes and says coquettishly: 'Well I might . . .'

'Would you sleep with me for a fiver?' he asks.

'How dare you,' she screams. 'What do you think I am?'

'We've already established that,' he replies. 'All we're discussing now is the price.'

Women in the dock

Daily Mail

Anti-abortion protesters march through Washington en route for the Supreme Court

Pro-life marchers mark legal landmark

Washington: Thousands of anti-abortion protesters marched from the White House to the Supreme Court, chanting prayers, shouting slogans and waving white crosses in an annual protest against the 1973 Supreme Court decision legalising abortion.

"Rejoice, rejoice: my mom was not pro-choice," many shouted as they walked through central Washington. "Abortion is not and never will be respectable," the march organiser, Nellie Gray, who is also president of March for Life Inc., said at a rally near the White House. "No one has the right to murder with impunity."

The marchers then knelt on the steps of the Supreme Court to pray as police in riot gear surveyed the crowd, estimated at 45,000. Later, 39 protesters were arrested after blocking a government building to demonstrate against foetal tissue research.

Activists on both sides were holding rallies, prayer vigils and demonstrations to mark Sunday's anniversary of the 1973 Roe vs. Wade ruling. Kate Michelman, president of the National Abortion and Reproductive Rights Action League, said the protesters were creating an atmosphere likely to provoke more shootings at US and Canadian abortion clinics, where four people were killed last year. *(AP)*

Pro-life marchers mark legal landmark - The Times

Preacher Flip Benham hails the baptism of Norma McCorvey in a Texas pool

Abortion crusader recants

By Martin Fletcher

AMERICA'S anti-abortion forces savoured a stunning propaganda triumph yesterday after the woman who won the historic 1973 Supreme Court ruling, establishing a woman's right to terminate a pregnancy, switched sides.

Norma McCorvey, who fought the case of Roe vs Wade using the pseudonym Jane Roe, announced that she had found God, left her job at a Dallas abortion clinic and signed on with Operation Rescue, the militant anti-abortion group whose leader, a fundamentalist preacher named Flip Benham, secretly baptised her on Tuesday night. He began working on her after his group moved its headquarters into an office adjoining the clinic in March.

"I think what I did with Roe vs Wade was wrong," said Ms McCorvey to the fury of abortion rights activists. Sarah Weddington, the lawyer who fought her case, called her a woman who "craved and sought attention".

Ms Weddington took up the case after Ms McCorvey claimed that she had been raped, believing that this would entitle her to an abortion in Texas. The Supreme Court gave the ruling in January 1973, after Ms McCorvey had given birth. In 1987, she made the headlines again when she admitted that she had made up the story about being raped.

Abortion crusader recants

The Times

EVENING STANDARD TUESDAY, 18 NOVEMBER, 1997 13

BRIAN SEWELL

Women are the crueller sex

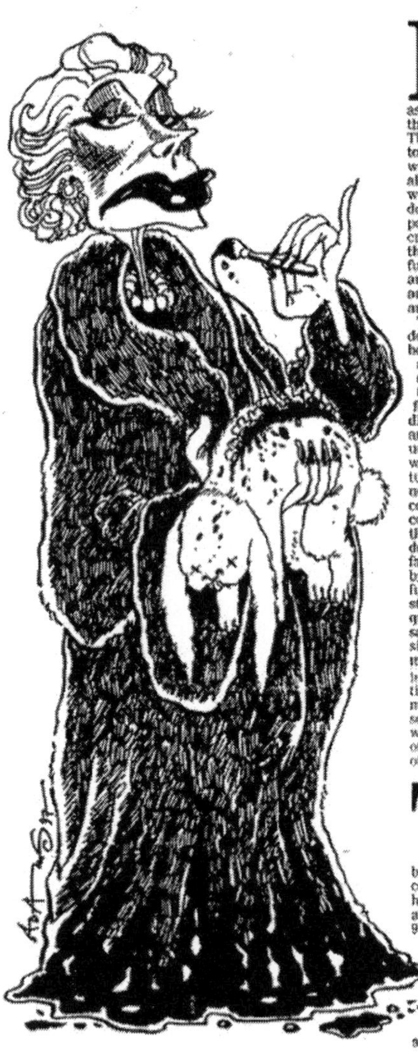

'The other concept of woman, as warm, kindly and compassionate, as the mother of us all, as the comforter for whom grown men cry on deathbed and in deep distress, still stands fairly firm but for some of us is blemished by their attitude to abortion, cosmetics and fur coats, for in all three, women demonstrate a measure of heartless selfishness quite alien to the image of woman as universal mother'

MEN OF a certain age, brought up to doff their hats to women, open doors for them, bow and scrape and put them into lifeboats first, cling to these conventions at the risk of being set aside as old fogeys and old buffers blind to the social revisions of the past 30 years. They are forbidden by political correctitude to think of women as the fair and gentle sex whom they must revere, nor are they allowed to see them as sexually willing wenches whose bottoms they may pinch. No doubt some polytechnic academic has composed a doctoral thesis on the paradox of the creature who in the mythology of men is on the one hand the devoted little woman, dutiful wife and loving mother of their children, and on the other is mopsy, doxy, strumpet and trollop happy to accommodate a man at any moment, even standing up in a canoe.

These concepts persist, for they are rooted deep in an inheritance that reaches far back beyond the mythology of ancient Greece, but against these millennia of entrenched traditional attitudes, we have set one generation of feminist argument and wrought a formidable change that leaves many a man disoriented. Though governed, as all men are to some considerable extent, by his unruly member, he may not utter certain words or sentiments, may not touch or gesture, for the concept of woman as doxy is now done for by law and politics. The other concept of woman, as warm, kindly and compassionate, as the mother of us all, as the comforter for whom grown men cry on deathbed and in deep distress, still stands fairly firm, but for some of us is blemished by their attitude to abortion, cosmetics and fur coats, for in all three, women demonstrate a measure of heartless selfishness quite alien to the image of woman as universal mother. To many men it is incomprehensible that in the 30 years since abortion was made legal, some five million foetuses, living human beings whose hearts are functioning and limbs are formed, far from the mere blobs of jelly of which pro abortionists so often speak, have been ripped from wombs with the compliance and authority of law and medicine. Are women quite so often sexually had against their will?

THAT an abortion may save a woman's sanity when she has been assaulted by a stranger, drunk, drugged and perhaps diseased, we may feel compelled to concede, but that abortion should be employed as a primary method of birth control — and that is the implication of this huge and growing number — is surely not acceptable. Convenience was the reason for 91 per cent of abortions in 1996 — unwanted babies dressed up in the statistics as supposed threats to the physical and mental health of mothers. These were babies that need not, and should not, have been conceived, but prevented with a moment's forethought and the necessary simple apparatus to keep egg and sperm apart.

It is time that we questioned the fancy that women are more compassionate and merciful than men. Are they indeed in any sense the gentler sex? They have for years ignored the cruel business of cosmetic testing on small animals that in cuddly woollen form they give as comforts to their children, their eyes closed to the tears wept by rabbits blind with pain deliberately inflicted; it is in the face of their massive indifference that this is now to end. Worse, the filthy trade in furs survives and increases solely for the vanity of women — a trade in wild animals indiscriminately trapped and, in animals bred for slaughter, fed on each others' bodies, kept in cages so small and conditions so vile that, in comparison, the farmer who breeds broiler chickens might think he runs a Ritz for his miserable hens.

Do women care nothing for such endangered species as the snow leopard? Nothing for a wild animal slowly dying of cold and hunger in a snare or trap? Is their vanity of such overwhelming importance to them that it overrides the compassion they should feel for the captive victims of the loathsome breeding trade in Canada, America, Russia, Scandinavia and even in this country? How do they think these animals are killed? Kindly, by a man trained in humane slaughter? Not at all — slaughter in this country and most others requires no training, no certificate of skill; the more fortunate animals receive a lethal injection, but these are few; some have their necks broken with a karate chop, others gasp their lives away with the stink of vehicle exhaust fumes in their nostrils. The least fortunate animals are electrocuted because that way their coats are best preserved — and how is that done? With one electrode jammed in the anus and the other in their jaws.

EIGHT years ago the Farm Animal Welfare Council observed that the systems employed in the farming of mink and fox do not satisfy some of the most basic criteria for protecting the welfare of cows and pigs and hens. Nothing has changed since then. The Ministry of Agriculture has shown no interest in the welfare of these essentially wild animals, inquisitive and intelligent predators whose strong natural instincts lead to great suffering when caged, with appalling signs of stress. In America, so considerable is the demand for fur that breeders are experimenting with a wider range of caged animals — beaver, wolverine and lynx now added to the mink and fox, for the estimated worldwide production of 25 million mink and three million fox each year is not enough to satisfy the demand — and the demand is made by women, not by men.

Perhaps we should not expect women to be troubled by the deaths of so many animals when they so readily trot off to the abortionist to rid themselves of children. Why should killing an animal, caged or in the wild, mean anything unpleasant to a woman whose response to an unwanted pregnancy is to have it liquidated? Men, who learn their reverence for women at their mothers' knees, have been misled by at least 3,000 years of propaganda and find it very difficult to acknowledge that women are, if not the physically tougher sex, certainly the more coldly selfish, calculating and manipulative, far the more capable of pulling down the shutters of their minds when something unpleasant stands in the way of ambition or desire. They have insidiously achieved abortion on demand and are unlikely to relinquish it, but they could retain something of their ancient reputation for kindness and compassion if they would unite against the fur — overnight their unity could end this trade in bloodstained vanity.

• *Keep Fur out of Fashion, a campaign by Respect for Animals. 0115 952 5440.*

Women are the crueller sex

Evening Standard Nov 18, 1997

Soul will not die

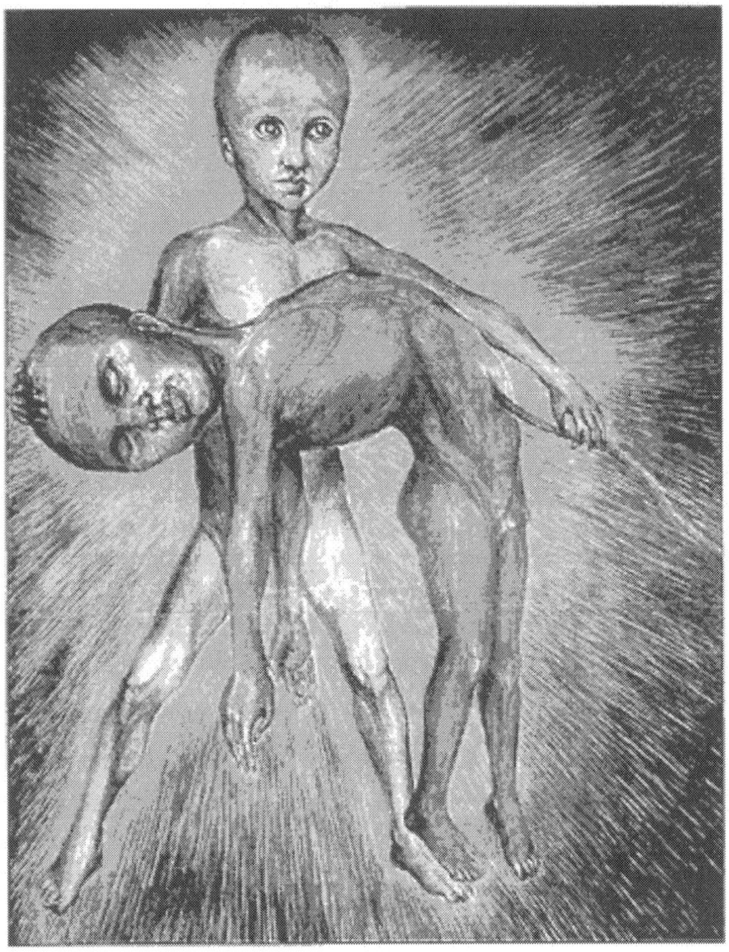

IF art fails to force comment then it's not art, as Picasso said – regular *Catholic TIMES* readers will be familiar with the stunning visual work of Catholic artist, Ann Bell, of Somerset, whose depiction of the Virgin of the Angels was featured on our pages recently.

Now Ann – moved by the recent scandals against the unborn – has produced her latest work designed to show that abortion can kill the body but not the soul of the child.

Defiantly pro-life, Ann is backing the campaign for the 1967 Abortion Act to be amended.

"It is surely time for the current flexible interpretation," she said, "to be tightened in the interests of family life and of the medical profession.

"It would be more appropriate to introduce an amended law that afforded protection to doctors and their pregnant patients. After all, each pregnant woman represents two patients."

Abortion

Kill the body - but not the Soul

Shocking new finding as birth rates in Britain hit an all-time low

1 IN 3 BABIES ARE ABORTED

A THIRD of pregnant women in some parts of Britain are having abortions as birth rates drop to an all-time low, shocking new figures show.

By **Sarah O'Grady**
Social Affairs Correspondent

Instead of the traditional average of 2.4 children, women in England and Wales are having just 1.64, according to the Office for National Statistics. The rate is the lowest since records began in 1924 and comes despite a huge rise in the number of multiple births over the past 10 years.

Yet in London one woman in three – 32.5 per cent – has an abortion after finding out she is pregnant. Even in the East of England, where the abortion rate is the lowest, 19.1 per cent of would-be mothers terminate their pregnancies. Rachel Heath, of Life, the UK's largest anti-abortion charity, said: "Unfortunately, we are not surprised by these numbers.

"We live in a society where most British universities will give a student money to fund an abortion but will not make free child care available if the young woman wants her baby. In a so-called civilised society women should not have to choose between their education or the life of their babies. We counsel women every day who are desperate to have their baby yet they feel the obstacles ranged against them are insurmountable.

"They give in to pressure from their parents or their partners and often feel that

TURN TO PAGE 6, COLUMN 4

FROM PAGE ONE

they cannot afford to bring a baby up. But these women are often not told of the physical and emotional damage they might suffer after an abortion.

"The procedure is not pleasant and it's a major medical operation. There are physical after-effects and emotional consequences, which we find women are not warned about.

"For example, some doctors have discovered a link between abortions and breast cancer which is worthy of more research and which women should be told about."

Tony Kerridge, of the Marie Stopes family planning agency, said: "As many more women are delaying a family, maybe these women choose a career rather than motherhood.

"But in no way can it be said that women are using abortion as a contraceptive. That is far too simplistic and women are not that irresponsible.

"Sex education in this country leaves a lot to be desired. There's a whole generation out there from 15 to 35 who are not properly informed of their contraceptive choices.

"We need to start educating young people at an early age about contraception. We should perhaps start when kids are 10 or 11 so the message gets fixed in their mind. The message we're sending out at the moment does not seem to be getting through to all age groups.

"We would always defend a woman's right to have an abortion. It is legitimate and has been sanctioned by law for 35 years."

The ONS report gives a detailed breakdown of population trends, using statistics from the 2001 census. As well as having fewer children, women are also leaving it later before starting a family, with the average age of a first-time mother increasing from 25.7 in 1991 to 27.1 in 2001.

The report also shows a 10 per cent rise in the number of births outside marriage, from 30 per cent in 1991 to 40 per cent in 2001, and a 22 per cent rise in the number of multiple births.

Under-25s had the highest number of births outside marriage – almost 90 per cent of births to teenagers and 63 per cent of births to women aged 20 to 24.

The highest teenage birth rates were in the North-east and Wales, both with 32.5 births per 1,000 to youngsters aged between 15 and 19, compared with a low of 22.1 per 1,000 in the South-east.

Couples in the North-east have the fewest children, with an average of 1.58, compared with a high of 1.74 in the West Midlands. The report also reveals a drop in the rate of pregnancies among girls aged 15 to 17, which stood at 43.8 per 1,000 conceptions in 2000, down three per cent on 1999. More than half (56 per cent) of all under-18 conceptions in 2000 led to births.

There was a 22 per cent rise in the number of multiple births between 1991 and 2001, from 12.1 per 1,000 to 14.8 last year, and married women were more likely to have a multiple birth than unmarried women, suggesting fertility treatments such as IVF could have been a factor.

There were 16.6 multiple births per 1,000 among married women, compared with 12.1 among their unmarried counterparts. There was also a two per cent drop in the number of live births in 2001 compared with 2000 – 595,000, down from 604,000.

SIMON HINDE: PAGE 17

1 in 3 Babies are Aborted

Daily Express - Friday 13th December 2002

ABORTION COULD LEAD TO BREAST CANCER

By **Alison Gordon**

SOCIAL AFFAIRS EDITOR

DOCTORS are to warn millions of women that having an abortion can lead to a greater risk of developing breast cancer.

The Royal College of Obstetricians and Gynaecologists is to alert doctors and patients to the worrying link, uncovered by researchers in America.

Exhaustive studies encompassing hundreds of thousands of women suggest that those who terminate pregnancies run a 30 per cent greater chance of breast cancer.

The findings are now causing alarm in Britain. The Royal College's warning – already on the Internet and to be issued via leaflets – will be echoed by the British Pregnancy Advisory Service, which is now relaying concerns to the 50,000 women who visit its doctors every year.

The US research, based on 28 separate studies, found that 24,500 cases of breast cancer were attributable to abortion. Now, following an independent assessment of the findings, the RCOG has agreed there is a risk of developing cancer after a termination.

The admission will fuel the debate on abortion and worry a large number of women. Around 180,000 abortions are performed annually in England and Wales and about 12,000 in Scotland – and at least a third of women have had a termination by the time they are 45.

Professor James Drife, vice-president of the RCOG, said last night: 'Concerns have been raised about the possible link between abortion and breast cancer.

'There is inconclusive research in this area but one analysis has indicated a possible increase in risk. This study cannot be rubbished or

Continued on Page 2

Abortion could lead to breast cancer The Mail Aug 13, 2000

has been swept along on the tide of … August 16.

Availability of abortion

From Mr Nicholas Richardson

Sir, Your leading article of August 8, "Hard choices", about the abortion debate [see also letters, August 7, 10, 15] rightly advocates "a bracing re-evaluation of difficult questions". It has indeed been taken for granted by most people for a long time that "NHS doctors would consent to abortions only if their refusal would result in significant harm".

Unfortunately, however, few people are aware of just how liberally the concept of "significant harm" has been interpreted in practice. Published statistics show that only some 2 per cent of abortions are carried out because of risk to the mother's life or a substantial risk that the child would be born seriously handicapped.

Some 98 per cent are performed on healthy women and healthy babies. Many abortions are due to much less strictly defined criteria, which often amount in reality to little more than the convenience of the mother, or the social pressures she is under.

These pressures can seem very strong at the time, but many women are unaware of the consequent dangers to their mental and physical health. There is now a very substantial body of evidence concerning "post-abortion trauma" — the severe and long-lasting psychological disturbance which affects the health of many women who have lost a baby in this way.

The time will come for a reassessment of the costs to society in terms of health and whether, after all, abortion is really the lesser of two evils. In the meantime, the shortage of children available for adoption by childless couples has led to increased demand for various forms of artificial and assisted conception, which in turn raises serious moral problems.

The recent and shocking case of the aborted twin has stirred consciences which have long been dormant. Surely it is high time that what had seemed to many a dead issue should again become a live debate.

Yours faithfully,
NICHOLAS RICHARDSON
(Chairman,
South Oxon Life Group),
The Old House,
72 High Street, Sutton Courtenay,
Abingdon, Oxfordshire.
August 9.

… Malvern and Lichfield and

Availability of abortion

Not a happy anniversary

THIRTY years ago this week, during the closing stages of the parliamentary debate on the Termination of Pregnancy Bill, the 29-year-old David Steel brandished a test-tube containing a foetus of six weeks' gestation. The waving around of an aborted foetus in the chamber of the House of Commons shocked some of the members present, but the Bill's youthful proposer had a point to make. He was, in effect, saying: see what a tiny thing this is that we are arguing about, how insignificant, how little resembling a human it is.

He got away with it. None of the Bill's opponents had the taste for trumping Steel's tawdry ace by bringing on to the floor of the House the all too human form of a foetus of 28 weeks' gestation — the limit for legal abortion as proposed by the legislators of 30 years ago

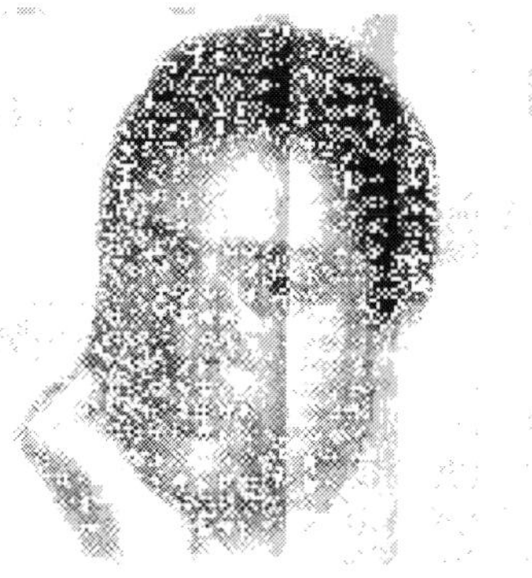

Dominic Lawson

When I was Editor of *The Spectator* I published an article on abortion by the writer Amanda Craig. Miss Craig expressed no opinions in her piece. All she did, one December day in 1990, was to witness seven abortions at an NHS hospital performed by a surgeon called Mr Paintin and report what he and a colleague said while going about their work . . . "'This is the bit people have fantasies about,' says Mr Paintin, squeezing and tugging with his long steel forceps. A dismembered arm half the size of a finger takes two or three attempts to pull out. . . . In the 18-week-old foetus, a complete 7cm torso with the left arm and hand still attached comes out . . . the semi-transparent hand, the size of a small fingernail, itself has fingernails. 'It takes skill to use this technique,' says Mr Paintin, panting slightly. 'You only acquire the expertise if you have a big caseload.' . . . Both the surgeons are relaxed and smiling as they work, discussing Mr Paintin's difficulties in buying a new house."

Not a happy anniversary.
The Times 1997.

Evening Standard

LONDON, FRIDAY, 12 SEPTEMBER 2003 www.thisislondon.co.uk Incorporating THE EVENING NEWS 40p

PICTURE EXCLUSIVE

PROOF BABIES SMILE IN WOMB

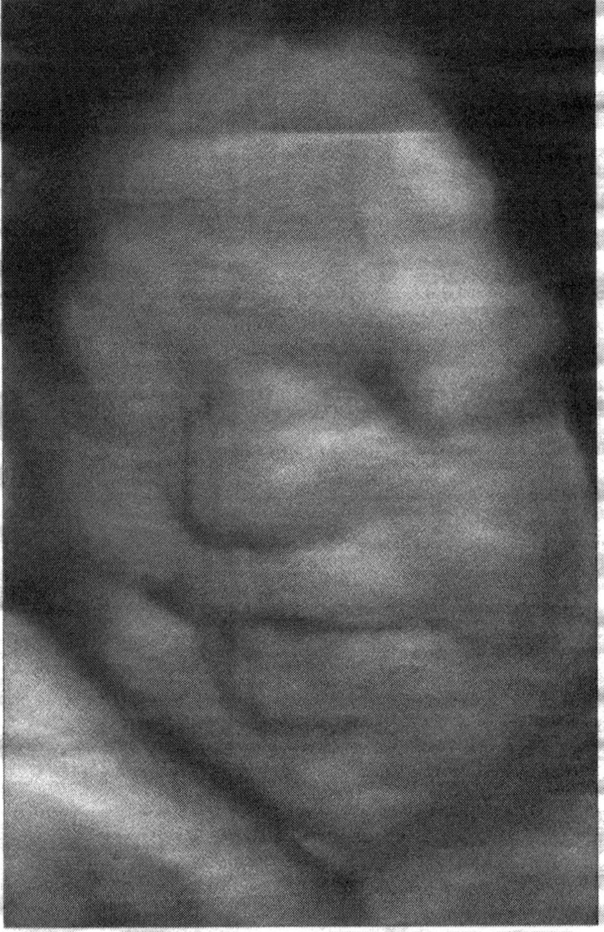

Happiness: an unborn baby smiles in the womb in a picture taken using new scanning techniques

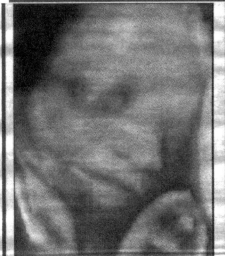

ASTONISHING new pictures show for the first time that babies smile in the womb.

By Isabel Oakeshott, Health Correspondent

Pioneering scanning techniques have allowed London obstetrician Professor Stuart Campbell to capture images which show that foetuses smile, yawn, blink and cry as early as 26 weeks after conception. Experts believe the breakthrough could lead to advances in baby health for a whole range of conditions. But anti-abortion campaigners are likely to seize on the development as further evidence against the case for terminations, which can legally be carried out as late as 24 weeks.

Full story and more pictures: Page 7

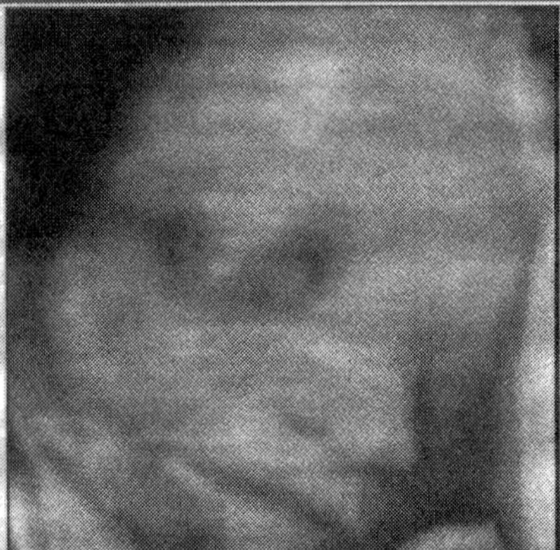

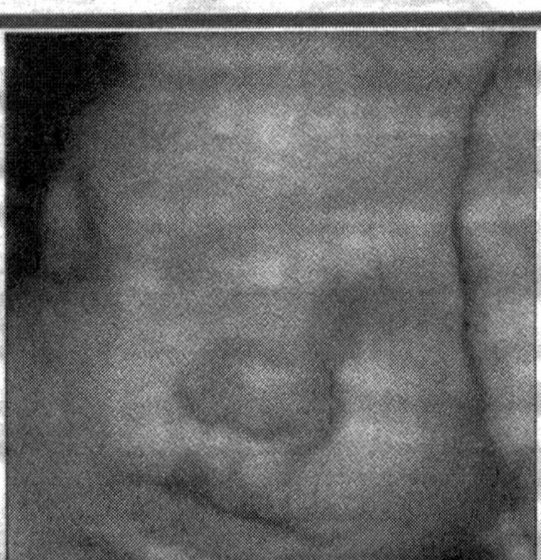

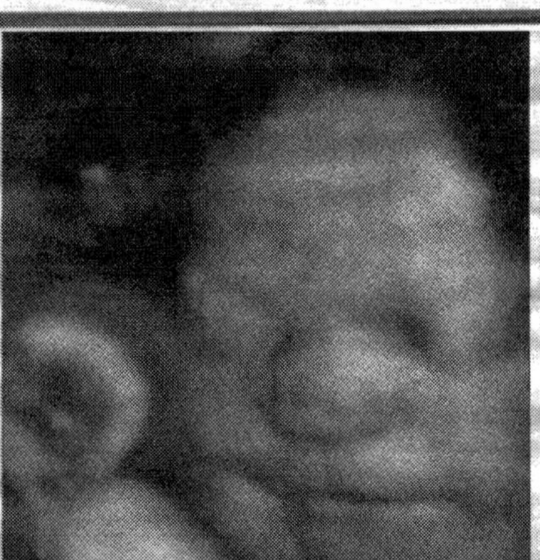

Life in the womb: these images, captured between 32 and 36 weeks after conception using new ultra-sound techniques, show a whole range of complex activities such as blinking, crying and smiling

Baby's first smile

Stunning scanner images

By Isabel Oakeshott
Health Correspondent

THESE astonishing pictures may revolutionise health care for unborn children.

For the first time, a foetus can be seen smiling in the womb months before it was thought they could form such expressions.

Until now, doctors thought infants did not smile until weeks after birth. They believed babies only learned the expression by copying their mothers.

The images will intensify the abortion debate, with pro-life campaigners claiming they prove foetuses feel emotion and pain

Ultra-sound techniques pioneered in London were used to create the pictures, some captured 26 weeks after conception. They reveal foetuses sucking fingers, blinking and crying just after the 24-week limit for terminations.

Pro-life groups praised the new pictures today. Paul Denon, a spokesman for the Society for the Protection of Unborn Children, said the development was "delightful".

He went on: "We earnestly hope they help persuade people that the unborn child is a human entity from the word go."

Obstetrician Professor Stuart Campbell said: "With this advance, many questions can be investigated." 'The techniques called 3D and 4D scanning, were developed by Professor Campbell at the Create Health Centre for Reproduction and Advanced Technology in London.

Pictures reveal foetuses move limbs at eight weeks. From 15 weeks, they make complex finger movements, while at 20 weeks, they yawn.

From 26 weeks, a whole range of more complex activities, such as blinking, finger sucking, smiling and crying can be seen.

Professor Campbell said: "It is remarkable that a baby does not smile for about six weeks after birth. Before birth, most babies smile frequently."

Obstetricians have been using ultrasound scans to study foetal activity for 20 years.

Babies who make breathing movements or vigorous arm and leg movements are assumed to be well oxygenated and healthy.

Professor Campbell said: "There are many questions that can now be investigated. Do babies with genetic problems such as Down's Syndrome have the same pattern of activity as normal babies?

"Does the foetus smile because it is happy, or cry because it has been disturbed by some event inside the womb?"

Consultant obstetrician Dr Maggie Blott said: "It is impossible to know whether it is an emotional response or a facial movement."

About 180,000 abortions are carried out every year in Britain, with around 600 taking place at 23 or 24 weeks.

In exceptional circumstances, terminations are legal beyond the 24-week cut-off point.

About 100 such abortions take place every year, usually because of serious birth defects which cannot be detected earlier.

So many questions left unanswered

COMMENTARY

by Geeta Nargund

UNTIL now, all we knew about what really goes on inside the womb was what we could see on a normal grainy ultrasound scanner — the kicking of the legs, punching of the fists and the foetal heart beat.

But for the first time, we see smiles and chuckles. They are seen playing with their umbilical cords, sucking their thumbs, sucking their lips and yawning. You can see grumpy and contorted faces, as if they are crying.

We see babies in the womb blinking, assumed until now to be a reaction to bright light or dust but why would they be blinking in darkness? This work will raise further concerns among the anti-abortion lobby, who will say that an aborted foetus at 24 weeks — the legal maximum term for abortion — is experiencing emotion and pain. (At 20 weeks foetuses can be seen yawning. From as early as eight weeks they are seen in human form with jumping movements).

These observations show it is not until 26 weeks that a range of complex activities such as blinking, sucking, smiling and crying can be observed. Anti-abortion campaigners will say the 24-week limit is too high (although that limit is based on the viability of a baby's life, rather than its degree of consciousness or feeling).

This equipment should be used with great care. The identification of minor deformities in the foetus can now also be picked up, which raises important moral questions. The pictures raise countless questions, among them why a foetus would smile yet, after birth, they don't smile for six weeks? More research is needed.

● ***Geeta Nargund is a consultant in Reproductive Medicine and Chief Executive of HER Trust. She is a colleague of Professor Campbell at the Create Health clinic.***

The Evening Standard Friday 12th September 2003

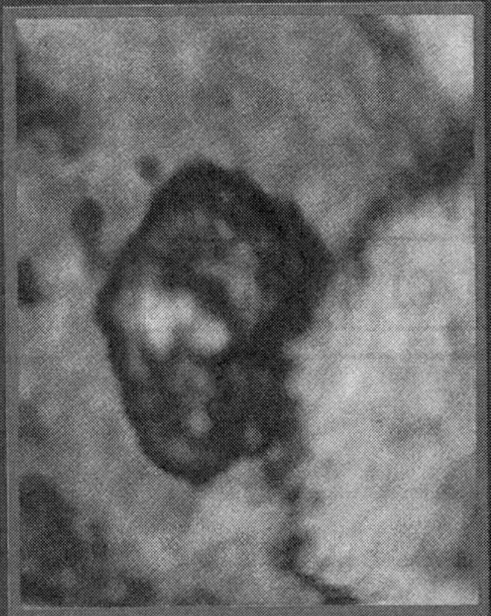

WEEK 7 LENGTH: 5mm (¼in): head and body only. I've grown to look like a small bean with a bumpy head that bends forward and is much larger than the rest of my body.
My tail is disappearing, my arms and legs protrude more and my hands and feet are paddle-shaped — each foot is a tiny fraction of a centimetre.
There are dark spots on the sides of my head, which are my eyes forming. Little openings on my face mark my nostrils, and my ears are developing. My heart is going at 150 beats a minute — faster than my mother's.

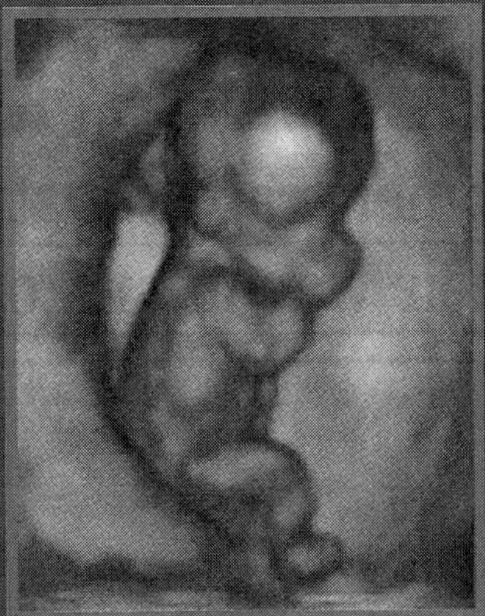

WEEK 12 LENGTH: 61mm (2½in). WEIGHT: 11g (½oz). I've acquired all the features that make me a human being. Plus, I've doubled in size over the past three weeks.
My fingers and toes have separated, my hair is growing and as my body lays down calcium, my bones strengthen. I have a lot of fun jumping about and stretching my arms and legs. My genital organs are discernible (if you're an expert, you can tell if I'm a boy or a girl) and my digestive system is capable of the contractions that push food through my bowels.

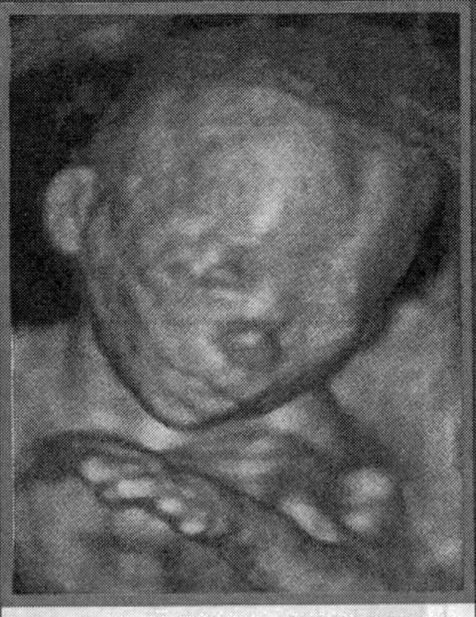

WEEK 17 LENGTH: 11cm (4½in). WEIGHT: 100g (3½oz). I can bend my fingers into fists and have a range of facial expressions: I can frown and grimace. There's fine hair, or lanugo, on my body to help regulate my temperature. My eyes, though still closed, are much larger and I have eyelashes, plus fingernails and toenails. I can do a lot with my hands — I like to put them in my mouth.
My chest rises and falls as I practise breathing movements and fluid in the womb passes into and out of my air passages.

JUST WA

THEY are the most extraordinary pictures ever seen of a baby in the womb, and are published in a new book, Watch Me Grow!, by leading obstetrician PROFESSOR STUART CAMPBELL. Here, he describes exactly what is happening, week by week . . . in the baby's own words.

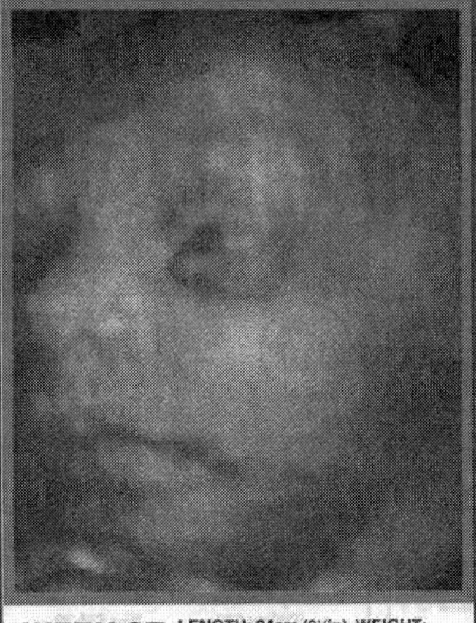

WEEK 27 LENGTH: 24cm (9½in). WEIGHT: 1kg (2lb 3oz). My eyes are now complete — the final layers of my retina in the back of them have formed.
My eyelids can now open some of the time, and my eyelashes are fully grown, and they are helping to protect my eyeballs from harmful matter. I am becoming more rounded and plump because of increased amounts of fat being deposited under my skin.
My lungs continue to grow and I have fully functioning tastebuds on my tongue and inside my cheeks.

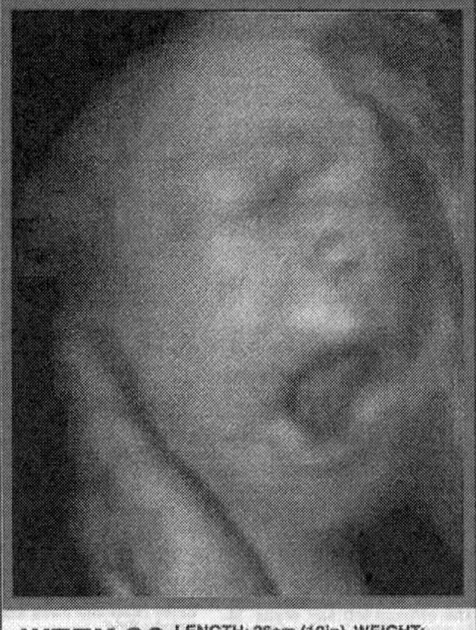

WEEK 29 LENGTH: 26cm (10in). WEIGHT: 1.25kg (2lb 12oz). Now I'm beginning to assert myself. I've only just got enough room to stretch my arms and legs, but my mother will normally feel as many as ten kicks in the course of a morning. Here I am yawning — which I have been able to do since around 11 weeks. My brain is getting pretty powerful: it controls my body temperature and breathing. The lenses of my eyes move during periods of quiet sleep and are more sensitive to light and dark, although I won't use this ability until I'm born.

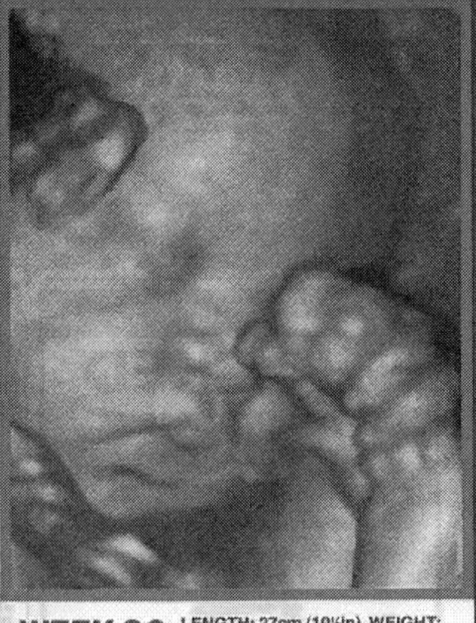

WEEK 30 LENGTH: 27cm (10½in). WEIGHT: 1.36kg (3lb). The hair that covered my body is disappearing. A few patches may be left at birth but will rub off after a few weeks. My skin looks less wrinkled because I've laid down more baby fat. My bone marrow has taken over the task of red blood cell production from my liver.
My skeleton is hardening more and more and my brain, muscles and lungs continue to mature. If I hear a noise, I will react to it with a kick. I increasingly open and close my eyes and I can breathe rhythmically.

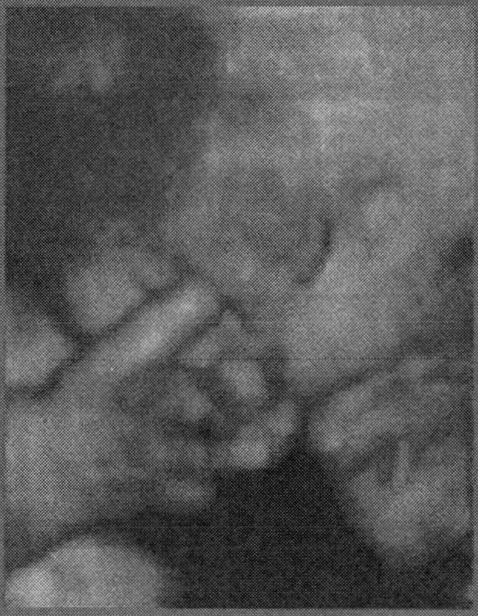

WEEK 18 LENGTH: 13cm (5in). WEIGHT: 150g (5¼oz). My respiratory system is among the last things to mature, but already tiny air sacs are developing in my lungs. Pads have formed on my fingertips and the unique swirls that will be my fingerprints begin to appear. I enjoy punching, kicking, turning and wriggling. My eyes are now in their correct position, although the lids will mostly stay closed until week 24. Undigested debris from swallowed amniotic fluid is collecting in my lower bowel. If I'm a boy, my prostate will be forming.

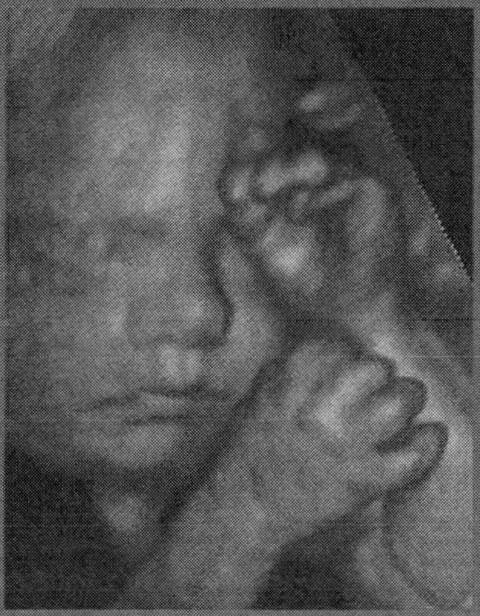

WEEK 23 LENGTH: 20cm (8in). WEIGHT: 455g (1lb). My skin is becoming less transparent as I begin to look more like a full-term baby, but is still quite wrinkly. I have quite distinct lips and there are tooth buds under my gum. My hearing is much more acute now because the bones of my inner ear have hardened. I can hear my dad's deeper voice more easily than my mother's higher pitched one. My eyes are formed now — the iris just lacks colour pigment — and my pancreas is developing. [A baby may still be legally aborted at this stage.]

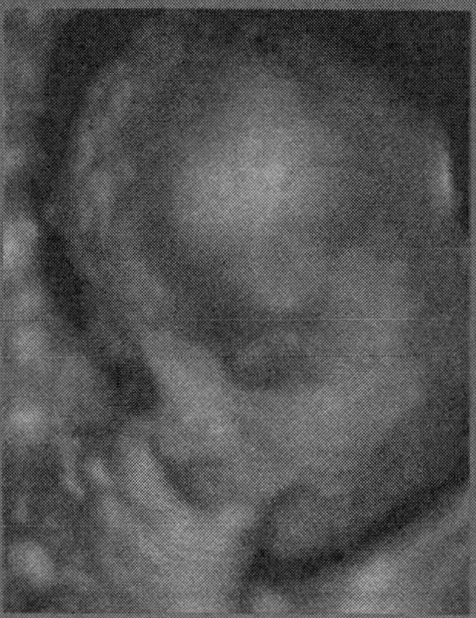

WEEK 25 LENGTH: 22cm (8¾in). WEIGHT: 700g (1lb 8oz). I am now more well-proportioned, though still skinny. Blood vessels continue to develop in my lungs, and my nostrils open. High in my gums, my permanent teeth begin, but these won't descend until my milk teeth fall out when I'm six. The nerves around my mouth are more sensitive now, and here I am sucking my thumb. My lungs are the only vital organs still fully to develop. If I'm a girl, my genitals have developed into a hollow tube. My umbilical cord is already thick.

TCH ME GROW!

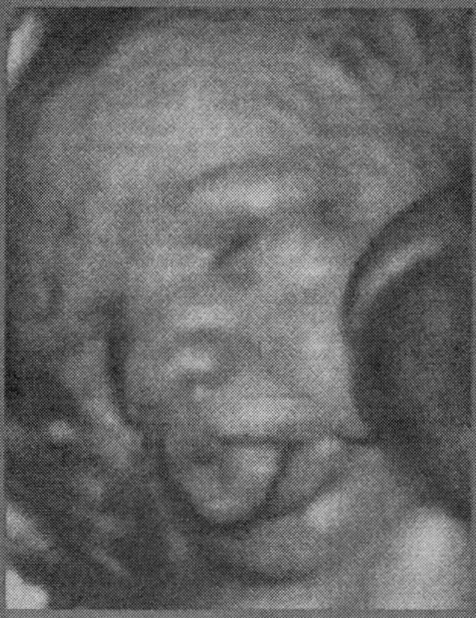

WEEK 33 LENGTH: 30cm (12in). WEIGHT: 2kg (4lb 6oz). Because of rapid brain growth, my head is now 9.5mm (⅜in) in circumference — in correct proportion to my body. My bones are fully developed, though soft and pliable, and I'm starting to store iron, calcium and phosphorous, essential for further bone development. My skin becomes pinker as I accumulate more fat. I am increasingly aware of my surroundings, including external noises and the things that are in my immediate environment, such as the amniotic fluid.

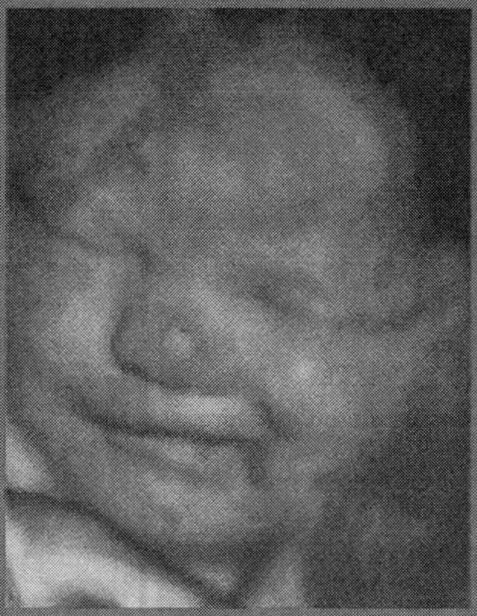

WEEK 35 LENGTH: 33cm (13in). WEIGHT: 2.55kg (5lb 10oz). I'm getting plumper and plumper now, as I acquire more body fat, which will later help to regulate my body temperature. There's hardly room to move around and I'm getting quite squashed.
My central nervous system is maturing and I'm increasingly awake and aware. My digestive system is almost complete, and my lungs are nearly fully mature. Like mine in this picture, some babies' heads will by now be engaged in the birth canal.

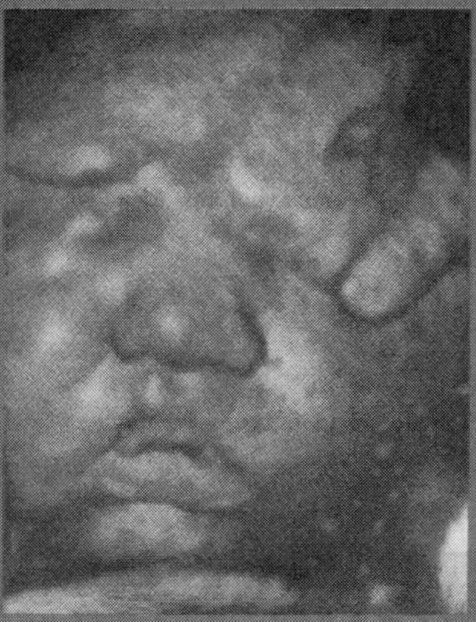

WEEK 38 LENGTH: 38cm (15in). WEIGHT: 3.25kg (7lb 2oz). I can be born at any time. My abdominal circumference is now slightly larger than my head and I have 15 per cent body fat. I have more than 70 reflexes to help me cope with the world outside the uterus. The placenta, which has sustained me all these weeks, is becoming less efficient, there is less amniotic fluid and the umbilical cord will soon finish its work. My first breaths of air will trigger my heart and arteries to transfer blood to my lungs.

WATCH ME GROW! by Professor Stuart Campbell (Carroll & Brown)

Daily Mail, Tuesday, June 29, 2004

Who can see pictures of tiny foetuses yawning and jumping and be CERTAIN abortion is not wrong?

STEPHEN GLOVER argues, in this deeply personal piece, that men's opinions are just as valid as women's in the abortion debate

AS A MAN, do I have a right to a view on abortion? Many women would say no. They might not mind if I were pro-abortion. They would not much like it if I were against.

Abortion, so we have been told so often that most of us men believe it, is ultimately a matter for women. Of course men can have a view, as any of us might have an opinion about the Maori question in New Zealand, whose outcome none of us is ever going to influence. But in the end, it is for women to decide. The issue is women's right to do what they want with their own bodies.

Women's bodies conceive and nurture babies, and bear the pain of birth. How can a man presume to pass any judgment in this sphere? Surely it must be a woman's right to decide whether or not she wishes to carry a baby to full term.

So, we men mostly keep quiet. We know that even an opinion tentatively expressed against abortion will call down the wrath not only of militant feminists but also of plenty of ordinary women who believe that this is *their* business. Many of us have accepted this.

Human

And then some new evidence appears which shakes us all, men and women. Disturbing photographs taken by means of a new technique show foetuses at 12 weeks walking and jumping in the womb. At 14 weeks to 15 weeks, they are photographed sucking their thumbs and yawning. In one sequence, a foetus of 17 weeks is seen sucking its little toe and then moving on to its big toe, as though coming to terms with its body.

They seem like little human beings. They *are* little human beings. Not even anti-abortionists realised that young foetuses are so highly developed at such an early stage in the pregnancy. One picture shows the face of a foetus aged 18 weeks with its eyes wide open. Why call it a foetus? It is a baby.

There were 185,000 abortions carried out in 2002, and there are estimated to have been some six million since the Abortion Act was passed in 1967. About 80 per cent of abortions are carried out before 13 weeks. Some 30 per cent occur between ten and 12 weeks when, as these pictures show, foetuses are capable of walking in the womb, and jumping around. In 2002, 2,573 abortions were carried out between 20 and 24 weeks, and some 114 at over 24 weeks.

The position of the Roman Catholic Church is that the abortion of a foetus of whatever age is wrong because even an embryo a few days old has the potential for human life. This is not an argument that has found much favour with our utilitarian lawmakers. The 1967 Abortion Act set the limit at 28 weeks. Later, it was reduced to its present 24 weeks.

The thinking was that until 28 weeks, revised to 24 as medicine advanced, a foetus could not survive outside its mother's womb. It was also believed that until this age, foetuses were so primitive that they could not be described as human. Now these photographs tell us that even at 12 weeks a foetus is quite a sophisticated little handful. But one which it is still entirely lawful to kill.

And yet the law does not say that foetuses have no rights. Even feminists do not claim it. The question is at what stage in the womb these rights are established. Only a very extreme person would argue that it should be legitimate to abort a baby at, say, 35 weeks. So it is accepted even by the pro-abortionists that the right of a woman to do as she pleases with her body must be circumscribed.

My own position is that of the Roman Catholic Church, not because I am a Catholic, but because it seems to me wrong to take away the life of a living organism which has the potential for human life. I accept, though, that many decent and thoughtful people think otherwise. And yet these same people do accept that at some stage the foetus acquires rights.

Newborn

Look at these pictures again, you people, and ask whether a 12-week-old foetus which jumps about in the womb, or one which yawns at 15 weeks, or another which has its eyes open at 18 weeks are not little human beings whom we should wish to protect with the same vigilance and love as we would bestow on a newborn baby. It is heart-rending to imagine such miniature perfection, so vulnerable and so alive, being vacuumed away into oblivion.

How could it be right to end the life of such a foetus? If its own mother's life were threatened and a choice had to be made, perhaps. But for our convenience? To maintain a lifestyle? To keep a job? To prevent it being born on account of some small defect which we don't like? It is difficult to think so. More difficult, I think, now that we have seen these pictures.

Abortion, like modern dying, is something most of us do not like to think about. The doctors will take care of it and never tell us exactly what goes on. We try to push it away. How often I have heard friends — usually men — say that they don't like abortion but they would not dream of interfering with a woman's right to chose. This is either cowardly or muddled. If we believe that abortion is wrong, we should argue against it, as we should argue against anything we think to be wrong.

Men have an equal right in this enterprise as women. Women bear the burden and the pain. They are stronger and braver than men — we all know that. But abortion is a human question, because it is literally about the right to life, and this is not a matter that concerns a single sex.

Misled

And women, too, are beginning to wonder whether they have not been misled by usually male doctors and usually male politicians into thinking that abortion is much less significant than it really is. There are women who are now in their 30s and 40s and 50s who had abortions almost without thinking when they were younger because they were told that it was no more meaningful than a check-up at the dentist. Now they know better, and some of them mourn. They can't be blamed.

Perhaps, though, those of us who look at these photographs and turn away as though nothing had been learnt are at fault. They tell us something we might have suspected, but did not precisely know, about the humanity of babies in the womb. To question abortion does not, as some militant feminists may tell us, make one a fundamentalist or an extreme right-winger or a women hater, though the few anti-abortionists who employ violent means to make their point deserve our contempt.

History tells us that good people can hold beliefs which subsequent generations think are misguided. There is a movement gathering force — of men and women, liberals and conservatives, Christians and humanists. Its credo is not so revolutionary. Who can look at these pictures of tiny foetuses yawning and walking and jumping, and be certain that abortion is not wrong?

JUST WATCH ME GROW — PAGES 20-21

The Times, Wednesday July 28th 2004

The Guardian Monday July 5 2004 5

Steel calls for abortion limit to be cut

Nicholas Watt
Political correspondent

David Steel, the former Liberal leader who introduced Britain's modern abortion laws, has called for a dramatic reduction in the legal limit for most terminations from 24 to 12 weeks.

In a change of heart, Lord Steel called for Britain to follow the example of Europe in the light of medical advances which allow premature babies to survive at 22 weeks.

Lord Steel's Abortion Act of 1967, which was regarded as one of the most significant social advances in the postwar period, legalised abortions until 28 weeks of pregnancy. Terminations were allowed with the agreement of two doctors if the mother's mental or physical state could be damaged by continuing with the pregnancy.

The 1967 limit was cut to 24 weeks in 1990 amid concerns that a 28-week-old foetus could survive outside the womb. Now Lord Steel feels it is time to go further.

"The Abortion Act achieved what it set out to do: which was the abolition of the criminal abortion and death from self-induced abortions. All that is past history. But the development of medical science plus the continuing problem of different access to abortion in different parts of the country suggests that we should follow what the rest of Europe has done since 1967. This is to move to a two-tier system where you can get an abortion on demand up to 12 weeks or so and then after that it is much more stringent."

Lord Steel told the Guardian in 1997 — on the 30th anniversary of his bill — that there was no need for a further reduction in the limit. He acknowledges that he has now changed his mind.

"There have been more and more stories of earlier foetuses surviving. There are these horrific stories of bungled abortions late on. Way back in 1967 the general view was that if an abortion had to happen it should happen as early as possible. The two doctor and registration requirement sometimes militates against that. I think it is perfectly reasonable to say let's have another look at the whole, given the advances in technology."

Lord Steel added that it would be best for a parliamentary committee to reflect on changing the law before introducing another bill on to the floor of the Commons. "Rather than go straight to a bill, I think a parliamentary committee is a good idea for further reflection provided they approach it in an objective manner."

John Reid, the health secretary, said he was personally in favour of cutting the limit. Stressing that any decision in the Commons would be made on a free vote, he told BBC One's Breakfast with Frost: "I voted personally before I was a minister for 18 weeks. But this is up to parliament to decide. When and if this is raised in parliament, everyone will be entitled to vote according to their conscience, it is such an important issue."

The Guardian, Monday, July 5th, 2004

THE TIMES

No. 68122 ■ THURSDAY JULY 8 2004 ■ www.timesonline.co.uk ■ 50p

WRESTLING JONNY
OWEN SLOT **SPORT**

FOOTBALLER'S WIFE
The final episode – payback time
NEWS PAGES 2, 3

Blair backs abortion review

MPs support move to rethink 24-week limit

By Philip Webster and Nigel Hawkes

MPs COULD vote within a year on lowering the 24-week legal time limit for abortions, after Tony Blair backed a rethink of the law to take account of scientific change.

The Prime Minister signalled his support for a Commons vote when he told MPs that "if the scientific evidence has shifted, then it is obviously sensible for us to take that into account". He also made it clear that MPs would be able to vote according to their conscience.

Mr Blair's stance took some MPs by surprise and Downing Street later insisted that the remarks did not signal a change of policy. However, there was growing support last night from MPs to reconsider an emotive issue which has not come before the Commons for nearly 15 years.

Ian Gibson, Labour chairman of the Commons Science and Technology Select Committee, told *The Times* last night that on scientific grounds alone there was good reason for the matter to be re-examined. "There has been such a big inflow of information since we last set the limit that, putting all the political issues aside, there is a case for looking at it again."

Advances in the care of premature babies mean that a handful now survive at 22 weeks' gestation. This change, and the photographs published in newspapers last week of foetuses moving and even appearing to walk in the womb at 12 weeks, are behind the calls for a rethink.

Ann Furedi, chief executive of the British Pregnancy Advisory Service, which is responsible for the great majority of abortions carried out for social reasons at over 20 weeks, said yesterday: "I am almost sure that the time limit is going to be looked at. Any review of the Act now is going to be seen as an opportunity to look again at time limits."

Ministers saw two potential opportunities for a new vote. A backbencher could bring forward a Bill to reduce the limit in the new session of Parliament in November or legislation could arise from a review of the Human Fertilisation and Embryology Act which set the 24-week limit in 1990.

The Department of Health announced the review because of the fast-changing science of in-vitro fertilisation (IVF). But pro-abortion groups now believe that it could be used to provide an opportunity to change the time limit. In 1990 MPs considered a number of options ranging from 18 weeks to the 28 weeks existing then. Mr Blair voted for 24 weeks and John Reid, now the Health Secretary, voted for 18 weeks.

Lord Steel of Aikwood, the former Liberal leader and architect of the 1967 Abortion Act that set the limit at 28 weeks, has called for Parliament to consider a lower limit because of the advance in technology. The limit was reduced to 24 weeks on a free vote in 1990 and some campaigners have called for it to be set as low as 12 weeks.

In 1990 anti-abortion campaigners failed to achieve their minimum aim, a reduction to 22 weeks. That was under a Conservative government and until now it has appeared unlikely that a Labour-dominated House would want to go

Continued on page 7, col 1

STEVE ALLEN/SCIENCE PHOTO LIBRARY

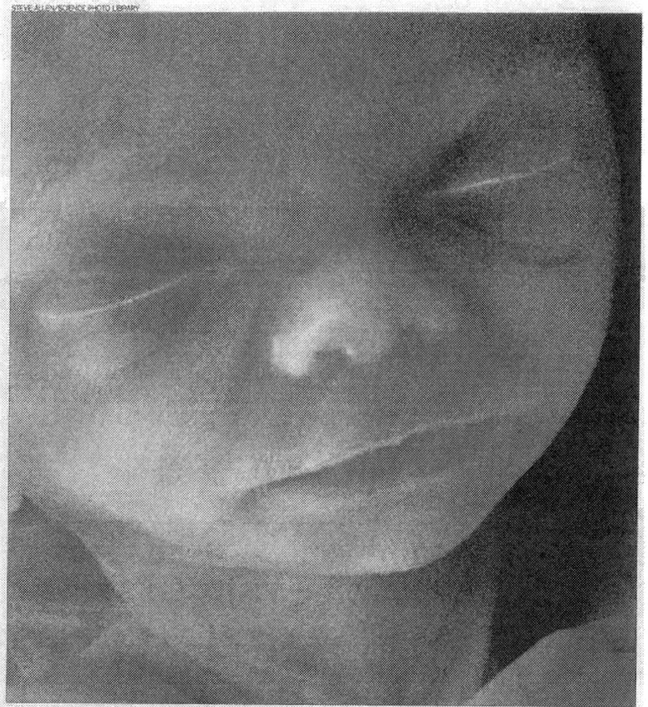

A foetus at 12 weeks, 6cm long and weighing 20g. Doctors believe that it can move its arms and legs, although the eyelids are sealed

Cash loses credit
Cash is no longer king. For the first time plastic has overtaken pounds and pence as the favourite way to pay, prompting the Bank of England to consider reducing the amount of currency in circulation. **NEWS** page 2

D-Day for M&S
The great battle of Britain's high street could be settled today when the board of Marks & Spencer decides whether to approve a £9.1 billion takeover proposal from Philip Green, the owner of Bhs. **NEWS** pages 10, 44

Cleric uproar
Pressure is growing on the Government to deport a fundamentalist Islamic cleric after he spoke openly of his support for suicide bombings in Israel and Iraq, saying that "martyrs" had no other option. **NEWS** page 9

Democrat divide
The Democratic campaign to win the White House has become a study in contrasts. John Kerry and John Edwards may share a first name, but there is little that they have in common as performers. **WORLD NEWS** page 31

Tennis ace's offer
Nick Bollettieri, whose Florida tennis academy has generated more grand-slam tournament champions in the past decade than any other outlet, has offered to assist any young British players that he can. **SPORT** page 88

Abortion: last hope for desperate

The Prime Minister signalled support yesterday for a new Commons vote on abortion when he told MPs that "if the scientific evidence has shifted then it is obviously sensible for us to take that into account". Recent ultrasound pictures of a foetus apparently "walking" at 12 weeks, thumbsucking at 14 weeks and smiling at 22 weeks, have reopened the abortion debate. Now that premature babies are surviving at 24 weeks of gestation, the Government is being asked to halve the time limit for social abortions to 12 weeks. *The Times* asked pro and anti-abortion campaigners to make their case

SCIENCE PHOTO LIBRARY

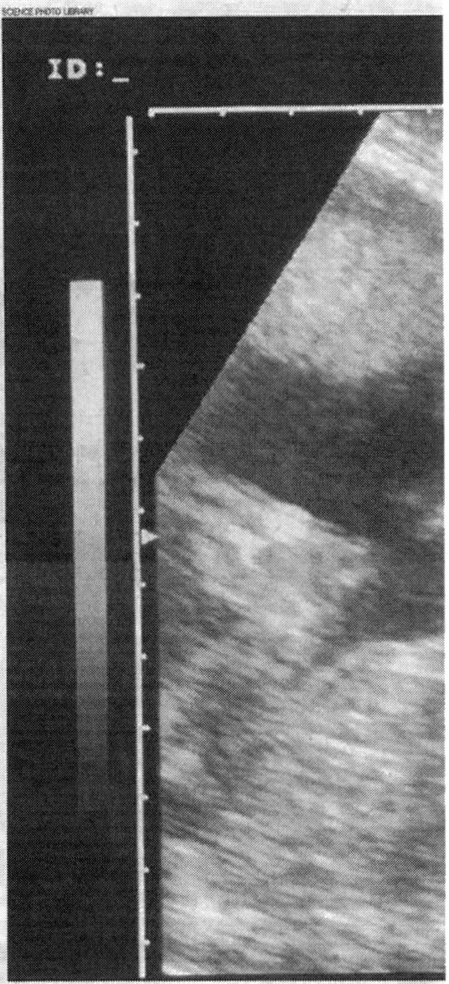

Brought into focus: the improved resolution of the ultrasound

FOR

By Anne Weyman

AT THE Family Planning Association our view is that abortion should be performed as early as possible and as late as necessary. Late abortion is rare. About 1 per cent of abortions take place after 20 weeks.

While we would argue in favour of speeding up the abortion process, we would oppose reducing the time limit for abortions from 24 to 12 weeks. Part of the difficulty that women face when they experience an unwanted pregnancy is getting access to abortion.

The Government's target for performing abortions is three weeks from GP referral to having the abortion. Many women have to wait longer. The target should be set at 72 hours once a woman has made her decision. If a 12-week limit were imposed, inadequacies in the system would mean women could find themselves exceeding that limit. There are huge geographical variations on service provision for abortion.

Nearly 90 per cent of abortions are carried out at under thirteen weeks' gestation, with nearly 60 per cent conducted at under ten weeks. But women who ask for late abortion are usually desperate. We recognise that it is a difficult decision time for them.

Many of these decisions will be made after tests for foetal abnormality, some of which cannot be done until quite late in the pregnancy. We should be providing more support to women needing late abortions, not removing it. We have recommended changing the 1967 Abortion Act to allow abortion on request within legal time limits.

The need for the signatures of two doctors for abortion should be abolished and the procedure treated like any other, where a woman makes a choice and then consents to treatment. Uncomplicated early abortion should be made available in settings such as GP surgeries and sexual health clinics. Trained nurses should be allowed to perform early abortion. We need an abortion service fit for the 21st century.

Anne Weyman is chief executive of the Family Planning Association, a charity that promotes sexual health, reproductive rights and choice.

AGAINST

By Jack Scarisbrick

I DO not believe that the life of an unborn child at 24 weeks is any more valuable than it is at 12 weeks. In much the same way I would not say that a ten-year-old child is worth more than a two-year-old.

Yet it is exactly this kind of distinction that those who want to halve the legal limit from the current 24 weeks to 12 are asking us to make.

This whole debate underlies our idiosyncratic approach to unborn children. What it is effectively saying is that as far as children are concerned, bigger is better. But just because a child is only 2in long, that does not mean that it is less important than a fully developed child. The smaller the child, the more protection it deserves.

While I welcome anything that will reduce the destruction of human life, all abortion is wrong. We know so much now about life in the womb that it is increasingly difficult for anyone to say that an unborn child at 12 weeks is not a real human being whose right to life should be protected.

I do believe, however, that if the limit is reduced to 12 weeks, it will reduce abortions and that is welcome. Many women will be able to hide that they are pregnant until after the 12-week limit. That will mean that by the time their pregnancy is obvious, it will be too late for their boyfriends, husbands or families to press them to have an abortion and a lot of lives will be saved that way.

We are in an extraordinary moral muddle. We are so enlightened when it comes to protecting children from sexual abuse, but until they are born nothing matters. We provide special loos and ramps and parking spaces for those born disabled, but at the same time we are ever more ruthless in our detection of abnormality and our destruction of the unborn disabled.

The 1967 Abortions Act effectively allows complete freedom of supply. Any doctor can abort any woman for the slightest reason.

This moral schizophrenia is something that we cannot live with. We really are in a hopeless moral mess.

Jack Scarisbrick is chairman of Life, an anti-abortion charity.

HOW A BABY GROWS

- At seven weeks an embryo is an inch long, with a tiny beating heart
- At three months the foetus is about 3in long, and fully formed
- At five months, a baby is 11in long and will weigh almost 1lb
- At six months, the eyebrows and eyelids are visible, and the baby has started breathing movements
- At seven months, a baby weighs more than 2lb and is about 15in long. Fingernails have developed
- At eight months a baby is gaining half a pound a week and has probably turned head down in preparation for birth
- At nine months, and ready to be born, a baby usually weighs between 6lb and 8lb, sometimes more, and is 18in to 22in long

women or wrong at any time?

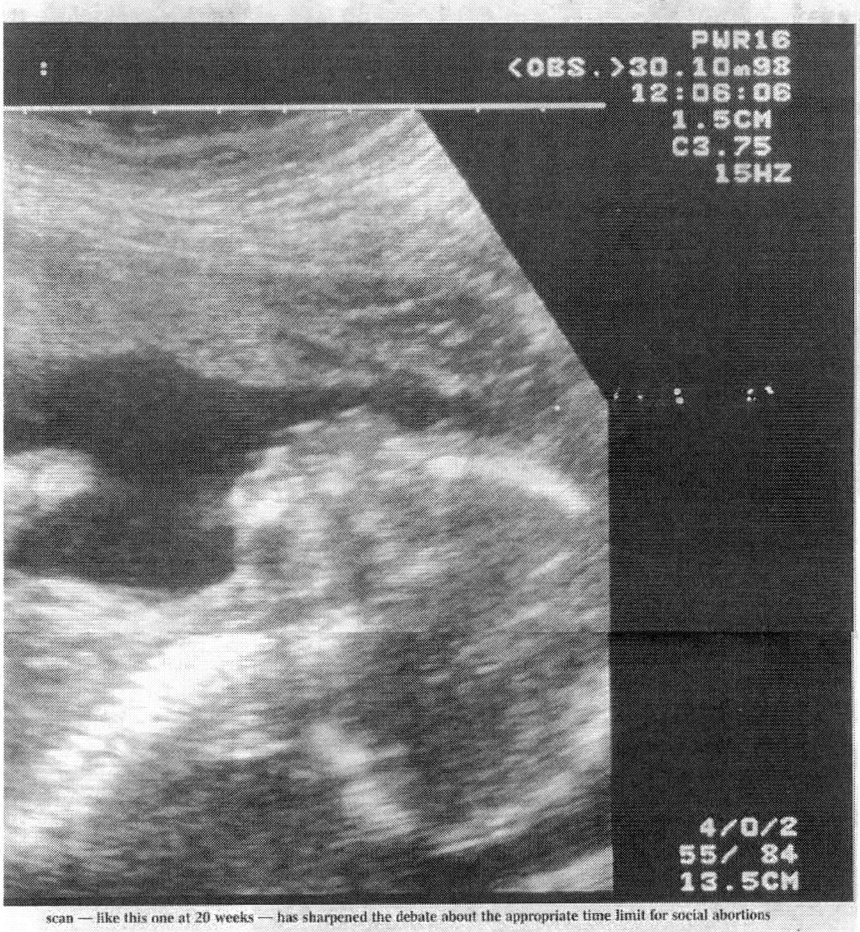

scan — like this one at 20 weeks — has sharpened the debate about the appropriate time limit for social abortions

Prime Minister backs review

Continued from page 1
further. Lord Steel has said that in 1966-67 the law on an upper time limit was based on the existing 28-week assumption of "viability" of a foetus contained in the Infant Life Preservation Act of 1929. As techniques advanced, the limit was cut to 24 weeks in 1990. Since then medical science has recorded survivals at 22 weeks. Opinion remains that abortions should be carried out as early as possible, Lord Steel added.

He said that any change should be carried out with care. Some severe abnormalities might not be detected until quite late in a pregnancy and mothers and their doctors should not be denied the option of a late abortion in such cases. "I am increasingly drawn to the continental experience of making early abortions [up to three months] easier and later ones more difficult, including bringing down the upper limit to 22 weeks."

Mr Blair told MPs: "I have not had an opportunity myself to study in detail the evidence that has been provided. But I am sure that if the situation does change then it would be advisable for us to have another look at the whole question."

His official spokesman said that Mr Blair's comments were not intended to signal a change in policy. "All he was intending to do was to underline that in the past and in the future this has been an issue which has been up to individual MPs, and that is the way it will be dealt with in the future."

The Department of Health said that it had no plans to change the law on abortion and that it was up to Parliament to do so.

But the review of the Human Fertilisation and Embryology Act, due to go to public consultation next year, could provide an opportunity for backbenchers to press for changes.

Opinions among gynaecologists are divided, but the number of late abortions is so small that those who do not wish to do them simply opt out. In 2002, the latest year for which figures are available, 2,753 abortions were carried out at between the 20th and the 24th week of gestation.

The British Medical Association said yesterday that it regarded the Abortion Act as a "humane piece of legislation" and that it had no policy on changing the time limits.

In 1929, the Infant Life Preservation Act defined viability as 28 weeks. Today substantial numbers of babies survive at 24 weeks, though the risk of developmental abnormalities is high.

Mrs Furedi made plain that the British Pregnancy and Advisory Service opposed any change. "We firmly believe that there is a need for abortion to be provided up to 24 weeks and that it would be inappropriate to lower the limit," she said. "Late abortion is a backstop — society might not like it but it is better than women being forced to have babies they don't want."

There were many reasons why women ask for late abortions, she said. Some had been deserted by partners, some were young women "in denial", yet others were women close to the menopause whose periods had become erratic so they did not realise they were pregnant.

Any change in the limits would be welcomed by anti-abortion groups. Life said: "Of course we welcome any measure which reduces the amount of destruction of unborn children."

Blair 'washed hands' in votes on time limits

By Greg Hurst
Political Correspondent

TONY BLAIR opposed moves to lower the time limit for abortions below the present 24 weeks when the issue last came before the Commons.

Mr Blair, then the opposition spokesman on employment, supported a move to reduce the limit from 28 to 24 weeks, which was carried overwhelmingly in a free vote by MPs. But he voted against attempts to bring the limit to 20 or 18 weeks, in a series of votes on amendments to the Human Fertilisation and Embryology Bill in April 1990.

Generally, Mr Blair has steered clear of entering the public debate on abortion, although he has faced pressure to do so, particularly from the Catholic Church. The late Cardinal Thomas Winning, former Roman Catholic Archbishop of Glasgow and leader of Scotland's Catholics, notably accused Mr Blair of hypocrisy when he was Leader of the Opposition. Cardinal Winning accused him of being personally opposed to abortion but unwilling to vote against it in Parliament, claiming that Mr Blair had "washed his hands" on one of the more serious moral issues of the time.

The late Cardinal Basil Hume, former Archbishop of Westminster, also urged Mr Blair when he became Prime Minister to give leadership to the Labour Party and convince its members and the nation that abortion was wrong.

Mr Blair's position is intriguing as his wife Cherie is a staunch Roman Catholic.

The Times, Thursday, July 8th, 2004

A.N. Wilson

Abortion: it's still licenced killing

THE Prime Minister adds his cliché to the abortion debate. "If scientific evidence has shifted then it is obviously sensible for us to take that into account."

What is this so-called new evidence which would make us alter our views on the question of abortion? Some new ultrasound pictures of the foetus showed us that a baby could move its legs after a mere 12 weeks in the womb, with gestures which resemble walking; at 14 weeks it could suck its thumb, and at 22 weeks it could smile. But the law still allows for the possibility of aborting this foetus at 24 weeks.

The strong implication of saying that we should "look again" is that the evidence has somehow changed. But it has not.

The fact that you can now see a foetus smiling is not new evidence. It would require a fantastic lack of imagination not to know that a foetus is human, whether or not you can actually see it nodding or smiling or waving its legs. The pro-abortion lobby can surely not have been positing their case on blindness and stupidity, can they?

I thought the whole strength of their case was a feminist one. A woman has "a right to choose what she does with her own body". No one has ever demonstrated the ground of this supposed right.

Nor does it make sense to describe a small embryonic being, which quite manifestly, if allowed to develop in the womb, would one day become a separate individual, as merely a part of someone else's body.

No "evidence", photographic or otherwise, could change the fact that something which is a human being after nine months in the womb was obviously a human being at nine weeks.

There are many cases when human beings have tried to justify killing other human beings. Sometimes these cases are extremely convincing, when you think a child is so disabled that it can not enjoy a happy life, or an old person has become so incapacitated that they would be better off dead.

In the past, in both these cases, medical types quietly killed their patients, with or without the connivance of families. The Catholic Church is opposed to abortion largely because it is the taking of a life which has not yet been baptised, that is, had the chance of becoming a Roman Catholic.

That Church, which historically has supported murders from the time of the Crusades to the campaigns of the IRA, has small credibility in its claim to respect the so-called sanctity of human life. The argument should be based on logic, not church bias.

We should surely be highly dubious about laws which allow the taking of human life, whether it is putting Granny out of her supposed misery or killing a child, born or unborn, because their arrival is going to cause inconvenience.

A state which licenses killing has a rum view of humanity; it classifies us all as potentially expendable. That is why I would make all abortion illegal except in cases which actually threatened the life of the mother.

● *AS another RC diocese in America bites the dust, protesters waving banners saying "You wrecked my life" weep all the way to the bank. Would so many cases have been brought against pervy priests if no money had passed to the so-called victims?*

Evening Standard, Friday, 9th July 2004

Daily Mail

MONDAY, NOVEMBER 28, 2005 www.dailymail.co.uk 40p

LIFESTYLE magazine

New controversy over the legal time limit for terminations

50 BABIES A YEAR ARE ALIVE AFTER AN ABORTION

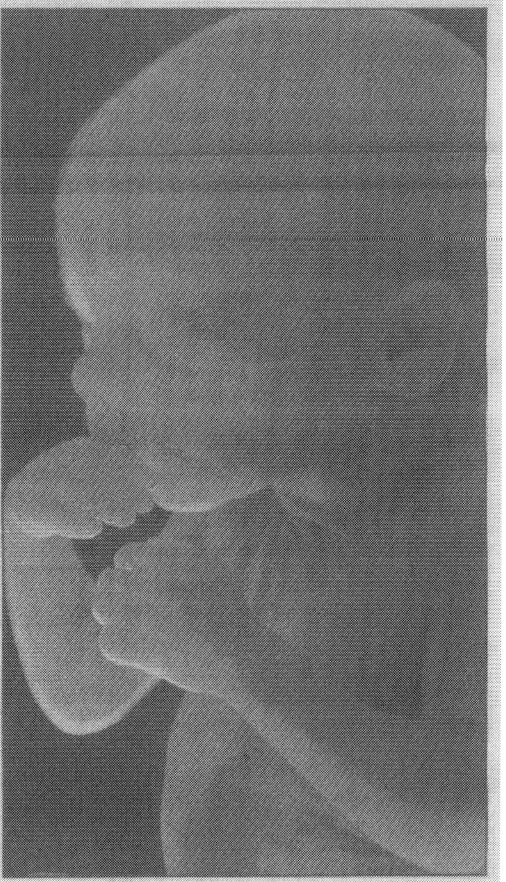

The miracle of life: A five-month-old foetus sucking its thumb

THE abortion debate was reignited last night after it emerged that 50 babies live through botched terminations in Britain every year.

By **Fiona MacRae**
Science Reporter

The figures are the first to show the true scale of a problem thought to have been confined to just a handful of babies.

Now some of the country's leading doctors will investigate how so many survived to be born after just 22 weeks of pregnancy. Shockingly, some of the babies may have gone through more than one attempted abortion.

The revelation triggered demands for the time limit for terminations to be cut. The procedure is currently offered 'on demand' up until the 24th week of pregnancy. The latest figures emerged from the Confidential Enquiry into Child Health (Cemach), which monitors pregnancy deaths on behalf of Britain's six royal colleges of medicine.

The study showed that, each year, up to 50 babies survive abortions carried out after 22 weeks. Doctors in Norwich

Turn to Page 6, Col. 1

Doctors who botch terminations accused of 'sub-standard medicine'

Demands for abortion time limit to be cut from 24 weeks

Continued from Page One

are treating a toddler born at 24 weeks after three botched terminations.

The boy, now aged two, has a range of medical problems. Cemach's report to the Department of Health could see Britain's abortion procedures being overhauled.

Currently, abortions at 22 weeks of pregnancy and above involve the fatal injection of a chemical into the baby's heart while it is still in the womb.

Any babies that survive the procedure, and are born alive, are entitled to medical care. However, anti-abortion campaigners claim that some are so unwanted that they are simply left to die within hours.

Last night, one of Britain's leading obstetricians accused the doctors who carried out botched abortions of 'sub-standard' medicine. Professor Stuart Campbell, who last year used sophisticated 3D scans to show very young foetuses 'walking in the womb', said the figures provided more evidence for the need to cut Britain's 24-week legal limit on abortion.

Mr Campbell, consultant at the Create Health Clinic in London, said: 'I am not anti-abortion but as far as I am concerned, this is sub-standard medicine.

'If viability is the basis on which they set the 24-week limit for abortion, then the simplest answer is to change the law and reduce the upper limit to 18 weeks.'

The investigation was welcomed by Dr Maggie Blott, one

'The answer is to change the law'

of Britain's top obstetricians. Dr Blott, of the Royal Victoria Infirmary in Newcastle, said strict guidelines covering the way abortions are carried out should prevent any live births.

'It shouldn't happen in the first place,' she said. 'The practises of these particular units should be looked at.

'People should be going in and saying, "Why are you having aborted babies being born alive? You shouldn't have aborted babies being born alive".'

The Cemach figures follow several studies which show that babies born at 23 and 24 weeks are capable of surviving.

A recent study of premature babies at University College Hospital London found that almost half of those born at 23 weeks survived.

At 24 weeks, the time limit for most abortions, 72 per cent of the babies survived.

Research published in August found that 31 babies survived botched abortions in the North West between 1996 and 2001.

Some of the babies were able to move around, breathe normally and even cry out. Many lived for more than an hour and one survived four-and-a-half hours.

Last night's revelation that dozens of babies face such a fate every year adds fuel to the arguments for reducing the cut-off point for abortions for so-called 'social' reasons.

Abortions beyond 24 weeks are meant to be allowed only if the baby has 'severe disability' or the mother's life is said to be at risk.

Each year more than 1,200 babies are aborted at between 22 and 24 weeks. Although some will have had severe disabilities, many will have been healthy.

The campaign group Life called last night for the abortion time limit to be lowered.

In Germany, abortions for non-medical reasons are only allowed up until the 12th week of pregnancy. In France, the cut-off point is ten weeks.

Life's Martin Foley said: 'It is time the Government looked at the whole issue of late-term abortions and they were stopped.

'An unborn child is a human being and is entitled to human rights including the right to life.'

Comment – Page 12

Gianna Jessen, of Tennessee, survived an abortion

TWENTY eight years ago, Gianna Jessen's mother had an abortion when seven-and-a-half months pregnant.

It failed and, 18 hours later, Gianna was born – alive.

Miss Jessen, of Tennessee, was born with cerebral palsy as a result of the botched abortion. She has defied doctors' predictions that she would never walk.

She has just completed her first marathon and travels the world to campaign against abortion.

'No baby that is capable of living should be aborted,' she said. 'There is life in the womb – and I am living proof of that.'

Miss Jessen's natural mother was 17 when she decided to have the abortion.

Gianna survived the injection into her mother's womb that was designed to kill her.

Weighing 2lb when born, she spent months in hospital fighting for life, before being placed in a foster home.

At 17 months she was diagnosed with cerebral palsy, caused by her brain being starved of oxygen during the abortion.

Miss Jessen, who is to run next year's London Marathon, said: 'If abortion is about women's rights, then what were my rights?'

A fatal injection to the heart

By **Science Reporter**

ABORTION in Britain is legal right up to until birth if it is thought the baby has a severe disability or the mother's life is at risk.

But termination for 'social reasons' – the effect of the pregnancy on the mental health and well-being of the mother – is legal only up to 24 weeks.

Terminations at 22 weeks and above involve a fatal injection of potassium chloride into the baby's heart. Doctors carry this out using ultrasound so they can check the heart has stopped before giving the mother drugs to induce labour.

However, the procedure is so delicate that in some cases the heart starts beating again and the baby is born alive.

In earlier abortions, hospitals or clinics use either a suction method or surgical scrape to clear the womb.

Concern that a 28-week foetus was capable of surviving outside the womb led to the time limit for terminations for social reasons being cut from 28 weeks to 24 in 1990. Then, the national survival rate at 23 weeks was less than 10 per cent.

But 15 years later, advances in medical technology mean many more premature babies are able to survive, fuelling calls for the time-limit to be reduced even further. Last year, a record 185,400 abortions were carried out in the UK.

Daily Mail, November 28th 2005

Beware of the love rat

Trickster: Mehtab Habib

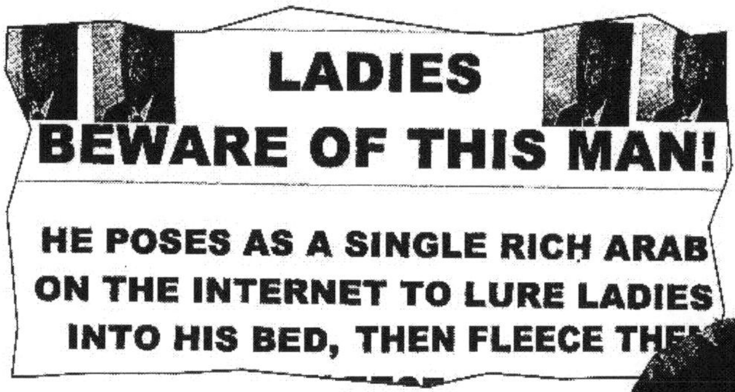

LADIES
BEWARE OF THIS MAN!
HE POSES AS A SINGLE RICH ARAB
ON THE INTERNET TO LURE LADIES
INTO HIS BED, THEN FLEECE

Warning: One of the posters put up by Miss Lamrabet

Victim's revenge on Internet suitor who turned out to be a married man

By **Andy Dolan**

IN search of love, the petite divorcee could hardly believe her luck when a dashing bachelor she met via an Internet dating website started wooing her.

As well as being handsome, the charming Arab said he was wealthy – heir to a £15million family fortune.

Within weeks, Mehtab Habib had wowed Karma Lamrabet with tales of his top publishing job, his £1million home and his regular business trips abroad.

They became engaged and he set a date for their wedding at his family's Dubai estate.

For 31-year-old accounts clerk Miss Lamrabet, it all seemed too good to be true. And sadly, it was.

After becoming suspicious, she did some frantic detective work – and discovered Habib was really a cash-strapped father of two from Reading with a pregnant wife.

So she set about taking revenge – by putting up 60 posters in his home town naming and shaming the 35-year-old love rat.

They were pasted on public toilets, bus stops, phone boxes, his

'Absolutely devastated'

car and through his neighbours' letterboxes.

The posters showed a picture of Habib with the warning: 'Ladies beware of this man!' and told how he had posed as a 'single, rich Arab' to win her heart.

'I was absolutely devastated when I found out that everything Mehtab had told me was a lie,' said Miss Lamrabet, of Raynes Park, South-West London.

'I thought I had found the perfect man to settle down with, yet it was all a sham.

'The posters were my way of warning other women what he was like – I would hate him to do this to anybody else.'

The couple met in February after she signed up to the Indianmatrimonials.com website in search of a Muslim 'soulmate'.

Habib told her it had been his mother's dying wish for him to marry a Muslim girl.

As their relationship developed, he showered Miss Lamrabet with expensive gifts and bombarded her with loving text messages.

Posing as a millionaire whose executive position at publisher Condé Nast took him worldwide, he boasted of magazine photoshoots with celebrity hairdresser Trevor Sorbie and promised the smitten divorcee a life of luxury and leisure.

Ironically, it was only when the trickster whisked Miss Lamrabet off for a romantic weekend in one of Monte Carlo's finest hotels that she began to suspect her 'fiancé' was not all he seemed.

'What he didn't bank on was that during that weekend I would start to feel uneasy about him,' she said.

'He demanded £5,000 so he could buy flights for all my family to our wedding in Dubai using a half-price discount through his company. I believe he was planning to take the cash and disappear – I just knew something was not right.'

When the couple returned to Britain, Miss Lamrabet discovered the address Habib had given her did not exist – but found him on an electoral roll Internet search at an address in Reading.

When she rang to confront him, she discovered she was speaking to his wife of 12 years, Errum, who was expecting his third child.

Miss Lamrabet caught up with the love cheat at a pre-arranged meeting in her local pub, where he confessed to his deception and begged forgiveness.

Yesterday Habib, who had worked for a month as sales executive for express courier firm Crossflight until recently leaving, said: 'I am not denying I had an affair with Karma. I was with her for a few months but she has said lots of wrong things about me.'

Mrs Mehtab said she was aware of the allegations, but 'we have two young children to consider'.

a.dolan@dailymail.co.uk

Karma Lamrabet: 'I thought I'd found the perfect man'

Beware of the love rat

Daily Mail May 3rd 2004

Daily Mail

MONDAY, MAY 3, 2004

40p

THE INDIAN IN THE CUPBOARD FOR JUST £2.60

It's the most complete beauty test EVER. Thousands of products tried by hundreds of ordinary women. Now we reveal their no-nonsense verdicts to help YOU build the perfect beauty regime ... PAGES 36–39

THE BEAUTY HANDBOOK

NEW ABORTED BABY STORM

The doctor: Consultant Michael Cohn

Mother of unborn infant with cleft palate was seven months pregnant

By **James Mills**

A BABY with a cleft palate was aborted at 28 weeks, it emerged yesterday.

Dr Michael Cohn agreed to terminate the pregnancy a full four weeks after the usual legal limit for abortion.

The only grounds for a termination after 24 weeks are if the infant has a 'serious handicap' or the mother's health is at risk. But doctors argue that in almost every case of cleft lip and palate, the

Turn to Page 5, Col. 2

The campaigner: Church of England curate Joanna Jepson

The Rev Joanna Jepson was herself born with a jaw defect

'Baby should not have died at 28 weeks, or any other age'

Dr Cohn: 'Immense pressure'

Continued from Page One

disfigurement can be corrected with surgery. Around 1,000 babies a year are born at 28 weeks and most go on to lead perfectly healthy lives.

The abortion, which took place in Herefordshire in 2001, is at the centre of a police investigation prompted by Church of England curate Joanna Jepson. She claims it was an 'unlawful killing'.

West Mercia Police initially refused her demands for an investigation last year, but she has since won a judicial review of the decision which will be heard this month in the High Court.

The parents in the case, who have not been named, are understood to be well-educated and in their 30s. The mother, it is understood, had been made aware of her baby's condition several weeks before the abortion.

Dr Cohn, 45, has not been suspended from his £80,000-a-year post.

He could be charged with wilfully failing to meet the requirements of the Abortion Act which carries a fine of up to £5,000. But prosecutors also have the option of a charge under Section 58 of the Offences Against The Person Act 1861, introduced to combat back-street abortionists, which is punishable with life imprisonment.

Miss Jepson, a 27-year-old Cambridge graduate who was herself born with a congenital jaw defect, claims cleft lips

'He is not a monster'

and palates do not justify a termination under the 1967 Abortion Act.

Last night she said: 'At 24 weeks a baby is deemed "viable" under law, so at a full four weeks later the abortion process is going to be far more painful for both the mother and the child.

'Babies are known to survive as early as 22 weeks, and at 28 weeks nearly all survive and go on to live healthy lives.

'Whatever the age the principle is still the same. This child was somehow deemed unfit to live simply for having a cleft palate. It is wrong that a person, whatever their age, should be denied the right to live for this reason.'

The medical profession rallied to the defence of Dr Cohn as the landmark case provoked strong opinions on both sides of the debate.

A colleague said the investigation – which also includes a second doctor who jointly authorised the procedure – was putting the married consultant and his three teenage children under immense pressure.

'This is absolutely devastating to the whole family.

'Mike is a family man with impeccable professional standards who has the utmost respect of his colleagues and patients.

'This case involves a complex set of circumstances and the decision to go ahead with the termination was ultimately taken by the mother after very careful consultation.

'These things are not entered into lightly but being the subject of a police investigation gives the impression that he is nothing more than a Victorian back-street abortionist.

'This is not the case. He is not a monster, but a thoughtful, caring professional making extremely difficult decisions to the best of his ability.'

The British Pregnancy Advisory Service said the circumstances of this particular abortion were likely to be less clear-cut than Miss Jepson claims.

A spokesman said: 'Some cleft lips and palates are more serious than others and are not always easily treated. The doctor's professional judgment should be trusted.'

The Royal College of Obstetricians and Gynaecologists, however, said most babies born at 28 weeks are 'viable' and that cleft palate was not a serious handicap.

Dr Maggie Blott, an obstetrician at the Royal Victoria Infirmary in Newcastle, said: 'From 28 weeks, we would expect 90 per cent to survive. We certainly deliver babies at 28 weeks if the mother has a life-threatening condition, and we assume they are going to survive.

'Cleft palate is not a serious handicap – the results from surgery on these are very good nowadays.

'I don't think I would support termination for cleft lip and palate.'

John Smeaton, national director of the Society for the Protection of Unborn Children, said: 'The key issue is that disabled people – whether they have a minor disability or a severe disability – all deserve a chance to live. There is quite dreadful discrimination in our laws which single out disabled people for destruction before birth.'

Dr Cohn has the full backing of the Medical Defence Union, of which he is a member.

The British Medical Association is also monitoring the case carefully as there could be far reaching implica-

'Not a serious handicap'

tions for abortion providers and mothers who discover late in pregnancy that their baby has a serious problem.

Miss Jepson asked West Mercia Police to investigate the abortion last year after she spotted the case whilst studying official statistics.

The curate of St Michael's Church in Chester is determined to press ahead with the case as she wants the court to provide a definition of 'serious handicap' which has not yet been defined legally.

What the battle is about

A CLEFT palate occurs when the tissues forming the roof of the mouth fail to join together properly.

In many cases it is accompanied by a cleft lip, also known as a 'hare-lip', in which the tissues forming the upper lip do not join.

Around one in 600 babies a year is affected in the UK. In almost all cases, corrective surgery lets them lead perfectly normal lives with no disfigurement.

Under the Abortion Act 1967, doctors are allowed to terminate a pregnancy after 24 weeks only if there is a serious threat to the mother's health, or if the baby would have a 'serious handicap'. Crucially, that term is not defined in law. This flexibility is needed to allow doctors and parents to make decisions according to the circumstances, campaigners claim.

The abortion time limit of 24 weeks was established as the point at which a baby could survive independently, outside the womb.

By 28 weeks, a baby would typically weigh 2.2lb. In the early 1980s, this was as small as a baby could be and still be considered 'viable'.

But medical advances are such that today, 90 per cent of them survive and go on to lead normal lives.

New aborted baby storm

Daily Mail May 3rd 2004

Daily Mail

THURSDAY, MAY 13, 2004 40p

LUCKY PAY PACKET
SEE PAGE 63

As school fixes a secret abortion for this 14-year-old girl, her furious mother asks:

WHOSE CHILD IS SHE ANYWAY?

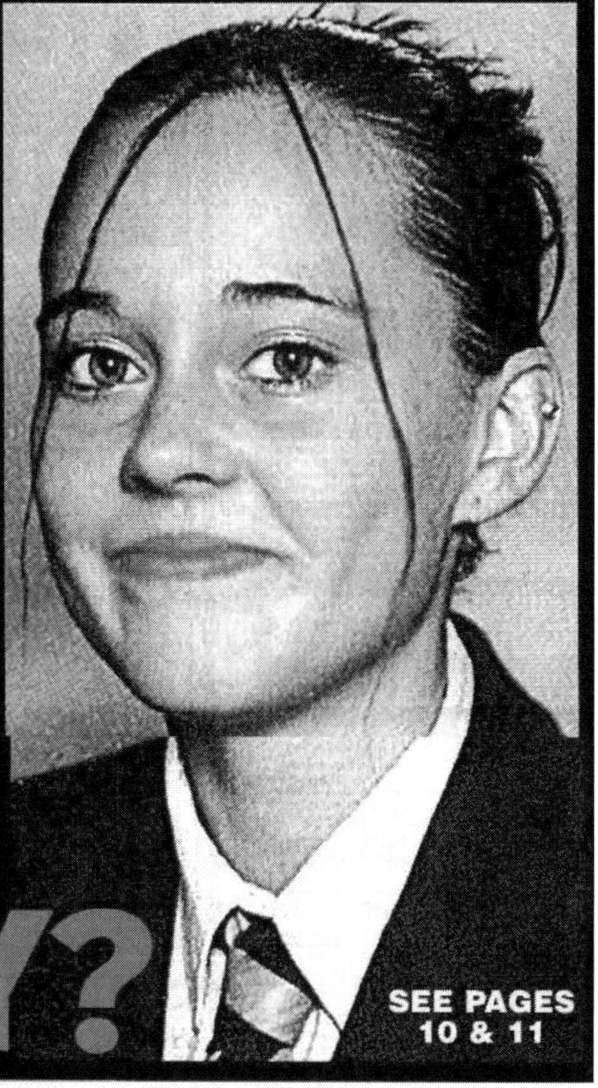

SEE PAGES 10 & 11

MAXINE OUT

But her £1m cover is blown by theft from civil servant's car

By **Stephen Wright**
Chief Crime Correspondent

MAXINE Carr was freed early from prison yesterday after serving just 21 months behind bars.

She was smuggled out of Foston Hall jail near Derby two days earlier than scheduled after confidential £1million plans for her release were wrecked by an astonishing security blunder.

On the eve of her release, documents outlining the Soham liar's new life – including where she was due to live under police protection – were stolen from a car belonging to a senior Home Office official. Also stolen from the female civil servant's car were papers containing details of her new bank accounts and National Insurance number, as well as the location of a number of police safe houses which had been made ready to accommodate Carr. It is believed the papers did not include her new name.

The shambles forced officials to bring forward her release.

Carr – who had been locked up for 635 days since her arrest on August 17, 2002 – was last night at a 'temporary secure address', believed to be a police

Turn to Page 5, Col. One

Page 10 * *

Daily Mail, Thursday, May 13, 2004

As 14-year-old struggles with remorse, her mother attacks a school's

My daughter's

A SCHOOL arranged for a 14-year-old girl to have an abortion without informing her parents.

Michelle Smith was left to visit doctors on her own after telling teachers she was frightened of breaking the news to her family.

Her mother found out only when one of her daughter's schoolfriends mentioned it when they met in the street.

An outraged Maureen Smith said last night that the experience had left her daughter traumatised and full of regret. She described the school's actions as 'deplorable'. 'I am absolutely outraged that my 14-year-old

By **Richard Price** and **Suzanne Finney**

daughter, who in the eyes of the law is only a child, was able to have an abortion without my knowledge,' said the care worker.

'This is one of the worst things she will go through in her life and I knew nothing about it. I wasn't there to help or protect her.

'I feel like my right as a parent has been taken away from me. I feel like I've had my heart ripped out, so God knows what my daughter is going through.'

'She had an appendix operation last year and I had to sign two consent forms, yet no one thought it necessary to tell me about this. If my daughter had been truanting from school or causing trouble in the classroom I would have been informed.

'Yet she can go ahead and have an abortion which will affect her for the rest of her life and I have no say and no rights as a parent.'

The schoolgirl, whose identity has been revealed with her mother's consent, went to a family planning clinic for a pregnancy test three weeks ago.

She was concerned after having unprotected sex and missing a period.

The clinic advised her to talk to her school, where she was referred to an 'outreach worker'. Michelle said she spoke to the health worker, who gives sex education lessons at the school, 'four or five days later'.

She was asked if she wanted to tell her parents, but responded: 'My mum would kill me.'

Michelle said she was worried her mother would feel 'let down' and the health worker agreed that an abortion should go ahead in secret.

She was referred to a hospital and took a 'chemical abortion' pill a fortnight ago.

She returned to hospital for the second stage of the abortion two days later, at seven weeks pregnant.

Michelle said: 'I feel like I wasn't ready to make a decision about the baby. If I had my chance again, I think I probably would have kept the child and would have let my mum know.'

When 37-year-old Mrs Smith found out and confronted the school, she was told that it did not have to give parents any information because of confidentiality rules. Brunts School in

'When she had her appendix out I signed two forms but nobody thought to tell me about this'

'Simply not old enough'

Mansfield said an 'outreach service' was made available to all pupils with the aim of reducing unwanted teenage pregnancies.

Deputy head Claire Allerton said a letter detailing the school's Community Child Health Service was sent to all parents every September.

The letter states that parental consent for consultations is not required 'other than in the rare circumstances when the young person is judged not to be sufficiently mature to take part independently'.

The deputy head said the teenager would receive 'all the support she needs' when she returns to class.

Campaign groups said the case highlighted how the Government was undermining family values and dismally failing to tackle soaring teenage pregnancy rates.

A girl under 16 can have an abortion without parental consent if a doctor deems her mature enough to make the decision. Department of Health guidelines state that she should be encouraged to inform her parents. But Michelle told doctors that she was worried her mother would feel 'let down' so they allowed the abortion to proceed in secret.

Mrs Smith, who also has a 16-year-old son, found out her daughter was pregnant before the final stage of the termination. After talks between mother and daughter and Dwain Smith, 14, the child's father, Michelle changed her mind. But by then it was too late to save the baby.

Mrs Smith, who was divorced from Michelle's father Peter, 38, four years ago, said: 'Of course I was upset that she had fallen pregnant. I had no idea she was even having sex.

'But we could have talked about it as a family and if she had wanted to keep the baby she would have had my full support. She is simply not old enough to make a decision like that on her own.'

Dwain, who has been dating Michelle for eight months, said: 'She had the abortion because it was the only thing we thought we could do.

'But now we realise just how serious it was and we both feel very upset and confused.'

Pressure groups attacked the actions of the teachers and health workers who helped arrange the abortion.

Josephine Quintavalle, of the campaign group Comment On Reproductive Ethics, said: 'This girl has been traumatised because the Government has set up a system which encourages

What the law says

MICHELLE Smith was able to go ahead with a secret abortion with the full backing of the law.

According to Department of Health rules, her doctors were not allowed to tell her mother because of patient confidentiality.

A termination for a girl under 16 can go ahead provided doctors believe it is in her best interests and she is competent to understand the moral, social and emotional implications.

If a girl as young as 11 or 12 sought an abortion without parental consent, doctors would spend more time talking to her because 'of concerns about possible abuse. In those circumstances, they would be allowed to raise the alarm if suspicious.

Abortion is legal if two doctors agree it would harm the mother physically or mentally to continue the pregnancy.

One in five abortions now involves a teenager, while pregnancies among under-18s rose by 7.3 per cent in the last year for which figures are available. In 2002, 175,000 women had a termination. Of these, 3,500 were under 16.

Daily Mail, Thursday, May 13, 2004 Page 11

'deplorable' decision to send the girl for a termination behind her back

secret abortion

Following the rules: Michelle's school

Support: Michelle and Maureen Smith

teenagers to have abortions behind their parents' backs.

'The first person a girl should turn to is her mother. What is the wisdom of having a law of underage sex if nurses and counsellors are complicit in covering up like this?'

Nuala Scarisbrick, trustee of the anti-abortion organisation Life, said: 'I feel desperately sorry for the mother who was deliberately deceived.

'Health authorities are sending workers into schools issuing "how to" advice on sex, dishing out condoms and morning-after pills, and if they don't work then they will carry out an abortion.

'There are three victims here: the girl, her mother and the unborn baby. They have all been let down by a system which does not work.'

A spokesman for Mansfield District Primary Care Trust, which organised the abortion, said it could not comment on individual cases but insisted standard procedure had been followed. The spokesman said:

'Let down by the system'

'If the patient is 16 or over, then that is the age of consent. If the patient is not 16 then the patient would be counselled by a clinician and an assessment would be made as to whether or not the patient was competent to make a decision regarding a termination of pregnancy.

'If the patient was found to be competent then a referral would be made to a gynaecologist. It would be the decision of the patient whether or not a parent was informed.'

Nottinghamshire County Council backed the school, adding: 'LEA guidance states that teachers are not legally bound to inform parents or the head teacher of any disclosure by pupils regarding pregnancy unless the school's confidentiality policy requires them to do so.'

Comment – Page 12

Whose child is she anyway?

Daily Mail May 13th 2004

Daily Mail

EXCLUSIVE

FRIDAY, MAY, 14, 2004 40p

The 14-year-old in the secret school abortion row and her distraught mother tell their full story – and reveal the role of a novice health worker ...

ABORTION ADVICE FROM GIRL OF 21

Picture: BRUCE ADAMS

Melissa Smith and boyfriend Dwain, both 14. He was the father of the child she lost

By **Richard Price** and **Steve Doughty**

THE scandalous truth about Melissa Smith's secret abortion emerged last night.

The 14-year-old, pregnant by a boy who is also only 14, had the operation arranged by an inexperienced school 'outreach worker' aged just 21.

The worker, Claire Chapman, did not even accompany Melissa

Turn to Page 2, Col. 3

Pregnant schoolgirl's adviser was aged just 21

Claire Chapman: 'Nothing will be said'

Continued from Page One

to the abortion clinic. Instead, in another telling sign of the times, she sent a text message wishing her good luck while the teenager sat alone in hospital for two hours.

After the abortion was over she sent another text saying: 'I hope it went well.'

Last night, Melissa's outraged mother Maureen spoke of her anger that the abortion was arranged without her knowledge by a woman barely out of her teens.

The family's lawyer has been instructed to investigate the possibility of criminal charges or a civil action, on the basis that Melissa did not properly consent to the operation.

'How can a 21-year-old think she knows my child

'I hope it went well'

better than I do?' said Mrs Smith, a divorced care worker from Mansfield.

'I don't believe in abortion, but if she had decided that is what she wanted I would have accepted it and helped her through it.

'The point is, as her mother, I should have been given the right to do that. Instead it was taken away from me.'

Melissa, a pupil at The Brunts School in Mansfield, discovered last month that she was pregnant by her boyfriend Dwain.

She had been supplied with contraceptive pills by a family planning clinic, but decided to take the risk after they were accidentally thrown away.

She took a pregnancy test at the clinic, and when it was positive said she did not want her mother to know.

'Samantha! Are you doing your homework?'

The clinic then referred her to the outreach worker, part of the school's Community Child Health Service, aimed at reducing unwanted teenage pregnancies.

Miss Chapman in turn referred her to hospital, where she took the first of a series of 'chemical abortion' pills to terminate her seven-week pregnancy.

Maureen Smith then learned about her daughter's pregnancy after the older sister of a schoolfriend told Melissa's grandmother.

At that point, Melissa changed her mind and said she wanted to keep the baby. But because she had taken the first abortion pill, the process could not be reversed.

Last night, Dwain Smith's mother, Sarah 29, was reported saying: 'Dwain and Mel have been seeing one another for about a year and I can tell you they love each other to bits.

'He insisted on going with Melissa's mother Maureen and I to help Mel through the termination.

'I shall never forget the look on his face or forgive these people for what they have done.'

She added: 'Dwain and Mel had even discussed names. He said that he had been secretly hoping all the while that it would be a girl and wanted to call her Chloe.'

At the school, Claire Chapman has had confidential discussions with hundreds of pupils since becoming a health worker last year.

According to her employers, Mansfield and District Primary Care Trust, her role is 'to discuss problems, offer pregnancy testing and free condoms'.

She advertises her services on a website promising 'a confidential service even if you are under 16 years of age. Nothing will be said to anyone including teachers, parents or friends'.

Last night, she said: 'There are lots of questions I would love to answer but I am not allowed to say anything.'

However, a spokesman for the health trust defended her, saying: 'The decision that termination of pregnancy is the most suitable treatment is only taken by two doctors, normally a family planning consultant and a gynaecologist in hospital, in line with the Abortion Act 1967.

'The health outreach worker's responsibility is to give much-needed support, particularly if the person is not able to disclose this information to the parents.'

Melissa's termination was carried out under the 1967 law that allows abortion – with the consent of the pregnant woman – if two doctors agree it would harm the health of the mother or other children to have the baby.

Angela Donen, the Smith family's lawyer, said, however, that the doctors who carried out the abortion appeared to have only the thinnest pretext of having obtained consent.

'According to her mum, Melissa changed her mind between taking the first pill and taking the second. If she had given consent, how come she changed her mind?'

If the doctors who carried out the abortion did not obtain proper consent from Melissa, they could be charged with unlawful killing.

Civil action could be taken on grounds of insufficient consent or failure to encourage her to tell her parents.

Although the abortion advice was given to the girl at school, head teacher Jerry

'No plans to change the law'

Dalton told parents: 'No teachers were aware of the student's situation.'

But a stream of critics said the teenager's aburtion had become a landmark in the remorseless process by which the state and its agents are stripping parents of rights over their children.

Tory health spokesman Simon Burns said: 'When this girl needed an operation for appendicitis, two signatures from her parents were required. But when the abortion happened, they were not even told.'

Religious leaders called for the Government, which constantly claims to be encouraging good parenthood, to act to restore the threadbare legal rights of families.

The Department of Health said: 'There are no plans to change the law on abortion.'

Comment – Page 12

r.price@dailymail.co.uk

How could it happen? Pages 8&9

Children's 'right' to sex guidance

By **Dan Newling**

CHILDREN are to be targeted in a nationwide publicity campaign for a confidential sex advice service.

They will be told they are entitled to help whatever their age.

It is understood there will be mailshots to schools and advertisements in teenage magazines.

Already the 'right to confidentiality' message is being displayed on Government-funded websites aimed at sexually active young children. One such website states: 'Under the Sexual Offences Act you still have the right to confidential advice on contraception, condoms, pregnancy and abortion, even if you are under 16.

'But remember, whatever your age, you shouldn't have sex until you are ready.'

The campaign is being co-ordinated by the Teenage Pregnancy Unit, part of the Department for Education and Skills. Last night, a spokesman for the department said the campaign was a response to recommendations made last year by the an independent advisory group.

He explained that some children simply do not feel comfortable talking about sexual issues with their parents, and may be dissuaded from seeking advice if they felt their parents would be told.

Last night, family campaigners reacted with anger to the planned campaign.

Norman Wells, of the pressure group Family and Youth Concern, said: 'The provision of controversial contraceptive advice or abortion services to young people without the support of their parents breaks down the relationship of trust within the family.

'When the things go wrong it's the family that has to pick up the pieces and the parents who have to live with the consequences.'

TV 59-62, Offers & Promotions 64, Letters 65, Coffee Break 66-68, City 83-85, Racing 86, 87 & 89

Abortion advice from a girl of 21

Daily Mail May 14th 2004

How could they let

In a heartbreaking interview, the 14-year-old whose school arranged a secret abortion and her distraught mother tell their full horrifying story

by **Helen Weathers**

TWO WEEKS ago at 11am, Maureen Smith was busy drying her hair as she prepared to go to work when the phone rang. At the other end of the line was her elderly mother Valerie, her voice so distressed she could barely speak. Her first words were: 'Sit down Maureen, you are going to have a bit of a shock.'

Maureen braced herself for the worst, thinking that maybe her father had died or that one of her two teenage children had been hurt in a terrible accident.

In the event, she was totally unprepared for her mother's next words: 'Melissa is pregnant and is going to have an abortion.' All Maureen could reply was 'What do you mean?' as she desperately tried to make sense of it all.

After all, her daughter was only 14 and Maureen never suspected for a second that she had been sleeping with her 14-year-old boyfriend, Dwain. And even if she was pregnant, what doctor would perform an abortion on a child so young without her mother's knowledge or consent?

Maureen listened, numb with shock, as Valerie, 61, told her how she had bumped into the older sister of one of Melissa's school-friends in the street earlier that day.

'You're Melissa's nan, aren't you?' said the young woman. 'Well, I think you should know Melissa's pregnant and she's going to have an abortion on Saturday. It's all been arranged and her school knows about it, but I think it's way out of order.'

The minute Maureen, 37, put the phone down she sent a text message to Melissa's mobile saying: 'Why didn't you tell me?' Her daughter sent back: 'I was scared. I felt I'd let you down.'

'I just couldn't stop crying,' says Maureen, speaking now for the first time. 'I felt as if my heart and soul had been ripped out. I couldn't understand why Melissa hadn't confided in me and I felt so hurt that she hadn't been able to turn to me for support.

BUT WORSE than that, I just couldn't believe it was possible for a 14-year-old child to have an abortion without her mother even knowing. It was inconceivable that Melissa's school could have kept that from me. I thought it couldn't possibly be true.

So I phoned the school to confront them. I said: "My daughter Melissa is pregnant and I understand the school has arranged an abortion."

'I wanted answers immediately. I was told someone would call me back in ten minutes and when after an hour no one had rung I phoned again, only to be told the person I needed to speak to was in a meeting.

'Even though I was furious, I was trying to stay calm because I knew I would get nowhere if I lost my temper. Eventually, someone called me back and told me they had known Melissa was pregnant, but couldn't tell me because it would have been a breach of patient confidentiality. I was flabbergasted.'

Maureen discovered Melissa had secretly taken a pregnancy test at her local family planning clinic in Mansfield. When it was positive, she told them she didn't want her mother to know, so her school was informed instead.

Melissa, who told the family planning clinic she wanted a termination, was then referred to a 21-year-old 'outreach health worker' who was part of the school's Community Child Health Service, aimed at reducing unwanted teenage pregnancies.

Maureen was also reminded by the school that a letter had been sent to parents in September stating that parental consent for consultations with the health worker was not required 'other than in the rare circumstances when the young person is judged not to be sufficiently mature to take part independently'.

'It was the first I had heard of it,' says Maureen. 'I certainly never received that letter and I know a lot of other parents who haven't either.

'Even if I had, I would have thought it referred to contraception, not abortions. I was absolutely horrified. In my mind Melissa wasn't mature enough to make that kind of decision. What 14-year-old is?

'Dwain's mother, Sarah, was as stunned as I was when I phoned her. She agreed to bring her son to my house after school so we could all talk about it.

'When Melissa walked in, the first thing I did was give her a big hug. I was devastated that she was pregnant so young, but I promised I'd help her, whatever she decided. She and Dwain said they'd been talking and wanted to keep the baby after all.'

But it was already too late. For that very morning, unknown to her mother, Melissa had been to King's Mill Hospital, in nearby Sutton in Ashfield, and received the first of a series of 'chemical abortion' pills which would terminate her seven-week pregnancy.

With just a schoolfriend for company, she had swallowed the pill and then waited for two hours before returning — deeply upset and shaking — for her English class at The Brunts School.

Melissa had thought she still had time to change her mind after taking that first pill — that is what she claims she was told by a hospital nurse — but even as she spoke to her mother and Dwain, the abortion pill was already working.

The next day, when Maureen phoned the hospital to cancel Saturday's appointment because Melissa wanted to go ahead with the pregnancy, she was told it was impossible.

The first pill had already cut off the foetus's blood supply and if Melissa didn't come in for the next set of pills, she would miscarry anyway in three to four weeks.

'On Saturday, May 1, a day which will be burned in my memory for the rest of my life, I had to drive my daughter to hospital for an abortion which I hadn't even known about and which none of us wanted.

'Melissa was terrified and her eyes kept welling up with tears as she realised the enormity of the situation and that there could be no going back.

'She had to swallow eight pills and for the next six hours I had to watch her screaming and crying in agony. Whenever I tried to comfort her, she screamed: "Don't touch me, leave me alone." I thought my heart would break.

'Before we left, a nurse told us the remains of what would have been my first grandchild would be cremated and the ashes scattered in the hospital gardens. It was just too much for me.

ALL I could see when I closed my eyes was that baby's face, or how I had imagined it would be had it been born. At 4pm I drove Melissa home. We were all so traumatised we couldn't even talk. Melissa rested and watched television while I sat and cried.

'The following Monday morning, Melissa's school phoned up and asked why she wasn't in class.

'It was then that all my anger spilled out. I shouted: "What do you mean, why isn't she in school? Don't you know? On Saturday she had an abortion which you arranged." And they just said: "Oh sorry, we forgot."'

In the two weeks since the abortion, Maureen's anger has not diminished. Indeed, she is so furious at what she regards as the deplorable actions of the school and the Government's policy to cut teenage pregnancies at all costs, she has agreed both herself and Melissa can be identified.

The family's misery is palpable. Maureen is never far from tears and Melissa holds her boyfriend Dwain's hand in mute despair, wishing she could turn the clock back.

Divorced care worker Maureen still can't quite believe the horrific events of the past few weeks and is appalled that when it came to the emotional and physical welfare of her own child, she was effectively stripped of her parental rights.

'When my daughter had an appendix operation last year I had to sign two consent forms, yet no one thought it necessary to tell me about this. Melissa is young and thinks she is coping, but how will she feel when she's older, knowing she had an abortion she didn't really want.

'Who decides that I have no right to know that my 14-year-old child is pregnant and to help her reach a decision, but that a young outreach worker who hardly knew her does?'

Like most parents, Maureen had no idea that a girl under 16 can have an abortion without parental consent if a doctor deems her mature enough to make the decision. Department of Health guidelines state that she should be encouraged to inform her parents.

Melissa now bitterly regrets not telling her mother in the first place. Chewing her lips and with her eyes welling up with tears, she says quietly: 'I was so shocked when I found out I was pregnant and terrified of what Mum might think. I just wanted to get rid of it without anyone finding out, but now I wish I hadn't.

'When I'd had time to think about it, I realised I wanted the baby.'

MELISSA is in many ways typical of thousands of young girls today. The product of a broken home, she was devastated when her parents split up four years ago after 16 years of marriage.

She felt resentful when six months after the break-up her mother started a new relationship, with a computer programmer.

Like too many of her peers, she started experimenting with sex at a young age.

Maureen readily accepts whatever blame may be apportioned to her. 'Melissa was very upset when I left her father, but we were very unhappy together and I thought it was for the best.

'My husband, Peter, had never worked and I was the one supporting the family, and then when he had a stroke at the age of 32 it put an enormous strain on the marriage.

'Melissa had always been a daddy's girl and blamed me for breaking up the family.

'She was very resentful when I started seeing Jeff and with hindsight I can see it was too soon. She felt pushed out and became very rebellious.'

When Melissa started seeing

> ***'When my daughter had an appendix operation I signed two forms. Yet no one would tell me about this'***

her do this?

...Melissa Smith, 14, with her boyfriend, Dwain, and mother, Maureen, who was not consulted about her abortion

Dwain, Maureen tried to talk to her about sex, but Melissa would brush off her efforts with the words: 'Stop it, I don't want to talk about it.'

'She was so embarrassed I thought that meant she wasn't interested in it at all, so I didn't think there was anything to worry about,' says Maureen.

But unknown to her mother, Melissa and Dwain had started sleeping together, sneaking off to a friend's house after school so they could be alone. She went to a family planning clinic and started taking the Pill.

She became pregnant when her mother accidentally threw out the pills, thinking they were paracetamol.

'My mum wasn't wearing her glasses and when she saw the pills she thought they were painkillers and said "These can be dangerous if you take too many" and threw them in the bin,' says Melissa.

'I didn't go back for more because I thought I might still be protected from the ones I had already taken. We took a risk. We didn't feel we were too young for sex. Almost everyone our age has sex these days.

'But when I found out I was pregnant, I was shocked and terrified of telling my mum, not because I thought she would be angry, but because I didn't want to upset her or my nan.

'So I told the family planning clinic I wanted an abortion. When I left, I met Dwain and told him I was pregnant, and he was just as shocked as me.'

Looking at these two youngsters side by side, fiddling with their fingers and staring out of the window, it is hard to see how anyone could have regarded them as mature enough to make such a far-reaching decision as having an abortion without their parents' love and support.

But that is exactly what happened. Melissa's school was informed by the clinic and one day, after her English class, the school nurse came to find her.

SHE then had a half-hour consultation with a young female outreach worker, who attended the school once or twice a week to give sex education lessons. The nurse and the health worker kept saying to me "You really must tell your mum", and one of them offered to call her for me, but I kept saying: "No, I want an abortion." I didn't really know what it involved. All I knew is that I wanted everything to get back to normal. We didn't talk about different options or whether I really wanted to keep the baby.'

An appointment was made for Melissa to see a doctor at King's Mill Hospital one Saturday three weeks ago. Again, she was insistent she wanted an abortion and didn't want her mother to know.

The following Monday, she was accompanied by the outreach worker to the hospital for a scan to confirm the pregnancy, and another appointment was made for her the following Thursday to receive the first of the chemical abortion pills.

'When I saw the scan, I didn't feel anything. I just felt numb. I just wanted it all to be over with. No one said "Do you want to change your mind?", but the outreach worker did say to me: "Are you sure you don't want to tell your mum?" I just said no.'

UNBELIEVABLY, Melissa went for the first 8.30am appointment for her abortion with just a schoolfriend for company. She claims the outreach worker told her she was unable to come with her. She did, however, send a text message wishing Melissa good luck — something most people would consider rather inadequate in the circumstances.

came along with me, but she had to leave because she had to go to school and I was on my own for two hours. I had to stay in case I was sick or fainted, but I felt all right apart from a terrible headache and went back to school. No one came to find out how I was.'

While patient confidentiality prevented Maureen being told about the abortion, it didn't stop Melissa's traumatised friend — who had accompanied her to the hospital — from confiding in her older sister. It was this girl who decided Melissa's family had a right to know.

Two weeks ago, Melissa went through with the abortion. A couple of days later, she received another text message from the outreach worker saying: 'I hope it went well.' She didn't bother to reply.

Watching this unhappy girl next to her devastated mother, it is impossible to conclude that either of them will easily put the trauma behind them. Maureen, who also has a 16-year-old son, Craig, feels so betrayed she is already talking of taking Melissa away from her school and finding somewhere else for her to complete her education.

Last night, a spokesperson for The Brunts School said they could not comment on individual conversations which may or may not have taken place with Mrs Smith.

They reiterated that a letter had been sent to all parents in September about the school's Community Child Health Service, informing them that parental consent was not required for consultations, except in rare circumstances, and that they are not aware of any other parents not receiving it.

Meanwhile, Maureen is struggling to make sense of what has happened: 'My children are my world. How can an outreach worker in her early 20s think she knows my child better than I do?

'I don't believe in abortion, but if she had decided that is what she wanted, I would have accepted it and helped her through it. The point is, as her mother, I should have been given that right.

'Instead, it was taken away from me. What my daughter went through was horrible, and to think I might not have been there when she needed me most defies belief.'

One fewer in the statistics for unwanted teenage pregnancies, but at what human cost?

■ *ESTHER RANTZEN, Page 13*

'We didn't feel we were too young for sex. Why are we? Almost everyone of our age has sex these days'

Picture: BRUCE ADAMS

How could they let her do this?

Daily Mail May 13th 2004

Abortion adverts to keep parents in dark

Secret abortion: 14-year-old Melissa Smith with her mother Maureen

By **Laura Clark**
and **Suzanne Finney**

MINISTERS are to spend millions on a campaign telling teenage girls they do not need parental consent for an abortion.

The 'right to confidentiality' advertising blitz will go ahead despite the escalating furore over 14-year-old Melissa Smith.

Controversy has erupted around the teenager following the revelation that a school 'outreach worker' arranged for her to have an abortion without telling her mother.

Now the Government is planning to launch a series of adverts to reassure teenage girls their parents will not be told if they seek an abortion.

The adverts will be directed at 'all under-16s, including those under 13' even though it is illegal for them to have sex.

Girls will be told they have the right to confidential advice on contraception, pregnancy and abortion.

The message will be spread through teenage magazines, posters, radio stations and billboards.

The campaign follows recommendations from the Government-funded Independent Advisory Group on Teenage Pregnancy, which discovered that many sexually-active youngsters were unaware they could be given advice in confidence.

It reported last year that some children were unwilling to approach doctors or health clinics because they feared their parents would be told.

The Teenage Pregnancy Unit has been planning the campaign since January, but officials could not say yesterday when it would begin.

Critics accused the Government of stripping away parental authority. Professor Jack Scarisbrick, chairman of the anti-abortion organisation Life, said the case showed Government policy was clearly failing.

He added: 'Advertising campaigns will only undermine even further parental authority and the very precious relationships that should exist between parent and child.

'The Government on the one hand criticises parents for failing to take seriously their responsibilities but on the other undermines their authority.

'This campaign is simply a quick fix that in the long term will further erode parental responsibility and familial trust.'

Simon Heffer – Page 23

Norman Wells, of Family and Youth Concern, said: 'The provision of controversial contraceptive advice or abortion services to young people without their parents' support breaks down the relationship of trust within the family.

'When things go wrong, it's the family who have to live with the consequences.'

Melissa Smith's mother said the campaign sent out entirely the wrong message to teenagers. Maureen Smith said: 'I know from my daughter's harrowing experience that girls of 14 and 15 are not old enough to decide on their own to have an abortion.

'It's all very well the Government educating children about their rights but what about parents' rights?

'I was the one picking up the pieces when my daughter was crying her heart out after aborting a child without fully understanding the consequences.

'It's about time the Government stopped wasting taxpayers' money and offered parents more support in educating our own children about sex rather than stealing those rights away and putting them in the hands of professionals who don't even know our children, yet have the ability to change their future.

'Instead the message seems to be, "It's OK to get pregnant because you don't have to tell your parents, we will arrange a termination and that will be the end of it". The reality is that something like that stays with you for ever.'

The Department for Education said the Teenage Pregnancy Unit already spends some £4million a year on advertising and helplines which promote the confidentiality message.

A spokesman said new materials were being drawn up in consultation with parents and pupils but was unable to disclose when they would be released and how much they would cost.

He added: 'The Teenage Pregnancy Unit works with parents and young people to make them aware of confidentiality issues, including helping teenagers approach their parents if they find it difficult.

'This is an important element of our drive to help young people resist pressure to have sex in the first place.'

Information about confidentiality is already available in literature and on websites from a range of organisations.

Web pages for the Brook Advisory Service, for example, say: 'Doctors, nurses and other health workers have a duty NOT to give out information about you without your consent, except in exceptional circumstances.

'This applies whatever your age. If you are under 16, doctors and other workers still have to keep what is said private.'

l.clark@dailymail.co.uk

Melissa's case heading for Europe

THE case of Melissa Smith's secret abortion is to go before the European Court of Human Rights, it emerged last night.

The 14-year-old's mother is determined to take legal action to save other families from the same ordeal.

Lawyers for Maureen Smith, a 37-year-old care worker from Mansfield, Nottinghamshire, said they would seek legal aid to go to the Strasbourg court.

They will try to prove Mrs Smith had her rights as a parent violated when she was kept in the dark about her daughter's pregnancy as a school outreach worker helped arrange an abortion.

Mrs Smith said yesterday: 'I want the law to recognise the importance of parental involvement in such a life-changing decision.

'As it stands, any underage girl deemed responsible and able to make a decision can terminate a child and her parents can be none the wiser.'

Her solicitors will also aim to establish that the family's privacy was invaded by care staff who guided Melissa through the abortion process.

Mrs Smith's lawyers say they can go straight to the European court because the principle of confidentiality for under-16s has already been tested in Britain in a case brought by sex-education campaigner Victoria Gillick in 1983.

Abortion adverts keep parents in dark

Daily Mail May 15th 2004

Daily Mail, Thursday, July 28, 2005

Shocking rise in abortions for under-14s

By **Jenny Hope**
Medical Correspondent

THE number of abortions among girls under 14 rose 6 per cent last year, official figures show.

Meanwhile, the total number of abortions in England and Wales hit a record high in 2004 of more than 185,000.

The rate of terminations has risen relentlessly since the mid-1990s, despite the fact that the morning-after pill is freely available from chemists.

The abortion rate was highest in women under 24, and there were 157 abortions among girls under 14 last year, up from 148 in 2003.

Government guidance advises doctors that they can perform abortions on under-16s without parental consent.

This caused an outcry last April after 14-year-old Melissa Smith had a termination arranged by her school without her mother's knowledge.

In December, Sue Axon, a mother of five from Manchester, won the right to challenge the Government guidance in the High Court.

Department of Health figures show that there were 185,400 abortions to residents in England and Wales in 2004. This was an increase of 2 per cent on 2003.

'This is a very vulnerable group'

Sixty per cent took place before ten weeks of pregnancy. About 1,900 were carried out on the grounds that the child would be born disabled. A third of the women had previously had at least one abortion.

There have been demands to lower the 24-week time limit for abortions after revolutionary scanning techniques showed a 12-week-old foetus 'dancing' in the womb and apparently sucking its thumb.

Babies born at 24 weeks have a high chance of survival. However, earlier this month the British Medical Association decided to retain its support for the status quo.

Last night, a spokesman for the Royal College of Obstetricians and Gynaecologists said the overall increase in abortions was 'disappointing'.

She called for more facilities allowing early terminations and an investigation into the availability of contraceptive services.

The family planning advice charity Marie Stopes International said: 'The rise among young people continues to be a concern. This re-emphasises the need for more focus on better sex education.'

Theresa May, Tory family spokesman, said: 'It is deeply concerning that the number of girls at 13 and under having abortions continues to grow.

'What is clear is that the Government's teenage pregnancy strategy is failing to stem the tide of teenage pregnancy.

'We urgently need to address both with parents and through the classroom the underlying problems which see young girls becoming pregnant.

'We need to educate and instill young girls with the self-esteem to resist the pressures which are clearly placed on them at such young ages, and equip them with the confidence to say no.'

The British Pregnancy Advisory Service said it was time to recognise that abortion is seen by women as a solution – not a problem – and the trend was set to continue. Chief executive Ann Furedi said: 'Women today want to plan their families, and when contraception fails they are prepared to use abortion to get back in control of their lives.'

Pro-life campaigner Patrick Leahy, of Student LifeNet, said: 'We are astonished that the overall abortion figures have increased again to a staggering total.

'Alarmingly, the number of under-14 abortions have also increased by 6 per cent. This is a very vulnerable group and we are shocked that the abortion rate for this age category is increasing year-on-year.

'It is clear now that the UK effectively has abortion on demand. The Government must take immediate steps to reduce this horrific number of abortions by at least half through cutting the abortion time limit.'

Anthony Ozimic, of the Society for the Protection of the Unborn Child, said women were being rushed into making the decision to have an abortion.

'The Government's approach of promoting early abortion is increasing the overall number of abortions,' he said.

'In this situation, the suggestion of changing the law to reduce the much smaller number of late social abortions is a distraction.

'It is policy, not legislation, that the Government should change. It should stop its ruthless attempt to rush women as quickly as possible through the abortion mill, in its frenzy to cut waiting times.'

j.hope@dailymail.co.uk

Left to cope alone

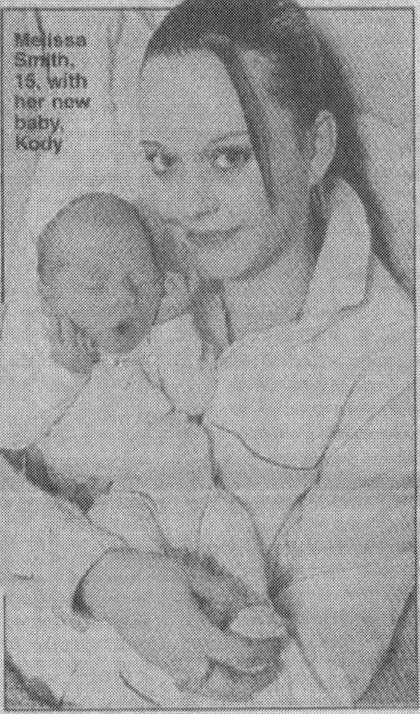

Melissa Smith, 15, with her new baby, Kody

MELISSA Smith was only 14 when she had a termination without her mother's knowledge.

The schoolgirl had sought the advice of 28-year-old outreach health worker Claire Chapman.

Asked if she wanted to tell her parents about the pregnancy, she replied, 'My mum would kill me', so Miss Chapman agreed that an abortion should go ahead in secret.

Melissa was left to visit doctors on her own.

She had taken the first of two 'chemical abortion' pills when her mother found out. She then changed her mind and decided to keep the baby, but it was too late.

Maureen Smith, 37, said: 'This is one of the worst things she will go through and I knew nothing about it. I wasn't there to help or protect her. I feel like my right as a parent has been taken away from me.'

Six months later, Melissa became pregnant again by the same boyfriend and gave birth last week. Her mother said she had been 'hell-bent' on replacing the baby she lost.

Shocking rise in abortions for under - 14s

Daily Mail, Thursday July 28 2005

Daily Mail, Saturday, May 8, 2004

Labour sex education can't curb abortions

By **Robin Yapp**
Science Reporter

LABOUR'S sex education programme has failed to reduce the number of women having terminations, it was revealed yesterday.

The number of such operations carried out in 2002 was more than 5,000 higher than when Tony Blair took power in 1997.

And the total of 175,904 abortions performed on residents in England and Wales was virtually unchanged from the previous two years.

One in five is now carried out on a teenager. In 2002, one in 50 girls aged 16 and 17 had a termination – the same proportion as women in their late 20s.

The statistics were disclosed by junior health minister Lord Warner in a written reply to a question in the Lords from Baroness Masham of Ilton.

They show that although the number of abortions fell for five successive years at the start of the 1990s to 154,315 in 1995, the annual total has since risen by more than 20,000.

'Women's desire to plan a family'

The rate was highest in 2002 – at 30 women in every 1,000 – among the 18 to 19 and 20 to 24 age groups. The figure for 16 and 17-year-olds was 20 per 1,000 – the same as for women aged 25 to 29.

There were 4.73million abortions on women in England and Wales between 1968 – when it was legalised – and 2002.

The cost to the NHS was put at £38million in 2002-2003 – £5.5million more than two years earlier despite more patients going private.

Professor Jack Scarisbrick, of Life, said: 'These abortion statistics show ever more clearly that Labour's policy has failed. It is making things worse with value-free sex education.

'The distribution of condoms to children, and making ever more explicit material available to them, can only encourage promiscuity.

'Abortion has caused the death of five million children in England and Wales – five times the number of dead we suffered in two world wars.

'We are being overwhelmed by women who have been traumatised by abortion, and sexual disease is rampant.'

Figures show that sexual infections amongst 16 to 19-year-olds are up 30 per cent since the launch of the Teenage Pregnancy Strategy in 1999, while pregnancies in the under-18s rose by 7.3 per cent between 2001 and 2002.

Paul Danon, for the Society for the Protection of Unborn Children, said: 'It seems these abortion figures desensitise us and we have become used to it. I fear it is being seen as another form of contraception.'

The British Pregnancy Advisory Service said: 'The current abortion rate demonstrates women's desire to plan their family and the ineffectiveness of the anti-choice campaign to convince people that abortion is evil.'

■ U.S. authorities yesterday rejected a drug company's request to sell a 'morning-after' contraceptive without a prescription.

The decision by the Food and Drug Administration went against the recommendation of scientific advisers, and was seen as another move in the backlash against a permissive society, led by Republicans nationwide.

r.yapp@dailymail.co.uk

Labour sex education can't curb abortions
Daily Mail May 8th 2004

Parents unaware of operations on children of 14

Under-age girls 'sterilised' to cut teen pregnancies

By **Adam Powell**

GIRLS as young as 14 are being 'sterilised' without their parents' knowledge as part of the Government's attempts to curb teenage pregnancy rates.

About 400 girls under 16 have been given contraceptive hormone implants which make them infertile for three years.

Britain has the highest rate of teen pregnancy in Europe and the Government has spent £63million on its strategy to tackle the problem, but has failed to stop the rise.

The revelation that it has adopted the tactic of contraceptive implants for such young girls outraged family values campaigners and sexual health experts.

They accused the Government of condoning sex at such an age rather than attempting to stop it, and increasing the risk of sexually-transmitted diseases, already rampant among the young.

There are also medical concerns about giving young girls large doses of synthetic hormone when they are undergoing their own hormonal changes.

Dr Trevor Stammers of the Family Education Trust said: 'I do not believe a doctor who does this to a girl under 16 without her parents' knowledge is acting in an ethically acceptable way.

'Doctors are giving carte blanche to men to have sex with under-age girls.' Doctors say the implants are the most effective method of preventing pregnancy and are especially popular among girls who do not want their parents to know they are having sex.

The fact that 400 girls have already received them came in a written parliamentary answer, along with the fact that a further 2,500 girls aged 15 or under have had injections which make them infertile for three months.

Shadow Children's Minister Tom Loughton, who obtained the figures, said the implants would encourage promiscuity.

'This will not help young people have a more responsible attitude to sex,' he said. 'It is no good guarding against teenage girls getting pregnant if you are in fact encouraging them, by the back door, to indulge in under-age sexual relations and open them up to diseases like chlamydia.'

Mr Loughton also suggested that the Government is endorsing such drastic measures to cut teenage pregnancies because it is falling behind its target of halving conception in under-18s by 2010.

In England, one in ten babies is born to a teenager. In 2002, there were 39,286 teen pregnancies recorded, of which nearly half ended in abortion. Meanwhile, teenagers suffering a sexual disease increased by a quarter between 1998 and 2001.

The current guidance from the Government and General Medical Council is that GPs must ensure only that the girl 'is capable to decide' on the treatment she is about to get.

They are, however, told that they should encourage teenagers to inform their parents.

A Government spokesman said: 'The decision on which kind of contraception to use is for the individual to make. We have to make sure that they have the information to make the choices for themselves.'

'A decision for the individual'

Comment – Page TEN

How the implant works

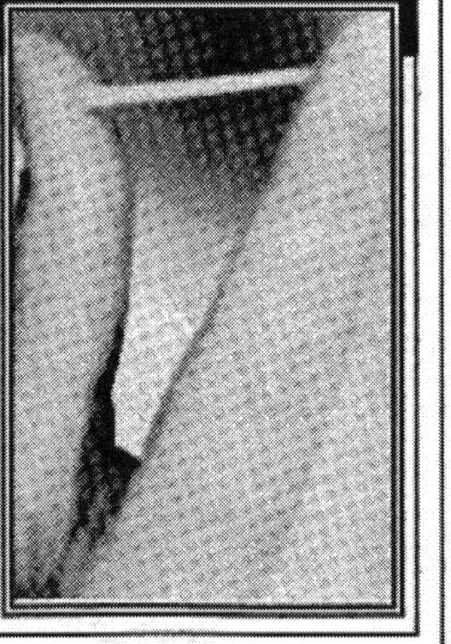

THE implant is a matchstick-sized plastic rod inserted just under the skin on the inside of the upper arm. It releases the synthetic hormone, progestogen, into the blood over three years.

Insertion takes just a couple of minutes under local anaesthetic. The rod, pictured right, is not usually visible but can be felt under the skin. Shortly after injection, tissue forms around it which keeps it in place.

It is particularly useful for females who cannot tolerate oestrogen, which is contained in most oral contraceptives, as well as those who have difficulty remembering to take a daily contraceptive pill.

Fertility is expected to return soon after the implant is removed and most women will ovulate within three months.

Supporters say its benefits are that it can be removed at any time, is very cost effective and is not affected by prescribed medication.

But it has disadvantages too. Some women may experience irregular bleeding patterns, weight gain, acne and headaches.

Under-age girls "sterilised" to cut teen pregnancies

Daily Mail May 3rd 2004

Pregnant teenagers live in different worlds: the rich have abortions, the poor have babies

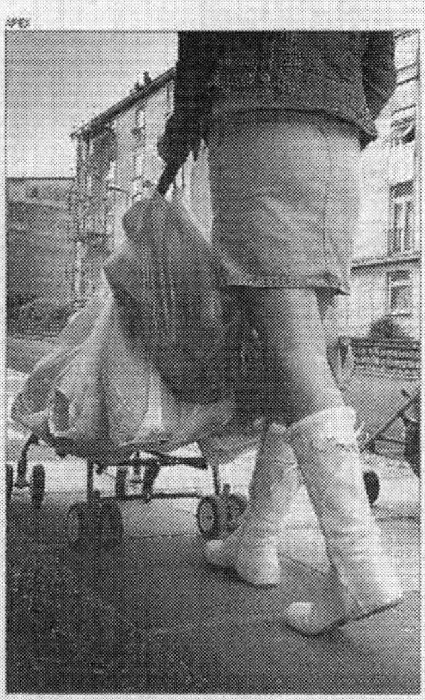

Baby love: Early motherhood is far more acceptable and "normal" in some deprived districts than in wealthier areas

PREGNANCIES RESULTING IN ABORTION

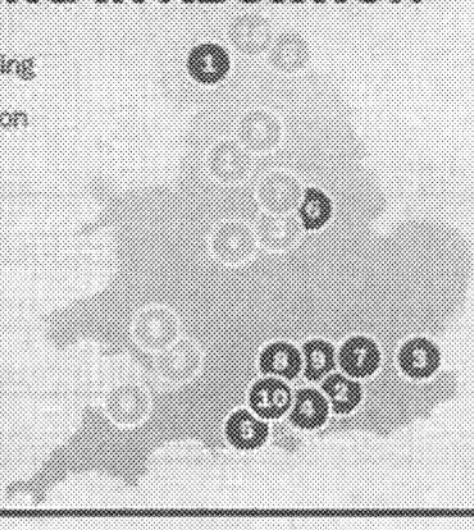

Highest proportions	Conception rate per 1,000 women aged 15-17	% leading to abortion
1 Eden	23.1	76
2 Epsom and Ewell	23.6	74
3 Rochford	29.5	72
4 Mole Valley	20.2	70
5 East Dorset	19.1	69
6 Rushcliffe	17.0	68
7 Kensington and Chelsea	36.2	67
8 Surrey Heath	20.8	66
9 Elmbridge	27.1	66
10 Hart	16.6	65

Lowest proportions	Conception rate per 1,000 women aged 15-17	% leading to abortion
1 Derwentside	41.8	18
2 Torridge	25.7	27
3 Merthyr Tydfil	65.8	28
4 Ashfield	53.6	30
5 Easington	61.5	30
6 Bradford	48.8	31
7 Stoke-on-Trent	64.1	31
8 Nottingham	69.9	31
9 Caerphilly	60.8	32
10 Rochdale	54.4	32

TEENAGERS in some affluent parts of the country are four times more likely to terminate a pregnancy than those in more deprived areas.

A study has revealed that almost half of pregnant girls aged between 15 and 17 opt for abortions, but there are huge variations in attitudes across the country.

Fewer than one in five conceptions in the Derwentshire district of Co Durham ended in the pregnancy being terminated, while 40 miles away in Eden, Cumbria, three in four resulted in an abortion.

Of the ten areas with the highest rate of abortions, eight were affluent parts of the South and Home Counties, while most teenagers who kept their babies came from the North and West.

The study, carried out for the Joseph Rowntree Foundation, also found that areas with a high abortion rate tended to have more extensive family planning provision and more women GPs.

Fewer abortions were carried out in the most socially disadvantaged areas despite the fact that they had the highest rates of conceptions among minors.

The authors said that teenagers' personal situations rather than their moral views on abortion informed their choice.

Those who saw their lives as insecure were more likely to accept motherhood as a positive change, while those who saw their lives developing through education or employment were more likely to abort.

> 'Fewer abortions took place in the areas that had the highest rates of conception among minors'

As well as Eden, the highest abortion rates were found in Epsom and Ewell in Surrey, Rochford in Essex and the Mole Valley in Surrey. All had more than 70 per cent of pregnancies ending in terminations.

After Derwentshire, the lowest percentages of abortions were seen in Torridge, Devon (27 per cent), Merthyr Tydfil, South Wales (28 per cent) and Ashfield, Nottinghamshire (30 per cent).

The researchers found that motherhood at an early age was more acceptable and "normal" in some neighbourhoods.

Interviews with 100 teenagers revealed that all those who chose an abortion had found it stigmatising, and many thought that they should keep their plans secret from parents. Some also said that they had been upset by doctors' attitudes.

Ellie Lee, co-author of the report, said: "When an unplanned pregnancy occurs, it is clear that most young women perceive the outcome as first and foremost their decision. Yet the evidence shows that their views are shaped by factors that include social deprivation, the attitudes of family and friends and the accepted norms of behaviour in the communities where they live."

Ms Lee said that the report indicated the need for more educational and career initiatives that helped to raise the expectations of young mothers.

"At the same time, we believe that young women who choose abortion should have their choice respected and have better access to services of a more consistent quality. Abortion needs to be de-stigmatised."

The findings follow a World Health Organisation report this month, which showed that more than 40 per cent of 15-year-olds in England and Wales said they had had sexual intercourse. Of 32 nations surveyed, only Greenland had a higher rate.

Anne Weyman, chief executive of the family planning charity fpa, said: "The difference in abortion rates across the social spectrum is not inevitable and it is essential young women receive advice and support from their family, friends and health professionals."

Patrick Cusworth, of the anti-abortion group Life, said: "We have long known that it is largely middle-class women who are going for abortions, despite the claims of those who promoted the Abortion Act in 1967 that it was primarily designed to help hard-pressed poor families.

"The truth is that the less affluent among us are more pro-life."

A TALE OF TWO TEENAGERS

Baby best thing to happen to me

For Jo, a 15-year-old living on a council estate on The Wirral, having a baby was an exciting new chapter in her life that helped to draw her away from drink and drugs.

She lives with her grandmother, but hopes to move in with her 17-year-old boyfriend. When she became pregnant, she was studying for her GCSEs and is now training to be a hairdresser.

"Before I was pregnant I was a bit mad. I was drinking, and stuff like that," she said. "I wasn't thinking about the future, do y'know what I mean? I was just being. I don't know how to explain it ... I'd been kicked out of one school already. I was quite naughty. We were just a pair of nutters.

"Now I'm just a better person all round, my boyfriend is a better person. It has been the best thing that's ever happened to me. If I hadn't had the baby I'm sure I would've been in jail."

A shock, but I wasn't worried

WHEN Emma fell pregnant at the age of 17 after a one-night stand, she was studying for her A levels and had a place at university to study law.

She was living with her parents, a nurse and a doctor, at the family home in Berkshire. She decided to have an abortion so as not to derail her future.

"Because we used a condom, I didn't really think anything more about the man. Then I missed my period and had a test.

"I just thought: 'Oh my God.' I wasn't worried about it because I knew it could be sorted out, but it was a real shock. I wasn't very happy about it at all."

She discussed the situation with her parents, but said the decision was easy. "It was my Mum who said to me: 'You've got to have an abortion.' I wouldn't have argued with her. I knew what the decision should be."

Pregnant teenagers live in different worlds: the rich have abortions, the poor have babies

The Times Wednesday June 30th 2004

Abortion kills

From Dominica Roberts

Sir: Contrary to Bruce Anderson's statement ('Abortion is a matter of aesthetics', 17 July), there is overwhelming and increasing evidence for the harmful effects, physical as well as mental, of abortion on women. A Californian study, comparing 173,000 Medicare records with death certificates, showed that women who had an abortion were nearly twice as likely to be dead within two years, many by suicide, as those who gave birth (*Southern Medical Journal*, August 2001). A Finnish study found similarly increased figures for suicides after abortion compared with birth or natural miscarriage (*British Medical Journal*, December 1996).

A study of every birth during one week in 1995 in the whole of France found an increased risk of prematurity for singletons (single, as opposed to multiple, births) of 30 per cent after one abortion and 90 per cent after two or more (*British Journal of Obstetrics and Gynaecology*, October 2001). A Bavarian study of 106,345 singleton births found an 80 per cent increase in prematurity after abortion (*European Journal of Obstetrics, Gynaecology and Reproductive Biology*, October 1998). Prematurity is, of course, a major cause of handicap.

There are many similar studies showing increased risks of infertility, ectopic pregnancy, need for psychiatric treatment, and so on. The link with breast cancer is at any rate likely enough to need serious research.

It is well known now that legalising abortion did not save women's lives. The maternity-related death rate was coming down all over the developed world well before 1967 because of better medical treatment — mainly antibiotics and blood transfusions — and continued to do so whether abortion was made easier or, in some countries, harder to obtain.

Roe *v.* Wade is being appealed in the US on the grounds of new evidence, not available then, that abortion harms women. Those who meant to help women by legalising abortion in 1967 in our own country should now overturn our law on the same grounds.

Dominica Roberts

Pro Life party, London SW3

From Mark Tinney

Sir: Bruce Anderson's article on abortion reminded me of something I have never understood — why is it that those who insist on a woman's right to kill a viable foetus because its arrival would be inconvenient are almost always the same people who are horrified by the idea of executing convicted murderers?

Mark Tinney

Laxfield, Suffolk

24 THE SPECTATOR 24 July 2004

Letters section The Spectator, 24th July 2004

www.telegraph.co.uk

Secret abortion for girls under 16

Doctors do not have to tell parents, say new guidelines

By Sarah Womack
Social Affairs Correspondent

DOCTORS can give abortions to children without telling their parents, the Government said yesterday as it issued new and explicit advice on treating unwanted pregnancies among under-16s.

The Department of Health document says that confidentiality must be maintained if the children insist on it.

Doctors should try to persuade them to tell their parents or another family member, but "doctors and health professionals have a duty of care and a duty of confidentiality regardless of patient age", the department says.

"This guidance applies to the provision of advice and treatment on contraception, sexual and reproductive health, including abortion."

The document infuriated pro-life campaigners who said it made a mockery of the concept of parental responsibility.

Ann Widdecombe, the Tory MP, said: "What worries me is the blanket description 'under-16s'. What about 10-year-olds? Surely the parents of 10-year-olds need to know if their children are sexually active, let alone having an abortion."

Paul Tully, of the Society for the Protection of Unborn Children, said: "In the vast majority of cases, the support that a teenage girl needs in these situations is the support of her parents."

The issue of confidentiality has been enshrined in decisions on contraception since 1986 when the Lords overturned Victoria Gillick's campaign to ban doctors from giving contraceptives to under-16s without parental consent.

But previous guidance on sexual health for under-16s did not mention abortion. The department said: "It did not mention abortion – just contraceptive services. This new advice, which does mention abortion, is much longer and clearer."

It has been issued as the number of under-age abortions is rising: from 3·7 to 3·9 per 1,000 girls last year, an increase of 5·4 per cent. It follows the controversy in May over a 14-year-old girl whose school arranged for her to have an abortion without her parents' knowledge.

Melissa Smith, from Mansfield, Notts, was asked by a community health worker at her school if she wanted to tell her parents but replied: "My mum would kill me." She was referred to hospital and took one of two "chemical abortion" pills.

Within days her mother, Maureen Smith, found out what was happening and the girl changed her mind. But it was too late. Michelle said that if she had her chance again, "I would probably have kept the child and let my mum know".

The new guidelines emphasise that, when a young girl wants an abortion but cannot be persuaded to involve a parent, every effort should be made to find another adult in the family to provide support or, failing that, a specialist youth worker.

Doctors should discuss the emotional as well as physical implications of sexual activity and pregnancy and the risks of sexually transmitted infections such as chlamydia, which can cause infertility.

Confidentiality should be overridden only when there is serious concern about the health, safety or welfare of the child.

Health professionals welcomed the document.

Dr Vivienne Nathanson, the head of science and ethics at the British Medical Association, said: "It is essential that competent young people's autonomy continues to be recognised and respected to ensure a good doctor-patient relationship based on trust, within which young people feel they are able to seek advice."

Anne Weyman, the chief executive of the Family Planning Association, said young people worried a great deal about the confidentiality of health services.

"In the absence of other support, this leaves them vulnerable to unplanned pregnancy or sexually transmitted infections. All health professionals have a duty of confidentiality to their patients."

Kathy French, a sexual health adviser at the Royal College of Nursing, said: "The biggest deterrents to under-16s seeking sexual health advice and using contraception have been addressed by the Department of Health.

"The RCN welcomes the guidance clarifying confidentiality and consent issues for young people when seeking advice and treatment related to contraception, sexual and reproductive health."

'Since the Telegraph changed owners do you think the chips taste any different?'

■ Report: Page 29

The Daily Telegraph 31-7-04
31
9 770307 123962
A B C D E F G ★

The Daily Telegraph, Saturday July 31st 2004

Secret abortions, junk ethics and the ruthless betrayal of our children

THE Melanie Phillips COLUMN

THE ASSAULT upon parents and corresponding attempts to nationalise childhood have just been ratcheted up another notch.

The Department of Health has issued new guidance telling doctors that they can provide abortions for children under the age of sexual consent without telling their parents.

When 14-year-old Melissa Smith was revealed last May to have had an abortion which was kept secret from her mother by a school community health worker, there was widespread outrage.

Melissa herself said she now wished her mother *had* been told, and that if she had been, she might have kept the baby.

Now, however, this secrecy is to be institutionalised. True, the law already states that a girl under 16 can have an abortion without her parents' consent.

At present, however, a GP could decide to involve her parents even if a girl insisted they were not to be told. But now, doctors are specifically being told not to do so.

This is nothing less than an open, systematic attempt to undermine the right of parents to exercise responsibility for their children's welfare. It simply cannot be in the best interests of a child for the state to tell doctors to go behind parents' backs.

The thinking behind it is that teenage motherhood must be avoided at all costs. Abortion is thus regarded as the prudent avoidance of disaster. But for a young girl, an abortion is also a disaster.

Guidance

An under-age mother is herself effectively still a child. Above all, a child needs the love, care and guidance of her parents. Instead, she is now to be fobbed off upon a doctor, impersonal school counsellor or poorly-trained social worker.

Such children are no longer regarded as children at all but as quasi-adults with the 'right' to make their own decisions.

Dismayingly, the medical profession goes along with such junk ethics. Thus Dr Vivienne Nathanson, head of ethics at the British Medical Association, said the new guidance clarified 'good practice' to protect 'competent young people's autonomy'.

But autonomy belongs to adults. That's because a decision such as whether to have an abortion requires an adult's understanding of all its implications. To say that children possess such understanding is to dismiss the very meaning both of childhood and of adult responsibility.

This is bad enough when a girl is 14. But what about sexually active ten-year-olds? Does Dr Nathanson really suggest that they, too, should enjoy the same rights to confidentiality as adults?

Even the law is muddying the distinction between childhood and adulthood, with the progressive erosion of the legal age of consent. For prosecutions of boys who have sex with under-age girls are rare. Generally, prosecutions only occur when an older man is involved — in which case the offence mysteriously mutates into 'sexual abuse'.

Teenage magazines — often read by much younger children — promote a menu of sexual activity which would not be out of place in a brothel.

Such magazines even hand out free condoms provided by birth control promoters who claim they are teaching children to think responsibly about contraception. But what they are actually teaching them to think about is having sex.

To see how far we have slid, look no further than the remarks made a couple of years ago by Professor David Hall, who was President of the Royal College of Paediatrics and Child Health.

Asked how doctors would deal with a problem in which a child of 12 was asking for contraception because she was sleeping with a 22- year-old man, Professor Hall replied that doctors would provide it because they would 'consider her very competent by the very act of having come to seek advice on contraception'.

This adultification of children has landed us with our current epidemic of dangerous and anti-social behaviour by young people.

Intoning the mantra of 'young people's autonomy', the adult world merely lays out the relevant information about sex, alcohol and illegal drugs and expects young teenagers to make 'informed' choices.

It is this degraded and irresponsible climate which has given us the highest teenage pregnancy rate in Europe, a galloping epidemic of sexually transmitted disease among young people, and one out of every five abortions administered to a teenager, with the rate of under-age abortions rising by more than five per cent last year.

What a disaster — and all the evidence is that it is being fuelled by the Government's strategy of funnelling more and more sex education and contraceptive and abortion advice to children.

The evidence is that where this programme is most vigorously promoted, the rates of sexual activity, pregnancy and disease are highest. Yet the response of officialdom is simply to redouble its efforts to provide even more of the same.

This is also undermining parents, depriving them of their crucial role in producing physically and emotionally healthy adults by setting boundaries for children and relaxing them as their offspring gradually develop the maturity to make their own way in the world unaided.

Instead, parents are seeing their rights taken away and given to their children.

The result is an erosion of parental responsibility. Yet this Government is forever lecturing parents on the need to take *more* responsibility for their children, with anti-social behaviour orders, parenting orders and the like pouring out of Whitehall.

But the truth is that this is not about parental responsibility at all. It is actually about telling parents what to do because officialdom knows best how to bring up children. So instead of parents providing guidance and support, that role is to be performed instead by agents of the state.

Destructive

And that means parents' own values are being substituted by the state's anti-family agenda. This sees sex as a recreational sport which has nothing to do with marriage and which carries no consequences that we should worry about except unwanted or teenage pregnancy.

At the same time, it sees nothing wrong with unmarried motherhood, which is just another valid lifestyle choice.

The only choice that is not valid is to promote marriage as superior for family life. So this agenda ruthlessly promotes the doctrine that all family lifestyles are morally equivalent.

Yet the truth is that children brought up by both their parents are far less likely to have sex under 16. The main protection against under-age sex and sexually transmitted disease is the married two-parent family.

The attack on the traditional family and the society which it underpins is a key part of the Sixties agenda. Only recently, Tony Blair blamed this agenda for producing the 'me' culture of personal irresponsibility.

Very true; and yet the remarkable fact is that it is Mr Blair's own Government which is enacting that Sixties agenda through attacking the family, liberalising soft drug use and promoting a sexual free-for-all in schools.

At the heart of that agenda lies the replacement of adult responsibility by a cult of permanent adolescence.

The Government's abortion guidance is but the latest instalment of a programme which infantilises adults and abandons children to a pretence of maturity, with consequences as tragic as they are destructive to our society.

m.phillips@dailymail.co.uk

Daily Mail, August 2nd 2004

The unmentionables

Judges are banned by the PC lobby from saying *evening, man and wife, girl,* or even *Mrs.* Oh, but they will allow the word *black*

By **Steve Doughty**
Social Affairs Correspondent

OUR courts surrendered to political correctness yesterday as judges were ordered to stop using everyday words and phrases such as 'immigrant', 'Asian', 'postman' and 'man and wife'.

Terms said to be tainted with racial prejudice include 'mixed race' and 'West Indian'.

'Asylum seeker' is also frowned upon as it is said to have become associated with people without a genuine claim to be refugees.

One of the few terms that has been passed by the language police is 'black'. Its associations are 'positive as a result of the political civil liberties movements in the 1960s and 1970s'.

In instructions that run to more than 300 pages, judges are told to take great care to avoid offending women.

Job descriptions such as 'postman', 'chairman' and 'fireman' must be replaced by 'non-sexist' equivalents. 'Man and wife' may not be used because it 'implies an evaluation of the sexes'.

Controversially, women are said to be 'disadvantaged in many areas of life'. Even the simple use of 'he' or 'she' should be avoided. 'They' is preferable because it is 'gender neutral language'.

The instructions are contained in an expanded version of the Equal Treatment Bench Book, published by the judges' training body, the Judicial Studies Board, to 'inform, assist and guide' judges and magistrates.

The board is headed by Lord Justice Keene, an Appeal Court judge and friend of Tony and Cherie Blair. He once worked in the same legal chambers as Mrs Blair and has invited the couple to use his 12th century chateau in the South of France.

'Should be exposed as charlatans'

The committee that produced the book includes another prominent Blairite, Judge Henry Hodge, husband of Children's Minister Margaret Hodge.

The purge of the English language was endorsed yesterday by the Lord Chief Justice Lord Woolf, who warned his more junior colleagues that 'if they don't appear to be acting fairly that is just not good enough'.

The Bench Book called on judges to stop the reporting of information about a court witness which would identify them as homosexual or lesbian.

'Employment can be lost, families devastated and relationships damaged by unnecessary and prurient court reporting,' it said. 'Courts and tribunals should be aware that these factors may place additional burdens on gay and lesbian witnesses and victims, and should consider what measures might be available to counteract them.'

The guidelines tell judges they should understand that transvestites may need to cross-dress in court. They are warned that it is particularly cruel to imprison such people because of the problems they are likely to face in jail.

The Bench Book claims that 'objective mainstream research' shows that children brought up by homosexuals do as well as those raised by heterosexuals. In reality, many academics say there is no worthwhile research on the subject, only claims made on slender evidence by the gay lobby.

The Bench Book also claims that one in ten of the population is gay – an estimate vastly higher than all recent evidence suggests.

Judges are given a hint that gay sex below the age of consent of 16 is acceptable. 'The vast majority of young gay men are aware of their sexual orientation before 16 and seek partners of about their own age,' it states, adding that there is 'no persuasive evidence that boys or girls can be seduced into homosexuality'.

Promiscuous gays should not be discounted as parents, judges are told. In gay relationships, it may be that 'the definition of fidelity is focused more on emotional and honest behaviour, than on sexual conduct'. The book adds: 'Judges should be careful not to judge gay relationships according to the principles of heterosexual married life.'

Critics called the guidelines offensive and skewed. Ruth Lea, of the Centre for Policy Studies think-tank, said: 'Some of this material is outrageously offensive to women, some of it is just wrong, and the people who produce this should be exposed as the charlatans they are.'

'Women are still not equal'

According to the guidelines, women are disadvantaged largely because many of them choose to give up work to bring up children. It is not innocuous, judges are told, to assume that women will have children and look after them – and such assumptions could affect compensation claims.

The committee chairman, Mrs Justice Laura Cox, said the statement on disadvantage to women was 'open to debate'.

But she added: 'I am one of only four women in the Queen's Bench Division among 70 judges, so women are still not equal in some sections of society.'

Criminologist Dr David Green, of the Civitas think-tank, said: 'If the courts pursue truth, they must sometimes give offence or be insensitive. Justice is more important than being sensitive to people's feelings.'

Comment - Page 12

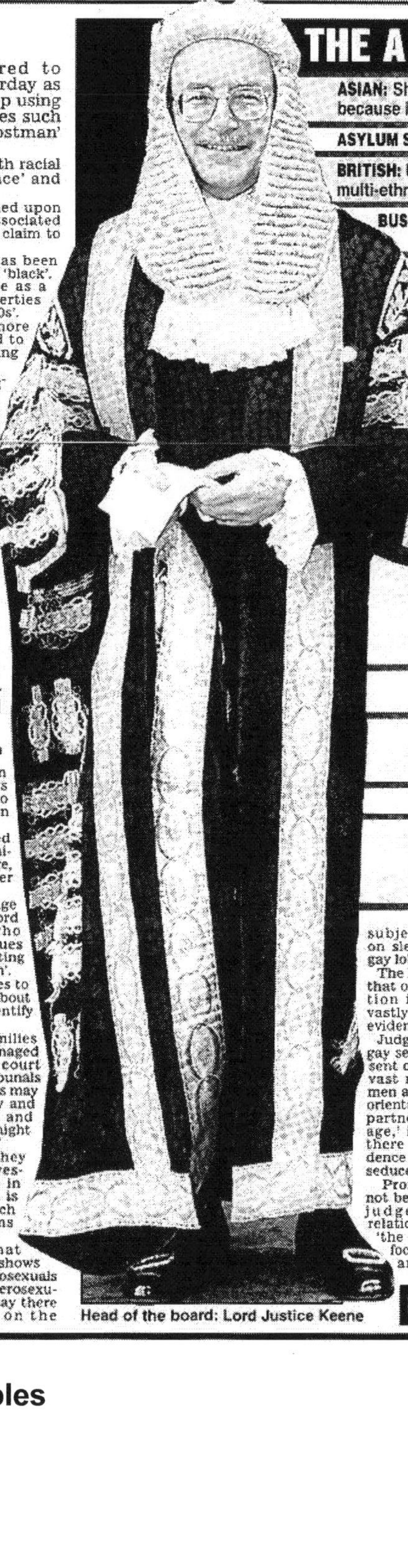

Head of the board: Lord Justice Keene

THE A TO Z OF POLITICAL CORRECTNESS

ASIAN: Should not be used by judges because it is a 'term of convenience'

ASYLUM SEEKER: *'Almost pejorative'*

BRITISH: Use only to 'include all in our multi-ethnic, multi-cultural society'

BUSINESSMAN: *'Implies an evaluation of the sexes'*

COLOURED: 'Offensive'

COMMON SENSE: *'Becomes problematical when there are parties from differing cultural backgrounds with their differing world views'*

EPILEPTIC: Use 'person with epilepsy'

ETHNICS: *Patronising, use 'minority ethnic' but not 'minority ethnics'*

EVENING: The notion of time can be relative. 'Evening can mean something completely different to a Scottish person and to a Spanish person'

GIRL: *See Businessman (but can be used for a child)*

HALF-CASTE: Offensive, use 'mixed parentage' but not 'mixed race'

HANDICAPPED: *'Insulting'*

HE, SHE, HIM, HER: Judges should use 'gender-neutral language' such as 'they' or 'them' instead

IMMIGRANTS: *'Highly inaccurate given the time the majority have been settled in the UK. The term is exclusionary and liable to offend'*

MAN AND WIFE: See Businessman

MENTAL HANDICAP: *Use 'learning disabilities or difficulties'*

MENTAL ILLNESS: Judges should say 'mental health problems' instead

MIXED RACE: *'Slightly pejorative to the extent that it focuses on the racial identity of the parents'*

MRS, MISS, MS: 'Given the history of marriage in the subordination of women it should come as no surprise that many women find it offensive to be referred to by reference to their marital status or their husband's name'

NORMAL: *To be avoided as a comparison with disabled people*

PEOPLE OF COLOUR: 'Popular in the USA, implies inferior status'

SLEEPING POLICEMEN: *'The 1989 Bar vocational evidence exam question with reference to sleeping policemen was failed by the vast majority of non ethnic-English students'*

SUFFER FROM AN ILLNESS: People must simply 'have' an illness

THE BLIND: *Use 'blind people' or 'people who are blind'. Similar rules apply to deaf people, who may also be 'deaf without speech'*

VISIBLE MINORITIES: 'Problematic' because it implies invisible minorities

WEST INDIAN: *'Colonial overtones'*

WHEELCHAIR BOUND: Use 'wheelchair user'

Melanie Phillips – Page 12; Superquango – Page 15

The unmentionables

Daily Mail May 13th 2004

WESTMINSTER NET PAGE CHARTS TREE OF ROMANTIC LINKS

Pupil passions and fantasy in gossip website at top school

Old girl: Dido studied at Westminster, top, but is not on the site

By Lech Mintowt-Czyz

WITH the advent of the Friends Reunited website, school gossip reached new heights.

For pupils unwilling to wait until they actually leave their alma mater, however, the latest internet trend is for sites which deal with current classroom tittle-tattle.

But one school's chat webspace has overstepped the mark.

Pupils from the £20,000-a-year Westminster School — including the sons and daughters of high-ranking politicians, lords and media figures — have found access to their site banned by teachers after it became a repository of sexual scandal and innuendo.

Highlights of the site include spider diagrams linking pupils known to have had close encounters with each other and a section where youngsters can rate their classmates' prowess.

The site, www.westminstertree.tk, has recorded some 17,000 visits and includes more than 600 photos of pupils in various states of apparent drunkenness and dress.

Users are invited to rate subjects out of 10 for attractiveness, and each year group has a breakdown of statistics, even down to the level of school houses, as well as charts with titles as delicate as, "Easy Ladies", "Super Studs", "Choosy" and "Desperados".

When the school — whose ex-pupils include Dido, Helena Bonham Carter, Sir Peter Ustinov and, appropriately enough, internet entrepreneur Martha Lane Fox — found out about the site it felt it had to act. Staff were horrified to discover that not only was the site full of pornographically detailed gossip, but pupils were also accessing it from the school library.

Access to the site from the boarding and day school's own computers was promptly blocked, but pupils have taken to accessing it from home.

Among those mentioned on the site are the son of a senior Tory MP and the daughter of a high-profile figure at a major public body.

Among the rated sexual encounters are edited comments such as "I could not resist ... huge ... all night long ... you have to try him" and "after a long period of frustration between the two they decided to hop on the good foot and do the bad thing".

The spider diagrams also name pupils said to have been in lesbian or gay relationships with each other.

Headteacher Tristram Jones-Parry said the school had investigated the possibility of closing the site. "I find it all rather silly and childish really," he said. "We believe we know the boy involved and I understand we have contacted him to ask him to tone the content down a bit.

"It is the sort of stuff you expect from a 13- or 14-year-old but this boy is 20 and is still concerning himself for some reason with his old school. It is rather sad, all in all.

"We have a filter that automatically blocks access to the site from school computers but that is all we can do."

One parent, whose son left the school in 2002 and has since seen details of two liaisons posted, said she was initially shocked, but added: "Schoolkids will be schoolkids."

Pupil passions and fantasy in gossip website at top school
Evening Standard 13th May 2004

WILL CHASTITY

Denise Pfeiffer: 'If you're close enough to have sex then you're close enough to get married'

Pictu[res:] DAVE CRUM[...]

Millions of young Americans have joined the growing abstinence movement. Now it's about to be launched in Britain by a group of concerned mothers. Is this the answer at last to our shameful record on teenage pregnancy?

by **Natalie Clarke**

ON THE face of it, they make an unlikely band of revolutionaries. But from their base in the Surrey stockbroker belt, a group of middle-class housewives have been carefully planning their strategy. This week, the uprising began.

They have watched with mounting horror as sexually transmitted infections spiral among teenagers, teenage pregnancy rates continue to cause alarm and young people succumb to the intense pressures placed upon them to have sex.

In the meantime, the authorities, schools and the Government look on blithely as the catastrophe unfolds before them, unable to do anything other than make contraception ever more available and sex 'education' even more graphic.

These women have decided enough is enough: it is time to act. And so Paula Jacobs and five friends announced this week that they are launching Britain's own version of the Silver Ring Thing — an American abstinence movement that encourages young people to make a 'pledge' of chastity until marriage.

Mrs Jacobs, a 42-year-old mother of three who lives in a village outside Guildford, hopes that thousands of British teenagers will follow the American example.

'Someone told me the definition of insane is doing the same thing over and over again and hoping that next time the result is going to change,' she says. 'Well, that's what's been happening here.

'We bombard teenagers with sexual imagery and throw contraception at them in the hope that sexually transmitted infections [STIs] and pregnancy will go down, but it hasn't happened.

'The Silver Ring Thing is not about teaching how to lessen the chances — it's about prevention.'

Mrs Jacobs, who has a daughter aged 18 and sons aged 16 and 14, adds: 'Teenagers today are under so much pressure to have sex. It's got to the point where they're emotionally removed from it.

'They go out, see a movie, then have sex — often on the first date. There's no waiting, no courtship, nothing to look forward to.

'They know it all after one date, yet they don't even know the person. They have no idea of the emotional value that comes from a close relationship, and that is a great tragedy.

'We just want teenagers to know they have a choice — to know they have the option.'

Mary MacAlister, 46, who lives with her husband Rodney, 49, a consultant, and children Martin, 16, and Lucy, 11, in Weybridge, Surrey, agrees. 'Society has handed our children such a problem,' she says. 'It's so confusing for them.

'My daughter has bought magazines and I have been horrified by the sexual content in them.

'I just want to get the message across to my children and to others that this is the world we live in, but it doesn't have to be *your* world.

'I'm very hopeful that when we do the Silver Ring Thing evening, the kids will be receptive to what we're saying. I suppose it's fair to say we're starting a kind of revolution.'

THE 'revolution' is taking the form of a nine-date tour of the UK and Ireland, starting in London on June 20, to spread the Silver Ring Thing message. There will first be a series of sketches and talks, before the audience are invited to make their 'pledge' to abstain from sex until marriage.

They will then buy a ring — at a cost of £10 — which they will wear as a symbol of their chastity.

As they place the ring on their finger, they also state, with great solemnity: 'I agree to wear a silver ring as a sign of my pledge to abstain from sexual behaviour. On my wedding day, I will present my ring to my spouse, signifying my faith and my commitment.'

The venue for the first event is a Baptist church in Bloomsbury, London. Mrs Jacobs and her friends hope up to 500 teenagers will attend the event. Their parents will also be welcome.

The show will then go north to Birmingham, Leeds and Glasgow, before heading across the Irish Sea to Belfast and Dublin and back over to Manchester.

The women became interested in the Silver Ring Thing after seeing a documentary about the organisation on television last year. They thought it was the answer to a desperate problem, so they contacted SRT's founder, Denny Pattyn, and asked for his help.

MRS JACOBS and the other women have spent the past few months working hard preparing for Mr Pattyn and his SRT to come over to Britain and bring their message to the inner cities.

This week 52-year-old Mr Pattyn, married with three daughters aged 15, 14 and 12, all of whom have taken the pledge and are actively involved in the Silver Ring Thing, flew to Britain to make preparations for the tour.

One of his greatest concerns is the epidemic of STIs in both Britain and the States as a result of promiscuity.

'The STI epidemic in America is a catastrophe,' he says. 'There are 65 million Americans living with an STI — the equivalent of the entire population of Britain.

'Medical experts tell me horrifying stories the whole time. That, for example, human papilloma virus (HPV or genital warts) is directly linked to 99.7 per cent of all cervical cancers.

'It is a crisis worldwide and Britain is no exception, having the highest teenage pregnancy rate in the Western world. The current strategy clearly isn't working.

'I personally believe it is morally right to abstain from sex until marriage, but even if you don't share that belief, you have to be worried about the dreadful impact of STIs.'

In Britain, the STI epidemic has reached critical levels. In the past seven years, for example, diagnoses of gonorrhea, as well as chlamydia, have more than doubled.

One in seven girls under the legal age of consent becomes infected with an STI.

Mr Pattyn, whose elder daughters Logan, 15, and Jessica, 14, will be taking part in the shows in Britain with him, points out that although the movement has its roots in Christianity, it wants to reach out to people of all faiths and those who hold no religious beliefs. 'We don't want to be perceived as evangelical and that the event is going to be a lecture.

'Silver Ring Thing evenings are cool and fun and full of life. We're in Britain to do the show and see what happens. If a groundswell begins, we will start a group here and give it more of a UK feel.' Mr Pattyn acknowledges that it is one thing to make a pledge at a social evening and quite another to keep it for years until marriage. To try to encourage fidelity to the pledge, they offer a 'follow-up' programme.

'One way of supporting the kids is, for example, to e-mail every kid who makes the pledge twice a week for two months to see how they're doing,' he says.

Mr Pattyn will be bringing over from America $50,000 worth of rings. 'The ring is important. It's a

CATCH ON HERE?

Pledged to purity: Roseanne Walters gave her daughter Kristina a silver ring for her 13th birthday

visible sign of the pledge and a constant reminder.'

Teenagers taking up the programme are supported by an 'accountability partner' — a friend with whom they can share their thoughts and worries.

And the programme emphasises that everybody deserves a 'second chance'. Those who have been sexually active are invited to attend and begin a 'Second Virginity' phase.

Mr Pattyn launched the Silver Ring Thing in Arizona nine years ago, after discovering that the area he lived in had the highest teenage pregnancy rate in his state. He then moved the programme on to Pittsburgh and then nationwide.

AROUND 100 events have been held across the country and nearly 22,000 American teenagers have bought a ring and made the pledge. On average, 75 per cent of attendees pledge at the end of the evening to refrain from sex before marriage.

Mr Pattyn says his organisation is collecting data as to how many teenagers keep their pledge and does not yet know how successful it has been.

But he can take heart from the fact that there has been a 20 per cent reduction in teenage pregnancies in the States over the past ten years, coinciding with the introduction of abstinence education.

Mrs Jacobs, whose husband of 18 years, Scott, 41, works in telecommunications, hopes for a similar result here. 'Even if a teenager abstains for two years longer than they otherwise would have, then it's worth it.

'I have had a heavy heart about all this for a long time and wanted to do something. My kids can't believe it, but they're very supportive.

'My daughter Allyson has had a lot of controversial conversations at school during the lunch hour — she is a firm believer in abstinence.

'But it's up to people to choose. We're not going to force people or tell them this is the way it has to be. It has to come from a willing heart.'

Mrs Jacobs and the other women are friends through their involvement in an inter-denominational church in Walton-on-Thames.

Another member of the group, Roseanne Walters, from Oxted, Surrey, has decided to put all her spare time into the Silver Ring Thing as a result of bitter experience. The 53-year-old mother of six, whose husband Michael, 59, is a partner in an accountancy firm, suffered the trauma of seeing two of her children's friends undergo abortions.

'One of the girls was just 15 when she fell pregnant, and a decision was taken to abort the baby.

'Another of my sons' friends wasn't long out of school and felt she could not support the baby.

'Neither relationship ended in marriage. It was a profoundly upsetting experience which illustrated all too well the downside of sexual liberalism.

'I was determined that my children would not go through that pain.

'I talked at length to them about abstinence, according to my own principles, and when my youngest child, Kristina, was 13, I gave her a ring to wear as a sign of chastity. I didn't know anything about the Ring Thing at the time — it just seemed appropriate.

'She believes totally in it, but she knows how difficult it is going to be, in the world we live in, to keep her pledge. But she has a goal and she is determined to reach that goal.'

Kristina, now 16, says there is great pressure among young people to become sexually active. 'You don't think TV and advertising makes a difference, but it accumulates and then you realise that it does.'

She supports the Silver Ring Thing but is not sure about making a public pledge. 'It's intimidating when you're in front of all those people. Maybe people shouldn't make the decision there and then.'

Alison Hunt, 46, from Cobham, Surrey, who is married to a general manager, is another member of the group. She is planning to take her 14-year-old son, Robert, to the first Silver Ring Thing show next month.

'I don't think we know the half of the pressures teenagers are under,' she says. 'I want to protect my son and others like him. The current thinking is that it's OK to have sex at any age.

'Teenagers get locked into this mentality, but the truth is that if they contract an STI, the consequences could live with them for the rest of their lives. I want my son to know he's got other options.'

The group, which is holding a fundraising dinner this weekend and is planning to start raising money in earnest over the next few months, has already acquired another avid supporter and helper in the form of Denise Pfeiffer, a 25-year-old part-time model and journalist from Leicester.

'The country has been crying out for this sort of thing for so long and I was thrilled that the Silver Ring Thing is coming to Britain,' she says.

'I made a personal decision to abstain from sex before marriage ten years ago when I was 15, and I follow the abstinence philosophy to the dot. I intend to wait until my wedding day before I have sex.

'There is nothing wrong in dating — it can be great fun. It's whether you've got the willpower to resist getting into a sexual relationship. My view is quite simple — if you're close enough to have sex, then you're close enough to get married.

RECENTLY I was discussing the subject with someone and they asked whether those who preach abstinence are saying that sex is a dirty thing. Not at all. The point of abstinence is to emphasise that it is a wonderful thing — in the right circumstances.'

So will the Silver Ring Thing enjoy the phenomenal success over here that it has done in the States, or has sexual permissiveness become too ingrained in teenage culture?

Is it simply too late? There are signs, in fact, that many young people are ready to embrace a change in attitudes.

It is the intention of the well-heeled revolutionaries from Surrey to help them along the way.

■ *www.silverringthing.com*

CASE STUDIES

JESSICA HOWIE (right), 25, is an online agony aunt working with teenage girls and the author of Sisters Unlimited: The Guide To Love, Life, Bodies And Being Yourself. She lives with her boyfriend in London.

I LOST my virginity at 14, which, looking back, was too early. I stayed in that relationship for six months, and after that I had sex with a few different guys. I wonder now what my motivations were for having sex that young.

Certainly, curiosity was a major part of the whole thing and wanting to grow up quickly. I was part of a group of girls who were into clubbing and make-up and we all wanted to have sex, though we didn't put pressure on each other. Later we all agreed that some of our experiences, while not terribly damaging, weren't great for our self-esteem either.

get attention from boys. If I got sex, that would bring me alive in some way. It was all about wanting to be appreciated rather than actually enjoying sex. The sex itself wasn't awful or traumatic, but it wasn't enjoyable or like I now know it can be.

I don't think there is an ideal age to lose your virginity — it is more about who you choose to have sex with. If I had been with a guy I trusted and respected, there would have been a sense of safety. That is more important than the age you are.

Now, if a 14-year-old girl tells me she has had sex, I am shocked, even though I did it myself. I won't say, 'Don't do it', but I will ask her to look at her motivation and self-esteem. You think you are mature and can handle it at that age but you are emotionally and sexually still so fragile.

I want to be open with my daughter about sex. It is important as a parent to show that sex can be fantastic and not shameful. If we are scared of encouraging our children, it just compounds the problem and they will go and do it in unsafe places.

If you go into a sexual relationship having had a positive attitude about sex instilled in you, you are much more likely to have a good feeling about it.

> **'I lost my virginity at 14, which was too early'**

SINEAD, 17, attends a sixth-form college in Leeds. She lives with her mother and two brothers.

MY MUM always said: 'Don't do it with just anyone, do it with someone you care about.' It is interesting that she never said: 'Do it with someone you love.' But that is because she did not love the man she lost it with at 16. She had loads of boyfriends after that.

I was 14 when I first had sex. It was a one-night stand; I was p***ed, in someone else's house. Afterwards I felt very ashamed of myself.

I wish I had not done it like that. I was young, but I felt old. Girls are more sensitive than boys and more likely to think of sex as a way to give and get affection. I liked the guy and wanted to get close to him. He was older than me and I felt flattered.

One of my friends had already done it and she wanted me to do it, too. It was as if she wanted me to be part of her club. I felt it was almost as if it was something to be got over. We were the first of our group, but not the first in the class. Someone later told me that girls give sex to get love and boys give love to get sex and I think that is true; at least, that is how it was with this boy. I didn't expect him to stay with me for ever or anything like that, but I hated it when he started avoiding me at school.

We had kind of been going out for a few weeks, but then, after I had sex with him, he dropped me. When I asked him why he had dropped me, he said there was no spark.

I felt used and stupid and I didn't want anyone to know. I told my best friends what had happened but when other girls asked me if I had done it, I just said: 'Maybe.' I didn't want anyone to know. I wasn't proud.

By the time I was 15, nearly all my friends had lost their virginity.

Sex is such an intimate thing. I've never heard of anyone who enjoyed it the first time. Now I have a great boyfriend. He has helped a lot because he's kind. Sometimes I think it's a shame I didn't wait for him.

I don't know what I would tell my daughter. I would definitely tell her to be careful, and not to do it just for the sake of it, but my mum going on to me about waiting didn't help. I think in the end you do what you want to do.

Will chastity catch on here?

Daily Mail May 13th 2004

More abortions

The number of abortions in England and Wales increased by 3.2 per cent last year. Department of Health statistics showed that there were 181,600 terminations carried out in 2003, up from 175,900 the previous year. The majority (87 per cent) were carried out before the foetus was 13 weeks old.

The Times Thursday July 22nd 2004

Page 6 * * * Daily Mail, Monday, March 28, 2005

Abortion laws creating our own holocaust, says cardinal

By **Steve Doughty**
Social Affairs Correspondent

ABORTION, euthanasia and baby sex selection have put Britain on the road to its own holocaust, the head of the Roman Catholic Church in England declared yesterday.

Cardinal Cormac Murphy-O'Connor raised the comparison with Nazi Germany in a strong Easter message intended to push the morality of life and death to the heart of the election campaign.

The Cardinal, who has already alarmed Tony Blair with calls for traditionally Labour-supporting Catholics to bear abortion in mind at the election, condemned laws that allow 'the strong to decide the fate of the weak'.

He added: 'That way lies eugenics, and we know from German history where that leads.

'We are already on that road, for what else is the termination of six million lives in the womb since the Abortion Act was introduced, and embryo selection on the basis of gender and genes?'

The Cardinal's warning, in a newspaper article, came a few days after a committee of MPs called for a relaxation of fertility laws so that couples having IVF treatment might choose their baby's sex or screen embryos to produce tissue-matched 'saviour siblings' to help seriously-ill children.

Cardinal Murphy-O'Connor said: 'There are now 180,000 abortions a year – the highest number ever – because these are 180,000 human lives considered not worth saving.

'Research embryos, surplus to in vitro treatment, are created, then discarded because they do not have the right tissue type; or because – as a parliamentary committee recommended this week – they are the wrong sex; or because they do not have the right genetic code to provide organs for one another; or because they are in some way disabled or imperfect.'

He asked: 'Have the millions of abortions carried out since 1967 corroded our consciences, as well as our institutions?'

The reference to Nazi Germany and to six million – the number of people, the vast majority of them Jews, killed in Nazi death camps – provoked unease among some Jewish leaders.

Holocaust references have been bandied around lightly in political campaigning in recent weeks.

'Undesirable but not murder'

London Mayor Ken Livingstone referred to the Holocaust in connection with the comparatively trivial question of the behaviour of the British media; Labour MP Kevin McNamara said Michael Howard's policy on Gypsies carried 'a whiff of the gas chambers'.

Rabbi Jonathan Romain, a spokesman for the liberal Jewish Reform Synagogues, said: 'It is somewhat disingenuous for the Cardinal to use the image of the six million without also acknowledging that the Jewish faith to which they adhered does permit abortion under various circumstances.'

He added: 'Judaism regards abortion as undesirable, but not murder. It is therefore possible to be both religious and pro-choice.

'Although abortion should not be undertaken lightly, it is an option for women who wish to terminate a pregnancy for a variety of valid reasons.

'These include severe deformity of the foetus, the physical or emotional health of the mother and instances of rape.'

Chief Rabbi Dr Jonathan Sacks, leader of Orthodox Jews, who usually take a more conservative position, made clear two weeks ago that he believes abortion is too often used as birth control and the law should be reformed.

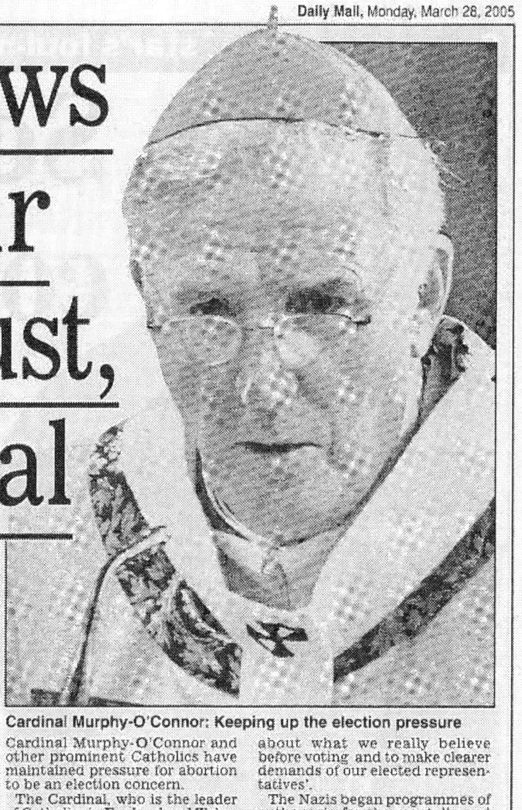

Cardinal Murphy-O'Connor: Keeping up the election pressure

Cardinal Murphy-O'Connor and other prominent Catholics have maintained pressure for abortion to be an election concern.

The Cardinal, who is the leader of Catholics in England and Wales, said it 'was among issues that are of concern to me that are also political issues because it has been politics that has to make judgments on it'.

The Most Reverent Vincent Nichols, Catholic Archbishop of Birmingham, said in his Easter message that 'we would all do well to think more deeply about what we really believe before voting and to make clearer demands of our elected representatives'.

The Nazis began programmes of euthanasia for the mentally and physically disabled in the 1930s, following Adolf Hitler's doctrine that such people were 'useless mouths'.

Many who survived until the war were wiped out in the Holocaust alongside Jews, Gypsies, homosexuals and other groups considered unfit to live.

s.doughty@dailymail.co.uk

Daily Mail, Monday, March 28, 2005

Abortions soar as careers come first

Rising rate among under-14s disappoints health officials, writes Alexandra Frean

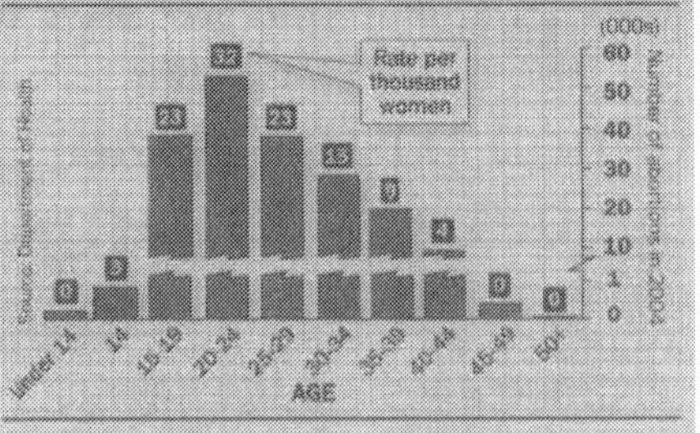

THE abortion rate hit a record high last year, according to government figures published yesterday that also show a sharp rise in terminations to girls aged under 14.

In 2004 the abortion rate rose by 2.1 per cent to 17.8 per 1,000 women aged 15 to 44, the highest recorded, according to the Department of Health. This resulted in 185,415 women resident in England and Wales having an abortion, compared with 181,600 in 2003.

The overall abortion rate among girls aged under 16 fell from 3.9 to 3.7 per 1,000, but the number of girls aged under 14 who had an abortion rose by 6 per cent last year to 157.

The findings provoked mixed reactions yesterday from people working in the family planning field. Some predicted that the rate would continue to rise as women increasingly regarded having a termination as a lifestyle choice.

Ann Furedi, chief executive of the British Pregnancy Advisory Service, Britain's leading abortion provider, noted that the rate was highest for those aged 18 to 24, at 31.9 terminations per 1,000 women.

This is part of a growing trend for women in this age bracket opting to end unwanted pregnancies, she said. Most women are at least 29 before they have a child and the increase in abortion rates of women aged 20 to 24 reflects that.

"Women today want to plan their families and, when contraception fails, they are prepared to use abortion to get back in control of their lives," Ms Furedi said.

"Motherhood is just one among many options open to women and it is not surprising that younger women want to prioritise other things. We should stop seeing abortion as a problem and start seeing it as a legitimate and sensible solution to the problem of unwanted pregnancy." She added that nowadays women who do want children want fewer of them later in life. Marriage was decreasing in popularity and unmarried couples were more likely than married couples to end an unplanned pregnancy, even if they were living together.

Ms Furedi said that women, particularly those in the professional classes, were increasingly reluctant to take breaks that could hinder their careers.

A spokeswoman for the Department of Health said that it was disappointed with the overall rise in abortions. She said: "We are working hard to reduce the demand for abortions by improving access to contraception and have committed an extra £40 million to improve access to contraceptive services." She said that the department would soon start a public information campaign to educate young people on the importance of safer sex as part of the Government's strategy to decrease teenage pregnancies.

> 'Motherhood is just one among many options open to women'

Anne Weyman, chief executive of the Family Planning Association, agreed that the figures highlighted the urgent need to improve NHS contraceptive services.

She also noted that the figures showed encouraging improvements to abortion services, which meant that more abortions (82 per cent in 2004, compared with 80 per cent in 2003) were being funded by the NHS.

This also enabled more women to have early abortions. In 2004, some 56 per cent of NHS abortions were carried out before ten weeks of gestation, up from 52 per cent in 2003.

Commentators were divided, however, about the significance of changes to the under-16 abortion rate, noting that as the numbers involved are so low, small increases or decreases in cases can produce big percentage swings.

The rate of abortions carried out because of the risk that a child would be born with a disability remained at 1 per cent. The figure was 1,900 in 2004, compared with 1,950 in 2003.

The figures also show that 42 women had terminations at 28 weeks or more gestation last year, compared with 49 women the year before. There were 18 cases that involved pregnancies of 32 weeks or more, compared with 22 in 2003.

The Times, Thursday 28th July 2005

This much I know

Sir Peter Ustinov, actor, 81, on the lessons he's learnt in life

Interview
Geraldine Bedell
Photograph
Yves Leresche

Being an exile is a huge advantage, if you handle it properly.

I have few regrets. But once, when I was making a film in Israel, I was collecting my breakfast from a buffet when I saw Ariel Sharon coming in the other direction with his tray. I stood back elegantly to let him past, and he went on like an express train. I have always regretted I didn't stick my foot out and send him and his breakfast sprawling.

Immediately I'm interested in something, I feel 10 years younger.

I only found out after my father died how consistently he had been unfaithful. He even stole a girlfriend of mine.

Children are close to the mystery of birth and old people are close to the mystery of death. Those in between are involved with the moment, so that their horizons are much nearer.

Comedy is tragedy that has gone wrong. It's one way of being serious.

When the little boys at my prep school in London wished to be unpleasant, they accused me of losing the First World War because my father was German. When they realised they'd gone too far, they claimed the German trenches had been much more sanitary than the French. But my mother was French, so it didn't really help.

An optimist is someone who realises how grim things are and resolves to try anyway; a pessimist is someone who finds it out anew every morning.

My half-Ethiopian grandmother would tell me the story of the crucifixion when I was a child on her knee. She would describe it as if she had been there, crying so copiously that the top of my pyjamas became wet with her tears and very cold. I've been suspicious of the Bible ever since.

Politicians are like milk that has been forced to float above cream.

I suspect if I'd married my third wife first I only would have been married once. But you can't tell.

Children are born completely without prejudice. So it shows that the basic material is very good.

Technology is developing so fast that the human mind is not ready to take it in. And just as in the 15th century, when explorers were discovering new lands, we are in desperate need of cartographers to make sense of it.

Russia is a country in which 60-year-olds are queueing to play Hamlet, but can't because some 80-year-old is still doing it. So if you're Russian you just carry on working.

Human beings can walk on the moon, but can't make successful airport baggage trolleys.

I tried to keep my second marriage going for so long because of the children. When it broke up, the children said to me, 'Why did you wait so long?'

Why was I always so aggressive about Mrs Thatcher? It's simple: I am a feminist and she isn't.

Education ends with death. Or after, according to your beliefs.

My father wanted me to be a lawyer. I told him I would be an actor, because it's really the same profession but less dangerous to our fellow men.

The only form of patriotism I can really stand is a feeling for the sap in your veins. I can't bear patriotism at anyone else's expense.

Tennis umpires have a code of conduct that makes no concessions to anything other than the stiff upper lip. Why shouldn't a man break his racket if he wants? It's his racket.

How do actors learn their lines? I've played King Lear twice, at four-and-a-half hours a time, and I still don't know.

At school we were asked to name a Russian composer on a general-knowledge paper. The answer was Tchaikovsky, because we had been studying him. I put Nikolai Rimsky-Korsakov and I was upbraided in front of the whole school for showing off.

The English believe the Germans don't have a sense of humour. But they do; it's just more intellectual.

There was a picture up in my first school of Jesus Christ pointing out the extent of the British Empire. No one would dream of putting up such a picture today, so it shows there is progress.

What would I like on my tombstone? Keep off the grass. **OM**

Lookat
Animal Farm with Sir Peter Ustinov will be shown on Channel 4 at 6.30pm tomorrow

'I only found out after my father died how consistently he had been unfaithful. He even stole a girlfriend of mine'

5 May 2002

Our Beloved Sir Peter Ustinov - on the lessons he's learnt in life.

Pierre Jourde, right, who told a court in Aurillac that he was attacked by local people after they discovered that his latest book was based on the lives of his neighbours in the hamlet of Lussaud

Neighbours beat up writer for novel that was just too close to home

Adam Sage
Paris

Five peasant farmers beat up a distinguished author for revealing in his novel the darkest secrets of their hamlet, including adultery, suicide, inbreeding and alcoholism, a court was told yesterday.

Pierre Jourde claimed that he was attacked by his neighbours in the Auvergne, central France, after setting his novel, *Pays Perdu* (Lost Land), in the local community. He changed names, but people in Lussaud recognised themselves as the drunken, lonely and uncouth characters he depicted, Aurillac Criminal Court was told.

Members of three of the five families who live in the hamlet were charged with assaulting Mr Jourde and racially insulting two of his children, whose mother is an Arab. The villagers lay in wait as the writer returned to the farm that has belonged to his family for three centuries. They hit him, threw stones, injuring his 15-month-old baby, and shouted "filthy Arabs" at his two sons on July 31, 2005, the court was told.

Mr Jourde said that he hit back at Paul Anglade, who is 72. "I hurt him," said the Professor of Literature at Grenoble University in eastern France and the author of six novels. "I punched him."

Pays Perdu — a grim comedy about peasant farming tradition — was published in 2003 to critical acclaim in Paris and indifference in Lussaud. But a nearby grocery put a few copies on its counter. Residents read the book and were outraged.

The work focuses on the funeral of a local girl but weaves in other stories — all known to Lussaud's 25 inhabitants but never mentioned to a wider public. Mr Jourde wrote, for instance, about the 1960s affair between two neighbours who have since returned to their spouses and whose children are married to each other.

He also denounced widespread alcoholism. "Rare are the houses where alcohol does not have its victims, its slaves," he wrote.

The novel tells of the Sunday church service, where "hymns are interpreted without pleasure by people without importance, gently moving their lips".

Jean-Marc Morel, the Mayor of Laurie, the district that includes Lussaud, said: "We knew this but we didn't speak about it. He brought out evil things and I don't know anyone who said he was right to do so."

'They lay in wait and threw stones, injuring his baby'

Mr Anglade said that the work insulted "our ancestors and here, you don't touch the ancestors". He accused the writer of betraying confidences. But Mr Jourde said that *Pays Perdu* was meant to convey a "globally positive" view of what he believes will be the last generation of French peasant farmers.

Virginie Dufayet, the state prosecutor, who is demanding the five are given six-month suspended sentences, said: "There was a smell of vengeance in this village."

Maître Gilles-Jean Portejoie, for the defence, told Mr Jourde: "You wrote about their lives and their vices. You didn't try to understand their motivations. You manipulated them, you played with them."

In 2002 Mr Jourde's scathing book *Literature Without Guts* won an award from the Académie Française, but infuriated French literary circles.

THE TIMES 45P

NEWSPAPER OF THE YEAR

No. 67596 THURSDAY OCTOBER 31 2002 5L www.timesonline.co.uk

'Half gay' Fleet fuelled admirals' fear of blackmail and treachery

By Steve Bird

A SECRET crackdown on homosexuality in the Fleet was ordered in the late Sixties after officials discovered that half of all sailors had indulged in gay acts and that no ship was immune from the risk of blackmail.

The problem was highlighted in 1969 when scores of sexually explicit photographs of British sailors were found in a flat in Bermuda. More than 400 sailors had been involved in "gross indecency" there, and the names of the men and their ships were written on the pictures.

At the same time, more and more drunken sailors were being lured into having sex with catamites, men masquerading as beautiful women, in Singapore.

The security concerns — which will revive old "hello sailor" jokes and Sir Winston Churchill's assertion that naval life was "rum, sodomy and the lash" — are disclosed in documents released by the Public Record Office yesterday under the 30-year rule. They say that homosexuals were at risk of being blackmailed because of "disgusting, infamous or immoral acts" that they would want to "keep hidden".

Admiral Sir John Bush, the Commander-in-Chief of the Western Fleet, responded by writing to all commanding officers, ordering them to "stamp out this vice". "There is, regrettably, ample evidence that homosexual practices are rife in the Fleet," he wrote in November 1969. "It can be assumed that the cases that come to official notice are but a small proportion of those who indulge in these practices." He adds that while he believes that many of the men were not "perverts", their behaviour was "thoroughly lax".

The scale of the problem had been outlined a year earlier in Captain Donald MacIntyre's *Report on Homosexuality in the Royal Navy*. That claimed that there was a risk of discharging on security grounds a "considerable" number of men who were otherwise loyal. There were even concerns that it could severely affect the manning of the Fleet.

He claimed that while 95 per cent of men remained heterosexual after adolescent gay encounters, a ship's enclosed male environment aggravated the "homosexual tendency". Recruits should be given fatherly advice and officers should be trained in blackmail risks and how to "detect and prevent" homosexuality.

"On one security side there are many difficulties," Captain MacIntyre said. "Senior naval officers have told me that they reckon that at least 50 per cent of the Fleet have sinned homosexually at some time in their naval service life."

A year later the Director of Naval Security advised leadership school lecturers to address the security issues of homosexuality, saying it was possible that gay servicemen would be more likely to "turn traitor" than to give in to blackmail. The Navy should therefore take no risks.

In the worst incident, a "large number" of naval ratings went to a male brothel in Bermuda where they were lavishly entertained and given presents for sexual favours. While there was no proof that the Bermuda flat was being run by a foreign intelligence organisation, it was feared that if such pictures were obtained by a foreign power, "we could be in trouble". The case led to three sailors and two Bermudians being jailed for indecency and to at least 40 sailors being discharged.

In Singapore, sailors visited male prostitutes who posed as women. A report outlining the lure of catamites said sailors went to the sex district as tourists but often got

Continued on page 2, col 6

Fears of 'half-gay' Fleet

Continued from page 1

drunk and ended up having sex with the male prostitutes. "Some of these 'girls' are very beautiful," the report said. "They dress well and smell delicious. They perfect the female walk, stance and mannerisms."

The ban on homosexuality in the Armed Services was lifted two years ago. Around 600 servicemen were sacked in the 1990s for homosexuality.

☐The Royal Navy feared the Pill would trigger an outbreak of promiscuity among servicemen and women in the Sixties.

The Roman Catholic Church, sailors' wives and senior officers tried to prevent it being given to single Wrens. They were overruled by Roy Hattersley, then a junior defence minister, who overturned the rule that it should be available only to married women or those intending to marry within three months.

Hello sailor

The Times - Thursday October 31st 2002.

THE TIMES Monday October 15 2007 2GM News | 25

Speaking out

Members of the Royal Navy at a gay parade in London last year

"The Germans had Stomach Battalions where a soldier with a tummy complaint was put into a battalion with others who had a similar ailment. Something similar might be worked out for gays"
General Sir Michael Gow (retired), former Commandant, Royal College of Defence Studies

"God help us if we have to fight a war"
Simon Heffer, now associate editor of *The Daily Telegraph*

"The British Armed Services are threatened not by foreign powers, but from within"
Gerald Frost, Editor of *Not Fit to Fight*, published by the Social Affairs Unit

"If the doors were opened to homosexuals, there would be a polarisation, people would be ostracised, there would be a sort of 'us and them' atmosphere ... Men don't like taking showers with men who like taking showers with men"
Air Chief Marshal Sir Michael Armitage (retired), former head of military intelligence

"We should follow the advice of the Armed Forces, which has always been that lifting the ban would adversely affect operational effectiveness"
Iain Duncan Smith, then Shadow Defence Secretary

Officers quit Navy after Forces lifted the ban on gays, secret paper reveals

Dominic Kennedy

The Royal Navy suffered a spate of protest resignations by lower-ranking officers after the ban on gays in the military was lifted, a restricted document obtained by *The Times* shows.

Soldiers were so reluctant to undress or be exposed in front of homosexual comrades that they suggested the provision of homosexual-only showers and lavatories, and RAF couples expressed worries that same-sex partners would be allowed to move into family quarters and influence their children.

The level of rank-and-file resistance to the scrapping of the ban on homosexuality in the Armed Forces is disclosed for the first time in a paper released under the Freedom of Information Act.

However, reported cases of bullying or harassment involving homosexuals in the services were described as very rare. And there had been only one complaint of an unwanted homosexual approach, in the RAF.

Overall, the Ministry of Defence concluded, the change has had no tangible impact on operational effectiveness, team cohesion or Service life.

The Government scrapped a prohibition on gays in the Armed Forces in January 2000 after the European Court of Human Rights ruled that the ban gravely interfered with private life. The Conservatives opposed the reform, saying that it would be unpopular with Services personnel and could undermine military effectiveness.

A review by the Service Personnel Board in 2002, headed "Restricted — Management", suggests that the change endured a bumpy ride.

A previously undisclosed rash of resignations from the Navy is described among the ranks of Senior Ratings, Warrant Officers and SNCOs: "This stratum of naval society is considered to be one of the most traditional and, correspondingly, there remains some disquiet in the Senior Ratings' Messes concerning the policy on homosexuality within the Service. This has manifested itself in a number of personnel electing to leave the Service, although in only one case was the policy change cited as the only reason for going." In the Navy, "no practical difficulties have been encountered, although it has been suggested that training in interrogation involving strip-searching might cause difficulties."

Junior ranks in the infantry continued to feel that homosexuality undermined unit or team cohesion.

Commonly held concerns were:

- "Heterosexuals do not want to share rooms with homosexuals;
- "Privacy should be mutually respected and soldiers should not be compelled to share accommodation with persons of a different gender or sexual orientation;
- "There is a strong feeling that toilets and showers should be separated as per male and female arrangements;
- "A perception that operational effectiveness might be undermined [by] living in close proximity with homosexuals on operations."

Privacy worried some Navy personnel, particularly in confined living conditions, and sailors were anxious about taking showers with gays. In the RAF, concerns were raised about children growing up next door to a same-sex couple.

However, few Services personnel decided to announce that they were gay. The review has never been repeated but tensions remain between the Armed Services about attitudes to homosexuality.

dkennedy@thetimes.co.uk

Officers quit Navy after Forces lifted the ban on gays...

The Times Monday 15th October 2007

Daily Mail, Tuesday, November 26, 2002

Homosexual? That's not quite the word...

By **Bill Mouland**

ACCORDING to the dictionaries, the word homosexual describes a person who is sexually attracted, often exclusively, to people of his or her own sex.

It was coined in 1869 by the Hungarian writer Karl Maria Kertbeny, who said it was a more suitable term than the word pederast that it replaced.

But now homosexual is being written out of the Government's vocabulary after complaints from the gay community that it is offensive and outdated.

Anti-discrimination laws being overseen by Equalities Minister Barbara Roche at the Department of Trade and Industry will use the term 'orientation towards people of the same sex'.

A spokesman said: 'When we were consulting there was a strong feeling that homosexual wasn't the way forward in defining sexual orientation.

'We found there were various concerns, for various reasons.'

Opposition to the word homosexual was discovered when Mrs Roche began a consultation exercise last year.

Consultation: Barbara Roche

Called Towards Equality and Diversity, it contained the Government's plans to bring in laws to tackle discrimination on the grounds of sexual orientation and religion by December next year.

Gay lobby groups and trades unions were among those who objected to the word homosexual and demanded a wider definition of sexual orientation to cover every group in society.

Mrs Roche, a 48-year-old barrister who is married with a daughter of 14, denied that it was an issue of political correctness.

'You are actually making a statement that these issues have moved on,' she said.

The consultation documents reveal that the word gay will remain as part of Government-speak. The Dictionary of Contemporary Slang, published by

'Offensive and outdated'

Bloomsbury, says that gay, which was regarded as non-discriminatory, overtook homo as the popular description of homosexuals in the late 1960s.

Over the years, however, a vast dictionary of words and expressions describing homosexuals has sprung up and the Internet is now sprinkled with websites dedicated to gay slang and its derivations.

It is thought the word homosexual gained mainstream credence in the late 19th century when it was used in U.S. medical journals. By the 1920s, it was in general usage.

The word gay, which has gained a wide acceptance, may owe its origins to 16th century theatre when young men or boys took women's roles in plays.

The word queer – as in odd – was first used in the early 20th century, while queen dates back to the 16th century when it was used to describe particularly effeminate young men.

Frog queens are French Canadian gays, or gays who fancy Frenchmen; fruits first became part of the American vocabulary in the early 20th century.

Lesbian owes its derivations to the Greek poet Sappho, who lived on the island of Lesbos and celebrated the love between women.

Nancy boy and pansy are both described as British-inspired, although poof was invented by the Australians in the early 1900s.

Some claim that the term faggot goes back to the days when homosexuals were burned at the stake, with faggots, or kindling sticks, used to light the fire. Others say it derives from the fagging system in boys' public schools.

Homosexual?

Daily Mail - Tuesday November 26th 2002

NEWS The Independent on Sunday 11 May 2003

Blair gives religious employers the right to sack gay workers

By Paul Waugh

Tony Blair was accused of caving in to evangelical Christians last night after it emerged that new government legislation will allow faith schools, churches, hospices and other religious employers to sack lesbian and gay staff.

Equal rights campaigners were furious when they discovered that regulations intended to combat discrimination in the workplace contain wide-ranging exemptions for any employer "with an ethos based on religion or belief".

The Lesbian and Gay Christian Movement said that the move would institutionalise homophobia in a way that "makes Section 28 look like a tea party". Others claimed that the exemptions exposed the "dangerous" influence church groups have over the Prime Minister.

The 2003 Employment Equality Regulations were originally drafted by ministers with the aim of achieving a historic breakthrough in combating harassment and bias in the workplace on grounds of sexuality or religion.

Drawn up to comply with an EU directive on workers' rights, they were meant for the first time to give protection to Muslims and to gays. An employer found to discriminate when hiring, promoting, demoting or training staff would be in breach of the law.

But *The Independent on Sunday* has learned that the statutory instruments slipped out to Parliament last week were watered down following direct intervention by Downing Street. A Whitehall source said the decision was made "at the highest level" and that Barbara Roche, the equalities minister, had been overruled.

One key clause inserted into the regulations states that an exemption applies when an employer acts "so as to comply with the doctrines of the religion – or so as to avoid conflicting with the strongly held religious convictions of a significant number of the religion's followers".

The wording of the clause is almost identical to that submitted by the Church of England. The Archbishops' Council's submission, which was leaked to the *IoS*, states that an exemption should apply "to comply with the doctrines of the religion or avoid offending the religious susceptibilities of a significant number of its followers".

Other major changes to the original draft, allowing discrimination against atheists or others who do not share the religious beliefs of their employer, were made following strong lobbying from evangelical groups. One of the biggest loopholes allows an employer to dismiss or fail to hire an individual if he is "not satisfied" that they fit his own "ethos based on religion or belief".

Critics claim that this would allow firms such as Stagecoach, run by Scottish evangelist Brian Souter, or Vardy, the North-east car dealership owned by millionaire Christian Peter Vardy, to discriminate freely.

Evan Harris, the Liberal Democrats' equality spokesman, condemned the new regulations, pointing out that they would actually weaken current employment rights of gay men and lesbians by institutionalising in law justifications for discrimination.

"When faced with pressure from those who wish to continue to harass and discriminate against people on the basis of lawful private behaviour or their sexuality in circumstances where sexuality is patently irrelevant to their ability to do the job, the Government has simply caved in," he said.

Keith Porteous Wood of the National Secular Society said the regulations were a "witch-hunter's dream come true". "Organisations with a 'religious ethos' employ around 200,000 people, most of them in jobs paid for out of the public purse. This includes over 100,000 teaching posts in faith schools," he said. "The Government has given in to religious pressure at every stage of this process."

The Deputy Prime Minister's Office said that religious employers were a special case "as they bring diversity to public life and delivery of services".

"We listened very carefully to responses in the last consultation and on reflection we decided it was right in very limited circumstances that the Government wouldn't interfere in matters of religious doctrine or strongly held religious convictions," said a spokeswoman.

The right to sack gay workers - Independent on Sunday 11 May 2003

Independent on Sunday
11 May 2003

'It is to gays what *Mein Kampf* is to Jews'

Peter Tatchell, campaigner for homosexual rights, describing his least favourite book, *The Bible*

Peter Tatchell - Gays against the Bible

Pressure grows on Williams to break silence in gay bishop row

Stephen Bates Religious affairs correspondent

The Archbishop of Canterbury is under growing pressure to break his silence over the planned ordination of a gay bishop in Reading.

Dr Rowan Williams is finding it increasingly difficult to stay out of a row between evangelicals opposed to Canon Jeffrey John being consecrated as bishop this autumn and liberal clergy supporting his appointment. Thousands of parishioners yesterday heard clergy across the country making clear from their pulpits where they stood, some in clearly agonised tones.

Canon John, 50, was selected for the suffragan bishopric by Richard Harries, the Bishop of Oxford, having given assurances that, although in a 27 year-long relationship, he had been celibate for many years.

A spokesman for the archbishop, who is known to be personally sympathetic to gays, said he had no immediate plans to speak out.

By contrast, sources close to David Hope, the Archbishop of York, second in the church hierarchy, said he was contemplating issuing a "cool it" call this week to the opposing factions who are threatening to tear the church apart,calling for quiet reflection to allow a consensus to be reached — or what one senior churchman called a ceasefire.

The Archbishop of York was Canon John's principal at St Stephen's House, Oxford, in the 1970s and is said to have reassured him then that being in a relationship would help to make him a better person.

Nine mainly evangelical diocesan bishops last week signed an open letter opposing the appointment of Dr John, canon theologian at Southwark Cathedral in south-east London. Eight others signed a letter to the Archbishop of Canterbury supporting the canon, with more expected to sign that letter this week.

Supporters of Canon John have pointed out that among the nine opposed to him are several disappointed candidates for Canterbury last year. They believe that some are motivated by frustrated ambition and wish to undermine the new archbishop, who has not received public support from any of them.

Archbishops from provinces in developing countries, mainly in Africa, have threatened to withdraw recognition from the Church of England if the consecration goes ahead. Archbishop Peter Akinola, primate of Nigeria, apparently said at the weekend that God's church was under "satanic attack".

Mr Akinola is reported to have said: "I cannot think of how a man in his right senses would be having a sexual relationship with another man, it is so unnatural, so unscriptural. This is unheard of ... and not what we can tolerate."

Meanwhile, after one Sunday newspaper's allegation that two gay bishops were appointed without fuss in the 1990s — with opponents of Canon John in attendance at their consecrations — gay campaigners asserted that the church had many more gay people on the episcopal bench than that. Richard Kirker, general secretary of the Lesbian and Gay Christian Movement, said: "If you include the 45 diocesan bishops, 71 suffragans and retired bishops, there must be at least a dozen."

At least 15 bishops are believed to be prepared knowingly to ordain gay clergy, with some dioceses more receptive than others. Previous surveys have estimated that up to 20% of clergy in London may be homosexual.

Unprecedentedly, Tony Sadler, the Archbishop of Canterbury's appointments secretary, the man responsible for shortlisting candidates for church posts, spoke on the record yesterday to deny that there was a liberal campaign to secure the election of a gay bishop.

Mr Sadler told the Sunday Times that he had put forward seven or eight names for the Reading bishopric by the Bishop of Oxford. "My understanding is that we are not in the business of discriminating on the grounds of sexual orientation. I put Jeffrey's name down on my list because his gifts and experience fitted the job description."

It is understood that the archbishop was not told of the bishop's choice until after it had been made, although he then endorsed it, as did Downing Street and the Queen.

Ironically, Canon John's name was previously rejected for the bishopric of Monmouth, vacated by Dr Williams when he moved to Canterbury. That bishopric was filled by the previous Bishop of Reading, Dominic Walker.

Dr Williams is known to believe the church's position on gays — that lay members can be in homosexual relationships but gay clergy must be celibate — is ultimately unsustainable, but that he does not welcome the debate erupting so soon after his appointment.

The Guardian Friday June 20 2003 The Guardian Monday 23 June 2003

Nigerian Anglicans stand firm against homosexuality

2 news.telegraph.co.uk

News

Picture: EMMA WILLIAMS

Bishop's anti-gay comments spark legal investigation

By Richard Alleyne

A BISHOP who angered homosexuals by suggesting they seek a psychiatric cure is to be investigated by police to see if his outspoken views amount to a criminal offence, it emerged yesterday.

The Rt Rev Dr Peter Forster, the Bishop of Chester, infuriated homosexuals both in and out of the Church of England when he said last week that they could and should seek medical help to "reorientate" themselves.

The Lesbian and Gay Christian Movement (the LGCM) accused him of putting forward an "offensive" and "scandalous" argument from a bygone age.

Cheshire Police have said that they are to investigate his comments, made in the local paper, the *Chester Chronicle*, after receiving a complaint that his views may incite people to turn against homosexuals.

In a statement released by the force, Assistant Chief Constable Graeme Gerrard said: "We are aware of the article in the *Chester Chronicle* and have received a complaint.

"We will examine the issues raised in the complaint and will speak to the reporter and the Bishop of Chester before considering any further action." A spokesman for the force added that it would send a copy of the article to the Crown Prosecution Service to see if any offence had been committed.

The bishop, who has in the past attacked the immorality of Britain and the ordination of homosexual bishops, spoke out after spending 18 months helping to write the Church of England report *Some Issues in Human Sexuality – A Guide to Debate*.

He told the newspaper that his research had led him to believe that homosexuals should seek medical help.

He said: "Some people who are primarily homosexual can reorientate themselves. I would encourage them to consider that as an option, but I would not set myself up as a medical specialist on the subject – that's in the area of psychiatric health."

Yesterday he refused to add to his views, but his spokesman said he would fully co-operate with any police inquiry.

Martin Reynolds, the communication director of the LGCM, welcomed the investigation into what he described as "scandalous" views. "These are irresponsible remarks that could inflame latent homophobia," he said.

"I am sure that the bishop is a very gentle man and his views are sincere. But many people in history who are gentle and sincere have said things that are evil.

"If he wants to say that homosexuality is a sin then he is entitled to his views but to say it is a psychiatric disorder is wrong.

"What is particularly worrying is that this man has spent 18 months researching this issue. We welcome the police investigation."

Mr Reynolds denied that the group had made the complaint but said it could have been one of their members.

It is not the first time that Dr Forster, 53, who is married with four children, has expressed strong views about sexuality.

He is part of the All Souls Day Group which has declared war on what it sees as a tide of liberalism engulfing the Church.

As a response it has called for all Anglican Church leaders to back the 1998 Lambeth conference, which condemned sexual activity outside marriage. The group also fiercely opposed the appointment of the openly homosexual Gene Robinson as the Bishop of New Hampshire, in America, which took place earlier this month. Dr Forster was one of nine bishops who signed a letter opposing the appointment of Dr Jeffrey John, a non-practising homosexual, as Bishop of Reading. Dr John later decided not to take up his appointment.

The Public Order Act 1986 covers so called hate crimes, which the Metropolitan Police define as "abusing people because of their race, faith, religion or disability – or because they are lesbian, gay, bisexual or transsexual".

The Bishop of Chester, Dr Peter Forster, said that homosexuals should seek medical help

The Daily Telegraph, November 10th 2003

Bishop recommends homosexuals seek psychiatric help.

Liberal fury as gay bishop stands down

BY JONATHAN PETRE
RELIGION CORRESPONDENT

CANON Jeffrey John, whose appointment as the Church of England's first openly homosexual bishop threatened a worldwide split among Anglicans, withdrew his acceptance of the post yesterday.

In a dramatic and unexpected move that dismayed his liberal supporters, he bowed to pressure from evangelicals and announced that he would seek the Crown's permission to step down as Bishop of Reading.

He said he was doing so for the sake of Church unity.

His decision was prompted by the Archbishop of Canterbury, Dr Rowan Williams, who spoke privately to him at a crisis meeting at Lambeth Palace on Saturday.

It followed weeks of behind-the-scenes talks among the Church's senior leaders, including the Archbishop of York, Dr David Hope, the Bishop of London, the Rt Rev Richard Chartres, and the Bishop of Winchester, the Rt Rev Michael Scott-Joynt.

Canon John's decision will defuse the immediate crisis but is bound to provoke a liberal backlash. A survey for *The Daily Telegraph* published on Saturday indicated that the General Synod was split down the middle on the issue.

The canon's withdrawal was welcomed by evangelicals in Oxford, as well as by the Bishop of Liverpool, the Rt Rev James Jones, and the Bishop of Carlisle, the Rt Rev Graham Dow.

Canon Jeffrey John: pressure

But the Dean of Southwark, the Very Rev Colin Slee, reflected the anger of liberals when he told his congregation that Dr John had been the victim of "appalling prejudice".

He said the news of his withdrawal was, for many in the Church, "a devastating blow to their hopes for progress and inclusiveness".

It also ensured "a nastier and more difficult battle" to come, he added.

Dr Williams, speaking on the steps of Lambeth Palace, said: "This has been a time of open and painful confrontation in which some of our bonds of mutual trust have been severely strained.

"We need now to give ourselves the proper opportunities honestly to think through what has happened and to find what God has been teaching us in these difficult days."

The Archbishop acknowledged that the appointment had caused great unhappiness and that there was an "obvious problem" in consecrating a bishop "whose ministry will not be readily received by a significant proportion of Christians in England and elsewhere".

But he said the episode should not preclude a Church debate on homosexuality and he attacked critics who had written him "unsavoury" letters displaying a "shocking level of ignorance and hatred towards homosexual people".

Canon John, a prominent gay rights advocate, had been in an active homosexual relationship but said he had been celibate for a number of years.

His appointment provoked protests from more than 100 members of the clergy and laity in the Oxford diocese and from nine diocesan bishops and several archbishops from the worldwide Church.

The Bishop of Oxford, the Rt Rev Richard Harries, responded vigorously to criticism of his choice of Canon John for the suffragan post and was supported by eight diocesan bishops.

But growing evangelical threats to withdraw loyalty and parish funds from the diocese, coupled with pressure from conservative archbishops in Africa and Asia, persuaded Dr Williams to act.

Canon John's decision will now raise questions about the future of Bishop Harries.

Pawn in bishops' game: Page 4
Editorial Comment: Page 19

Gay Bishop Stands Down

The Daily Telegraph Monday 7 July 2003

£1.40 (IR £2)

THE INDEPENDENT
ON SUNDAY

The gay scene by Charles Parker

'It was intoxicating. In the backroom I saw 25 naked men packed tightly together'

It's very dark, that's the first thing that always strikes me. Sometimes you bump into a sweaty body in the shadows or feel a strong hand give your crotch an eye-watering squeeze before your eyes have even adjusted. A voice might whisper an instruction in your ear – not exactly sweet nothings, but then I'm not talking about that kind of place. This is not mainstream, inclusive, gay nightlife. These are "hardcore" gay clubs in central London, often in converted railway arches or basements: spots where illicit sex might have occurred even before it was commodified.

You arrive any time after 11pm, queue at the discreet entrance, have your bag (cursorily) frisked by the doorman and then pay your £4 entrance fee. The next thing you do is take off all your clothes, with the exception of your underpants – this is "underwear night" – and shoes, if you don't fancy walking on sticky surfaces or broken glass.

Inside the black-painted interior a row of near-naked men sit chatting casually on stools at a long bar. Their ages range from late teens to anything above 70 (a baseball cap, pierced nipples, etc can do a lot to disguise age). More men are strutting on the modest dance floor. There are guys of all shapes and colours (black men are common, and Asian men increasingly part of the mix). You don't have to be young, skinny or good-looking to have casual sex. You don't even have to be gay – I know a married man with children who has enjoyed this kind of night out.

To find the real action in this club you have to move to the (even) darker room off the dance floor. However many times I see it, I still find the sight of a "backroom" intoxicating: a crowd of maybe 25 or more naked men packed tightly together in the shadowy light and engaged in a range of sexual acts ranging from one-to-one kissing, to group masturbation, to full-on anal sex.

Generally you can engage as little or as much as you want. You can squeeze between the bodies, watch the ecstatic faces, touch what you like and be touched (or more) in return.

Gay clubs of all kinds are flourishing in Britain
KAREN ROBINSON/REX

If you find someone you really fancy and the feeling seems mutual, you can make a little space for yourselves. Few words pass between men in this situation – the anonymity is part of the deal (and the pleasure).

Poppers (amyl nitrate, a chemical mix that is sniffed to get a quick and pleasurable high) is a shared part of the ritual. Many people bring condoms with them, but given the frantic nature of the couplings it does not surprise me to hear that some people have anal sex without them. Once people have had their pleasure they usually leave quickly. The more virile ones stay on until closing time. Nobody seems to be on cleaning duty.

Why do we do it? For all the assimilation of mainstream culture by gay men and the acceptance we have gained in return, there is still a deep-rooted desire among many homosexuals to engage in anonymous sex. Some of this might be the result of years of subterfuge, the need to be secret and quick for fear of prosecution or worse. That anxiety has largely disappeared, but there remains an element of danger that is thrilling (you don't know who you're dealing with; you never know what you might catch).

Clearly, it has nothing to do with love – for many of these men that is a separate, but parallel, experience. But there is a great feeling of male camaraderie and liberation about being able to touch someone you don't know in the most intimate way possible. Compliments are often paid during or after sex, something that can be flattering and confidence- building – particularly for men who may feel inadequate in many other aspects of their lives.

There have been clampdowns on open-air sex in the capital, but Hampstead's West Heath is still thriving, and on a summer night a gangbang of a dozen euphoric men is not an unusual sight. Any attempt to outlaw it completely will only drive it further underground – after all, it's a very old culture: as far back as 1726, when the infamous Margaret Clap's "Molly house" was raided in London, a witness at her trial described a scene of "between 40 and 50 men making love to one another".

Some people might find all this distasteful, to say the least. And there's certainly an element of irresponsibility among gay men (or more frighteningly, deliberate attempts to spread infection), which is alarming. That risk must be part of the thrill for some, but those of us who want to protect ourselves know how to. As long as the heat of the moment is not a distraction.

For the most part, this is just good dirty fun by a bunch of guys well away from the public gaze. Surely, only the most bitter killjoy would want to put an end to that?

The Gay Scene By Charles Parker (It Was Intoxicating......)

The Independent On Sunday 4th April 2004

THE TIMES WEDNESDAY JUNE 30 2004

B&B bans gays from sharing

A hotelier has angered the Scottish tourist board by refusing to let double rooms to male couples, Alan Hamilton writes

A GAY couple from the soft and forgiving south have fallen under the dark shadow of Calvin and Knox that still looms over the sterner reaches of the Presbyterian north.

Stephen Nock, 34, and his male partner, from London, had been looking forward to a four-day walking holiday in Wester Ross, Scotland, until the owner of the Cromasaig guest house in Kinlochewe rejected their request to book his double room because their relationship was "unnatural".

The failed booking developed into an exchange of angry e-mails between Mr Nock and Tom Forrest, owner of the guest house, which enjoys a recommendation and a three-star rating from VisitScotland, the former Scottish Tourist Board.

Instead of a polite confirmation of his booking, Mr Nock received an e-mail explaining that two gents sharing could book only a twin room.

Mr Nock was moved to threaten a complaint to the tourist authorities when the guest house informed him: "We do not have a problem with your personal sexual deviation, that is up to you. You are welcome to our twin room if you wish, but we will not condone your perversion."

Incensed that he and his partner had been denied the £22-per-person-per-night double bed, Mr Nock replied, suggesting that the proprietor of the guest house was bigoted and homophobic.

Mr Forrest countered at once. "Bigot? No. Respect for our other guests. Homophobic? No. I have no hatred or fear of poofs, etc — I just do not approve of unnatural acts being performed in my home."

Mr Nock, a campaigns officer with Voluntary Service Overseas who has lived with his partner for five years, was surprised and stung by Mr Forrest's stance and has asked VisitScotland to remove Cromasaig from its list of recommended accommodation.

"My partner and I have never encountered anything like that before from any establishment. It really depressed me. There's still so much prejudice. I would hate for other couples to approach his B&B and get the same abuse."

VisitScotland has asked Cromasaig not to discriminate against future guests on the basis of sexual orientation but Mr Forrest, who has run the establishment for 11 years, retains his stance, refuses to be told which guests to accept and has posted a notice on his website saying that his double room will be let only to heterosexual couples or single guests.

"I stand by exactly what I said," Mr Forrest said yesterday. "I do not go along with this word 'gay'. They are not happy in that situation. I called them poofs and will continue to call them that. Gay is a word that means happy to me."

> 'You are welcome to our twin room if you wish but we will not condone your perversion'

Mr Forrest, who admits to having received more than 80 abusive e-mails from "poof organisations", said: "We run a respectable B&B and we have families coming to stay. I have had bent people to stay but they have had a twin room and respect our wishes."

Barbara Clark, of VisitScotland, said that an investigation was under way. "We are looking into the incident but are confident this kind of appalling attitude is not mirrored across the vast proportion of Scotland."

John Knox, in his 16th-century tract *The First Blast Of The Trumpet Against The Monstrous Regiment Of Women*, was not taking a view about gays, it was women ministers he was against. Today, the Kirk has lots of them and now has its first female Moderator.

CENTRE PRESS

Old attitudes: Cromasaig guest house in Kinlochewe, Scotland

B&B bans gays from sharing

The Times Wednesday June 30 2004

The Guardian Wednesday October 13 2004 5

Evangelicals call Williams a prostitute

Stephen Bates Religious affairs correspondent

Conservative evangelicals flexed their muscles yesterday by denouncing the Church of England and its leader, the Most Rev Rowan Williams, Archbishop of Canterbury, as sinful and corrupt, and threatening to refuse to recognise the authority of liberal bishops.

They warned that they might seek the ecclesiastical oversight of more theologically congenial bishops from the developing world if the church did not offer them the chance to align with bishops of their own stamp in England.

The complaints came in the run-up to next week's publication of an international commission reviewing the structure of the Anglican communion in the wake of the gay bishops dispute.

Supporters of the evangelical pressure group Reform, meeting at their conference in Derbyshire, overwhelmingly supported its plans to start disengaging from liberal bishops and refusing to pay funds to their dioceses, to indicate their disapproval of what they see as the church's slide into acceptance of sexual immorality.

Dr Williams was denounced as a theological prostitute by the Very Rev Phillip Jensen, the controversial Anglican dean of Sydney, addressing the 200 clergy and lay members attending the conference.

He and his brother Peter, Archbishop of Sydney, have led the way in aggressive low church conservatism.

Dean Jensen was applauded as his sweeping denunciation of the Church of England took in the Prince of Wales — a "public adulterer"; King's College Chapel in Cambridge, attacked as a "temple to paganism" for selling the records and compact discs of its famous choir in the ante-chapel; and women priests because, "as soon as you accept women's ordination everything else in the denomination declines".

But the dean reserved his strictest condemnation for Dr Williams, because he holds liberal private views about homosexual relationships, even though he has struggled to uphold the church's unity by maintaining its traditional opposition to ordained gays.

"That's no good. That's total prostitution of the Christian ministry," the dean declared, to applause and cries of "Amen".

"He should resign. That's theological and intellectual prostitution. He is taking his salary under false pretences."

Reform is developing links with the Anglican church in the developing world in readiness for the outcome of the report of the commission headed by Archbishop Robin Eames, set up a year ago in response to the decision by the US Episcopal church to ordain its first openly gay bishop, Gene Robinson, to lead the diocese of New Hampshire.

Bishop Robinson was elected by parishioners in the state, even though he was known to be living with his partner, in defiance of traditional church practice.

Evangelicals now want the commission to discipline the US church, or at least those of its bishops who supported Bishop Robinson's appointment, until they repent, though there is at present no mechanism for the worldwide church to do so.

In England the first targets of conservative evangelicals are likely to include the eight diocesan bishops who publicly supported the appointment of the celibate gay cleric Jeffrey John to the suffragan bishopric of Reading last year.

Dr John was later forced to give up the appointment, because of evangelical protests, but he has subsequently been made Dean of St Albans.

Reform members are already beginning to demand answers from their diocesan bishops about where they stand on the gay issue before deciding whether to continue to support them.

But some at the conference believed that shunning bishops was not going far enough. Ian Seymour, a churchwarden in Arborfield, Berkshire, said: "The Church of England is over, its days are numbered.

"If our rector was an adulterer, a drunk or a liar, he would be removed, but if he was in a same sex relationship he would be cherished.

"The institution is sinking — new groupings will emerge."

Archbishop of Canterbury - "a theological prostitute"

The Guardian, Wednesday October 13th 2004

African bishops threaten split over homosexuality

AFRICAN BISHOPS condemned the Anglican Church's stance on homosexuality yesterday and said that they would stop sending priests to be trained in countries where same-sex relationships were accepted.

The 300 Anglican bishops who met in Nigeria for the first African bishops convention said homosexuality was an "unAfrican" practice and warned that congregations would turn away from a church that condoned it. Only the Archbishop of Cape Town, Njongonkulu Ndungane, offered any dissent, saying his church was committed to its entire congregation, including homosexuals.

Their statements highlight the growing divide between the Anglican Church in Africa, which makes up more than half the world's 70 million-strong Anglican population, and the West.

African bishops were particularly angered by their American colleagues' decision to ordain an openly gay bishop, Gena Robinson, last year, and complained that the church has not been strong enough in condemning homosexuality. They are also outraged that some Anglican churches have given blessings for same-sex marriages.

Bishop Peter Akinola, chairman of the Council of Anglican Provinces in Africa, said it was time the African church reduced its dependency on the West. He added: "You now have men and men cohabiting, which is against the African way of life. The Western world is embroiled in a new religion which we cannot associate ourselves with."

In contrast to Europe, where homosexuality is becoming more accepted, many

BY MEERA SELVA

African countries are firming up their stance against same-sex relationships. Homosexuality has long been illegal in many African countries but now even places such as Zanzibar, which had been more tolerant of the gay community, has recently passed laws imposing a mandatory 25-year jail sentence for any men caught having sex with each other.

Even relatively liberal societies like Kenya take a firm stance on the subject. Jomo Kenyatta, the first president of Kenya, once famously said there was no African word for homosexuality.

The Rev Joseph Ogola, dean of the Anglican Church in Kisumu, western Kenya, said: "I don't like the idea of gay bishops. It is against the Bible. I accept we live in a changing society and have to accept that people value their own freedom, but that should not be linked to the church. They should branch off and start their own religion."

The Anglican Church in Africa currently receives almost three quarters of its funds from the West, but bishops from Nigeria and Kenya have said they would refuse to accept financial support from American churches that did not share their views on homosexuality. They warned that African congregations would convert to Islam or other religions if they felt the Anglican Church took too liberal a stance on the matter.

The Anglican Church in Africa is growing at a faster rate than anywhere else in the world, with 17.5 million members living in Nigeria alone, and the issue threatens to tear the global church apart.

Last week, the church published the Windsor report which criticised American Anglicans for ordaining a gay bishop, but African bishops felt it did not go far enough in condemning homosexuality.

They were further outraged by comments from Frank Griswold, leader of the Anglican Church in the United States, who said last week that he did not believe the blessing of same sex-marriages should be banned.

South African bishop Johannes Seoka, left, and Nigerian bishop Peter Akinola address the convention *Reuters*

The Independent, Thursday 28th October 2004

The Christmas compromise

You would have to come from a different planet not to have noticed that the season of Christmas is now upon us! The crowded shops, the lack of parking space, the gaudy decorations and the stressed looking shoppers counting down how many shopping days are left and will they have enough time to get everything, and how are they going to recover from the debts that inevitably follow.

Then preach the righteous voices, "Christmas has become too commercialised. Everyone's forgotten what the true meaning of Christmas is all about!" True! People have forgotten what the true meaning is all about, but I am not referring to the birth of Jesus Christ (peace be upon him).

When Christianity swept through Europe, pagan religious systems were firmly embedded in the hearts and minds of the people. Unlike Islam, which wiped the slate clean in preparation for pure monotheism, Christianity chose the path of compromise. To win numbers, preachers and priests allowed worshippers to stick to their old pagan religious routines and rituals as long as Jesus (peace be upon him) was incorporated somewhere within them.

Christmas is merely one such pagan festival amongst many adopted by early Christians.

History testifies that Christmas was not even heard of as such even up until the third century after Christ, and it was well into the fourth century before the Christian church began to observe such a festival.

There is no Christian scripture that claims Jesus (peace be upon him) was born on 25th December, or at any other winter date. Indeed, scripture tells us that on the night of the birth, the Palestinian shepherds were outside on the hills guarding their sheep. It is true, the Palestinian shepherds used to do that, but not in the winter. We are also told of a nationwide consensus at the time of the birth, which involved every man, woman and child travelling back to their home town. Again, this would not have occurred in winter.

So, what was happening on 25th December that made Christians pick that date for the birth of their saviour?

Well the date coincided with the Winter Solstice (shortest day of the year) on the old Julian calendar of Ancient Rome, and it was Rome that became the centre of the Christian church in Western Europe. At this time of year, Rome enjoyed five days of drunken revellry celebrating the festival of SOL INVICTUS (the Unconquerable Sun), an incarnation of the Sun-god supposedly born on the night of the winter solstice.

The Christian church felt no shame in using expressions from the pagan rituals of this time in their own Christmas liturgy. Many comparisons were made between Sol Invictus and Jesus Christ and it is interesting to note that the Christians preferred for their Sabbath, Sunday (DIES SOLIS) taken from the god's name, as opposed to the Jewish Saturday. It is a Sunday, too, which is taken at Easter as the day of Christ's Resurrection from the dead.

Rome, though, along with Ancient Egypt and Greece, was heavily influenced by the Ancient Babylonian religion, the main theme of which was a MOTHER-GODDESS, whose husband, the SUN-GOD sacrificed himself for the salvation of their followers and was resurrected again in the form of their DIVINE SON, born at the winter solstice, (a similar concept to the Christian idea of Mary and the role of Jesus as Saviour).

The influence of Babylon reached Northern Europe where still today in Nordic languages, 'Yule' is the word for Christmas. Chocolate Yule Logs pack the supermarket shelves this time of year and many Christmas cards will have the inscription, "Greetings this Yule-tide". Where does the word come from? 'Yule' is the Ancient Babylonian word for 'infant'! In some myths the Mother-goddess changed into a tree before giving birth, the divine child being a branch of that tree, hence Yule Log and the idea of the Christmas Tree seen at this time and also present in the celebrations of Ancient Egypt and Rome (although I suspect with a loss less tinsel!)

Up until the last century the boar and the goose were the traditional meats eaten for Christmas Dinner in Europe. There is even a little poem still chanted at this time of year:

"*Christmas is coming,*
the goose is getting fat,
Please put a penny
in the old man's hat".

One legend holds that it was a boar that killed the Sun-god and so the creature was sacrificed each year at this mid-winter time. As for the goose, this was regarded as a sacred bird in Rome, Egypt and of course, Babylon.

The Christmas carol, the '*twelve days of Christmas*' is still popular but it likely refers to the twelve days of feasting and drunkenness that took place around the Winter solstice in Europe.

However the celebrations in the pre-Christian pagan world were not all connected to the worship of the sun. For the Sabeans of Arabia their favoured object of worship was the Moon-god and its birth was celebrated on the 24 December. What is very striking is that on the last day of the year Egypt and Scotland shared a festival for the Moon-god. The celebration in Scotland is supposed to be linked to the Christian Christmas celebrations and is called Hog-manay, but in the language of ancient Babylon, Hog-manai means feast of the Numberer - the Numberer being another title for the Moon-god.

It is incredible for Muslims to understand how a monotheistic 'People of the Book' could be persuaded all those centuries ago to make such compromises with not just the practises of pagan religions but their very belief systems. But then maybe it is not so surprising for even today the church is back-tracking on its previous Biblical stance against homosexuals and people who live together without being married. Adjusting to the climate of the times, as they did with the popularity of mid-winter partying just three centuries after Christ, many church members including priests, judge that speaking against the sins of adultery, fornication and homosexuality would drive people away from that religion. We thank Allah for the clarity of Surah *Al-Kafirun* [109].

Farah McGee

ISSN 0965-3384
245
9 770965 338005

Published by Q-News International Ltd, Dexion House, 2-4 Empire Way, Wembley, Middx HA9 0XA
Tel: 0181 903 0819 Fax: 0181 903 0820 Registered as a newspaper at the Post Office. ISSN 0965 3384

The Origins of Christmas

Q-News 6-12 December 1996

The Prince of Wales explains how the Muslim critique of materialism helped him to rediscover the sacred

Islamic spirituality and the decline of the West

I start from the belief that Islamic civilisation at its best, like many of the religions of the East — Judaism, Hinduism, Jainism and Buddhism — has an important message for the West in the way it has retained an integrated and integral view of the sanctity of the world around us. I feel that we in the West could be helped to rediscover the roots of our own understanding by an appreciation of the Islamic tradition's deep respect for the timeless traditions of the natural order.

I believe that process could help in the task of bringing our two faiths closer together. It could also help us in the West to rethink, and for the better, our practical stewardship of man and his environment — in fields such as healthcare, the natural environment and agriculture, as well as in architecture and urban planning.

Modern materialism is unbalanced and increasingly damaging in its long-term consequences. Yet nearly all the great religions of the world have held an integral view of the sanctity of the world. The Christian message with, for example, its deeply mystical and symbolic doctrine of the Incarnation, has been traditionally a message of the unity of the worlds of spirit and matter, and of God's manifestation in this world and in mankind.

But during the past three centuries, in the Western world at least, a dangerous division has occurred in the way we perceive the world around us. Science has tried to assume a monopoly — even a tyranny — over our understanding. Religion and science have become separated, so that now, as Wordsworth said, "Little we see in nature that is ours". Science has attempted to take over the natural world from God; it has fragmented the cosmos and relegated the sacred to a separate and secondary compartment of our understanding, divorced from practical, day to day existence.

We are only now beginning to gauge the disastrous results. We in the Western world seem to have lost a sense of the *wholeness* of our environment, and of our immense and inalienable responsibility to the whole of creation. This has led to an increasing failure to appreciate or understand tradition and the wisdom of our forebears, accumulated over the centuries. Indeed, tradition is positively discriminated against — as if it were some socially unacceptable disease.

In my view, a more holistic approach is needed now. Science has done the inestimable service of showing us a world much more complex than we ever imagined. But in its modern, materialist, one-dimensional form, it cannot explain everything. God is not merely the ultimate Newtonian mathematician or the mechanistic clockmaker. As science and technology have become increasingly separated from ethical, moral and sacred considerations, so the implications of such a separation have become more sombre and horrifying — as we see in genetic manipulation or in the consequences of the kind of scientific arrogance so blatant in the scandal of BSE.

I have always felt that tradition is not a man-made element in our lives, but a God-given intuition of natural rhythms, of the fundamental harmony that emerges from the union of the paradoxical opposites that exist in every aspect of nature. Tradition reflects the timeless order of the cosmos, and anchors us into an awareness of the great mysteries of the universe, so that, as Blake put it, we can see the whole universe in an atom and eternity in a moment. That is why I believe Man is so much more than just a biological phenomenon resting on what we now seem to define as "the bottom line" of the great balance sheet of life, according to which art and culture are seen increasingly as optional extras in life.

This view is quite contrary, for example, to the outlook of the Muslim craftsman or artist, who is never concerned with display for its own sake, nor with progressing ever forward in his own ingenuity, but is content to submit a man's craft to God. That outlook reflects, I believe, the memorable passage in the Koran, "whithersoever you turn there is the face of God and God is all-embracing, all knowing". While appreciating that this essential innocence has been destroyed, and destroyed everywhere, I nevertheless believe that the survival of civilised values, as we have inherited them from our ancestors, depends on the corresponding survival in our hearts of that profound sense of the sacred and the spiritual.

Traditional religions, with their integral view of the universe, can help us to rediscover the importance of the integration of the secular and the sacred. The danger of ignoring this essential aspect of our existence is not just spiritual or intellectual. It also lies at the heart of that great divide between the Islamic and Western worlds over the place of materialism in our lives. In those instances where Islam chooses to reject Western materialism, this is not, in my view, a political affectation or the result of envy or a sense of inferiority. Quite the opposite. And the danger that the gulf between the worlds of Islam and the other Eastern religions on the one hand and the West on the other will grow ever wider and more unbridgeable is real, unless we can explore together practical ways of integrating the sacred and the secular in both our cultures in order to provide a true inspiration for the next century.

Islamic culture in its traditional form has striven to preserve this integrated, spiritual view of the world in a way we have not seen fit to do in recent generations in the West. There is much we can learn from that Islamic world view in this respect.

There are many ways in which mutual understanding and appreciation can be built. Perhaps, for instance, we could begin by having more Muslim teachers in British schools, or by encouraging exchanges of teachers. Everywhere in the world people want to learn English. But in the West, in turn, we need to be taught by Islamic teachers how to learn with our hearts, as well as our heads. The approaching millennium may be the ideal catalyst for helping to explore and stimulate these links, and I hope we shall not ignore the opportunity this gives us to rediscover the spiritual underpinning of our entire existence.

This is an extract from the Prince's speech yesterday at Wilton Park.

Islam and the Prince of Wales

The Times - Saturday, December 14, 1996

My journey to Islam

Islam is by far the most misunderstood religion in the world today thanks to centuries of medieval-style propaganda successfully peddled by bigots and Christian zealots. So I should not have been entirely surprised by the almost hysterical reaction in the mainstream media to news that I am considering becoming a Muslim. Some of the comments were bitchy and snide, other journalists asked me stupid questions showing a distinct lack of research or understanding. One even accused me of suffering from Stockholm Syndrome as a result of spending ten days in the hands of the Taliban!

My spiritual journey, like that for many converts/reverts, was meant to be a personal affair between myself and God. Sadly it has now become a very public issue and so I have decided to share with *Q-News* readers my feelings and thoughts on Islam to prevent any more misunderstandings or misconceptions.

Yes, my journey did begin in the unlikely surrounds of an Afghan prison where I was being held by the Taliban facing charges of entering their country illegally disguised in the all-enveloping burqa. One day, during my captivity I was visited by a religious cleric who asked me what I thought of Islam and if I would like to convert. I was terrified. For five days I had managed to avoid the subject of religion in a country led by Islamic extremists. If I gave the wrong response, I had convinced myself I would be stoned to death. After careful thought I thanked the cleric for his generous offer and said it was difficult for me to make such a life-changing decision while I was in prison. However, I did make a promise that if I was released I would study Islam on my return to London. My reward for such a reply was being sent to a ghastly jail in Kabul where I was locked up with six Christian fanatics who faced charges of trying to convert Muslims to their faith. (After being bombarded with their bible readings, happy clappy Christian songs and prayers twice a day, I think we can discount the accusations of Stockholm Syndrome.)

Several days later I was released unharmed on humanitarian grounds on the orders of Mullah Omar, the Taliban's one-eyed spiritual leader. My captors had treated me with courtesy and respect and so, in turn, I kept my word and set out to study their religion. It was supposed to be an academic study but as I became more engrossed with each page I turned so I became more impressed with what I read. I turned to several eminent Islamic academics, including Dr Zaki Badawi, for advice and instruction. I was even given several books by the notorious Sheikh Abu Hamza Al-Masri who I spoke to after sharing a platform at an Oxford Union debate. This latter snippet was seized upon by some sections of the media in such a ridiculous fashion that outsiders might have thought I was going to open a *madrassa* for Al-Qaeda recruits from my flat in Soho!

> THE QURAN MAKES IT CRYSTAL CLEAR THAT ALL MUSLIMS, MEN AND WOMEN ARE ENTIRELY EQUAL IN WORTH, SPIRITUALITY AND RESPONSIBILITY. ALLAH ORDAINED EQUALITY AND FAIRNESS FOR WOMEN IN EDUCATION AND OPPORTUNITY. FAIR PROPERTY LAW AND DIVORCE SETTLEMENTS WERE INTRODUCED FOR MUSLIM WOMEN 1500 YEARS AGO.

Thankfully the support and understanding I have been given from my brothers and sisters (for I regard them as that) has been unstinting and comforting. Not one of them has put pressure on me to become a Muslim and every convert/revert I've spoken to has told me to take my time. One of the big turning points for me happened earlier this year when the Israelis began shelling The Church of the Nativity in Manger Square - one of the most precious monuments for Christians. Every year thousands of school children re-enact the Nativity at Christmas time, a potent symbol of Christianity. Yet not one Church of England leader publicly denounced the Israelis for their attack. Our Prime Minister Tony Blair, who loves to be pictured coming out of church surrounded by his family, espousing Christian values, was silent. Only the Pope had the guts to condemn this atrocity. I was shocked and saddened and felt there was no backbone in my religious leaders. At least with Islam I need no mediator or conduit to rely upon, I can have a direct line with God anytime I want.

While I feel under no pressure to convert/revert by Muslims, the real pressure to walk away from Islam has come from some friends and journalists who like to think they're cynical, hard-bitten, hard-drinking, observers of the world. Religion of any form makes them feel uneasy, but Islam, well that's something even worse. You'd think I had made a pact with the devil or wanted to become a grand wizard in the Ku Klux Klan. Others feared I was being brainwashed and that I would soon be back in my burqa, silenced forever like all Muslim women. This, of course, is nonsense. I have never met so many well-educated, opinionated, outspoken, intelligent, politically aware women in the Muslim groups I have visited throughout the UK. Feminism pales into insignificance when it comes to the sisterhood, which has a strong identity and a loud voice in this country. Yes, it is true that many Muslim women around the world are subjugated, but this has only come about through other cultures hi-jacking and misinterpreting the Koran. (Saudis take note).

I wish I had this knowledge (and I'm still very much a novice) when I was captured by the Taliban because I would have asked them why they treated their own women so badly. The Quran makes it crystal clear that all Muslims, men and women are entirely equal in worth, spirituality and responsibility. Allah ordained equality and fairness for women in education and opportunity. Fair property law and divorce settlements were introduced for Muslim women 1500 years ago - may be this is where Californian divorce lawyers got their inspiration from in recent years! The Quran could have been written yesterday for today. It could sit very easily with any Green Party manifesto, it is environmentally friendly and it is a true inspiration for the 21st century, yet not one word has changed since the day it was written unlike other religious tomes. "It's more punk than punk," musician Aki Nawaz of the band *Fun-da-Mental* recently told me. And, of course he is right.

Yvonne Ridley

Journalist Yvonne Ridley - On a woman's right to choose.

Q News - July/August 2002

Faith plays minor role in lives of most white Christians

BY NIGEL MORRIS
Home Affairs Correspondent

ALTHOUGH MOST white Britons call themselves Christian, most admit religion plays little part in their lives, a government study shows. But a strikingly different picture emerges in black and Asian communities, who say that their faith is a crucial part of their identity.

And in a sign that Britain's religious map is likely to change dramatically over the next decade, the numbers of young Muslims, Sikhs and Hindus who stressed the importance of their religion far outstripped the young Christians who professed a similar strength of faith.

The first detailed Home Office survey of the nation's belief found almost four out of five people expressed a religious affiliation, a result some officials regarded as surprisingly high in an increasingly secular society.

The highest number (74 per cent) called themselves Christian, with Muslims (2 per cent) and Hindus (0.8 per cent) the largest of other faith groups. Almost 22 per cent, nearly all white, said they had no faith.

But there are signs religious affiliation made little difference to the lives of its white adherents. When asked what they considered important to their identity, religion was cited by only 17 per cent of white Christians, behind family, work, age, interests, education, nationality, gender, income and social class. For black people, 70 per cent of whom say they are Christian, religion is third, and Asians placed it second, only behind family. People of mixed race ranked their religion seventh.

Nearly all people who called themselves as Christian (98 per cent) were white, and 2 per cent were black. The majority of respondents who were Muslim were Asian (76 per cent), and most Hindus (83 per cent) and Sikhs (88 per cent) also described themselves as Asian.

Signs of a rapid demographic change in Britain's religious make-up emerged. Just 18 per cent of Christians aged 16 to 24 viewed their religion as important, but 74 per cent of young Muslims, 63 per cent of young Sikhs and 62 per cent of young Hindus said they did.

Followers of Islam, the country's fastest-growing religion, tended to live in more deprived neighbourhoods than other faiths. Muslim respondents were also more likely than any group to never have had a job.

Fewer Christians and Muslims had degree-level qualifications than those of other religions; Hindus and Jews had more higher qualifications than the national average. Highest levels of home ownership were among Sikhs (88 per cent), Hindus (76 per cent), Jews (74 per cent) and Christians (74 per cent), with the lowest among Muslims (52 per cent), nearly one quarter of whom rented local authority accommodation.

Most people believed ministers and employers were doing enough to defend and respect religious rights and customs. But in a sign of growing discontent among ethnic-minority youths, some young Muslims and Sikhs said the Government was doing too little. One-fifth of Christians of all ages accused the Government of doing too much to protect religious freedoms.

More than two-thirds of people surveyed were allowed to take time off work for religious ceremonies and festivals. But most said their employers did not provide prayer facilities. Researchers found no apparent link between religious affiliation and participation in the local community, such as by contacting councillors or signing petitions.

A Home Office spokesman said the research, based on nearly 15,500 interviews, was aimed at ensuring government policy reflected social change and tapped into the talents of the ethnic minorities. He said: "We are committed to building stronger and more cohesive communities and to reach out to people at risk of social exclusion."

Fiona Mactaggart, the Home Office minister, said: "For many people, their religious affiliation is important to their sense of identity. Our job is to take account of this in our policy-making. It is encouraging that most people questioned felt the Government was doing enough to tackle religious discrimination.

"Mutual understanding is important for building strong, active communities in which citizens have the power to shape their future."

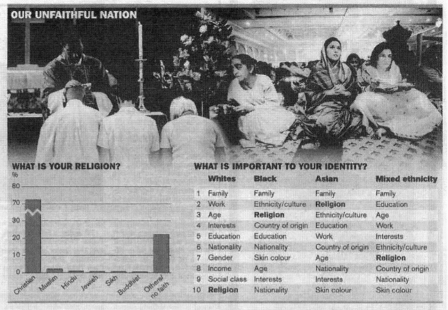

OUR UNFAITHFUL NATION

WHAT IS YOUR RELIGION?

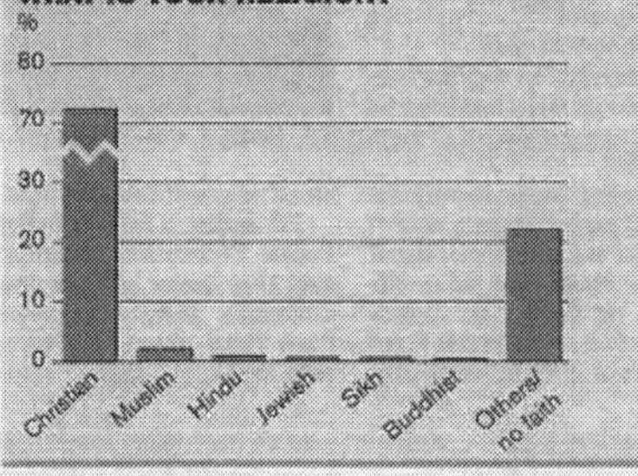

WHAT IS IMPORTANT TO YOUR IDENTITY?

	Whites	Black	Asian	Mixed ethnicity
1	Family	Family	Family	Family
2	Work	Ethnicity/culture	**Religion**	Education
3	Age	**Religion**	Ethnicity/culture	Age
4	Interests	Country of origin	Education	Work
5	Education	Education	Work	Interests
6	Nationality	Nationality	Country of origin	Ethnicity/culture
7	Gender	Skin colour	Age	**Religion**
8	Income	Age	Nationality	Country of origin
9	Social class	Interests	Interests	Nationality
10	**Religion**	Nationality	Skin colour	Skin colour

...and single Britons have lax sexual morals

BY MAXINE FRITH
Social Affairs Correspondent

SINGLE MEN and women in Britain have some of the most lax sexual morals in the world, an international survey claims.

Britons are the most likely to believe it "normal" for a thirtysomething to have had at least 10 lovers, and are among the least fervent believers in monogamy. Views on fidelity and sexual liberation were found in a poll of more than 10,000 people for the marketing agency Euro RSCH Worldwide.

Adults from the UK, France, Germany, United States and China were questioned about their sexual mores for the survey. Nearly six out of 10 Britons (59 per cent) said it was normal for a person in their 30s to have had 10 or more lovers, compared with 30 per cent of French and 17 per cent of Chinese.

The Americans came close to Britain in the "10 or more" belief. But more than half of Americans and 70 per cent of Chinese say monogamy is a natural state for humans, while just 42 per cent of Britons agree.

Also in Britain, only 63 per cent of men and 47 per cent of women expect regular sex with their partners, the lowest proportions in the world.

The Independent, Wednesday August 18th 2004

WILLIAM DALRYMPLE

The demonising of Islam

Islamophobia has become more acceptable since 9/11, with increasing numbers of Muslims insulted and assaulted. This is not the way to respond to terror

SINCE 11 September 2001 there has rightly been a great deal of scrutiny of the failings of the Muslim world. Much has been written about the absence of freedom and a civil society in almost all Muslim countries, as well as the failure of Muslim elites to bring either mass education or economic prosperity to their people. There has been much questioning as to why so many of the world's conflicts, and so much of its terrorism – including last week week's atrocity in Russia – is associated with Islamist groups and a great deal of reflection on the difference between the tolerant pluralistic and intellectual past of Islam and its often intolerant and violent present.

"In the Court of the Lions I Sat Down and Wept" is a fine essay by the Lebanese novelist Hanan al-Shaykh on just this subject. Al-Shaykh is writing about her feelings on visiting the Alhambra and her depression on feeling that, "we Arabs have no connection with the Arabs of Andalucia, with those who, having borrowed the pens and chisels of angels, have carved and embellished to such melodious perfection. Why is it that we didn't complete our cultural journey, and how is it that we have ended up today in the very worst of times? What is it that made our predecessors pore over their desks, writing down and recording the marvels of mathematics and science and searching out the skies in order to discover their secrets, and, driven by the love of knowledge, to study medicine and to devise medicaments even from the stomach of bees...?"

This soul searching, which has taken place both within the Islamic world and among the wider Muslim diaspora, has been for the good: few Muslims would now dispute that much has gone badly wrong with contemporary Islam, and particularly with the way that the Gulf Arabs have used their petrodollars to spread around their particularly narrow and intolerant Wahhabi brand of Islam – the brand which flourished in Taliban Afghanistan and which has spread to the surrounding regions. We have seen the tragic results in Beslan last week.

But at the moment, in the aftermath of the horrors in Abu Ghraib and Guantánamo Bay and the entirely avoidable and barely reported massacres of ordinary Iraqi civilians in Fallujah, it is highly debatable whether now is the time for putting only the wider Muslim world on the psychiatrist's couch. At this point, we in the West should also be engaged in some introspection.

For what Abu Ghraib and the behaviour of American troops in Iraq and Afghanistan has shown yet again is the continuing tendency of the imperial Christian West to treat "the Other" as *Untermensch* – subhuman. For much of the history of Christendom it was the Jews who suffered the brunt of European bigotry. But it is increasingly apparent that just as Islam is now replacing Judaism as Europe's second religion, so Islamophobia is replacing anti-Semitism as the principal Western statement of bigotry. It is worth asking whether the United States and UK defence secretaries, Donald Rumsfeld and Geoff Hoon, would still be in their jobs if it were another ethnic or religious group which had been subject to the murder, rape and sexual humiliation in Abu Ghraib. Had it been, say, Irish Republicans who had

been systematically tortured by British forces, would British ministers get away with suppressing damning Red Cross reports and with claiming ignorance of the horrors they contain?

Earlier in the summer, on a lecture tour in the United States, I came across the full force of Middle-American views of Muslims. Following the beheading of the kidnapped American Nick Berg, Rush Limbaugh – self-styled "champion of the underdog" – went on air to reassure Middle America that "they are the ones who are perverted. They are the ones who are dangerous. They are the ones who are subhuman. They are the ones who are human debris – not the United States of America and not our soldiers and not our prison guards."

Nor do the British have any right to sneer at the Americans. When Robert Kilroy-Silk was sacked for writing that the Arabs were "loathsome" – "suicide bombers, limb amputators and women repressors" – 97 per cent of callers to the *Express* newspaper (about 22,000 people) agreed that the BBC had been too harsh in firing him. It is still clearly acceptable to people in the UK to make the sort of racist asides about Arabs and Muslims that would now be considered quite unacceptable if made about Jews, Catholics or black people.

Consider this letter I received a couple of months ago from William Roff, formerly professor of history at Columbia University in New York who now supervises students in Islamic and Middle Eastern studies in Edinburgh:

"Within the past few years, four of my Malaysian students have been subjected to racist violence directed against them as 'Pakis' or Arabs (and Muslims). One had emerged from Friday prayers at a mosque in Dundee when he was hit in the face by a stone and nearly lost an eye. Another, living in a village with his young family, had obscene graffiti scrawled on the house and excrement pushed through the letter box. A third lived with his wife and young children on an Edinburgh housing scheme, where they were so harassed by vituperation and threats of violence that they were forced to move into central Edinburgh, at a much higher rent which required him to take a job and prevented him completing his thesis. The fourth, a month or so ago, returned to Edinburgh from fieldwork with his wife, a toddler and a baby, and had a brick thrown through the bedroom window. Such incidents testify to a culture of active racism in Britain that is the product of levels of ignorance inadequately addressed by educational authorities and fostered by the sneering, casual racism of much of the tabloid press."

Last month, the BBC aired a chilling programme about the British National Party that seemed to confirm how widespread this sort of thing has become. An undercover journalist filmed the BNP leader Nick Griffin calling Islam a "wicked, vicious faith" that "has expanded through a handful of cranky lunatics" and "is now sweeping country after country" because "the Koran tells Muslims it is acceptable to rape white women and children". Interviewed on *Newsnight*, Griffin refused to apologise for his remarks, and instead ranted at the programme's host, Gavin Esler, for 15 minutes about how Islam was spread by rape. The BNP is undergoing something of a renaissance in the country and at the European elections in May it received no fewer than 800,000 votes.

What is most alarming is the way that this sort of neo-Nazi activity is being aided and encouraged by the Islamophobic scaremongering of even the most intelligent sections of the right-wing British press. Last month the *Spectator* published a cover story entitled "The Muslims are coming", which argued that most Muslims, not just the extremist fringe, "are open about their desire for Islam to conquer the West". The story was illustrated by a picture of the Islamic crescent hoisted atop the Arc de Triomphe, Big Ben and the leaning tower of Pisa.

At around the same time, the *Sunday Telegraph* ran a series of virulently Islamophobic pieces by a writer who used the pseudonym Will Cummins – who later turned out to be a senior press officer of the British Council. "Christians are the original inhabitants and rightful owners of almost every Muslim land," he wrote, "and behave with a humility quite unlike the menacing behaviour we have come to expect from the Muslims who have forced themselves on Christendom, a bullying ingratitude that culminates in a terrorist threat to their unconsulted hosts." He was finally sacked last week. But the *Sunday Telegraph* has refused to rule out publishing further contributions from the author, and its editor, Dominic Lawson, was quoted in the *Guardian* as saying he did not regret printing them.

Since then the *Mail on Sunday* has published a number of equally Islamophobic pieces by the political commentator Peter Hitchens. One of them, headlined "Islam is a threat to us all", began: "Soon it will be illegal to say this, so I had better do it now. Islam, yes even 'moderate' Islam threatens our freedom and civilisation." All this comes on top of the usual rabble-rousing *Daily Mail* stories about Muslim asylum seekers receiving lavish benefits and indulging in wanton criminal activity.

Such offensive prejudices against Muslims – and the spread of idiotic stereotypes of Muslim behaviour and beliefs – have been developing at a frightening rate since 9/11. It is especially ironic that much of the criticism of Muslims comes from conservative commentators given that British Islam has successfully preserved the traditional conservative values that in this country once used to be associated exclusively with Christianity: an emphasis on the family, chastity before marriage, respect for elders and weekly attendance at religious services, as well as sitting down to various important religious feasts.

Articles such as those by Cummins and Hitchens form a worrying and dangerous parallel with the sorts of things people were writing about Judaism in the Twenties and Thirties. A couple of weeks ago on Radio 4's *Today* programme, Hitchens was arguing that "Islamophobia" was a foolish term. Well, it may be foolish to Hitchens, but it is sadly only too full of meaning for Professor Roff's students or those who come across BNP thugs in the dark streets of Bradford. If you have hysteria about a newly immigrated community whipped up by irresponsible journalism you cannot be surprised when that precipitates acts of racial violence.

Racism is not static. It changes and moves its targets. In Elizabethan times, Catholic missionaries, if found, would be hanged, drawn and quartered. Even two generations ago, mutterings about Left Footers were still common and a glass ceiling kept even the most well-born Catholics from the most senior jobs in the Establishment. Today that prejudice seems as dead and as distant as the age of the dinosaurs – except possibly for a few antediluvian corners of Belfast and, possibly, Glasgow. Elsewhere, to be a Catholic is now often rather chic: the last two editors of the *Daily Telegraph* have been Catholics, as is the Prime Minister's wife – something that would have seemed an impossible dream to our grandparents' generation.

Anti-Semitism is probably following a similar trajectory. In the aftermath of the mass immigration of European Jews fleeing Nazi and Russian persecution during the inter-war years, anti-Semitism was once the most virulent form of prejudice in this country, and even now is far from dead, but with British Jews well integrated into British society there are now much more obvious and inviting targets for religious and racial prejudice. Desecrations of British Jewish cemeteries and synagogues are not unknown, but they are no longer common; and while the pre-war Blackshirts attacked the newly arrived East End Jews, their modern equivalents now go "Paki bashing".

The fact is that Muslims in Britain have become used to endless abuse, discrimination and violence. Little of this gets reported, either to newspapers, monitoring groups or the police. Eighteen months ago I was wandering past a mosque near Brick Lane in the East End when I came across a group of elderly Bangladeshis sweeping up broken glass, the result of a thrown brick. It emerged that such vandalism was considered by them so routine that they never bothered reporting it to anyone, least of all the police. In the course of writing this article, I found it impossible to find any statistics on incidents of Islamophobic violence, whereas accurate and up-to-date statistics on anti-Semitism are readily available on a variety of websites.

British Islam has preserved the traditional conservative values once associated exclusively with Christianity

The massacre of 8,000 Muslims at Srebrenica in 1995 never led to articles about Christianity's history of violence. Yet every abominable act of al-Qaida terrorism brings to the surface a raft of criticism about Islam as a religion, and dark mutterings about the sympathies of Western Muslims. Meanwhile, British Muslims remain firmly on the margins of our national life. Considering the size of our Muslim community, it is scandalous that there are only four Muslim schools in the state sector. It is even more alarming that there are only four Muslim peers, two Muslim MPs and a single lonely British Muslim MEP. One of Tony Blair's most senior Downing Street advisers recently told me that Labour did not take Muslim sentiment seriously as there was yet to emerge a serious Muslim lobby, capable of reacting in a politically coherent manner.

Even the Vatican seems to have been affected by this fashionable hostility towards Islam. In one month we have seen the International Catholic-Jewish Liaison Committee, led on the Catholic side by Cardinal Walter Kasper, abandon its support of the Palestinians and equate anti-Semitism with anti-Zionism (the document describes anti-Zionism as "a more recent manifestation of anti-Semitism"); while Cardinal Joseph Ratzinger tells *Le Figaro* that Turkey should not be admitted to the European Community in order to protect European identity from the supposed dangers of Muslim influence. Yet perhaps the most worrying thing about this increasingly widespread Islamophobia is the extent to which it has gone largely unrecognised and uncriticised: indeed, despite centuries of prejudice and violence against Muslims, the term Islamophobia was only coined within the last decade.

Meanwhile, Blair's neo-conservative chums in Washington, immune to the justifiable fears of the Muslim world, still talk blithely of moving on next year from Iraq to attack Iran and Syria. To add petrol to the flames, they invited Franklin Graham, the Christian evangelist who has branded Islam a "very wicked and evil" religion (Christianity and Islam, he writes, are "as different as lightness and darkness") to be the official speaker at the Pentagon's annual Good Friday service – and this immediately prior to Graham's departure for Iraq to attempt converting the people of Baghdad to Christianity.

All the while, the paranoia and bottled-up rage in the Muslim world grows more uncontrollable. Angry young men volunteer for suicide bombings and attacks by Islamic militants gather pace, with ever wider global reach and technical sophistication. No wonder we feel scared.

The "war" on terrorism cannot be won unless we win the battle for Muslim hearts and minds. It is decent, moderate Muslim opinion – not torture chambers – that will be our best defence against the spread of Islamist radicalism. Yet at the moment we seem to be doing all we can to persuade the people of the Middle East that we are all hypocrites, sadists and liars. In one summer, the abuses of Abu Ghraib, the mass murders of Iraqis in Fallujah combined with the betrayal of the Palestinians by Bush and Blair – allowing illegal settlers to annex great chunks of the West Bank – has succeeded in inflaming even the most moderate Muslim opinion. The Islamic world is now united against the West more forcefully than at any time since Suez. Unless we change our ways, it is not just Iraq that we stand to lose, it is the entire war on terror. Bin Laden must be delighted.

⁂ *William Dalrymple's most recent book,* White Mughals *(Harper Perennial) won the Wolfson Prize for History. A stage version by Christopher Hampton has just been commissioned by the National Theatre.*

The Tablet 11th September 2004 by **William Dalrymples**

Muslims are right about Britain

John Hayes says Islamic moderates are correct to despise our decadent culture of gay rights and lager louts

Many moderate Muslims believe that much of Britain is decadent. They are right. Mr Blair says that the fanatics who want to blow us up despise us, but he won't admit that their decent co-religionists — who are the best hope of undermining the extremists at source — despair of us. They despair of the moral decline and the ugly brutishness that characterise much of urban Britain. They despair of the metropolitan mix of gay rights and lager louts. And they despair of the liberal establishment's unwillingness to face the facts and fight the battle for manners and morals.

They are not alone. The *Windrush* generation of Caribbeans came to Britain with the most traditional of values — proud Christians with dignity and a sense of duty — the kind of people so steeped in our history that they gave their children names like Winston, Milton and Gladstone. As vice-chairman of the British Caribbean Association, I recently had the chance to ask such people why so many young British blacks had got into trouble with the law. They unequivocally blamed the licence they encountered almost as soon as they arrived here, which made it so hard to inculcate their standards in the next generation.

The alienation felt by young blacks and Asians is not a result of any intolerance shown towards them, but of the endless tolerance of those who would allow everything and stand up for nothing. It is the excesses permitted by a culture spawned by the liberal Left that have produced a generation that feels rootless and hopeless. The young crave noble purposes as children need discipline; neither get much of them in modern Britain and the void is filled by disrespect, fecklessness, mindless nihilism or, worse, wicked militancy.

It is unreasonable to expect Muslim leaders to put right what's wrong in their communities if we are not going to be honest about what's wrong with ours.

Some of rural Britain (including the area in which I live and represent) still has strong communities. There, many of the old-fashioned values lost elsewhere prevail. Beyond these heartlands, much else is ailing. A sickening decadence has taken hold. People's sense of identity has been eroded as our traditions and the institutions that safeguard them have been derided for years. People's sense of history has been weakened by an education system that too often emphasises the themes in history rather than its chronology, and which indoctrinates a guilt-ridden interpretation of Britain's contribution to the world. People's sense of responsibility has been undermined by a commercial and media preoccupation with the immediate gratification of material needs, regardless of consequences — we want everything and we want it now, so we spend and borrow, cheat and hurt. People's self-regard has diminished as, robbed of any sense of worth beyond their capacity to consume and fornicate, they feel purposeless. We have forgotten that pleasure is a mere proxy for the true happiness which flows from commitment and the gentle acceptance that it is what we give, not what we take, that really matters.

The vulnerable are the chief victims of decadence. Children suffer when families break down. The old suffer as their needs are seen as inconvenient and their wisdom is no longer valued. For the rich, decadence is either a lifestyle choice or something you can buy your way out of. But for the less well off — stripped of the dignities which stem from a shared sense of belonging and pride — the horror of a greedy society in which they can't compete is stark. The civilised urban life that was available to my working-class parents is now the preserve of those whose wealth shields them from lawlessness and frees them from the inadequate public services that their less fortunate contemporaries are forced to endure.

'This is the worst drought we've had for 50 years!'

Safely gated, the liberal elite do not merely turn a blind eye — though that would be bad enough. They voyeuristically feed the masses with *Big Brother* and legislate to allow 24-hour drunkenness. In answer to the desperate call for much-needed restraint, we hear from those with power only the shrill cry for ever more unbridled liberty.

Politicians who should know better fear debates about values, preferring to retreat to morally neutral, utilitarian politics, as uninspiring as it is unimaginative. It is the kind of discourse which leaves those who aspire to govern reduced — in the heat of a general election campaign — to debating how efficiently their respective parties can disinfect hospitals. Most Church leaders have also given up the fight. Many have convinced themselves that to be fashionable is to be relevant and that being relevant is more important than being right. Is it any wonder that the family-minded, morally upright moderate Muslims despair?

So, with little understanding of the past, little thought for the future, little respect for others and virtually no guidance from those appointed or elected to give it, many modern Britons — each with their wonderful, unique God-given potential — are condemned to be selfish, lonely creatures in a soulless society where little is worshipped beyond money and sex.

The roots of this brutal hedonism are in soulless liberalism. Against all the evidence, the liberal elite — who run much of Britain's politically correct new establishment — continue to preach their creed of freedom without duty, and rights without obligations. Pope John Paul II — perhaps the greatest figure of our age — said 'only the freedom which submits to the truth leads the human person to his true good'. Freedom without purpose is the seed corn of social decay. It is through the constraints on self-interest and the restraint that good Muslims revere that we can rebuild civil society. The most fitting response to the terrorist outrages would be the kind of moral and cultural renaissance that would make Britons of all backgrounds feel more proud of their country.

John Hayes is Conservative MP for South Holland and The Deepings.

LETTERS

Our 'decadent' society

From Brian Binley MP and others

Sir: As Conservative MPs elected at this year's general election we represent a new generation unencumbered by the political baggage of the past. In this spirit we enthusiastically endorse the rejection articulated by John Hayes ('Muslims are right about Britain', 6 August) of the liberal establishment's assumptions about our society. For too long politicians of the centre and centre-Left — including some who curiously wear the badge of Conservatism — have ignored the common-sense opinions of the hard-working, patriotic majority of Britons who retain their belief in traditional values. In a recent Centre for Social Justice pamphlet, Iain Duncan Smith suggests that 'it is noteworthy — even remarkable — that [what he calls] Britain's conservative majority has persisted in the face of a largely hostile broadcast media and hesitant Church leaders'.

Some liberals remain in denial, unwilling to face the decadent consequences of years of their ideas being put into practice. But whether it is lawlessness, family breakdown, the menace of drugs, binge-drinking, teenage pregnancies or merely the coarse brutishness which, as Mr Hayes suggests, has infested popular culture, the results of years of woolly-minded liberal thinking (with the licentiousness it has created) are plain to see. Conservatives can choose either to help prop up the failed ideas of the liberal elite, or answer the people's plea for certainty, order and decency. Choosing the latter is the key to success.

Brian Binley MP, Peter Bone MP, David Burrowes MP, Philip Davies MP, Robert Goodwill MP, Mark Harper MP

Muslims are right about Britain

The Spectator 6th August 2005 and 13th August 2005

UNFINEST HOUR
'A potent blend of moral outrage and scrupulous research, exposing the culpability of those apparently civilized and intelligent British politicians who betrayed the people of Bosnia'
Francis Wheen, Guardian, Books of the Year
BRITAIN AND THE DESTRUCTION OF BOSNIA
Brendan Simms

Brendan Simms has asked for a government. inquiry into the abject role played by John Major, Douglas Hurd and Malcolm Rifkind during their time in office.

'A SCORCHING POLEMIC ... AGAINST BRITISH INACTION IN THE FACE OF SERB ATROCITIES ... QUITE RIGHTLY MINCES NO WORDS AND TAKES NO PRISONERS'
Cal McCrystal, *Financial Times*

'Outstandingly good ... liberating and exhilarating ... A powerful exposition of just how disastrously Whitehall got it wrong ... Every Foreign Office official, every MP and every pundit should be obliged to read it' Noel Malcolm, *Sunday Telegraph*

'Britain's refusal to act in the former Yugoslavia left the Serbs free to butcher thousands of Bosnians ... Simms's attention to telling detail and cool, literate anger make *Unfinest Hour* the best epitaph for the wretched years of the Major administration I've read to date' Nick Cohen, *Observer*

'This is a book about how the British establishment grovelled before Serbia's murderous dictator Slobodan Milosevic ... Talk about a low, dishonest decade! Reading it made me want to throw my passport on the nearest rubbish heap, so total is the indictment of ... the British state' Marcus Tanner, *Independent*

'The best sort of polemical book: hard-hitting, well researched and stimulating, with a preference for analysis over sensation'
Alan Judd, *Sunday Times*

ISBN 0-140-289-836
9 780140 289831
U.K. £8.99
CAN. $20.99
Get closer to Penguin at
www.penguin.com
Penguin
Politics/Current Events

ABOUT THE AUTHOR

Brendan Simms is Director of Studies in History at Peterhouse and Newton Sheehy Lecturer in International Relations at the Centre for International Studies, University of Cambridge. He is also the author of *The Impact of Napoleon* and *The Struggle for Mastery in Germany, 1779–1850.*

If you have shown yourself weak at a time of crisis, how limited is your strength!
Rescue those being dragged away to death, and save those being hauled off to execution.
If you say, 'But this person I do not know', God, who fixes a standard for the heart, will take note; he who watches you will know; he will repay everyone according to what he does.

Proverbs 24: 10–12

From preface of 'Unfinest Hour':

Remorseless and baffling, Breivik'

Gunman claims he struck for his country, and that his 77 victims were not innocent. **Helen Pidd** on day two of the terror trial in Oslo

Yesterday was the day Norwegians hoped they might begin to understand how Anders Behring Breivik became the worst mass murderer in the country's recent history.

Almost nine months after killing 77 people in three brutal hours, Breivik took to the stand at Oslo central criminal court to describe what he called "the most sophisticated and spectacular political attack committed in Europe since the second world war".

Just when it seemed he was taking responsibility for his actions, or showing a hint of remorse, Breivik would deliver a callous endnote. "I know it is gruesome what I have done and I know that I have caused an incredible amount of pain to thousands of people," he said at one point, before adding: "But it was necessary." And: "I would do it again."

In a pre-prepared statement, which the court allowed him to read out for more than an hour – a highly unusual concession granted only because he refused to give evidence at all otherwise – he insisted it was "goodness, not evil" that had prompted him to act in order to prevent a "major civil war".

The persona that emerged during day two of Breivik's 10-week trial was a rambling, repetitive obsessive, fixated on a threat he never truly managed to articulate, but which involved "cultural Marxists", whom he claimed had destroyed Norway by using it as "a dumping ground for the surplus births of the third world".

Norwegians would be a minority in their own capital city within five to 10 years, he said, and he blamed liberal politicians for allowing immigration as well as "feminism, quotas ... transforming the church, schools".

Often Breivik came across as exactly the kind of "pathetic and mean loser without integrity" that he insisted he was not.

He admitted he had exaggerated the size and reach of the Knights Templar, the shadowy anti-Islamist network he claimed to have joined in London in 2001, because it wouldn't have sounded so impressive to tell of "four sweaty guys in a basement".

You "gild the lily" in order to "maximise the propaganda effect", he said.

He said he regretted creating a "pompous" backstory, and posting pictures of himself wearing a pseudo-uniform cobbled together from eBay, because it had created the impression he was insane.

He repeated over and over again that he knew exactly what he was doing when he planned the attacks.

His targets were not random. The young people he shot dead on the island of Utøya during a Norwegian Labour party summer camp, some of them as young as 14, were "not innocent, non-political children", he said. "These were young people who worked to actively uphold multicultural values. Many had leading positions in leading Labour party youth wings."

The summer camp was like those run by the Hitler Youth, he added.

He told prosecutors he would have preferred to attack a conference of Norwegian journalists, but he had not been able to carry out that "operation".

Some of the survivors were in the courtroom. It was sheer luck that none of Breivik's thousands of bullets hit Tore Sinding Bekkedal, a 26-year-old activist in the Norwegian Youth Labour party (AUF), but Bekkedal said he didn't want the man who murdered so many of his friends to consider him a benign force.

"I don't want him to consider me innocent," said Bekkedal during a break in court yesterday. "I want to be a threat to his world model, I really do. I want to work for tolerance in society. I think that's a great thing to be working for. There is no enemy I'm more grateful for than Breivik."

During cross-examination, prosecutors tried to tease out exactly when Breivik was radicalised. His answers produced a confusing picture of a teenager who once "had a best friend who was a Muslim".

He said he awoke to the threat of multiculturalism when immersed in Oslo's hip-hop scene and after being attacked by "Muslims" (he claimed a gang broke his nose – a claim the prosecution may test with an x-ray).

Like many who came of age in the late 1990s, much of Breivik's education came via the internet. He admitted he had relied extensively on Wikipedia to produce the 1,801-page "compendium" setting out his manifesto before the attacks last year.

He read the English media, misconstruing a Times article from February 2010 to claim that the newspaper reported that a survey had found "3/5 Englishmen believe that the UK has turned into a dysfunctional society as a result of multiculturalism".

He noted that "Sarkozy, Merkel and Cameron have all said that multiculturalism has failed". He had studied recent history and was disgusted to see what happens "any time nationalist parties take power". He cited as an example the partial EU boycott after the far-right Freedom party entered Austria's government.

Breivik insisted he was not alone in fighting against mass immigration. He singled out neo-Nazis who killed nine immigrants and a policewoman in Germany, and Peter Mangs, suspected of a seven-year killing spree in Sweden.

It was important, he said, that these "heroic young people" should be celebrated for sacrificing their lives for the "conservative revolution".

He also declared himself inspired by al-Qaida, which he described as the most successful militant organisation in the world, and claimed al-Qaida was now emulating the "one-man cell" model he had operated on 22 July with such deadly success.

At the start of yesterday's court session, one of the five judges was dismissed after it emerged he had posted a message on Facebook last year saying "death penalty is the only just thing to do in this case". Thomas Indebro, 33, one of three ordinary Norwegians sitting as lay judges alongside two professionals, was replaced.

Breivik has four more days to explain his attacks. He denies criminal guilt, saying he was acting out of "necessity". Yesterday court interpreters issued a correction to their translation of Breivik's not guilty plea on Monday.

He is not claiming to have acted out of "self-defence", as originally reported, but is using a defence under Norwegian law that states: "No person may be punished for any act that he has committed in order to save someone's person or property from an otherwise unavoidable danger when the circumstances justified him in regarding this danger as particularly significant in relation to the damage that might be caused by his act."

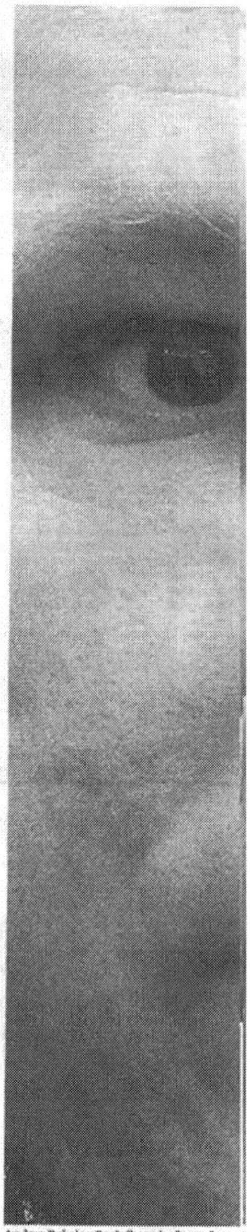

Anders Behring Breivik spoke for an hour

Reality check The killer's claims

Claim "Three out of five Englishmen believe that the UK has turned into a dysfunctional society as a result of multiculturalism." Breivik claimed to be quoting from a survey in the Times newspaper on 9 February 2010.
Fact Breivik appears to be inaccurately citing its lead story on that date, based on a Populus poll, which makes no reference to multiculturalism. It reads: "Nearly three-fifths of voters say they hardly recognise the country they live in." But the target of their ire does not appear to be immigrants. The Times says: "Voters' main fire is directed at political institutions: 73% say politics is broken in Britain and 77% say there are far fewer people in public life that they admire than there used to be. The poll suggests anger at MPs who have had to repay expenses. A third say that they will vote against their local MP if he or she is required to repay money."

Claim Breivik asked his audience to look at Luton "and the more than 1,000 Islamic no-go zones where police do not dare pass through". The city was, he said, living in "warlike conditions".
Fact Bedfordshire police said in a statement that "no-go areas do not exist in Bedfordshire". According to the 2001 census, 60% of inhabitants in Luton are Christian and 15% are Muslim. A 2009 Office for National Statistics report estimates that Asian or Asian-British people make up 18.9% of the local population. It has, however, been cited as a home to some people with extremist views. The Muslim group al-Muhajiroun was based there before it was banned. A Muslim protest in March 2010 was staged against soldiers returning from the Iraq war. The English Defence League has staged protests there.
Claim "Norwegians are becoming a minority in their capital city."

Contact

For missing sections call **0800 839 100**. For individual departments, call the Guardian switchboard: **020 3353 2000**. For the Readers' editor (corrections & clarifications on specific editorial content), call **020 3353 4736** between 10am and 1pm UK time Monday to Friday excluding public holidays, or email **reader@guardian.co.uk** Letters for publication should be sent to **letters@guardian.co.uk** or the address on the letters page

Guardian News & Media, Kings Place, 90 York Way, London N1 9GU. 020 3353 2000. Fax 020 7837 2114. In Manchester: Centurion House, 129 Deansgate, Manchester M3 3WR. Telephone Sales: London 020 7611 9000; Manchester 0161 908 3800. guardian.co.uk. The Guardian lists links to third-party websites, but does not endorse them or guarantee their authenticity or accuracy. Back issues from Historic Newspapers: 0870 165 1470. guardian.backissuenewspapers.co.uk. The Guardian is published by Guardian News & Media, Kings Place, 90 York Way, London N1 9GU, and at Centurion House, 129 Deansgate, Manchester M3 3WR. Printed at Guardian Print Centre, Rick Roberts Way, Stratford, London E15 2GN; Guardian Print Centre North, Longbridge Road, Manchester M17 1SN; and at Carn Web, 2 Esky Drive, Carn, Portadown, Craigavon, County Armagh BT63 5YY. No. 51,513. Wednesday 18 April 2012. Registered as a newspaper at the Post Office

testimony leaves Norway no wiser

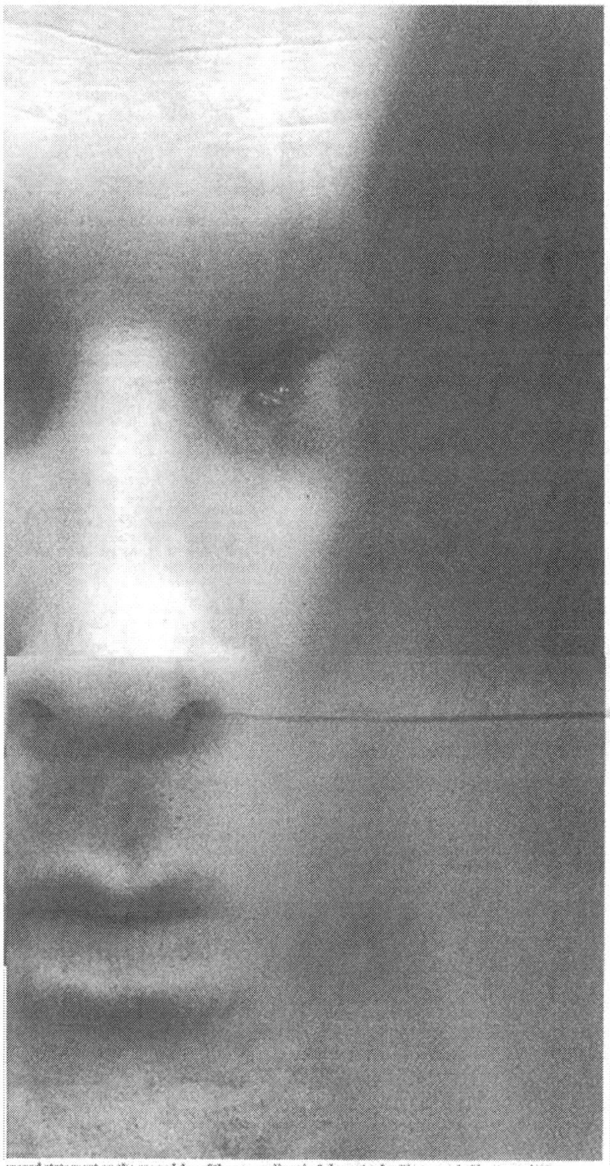

epared statement on the second day of the proceedings in Oslo yesterday Photograph: Lise Aserud/AP

The victims

'It's hard to explain ... it's really hard to see yourself getting blown away'

Helen Pidd

Propped up outside Oslo's central court yesterday afternoon, Eivind Thoresen reflected on all that he had heard in Anders Behring Breivik's evidence. "It's really hard to explain, but I feel really empty inside," said the 26-year-old.

Almost nine months ago, Breivik blew Thoresen up when he was passing through Einar Gerhardsen's Square, just a few minutes' walk from the courtroom. Not that Thoresen could walk there now; ever since the moment Breivik detonated the bomb in Oslo's government district last July, Thoresen has been reliant on crutches. He has just gone through his fifth operation after doctors found another metal splinter in his leg from the van Breivik had packed with explosives.

Yesterday, Thoresen was in court when prosecutors showed harrowing CCTV footage that showed him literally being knocked off his feet.

"It's really hard to see yourself getting blown away," he said.

Thoresen said he was no closer to understanding Breivik's motives. He was just an ordinary Norwegian in the wrong place at the wrong time.

Eivind Thoresen, below, said he was just an ordinary man in the wrong place at the wrong time

"He had a target, a political target. I was not one of them," he said.

"I don't think he will apologise to me or anything like that."

Families were keen to stress that the man who killed their loved ones had no legitimate mandate for what he did.

"I think it's important to underline that we don't view Breivik as a politician in this matter. He is a mass murderer," said Trond Henry Blattmann, whose 17-year-old son, Torjus, was killed on Utoya.

Tore Sinding Bekkedal, 26, who survived the Utøya attacks physically unscathed, said he appreciated the opportunity to get "a more detailed image of the defendant". It was right to let Breivik read out his pre-prepared statement, he said.

"Of course it was incredibly boring and silly, but it is a major part of building up an image of his political views and his personality and so on and so forth," Bekkedal said. "There was nothing in his speech that you can't read in the comments field of any newspaper website. It was predictable nonsense, the kind of stuff that you see all the time. I was almost glad to be bored at some points because it's a sign that the normal court procedure is going on."

More on the Breivik trial at guardian.co.uk/world ›

Fact According to a Statistic Norway report in January 2011, the number of immigrants and Norwegians born to immigrant parents accounted for 12.2% of the total population in Norway on 1 January 2011, with immigrants from Poland making up the largest group, followed by Swedes, Germans and Iraqis. It adds: "During 2010, the number of Norwegian-born to immigrant parents increased from 93,000 to 100,400 persons. Those with Pakistani parents made up the largest group of all Norwegian-born to immigrant parents, with 14,400. Norwegian-born to Somali parents were the second largest group (7,800), followed by those with parents from Vietnam (7,400), Iraq (6,600) and Turkey (5,900)." Of the 599,200 inhabitants of Oslo, 28.4% were immigrants or Norwegians born to immigrant parents.

'Norwegian people are becoming a minority in their capital city'

Claim The liberal left boycotts democracy when nationalists take power. "For example, when [Jörg] Haider came to power in Austria, 14 countries in the EU boycotted Austria." **Fact** The "boycott" referred to by Breivik appears to be a reference to the diplomatic sanctions imposed by 14 members of the European Union, led by France and Germany, on Austria in February 2000 after the Freedom party and its leader, Haider, entered the ruling coalition in Vienna as a junior partner to Schuessel's People's party. The EU members acted, according to the German foreign minister, Joschka Fischer, because "this is the first time an anti-European, xenophobic party with a very dubious relationship with the Nazi past has come into the government of a member state". The boycott lasted seven months.
Caroline Davies

The Guardian 18 April 2012

Violent: A scene from Call Of Duty

Breivik: I perfected my shooting skills playing video games for 16 hours a day

Deadly training: Anders Breivik

From **Christian Gysin** in Oslo

ANDERS Breivik became a deadly marksman after honing his shooting skills on a violent computer game, he told his trial yesterday.

The mass killer even bought a gun-sight similar to one featured in the game, Call Of Duty – Modern Warfare, and attached it to the hunting rifle he used for his rampage on a Norwegian island.

The killer told the court: 'The game [Call Of Duty] teaches about target acquisition and you have to practise within a specific time.

'It's a war simulator that shows you how to shoot at people. It helps you acquire experience of sights and targeting. You could give it to your grandmother and she would be able to become a super marksman.' The right-wing extremist admitted he took a year off work just to play video games.

And he told how he gave his hunting rifle, pistol and 'getaway' vehicle names taken from Norse mythology. He called the pistol 'Thor's Hammer'.

Breivik also claimed that he planned to capture former Norwegian prime minister Gro Harlem Brundtland, 72, on the island of Utoya, and behead her on camera.

He took a digital camera with him, he said, along with a knife, bayonet and plastic handcuffs, but changed the plan after finding the camera did not have enough battery life.

Details of Breivik's fixation with video games were revealed yesterday during cross-examination on the fourth day of his trial for the killing spree on July 22 last year that left 77 dead – eight in Oslo and 69 on Utoya.

Breivik, 33, was asked about his interest in computer games and told the court that between the summer of 2006 and December 2007 he took a 'sabbatical' from working and played the games for around 16 hours a day.

Initially Breivik concentrated on playing fantasy game World Of Warcraft before turning to more violent forms of computer 'entertainment'.

He told the court: 'I wanted to take a year off to play World Of Warcraft. It is not violent at all. It's just fantasy. It's a strategy game.

'During that year I played perhaps 16 hours a day and played an entire year. I was just playing and sleeping... it was a dream I had.

'Some people like to play golf, some like to sail, I played WoW. It had nothing to do with 22/7.' But Breivik then told how he began playing Call Of Duty – Modern Warfare, a version of which was the bestselling video game in Britain last year.

It is described as a 'first person shooter video game' and Breivik admitted that by playing it he honed his gun and targeting skills.

He would later use those same 'skills' to kill 69 innocent people, mostly teenagers, on Utoya.

Breivik also admitted visiting an Oslo pistol club 25 times to improve his handgun skills, but said the game, and its holographic weapon-sight, were a great help to him.

'I used a similar holographic aiming device [sight] at Utoya and the game is such a good war simulator, [it] is so good that it is used by armies all around the world.'

A holographic weapon-sight is a non-magnifying gun attachment that allows the user to look through a glass optical window and see his target image superimposed at a distance.

The sight provides a red circle image with a red dot inside the ring identifying the target.

Breivik also told the court he planned to kill far more than his 69 victims, as he was aware around 564 people were on the island. He hoped many more would have fled into the water and drowned. 'My goal was to kill them all,' he said. The trial continues.

David Gillard

first night review

Battleaxe: Anne Widdecombe as Duchesse de Crackentorp

LA FILLE DU REGIMENT

Royal Opera House

STRICTLY no singing (which is probably just as well, given the reports of her trilling in panto last year).

But last night the doughty Ann Widdecombe made a rather unlikely debut with the Royal Opera in the cameo speaking role of the haughty Duchesse de Crackentorp in Donizetti's effervescent comedy.

The part was first performed in Laurent Pelly's joyously knockabout production by the divine Dawn French five years ago.

Widdy is, of course, no new Dawn. As an actress, she inhabits more of a twilight zone, somewhere between a creature of the night (old bat), grumpy Lady Bracknell and diminutive pocket battleaxe.

She speaks mainly in grotesquely accented French, but manages a few gags about Cornish pasties, the Olympics and 'Strictly'. There's even a suitably Parliamentarian 'Order, order!'

Mugging, stamping and glaring, she is endearingly dreadful, though the benevolent Covent Garden audience gave her an affectionate ovation. Widdy's a trouper, that's for sure.

There were rather more meaningful cheers for the singers in this wonderful ensemble evening. Donizetti's tuneful farce calls for elaborate vocal cascades, including the celebrated string of top Cs in the showpiece tenor aria. We were not short-changed.

The story tells of the romantic adventures of a feisty battlefield orphan, adopted by a regiment during the Napoleonic Wars. Director Pelly here updates the action to the First World War, and treats the piece like a Gilbert and Sullivan operetta, full of chorus capers and visual gags.

The Italian soprano, Patrizia Ciofi, makes her role debut here as Marie, the daughter of the regiment of the title, with South African coloratura tenor Colin Lee as her Tyrolean lover, Tonio.

Miss Ciofi, like the French soprano Natalie Dessay before her, turns Marie into a lovable scamp, as adept at peeling bucketloads of potatoes and ironing the regiment's shirts as she is at spinning her vocal delights.

And though Lee doesn't quite eclipse memories of bel canto king Juan Diego Florez, he is a likeable and nonchalant Tonio, accomplishing his tour de force of nine consecutive top Cs with gleaming assurance.

Ann Murray, Alan Opie and Donald Maxwell add accomplished support, and conductor Yves Abel ensures that the orchestral fireworks blaze brightly.

Daily Mail 20 April 2012

Don't ridicule me, killer Breivik tells prosecutor

Bo Wilson

MASS killer Anders Breivik today told his prosecutor not to ridicule him as she attempted to show that his alleged Europe-wide network of Right-wing extremists does not exist.

The Norwegian, who began the third day of his trial by giving a fist salute, appeared irritated by her questions and repeatedly refused to name other members of the network.

The prosecution has said it does not believe that Breivik's so-called "Knights Templar" group exists "in the way he describes it". Breivik insists it does, and said police simply had not done a good enough job in uncovering it.

The issue is of key importance in deciding on his sanity, which will determine whether the Oslo court gives him a prison sentence or compulsory psychiatric care for his bombing and shooting massacre.

Breivik, who killed 77 people last July, gave few details. Public prosecutor Svein Holden told him the purpose of her questions was to shed doubt on the existence of the purported network.

He said he hoped she would "ridicule me less and stick to the events". The prosecutor asked him: "Why are you smiling?" He replied: "Because you're asking me questions you know I'm not going to answer."

Irritated: Breivik at court in Oslo today

The judge told him he had the right to remain silent – but not answering questions could be held against him.

Breivik said: "Anyone could do what I did. Not everyone is born with a backbone but you can develop one."

The killer told the court he met a Serbian nationalist in Liberia in 2001 and also travelled to London for meetings but refused to elaborate. He claims to have carried out the attacks on behalf of the Knights Templar group, which he describes as a militant nationalist group fighting Muslim colonisation of Europe.

The prosecution showed the court an excerpt from his 1,500-page manifesto in which he said he had contacts with "Serbian cultural conservatives".

Breivik wrote in it that they did a "complete screening and background check" to ensure that he was of "the desired calibre".

He claimed the group was considering "several hundred" individuals across Europe for a training course.

Breivik admits he set off a bomb outside the government headquarters in Oslo, killing eight, then drove to Utoya island outside the capital and massacred 69 people in a shooting spree at the governing Labor Party's youth summer camp.

Yesterday he boasted it was the most "spectacular" attack by a nationalist militant since the Second World War.

He said his victims, mostly teenagers, were legitimate targets because they were the representatives of a "multiculturalist" regime he claims is deconstructing Norway's identity by allowing immigration. The trial continues.

Daily Mail 20 April 2012

I fled Breivik after he sh

Student tells court how killer found her hiding behind a piano

Mark Wilkinson

A STUDENT who was shot four times by Anders Breivik told of her incredible battle for survival.

Ina Rangønes Libak was shot in the face, both arms and in her chest by the gunman but managed to run away before he could kill her.

She told his trial in Oslo how Breivik found her hiding behind a piano in a café on the island of Utøya last July.

The 22-year-old said she felt sure she was going to die, saying: "I remember all the shots that hit me. I think I was first shot in the arms and I thought, okay, I can survive this, it's okay if you're shot in the arms. Then I was shot in the jaw. I thought, this is a lot more serious. Then I was shot in the chest and I thought, okay, this is going to kill me."

But somehow she managed to run away down a corridor. "I started to feel that I am stumbling, falling, I don't have full control over my body and I'm thinking, okay, I'm going to die. This is how it feels to die." Outside the café, she and others tried to use rocks and clothes to stem the bleeding.

Ms Libak told the court that despite the danger her friends stayed by her side: "None of them chose to save their own lives and run. They said we are all together in this." The group held their breath as Breivik approached, eventually coming to within two metres but he failed to spot them.

It was only when she made it onto a

ot me four times

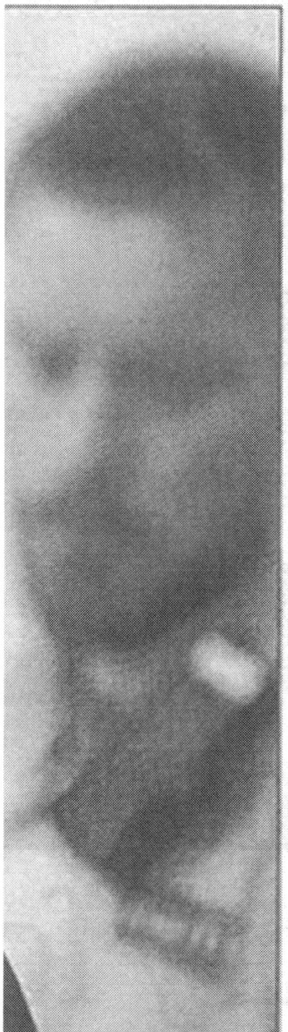

Gun rampage: Anders Breivik listening to the evidence at the Oslo court today

boat to take her to the mainland that Ms Libak thought she might survive.

She spent almost a month in hospital but has recovered enough to continue her course in international environment and development studies, and take all her exams. Breivik admits the 69 killings on Utøya, and eight more in a bomb attack in Oslo.

The trial's outcome hinges on whether the court finds Breivik to have been sane or not, as it could determine whether he is sent to prison or to a psychiatric institution.

A teenager told the trial how she only lived because she hid under another victim's body. Ingvild Leren Stensrud, 17, told the court of the "dreadful seconds" as she waited for Breivik to leave the building where he had shot 13 people dead. She then used a dead girl's phone to try to call emergency services.

When she couldn't get through, she called her mother and told her she had been shot, but hung up because she did not dare speak any longer.

The girl said: "I did not dare to talk too loud with my mother. I do not think they (her family) understood what was going on. I just had to hang up."

She explained that "mobile phones were ringing everywhere but no one was picking up".

The victim said there were a number of dead and injured people around her and she was afraid she was going to bleed to death.

Ms Stensrud also claimed she heard Breivik shouting with joy while he was shooting. The killer has denied this allegation. The trial continues.

Evening Standard 16 May 2012

THE INDEPENDENT
MONDAY 16 APRIL 2012

INSIDE THE MIND OF ANDERS BREIVIK

As the trial of one of Europe's worst serial killers begins, the psychiatrists who have got to know him speak out. **Lene Wold** reports

They met for the first time on 19 February: Terje Torrisen, the Norwegian psychiatrist given the task of assessing the sanity of a mass murderer, and Anders Behring Breivik, the man who today goes on trial for one of the most shocking crimes in European post-war history.

Breivik was well-mannered and co-operative, according to Mr Torrisen: "My first impression was that he was a polite man. He was answering all of our questions and did whatever he could to make the process as smooth as possible."

Throughout the 24-hour-a-day observation Mr Torrisen and the rest of his team were able to watch and analyse how the self-confessed mass murderer eats, sleeps and interacts with others. When Breivik sleeps alone in his cell – or spends time weight-training, or reading world history – the team has always been around him, scrutinising his behaviour for more than 200 hours, building up the most complete profile of Norway's worst-ever serial killer.

"He's not like a normal person," Mr Torrisen told *The Independent*, seemingly stating the obvious by adding that Breivik has an extreme personality. "During conversations, he is friendly," Mr Torrisen explained. He said Breivik spends a lot of time, as he has done during his handful of public appearances, talking about his own thoughts and political opinions. He "smiles every time he discovers himself in newspapers or on television," Mr Torrisen said.

Breivik has told the psychiatrists and doctors that he is "incredibly proud" of what he has done, and that "the operation was a major ego boost, in a way *I am probably a little attention-whore*".

Last week, Mr Torrisen and Agnar Aspas, the other analyst to assess Breivik's mental state, delivered a report about his mental health to the court in Oslo. The report was commissioned after an earlier assessment declared him insane. According to newspapers in Norway, the new report – still confidential – concludes that Breivik has a narcissistic and antisocial personality disorder – a diagnosis that has certain similarities with other psychopaths. It concludes, however, that he is mentally fit enough to face trial.

Most people who have met Breivik in prison say he seems happy, a person who wants to talk about his ideology like religious people talk about Jesus. On the one hand, he is an educated and polite man who hangs up the jackets of all his visitors, learns their names and questions their well-being. But he is also a heartless killer who discusses his mass murder as a formality; he blushes when he talks about his executions, doctors say.

Because of a lack of empathy for his victims the first forensic psychiatrists diagnosed Breivik with paranoid schizophrenia, and declared him to be criminally insane.

According to Dr Randi Rosenqvist, who has assessed Breivik, the mass murderer found it "funny" that he had been classified as being a schizophrenic. "I asked what he thought about the investigators' conclusions, and he answered almost in a humorous way that he 'didn't recognise himself at all'," Dr Rosenqvist wrote in her report.

She said that Breivik compared his new life in prison to being in a "kindergarten", where he can ring on a bell to get cigarettes.

But Breivik did not like the fact that he had been declared insane. He wrote a 35-page letter to several newspapers, listing 200 points that explained why the diagnosis was wrong.

"I must honestly admit that this is the worst thing that could have happened to me. It is the ultimate humiliation. Sending a political activist to a mental hospital is more sadistic and crueller than killing him. It's a fate worse than death."

His defence lawyer Geir Lippestad said that Breivik was "very satisfied" when he heard about the conclusions of the second examination.

But while psychiatrists and psychologists struggle to understand the personality of the man behind the attacks on Oslo and Utoya in July last year, people in Norway seem more interested in bringing him to court.

"The discussion around Breivik has been too concentrated around his mental state and not the right-wing extremist network that triggered and inspired him," Eivind Rindal, a survivor from Utoya said.

He hoped that the trial, which starts today and which is due to last for the next 10 weeks, will herald the start of a debate about the dangers of extremism in Norway and Europe, and not spark more attention about Breivik's health.

"We might never understand him, but we are going to judge him," commented Mr Rindal.

"He's not a normal person. He smiles every time he sees himself in the newspapers, or on television"
TERJE TORRISEN
Psychiatrist who assessed Anders Breivik

Ahead of his trial at a courthouse in Oslo, top left, a report on Anders Breivik declared he was mentally fit to face the charges
STOYAN NENOV/REUTERS

I'M STILL HAUNTED A SURVIVOR'S TALE

Kristian Kragh Lundø wanted to save the world; but that was a year ago. These days, mostly, he is trying to save himself. The 18-year-old is pursued by demons – well, one in particular that looms when he sleeps; threatens to return when he drops his guard. The trial of fanatical, right-wing gun and bomb attacker Anders Behring Breivik, beginning today, brings the prospect of healing; but also recollection of the horror he unleashed.

A year ago, Kristian, was a regular Norwegian teenager. His plans were no more ambitious than to enjoy a few sunny summer days at the small island of Utoya with his friends during a camp organised by the Norwegian Labour party. "We heard three shots fired, but like everyone else, we thought it was just someone making a bad joke," he says.

"Then we heard more shots and some youths came running towards us. I could tell how frightened they were by the terrified look on their faces. The sound of the shots came closer. Projectiles flew everywhere around me. I heard the buzzing sound that bullets make when they are really close to your body.

"In the period after the attack, I had trouble sleeping. When I slept, I had nightmares where memories from the island haunted my dreams. I realised that I had to take control over my own destiny if I wanted to move past what happened. That was an important step in handling the grief. I try to begin every day with a smile and with time it's gotten easier.

"I have visited Utoya once since the atrocities. I went back on the national memorial day a month after the attacks because I felt a need to. I wanted to show my parents where I had been. I needed to see the place where some of my friends had lost their lives."

CHARLOTTE SUNDBERG

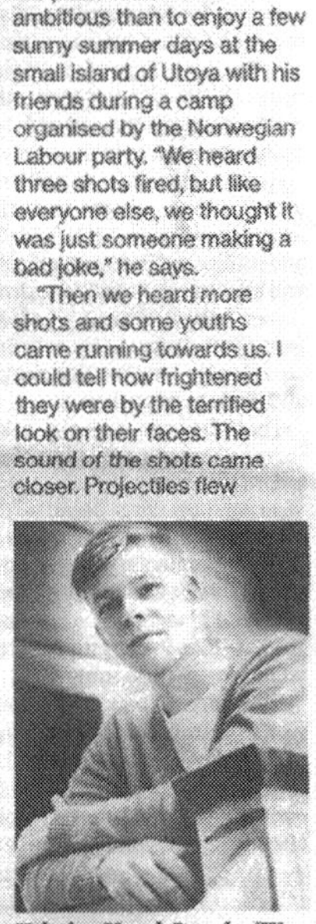

Kristian Kragh Lundø: 'We thought it was a bad joke'

The Independant 16 April 2012

Sentence me to death or set me free: Breivik pleads with court

Killer shows strain on day of tough questioning – as doubt is cast on claims he had English mentor

By TONY PATERSON

Norway's self-confessed mass killer, Anders Behring Breivik, angrily dismissed the prospect of a lengthy jail term as "pathetic" yesterday and insisted that the death penalty or acquittal were the only "logical" legal responses to his slaughter of 77 people last year.

The 33-year-old right wing fanatic's outburst came after tough questioning from prosecutors on the third day of his trial for carrying out Norway's worst acts of violence since the Second World War. He killed eight in an Oslo bomb blast and shot dead 69 young people attending a Labour Party summer camp last July.

"If I had feared death, I would not have dared to carry out this operation," Breivik boasted to the court in support of his death penalty plea. Observers said his angry and illogical remarks showed that he was beginning to feel the strain of cross examination. Norway abolished the death penalty in 1979.

His outburst followed detailed questioning about his claims to belong to a militant anti-Islamic terrorist organisation called the "Knights Templar" which prosecutors do not believe exists.

Breivik told the court yesterday that prior to carrying out his 2011 massacre, he was "ordained" in London by the group. Pressed about its authenticity, Breivik snapped back at examining prosecutor Inga Bejer Engh, saying "it was not an organisation in the conventional sense" but a group made up of "independent cells".

He then gave the court a brief glimpse into the bizarre and seemingly infantile fantasy world of the so-called "Knights Templar" in which Breivik claimed his English "mentor" was codenamed after the 12th-century crusader "Richard the Lionheart" and Breivik himself was ordained "Sigurd" after a 12th-century Norwegian monarch.

Anders Behring Breivik walks to take his seat in the witness box on day three of his murder trial in Oslo yesterday

Breivik is said to have attended a meeting of the "Knights Templar" in a café in London in the spring of 2002. He told the court that one of the group's founding members was a Serb nationalist "war hero" who he met in Liberia in 2002. In his manifesto Breivik described the group's members as "brilliant political and military tacticians of Europe".

His descriptions echoed the "manifesto" Breivik posted online shortly before he carried out his devastating attacks. It included a theatrical photographic portrait of him dressed in a black tunic which was covered with sinister pseudo insignia including a death's head pierced by a medieval sword.

The outcome may hinge on whether the Knights Templar group exists or is in Brevik's imagination

Under detailed questioning about the group, he insisted he had not made up anything but refused to comment further. "It is not in my interest to shed light on details that could lead to arrests," he said.

Relatives and friends of Breivik's victims sat behind a bullet proof glass screen as they witnessed the killer making his claims. "I think what we are watching is the revelation of some sort of fantasy or dream," said Christian Bjelland, of the survivors' support group.

Whether the "Knights Templar" exist or are merely a figment of Breivik's imagination is likely to be one of the key factors which will determine the outcome of the trial. If judges rule the group is a fantasy organisation, it will support the conclusion of one psychiatric report which argues that Breivik is a schizophrenic who should spend the rest of his life in care.

However a second psychiatric report recently found Breivik to be sane. If judges accept these findings, he could face a maximum 21-year jail term followed by a custody arrangement which would almost certainly keep him in prison for much longer. Breivik has told his lawyers that he will do all he can to prove to the court that he is sane, not least because a verdict of insanity would completely undermine all his claims.

Leonard Cohen with his former manager and lover, Kelley Lynch

Cohen's ex-manager jailed for harassment

By GUY ADAMS
in Los Angeles

There ain't no cure for love but an 18-month prison sentence might go some way towards persuading Leonard Cohen's former mistress and business manager to consign their tattered relationship to the dustbin.

Kelley Lynch, who worked with Mr Cohen for 17 years before being sacked in 2004, is now behind bars after a court in Los Angeles found her guilty of violating restraining orders by sending him thousands of abusive emails and phone messages. Her sentencing brings to a temporary close a bizarre scandal in which the 77-year-old singer was defrauded of millions of dollars.

A judge said that Lynch, 55, continued to show "no remorse" after being found guilty last week of violating protective orders and of harassment. The court heard how she left hundreds of explicit phone messages with his friends and family.

Lynch's campaign of harassment began in 2004 when Mr Cohen suddenly sacked her, saying that she had stolen \$5m (£3.1m) from his bank accounts and other investments. A court in Los Angeles agreed, ordering Lynch – who for a brief period had also been the singer's lover – to pay him \$9.5m in compensation. However, she failed to pay. In 2008, Mr Cohen toured for the first time in 15 years, apparently to pay the debts he was saddled with.

The Independent 19 April 2012

'They were not innocent. I acted in defence of my culture. I would do it again'

By David Blair in Oslo

ANDERS BEHRING BREIVIK, flushed with boastful self-righteousness, claimed yesterday that "goodness not evil" had caused him to murder 77 Norwegians, declaring: "I would have done it again."

The far Right killer showed no contrition or humility when the court in Oslo allowed him 65 minutes to read a personal statement on the second day of his trial.

Breivik came close to arguing that he killed 67 members of the youth wing of the Norwegian Labour Party, most of them teenagers, out of justified retribution. They were "not innocent", he said, but "young people who were actively working to uphold multiculturalism". Their organisation was comparable "to the Hitler Youth".

Yet the man who said his crimes were designed to save Europe from destruction at the hands of radical Islam came out as an admirer of al-Qaeda. Osama bin Laden's creation was the "most successful revolutionary force in the world", said Breivik, and European ultra-nationalists had much to learn from its cell structure and "cult of martyrdom".

He disclosed that his own rampage through Oslo on July 22 last year had been a "so-called suicide attack" that he had not expected to survive.

Yesterday's session consisted of nothing but Breivik stating his views and being cross-examined. As such, this hearing before a hushed and subdued court provided the first public insight into the world view and mentality of one of the worst killers in Europe's modern history. Crucially, it will also help the court to rule on the contested question of his sanity, which will decide whether he goes to prison or a mental institution.

On Monday, Wenche Elizabeth Arntzen, the presiding judge, said that Breivik's statement would take 30 minutes. In the event, he was afforded over an hour. Justice Arntzen interrupted four times to demand restraint, but Breivik was never silenced. Norwegians had to listen as he claimed that a concern for "human rights and international law" had led him to detonate a car bomb in the centre of their capital, before carrying out the Utoya island massacre.

"This was the most sophisticated and spectacular political attack committed in Europe since the Second World War," boasted Breivik. "If one can force the Norwegian Labour Party to change their immigration policy by executing 77 people, that will contribute to holding our values and culture."

Reading a 20-page statement that he had spent months preparing in prison, Breivik looked directly at the judges. "I acted in defence of my culture and of my people and so I ask to be acquitted," he said.

Earlier, he had turned on the media, denouncing "100 per cent of" the world's news organisations for "pumping out multicultural propaganda 24 hours a day". Inexplicably, they were also portraying him as a "pathetic and mean loser without integrity".

With a special tone of indignation, Breivik added: "It has been suggested that I'm a child-killer despite not being indicted for killing anyone under the age of 14."

He would have preferred to bomb a journalists' conference in Oslo, but "unfortunately" that attack had been impossible to organise in time.

Numerous figures from history had inspired his struggle as a "Knight Templar", said Breivik, singling out Sitting Bull, the native American chief who defeated General Custer at the Battle of Little Bighorn, and Enoch Powell, the late Conservative politician.

Recalling Powell's infamous speech from 1968, Breivik said: "Enoch Powell predicted that rivers of blood would flow through our streets. Unfortunately no one listened to him, or to the other Enoch Powells in Europe."

Britain came up repeatedly during Breivik's testimony. Luton was a city where the indigenous population "and even emergency vehicles" were unable to enter large areas, allegedly because of the depredations of Muslim immigrants.

"And three out of five Englishmen believe the UK has turned into a dysfunctional society because of multiculturalism," added Breivik, citing an opinion poll which he said had appeared in *The Times* in 2010.

The "Knights Templar" had been founded in London in 2002, he claimed, although the prosecution believe it to be a figment of his imagination.

Turning to American inspirations, Breivik lamented that Europe had never possessed "an anti-Communist like McCarthy to prevent Marxists from infiltrating universities and schools". He added: "McCarthy was far too moderate. He thought about deporting all American Communists to the Soviet Union, but unfortunately he did not do so."

After venting his phobies unchallenged, Breivik, 33, finally faced cross-examination. Inga Bejer Engh, the softly spoken prosecutor, did not attempt a bruising confrontation in the style of the Old Bailey. Instead, she politely and persistently tied Breivik in knots.

"Who gave you the authority to take the lives of Norwegians?" she asked. Breivik squirmed around this question for the best part of 20 minutes before confessing that he gave himself the "mandate" to kill Norwegians in order to rescue them.

As for Breivik's own past, Ms Engh forced him to admit that all of his various business ventures were hopeless failures until, at last, he set up an internet company selling fake diplomas, yielding a profit of £436,000. Peddling forged certificates was, he admitted, "morally despicable".

Along the way, Breivik had also evaded taxes, dodged Norway's compulsory military service, invented a story about having his nose broken by a Muslim, and lied about gaining a business degree from an American university.

After dropping out of secondary school, the killer claimed to have spent 15,000 hours in private study to remedy his lack of formal education. "And what," asked the prosecutor, "was your main source of information?" Breivik's answer was emphatic: "Wikipedia," he said. "The English articles there contained a lot of information."

When he became an ultra-nationalist, he described himself as rising to be "commander of a cell" of the "Knights Templar". Under questioning, he admitted that he was the sole member of the cell he commanded. There were, apparently, two other "one-man cells" in Norway.

The aim was to defend Christian civilisation from the incoming tide of Muslim migrants. But Ms Engh brough Breivik's flow of rhetoric to an abrupt halt by asking: "Do you consider yourself a Protestant?" After a long pause, he replied: "I have not been a religious person, but there's a proverb that there are no atheists in the trenches. I'm a member of the Church of Norway, but I'm more drawn towards the Catholic church."

Again and again, Breivik returned to the subject of his lack of education. "It's important to signal that one is not without knowledge," he said. "You could see me as a salesman: I sell ideology, a view of life."

Devoid of shame about massacring defenceless teenagers, Breivik appears tormented by his failure to go to university. The case continues.

Judge who called for death penalty is sacked

One of the three lay judges trying Breivik was dismissed yesterday because he posted a comment on Facebook calling for him to be executed. "The death penalty is the only just sentence in this case," read the message posted by Thomas Indrebo on July 23 last year, the day after Breivik killed 77 people.

Judge Wenche Elizabeth Arntzen ruled that he should be replaced by lay judge Elisabeth Wisloff, one of two back-ups.

Breivik is being tried by two professional judges and three lay judges for the crime of mass-killing with the aim of terrorising a population. It is they who will rule on whether he faces a maximum prison sentence of 21 years, or compulsory psychiatric treatment.

Richard Orange, Oslo

Anders Behring Breivik in court yesterday. During his statement, he cited, from left, Enoch Powell for his 'rivers of blood' speech, Senator Joe McCarthy, the anti-Communist whom he described as too moderate, and Sitting Bull, the Native American chief

New blow for Sarkozy as Chirac 'backs rival'

By Henry Samuel in Paris

JACQUES CHIRAC will vote for the Socialist presidential candidate in elections on Sunday rather than his fellow conservative Nicolas Sarkozy, a close friend has confirmed.

The support will be unwelcome news for Mr Sarkozy, who is tipped to lose heavily to François Hollande in a second round run-off, as his predecessor in the Elysée Palace is now polled as one of France's best-loved political figures, despite a corruption conviction.

Mr Chirac's wife, Bernadette, has been campaigning for Mr Sarkozy, even speaking in campaign rallies. Mr Chirac suffers from Alzheimer's disease and is now rarely seen in public.

When the 79-year-old former president first publicly suggested he would back Mr Hollande last June, he and his family subsequently sought to laugh it off as a joke. But on Tuesday, the French historian Jean-Luc Barré, who helped Mr Chirac to write his memoirs, told *Le Parisien* newspaper that he was deadly serious in backing Mr Hollande, who, like him, has built his rural power base in the south-central Corrèze region.

"Jacques Chirac is true to himself when he says he will vote for François Hollande," Mr Barré said. "I visit him frequently. After four years of discussions I believe I'm one of those who knows best how he thinks."

Relations between Mr Chirac and Mr Sarkozy have been notoriously chequered. After idolising the man who gave him his first political break, Mr Sarkozy held up his former mentor as his antithesis – a feckless *roi fainéant* (idle king) who "fiddles the locks of Versailles while Paris burns".

He famously betrayed Mr Chirac by resigning as his campaign manager in the 1995 presidential election and backing his rival, Edouard Balladur. At the time, he was very close to Mr Chirac's son Claude. When Mr Sarkozy dropped the Chirac clan, Mrs Chirac is said to have cried: "And to think he saw us in our nightshirts."

Despite, that, she has become a staunch supporter during this campaign, declaring that Mr Hollande "doesn't have the build of a French president".

Mr Chirac broke his silence on his one-time protégé last year when he described him as "nervous", "impetuous" and untrustworthy in his memoirs, saying he did not share the same "vision of France". Meanwhile, he heaped praise on Mr Hollande, saying he had the stuff of a true "statesman".

However, a spokesman for the office of the former president said: "Nobody is entitled to express themselves in the name of Jacques Chirac, who will make no public declaration in this election."

Mr Sarkozy said he was "sad" that others were seeking to speak in Mr Chirac's name.

Assange starts his TV show with a terrorist

By Tom Parfitt in Moscow

JULIAN ASSANGE interviewed the Hizbollah chief Hassan Nasrallah in the first episode yesterday of his provocative new show on RT, the Russian-government's English-language propaganda channel.

Nasrallah, considered a terrorist by the US and Britain, spoke to the WikiLeaks founder via a video link from a secret location in Lebanon in his first appearance on a foreign TV station in three years.

Mr Assange, 40, who is on bail in Britain while he fights extradition to Sweden on sex crime allegations, had promised a "notorious" first guest on his 12-episode show, *The*

The Daily Telegraph 18 April 2012

Execute me or set me

Killer says jail is 'pathetic punishment' for massacre

He claims he has sacrificed himself to inspire others

Helen Pidd Oslo

PHOTOGRAPH: LISE ASERUD/AP

Anders Behring Breivik would rather be executed than receive Norway's "pathetic" maximum punishment of 21 years in jail for the bomb and gun attacks that left 77 dead last summer, he told a court yesterday.

"There are only two just and fair outcomes in this case," he told Oslo central court: "Acquittal or capital punishment."

He said he didn't want to be killed, but said he would "respect" the decision. "I consider 21 years of prison as a pathetic punishment," he said, later describing himself as a "militant Christian" who believed in the afterlife.

Norway abolished the death penalty in peacetime in 1905 and for war crimes in 1979. On Tuesday, one of the five original judges trying the case was dismissed after it emerged he had written on Facebook that the death penalty was the "only just thing to do" with Breivik.

During his second day in the witness box, the 33-year-old was questioned about his claims to be part of a militant anti-Islamist network founded in London in 2002 called Knights Templar, which the prosecution does not believe exists. Breivik is adamant that it does - and that police haven't tried hard enough to uncover it.

He also claimed yesterday he knew of two other "one-man cells" in Norway that could attack at any time.

Declaring himself an "anti-Nazi", Breivik said Knights Templar had made a conscious decision to distance itself from national socialism "because it was quite blood-stained". He added: "We felt it completely essential to do so. For the extreme right to ever be able to prevail in Europe in the future, one had to distance oneself from the old-school ideology."

The difference between him and Hitler, he said, was that "the pillar of National Socialism is expansionism; I am an isolationist". He was also "more liberal on ethnicity" than the Nazis, he added, suggesting he could accept it if "around 2%" of Norway's population was "non-indigenous".

The Knights Templar cultural identity was imported from Serbia, he said. The Serbs who died during the Nato bombing of Kosovo in 1999 had a "crusader" mentality to which he aspired. Questioned about his radicalisation, he said that the Serbian bombing was for him "the straw that broke the camel's back".

Breivik claims he travelled to London in April 2002 to meet three other "militant nationalists" to form the network, which borrowed the methodology of al-Qaida.

Establishing whether Knights Templar exists beyond Breivik's imagination is of key importance in legally determining his sanity, and whether he is sent to prison or compulsory psychiatric care for the massacre on 22 July last year.

Though the longest sentence the court could impose is 21 years, Breivik could be locked up for life if there was "considerable danger" he could strike again. The court always fixes a timeframe that may not exceed 21 years, but when that expires, the offender may be reassessed.

The prosecution spent the morning session asking Breivik about trips he made to Liberia and London in 2002. Breivik was questioned in detail about the three people he claimed to have met in London, but refused to reveal any details, including the identity of the "English protestant host" who became his "mentor". That man is named in his 1,801-page manifesto as Richard the Lionheart.

He claimed that his visit to Liberia was made to visit a Serbian war "hero" wanted for war crimes. He refused to reveal the man's name.

free, Breivik tells Norway court

Expert view A life of fantasy

Anders Behring Breivik has no coherent ideology. Instead, he appears to have picked bits of numerous rightwing philosophical strands and attempted to weave them together as his own.

Breivik comes from a conservative Christian background, into which he has incorporated nationalist and racist ideologies, adopting the politics and language of the "counter-jihad" movement that believes Islam is a major threat to western civilisation.

In targeting government buildings and the youth wing of Norway's ruling Labour party, Breivik was attacking those he blamed for the rise of Islam. Some 375 pages of his "manifesto" were quotes from other people.

Breivik is not a neo-Nazi. Rather, he reflects the changing face of the modern far-right. He has drawn from the Serbian conflict and the activities of the Serb paramilitary groups the White Eagles and the Tigers.

I do not believe Breivik's Knights Templars exist. Perhaps he got the idea from Paul Ray, one of the founders of the English Defence League, who claims to run the Ancient Order of the Templar Knights. Or from Swedish author Jan Guillou's Templar knight Arn, who kills "for king or country".

Breivik's political rantings reflect a life of fantasy. From dressing up in uniforms to falsifying certificates, here was a man always desperate to be somebody else. **Nick Lowles**
The author is director of Hope Not Hate

Breivik indicated that he saw himself a martyr who had "sacrificed himself" in order to inspire others. True role models can achieve credibility through "an action, an operation" he said, comparing himself with "keyboard warriors" who spread their message via the internet.

Asked by the prosecutor if he had gained credibility among such groups since the 22 July attacks, Breivik agreed, before adding: "It would be incorrect of me to say anything about that, but what is true is that there are many keyboard warriors who have tried to promote things that can improve us ... but they face serious problems because it's difficult to promote martyrdom when you fear death yourself and you are afraid to fight yourself."

'For the extreme right to prevail, one had to distance oneself from the [Nazi] ideology'

He contrasted his "operation" with the leftwing German terrorist group known as the Red Army Faction, or Baader Meinhof gang, who he said were atheists who did not want to die because they "didn't believe in the afterlife". He added: "That's what's unique about both militant nationalists and militant Islamists ... we do believe in an afterlife, at least many of us [militant nationalists] do, because we are Christians."

Breivik admits he set off a bomb outside the government headquarters in Oslo, killing eight, then drove to Utøya island outside the capital and massacred 69 people in a shooting spree at the governing Labour party's youth summer camp. He said his victims, mostly teenagers, were not innocent but legitimate targets because they were representatives of a "multiculturalist" regime he claims is deconstructing Norway's national identity by allowing immigration.

The Guardian 19 April 2012

International

Breivik planned to film beheading of former PM

Gro Brundtland visited Utøya just before massacre

Anti-Muslim fanatic had planned three car bombs

Helen Pidd Oslo

Anders Behring Breivik has told a court that his "primary target" in last year's terrorist attacks was a former prime minister whom he planned to behead, posting the footage on the internet – and that he anticipated all 564 people on Utøya would die in his "operation".

Giving evidence on the fourth day of his trial, the 33-year-old said he would have preferred to carry out three bomb attacks rather than target Utøya, where the Norwegian Labour party was holding its annual youth summer camp on 22 July last year. In the end, he went on the rampage on the island after planting one bomb in Oslo's government district, killing eight people.

Breivik claimed he was "forced" to carry out the massacre on the island, which left 69 dead, because Norwegian and EU regulations had made it difficult to acquire sufficient bomb-making equipment.

Bombing was much easier on the emotions than pulling a gun trigger, he said. "It's easy to press a button and detonate a bomb. It's very, very difficult to carry out something as barbaric as a firearm-based action."

To do so, he claimed, was not natural. 'It is contrary to human nature to execute something like this," he said. "You have to work on yourself for a very long time to make yourself do this ... to hammer away at your emotions."

His original plan for the attack on Utøya was to time his arrival on the island with a visit from Gro Harlem Brundtland, a former Labour prime minister of Norway. Breivik told the court he planned to handcuff her, before "decapitating" her using a bayonet on his rifle and then filming the execution on an iPhone.

"The plan was to chop her head off with [the bayonet] while reading a text and then upload the film to the internet," he said.

Brundtland was his main target, said Breivik, adding that he nonetheless expected everyone else on the island to die. "The objective was not to kill 69 people on Utøya. The objective was to kill all of them," he said, explaining that he planned to scare the campers into the water.

"The main goal was to use the water

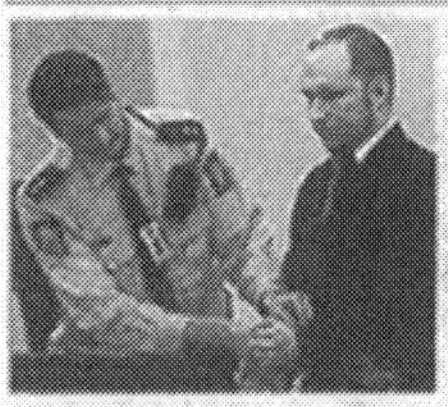

Breivik claimed he was 'forced' to carry out the Utøya massacre because he could not source enough fertiliser to make three bombs

as a mass destruction method. Basically, I assumed most people would drown," adding that "it's hard to swim if you have death anxiety".

Brundtland survived, having left the island by the time Breivik arrived.

Breivik insisted those he killed on Utøya, some as young as 14, were "legitimate targets". He said: "I am not a child murderer. I believe that all political activists who choose to fight for multiculturalism ... and have leadership positions are legitimate targets."

He admitted he would rather have bombed the parliament or the Labour party congress, but that it took him far longer than he anticipated to make the bomb, and by the time he was finished, parliament was in recess.

Breivik revealed his original plan was

Princess Mette-Marit, left, Eskil Pedersen, the Labour youth movement chairman, and Gro Harlem Brundtland, front Photograph: Jörg Carstensen/EPA

to also bomb two other targets in the Norwegian capital: the Labour party's office and a third target, possibly the royal palace, the parliament or the headquarters of the newspapers Aftenposten and Dagsavisen.

"I settled on the palace in a setting where the royal family wouldn't be hurt," he said. "Most nationalists and cultural conservatives are supporters of the monarchy, including myself."

The anti-Muslim fanatic said the three bombs would be followed by several shooting massacres, if he survived. He decided against multiple bombs because building one was "much more difficult than I thought".

Yet Breivik also said that "if it hadn't been for the EU and Norway's rules on explosives ... there would have been three car bombs". It was very difficult to source the sufficient amount of fertiliser required to make a bomb, he claimed. In order to acquire the necessary amount, he had to rent a farm with the requisite area of land so that the fertiliser companies would not get suspicious and "flag" him to the security services.

It was from a farm about 140km northeast of Oslo, that he made the bomb, which killed eight in the capital's government district.

Earlier Breivik revealed that he had practised shooting by playing the computer game Call of Duty: Modern Warfare.

The court also heard Breivik took what he called a sabbatical for a year between the summers of 2006 and 2007, which he devoted to playing another game, World of Warcraft (WoW), "hardcore" full time.

But he insisted WoW had nothing to do with the attacks. He said: "Some people like to play golf, some like to sail, I played WoW. It had nothing to do with 22 July. It's not a world you are engulfed by. It's simply a hobby."

The Guardian 20 April 2012

Comment editor: Becky Gardiner
Telephone: 020 3353 4995
Fax: 020 3353 3193
Email: comment@guardian.co.uk

Jonathan Freedland

Breivik is a terrorist, so why treat him like the chancellor?

We comb over every word from Oslo, but disregard al-Qaida's rants. The lack of consistency speaks volumes

Does Abu Qatada play World of Warcraft? Did he once, like Anders Behring Breivik, dedicate a sabbatical year to "hardcore" playing of the game? We don't know. Perhaps we will find out when Abu Qatada, often described as the spiritual leader of al-Qaida in Europe, finally faces trial. But I wouldn't bet on it.

For when alleged jihadists like Abu Qatada have been brought to trial, they don't quite get the treatment accorded to Breivik this week. If they are allowed to testify for five solid days, given an extended opportunity to expound their worldview, then the world's press do not hang on their every word, reporting in tweet-sized nuggets the nuances of their philosophy. Nor are their personal life histories, their psychology and video game habits, probed and debated.

Of course comparisons are tricky, not least because those who have staged the most lethal acts of jihadist violence - in New York, Madrid or London - have rarely lived to stand trial. But take this contrast. In Oslo, the court has been listening to a man who planted a bomb that killed eight and who went on to murder another 69 people, mostly teenagers, on the island of Utøya - a death spree Breivik described yesterday in terms that stop the heart. There has been copious discussion of Breivik's psyche and especially his views, starting with his courtroom lament that Norway had become "a dumping ground for the surplus births of the third world".

Contrast that with the airline bomb plot of 2006, in which an al-Qaida cell in Britain planned to blow seven transatlantic jets out of the sky. News reports of that trial offered a scant few lines about the conspirators' individual motives, with most of the coverage focused on operational details, the mechanics and scale, of the planned attack. My Guardian colleague Vikram Dodd, who covered that London trial, was struck when he heard a Radio 5 Live phone-in this week that was regularly interrupted by snippets from Breivik's statement. "The grammar of the coverage was as if this was the chancellor giving his budget," says Dodd.

More than one caller to that programme, while quick to insist they disagreed with Breivik's methods, did rather think the Norwegian had a point about multiculturalism run riot. "I can understand where this guy's coming from," said Tom from Dover. Several readers of a Guardian article sought to post comments in the same vein, calling for "a complete stop of immigration from Muslim countries" and suchlike. To listen to it, you'd think Breivik had simply wanted to start a debate, that he'd perhaps written a provocative pamphlet for Demos, rather than committed an act of murderous cruelty.

It was to avoid precisely this problem that the US Congress acted to relocate the prospective trial of Khalid Sheikh Mohammed, the alleged principal architect of the 9/11 attacks, from federal court in Manhattan to a military tribunal at Guantánamo. They did not want him enjoying the platform so gleefully exploited by Breivik. Perhaps they understood what the latter wrote in his 1,801-page manifesto, posted before the Utøya killings: "Your trial offers you a stage to the world."

The comparison is not so far-fetched. Breivik has expressed his admiration for al-Qaida's willingness to "embrace" death and was keen to adopt the organisation's methods: his ultimate goal last July was to behead Norway's former prime minister and post the video online. Like al-Qaida, he believes in acts of spectacular violence as a first step to changing the world, seeks to purge his own people of those deemed weak in the face of the enemy, yearns for a pure, past golden age that never existed, and dreams of apocalypse. Above all, he wants those he regards as his people to be unsullied by contact with inferior others. In this, Breivik and al-Qaida are kindred spirits.

What, then, is the right way to bring such people to justice? The cost of the Norwegian approach is that, by treating Breivik like any other defendant, the courts have given him that global megaphone. That represents a perverse reward for his actions: he would never have got such a hearing had he confined himself to ranting on a blog. More alarmingly, the Oslo trial has surely supplied an incentive to any would-be Breiviks: kill as he killed and you too will get the attention of the world.

And yet, by trying Mohammed behind closed doors, the US too has handed the forces of terror a kind of victory. They have declared there are limits to the open society, that the rule of law is not strong enough to cope with every eventuality. In a small way, they have conceded ground to the terrorists' view of the world. How much more appealing is the message of the Norwegian PM last summer, who declared his country would respond to Breivik with "more democracy, more openness and greater political participation".

Whichever approach we take to such crimes, Oslo's or Washington's, one duty is surely clear: we have to be consistent. We cannot apply different standards to terrorists depending on whether they are fanatics of the white supremacist or jihadist variety.

And yet we do just that. Scott Atran, an eminent anthropologist who has briefed American officials on the nature of terrorism, explains that we adopt radically different approaches depending on whether we believe the threat is from within or without.

Outside attackers, like the 9/11 hijackers, are treated only in terms of the impact and consequences of their actions; those who come from "our side", as the Norwegians see Breivik, are examined for their intentions, what made them act the way they did. Witness the case of Robert Bales, the US soldier who murdered 16 civilians in Afghanistan. "When it all comes out, it will be a combination of stress, alcohol and domestic issues - he just snapped," said the US military spokesman. It was personal, not political. Had it been an Afghan soldier killing Americans, it would have been the other way around.

It's clear why we might do this. We can unite against an outside enemy; if the threat is from within, we want to believe it amounts to no more than a single, lone madman. "People don't want to probe," says Atran. "They want to be reassured." But this division, instinctive as it might be, is not really defensible. Terrorist murder is terrorist murder, and we need to treat it that way - even when the killer looks like us.

Outside attackers are treated only in terms of the impact and consequences of their actions

Twitter: @j_freedland

The lengths we will go to

Muriel Gray

Running a marathon requires total dedication - from us sausage-banging supporters too

Tomorrow, millions will enjoy the festive spectacle that is the London marathon. TV pictures will cut between elite, beautiful Kenyans dodging the camera motorbikes, pantomime horses shaking buckets, and thousands of heads bobbing like popcorn on a griddle. They win the attention and admiration they so rightly deserve.

But on the other side of the barriers, standing steadfastly in all weathers, are the legions of camera-clutching, inflatable sausage-banging supporters - the men, women and children who have lived with their loved one through the gruelling months, sometimes years, of training. I'll be one of them. Our family has supported my husband through a decade of marathon running that's taken him from never having run at all to being a sub-three-hour competitor who's raised thousands of pounds for charity. However, despite our palpable pride, one feels duty-bound to pass on lessons learned in living with a runner that may inform those inspired to embark on a similar course.

The first sign of impending maratho ambition is the bathroom bulging with runners' magazines. These are apparently released monthly, yet are so uniformly identical in banal content with "Ten top tips for nutrition" and " turned my life around" regurgitated in every issue that their continuing sales remains a publishing miracle.

Your runner, following the brutal schedule impelled by these hectoring glossies, will then be virtually absent from family life. In their first marathon they will be nervous and slow, and this is the peak of your career as a supporte It's back there waiting for the five-hou plus runners, cheering on bearded me dressed as nurses and runners spewin up on the kerb, where the most uplifting events occur. The London Maratho after the 7/7 bombing atrocity was mar shalled largely by armed special branc officers poorly disguised as stewards. At that event we applauded a runner whose heartbreaking T-shirt revealed h was competing in memory of a recentl deceased young wife. Yards from the finish his toddler son was handed to him from the crowd and placed on his shoulders. It was too much. The man collapsed, and was utterly distraught. Quickly, the muscle-bound cop picked up the child, put him on his shoulders, lifted the man to his feet and helped hi limp over the finish line. Unforgettable

By the next marathon, however, your runner will speed up into a different group and the tears dry. Mid-range runners are serious, always in pain, and Superman capes are few and far between. This is when the danger of the marathon abroad creeps in. Never, ever believe you will have a "romantic weekend" in Paris to support someone running. You will spend half a day queueing to register in a concrete conference centre, and the other half searching for a shop that sells Vaseline. That evening you will pass every enticing French restaurant to find a touristy Italian that serves a Desperate Dan-size plate of bland pasta. Race day will find you running, wide-eyed with panic, to find the 18-mile marker in time, to stan with torn strips of Le Monde taped to a garden cane held above your head for hours to hand over the disgusting energy gel pack he's banking on.

Should they go sub-three, forget getting dewy eyed. Now it's just skinny men in running-club vests ignoring the clapping, and frowning as they tap GPS watches.

Yet every single moment is priceless. The marathon is a celebration of life's truly excellent things; ambition, self-discipline, health, dedication, love and remembrance. Just remember that thos of us waiting in the rain under the alpha bet family meeting signs, bursting with pride and ready with the sweatshirts, are all a part of it too. We love you.

Muriel Gray is an author and broadcaste

The Guardian 21 April 2012

Brides who take the tube diet to slim down for their wedding
Page 30

World

I was inspired by al-Qaeda to expand boundaries of terror, Breivik tells court

REUTERS; AP; AFP / GETTY IMAGES

Sitting facing the judges, Anders Breivik appears relaxed in the witness box yesterday. Behind him were two rows of survivors and relatives of his victims

Norway
David Charter Oslo

The man who claims to have massacred 77 people in the defence of Western values said yesterday that he drew inspiration for his "gruesome but necessary" killings from atrocities carried out by al-Qaeda.

Anders Behring Breivik used his first day in the witness box at his trial for terrorism and murder to paint himself as a martyr who was prepared to die carrying out attacks that were "based on goodness not evil".

Breivik, 33, who killed eight people in an Oslo bomb blast before embarking on a shooting spree at a young people's holiday camp that claimed 69 more lives, gave his customary right arm salute when he entered the courtroom.

Proceedings were delayed for an hour after revelations that one of the three lay judges had said on Facebook the day after the July 22 killings that the death penalty was the only fair outcome in the case. The judge was replaced.

For the first time Breivik showed a hint of regret — but only that he had been foiled in his plans to carry out his slaughter at a conference of journalists rather than at the gathering of the Young Labour Party activists on the island of Utoya.

He was questioned about the extent of the Knights Templar organisation that he once claimed was widespread in Europe. Yesterday he said it amounted to three active cells, each of one person, of whom he was one. There were also insights into his radicalisation as he claimed to have been in 20 confrontations with Muslims, one of which resulted in his nose being broken.

"Al-Qaeda is the most successful militant group in the world and I believe militant nationalists in Europe have a great deal to learn from them," he told the court. "We have attempted to introduce new traditions for militant nationalists in Europe and we have taken a bit from al-Qaeda and Islamists including the use of martyrdom. The resistance movement since the Second World War has been pathetic and we have to introduce new traditions."

These new traditions included atrocities so shocking that they pushed the boundaries of terror, he said, adding that he would do the same again.

He said that 9/11 created al-Qaeda to an extent and there was a leap forward in terms of methods. "In the beginning people were shocked."

Sitting facing the judges, with his back to two rows of survivors and relatives of victims, he appeared relaxed and was conversational with prosecutors. Allowed to make a 30-minute statement, he was warned several times to hurry up by Judge Wenche Elizabeth Arntzen, but each time went back to his prepared text. The statement took 73 minutes to read out.

As Breivik's statement overran, Mette Yvonne Larsen, a lawyer for the families, said: "I have had so many messages from relatives who are reacting to the fact that he is speaking this way, I have to ask him to show more consideration and stop now." The defence and prosecution insisted, however, that he be allow to continue.

He sought to justify his actions as a blow against multiculturalism which he said was destroying his country. "There are claims that I carried out the attacks because I was a pathetic and mean loser," Breivik said, reading in his quiet, thin voice from his notes. "They say I am insane and because of this I should be ignored and forgotten … They also claim I am narcissistic, that I have an incestuous relationship to my mother, that I like red sweaters, that I am a paedophile.

"This is only lies and propaganda and the answer is clear — I have carried out the most sophisticated, spectacular political attack committed in Europe since the Second World War."

At one point Breivik referred to an article from *The Times* in February 2010 which he said reported that "three out of five Englishmen believe that the UK has turned into a dysfunctional society as a result of multiculturalism".

Breivik also referred to Enoch Powell's "rivers of blood" speech about immigration made in 1968. "Unfortunately nobody listened to him or any of the Enoch Powells in Europe. Everyone has been censored and ignored and what do we see? Rivers of blood have flowed through Belgium, Toulouse, Madrid, and rivers have flowed from those who tried to save their culture through Oslo and Malmo."

One of the survivors of the island, Tore Sinding Bekkedal, who watched Breivik's evidence, said: "I have a difficult time being offended by things he says because, after all, he has killed friends so that sets the bar very high. This was a political assassination so his political views are a very relevant part of the court's judgment."

The trial continues.

Exclusive to subscribers
Audio exclusive
A survivor's story
thetimes.co.uk/norway

Killer wants to be found sane

Behind the story David Charter

The first thing that Anders Behring Breivik said yesterday was that he would tone down his rhetoric "out of concern for the relatives and victims".

He then proceeded to make a mockery of this absurd claim, comparing the Young Labour activists he slaughtered to the Hitler Youth and insisting that he acted out of "goodness, not evil" while those in court shook their heads in disbelief.

But Breivik's statement of concern was not really intended for the watching relatives or survivors.

A phalanx of psychologists is in court trying to assess the state of his mind. If judged to be sane, as he wishes, he will be sent to jail. If he is insane, he will be locked up in a secure hospital and treated.

Being labelled insane, Breivik has said, would be "a fate worse than death". Moreover, he believes that a verdict of sanity will give his hateful ideology greater legitimacy.

Breivik also repeatedly said in court that his 1,500-word manifesto was deliberately "pompous" in an attempt to inspire others. The subtext is that he has become self-aware and does not suffer from crazed delusions. But is he sane?

Paul Grondal, a forensic psychologist who is following the trial, said: "He is not obviously hallucinating, he does not have thought distractions, but he may have delusions which are very hard to detect."

Asked whether Breivik's claim to have toned down his rhetoric out of respect showed empathy and helped to demonstrate his sanity, Mr Grondal added: "He is talking about doing this but whether he is able to present a genuine empathetic feeling, I doubt it very much. I think it is all intellectual, all in his head."

Inside today
He is a test case for zero empathy
Simon Baron-Cohen, page 21

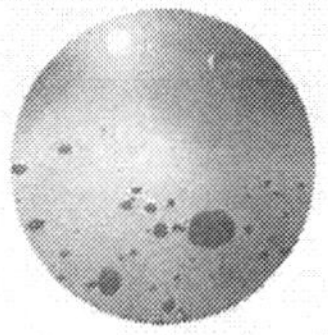

The science tycoons who want to make trillions from space mines
Page 43

World

Calm Breivik tells brutal story of his cold-blooded murder spree

Norway
David Charter Oslo

Some played dead while others were simply paralysed with fear and could only watch in terror as Anders Behring Breivik reloaded his pistol. No matter, he shot them all.

Bereaved relatives filled the public seats in Oslo's court 250 yesterday for a traumatic account of the day when a self-proclaimed ultra-nationalist, who claimed to love his country above all else, gunned down their children in cold blood.

Before the court heard Breivik's account of the killings, the families received a warning from him about the detailed nature of the testimony he would deliver. Breivik's admits to carrying out attacks that killed 77 people but has pleaded not guilty on the grounds of "necessity" in his one-man crusade against multiculturalism.

"I recommend everyone who does not need to listen not to listen because some of the descriptions will be horrendous," said Breivik from his seat in the witness box, with his back to the bereaved sitting a couple of yards away.

Nobody left the courtroom at that point. But while all maintained a quiet and humbling dignity, what followed would be too much for some to bear.

Disguised as a police officer, Breivik tricked his way onto Utøya island, a holiday camp for young Labour Party activists, on the pretence of providing protection after the terrorist bomb in Oslo that he had earlier detonated. He killed 69 people on the island, most of them under 20.

His first target was Trond Berntsen, an unarmed security guard. "My whole body tried to revolt when I took the weapon in my hand. There were 100 voices in my head saying, 'Don't do it, don't do it'," Breivik told the court.

"I pointed the weapon towards his head and shot him. Then Monica Bosei [the head of security] started to run so I directed the weapon towards her and shot her once in the head and she fell. Then I shot him [Berntsen] twice in the head and went over to her and shot her twice in the head."

It was a pattern that he repeated many times with the young holidaymakers. At the island's café, he found many already in total confusion.

"People ran in all directions and I thought, 'I am going to go into that building and execute as many as possible'." He killed "six or seven" in the first room but could not remember the exact number. "In a corner I saw that some were just paralysed. They were unable to run. This was something you never see on TV. It looked really odd. I took the magazine out of my pistol and put new magazines in while these two people were just standing there and just shot both of them in the head."

Breivik took about 90 minutes to detail the shootings in chilling, matter-of-fact detail. His testimony was not broadcast, but outside the court Norwegians were placing roses on the security railings.

"I heard many people screaming and begging for their lives. I don't really remember what they were saying," he recalled, leaning back in his chair. Breivik looked slightly flushed but was otherwise calm and expressionless. Relatives wiped away tears and comforted each other behind his back.

"One person I remember well. He tried to dodge the bullets by zig-zagging, so I shot him in the body a lot of times."

Breivik then told how he moved to the campsite. "This person had just got out of a tent, listening to his iPod. He has no idea what the hell was going on. So I just went over to him and shot him in the head."

After phoning police to surrender, Breivik encountered another dozen or so youngsters at a pump house. "I remember one person there very well. He came from somewhere in the Middle East. He said: 'Please, mate' or something like that. I shot everyone there."

After sparing a boy crying hysterically because he looked under 16, Breivik claimed that he considered suicide rather than surrender. "I thought: do I really want to survive this? I will be the most hated person in Norway." But he said he decided he could spread his extremist ideas better if he lived.

Earlier, Breivik said that "in normal circumstances, I am a nice person". He said he suppressed his emotions in preparation for the attack using meditation based on the Bushido tradition of Japanese samurai.

Christin Bjelland, a spokeswoman for a support group set up for survivors and their families, said: "I am going back to my hometown tonight. My husband, he is going to drive me out to the sea, and I am going to take a walk there and I am going to scream my head off."

The case continues.

FABRIZIO BENSCH / REUTERS

Dogged prosecutor who deflated pompous misfit

Profile Inga Bejer Engh

Criticised at first for her gentle style of questioning, the high-flying district attorney given the task of prosecuting Anders Behring Breivik believes that her methods are the best way of exposing the mind of the mass killer (David Charter writes).

The persistent questioning of Inga Bejer Engh, 41, has slowly stripped bare Breivik's grandiose portrayal of a pan-European nationalist revolution. Under her insistent probing, Breivik admitted that his 1,500-page manifesto was deliberately "pompous" to "sell a dream" as it became clear that the 50-strong network of Knights Templar was actually the product of a misfit's warped imagination.

As Ms Engh searched for more details about the alleged founding meeting of his mythical organisation, Breivik eventually snapped that it was actually "four sweaty guys in a basement".

Ms Engh has prosecuted many murder trials in the ten years since she left the UN headquarters in New York where she worked in international law. But she acknowledges that the July 22 case that she shares with co-prosecutor Svein Holden is of a different order.

"When I got the offer I answered yes right away because I think it is an important case and I wanted to be a person who influenced the process and make sure it is a good process," she said yesterday. "It is a huge responsibility, to pick what we think are the most relevant issues and try to present them to the court. But it is what I do for a living."

Ms Engh, whose husband is caring for their two young children during the trial, added: "This case has not left my thoughts."

Asked whether she is mindful of the feelings of the bereaved during her questioning, she said: "It is going to be awful but I have to go through it and this is what this case is all about. We simply have to go through it."

The Times 21 April 2012

Daily Mail
COMMENT

A 13-year affront to Western civilisation

WITH the Paris atrocities still fresh and raw in Western minds, many may think this is not the moment to plead the cause of a prisoner suspected of involvement in Islamist terrorism.

But as David Cameron visits Barack Obama in Washington, this paper believes there could be no more fitting time to highlight the plight of Shaker Aamer, who has been held in Guantanamo Bay without trial for a shameful 13 years.

Yes, the Mail accepts that Aamer – a Saudi citizen whose home is in London where his British wife and family still live – may be a wicked and dangerous man. Certainly there are disturbing questions about what he was doing in Afghanistan before he was captured in 2001.

But as millions have rallied to proclaim after the horror of the Charlie Hebdo killings, freedom under the law is the very cornerstone of our civilisation.

It includes not just the right to print offensive cartoons, mocking beliefs held sacred by billions, but the fundamental principle that even those suspected of vile crimes are entitled to their day in court.

Indeed, though it grieves us to say this, as firm admirers of so much about the United States, Aamer's continued incarceration without trial is a deep stain on our ally's moral authority.

Add the horrifying evidence that he and other detainees have been repeatedly tortured – possibly with the complicity of British security agencies – and this is almost as much an affront to the values we hold dear as the deranged jihadis' murderous rampage in Paris.

In Washington, therefore, Mr Cameron should have no hesitation in demanding that Aamer must either be tried or released to rejoin his family in Britain.

And while he's about it, he should press the President to honour his six-year-old promise to close Guantanamo Bay. For every day this recruiting sergeant for Islamist terrorism remains open is another day of ignominy for the West.

Trust the viewers

THERE are plenty of respectable reasons Mr Cameron could have given for not wishing to appear in an election debate with Messrs Miliband, Clegg and Farage.

He could have argued that the acting skills required for a TV talent show offer no guide to a politician's fitness for government – as witness Nick Clegg's triumph in the first debate of 2010.

He could also have said, with some justice, that such contests are unfair on incumbent prime ministers, inevitably putting them on the defensive while inflating the stature of untested outsiders such as Nigel Farage.

But instead, he wriggled and writhed – before coming up with the cock-and-bull excuse that his conscience wouldn't allow him to take part in a four-way debate that excluded the Greens!

Does he expect anyone to believe him?

Mr Cameron should have more faith in voters' intelligence. Either he should be honest about his reasons for staying away from a contest whose odds he fears are stacked against him. Or, better, he should agree to take part in the only fixture of the election campaign guaranteed to engage millions of voters.

Given his impressive economic record, and the pitifully low calibre of his rivals, he might even beat the odds.

Question of values

WHAT in the name of sanity does the schools regulator think it is up to, asking 10-year-olds if they know what lesbians do, whether their friends feel trapped in the wrong body or if anyone in their school has two mums or dads?

If this is how Ofsted inspectors see their job of checking that pupils are learning 'British values', is it any wonder that this country is sliding relentlessly down the world education league tables?

I abominate the Charlie Hebdo murderers. I also believe the magazine's malign and bigoted

by Stephen Glover

A FEW minutes after gunmen burst into the offices of Charlie Hebdo last week, murdering journalists and cartoonists, the BBC's resident correspondent in Paris was asked on Radio 5 Live for his opinion on the French satirical magazine.

The two words Hugh Schofield found to describe Charlie Hebdo were 'pretty mediocre'. That was almost the last I heard of him for a few days as incoming BBC correspondents from London and elsewhere swamped the airwaves. Was he ostracised for telling the truth that no one has since dared to utter?

For obvious reasons, Charlie Hebdo has quickly assumed heroic status. Whatever shortcomings it may have had were instantly set aside as millions of people privately and publicly declared *'Je suis Charlie'*.

Militant

How many of these people, as well as those who will sample this week's five-million print run of the magazine in six languages, know exactly what this avowal involves? I, too, 'am Charlie' if it means I fervently support free speech within the law, and abominate the terrorists who brutally took 12 innocent lives and who want to destroy what offends them.

But I am very definitely 'not Charlie' if the proposition entails embracing what I take to be the core values of the magazine, which seem to me to be bigoted, intolerant and often puerile.

The new cover, which depicts the Prophet Mohammed, deliberately sets out to stir things up further.

Not many among the millions of people who have identified with Charlie Hebdo can be aware that its *raison d'etre* is a hatred of all religion. Stephane Charbonnier, the magazine's editor who was murdered last week, once asserted that his magazine was 'above all secular and atheist'.

That was a very revealing thing to have said. His atheism, and that of his colleagues, was not the easy-going sort of non-belief so widespread in the modern West, which can happily co-exist with religious faith. No, it was a militant, campaigning credo which wished to mock, attack, defile and excoriate religion in all its forms.

Incidentally, this is one of many things that distinguish Charlie Hebdo from Private Eye, to which it is often lazily compared. Richard Ingrams, who edited the satirical magazine from shortly after its foundation in 1962 until 1986, has become a Catholic. His successor, Ian Hislop, is at the very least well-disposed towards the Church of England.

Over the past week, we've heard a lot about the various cartoons depicting the Prophet Mohammed which have been published by the magazine over the years and given so much offence to many Muslims. One such example showed the Prophet naked and in various pornographic poses.

We've also read about one issue of the magazine which was supposedly edited by the Prophet Mohammed. Is this funny? It seems to me the sort of juvenile idea that might be discussed by the editors of a low-grade student publication after too many drinks before being unanimously jettisoned.

Shocking

What is perhaps less well-known is that Charlie Hebdo is at least as hostile — if not even more so — towards Christianity. The last Pope, Benedict XVI, was regularly lampooned. One cover showed him holding a condom above his head, and intoning the words from the Eucharist, 'This is my body'.

A recent cartoon showed the Virgin Mary (especially venerated in the Roman Catholic world) giving birth to Christ. More shocking still, another recent cover story about gay marriage was illustrated with a cartoon of a naked Jesus sodomising a bearded God while, in turn, being sodomised by a representation of the Holy Ghost. Like most of Charlie Hebdo's cartoons, it's not even clever.

I am sorry to have to describe these obscenities in such minute detail, but there is no other way of conveying just how unbelievably awful these cartoons are. By the way, it's worth pointing out that sodomy and bare bottoms are a constant obsession in many of them.

Whether in the case of Islam or Christianity — and the magazine sometimes also extends its *animus* towards the Jewish faith — the purpose is to shock and dishearten those of religious persuasion. There is no pity or respect or kindness. Charlie Hebdo hates all religion, and mocks all its adherents.

I can only imagine how ordinary Muslims feel when they see everything that they hold most sacred being held up for ridicule. As someone who calls himself a Christian, I can sense some of the pain and outrage that Christians much more devout and holy than me must experience when they see or read about these appalling images, which are intended to cause pain.

Here, of course, we come to a parting of the ways. Christians and, I believe, most Muslims, recognise that as we live in a free society we are required to put up with even the most hurtful insults to our faith. The Kouachi brothers (who committed the Paris murders) and their deluded supporters think otherwise, and many innocent people, including the journalists of Charlie Hebdo, have paid a terrible price.

It's obviously insane and immoral to kill someone because one is offended by an image and I abhor what happened in Paris in the name of Islam. But it's *not* insane or immoral to be offended by an image whose purpose is to vilify our beliefs and make us unhappy. It's simply natural and human.

None of us, not even the journalists and cartoonists who have worked and still work for Charlie Hebdo, would like to see those closest to us depicted in the coarsest and cruelest fashion. For the pious Christian, Jesus Christ is in a way more precious than their dearest relative. So is Mohammed for the pious Muslim, and presumably the Lord Buddha for the pious Buddhist.

Blinkered

The militantly atheistical Charlie Hebdo cannot grasp this simple truth. Convinced that all religion is a form of deviance, it lacks the imagination or human sympathy to understand the value of the sacred for religious people, of whom there are thousands of millions on this earth.

Far from being sophisticated or enlightened, in some respects the magazine resembles a narrow and monomaniacal sect that actually works against the precepts of freedom. Ironically, in this it is more similar to its blinkered Islamist opponents than it could ever dream — though, of course, without the violence.

Like almost everyone else, I was greatly moved by the sight of people standing in demonstrations with their pens aloft, signifying that the word is mightier than the sword. Even if it isn't, it should be.

Freedom of speech and thought is a priceless treasure which must be defended against the depredations of the violent Islamists. In that sense, I am happy and proud to say *'Je suis Charlie'* so long as Charlie stands for democracy and mutual respect.

It's clear to me, however, that its true values are rather different. Many millions of people in the West may think they identify with the magazine. But I've come to understand that deep down it's sometimes intolerant and malign.

Daily mail 15 January 2005

2012 LONDON'S OLYMPIC YEAR | **WEST END FINAL**

London Evening Standard

Vegazzled
Get down to earth with summer's vegetable fashion
Trends
Pages 32 & 33

Monday 16 April 2012 | FREE | NEWSPAPER OF THE YEAR | standard.co.uk

OLD HARROVIAN MURDERED AFTER DEMANDING BIGGER CUT OF £800M DEAL

POISONED BRITON 'GOT TOO GREEDY'

CHINESE LEADER'S WIFE FEARED HE'D EXPOSE CORRUPTION

Tom Harper
Investigations Reporter

A BRITISH businessman was murdered in China after he "became greedy" and demanded a bigger slice of the profits from a secret £800 million deal run by the wife of a Communist party official, it was claimed today.

The death of Old Harrovian Neil Heywood, 41, has caused political uproar in the country but this is the first time details of a possible motive have emerged. He was allegedly killed with a cyanide-laced drink in a secluded hilltop hotel in the city of Chongqing last November.

Gu Kilai is accused of arranging the death of Mr Heywood after meeting him at the hotel. Mr Heywood is alleged to have helped Ms Gu and her husband Bo Xilai, the mayor of Chongqing, siphon away money to offshore accounts.

She now faces a possible death sentence for "intentional homicide". Mr Bo, once tipped for a place on the Politburo that runs the country, is under house arrest and faces a Communist Party investigation for "serious disciplinary breaches".

Wang Kang, a well-connected Chongqing businessman, said today: "Bo and Gu had not been a proper husband and wife for years. Gu and Heywood had a deep personal relationship and she took the break between them to heart. Her mentality was, 'you betrayed me, and so I'll get my revenge'."

A city official, Xia Deliang, has also been arrested and allegedly confessed that he prepared the poison and handed

Continued on Page 9

Defiant: Anders Breivik gives a far-Right salute as he appears in a packed Oslo court charged with murdering 77 people. He pleaded not guilty, saying he was acting in self-defence **REPORT: Page 5**

I KILLED 77 IN SELF-DEFENCE

Boris 'is a Mayor for the wealthy'

EXCLUSIVE POLL

Pippa Crerar City Hall Editor

THE VAST majority of Londoners believe Boris Johnson is a "Mayor for the rich", an exclusive poll reveals today.

Almost eight out of 10 – 78 per cent – believe the Conservative Mayor is fighting on behalf of the wealthy more than any other group, including commuters and the poor.

But the extraordinary Evening Standard survey shows many Londoners are supportive of this stance – as Mr Johnson has consolidated a six-point lead over Labour rival Ken Livingstone.

The survey by YouGov puts Mr Johnson on a 53 to 47 lead overall.

Only four per cent of people polled said Mr Johnson would focus on the poor, compared with 40 per cent for Mr Livingstone, who was also seen as "particularly keen" to help Muslims,

Continued on Page 7

Evening Standard 16 April 2012

20p

Britain's first and only concise quality newspaper

i

The essential daily briefing

FROM *The* INDEPENDENT

Email: i@independent.co.uk
Facebook: facebook.com/theipaper
Twitter: @theipaper
Text: 07786 200 100
Begin messages with: 'THEI'

TUESDAY
17 APRIL 2012
Number 434

Cameron to put charity tax cap plan out 'for consultation' P9

Attendance at nursery to be recorded in truancy crackdown P5

Breivik pleads 'self-defence' over massacre

Breivik gestures as he arrives at court in Oslo yesterday REUTERS

- Killer breaks down only during airing of own video
- Flashes right-wing salute at start of Oslo trial
- Refuses to recognise authority of the court judge
- Accepts killing 77; denies criminal responsibility

P4

The Independent 17 April 2012

THE INDEPENDENT
• SATURDAY 21 APRIL 2012

21.04.2012
Contents

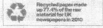

Recycled paper made up 77.4% of the raw material for UK newspapers in 2010

'ALL THE VOICES IN MY

After a week of testimony that has made Norway recoil, Breivik's account of his crimes reaches a harrowing new low. By Tony Paterson

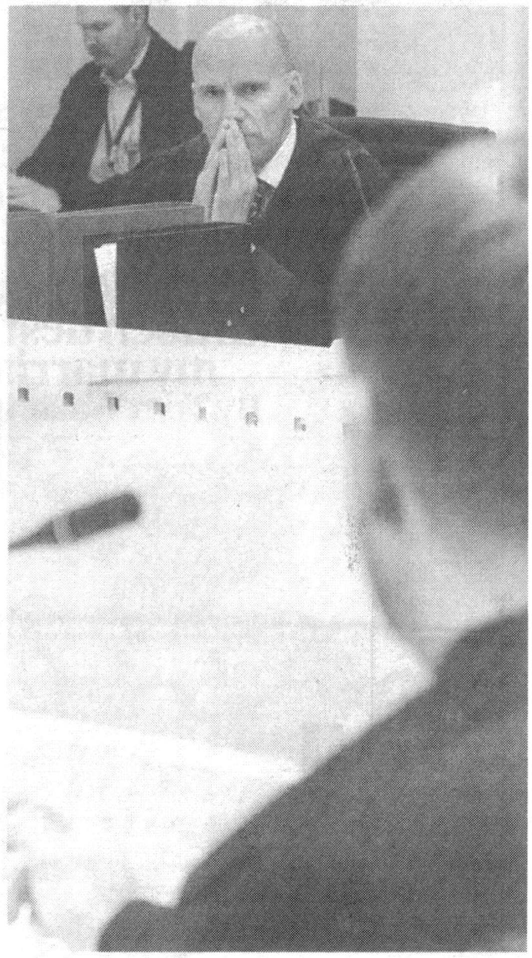

Relatives of the victims of Anders Behring Breivik wept and hugged each other in court yesterday as the Norwegian mass killer described in harrowing detail how he shot dead scores of teenagers who "begged for their lives" as he hunted them down at a Labour Party summer camp on an idyllic fjord island.

Lawyers had warned in advance that day five of Breivik's trial on charges of carrying out Norway's worst acts of violence since the Second World War would be the hardest so far for survivors and relatives of the dead. The far-right killer exceeded their worst expectations. He left out none of the chilling details in his grisly account of the mass slaughter he inflicted on his 69 terrified, mostly teenaged victims at the Utoya summer camp on 22 July last year.

Recalling how he used an automatic pistol and hunting rifle with a telescopic sight to gun down his prey – sometimes at point-blank range – he fell into the present tense when describing the horror he induced as, gun in hand, he walked into a café on the island where a group of terrified teenagers had sought refuge.

"Some of them are completely paralysed. They cannot run. They stand totally still. Two of them are curled up. This is something they never show on TV," Breivik said. "It was very strange." He explained how he had to reload after running out of ammunition: "They were begging for their lives. I just shot them in the head."

Many of the victims' relatives were sitting only a few feet behind the 33-year-old as he described the massacre. His words brought several of them to tears. A father who lost his son closed his eyes and squeezed them shut.

> "Some are completely paralysed. They cannot run. They stand totally still. Two are curled up"

Breivik described how, disguised as a policeman, he took a ferry to the Utoya summer camp some 45 minutes by car from Oslo, after he had detonated a bomb in the centre of the Norwegian capital which killed eight people.

Remembering how he had taken along a supply of drinking water to cope with the "dry throat" he would suffer through stress, he said he was plagued by doubt and feelings of revulsion when confronted by his first two victims, Monic Boesei, a camp organiser, and Trond Berntsen, the island's security guard. "My whole body tried to revolt when I took the weapon in my hand.

Change to the cover price of The Independent

Letter from the Editor

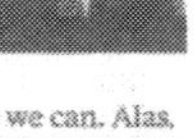

I know some of you are becoming irked by the repeated message in this space every day this week to alert our readers to the fact that we will soon be putting our price up. Sadly, not all of you read the paper every day, and we don't want anyone to receive a rude shock when they next buy *The Independent*.

It is almost four years since the paper last raised its price. During that period, we have been living through a prolonged economic storm. Inflation has been high, the recession severe and lengthy. Newsprint, transportation and other production costs continue to rise, seemingly permanently. Advertising revenues across the industry are not what they were. Despite that, we have avoided asking for more from you for as long as we can. Alas, we cannot put the fateful day off any longer – so, unfortunately, from Monday 23 April, *The Independent* will increase its cover price, to £1.20, bringing it into line with other newspapers.

This will apply only to Monday to Friday. The price of our excellent and soon-to-be-improved Saturday package will remain unchanged, at £1.60.

Our proprietors continue to believe in us, and there are more exciting changes planned for the months ahead. From next Saturday, we will be offering refreshed supplements and a flagship arts, books, listings and culture magazine: *Radar*. From its name you can guess that *Radar*'s aim is to give you advance notice of everything that's worth knowing in that space. It combines the strengths of the existing Arts & Books section – most of which will move next week from its current Friday slot – and our old listings supplements. We will, though, still help you choose which films to go out and see on a Friday night.

The Independent recently added to its award-winning team of writers two of the brightest young stars in the journalistic firmament: Owen Jones and Laurie Penny. They are now joined by more talent, wooed from the competition – the brilliantly funny Grace Dent.

We are also developing new digital products – but don't worry, our printed newspapers remain at the core of our operations.

We value you, our readers, greatly. We make special efforts to keep in contact with you and we want you to continue to read our superb journalism. So our existing, pre-price-rise subscription offer still stands: £5 per week for all editions of *The Independent* and *The Independent on Sunday* – worth £9.60 – now with free iPad access, which would normally cost £9.99 a month. (You can use prepaid vouchers at the newsagent. For more information and to sign up, go to independent.co.uk/subscriptions.)

Judging by the emails and letters I've received so far, most of you are accepting of the increase. It's a sum worth paying, is the common theme, for a newspaper that is neither dogmatically left nor right, and that believes passionately in presenting the world as it really is, without bias or favour.

Thank you for that encouraging support. For my part, I must repeat how sorry I am that your *Independent* will cost more. We fully appreciate that you, our readers, face the same sort of financial squeeze as we do, and possibly an even worse one.

In particular, for those many of you who have been with us from the start in 1986, I hope you will keep the faith in such difficult times. More than ever, I think we're all agreed, *The Independent*'s unique, objective voice needs to be heard.

Best wishes

Chris Blackhurst, Editor
c.blackhurst@independent.co.uk

the Independent 21 April 2012

China rules the world

Martin Jacques The American failings that allowed a new superpower to rise

Hari Kunzru in NY

Taking a hit on the "cultural crack pipe" with Kraftwerk

Will Self

A journey into London's sewers in our food column

NewStatesman

Current affairs and newspaper magazine of the year

23 April 2012/£3.50 www.newstatesman.com

The most shocking thing about Anders Behring Breivik? How many people agree with his opinions.

INSIDE Why it's time to put mainstream Islamophobia on trial

16 >

9 771364 743131

New Stateman 23 April 2012

Gary Younge Polly Toynbee Aditya Chakrabortty Julie Bindel George Monbiot

Tuesday 17.04.12
Published in London
and Manchester
£1.20

9 770261 307521 16

theguardian

guardian.co.uk

Four Matildas into one musical
How the stars share the glory, in g2

'We've got to nail this now'
Coe's Olympics sprint. Interview, page 14

Those revolutionary pre-Raphaelites
British art that changed the world, page 7

Gas fracking gets the green light

Experts say controversial drilling can be extended in the UK even though it causes earthquakes

Fiona Harvey
Environment correspondent

Ministers have been advised to allow the controversial practice of fracking for shale gas to be extended in Britain, despite it causing two earthquakes and the emergence of serious doubts over the safety of the wells that have already been drilled.

The advice of the first official British government report into fracking, published today, is all but certain to be accepted by ministers, with the result that thousands of new wells could be drilled across the UK.

The experts say hydraulic fracturing, whereby a well is drilled hundreds of metres deep and pumped full of water, sand and chemicals in order to release methane gas, should be allowed on a wide scale, although they accept that two small earthquakes in Blackpool last spring were caused by the first stages of fracking activities in the only British plants operating.

The government's own data revealed serious questions around the safety of fracking in areas of known seismic activity, such as the two wells in Lancashire, because of evidence that the resulting earthquakes have damaged the integrity of at least one well. There is also apparent confusion over which government agencies should be overseeing the process to ensure its public safety, with the responsibility shared among several bodies that appear not to be co-ordinating.

The report, written by Peter Styles, professor at Keele University, Brian Baptie of the British Geological Survey, and Christopher Green, an independent fracking expert, found that fracking "should include a smaller pre-injection and monitoring stage", which did not take place at the existing sites, and called for "an effective monitoring system to provide near real-time locations and magnitudes of any seismic events [as] part of any future fracking operations".

Styles warned that further fracking in the Blackpool area was very likely to lead to further tremors: "The similarity of the seismic events suggests this is a highly repeatable source."

Andy Atkins, the executive director of Friends of the Earth, said: "We don't need earth tremor-causing fracking to meet our power needs - we need a seismic shift in energy policy. There should be a full scientific assessment of all the impacts of fracking - a short consultation on one of the problems is completely inadequate."

In the US, fracking has been associated with the contamination of water supplies and soil, and the danger of explosions.

But Mark Miller, the chief executive of Cuadrilla Resources, which drilled the British earthquake sites, said: "We are pleased the experts have come to a clear conclusion that it is safe to allow us to resume hydraulic fracturing, following the procedures outlined in the review."

In April last year, around Cuadrilla's main Blackpool site, there was a tremor measuring 2.3 on the Richter scale and in May one measuring 1.5. These tremors are enough to be felt but do not in themselves cause serious damage.

The report, titled Preese Hall Shale Gas Fracturing: Review and Recommendations for Induced Seismic Mitigation, concluded that both earthquakes were related to the drilling. The report also revealed another concern - instruments showed the second tremor had caused "deformation" to the structure of the well.

This is of concern because if the integrity of a well is compromised, it could cause future problems with leakage and contamination, and raises longer term concerns about the design and viability of such wells, according to Mike Hill, an industry expert. He is worried that the monitoring of the cement casings for the fracking wells is inadequate, as officials have been unable to provide detailed information on their monitoring.

Green, one of the authors of the report, said: "We have indicated we would like further tests to be done to check the well integrity by the Health and Safety Executive."

David Mackay, chief scientific adviser at the Department of Energy and Climate Change (DECC), said: "This comprehensive independent expert review of Cuadrilla's evidence suggests a series

Continued on page 4 »

'I acknowledge the acts. But I do not plead guilty' - Breivik defiant as massacre trial opens

Anders Behring Breivik makes a closed-fist salute before saying he was not pleading guilty at the opening of his trial in Oslo Photograph: Hakon Mosvold Larsen/AP

Helen Pidd Oslo

A taped phone call went some of the way to establish the full horror of what Anders Behring Breivik did in just three hours one afternoon last summer. "He's coming, he's coming," said Renate Taarnes in a terrified whisper. The room at Oslo's central criminal court was silent as she explained to the telephone operator that she had barricaded herself in a toilet in the cafe on the island of Utøya after hearing shooting. By the time the 22-year-old emerged from her hiding place 12 of her friends were lying dead on the cafe floor.

Taarnes's emergency call was deemed too harrowing to be broadcast on the live TV feed which was covering the first day of Breivik's 10-week trial. But as the recording played inside the courtroom the defendant appeared untroubled. He knew it was he who fired those shots, he who prompted those screams. His face gave little away.

Breivik's small, narrow eyes stared straight ahead. His jaw, framed by a thin, angular beard, did not drop. It was only the bulge of his Adam's apple as he gulped down saliva which suggested he was finding the experience emotionally taxing.

From the moment he entered the court yesterday morning, Breivik appeared defiant. After being released from his handcuffs the 33-year-old greeted waiting photogra-

3 »

Continued on page 3 »

US and China unite in war games as cyber hostilities mount

Nick Hopkins

The US and China have been discreetly engaging in "war games" amid rising anger in Washington over the scale and audacity of cyber-attacks on western governments and big business co-ordinated in Beijing, the Guardian has learned.

US state department and Pentagon officials, and their Chinese counterparts, were involved in two war games last year designed to help prevent a sudden military escalation if either side felt targeted. Another is planned in May.

Although the exercises have given the US a chance to vent its frustration at what appears to be state-sponsored espionage and theft on an industrial scale, China has been belligerent. "China has come to the conclusion that the power relationship has changed, and it has changed in a way that favours them," said Jim Lewis, a senior fellow and director at the Centre for Strategic and International Studies (CSIS) thinktank in Washington.

"They see the US as a target. They feel they have justification for their actions. They think the US is in decline."

The war games have been organised through the CSIS and a Beijing thinktank, the China Institute of Contemporary International Relations. This has allowed officials and US intelligence agencies to have contact in a less formal environment.

Known as Track 1.5 diplomacy, it is the closest governments can get in conflict management without full-blown talks.

"We co-ordinate the war games with the [US] state department and department of defence," said Lewis, who brokered the meetings, which took place in Beijing last June and in Washington in December.

"The officials start out as observers and become participants ... it is very much the same on the Chinese side. Because it is organised between two thinktanks, they can speak more freely."

In the first exercise, both sides had to describe what they would do if they were attacked by a sophisticated computer virus such as Stuxnet, which disabled centrifuges in Iran's nuclear programme in 2010. In the second, they had to describe their reaction if the attack was known to have been launched from the other side.

"The two war games have been quite amazing," said Lewis. "The first one went well, the second one not so well.

"The Chinese are very astute. They send knowledgeable people. We want to find ways to change their behaviour ... [but] they can justify what they are doing. Their attitude is, they have

10-11 »

Continued on page 11 »

The Guardian 17 April 2012

THE TIMES

Tuesday April 17 2012 | thetimes.co.uk | No 70549 2GM Max 12C, min -3C

Still only £1

How to cure a headache

Dr Mark Porter reveals his remedy Times2

Poll shock as new U-turn looms

Labour opens largest lead since general election

Sam Coates, Frances Gibb
Roland Watson

Labour has opened a nine-point lead over the Conservatives after David Cameron's worst month in office.

Furious opposition to the Budget and the Government's handling of the fuel tanker drivers' dispute have led to a sharp drop in satisfaction with the coalition, with 61 per cent saying that it is going "badly".

A Populus poll for *The Times* puts Labour on 42 per cent, up four points on March, its highest share of the vote in this Parliament. The Conservatives slipped back one point to 33 per cent, its joint lowest poll rating in coalition, while the Lib Dems remain unchanged on 11 per cent.

The Prime Minister faces further trouble this week after a leak to *The Times* revealed that other members of the 47-strong Council of Europe have forced him to water down proposals to overhaul the European Court of Human Rights in Strasbourg.

The latest draft of the agreement, to be signed this week when representatives from the council gather in Brighton, shows that key British proposals have been dropped or watered down, meaning that the court is unlikely to receive new powers to reject cases and curb its backlog.

Draft 4 of the communiqué sent to member states last Thursday shows how specific British proposals have been crossed out in red and replaced with new, bland commitments that can be agreed at the meeting chaired by Ken Clarke, the Justice Secretary.

- British plans to limit the court's scope to take cases already heard in national courts have been diluted.
- A second UK reform to allow states to ask the European Court for preliminary or advisory opinions, stopping many cases ever reaching Strasbourg, has been substantially watered down.
- Requirements for any legal changes on the scope of the court to take place before the end of 2013 have been removed.

The document does, though, agree that the core principle that gives states discretion on interpreting human rights laws — the so-called "margin of appreciation" — should be included in the preamble to the European Convention on Human Rights.

Sources close to Mr Clarke insist that the Government is happy with the

Continued on page 5, col 5

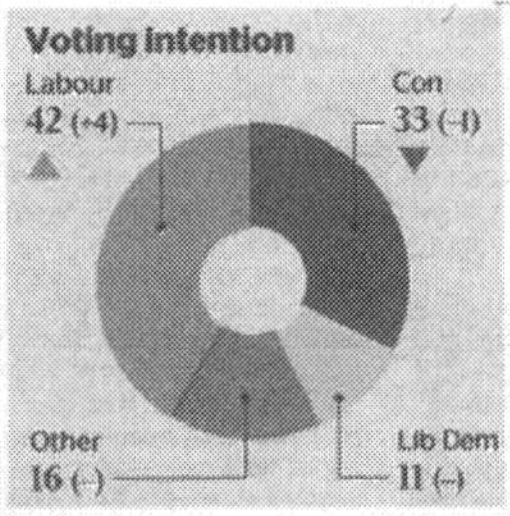

Stop sending patients home late at night, hospitals told

Chris Smyth Health Correspondent

Hospitals have been ordered to end the "obviously unacceptable" practice of sending vulnerable patients home in the middle of the night.

Professor Sir Bruce Keogh, medical director of the NHS, demanded that all hospitals review how they discharge patients and explain what action they are taking by next month.

After revelations by *The Times* that elderly patients were among thousands being sent home at night, Sir Bruce said that hospital boards must "take ownership of this issue".

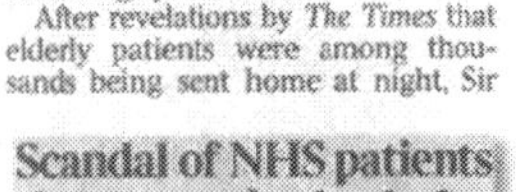

Scandal of NHS patients thrown out in the dark

How The Times reported the scandal of late-night discharges last Thursday

David Cameron will today ask nurses for ways of making the NHS more responsive to patients at a meeting in No 10 which is likely to consider how to ensure that hospital discharges are safe and convenient.

In a letter to the medical directors of England's ten strategic health authorities, Sir Bruce wrote: "The issues highlighted by the recent media reports are central to the drive to put quality at the heart of the NHS. As health professionals we agree that patients should be treated with compassion, so it is simply not acceptable to send people home from hospital late at night when they may have no family members nearby to support them."

Last week *The Times* revealed NHS data that showed hundreds of thousands of patients were sent home from hospital in the middle of the night. Almost 240,000 patients a year were discharged between 11pm and 6am, according to the 100 of England's 170 hospital trusts which replied to requests under the Freedom of Information Act.

"While some patients may of course choose to be discharged during these hours, the examples highlighted of elderly patients being left to make their way home by themselves in the middle of the night are obviously unacceptable, and need to be addressed urgently," Sir Bruce wrote in the letter, sent out over the weekend.

"Discharge or care transfer is of course an essential part of care management in any setting. It ensures that

Continued on page 10, col 4

Anders Behring Breivik gives a clenched-fist salute at the start of his trial for 77 murders. Leading article, page 2; News, 6-8

Breivik impassive as court hears desperate phone call from Utøya

Leading articles

Breivik's Bombast

A mass killer is exploiting due process to expound a poisonous, paranoid ideology. His trial is not about his rights but about the victims he pitilessly slaughtered

The trial of Adolf Eichmann in Jerusalem half a century ago gave currency to the phrase "the banality of evil". In an age of digital communication, the appearance of Anders Behring Breivik in an Oslo courtroom likewise risks focusing appalled public fascination on the personality of a mass killer. But, while the nature of human evil is indeed intractable, the trial is not primarily about Breivik, whose responsibility for the deaths of 77 people is not disputed. It is about his victims.

On a July day last year, Breivik planted a car bomb outside government buildings in Oslo. It killed eight people and wounded 209. He then made his way to the island of Utøya, and a youth camp of the governing Labour Party, and killed another 67 people and wounded 33. Two more died in trying to escape him.

Breivik does not so much admit his acts as exult in them. Arriving at court yesterday he smiled and gave a clenched-fist salute. As a recording of his victims' screams was played, he sat impassively. His tears were reserved for a screening of his own video, inveighing against Islam and multiculturalism, which he had posted on the internet before the attacks. Responding to the indictment, he acknowledged the killings but did not admit guilt, claiming that he had acted in self-defence.

This behaviour raises a dilemma, which may prove intractable, for a free society. The principle of due process is central to a democracy, to the disinterested application of law and to the notion of justice. Norway's legal system exemplifies it. But this is not a normal case in which it is the task of a jury and judge to determine guilt according to the evidence. Breivik is exploiting the scrupulousness of the proceedings in order to turn them into a malevolent pantomime. He has the opportunity to do more. There is no question about his culpability, only his sanity; he will spend many years either in a psychiatric institution or in prison.

The maximum jail term is in principle 21 years, but it could and surely would be extended to the rest of his life if he were jailed. Given that in practice these are the sole questions that the court has to decide, it is troubling to anyone of human sympathy that the victims' families will be subjected to a grandstanding rant by a fanatic.

When Radovan Karadzic, whom Breivik reveres as a hero, cross-examined in his own trial the families of victims of the Srebrenica genocide, he insulted them and lied about the crime of which he stands accused. In Breivik's trial, something similar is all too likely to happen. As far as possible within the constraints of the legal system, the court authorities should prevent Breivik from compounding atrocity with calumnies against the victims and inflammatory denunciations of their ideals.

The defendant's testimony will not be televised in this case. That is beyond argument the right decision. Whatever the psychological roots of Breivik's barbarism, its public manifestation is a pitiless and brutal xenophobia stoked by demented conspiracy theory. Contrary to his fantasies, he was not driven to it by injustice, nor is the democratic state that he loathes an exemplar of oppression. Breivik is a spectacular instance of what Richard Hofstadter, the American sociologist, termed 50 years ago the paranoid style in politics. He combines small-minded suspicion, wild exaggeration and imperviousness to feeling and sympathy.

Breivik would never gain public attention by normal political means for such poisonous sentiments. He must not get it by the expedient of mass murder. It would be an affront to the victims and a public danger in encouraging extremists with grievances to pursue them by similar means. There will be much soul-searching in Norway during this trial. The values of a distinctively tolerant society are vindicated in extending them to Breivik. But that is where obligations to him end.

Diplomatic Impunity

Britain remains indefensibly quiet over the death of Neil Heywood

Almost certainly, many of China's powerful figures would prefer not to be discussing the scandal surrounding the death of the British businessman Neil Heywood. But now that they are, they seem almost to be enjoying themselves.

Bo Xilai, formerly the Communist Party boss of Chongqing, has fallen from grace and disappeared. Gu Kailai, his wife, has been arrested on suspicion of murder. Chinese state-controlled media are covering this saga extensively, making it a safe assumption that they are being encouraged to do so. Wen Jiabao, the Prime Minister, has warned gravely that corruption is the greatest threat to the Communist Party's survival.

He is, of course, quite right, even if Chinese officialdom's emerging default pose of naive self-flagellation must strain credulity. The minutiae of Mr Bo's and Ms Gu's lifestyle — complete with delicious detail such as the red Ferrari driven around Beijing by their Harrow-educated son, Bo Guagua — are perhaps a surprise to most of those in China. But they surely cannot come as much of one to his erstwhile peers in the Chinese elite.

The extent to which Chinese authorities are making hay with the Heywood case, nonetheless, stands in stark contrast to the near silence from Britain. William Hague and the Foreign Office have commented only rarely, and with great reluctance. This cannot be excused as a polite wariness of meddling in another country's due process. Chinese justice is opaque at the best of times and this is a murder investigation already deeply politicised. Mr Heywood deserves better.

The Foreign Office has a string of questions to answer and no excuse for keeping the answers to itself. Was there no British suspicion of foul play at the time of Mr Heywood's death? Why, then, did a consular official attend his (remarkably swift) cremation? Jeremy Browne, a Foreign Office minister, was by chance in Chongqing when the body was discovered and met Mr Bo. According to the Foreign Office, he was not even informed that a British citizen, very close to the man he was meeting, had been found dead. Why on earth not?

What does the Foreign Office know about Mr Heywood's involvement and subsequent disagreement with Mr Bo and Ms Gu? In the absence of official comment, rumours already abound, from illicit romance to blackmail to business deals gone sour. What does the Foreign Office believe about the circumstances of his death? Are there fears that it is being exploited for a politically useful show trial? Are such concerns being shared?

Wang Lulu, Mr Heywood's widow, is Chinese. His children have British nationality. Can it be true, as has been reported, that Ms Gu visited Mr Heywood's widow days after his death and, accompanied by armed policemen, secured her agreement that he had died of alcohol poisoning and should be cremated without an autopsy? Has Ms Wang been offered passage to the UK? Has she the freedom of movement to accept it, if so?

Faced with such questions in almost any other country in the world, the British Government's demand for answers would be vocal and righteous. China is going through a period of sudden and enormous political upheaval and may yet emerge as a more open, freer, better-governed country, with a far greater respect for the rule of law. Faced with a grim opportunity to be at the heart of this transformation, Britain should be encouraging it loudly, not meekly holding its tongue.

Opera; Glass's

The American composer's opera, getting a London premiere, is assured a long run

Every once in a while an opera comes along that is so novel, so daring, so adventurous and so very, very long that after the first four hours have passed audiences can't help wondering if maybe they are patsies in some *Candid Camera* stunt, and the TV crew is peeking at them from the wings and shrieking in disbelief: "Can you believe it? They're actually still sitting there pretending to be interested!"

Some composers equate length with musical machismo. Wagner's *Ring Cycle* is so long that by the time it is over the seasons have changed. Twice. Some operas are so challenging that they show up in public more rarely than even J. D. Salinger did. Operas such as *Einstein on the Beach*, which, almost four decades after the composer Philip Glass and the director Robert Wilson created it, is finally getting its British premiere (see Times2). Though fêted by many as the first great American opera, *Einstein* has had only four runs since its New York debut in 1976. Its being five hours long might have something to do with that. Without intervals. Or a plot.

Four runs may not be many, but at least *Einstein on the Beach* does occasionally get performed. Kaikhosru Sorabji, the Chingford-born composer, wasn't so lucky with his *Symphonic Variations*. At nine hours, it has never been performed in full.

But if you have real stamina and a sturdy faith in your own longevity, you could take a pew at St Burchardi's Church in the German town of Halberstadt. Here, in 2003, they fired up the organ to perform John Cage's work, *As SLow aS Possible*. The piece has no specified length. So St Burchardi's has settled on a running time of 639 years. The first three notes took a year and a half. It makes *Parsifal* sound friskier than a fandango. Relatively speaking, as Philip Glass's Einstein might say.

News Breivik trial

'There is shooting, there is panic. He's coming . . .' More shots, the call ends

A woman's attempt to raise the alarm brought the horrors on Utøya into the courtroom, **David Charter** reports

A chilling three-minute phone call captured the raw terror of Norway's worst peacetime massacre at the start of the trial of Anders Behring Breivik yesterday.

Breivik, 33, had already shown his defiance by refusing to stand for the judges, giving a clenched-fist salute as his handcuffs were removed and announcing that he did not recognise the court. He entered a plea of not guilty on the ground of "self-defence" to the charge of terrorism and killing 77 people last summer.

Several relatives of the slaughtered left the packed public gallery of the court in Oslo following a warning from the judges that a short police recording would be played.

Others wept and consoled one another just yards from an impassive Breivik as the dramatic phone conversation between 22-year-old Renate Taarnes and an uncomprehending local police officer was relayed.

"There were shots on Utøya," said Miss Taarnes, her voice racing and urgent, as soon as she got through.

This was early on in Breivik's one-man killing spree on the tiny holiday island of Utøya, where more than 500 young people were at a summer camp for Young Labour Party activists.

"What are you saying?" the police officer asked. "Shots have been fired on Utøya," came the panicky reply.

"Anyone injured?" the officer asked, still not grasping that this would become the most intimate evidence of the atrocities that have indelibly marked July 22 in the Norwegian calendar.

"Yes, I have seen several people injured. There is shooting all the time. There is complete panic here," Miss Taarnes said.

"What was your name?" At this point Miss Taarnes whispered: "He is inside." A shot is heard. Then another. There were screams audible in the background and then a volley of gunfire.

The officer continued to ask questions but Miss Taarnes was clearly trying to keep as quiet as possible. More single shots rang out in the background. In the café on the other side of the door, Breivik killed seven people and wounded several more as they fled.

Extremely quietly, Miss Taarnes whispered: "There is someone walking around shooting." More shots. "You're still there?" Her voice barely audible, she replied: "Yes . . . he is just outside."

All the while, Breivik sat emotionless in court, staring either straight ahead or down at his desk.

"He's coming . . . He's coming, quickly." After more shots, the call ended. Miss Taarnes survived, but her boyfriend was among the 69 who did not.

The court heard two more recordings yesterday, both from Breivik himself calling the police to offer his surrender towards the end of the day.

"I have just carried out an operation on behalf of the Knights Templar of Norway and Europe and since the operation has been completed it is acceptable to surrender," he said in the second call.

Breivik declared that he was from the Norwegian anti-communist resistance movement against the Islamisation of Europe. In his mind, and in his 1,500-page manifesto, Breivik was licensed by these movements to carry out the execution of Category A and Category B traitors — those in political positions who have allowed immigration, which has put the West at the mercy of Islam.

"I do not recognise the Norwegian courts," he said in court. "You have received your mandate from political parties which support multiculturalism. I do not acknowledge the authority of the court." Asked later in the proceedings for his plea, he replied: "I acknowledge the acts but I do not plead guilty. I claim self-defence."

The prosecution began its outline by emphasising the importance for Breivik of the alleged foundation in London in April 2002 of the Knights Templar, the organisation which he claims to be representing in his war against multiculturalism and Islam.

"His membership in this network is of great importance to how he led his life," said Svein Holden, one of the two main prosecutors. "One of its main aims is to deport Islam out of Europe. In our opinion no such network exists."

Breivik was portrayed by the prosecution as a misfit from an early age, who failed to find a girlfriend or a steady job.

"The sale of fake diplomas generated considerable income for Breivik and a lot of it was not subject to tax because he established his company in a tax haven," Mr Holden said.

Breivik was said to have played World of Warcraft, an online combat game, full-time for a year from the summer of 2006 to the following summer. He described this as a "gift to martyrdom" which helped to prepare him mentally to slaughter his victims.

With screams and shooting audible in the background, Renate Taarnes struggled to get her message across to police

A tear, but not for the dead

Analysis A flicker of emotion

Impervious to the hour-long litany of the names of the dead, smirking slightly at video footage of the bomb that blew victims off their feet in Oslo, Anders Behring Breivik showed recognisable emotion only once in the courtroom yesterday (David Charter writes).

It happened when the prosecution played his 12-minute home video showing images of the Crusades and pictures of his heroes, such as El Cid and Vlad the Impaler.

Just as the courtroom was allowing itself a smirk at his expense for a change, Breivik began blinking rapidly and his bottom lip started trembling. He seemed to wipe away a tear.

Asked later how this could be the only sign of emotion in a man who listened impassively to details of all the teenaged victims he shot in cold blood, his lawyer, Geir Lippestad, said: "Part of the explanation may be that he committed these acts which he characterised as horrendous but necessary to prevent war in Europe, and he only has empathy when these sentiments come up."

Tore Sinding Bekkedal, 24, one of the survivors of the island who attended court, said: "To me it was a childish, boring, PowerPoint presentation. But he seemed to attach some emotional significance to it. I just thought it was stupid."

77 victims of Breivik's rampage

HANNE EKROLL LØVLIE 30 MINISTRY VICTIM

HANNA ORVIK ENDRESEN 61 RECEPTIONIST

IDA MARIE HILL 34 DIED IMMEDIATELY

KAI HAUGE 33 OWNED BAR AND RESTAURANT

ANNE LISE HOLTER 51 DIED IN RECEPTION

JON VEGARD LERVÅG 32 WAS CLOSE TO VAN

TOVE ÅSHILL KNUTSEN 56 ON WAY TO SUBWAY

KJERSTI BERG SAND 26 JUSTICE DEPT WORKER

DIDERIK OLSEN 19 SHOT BY PUMP HOUSE

ALEKSANDER AAS ERIKSEN 17 SHOT BY CAFÉ

MONA ABDINUR 18 SHOT IN CAFÉ

BANO RASHID 18 SHOT ON 'LOVE PATH'

ISMAIL HAJI AHMED 19 SHOT BY PUMP HOUSE

PORNTIP ARDAM 21 SHOT BY PUMP HOUSE

Breivik trial News

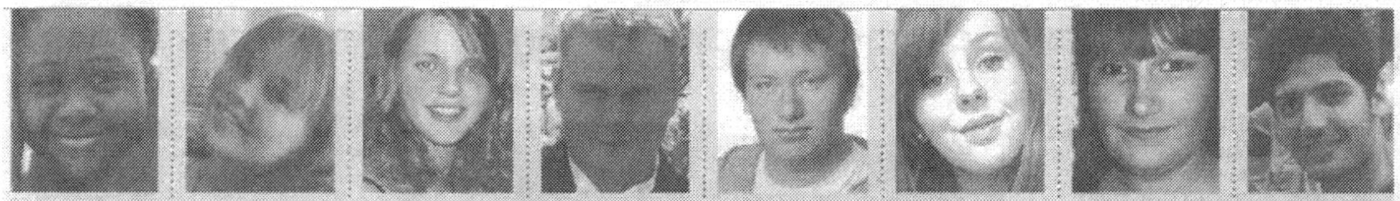

MODUPE ELLEN AWOYEMI 15 SHOT ON ESCARPMENT

CARINA BORGUND 18 SHOT BY COVE

MARIANNE SANDVIK 16 SHOT BY PATH

RUNE HAVDAL 43 GUARD ON THE ISLAND

HENRIK RASMUSSEN 18 AT PUMP HOUSE

SYNNE RØYNELAND 18 SHOT BY WATER

TINA SUKUVARA 18 SHOT BY PUMP HOUSE

KARAR MUSTAFA QASIM 19 SHOT BY COVE

ANDRINE ESPELAND 16 SHOT BY WATER

ANDREAS DALBY 17 FELL OFF CLIFF

SHARIDYN SVEBAKK-BØHN 14 SHOT BY PATH

ÅSTA SOFIE HELLAND DAHL 16 SHOT ON PATH

MONICA ISELIN DIDRIKSEN 18 SHOT ON PATH

SILJE STAMNESHAGEN 18 SHOT ON PATH

ROLF PERREAU 25 SHOT OUTSIDE CAFÉ ENTRANCE

THOMAS ANTONSEN 16 SHOT ON PATH

HANNE BALCH FJALESTAD 43 SHOT AT CAFÉ

IDA BEATHE ROGNE 17 SHOT IN CAFÉ

HENRIK ANDRÉ PEDERSEN 27 SHOT IN CAFÉ

ESPEN JØRGENSEN 17 BY PUMP HOUSE

STEINAR JESSEN 16 SHOT OUTSIDE CAFÉ

VICTORIA STENBERG 17 BY PUMP HOUSE

RONJA SØTTAR JOHANSEN 17 SHOT IN CAFÉ

EVEN FLUGSTAD MALMEDAL 18 SHOT BY WATER

INGRID BERG HEGGELUND 18 SHOT BY COVE

GIZEM DOGAN 17 SHOT IN WOODS EAST OF SCHOOL

KEVIN DAAE BERLAND 15 SHOT BY WATER

TORE EIKELAND 21 SHOT ON PATH

MARGRETHE KLOEVEN 16 SHOT IN CAFÉ

ELISABETH TRONNES LIE 16 SHOT IN CAFÉ

SYVERT KNUDSEN 17 SHOT BY WATER

MARIA JOHANNESEN 17 SHOT ON PATH

TROND BERNTSEN 51 SHOT NEAR PIER

ANDREAS EDVARDSEN 19 SHOT 3 TIMES

JOHANNES BUØ 14 YOUNGEST VICTIM

SONDRE KJOREN 17 SHOT IN CAFÉ

TAMTA LIPARTELIANI 23 SHOT BY WATER

GURO VARTDAL HAVOLL 18 SHOT IN CAFÉ

SIMON SAEBØ 18 SHOT CLOSE TO SECLUDED PATH

FREDRIK LUND SCHJETNE 18 BY PUMP HOUSE

SVERRE FLÅTE BJØRKAVÅG 28 BY PUMP HOUSE

SILJE MERETE FJELLBU 17 SHOT IN CAFÉ

SONDRE DALE 17 SHOT BY THE WATER

LENE MARIA BERGUM 19 SHOT IN CAFÉ

EVA KATHINKA LUTKEN 17 SHOT ON PATH

RUTH NILSEN 15 SHOT BY THE PUMP HOUSE

HÅKON ØDEGAARD 17 DROWNED

GUNNAR LINAKER 23 OUTSIDE CAFÉ

TORJUS BLATTMANN 17 SHOT BY COVE

HANNE FRIDTUN 21 SHOT BY PUMP HOUSE

SNORRE HALLER 30 SHOT OUTSIDE CAFÉ

KARIN ELENA HOLST 15 SHOT BY WATER

EMIL OKKENHAUG 15 BY PUMP HOUSE

HÅVARD VEDERHUS 21 AT PUMP HOUSE

BIRGITTE SMETBAK 15 SHOT BY CAFÉ

TARALD KUVEN MJELDE 18 SHOT ON PATH

MONICA BOSEI 45 SHOT NEAR PIER

ISABEL SOGN 17 SHOT BY THE COVE

BENDIK ELLINGSEN 18 SHOT IN CAFÉ

EIVIND HOVDEN 15 SHOT IN CAFÉ

JAMIL RAFAL YASIN 20 SHOT BY WATER

ANDERS BEHRING BREIVIK KILLED 77 INDIVIDUALS 8 IN THE OSLO BOMBING 69 ON THE ISLAND OF UTØYA RESEARCH BY DAVID KEEGAN

LEILA SELACI 17 SHOT IN FRONT OF CAFÉ

ANDERS KRISTIANSEN 18 SHOT ON PATH

There was a gasp in court as the prosecution showed CCTV footage of the bomb concealed in a white van that Breivik parked right in front of the main government building in Oslo.

Five minutes after Breivik walked calmly away, a man could clearly be seen strolling into the building past the van the moment before the explosion. He was later named as Jon Vegard Lervåg, the first named victim on the indictment.

As the explosion was shown in silence from different angles from various CCTV cameras, Breivik watched intently and gave a smirk when film was shown of glass blowing out of windows on the other side of the building.

The names of each of his victims was read out, together with brief details of where and how they died, starting with

A sticker worn in the courtroom by a survivor of the island massacre

Inside today

A mass killer is exploiting due process

Leading article, page 2

his victims in Oslo, who were killed by shrapnel and the shock wave of the huge exploson.

At the reading of the names and dates of birth, Breivik showed no emotion but lowered his eyes and seemed to be following the indictment on a piece of paper in front of the lawyer seated next to him.

The details were perfunctory and devastating. Many of the dead had been shot at least three times, often twice in the head, and in the throat. Many were also shot in the back.

"Ida Beathe Rigne, born November 8, 1993. She was in the big hall of the café and was shot at least twice with a pistol and a rifle," the official said.

"One shot entered the right side of the face, penetrating the brain, the other entered the right cheek. She died of injuries to the head and face …

"Andreas Edvardsen, born November 30, 1992. He was on Lovers' Path and was shot three times with a pistol and/or rifle, of which one shot was to the head and one to the neck …" It went on for almost an hour.

Geir Lippestad, for the defence, told the court that his client had a basic right to be heard. Breivik will give evidence today for five full days under questioning from the prosecution and defence. "He has his basic right as a defendant under Norwegian law and also a human right," Mr Lippestad said.

"More importantly, his evidence is also the most important piece of evidence for the court to decide on an independent basis whether he is legally sane and can be punished."

Norway has a maximum jail sentence of 21 years, which can be extended if the convict is deemed a violent threat to public safety.

Last week, a psychiatric assessment found that Breivik was sane, contradicting a first analysis that declared that he was a paranoid schizophrenic who was psychotic at the time of the killings.

Depending on what the five judges decide, Breivik could either be jailed or committed to a secure psychiatric hospital.

News Breivik trial

The court where lawyers shake hands with a murderer

David Charter
Commentary

It was, in many ways, just like any normal trial. Lawyers and court officials greeted each other as they arrived and mingled in the intimate Oslo courtroom. And once Anders Behring Breivik had performed his brief right-handed salute for the cameras, most of those around him also took the trouble to shake him by the hand. It seemed a disconcerting courtesy for a man sworn to destroy everything the country stands for.

"Oh, they always shake hands in a Norwegian courtroom," said Olav Rønneberg, a reporter from NRK, Norway's state television station. "Whether you are a murderer, a robber, or a rapist, they always shake hands."

This is exactly what the Norwegians did yesterday. They staged a regular trial in the full glare of the world's media with a minimum of fuss and a calm adherence to their cherished values of fairness and transparency.

Not for the Norwegians any rushed parliamentary measures to eavesdrop on radicals or seize control of the internet. They are determined to defeat the extremism of Breivik with normality.

It was truly humbling to watch the dignity of the bereaved relatives and the survivors of Breivik's massacres from my seat in the fourth row of court 250.

I wondered if any would shout out at the man who had coldly murdered their children, 56 of whom died from a bullet to the head. I wondered if a vengeful father or brother would leap the low barrier to land a blow on Breivik, who sat unprotected just three yards away.

FABRIZIO BENSCH / REUTERS

Norwegians are sticking to their values of fairness and transparency

But they kept to their allotted rows, watching on with private thoughts and wiping away the occasional tear.

Some wore badges stating politely in English: "No interviews please." Those who were willing to speak to journalists were articulate and thoughtful.

"I think it is very important to hear what he has to say," said Bjørn Ihler, 20, who escaped from the island of Utøya. "It is important because these ideas are not just Breivik's ideas, he shares them with a lot of people. We have to do whatever we can to fight extremists from all sides because extremists like this destroy so many lives."

Tore Sinding Bekkedal, 24, who hid in the boys' toilets next door to where Renate Taarnes called the police, said: "It was difficult to hear the run-through of events, of course, but it is a necessary evil to have a proper trial."

One of the main Norwegian newspaper websites had a button to switch off its reporting of Breivik, while the national television coverage of the opening statements respectfully bleeped out any gory details. Across the country 17 courtrooms showed the trial live for those relatives unable, or too distraught, to attend the media circus in Oslo, with warnings before the most upsetting moments. Norway took evil in its stride.

The Times 17 April 2012

World

Breivik reveals plot for beheading Labour leader

Norway
David Charter Oslo

The full murderous ambitions of Anders Behring Breivik became chillingly clear yesterday when he told his trial that he planned to behead a former Norwegian Prime Minister and kill all 569 young people on Utøya island.

Unrepentant and matter of fact, the self-styled Knight Templar said he thought that if he shot a few people on the island the rest would run into the lake and drown. A shocked silence gripped the Oslo courtroom as he listed the targets he considered before a chain of circumstances led him to the tiny island owned by the AUF, the Labour Party youth movement.

Breivik, 33, who pleads not guilty to charges of terrorism and the murder of 77 people on July 22 last year, told how he pumped himself up on steroids and bought exploding hollow-nosed bullets for his assault on the island.

He also detailed his plan against the Labour leader who served three terms as Prime Minister up to 1996.

"I planned to send film to supporters or upload on the internet the execution of Gro Harlem Brundtland," he told the fourth day of his ten-week trial. "I had a bayonet on my rifle and I had a knife and the plan was to chop her head off while filming it."

He then intended to kill the leader of the AUF, Eskil Pedersen.

"The plan was to frighten the rest of the AUFers by shooting some people and to use the water as the weapon of mass destruction. People would basically drown. The objective was not to kill 69 people … the objective was to kill them all."

Ms Brundtland, who is 73 today and was Norway's first woman Prime Minister, was on the island that morning but left before Breivik arrived. Mr Pedersen escaped with several others on the ferry to the mainland.

Breivik remained adamant that his actions were necessary to draw attention to his fight against multiculturalism and the supposed Islamisation of Norway. He blamed journalists for making it impossible for him to convey his message peacefully, and at one point blamed the European Union for the shootings because it had made it harder to buy explosive materials, thwarting his original plan for three large bombs.

"I did not expect anyone under 16 to be on the island," he said as bereaved relatives comforted each other in the public gallery. "I also thought that to kill a person under 18 would be criticised so I wanted to do everything I could to focus on people above the age of 18. But in practice they turned around so it was not feasible to use facial features to determine people's age." Two of the dead were 14, seven were 15 and eight were 16.

He said that he pressed on to attack the island because the bomb he planted in Oslo, which he intended to kill the whole Goverment, killed only eight people. He said: "I decided it was necessary to carry out the entire operation."

Breivik added that the island became a target only because his plans to strike elsewhere fell through. He had contemplated blowing up a petrol tanker in central Oslo during the May Day parade, which would have killed several thousand people. Other targets he considered but dismissed were the Royal Palace and Labour headquarters. Plans to attack conferences of journalists and of the Labour Party were "delayed", so he turned to Utøya. Breivik said that he named his weapons.

"El Cid was the biggest hero in Spain and he had a sword that he gave a name to: he is not the only one," he said, smiling at the thought. "I did the same. The rifle I called Gungnir, that is the name of the imaginary spear of Odin that returns after you have thrown it."

He had named his Glock pistol Mjollnir, the hammer of Thor.

"The support vehicle I gave the name Sleipnir, the name of the eight-legged horse of Odin. I marked all three with runes."

John Hestnes, head of a support group for survivors of the bomb, said: "Now we are starting to see what an evil man he is — cynical, cold and structured as he explains in the smallest detail what he planned. This is starting to become very tough for the survivors and family members to bear."

The trial continues.

ALLOVER NORWAY / REX FEATURES

Breivik said that he planned to use Utøya lake as a weapon of mass destruction

● Breivik immersed himself in online war games to hone his mental and physical skills for carrying out the Norway atrocities (David Charter writes). He played the popular fantasy game *World of Warcraft* "perhaps 16 hours a day for an entire year" from summer 2006.

Closer to the attacks, he played *Call of Duty: Modern Warfare* for more than six hours a day from November 2010 to February 2011 to train himself as a marksman.

"One of the reasons why that year [on *World of Warcraft*] was quite practical was because I knew there would be an upcoming action and it was quite convenient for me to isolate myself during that period," he told the court. "I could not have a network close to me, I could not have friends close to me . . . I thought it was important to do it to prepare myself mentally for sacrificing my life."

Breivik said he played *Call of Duty* to plan his escape if he was confronted with armed police after planing the Oslo bomb. "I trained to force my way through the weakest flank in a frontal attack on a total of six persons," he said.

Breivik said that he planned to film the murder of Ms Brundtland

The Times 20 April 2012

THE TIMES

Max 12C, min 0C

Thursday April 19 2012 | thetimes.co.uk | No 70551

Only £1

Coren dives in
Our man makes his Olympics debut in the pool, News, page 4

Britain threatens exit from European Court of Human Rights as Home Office mix-up over deadline lets Abu Qatada win again

Europe's court jesters

Sam Coates, Richard Ford
Frances Gibb

Britain's relationship with the European Court of Human Rights was put on notice last night after the court halted deportation proceedings against the radical Islamist cleric Abu Qatada.

David Cameron vowed to force him out of the country "no matter how difficult" after Abu Qatada's lawyers challenged the removal process.

"I am absolutely clear, the entire Government is clear, and frankly I think the country is clear, that this man has no right to be in our country," the Prime Minister said last night.

The row erupted on the eve of a conference in Brighton intended to curb the court's influence on Britain after a series of rulings that have infuriated senior government ministers.

But Sir Nicolas Bratza, the British judge who heads the court in Strasbourg told *The Times* that "no magic wand" would emerge and that attempts

The court is being played by defendants

Leading article, page 2

to alter the balance of power between the court and Parliament would fail.

Abu Qatada's lawyers lodged an appeal on Tuesday, blind-siding the Home Office which believed that the deadline for appeals to the court had expired 24 hours earlier. The Home Secretary denied that her officials muddled up their dates and insisted that Abu Qatada's re-arrest was legal.

Ministers refrained from publicly attacking the move, but officials sent a robustly worded letter to the court accusing Abu Qatada's lawyers of a deliberate attempt to thwart British legal process.

A senior government source told *The Times* that severe consequences would follow if Strasbourg revisited the decision. "Of course this is likely to be a

Continued on page 7, col 5

EUROPEAN COURT OF HUMAN RIGHTS
COUR EUROPÉENNE DES DROITS DE L'HOMME

Sir Nicolas Bratza, president of the court, centre-front, said that "no magic wand" would emerge from today's conference

Does May know what day it is?

Richard Ford Home Correspondent

Theresa May was facing mounting questions last night over whether it was a Home Office blunder which had thrown the deportation of Abu Qatada into disarray.

The European Court of Human Rights said that the deadline for the cleric's appeal was midnight on Tuesday, April 17 and that it was lodged an hour before. But the Home Office insisted that the deadline fell 24 hours earlier.

Lawyers for Abu Qatada, now in Bel-

The appeal 'is a delaying tactic from Abu Qatada'

Theresa May

marsh top-security jail in southeast London, claim in his appeal that the court was wrong when it ruled three months ago that he would not be at risk of torture if returned to Jordan.

The ruling was delivered in Strasbourg on Tuesday, January 17 and stated that it did not become final until "three months after the date of judgment".

Mrs May said yesterday: "I am sure that we got the deadline right, because you look at the treaty, and what the treaty says is that it is three months from the date of the judgment.

"As you would expect, we have been in touch with the European court over the last three months to check our understanding. They were absolutely clear that we were operating on the

Continued on page 6, col 1

IN THE NEWS

Murder and defiance in Syrian farming town

The regime of President Assad has brought horror to the town of Tal Rifaat, but it's 35,000 people will not submit to his thugs. *Times* writer Martin Fletcher reports from inside Syria. **World, page 31**

Tailored cancer care

Breast cancer will soon be treated as ten different diseases, giving women more personal care. **News, page 9**

Grand Prix protests

Formula One faced pressure to cancel the Bahrain Grand Prix amid growing pro-democracy protests. **Sport, page 72**

Tesco's £1bn gamble

Tesco will invest £1 billion to overhaul its British business in an attempt to restore sales growth. **Business, page 39**

Inside today

Chelsea's old boys shut out Barcelona

Sport, page 80

The Times 19 April 2012

The INDEPENDENT

Saturday Edition

ISSUE NO.8,810
£1.80

SATURDAY 3 JANUARY 2015

WWW.INDEPENDENT.CO.UK

From Russia with love: the mystery of Nick Clegg's great aunt Moura P.16

IN THE MAGAZINE

We are Malala
Her classmates' new life in Wales

The real Peter Cook
His closest friends recall a comic genius

Ron Paul
Me and Mo Mowlam

IN RADAR

2015's hottest tickets
Our critics' guide to the cultural highlights

IN VOICES

The joy of darts!
Howard Jacobson goes potty for the oche

THE BEST WRITING

Janet Street-Porter
What my divorces have taught me

Boyd Tonkin
HarperCollins and the erasing of Israel

Paul Scholes
on Gerrard's goodbye

Prince Andrew with Jeffrey Epstein in Central Park in New York in 2011 NI SYNDICATION

Twitter and Facebook 'allowing Islamophobia to flourish'

EXCLUSIVE
OLIVER WRIGHT
WHITEHALL EDITOR

Twitter and Facebook are refusing to take down hundreds of inflammatory Islamophobic postings from across their sites despite being alerted to the content by anti-racism groups, an investigation by *The Independent* has established.

The number of postings, some of which accuse Muslims of being rapists, paedophiles and comparable to cancer, has increased significantly in recent months in the aftermath of the Rotherham sex-abuse scandal and the murder of British hostages held by Isis.

The most extreme call for the execution of British Muslims – but in most cases those behind the abuse have not had their accounts suspended or the posts removed.

Facebook said it had to "strike the right balance" between freedom of expression and maintaining "a safe and trusted environment" but would remove any content reported to it that "directly attacks others based on their race". Twitter said it reviews all content that is reported for breaking its rules which prohibit specific threats of violence.

Over the past four months Muslim groups have been attempting to compile details of online abuse and report it to Twitter and Facebook. They have brought dozens of accounts and hundreds of messages to the attention of the social-media companies.

But despite this, most of the accounts reported are still easily accessible. On New Year's Eve the author of one of the accounts reported wrote: "If whites had groomed only paki girls 1 It would be a race hate crime. 2 There would be riots from all Muslim dogs."

Other examples of extremist postings on Twitter include:

■ A user posted an image of a girl with a noose around her neck with the caption: "6 per cent of white British girls will become sex slaves to the Islamic slave trade in Britain".

■ A tweet which reads: "Should have lost World War Two. Your daughters would be getting impregnated by handsome blond Germans instead of Pakistani goat herders. Good job Britain."

On Facebook a posting in response to the beheading of Westerners in Syria is also still easily accessible despite being reported to the company weeks ago. It reads: "For every person beheaded by these sick savages we should drag 10 off the streets and behead them, film it and put it online. For every child they cut in half… we cut one of their children in half. An eye for an eye."

When the comments were reported, Facebook said that

Continued on P.5 →

Prince Andrew accused of abusing teenage girl

PAUL PEACHEY, CAHAL MILMO AND ANDREW BUNCOMBE

The Royal Family was pulled into an international sex scandal after a woman claimed to have been repeatedly abused by Prince Andrew while held as a "slave" to wealthy men.

Buckingham Palace dismissed as "categorically untrue" the allegations made in US legal documents that the fifth in line to the throne had sex with a teenage girl in London, New York and at an orgy in the US Virgin Islands attended by underage girls.

The claims were made in court documents filed as part of legal action by a group of women who said they were abused by Jeffrey Epstein, a financier and former friend of the Prince, who was convicted of soliciting sex with an underage girl in 2008. Reports suggested the woman was aged 17 at the time of the alleged incidents with Prince Andrew, which would make her below the age of consent in Florida.

The papers said she was invited to Epstein's Florida mansion as a 15-year-old before becoming his "sex slave" from 1999 to 2002. She claims she was then passed around "politically connected and financially powerful people" that included the Prince. She

Continued on P.6 →

The Independent 3 January 2015

The British Teenager

The Sun newspaper is Britain's biggest tabloid and for decades it used to feature a daily 'Page 3' girl – a topless beauty. So it speaks volumes that the paper saw fit to expose in 2004 the unwholesome reality of teenage sexual promiscuity and its attendant problems. Its editorial of Monday 13 September 2004 spoke of 'Wasted lives'. Such an opinion was no more than the Muslim imams of Norway had expressed in 2003 (see above) but which incurred the wrath of the Prime Minister of Norway for their 'holier-than-thou' 'extremist' attitude which Mr Bondevik found divisive – when in fact it was pure Islamophobia. This was followed by the Daily Mail criticising the drinking culture of British youth, especially when on holiday abroad. No more than the imams of Norway had signalled – the Quran forbids the drinking of alcohol because the harm it does outweighs the benefits. Drinking in Norway by its youth is at levels that make the British look like teetotallers by comparison. But any criticism from a Muslim organisation will be taken as a criticism of 'our values.

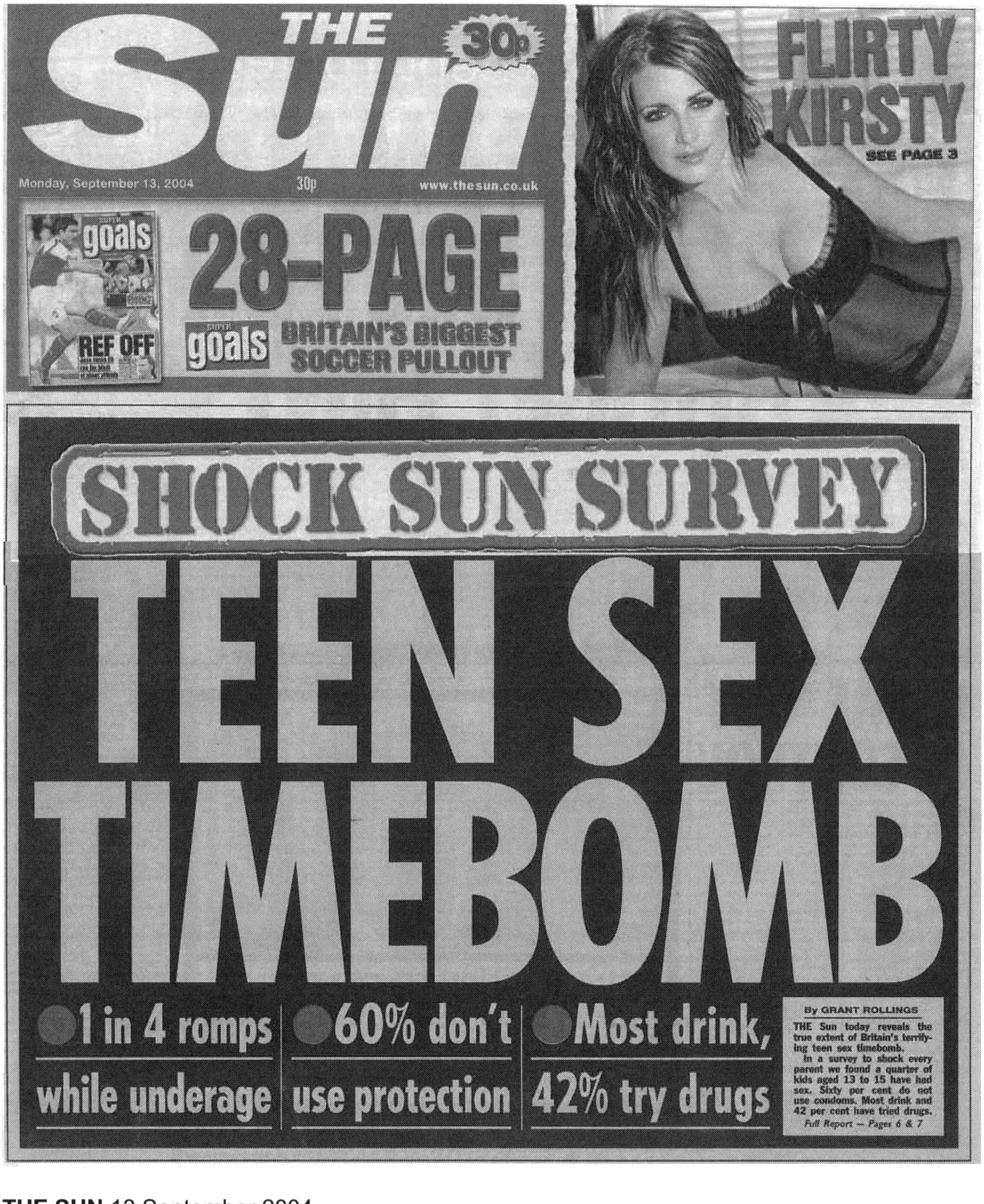

THE Sun 30p

Monday, September 13, 2004 30p www.thesun.co.uk

super goals

REF OFF

28-PAGE super goals BRITAIN'S BIGGEST SOCCER PULLOUT

FLIRTY KIRSTY

SEE PAGE 3

SHOCK SUN SURVEY

TEEN SEX TIMEBOMB

- 1 in 4 romps while underage
- 60% don't use protection
- Most drink, 42% try drugs

By GRANT ROLLINGS

THE Sun today reveals the true extent of Britain's terrifying teen sex timebomb.

In a survey to shock every parent we found a quarter of kids aged 13 to 15 have had sex. Sixty per cent do not use condoms. Most drink and 42 per cent have tried drugs.

Full Report — Pages 6 & 7

THE SUN 13 September 2004

Sun SURVEY REVEALS WHAT

WHO'S HAD GAY SEX? ✱
13–15s 7%
16–19s 11%

WHO'S HAD A ONE NIGHT STAND? ✱
13–15s 42%
16–19s 32%

WHO'S HAD UNPROTECTED SEX? ✱
13–15s 60%
16–19s 46%

WHO'S HAD AN STI?
13–15s 6%
16–19s 10%

WHO'S WORRIED ABOUT HIV/AIDS?
13–15s 28%
16–19s 54%

WHO'S HAD SEX WHILE DRUNK?
13–15s 23%
16–19s 26%

DO YOUR PARENTS KNOW YOU'VE HAD SEX? ✱
13–15s 24%
16–19s 45%

WHO'S BEEN IN TROUBLE WITH THE POLICE?
13–15s 42%
16–19s 10%

HAVE YOU SHOPLIFTED?
13–15s 27%
16–19s 22%

Teens in grip of sexual CRISIS

—SARAH GILL, SEX HEALTH EXPERT

By GRANT ROLLINGS & HARRY MacADAM

OUR teenagers are in the grip of a massive sexual health crisis, an expert warned last night.

Gynaecologist Dr Sarah Gill spoke out after a Sun survey exposed a horrifying teen culture of sex, drugs and alcohol in Britain today, including rampant underage sex.

The sex health expert said: "It is very important The Sun is highlighting this issue. We are in a huge sexual health crisis. The chance of picking up a sexually-transmitted infection is much higher than ten years ago.

"It is going to keep getting worse if people maintain the attitudes shown in this survey."

Our shock study revealed **A QUARTER** of 13 to 15-year-olds have had sex. And a staggering 60 per cent of those have had unprotected sex.

By 15, sexually-active teens will have already slept with more than two people. And by 19 they will have had more than four partners.

Experts predict an explosion in sexually-transmitted infections and an infertility timebomb.

Teens are not taking the dangers of sex seriously. Only one third of 13 to 15-year-olds are worried about HIV/Aids.

Disturbingly, it is the youngest age group who are taking the greatest risks.

Over a quarter of Britain's 13-15 age group have had sex and one in six of that total age group has had sex without contraception.

Sexually-active teens aged between 13 and 15 lose their virginity at an average age of just 13 years and three months.

Damaging

Half of the 16-19 age group have slept with someone and **HALF** of those have had unprotected sex. **42 PER CENT** of the sexually-active 13 to 15-year-olds admitted a one-night stand.

The decision to ignore warnings about sexual diseases is damaging the health of youngsters. Ten per cent of boys have had an infection.

A similar number have been drunk while having sex and ten per cent of sexually-active teens have slept with someone of the same sex.

The Sun survey also showed that drug and alcohol abuse is **WORST** among youngest teens.

A massive 42 per cent of 13 to 15-year-olds have tried cannabis. A staggering 96 per cent of all teens drink with 45 per cent of them boozing at least once a week.

Also, when 18-30 year-olds were asked if they would fight for Queen and country, only a **FIFTH** said they would do so unconditionally.

And 34 per cent believe this country is racist.

More than half say they do not trust the police and a third believe Britain is stuck in the past. Despite this a whopping 80 per cent of youngsters said they were proud to be British.

The sex and drug survey was carried out by Dubit, a market research company that specialises in talking to young people. The firm also carries out statistical work for the Home Office. It polled 611 13 to 19-year-olds in all regions of the UK. The data is weighted to ensure it is representative of the youth population.

● The responses asterisked are from teens who have had sex. The others are for the whole of the survey group.

The Sun Says — Page Eight

HAVE YOU CONSIDERED SUICIDE?
13–15s 16%
16–19s 36%

HAVE YOU DRUNK ALCOHOL?
YES 96%

WHO'S TAKEN SPEED?
13–15s 9%
16–19s 8%

WHO'S TAKEN ECSTASY?
13–15s 8%
16–19s 5%

WHO'S USED COCAINE?
13–15s 5%
16–19s 4%

TOMORROW: TEENAGE CONFESSIONS

THE SUN 13 September 2004

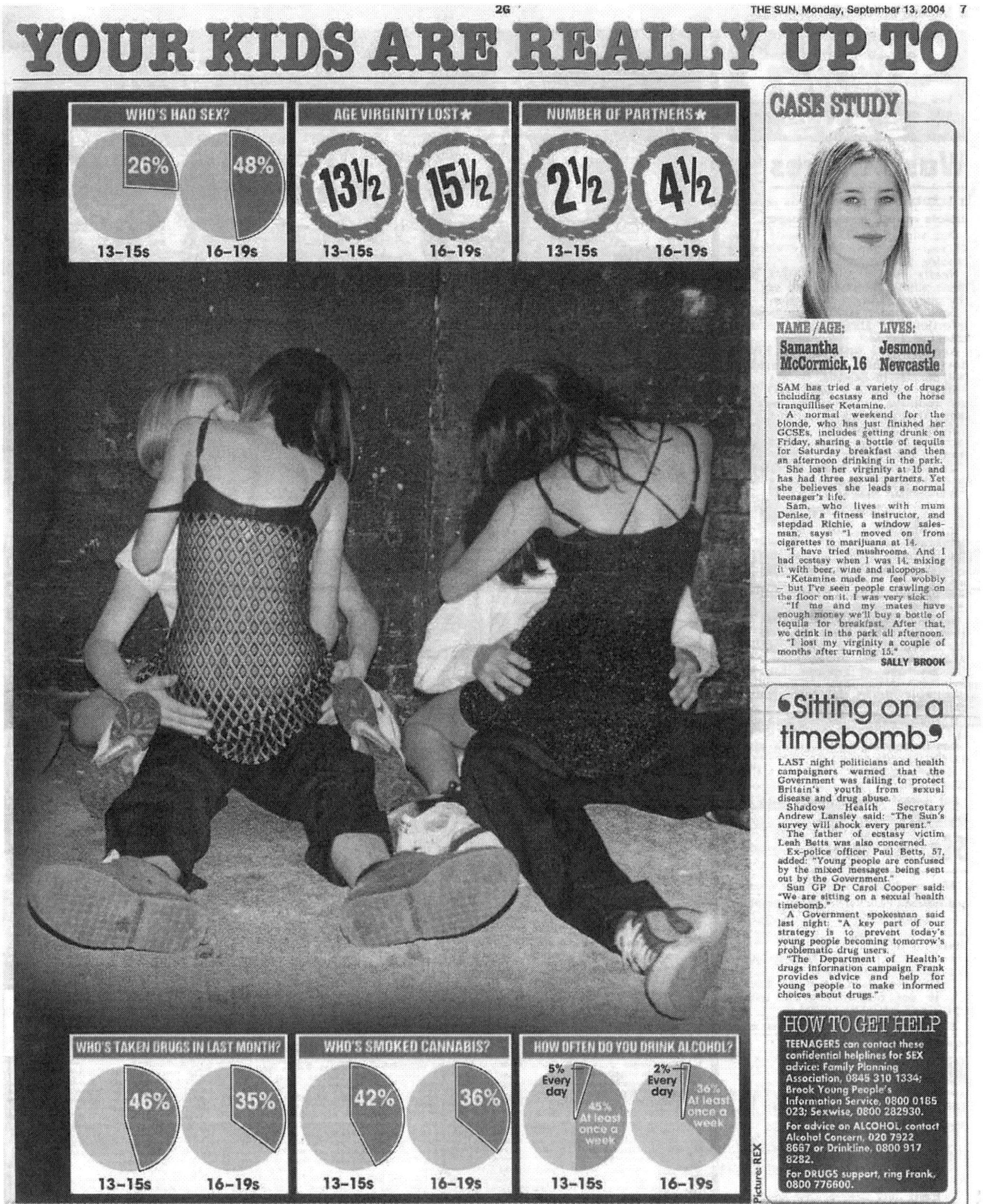

2G THE SUN, Monday, September 13, 2004 7

YOUR KIDS ARE REALLY UP TO

CASE STUDY

NAME/AGE: Samantha McCormick, 16

LIVES: Jesmond, Newcastle

SAM has tried a variety of drugs including ecstasy and the horse tranquilliser Ketamine.

A normal weekend for the blonde, who has just finished her GCSEs, includes getting drunk on Friday, sharing a bottle of tequila for Saturday breakfast and then an afternoon drinking in the park.

She lost her virginity at 15 and has had three sexual partners. Yet she believes she leads a normal teenager's life.

Sam, who lives with mum Denise, a fitness instructor, and stepdad Richie, a window salesman, says: "I moved on from cigarettes to marijuana at 14.

"I have tried mushrooms. And I had ecstasy when I was 14, mixing it with beer, wine and alcopops.

"Ketamine made me feel wobbly – but I've seen people crawling on the floor on it. I was very sick.

"If me and my mates have enough money we'll buy a bottle of tequila for breakfast. After that, we drink in the park all afternoon.

"I lost my virginity a couple of months after turning 15."

SALLY BROOK

'Sitting on a timebomb'

LAST night politicians and health campaigners warned that the Government was failing to protect Britain's youth from sexual disease and drug abuse.

Shadow Health Secretary Andrew Lansley said: "The Sun's survey will shock every parent."

The father of ecstasy victim Leah Betts was also concerned.

Ex-police officer Paul Betts, 57, added: "Young people are confused by the mixed messages being sent out by the Government."

Sun GP Dr Carol Cooper said: "We are sitting on a sexual health timebomb."

A Government spokesman said last night: "A key part of our strategy is to prevent today's young people becoming tomorrow's problematic drug users.

"The Department of Health's drugs information campaign Frank provides advice and help for young people to make informed choices about drugs."

HOW TO GET HELP

TEENAGERS can contact these confidential helplines for SEX advice: Family Planning Association, 0845 310 1334; Brook Young People's Information Service, 0800 0185 023; Sexwise, 0800 282930.

For advice on ALCOHOL, contact Alcohol Concern, 020 7922 8667 or Drinkline, 0800 917 8282.

For DRUGS support, ring Frank, 0800 776600.

THE SUN 13 September 2004

8 THE SUN, Monday, September 13, 2004

THE SUN SAYS

Wasted lives

A SEXUAL health timebomb is about to explode among our young teenagers.

Our survey into the lives of 13 to 15-year-olds makes deeply alarming reading for parents.

Nearly one in four in their early teens admits to having had sex. But the majority use no protection.

Small wonder sexually-transmitted infections are almost as common as catching a cold.

And hardly a surprise that Britain has the highest rate of teenage pregnancies in Europe.

Many youngsters say they don't use condoms because they have sex while they're drunk or on drugs.

Make no mistake, there is a terrible price to be paid for this wanton behaviour.

Diseases caught young in life can cause infertility later in life.

Worse than that, AIDS kills.

Chastity

In America, more and more teenagers are taking a pledge of chastity until after they are married.

Here, we bombard under-16s with sex, go soft on cannabis and send the message with 24-hour drinking that alcohol is cool.

Sex education in schools has been questionable for years. So, too, has the teaching of morality both at school and in the home.

A low age of consent, for both heterosexuals and homosexuals, inevitably draws in even younger children.

If youngsters do not learn to value self-restraint, there is little to stop them descending to the levels of the animal world.

Many teenagers clearly don't think clean living is cool.

But neither is an unwanted baby or a lingering death from AIDS.

Amanda Platell

Who will tell the truth on teenage sex?

ONE in four teenagers now has sex, many as young as 13 years old. The majority of these sexual encounters are unprotected and 42 per cent are one-night stands. Most of these barely pubescents also drink and 42 per cent take drugs.

The results are from a phone poll of teenagers. While there can be an element of boasting in self-reporting surveys, if the problem is even half as bad as these kids say, it is still shocking.

Is it any wonder there has been a decline in the mental health of our young, with a 70 per cent increase in anxiety and depression, and one in five girls suffering emotional problems?

And what do we do about it? We wring our hands and secretly console ourselves it's not our nice kids, surely. Yet a new study covering three generations of 15-year-olds in 1974, 1986 and 1999 claims this decline respects no social or ethnic boundaries and is independent of whether children come from divorced, single or married families.

But the most staggering fact is the deafening silence on the issue of teenage sex and drugs. Politicians are struck dumb about the absence of moral values in a whole generation of teenagers.

It is left to black community leaders to speak out. Garth Crooks, the BBC sports commentator and former Tottenham Hotspur player, put us all to shame with his speech to the London Schools and Black Child conference: "Street culture will become a deadly virus ripping indiscriminately through our next generation, robbing millions of their potential." He condemned the gangsta-rap culture and the decline in cultural values. And he's right. But who in the Establishment has the guts to speak out, to say to kids that promiscuity and drugs only bring unhappiness? I vaguely remember such a speech by Tony Blair ... once.

Public figures fear that, by taking a moral stand, they'll be branded out of touch, which is instant death to any politician. Just ask the Tories.

So they don't line up to condemn the culture of cannabis-taking at school. Yet last Friday saw the death of our youngest heroin victim. Matthew Girvin, 13, started on dope and quickly progressed to heroin. With the government downgrading cannabis to category-C, why should kids think drugs are wrong?

It is my generation who are most culpable. We drank, many of us took drugs, the Pill brought us freedom from unplanned pregnancies. But with it came an "anything goes" attitude and a belief it was wrong to judge others' sexual mores.

NOW few young girls worry about getting pregnant. With no reprobation on teen pregnancy, none really on abortion and the readily available morning-after pill, what's there to worry about? The terrible thing is that all this "freedom" has not been emancipating but enslaving, forcing kids into behaviour that their minds and their bodies are not ready for. No wonder they're depressed.

And who is there to guide them? Where are the cool Beyoncé-like role models who could make a difference when teenage girls and boys need them most? Who is there to enable these kids to say: "No"?

Pop stars make money out of teenagers but are prepared to put nothing back. Britney Spears' extolling the virtues of virginity turned out to be nothing but a cheap publicity stunt that just deepened the cynicism.

And maybe we haven't even got the whole truth from these surveys. Bob Geldof's 15-year-old daughter, Peaches, said at the weekend: "People should open their eyes to what's actually happening. Most of my friends lost their virginity at 13."

Out of the mouths of babes.

Oh, do shut up

WHEN did we become a city of hooters? For weeks the road outside my home has been dug up to replace water pipes. It has meant temporary lights, queues and terrible tempers. It has proved how selfish some motorists are. The hooting is bad enough. But they do it right outside the busiest hospital in north London. Sick people deserve a bit of peace and quiet.

THE SUN 13 September 2004 **EVENING STANDARD** 14 September 2004

Abortion rate across England and Wales climbs to new record

By John von Radowitz

THE ABORTION rate in England and Wales reached an all-time high last year.

Government statistics revealed last night that 181,600 women terminated pregnancies last year, up 3.2 per cent from 2002. The figure represents a rate of 17.5 abortions per 1,000 women aged 15 to 44, the highest ever recorded.

In 2002, the total number of abortions had actually fallen by half a per cent to 175,900.

The vast majority of women seeking abortions last year were in the 20 to 24 age bracket. A total of 51,124 women in this group had terminations.

But there was also a high number of teenage abortions. A total of 37,043 took place among girls of 15 to 19; higher than the 36,018 recorded for the 25 to 29 age group.

A statement from the Department of Health said: "The figures are disappointing. However, no contraception method is 100 per cent effective and there will always be women seeking an abortion as they are legally entitled to do." The DoH bulletin said abortion rates for 2003 in all age groups were higher than those for 2002. The greatest rate of increase was for the 20 to 24 age group, at about 31 per 1,000 women.

Three quarters of abortions were carried out on single women, and the number carried out for medical reasons rose from 14 per cent to 17. More than half the total number of terminations, about 58 per cent, were carried out at under 10 weeks of pregnancy, and a further 29 per cent at 10 to 12 weeks.

Anne Weyman, chief executive of the Family Planning Association, said: "It is good news that more abortions are taking place under 10 weeks and that there are higher rates of medical abortion. It is encouraging to see access to abortion speeded up and women being given a choice of methods.

"But again we see more figures exposing the desperate need for investment in NHS contraceptive services, including support for the professionals trying to run them.

"Access to good quality, widely available services is essential in preventing unplanned pregnancies. However, despite saving the NHS an estimated £2.5 billion a year, contraception is still treated as the Cinderella service of public health. Providing individuals with access to the full range of contraceptive methods should not be regarded as a luxury service when it is each person's right to be able to control their own fertility and safeguard their sexual health."

The Department of Health said a key aim of both the Government's sexual health and HIV strategy and its teenage pregnancy strategy, was to reduce unplanned pregnancies.

It added: "Provision of good quality contraceptive services is key in achieving this. In 2003/04, we allocated £200,000 to the RCN for training, and in 2004/05 we will be allocating £500,000 to contraceptive services and £160,000 for national projects.

"We have also convened a group of key experts, including representatives from the Faculty of Family Planning and Reproductive Healthcare, the Royal College of General Practitioners and the Family Planning Association to develop an action plan to support contraceptive services at local level."

Yesterday's figures showed 9,100 pregnancies were terminated among visitors, mostly from Northern Ireland and the Irish Republic.

THE INDEPENDENT 28 August 2004

BINGE

Yesterday Mr Blair defended 24-hour drinking by saying that those who go to the theatre and want a nightcap should not be 'inconvenienced'. Look at these pictures and ask yourselves what planet he's on

Arguing all the way to the cells: One of those who have made once genteel Brighton hell at night

Another black Friday in Cardiff: This man is almost comatose with alcohol in St Mary Street

Late-night Leeds: She's out of her head, has lost her bag, and is in danger of all kinds of assault

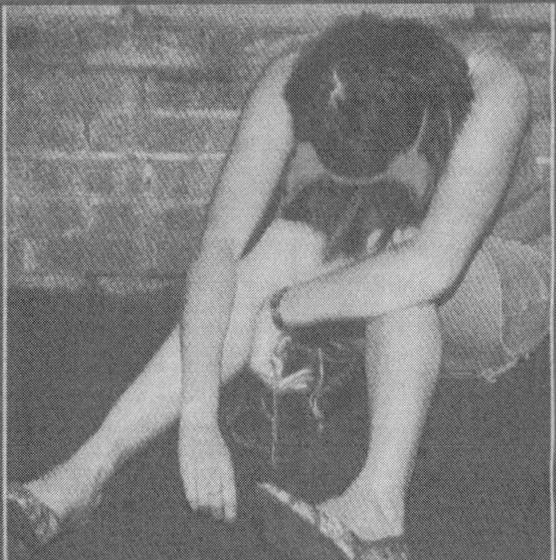

What's the opposite of ladylike? Too drunk to stand up in Nottingham

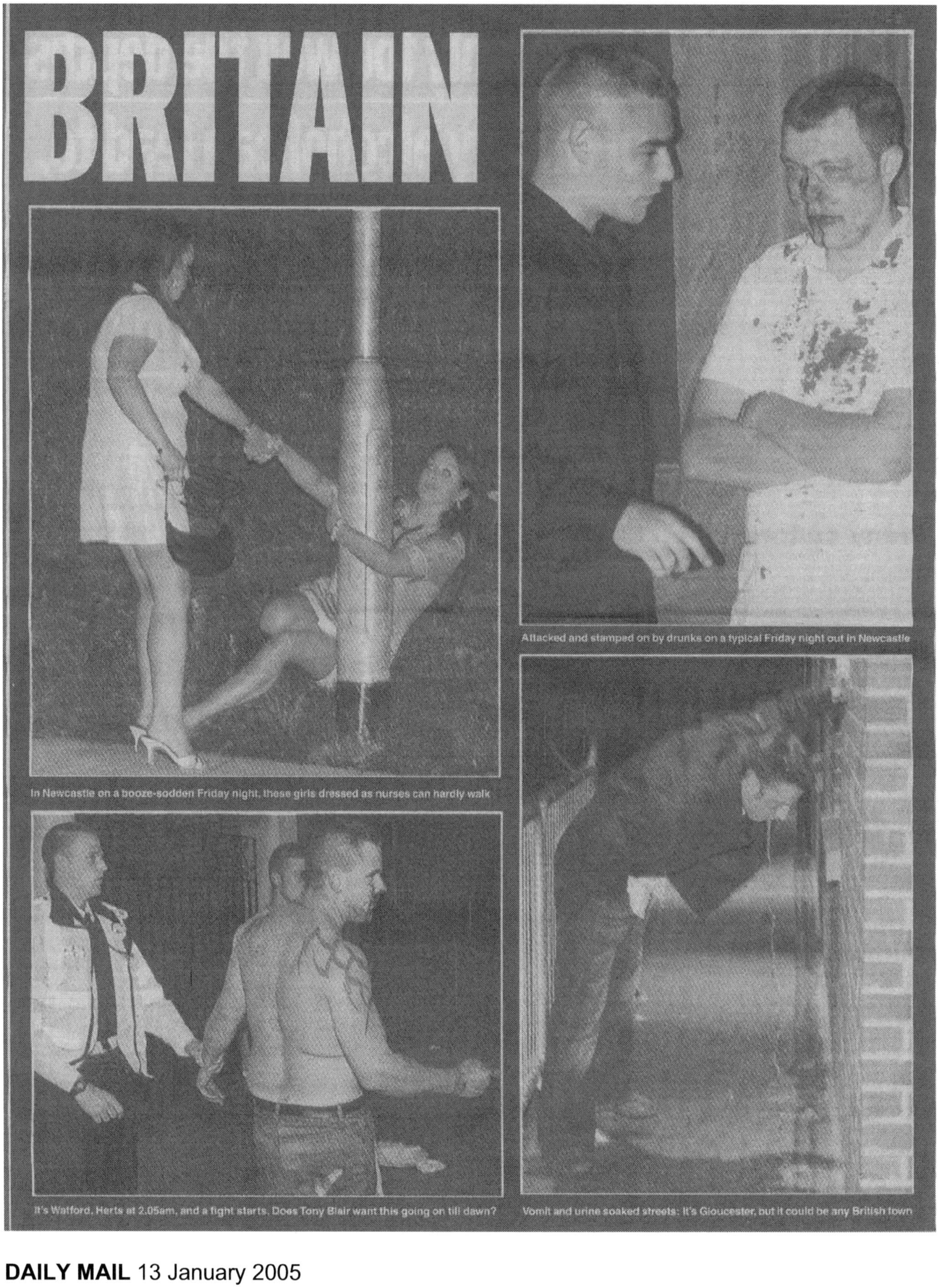

BRITAIN

In Newcastle on a booze-sodden Friday night, these girls dressed as nurses can hardly walk

It's Watford, Herts at 2.05am, and a fight starts. Does Tony Blair want this going on till dawn?

Attacked and stamped on by drunks on a typical Friday night out in Newcastle

Vomit and urine soaked streets: It's Gloucester, but it could be any British town

DAILY MAIL 13 January 2005

‘LUNACY’ OF 24-HOUR DRINKING

Daily Mail, Wednesday, August 10, 2005 Page 11

but judges and police warn of a terrifying descent into brutality and barbarism

into ‘Faliraki UK’

From a judge, the damning verdict

AMONG the wealth of evidence submitted to the Home Office was a damning assessment from a Crown Court judge, Charles Harris, QC. Here, we publish his testimony in full.

I ONLY try a modest amount of crime, which I do in three pretty different places.

Warwick, an old county town , which takes a lot of work from South-East Birmingham, Northampton, a largely ruined old county town which gets custom from itself and places like Kettering and Oxford, which needs no description.

At all three, the lists contain a substantial quantity of violence, from S18 (Section 18 of the Public Order Act, prohibiting threatening or insulting behaviour) to affray, with offences often allocated with little apparent relationship to their seriousness.

It is very rare for any of these offences of violence to be committed by someone who has not been drinking. Sometimes the quantity of alcohol is simply beyond belief.

A gallon is common, 12 pints by no means rare. Often these quantities of beer are diluted by various additions of spirits. It is becoming common, too, for cocaine to be taken as well.

It is not just the illiterate and inarticulate underclass which does this, quite bright people in well-paid jobs do it too (with a surprising number of women). Their sole idea of fun is to get as

Judge Charles Harris, QC

drunk as possible in bars where this can be done as easily as possible. This is the object of their evenings of pleasure, which last as long as they have money and can find places to spend it. Often they fight in the pubs, generally over

An eruption of blind savagery

some vestigial or imagined provocation. If not, they roam the streets in malign, short-fused and generalised hostility, until some victim presents himself.

Perhaps he once went out with a girl the intoxicated thug knew, perhaps he has a telephone he wants, perhaps he is simply in the way on the pavement.

There follows a brief and ill-expressed altercation, and then an eruption of blind savagery. Someone falls down, and he is not then left, vanquished, as an animal would leave a rival. He will be repeatedly kicked. It is quite astonishing how many survive this with only modest injury.

For a while these people are simply savages, angry, blind and brutal. They are in this condition because of what they have been drinking. They are so ill-educated or made crude by inadequately civilising influences in their homes that they seem unable to drink in an acceptable 'continental' fashion. The more there is to drink, and the more time to drink it, they will keep drinking. If it was not for the widespread availability of alcohol, I believe that crimes of violence would be at very modest levels indeed.

But there is no attempt made by the Government to lessen public drinking. No 'Don't drink and drive' type campaigns are waged against those who drink and prowl (and often walk into contact with cars, for which the drivers are then blamed).

The situation is already grave, if not grotesque, and to facilitate this by making drinking facilities more widely available is close to lunacy. It simply means that our town and city centres are abandoned every night to tribes of pugnacious, drunk, noisy, vomiting louts.

The cost to the health service must be vast. The cost of those who try to live civilised lives in urban surroundings is huge. The take by the Government in alcohol tax is no doubt excellent.

In my view we should express a very high level of concern indeed, and suggest that what is needed, as a start (the subject is a large one) is a lot less provision of drinking facilities, not a lot more.

DAILY MAIL 10 August 2005

THE SPECTATOR 4 March 2006 **SEX AND SOCIETY**

Why foreigners love us

Rod Liddle doesn't mean to give offence, but suggests that one of Britain's strongest appeals as a tourist destination is that our women put it about

An opinion poll of young European men recently asked which of the Continent's women they would most like to sleep with. Italian and French girls took the honours, but there was a strong showing from the Swedish ladies, which shows that a lot of gentlemen really do prefer blondes, even if they're likely to harangue you about Third World debt and gender inequalities before, after or even during the act of intercourse. British girls were nowhere in sight, but we should not reflect too sadly upon this — because there was another question a little further down the page, and our babes won by a mile. It asked, which country's women have you *already* slept with? Absolutely no contest.

This propensity of British girls to give of themselves, selflessly, over and over again, their minds seemingly unpoisoned by even the vaguest notions of discrimination, is excellent news for our tourism industry, which over the last few years has shown greater growth than any other in Europe. Youth tourism (meaning for those under the age of 35 — you may have noticed that the definition of 'youth' has gloriously expanded in recent years, perhaps in line with the increasing age of our population) constitutes a respectable 20 per cent of the world market. Aside from being lucrative, it also, according to the World Tourism Organisation, 'plays a highly important social integration function', a concept which British girls have taken to their hearts in a most committed and literal fashion. So about this time each year, when Europe's young men mull over their holiday options, their limited budgets mean that they are apt to forget that what they really yearn for is to sink back into the fragrant, sophisticated embrace of a Collette or Gina; they are rational, they go for what is achievable — a quick knee-trembler by the bins behind the local KFC from a Kylie or a Kelis. They may indeed end up with a pig in a poke, but at least it will be an amenable and accommodating pig. A guaranteed poke in a pig, in fact.

The question which British tourism chiefs should be asking one another is why this should be the case, why British women are so much more accommodating than the girls of Spain, Luxembourg or Belgium. After all, one should always very carefully look a gift horse in the mouth.

In fact, this is a comparatively recent phenomenon. British girls were not always 'easy', as they say; ease of access has been thrust upon them somehow during the last 30 or 40 years and with a wholeheartedness that is not yet apparent on the European mainland. It has been a quite remarkable social change and one not frequently commented upon, except obliquely, perhaps for reasons of political correctness. It is, of course, a woman's right to choose to have an infinite number of sexual partners if she so wishes, and not one which we ought to question. And so, over the last half-century or so, the average number of sexual partners enjoyed by women in their mid-twenties has risen from zero or one to 12 or 14. The number of sexual partners enjoyed by similarly aged men has increased too, although not nearly so dramatically. From which one

Fans of Tessa Jowell waiting for the outcome of Italian police inquiries.

can perhaps deduce that there is a gap between doing and admitting; men still admit to having had more sexual partners than women, but the gap is narrowing by the year. The real social change, then, has not been in male behaviour — which is much as it ever was — but in female behaviour. The old, traditional notion that women were the 'gatekeepers' to sexual intercourse has dissolved, for one reason or another. British women are not guarding their gates with anything like the discipline or rigour which they once did or, so it would seem, women still do 20 miles away across the Channel.

The reasons cited for such a change and discrepancy usually fit the political prejudices of the people advancing them. The decline of the Established Church in Britain and as a result the winnowing away of such notions as deferred gratification (a formerly potent, Protestant-derived ethic now almost extinct in every walk of British life) and the consequent absence of any ideological justification for sexual virtue and virginity, for example. But there's not much doubt that this is in the mix somewhere. Weddings now seem to be viewed as enjoyable, if expensive, social gatherings which can be repeated with impunity every four or five years or so. We might also aver that the pull of the Roman Catholic Church in Spain, France and Italy has declined far less markedly. But it is hard to make a case for Britain as a more secular country than, say, Holland and Denmark, or even the Protestant tranche of Germany.

The fashionable explanation these days is alcohol or, to use the government-approved buzz phrase, 'binge-drinking'. Or, to use the gender-appropriate term from the glossy magazines — the 'ladette' culture of young women drinking vast amounts of alcohol and then, having chemically removed their inhibitions, physically removing their clothes at the drop of a hat. We are told ad infinitum by bourgeois commentators that over here we do not have a culture which properly understands or appreciates alcohol; instead of enjoying a nice glass of Sancerre with our meal at an agreeable pavement café, accompanied by, say, a plate of olives and some peasant-recipe crusty bread, we swallow vast gallons of acrid plonk with a bag of Walkers and then throw up in the bushes and stagger home with an ill-considered partner. But these dark ruminations ignore two crucial factors. Firstly, British women do not succumb unwittingly to the depredations of Wikid and Archers and so on and then helplessly surrender their virtues. They drink vast quantities in order to partake of ad-hoc sexual intercourse: the intention was there at the beginning of the evening — and if you doubt that, look at what they chose to wear when they were still sober. Alcohol may lubricate the romantic, moist rummagings by the bins behind the KFC,

'No giving up smoking at the bar, please.'

but I would argue that the motive was present already, m'Lud.

It is hard, too, to blame radical feminism. Sure, what began as a movement almost pathologically distrustful of men has evolved into an ideology which has embraced us beyond our wildest dreams. I well remember a former girlfriend of mine informing me sadly, by means of an explanation for her outrageous act of infidelity with a close friend, that she had been 'programmed by the patriarchal society never to say no to a man' and hence she'd been coerced by the white male hegemony into shagging my mate. On a dhurrie. She had not meant to, but she had. That was back in about 1981, the time of the Greenham Common women and organisations called 'Neasden Wimmin Against Everything' and so on, a time when one simply did not demur in the face of feminist arguments about, well, anything. Since then the thesis has evolved from 'We can't say no!' to 'Why the hell should we say no?', which is, frankly, fine by me. But again, it is difficult to make the argument that feminism was any more strident in Britain than it was in Germany or Holland.

It may, in the end, prove to be a combination of all of these factors, allied to perpetual exposure to a popular press and televisual media that are obsessed with sexual intercourse in all of its increasingly diverse manifestations. Sex lurches towards us from every conceivable, sulphurous angle. Even Tories have sex these days, quite openly: what is the world coming to?

My suspicion is that British girls 'put out', as the Americans have it, because they are expected to and because there is no reason not to. They are doing what society — and Italian male tourists — expect of them, without fear or favour. If you think they are wrongheaded in their behaviour, then think quickly and invent a reason for them to change their behaviour. Meanwhile, the rest of Europe can lie back and simply enjoy.

DAILY EXPRESS

WE'RE BACKING BRITAIN — express.co.uk — TUESDAY, JULY 23, 2019 65p

STRICTLY'S SISTER ACT

NEW JUDGE IS REVEALED: SEE PAGE 7

Hottest July day ever on the way

SEE PAGE 9

FANTASIST WHO MADE A MOCKERY OF JUSTICE

Police blasted over £2million inquiry into VIP sex abuse lies

By **John Twomey** and **Paul Jeeves**

POLICE chiefs were in the dock last night after a self-confessed paedophile was found guilty of falsely accusing VIPs of child murder and abuse.

Former children's nurse Carl Beech was on suicide

TURN TO PAGE 4

Cool dude Rod wears it well

SEE PAGE 3

DAILY EXPRESS 23 July 2019

Fantasist Carl Beech. The story of Carl Beech and the gullible Metropolitan Police who believed his pathological sex-abuse lies regarding senior British figures rocked Britain in 2019. The British Press, in particular the Daily Mail, expertly tore apart a pathetic Metropolitan Police force who covered up for their amateurish efforts when trying to investigate the allegations of Carl Beech. Eventually Carl Beech got a very long prison sentence, but not before the lives and reputations of his victims had been destroyed as for two years the Met Police believed him. But Norway's own Carl Beech – the registered mental patient Heidi Schøne - was never exposed by the Norwegian Press for the fantasist she so very obviously was. That job was left to the Muslim London Solicitor himself: 25 years of very exhausting litigation in the Norwegian and English courts. The 'free press' of Norway were in fact enslaved to bigotry due to their isolated, inbred attitudes and aversion to the 'Muslim man'.

FROM PAGE ONE

His vile sex ring lies smeared innocent men. How did police ever believe him?

watch as he faced a lengthy prison sentence for tricking the Yard into believing bizarre lies about a non-existent Westminster child sex ring.

In one of the most controversial inquiries in the history of the Metropolitan Police, a team of experienced Yard detectives took the pervert at his word.

Describing his claims as "credible and true," they launched Operation Midland – a £2million investigation which resulted in no arrests.

But many legal experts were astounded that Beech – who served as a school governor and NSPCC volunteer – was taken seriously.

One commented: "His statements about the VIPs sex ring were not only bizarre, they were simply incredible and untrue. They were transparently false."

Despite the debacle and waste of

Det Supt Kenny McDonald led hunt

taxpayers' money, no police officer has been disciplined over Operation Midland.

There were calls for them to be investigated last night led by the son of the late Lord Janner.

Daniel Janner QC, whose father Lord Janner of Braunstone QC faced allegations before he died, said police must be held accountable.

He said: "The policemen who put out that Carl Beech's lies were 'credible and true' in 2014 should be prosecuted for the crime of misfeasance in a public office."

Beech – then known only as Nick – told a stream of malicious lies leading to heavy-handed police raids on the homes of Second World War hero Lord Bramall, now 95, the late Lord Brittan and former Conservative MP Harvey Proctor.

The three men, and a series of others named by Beech including

Lord Janner faced accusations

Sir Edward Heath was named

Lord Brittan was investigated

Harvey Proctor is suing police

Sir Edward Heath, were completely innocent. But their reputations were dragged through the mire.

Mr Proctor lost his job and his home after he was falsely identified by Beech as being one of the sadistic murder gang.

The former MP blasted the Met describing Operation Midland as a "truly disgraceful chapter in the history of British policing". He is suing the force for £1million.

Lord Bramall and others have already received substantial payouts from the public purse.

Beech, 51, initially made his bizarre allegations through the now defunct Exaro news agency and won support from Labour's deputy leader Tom Watson, then an influential backbencher, the BBC and other news outlets.

He repeated the outrageous lies in a series of interviews with the Yard between 2012 and 2015.

Over hours of tearful interviews, Beech claimed that his late stepfather, an Army major, raped him, then passed him on to other officers including generals.

At a now notorious Scotland Yard press conference, Detective Superintendent Kenny McDonald described Beech's allegations as "credible and true" even though there was no corroboration.

He alleged he had been tortured at military bases and subjected to savage sex abuse by other establishment figures in the 1970s and 1980s. Beech named Sir Edward, Mr Proctor and Jimmy Savile as well as former heads of the security and intelligence services and other VIPs figures as members of the fictitious sex ring.

The fantasist claimed to have witnessed the rape and murder of a boy who could have been a missing teenager called Martin Allen.

Beech said another youth was beaten to death by the gang and a third was deliberately mowed down by a car and killed.

After Operation Midland collapsed, retired judge Sir Richard Henriques was brought in to investigate the way the Yard carried out Operation Midland.

Damningly, Sir Richard said Beech's claims should have been probed "without any of the men named by Nick ever knowing about it".

Stung by the collapse of the operation, the Met's then Commissioner Sir Bernard Hogan-Howe called in Northumbria Police to investigate

SEVEN MAJOR FABRICATIONS

THE CPS was able to show seven key claims which Beech had fabricated or lied about.

● *Lie:* He had a fear of swimming after being tortured at pools by his abusers.
Reality: He enjoyed swimming and did so all over the world, from theme parks to snorkelling on honeymoon.

● *Lie:* He suffered electric shock treatment, fractures and puncture wounds.
Reality: His ex-wife never noticed any marks and his only injury on file was a skiing accident aged 15.

● *Lie:* Former MP Harvey Proctor threatened to cut his genitals with a penknife.
Reality: His wife said the knife was stored in Beech's "happy memories" box.

● *Lie:* He was regularly taken out of school and abused.
Reality: School reports showed good attendance and he received an award for 100 per cent punctuality.

● *Lie:* Beech sketched abuse locations based on memories "flashing up in his head".
Reality: He researched the sites on the internet.

● *Lie:* He saw the murder of three children including "Scott" and another allegedly killed by Harvey Proctor.
Reality: Scott did not exist and Beech manufactured all claims about Mr Proctor.

● *Lie:* Witness "Fred" was in email contact with Beech and contacted police to express fears over co-operating with the investigation.
Reality: "Fred" never existed and Beech sent the emails.

'Swimming fear'...Beech takes dip

'CASE SHOWS WHAT CAN GO WRONG'

COMMENT

JENNY WILTSHIRE

Head of general crime at Hickman & Rose solicitors

THIS shocking case illustrates the serious problems that can occur when the police assume that someone who claims to be a victim of crime actually is one.

Officers have a duty to investigate allegations of criminality dispassionately by pursuing lines of inquiry that may support or undermine what they have been told. This case shows what can go wrong when they initially accept false claims as fact.

In my view the problems begin with the practice, widespread in the criminal justice system, of using the word "victim" to describe anyone making a complaint. From this uncritical start, police too often proceed on the assumption that a suspect is guilty, rather than innocent until proven guilty.

We should all be grateful that the police and CPS eventually treated Beech as a suspect rather than a victim.

However, this was not before irreparable damage was done to the reputations of those he named as perpetrators, some of whom were no longer alive to defend themselves.

In my view the problems this case highlights are now so endemic in the criminal justice system that new legislation is needed to maintain suspects' anonymity until they are charged.

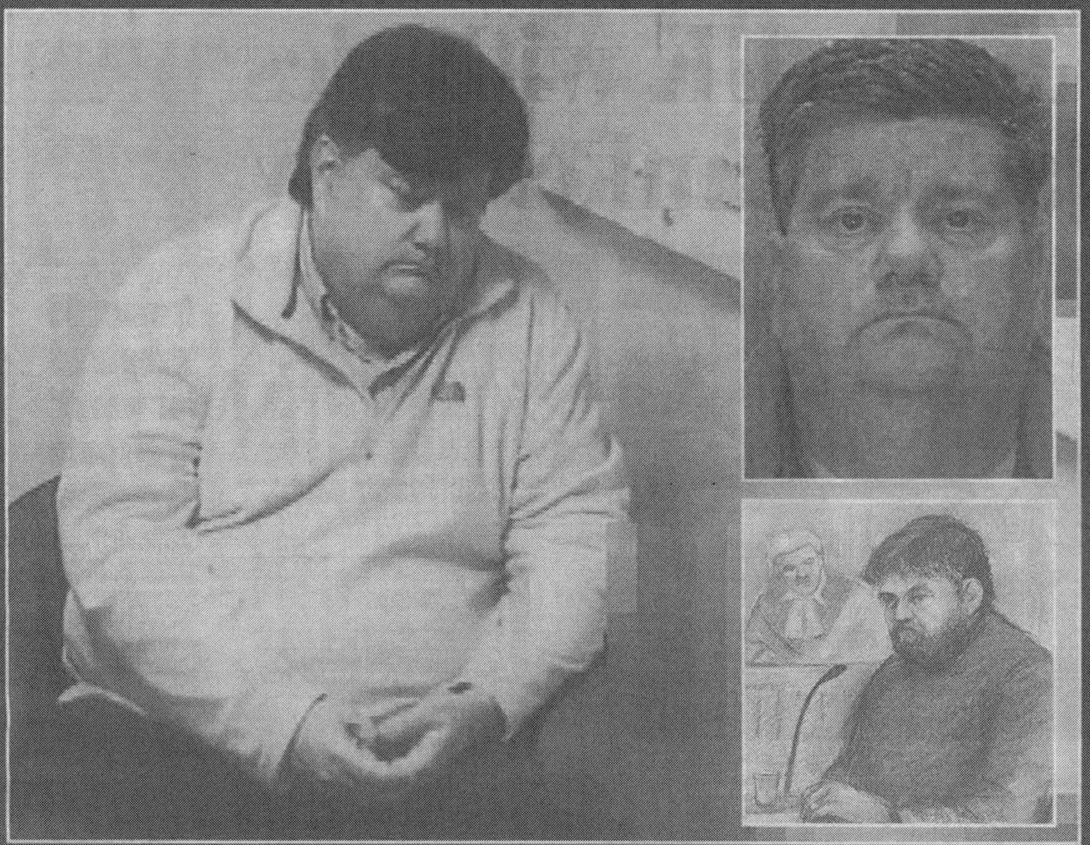

Carl Beech during his tearful interviews where he invented the allegations and at the time of his arrest, top, and court sketch of him in the dock yesterday

Beech. He was due to go on trial for downloading vile images of child sex abuse but fled to Sweden.

He was later extradited and charged with 12 counts of perverting the course of justice. He was further accused of defrauding taxpayers out of £22,000 in a false criminal compensation payout after saying Savile had raped him.

Yesterday, a jury at Newcastle found him guilty of all 12 counts of perverting the course of justice and of fraud.

He is due to be sentenced on Friday.

Beech, of Quedgeley, Glos, denied all the charges against him.

After the verdicts, the Met's Deputy Commissioner Sir Stephen House admitted the force "did not get everything right".

Yesterday, the Independent Office for Police Conduct cleared three officers who were investigated over misconduct allegations relating to applications for search warrants.

Sir Stephen said in a statement: "It must be remembered also that the work of Operation Midland was carried out against a backdrop of intense scrutiny and allegations that in the past the Met had covered up sensitive allegations about prominent people.

"It remains true that investigating allegations of sexual offences is a very complex and challenging area of police work. Those complexities are compounded where those allegations stretch back many decades."

OPINION: PAGE 12

Boy who enjoyed a privileged childhood in leafy suburbia

WHILE fraud Carl Beech told the world he had seen unimaginable horrors in his childhood, the truth is he had a very privileged upbringing.

As an only child living in leafy Kingston-upon-Thames in south-west London, he was given his own horse and a dog.

There were summer holidays in Malta and Tunisia, a ski trip to Austria when he was 15, and he and his mother Charmian, an ex-nurse who became a vicar, formed a tight bond.

He claimed the abuse began after her brief marriage to his stepfather, the late Major Ray Beech. They parted after four months in 1976 due to his drunken domestic violence.

Beech, 51, claimed in adulthood his stepfather, who retired from the Army on health grounds, raped him and passed him on to his superiors to be exploited by paedophiles at the top of British society.

Many observers now doubt that accusation of abuse by his stepfather, given the way he subsequently changed his story in blogs.

Beech told police the alleged VIP paedophiles "The Ring" punished him when he broke their instruction not to have school friends by murdering a boy at his school. But Northumbria Police found two friends from the Tudor School in Kingston who recalled happily spending time in the library with him.

Steven White said under oath. "I think we bonded. We were all probably socially awkward, spending time in the library and talking." Jonathon Budd remembered him as "a good kid" who his parents liked.

Beech became a paediatric nurse, working at children's hospitals in Birmingham and London, before becoming an NHS manager and a Care Quality Commission inspector.

He married now ex-wife Dawn, a nurse, and they had a son. Beech began writing online about child sex abuse he claimed to have suffered. He had 57 blogs and wrote a fictitious memoir, full of horrifying detail, which left observers convinced he was actually inspired by his own perverted desires.

Police found he had downloaded indecent material. He also set up a camera to film a boy using a toilet and took covert photos of boys. After he was charged with making indecent images, voyeurism and perverting justice he went on the run to Sweden where police found him.

Beech as a schoolboy

A CLASSIC CAR OBSESSION

CARL Beech used a criminal injuries payout to buy a £34,000 "muscle car".

The fraudster was obsessed with the Ford Mustang Drophead convertible, which he drove on a US trip in 2012.

Back home, he ordered a brochure to gaze at the white convertible model.

In August 2013 he made a special trip to see one and told police he needed cash to pay his counselling fees.

A payment of £22,000 was approved in March 2015 and Beech ordered the car the same day. He used £10,000 as the deposit – and the fees were never paid.

Swimming pool videos of children

By **Paul Jeeves**

TWISTED Beech toured swimming pools across Europe recording videos of young boys using an underwater camera, it was revealed yesterday.

He took 59 videos using a waterproof GoPro camera strapped to his head as he swam beneath the surface.

Of 59 video clips, 53 were stored on a MacBook, one of several electronic devices which were seized from his home.

The images were not part of the collection which Beech amassed.

However, the fact he kept them showed he had "a fascination for filming boys underwater," claimed prosecutors during legal argument not seen by the jury. They wanted to play the footage to show Beech had no problem putting his head under water.

He told the trial that he could not submerge his head without a mask or nose clips because of a particular form of abuse.

He claimed Jimmy Savile and Lord Brittan had raped him as his head was held underwater.

Police acted maliciously, says ex-MP

By **Henry Clare**

FORMER Conservative MP Harvey Proctor, falsely accused of murder and child rape by fantasist Beech, has described the investigation as "a truly disgraceful chapter in the history of British policing".

Mr Proctor, who is gay, said Metropolitan Police's Operation Midland was "rogue, malicious and apparently homophobic".

He said his reputation had been ruined and he had had to leave his job as secretary to the Duke and Duchess of Rutland.

Mr Proctor also criticised Labour deputy leader Tom Watson who he said "gave oxygen" to the claims by holding talks with Beech.

He said: "It is time for an apology from him to me and everyone named or implicated in this truly disgraceful chapter in the history of British policing."

The 72-year-old, who was MP for Basildon and Billericay, has launched a civil action against the force and has called for an independent investigation.

A Met Police spokesman said the force would not "comment outside of the legal process".

DAILY EXPRESS 23 July 2019

DAILY EXPRESS
One Canada Square, London E14 5AP
Tel: 020 8612 7000 (outside UK: +44 20 8612 7000)

Case that proves police must learn lessons now

THE ABC rule is supposed to be a founding police principle: "Assume nothing. Believe no one. Challenge everything." Tragically, the case of Carl Beech proves that it can easily be overriden by a convincing liar.

Claiming to have news about a VIP paedophile ring at the heart of Westminster, Beech led officers a merry dance.

Known by the alias "Nick", his grisly claims were that several Establishment figures had been involved in historic sexual abuse, including late prime minister Edward Heath, as well as ex-MPs Harvey Proctor, Greville Janner, Leon Brittan and elderly military figures.

There were raids on the homes of the blameless. The police – no doubt chastened by the Jimmy Savile case, and trigger-happy after Operation Yewtree that investigated him and others – started Operation Midland, wasting £2million following up Beech's false allegations.

The farrago resulted in no arrests – apart from that of Beech himself, now convicted of perverting the course of justice and fraud.

An inevitable twist found Beech to be a paedophile, and latterly he evaded British law in Sweden. No doubt, "lessons will be learned". But they need to be learned and implemented quickly.

Time to stay and fight on

AS Boris Johnson prepares to take power, some colleagues are trying to scupper his premiership by making pre-emptive exits. Yesterday the Foreign Office minister and Remainer Alan Duncan resigned – not exactly out of principle, but more that he could table a no-confidence motion in our likely new prime minister.

His initiative follows noises off from Chancellor Philip Hammond and Justice Secretary David Gauke, who both intend to quit a Johnson-led government.

They may consider their intentions to be noble. But much of the reason for Mr Johnson's appointment is to bring forward the democratic mandate to leave the EU.

To try and stop this process is disruptive at best, and anti-democratic at worst. It also means the Tories will be even more divided. Stay, and fight the good fight.

Motsi's Strictly sparkling

DAME Darcey Bussell was a class act on blockbuster TV show Strictly Come Dancing, now in its 17th series. So we salute Motsi Mabuse, her replacement, whose undoubted talents will step up to the judge's bench and follow Darcey with aplomb.

The elder sister of Strictly Come Dancing star Oti, Motsi is a former South African champion and since 2011, a judge on Strictly Come Dancing's German version, called Let's Dance. "I hope to add my own bit of sparkle to the show," she said.

We'll definitely tune in.

How Boris could play a political masterstroke

TOP JOB: Mr Johnson is more of a mainstream Conservative than a rabble-rousing populist

Stephen Pollard
Political commentator

SINCE Neil Armstrong first set foot on the Moon 50 years ago, more people have walked on it than have entered 10 Downing Street as a new prime minister.

So when Boris Johnson walks through the door tomorrow – assuming every prediction is correct – it will be a huge and rare moment.

He hasn't yet taken office but he is already being relentlessly attacked as a British version of Donald Trump: a Right-wing populist who will say and do anything to secure power.

I'm no particular fan of Mr Johnson. But while there are sensible reasons to worry about his suitability to be PM, the idea that he is some kind of British Trump is simply ridiculous and reveals far more about those making the accusation than it does about Mr Johnson.

Both in his record as Mayor of London and throughout the leadership campaign he has behaved as a mainstream liberal Conservative – far more of a "wet" (to use the old Thatcherite terminology) than the likes of Jacob Rees-Mogg and the Right of the Tory party.

For one thing, you do not win elections as mayor in a liberal and ethnically diverse city like London if you are not seen as being a champion of diversity.

One of Boris Johnson's very first decisions as foreign secretary was to lift the ban on British embassies flying the rainbow flag of gay pride.

HE HAS repeatedly made clear that he is in favour of more, not less, immigration – with one reason for his support for Brexit apparently being his desire to see immigrants from outside the EU get a fair crack of the whip.

As he put it during his time as mayor: "I'm probably about the only politician I know of who is actually willing to stand up and say that he's pro-immigration."

It's often forgotten that when he compared women who wear the burqa to letterboxes, he was actually defending their (and anyone else's) right to wear what they want – although his language may have been misguided. Whatever else he may be, Mr Johnson is not an idiot. He knows there are two groups which threaten his time as prime minister, both of which he has somehow to win over.

On the one hand are the hardline Brexiteers in the Commons who see No-deal as some kind of test of ideological purity. We can argue about the problems of leaving without a deal until the cows come home (or, until October 31) but at a time when the Conservative Party had to be led by a Brexiteer, he was the effective leader of the Leave campaign. If there is one person capable of persuading those hardline colleagues to agree to some sort of deal, surely it is Boris Johnson.

Whether and for how long he remains as PM will depend on this. Then, if he delivers Brexit he will also neutralise the Brexit Party, aiding the Tories' electoral prospects.

There is another group he needs to woo if the Conservatives are to return to election-winning support: floating Labour voters. The sort of voters, that is, who David Cameron was able to prise away from Labour in 2010 and 2015.

He has one huge asset in doing this: Jeremy Corbyn, who is anathema to such centrist voters. These are the people who voted for him in 2008 and 2012 to be Mayor of London. But if he governed as a Right-wing populist he would not stand a chance of winning their votes come the next election.

We have already seen how he will run his administration, because it's how he ran City Hall as mayor. He describes it as being a company chairman who decides overall strategy and lets the rest of his team bring it to fruition. In this vein, he is surely likely to appoint people with particular skills and drum up two or three flagship policy ideas that will define his government beyond Brexit.

Last week, for example, he pledged to end the injustice of families having to sell their homes to pay for dementia care.

'You don't win elections in London if you're not a champion of diversity'

WHAT could be a better legacy than being the first prime minister to actually move towards a sustainable settlement of our social care crisis?

But as events in the Strait of Hormuz show, even the best-laid plans can be hit by events. Boris Johnson faces a difficult enough time as PM with a majority of four – which will almost certainly be just three after the Brecon and Radnor by-election on August 1.

Now there are rumours of Tory MPs defecting to the LibDems. God help us if they open up the possibility of Jeremy Corbyn as PM.

Mr Johnson may be far from perfect. But if he plays his cards well, he could grab the centre ground and appease the Brexit lobby. That really would be a political masterstroke.

DAILY EXPRESS 23 July 2009

DAILY NEWSPAPER OF THE YEAR

THE TIMES

Tuesday July 23 2019 | thetimes.co.uk | No 72906

£1.80 Only £1.10 to subscribers

Swim! Cycle! Run!
How to be a triathlon nut
INSIDE TIMES2

Dr Mark Porter
When you need to steer clear of antibiotics

Put away the duvet: Britain expects hottest night on record

Harry Shukman

A tropical plume of air moving over Britain threatens to disrupt the sleep of millions and break the record for the hottest night ever.

Forecasters are predicting that temperatures will reach 25C in southern England between 8pm tonight and 8am tomorrow, beating the previous overnight record of 23.9C set on August 3, 1990.

"There is a chance we could be knocking on the door of that record," Nicola Maxey, a Met Office spokeswoman, said. "We have got tropical air coming in from the Atlantic and warm air coming up from the continent."

Other records could also fall this week. The hottest July day was in 2015, when 36.7C was measured at Heathrow. Britain's hottest day of all was 38.5C, recorded at Kew Gardens, south-west London, in August 2003.

"On Wednesday there is a cool incursion of air coming in from the west but on Thursday we are back to very widespread high temperatures before the end of the week," Ms Maxey said.

The humidity could make the weather feel several degrees warmer and Public Health England has issued a level three heatwave warning until Friday. Only level four, which is called in an emergency, is more severe.

The agency urged people to check on friends and neighbours who are less able to look after themselves and advised people to stay inside between 11am and 3pm, and keep themselves hydrated. Experts also said pollen levels could be "extremely hazardous".

Andy Whittamore, the clinical lead at Asthma UK, said: "Plan any outdoor activities for earlier in the day when the air quality tends to be better."

Heatwaves are determined by the Met Office when temperatures in the same area remain high for three days.

Forecast, page 53

Watson has to apologise, say victims of abuse lies

Police also criticised by VIPs for backing fantasist

Sean O'Neill Chief Reporter

Police and politicians who promoted lurid claims of an establishment paedophile ring faced condemnation last night after the man behind them was found guilty of making false allegations.

Tom Watson, Labour's deputy leader, was urged to make a full apology to public figures named by the paedophile Carl Beech, who was convicted of 13 charges of perverting the course of justice and fraud.

Scotland Yard, which conducted a £2.5 million investigation into his claims of child murder, rape and torture, was criticised by Field Marshal Lord Bramall, who said the lies about him had done "irreparable damage".

Carl Beech said he had been abused by politicians, military officers and spy chiefs

Lord Bramall, 95, the former head of the armed forces, told *The Times*: "It was Beech's outrageous and totally untrue allegations which perverted the course of justice. However, the incompetence of the Metropolitan Police and the improper way it accepted his allegations unquestioningly and at face value lent them an unwarranted credibility."

Beech, 51, from Gloucester, had been the star witness in Scotland Yard's Operation Midland investigation into his claim that he had been abused for years by a VIP ring made up of politicians, military officers and spy chiefs.

The former paediatric nurse, NHS manager and NSPCC volunteer faces a lengthy jail term for a determined campaign of lies and deceit which he hoped would lead to people being convicted of crimes that never happened.

The trial had examined the Metropolitan Police's decision in 2014 to regard Beech — then known by the pseudonym "Nick" — as truthful.

Acting under a policy of always believing the victim, Met detectives accepted his stories of being tortured by snake bites, flown abroad on private planes to be abused, having his dog kidnapped by MI5 and witnessing three separate murders of children. The Met publicly described Beech's allegations at the time as "credible and true".

Many of those accused by Beech, including the former prime minister Edward Heath, Greville Janner and Jimmy Savile, were dead. But he also named Lord Bramall, the former home secretary Leon Brittan and the former MP Harvey Proctor, leading to them being questioned and having their homes searched.

Just days after Brittan's death in January 2015, before his name was cleared, Mr Watson wrote in a newspaper that it was "a travesty that [he] will never be asked the truth". The article was deeply upsetting for the former Conservative

Continued on page 2, col 3

Jo Swinson at an event in central London yesterday where she was revealed as the new Lib Dem leader. She pledged to do whatever is needed to stop Brexit

New Lib Dem leader 'could steal votes from Tories'

Steven Swinford Deputy Political Editor

Boris Johnson risks losing millions of Tory voters to the Liberal Democrats under their new leader Jo Swinson because of his no-deal Brexit strategy, a cabinet minister has warned.

David Gauke, the justice secretary who will resign tomorrow, told *The Times* that no-deal will "play into the hands" of the Lib Dems, who now have an "energetic and passionate" leader.

Ms Swinson, 39, yesterday became the first woman to lead the Liberal Democrats as she was elected with nearly two thirds of the votes cast by party members. In a speech she appealed to disaffected Conservative and Labour voters as she said that she would do "whatever it takes" to stop Brexit.

Mr Johnson, the favourite for the Tory leadership, held meetings with cabinet ministers prepared to quit over his "do or die pledge" to leave the EU with or without a deal.

They included Philip Hammond, the chancellor, Rory Stewart, the international development secretary, and Mr Gauke. Mr Stewart said Mr Johnson had asked if he was prepared to serve in his cabinet, while Mr Gauke said he had had a "very friendly" conversation.

Theresa May hosted a farewell reception last night for Tory and DUP MPs in Downing Street. The prime minister urged them to have a break over the parliamentary recess and be loyal to her successor as she warned of the threat posed by Jeremy Corbyn.

Mr Gauke said that Ms Swinson and the resurgent Lib Dems must not be underestimated. He said: "If we were to narrow our support to purely being those in favour of a no-deal Brexit I think we would be significantly out of touch with a lot of people who have traditionally voted Conservative — those who live in London, the home counties, and various other relatively affluent parts of the country.

"It is important the Conservative Party appeals to voters in the centre ground. It's a position that would play

Continued on page 2, col 5

THE TIMES 23 July 2019

News

BRITAIN'S MOST TRUSTED NATIONAL NEWSPAPER

TODAY'S EDITION

NEWS

LIFE LESSONS
Acupuncture and reiki have been soothing nerves at a primary school
PAGE 8

SPORT

ROUGH PATCH
Golfers say the major competitions now come too thick and fast
PAGE 58

TIMES2

BAD DATE
William Dameron's image was used to scam strangers on the internet
PAGES 2-3

COMMENT
Boris Johnson has tried to keep everyone happy. In power he will have to choose who to betray
RACHEL SYLVESTER, PAGE 21

Nissan refuses to clean up car

Nissan has refused a government request to make thousands of highly polluting cars less toxic. The Nissan Qashqai produces 17 times the legal limit for nitrogen oxides but the carmaker said it wanted to focus on developing new models. **Page 4**

Victim tells of moped ordeal

Two masked men on a moped robbed a finance director on her doorstep and dragged her husband out of his car at knifepoint. Ratun Lahiri, who lives in Hampstead, north London, said the attack had made her scared to leave her house. **Page 5**

Oxford's £4bn science drive

Oxford university is to take on Cambridge's prowess in science and technology with a vast investment programme to build two innovation hubs. It is hoped that the £4 billion deal will lead to thousands of high-tech science spinouts. **Page 8**

Hong Kong chief accused

The chief executive of Hong Kong has been accused of collusion after suspected triad gang members attacked protesters travelling home by train from an anti-government rally. Carrie Lam denied the police had turned a blind eye. **Pages 26-27**

Big firms face activist threat

Dozen of Britain's biggest companies, including Centrica, Kingfisher and Next, are at risk of being besieged by activist investors because they are producing weak shareholder returns, a City stockbroker has warned. **Page 33**

Free-to-air TV plea by Lord's

One of the summer's two Lord's Test matches should be shown on free-to-air television every year to capitalise on the success of the World Cup final, the chief executive of MCC, which owns the ground, said. **Page 64**

THE WEATHER

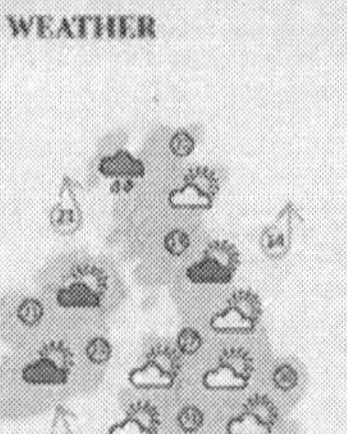

Cloudy with patchy rain in the northwest. Elsewhere, largely dry and sunny. **Full forecast, page 53**

Mountains, moors and heaths offer £20bn in green benefits

Philip Aldrick Economics Editor

Britain's mountains, moorlands and heaths are worth £20.1 billion for their ability to absorb carbon, remove air pollution and provide recreational activities, according to the Office for National Statistics.

The ONS is mapping environmental assets as part of a government project to "improve understanding of our natural capital".

It estimated in 2015 that the entirety of Britain's green spaces was worth £761 billion in terms of carbon sequestration, the removal of pollution, and recreation. The statisticians are now conducting a more thorough analysis of each habitat type to better measure how the ecosystem is changing.

Valuing natural capital has become a critical issue because without a price markets automatically treat the environment as worthless. Costing natural services helps to correct that mistake and improve decision-making.

The natural capital accounts are distinct from the land value of all the homes in the UK, which the ONS has calculated at £4.1 trillion.

Natural accounts are required by the European Union but Theresa May has also made them a feature of the 25 Year Environment Plan that she unveiled last year.

The plan is focused on "protecting and enhancing [natural landscapes and habitats] for the next generation". It follows work by the World Bank, which has estimated the value of the world's untouched ecosystems at $33.7 trillion (£27.2 trillion).

The ONS said that the value of the carbon capture provided by mountains, moorlands and heaths was £10.6 billion in 2017. Grassland absorbed carbon dioxide but wetland emitted it. The removal of pollutants from the atmosphere was worth £391 million in health benefits and the recreational service of unspoiled walks was worth £9.2 billion, the ONS said.

The value put on carbon sequestration will increase as the government pursues its target to achieve "net zero" emissions by 2050, it added.

Wind power generated from the land also contributes to its natural value but the ONS could not quantify the effect of this because it is updating its methodology. It added that electricity generated by wind from the habitats had increased more than 24-fold since 2003.

The statisticians are also working on a way of calculating the cultural services "provided by aesthetic appreciation and heritage value". At the moment the estimate is extrapolated solely from the amount people spend on petrol and recreational activities such as game hunting.

In 2017, almost 37 million people spent more than 46 million hours in Britain's mountains, moorlands and heaths. Since 2009, the recreational value of the habitats has decreased because fewer people are visiting. The biggest driver of the decrease has been a decline in spending on car running costs.

The country's mountains, moorlands and heaths cover 36,642 sq km, 15 per cent of the 244,654 sq km that make the whole UK landmass.

Rise in jury-dodging down to online chat, judge warns

Jonathan Ames Legal Editor

Hollywood may have given jury service a worthy sheen in *12 Angry Men* but in reality citizens often dread the call-up and will produce a torrent of reasons not to attend.

Now a senior judge has become exasperated with the excuses, which he claims have become more unified with the help of the internet.

Judge Andrew Menary, QC, the recorder of Liverpool, blamed online chat rooms for fostering the view among the public that they can produce standard reasons that will allow them to avoid their duty.

He expressed his frustration as he handed a 70-year-old man the maximum fine of £1,000 for producing a string of unacceptable excuses for failing to attend Liverpool crown court.

Barry Grimes of Bromborough in the Wirral refused to serve as a juror then failed to attend his contempt of court hearing, according to BBC News.

Grimes failed to attend court for jury service that was initially scheduled for January 2018. His jury service was deferred until this month, but again Grimes was absent. He is understood to have told officials that he was incapable of sitting for long periods and that he was unable to concentrate. However, when told that he would need to provide a valid medical certificate, Grimes said that he was generally unfit and would not attend.

On another occasion, Grimes said that the scheduled jury service conflicted with a pre-booked holiday but the judge also rejected that excuse.

In the judge's view, Grimes "displayed a wholly unpleasant and unnecessary attitude" and his approach was "a quite deliberate contempt of court".

Grimes has 28 days to pay the fine. If he fails, he could be jailed for 14 days.

Fining Grimes, Judge Menary bemoaned what he said was a rising frequency of people ignoring jury summonses and refusing to sit. He claimed that many were turning to chat rooms for tips on dodging doing their duty.

One web chat room called OverclockersUK, and a Yahoo chat forum, for example, list tips for avoiding jury service.

Prospective jurors who feel that they should be let off the hook must contact the jury central summoning bureau for a deferral or to be excused entirely.

CONTINUED FROM PAGE 1
New Lib Dem leader

into the hands of the Liberal Democrats. I don't think we should underestimate Jo Swinson. I think she's capable, she's a very good communicator. I think she will be energetic and a passionate advocate for her party's views."

He said if Mr Johnson called an election on a no-deal platform "I think that is going to draw millions of traditional Conservative voters away from us".

Mr Gauke warned that Britain would face a recession if it left the EU without a deal. He said: "We will see the pound falling significantly which, if not immediately, plays into living standards. The cost of lots of goods [would] go up significantly, not least petrol but also food.

"We are likely to see unemployment rises in particular sectors and we are likely to see the public finances taking a hit as tax receipts will fall. If we have left in no-deal circumstances we will almost certainly be in recession, which is generally not a good time for an incumbent government to go to the country."

He said that he wants Mr Johnson to succeed in striking a deal with the EU, but does not believe it is possible before October 31. Mr Gauke also warned that a no-deal Brexit risks breaking up the Union, fuelling support for a united Ireland and a second independence referendum in Scotland.

I'll scupper Brexit, page 11
Leading article, page 25

CONTINUED FROM PAGE 1
'Outrageous' abuse lies

minister's family. Mr Proctor, 72, said Beech had "lied, lied and lied again and his breathtaking lies were facilitated, enhanced and given credibility by the Met Police". He also called on Mr Watson to "put right past wrongs" with a public admission. He said: "It is time for an apology from him to me and everyone named or implicated in this truly disgraceful chapter in the history of British policing".

Greville Janner's son, Daniel, said that Mr Watson had politicised a police inquiry for "personal political advancement, riding on a bandwagon of public frenzy which he had whipped up".

Scotland Yard said its officers had behaved "in good faith" and none faced misconduct proceedings. Deputy commissioner Steve House said: "Operation Midland was carried out against a backdrop of intense scrutiny and allegations that in the past the Met had covered up sensitive allegations about prominent people."

Beech's crimes were exposed by a Northumbria police investigation. He will be sentenced on Friday at Newcastle crown court on the 13 charges for which a jury took four and a half hours to find him guilty. He will also be sentenced for separate offences of downloading child abuse images, voyeurism and absconding to Sweden.

Mr Watson said he had apologised to Lord Brittan's family and, although he recognised Mr Proctor's hurt and anger, would not apologise to him. He said he had met Beech once. "It was not my role to judge whether victims' stories were true. I encouraged every person that came to me to take their story to the police. That is what I did with Nick."

Police in the dock, pages 6-7
Leading article, page 25

What Tom Watson said

In PMQs in 2012: "[I] want to ensure the Met … investigate clear intelligence suggesting a powerful paedophile network linked to parliament and No 10."

Letter in 2014 demanding rape claim be investigated: "I am driven to the unpalatable conclusion that the identity of the alleged perpetrator — Leon Brittan — may have influenced the case."

Sunday Mirror article in 2015 after Leon Brittan's death: "Yesterday, one survivor said to me that Brittan … was 'as close to evil as a human being could get in my view' … I believe the people I've spoken to are sincere."

News VIP abuse scandal

How police found themselves in

Sean O'Neill Chief Reporter

Carl Beech was the sole defendant, and spent seven days in the witness box at Newcastle crown court, yet somehow he was a peripheral figure in this extraordinary case.

On the trial's opening day Tony Badenoch, QC, said that he would prove Beech's story of child murder, rape and torture to be "incredible and untrue". From that moment the Metropolitan Police was also in the dock.

As the prosecutor dissected Beech's myriad lies, including stories of being flown to Paris on a private Boeing 747 by his abusers, bitten by snakes while trapped in a cupboard, and having his dog kidnapped by MI5, it seemed astonishing that Scotland Yard had once declared these claims "credible and true".

When the Met finally abandoned its £2.5 million inquiry into Beech's allegations, the task of investigating him was given to Northumbria police. Its team challenged almost everything that the Met had accepted.

Beech claimed that he was taken out of school weekly to be abused. Detectives found school records back to the 1970s that described a model pupil with prizes for good attendance.

Officers interviewed Dawn Beech, who had been married to Beech for 22 years. Never once had he spoken to her about being abused by powerful men.

They seized his computers, identifying him as the owner of an encrypted email account sending bogus witness accounts, and confirmed that three murders he said he was "forced to watch" never happened.

Rather than being an abuse survivor, Beech was a paedophile. He wrote hundreds of pages of a child sex fantasy, disguised as a memoir, watched illegal videos and collected indecent images. Yet for more than a year the officers on Operation Midland, and their commanders, treated Beech's lies as truth. The answer to why they swallowed his fantastical story is found in the hysteria that took hold in the aftermath of the exposure of Jimmy Savile's crimes.

Haunted by the failure to bring Savile to justice, the Met set up Operation Yewtree and predators such as Max Clifford and Rolf Harris were jailed.

In late 2014 the Met was looking for other prosecutions and officers actively sought out Beech — then known as "Nick" — when his story appeared on the website Exaro News. Exaro introduced Beech to the Labour MP Tom Watson, who stoked pressure for investigations. Beech's lurid story became mainstream news in November 2014 when the BBC led news bulletins with an anonymised interview with "Nick".

The Met saw "Nick" as a star witness. He had a personal liaison officer and was driven around alleged crime scenes as he named the 12 members of "The Group". No one at the Met seems to have considered the sheer implausibility of a story about senior men in MI5, MI6, parliament, the military and showbusiness gathering at the Dolphin Square apartments in Pimlico or the Carlton Club for brutal child sex orgies.

Nor did they seem to realise that Beech had been to police before. In late 2012, only 17 days after the ITV documentary that exposed Savile, he contacted Operation Yewtree and was referred to Wiltshire police. He told how he had been abused by his stepfather and a group of men including military officers, two Saudi princes and Savile.

The case was closed as "undetected" but Beech claimed £22,000 in criminal injury compensation.

The story he told the Met in 2014 was strikingly different. The abusers now included politicians, intelligence chiefs and the former head of the army. The Met did not seem to question the inconsistency and, in December 2014, called a press conference to say it was investigating three murders and appealing for victims of The Group to come forward.

It was at this event that Detective Superintendent Kenny McDonald described Beech's claims as "credible and true". At the packed news conference, this newspaper was sceptical, asking if police were aware that the muckraking magazine *Scallywag* published similar sensationalist reports in the 1990s. The next day *The Times* reported that "the murders may never have taken place".

The Met blundered on through the lives of those that their witness had accused — frail men unprepared for the assault that officers would unleash.

Field Marshal Lord Bramall, 95, a D-day veteran and former head of the armed forces, had his home searched for 20 hours by ten officers.

The former home secretary Lord Brittan of Spennithorne was ill with cancer when the police questioned him about false allegations. He died aged 75 before his name was cleared.

The former MP Harvey Proctor, 72, had his home searched for 27 hours by 15 police officers, who took away computers and paperwork but found no evidence of any crime. News of the search quickly appeared on the Exaro website.

But the Met had not examined Beech's computers, which would have shown his research into the men he accused. It was Mr Proctor who exposed Operation Midland's failings in August 2015, denouncing the investigation as "so far-fetched as to be unbelievable".

The Met was stung and Midland began to unravel. In September 2015 the police assertion that Beech's claims were "true" was withdrawn and Mr McDonald stepped aside. In January 2016, as Lord Bramall was told the case against him had been dropped, detectives confronted Beech about his evidence. He walked out of the interview.

Midland closed down in March 2016 as Mr Proctor was told he had no case to answer. But an investigation into Beech was ordered only eight months later when Sir Richard Henriques, a retired judge, produced a damning report, detailing 43 failings by the Met.

Northumbria police seized Beech's computers — loaded with evidence of his deception. When faced with the evidence the once talkative Beech gave "no comment" interviews.

Leading article, page 25

Hook, line and sinker

- Scotland Yard followed a policy of always believing the victim rather than keeping an open mind
- It declared Beech's story "credible and true" four weeks into inquiry
- His ex-wife, who had crucial evidence, was not interviewed
- His collection of child abuse images was not discovered
- Police were unaware that Beech had researched places and people before making allegations
- They believed that MI5 had shot his horse and kidnapped his dog
- Accepted that Harvey Proctor and Edward Heath — political foes — were part of same child-sex gang
- Did not discover that a penknife he said he had been threatened with was his grandmother's fruit-knife
- Beech's claim to have been taken out of school was not checked
- Claim that he hated water could have been easily disproved by his photo album, which showed him at pools and beaches around the world

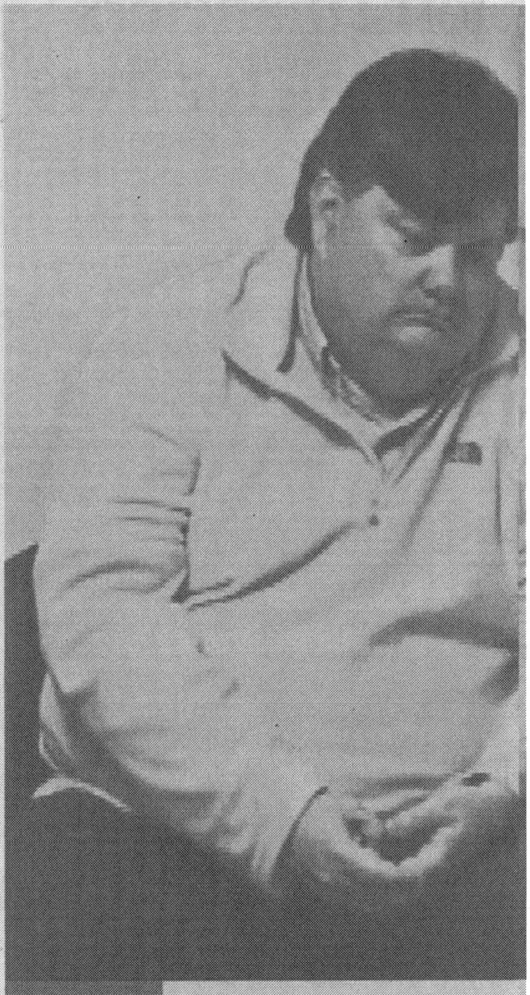

An expert in deception and invention

Behind the story

Carl Beech was an NSPCC volunteer on a child safety project at the same time he was lying to police about being the victim of a powerful paedophile gang (Sean O'Neill and Fiona Hamilton write).

Beech, 51, visited 33 primary schools in Herefordshire between 2012-15 to talk about recognising and reporting child abuse.

He had a high-level DBS check before being accepted as a volunteer on the Speak Out, Stay Safe programme and told the charity he was an abuse survivor whose allegations were being investigated by police. The NSPCC accepted his word and became, along with the police, politicians and sections of the media, victims of his skill at deception.

A former nurse, school governor and NHS manager, Beech's image as a respectable, professional, family man was a key factor in persuading people he was telling the truth. His 20-year marriage was coming to an end when he began making his public claims about being an abuse victim. He and his wife Dawn met at nursing school in the late 1980s and after the split their only son lived with his father.

Beech seemed to be coping well despite the break-up, taking a new job as an inspector for the Care Quality Commission. Yet he was also constructing his lurid account of physical and sexual abuse.

The ordeal began, he claimed, when he was aged eight and his mother Charmian — later a Church of England vicar and diocesan safeguarding officer — married Major Raymond Beech in Salisbury in 1976.

It was her second marriage but lasted just four months before she moved out and obtained a restraining order. The military's file on the major describes a "dangerously explosive" alcoholic who assaulted his wife, tore up her clothes, smashed furniture and threatened to sexually assault her.

Relatives of Major Beech, who died aged 60 in 1995, dismiss the claim he abused his stepson as "fantasy". But the court heard that in 1990 Beech wrote to his mother telling her for the first time he had suffered sexual abuse from his stepfather.

There is no doubt Beech embellished his account greatly over the years, adding detail from internet conspiracies and stealing the stories of genuine survivors.

Secretly, Beech was also accessing paedophile material online. Hereford crown court heard earlier this year that police found 333 illegal images — including 36 of the most serious category — on his computers after a search of his home in November 2016. They also found more than 300 "indicative" images, many taken by himself of children near his home or in swimming pools.

Until last-minute guilty pleas in January, Beech had planned to claim in his defence that his son could have downloaded the illegal material.

Key players in a scandal that wrecked reputations

TOM WATSON

Labour's deputy leader has been accused at the child abuse public inquiry of having stoked "a moral panic". Mr Watson, 52, piled pressure on the Crown Prosecution Service and the police to ensure that Lord Brittan of Spennithorne was interviewed over a rape allegation, despite his frail health. Beech described Mr Watson as "part of the little group that was supporting me".

LORD HOGAN-HOWE

The Metropolitan Police Commissioner at the time now sits as a crossbencher in the House of Lords. Lord Hogan-Howe, 61, commissioned a report by Sir Richard Henriques that cleared him of any culpability for the botched investigation.

dock over fantasist's web of lies

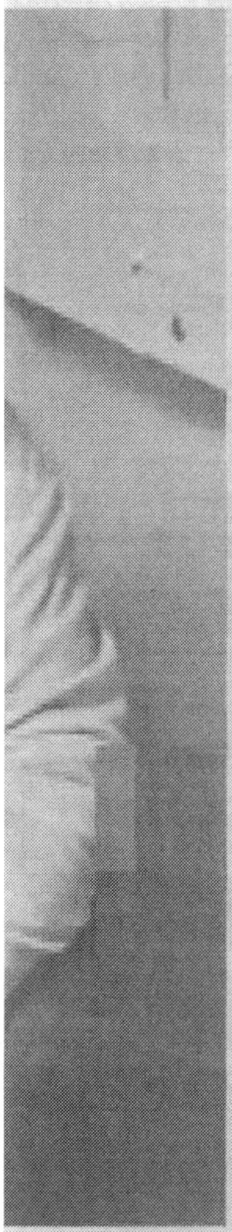

Fugitive tried to start new life as B&B owner in Swedish wilderness

David Brown
Chief News Correspondent, Overkalix

Drifts of snow on the mud track where he had parked his car lay 5ft deep as Carl Andersson struggled to clear a path to his new home on the banks of the frozen Kalix River.

His purchase in January last year of a decrepit wooden house on the edge of the Arctic Circle was a chance to make a fresh start away from the trouble in Britain as he approached 50.

Anna-Lisa Andersson, no relation, recalled Andersson arriving at her guesthouse in Overkalix, a village which has a population of fewer than 1,000. "He said he liked the snow, the wind, the cold and the loneliness," Ms Andersson said. "He told me he was looking for a new place, a new life."

The drifts eventually melted. By the time the snow returned later that year, the villagers' sense of trust had been betrayed after they gradually uncovered the truth about the stranger they had welcomed into their lives.

He was Carl Beech. And the trouble in Britain he was fleeing was criminal and of his own creation. He had made a series of lurid and utterly fantastical allegations of paedophilia which had devastated the lives of elderly, well-known men.

He had taken early retirement from the NHS in 2017, receiving a £59,000 lump sum and a monthly pension of £752. He had given the lump sum to his mother, the Rev Charmian Beech, 74, and she repaid £39,000 so that he could buy a £17,500 house five miles from the centre of Overkalix which he planned to turn into holiday accommodation.

Overkalix's remoteness and the bitter conditions in winter necessitate a close sense of community, so Ms Andersson was happy to help her future business competitor settle in as he attended local Swedish-language classes for immigrants.

"He is a nice man," she said. "I was helping him with his new life. Helping him to refurbish the house. I got him the people to do the work."

Nathalie Navez, 37, befriended the man she knew as Andersson on the Facebook page for Overkalix. She and her husband, Vincent van Vytven, 38, are also outsiders, having moved from Belgium to run a holiday chalet business on the outskirts of the village.

"We were not interested in his past," Ms Navez said. "When you come to the north you have a blank sheet; you start again. He told us he was fed up with the stress and the people at home."

Ms Navez and her husband were surprised when their new friend's mother, Charmian, 74, and aunt, Diana, 71, drove 2,000 miles to Overkalix to visit him rather than take a flight. Both women were Church of England vicars.

She recalled their friend saying that his mother and his teenage son both wanted to live with him in Sweden.

At the end of June, he went travelling with Claudio Comi, an Italian travel blogger. The pair were pictured together on July 1 in the 24-hour daylight in Batsfjord, Norway.

The last time that Ms Navez and her husband saw the Briton was when they went together to an event to mark the solar eclipse on July 13. Mr van Vytven said. "He said to us, 'I am having some stressful things right now. I need some time. I will text you when it is clear.'"

Then he stopped replying to messages or answering calls.

Christina Gaversten, 73, a retired teacher, met him soon after he moved to the opposite side of the road from the home where she had been born. "I told him that I am here to help him come into the society," she said. "I haven't so many friends so it was nice."

When her new friend's mother and aunt arrived in early June they visited her home for coffee. "His mother told me her surname was Beech and I said to Carl, 'But your name is Andersson.'" she recalled. "He said he had taken his grandmother's name who was from Denmark."

The next month he told Ms Gaversten that a friend from France would be visiting and they would both be travelling to the north of Sweden and into Norway. His mother had repaid her son the rest of the lump sum he had given her and a further £3,000 as he moved around Sweden.

Property records showed that on July 29 he had bought a second property in Kiruna, a mining town 150 miles from Overkalix deep in Swedish Lapland.

When he failed to return to Overkalix, Ms Gaversten began her own research on her English friend but could find no trace of him on Google. Then she recalled talking to his mother and began searching for "Carl Beech".

Carl Beech's house at Overkalix, where neighbours read online about his past

The results from conspiracy theory websites which had ignored court orders not to publish his name made disturbing reading.

At 5.50pm on October 1 he was seized by police at Gothenburg's central railway station as he tried to return to the far north of the country. He was arrested under his real name.

He later claimed that after moving to Sweden he adopted the surname Andersson to "get away from Beech" but offered no explanation for using other aliases including Oscar Andersson, Samuel Williams, Samuel Karlsson and Sam Anders. Three days after his arrest he shuffled, handcuffed and unkempt, into the court of international and organised crime in Gothenburg and agreed to be extradited.

His conviction yesterday at Newcastle crown court for the lies he told, claiming to be the victim of an establishment paedophile ring, may finally help his friends in Overkalix begin to understand the mysterious Englishman they welcomed into their lives.

STEVE RODHOUSE

The most senior officer at the press conference where Beech's lurid allegations were declared to be "credible and true". Mr Rodhouse, 47, is now director-general of operations at the National Crime Agency.

KENNY MCDONALD

The senior investigating officer in Operation Midland also declared Beech's allegations to be "credible and true". The detective superintendent retired weeks before the start of Beech's trial. The police watchdog said five officers involved in Midland had been cleared of misconduct.

EXARO NEWS

The now defunct "investigative" website that first published Beech's allegations and promoted his claims. One of its reporters, Mark Conrad, contacted Beech after seeing his blog about being a survivor of child abuse and built a relationship with him. Conrad, who is now a contributor to Byline Times, told police that he had helped Beech to set up an encrypted email account so they could communicate securely. Beech would later use encrypted emails to send bogus witness accounts to police. Exaro's former editor, Mark Watts, said yesterday that Beech's convictions should be considered "unsafe".

Clockwise from top: Carl Beech in a police interview; the former MP Harvey Proctor; Lord Brittan of Spennithorne; Lord Bramall; the Labour MP Tom Watson; and the police officer Kenny McDonald

HARVEY PROCTOR

The former Conservative MP was wrongly accused by Beech of involvement in child murder and rape. Mr Proctor, 72, is seeking damages from the Met over the injury to his health and the loss of his home and job.

LORD BRAMALL

The former head of the Armed Forces had his home searched by ten officers and was subjected to hours of police interviews. Lord Bramall, 95, has since received £100,000 compensation from the Metropolitan Police. He told police that the accusations were "monstrous" and that he was "absolutely astonished, amazed and bemused" police were taking them seriously.

LEON BRITTAN

The former home secretary died aged 75 from cancer while still under investigation by police over the false allegations in 2015. His widow, Lady Brittan, received a personal apology from Lord Hogan-Howe as well as compensation.

Leading articles

Daily Universal Register

UK: Jeremy Hunt, the foreign secretary, or Boris Johnson to be announced as the leader of the Conservative Party to replace Theresa May.

Nature notes

Two spectacular, but elusive butterflies are now flying about in woods. One is the white admiral, which has dark brown wings with a broken white bar slanting right across them on either side. It soars and glides dramatically between the trees and lays its eggs on honeysuckle. The other is the purple emperor. This flies high and fast among the treetops, but comes down to feed on sap in tree trunks and on salt in dung on the ground, where it opens and shuts its iridescent purple wings. Much easier to see in the next few months will, it seems, be painted lady butterflies, which have pale orange wings marked with black and white. These are immigrants that have been arriving in large numbers, nectaring on thistle, and coming into gardens. They are laying eggs, so their numbers will soon increase further, portending a great "painted lady summer", perhaps matching the glory of the invasion year of 2008. DERWENT MAY

Birthdays today

Daniel Radcliffe, *pictured*, actor, the Harry Potter film series (2001-11), 30; **Prof Christopher Andrew**, former official historian, MI5, *The Secret World: A History of Intelligence* (2018), 78; **Alan Barnes**, saxophonist, composer, *The Sherlock Holmes Suite* (2007), 60; **Jo Brand**, comedian, 62; **Sir Ross Cranston**, High Court judge (2007-17), Labour MP (1997-2005), 71; **David Essex**, singer-songwriter, *Rock On* (1973), and actor, *Silver Dream Racer* (1980), 72; **Alex Fraser**, chief executive, London Institute of Banking and Finance, 60; **Graham Gooch**, cricketer, former England captain and coach, Test career 1975-95, 66; **Martin Gore**, musician, Depeche Mode, 58; **Prof Edward Gregson**, composer, 74; **Woody Harrelson**, actor, *Cheers* (1985-93), *The People vs. Larry Flynt* (1996), 58; **Fran Healy**, singer-songwriter, Travis, *Why Does It Always Rain on Me?* (1999), 46; **Mike Hulme**, professor of human geography, University of Cambridge, 59; **Alison Krauss**, singer, *Raising Sand* (2007), 48; **Andrew Langdon**, QC, chairman of the Bar Council (2017), 56; **Sergio Mattarella**, president of Italy, 78; **Len McCluskey**, general secretary, Unite, 69; **Judit Polgár**, chess grandmaster, title achieved at the age of 15 years and 4 months, 43; **Lord (Richard) Rogers of Riverside**, architect, *One Hyde Park* (2009), 86; **Robin Simon**, founding editor, *British Art Journal*, 72; **Mark Skipper**, chief executive, Northern Ballet, 58; **Slash** (**Saul Hudson**), guitarist, Guns N' Roses, 54; **David Strettle**, rugby union player, England (2007-13) and Saracens (2010-15, 2018-19), 36; **Dame Mary Tanner**, European president, World Council of Churches (2006-13), 81; **Prof Mark Williams**, director, Oxford Mindfulness Centre (2008-13), 67; **Prof Michael Wood**, historian and broadcaster, 71.

On this day

In 1998 a team of scientists announced in the science journal *Nature* that they had produced three generations of cloned mice.

The last word

"He sows hurry and reaps indigestion."
Robert Louis Stevenson, novelist, *Virginibus Puerisque* (1881).

THE TIMES

Liberal Revival

Jo Swinson has won the leadership of the Liberal Democrat Party on a surge of support for opposing Brexit. Now she has to find a wider appeal

On the more trying days of coalition government after 2010, the late Paddy Ashdown liked to reflect on the lowest point of his time as leader of the Liberal Democrat Party. Do not complain about ministerial office, he would say, when he could recall the party's popularity marked by an asterisk which denoted "support within the margin of error of zero". Mr Ashdown's point was that Liberal Democrats are a resilient bunch.

That was an important virtue when, in 2015 and again in 2017, the party suffered the electoral punishment that is the common fate of junior parties in coalitions. Sir Vince Cable took over unopposed as the reluctant new leader and the party seemed to be all but over. Yesterday the Lib Dems chose Sir Vince's deputy, Jo Swinson, as their leader over the former energy secretary Sir Ed Davey. Ms Swinson inherits a party in ruder health than could have been expected.

The Lib Dems came second in the May 2019 European parliament elections, beating the Conservatives and Labour, and made most progress in the local elections. In a political contest splitting four ways, Ms Swinson takes up her new post as a significant political figure, one who may well help to determine the nature of the next government. It was for that reason important that she used her acceptance speech to clarify that she did not like the idea of a coalition with either the Labour Party or the Scottish National Party.

For the moment Ms Swinson only really has one policy. The cause that has propelled the Lib Dem recovery is the same one that dominated the hustings — opposition to Brexit. With the Tories committed to delivering Brexit, the Brexit Party angry that it has not yet happened and Labour unable to make up its mind, the way has been cleared for the Lib Dems to speak with clarity for the cause of remaining in the European Union. Sir Ed tried to make "decarbonising capitalism" a talking point but Ms Swinson's point that the Lib Dems were "the obvious rallying point" for those opposed to Brexit was the central question.

Ms Swinson will only capitalise, though, if she is able to widen the appeal of her party beyond the residual minority who do not accept Brexit. If the new prime minister is successful in taking Britain out of the EU, then clarity on staying in will lose much of its relevance. The Lib Dems will probably become the first party to advocate that Britain should reapply for membership. Even for Remainers that will be a big hurdle and politics will to some extent move on.

The task for Ms Swinson is to define the kind of Liberal Democrat Party that she wishes to lead. Even three decades after the fact, the party bears the marks of its uneasy merger of classical liberals and social democrats.

The new leader made an immediate pitch for the liberal vote when she praised immigrants, feminism and action on climate change. She also paraded the usual litany of liberal bogeymen such as Messrs Trump and Farage. There are bigger questions that need to be answered, however. Is the party to be liberal on economics and in favour of reform of public services, in the manner of the Orange Book liberals, such as the former MPs David Laws and Sir Danny Alexander, or will its statist wing prevail?

Ms Swinson will have to be clear on her plans for working with other small parties as well as the conditions under which her party might lend its support to an administration led by a Conservative or Labour prime minister. David Steel's advice to the Liberals in 1981 to go back to their constituencies and prepare for government was soon mocked by events. Ms Swinson told her party that she stood before them as a possible prime minister. That, too, is probably hyperbole but one of Brexit's many revolutions has been to make the Lib Dems matter again.

China without Charm

The use of gangsters to bludgeon democrats in Hong Kong is an act of desperation

The Chinese leadership believes it can conquer hearts and minds across the globe with elaborate investments in deep-sea ports and high-speed rail lines. Sadly it does not have much of that synthetic charm left over for Hong Kong. In that unhappy territory, pro-Beijing gangsters this week broke the bones of democracy activists with steel batons, safe in the knowledge that their savagery would be immune from arrest or investigation.

Since the 1997 British handover, Beijing has tightened its grip on what is now known as a special administrative region. It was always clear that China resented this "specialness" but grudgingly accepted it as long as Hong Kong was a magnet for investment. Today many mainland cities, such as Shanghai, are more prosperous and the commercial argument for Hong Kong's exceptionalism has weakened. As for the territory's semi-autonomous status, this plainly clashes with the absolutist tendencies of President Xi. In 2014 the frustration of young Hong Kongers bubbled over in the street protests of the umbrella movement. This was quashed partly with the use of triad gangs, hired to do Beijing's dirty work. One critical journalist was severely injured by a gangster on a motorcycle wielding a meat cleaver.

The demonstrators have learnt from the failed 2014 protests. This time they have a single primary aim: to have the Hong Kong administration formally withdraw an extradition bill that would allow the mainland to interfere even more with the territory's judiciary. For the most part the protest leaders have maintained discipline; debris was cleared and Hong Kong's business activities were not seriously impaired. This week, however, a handful of protesters pelted the walls of the Beijing representative's office in Hong Kong with eggs and stones. Beijing was furious. The triads did their bidding and stormed the urban railway to beat people at random. The police appeared only after the gangs had melted away.

Beijing fears that Hong Kong could turn into a "coloured revolution" such as that experienced in the former Soviet Union. A successful uprising in Hong Kong could encourage the downtrodden Uighur Muslims of Xianjing province or the separatists of Tibet. To remove that threat it is pursuing a kind of hybrid warfare that largely sidesteps the alternately passive or brutal Hong Kong police. It no doubt calculates that thugs administering a short sharp shock to noisy democrats is better than bringing the Chinese army out of their barracks and on to the streets. And it reckons that neither the Hong Kong chief executive, Carrie Lam, nor the West, will raise much of a fuss.

But China is making a nonsense out of its pledge to abide by "one country, two systems". Every weekend for the past six weeks it has shown its reluctance to tolerate any system that voices independent thought or seeks to democratise a dysfunctional local government. By handing the state monopoly of force over to criminal gangs to enforce "order", Beijing displays the fragility of its rule. Its behaviour in Hong Kong is an act of self harm. Those in independent Taiwan who call for a closer political relationship to the mainland can no longer persuade young people that it is possible to breathe free in a union with China. And those in the West who argued that unfettered trade with Beijing was the surest way of liberalising the communist regime have also been wrong-footed. Day by day, China's mask is slipping.

Web of Lies

False claims about a paedophile ring were fanned by the police and Tom Watson

Wrong, malicious, false and horrendous were the words that the former MP Harvey Proctor used to describe the gruesome allegations levelled against him by Carl Beech. In 2014 Beech, a former hospital manager, accused Mr Proctor and a string of other high-profile men of the murder, abuse and rape of children in the 1970s and 1980s. Now we know he made it all up.

A ten-week trial at Newcastle crown court has found Beech guilty of fraud and fabricating evidence. His lies launched a mammoth investigation, Operation Midland, that cost the Metropolitan Police £2.5 million and irreparably damaged the reputations of innocent men. Initially, Beech's identity remained cloaked, but his alleged abusers' names became known when their properties were raided by the police. The officer leading the investigation gave Beech's account additional clout when he called it "credible and true" on television.

The crown court's verdict is welcome but it comes too late for some. Of the 12 men whom Beech falsely accused, eight are dead, including the former prime minister Edward Heath and Leon Brittan, the former home secretary. Brittan lived long enough to witness the trashing of his reputation, but died before his name was cleared. Not the least of those responsible for this behaviour was Labour's deputy leader, Tom Watson, who met Beech and pressed police to pursue his allegations. Days after Brittan's death, Mr Watson wrote an article in the *Sunday Mirror* in which he quoted a "survivor", thought to be Beech, who had told him that the late politician was "as close to evil as a human being could get".

All the living victims of Beech's sordid accusations deserve apologies from detectives who dragged them through hell. They also deserve an apology from Tom Watson.

THE TIMES 23 July 2019

FANTASIST 'NICK' GUILTY

WITCH-HUNT

Liar triggered VIP paedo probe

Fury . . Hogan-Howe, left, Watson and Beech, right

By ROBIN PERRIE & MIKE SULLIVAN

FANTASIST Carl Beech was facing jail last night for his VIP paedophile lies – as furious victims blasted cops and Labour's Tom Watson over the scandal.

Beech, 51, cost the taxpayer £4million with his bogus claims of rape and murder committed by politicians, military top brass and security service chiefs.

Beech — known as "Nick" before his anonymity was taken away by a judge — was yesterday convicted of perverting the course of justice after a ten-week trial.

The Met, headed at the time by Lord Hogan-Howe, was accused last night of presiding over a "total and utter cock-up". Beech was

Continued on Page Two

WHITEWASH

But cops & Watson dodge rap

THE SUN 23 July 2019

WITCH-HUNT LIAR

Continued from Page One

also convicted of fraudulently claiming compensation after lying he had been abused by disgraced TV personality Jimmy Savile.

As he was hauled off to cells to await sentencing:

● EX-MP Harvey Proctor — who had been accused of rape and murder — laid into the Metropolitan Police and slammed them as "lapdogs";

● THE son of another victim, Lord Janner, dubbed Labour's deputy leader Mr Watson "Britain's chief paedo-finder general" and said: "He should resign.";

● MR Watson desperately tried to defend his role in the scandal — but failed to pacify his accusers;

● THERE was fury over the police watchdog's decision to clear cops of blame without them ever being interviewed;

● THE mother of one of paedophile Beech's victims said he was "sick";

● MORE details of Beech's escape to Sweden emerged, where he posed as a wealthy bed and breakfast owner in a remote village;

● BEECH'S lies about his childhood of trauma were exposed — in reality he enjoyed a comfortable, middle-class upbringing;

● IT was revealed that he was obsessed with Ford Mustangs and made his fraudulent compo claim just so he could buy one;

● THE police probe into Beech's claims involved one officer travelling to Australia.

Cops eventually scrapped the Operation Midland probe into his allegations, before investigating Beech himself. In November 2016 officers raided the rented three-bed semi he shared with his teenage son in Gloucester.

They seized a number of computer devices and found hundreds of sickening pictures of child abuse.

At first he denied being responsible — and even hinted it was all down to his son before going on the run.

Beech, a former Care Quality Commission inspector, will be sentenced at Newcastle crown court on Friday.

He will also be sentenced for possession of child abuse images, voyeurism and fleeing to Sweden.

Fantasist . . . Beech

BID TO EASE GP AND A&E WAITS

THE PHARMACIST WILL SEE YOU NOW

By SHAUN WOOLLER

Sick seen same day

MILLIONS of sick Brits will be offered same-day appointments with pharmacists to ease pressure on A&Es and GPs.

Health chiefs say waiting rooms are clogged by patients with minor illnesses such as colds, earache and sore throats.

These can often be treated quickly with over-the-counter medication sold by highly-trained chemists in shops such as Boots and Lloyds.

But many wait hours to be seen in A&E or weeks to secure an appointment with their family doctor. The NHS Community Pharmacist Consultation Service could treat 20million people a year.

Anyone phoning NHS 111 over minor conditions will be offered a booked appointment at their pharmacy.

And if the pilot scheme proves successful, it will be expanded to include referrals from GPs and A&Es. It is estimated up to six per cent of GP consultations – 20million a year – could be safely transferred to a pharmacist.

Pharmacists undergo five years of training, giving them expert knowledge of medicines. But they will receive training to identify cases of sepsis, patients at risk of suicide and heart disease.

Their expanded role is part of a five-year contract struck between their trade body and the Health Department.

Health Secretary Matt Hancock said: "Pharmacies are a vital and trusted part of our NHS. And this five-year deal will ensure more people get support in the most appropriate setting, which in turn will relieve pressure on the wider health service."

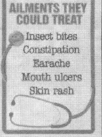

Jab . . . pharmacist at work

NHS chief pharmaceutical officer Keith Ridge said: "This deal provides the accessible and convenient health care the public want."

Prof Helen Stokes-Lampard, of the Royal College of GPs, said: "Pharmacists must not be seen as substitutes for GPs – so efforts to recruit and retain existing GPs must be redoubled."

shaun.wooller@the-sun.co.uk

AILMENTS THEY COULD TREAT

- Insect bites
- Constipation
- Earache
- Mouth ulcers
- Skin rash

PAY RISE FURY

THERESA May was yesterday accused of short-changing public sector workers despite a £1.4billion pay rise for teachers, soldiers and the police.

Low-paid soldiers, sailors and airmen will get as much as six per cent, while teachers will get 2.75 per cent or an average £1,000 jump.

But the Treasury admitted the money would come from "existing" budgets in government departments.

The National Education Union stormed: "The Government is loading further costs of £280million on schools."

HUAWEI 5G IS NOW ON HOLD

MINISTERS have dodged making a decision on whether to let Huawei work on Britain's 5G networks.

They want to see if the Chinese firm is on a US trade blacklist.

DOCS CUT TIME

ONE in three senior NHS doctors are cutting overtime and weekend work in a row over pensions, officials say.

Some GPs and consultants have quit, meaning more patients face possibly fatal delays for ops and scans.

Health Secretary Matt Hancock is to consult over proposals to change NHS pension rules. He said: "Too many of our most experienced clinicians are reducing hours or leaving the NHS early due to frustrations over pensions."

The British Medical Association warned that the proposals would do little to improve the "ridiculous, but serious" crisis many NHS doctors were facing.

Winner . . . Swinson

Lib Dem chief call to rivals

By MATT DATHAN

JO Swinson issued a "come and join us" plea to Tory and Labour MPs yesterday after being unveiled as the first female Lib Dem leader.

She romped to victory over rival Sir Ed Davey, winning nearly two-thirds of the members' votes.

And she said: "As your leader, I will do whatever it takes to stop Brexit."

Ms Swinson made a direct appeal to Tory MPs who want to stop Brexit and Labour moderates despairing at Jeremy Corbyn's leadership.

She also hinted she would be prepared to take the Lib Dems back into coalition, saying: "This is the time for working together, not the time for tribalism."

She said the Lib Dems should be aiming to win the next general election.

CORRECTIONS & CLARIFICATIONS

THE Sun aims to have the highest standards and we abide by the rules in the Editors' Code of Practice.

The Sun is a member of the Independent Press Standards Organisation. To make a complaint to us go to www.thesun.co.uk/ipso, email editorialcomplaints@the-sun.co.uk, or write to Editorial Complaints, The Sun, 1 London Bridge Street, London SE1 9GF.

ipso Regulated

Migrants all at sea

SAJID Javid said more than 1,000 migrants tried to cross the Channel this year and just a handful have been sent back.

Crossings since January are twice the figure for the whole of last year.

The Home Secretary said in 2019 "there has been 1,150 attempts". He said 725 arrived in the UK and 425 were intercepted in France.

Only 582 attempted it in the whole of 2018.

He told MPs that just 53 have been returned.

THE SUN 23 July 2019

'NICK' GUILTY

FURY AT BUNGLERS

The liar, the witch-hunt ...and the perv probe

●COPS RUINED LIVES
●WATSON 'MUST GO'

By ROBIN PERRIE, MIKE SULLIVAN and CHRIS POLLARD

MET officers who fell for Carl Beech's lies about a murderous VIP paedophile ring were yesterday accused of incompetence and astonishing gullibility.

Beech, whose fantasies triggered a multi-million pound Scotland Yard inquiry that smeared innocent public figures, was yesterday found guilty of perverting justice.

His victims and their families blasted the Met's botched Operation Midland – described by one ex-detective as a "total cock-up".

Deputy Labour leader Tom Watson was also accused of fuelling a witch-hunt by making Parliamentary speeches to bolster Beech's lurid accusations.

Ex-MP Harvey Proctor, 72, whose house was raided over Beech's claims he murdered a boy, said: "Tom Watson gave oxygen to his claims. He put pressure on the police to act on Beech's fantasies.

"It's time for him to apologise to me and everyone named in this truly disgraceful chapter in the history of British policing.

"It is time for the torchlight to take a closer look at Mr Watson."

Mr Proctor also blasted the police and Bernard Hogan-Howe, the Met Commissioner who launched Operation Midland.

He said: "The Metropolitan Police were lapdogs to Mr Watson's crude dog whistle. The Met should also apologise for squandering millions with incompetence and negligence."

Also wrongly accused was Labour peer Lord Janner, who died in 2015. His son Daniel Janner QC said: "Tom Watson should resign.

"He appointed himself Britain's chief paedo-finder general and created a moral panic."

Convicted paedophile Beech, 51, was yesterday found guilty at Newcastle crown court of perverting justice. He was also found guilty of fraud over compensation claims relating to abuse allegations.

The former nurse and social services inspector will be sentenced on Friday.

Vicar's son Beech, father of a teenage son, dreamed up his tales of rape, torture and murder when the Jimmy Savile scandal broke.

At the time, in late 2012, his 20-year marriage had ended and he was deeply in debt.

He told a counsellor he had been abused as a child by Savile – and logged a claim for compensation.

Beech was interviewed but officers found his story unconvincing.

So he invented new allegations – claiming he was one of many young victims of a secret VIP paedophile ring.

Beech said these men kidnapped and raped boys in the 1970s and 80s. He said three boys were murdered – one victim being deliberately run over in the street.

Among the alleged abusers were prominent Tories, former PM Edward Heath, ex-Home Secretary Leon Brittan and MP Proctor.

Beech also named former Army chief Field Marshal Lord Bramall, ex-MI6 head Sir Maurice Oldfield and ex-MI5 chief Sir Michael Hanley. He claimed he was passed on to the ring by stepfather Raymond Beech, the first to abuse him.

Beech started writing an internet blog about his "experiences". They were picked up by online journalists – and brought to the attentions of Watson.

In 2014 Watson met Beech, whose allegations became wilder – including a claim Proctor tied a boy to a table, raped him and then stabbed him to death.

A Sunday newspaper published his allegations using the pseudonym "Nick."

In October 2014 Beech was interviewed by the Met and Operation Midland was a launched. Detective Superintendent Kenny McDonald publicly described "Nick's" claims as "credible and true" – despite the fact they had not been fully investigated.

Officers raided the homes of Brittan, who was to die before his name was cleared, Proctor and Lord Bramall. Twenty officers worked full-time for 16 months on the case. They took 370 witness statements, launched 1,700 actions and produced 1,860 documents. Not a single arrest was made.

In 2016 Operation Midland was scrapped. Northumbria Police were tasked to investigate Beech himself and discovered gaping holes in his story which the Met failed to find.

Ex-Met detective superintendent Michael Hames said of Operation Midland: "It was a total and utter cock-up. What I find extraordinary is how the police believed the lies told by Beech."

But yesterday it emerged the officers who led Operation Midland were cleared of blame without ever being interviewed.

The Independent Office of Police Conduct ruled there was no disciplinary case to answer for McDonald and Deputy Assistant Commissioner Steve Rodhouse.

Its decision was based on a "comprehensive" analysis of reports and case notes rather than interviews with the pair.

Watson yesterday defended his role, saying: "I felt it was my duty to respond to the claims that had been made to me."

robin.perrie@the-sun.co.uk

The Sun Says – Page 12

Guilty . . fantasist Carl Beech, aka 'Nick'

THE COMPO CABIN: PAGES 8 & 9

CONNED BY SICK FANTASIST

THE BELIEVERS

LABOUR MP TOM WATSON

LABOUR'S deputy leader told Parliament in 2012 about a paedo network with links to government. Had to apologise to Lord Brittan's family for calling him "evil". Beech's victims have called for him to resign.

POLICE CHIEF HOGAN-HOWE

THE Met Commissioner was in charge at the height of Operation Midland and had to apologise to those accused by Beech. A probe cleared him of any personal blame over the botched investigation.

DETECTIVE KEN McDONALD

DET Supt McDonald had day-to-day charge of Midland probe. He called Beech's claims "credible and true" even before officers investigated them. He had health problems and retired weeks before Beech's trial.

THE EXARO NEWS AGENCY

BEECH'S claims of abuse on an obscure blog were highlighted by little-known news agency Exaro part-owned by Jerome Booth, *right*. Beech named some abusers after a reporter showed him photos of prominent men.

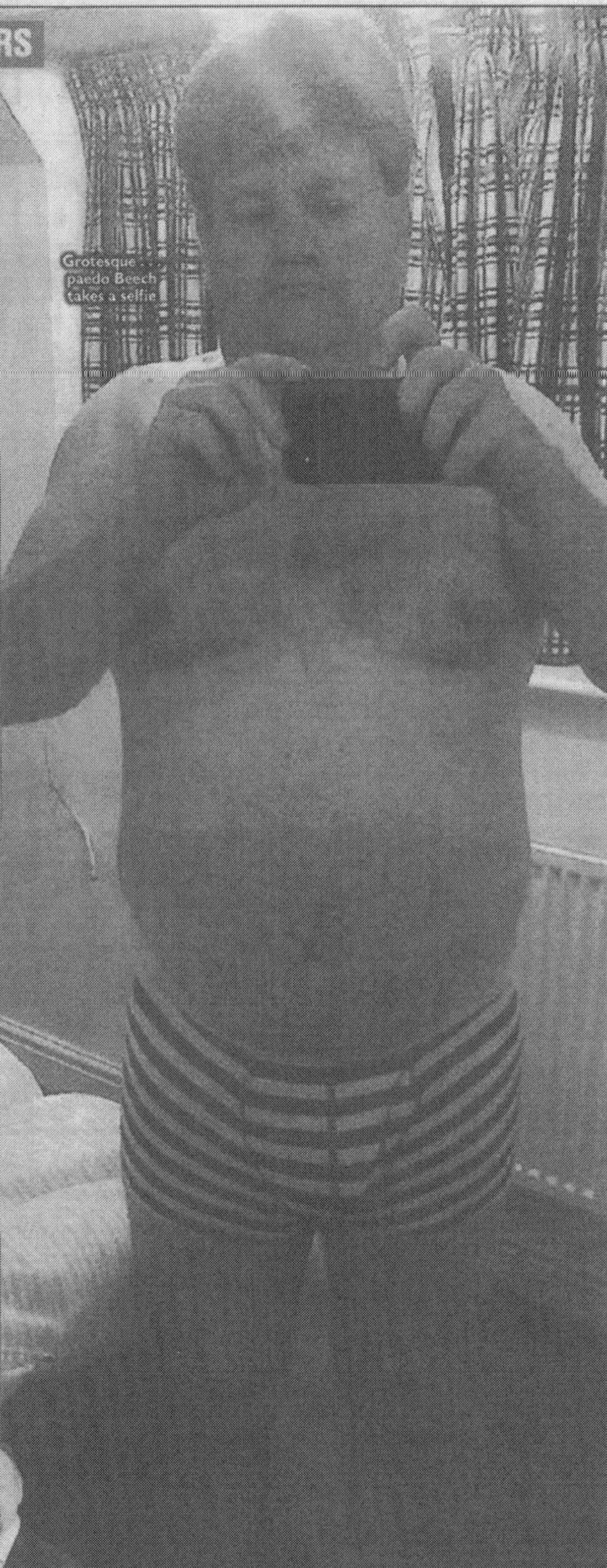

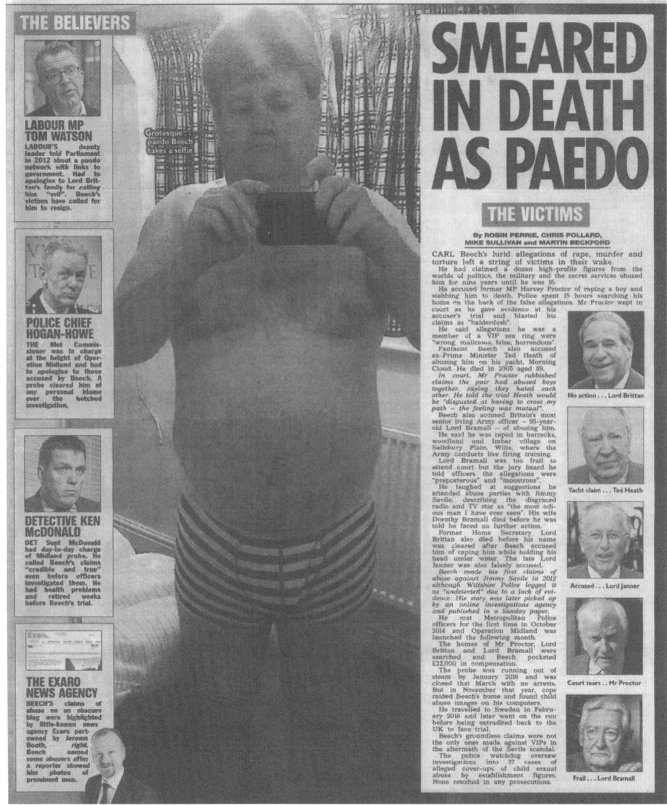

Grotesque ... paedo Beech takes a selfie

SMEARED IN DEATH AS PAEDO

THE VICTIMS

By ROBIN PERRIE, CHRIS POLLARD, MIKE SULLIVAN and MARTIN BECKFORD

CARL Beech's lurid allegations of rape, murder and torture left a string of victims in their wake.

He had claimed a dozen high-profile figures from the worlds of politics, the military and the secret services abused him for nine years until he was 16.

He accused former MP Harvey Proctor of raping a boy and stabbing him to death. Police spent 15 hours searching his home on the back of the false allegations. Mr Proctor wept in court as he gave evidence at his accuser's trial and blasted his claims as "balderdash".

He said allegations he was a member of a VIP sex ring were "wrong, malicious, false, horrendous".

Fantasist Beech also accused ex-Prime Minister Ted Heath of abusing him on his yacht, Morning Cloud. He died in 2005 aged 89.

In court, Mr Proctor rubbished claims the pair had abused boys together, saying they hated each other. He told the trial Heath would be "disgusted at having to cross my path – the feeling was mutual".

Beech also accused Britain's most senior living Army officer – 95-year-old Lord Bramall – of abusing him.

He said he was raped in barracks, woodland and Imber village on Salisbury Plain, Wilts, where the Army conducts live firing training.

Lord Bramall was too frail to attend court but the jury heard he told officers the allegations were "preposterous" and "monstrous".

He laughed at suggestions he attended abuse parties with Jimmy Savile, describing the disgraced radio and TV star as "the most odious man I have ever seen". His wife Dorothy Bramall died before he was told he faced no further action.

Former Home Secretary Lord Brittan aleo died before his name was cleared after Beech accused him of raping him while holding his head under water. The late Lord Janner was also falsely accused.

Beech made his first claims of abuse against Jimmy Savile in 2012 although Wiltshire Police logged it as "undetected" due to a lack of evidence. His story was later picked up by an online investigations agency and published in a Sunday paper.

He met Metropolitan Police officers for the first time in October 2014 and Operation Midland was launched the following month.

The homes of Mr Proctor, Lord Brittan and Lord Bramall were searched and Beech pocketed £22,000 in compensation.

The probe was running out of steam by January 2016 and was closed that March with no arrests. But in November that year, cops raided Beech's home and found child abuse images on his computers.

He travelled to Sweden in February 2018 and later went on the run before being extradited back to the UK to face trial.

Beech's groundless claims were not the only ones made against VIPs in the aftermath of the Savile scandal.

The police watchdog oversaw investigations into 37 cases of alleged cover-ups of child sexual abuse by establishment figures. None resulted in any prosecutions.

No action ... Lord Brittan

Yacht claim ... Ted Heath

Accused ... Lord Janner

Court tears .. Mr Proctor

Frail ... Lord Bramall

THE SUN 23 July 2019

'NICK' GUILTY

EXCLUSIVE: LAIR OF THE COM

●Fugitive bought up luxury hut in Lapland

●He paid for it with cash from taxpayers

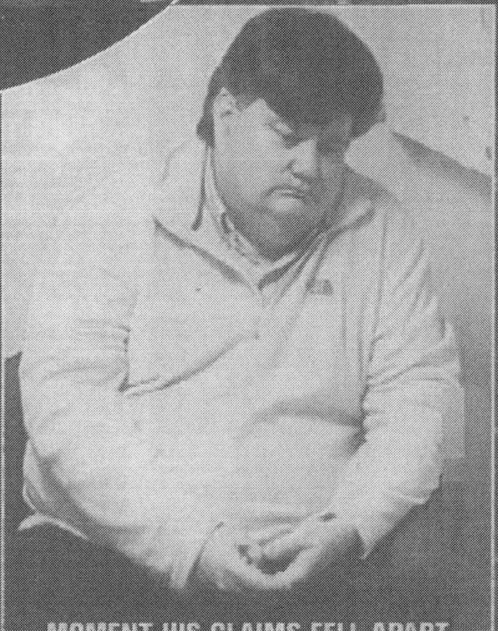

MOMENT HIS CLAIMS FELL APART

Ex-hospital manager Beech being interviewed by police in January 2016

NORTHERN LIGHTS

Sights . . . Beech promised 'dancing lights'

EXCLUSIVE from CHRIS POLLARD in Overkalix, Sweden

SEX-abuse liar Carl Beech fled to a remote village in Lapland and posed as a luxury guesthouse proprietor to dodge justice.

The fugitive, who had swindled £22,000 compensation from the UK taxpayer, conned locals into believing he was a successful businessman.

With an international arrest warrant hanging over him, Beech bought a secluded woodland cabin for £17,000 and spent months turning it into a fairytale cottage.

But the brazen conman ran up debts of at least £13,000 with traders – and mysteriously refused to pose in any photos with friendly locals – before vanishing.

One said after he was rearrested: "I had a feeling something fishy was going on."

Beech skipped bail in February last year after cops failed to monitor him as he awaited trial on a string of child sex offences.

He caught a train to Paris then travelled 2,000 miles to the village of Overkalix – population 900 – in Swedish Lapland.

There he planned to open a luxury Arctic Circle guesthouse, called 66 Degrees North, with views of the Northern Lights.

He bought a property overlooking the Kalix River, plus five small outbuildings, for around £17,000.

He also planned to buy a large house across the road plus several cabins by the riverside, including a luxury villa for his mum.

Former hospital manager Beech, 51, even ran two Facebook pages and an Instagram account to promote his plan.

Local tradesmen were hired to help, including plumber Patrik Elemalm, 47, who installed a new bathroom and renovated the pipework for £4,500.

Patrik said: "He seemed very odd. I always wondered why an Englishman would want to buy a house in Overkalix. This is a very quiet and secluded community."

Beech had evaded UK cops but knew a criminal trial was pending.

Patrik went on: "One day he came in ranting we were taking too long. He was furious, very rude and aggressive. I had to send another workman to calm him."

He said he then "vanished like a ghost", ignoring repeated requests to pay, adding: "I can't afford to lose this kind of money."

Carpenter Pär Andersson, 48, is owed £8,500 for "a lot of work" on the bathroom, corridor and bedrooms. He said: "It seemed very strange he was here.

"We've had people from other countries move here, but never an Englishman of his age. He said he had been to Overkalix on holiday and fell in love with it.

"At some point his mother came and she wanted us to build her a luxury cabin. She wanted us to go ahead with it straight away." But Pär said it cost £85,000 and Beech had to settle the original bill first.

He went on: "I was right to be cautious. It will be very difficult to get my money back."

Beech used various names to hide his identity, including Andersson, Karlsson and Oskar – and posted updates on his "business".

He wrote in February: "Follow us on an exciting journey to create 66 Degrees North bed and breakfast in the heart of Swedish Lapland."

Future guests were invited to "see the various activities you can do and meet the local wildlife", including lynx, moose and reindeer. He added: "When we open, come and stay, see for yourself."

On April 2 he wrote: "The Northern Lights have been dancing around the sky for the last three nights. Just amazing every time you see them, so lucky."

He also quipped on another occasion: "I don't need therapy, I just need Sweden."

On April 30 he posted pictures of a bonfire festival in Overkalix, writing: "Great to see a thriving community spirit."

He also thanked neighbour Christina Gëversten-Stål for "making me feel so welcome". She told The Sun: "He seemed very polite and I tried to introduce him to the local community.

"Then one day he said he was going with a friend to Norway on holiday, and never came back.

"I was shocked when I heard what he was accused of."

Beech, who was taking Swedish lessons, also introduced himself as Oskar to an Italian traveller, Claudio Comi.

Claudio, who helped Beech redecorate his cottage, posted some pictures of the property on Facebook. But Beech refused to pose for any photos himself, telling him: "I never have my picture taken."

Claudio said: "We kind of guessed he was not who he was telling us he was."

Another neighbour, Sonja Isaksson, recalled: "He seemed nice.

"He said he wanted to buy more property and make this a tourist destination. Then we started seeing an unmarked police car watching the house."

Property records show Beech bought a second property in Kiruna, 150 miles from Överkalix, but is thought to have never visited it.

He feared the net was closing in

THE LIAR WHO FLED COPS

I don't need therapy, I just need Sweden
Idyllic ... Beech's cabin and the outbuildings

HE WAS LYING SPITEFUL CHILD

EXCLUSIVE by CHRIS POLLARD ROBIN PERRIE and PAUL SIMS

CARL Beech grew up a "spiteful brat" who used lies and deceit to get his way, stepbrother Charles says.

Care worker Charles was 12 when in 1976 his dad Raymond Beech married Carl's mum Charmian, a vicar.

He said: "Carl was eight and very difficult to get on with. He was an only child and he'd always had his mother. Suddenly her attention was split and he resented it.

"He was a spoilt brat, he was sneaky. And he was a liar from day one.

"He was always doing spiteful little things and blaming them on us. His mother would always side with him."

Beech told police and his trial that Raymond, a major in the Royal Artillery, sexually abused him and then passed him on to a VIP paedophile ring, that included former PM Edward Heath.

Charles said: "The closest Carl ever got to Heath was seeing him on the telly.

"To suggest he was suffering childhood abuse and keeping quiet about it just seems ridiculous. He would whinge and whine about the smallest things.

"I can absolutely believe he has grown up to be an adult who would deceive and make stuff up for his own ends."

Charles is angry about the way police investigated the claims made against Raymond, who died in 1995.

He said: "Detectives came to my house on several occasions asking all sorts of questions. They also hassled my sisters.

"They asked lots of strange questions but never once did they ask, 'Did your father abuse you?'

"We only found out what was going on because we read about it in The Sun.

"My father could be a difficult man. But he was not a child abuser."

Charmian split with Raymond after a few months of marriage. She and Beech moved from Wilton, Wilts, to Kingston-upon-Thames in South West London.

His mother continued to dote on him, buying him a dog and later a horse. There were also plenty of foreign holidays.

After school Beech trained as a nurse. In 1988 he met fellow trainee Dawn Morgan, 19. They wed in 1992 and in 2002 they had a son, now 16. They divorced in 2012. Dawn told her ex's trial there were problems over "intimacy" and his personal hygiene.

Beech, later revealed as a paedophile, went on to work on a paediatric ward.

He was also a school governor and an NSPCC volunteer who warned kids about the dangers of child abuse.

After taking NHS redundancy Beech got a job as an inspector of health and social services. Outside work he had started devoting his time to writing online about the abuse he claimed to have suffered.

'SPOILED BRAT'

Beech as a child. His mum doted on him

PO CABIN

on him in August, and fled. He checked in to several cheap hostels in the Swedish city of Gothenburg under false names. He was eventually arrested at its central train station on October 1.

Vincent Van Uytven, who runs a holiday resort in Overkalix, was the only local to hear from Beech after his disappearance.

He messaged Vincent on August 16: "I'm just dealing with a few things and getting stressed."

Vincent said: "He said he would get back to me again later, but that was the last I heard. I had a feeling something fishy was going on."

chris.pollard@the-sun.co.uk

Remote spot . . . where Beech holed up

PERV FILMED LAD

THE mum of a lad who was spied on by Carl Beech said of the paedo: "He's sick."

The pervert had rigged up a camera to make footage of the boy using the toilet.

Beech stored the video on his computer so he could watch it over and over again — alongside hundreds of child abuse images.

The mum of the teenager who was filmed said: "Carl was a governor of two schools, had been an NHS nurse and was a single parent. He was trusted.

"There weren't any warning signs that he was a danger.

"To me, he was a good dad. That was the impression he gave. There was nothing unusual. I never had any concerns.

"The first time I knew anything was wrong was when CID said they had found images of my son on his phone and laptop. When I saw the pictures, reality set in. There were images of my son in his underwear and one of him using the toilet."

She added: "It has really affected my son. He's withdrawn and will not talk about it.

"They need to lock up Carl and throw away the key. I thought I could trust him. He isn't what you think. He's sick."

THE SUN 23 July 2019

THE Sun SAYS

Paedo shame

SHAME on the Met Police, its appalling former chief Bernard Hogan-Howe and the staggering incompetence of the cops who swallowed Carl Beech's warped fantasies.

His preposterous lies always sounded like a round-up of the paedophile conspiracy theories which nutters circulate on the web. So they have proved.

What does it say about the calibre of our detectives that they were so gullible?

That they called his flawed, inconsistent claims "credible and true" before investigating them? That bosses blew £2.5million on Operation Midland only to find (surprise, surprise) zero evidence?

And that they put the men Beech falsely accused through sheer hell, along with their distressed families?

How has Hogan-Howe retired to the Lords when his Met career is solely remembered for the failures of Midland and Operation Elveden, the politically-driven and equally fruitless witch-hunt into innocent Sun journalists?

How, too, is Tom Watson still an MP today, let alone Labour's deputy leader?

It was he who in 2012 ignited a moral panic with his grandstanding allegation of "a powerful paedophile network linked to Parliament and No 10". It was drivel.

But Watson then indulged Beech, cynically promoting his lies about Tories including Leon Brittan, a blameless old man the MP disgracefully branded "as close to evil as any human could get".

It was a repugnant, baseless slur typical of this most unscrupulous and tribal of politicians. Watson let himself become "a vehicle for conspiracy theorists and a patsy for fake news", according to a lawyer for one accused former Tory.

He is a disgrace to our Parliament and should have no place in it.

Yet somehow Watson remains Labour moderates' great hope to save them from Corbyn and his racist extremists.

God help them if he is all they have.

Duncan donut

YOU won't have heard of Alan Duncan MP, which is what drives him mad.

He is a pompous pipsqueak, insignificant yet monumentally self-important.

Yesterday, after quitting as a Tory minister, he launched a deranged attempt to stop Boris Johnson becoming PM.

Imagine it: A Tory flouncing out of Government trying to block a fellow Tory, elected by Tory MPs and members, because he doesn't like him.

Throwing his toys out of the pram, as with Brexit, because the vote went against him. Abandoning the Foreign Office amid multiple international crises because he must get **HIS** way.

What did we do to deserve these childish idiots at Westminster?

How did the Chancellor go from steadfastly backing Theresa May over "No Deal is better than a bad deal" to vowing to topple the Government if Boris carries out the same policy?

The Sun has no desire for an election.

But the Tories could at least use it to boot out the juvenile, self-centred chancers destroying them from within.

LIAR WAS USED AS A POLITICAL TOOL

The only thing 'credible and true' about VIP claims is fact Tom Watson used them to boost career

SHAMEFUL... Labour's Tom Watson at the time of false paedo claims

By ROSS CLARK

IS there any phrase in the English language now as notorious as "credible and true"?

Those were the words uttered by Det Supt Kenny McDonald as officers from the Metropolitan Police were let loose raiding the homes of elderly politicians searching for evidence to back up the allegations made by a mysterious man called "Nick".

Nick, it was claimed, had been abused by a paedophile ring of wealthy and powerful men in the 1970s and 1980s, including the former Prime Minister Sir Edward Heath.

On one occasion, he claimed Harvey Proctor, then a Conservative MP, had threatened to cut off his testicles with a pen knife, before being talked out of it by Heath.

One of Nick's pals had apparently been deliberately run down and killed by the gang in a warning to Nick not to make friends.

Now we know exactly how "credible and true" these allegations were. They were fantasies cooked up by Nick himself, cynically played in an atmosphere already high with emotion following the revelations in 2012 of Jimmy Savile's activities.

Yesterday, Carl Beech – to use Nick's real name – was convicted of fraud and perverting the course of justice after his tales were exposed as a total sham.

He had no injuries to suggest he had been abused in the way he described. He had never mentioned his supposed ordeal once to his former wife. His accounts simply did not add up and parts seemed to have been lifted from a misery memoir written by someone else.

Attracting liars and fantasists

Pleasing though it is to see Beech convicted, he leaves a horrible trail of destruction in his path. Untold damage has been done to the lives of those he falsely accused. Lord Bramall, a Field Marshall who took part in the Normandy landings, saw his wife die with allegations still hanging over his head.

Lord Brittan, Home Secretary in Mrs Thatcher's government, died while under investigation, and his widow watched as their home was raided by police.

Harvey Proctor lost his home and his job when the allegations emerged.

That Beech is a despicable individual who deserves a long term in jail goes without saying. But there are plenty of others whose role in this affair leaves them in disgrace.

Obviously police have to investigate when allegations of child abuse are made, but the enthusiasm with which former Met Commissioner Lord Hogan-Howe threw resources into Operation Midland – the inquiry into Carl Beech's allegations – raises questions into just how objective some of our senior police officers are.

Surely it could not have taken long to establish that aspects of Beech's claims were outlandish. Yet police lavished £2.5million on the investigation, guided, it seems, by a doctrine that people claiming to be victims of sexual abuse must always be believed.

True, there was a time when genuine victims tended not to be believed, and in some cases were sent back to live with their abusers. That was a very great wrong but it cannot be righted by going to the opposite extreme and automatically believing the stories of people claiming to be victims, however fantastical they prove to be.

Yes, child abuse is a horrible crime which can scar its victims for life but so, too, is making false allegations against innocent people.

Sadly, this kind of behaviour has been encouraged through compensation schemes which seem to hand out money willy-nilly to anyone who makes a claim they were abused as a child.

Unbelievably, Beech was awarded £22,000 in compensation for his supposed ordeal even before his claims were tested in court. He spent the money on a Ford Mustang.

How can the Criminal Injuries Compensation Scheme, which handed over the money, not see that it is attracting liars and fantasists?

But there is one figure in the Carl Beech scandal who deserves to be singled out for particular condemnation.

When allegations about a Westminster paedophile ring first came to light, Tom Watson – now Labour's deputy leader leapt upon them with relish.

He could see many of the names being touted as alleged abusers were Conservatives and sensed the opportunity to damage his opponents.

He used Prime Minister's Questions as a forum to repeat allegations, and invited Beech to his Westminster office, politicising his claims and helping to put pressure on police to set up a wider inquiry.

He called Lord Brittan "evil". He has at least apologised for those words, writing a letter to Lady Brittan, but for his wider role in Operation Midland he still refuses to say sorry.

But a letter to Lady Brittan is not enough. If he had any decency he would recognise the pain and havoc he has caused to innocent lives and resign as Labour's deputy leader – and as an MP, too.

Daniel Janner QC, the late Lord Janner's son, put it best shortly after Beech was convicted yesterday.

He said: "Tom Watson should resign. He appointed himself Britain's chief paedo-finder general and created a moral panic. His motive was personal political advancement riding on a bandwagon of public frenzy which he had whipped up. He should hang his head in shame."

Finally a statement in this sorry mess that *is* credible and true.

● Ross Clark is a columnist for The Spectator.

See The Sun Says

THE SUN 23 July 2019

NEWS BRIEFING

NEWS

Boris plans to borrow to fund tax pledges

Boris Johnson is prepared to turn on the spending taps by borrowing money to help the squeezed middle classes if he is confirmed as the new Tory leader today. The former foreign secretary is in favour of a policy of "fiscal loosening" that would reverse the tight controls on public spending imposed by Philip Hammond. He is determined to honour promises to give tax breaks to everyone who earns less than £80,000.
Page 4

WORLD

Britain joins maritime protection force in Gulf

Jeremy Hunt announced yesterday that Britain will join a European-led marine protection force to guard against Iranian threats in the Gulf, as he described Tehran's hijacking of a UK-flagged tanker as an act of "state piracy". The Foreign Secretary said he wanted to "keep diplomacy going", but the seizure last week by Iran of the Stena Impero meant the UK had to take more robust action. "If Iran continues on this dangerous path, they must accept the price will be a larger Western military presence in the waters along their coastline," he said.
Page 15

MATT

NEWS

Nessy hunt is asking for trouble, says RNLI

Conspiracy theorists risk hypothermia and drowning if they follow through with a plan to "storm" Loch Ness in search of its mythical monster, the RNLI has warned. More than 40,000 people have signalled their interest in storming the loch to find the fabled monster, prompting a safety warning.
Page 13

ISSN 0307-1235

Fantasist whose lies should never have been believed

The conviction of Carl Beech, centre, yesterday on charges of perverting the course of justice has piled pressure on Tom Watson, left, and Lord Hogan-Howe, right, over their roles in pursuing his baseless allegations

Tom Watson and Scotland Yard face serious questions as paedophile's deception and manipulation exposed

By **Martin Evans** *and* **Robert Mendick**

A FANTASIST who accused some of the country's most high-profile figures of child torture, rape and murder was yesterday found guilty of inventing the Westminster VIP paedophile ring amid serious questions over the roles of both Scotland Yard and Labour MP Tom Watson in his deceit.

Carl Beech, 51, a highly manipulative paedophile, was found guilty of 12 counts of perverting the course of justice and one count of fraud by a jury at Newcastle Crown Court, following a ten-week trial.

Beech now faces a lengthy prison sentence after prosecutors proved he had repeatedly lied to police, who had fallen for his claims.

The conviction of Beech prompted calls last night for Scotland Yard – which spent 18 months and £4million investigating the allegations – to be placed in the dock, after it emerged that all of the officers involved in the debacle had been formally cleared of wrongdoing by the police watchdog.

Mr Watson's role in fuelling the "witch hunt" is also under intense scrutiny and he is even under pressure to resign after it emerged the deputy Labour leader urged Beech to take his allegations to the police after meeting him in July 2014.

Beech, a former paediatric nurse, told detectives he and other boys had been raped and abused by an organised gang that included Sir Edward Heath, the former prime minister, Lord Brittan, the former home secretary, Harvey Proctor, the former Tory MP, Field Marshal Lord Bramall, the former head of the Army, Lord Janner, the former Labour MP, Sir Maurice Oldfield, the former head of MI6, Sir Michael Hanley, the former director of MI5, General Sir Hugh Beach and Field Marshal Sir Roland Gibbs.

Swallowing his lies, the Metropolitan Police launched the disastrous Operation Midland, which saw the homes of some of those accused raided and their reputations left in tatters.

Speaking after yesterday's verdict – which took the jury just four hours of deliberations – Lord Bramall, 95, castigated the Metropolitan Police.

The D-Day veteran said: "I am naturally delighted that after four years someone has at last been brought to book for the appalling travesty of justice which I and my whole family and others have had to endure.

"It is of course not only the outrageous, totally untruthful allegations by Carl Beech which perverted the course of justice but also the incompetent and improper way the Metropolitan Police Service handled them at their unquestioned face value which lent them unwarranted credibility."

Mr Proctor, who lost his home and job as a result of the false accusations, said Mr Watson also had questions to answer. He said: "The Metropolitan Police were lapdogs to Mr Watson's crude dog whistle. It's time for the torchlight to take a closer look at Mr Watson. It is time for an apology from him to me and everyone named or implicated in this truly disgraceful chapter in the history of British policing.

"All he had to do was lie. Mr Beech lied, lied and lied again, and his breathtaking lies were facilitated, enhanced and given credibility by the Met Police without corroboration."

Joan Harborne, the ex-wife of Major Raymond Beech – Beech's late stepfather who was the first person falsely accused – said: "We tried to give them evidence that would prove what Carl was saying was not true, but it was as if they did not want to listen."

Sir Richard Henriques, a retired High Court judge, found more than 40 mistakes in the way the force had handled the inquiry. Sir Richard told *The Daily Telegraph* yesterday: "Within a very few days of receiving all the documents ... I concluded that the allegations were fabricated, incredible and untrue."

Five officers were referred to the Independent Office for Police Conduct for potential misconduct. None of the officers involved has been sanctioned.

Lord Hogan-Howe, the then Met Commissioner, retired from the force in February 2017 and was elevated to the House of Lords as a cross-bencher.

Deputy Assistant Commissioner Steve Rodhouse, who had overall responsibility for the investigation, left the Met in May 2018 to take up a £214,722-a-year job as director-general of operations at the National Crime Agency. Det Supt Kenny McDonald, who was head of Operation Midland, retired in August 2017 on full pension.

Lincoln Seligman, the godson of Sir Edward Heath, said: "Those who were being investigated by the police watchdog have been let off scot-free."

The trial heard how as Beech was lying to police, he was also committing his own paedophilia offences, downloading appalling child abuse images and filming a young boy urinating.

Mr Watson said he only met Beech once and added: "During that meeting 'Nick' said very little and did not name any of his alleged abusers. I reassured Nick that the police had made clear that all allegations of historic sex abuse would be taken seriously and treated sensitively. It was not my role to judge whether victims' stories were true. I encouraged every person that came to me to take their story to the police and that is what I did with Nick."

Reports: Pages 10-11

THE DAILY TELEGRAPH

A saga of lies, staggering police incompetence and shocking political gullibility

Editorial Comment: Page 19

THE DAILY TELEGRAPH 23 July 2019

Trail of deceit Carl Beech and tissue of lies that ruined lives

- **October 2012** Carl Beech tells Wiltshire Police he was sexually abused as a child by his stepfather, Major Ray Beech, and Jimmy Savile. The police later mark the case as "undetected" and take no further action.

- **July 8 2014** Beech meets Tom Watson, left, at his Commons' office. Mr Watson says Beech did not name names but did mention that a VIP gang had murdered a child. Watson encourages Beech to go to the police.
- **November 2014** Operation Midland is launched into claims of "possible homicide" linked to an alleged VIP paedophile ring. On Dec 18, Detective Superintendent Kenny McDonald calls Beech's claims "credible and true".
- **March 4 2015** Police raid the homes of former Conservative MP Harvey Proctor, the homes of Lord Brittan's widow Lady Brittan and Field Marshall Lord Bramall, whose wife is a dementia sufferer.
- **August 25 2015** Mr Proctor holds a press conference in which he denounces "Nick" and the police. Mr Proctor says Beech alleges that Sir Edward Heath prevented Mr Proctor from castrating him.
- **January 15 2016** After 10 months as a suspect, Lord Bramall is told he faces no further action. Mr Proctor is told on March 21 2016 he will face no further action, and Operation Midland is closed without a single arrest.

How Tom Watson sparked police inquiry

Why was a paedophile whose claims of abuse and murder were not supported by any shred of evidence believed for so long?

By Robert Mendick and Martin Evans

CARL BEECH, a narcissist, fantasist and now a convicted paedophile, must have been cock-a-hoop. Tom Watson, then a backbench MP and soon to be elected the Labour Party's deputy leader, had granted Beech an audience.

This was Beech's opportunity to tell Mr Watson of the sexual abuse he had suffered at the hands of a murderous paedophile gang that had operated from the Palace of Westminster.

The meeting would set in chain the perfect storm. Scotland Yard's finest detectives would believe every word Beech told them of three murders and unimaginably depraved child sexual abuse committed by a gang that included a former prime minister and a home secretary, the ex-chiefs of MI5 and MI6, the former head of the Army, numerous MPs and Jimmy Savile.

It didn't matter that there wasn't a shred of evidence to back up Beech's crazy claims. Mr Watson had already stood up in Parliament and said a powerful Westminster paedophile ring needed investigating while police were stuck on a mantra that "victims must be believed".

Yesterday, victims of Beech turned on not just the police but also Mr Watson for his part in their hell. Harvey Proctor, the former Conservative MP falsely accused by Beech of murder, torture and rape, said: "The Metropolitan Police were lapdogs to Mr Watson's crude dog whistle. It is now beyond doubt that all of these allegations could never have been true and only someone with spectacular bad judgment could think that they might be."

He called on Mr Watson to apologise.

Field Marshal Lord Bramall, 95, a D-Day veteran, said: "It is of course, not only the outrageous, totally untruthful allegations by Carl Beech which perverted the course of justice but also the incompetent and improper way the Metropolitan Police Service handled them at their unquestioned face value which lent them unwarranted credibility."

Lincoln Seligman, godson of Sir Edward Heath, said: "What I find astonishing is that senior police officers in the Metropolitan Police and politicians like Tom Watson, and some elements of media, believed Beech and made frequent public statements to that effect."

Andi Lavery, 47, a genuine victim of abuse who was raped as a five-year-old child by a Catholic priest and some of whose own account Beech had stolen, was scathing. "Tom Watson weaponised child abuse," he said, adding: "Beech is a psychopath, he reminds me of Harold Shipman – he is so mundane, yet there within Beech is the banality of evil."

Daniel Janner QC, whose father Lord Janner was also accused of abuse by Beech, said: "Watson had politicised a police inquiry. He showed no regard for the presumption of innocence. He hounded Lord Brittan, a dying man, to his grave."

Beech, now aged 51, spoke to Watson "at some length" in his private office at that fateful meeting in July 2014. Beech would later tell police that "Mr Watson formed part of the little group supporting me and putting my information out there to encourage other people to come forward".

Mr Watson was a powerful ally for Beech. The MP had previously taken on the police and newspapers, pursuing the *News of the World* for its systemic phone hacking and holding the Met to account over its failure to investigate fully the extent of journalists' crimes.

Here was a new crusade for Mr Watson: the pursuit of VIP child abusers. In October 2012, two years before his meeting with Beech, Mr Watson had stood up in Parliament and declared the existence of "clear intelligence suggesting a powerful paedophile network linked to Parliament and No10".

The claims, in the wake of the furore over the failure of police to bring to justice Jimmy Savile, the BBC broadcaster and serial paedophile, had a devastating effect: Scotland Yard devoted millions of pounds to hunting gangs that didn't exist and Theresa May, as home secretary, was bounced into setting up the Independent Inquiry into Child Sexual Abuse that will cost the taxpayer north of £200million.

Against this background, Beech was desperate to be listened to. In the same month as Mr Watson was making that claim, Beech, a middle-class, middle-aged professional working in the NHS, had contacted Wiltshire Police.

He told detectives that for several years when he was a young boy, his stepfather, a major in the Army, had taken him to Wilton barracks, where he and other men had raped and abused him. He also claimed to have been one of Savile's many victims.

Wiltshire Police interviewed Beech but with his stepfather, Raymond Beech, having died in 1995, and Savile long gone, it was decided little more could be done. Sources have told *The Daily Telegraph* that detectives thought Beech's story implausible.

Beech began a blog, detailing his supposed ordeal. He stole the accounts of genuine survivors of abuse and added his own from the depths of his twisted imagination.

Exaro, a controversial news agency that later closed down, spotted Beech's blog and one of its journalists, Mark Conrad, made contact. Exaro began publishing Beech's increasingly lurid claims, giving him the pseudonym "Nick" to preserve his anonymity. It also peddled Nick's ever more extreme stories to tabloid newspapers for cash.

The meeting between Beech and Watson was set up for July 8 2014. Mr Conrad and a social worker, Peter McKelvie, who was a member of a victims' panel with the national child abuse inquiry, accompanied Beech.

Over the course of two hours, Beech laid out his story of how he had been abused by the gang. Mr Watson was impressed. "It was a very, very traumatic and difficult conversation, as you would imagine," Mr Watson told *The Guardian* a month later. "He only told me about one murder. He spoke very slowly, very intermittently, and I didn't need to hear any more."

Yesterday in a statement, Mr Watson said he only met Beech once and at that meeting "Nick said very little and did not name any of his alleged abusers". Mr Watson added: "It was not my role to judge whether victims' stories were true. I encouraged every person that came to me to take their story to the police and that is what I did with Nick."

Mr Watson said in his *Guardian* interview, "What I'm certain of is that he's not delusional. He is either telling the truth, or he's made up a meticulous and elaborate story. It's not for me to judge."

In November 2014, Beech gave an interview to Tom Symonds, the BBC's home affairs correspondent, which made headline news. "They had no fear at all of being caught, it didn't cross their mind," Beech unchallenged told the BBC, adding: "[The gang] created fear that penetrated every part of me, day in day out."

The Met bought Beech's story book, line and sinker. Det Sgt James Townly interviewed Beech initially and in all he was questioned for 20 hours. Operation Midland, a homicide inquiry, was launched, based solely on Beech's unsubstantiated testimony of witnessing three child murders.

Nobody at Scotland Yard would bother to check if the claims could possibly be true. His mother, for example – a Church of England vicar who would have known if her son was picked up weekly by the gang and returned after being raped – was not interviewed for at least six months. Beech's wife was also not approached.

'Watson had politicised a police inquiry. He showed no regard for the presumption of innocence. He hounded Lord Brittan, a dying man, to his grave'

Checks would have shown that children he claimed had been murdered were still alive. Officers flew to Australia to see if a former classmate of Beech's was alive. He was.

Beech had claimed that Sir Michael Hanley, then the head of MI5, had on one occasion arrived at his school and told him his dog had been kidnapped as a warning. Beech also told police that he had witnessed the gang – he called them The Group – shoot his horse Sam, although he had no idea what happened to the body, or what his mother, who was paying for its stabling, thought.

On Dec 18 2014, Det Supt Kenny McDonald declared at a press briefing: "Nick has been spoken to by experienced officers from the child abuse team and from the murder investigation team and they and I believe what Nick is saying is credible and true."

Just over a month later, Brittan, who had been terminally ill with cancer, died at the age of 75. Although while alive he had not been named in connection with Beech's allegations, he knew full well he was at the centre of the false claims. Brittan, once the leading libel QC in the country, also knew that as soon as he died, he would be outed as a member of the fictitious paedophile gang because the dead cannot sue for defamation.

Mr Watson had already been in pursuit of Brittan over another false claim, this one an allegation of rape dating back to 1967 made by a woman known only as "Jane".

Her claims had been investigated by a team led by Det Chief Insp Paul Settle, head of the Met's paedophile squad, who had concluded that her story was fantasy and closed the case in 2015. Mr Watson intervened, writing to Alison Saunders, the Director of Public Prosecutions, to complain that the case had been closed without Brittan being questioned.

Police caved in and Brittan, while dying, was interviewed under caution. The case was dropped a second time but police never bothered to tell Brittan before his death. Mr Settle, the one police officer who would have exposed Beech's lies, was put on effective gardening leave, his career over. Mr Settle told *The Telegraph*: "The reason I have nothing but contempt for Tom Watson is that he presented himself as an honest broker but he wasn't anything like that."

'The reason I have nothing but contempt for Tom Watson is that he presented himself as an honest broker. But he wasn't anything like that'

Four days after Brittan died, and with his widow and family still grieving, Mr Watson twisted the knife. Brittan was, he said quoting a "survivor" of child abuse, "as close to evil as a human being could get". His spokesman last night declined to say if he was quoting Beech.

Mr Watson didn't stop there. "Former home secretary Leon Brittan stands accused of multiple child rape. Many others knew of these allegations and chose to remain silent. I will not. The police," he concluded in the article published in the *Sunday Mirror*, "must continue their investigations."

The Met duly obliged – despite the absence of any corroboration, including actual murder victims. Officers sought a private hearing at Westminster magistrates' court where they obtained search warrants, insisting Beech's testimony was consistent. It had in fact been anything but.

Shortly after dawn on March 4 2015, Lord Bramall, then 92, was woken at his home in Crondall, Hants. His wife, suffering from dementia, was terrified. She would die a few months later without ever knowing Beech's claims were lies. He was greeted by around 20 officers who told him they had a search warrant. He would remain under suspicion for another 10 months.

At around the same time, 150 miles away at Belvoir Castle, Leics, a similar number of officers were raiding the

Calling the shots Key figures in the investigation

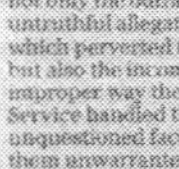

Lord Hogan-Howe Commissioner of the Met throughout Operation Midland, he distanced himself from the day-to-day running. When it began to unravel, he said he was sorry for any distress caused to the accused, but refused to apologise for the investigation. Later issued a personal apology to Lord Bramall, Lady Brittan and Harvey Proctor. Retired in Feb 2017 and was elevated to the Lords that year.

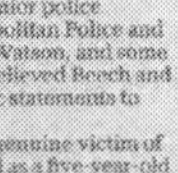

Dep Asst Commissioner Steve Rodhouse In overall charge of Operation Midland. Was present at the press conference in Dec 2014, when the phrase "credible and true" was first used. Was the subject of a voluntary referral to the Independent Police Complaints Commission in Nov 2016. Left the Met in May 2018 to join the National Crime Agency as director general of operations on a salary of £214,723 a year.

Asst Commissioner Patricia Gallan Along with Mr Rodhouse was in overall charge of Operation Midland. Retired on a full pension last year.

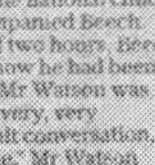

Det Supt Kenny McDonald The initial head of the investigation, described Beech as "credible and true". Replaced as head in Oct 2015, months before it was closed down. Retired in May.

Det Chief Insp Diane Tudway Responsible for signing the application for search warrants. Believed to be off sick.

Det Insp Alison Hepworth Was part of the team that investigated Beech's claims. Now retired.

Det Sgt Eric Sword Retired in 2017 while still under investigation over alleged wrongdoing during the operation.

Det Sgt Danny Chatfield Liaison officer for Carl Beech. Still serving in Scotland Yard.

Det Sgt Matt Flynn Led the search at Mr Proctor's home in 2015. Still serving.

Det Sgt James Townly The first Scotland Yard officer to interview Beech in Oct 2014. Still serving.

Martin Evans

Beech used his 'respectable' background to trick police

By Martin Evans CRIME CORRESPONDENT

AS A school governor, a former children's nurse and an NSPCC volunteer, Carl Beech used his credentials to fool police officers into launching a disastrous investigation.

Born in Wrexham in 1968, Beech was the only son of Robert and Charmian Gass, who were both nurses.

His parents split up shortly after his birth and in 1976 his mother married army officer Raymond Beech and the family moved into military accommodation at Wilton Barracks in Wiltshire.

Major Beech, who already had three children from his first marriage, was an uncompromising disciplinarian who was nevertheless prone to violence when drunk and his relationship with his stepson was difficult from the outset.

The marriage only lasted a few months and Charmian and her son moved to Kingston Upon Thames.

It was while training at the Royal Berkshire Hospital in Reading in 1988 that Beech met fellow nurse Dawn Morgan and the pair married in 1992 when he was 24.

The couple relocated to Gloucester, where Beech was employed at the local hospital. The couple had a son in 2002 and Beech was appointed chair of governors at Beech Green Primary School.

He eventually moved into hospital management at Gloucestershire Hospitals NHS Trust.

All of this was to prove key when helping to convince the police that his allegations of VIP paedophile abuse were "credible and true".

On the surface he was a devoted family man but he spent well beyond his means and the family were often in financial difficulty.

In 2011 his marriage broke down and he moved into a house with his son.

But with his mother having been ordained as a Church of England vicar, she was less able to bankroll his spending and his debts began to mount.

The financial motive may explain why in 2012 Beech went to Wiltshire Police, claiming to have been abused.

He set up an organisation for child abuse survivors and claimed to have worked as a volunteer for the NSPCC.

But throughout this period Beech was accessing appalling videos and images of child abuse.

When his lies began to unravel Beech fled to Sweden, where he planned to run a guesthouse with his mother.

November 8 2016
A report by retired High Court judge, Sir Richard Henriques, finds that Scotland Yard made "numerous errors" in Operation Midland and that a major factor was "the culture that 'victims' must be believed".

July 3 2017
Beech is charged with five counts of possessing indecent images and one count of voyeurism following a raid on his house in Gloucester by Northumbria Police.

February 2018
Beech grows a beard as a disguise and flees to Sweden where he buys a £20,000 property, right, in the Arctic Circle, and plans to open a bed and breakfast.

July 3 2018
Beech is charged with 12 counts of perverting the course of justice and one count of fraud.

October 1 2018
Beech is arrested at Gothenburg train station by Swedish police, who have tracked his mobile phone. He is extradited back to the UK.

January 22 2019
Beech pleads guilty to voyeurism, making indecent images of children, and possessing indecent images. Hereford Crown Court hears how he covertly filmed a teenage boy urinating.

July 22 2019
After a 12-week trial, a jury convicts Beech after just four hours of deliberation of all 12 counts of perverting the course of justice and one fraud charge.

after falling for the vile lies of a fantasist

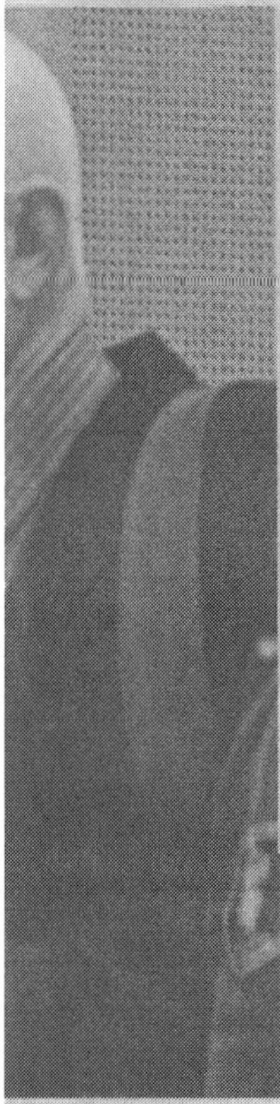

apartment of former Tory MP Harvey Proctor, whom Beech had named as one of Lord Bramall's co-conspirators.

Officers also raided the London and North Yorkshire homes of Lady Brittan, shortly after her husband's funeral and while she was still in deep grief. Van loads of personal possessions were taken and police absurdly asked if soil in her garden in Yorkshire had been recently disturbed.

During the search of Mr Proctor's home, Beech was telephoned by police and told the raid was taking place. Beech called Exaro and the details were published on its website that day.

Lord Bramall was asked by detectives if he could swim, as if this might prove his involvement in a pool sex party. On Aug 24 2015, Mr Proctor was questioned under caution, during which the full extent of the allegations against him were set out.

Beech had told police that in 1980, at a property in central London, he had witnessed Mr Proctor raping a 12-year-old boy before strangling him to death. On another occasion he claimed he had seen a boy beaten to death during a sex game, and told officers he had also seen Heath physically restrain Mr Proctor in order to prevent him cutting the genitals off a young boy with a penknife.

He had also claimed a boy in his school called Scott had been run over and killed by the gang. Police failed to check if any child called Scott had ever turned up dead or reported missing. He hadn't.

Mr Settle, by now *persona non grata*, said the detectives had lost sight of what they were supposed to be doing. "The policy of believing victims meant they were only interested in finding evidence that supported his claims," he said. "Anything that did not fit that narrative was discounted, which is no way to run an investigation."

By January 2016, after almost a year under investigation, Lord Bramall was informed by the police that he would face no further action. He was told there was "insufficient evidence" to proceed, rather than explicitly being cleared of any wrongdoing.

Two months later, Mr Proctor was formally cleared of any wrongdoing, and the Met Commissioner asked retired High Court judge Sir Richard Henriques to carry out a review into Operation Midland.

His findings – while heavily redacted – were scathing. Sir Richard identified 43 separate mistakes by the Met, including misleading a judge when applying for a warrant to search the suspects' homes. It had taken Sir Richard "a matter of days" to realise Beech was a fantasist. Sir Richard said

Carl Beech, far left, at an extradition hearing in Sweden last year. During his trial, he maintained his lies against Field Marshal Lord Bramall, top, and Harvey Proctor, right, while Lady Brittan, centre, had her homes raided. Above, Beech makes merry by the pool in snorkelling gear while on holiday, even though he claimed the abuse had left him with a lifelong fear of water

officers had searched Lady Brittan's home in North Yorkshire "as if they were looking for bodies or body parts".

Following the publication of the damning Henriques report, the Met confirmed it had passed the case to another force and Northumbria Police began investigating Beech for perverting the course of justice. Scrutiny had finally turned to Beech.

As part of that investigation, detectives seized a number of computers and other devices from Beech.

It was during these searches that they discovered more than 350 indecent images of children, including 36 of the most serious category A. One device also contained a video of a young boy urinating.

In July 2017, Beech was charged with five counts of possessing indecent images and one count of voyeurism and summoned to appear before Worcester Crown Court.

But because he had claimed to have suffered sex abuse himself, he retained his right to anonymity.

In July last year, just weeks before his trial was about to get going, the Crown Prosecution Service, which had been examining a file of evidence from Northumbria Police, announced he was also to be charged with 12 counts of perverting the course of justice.

He was also charged with one count of fraud in relation to the £22,000 he had received from the Criminal Injuries Compensation Authority for the abuse that had never taken place.

Northumbria Police had also discovered that Beech had used an encrypted email address to create a fake profile for a witness called "Fred" in an attempt to corroborate his claims.

This was something their colleagues in the Met had clearly failed to spot.

Beech's trial for possessing indecent images had been due to begin on July 30 last year, but he was nowhere to be seen. He had gone on the run. A warrant was issued for his arrest and an international manhunt began.

Beech had fled to Sweden, planning a new life in a small village in the Arctic Circle, using the false name Stephen Anderson. He bought a house in Overkalix with a plan to open a bed and breakfast business.

He skipped town, travelling through Sweden under a variety of aliases, staying at hostels or sleeping on trains.

Acting on a European Arrest Warrant, Swedish police tracked Beech through his mobile phone to Gothenburg station, where he was finally apprehended on Oct 1 2018.

On Jan 21, 18 months after he was first charged, Beech finally appeared at Hereford Crown Court, charged with four counts of making indecent images, one of possessing indecent images and one of voyeurism.

> *The prosecution case described Beech as a sophisticated paedophile for whom lying was as natural as having a morning cup of tea*

Hidden behind a fake calculator app on his computer were pictures of young boys, some of them undressed, one of whom was lying face down on a bed, blindfolded and handcuffed.

A camera belonging to Beech contained photographs of young boys playing football with their shirts off, which he had taken surreptitiously from a window of his Gloucester home. There was also evidence that he had been watching appalling child abuse videos online, including ones featuring the rape of babies.

Beech pleaded guilty and was remanded in custody and ordered to immediately sign the sex offenders' register. The man who had spread so many lies about being a victim of abuse had finally admitted to being a paedophile himself.

Beech's trial for perverting the course of justice and fraud began at Newcastle Crown Court on May 7, with him pleading not guilty to all charges.

With astonishing arrogance and cruelty he kept up his lies, meaning the true victims in the case – those he had falsely accused, including Mr Proctor and another military figure, 96-year-old Gen Sir Hugh Beach – were forced to give evidence and undergo painful cross-examination.

When Beech entered the witness box, during three days of cross-examination, prosecutor Tony Badenoch QC systematically exposed every lie he had told the police.

The jury was told that the day Beech's £22,000 criminal injuries compensation claim was approved, he put down a £10,000 deposit for a white Ford Mustang convertible.

It was also revealed that Beech had been penning a so-called "misery memoir", which he no doubt hoped would make him rich. Entitled "Too Many Secrets: Surviving a Child Sex Ring", it contained a series of wild allegations of sexual abuse relating to himself and his "best friend", John.

At one point Beech claimed to have been beaten so badly that he had been hospitalised. However, there were no medical records to support this.

Among the more outlandish claims Beech made during his evidence were that he had been subjected to a series of cruel punishments by his abusers, which included being bitten by a snake, stung by angry wasps and electrocuted. He drew a body map that purported to accurately chart the many scars and wounds that he bore as a result of his years abuse.

The only problem was that when a doctor examined him before the trial, there were no marks on his body.

He also told the jury that he had been left with a lifelong fear of water after having his head shoved under it as he was raped over the bath as a boy.

But the prosecution exposed the lie with holiday snaps that showed Beech swimming and even snorkelling.

He told police he was removed from school every Friday by his abusers, but his records showed him to have had an excellent attendance.

Beech handed police a penknife that he claimed he had kept from the time when Mr Proctor had threatened to cut off his genitals. But Beech's ex-wife told the jury that the penknife had actually belonged to his grandmother.

They were all claims that could easily have been checked by the Met.

Summing up the prosecution case, Mr Badenoch described Beech as a "sophisticated paedophile" for whom lying was as natural as having a morning cup of tea.

The jury was also told that his story bore many similarities to child abuse memoirs written by the author Timmy Fielding.

Mr Badenoch suggested that there may have been a financial motive behind Beech's lies, but the real reason he decided to destroy the lives and reputations of so many innocent men may never be fully known. But there's no question Beech enjoyed the attention afforded him by Tom Watson, a questionable news website and some overeager Scotland Yard detectives who had forgotten to bother with the truth.

Who are the victims? The high-profile men accused of belonging to The Group and abusing young boys

Sir Edward Heath
Served as prime minister from 1970 to 1974. Died in 2005, aged 89. Beech claimed he first met Heath when he was taken to the Carlton Club in London in the late Seventies. He told police the former prime minister had abused him aboard his yacht, Morning Cloud. He also claimed Mr Heath had intervened to prevent Harvey Proctor castrating him with a penknife.

Lord Brittan
Home Secretary from 1983 until 1985. Died 2015 aged 75 while still under suspicion. Beech claimed to have met him for the first time at the Carlton Club and said he had repeatedly subjected him to abuse. Beech lied to police, telling officers the former home secretary had raped him over a bath and had also been present when boys were murdered. Scotland Yard detectives raided Lady Brittan's home after her husband had died. They later paid her £100,000 in compensation.

Michael Hanley
Former director general of MI5. Died in 2001 aged 82. Beech told police Mr Hanley had been one of the cruellest of the abusers and would mete out punishment when he broke the rules. He claimed Mr Hanley had once kidnapped his dog, had set wasps on him and had thrown him in a cupboard with a snake.

Harvey Proctor
Tory MP between 1979 and 1987. Beech told police Mr Proctor had been the most sadistic of the group, claiming he liked to inflict pain while he was carrying out the abuse. He lied to police, claiming to have seen Mr Proctor murder a boy during a sex game. Mr Proctor's home was raided by police and as a result he lost the property and his job. He is currently suing Scotland Yard.

Lord Bramall
Former head of the Army and D-Day veteran. Beech claimed Lord Bramall had first abused him at Wilton Barracks where his stepfather was a major. He also accused the retired general of being present at pool parties where children were abused. Lord Bramall's home was raided by police at a time when his wife was suffering from dementia. She died while her husband was still under suspicion. He was later paid £100,000 in compensation.

General Sir Hugh Beach
Former deputy commander in chief of UK land forces. Beech claimed Sir Hugh had been one of the senior army figures who had abused him at various military establishments around the UK. Now 96, he gave evidence during the trial via video link in which he described the allegations as "beyond grotesque".

Lord Janner
Former Labour MP and Peer. Died in 2015 aged 87. Beech claimed he had first met Janner at the Carlton Club, an allegation that caused the police to become suspicious because as a Labour politician he would not have been welcome at the Conservative Party gentleman's club.

Maurice Oldfield
Former head of MI6, who died in 1981, aged 63. According to Beech, Mr Oldfield was part of the "inner circle of abusers". He told police Mr Oldfield tortured him with spiders, wasps, snakes and darts. Mr Oldfield, who served in the intelligence corps during the Second World War, later became the head of MI6 and was reputedly one of the models for John le Carré's fictional character, George Smiley.

Field Marshal Roland Gibbs
Former Chief of the General Staff. Died in 2004 aged 83. Beech claimed Gibbs had been among the senior military officials who had abused him at bases around the country.

Major Raymond Beech
Beech's stepfather. Died in Brighton in 1995. His marriage to Beech's mother, Charmian, lasted less than a year, but during that time, Beech said he was regularly abused. Beech also accused his stepfather of introducing him to members of The Group, including his military superiors. Beech hired a private detective to make sure his stepfather was dead before going to the police with his allegations.

Letters to the E

THE DAILY TELEGRAPH

ESTABLISHED 1855

A shameful episode for the police

The conviction of Carl Beech for fabricating allegations of an Establishment paedophile ring marks the end of a saga of lies, staggering police incompetence and shocking political gullibility. It has shredded the reputations of innocent people, several of whom have died and cannot defend themselves.

Beech, who was given the pseudonym "Nick" while his claims were investigated, was found guilty of 12 counts of perverting the course of justice and one of fraud over a £22,000 criminal compensation payout. However, he is not really a fraudster but a fantasist, and should have been recognised as such from the moment he began touting his story around to credulous listeners.

He alleged that he was the victim of a Westminster-based paedophile network that included a former prime minister, an ex-home secretary and various heads of the intelligence services and the military. Not only had they abused children, he claimed, but they had taken part in murder, and dark forces had covered it all up.

The context for what then transpired was the failure of the police properly to investigate the late Jimmy Savile, a prolific sex offender. In Oct 2012, Tom Watson, now Labour deputy leader, told MPs that he knew of the existence of "clear intelligence suggesting a powerful paedophile network linked to parliament and No 10". This referred to another case but alerted Beech to a potentially friendly ear after failing to interest Wiltshire Police in his story.

He was urged by Mr Watson to go back to the police who were, by now, committed to believing any sex abuse complaint, however outlandish. Basic checks that would have disproved Beech's lurid claims were not carried out. A homicide inquiry was set up solely on the basis of his unsubstantiated allegations and, against this backdrop, Theresa May as home secretary instigated a public inquiry into historic sex abuse. One senior police officer even called this farrago of obviously fanciful tales "credible and true". They were neither.

This was a shameful episode for the police, though they still insist they did everything right; and Mr Watson must share culpability. Many observing him on this matter formed a clear impression of a scandal at the heart of the Tory establishment, and Mr Watson did little to disabuse them as the lives of innocent people were dragged in and destroyed. He should apologise today in the Commons.

Ineptitude over Iran

To describe the Government's handling of the events that resulted in Iran's illegal seizure of a British oil tanker as totally inept would be an understatement. The warning signs that Tehran was likely to attempt an act of piracy against British shipping in the Gulf had been evident ever since a detachment of Royal Marines earlier this month intercepted an Iranian tanker suspected of shipping oil to Syria. Not only did Iran respond by threatening to seize a British ship, but the frigate HMS Montrose had already been obliged to intervene when Iran's Revolutionary Guard Corps harassed the BP-owned tanker British Heritage.

And yet ministers failed to take adequate measures to protect British shipping. Theresa May has even been accused of turning down an offer from Donald Trump of US protection for British ships in the Gulf which, given the chronic shortage of available Navy vessels to do the task, might well have prevented the British-flagged tanker Stena Impero from falling into Iranian hands

We accept letters by post, fax and email only. Please include name, address, work and home telephone numbers.

111 Buckingham Palace Road, London SW1W 0DT

FAX
020 7931 2878

EMAIL
dtletters@telegraph.co.uk

FOLLOW
Telegraph Letters on Twitter @LettersDesk

The Iran debacle has exposed our politicians' lack of military sense

SIR – Acting in haste on behalf of the EU to seize a foreign tanker was bound to have consequences, especially as the Royal Navy has so few usable ships. Refusing help from the United States to escort our tankers through the Strait of Hormuz (report, July 22) compounded the folly.

As a staff college instructor, I do not recall any military student suggesting such a foolish course of action to deal with a similar challenge. Are our ministers properly trained for their critical roles?

Group Captain DRE Evans (retd)
Cardiff

SIR – Iran's hijacking of British ships highlights the folly of investing a large part of the Navy's budget in two huge, cumbersome, vulnerable aircraft carriers. A fleet of frigates and small boats would be far more effective.

Brian Sanders
Brighton, East Sussex

SIR – To my knowledge, Jeremy Hunt wasn't part of the Cabinet that bought two white-elephant aircraft carriers. It was the legacy of Gordon Brown's Labour government. I live close to Rosyth, where they were assembled.

Ian Kelman
Dunfermline, Fife

SIR – Sir Alan Duncan is leaving the Foreign Office because of his dislike of Boris Johnson, but it would have been more to his credit at this time of crisis if he had remained in his post to assist Mr Hunt in negotiations with Iran.

A lot of MPs are motivated more by their own pride than that of their country.

Colin Eldred
Eastbourne, East Sussex

SIR – If HMS Montrose had been close to the tanker abducted by Iranian forces (Letters, July 22), what action could it have taken?

Would it have shot down the helicopter and fired on the gunboats? Or could it have sent out boarding parties? Any action like this would have resulted in considerable loss of life, and the event would have beco a major international incident.

David Vaudrey
Doynton, Gloucestershire

SIR – Were our tankers to carry hea armed specialists to repel gunboats suggested in yesterday's letters, we would risk starting a new Gulf war.

Instead, they should be fitted wit water jet system of the kind used to repel Somali pirates. Pointing the je upwards as well as outwards, creati mists over the decks, would also de helicopters from lowering gunmen

Nick Rose
Chichester, West Sussex

SIR – When the media reports majo incidents – whether criminal, medi educational or otherwise – a servin professional briefs the public.

For defence issues, only politicia and retired admirals seem to addre the public. Have the Armed Forces been struck dumb?

Christopher Samuel
Haslemere, Surrey

Electric scooters

SIR – Electric scooter enthusiasts (Letters, July 22) would do well to look at cities already blighted. In Stockholm, you find dumped hire-scooters littering busy footways.

More dangerously, their riders navigate among both pedestrians and moving vehicles, day and night. For now, Londoners will be safer and healthier sticking to Shanks's pony.

Vivian Bush
Beverley, East Yorkshire

SIR – Having just returned from San Diego, California, and spent time in Austin, Texas, I would warn those rushing to legalise electric scooters in London: they are a menace to all – from pedestrians to motorists, and of course to the riders themselves.

They litter the streets – the flotsam and jetsam of the Eco Age – and are a nuisance to everyone save the Silicon Valley masters who profit from their existence.

The solution to London's travel woes they are not.

Martin Killick
Fort Worth, Texas, United States

High-street homes

SIR – Dorothy Alexander (Letters, July 20) asks whether redevelopment could permit commercial and residential properties to exist side by side to prevent town centres being deserted after shops close.

When shops are converted to residential use, they should incorporate a garage with an easily replaced frontage, in order to accommodate any subsequent upturn in the demand for retail premises. This would relieve housing needs, solve parking problems, and allow for rapid reconversion if required.

Bruce Denness
Whitwell, Isle of Wight

Vibrant verges

SIR – Your report (July 20) on the planting of verges using non-native seeds and its potential harm to invertebrates was a little concerning.

I ran into very slow-moving traffic on the anti-clockwise M25 recently when returning from holiday. My frustration at the delay turned to delight when I looked at the roadside and saw miles of wildflowers with oxeye daisy, scabious and teasel being visited by many butterflies.

I assumed this attractive display occurred spontaneously, but would be interested if anyone knew otherwise.

Janet Newis
Sidcup, Kent

Profligate genius: Brunel beside the launching chains of the SS Great Eastern, 1857

What Brunel would have liked about HS2

SIR – Isambard Kingdom Brunel may have been a great engineer, but he also had a penchant for spending other people's money.

The same can be said of those in charge of HS2. The Stephensons had a much more down-to-earth approach than Brunel, and their work has stood the test of time.

Terry Morrell
Willerby, East Yorkshire

SIR – As the estimate of the cost of HS2 drifts from £60 billion to £90 billion, it's worth trying to understand what these numbers actually mean.

This increase takes the amount to be paid by every British taxpayer (of whom there are roughly 30 million) from £2,000 to £3,000. The average salary in Britain is roughly £28,(– on which the tax payable is, as i happens, around £3,000. So wha proposed is that every taxpayer i Britain contributes a year of thei work to build HS2.

These calculations are fairly rough and ready, but I'd suggest they are not 50 per cent out, as th (already revised) HS2 estimate h proved to be. Let's also rememb that this money is to be spent on project which the Government's own economic affairs committe described as relying on "evidenc that is out of date and unconvincing", adding: "The analysis presented to justify the project is seriously deficient."

John Stewart
Terrick, Buckinghamshire

The rise of Lyme disease must not be ignorec

SIR – Your report (July 18) on Lyme disease and its possible origins needs amplification.

Down the years, I have walked in the Highlands, the Pennines, the North York Moors, the Peak District, France, Belgium, Florida, Vermont and California, and was never bitten by a tick. However, a year ago, in my garden, two miles from Stansted Airport, I was bitten by a tick and acquired the disease. I am still suffering the effects: they are nast When I asked the doctor if there w any more cases in the village, pati confidentiality was cited.

I suggest that Lyme disease is m widely distributed than acknowle by the medical profession. BBC Scotland's recent *Disclosure* programme about it should be see every doctor in Britain.

Alan Davidson
Elsenham, Essex

Compromising now would be a ca

THE DAILY TELEGRAPH 23 July 2019

After judge's bombshell intervention, victims of VIP abuse fantasist demand...

NOW TURN FULL FORCE OF LAW ON 'NICK' POLICE

By **Stephen Wright, Jack Doyle** and **Glen Keogh**

VICTIMS of VIP child abuse fantasist 'Nick' last night called for a fresh criminal probe into Scotland Yard's bungled inquiry.

Their demand follows a sensational intervention from a retired High Court judge who said police may have broken the law with £2.5million Operation Midland.

Writing in yesterday's Daily Mail, Sir Richard Henriques suggested detectives had used false evidence to obtain warrants to raid the homes of high-profile figures.

Harvey Proctor, who was accused by Nick, called for another force to investigate the Met's actions.

The former Tory MP was backed yesterday by a string of politicians and Lord Macdonald, a former director of public prosecutions.

He called for a full investigation into how warrants were obtained against 'highly distinguished and completely

Turn to Page 2

Daily Mail COMMENT

There was no secrecy for the true victims of 'Nick's' vile lies. Now there should be none for the officers who trashed their good names in such cavalier fashion.

DAILY MAIL 31 July 2019

Weather

Go to: dailymail.co.uk/weather for UK and world 5 day forecast

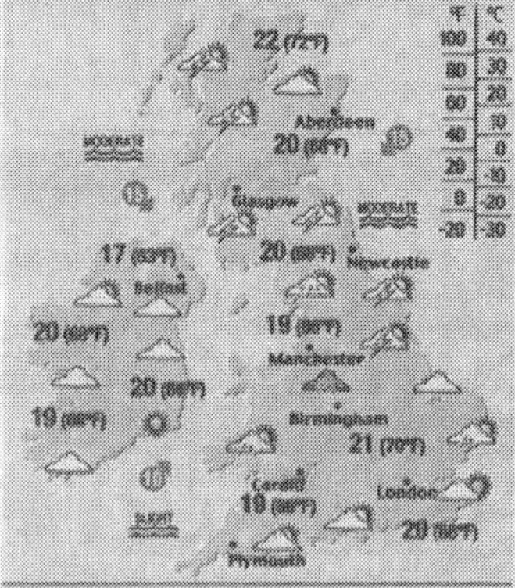

Summary: Rain for many

UK TODAY: It is forecast to be cloudy with showers for central, northern and eastern areas, some thundery later. Mostly dry with variable cloud in the south and west. Moderate northwesterly winds. Max 23c.

Today's weather

	9am	12noon	3pm	6pm	9pm
London	18c	21c	23c	22c	20c
Plymouth	17c	18c	18c	18c	16c
Cardiff	16c	18c	18c	18c	16c
B'ham	17c	18c	19c	19c	17c
M'chester	17c	18c	18c	18c	17c
Newcastle	16c	18c	18c	18c	16c
Glasgow	18c	20c	20c	20c	18c
Aberdeen	17c	19c	19c	18c	16c
Belfast	15c	16c	17c	18c	18c

5 day forecast

	Thu	Fri	Sat	Sun	Mon
London	24c	25c	26c	25c	24c
Plymouth	21c	22c	21c	20c	19c
Cardiff	23c	25c	24c	22c	22c
B'ham	22c	23c	23c	23c	22c
M'chester	21c	23c	23c	22c	22c
Newcastle	20c	19c	20c	20c	21c
Glasgow	20c	21c	21c	20c	20c
Aberdeen	19c	19c	19c	18c	18c
Belfast	20c	21c	20c	21c	20c

Yesterday

24 hours to 7pm	Sun (hrs)	Rain (ins)	Temp (min)	Temp (max)
Aberdeen	10.4	0.00	13	24
Aberporth	0.1	0.24	15	18
Belfast	2.5	0.01	14	20
Birmingham	4.3	0.64	14	20
Bournemouth	2.5	0.33	16	22
Bristol	3.2	0.42	16	20
Cardiff	2.2	0.35	16	20
Durham	3.7	0.03	11	21
Edinburgh	4.3	0.02	11	21
Glasgow	3.1	0.02	12	22
Hull	7.3	0.01	13	24
Ipswich	7.8	0.02	17	22
Leeds	5.4	0.31	14	23
Lincoln	7.1	0.02	15	24
London	2.4	0.15	17	20
Manchester	5.5	0.09	14	23
Southampton	3.8	0.11	17	21
St Andrews	5.9	0.00	12	21
Stornoway	3.1	0.02	15	18

Information supplied by Meteogroup

Moon and Sun

MOON rises: 4.09am, sets: 8.42pm
Sun rises London: 5.22am, sets: 8.30pm
Manchester rises: 5.22am, sets: 9.07pm
HIGH TIDE London Bridge: 2.11pm
Liverpool: 11.37pm

Extremes (24 hrs to 7pm y'day)

Warmest: East Park, Hull, 27c (81F). Coldest: Kielder Castle, Northumberland, 7c (45F). Wettest: St. Mary's, Isles of Scilly, 1.23ins. Sunniest: Aberdeen, Aberdeenshire, 10.4hrs.

Europe forecast

	today	c	f	tomorrow	c	f
Amsterdam	thunder	21	70	rain	21	70
Brussels	fair	22	72	fair	23	73
Frankfurt	sun	26	79	fair	26	79
Geneva	fair	25	77	sun	26	79
Lisbon	sun	28	82	sun	26	79
Madrid	sun	35	95	sun	35	95
Paris	fair	24	75	sun	26	79
Rome	sun	30	86	sun	29	84

Around the world yesterday

Noon local time

	weather	c	f		weather	c	f		weather	c	f
Algiers	Fair	30	86	Florence	Sunny	29	84	New Delhi	Cloudy	32	90
Amsterdam	Sunny	27	81	Geneva	Sunny	25	77	New York	Fair	33	91
Athens	Sunny	32	90	Gibraltar	Sunny	28	82	Nice	Fair	26	79
Auckland	Fair	16	61	Guernsey	Showers	18	64	Oslo	Rain	12	54
Bahrain	Sunny	46	115	Helsinki	Fair	16	61	Palma	Sunny	30	86
Barcelona	Fair	30	86	Hong Kong	Fair	32	90	Paris	Cloudy	23	73
Basra	Sunny	47	117	Innsbruck	Fair	26	79	Perth	Sunny	20	68
Beijing	Cloudy	30	86	Istanbul	Fair	28	82	Prague	Cloudy	26	79
Beirut	Sunny	30	86	Jersey	Fair	18	64	Rhodes	Sunny	30	86
Belfast	Cloudy	18	64	Larnaca	Sunny	32	90	Riga	Rain	19	66
Belgrade	Fair	27	81	Las Palmas	Cloudy	24	75	Rome	Sunny	29	84
Berlin	Showers	22	72	Lisbon	Sunny	24	75	Singapore	Fair	30	86
Biarritz	Cloudy	20	68	London	Showers	18	64	Stockholm	Fair	17	63
Brisbane	Sunny	22	72	Los Angeles	Cloudy	22	72	Strasbourg	Sunny	29	84
Brussels	Sunny	24	75	Luxor	Sunny	39	102	Sydney	Cloudy	14	57
Bucharest	Fair	27	81	Madrid	Sunny	27	81	Tangier	Sunny	25	77
Budapest	Fair	29	84	Malaga	Sunny	25	77	Tel Aviv	Sunny	31	88
C'hagen	Fair	22	72	Malta	Sunny	31	88	Tenerife	Sunny	26	79
Cairo	Sunny	35	95	Melbourne	Cloudy	11	52	Tokyo	Sunny	33	91
Cape Town	Showers	16	61	Mexico City	Fair	21	70	Toronto	Cloudy	31	88
Casablanca	Fair	24	75	Miami	Cloudy	32	90	Tunis	Sunny	32	90
Corfu	Sunny	30	86	Milan	Sunny	30	86	Vancouver	Fair	21	70
Dubai	Sunny	43	109	Montreal	Fair	29	84	Venice	Sunny	28	82
Dublin	Showers	18	64	Moscow	Cloudy	14	57	Vienna	Sunny	28	82
Dubrovnik	Sunny	26	79	Mumbai	Rain	28	82	Warsaw	Fair	30	86
Faro	Sunny	30	86	Nairobi	Cloudy	19	66	Wellington	Showers	12	54

KUROSU

EVERY day in the Mail you can play Kurosu, the most addictive brainteaser since Sudoku. There are only two rules:
1: Fill in each space with either a nought or a cross so there are no more than two consecutive noughts or crosses in any row or column. Important note: diagonals don't count.
2: Each row and column must contain three noughts and three crosses.

Today's difficulty rating ★★☆

X		O			X
	O				
O			X	O	
		X			
	X	O	O		X
O					O

PLAY more Kurosu and 28 addictive puzzles like them every day on your smartphone or tablet with Mail Plus, your Mail newspaper on your screen. Get a FREE trial today at *dailymailplus.co.uk*
Solution on Puzzles & Prizes back page.

Continued from Page One

innocent' individuals. The Independent Office for Police Conduct (IOPC) was also under intense pressure last night for refusing to reopen its inquiry into five Scotland Yard officers involved in the case. It insisted it had already investigated them and found 'no suspicion of criminality'.

New Home Secretary Priti Patel will haul in the head of the watchdog to demand answers about the case. Miss Patel will challenge Michael Lockwood, its £175,000-a-year director general 'as soon as possible', a source close to the Home Secretary said.

The scandal surrounding Scotland Yard's investigation into Nick, real name Carl Beech, was dramatically reignited by Sir Richard's broadside yesterday.

He said detectives did not have the right to search the properties of former armed forces chief Lord Bramall, the widow of ex-home secretary Leon Brittan and Mr Proctor. This, he said, was because their description of Beech as a 'consistent' witness was false, effectively fooling a judge into granting the warrants.

Sir Richard, the author of a scathing review of Operation Midland for Scotland Yard in 2016, also alleged 'the course of justice was perverted with shocking consequences' during the investigation.

He said he found it astonishing no officer had been brought to book over the fiasco and that a 'criminal investigation should surely follow'.

Beech was jailed for 18 years last week over his bogus claims of child rape and murder. With the Home Office under huge pressure to order a new probe:

- Lord Bramall, Mr Proctor and the family of late Labour peer Greville Janner – also falsely accused – led furious calls for Scotland Yard to release the full, unredacted Henriques report;
- But the Met again refused to release to do so, citing 'the confidentiality of complainants, witnesses and those accused';
- Former Met commissioner Lord Hogan-Howe, whose officers carried out raids on VIPs during Operation Midland, refused to answer questions from a Daily Mail reporter.

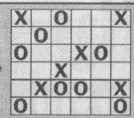

Jailed: Carl Beech is serving 18 years

Report: Sir Richard Henriques

Mr Proctor said: 'I take no satisfaction in having my view [confirmed] that the Metropolitan Police force were wrong in the way that they investigated Nick.'

'An attempt to pervert justice'

Lord Macdonald QC told BBC Radio 4's World at One that if 'the courts were misled then criminal investigations should follow'.

He added: 'The police didn't set out to investigate Carl Beech's allegations, they set out to prove them. A cursory investigation of this man's allegations at an earlier stage would have exposed him as a fantasist, as a liar, as someone who was engaged in an attempt to pervert justice.'

Scotland Yard said the IOPC had looked into allegations about how the search warrants were handled and it was found that the three officers involved had no case to answer.

This came after it had referred potential conduct matters relating to five officers which had been identified in Sir Richard's report.

A spokesman said: 'None of the five officers involved in the original referral or the three officers subject to investigation were found to have cases to answer in relation to any of the allegations.'

All those involved in the allegations which were referred to the IOPC have either retired or moved to other jobs and are no longer serving Met Police officers. A Home Office spokesman said: 'The Home Secretary looks forward to meeting with a number of policing partners, including Michael Lockwood of the IOPC. It is right that allegations relating to the seeking of warrants as part of Operation Midland were referred to the IOPC – the public need to have confidence that the police are exercising their powers in a correct and proportionate way.'

But Lincoln Seligman, godson of former PM Edward Heath who was also wrongly accused, said: 'For so many senior and junior police to choose to believe Beech without corroboration or other evidence is astonishing.

'It suggests a lack of education or training in both analysing evidence and in the importance of the presumption of innocence. Or a wilful and reckless disregard for both.

'Given that the IOPC have already cleared every officer involved something stronger, genuinely independent and less myopic is needed.'

Comment – Page 18

Give us the full report
SEE PAGES 6-9

North Korea launches 'multiple' missiles

Mail Foreign Service

NORTH Korea defied an international embargo yesterday by launching a series of unidentified missiles.

The exercise is thought to be another attempt by Pyongyang to pressure Washington into restarting nuclear negotiations.

North Korea is banned by the UN Security Council from engaging in any sort of ballistic missile launches and is under 11 rounds of sanctions. But it is unlikely to face further action unless the missiles travel a significant distance.

The 'multiple' launches were fired from the Hodo peninsula on North Korea's east coast, according to reports in South Korea. Military chiefs in Seoul said they were monitoring the situation in case of additional launches and maintaining a readiness posture.

The launches come a week after Kim Jong-un's communist dictatorship test-fired two short-range ballistic missiles into the sea. Observers suggested this was a warning shot to remind the White House what may happen if talks with the US are abandoned. The weapons flew between 270 and 430 miles before landing off the east coast.

Takeshi Iwaya, Japan's defence minister, said this was probably a violation of Security Council resolutions because of the distance the missiles travelled.

Kim claimed that the missiles were launched under his personal supervision. He said that they were a 'solemn warning' in response to military drills planned by the South and the US forces based there.

'North Korea appears to be thinking its diplomacy with the US isn't proceeding in a way that they want.

So they've fired missiles to get the table to turn in their favour,' said Kim Dae-young, from the Korea Research Institute for National Strategy.

Clarifications & corrections

All our journalists observe the Editors' Code of Practice and the Mail is a member of the Independent Press Standards Organisation (IPSO). We aim to correct any errors as promptly as possible.

- *To report an inaccuracy, please email corrections@dailymail.co.uk.*

ipso Regulated

To make a formal complaint go to www.dailymail.co.uk/readerseditor. You can also write to Readers' Editor, Daily Mail, 2 Derry Street, London W8 5TT or contact IPSO directly at ipso.co.uk

IF YOU CAN'T GET YOUR DAILY MAIL ...
If the Mail was sold out at your retail outlet please let us know by emailing **availability@dailymail.co.uk** and we will endeavour to ensure it doesn't happen again.

GIVE US THE

Bramall leads calls for Met to publish judge's inquiry into VIP abuse probe

By **Glen Keogh** and **Stephen Wright**

LORD Bramall last night led furious calls for Scotland Yard to release an unredacted version of Sir Richard Henriques' report into its shambolic 'Nick' investigation.

The former head of the Armed Forces said it was imperative the document was published immediately and 'in its entirety' to ensure there could be no repeat of the Operation Midland scandal.

Sir Richard's investigation into the Yard's handling of Nick – carried out three years ago – identified 43 failings as police probed his bogus allegations of murder and child rape against Establishment figures.

But when the retired high court judge's report was published more than 80 per cent of its 491 pages were redacted.

At the time, Metropolitan Police commissioner Sir Bernard Hogan-Howe insisted this was necessary for 'data protection' and because the report contained 'sensitive information'.

But in a devastating intervention in yesterday's Daily Mail, Sir Richard spoke out to renew his criticism of the force and to call for a criminal investigation into how Met officers had obtained search warrants in the case.

That led to fresh demands yesterday for Scotland Yard to finally release the judge's original report in full. Lord Bramall, Harvey Proctor

'The public has a right to know the truth'

and the family of late Labour peer Greville Janner all demanded its publication.

Despite this, Scotland Yard again insisted it was not yet ready to meet the requests, citing 'the confidentiality of complainants, witnesses and those accused'. The force said it was still reviewing whether more of the report could be published.

Nick – whose real name is Carl Beech – has been jailed for 18 years for perverting the course of justice and fraud.

In a statement yesterday, 95-year-old Lord Bramall, the former field marshal who was falsely accused by Beech and had his home raided, said: 'It was much to Sir Bernard Hogan-Howe's credit that he commissioned the independent review into investigations of historical sexual abuse by the Metropolitan Police Service led by Sir Richard Henriques following the spectacular collapse of Operation Midland. However the decision to only release a redacted version of the report undermined its impact.

'Following the comments made by Sir Richard Henriques in the Daily Mail, the report in its entirety should be released to the public immediately.'

Daniel Janner QC, son of falsely accused Labour peer Lord Greville Janner, said: 'The report must be published in full. The police are still protecting their own from the risk of being prosecuted for perverting the course of justice. The public has a right to know the truth if trust in the police is to be restored.'

The solicitor of former MP Mr Proctor, who had his home raided during Operation Midland, said: 'It is clear that justice requires the full report to be available to the victims of Beech's crimes, and for public scrutiny.'

In an explosive intervention in the Mail yesterday, Sir Richard, who acted for the prosecution in the trials of James Bulger's killers and Harold Shipman, alleged that the 'course of justice was perverted with shocking consequences' in the Nick case. He said officers misled a district judge in obtaining search warrants to raid the homes of Mr Proctor, Lord Bramall and Leon Brittan by insisting Beech had been a 'consistent' witness.

Sir Richard's report was ordered in February 2016, with a redacted version published nine months later. He said it took him 'a matter of days' to realise Beech was a fantasist and he criticised officers who took part in the raids on the homes of elderly men 'as if they were looking for body parts'.

Sir Richard also examined Wiltshire Police's Operation Conifer investigation into sex abuse allegations against former prime minister Edward Heath.

He concluded that the 'vast majority' of 400 complaints made as part of a national inquiry into historic child abuse claims were without merit.

In a statement, the Met said: 'The MPS is reviewing Sir Richard's report to ascertain whether more of it could be published. However, the MPS has tostrike a balance between its commitment to transparency and its legal and moral duties to protect the confidentiality of complainants, witnesses and those accused.

'The report contains sensitive personal information and explicit descriptions of sexual offences that it would neither be right nor lawful to publish. Nor would it be appropriate to publish or repeat information from investigations where the allegations were dropped without charge or defendants acquitted.'

Moment police heavy mob moved in on Brittan's home

EXCLUSIVE PICTURE

THIS is the astonishing scene on the drive of Leon Brittan's home when a Scotland Yard search team turned up mob-handed six weeks after he died.

Officers brought two minibuses, two vans and at least two cars to the former home secretary's weekend retreat. A district judge had granted them a search warrant after being supplied with false information.

Over two days the detectives turned the property upside down looking for evidence that the peer had been part of a murderous VIP paedophile gang.

According to sources, they emptied the attic and took away private letters, copies of speeches and treasured

By **Stephen Wright**
Associate News Editor

pictures. They removed footwear for 'DNA testing'.

The exclusive picture obtained by the Daily Mail was taken from a first-floor window during the raid that also saw officers carry out a finger-tip search of the garden in the hunt for 'disturbed earth'.

The search warrant was granted on the uncorroborated word of Carl Beech, a paedophile and serial liar. Police told the judge he was a consistent and credible witness. At the same time as the North Yorkshire raid in early March 2015, officers on Operation Midland raided Lord Brittan's home in central London, which he shared with his wife of 34 years, Lady Brittan. The peer had died there of cancer aged 75 on January 21.

Last week, in a victim impact statement read to court after Beech was imprisoned for 18 years for his lies and other offences, Lady Brittan laid bare her suffering.

She said: 'The experience of having my house in London searched by a dozen police officers for 12 hours was traumatizing. The impact of these allegations and their consequences on my wider family were significant.'

FULL REPORT

I was ruined on a lie. We must have an inquiry

Anger: Harvey Proctor yesterday

by Harvey Proctor

WHEN I drew back my bedroom curtains at 8am on that fateful day in March 2015, there was a police van sitting right outside.

It wasn't unusual. I worked as a private secretary on the Duke of Rutland's estate in Leicestershire, and liaised regularly with the local police over the fire and burglar alarms at Belvoir Castle.

But then the doorbell rang. When I opened the door, a Detective Sergeant from the Metropolitan Police Murder Squad stepped inside with a search warrant, followed by 18 stern-looking police officers in their forensic blue uniforms. And so began a Kafkaesque nightmare of deceit and injustice that would see me lose my home, my job and my reputation – thanks to a treacherous miscarriage of justice.

I am now 72 and it is more than four years since my descent into hell began. The ordeal still casts its shadow over me: I have been diagnosed with post-traumatic stress disorder and have lost countless friends.

But former High Court Judge Sir Richard Henriques's blistering denunciation in the Mail yesterday of the police's witch-hunt against me and others has given me some cause for comfort. It confirmed every misgiving I'd had about the inquiry. I had known it was morally dubious. And now, thanks to Sir Richard's intervention, it amounted to a perversion of justice.

There can only be one result: A formal inquiry must be held. For too long, the gross and defamatory lies of Carl Beech (the paedophile fraudster known as Nick) – peddled by the now defunct website Exaro and Labour's deputy leader Tom Watson – were given unchallenged currency and credence.

Back in 2014, when I first read about Nick's horrific claims of a VIP paedophile ring of politicians and leading British figures, I was appalled like every one else. But I never imagined that I would one day find myself at the heart of the ensuing investigation.

That spring day, as I watched officers turn my home inside out, I thought their actions might be linked to the charges of gross indecency that had been brought against me in 1987, for having consensual sexual relations with someone under the age of 21, which was then illegal. I pleaded guilty to the charges and did not seek re-election as a Member of Parliament.

But in those interminable 15 hours during which boxes full of my possessions were removed from my home, I did not learn anything about what I was supposed to have done. All I was told was that I was connected to the gruesome crimes that Nick had revealed to the Met. But I had no idea how.

I had no idea where or how I was supposed to fit into Nick's narrative. When I asked if the officers would keep my name out of the Press until I knew what I was accused of and could defend myself, the Detective Sergeant assured me that my identity would be protected.

YET two hours before his officers left, a journalist from Exaro, called Mark Conrad, emailed my office and asked if I would like to provide a statement.

It was disgraceful, as was the fact that during the four long months between the police search and the day my solicitor outlined the full case against me, I had no idea of what crime I was accused.

He broke the news to me carefully in his offices. Since the charges were so gruesome – the rape, torture and murder of three children – he was worried that I might break down and harm myself if I had been alone.

It was a sensible move. Accused of these horrific crimes, I didn't think life was worth living. Thankfully, my partner Terry, my brother Greville and a handful of friends stood by me.

They wholeheartedly supported me through the dark days when I was portrayed as a vile fiend – not just by the Met and Beech – but by an over-zealous and self-serving Tom Watson, who used parliamentary privilege to spout Beech's unfounded claims.

'The truth will out,' Terry kept telling me. I had to believe him.

The police, meanwhile, under the guise of Operation Midland, were bent on squeezing a 'confession' out of me.

Incredibly, they never sought to investigate Beech's credibility as a witness. Nor did they find any evidence to support his claims. It was as if the police, the institution dedicated to maintaining law and order, were determined to bring down members of the Establishment – or at least tarnish its reputation.

Sir Richard's intervention is timely and the events of the past few weeks – Beech's sentencing to 18 years on 12 counts of perverting the course of justice and one count of fraud – is certainly a battle won. Hopefully, I will be able to win a second battle, for fair compensation in November, when I take the Met to court. Their wrongful actions have ruined my life.

As Sir Richard made clear, a formal inquiry must be held into whether officers knowingly provided false evidence to obtain search warrants. Those found guilty must be prosecuted with the full strength of the law.

Meanwhile, we already know Tom Watson, who spent so much time and energy amplifying Nick's accusations, has peddled lies. If he wants to save a shred of respectability, he must resign from public office. And if he doesn't, I shall stand against him in the next election. His support for this calculated, menacing miscarriage of justice cannot go unpunished.

Trauma: The late Leon Brittan with his wife Diana

DAILY MAIL 31 July 2019

Home Secretary to call in head of police watchdog

£175,000 boss faces grilling over decision to clear Met officers of misconduct

By **Jack Doyle** Associate Editor

HOME Secretary Priti Patel is to personally interrogate the boss of the police watchdog accused of bungling its probe into the VIP child abuse inquiry.

Miss Patel, who has been in post for less than a week, plans to haul in £175,000-a-year Michael Lockwood 'as soon as possible'.

The Independent Office for Police Complaints yesterday refused to reopen its misconduct investigation into officers involved in the debacle, despite damning allegations from former high court judge Sir Richard Henriques.

In an article for the Mail, Sir Richard accused police of providing false evidence to obtain search warrants. This allowed them to raid the homes of D-Day hero Lord Bramall, ex-Tory MP Harvey Proctor and former home secretary Lord Brittan's widow.

Sir Richard suggested the officers involved should face a criminal investigation. However, the IOPC responded by saying it had already concluded there was 'no suspicion of criminality'.

Last night a source close to Miss Patel told the Mail: 'Priti will be meeting the head of the IOPC as soon as possible. Top of the agenda will be seeking an explanation as to why there were no proceedings against officers if there was indeed evidence of misconduct.' Ken MacDonald, the former head of the Crown Prosecution Service, accused the watchdog of conducting a 'cursory investigation' into the most senior officers, who were not even interviewed.

He told BBC Radio 4's World at One: 'They will have to explain how they missed so much of the material that Sir Richard seems to have ferreted out. Certainly, if he is right in his conclusions, it calls into question the rigour in which the IOPC have pursued this case and that would be very troubling.' He called for a 'full investigation' into how warrants were obtained, adding: 'If the courts were misled then criminal investigations should follow.'

Tory MP Nigel Evans said: 'They should look again at all the processes that were followed... if people have hidden evidence or misled a judge which has led to £2.5million being wasted and lives being destroyed.'

Misconduct allegations were first referred to the IOPC's predecessor, the Independent Police Complaints Commission, in 2016 but the probe was not completed until earlier this month. Sir Richard said he was 'surprised' by the length of the investigation, and warned it meant officers could not recall which documents they had seen before making warrant applications.

He said it was 'significant' that a relatively junior officer – a detective sergeant – with 'limited knowledge' of the investigation had signed the applications and applied in person to the judge.

Sir Richard also said detective chief inspector Diane Tudway, the chief investigating officer, was aware of several matters which undermined the credibility of key witness Carl Beech – and 'knew full well that they had not been brought to the attention of the district judge'.

'Knowingly misleading a district judge is far more serious than mere misconduct,' he said. 'The IOPC should in my judgment have investigated whether a criminal act had been committed.'

He also criticised the watchdog for failing to explain why two senior officers were exonerated without being interviewed.

Former deputy assistant commissioner Steve Rodhouse has since been promoted, while detective superintendent Kenny McDonald – who called Beech's allegations 'credible and true' at the start of the inquiry in 2014 – retired on the eve of the witness's own criminal trial this year.

The IOPC rejected Sir Richard's claims in a statement published at lunchtime, saying it had conducted a 'careful assessment' in which 'no suspicion of criminality was identified'.

The watchdog said investigators 'did not identify any information to suggest officers deliberately withheld evidence' with the intention of 'misleading' the district judge who approved the search warrants.

Lord Bramall branded the decision 'completely ridiculous'.

j.doyle@dailymail.co.uk

New broom: Priti Patel

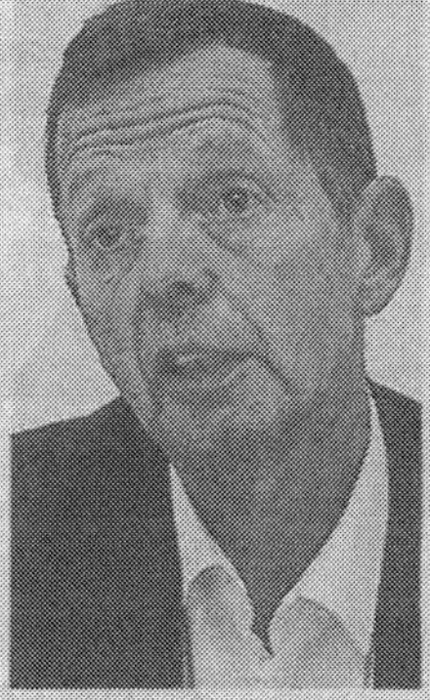

Boss: Michael Lockwood

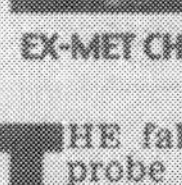

COMMENTARY by **Phil Flower**

EX-MET CHIEF SUPERINTENDENT

A GUARDIAN NOT FIT FOR PURPOSE

THE fallout from the bungled probe into lurid and now-rubbished claims of historic child abuse by VIPs continues to inflict serious damage to the police.

But nothing has been as devastating as the condemnation of former High Court judge Sir Richard Henriques, who accused top officers of allowing the course of justice to be perverted through their mishandling of the ridiculous allegations made by the fantasist and paedophile Carl Beech.

Sir Richard's attack is so powerful not only because of his judicial status but also because in 2016 he conducted an inquiry into how the police tackled the case, highlighting no fewer than 43 blunders.

He now believes that the police's potentially illegal behaviour and incompetence were so serious that 'criminal investigations should swiftly follow'. As a former detective, I agree.

Last week, as Beech was sentenced to 18 years in prison, the Independent Office for Police Conduct (IOPC) finally published its report into the saga, formally clearing three officers of any misconduct in the case.

It was a decision that both Richard and the wider public found incomprehensible.

Indeed, as Sir Richard has pointed out, because police were fully aware of the glaring inconsistencies in Beech's testimony, they may have broken the law when seeking to obtain warrants to raid the homes of those accused of abuse. I share much of Sir Richard's exasperation with the IOPC. As most police officers will tell you, the organisation is simply not fit for purpose, being top-heavy with senior managers and short of hard-nosed investigative experience.

A key part of the problem lies in how it was established.

The IOPC was launched after the Independent Police Complaints Commission (IPCC) was thought to have lost its credibility after a string of controversies, not least its investigation of the shooting by police of 29-year-old Mark Duggan in 2011, which was accused of having inconsistencies and omissions and which was dismissed by Duggan's family as a 'whitewash'.

It was designed to be independent, with fewer conflicts of interest. Officers did not themselves carry out investigations into allegations of misconduct.

In the understandable desire for impartiality, the effectiveness of the IOPC has been lost. Misconduct cases are among the toughest of all to resolve because the small minority of corrupt officers are precisely the ones who know the tricks to mislead inquiries into their behaviour.

The IOPC moans about lack of resources to do its job properly, but this is unconvincing. In the last financial year, the organisation spent £72.6 million.

Too much of this sum is squandered on bureaucracy, not enough on hardened investigators. What we need now is radical reform. My solution would be to put stipendiary magistrates – who really understand the criminal justice system – in charge of investigations, bolstered by more investigators with real police experience.

Most of the police are decent. Like me, they loathe the way the force has been dragged through the mud by the deceitful incompetence of a few.

Now their watchdog must have the teeth to prove it.

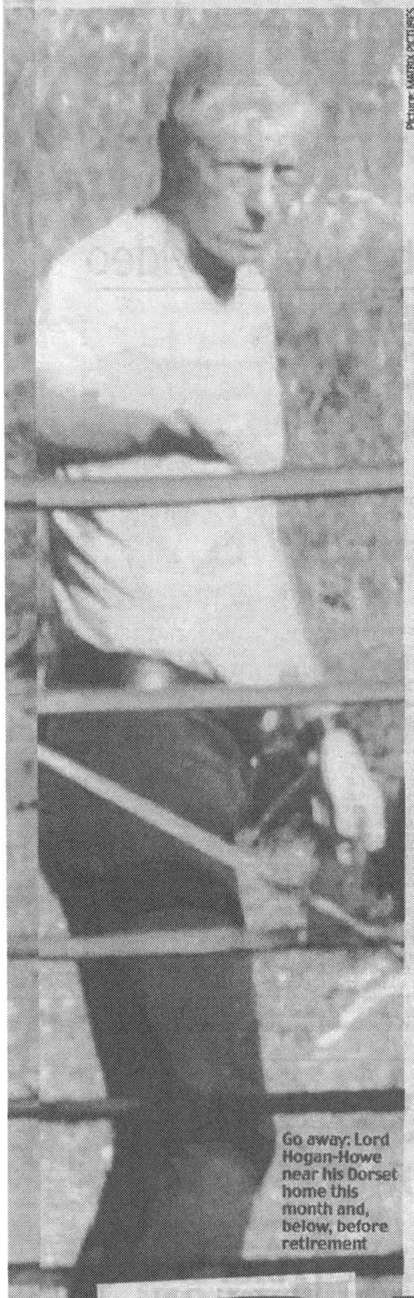

Picture: MATRIX PICTURES

Go away: Lord Hogan-Howe near his Dorset home this month and, below, before retirement

10 QUESTIONS THAT HAVE TO BE ANSWERED

By **Stephen Wright**

ASSOCIATE NEWS EDITOR

THE bombshell 1,200-word statement by former High Court judge Sir Richard Henriques, attacking Scotland Yard and police watchdogs, included devastating allegations about the conduct of senior officers. Here are the key questions about Operation Midland that must now be answered:

1 Why did the Metropolitan Police Service take nine months to correct the use of the phrase 'credible and true' by a senior officer to describe Carl Beech – aka 'Nick' – at the start of Operation Midland?

The use of this phrase by Detective Superintendent Kenny McDonald in December 2014 undermined the principle of 'innocent before proven guilty' and set the tone for the bungled investigation.

2 What role did 'gold commander' Steve Rodhouse, the Met deputy assistant commissioner in charge of Operation Midland, have in the decision to raid the homes of Lord Bramall, Lord Brittan and Harvey Proctor?

Sources say it is vital that there is transparency at Scotland Yard about the level of involvement by such a senior officer in the application for search warrants.

3 Was then Met chief Sir Bernard Hogan-Howe briefed ahead of the raids and did he raise any concerns?

The tough-talking Yorkshireman has distanced himself from the running of Operation Midland but senior Yard sources say there needs to be clarity on what he knew, and when, about the unprecedented triple murder inquiry involving a former prime minister and home secretary.

4 Sir Richard Henriques said in his devastating article in the Daily Mail there were a number of major inconsistencies in Beech's accounts which were contained in a police document prior to the application for the search warrants. Who compiled this document and who saw it?

This is a critical issue at the heart of Sir Richard's claim that officers applying for search warrants did not act with due diligence and good faith.

5 Why, in the words of Sir Richard, was a 'comparatively junior officer' with limited knowledge of the investigation 'detailed or required to sign the three applications' for search warrants that portrayed Beech as a credible and consistent witness?

According to the former High Court judge, the officer – a detective sergeant – was accompanied to court by his boss DCI Diane Tudway who had access to the document highlighting the fantasist's 'several inconsistencies', but did not raise it with the district judge who granted the search warrants.

6 Why was Sir Richard not supplied with 'all relevant documentation' by the Met during his 2016 review of Operation Midland?

This is a potentially very serious matter, involving possible criminal conduct because Sir Richard said he was not given the three applications for search warrants and had to obtain them from court.

7 Why did the Independent Office for Police Conduct clear DAC Rodhouse and Det Supt McDonald of potential misconduct within a few months – all without interviewing them?

This is another critical issue which, according to critics, goes to the heart of whether the watchdog is fit for purpose.

8 Why did it take the IOPC two years to investigate the three officers accused of misleading a district judge over the application of the search warrants?

Critics claim this is fundamental because all the officers under suspicion had retired by the time the watchdog inquiry had finished this month.

9 Why did a lowly detective constable, not a high-ranking officer, interview former head of the Armed Forces Lord Bramall under caution for 100 minutes?

An excruciating video of the D-Day hero being asked a series of ridiculous questions – including whether he knew Jimmy Savile and whether he could swim – was played to jurors at Beech's trial. Friends of Lord Bramall say the choice of junior interviewing officer, who appeared woefully out of his depth, heaped further humiliation on the Normandy veteran.

10 How on earth could the Met spend £2.5million investigating Beech's murder and abuse allegations? These included ludicrous claims he was used as a 'human dartboard' by the heads of MI5 and MI6, had his dog kidnapped by a top spy, had his horse shot by the VIP paedophile gang, suffered snake and wasp torture and was forced by Lord Bramall to eat his vomit.

This is the most simple yet damning question of Operation Midland. A man whose fantastical claims would not have looked out of place on the front of the Sunday Sport newspaper in the 1980s, were probed by the Met for 18 months.

... and the ex-Met chief's reaction? Get off my land!

HE is the former Met Police boss at the centre of a storm over controversial raids on VIPs during the disastrous police inquiry into alleged abuse.

But yesterday when the Mail approached Lord Hogan-Howe over claims of a possible perversion of justice he refused to comment.

He tetchily stated: 'Leave my property immediately!' Lord Hogan-Howe – commissioner at Scotland Yard from 2011 until 2017 – refused to answer any questions about the devastating claims by ex-High Court judge Sir Richard Henriques. The horse-loving peer was approached at his remote home in a Dorset village. He had just received an item from a parcel delivery driver when he lost his cool. The reporter waited until the driver had left and was out of earshot before walking up to the door of his converted barn with stunning Jurassic Coast views.

When he introduced himself, making it clear he was from the Daily Mail, Lord Hogan-Howe interrupted abruptly.

He pointed with his left hand to the gateway at the end of his gravelled drive and told the reporter to go away. The journalist said it was important he was given every opportunity to respond to Sir Richard's allegations about a possible perversion of the course of justice.

But Lord Hogan-Howe, 61, who has forged a lucrative career in business since leaving the Met, refused to listen and talked over the top of the reporter, adding: 'I have told you to leave my property. Leave my property immediately!'

DAILY MAIL 31 July 2019

Daily Mail
COMMENT

Victims of Met fiasco deserve the truth

EDWIN Bramall has given a lifetime of service to his country, from the day as a young officer that he took part in the D-Day landings to his retirement with the rank of Field Marshal.

That this distinguished soldier should have been humiliated by having his home searched as part of a police investigation into child sexual abuse – and then interrogated like a common criminal – is a national disgrace.

Reputations have been dragged through the mud as a result of Operation Midland, the hopelessly shoddy investigation conducted by the Metropolitan Police into allegations concerning a VIP paedophile ring made by the fantasist Carl Beech, known as 'Nick'.

Even more grave is the disclosure that the inquiry was mishandled from the outset.

Thanks to an article in this newspaper yesterday by former High Court judge Sir Richard Henriques, we have learned that officers engaged in Midland withheld evidence showing how Beech's fantastical claims were riddled with inconsistencies in order to gain court approval for warrants to search individuals' homes.

Yet, the police watchdog, the IOPC, quietly cleared them after what former DPP Lord Macdonald calls a 'cursory' process.

So where is Sir Richard's full, un-redacted report? So far, the Met is refusing to release it – a fresh scandal adding to those of the Midland fiasco and IOPC whitewash.

There was no secrecy for the true victims of 'Nick's' vile lies. Now, there should be none for the officers who trashed their good names in such cavalier fashion.

As a first step, Sir Richard's report needs to be published in full, and now.

Nothing else will do if the reputation of the Metropolitan Police is not to be damaged beyond repair by this appalling witch-hunt, a grave warning of what happens when police pander to hysteria.

Pluck's not enough

POSING with chickens, the Prime Minister yesterday sought to comfort farmers facing crippling EU tariffs in the event of a No Deal Brexit.

But as the pound traded at British airports for 0.78 euros, the realities of this frightening scenario are coming home to roost.

Indulging in stunts while touring the Union, rowing with the Irish premier on the telephone and engaging in macho talk of a 'Brexit war cabinet' may play well with hardliners. But megaphone diplomacy is rarely helpful. Mr Johnson should ditch Churchillian rhetoric and engage in sensible talks with our most important trading partner.

Yes, precautionary planning for No Deal should be pursued, but not recklessly. Every sinew must be strained to reach a deal. That is as true for EU leaders as it is for Boris.

Campbell clears off

THIS newspaper is no fan of Alastair Campbell. In promoting the invasion of Iraq in 2003, based on non-existent WMD, Tony Blair's media henchman proved himself an accomplished pedlar of fake news.

But Campbell knows how to win general elections – having helped in three victories. Now, he is quitting his old party in despair over the leadership of Jeremy Corbyn.

Labour, he warns, risks destruction unless it junks its far-Left politics – and that means junking Mr Corbyn. In saying so, he is merely reflecting the view of many Labour MPs.

With his dithering over Brexit, dissembling over anti-Semitism and discredited socialist thinking, this creaking Marxist is leading Labour towards the precipice.

The diehards surrounding him will no doubt shoot Campbell the messenger.

The fact that Labour's 'conscience' is a man who employed mendacity and bully-boy tactics in attacks on the Press shows how far the party has sunk.

AS WOODFORD INVESTORS ARE BETRAYED AGAIN

Why the fat-cat fund boss who shames the City must be forced to step down

by Alex Brummer

CITY EDITOR

EACH year, Britain spends £1.7billion to ensure that our financial system — the most important in Europe — is clean, fair, and works in the best interests of us all.

For this staggering sum, provided by the taxpayer and financial industry, we surely have a right to expect a Rolls-Royce system of regulation.

How, then, can we explain the flaccid, near negligent response by the regulator and the Bank of England to the meltdown inside the investment empire of Neil Woodford?

Indeed, I find it almost inexplicable that Woodford has not been discharged from his job. Why is he being allowed to soldier on, raking in fees of around £100,000 each working day, while his clients are denied access to their money?

Unscrupulous

The Woodford saga is one I have written about regularly since June, when his main fund, Global Equity Income, was frozen because it did not have enough ready cash to pay departing savers due to so many of its holdings being illiquid (hard to sell).

I make no apology for returning to it after news emerged this week that 291,520 savers — myself included — either directly or indirectly exposed to Woodford funds via the Bristol-based investment platform Hargreaves Lansdown, will not be able to get their hands on £1.6billion of their own money until at least December.

What really sticks in the craw is that, while small investors are being made to wait and worry, not only are Woodford and his firm continuing to charge fees — amounting to some £12million by the end of the year — he has also been cashing in his investments.

The shameless financier revealed he sold 1.75million shares in his publicly quoted Patient Capital Trust Fund, in total worth £1million, to meet a personal tax bill.

In so doing he drove the shares in Patient Capital, which have fallen 30 per cent this year, down further, hurting all his fellow investors.

He only told the Trust board on Saturday — three weeks after he ditched the shares.

Woodford has become super-wealthy — with the houses, cars and a lifestyle to match — on the back of ordinary savers, and he is still able to get his hands on resources.

The muggins in his main fund, however, are totally trapped. They are unable to release funds to pay *their* tax bills, meet social care costs for a family member, organise a wedding or buy a house.

They are the innocent victims of the unscrupulous greed of Woodford and his sponsors, Hargreaves Lansdown.

Once lionised by the City as Britain's savviest stock picker, Woodford has not been seen in public since the scandal erupted. He's confined his excuses to online postings.

There has been absolutely no recognition by him or by the City regulators of the damage being done to the reputation of our investment industry.

If I sound angry and aggrieved it is because I, like several colleagues and members of my family, have reasons to be worried. We are among those who trusted the loaded advice of Hargreaves Lansdown.

I committed some of my retirement funds to Woodford's flagship Equity Income Fund and to the separate, but as it turned out far too closely related, Patient Capital Trust.

We can't access our money, but Woodford continues to ruthlessly exploit us, refusing to waive fees in defiance of admonition from Andrew Bailey, the head of the City watchdog, the Financial Conduct Authority (FCA) — or, as Private Eye has dubbed it, the Fundamentally Complicit Authority. Savers could be forgiven for thinking the magazine may have a point.

As this appalling spectacle plays out, the City's biggest potential embarrassment since the financial crisis, it is clear the regulators have totally misjudged the public mood.

What we have witnessed since the build-up of trouble within the Woodford empire began, is fumble after fumble by those charged with safeguarding our investments.

Yet there was no shortage of evidence of alleged rule-breaking and conflict of interests, which justified a far more robust approach from the regulator from the start.

Stocks held by his Equity Income Fund were sold on to an interconnected company (Patient Capital Trust) — something frowned on by regulators — and unlisted stocks were transferred to the Guernsey Stock Exchange, where few dealings are done, so it could be claimed they were 'quoted' somewhere.

Several directors of Patient Capital were also directors of companies in which funds were invested, while the relationship between Woodford's firm and Hargreaves Lansdown was far too intimate.

Dangers

And not enough attention was paid, until it was too late, to the necessity of keeping a generous cash or 'liquidity' cushion to protect against a run on the funds by savers.

Yet, for several years now, the Bank of England and its deputy governor, Jon Cunliffe (along with Bailey, one of the candidates to succeed Mark Carney as governor), have regularly warned of the dangers of 'open funds', such as those Woodford managed, where investors are entitled theoretically to withdraw their cash instantly.

The FCA has been aware of the weaknesses in the system, but reforms of fees and governance have been hampered in part by fierce lobbying by the fund management industry.

Despite all this, instead of raising red flags as warnings of unorthodox dealings and a lack of cash in Woodford funds grew, the FCA was silent.

At the same time, Hargreaves Landsdown continued to support Woodford — even after problems became public — by including his funds among its top recommendations.

So, if ever there was a time for the FCA to seize the moment to protect savers, it is now. But its main response to date has been to announce an inquiry into what went wrong — a worthy exercise, but one that will do nothing to address the immediate pain of savers.

Failed

It is not too late to do more. The FCA together with the Bank of England, which has overarching responsibility for preserving financial stability, need to act decisively. Woodford should be summoned from his hideaway and ordered to suspend the average 0.6 per cent fee he charges savers for managing their money.

He won't be left short. Managing other people's cash is hugely rewarding, with profit margins of close to 50 per cent. Since he founded his firm in 2014, Woodford and his main associates have extracted £100million in dividends.

Should Woodford defy the FCA's request to waive the fees, the FCA should remove his licence as an 'approved' person to work in the City.

In previous financial scandals, such as Equitable Life and the Libor interest rate scam at Barclays, regulators moved ruthlessly to clean the stables by removing top executives.

They may lack a clear legal basis for asking Woodford to step down, but the FCA and the Bank of England have sufficient moral authority to force his departure.

The duty of the regulator is to us, the customer, so that the ordinary citizen can invest for the long-term with confidence and know precisely how and when they can access their own money.

In this, regulators have failed miserably and the scandal continues unabated.

DAILY MAIL 31 July 2019

Daily Mail
TUESDAY, JULY 30, 2019
www.dailymail.co.uk
70p

Memo to Meghan: Brits prefer true royalty to fashion royalty

by SARAH VINE SEE PAGES 12-13

'NICK' POLICE SEARCHES BROKE LAW

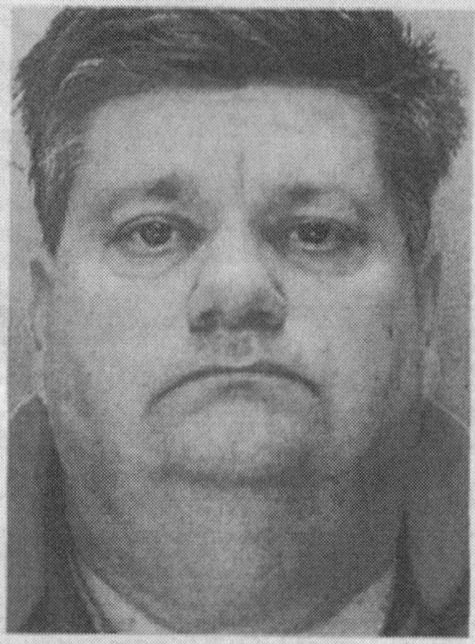

Lies: Carl Beech's claims led to witch-hunt

- Bombshell as judge behind inquiry reveals 'perversion of justice'
- He tells Mail: Officers got search warrants using false evidence...
- ...but says his damning findings were ignored by police watchdog

Intervention: Sir Richard Henriques

By **Stephen Wright**
Associate News Editor

POLICE broke the law in the bungled probe into VIP child abuse fantasist Nick, a former High Court judge says today.

Sir Richard Henriques said officers used false evidence to obtain search warrants to raid the homes of retired Armed Forces chief Lord Bramall, the widow of ex-Home Secretary Lord Brittan and ex-Tory MP Harvey Proctor and should now face a criminal investigation.

In an astonishing intervention, he tells the Daily Mail that Scotland Yard detectives did not have the right to search the properties because their description of Nick – real name Carl Beech – as a 'consistent' witness was false, effectively fooling a judge into granting the warrants.

He also alleges the 'course of justice

Turn to Page 4

EXCLUSIVE

DAILY MAIL 30 July 2019

'JUSTICE WAS PERVERTED – WITH SHOCKING CONSEQUENCES'

Continued from Page One

was perverted with shocking consequences' and says he finds it astonishing that no officer has been brought to book over the fiasco. He says a 'criminal investigation should surely follow'.

Last week it was confirmed that not one officer would face misconduct proceedings over the case, following a watchdog investigation branded a 'whitewash' by critics.

In 2016 Sir Richard wrote a scathing report for Scotland Yard about its £2.5million investigation into Beech's allegations. His report, which identified 43 blunders, was heavily redacted and has never been fully made public.

But his 1,200-word statement in today's Mail will pile pressure on ex-Metropolitan Police chief Sir Bernard, now Lord Hogan-Howe, and the officer who led Operation Midland, ex-deputy assistant commissioner Steve Rodhouse, who has been promoted to one of the top jobs in British policing.

In other bombshell claims, Sir Richard:

- Says the Metropolitan Police has 'sought to protect itself from effective outside scrutiny' over Operation Midland;
- Alleges that during his hard-hitting 2016 investigation, the Met did not give him 'all relevant documentation'; and
- Attacks police watchdogs for clearing two senior officers of misconduct without interviewing them.

Sir Richard's broadside at the Met and police watchdogs comes days after vicar's son Beech, 51, was jailed for 18 years for telling a string of lies about alleged VIP child sex abuse and serial murder.

At his ten-week trial, jurors heard the fantasist told officers that he was used as a human dartboard by the former heads of MI5 and MI6, that his dog was kidnapped by a spy chief, and that the paedophile ring shot dead his horse.

The court also heard Beech is now a convicted paedophile after child porn offences came to light when an independent police force, at Sir Richard's behest, started investigating him on suspicion of making false claims about a murderous Establishment paedophile ring.

In the wake of his convictions last week, Scotland Yard chiefs faced intense criticism over its staggering incompetence and 16-month investigation launched on the word of a pathological liar.

But shortly after he was found guilty last Monday, the Independent Office for Police Conduct (IOPC) announced three officers accused of misconduct over search warrant applications had been cleared.

The IOPC said the officers, led by senior investigating officer detective chief inspector Diane Tudway, acted 'with due diligence and in good faith at the time'.

But Sir Richard tells the Mail the finding is 'in conflict' with his review of Operation Midland in 2016 and he maintains 'the opinion that the three search warrants authorising the searches of the homes of Lord Bramall, Lady Brittan and Harvey Proctor were obtained unlawfully' from a district judge. This is because, he says, Beech's allegations had changed since he first contacted police in 2012 and were not 'consistent'.

He continued: 'I remain unable to conclude that every officer acted with due diligence and in good faith. When the applications were made officers leading the investigation were fully aware of six matters in particular which undermined Beech's credibility.'

In another damning revelation, Sir Richard said that during his

'Met sought to protect itself'

review for the Met, he was not – as promised at the outset – given 'all relevant documentation'.

He said Mrs Tudway – who was promoted to superintendent while under investigation for alleged misconduct and retired just before Beech's trial – was aware of several matters which undermined Beech's credibility and 'knew full well that they had not been brought to the attention of the district judge'. He added: 'Knowingly misleading a district judge is far more serious than mere misconduct. The IOPC should in my judgment have investigated whether a criminal act had been committed.'

He also lambasted the watchdog for offering no explanation as to why two senior Operation Midland officers – Rodhouse and ex-detective superintendent Kenny McDonald, who called Beech 'credible and true' at the start of the inquiry in 2014 – were exonerated without being interviewed by watchdogs.

'Through the device of deploying an officer with an incomplete knowledge of the investigation to sign the applications and to make the applications, the Metropolitan Police has sought to protect itself from effective outside scrutiny,' he concluded.

Last week Met Deputy Commissioner Sir Stephen House said he believed all five officers probed by police watchdogs over Operation Midland 'worked in good faith'.

They cooperated fully with both the Henriques' Review and the Independent Office for Police Conduct investigations, he added.

Comment – Page 18

Lies: Carl Beech, pictured during a police interview

Warrants: How they work

IF police want to search a suspect's home, they have to apply to the local magistrates' court for a search warrant.

The court will only grant it if satisfied there are reasonable grounds to suspect an offence has been committed – and that material of substantial value to an investigation is likely to be recovered. Once a warrant has been granted, police have three months to carry out the search – or one month if issued under the Misuse of Drugs Act.

When a police officer attends a search, they must provide a copy of the search warrant. If the homeowner is present, they must ask permission to search the property – unless the search would be hindered by doing so.

Sir Richard Henriques: Officers knew of inconsistent evidence

The court was given false and misleading evidence... a criminal inquiry must now follow

Shattering verdict of top judge who ran VIP abuse case review

by SIR RICHARD HENRIQUES

RETIRED HIGH COURT JUDGE

ON MONDAY, July 22, the Independent Office for Police Conduct (IOPC) published its findings into how the Metropolitan Police handled the investigation into allegations made by Carl Beech, namely that the Operation Midland officers involved in applying for search warrants acted 'with due diligence and in good faith at the time'.

That finding is in conflict with my own finding set out in my review handed to Sir Bernard Hogan-Howe, as he was then, on October 31, 2016.

That section of my review has not as yet been disclosed to the public or to those named and falsely accused by Beech, previously known by the pseudonym 'Nick'.

I concluded in my review – and maintain the opinion – that the three search warrants authorising the searches of the homes of Lord Bramall, Lady Brittan and Harvey Proctor were obtained unlawfully.

All three applications stated that Beech had remained consistent with his allegations.

Beech had not been consistent. His allegations made to the Wiltshire Police in 2012 were fundamentally inconsistent with those he made to the Metropolitan Police in 2014 and with blogs published by Beech in 2014.

Beech told Wiltshire Police that he was first raped by an unnamed lieutenant colonel. He told the Metropolitan Police that he was first raped by his stepfather.

The identities of subsequent named alleged rapists were inconsistent. The alleged locations were inconsistent, persons allegedly present were inconsistent, the alleged accompanying acts of violence were inconsistent and Wiltshire Police were never informed of three alleged child murders.

These numerous inconsistencies were within the knowledge of those officers leading the investigation. A document highlighting Beech's 'inconsistencies' was in existence prior to the application for search warrants. The Wiltshire interviews had been handed to the Metropolitan Police in May 2013.

The description of Beech as having been consistent was false and misleading and persuaded the district judge to grant the applications, as did the fact 'that this has been considered at deputy assistant commissioner level'.

I remain unable to conclude that every officer acted with due diligence and in good faith. When the applications were made officers leading the investigation were fully aware of six matters in particular which undermined Beech's credibility.

They are set out in my review at some length and should have been brought to the attention of the district judge in the event of any application being made.

In particular there was compelling evidence that Beech had never been injured in the manner he had asserted, that he had never been absent from home as alleged, nor removed from school as alleged, there was no evidence that any one of the three children allegedly murdered had in fact been murdered, and no corroboration of any single allegation not withstanding a public request for information made on December 18, 2014.

NONE of these matters were disclosed to the district judge as they should have been.

Every search warrant application contains the words 'this application discloses all the information that is material to what the court must decide including anything that might reasonably be considered capable of undermining any of the grounds of the application'.

In order to obtain a search warrant, an applicant must establish that he or she has reasonable grounds to believe that an indictable offence has been committed.

I concluded in 2016 – and I remain of the view – that the officers responsible for the three applications did not in fact fully believe that there were reasonable grounds to believe Beech's allegations.

If such reasonable grounds had existed, and had officers believed in their existence, I have no doubt Harvey Proctor would have been arrested on suspicion of having committed three child murders.

When I was asked by Sir Bernard to conduct my review, I was assured that I would receive all relevant documentation. I was not in fact supplied with the three applications for search warrants.

Nor were the applications listed on a list of relevant documents supplied to me. It was necessary to approach Westminster Magistrates' Court direct in order to obtain the written applications.

It is significant a comparatively junior officer – a detective sergeant with limited knowledge of the investigation and with no knowledge of the content of the Wiltshire interviews (having chosen not to read a summary provided to him) – was detailed or required to sign the three applications and to apply in person to the district judge.

Indeed, the detective sergeant told the IOPC that he was unaware of the inconsistencies in Beech's accounts and had not read the Wiltshire interviews.

The senior investigating officer, however, attended before the district judge and had herself reviewed the written applications.

She had access to the Wiltshire interviews and to the document highlighting Beech's several inconsistencies.

She was present at the application when the more junior and less well informed officer gave evidence on oath in support of the applications. The senior investigating officer was aware of the several matters referred to earlier which undermined Beech's credibility and knew full well that they had not been brought to the attention of the district judge.

The consequence of obtaining and executing these three search warrants and then informing Beech thereof must not be underestimated. Beech immediately informed Exaro, the online news agency, which resulted in the avalanche of dreadful publicity which has blighted the lives of Lord Bramall, Lady Brittan, Harvey Proctor, nine other named individuals and their families and friends.

If any police officer drafted, reviewed, promoted or signed an application for a search warrant stating that Beech had remained consistent whilst knowing he had not been consistent, such an officer would be guilty not only of misconduct, but also of intending to pervert the course of justice.

I was surprised to learn that the criticism made by me in my review had been assessed to amount to misconduct only by the IOPC. Knowingly misleading a district judge is far more serious than mere misconduct.

The IOPC should in my judgement have investigated whether a criminal act had been committed, and if so by whom.

I was also surprised by the length of time taken to complete the IOPC investigation.

I was informed by Sir Bernard that the matter would be referred to the Independent Police Complaints Commission (as the IOPC was previously known) in November 2016 and the investigation was not completed until July 2019. Whilst the IOPC apologised for the time taken to conclude the matter, such delay undoubtedly resulted in 'officers being unable to specify which documents each had sight of and knowledge of at what time'.

Finally, there was no explanation from the IOPC as to why the two most senior officers were exonerated without interview, not least since the district judge relied on the fact the search warrant applications had been considered at deputy assistant commissioner level.

Through the device of deploying an officer with an incomplete knowledge of the investigation to sign the applications and to make the applications, the Metropolitan Police has sought to protect itself from effective outside scrutiny.

The fact remains, however, that Beech had not remained consistent, the Metropolitan Police informed the district judge that Beech had remained consistent and 'he is felt to be a credible witness who is telling the truth'.

Thus the course of justice was perverted with shocking consequences. A criminal investigation should surely follow.

■*Sir Richard did not request or receive a fee for this article.*

LIVES LEFT IN RUINS PAGES 6-7

DAILY MAIL 30 July 2019

Page 6 ABUSE POLICE IN THE DOCK Daily Mail, Tuesday, July 30, 2019

LIVES TRASHED,

Laid bare in their own haunting words, torment of innocent VIPs and families who faced shock of police raids

By **Glen Keogh**

THE devastating toll of the Operation Midland investigation was starkly laid bare by those who had their homes raided over false allegations of murder, child rape and torture.

The trial of fantasist Carl Beech heard how officers searched the home of Britain's most distinguished living war hero while his wife suffered with dementia.

One detective allegedly leaked news of the search of an ex-MP's home to his accuser, who handed the information to discredited news website Exaro. And the grieving widow of a former home secretary was 'traumatised' as their two properties were searched only six weeks after his death.

As retired judge Sir Richard Henriques calls for a criminal investigation into how the search warrants were obtained, the Mail outlines the impact of the raids in March 2015.

PROCTOR: IT WAS KAFKAESQUE

ON March 4, 2015 officers from the Metropolitan Police's murder squad raided former Tory MP Harvy Proctor's home on the Duke of Rutland's private estate.

They spent 15 hours searching his grace-and-favour home in the grounds of Belvoir Castle in Leicestershire.

Mr Proctor told Newcastle Crown Court during Beech's trial that police would initially not give him details of what he was accused of other than saying it was to do with allegations of historic child abuse.

In fact, police were probing at least two murders said to have been committed by Mr Proctor.

The details they had been fed – described at one stage as 'credible and true' – included an allegation that Mr Proctor had attempted to castrate Beech with a pen knife and was only stopped from doing so when 1970s prime minister Sir Edward Heath intervened.

Mr Proctor was assured during the search his name would not find its way into the media. He had to be talked out of taking his own life in the late 1980s when he admitted gross indecency for having sex with underage men after being exposed by newspapers.

The following morning after the raid he awoke to coverage on TV news. He told Beech's trial: 'When I awoke at 7am on the dot I looked up at the TV screen to see my face looking back at me and a story running at the head of the BBC news that my house had been searched in connection with historic child sexual abuse including child murders.

'It was a Kafkaesque situation – a horrendous, irrational nightmare.' A detective taking part in the raid on Mr Proctor's home is then said to have phoned Beech to update him. Beech passed details of the raid to reporters at Exaro, who ran the piece and caused Mr Proctor's name to become public knowledge.

As a result of the raid and the following publicity, Mr Proctor lost his job and the home that went with it. After receiving death threats, he moved with his partner to Spain 'away from the country I love' before quietly returning to Britain to live in a converted shed provided by a friend which had no running water.

He is now back living in a property owned by the Rutland estate.

He added: 'I suffer severe depression and sometimes weep when reminded of what I have lost as a result of the police action.'

Mr Proctor is pursuing a civil claim against the Metropolitan Police and Beech. In an interview with the Mail in 2018, Mr Proctor said: 'When the police raided my home in March they arrived at 8am. I was given no prior warning. There were at least 15 of them. They searched my home for 15 hours.

'They assured me my identity would not come out. But even before they left, the Press were telephoning my office.'

Searched as widow grieved: London home of ex-home secretary Lord Brittan and wife Diana, above

'Horrendous, irrational nightmare': Former MP Harvey Proctor

BRAMALL: CHILD SLUR SO INSULTING

AS Field Marshal Lord Bramall sat down to have breakfast with his wife of 66 years, 20 police descended on their home in a village on the Hampshire-Surrey border.

The former head of the Armed Forces and war hero, 95 and wheelchair-bound, said the visit was so unexpected that he immediately invited the police inside when they knocked on the door.

In an interview with the Sunday Times, he described how he was told 'accusations had been made'.

When Lord Bramall replied 'Against who?' he was informed 'Against you.' His wife Avril was in the advanced stages of dementia and did not understand what was taking place. She died before he could be exonerated.

Lord Bramall described how the officers arrived in overalls and spent ten hours searching 'absolutely everything' in the house.

His daughter Sara arrived and she was asked whether he had any grandchildren before one officer added: 'Are you afraid of leaving them alone with him?'

He told the newspaper: 'Can you think of anything more insulting?'

The officers left with an old visitors' book and copies of two speeches Lord Bramall had made.

In an interview with the Mail last week, his son Nicholas said: 'They went behind every picture in the house. They ripped the place apart. There was a bus-load of police in white suits. My parents live right in the middle of the village. They weren't being subtle.

'Most of the officers went down the pub for lunch and it wasn't long before the local paper got onto Dad. The trouble with all allegations, particularly paedophilia, is it sticks, doesn't it? It's just such an overwhelmingly awful thing.'

Lord Bramall received £100,000 compensation from the police for their handling of the raid.

Nicholas said: 'They over-reacted and got it spectacularly wrong and Dad and other people had to pay the price.' His wife Pip added: 'He [Lord Bramall] said the police had raided his house and were there now. They were going through everything and he wasn't allowed to move. He said he'd been accused of something involving a minor 40 years ago but they wouldn't say what it was.

'Mum was very confused. It was so unpleasant for her. She was sort of shunted from one room to another. She knew something was wrong, but wasn't quite sure what it was. It affected her quite badly. She used to say, "What have I done, what have I done?"'

LADY BRITTAN: MY SEARCH TRAUMA

HOMES in Yorkshire and London belonging to the former home secretary were raided by police six weeks after his death from cancer.

HOMES INVADED

Humiliated: Lord Bramall outside the home raided by police

The key figure in Margaret Thatcher's cabinet was alone in hospital, terminally ill, when the allegations concocted by 'Nick' became global news. The politician died in January 2015 and his grieving widow Diana had to contend with huge media interest in the allegations made by Beech.

A short time later, police raided Lord Brittan's homes in Pimlico, central London and Leyburn, North Yorkshire.

In a victim impact statement read at the sentencing of Beech last week, Lady Brittan said their London home was searched for 12 hours and the Yorkshire residence, which was being let, for two days.

She said: 'The experience of having my house in London searched by a dozen police officers for 12 hours was traumatising.' Describing the Yorkshire raid, she added: 'The whole house was turned upside down, and questions were asked about "newly-turned earth".

'Van-loads of personal effects were removed. The elderly couple resident in the house were shell-shocked by the nature and extent of the search. They were also subjected to very intrusive questioning about my husband and my family. I feared the two searches would be made public. And a few days later they were. The impact of these allegations and their consequences on my wider family were significant. My younger daughter, who lives in Australia, advised me shortly after my husband's death not to go on the internet and in particular the website Exaro because she said, 'You will find it very upsetting.'

She added: 'My husband's name has now been cleared, but he will never know this.'

Lady Brittan was paid £100,000 compensation by police.

STEPHEN GLOVER PAGE NINE

HOW TRAVESTY OF JUSTICE UNFOLDED

2012

OCT 5 Operation Yewtree investigation into Jimmy Savile and other celebrities launched.

OCT 24 Tom Watson makes statement in Commons about VIP paedophile ring.

OCT 30 Beech contacts Met to say he was abused by late stepfather and Savile. Case referred to Wiltshire police.

2013

MAY 3 Wiltshire police close probe into original Beech claims because of no evidence.

SEP 21 Beech asks for a crime number to begin a Criminal Injuries Compensation claim.

2014

JUL 12 Exaro news website runs claims of sex abuse parties at Dolphin Square, Westminster.

OCT 6 Beech, now known as 'Nick', emails the Yard, about alleged VIP child sex abuse.

OCT 22 First taped police interview with Beech.

NOV 14 Operation Midland formally launched.

DEC 18 Det Supt Kenny McDonald describes Beech's claims as 'credible and true'.

2015

JAN 21 Lord Brittan dies.

MAR 4 Police search homes of Field Marshal Lord Bramall, Harvey Proctor and Lord Brittan.

APR 30 Lord Bramall first interviewed under caution.

JUN 18 Mr Proctor questioned under caution by police.

JUL 31 Lord Bramall re-interviewed days after wife dies.

AUG 24 Mr Proctor questioned again; the next day he publicly denounces Operation Midland.

SEPT 5 Daily Mail reveals Beech is a suspected serial liar and fantasist, but police too scared to close down inquiry.

2016

JAN 15 Lord Bramall cleared.

FEB Sir Richard Henriques ordered by Met Commissioner Sir Bernard Hogan-Howe to start independent inquiry into Operation Midland fiasco.

MAR 21 Mr Proctor cleared. Operation Midland scrapped.

SEP 28 Lord Hogan-Howe tenders resignation.

OCT 31 Report into Operation Midland makes 43 criticisms but 85% is redacted.

VIP abuse police raid home of shamed Tory

From the Mail, March 6, 2015

NOW PUT VIP ABUSE 'FANTASIST' IN DOCK

From the Mail, Nov 9, 2016

NOV Northumbria Police begin investigation into Beech for perverting the course of justice and raid his home.

2017

MAR 8 Police watchdog clears two senior Met officers of wrongdoing.

SEP Lord Bramall and widow of Lord Brittan receive £100,000 compensation each.

2018

FEB 7 Beech revealed as having been charged with child porn and voyeurism offences.

JUL 2 Charged with perverting course of justice and fraud.

JUL 31 Fails to appear for trial at Worcester Crown court over paedophile allegations after fleeing to Sweden – extradited.

2019

JAN 21 Jury sworn in at Hereford Crown Court to hear Beech trial on child porn charges.

JAN 22 Beech changes plea to guilty.

MAY Beech's trial for perverting the course of justice and fraud begins in Newcastle.

JULY 22 Beech found guilty. Three former officers on Operation Midland cleared of alleged misconduct by watchdog.

JULY 26 Beech jailed for 18 years.

JULY 30 Sir Richard calls for criminal probe into how search warrants were obtained.

DAILY MAIL 30 July 2019

Daily Mail
COMMENT

Criminal probe must lay bare Met failings

DISHONEST police officers conspiring to lie deliberately to a court in order to obtain authorisation for raids on the homes of innocent citizens using the full, blunt force of the State?

One might be forgiven for thinking this chilling scenario could only occur in some failed banana republic or Third World dictatorship.

In fact, eminent retired High Court judge Sir Richard Henriques tells the Daily Mail today it may, shamefully, have happened in 21st Century Britain.

In an unprecedented intervention, he accuses Scotland Yard of unlawfully securing search warrants while investigating malign claims of a VIP paedophile ring which raped and murdered children in the 1970s and 1980s. Desperate to believe deranged allegations by a man known as 'Nick', he fears detectives may have acted illegally.

Disturbingly, he says police ignored glaring inconsistencies in the fantasist's assertions (including that three close friends were killed by the child-sex gang).

Then by submitting 'false and misleading' statements to court, he says, they persuaded a judge to grant warrants against three prominent figures.

This empowered the Metropolitan Police to ransack the homes of former Home Secretary Lord Brittan, war hero Field Marshal Lord Bramall and ex-Tory MP Harvey Proctor. Their lives were ruined, their reputations trashed.

Sir Richard doesn't mince his words: These officers 'perverted the course of justice with shocking consequences'.

He is similarly unequivocal about the next step: A rigorous criminal investigation.

Why are Sir Richard's words so explosive? First, he is an Establishment mainstay. He has put his neck on the line to lift the lid on wrong-doing at the heart of the police.

Next, he wrote the (heavily-censored) 2016 report which laid bare Operation Midland's appalling failings, and how police dragged the blameless through the mud.

Even a cursory investigation would have discovered the smears were the inventions of a twisted imagination.

Last, Sir Richard is livid officers have got off scot-free. Mere hours after 'Nick' – real name Carl Beech – was convicted of lying to police, a watchdog sneaked out that three officers had been cleared of misconduct.

Not a soul has been punished for the outrage. Met police chief Bernard Hogan-Howe, ultimately in charge of the massive botch-up, was rewarded with a place in the House of Lords.

Detective Superintendent Kenny McDonald, who declared on TV the grotesque claims were 'credible and true', retired on a gold-plated pension.

And what of the real victims? D-Day veteran Lord Bramall, 95, saw his wife die with the sickening allegations still hanging over his head. Lord Brittan went to his grave without his name being cleared. And Harvey Proctor lost his home and job.

Truly, this has been one of the blackest episodes in Scotland Yard's history. Serious questions need answering about how the shamed force got it so profoundly wrong.

Today, the Mail demands action. Sir Richard's report must be published immediately – unredacted. MPs should launch an urgent inquiry into why the Met was so pathetically gullible – and gung-ho.

And it is vital an independent police force investigates if the Yard perverted the course of justice during the costly witch-hunt.

It is instructive that the distinguished judge has spoken out in the Mail as a means to expose the horrendous injustice – highlighting the importance of a free Press in holding the powerful to account.

For it is crucial to maintaining public trust that we get to the bottom of this scandal.

If people of the monumental standing of Lord Bramall can be fitted up by a rogue police force acting as the arm of the State, surely it could happen to any one of us.

Is Boris's economic plan more Bertie Wooster than rocket booster?

by Ruth Sunderland

ON A whirlwind charm offensive to leading City power-brokers, Boris Johnson has been cajoling them with the glorious word 'Boosterism' to describe the principles behind his Government's economic policies.

How typical of Johnson to use a word that vividly encapsulates his vision for a 'turbo-charged' Britain and which also is redolent of P.G. Wodehouse's classic creation, Bertie Wooster. For Johnson has often been compared to Wooster, the raffish gadabout with a public school accent and who uses flamboyant language.

But make no mistake, a canny Johnson is trying to give rocket fuel to his own administration and quickly brand it in the public's mind as an on-the-road-to-success story.

For the moment, Boris's Boosterism refers to the list of spending commitments he has been showering on the electorate like confetti in the five days since he became prime minister.

He is desperate to boost the financial security of Britain in case of a No Deal EU exit by pumping billions into a host of projects and sectors.

The cost of all this is mind-boggling. Indeed, just one of numerous proposals under consideration, for example, is to spend £100billion to help bridge the North/South divide.

Honed

As a student of history — ancient and modern — Johnson knows that all great governments have been identified with their own economic philosophy.

We have had Thatcherism — when Margaret Thatcher brilliantly honed the principles of 'Monetarism' to fit her own ideals. Thatcherism treated money supply as the main factor influencing the economy, and monetary policy as the key instrument of government decision-making.

Then there was the equally successful Reaganomics — named after U.S. President Ronald Reagan's obsession with cutting taxes and public spending, and reducing government control of business and industry.

Their opposite is Keynesian economics, based on the ideas of British thinker John Maynard Keynes, who believed that, in a recession, an economy can be made to grow and unemployment reduced by increasing government spending and reducing interest rates.

Thankfully, so far, we have been spared Corbynomics — the policy of bankrupting a country, Venezuela-style.

The big question is whether Boris's Boosterism will go down in history as one of these successful creeds that will be studied by future generations of economics students, or will be seen as a reflection of the PM's lack of attention to detail and amounts to little more than wishful thinking.

Inevitably, his critics see it as closer to Woosterism. Johnson, like Bertie Wooster, is long on cheer but short on pragmatism.

At the risk of sounding more Jeeves than Wooster, the fundamental problem facing the Government is that the current risks to Britain's prosperity are grave. Of course, Johnson would argue that spending and a mood of optimism are tools to help create confidence and success.

Slogans aside, it will be far harder for Johnson to extricate our economy from the damage of a No Deal Brexit than for Bertie Wooster to escape the clutches of a malign aunt or an engagement to Madeline Bassett.

In fact, Boosterism is not a new word. It was coined in 19th-century America. To encourage the building of railroads in dusty, lawless outposts in the Wild West, town representatives made all sorts of exaggerated claims about how they would boost the local economy beyond residents' rosiest dreams.

Mistake

Often the hyperbole crashed, leaving investors broke and livelihoods devastated.

It's worth remembering that Johnson's hero and role model, Winston Churchill, was a great wartime leader but utterly wrong-headed when it came to the economy.

His personal finances were rackety and, as Chancellor in the 1920s, he put Britain back on to the gold standard — a fateful decision that had deeply damaging repercussions for the UK economy and which he later acknowledged was his biggest mistake.

Of course, we are not facing economic perils as great as then, but the stakes with Brexit are terribly high. The Tory Party has a hard-won reputation for economic competence. The risk is that Johnson, with his relentlessly upbeat promises, might squander it.

Yes, Boosterism sounds far cheerier than austerity. But over the past nine years, Chancellors Osborne and Hammond made great strides to get the nation's books in better order.

With Johnson's oft-repeated mantra of wanting a 'turbo-charged' government, his strategy marks a dramatic reversal of direction. Can it succeed?

If, and I accept it is a big 'if' considering the way he often changes his mind, Johnson is serious about fulfilling all his Boosterism promises, he will need to raise taxes or cut public spending, both of which will be difficult for a government with a gossamer-thin Commons majority.

The only other option is to borrow more. And if Johnson proceeds to upset the nation's balance sheet, the Tories would not be able to moralise about Jeremy Corbyn and John McDonnell being economic illiterates.

The fact is that the British economy has performed remarkably well since the financial crisis and the European Union referendum. If the Government achieves an orderly Brexit, this process could continue.

But warnings over No Deal are coming thick and fast. The independent Office for Budget Responsibility says it would plunge the country into recession and cause borrowing to mushroom by £30billion a year. The National Institute for Social and Economic Research says that, already, the risk of a No Deal departure may have pushed us into recession.

And if you think these are just the gloomy prognostications of discredited experts, then look at the real world.

Sterling has fallen sharply against the dollar and the euro — an indication that the foreign exchange markets are sceptical about Britain. The owners of Vauxhall have said they will pull out of the UK, with the loss of 1,000 jobs, if Brexit hits their profits.

Infectious

Having said all of that, it would be foolish entirely to discount Boris the Booster's big idea.

Negativity certainly *does* act as a dead hand, quelling dynamism in the economy.

Johnson is right in his instinct that positive thinking, optimism — call it what you will — can be a hugely powerful force. Confidence is attractive and infectious. Optimism fuels the entrepreneurial spirit.

Boosterism can certainly work, providing there are sound economic underpinnings. As any businessman or woman will tell you, though, optimism must be underpinned with capital, know-how and a sound business plan.

There is a fine line between Boosterism and Woosterish — or Johnsonian — delusion.

Or to quote Wodehouse himself, in Jeeves In The Morning: 'It was one of those cases where you approve the broad, general principle of an idea but can't help being in a bit of a twitter at the prospect of putting it into practical effect.'

DAILY MAIL 30 July 2019

Daily Mail
TUESDAY, JULY 23, 2019 www.dailymail.co.uk 70p

D-DAY FOR BORIS

Today he's set for No 10. So can he emulate his hero Churchill and turn Brexit into HIS finest hour?

STEPHEN GLOVER: PAGE 18

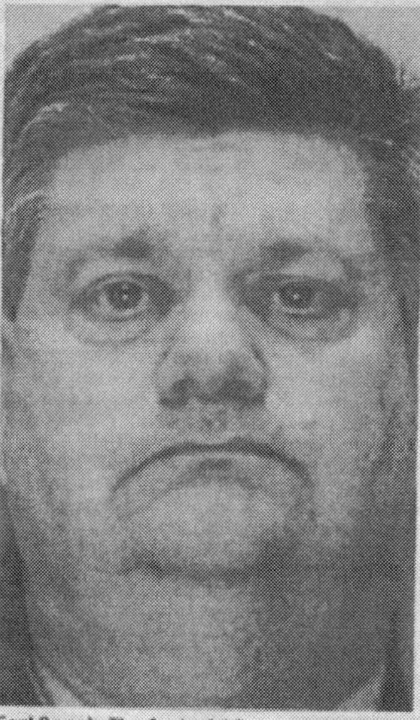

Carl Beech: The fantasist known as Nick

Aided by police, 'Nick' destroyed lives with sex abuse lies. Now he's been convicted of peddling a monstrous fantasy – as Labour's deputy faces calls to quit for his part in a...

Tom Watson: He has refused to apologise

PERVERSION OF JUSTICE

SCOTLAND Yard was in the dock last night for launching a VIP paedophile probe based on the serial lies of a fantasist.

By Stephen Wright and Glen Keogh

Carl Beech, also known as 'Nick', was convicted yesterday over outlandish allegations that led to a disastrous investigation in which homes were raided and lives ruined without a shred of evidence.

D-Day veteran Lord Bramall, 95, was among the victims and endured a police search and interview under caution.

Railing at the Yard's 'incompetence', the field marshal said it was ridiculous that the officers involved had managed to retire without facing any disciplinary action. He added: 'The police contributed to the perversion of justice. They didn't go out to pervert the course of justice but the way they handled uncorroborated evidence lent more credibility to Beech's statements than they deserved.'

Labour's deputy leader Tom Watson also faced calls to quit after meeting

Turn to Page 2

DAILY MAIL 23 July 2019

Continued from Page One

Beech, 51, in his Westminster office just months before he made his claims to Scotland Yard in late 2014. Mr Watson, who has refused to apologise, was accused of creating a 'moral panic' around alleged Establishment sex abuse.

Lord Bramall's son claimed that ex-Met chief Lord Hogan-Howe had indicated to his father that he didn't believe he was involved in the paedophile ring before officers raided his home but police were under pressure after the Jimmy Savile scandal. The former police chief denies this.

Former Tory MP Harvey Proctor, another victim of Beech's lies, said the bungled probe was 'a truly disgraceful chapter in the history of British policing'.

Mr Proctor, falsely accused of being a serial child killer, demanded a 'fully independent investigation' into what he called a 'rogue, malicious and apparently homophobic' inquiry. He also demanded an apology from Mr Watson.

Lincoln Seligman, godson of Ted Heath, who was also accused by Beech, said the impact of his 'ludicrous lies' had affected him, his family and friends of the late former prime minister very deeply.

'What I find astonishing is that

'Malicious and homophobic'

senior police officers in the Metropolitan Police and politicians like Tom Watson, and some elements of media, believed Beech and made frequent public statements to that effect,' he added.

'I and my family take great comfort from this verdict which makes clear beyond doubt that Sir Edward was always innocent of these wicked accusations.'

The scandal surrounding the VIP child sex ring case deepened after the police watchdog announced that not one officer involved in the Operation Midland inquiry would face disciplinary action.

At his ten-week trial for lying about the VIP child abuse gang, jurors heard that Beech told officers that he was used as a human dart board by the former heads of MI5 and MI6, that his dog was kidnapped by a spy chief, and that the paedophile ring shot dead his horse.

The court also heard that Beech is now a convicted paedophile after child porn offences came to light when an independent police force started investigating him on suspicion of making false allegations.

Yesterday – after deliberating for under five hours – jurors at Newcastle Crown Court convicted him of 12 charges of perverting the course of justice and one count of fraud.

In the wake of the verdicts:

■ Mr Watson remained defiant, saying it was not his role to judge whether Beech was telling the truth;

■ Two former journalists at defunct news website Exaro, which gave prominence to Beech's claims, faced demands to be prosecuted;

■ Scotland Yard said the phrase 'credible and true' to describe Beech was not discussed before it was said by a senior officer;

■ Legal sources said Beech could receive a sentence of between ten and 15 years;

■ New details emerged of how the paedophile fantasist went on the run in Sweden after being charged with child sex offences and lying about VIP child sex abuse.

Lord Hogan-Howe, who was in charge of the Met during the bungled inquiry, said the 'investigations of claims of historical child abuse were complex and of great public interest at the time'.

He added: 'There are clear lessons to be learned from this investigation which caused damage to those who were investigated. I also believe that damage was made worse by the publication of the suspects' identities before charge.

'In terms of my apology to Lord Bramall, I have a different recollection of this conversation which tried to convey why apparently incredible claims had to be investigated by the police.'

The Independent Office for Police Conduct said it had cleared three Met detectives following an investigation into how the force applied for search warrants in the case of Beech. IOPC interim director general Jonathan Green said: 'The allegations Nick made were grave and warranted investigation.'

Comment – Page 18

Vile lies of a pervert

SEE PAGES 8-15

Paedophile's NSPCC role saw him visit children as young as four

By **Glen Keogh** and **Simon Trump**

CONVICTED paedophile Carl Beech's astonishing level of officially-sanctioned access to young children can today be laid bare.

The fantasist, who admitted possessing indecent images of children of the 'gravest kind', has repeatedly sought access to young people.

As recently as 2017, Beech was able to visit children as young as four in primary schools on behalf of the NSPCC to speak about child abuse. As part of the charity's Childline service he delivered assemblies on how young people can stay safe online and in person.

The fantasist started in the role in November 2012, shortly after making his first bogus claims of abuse to police.

Beech's ties with children stretch back to at least 1993 when, as a 25-year-old married man, he specialised as a paediatric nurse on a children's ward at St Mary's Hospital in Paddington, London.

He later worked on a children's unit in Cheltenham, Gloucestershire.

By 2006, Beech had become chairman of governors at his son's primary school in Gloucester and incredibly he also became safeguarding representative. He was even interviewed by Ofsted, the education watchdog, during an April 2013 visit.

He went on to become vice-chairman of governors at a secondary school in the same area between 2014 and 2017.

During the trial, Beech's hypocrisy, given his own sexual interest in young boys, was described as 'breathtaking.'

The prosecution pointed to an incident in 2014 when Beech wrote to his counsellor about a teacher arrested on suspicion of gathering child abuse images similar to those he had been collecting. In an email, he said: 'I don't think I have been this cross before, it is a new feeling.'

Last night an NSPCC spokesman said: 'We severed all ties with [Beech] in February 2017', adding that it was a 'mutual' decision 'taken after he had been out of contact with us for some time'.

'We did not find out until February 2018 that he had been charged in connection with the possession and distribution of indecent images of children.'

Imperial College Healthcare NHS Trust, which runs St Mary's, confirmed Beech worked there in 1993 and 1994.

Clarifications & corrections

■ FOLLOWING an article on July 18 about Britain's biggest privately run care homes, we are happy to clarify that Dermot Desmond, JP McManus and John Magnier, Barchester Healthcare's long-term investors for over 20 years, have at all times acted in good faith in respect of Barchester's business. We have also been asked to point out that, since the Company's debt has been provided predominantly by its major shareholders rather than banks, the future of Barchester Healthcare is not 'uncertain' as our article may have implied. We apologise for any contrary impression given.

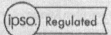

ipso. Regulated

■ *To report an inaccuracy, please email corrections@dailymail.co.uk. To make a formal complaint go to www.dailymail.co.uk/readerseditor. You can also write to Readers' Editor, Daily Mail, 2 Derry Street, London W8 5TT or contact IPSO directly at ipso.co.uk*

DAILY MAIL 23 July 2019

Daily Mail, Tuesday, July 23, 2019

Paedophile mummy's boy who got twisted sexual kicks from his wicked lies

Remarried: Charmian Beech

HIS VICAR MOTHER

by Paul Bracchi and Stephen Wright

CARL Beech was introduced to the world on a primetime BBC News bulletin in 2014 as a shadowy silhouette under the now infamous pseudonym 'Nick'.

He had a sensational story to tell. At the age of seven, he said, his own stepfather had farmed him out to paedophiles – and the paedophiles in question were among the most powerful and influential figures in society.

'Give me some idea of the kind of people,' he was asked during the interview. 'Military?'

'Yes,' he replied, his words spoken by an actor, 'others from law enforcement, the political establishment ...'

The abuse, he claimed, took place in hotels, apartments and private clubs around London, adding, chillingly: 'We weren't smuggled in under a blanket through the back door. It was done openly. They had no fear at all of being caught.'

Beech had given the Metropolitan Police the names of his abusers. He singled out former prime minister Edward Heath, ex-home secretary Leon Brittan and Harvey Proctor, once a Tory MP.

Two senior Army generals were also implicated along with the former heads of MI5 and MI6. Almost the entire top tier of the security establishment back in the Seventies and Eighties, in other words, were involved in the depravity that culminated, Nick claimed, in three ritualistic murders.

Mr Proctor, he said, had strangled a fellow victim in front of his very eyes, having first stabbed him with a penknife.

He was prevented from taking the penknife to the young Carl's genitals only by the intervention of the 'other [adult] male present'. That person was Heath.

At one point during his recorded testimony with officers from Scotland Yard, Beech broke down in tears. Surely, though, detectives should not have accepted at face value Beech's fantastical account without evidence to corroborate it.

There was none. Not now. Not then. Nevertheless, his story, they concluded in a formal statement, was not only *credible* it was also *true*.

The decision to believe him unequivocally resulted in a £2million, 16-month investigation (Operation Midland) which closed without a single arrest. By then reputations had been trashed, homes raided and lives ruined.

POST-SAVILE HYSTERIA

Beech ruthlessly exploited the hysteria of the post-Savile era when the country was gripped by collective guilt over the institutional failings that allowed the now notorious DJ to abuse at will.

It's still hard to believe he was taken so seriously for so long.

The irony is that the 'star witness' was himself a danger to children. At the time he was 'helping' detectives, he was viewing child pornography, making him a paedophile *and* a dangerous fantasist.

Money was one motivating factor in all this. Beech, now 51, was awarded £22,000 in criminal injuries compensation by falsely claiming he had suffered serious injuries as a result of having been sexually and physically abused as a child.

He also intended to make a living on the international 'survivor' speaking circuit. But the thing he craved most was attention. Going on TV, providing 'exclusives' for the now defunct – and disgraced – 'investigative' website Exaro, and working hand in hand with the police who praised him for his bravery, made up for the inadequacies in his own life.

Beech might have had a good job as a £45,000-a-year inspector with the Care Quality Commission, the independent health regulator, but he was a loner with no friends and a failed marriage.

Beech may have also been attempting to assuage the guilt of his own paedophilia by creating an alternative reality in which he was the victim.

The prosecution – and a leading psychologist who followed the case – are convinced this gave him a form of sexual gratification.

THE TEENAGE LONER

Either way, Beech's web of narcissism-driven lies would have been exposed at the very beginning – but for the wilful blindness of the Metropolitan Police. So, who is Carl Beech?

His mother Charmian, a community nurse (who became a Church of England vicar in 2001 after 37 years in the NHS) and his late father, a jeweller, separated when he was a baby.

Charmian remarried in 1976 when Carl was eight. Her new husband, Raymond Beech, was a major in the Royal Artillery; he was the person who is said to have begun abusing him, physically and sexually, after the family moved into officers' accommodation on an Army base in Wiltshire.

Raymond Beech was not a pleasant man. His Army records show he had a drink problem and was retired on mental health grounds after evidence came to light that he had been violent, not just to Charmian, but to a previous wife and a live-in lover. There is no suggestion whatsoever of sexual abuse, however. Major Beech died in 1995 when Carl was 27.

Mother and son settled in Kingston-upon-Thames, south-west London, where neighbours remember a 'big, well-built boy,' without many friends.

Contemporaries at school paint a picture of a mummy's boy who went plane-spotting on his own and loved horses and his English setter dog. It was on Coombe Hill in Kingston, that Beech would later say that he witnessed the hit-and-run murder of a boy he remembered only as Scott.

It was apparently carried out by members of the paedophile gang – or the Group as he referred to them – because Scott had disobeyed an order from his abusers. Funnily enough, there was no report anywhere of a boy going missing; not at the local police station, not at local schools, and not in the local paper.

On leaving school, where his attendance was exemplary, Beech worked briefly as an estate agent before following his mother into the nursing profession.

A SELFISH HUSBAND

He trained at the Royal Berkshire Hospital where he met future wife Dawn, also a nurse. They married in 1992; he was 24; she was 22. He then moved to St Mary's Hospital, Paddington, where – disturbingly – he worked on the children's ward. His career in paediatrics also took him to Swindon and the Great Western Hospital where he later took up a managerial post with the

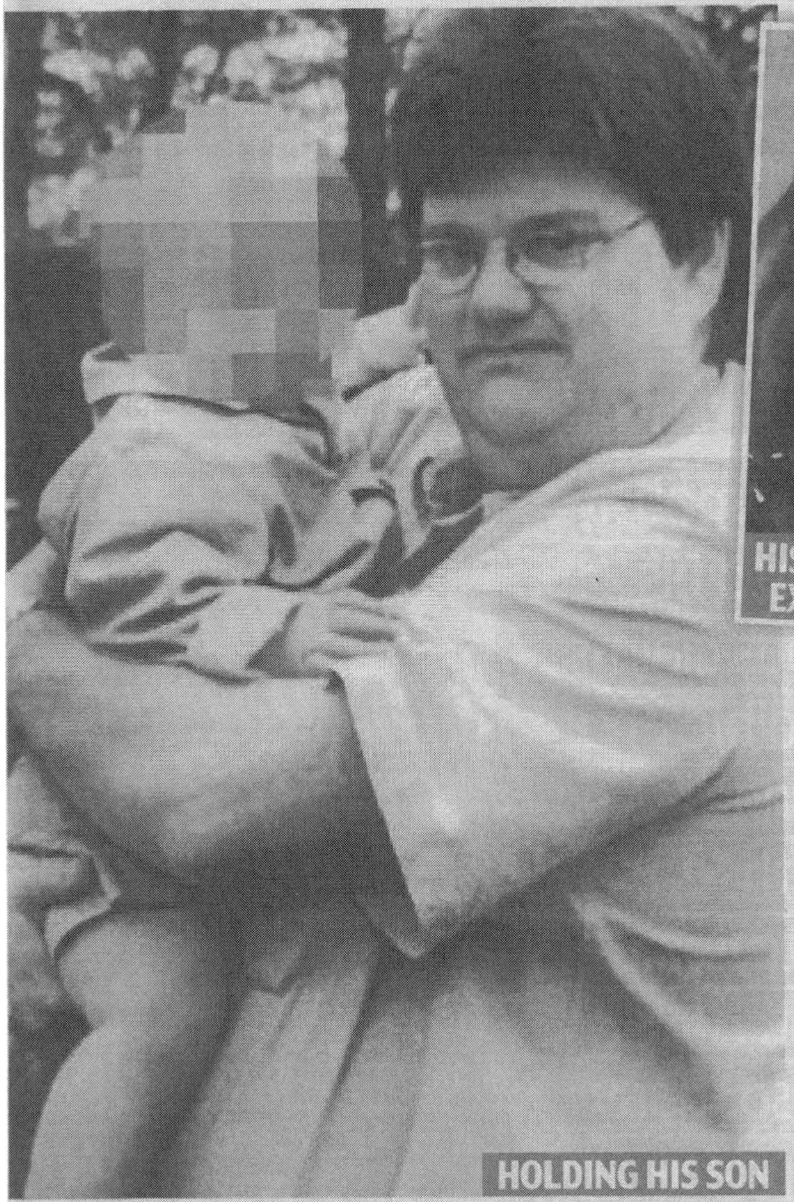

Father: Carl Beech with his son
Above: Former wife Dawn

Patient Advice and Liaison Service. He and his wife, who had now had a young son, rented a three-bed house in Gloucester. According to one relative Beech was 'selfish, controlling and mean'. 'He didn't speak very much,' said the relative. 'You had a job getting into any conversation with him.

'I don't think it was shyness. I think he thought he was a cut above us – intellectually superior. Dawn was so different. Happy, full of life, the complete opposite.

'I suppose she loved him in her own way. But they weren't a good match.'

His discontentment with his own life manifested itself in delusions of grandeur and a string of expensive purchases, including a luxury motor home (and later a Ford Mustang) which, at one point, left the couple with debts of around £70,000.

Beech visited the Southampton boat show every year and talked of flying lessons. There is one further telling detail to add about his marriage. 'He told Dawn he'd been abused by his stepfather,' revealed a family member.

'She believed him then but she doesn't now. But he never mentioned anything about being abused by VIPs or ritualistic murders.

'When we heard about the allegations years later we just laughed and thought "what a load of rubbish". His lies just got bigger and bigger.'

To everyone's astonishment, the marriage lasted 17 years. In 2012, the year their divorce was finalised, Beech started a new job with the CQC watchdog body.

More worryingly, given his recent exposure as a paedophile, he was from 2012 to 2017 a volunteer for the NSPCC's 'Childline schools service' – going into schools to deliver workshops and assemblies for children about the dangers of abuse and how to keep themselves safe in person and online.

MALEVOLENT FANTASIST

Savile had died in 2011 and the truth about his past had now emerged. Beech wasted no time in contacting Operation Yewtree – the investigation into the DJ led by Scotland Yard – and was referred to Wiltshire Police.

In his statement, he told how his stepfather had shared him among a group of paedophiles and one of them, he said, was Savile. But there was no mention of a VIP ring. After investigating his allegations, police took no further action.

Four months later, Beech submitted an application to the Criminal Injuries Compensation Authority as a victim of abuse.

He received £22,000 and used some of the money as a cash deposit on a brand new white convertible £34,000 Ford Mustang. Beech also started blogging about his childhood 'experiences' under the Twitter handle 'CarlSurvivor', writing poetry about his 'ordeal'.

The final few lines of one passage read: 'I'm taken upstairs, put on the bed/ Raped by each one of them, the sheets turn red/ It's the last one who helps me get clean/ But I'm still dirty, survivors know what I mean/ As a child this was part of my daily life/The hurt pain and terror and threat of the knife/.'

Not a whisper, though, of MPs or the involvement of M15 and M16.

Nor, initially, was there on the website he founded, RAVSCA (Raising Awareness for Victims & Survivors of Child Abuse) which brought him to the attention of 'investigations' website Exaro. Before Beech went to Exaro, remember, there was nothing in his online accounts – or his testimony to Wiltshire Police – which suggested that some of his abusers were MPs or men in the top echelons of the secret services.

An Exaro reporter helped him 'fill in the blanks' by showing him pictures of potential suspects; previously, he could only 'identify' two of his abusers (Savile and his stepfather). Now, hey presto, he had a list of 12. His dealings with Exaro produced a series of explosive front page exclusives for the Sunday People. The first was published in July 2014 under the headline: 'We Were Raped By MPs In Flats Near Commons'.

The second hit the news stands a few months later: 'Police Probe "Abuse" At MPs' Luxury Block.'

Exaro took their 'star source' to the Metropolitan Police who, unlike Wiltshire Police, took him seriously. Beech was given the pseudonym 'Nick' and Operation Midland was set up.

Beech now introduced the concept of a VIP ring in his blog. Not everyone took his 'revelations' at face value, however.

THE FIRST SUSPICIONS

One of them was Ian McFadyen, a survivor of childhood abuse, who said: 'I rumbled he was not what he seemed after he took a post I had written about the abuse I suffered, being raped over a bath at school by a master, and then presented it as his own only a few days later, except he had added an extra dimension of violence just for good measure.'

But Beech, or Nick as he was now widely known, continued to lap up the media interest, particularly his TV interviews with the BBC and other broadcasters when he appeared in silhouette with a disguised voice.

There is only so long, though, that such a high-profile murder investigation can be sustained without a shred of evidence. By September 2015 questions were beginning to be asked about the anonymous source fuelling the inquiry.

In a major article, which raised serious doubts about his account, the Mail summed up the growing disquiet: 'Nick: Victim or Fantasist?' Operation Midland was finally wound up in March 2016.

Eight months later, officers from Northumbria Police, the outside force brought in to investigate the fiasco, raided Beech's home in Gloucester.

They found more than 362 indecent images of children on three laptop computers, a USB stick, camera memory card – and an iPad left on the passenger seat of his Mustang parked outside. The names of the files recovered by police including: 'Man and two boys 12 years of age', 'Little boy and man' and '13-year-old with ten-year-old'.

CHILD PORNOGRAPHY

The filth was obtained on the 'dark web' with special software installed on one of Beech's computers. Police discovered he had also begun writing his memoirs, Too Many Secrets: Surviving a Child Sex Ring, under the pen-name Charles Chassereau.

There were striking similarities, it later emerged, between the 'experiences' described in his autobiography and an account of abuse contained in two books by an American author.

At Beech's home, the curtains remained drawn after the raid. 'His mother told us he had a breakdown,' said a neighbour. 'He cut a pretty sad figure. Then he was gone.'

While on bail, Beech fled to Swedish Lapland and hid out in a remote forest cabin, which he told neighbours he was renovating.

He gave his name as 'Anderson' to workmen employed to renovate the cottage before disappearing, owing them nearly £15,000.

CORNERED IN LAPLAND

A specialist fugitive unit in Sweden worked closely with Northumbria Police and the National Crime Agency to secure his extradition and arrest. He was sent back to Britain where he pleaded guilty earlier this year to making and possessing child abuse images – including 'some of the gravest kind' – as well as voyeurism for covertly filming a young boy.

Beech, who tried to blame his own son, was removed as a school governor and from the CQC.

During the prosecution opening at Newcastle Crown Court, where Beech stood trial for perverting the course of justice and fraud, Tony Badenoch QC said: 'The fact Carl Beech is a paedophile may help explain how he was quite so able and willing to conceive of, and then relay, to a captive audience such detailed and graphic stories of the sadistic sexual abuse of young boys at the hands of much older men.'

He got a sexual kick out of it, in other words.

Consultant clinical psychologist Roy Shuttleworth certainly believes this was the case. 'In one way or another I believe he gained sexual gratification from the stories he was telling which extended to him giving evidence in court. In my professional opinion, I think he got a thrill out of it.'

In his devastating critique of Operation Midland, published in November 2016, former High Court judge Richard Henriques identified 43 basic failings in the police investigation. But the very first, the most fundamental, was 'believing "Nick" at the outset'.

Finally, after leading detectives on a merry dance for 16 months, Beech has been held to account for his wicked lies.

But not a single officer has been disciplined. In fact, three detectives investigated over the debacle were allowed to retire before the Independent Office for Police Conduct had even concluded its inquiry.

Isn't this as grave a scandal?

Additional reporting: EMINE SINMAZ

DAILY MAIL 23 July 2019

Timeline of police fiasco

- Met backs claim that VIP abuse ring killed three boys — *December 19, 2014*
- I'M VICTIM OF A WITCH HUNT, SAYS ABUSE PROBE EX-TORY MP — *August 26, 2015*
- VIP ABUSE INQUIRY IS STARTING TO UNRAVEL — *September 5*
- NICK: VICTIM OR FANTASIST? — *September 19*
- WHY DID MET LET WATSON TAKE OVER? — *October 12*

INCREDIBLE

They infamously described his ludicrous claims as 'credible and true', and wasted 16 months and £2.5m trying to prove it. How COULD so many senior police be so gullible?

By **Stephen Wright**
ASSOCIATE NEWS EDITOR

Met chief: Bernard Hogan-Howe was rewarded with a peerage

QUITE simply, it has rewritten the rule book for shambolic police investigations.

Diabolical would be a more appropriate word to describe Operation Midland – the £2.5million inquiry into an alleged murderous, VIP paedophile ring involving a former prime minister, ex home secretary, one-time armed forces chief and heads of the security services.

Haunted by police failings in the Jimmy Savile case, obsessed with the idea that any abuse allegations should automatically be believed and under ferocious pressure from the likes of Labour deputy leader Tom Watson, officers abandoned common sense.

But as the rudderless investigation descended into a black comedy, it appeared detectives were auditioning for a 21st century revival of the Keystone Cops.

Imagine the scenes at the North Yorkshire home of former home secretary Leon Brittan where, just six weeks after his death, a line of officers did a fingertip search of his garden looking for signs of 'disturbed earth'.

Detectives searching this property and his London house later took away dozens of items for further investigation – including a

'Fingertip search of his garden'

Teletubbies video. In an excruciating 100-minute police interview, D-Day veteran Lord Bramall was asked if he could swim, if he ordered his accuser to eat his vomit, whether he chose to molest him on Remembrance Days and if disgraced TV presenter Savile was an accomplice.

If that wasn't bad enough, police calmly carried out a follow-up interview shortly after his wife of 66 years had died. Within days of receiving Beech's allegations, it should have been clear they were the work of an attention-seeking fantasist.

But detectives on Operation Midland took 370 witness statements, launched 1,700 'actions' and produced 1,860 documents. The inquiry involved a minimum of 20 police officers full time.

In November 2012, Beech contacted Metropolitan Police officers on Operation Yewtree, the force's umbrella investigation into spiralling claims against Savile and other celebrities.

His complaint was referred to Wiltshire Police and Beech was interviewed the following month, when he gave more details of supposed abuse by Savile, his late stepfather and others.

He made no mention of VIPs, recollections were sketchy, and he struggled to answer basic questions. In May 2013, the Wiltshire probe was shelved due to insufficient evidence. A file saying so was returned to the Met.

After being snubbed by detectives, Beech began blogging on the internet about his alleged child sex abuse. In August 2014 he appeared in silhouette and with a disguised voice in an obscure satellite TV documentary under a different name claiming he was abused by Savile.

By the time the programme was broadcast, Beech was also in contact with Mark Conrad, a reporter from a hitherto unknown investigations website, Exaro.

Beech now named Tory ex-MP Harvey Proctor as being among his tormentors. His growing allegations caught the eye of a detective from Scotland Yard's Operation Fairbank inquiry into alleged historic child sex abuse by politicians and other public figures.

By now Beech was using the pseudonym 'Nick' and had a bombshell tale to tell: he said he had witnessed the sadistic murder of three boys by various high-profile figures. In October 2014, Beech provided Detective Sergeant James Townly with a list of 12 alleged abusers, including Lord Bramall, Sir Edward Heath, Lord Brittan, Mr Proctor, Labour peer Lord (Greville) Janner, ex-MI5 boss Sir Michael Hanley and ex-MI6 chief Sir Maurice Oldfield.

Police should not have taken such a list seriously – especially given Beech had made no mention of VIPs two years earlier. The decision not to check against Wiltshire Police files was a major blunder.

But they did take him seriously, almost certainly as a consequence of a new policy directive issued in November 2014, when Her Majesty's Chief Inspector of Constabulary Sir Tom Winsor stated that 'the presumption that a victim should always be believed should be institutionalised'.

Deputy Assistant Commissioner Steve Rodhouse, perhaps smarting from overseeing a bungled previous inquiry into Savile, formally opened an investigation and briefed senior officers, including Yard chief Sir Bernard Hogan-Howe and Assistant Commissioner Patricia Gallan.

Within months of the probe commencing, a leading criminal psychologist was warning that Beech was very likely to be a fantasist.

The basic detective's rule of 'assume nothing, check everything' was thrown out of the window in December 2014 when Detective Superintendent Kenny McDonald held a press conference at Scotland Yard to describe allegations made by 'Nick' as 'credible and true'.

At that point officers hadn't interviewed a single suspect, didn't know who the alleged murder victims were, and hadn't found a body. Sources claim Yard chiefs were so concerned about 'undermining victim confidence' in the police that they decided against asking Beech for permission to look at his computers and electronic devices.

Had they done so, they would established very quickly that he had carried out internet research to identify his victims and fabricate his story, and downloaded appalling child porn including images of children being raped.

It should not have taken long to establish that Heath and Mr Proctor were sworn enemies, yet Beech suggested that they were part of the same paedophile ring.

The suggestion that Sir Michael kidnapped Beech's dog as a warning to comply with the abuse gang's wishes was similarly outlandish.

Mr Proctor firmly believes that the fantasist effectively ended up running Operation Midland: calling the shots, putting pressure on

Off the case, detective who said VIP abuse claims were 'credible'
October 20

VIP ABUSE INQUIRY: WAR HERO CLEARED
January 16, 2016

NOW SAY SORRY TO HOUNDED HERO
January 18

HUMILIATION OF THE YARD
March 22

NOW PUT VIP ABUSE 'FANTASIST' IN DOCK'
November 9

AND UNTRUE

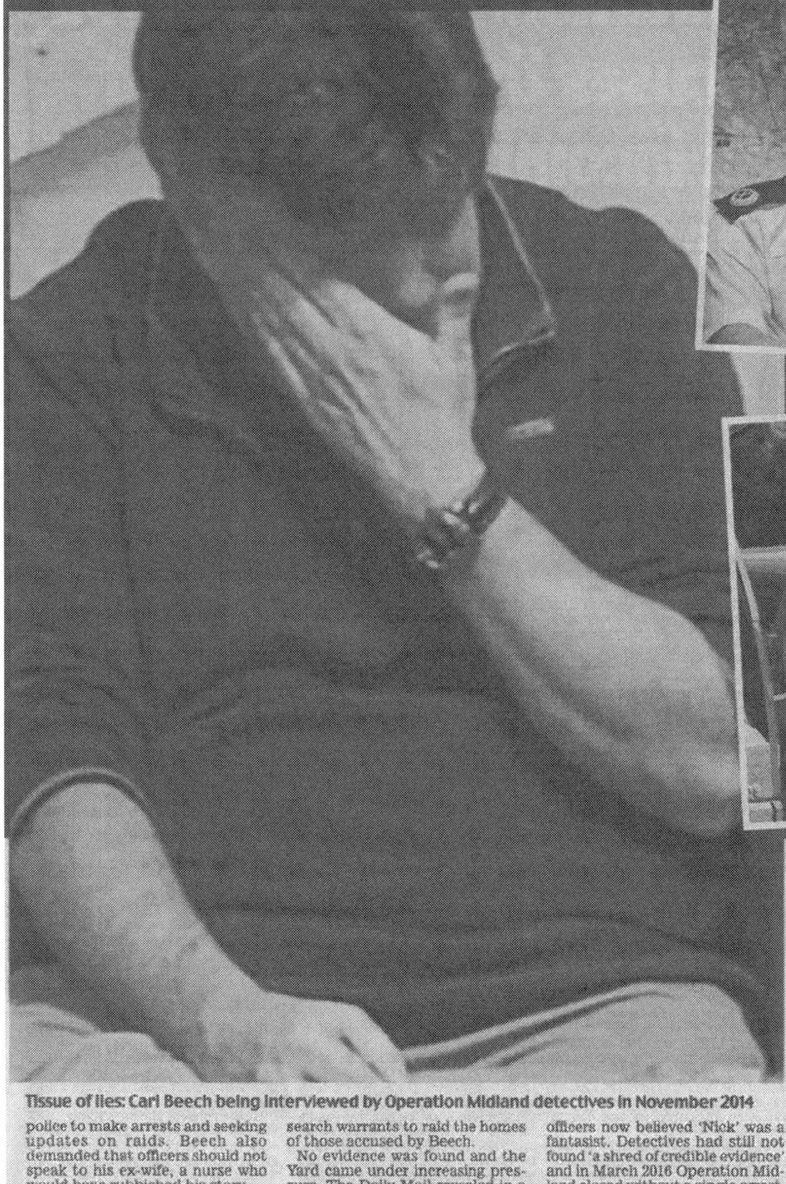

Tissue of lies: Carl Beech being interviewed by Operation Midland detectives in November 2014

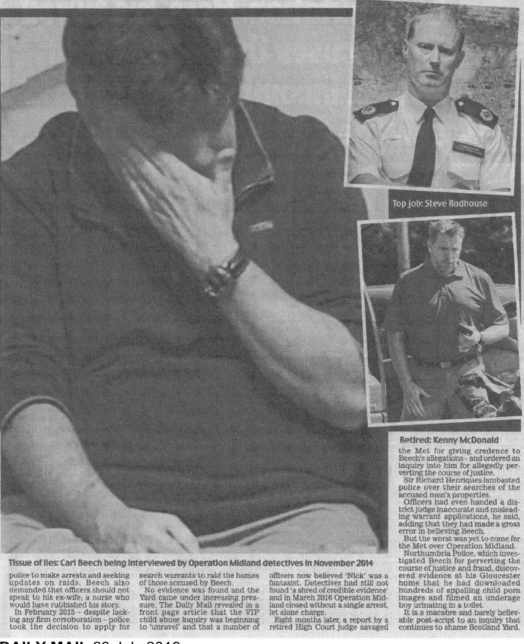

Top job: Steve Rodhouse

Retired: Kenny McDonald

police to make arrests and seeking updates on raids. Beech also demanded that officers should not speak to his ex-wife, a nurse who would have rubbished his story.

In February 2015 – despite lacking any firm corroboration – police took the decision to apply for search warrants to raid the homes of those accused by Beech.

No evidence was found and the Yard came under increasing pressure. The Daily Mail revealed in a front page article that the VIP child abuse inquiry was beginning to 'unravel' and that a number of officers now believed 'Nick' was a fantasist. Detectives had still not found 'a shred of credible evidence' and in March 2016 Operation Midland closed without a single arrest, let alone charge.

Eight months later, a report by a retired High Court judge savaged the Met for giving credence to Beech's allegations – and ordered an inquiry into him for allegedly perverting the course of justice.

Sir Richard Henriques lambasted police over their searches of the accused men's properties.

Officers had even handed a district judge inaccurate and misleading warrant applications, he said, adding that they had made a gross error in believing Beech.

But the worst was yet to come for the Met over Operation Midland.

Northumbria Police, which investigated Beech for perverting the course of justice and fraud, discovered evidence at his Gloucester home that he had downloaded hundreds of appalling child porn images and filmed an underage boy urinating in a toilet.

It is a macabre and barely believable post-script to an inquiry that continues to shame Scotland Yard.

Officers escape sanction

NOT one police officer will face misconduct proceedings over the disastrous £2.5million inquiry into Carl Beech's allegations.

Five officers were referred to the Independent Office for Police Conduct over fears they failed in their 'duties and responsibilities'. But last night it confirmed that no one on Operation Midland or those who supervised it would face any disciplinary action.

In any event, three detectives retired before the inquiry concluded – including senior investigating officer Detective Superintendent Diane Tudway.

Two further officers, Det Supt Kenny McDonald, who described Beech as 'credible and true', and Deputy Assistant Commissioner Steve Rodhouse were cleared of misconduct in March 2017.

This was despite a scathing 2016 report into Operation Midland by retired High Court judge Sir Richard Henriques who identified 43 separate blunders.

However he absolved then Metropolitan Police Commissioner Sir Bernard Hogan-Howe and his Assistant Commissioner Patricia Gallan, who had oversight of Operation Midland, of any blame.

Bizarrely, Mr McDonald's now infamous 'credible and true' comments, which critics said prejudiced Operation Midland, were not even examined by watchdogs. He retired with an estimated £250,000 pension pot weeks before the Beech trial.

Mr Rodhouse is now a £175,000-a-year director general at the National Crime Agency. Miss Gallan retired last year with an estimated £400,000 pension. Mrs Tudway was promoted to superintendent and retired on the eve of Beech's trial.

Detective Sergeant James Townly, who conducted around 20 hours of interviews with Beech, now works in counter-terrorism. Sir Bernard was given a peerage.

DAILY MAIL 23 July 2019

Aged 21, Lord Bramall led a platoon onto the Normandy beaches and rose to head our Armed Forces – only for the claims of a fantasist to shatter his reputation. Here, his furious son accuses the ex-Met chief of rank incompetence that saw the father he adores...

THROWN TO

by Rebecca Hardy

A FEW weeks ago, Field Marshal Lord Bramall, a man of impeccable character who has served this country with distinction in war and in peace, asked his son Nicolas: 'I'm not a bad chap, am I?

'Dad puts on a very brave face but what he's going through internally — I'm not sure,' says Nicolas. 'There's been a lot of suffering and I don't think that should be underestimated.

'Look, I don't want to make out Dad's a shrinking violet. He's not. He's as tough as they come, but the longer this monstrous business has gone on…' He shakes his head part in anger, part sadness.

'I find it mind-boggling the police could have got it so wrong. They took the word of a complete fantasist and threw Dad — a man who's been a wonderful servant to this country — to the wolves without a single piece of evidence.

'I think this has affected him more the longer it's gone on. The very fact you've been so publicly accused of paedophilia, rape and torture when it's absolute rubbish is enough to finish anybody, isn't it? The trial has been particularly hard for him.'

Lord Bramall did not attend the ten-week trial, where Carl Beech, persisted in making outrageous slurs against the war hero, and which ended yesterday, with Beech being convicted of 12 counts of perverting the course of justice, and another of fraud.

For Lord Bramall was not well enough to endure appearing at the trial. When I met this delightful old soldier 18 months ago, he needed sticks to walk owing to a degenerative neurological condition. Now he is wheelchair bound.

'Our concern was that this might not be sorted before he dies. It has dragged on and on,' says Nicolas. 'We hoped Nick/Carl Beech, whatever his name is, would plead guilty. Instead he's had such a platform for his poison. It doesn't help a 95-year-old chap, does it? When we last saw Dad he was quite emotional.

'He started going through the story all again: "The police came to the door. I greeted them. I thought it was a security issue, maybe a threat or something."'

Lord Bramall was having breakfast with his frail wife Avril, who was suffering with Alzheimer's disease, at his home in Hampshire when police knocked on his door on March 4, 2015.

More than 20 officers in white overalls spent ten hours examining every inch of the house, leaving with an old visitors' book and copies of two speeches Lord Bramall had made, one to Sandhurst cadets and another about a fellow Army commander.

'They went behind every picture in the house — every picture. They ripped the place apart,' says Nicolas. 'There was a busload of police in white suits. My parents live right in the middle of the village. They weren't being subtle.

'Most of the officers went down the pub for lunch and it wasn't long before the local paper got onto Dad.

HOGAN-HOWE [Sir Bernard Hogan-Howe who was Met Commissioner at the time] actually came down to see Dad twice. He said from very early on he'd never really believed Dad had been involved, but the police were under such pressure, after the Jimmy Savile scandal, to show no-one was above the law.

'That was the key to this: it doesn't matter who they are or what they've achieved, we'll get them. They were absolutely seduced by the idea that they had a top-level paedophile ring.'

Nicolas's disgust is writ large upon his face. The very suggestion his father was involved in a VIP paedophile ring with, among other prominent men, former Prime Minister Sir Edward Heath, ex Tory MP Harvey Proctor, former head of MI5 Michael Hanley, former head of MI6 Maurice Oldfield and former Home Secretary Leon Brittan would be laughable, if it wasn't so downright devastating.

'The trouble with all allegations, particularly paedophilia, is it sticks, doesn't it? It's just such an overwhelmingly awful thing.

'Once it's out there you can't bring it back and people believe there can't be any smoke without fire. I've even had a few letters — nasty letters — from people saying he's as a guilty as…' The sentence tails into a furious silence.

'The question I've always asked myself is this: here's this chap who has accused a prime minister, a home secretary, the head of the British armed forces, the head of MI5 and the head of MI6.

'Surely to God when this came up old Hogan-Howe or someone would have said, "Hang on a minute. Let's look at this bloke."

'If only for self-preservation you'd think they'd think, "Before we start raiding these houses, we really need to be certain that this chap is who he says he is."

'But they didn't make sure. They took his story and ran with it. Nobody thought to look on his computer, look into his life or interview his wife. They just couldn't wait to get stuck into Dad.'

A thoroughly likeable man who shares his father's sense of humour and passion for cricket, Nicolas, 66, loves his father 'hugely'.

It is why he is speaking now. 'I've agonised how best to support him. I feel angry about it. I'm his son. I feel I should stand up and be counted. We need to draw a line under this business. Dad was always there for us [Nicolas has a sister, Sara] whenever he could possibly be. He was a hard act to follow, but the great thing he said to me was, "I don't mind what you do Nick, but try to do it well."'

Nicolas is a successful landscape gardener and lives in Dorset with his second wife, Pip. The past four years have, he says, 'been hell' for his father and hugely upsetting for his family, which includes Nicolas's son Alexander, 40 — a talented fashion photographer who photographed Princess Eugenie's wedding last year — and his 38-year-old daughter Charlotte, who between them have five children.

WHEN the police were rummaging through Dad's house, they actually said to my sister, who was there, "Are you happy for him to see your grandchildren?"' Nicolas looks truly outraged, as well he should.

'This is a man who has achieved just about everything you could possibly achieve in one life. He was captain of the Eton [cricket] XI, he was a boxer, a very good artist — he had two pictures in the Royal Academy at the age of 16.

'He landed in Normandy at the age of 21 in charge of a platoon, was wounded twice. He fought his way through Holland towards Berlin, won the Military Cross. He got to the top of the forces, was made a Knight of the Garter. He had a lovely wife, never let his kids down. There was never a whiff of scandal — not men, women, boys or corruption. He's just been a wonderful public servant.

'But he's been dragged through four years of hell because the police are basically incompetent.

'That's the bottom line. They were totally incompetent.

'They overreacted and got it spectacularly wrong and Dad and other people — Dad's family, Lady Brittan [Lord Brittan's widow] — had to pay the price.'

Alexander, who's particularly close to his grandfather, would like to see Nick 'take a long walk off a short pier'.

Nicolas adds: 'I've often said to Dad, "Aren't you p****d off with Nick?" He always replies: "No, it's the Met. They've made a complete arse of the whole thing."

He's tried to keep his sense of humour but…'

Nicolas leans forward in his armchair. 'Do you know the thing that hugely bothers Dad? When he's dead his great-grandchildren will Google him — or 'goggle' him as he puts it — and all of this will come up. This is what really upsets him. In future years, when people do military research, there'll be all this stuff about these heinous crimes. You can't get rid of it, can you? It's there for ever.' Nicolas was at work when his wife Pip was called by a distressed Lord Bramall that March morning.

'He was upset,' she says today. 'He said the police had raided his house, and were there now. They were going through everything and he wasn't allowed to move. He said he'd been accused of something involving a minor 40 years ago but they wouldn't say what it was.

Picture: TONY HARRIS/PA

Military legend: He led the Army and our Armed Forces

Supportive: Nicolas with his parents Edwin and Avril Bramall — whose lives were broken apart by the false claims

Long career: In the Home Guard at 17

THE WOLVES

Incredulous: Lord Bramall during his police interview

Mum was very confused. It was so unpleasant for her.

'As police went through the house, she was sort of shunted from one room to another.

'She knew something was wrong, but wasn't quite sure what it was. It affected her quite badly. Do you remember she used to say, "What have I done, what have I done?"'

Pip turns to her husband who nods. 'It was so upsetting,' he says. Nicolas was 'shocked, absolutely shocked', when, after being unable to reach him on his mobile, Pip went to tell him at work. 'Dad is the least sort of paedophile man you could meet. I felt complete shock. We needed to support him.

'The Bramalls closed ranks. From day one we were all in this together. I never doubted him for a second.'

Lord Bramall's lawyer badgered the Metropolitan Police for details of the accusations against him.

Shamefully, he was kept waiting until April 30, almost two months after that first traumatic raid, and was then interviewed under caution by a detective constable. The allegations were so preposterous — paedophilia, torture, rape — he ended up banging the table.

Beech alleged his stepfather Major Ray Beech sexually abused him and took him to Lord Bramall's office in Erskine Barracks, Wiltshire, in 1976 when he was in charge of the UK land forces.

'Some of the abuse was supposed to have taken place at a pool party, so Dad was asked if he could swim. He said he jolly nearly had to at Normandy.

'The interview was conducted by a detective constable. You'd think interviewing a Field Marshal you'd get one of your heavyweights in, wouldn't you?

'The questions were so banal. Dad ran rings round him. At one point, Dad said something like, "Did he tell you I was circumcised?" 'The detective constable looked at his notes, saw nothing there, so asked, "Are you?" Dad said, "I'm not telling you." Nicolas chuckles, but in truth there has been little to laugh about in the past four years.

'You've met Dad. He's not someone who would run away from the sound of a gun, but when you're accused of heinous crimes like that, it's a very lonely place,' he says. 'It takes a lot of courage when all these allegations are out there to stand up and show your face. He didn't want to cause embarrassment to anybody.'

So much so Lord Bramall offered not to attend that June's high-profile Order of the Garter service where recipients of this, the oldest British order of chivalry, gather at Windsor for lunch with the Queen, followed by a service at St George's chapel.

'He was encouraged to go and I think the Queen was very glad he went. Dad's never shied away. He's always looked people in the eye.

'All his peers have been very supportive. His aides-de-camp went en masse to the police and said, "This is ridiculous." A lot of them appeared in court. They had gatekeepers at his office at the barracks signing people in and out.

'The thought of a major bringing his son to the commander of the British Armed Forces and saying, "Help yourself. I'll pick him up in a couple of hours," was ridiculous.'

A second police interview took place in July 2015 at Lord Bramall's home. By now, his wife of 66 years was terribly ill. He worried about missing a moment of the precious time they had left together. As it was, she sadly died before that interview.

'I believe this whole thing very much affected her,' says Pip. 'She sensed all this chaos and all these changes around her when what she needed was a quiet predictable life.

'They were devoted to each other. To have died with all this going on...' Pip is truly distressed by her mother-in-law's suffering. It was ten months before officers leading the now utterly discredited Operation Midland finally told Lord Bramall there was 'insufficient evidence' to charge him.

'There was never evidence of any form,' says Nicolas. 'Nothing. Just this man's word and the police fell for it hook, line and sinker, but they wouldn't put their hands in the air, say "We've got it wrong" and clear Dad's name.

'An apology did eventually come [in October, 18 months after the raid], but it was fairly mealy-mouthed. 'I was always saying to Dad, "This is awful". I was perhaps more indignant than him in the beginning. He'd say, "If you've landed on the beaches of Normandy, you've been through worse than this." But I don't think he'd say that now.

'Since the trial began he's endured a bombardment of unpleasant accusations — rape, torture, paedophilia. Nick's persisted in the accusations against Dad in a lot of detail.

'It makes me so angry.

'Dad's achieved just about everything any man could possibly achieve in life. It should be his sort of pipe and slipper time to relax and be proud of all he's done.

'Instead, he now gets quite watery-eyed and keeps saying, "I'm not a bad chap, am I?"'

'Dad? A bad chap?' Nicolas repeats disbelievingly. 'He's a good guy.' He is.

DAILY MAIL 23 July 2019

Labour No 2 told: Quit as MP for your smearing of the innocent

Hysteria: Watson is accused of fuelling a moral panic

By Glen Keogh

TOM Watson was last night told to quit as an MP as he was accused of fuelling a 'moral panic' and a climate of Establishment hysteria over child sex abuse.

The Labour deputy leader met Carl Beech in his Westminster office just months before he made his outlandish claims to Scotland Yard in late 2014.

The following year Mr Watson personally met a Metropolitan Police detective sergeant to discuss Beech's fantastical claims following an initial phone discussion, it can now be revealed.

Last night, Mr Watson was slammed by victims of Beech's lies and accused of furthering his own career by making political capital out of their misery.

Daniel Janner QC, son of the late Labour peer Greville Janner, called on Mr Watson to resign and criticised him for taking the 'moral high ground' against anti-Semitism in the Labour Party, having helped smear innocent men as paedophiles.

Former MP Harvey Proctor, who Beech accused of murdering a child, called on Mr Watson to apologise.

But, in a 1,400 word statement last night, Mr Watson refused to apologise to victims of Beech's allegations and sought to defend himself, saying it was not his role to judge whether victims' stories were true. Referring to Beech by the pseudonym he was using at the time of their meeting, he said: 'I encouraged every person that came to me to take their story to the police and that is what I did with Nick.'

Mr Watson's direct role in the Beech case began in 2014 when he welcomed the former health worker to Westminster, knowing he had made allegations, including the murder of a child by members of an Establishment paedophile ring.

The pair spoke 'at length'. Mr Watson would later be described by Beech as being part of a 'little group', alongside a journalist from the now-disgraced investigative news website Exaro and a retired social worker, who helped him 'put my information out there'.

'Whipped up a public frenzy'

Shortly after this, Beech contacted the Metropolitan Police with his lurid claims.

The MP initially retained a degree of scepticism. He said: 'What I'm certain of is that he's not delusional. He is either telling the truth, or he's made up a meticulous and elaborate story. It's not for me to judge.'

His role, he would later say, was to offer 'Nick' 'a degree of protection' to make his allegations. Mr Watson had been basking in the praise he received for helping to expose the tabloid phone-hacking scandal which ultimately led to the closure of the News of the World.

In 2012, as the row over the late Jimmy Savile's paedophile crimes raged, he intervened during Prime Minister's Questions with the headline-grabbing statement that there is 'clear intelligence suggesting a powerful paedophile network linked to Parliament and No10'.

Mr Watson had been contacted by self-styled abuse 'whistleblower' Peter McKelvie – also part of Beech's 'little group' – who said he had evidence of a paedophile ring.

On his own admission, the Labour MP now found himself receiving an 'avalanche' of historic child sex abuse complaints from alleged victims.

Months before meeting Beech, Mr Watson spoke to a woman who said she had been abused by the former home secretary Lord Brittan. Mr Watson wrote to Alison Saunders, the Director of Public Prosecutions, complaining that the peer had not been interviewed by Scotland Yard over an alleged 1967 attack. In fact, police had already concluded there were no substance to the allegations made by a woman known as 'Jane', a Labour activist suffering from mental health issues.

When Lord Brittan died in early 2015 under a cloud of accusations, Mr Watson traduced the former peer when he could no longer defend himself.

Repeating an unsubstantiated quote from a 'survivor', he wrote that Lord Brittan was 'as close to evil as a human being could get in my view'.

There was never any evidence to back up the claims and Mr Watson apologised to Lady Brittan in late 2015. He later admitted he had let his self-appointed status as child abuse campaigner take over his life.

Last night barrister Mr Janner, added: 'His motive was personal political advancement riding on a bandwagon of public frenzy which he had whipped up.'

Defiance of the pair who 'peddled lies'

'Masquerade': Mark Watts (left) and Mark Conrad

JOURNALISTS behind the disgraced investigations website that peddled paedophile fantasist Carl Beech's lies should be prosecuted, one of his victims said last night.

Harvey Proctor called for an investigation into the senior figures behind Exaro, including Mark Watts, the site's former editor-in-chief, and Mark Conrad, a reporter who accompanied Beech to his police interview after showing him 42 images of potential 'abusers'.

Exaro – now defunct – produced a string of 'exclusives' on the existence of a paedophile ring operating in Westminster, largely based on the testimony of Beech. Mr Proctor said: 'Mark Watts and Mark Conrad [were] masquerading as journalists... they reported manufactured and manipulated information.'

Yesterday Mr Watts insisted that Beech's convictions were unsafe.

Mr Conrad, a friend of Labour deputy leader Tom Watson, was interviewed by Northumbria Police at his home over three days earlier this year regarding his dealings with Beech.

He admitted he had doubts about Beech's allegations, but insisted: 'I have nothing to apologise for.' Exaro closed down in 2016.

ONE prominent individual was conspicuous by his absence when the paedophile con-artist formerly known only as 'Nick' was convicted at Newcastle Crown Court of perverting the course of justice by making false and malicious allegations of sex crimes and murder against a series of high-profile public figures.

We would never have heard of the man whose real name is Carl Beech had it not been for Labour's deputy leader Tom Watson, the self-appointed Nonce Finder General. I have maintained all along that Watson should have been in the dock alongside Beech.

Seven years ago he embarked on a vicious vendetta, smearing Conservative politicians and other Establishment figures as kiddie-fiddlers and serial rapists, without a single shred of hard evidence.

Watson was Beech's enabler and cheerleader, using this evil fantasist's farrago of fabrications as a nuclear weapon in his seek-and-destroy mission, defaming leading Tories by accusing them of some of the most disgusting crimes imaginable.

His disgraceful behaviour has ruined the lives of distinguished public servants and their families. Watson's victims included not just former Tory treasurer Lord McAlpine but ex-Home Secretary Leon Brittan and the war hero Lord Bramall, ex-head of the Armed Forces.

In 2012, two years before he discovered 'Nick', Watson hid behind Parliamentary privilege to claim there was a 'powerful paedophile network linked to Parliament and No 10'.

Watson made wild, unsubstantiated allegations of sex abuse at a North Wales children's home, which sparked a media frenzy and emboldened soppy Sally Bercow, the Speaker's wife, to name Lord McAlpine on Twitter as one of the guilty men.

McAlpine was wholly innocent and successfully sought redress for defamation from Bercow and broadcasters stupid enough to repeat and embellish these false allegations.

HE WAS not in the best of health when these vile accusations surfaced and died just over a year later. Who can tell whether this disgraceful assault on his reputation hastened his death?

While Watson hadn't named McAlpine, he might just as well have led a torch-lit procession along Whitehall, burning effigies of top Tories.

That's why I dubbed him The Nonce Finder General.

The McAlpine scandal didn't, however, give him pause for thought. Soon he was back in the saddle, flaming torch in hand, widening the scope of his Inquisition.

Watson wrote to the then Prime Minister David Cameron, suggesting that organised abuse of children may have taken place in Downing Street during the Thatcher years.

Menacingly, he charged that anyone counselling caution about these claims was a 'friend of the paedophile'.

It was a classic case of trying to attribute guilt by association.

When Nick fell into his lap in 2014, Watson worked closely with a so-called (now discredited and defunct) 'news' agency, one of whose reporters conveniently showed Nick pictures of prominent figures to help him identify his 'abusers'.

Watson badgered the police and the Crown Prosecution Service to investigate. Brittan and others had their homes raided and were interviewed under caution, though never charged.

According to the Labour-supporting Sunday Mirror, Watson said he had been in contact with someone who alleged a former 'top minister in Margaret Thatcher's government' had 'regularly abused boys'. After Brittan died, without

DAILY MAIL 23 July 2019

Daily Mail, Tuesday, July 23, 2019 Page 15

LITTLEJOHN

richard.littlejohn@dailymail.co.uk

Labour's Deputy championed the cause of fantasist 'Nick' — the malignant mud-slinger behind a vicious vendetta. LITTLEJOHN'S withering verdict...

NOW PUT WATSON IN THE DOCK

his name having been cleared (even though Scotland Yard had concluded months earlier that he was entirely innocent), Watson continued to repeat allegations that the former Home Secretary was guilty of multiple child rapes.

He also claimed to have spoken to a man and a woman who said they had been raped by Brittan. My suspicions were aroused when it was revealed that the woman in question was a Labour activist with mental health problems.

At one stage the Yard, still smarting from their failure to nick Jimmy Savile while he was still alive, appeared to be taking their marching orders directly from Watson. Under the Home Secretary Theresa May's favourite Plod, Commissioner Bernard Hyphen-Howe, the police set up the heavy-handed, over-zealous, ruinously expensive Operation Midland, which mounted dawn raids, dragged the reputations of innocent men through the mud and left their families distraught.

Midland was eventually wound up ignominiously without a single arrest being made.

The Met even declared that the most lurid, and indeed ludicrous, allegations were both 'credible and true' — despite Nick's claims being a pack of lies.

This shameful miscarriage of justice was egged on by a credulous Mother Theresa herself. She pronounced Watson's allegations as 'just the tip of the iceberg' and ordered a full-scale Paedos In High Places public inquiry be established. This is still lumbering on and could last for many more years, costing at least £100 million.

In the process, innocent civilians became collateral damage — none more so than a young couple who had the misfortune to live in the same property as former Tory MP Harvey Proctor, another Conservative figure who found himself in the frame. During a police raid on Proctor, they were told that if they didn't vacate the premises immediately, their three-month old daughter would be taken into care. The Old Bill had even taken along a social worker with a child's car seat.

I'm not going to name them again, because they've suffered enough. But everyone involved in this witch hunt should be thoroughly ashamed of themselves.

All of this madness, all this tyranny, all this outrageous abuse of police power, all this waste of taxpayers' money, all this misery inflicted on blameless men and their families, can be laid at the door of Watson. Yet the man himself has never been called to account, and even after yesterday's verdict on Nick, remains shamelessly unrepentant.

Incredibly, he is now being touted in the political world as the saviour of the Labour Party, a voice of moderation prepared to take on Jeremy Corbyn and his cohort of anti-Semites.

Ever since Watson shed an entire forest of timber and bought a new wardrobe — something which, I'm told, generally happens when formerly married men take up with a woman half their age — some sections of the media have been carrying laudatory profiles of him, apparently oblivious to his previous.

His opportunist public criticism of Labour's endemic anti-Semitism is at odds with the fact that Leon Brittan, one of his principal targets, was one of this country's most prominent Jewish politicians.

And he seems not to have been troubled by the fact that the false allegations against Brittan first surfaced in the 1980s and were discredited by none other than Left-wing investigative journalist Paul Foot, who maintained they were motivated by, er, anti-Semitism in the security services.

Then there was Watson's bromance with anti-Press campaigner Max Mosley, son of Fascist leader Oswald Mosley, who gave Watson a £540,000 donation — money Watson refused to return even after the Mail exposed his benefactor's dubious, racist past.

THIS is also a man who wants to shackle our Free Press, bringing it under State control, yet has no compunction about using his own position and Parliamentary privilege to peddle false allegations of hideous crimes against his political opponents.

It's also forgotten — or conveniently overlooked — that while Watson refuses to accept the legitimate result of the EU referendum in which 'only' 52 per cent voted Leave (and is leading demands for a second People's Vote), he was elected as Labour's deputy leader with just a cigarette paper-slim 50.7 per cent share of the vote.

I haven't heard anyone suggesting that particular vote should be re-run, least of all Watson himself.

So we can add ocean-going hypocrite to the list of charges against him.

All this explains why, unlike the Boys In The Bubble, I'm not buying in to the reinvention and sanitisation of slimline Tommy Watson, the previously obese MP who once spent so much of his parliamentary expenses on food at Marks & Sparks they gave him a free pizza wheel.

I stand by my earlier assessment of Watson as mad, bad and dangerous, a malignant mud-slinger, utterly unfit for high office, who conspired to exploit a fantasist to promote his ghastly politically-motivated crusade.

We now know that 'Nick', aka Carl Beech, is himself a serial paedophile, guilty of the very crimes which he falsely accused other, innocent men of committing.

Of course, the great irony in all this is that the one nonce the Nonce Finder General failed to expose was Nick the Nonce, sitting right under his nose.

LITTLEJOHN'S COLUMN RETURNS ON FRIDAY

DAILY MAIL 23 July 2019

Daily Mail
COMMENT

Don't let disloyalty destroy the new PM

BY the time you read this column, or very soon afterwards, we will know the identity of the United Kingdom's next Prime Minister, bringing to an end a protracted Tory leadership contest.

And it's no exaggeration to say his mission is the most daunting of any Downing Street incomer since at least 1979 – arguably since 1940.

The country is angry, fractious, and deeply divided over Brexit – some because it hasn't happened yet, others because it's happening at all.

Theresa May tried valiantly to heal the schism, with a withdrawal deal that was both pragmatic and honourable.

Ultimately it was savaged in the Commons, bringing her premiership to a humiliating end. She deserved better.

So can her replacement succeed where she failed, or will he also be broken on the Brexit wheel?

The omens aren't encouraging.

Overwhelming favourite Boris Johnson has pledged to take Britain out of the EU by October 31, with or without a deal.

But how? He has little or no working majority and militant forces are ranged against him on all fronts.

In Brussels, they say there can be no re-opening of the withdrawal agreement, and no change to the Irish backstop – the rock on which Mrs May's deal foundered.

Yet the intransigence of the EU may prove a minor obstacle compared with the backstabbing and wrecking tactics of MPs at home. And not just from opposition parties.

Already several Tory ministers are threatening to resign if Mr Johnson wins, in protest at his declaration that No Deal must remain on the table.

Some will see this as a principled stand. Others as an act of treachery.

The party membership has just selected its new leader, but before he's even in place, the rebels are trashing their decision.

Outgoing Foreign Office minister Alan Duncan even called for a no confidence vote in his own government. Could there be more flagrant disloyalty?

If the party is to move forward – indeed to survive at all – it must strive at every level to find consensus.

Let's assume that Mr Johnson has indeed won. Yes, he's gaffe-prone and sometimes appears anything but the *homme serieux* Britain needs at this critical time.

But for all his flaws, he is a remarkable individual – clever, engaging and deeply patriotic. Is it just possible that he could solve the backstop conundrum and untie the Brexit knot?

The Irish are beginning to fret about No Deal and may be ready to compromise. Perhaps Mr Johnson can pull off a miracle.

One thing is certain, however. Without the full support of his party, he is doomed to fail. The rebels must take a long hard look at themselves and ask whether they really want the likely consequences of that failure – Prime Minister Corbyn and Chancellor McDonnell – on their conscience.

A grotesque fiction

EXPLOITING the moral panic that followed the Jimmy Savile scandal, Carl Beech concocted a grotesque fiction about a supposed VIP child-sex ring.

It was promoted by a now defunct news website, fuelled by the BBC, swallowed whole by a pathetically gullible Scotland Yard and manipulated for political motives by Labour's deputy leader Tom Watson.

Of those maliciously accused, Lord Brittan was hounded to his grave, and elderly Field Marshal Lord Bramall had his home ransacked and his good name smeared.

Beech is now bound for prison, where he belongs. But why has no one else – no police officer, no accomplice or accessory, and certainly not Mr Watson – been punished for allowing this outrage to happen?

If we are to learn from this appalling miscarriage of justice, the guilty must be held to account.

Just like his hero Churchill, Boris is rackety, feckless and gaffe-prone. But this could also be HIS finest hour

by Stephen Glover

TODAY, barring accidents, Boris Johnson will be pronounced the winner of the Tory leadership contest. Tomorrow afternoon, he will be driven to Buckingham Palace, where he will kiss hands with the Queen. He will be Prime Minister.

Like his hero, Winston Churchill, he has lived all his adult life yearning for this prize. Like his hero, he has been written off countless times. And, like his hero, he assumes power at a critical moment in our history.

The dangers are obviously not as great as they were when Churchill became PM on May 10, 1940, with the humiliating evacuation of Dunkirk and the capitulation of France, Britain's main ally, only weeks away. But they are bad enough.

Flawed

Britain is divided and isolated. We are being driven mad by Brexit. One might almost say that, although Churchill's task in 1940 was enormous, at least he knew what he had to do. It is hard to see how any politician can lead us out of the mess we're now in and bring our country together again.

Can Boris save us? Or will he be driven ignominiously out of No10 in months, even weeks? Like many, I ask myself these questions constantly. And I must admit — again, I suspect, like many people — that there is no easy answer. But I hope.

One way to weigh Boris's weaknesses and strengths is to strip away the layers of gilt that have been lovingly applied to the figure of Churchill and to see the magnificent wartime leader for the flawed human being he was.

I don't suggest that Boris is remotely equal to his hero. But when considering our new Prime Minister's failings (which have been catalogued by his many detractors), it is comforting to recall that Churchill also came to the highest office bearing a long charge sheet.

He had been responsible for the Dardanelles fiasco in World War I, in which nearly 50,000 Allied lives were lost. His stint as Chancellor of the Exchequer in the Twenties was a near disaster.

Always his judgment was being impugned: over his bigoted opposition to virtual home rule in India in the Thirties, and his rash championing of Edward VIII during the 1936 abdication crisis when public opinion was firmly against the King marrying American divorcee Wallis Simpson.

It's true that, by 1940, Churchill's political career stretched back over four decades, whereas Boris's has been much briefer, and so he has had less scope for political gaffes. Still, he managed to pack in quite a few during his two-year spell as Foreign Secretary.

In his biography of Winston Churchill, Boris describes the great man as 'eccentric' and 'over the top' — words that could as well be used of himself. 'Rackety' would be another way of describing what they have in common.

Unlike Boris, Churchill had no appetite for extra-marital sex, but he drank much more prodigiously. He was far more feckless with money, though he earned even greater amounts as a newspaper columnist.

In May 1940, many in the parliamentary Tory Party regarded the country's new leader as flashy, unreliable and lacking in judgment. Rab Butler — then a junior minister and, much later, very nearly Prime Minister — described Churchill as 'the greatest adventurer of modern political history' and 'a half-breed American'.

Sound familiar? My point is that Churchill has been deified, and so his faults and all the rude things said and thought about him by members of his own party, as well as by Labour, have been airbrushed out. Might Boris also succeed despite being written off by nearly half the country and *bien pensant* intellectuals?

There is another similarity. In May 1940, Winston Churchill was opposed by a knot of conspirators in his own party, such as Lord Halifax and Rab Butler, who wanted to put out feelers to Hitler via the Italian leader Benito Mussolini and sue for peace. His most deadly adversaries were on his own side.

And so it is with Boris. The Tory Party is in disarray. All discipline has broken down. Philip Hammond has petulantly said he will resign as Chancellor to avoid being sacked, while Boris-hating Sir Alan Duncan childishly quit his job as a Foreign Office minister in the midst of a worsening international crisis involving Iran. Where is duty?

Meanwhile, Iain Duncan Smith, who, in a couple of days, could be Deputy Prime Minister in a Johnson administration, publicly accuses the Government — and, by implication, Jeremy Hunt, Boris's rival and Foreign Secretary — of a 'major failure' over its Iran policy.

Respect

Actually, the treachery within the Tory Party is even more rampant than it was in May 1940, when many MPs who were suspicious of Churchill at least showed a measure of respect for their new leader and were prepared to give him a chance.

Sir Alan Duncan has tried to table an emergency Commons motion on whether Johnson should become Prime Minister. Fortunately, he was rebuffed by Speaker John Bercow, who was sensible for once in his life.

Despite this setback, ultra Conservative Remainers (perhaps including erstwhile Eurosceptic Mr Hammond) may try to bring down Boris even before he starts talking to the EU.

An iron rule of politics is that voters abhor divided parties. A decisive early vote of No Confidence in Boris is almost bound to precipitate a general election, in which the Tories would be viewed as a fractious rabble who failed to honour the Leave vote in the referendum.

One difference between then and now: in May 1940, Churchill formed a coalition with Clement Attlee's Labour Party, whereas Boris will confront Jeremy Corbyn, whose only concern is to achieve power so that he can unleash his Marxist experiment on Britain.

Ambition

Does our new Prime Minister have the political guile, force of personality and greatness of spirit to see off these threats and find his way through a bewildering maze to reach a reasonable accommodation with Brussels?

It is certainly a tall order. So it would be even for Winston Churchill, who, after all, proved himself a disappointing peacetime leader after he was returned to office in 1951.

But Boris, facing as he does the most perilous state of affairs that has bedevilled any prime minister since Churchill in 1940, can reasonably take comfort in the knowledge that his hero was prematurely written off by critics later forced to eat their words.

Maybe he will rise above the pygmies planning to bring him down. For all his faults, he has one striking advantage that he definitely shares with the wartime leader. He has craved the highest office in the land since he was a child.

All-encompassing ambition is rare, even in leading politicians. It amounts almost to a mystical sense of personal destiny. Churchill certainly had it. He wrote later of that moment in May 1940: 'I felt as if I were walking with destiny, and that all my past life had been but a preparation for this hour and for this trial.'

Such rare men are difficult to stop. Is Boris one of them? I don't know. But it seems to me his obsessively wanting to lead our country probably constitutes the best hope we have that he will make a decent job of it.

DAILY MAIL 23 July 2019

As Lord Bramall dies at 95, not one of the detectives who hounded him over false sex abuse claims has been punished

Ordeal: Lord Bramall's home was raided by police

THE HERO WHO DIED WITHOUT JUSTICE

THE war hero hounded by police over false child abuse claims has died without a single officer being held to account.

By **Stephen Wright**
Associate News Editor

The final years of Lord Bramall, who was wounded in the D-Day landings, were ruined by Scotland Yard's disgraceful inquiry. Indulged by incompetent police, a wicked fantasist nearly ruined the reputation of the infantryman who rose to head of the Armed Forces.

The field marshal's home was raided on the uncorroborated word of 'Nick', real name Carl Beech, and he was subjected to a humiliating 100-minute interview under caution. Beech was jailed for 18 years in July but Lord Bramall, who was 95, said police should have been in the dock too.

He accused Scotland Yard of perverting the course of justice and of raiding his home for public relations

Turn to Page 4

DAILY MAIL 13 November 2019

Continued from Page One

reasons. His wife of 66 years was terminally ill when 20 officers carried out the search in 2015.

In his last newspaper interview in July he said he was investigated for almost a year even though the then head of the Metropolitan Police, Bernard Hogan-Howe, knew he was innocent.

A harrowing victim impact statement penned by the peer – spelling out how Beech's lies and Scotland Yard's shocking inquiry into them had wrecked his life – was read out at Newcastle Crown Court as his accuser was sentenced.

Last night the widow of former Tory home secretary Leon Brittan, also falsely accused of child sex abuse by Beech, led tributes to Lord Bramall.

Lady Diana Brittan said: 'I got to know [him] in difficult circumstances but he was a truly remarkable man and he became a close friend. He faced a great many challenges in his later life but, even in his nineties, he had a great strength of character that carried him forward and supported those around him.

'He was a deeply compassionate individual who was totally devoted to serving his country, both as a soldier and as a public servant.'

Lord Bramall died at home a few days after being released from hospital, where his health had declined sharply in recent weeks. He lived to see the 100th anniversary of the Armistice Day celebrations on Monday.

Under pressure from Labour's deputy leader Tom Watson, Scotland Yard officers led by former Met deputy assistant commissioner Steve Rodhouse took Beech's lies seriously and ruined Lord Bramall's final years.

After Operation Midland closed without any arrests or charges in 2016, the war hero received a belated apology from the Met and £100,000 compensation.

Last night Met commissioner Cressida Dick, who endorsed the launch of Operation Midland and has admitted errors of her own in overseeing the early stages of the inquiry, said she was 'very sad' to hear of Lord Bramall's death.

'I met him recently to apologise personally for the great damage the Metropolitan Police investigation into Carl Beech's false allegations has had on him and his family,' she said last night.

'It was very humbling to be in his company and hear first-hand his experience. He was a great man, a brilliant soldier and leader, and much loved family man. He was a true gentleman and will be hugely missed.'

In his impact statement, Lord Bramall

'Brilliant soldier and leader'

wrote: 'Of course, it is a matter of public record that the Metropolitan Police apologised to me for their conduct towards me and the then commissioner stated that I was innocent of the allegations against me. Despite this, mud sticks.'

His death will reignite the row over the 'whitewash' report by the police watchdog which cleared five Operation Midland officers of misconduct – four of whom were not even interviewed in person.

Sir Bernard, who as Met chief oversaw the shambles, has been made a peer; Mr Rodhouse has been promoted to head of operations at the National Crime Agency; and Diane Tudway, who was in day-to-day charge of Operation Midland, was promoted to superintendent while under investigation for alleged misconduct and retired from the force

Retired High Court judge Richard Henriques wrote a scathing article in the Daily Mail this summer about Operation Midland, alleging that police had broken the law to search the homes of the war hero and other VIPs.

In a second article in October, Sir Richard attacked the 'flawed' Independent Office for Police Conduct inquiry into the five officers, highlighting 'gross and inexcusable delays'. In 2016 he wrote a report identifying 43 major errors in £2.5million Operation Midland.

Paying tribute to Lord Bramall, chief of the defence staff General Sir Nick Carter said: 'He was a remarkable soldier who served our country with great bravery and dedication over many decades, inspiring his many subordinates, and overseeing significant change as a chief of staff that we still benefit from today.

'We will all miss his wisdom, his generosity and his rifleman's lightness of touch.'

Comment – Page 18

DECORATED BY MONTY

Honour: Field Marshal Montgomery pins on his Military Cross in 1945

PROUD BESIDE THE QUEEN

Distinguished position: Watching the VJ Day

HOU A FA

Before he was twice. He went Forces. Yet Lord Carl Beech's swallowed by

by Robert Hardman

SHORTLY after landing on the D-Day beaches in June 1944, Lieutenant Edwin Bramall was on his way back home again. A German 88mm field gun had opened up on his company's flank near the village of Maltot, killing many of his comrades. Bramall was the only survivor in his immediate group and was so badly wounded that he had to be evacuated back to England and thence to a hospital in Edinburgh.

Just five weeks later, however, he was back in the thick of the action in Normandy only to be wounded and hospitalised again, this time with shrapnel in his shoulder. A mere three days later, he had discharged himself and was leading his platoon into action once more. And he had not even come of age.

Towards the end of 1944, young Bramall spent his 21st birthday in a snow-covered Belgian slit trench, celebrating the fact that he had just been awarded the Military Cross for his assault on a forest infested with German snipers and mortars. He fought on into Germany, witnessed the horrors of Belsen concentration camp and ended the war in Hiroshima where he saw, at first hand, the aftermath of atomic warfare.

Yet, for all these experiences – the like of which few of us could possibly imagine – nothing would prove as wounding as an attack that came towards the very end of his life.

At least Field Marshal Lord Bramall KG GCB OBE MC, who has died at the age of 95, has gone to his Maker safe in the knowledge that the man who tried to destroy him with fabricated accusations is now behind bars and wholly discredited.

It was just a pity that he did not survive to see the police officers behind this monstrous ordeal brought to justice, too.

'Dwin' Bramall, devoted husband, father and grandfather, was one of the outstanding military figures of the last century.

He not only rose to the very top of the Army – just in time for the Falklands War – but went on to direct national defence strategy, run umpteen national organisations and reshape conventional military thinking with a sharp, original, questing brain.

Yet none of this mattered a jot when a demented fantasist and serial liar known as 'Nick' – real name Carl Beech – made a series of ludicrous claims about child abuse at the hands of an Establishment cabal

One of the names on Beech's list was Lord Bramall.

Equally staggering was the extent to which credulous, box-ticking Metropolitan Police high-ups – urged on by the former deputy leader of the Labour Party Tom Watson and embarrassed by the unchecked paedophilia of the late Jimmy Savile – gave Beech credence.

They even called his claims 'credible and true', despite a manifest lack of substance. It remains a saga with terrifying implications for all of us. In March 2015, a team of officers from the Met swooped on the Bramalls' Hampshire home unannounced and ransacked it.

It was an especially harrowing experience since the field marshal was also caring for his wife of 66 years, Avril, who was suffering from Alzheimer's.

The police found nothing. Seven weeks later, he was interviewed for two hours, at the end of which the police remained as clueless – literally – as they had been after the raid. With exquisite tactlessness, the police summoned him to a second interview just days after Avril's death. It proved equally futile.

Yet, it was not until the following year that Scotland Yard finally conceded that they had found nothing to go on. So, Avril died never knowing for sure that her husband was entirely blameless of these repulsive charges.

It was a further ten months before the Met Commissioner, Sir Bernard Hogan-Howe, finally deigned to apologise – and only then after a sustained campaign by family supporters, the Daily Mail and a deeply sympathetic public.

It later transpired that the Met had paid a substantial six-figure sum of damages for its ineptitude. Yet no amount could atone for the hurt felt by a great servant to his country.

In July, as Beech finally received a hefty 18-year prison sentence for his monstrous lies, Lord Bramall issued a lengthy statement via his solicitor. He had been dismayed by the impact of the police raid on his sick wife and also the reverberations around a tiny rural village.

The 20-strong police squad had made sure that everyone knew exactly what they were up to at the Bramalls' home, especially when some of them adjourned to the local pub for lunch.

Under interview, he wrote, the officers had failed to give him details of the claims against him. He was too modest to add that he was interviewed by such a junior policeman that the entire process had to be repeated, not that it yielded any further information. For this was a witch-hunt devoid of a witch.

As Lord Bramall told the court, he felt grievously let down by a nation for which he had risked everything. 'Above all what, really upset me is this,' he wrote. 'My record of public service speaks for itself. In service of my Queen and Country I have done all that has been required of me.

'I have suffered both physically

iversary parade

GRILLED BY DETECTIVES

WITH HIS LOVING FAMILY

Quiz: A still from his police interview, aged 91, and (right) with his late wife and son

NDED BY NTASIST

21 he'd survived Normandy – on to the very top of our Armed Bramall died still scarred by ludicrous accusations that were police... who remain unpunished

'NICK', HIS ACCUSER

Lies: Beech, initially known only as Nick, was eventually jailed for perverting the course of justice in July

and emotionally as a result and did so without regret or complaint. I thought I could be hurt no more. I can honestly say however I was never as badly wounded in all my time in the military as I have been by the allegations made by 'Nick'.

These are devastating words for a police force still desperately trying to bury one of the most ignominious chapters in its history.

Despite the Met's grudging apology, Lord Bramall warned, 'mud sticks'. He was particularly distressed that some of his descendants might look up their ancestor on the internet 'and instead of seeing that which I achieved, find out about that which I was accused of.' He concluded: 'For those of us that have climbed the highest, we face the greatest fall.'

'Dwin' Bramall climbed to the top in so many regards. With a peerage and two knighthoods – including a Knight of the Garter, Britain's oldest order of chivalry – he was a trusted confidant of the Royal Family.

I well remember attending the 50th anniversary commemorations of VE Day where Lord Bramall was about to welcome the Queen to Hyde Park in his capacity as Lord Lieutenant of Greater London. He had noticed that one of the spurs on his uniform was coming loose and was mortified.

Then he had a bright idea. He asked if one of the photographers in the press pen might have a toolkit and an obliging snapper got down on all fours to whack the errant spur back into place, for which the field marshal was profusely grateful.

He was clearly cut out for success at an early age. It was just a question of what sort of success. His father's family had once been prosperous cotton traders – distantly related to the Tory prime minister Robert Peel – but the money was running low by the time Edwin was sent to Elstree prep school and then to Eton.

There he excelled at cricket, scoring the winning run in the 1942 Eton-Harrow match, and also at art. At the age of just 16, he had two paintings accepted for the Royal Academy's summer exhibition.

Bramall was deemed well up to scratch for university entrance to Oxford but, by then, war had intervened. Commissioned in to the King's Rifles (later the Green Jackets) in 1943, he served with the regiment through one bloody battle after another right across Europe until the German surrender in May 1945.

He was then assigned to the airborne forces preparing for the invasion of Japan, only to be spared that grim prospect by the atomic bombs which landed on Hiroshima and Nagasaki.

Bramall later reflected that he had witnessed not dissimilar destruction in Hamburg, as well as the horrors of the Nazi concentration camp at Belsen; they were all images that would remain with him for life.

With the war over, he was finally offered that place at Oxford but, instead, opted to remain in the

Turn to Page 6

DAILY MAIL 13 November 2019

Daily Mail
MONDAY, OCTOBER 7, 2019 www.dailymail.co.uk 70p

WORLD EXCLUSIVE

ELTON

How mum tried to spoil the happiest day of my life

'ME' – the rock memoir the whole world's talking about

SEE PAGES 14-17

EXCLUSIVE
By **Stephen Wright**
Associate News Editor

JUDGE BLASTS 'NICK' POLICE WHITEWASH

Fury at watchdogs who cleared officers of misconduct in sex abuse fantasist case

THE police watchdogs who cleared five 'Nick' scandal detectives are savaged by a former High Court judge today.

Richard Henriques says 'no effective interrogations' were carried out during the 'flawed' inquiry by the Independent Office for Police Conduct.

Calling on Home Secretary Priti Patel to take action, he expresses alarm at the watchdog's 'lack of knowledge of criminal procedure'.

In an article in today's Daily Mail, Sir Richard accuses the agency of 'gross and inexcusable delays' in a 'lamentable and inadequate' inquiry.

His bombshell comments come as the IOPC prepares to publish a report explaining why it exonerated the officers involved in a disastrous VIP child sex abuse probe.

Sources familiar with the dossier call it a 'disgraceful whitewash' – 'sloppy, partial and full of errors'.

Sir Richard, who spent several

Turn to Page 2

DAILY MAIL 7 October 2019

Now Trump faces new whistleblower

US President lashes out as crisis grips White House

Mail Foreign Service

THE White House was plunged into further crisis yesterday after a second whistleblower came forward as part of the impeachment investigation into Donald Trump.

The case involves an alleged security breach in a telephone call between Mr Trump and his opposite number in Ukraine, which occurred last month.

He had reportedly tried to push Volodymyr Zelensky into 'digging up dirt' into his potential opponent in next year's election, Joe Biden.

Mr Trump last night heard there are 'multiple whistleblowers' lining up to point the finger at him. The second whistleblower is also from the US intelligence community, according to their lawyer Mark Zaid. He said the individual had 'first-hand knowledge' of Mr Trump's dealings with Ukraine – sparking rumours it is somebody within Trump's inner circle.

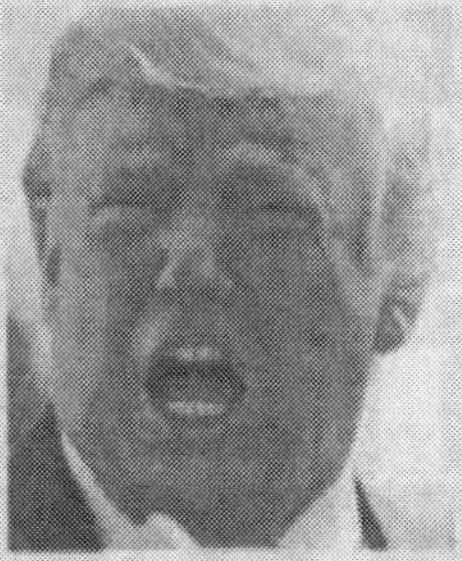

Furious: Mr Trump

The lawyer also represents the first whistleblower who filed a complaint about the July 25 phone call between Mr Trump and Mr Zelensky.

As a result, leading Democrat Nancy Pelosi launched formal impeachment proceedings on September 24.

A senior figure in Mr Zaid's firm, Compass Rose Legal Group, said there were in fact 'multiple' whistleblowers.

Andrew Bakaj said on Twitter: 'I can confirm that my firm and my team represent multiple whistleblowers in connection to the underlying August 12, 2019, disclosure to the Intelligence Community Inspector General.'

Rather than hide away, a typically bullish Mr Trump asked China to investigate Mr Biden's son Hunter on Friday.

This second appeal to a foreign government saw the knives come out for Mr Trump from his own party, with Republican governor Mitt Romney calling the President's appeal 'brazen and unprecedented', as well as 'wrong and appalling'.

But yesterday, Mr Trump reiterated on Twitter his wish to see a probe into the Biden family. He said: 'It is INCREDIBLE to watch and read the Fake News and how they pull out all stops to protect Sleepy Joe Biden and his thrown out of the Military son, Hunter, who was handed $100,000 a month (Plus,Plus) from a Ukrainian based company, even though he had no experience in energy, and separately got 1.5 Billion Dollars from China despite no experience and for no apparent reason.

'There is NO WAY these can be legitimate transactions? As lawyers & others have stated, as President, I have an OBLIGATION to look into possible, or probable, CORRUPTION!'

'Brazen and unprecedented'

There is no evidence of any wrongdoing from either Joe or Hunter Biden. No details have yet been released about the second whistleblower's claims.

Mr Biden, whose son Hunter sits on the board of a Ukrainian oil company that has faced corruption allegations, is the favourite Democrat to run in next year's election.

In a Washington Post article, released Saturday, Mr Biden accused Mr Trump of 'frantically pushing flat-out lies', in the hope it would 'undermine my candidacy for the presidency... Enough is enough.'

Continued from Page One

months investigating Scotland Yard over Operation Midland before demanding five officers face a misconduct probe, also reveals that the IOPC waited 20 months before taking a statement from him.

He says the official who belatedly contacted him 'readily conceded her lack of relevant education, training and experience'. He stresses that the woman, who the Daily Mail has decided not to name, should not be made a scapegoat for the serious failings in the case.

Instead he directs the blame higher up the organisation which is led by Michael Lockwood, an accountant who headed a suburban London council.

Last week the appalling failures of what is now considered to be one of Scotland Yard's most disgraceful investigations were laid bare when Sir Richard's damning 2016 report on Midland, previously heavily redacted, was published.

It documented how officers made 43 major errors and wasted £2.5million probing bogus claims of VIP child abuse and murder by Nick – the convicted paedophile Carl Beech who is serving 18 years for perjury and other offences.

Yet Steve Rodhouse, the officer who oversaw the shambles, remains in his £240,000-a-year job at the National Crime Agency. Sir Richard's scathing commen-

JUDGE'S ATTACK
PAGES 8-9

tary in the Mail today will make uncomfortable reading for Miss Patel, who has faced calls to set up a rigorous, fully independent investigation into the conduct of blundering detectives.

There have been repeated demands for Mr Rodhouse, described as an 'embarrassment' by a Home Office official, to be removed from his job. Also caught up in the affair is Met Commissioner Cressida Dick, who oversaw the setting up of Midland in November 2014 and who has refused to answer questions from the Mail about her role.

The IOPC's decision to exonerate all five officers looked even more extraordinary last week following the publication of Sir Richard's report. It revealed that Mr Rodhouse thought parts of Nick's account may have been fabricated yet still kept to a strategy of declaring publicly that police believed him.

Geoffrey Robertson QC, who is representing Harvey Proctor, a Tory ex-MP who was falsely accused by Nick, said the Henriques report revealed that 'Operation Midland was conducted incompetently, negligently and almost with institutional stupidity'.

In his article today, Sir Richard says that he finds 'it difficult to conceive that no misconduct or criminality was involved by at least one officer' on the 16-month inquiry, which ended without any arrests or charges.

He concludes by warning: 'Maintenance of law and order depends upon the effective oversight of those invested with power. Who guards the guards themselves? A malfunctioning police force has not received the necessary oversight.'

Comment – Page 18

Clarifications & corrections

All our journalists observe the Editors' Code of Practice and the Mail is a member of the Independent Press Standards Organisation (IPSO). We aim to correct any errors as promptly as possible.

■ *To report an inaccuracy, please email corrections@dailymail.co.uk.*

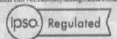

ipso. Regulated

To make a formal complaint go to www.dailymail.co.uk/readerseditor. You can also write to Readers' Editor, Daily Mail, 2 Derry Street, London W8 5TT or contact IPSO directly at ipso.co.uk

WHERE'S CRESSIDA?

Pressure grows on Yard Commissioner after her failure to publicly face music over VIP sex abuse scandal fallout

By **Stephen Wright**
Associate News Editor

DAME Cressida Dick is under mounting pressure to make a full statement about her role in the bungled VIP child abuse inquiry after ex-High Court judge Sir Richard Henriques said watchdogs should have interviewed her about it.

In today's damning Mail commentary, Sir Richard insists the Scotland Yard chief should have been quizzed about her knowledge of the case.

His remarks came as criticism intensified over Dame Cressida's role following Sir Richard's scathing report into her force's handling of the VIP sex ring allegations.

Yesterday the Sunday Telegraph quoted a senior Government source as saying: 'It's clear that the report raises serious questions about leadership, yet the public have heard very little from Cressida Dick on this, which has worried people in senior levels of the Government.

'There are concerns that she has washed her hands of this.' The criticism was fuelled when the full humiliating details of Sir Richard's 2016 report on Operation Midland were released on Friday and it was Dame Cressida's deputy, Sir Stephen House, who made a Press statement about the case and fielded questions.

Pressure: Dame Cressida Dick

The Metropolitan Commissioner was at an annual memorial service for a murdered police officer elsewhere in London but sources pointed out that it was her force's decision to release the report on Friday morning.

Dame Cressida was an Assistant Commissioner in charge of specialist crime and operations in the Met in October 2014 when 'Nick' – real name Carl Beech – was interviewed at length about outlandish allegations he made.

He claimed the heads of MI5 and MI6 used him as a human dartboard and that D-Day hero Lord Bramall fraternised with Jimmy Savile and ordered him to eat his own vomit.

He also falsely alleged former prime minister Ted Heath and ex-Home Secretary Leon Brittan were in a gang that murdered three boys.

Dame Cressida oversaw the setting up of Operation Midland under Deputy Assistant Commissioner Steve Rodhouse in November 2014, and was also in post a month later when a senior detective described Nick as giving a 'credible and true' account.

Scotland Yard confirmed Dame Cressida was not interviewed by Sir Richard as part of his 2016 investigation into Operation Midland.

He was not made aware of her crucial role overseeing the early stages of the investigation, as she had left to join the Foreign Office by the time he was commissioned to write his report. She rejoined the Met later.

Her name did not feature in his report and her involvement overseeing Operation Midland was not widely known until last month when the Daily Mail revealed it. Commenting on the police watchdog's inquiry into Operation Midland officers, Sir Richard writes today: 'Emails between officers should have been examined. DAC Rodhouse's immediate superiors – Assistant Commissioner Cressida Dick and her successor Patricia Gallan – should have been interviewed about their roles in the investigation, the briefings they received and their responses.'

A Met spokesman confirmed she had received briefings on the operation. Former Tory MP Harvey Proctor, who was falsely accused of serial murder by Beech, 51, has alleged Dame Cressida neglected her duty. MPs on the home affairs committee have indicated they want to question her.

10 questions this officer must answer

EX-YARD Deputy Assistant Commissioner Steve Rodhouse was in charge of the disastrous sex abuse probe sparked by fantasist Carl Beech, also known as 'Nick'. Today he has a top job at the National Crime Agency after he was cleared in four months by police watchdogs without even being interviewed. Here are the questions ex-judge Sir Richard Henriques says he SHOULD have been asked...

1 Why did you not read either Carl Beech's police interviews or his blogs, and how was it possible to accurately assess his credibility without considering them?

2 Why did you agree with Det Supt Kenny McDonald in saying that 'if asked we will say that we do believe Nick (Beech)' when neither of you had met Beech or read his interviews and blogs?

3 Why on that same day did you write in a log that a full investigation was required to establish Beech's credibility?

4 Having concluded that it was inappropriate for Mr McDonald to have used the words 'credible and true' to publicly describe Beech's allegations, what steps did you take either immediately or thereafter to correct his error?

5 Did you consult or communicate with your immediate superior at the time, Assistant Commissioner Cressida Dick, concerning Mr McDonald's error and possible means of correcting it?

6 Why did the error remain uncorrected and in the public domain from December 18, 2014, until corrected on September 21, 2015?

7 Was it appropriate for you to authorise the applications for search warrants for the homes of Lord Bramall, Harvey Proctor and the late Lord Brittan having not read any police interview with Beech or his blogs?

8 Why did you not review the applications before they were presented to court?

9 The district judge relied on the fact that the applications had been considered at deputy assistant commissioner level. Having read no interview, no blog and no application, was your oversight sufficient and responsible?

10 Why, when Operation Midland ended, did you state 'we have found no evidence of Nick (Beech) wilfully misleading the investigation team or perverting the course of justice'? This is singularly inaccurate as Beech's subsequent convictions demonstrate.

HOW IS THIS MAN STILL IN A JOB?
He drove the botched 'Nick' inquiry – and was damned in the judge's scathing report. His punishment? To be promoted to run Britain's 'FBI'... on £245,000 a year

Cleared in months: Former DAC Steve Rodhouse

DAILY MAIL 7 October 2019

In July this judge made the bombshell claim that detectives broke the law while probing false claims of VIP sex abuse. Today, he blasts the police watchdog who ruled not ONE officer should be punished over the scandal

Lamentable. Inadequate. Inexcusable.

by Sir Richard Henriques

RETIRED HIGH COURT JUDGE

THE tardy publication of the Independent Office for Police Conduct report exonerating all five officers involved in the application for search warrants at the homes of Lord Bramall, Lady Brittan and Harvey Proctor should give rise to the most serious public disquiet.

Whilst all five, absent any proper investigation, must be presumed innocent, the responsibility of the IOPC was to carry out a high quality investigation in a timely manner. The delay in reaching their findings of almost three years is gross and inexcusable and goes some way to inhibiting any further investigation.

The investigative process itself was minimal, unprofessional and the decision-making was flawed. The complaint was referred by the then Met commissioner Sir Bernard Hogan-Howe, at my request, to the police watchdog, then named the IPCC, in November 2016. I had concluded the search warrants had been obtained unlawfully and I called for a vigorous investigation into the decision to apply for them.

No such vigorous investigation has taken place. Neither Deputy Assistant Commissioner Steve Rodhouse nor Detective Superintendent Kenny McDonald have been asked a single question in interview as 'subjects' (potential suspects) – written answers having been accepted without questioning.

Both were exonerated within four months and were later interviewed as potential witnesses against the more junior officers.

A decision was taken to investigate all five officers for misconduct as opposed to gross misconduct or criminal conduct, notwithstanding the fact that false documentation had been placed before a district judge on oath, in order to obtain the warrants. Their source, Carl Beech, was described as having remained consistent 'and he is felt to be a credible witness who is telling the truth'.

But he had not remained consistent and officers failed to disclose seven factors that undermined his credibility.

The investigation of the three more junior officers proceeded so slowly that all of them had retired by the time any decision was reached. Had disciplinary measures been ordered they could no longer have been imposed. Both Detective Inspector Alison Hepworth and Detective Sergeant Eric Sword submitted written answers to questions which were accepted with no cross examination.

The only officer to be questioned face to face was Detective Chief Inspector Diane Tudway who by reason of the passage of time 'was unable to recollect what information was available at what time'. No attempt was made to establish what material was available to each officer. This could have been simply achieved by reference to available logs and other documentation. It follows that no effective interrogation of any officer was carried out.

HAVING agreed with Sir Bernard on October 31, 2016, that this matter should be investigated by the IPCC, I anticipated contact from a senior watchdog official in the early stages of its inquiry, to question me in detail about my concerns over the officers' conduct.

I was not contacted until July 2018 – 20 months later – when the 'lead investigator' asked me to make a statement by telephone.

She informed me she had no legal training, was not fully aware of the process for obtaining warrants and initial attempts to create a statement failed. I agreed to write my own statement and submitted it electronically.

I was shocked to learn that the two most senior officers in Operation Midland – DAC Rodhouse and DSU McDonald – had been exonerated more than a year earlier and that 'mere misconduct' was being investigated in preference to gross misconduct or criminal misconduct.

In the final paragraph of my report on Operation Midland I wrote: 'At the conclusion of my interview with the officers on 16/17 August 2016, I formed the view that notwithstanding the many mistakes I have enumerated above (43), the officers had conducted the investigation in a conscientious manner and with propriety and honesty.'

It appears that the IOPC used these words to justify their findings exculpating all five officers.

In the preceding paragraphs I had called for a vigorous investigation to be conducted by those with appropriate investigative powers. Prior to any such investigation the officers were presumed to be innocent. Such presumption may or may not have survived a full and proper investigation.

No 'subject' is to be tried for misconduct or criminal conduct without proper investigation. My concluding observation should not have been used as a basis for failing to carry out a high quality and timely investigation. I did not have the authority to carry out any disciplinary investigation myself. Written responses from four of the officers should have been tested by cross examination. All five officers should have been interviewed and cross examined. Junior officers should have been interviewed before the senior officers were exonerated.

There is no justification for the officer in charge of Operation Midland, DAC Rodhouse, to have been exonerated after four months, more than two years before the junior officers were cleared.

Other Midland officers should have been interviewed. Emails between officers should have been examined. DAC Rodhouse's immediate superiors, then Assistant Commissioner Cressida Dick and her successor Patricia Gallan, should have been interviewed about their roles in the investigation, the briefings they received and their responses. DAC Rodhouse and DCI Tudway in particular had numerous difficult questions to answer. In the context of these facts it is crucial to observe the presumption of innocence.

It is possible that senior officers delegated the drafting, reviewing and presentation of the search warrant applications to fully informed junior officers who were responsible for the errors.

It is also possible the senior officers knew full well that no judge would grant the applications if they were accurately drafted setting out the undermining factors – and that junior officers with incomplete knowledge of the operation were deployed to make the applications.

CLOSE examination of logs, minutes from office meetings, policy files, weekly briefings, 'Gold Group' minutes, and emails would have resolved such issues and still could. I readily conclude that one or more of the five officers may not have committed misconduct in the application for warrants.

However I find it difficult to conceive that no misconduct or criminality was involved by at least one officer. Beech was not consistent. There were numerous undermining facts omitted from the applications. A rigorous and timely investigation – headed by a serving or retired chief constable from an outside force – would have detected the misconduct or criminality.

This has been my first contact with either the IPCC or the IOPC.

Whilst I have been treated with the utmost courtesy, I have been alarmed by the lack of knowledge of relevant criminal procedure. The 'lead investigator' readily conceded her lack of relevant education, training and experience. She should not have been tasked with this highly-sensitive case.

She must not be made a scapegoat for failings in the IOPC under its director-general Michael Lockwood, an accountant with many years in local government.

It is a matter of profound regret that one of the most unsatisfactory and error-ridden criminal operations in history should be followed by such a lamentably slow and inadequate process.

Maintenance of law and order depends upon the effective oversight of those invested with power. Who guards the guards themselves? A malfunctioning police force has not received the necessary oversight. Those acting for people shamefully and adversely affected by this chain of events need no assistance from me. The Home Secretary will wish to address these shocking failures.

Sir Richard Henriques neither sought or received payment for this article.

DAILY MAIL 7 October 2019

Daily Mail

COMMENT

Is anyone policing the police in Britain?

THE Roman poet Juvenal once asked the rhetorical question: 'Quis custodiet ipsos custodes?', or 'Who guards the guards?'

That is pertinent indeed as the stench from one of the most disgraceful chapters in the Metropolitan Police's history lingers and spreads. Today, it is posed by Sir Richard Henriques in a damning condemnation of the Independent Office for Police Conduct (IOPC).

After the eminent retired High Court judge wrote a damning 2016 report exposing the abysmal failings in Scotland Yard's bungled VIP child-sex ring investigation, the watchdog was tasked with scrutinising the conduct of five officers.

Not only had detectives declared the deranged allegations 'credible and true', they duped a judge to secure illegal search warrants. By giving myopic credence to a paedophile's preposterous fantasies, the Met destroyed innocent lives and cost taxpayers £4.5million.

Now, as the IOPC's report is – finally – published today, Sir Richard dismisses it as an 'alarming' whitewash. In a crushing verdict, he brands its inquiry late and lamentably inadequate, hampering further criminal investigations into the outrage.

Incredibly, despite his unrivalled knowledge of the case, he wasn't interviewed for nearly two years – and then only on the phone by someone barely out of short trousers. That not a single officer has been punished for this entire cavalier and calamitous scandal truly beggars belief.

Certainly not the then Met chief Bernard Hogan-Howe, who was rewarded with a place in the Lords. Nor Deputy Assistant Commissioner Steve Rodhouse, promoted to a gold-plated post at Britain's 'FBI'.

And definitely not Operation Midland's original leader, Cressida Dick, now Met Commissioner. Cravenly, she's vanished, leaving her unimpressive No 2 Sir Stephen House to read out churlish statements.

Preservation of law and order is contingent on effective oversight of those handed power. Here we have a dysfunctional force supervised by a dysfunctional watchdog.

Who guards the guards indeed? Home Secretary Priti Patel must reflect upon this 2,000-year-old question urgently.

Grow up, Brussels

AFTER legislating to block a No Deal Brexit, smug Remain MPs patted themselves heartily on their backs.

But with supreme irony, their plot to make a clean break from the EU impossible has made this outcome much more likely.

To sort out the Irish backstop, Boris Johnson submitted sensible plans based on difficult and generous concessions, winning cross-Commons support. But Eurocrats, with no imperative to negotiate, just sneer contemptuously. They want capitulation.

They're gambling on pro-Remain parties winning a general election – and revoking Article 50. But that's a dangerous assumption – one poll puts the Tories 15 points ahead.

If Boris won a majority, it's unlikely such a benevolent offer would stay on the table. Therefore, to avoid a No Deal Brexit that would cause everyone economic pain, compromise is essential. Now's the time for the EU's posturing juveniles to grow up.

Tackle this unfair tax

IT'S wholly conceivable that Britain will soon be asked to vote in a general election.

If so, the Mail respectfully suggests the Tories find room in their manifesto for a promise to reform iniquitous inheritance tax. Rising house prices and a threshold freeze mean what was intended as a levy on the rich now wallops the middle classes.

Yesterday, the Housing Secretary conceded it's 'unfair'. Actually, it's more than unfair. Re-taxing the same money after someone's death verges on immoral.

Addressing this unpopular tithe would help millions... and help hoover up countless precious votes.

Why a horseshoe bat in Kent exposes the sheer folly of today's mass eco-protests

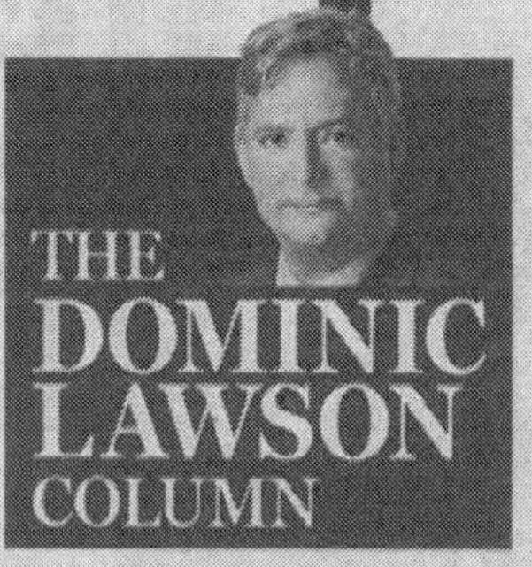

AND now for some good news. One of Britain's and Northern Europe's rarest and most elusive mammals has been discovered living in the East of England for the first time in 115 years.

Revealing this happy development, the Guardian said: 'The return to Kent of the greater horseshoe bat has delighted and astounded conservationists.'

But what is the reason for the unexpected return of this creature with its 'distinctive, alien-like ultrasonic warbling signals'? According to a spokesman for the Bat Conversation Trust, it seems possible that 'the species is now able to expand its range into Kent due to climate changes'.

But isn't climate change meant to be an ecological disaster for every living thing on the planet? That's the Guardian's usual line, and it is definitely the view of the eco-protest group known as Extinction Rebellion, which from today is launching 'mass-disruption' in our capital city as part of its attempt to bully politicians to make the UK 'net carbon zero by 2025'.

Furnace

Actually, I wonder why they bother, since the co-founder and leader of Extinction Rebellion, Roger Hallam, told the Sunday Times: 'We're all going to be dead soon, so there's nothing else to do.'

In like spirit, the 16-year-old Swedish schoolgirl Greta Thunberg declares that unless we immediately switch to a form of existence not seen since before the Industrial Revolution, she and others of her age will not grow up to have children of their own because Earth will very soon be an uninhabitable furnace.

The same approach is championed in America by the no less charismatic 29-year-old Congresswoman Alexandria Ocasio-Cortez, who declaims: 'The world is going to end in 12 years' — not 11 or 13 years, she's most precise — 'if we don't address climate change.'

The only problem with this is that it isn't true. Not remotely so. What *is* true is that if, in line with Hallam's demands, we revert to what he enthusiastically describes as 'a peasant orientation which obviously has been completely lost in Western society', we will indeed witness a shortening of life expectancy and even the prospect of mass starvation (we might have to beg for food aid from rapidly industrialising China).

But what about our friends in the animal kingdom? Are they truly at imminent threat of global wipe-out as a result of the CO2 we emit?

Despite Extinction Rebellion's message, the Intergovernmental Panel on Climate Change — the UN body guided by the scientists in the field — says nothing of the kind. Its most recent report declares: 'Overall, there is very low confidence that observed species extinctions can be attributed to recent climate warming, owing to the very low fraction of global extinctions that have been ascribed to climate change and the tenuous nature of most [such] attributions.'

Greener

In terms of the future, having modelled the effect of anticipated global increases in CO2 emissions from rapidly growing economies of the most populous nations, the IPCC states: 'There is low agreement concerning the fraction of species at increased risk ...and the timeframe over which extinctions could occur.'

But what's the story to date? What you won't hear so much about is that a certain amount of warming is, on balance, a good thing for species, including humans.

As a result partly of man-made CO2 emissions, Earth has actually become greener. Dr Ranga Myneni of Boston University has demonstrated by analysing data from satellite images of the planet, that 31 per cent of the global vegetated surface of the Earth has become greener over the past three decades, and only 3 per cent has become less green. It's not called the 'greenhouse effect' for nothing.

But what about Africa, said to be the biggest likely victim of climate change?

While increased temperatures might save tens of thousands of lives a year in Northern Europe, where cold bears off so many mostly elderly people in winter, they are less likely to be a boon nearer the Equator. Yet it turns out those satellite images have also shown a marked greening in dry areas such as the Sahel in Africa.

As best-selling science writer Dr Matt Ridley observed: 'The decline of famines in the Sahel in recent years is partly due to more rainfall caused by moderate warming and partly due to more carbon dioxide itself: more greenery for goats to eat means more greenery left over for gazelles, so entire ecosytems have benefited.'

Perverse

The key fact to bear in mind is that CO2 is not, in itself, a pollutant; nor detrimental to the air we breathe. The problem for us is the sooty particulates that come out of the exhaust of vehicles powered by internal combustion engines. They really do kill.

Diesel engines produce far more of these dangerous emissions than petrol ones — yet because of the fixation with 'man-made climate change', the British government massively incentivised, through the tax system, a switch to diesel from petrol because the latter produced more CO2 per unit of energy.

What a perverse, self-annihilating strategy. I'm glad I've got an 11-year-old hybrid petrol-electric car, though I don't delude myself that it will 'help save the planet'.

Of course, the Extinction Rebellion demonstrators are against all forms of motorised transport; indeed, every modern form of travel. As even a reasonably supportive article in the New Internationalist explained, under the policies of Extinction Rebellion: 'Energy would be strictly rationed, dedicated to survival ...expect massive disruption in the way food is grown, processed and distributed ...there would be virtually no private car use, aviation, haulage or shipping.'

We would be living in an eco-fascist dystopia. In short: completely bats.

HERE'S A THOUGHT: LET'S BIN RADIO 4'S 'GOD SLOT'

COMPETITIONS have been run to find the most dispiriting regularly heard words in the English language. 'Unexpected item in the bagging area' would win, for many. Others might nominate 'See it. Say it. Sorted.'

But for my part, 'And now it's time for Thought for the Day with Indarjit Singh' can hardly be bettered (or rather, worsened). That has always had me lurching with unwonted energy for the radio off-switch.

So it was not with the deepest regret that I read Lord Singh has quit Radio Four's Thought For The Day.

He does so in protest at what he sees as censorship by the 'politically correct thought police' of the BBC: they stopped him devoting his radio sermon last November to the 'martyrdom of Guru Tegh Bahadur', apparently because they thought it would offend Muslims.

To think we had been denied such a thrilling episode of Thought For The Day!

In fact the so-called 'God Slot' is reliably soporific, no matter which of the regular speakers is called upon. And that is not just because the BBC, as we now learn from Lord Singh, is determined to block anything that might cause a little religious controversy.

The trouble is that all the sermonisers read from a prepared script. These are trite lectures, delivered with not a scintilla of spontaneity.

Perhaps the only Thought For The Day preacher who managed to sound as if he was talking to us, rather than at us, was Rabbi Lionel Blue.

Alas, ill-health took him off the airwaves in 2012 (he sounded painfully out-of-breath in his final broadcast, and died in 2016).

It was no accident that Rabbi Blue, with his wonderfully conversational and intimate style, was the only Thought For The Day speaker whom even the most secular listeners engaged with — and missed.

So it's not just the absence of Lord Singh's sermons I suspect the nation can endure without going into a state of mourning — but the whole lot of the current Thought For The Day crew.

DAILY MAIL 7 October 2019

HORRIFYI

Son of vilified war hero condemns police after Mail exposé... and says Met MUST come clean

By **Stephen Wright, Glen Keogh** and **Jemma Buckley**

'NICK': THE DAMNING DOCUMENT

The Mail yesterday

LORD Bramall's son last night called on the head of Scotland Yard to order an independent criminal probe into alleged misconduct in the Met's bungled VIP child sex abuse inquiry.

Urging Met Commissioner Cressida Dick to call in an outside force, he said her officers had shown a 'staggering level of incompetence' in Operation Midland and also appeared to have 'acted illegally'.

Nick Bramall spoke out a day after details emerged of a damning document that showed police should never have raided the home of his 95-year-old father – a former head of the Armed Forces. The raid was over false paedophile allegations made by the fantasist known as 'Nick', whose real name is Carl Beech.

'We want an honest conclusion'

A Mail investigation revealed that an application seeking permission to search Lord Bramall's home was riddled with falsehoods.

Last night, Mr Bramall was scathing of the Met, saying: 'Their having listened to and believed the uncorroborated ramblings of Carl Beech was bad enough.

'Now we discover that the injustices served on those falsely accused has been compounded by contempt for the law. The latest developments about the misleading evidence given in order to secure a search warrant is horrifying. They must come clean.'

His comments come a week after retired judge Sir Richard Henriques – who in 2016 wrote a scathing report on Operation Midland – said officers gave the judge false evidence to obtain the search warrants to raid the homes of Lord Bramall and two other VIPs and should face a criminal investigation.

Met Deputy Commissioner Sir Stephen House said last night: 'The Met has already published a redacted version of Sir Richard's report pending the investigation of Carl Beech. We will publish as full a version of the report as possible, as soon as we can now proceedings are complete.'

But Mr Bramall, 67, a successful landscape gardener in Dorset, added: 'Sir Richard's report must be published in full. He went to the trouble to write a very thorough report into Operation Midland and yet much of it has been withheld.

'This whole sorry business continues with four years of my father's life ruined. He is not a well man and we want an honest conclusion before it's too late. To that end Commissioner Dick should order a criminal enquiry, carried out by an independent force otherwise much of the respect for the Met will be lost.'

Speaking in the wake of the latest revelations, former Director of Public Prosecutions Lord Macdonald QC said: 'This scandal is growing by the day. Police officers are under an absolute duty to be frank, open and truthful when they are applying for a search warrant.

'But the document uncovered by the Mail... omitted crucial information that completely undermined their own case. Misleading a court in this way is not only a disgrace, it is probably criminal.

'Public confidence demands an independent inquiry into the handling of Operation Midland.'

Tory MP Nigel Evans joined the demands for a fully independent inquiry. He said: 'Quite frankly, huge errors were made. I think it would be very wise of Cressida Dick to ensure this is independently looked at by an outside force.'

Daniel Janner QC, whose father Lord Janner was falsely accused of abuse by Beech, said: 'An outside police force should be brought in immediately. Cressida Dick needs to act decisively if faith in the police is to be restored.' Yesterday the Mail revealed how detectives claimed in a secret search warrant application that they had no reason to doubt claims made by Beech. The document was presented to a judge who approved the raid on Lord Bramall's home in March 2015.

But an investigation by this newspaper has established that police were aware of at least eight factors that raised serious questions about the claims made by Beech, a 51-year-old former nurse.

The revelations about the warrants for raids on Lord Bramall, former home secretary Lord Brit-

Now bitter blame game breaks out

By **Stephen Wright**
ASSOCIATE NEWS EDITOR

THE police chief who led the bungled inquiry was under mounting pressure last night after his former Scotland Yard boss distanced herself from the decision to raid the homes of high-profile figures including Lord Bramall.

Ex Met assistant commissioner Patricia Gallan said Operation Midland gold commander Steve Rodhouse had 'operational control' and 'oversaw' the investigation into an alleged Establishment paedophile ring.

She added: 'I did not approve the raids nor was my permission or advice sought before the execution of the Section 8 warrants.'

Her intervention placed former Met deputy assistant commissioner Mr Rodhouse – now the £175,000-a-year director general (operations) at the National Crime Agency – firmly at the centre of the Operation Midland search warrants scandal.

Miss Gallan's comment came in response to a series of questions from the Daily Mail that she answered before sex abuse fantasist 'Nick', real name Carl Beech, was convicted of perverting the course of justice and fraud last month. As an assistant commissioner in the Met – the third most senior rank in the force – she had oversight of Operation Midland and received regular briefings from Mr Rodhouse.

She also updated former Scotland Yard boss Lord Hogan-Howe on the progress of the 16-month inquiry which ended without any arrests or charges in March 2016.

Miss Gallan told the Mail that upon taking her post as assistant commissioner in February 2015 and being briefed on Operation Midland 'by the gold commander', she 'ordered an immediate review of what was by that stage a long-running investigation'.

She said she raised concerns about the use of the phrase 'credible and true' by a senior Met officer to describe key witness 'Nick' at the start of Operation Midland. She added: 'I cannot speak for the views of the investigators in this case.

'My view then and now is that it is for the courts, not the police to decide on the truth or otherwise of a witness. It is the role of the police to investigate and then to present the evidence to the CPS who must decide whether there should be a prosecution.'

Asked how often Lord Hogan-Howe was updated on Operation Midland, Miss Gallan said the chief 'would have been briefed as and when appropriate as per any other significant investigation'.

'Not for the police to decide on the truth'

Miss Gallan's willingness to answer questions was in sharp contrast to Mr Rodhouse, who declined to answer any of ten questions put to him by the Daily Mail last month.

These included whether he approved the use of the phrase 'credible and true' by Det Supt Kenny McDonald in December 2014 and whether he approved the raids on the homes of Lord Bramall, Lord Brittan and ex-Tory MP Harvey Proctor in March 2015.

Yesterday the Mail revealed how the emergence of the search warrant application for the raid on the home of former Armed Forces chief Lord Bramall put Mr Rodhouse at the centre of the Operation Midland row.

The document revealed that a district judge approved the police request after being assured its implications had been 'considered at DAC level' – deputy assistant commissioner, Mr Rodhouse's rank at the time.

Following the scathing report into Operation Midland by ex-High Court judge Sir Richard Henriques in November 2016, which cleared Miss Gallan of any blame, Mr Rodhouse was referred to the police watchdog for potential breaches of 'duties and responsibilities' in the investigation.

Along with Mr McDonald he was cleared in March 2017. The watchdog said there was no evidence to indicate 'bad faith, malice or dishonesty' by the officers and Operation Midland was 'carried out diligently'.

NG

Family togetherness: Nick Bramall with his mother and father pictured in 2000

tan and ex Tory MP Harvey Proctor piled pressure on Home Secretary Priti Patel to order a fresh inquiry.

Last week she demanded a full explanation of the police watchdog's decision to clear three Operation Midland officers. Two more senior officers were exonerated two years ago.

Last month vicar's son Beech was jailed for 18 years for telling lies about alleged VIP child abuse and murder.

■ The Met Police gave nearly £1million to another force while investigating Beech. A Freedom of Information request showed they reimbursed Northumbria Police £951,982 for probing his fabrications.

Comment – Page 16

at Yard

Accusations: Steve Rodhouse was a leading figure in the VIP probe

I admire our police, but I fear the Met's trying to cover up its mistakes, not admit to them

By **Lord Blunkett**

FORMER HOME SECRETARY

THE Metropolitan Police, in the way it conducted its investigation into Establishment figures accused of terrible sex abuse, has made appalling mistakes.

We now realise how grossly mishandled the case was from start to finish – from the first unsubstantiated claims by the paedophile fantasist Carl Beech, known to police as 'Nick', up to the continued refusal of the Met to admit their dreadful errors and apologise.

You might expect me, as a former Home Secretary, to rant and rave about this deplorable perversion of the mechanics of justice. And believe me, I do deplore it. There is no exaggeration in saying that the whole integrity of the criminal justice process has been called into question.

But my chief feeling is one of sorrow, not anger. I'm a great admirer of Britain's police and it saddens me to see the Met in such a mess. In no way do I condone or minimise any of the mistakes, but I understand how they came about. I should do: I am a politician, and I've committed mistakes of my own.

The most important rule whenever errors are made, however, is to acknowledge them. Own up. Come clean. Unless you admit to the mistakes, you cannot learn from them. And it is imperative that the Met learn from their mistakes with 'Nick', because if they don't then the same dire situation might arise again.

In cases of alleged abuse, our understandable inclination as a society is now to tend to believe the alleged victims. This was not always so. In the past, sexual horror stories were too easily dismissed, and some very well known figures were able to get away with awful crimes.

Because of the cases over the past 20 years or so, the pendulum of public opinion has swung the other way. Our instinct is now to side with the apparent victim. But justice is not a pendulum, and the police must not veer wildly from side to side. That's how catastrophes occur.

The fundamental basis of policing is to follow the evidence. The facts must always be tested and interrogated, as investigating officers examine in detail whether the allegations stack up. It is methodical, painstaking work, and it can be wrecked if there is a prior assumption by police about a suspect's guilt.

In this case, some officers had clearly decided to believe Beech's claims, no matter how outlandish and despite a catalogue of blatant lies that should have exposed him at once as dishonest. This led to severe consequences for several people who should never have been serious suspects – including my fellow former Home Secretary, Leon Brittan, who died before his name could be cleared.

HE and others were bundled on to a rollercoaster of events from which they could not escape, treated as figures of public shame.

The shoddiness of the evidence which enabled police to get a search warrant and raid the home of Field Marshal Lord Bramall, regarded as our greatest living soldier, defies belief. The police application put before Judge Howard Riddle now appears to be filled with contradictions and falsehoods.

At the top of the form, Beech was described as 'a credible witness who is telling the truth' and whose 'account has remained consistent'. In fact, as the Mail has revealed, his stories were riddled with holes that police were purposefully ignoring – such as unsubstantiated claims that one of Beech's schoolmates disappeared (supposedly strangled by a prominent MP) and that Beech himself missed many days of school because of sexually inflicted injuries. Both these lies were easily disproved, yet there was no mention of them in the request for a warrant.

The officer making that request was a detective sergeant. It would be wrong to scapegoat that man. The problem lies not in individuals or 'bad apples'. When the application for a warrant was filed, it was considered by very senior officers – and Deputy Assistant Commissioner Steve Rodhouse was gold commander in charge of the investigation.

Why haven't he and other high-ranking figures in the force come forward? I'm deeply concerned that the Met appears to be trying to cover up its mistakes, rather than acknowledging them.

By now, these officers should have taken responsibility and apologised profusely for the enormous hurt and damage caused. We shouldn't still be waiting for their contrition – we should already be seeing mechanisms put in place to ensure nothing of the like can ever happen again.

Instead, there is a surly evasiveness from all concerned in the force. Lord Bramall and his family have not received anything like the apology they deserve, and nor have the other victims. As Home Secretary, I was faced with systemic problems in some parts of police forces. In 2001, I had to ask Chief Constable Paul Whitehouse to resign over his failure to ensure murders in Sussex were being properly investigated.

When the country was rocked in 2002 by the murder of two ten-year-old girls in Soham, I was confronted by desperate failures of record-keeping and communication between police in Humberside and Cambridgeshire.

Sorting these issues out wasn't easily done. When challenged, the police force has a tendency to become overly defensive. But that helps nobody. I'll say it again: when mistakes are made, the important thing is to learn from them, not to try and hide them.

That's why it is essential the report into the Carl Beech case by retired High Court judge Sir Richard Henriques is published without redactions – and, if it really is impossible for some information to be made public, we have to be told the underlying reasons. It is no longer acceptable for passages in this report to be blacked out without explanation.

WE need to know there are good operational reasons, and that it isn't simply a matter of withholding material that would prove embarrassing.

At the same time, the Met's Commissioner Cressida Dick must now break her silence and make a statement. I am a great admirer of hers. She's done an outstanding job in many areas over recent months. But this is too big a business to be ignored, and the Commissioner cannot simply continue to behave as though it's someone else's responsibility. And the same goes for Priti Patel, the new Home Secretary, whose silence is anything but golden.

I do not believe it is appropriate to launch a wholescale investigation into the Met. This scandal is not on the scale, for example, of corruption in the West Midlands fraud squad during the Seventies, when wrong-doing infected the force root and branch.

But the specific circumstances of this case have to be examined impartially. It is not enough to put the probe in the hands of an inexperienced investigator just a few years out of university, which has been the response of the Independent Office for Police Conduct.

I'd suggest it is more appropriate to hand the investigation to the National Crime Agency – except that Steve Rodhouse, the former Deputy Assistant Commissioner was gold commander in charge of this investigation and is now No 2 at the NCA. Ironically, for the past 18 months they have been investigating the failings of the South Yorkshire police in respect of historic child abuse cases.

Clearly an alternative independent outside body is needed in this case. That all goes to show how hard it's going to be to unravel this mess.

But one thing shouldn't be hard. An unequivocal apology has to be offered, sincere and unreserved, to all the people whose lives were turned upside-down and whose reputations were smeared because of Carl Beech's lies.

Let's hear that apology right now. Until we do, there can be no lessons drawn from these terrible events.

DAILY MAIL 7 August 2019

Daily Mail

COMMENT

Met's honour on trial over VIP sex fiasco

BUNKER mentality has set in at Scotland Yard as the Metropolitan Police seeks to play down its disastrous mishandling of Operation Midland – the inquiry into a non-existent VIP sex abuse ring that resulted in the homes of totally innocent people being raided by officers using search warrants obtained by deceiving a judge.

As former home secretary David Blunkett states in this newspaper today, the Midland fiasco is an appalling stain on the Met, and will remain so until it does the decent thing and admits its culpability. Yet, Commissioner Cressida Dick remains silent, refusing to commit to an independent inquiry into misconduct bordering on criminality.

Stonewalling is a common tactic of modern officialdom. But be assured: the Mail will be unrelenting in its pursuit of the truth about this disgraceful affair.

Not only in the cause of rooting out wrongdoing by the powerful – a vital ingredient of democracy – but in deference to those who have suffered.

One of them is Field Marshal Lord Bramall, now 95 years of age. This D-Day veteran has suffered not only terrible 'indignity' but also 'injustice', says his son.

The police deserve our support and respect in normal circumstances. But this is conditional upon them observing the highest standards of behaviour – and admitting their failings.

Edwin Bramall is holder of the Military Cross, an honourable man. The Met should learn from him how honourable men and women behave.

Battle of the Doms

TORY arch Remainer Dominic Grieve warns that the Queen may have to sack Boris Johnson if he refuses to quit Number 10 following a no confidence vote designed to sabotage Brexit.

The proposed replacement: a figurehead prime minister leading an unholy rainbow alliance of Labour, the Lib Dems, Tory rebels and the SNP – which is being bought off with the promise of a second independence referendum.

Febrile speculation is to be expected in the summer months, as MPs plot away on their Provencal patios. But does the country need a lash-up administration concocted over the phone to frustrate the result of the 2016 EU referendum?

Equally unsettling are the comments of Dominic Cummings, Mr Johnson's chief (unelected) adviser, a man who delights in upsetting apple carts. He claims that, even if the Government falls in early September, it can cling on until after Brexit has been achieved on October 31.

This 'Battle of the Doms' threatens to drag us into a constitutional quagmire that will simply exacerbate ill-feeling in the country. Cooler counsel should prevail.

The Prime Minister is pursuing a policy of seeking a deal with the EU while planning in detail for the opposite eventuality. This is to convince our European partners – who will also suffer in a No Deal world – of his seriousness of purpose. He should be allowed to get on with it.

Mr Johnson's best hope of political survival lies in pursuing this policy sincerely. If this country is to quit the EU with No Deal, it should not be due to any unwillingness on his part to negotiate. The stakes are too high for testosterone politics.

■ IN a fine example of upbeat 'boosterism', new Transport Secretary Grant Shapps promises to reverse seven successive years of worsening punctuality on the railways – while ignoring the little matter of his party's responsibility for them since 2010. Still, we wish Mr Shapps well in making the trains run on time. Certainly, he can do no worse than his ill-starred predecessor Chris Grayling – who was no Il Duce. Promises like this can come back to haunt politicians. But we take Mr Shapps at his word – and hope he can indeed make life a little easier for the long-suffering travelling public.

Why I fear the future of Britain (and Boris) is now in the hands of an unelected Svengali

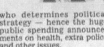

by Peter Oborne

DOMINIC Cummings, who is today installed in Downing Street as arguably the second most powerful man in Britain, first came to public attention when played by Benedict Cumberbatch in Channel 4's Brexit: The Uncivil War.

The drama told the behind-the-scenes story of Vote Leave's successful campaign in the 2016 EU referendum.

Cumberbatch interpreted Cummings, the campaign director, as a sinister anti-hero and *eminence grise* controlling events.

Boris Johnson, officially the leader of Vote Leave, was given little more than a walk-on role, portrayed as a slightly bumbling idiot figure who travelled the country to address public meetings according to a script written for him by the much more committed Cummings.

Johnson the monkey. Cummings the organ grinder.

Contemptuous

Three years later, and life is copying art. With one crucial difference. Cummings is no longer in the shadows, operating behind the scenes — this Svengali is out in the open.

Indeed, he seems to relish being seen in public, striding ostentatiously into Downing Street every morning.

Now, we are all familiar with his shaven head, scruffy T-shirts, crumpled appearance and contemptuous and appraising eyes, his newspapers and bundles of documents carried in a Vote Leave bag.

According to some papers, and many ministers and civil servants I have spoken to recently, this is the man who is truly running Britain. It's Cummings who oversees the No10 grid which controls the timing of announcements and public events.

It's in this capacity that he dispatches the PM up and down Britain, photographed in hospitals, sharing selfies with nurses, and on construction sites wearing a hard hat. It is also Cummings, not Johnson, who determines political strategy — hence the huge public spending announcements on health, extra police and other issues.

Indeed, it looks very much as if Johnson has become the public face of Cummings.

And this, I am afraid, is profoundly disturbing. No one ever voted for Cummings, he has little experience of life outside politicking yet he has been given unprecedented power at a moment of immense crisis in the national fortunes.

Within hours of Johnson becoming Tory leader two weeks ago, newly anointed special adviser Cummings called 'his' staff together in the magnificent Downing Street first-floor state room.

He told them that he plans to deliver Brexit 'by any means necessary'.

It is a phrase that could not be more chilling, given that it was coined in the Sixties by extremist black rights activist Malcolm X when he rejected the peaceful approach of civil rights leader Martin Luther King.

Cummings's use of this dangerous and inflammatory language was, in my view, not accidental. He used the term no fewer than six times in his speech that day.

Unlike Malcolm X, Cummings was not advocating violence, but there's certainly a touch of gangsterism about his reported threat to advisers who talk to journalists.

At a 7.55am meeting on Monday, he apparently told them they would be sacked without any right of appeal if they leaked information that damages the Government's Brexit policy.

He would, he said, be able to persuade journalists to reveal their sources. 'My worth to journalists is far greater than yours... they will rat you out. You have no rights,' he added.

And Cummings is certainly advocating ripping up the metaphorical rule book of the British state as it has existed for centuries. This became crystal clear over the weekend in the wake of a No 10 briefing in which Cummings told colleagues Johnson plans to stay in office even if he is voted out and defeated in a Commons confidence motion.

A Prime Minister would normally quit within minutes of such a humiliation. It goes without saying that such conduct would be a two-fingered salute to our entire system of government.

Experts say it could at once drag the Queen into politics because ultimately it would be her constitutional duty to order Johnson to step down.

But smashing the status quo is what Cummings is all about. He is, in truth, a far more revolutionary figure even than Labour leader Jeremy Corbyn.

This is a man who is utterly disdainful of the conventions of British public life.

He despises our tried and tested system of representative democracy, so much so that he was found in contempt of Parliament after refusing to appear in front of MPs on the Digital, Culture, Media and Sport committee who were investigating fake news during the Referendum campaign. (He said he offered to appear, but was rebuffed.)

Shame

Cummings is known for his loathing of the Civil Service. He has also been accused of telling lies to advance his political project. For example, the now infamous '£350 million for the NHS' slogan on the side of the Vote Leave bus is believed by many to have been his handiwork.

Those who support him say this revolutionary approach is justified because Brexit cannot be delivered in any other way. Conventional means were tried and failed during Theresa May's three-year premiership.

I disagree. Margaret Thatcher, the most radical Tory leader of the past century, was always respectful of Parliament, the Civil Service and the Monarchy.

Certainly, she used advisers. But she never became their creature, or as dependent on them as Johnson, to his shame, appears to be on Cummings.

The same applies to Winston Churchill, upon whom Johnson appears to model himself. Churchill was his own man. He had no need of an adviser to dictate to him what he thought and did.

There is no constitutional outrage in Johnson doing and saying what he is told to do by Cummings. That's a matter for him, even if it is embarrassing and undignified.

Arrogance

But what a bitter irony that Brexit — which was supposed to 'take back control' — has ended up with Government policy so much in thrall to an unelected official.

By the way, don't believe the fawning comments and profiles of Cummings by some journalists who kowtow to him because they need access and rely on his information.

Yes, he's got lots of clever theories and has run successful political campaigns, but has little experience of real life.

He's the supreme example of the type of nerdy political obsessives who have done so much damage to British politics over the past 25 years.

Indeed, one factor worries me more than anything else. There is a precedent for the Cummings/Johnson partnership that governs Britain as Brexit looms.

Tony Blair was also a creature of his powerful adviser, Alastair Campbell. They showed equal arrogance and contempt for Parliament.

They, too, were indifferent to truth. They, too, had little integrity. The Blair/Campbell double act ended in the tragedy of the Iraq war, the unnecessary deaths of countless Iraqis, 179 brave British service personnel and ultimately the rise of Islamic State.

We can only hope that the double act of Boris Johnson and Dominic Cummings has a happier outcome.

DAILY MAIL 7 August 2019

Daily Mail

TUESDAY, AUGUST 6, 2019 www.dailymail.co.uk 70p

Brave Barbara's plea to Boris – end the dementia care scandal now!

SEE PAGE FOUR

'NICK': THE DAMNING DOCUMENT

Behind bars: 'Nick' fantasist Carl Beech

EXCLUSIVE: Mail discovers police form used to authorise raid on VIP's home was riddled with falsehoods

By Stephen Wright
Associate News Editor

A FILE showing police should never have raided the home of Britain's greatest living soldier can be revealed today.

Detectives claimed in a secret search warrant application that they had no reason to doubt VIP child abuse and murder claims made by the fantasist 'Nick'.

Signed by a detective sergeant, the document was presented to a judge who approved the raid in March 2015 on the home of Lord Bramall, a D-Day veteran and former head of the Armed Forces.

But an investigation by this newspaper has established that police were aware of at least eight factors that raised serious questions about the outlandish claims made by Nick,

Turn to Page 2

DAILY MAIL 6 August 2019

Continued from Page One

whose real name is Carl Beech. A key factor was that despite extensive efforts police found no evidence to back up Beech's claim to have suffered physical abuse and injury and to have been absent from school.

Yet officers told district judge Howard Riddle that the 51-year-old former nurse was a 'consistent' and 'credible' witness.

In the document, which has been seen by the Daily Mail, Judge Riddle wrote that he was assured the implications for the application for the proposed raid had been 'considered at DAC level'.

This was a reference to Steve Rodhouse, a deputy assistant commissioner with Metropolitan Police and 'gold commander' of the bungled £2.5million investigation.

The revelations about the warrants for raids on the homes of Lord Bramall, former home secretary Lord Brittan and ex Tory MP Harvey Proctor, will pile pressure on Home Secretary Priti Patel to order a fresh inquiry into the fiasco.

Last week she demanded a full explanation of the police watchdog's decision to clear three Operation Midland officers.

Two more senior officers – including Mr Rodhouse – were controversially exonerated two years ago.

Victims of Beech's lies, and their families, are furious that no police officer has been held to account over the Met's disastrous investigation.

Today the Daily Mail can also reveal that a rookie worker at the Independent Office for Police Conduct, who was in her late 20s, was the 'lead investigator' during the two-year probe that cleared the three officers of misconduct last month.

The latest developments come a week after a former High Court judge said that police broke the law with Operation Midland.

In an astonishing intervention, Sir Richard Henriques told the Daily Mail that officers used false evidence to obtain the search warrants and should now face a criminal investigation.

He said that detectives did not have the right to search the properties because their description of Beech as a consistent witness was false, effectively fooling a judge into granting the warrants.

He also alleged that the 'course of justice was perverted with shocking consequences', saying he found it astonishing that no officer has been brought to book.

In 2016 Sir Richard wrote a scathing report for Scotland Yard about Operation Midland. It identified 43 blunders, was heavily redacted and has never been fully made public.

In the wake of the Mail's revelations last week, a string of distinguished law enforcement figures – including former Met chief Lord Stevens, and former director of public prosecutions Lord Macdonald, have called for an unredacted version of the dossier to be released.

Sir Richard's broadside at the Met and police watchdogs came days after vicar's son Beech was jailed for 18 years for telling a string of lies about alleged VIP child sex abuse and serial murders.

At his ten-week trial, jurors heard the fantasist told officers that he was used as a human dartboard by the former heads of MI5 and MI6, that his dog was kidnapped by a spy chief, and that the paedophile ring shot dead his horse. The court also heard that Beech is now a convicted paedophile after child porn offences came to light when an independent police force, at Sir Richard's behest, started investigating him on suspicion of making false claims about a deadly Establishment paedophile ring.

In the wake of his convictions, Scotland Yard chiefs faced intense criticism over staggering incompetence in 16-month investigation launched on the word of a pathological liar.

But shortly after Beech was found guilty, the Independent Office for Police Conduct announced the three officers accused of misconduct over search warrant applications had been cleared.

The watchdog said the officers, led by senior investigating officer detective chief inspector Diane Tudway, acted 'with due diligence and in good faith at the time'.

But Sir Richard told this newspaper the finding was 'in conflict' with his review of Operation Midland in 2016.

Following Beech's convictions, Met Deputy Commissioner Sir Stephen House said he believed all five officers probed by police watchdogs over Operation Midland 'worked in good faith'.

They cooperated fully with both the Henriques Review and the Independent Office for Police Conduct investigations, he added.

Comment – Page 16

EIGHT reasons why police raids should never have taken place

1 Despite extensive inquiries into Beech's background, police had found no evidence of physical abuse, injury or proof that he been absent from school as he had alleged.

2 No witnesses had come forward despite extensive media coverage.

3 There was no record of the supposed hit and run murder of a school friend called Scott in south west London in 1979, as Beech had claimed.

4 Officers on Operation Midland had traced seven out of eight boys called Scott from Beech's primary school, while the last one was known to have moved to Australia (and could not have been killed).

5 Police had concluded that a supposed witness to the abuse called 'Fred' was either unwilling to engage or was an invention of Beech. It later turned out that 'Fred' was a bogus witness created by the fantasist.

6 There was no identity for 'boy 3', who was supposedly strangled to death by Harvey Proctor.

7 Officers on Operation Midland had access to an interview he had conducted with Wiltshire Police in 2012, where he made no mention of VIP child sex abuse, torture and murder.

8 In blogs on the internet, before he went to the Met in 2014, he did not mention murders by high-profile figures.

PERVERSION OF JUSTICE

INCREDIBLE AND UNTRUE

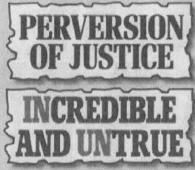

From the Mail, July 23

'NICK' POLICE SEARCHES BROKE LAW

July 30

NOW TURN FULL FORCE OF LAW ON 'NICK' POLICE

July 31

WARRANT FOR DISGRACE

SEE PAGES 6-9

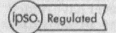

INSIDE: Puzzles & Prizes 41-44, TV & Radio 52-55, Calner 56, Letters 58 & 59, City & Finance 67-70

DAILY MAIL 6 August 2019

WARRANT F

In shocking detail, shameful document police submitted to authorise raid that ruined life of war hero Lord Bramall

By **Stephen Wright**
ASSOCIATE NEWS EDITOR

THE secret court document seen by the Daily Mail – which blows open the 'Nick' search warrants scandal – was part of a two-stage process which gave police permission to raid the home of Britain's greatest living soldier, Field Marshal Lord Bramall.

The first involved a detective completing a confidential form and the second involved three murder squad officers going before court to get official permission to storm his house.

The document sets out the astonishing nature of the claims and reveals that police even sought to rely on an independent consultant to back up their star witness's allegations.

It also shows that when asked if there was anything that might undermine their request for a search warrant, the Met simply answered N/A – not applicable. In fact, police were aware of several factors that raised questions about the claims made by Nick, real name Carl Beech.

Before detectives could raid the home of the former head of the Armed Forces, now 95, in March 2015, an officer had to complete a standard 'Application for Search Warrant' form (Criminal Procedure Rules, rule 6.30; section 8, Police and Criminal Evidence Act 1984). The document includes nine sections which need to be filled out by police, and a final one – to be signed by the presiding judge – granting them authority to execute the warrant.

'To the best of my knowledge'

Police had to answer a series of questions about the offence(s) under investigation, background details of the case and why officers believed crimes had been committed, the material being sought by police and the premises officers were seeking to search.

Critically the officer signing the warrant – in this case Detective Sergeant Eric Sword – was asked under section eight ('duty of disclosure') whether there is 'anything of which you are aware that might reasonably be considered capable of undermining any of the grounds of this application, or which for some other reason might affect the court's decision?'.

It adds: 'Include anything that reasonably might call into question the credibility of the information you have received and explain why you have decided that that information still can be relied upon.'

This is a crucial section because judges are warned that they must exercise their power 'with great care and caution' and must not allow police to engage in 'a fishing expedition'.

In this box, the Met said 'N/A' and Mr Sword, now retired from the force, signed a declaration in section nine saying that 'to the best of my knowledge and belief' ... 'the content of this application is true'.

After filling in the form on February 27, 2015, detectives went before Westminster Magistrates' Court in central London on March 2, 2015 to answer questions about the search warrant application.

District judge Howard Riddle ruled that the search of Lord Bramall's home could go ahead after hearing that the 'victim' (Carl Beech) was 'consistent' and 'credible' and that a Met Deputy Assistant Commissioner had 'considered' the application. Two days later on March 4, 2015, police raided Lord Bramall's home in Surrey as raids took place at homes of the recently deceased Lord Brittan, and former MP Harvey Proctor.

At the top of the search warrant application the Met says of Beech: 'His account has remained consistent and he is felt to be a credible witness who is telling the truth.'

Approving the request to raid Lord Bramall's home, Judge Riddle said: 'I am satisfied that the police are fully aware of the sensitivities and the need for a proportionate approach. This has been considered at DAC level.'

Grotesque allegations: Lord Bramall

Persuaded: Judge Howard Riddle

Here we set out the key passages of the application by the Met to search Lord Bramall's home – and, alongside them, the devastating evidence that undermines the police claims

Nick the liar

IN his 1,200 word statement last week, former High Court judge Sir Richard Henriques insisted that Beech had 'not been consistent', dating back to when the fantasist had first made claims of historic child sex abuse to Wiltshire Police in 2012.

Therefore he WAS known to police.

Sir Richard said: 'His allegations made to the Wiltshire Police in 2012 were fundamentally inconsistent with those made to the Metropolitan Police in 2014 and with Beech's blogs also published in 2014.

'The identities of subsequent named alleged rapists were inconsistent. The alleged locations were inconsistent, persons allegedly present were inconsistent, the alleged accompanying acts of violence were inconsistent.'

Passing the buck

THIS suggests that police were already seeking to pass the buck over who was giving credibility to Beech.

The 'independent counsellor' is Beech's counsellor, Vicki Paterson, to whom he gave a body map detailing dozens of alleged injuries.

The warrant then reveals her verdict was rubberstamped by another 'consultant', Dr Elly Hanson.

Neither Ms Paterson or Dr Hanson would have had access to his medical records to corroborate his story.

Did Scotland Yard overstate the importance of the pair's professional views to bolster their case?

No evidence

SIR Richard was damning of police on this issue.

He argues powerfully that there was no compelling evidence to suggest that Beech had ever been injured in this way, or absent from school.

Crucially, he says that, at the time of the warrant being applied for, there was no evidence that any of the three children cited here had indeed been murdered.

OR DISGRACE

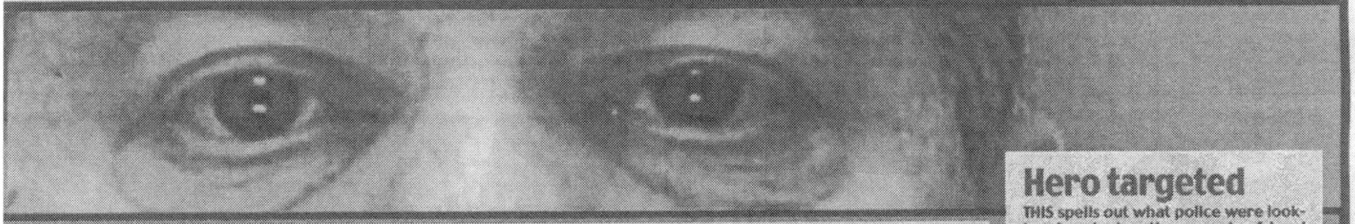

APPLICATION FOR SEARCH WARRANT

(Criminal Procedure Rules, rule 6.30; Section 8, Police and Criminal Evidence Act 1984)

Application to: District Judge Howard Riddle at Westminster Magistrates Court

This is an application by: DS Eric Sword, Westminster Court

1. The offence(s) under investigation The victim in this matter has been interviewed at length by experienced officers from the child abuse investigative team.

His account has remained consistent and he is felt to be a credible witness who is telling the truth.

Enquiries made relating to the victim find nothing to suggest any links to those that he accuses, suggesting his allegations are malicious. The victim is not known to police.

Prior to police involvement these allegations were detailed to an independent counsellor by the victim who also supports his account as being credible. At the request of police a qualified consultant Dr Elly Hanson was asked to give an opinion if the counsellor was able to make an accurate judgement of the victim's credibility.

Dr Hanson (sic) views were that the counsellor was able to make an accurate judgement of the victim's credibility.

2. The investigation The victim contacted police in late 2014 detailing allegations of serious sexual assault. He stated that he had been present when three separate males had been murdered by his group of abusers. He states this abuse was often carried out when he was in the company of other boys of a similar age who were also abused.

He states that from the age of 7 until he was 16 he was subject to regular sexual assaults by persons introduced to him by his stepfather, a major in the British Army.

He named various high-profile individuals as his abusers and those that are subject to these applications are Lord Edwin Bramall, Lord Leon Brittan (recently deceased) and Keith Harvey Proctor. The victim alleges that he was present at the scene of three murders and he names Harvey Proctor as being involved in two of these offences and Leon Brittan as being present during one of them.

Lord Edwin Bramall

Between 1975-1984 it is alleged that he abused the victim on numerous occasions, including sexual assault, buggery, and torture. This included the victim being tied up, beaten and burned with a lighter by his group of abusers.

The alleged offences involving Bramall are said to have been committed in the following locations: unknown residential premises in Wiltshire Army barracks in Wilton, Wiltshire (Erskine), Imber Military training village in Salisbury, Army barracks in Bicester – other unknown military establishments. He is also alleged to have been present at pool parties where boys were abused – believed to be the Dolphin Square complex in Pimlico.

3. Material sought. What are you looking for?

Documents, journals or records detailing action by named individuals in relation to the abuse of the victim or others. Still images of the victim or any other child of an indecent nature.

8. Duty of disclosure Is there anything of which you are aware that might reasonably be considered capable of undermining any of the grounds of this application or which for some other reasons might affect the court's decision? Include anything that reasonably might call into question the credibility of information you have received and explain why you have decided that that information still can be relied upon.

(ANSWER IN A BOX) N/A

9. Declaration

To the best of my knowledge and belief:

a) This application discloses all the information that is material to what the court must decide, including anything that might reasonably be considered capable of undermining any of the grounds of the application and

b) The content of this application is true

Signed: **DS Eric Sword** Date: **27/2/15** Time: **11.50**

10. Authorisation

Authorising officer's name: **Alison Hepworth (DI)**

Date: **27/2/15** Time: **13.00**

Decision

The applicant satisfied me about his or her entitlement to make application

The applicant confirmed on oath or affirmation the declaration in box 9

I am satisfied that the police are fully aware of the sensitivities and the need for a proportionate approach without press involvement. This has been considered at DAC level. I am satisfied the access material (sic) are met and have been properly considered.

I am satisfied that interference with the private life of the parties is justified, necessary and proportionate.

Name: **HCF Riddle** Date: **2 March 2015** Time: **12 noon.**

NOTES FOR GUIDANCE

11. Information that might undermine the grounds of the application

Information that might undermine any of the grounds of the application must be included in the application, or the court's authority for the search may be ineffective.

The applicant must inform the court if there is anything else that might influence the court's decision to issue a warrant. This may include whether there is any unusual feature of the investigation or of any potential prosecution.

Hero targeted

THIS spells out what police were looking for during the search of Lord Bramall's home – effectively seeking permission to turn the war hero's house upside down.

Doubts dismissed

THIS is a crucial section of the form and, according to Sir Richard, clear evidence that the police misled a district judge into approving the search of Lord Bramall's home. He said officers leading the investigation 'were aware of six matters in particular which undermined Beech's credibility'. But they dismissed this by writing N/A - or not applicable. A quite staggering entry.

Signed off by junior

ACCORDING to Sir Richard, DS Sword was 'a comparatively junior officer' who had a 'limited knowledge of the investigation and with no knowledge of the content of the Wiltshire interviews (having chosen not to read a summary provided to him)'. However the warrant makes clear it was authorised by a more senior investigating officer, Alison Hepworth.

Boss in firing line

CONCLUDING remarks by District Judge Howard Riddle makes clear that the implication of the search warrant had been considered at DAC level'. This places Steve Rodhouse, then a Deputy Assistant Commissioner firmly in the firing line.

An 'unusual' case

THIS advisory guideline for warrant applications gets to the very heart of the charge against Scotland Yard: that it was fully aware of the glaring flaws in Beech's story yet ploughed on with the search warrant application in the vain hope that something would turn up to justify the distress caused to Lord Bramall and his elderly wife.

Clearly the entire case was 'unusual' as it was a triple murder probe based on the word of one man.

DAILY MAIL 6 August 2019

OPERATION MIDLAND: THE MET'S CHAIN OF COMMAND

COMMISSIONER Sir Bernard (now Lord) Hogan-Howe
Former Met chief, the buck stopped with him

ASSISTANT COMMISSIONER Patricia Gallan
Formal oversight of Midland, says she never approved raids

DEPUTY ASSISTANT COMMISSIONER Steve Rodhouse
Gold Commander who was in charge of all key decisions

DETECTIVE SUPERINTENDENT Kenny McDonald
Called 'Nick' 'credible and true'. He supervised inquiry team

DETECTIVE CHIEF INSPECTOR Diane Tudway
Senior Investigating Officer who was in daily charge of Midland

DETECTIVE INSPECTOR Alison Hepworth
Reviewed and authorised search warrant application

DETECTIVE SERGEANT Eric Sword
Signed search warrant application for the court

So who WAS to blame for breaking law?

By **Stephen Wright** Associate News Editor

■ Top officer in spotlight for raid on Bramall home
■ Inspector 'reviewed and authorised' warrant
■ Application to judge signed by detectives

THE emergence of the search warrant application for the raid on the home of former Armed Forces chief Lord Bramall puts one of the country's most senior police officers at the centre of the Operation Midland scandal.

The previously secret document – seen by the Daily Mail – reveals that a district judge approved the police request to storm the property of the D-Day hero after being assured its implications had been 'considered at DAC level' – deputy assistant commissioner.

At the time, Steve Rodhouse held that rank with the Metropolitan Police and was gold commander of Operation Midland.

He had a crucial role in running the 16-month investigation, including decisions over raids and interviews with suspects.

Also coming under renewed scrutiny is Alison Hepworth, the former detective inspector and 'authorising officer' who reviewed and authorised the Bramall search warrant application on February 27, 2015. It went before District Judge Howard Riddle in London on March 2.

Miss Hepworth was at the behind-closed-doors hearing at Westminster magistrates' court with the senior investigating officer on Operation Midland, Detective Chief Inspector Diane Tudway, and fellow murder squad officer Detective Sergeant Eric Sword – who signed the search warrant application.

'Facing awkward questions'

Last week a former judge said police broke the law in the bungled probe into VIP child abuse fantasist Nick. Sir Richard Henriques said officers used false evidence to obtain search warrants.

As the officer in overall charge of the shambolic murder inquiry, it is Mr Rodhouse who faces awkward questions. Over the years, he has repeatedly refused to comment on whether he approved the use of the phrase 'credible and true' to describe Carl Beech – then known as 'Nick' – whose lies about child abuse and murder triggered Operation Midland in December 2014.

The phrase – originated by Det Supt Kenny McDonald – went uncorrected by police for nine months, until after the Daily Mail exposed Beech as a suspected serial liar in September 2015.

It was not until January 2016 that Mr Rodhouse informed Lord Bramall's lawyer that there was 'insufficient evidence' to charge the former head of the Army with paedophile offences.

But Mr Rodhouse's letter announcing the end of the investigation into Lord Bramall sought to absolve Scotland Yard and blamed the media for his ten-month ordeal which included the March 2015 breakfast raid. He also left open the prospect of a further inquiry, should new information emerge. The legalistic tone of the letter infuriated Lord Bramall's family and friends, who said that the Met should have been generous enough to say that it had 'not found a shred of evidence'.

They called for a 'proper' apology from the Met after the uncorroborated allegations made by Beech came to nothing.

The force later paid Lord Bramall £100,000 in damages.

When Operation Midland formally closed in March 2016, with no arrests or charges, Mr Rodhouse insisted the investigation had been 'handled well'.

He also refused to apologise to former Tory MP Harvey Proctor, one of those falsely accused of serial child abuse and murder.

At a press conference, he stopped short of saying he was confident there never was a VIP paedophile ring and instead stated the evidence had not reached the threshold for charges. He added: 'Our role here has been to investigate some serious allegations of crime. We've conducted a very detailed inquiry and our role really has been to assess whether or not there's enough evidence to ask the CPS to level charges.

'My conclusion today is we haven't reached that threshold. We've had a long investigation, a detailed investigation into some serious allegations of crime. It's absolutely right that we fully investigated it.'

'Not a shred of evidence'

Following the scathing report into Operation Midland by High Court judge Sir Richard in November 2016, Mr Rodhouse was referred to the police watchdog for potential breaches of 'duties and responsibilities' in the investigation. Along with his senior colleague Mr McDonald he was cleared in March 2017. The watchdog said there was no evidence to indicate 'bad faith, malice or dishonesty' by the officers and Operation Midland was 'extensive and carried out diligently'.

Mr Rodhouse has been promoted to a £175,000-a-year post at the National Crime Agency, Britain's version of the FBI, where he is director general (operations) under Lynne Owens, his old boss at the Met and Surrey Police.

Lady Brittan received £100,000 damages from the Met over the bungled Operation Midland searches of her two homes in March 2015 – just six weeks after her husband Leon's death.

Mr Rodhouse had previously been criticised over his handling of a separate, equally disastrous, Scotland Yard rape inquiry into Lord Brittan.

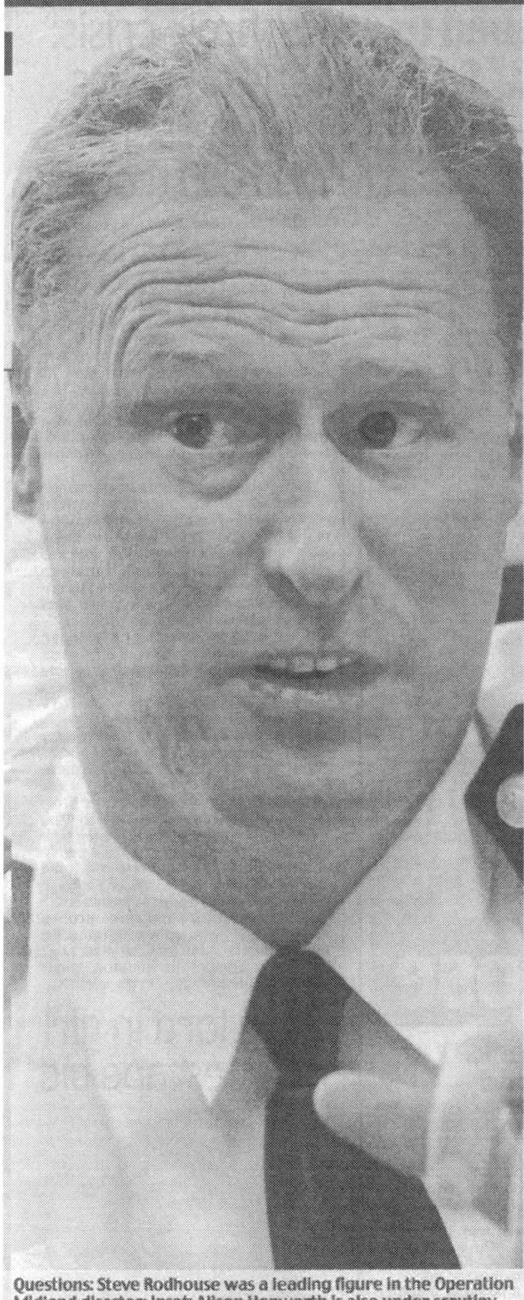

Questions: Steve Rodhouse was a leading figure in the Operation Midland disaster: Inset: Alison Hepworth is also under scrutiny

SOMETHING ROTTEN AT THE HEART OF THE MET

Daily Mail COMMENT

SEE PAGE 16

Watchdog's lead investigator was a recent graduate in her twenties

By **Jemma Buckley** and **Stephen Wright**

THE lead investigator of the police watchdog probe into Scotland Yard's handling of Carl Beech's claims was handed the role just a few years after graduating from university, it emerged last night.

Despite Operation Midland being widely regarded as one of the most shambolic police investigations in living memory, the watchdog has absolved the police and ruled that not a single officer will face misconduct proceedings.

Now it has emerged that the lead investigator was put in charge of the vastly complex case when she was in her late 20s and with only a few years' experience. Now 30, she has a degree in International Political Studies.

She also gained a master's degree in Intelligence and International Security from King's College London in 2013.

The revelation that such a young official – whom the Mail has chosen not to name – was leading inquiries on such a sensitive case raises serious further questions about the probe by the Independent Office for Police Conduct.

Lead investigators are required to be educated to degree level or equivalent and are responsible for tasks such as conducting interviews, taking statements, visiting incident scenes, recommending if disciplinary or criminal proceedings are necessary and writing reports.

They are the main point of contact for complainants and bereaved families. They also draft the scope of the investigation and report to a team leader who is responsible for making key decisions, including outcomes of the investigations. The IOPC is

'No case to answer'

already under pressure after last week's sensational intervention from retired High Court judge Sir Richard Henriques who said police may have broken the law during Operation Midland, suggesting detectives had used false evidence to obtain warrants.

The IOPC investigated the actions of three officers involved in applying for search warrants.

After more than two-and-a-half years, the IOPC ruled the officers had 'no case to answer' and had 'acted with due diligence and in good faith at the time'.

The IOPC has refused to reopen its inquiry into those officers. It has insisted it has already investigated them and found 'no suspicion of criminality'.

The IOPC is the watchdog which oversees the police complaints system. It states its mission is to 'improve public confidence in policing by ensuring the police are accountable for their actions and lessons are learnt'. While police forces deal with the majority of complaints against their officers and staff, they must refer the most serious cases to the IOPC, regardless of whether there has been a complaint.

Ultimate responsibility for rulings made by the IOPC lie with its £175,000-a-year director general Michael Lockwood.

He is the former chief executive of Harrow Council and in 2017 led recovery work as part a government task force following the Grenfell Tower tragedy.

Mr Lockwood is a qualified accountant. By law, the director general of the IOPC can never have worked for the police.

Last Thursday he was hauled in front of Home Secretary Priti Patel who demanded a full explanation of the watchdog's decision to clear the three officers. He has been asked to provide a full written explanation to the Home Office. Misconduct allegations around Midland were first referred to the IOPC's predecessor – the Independent Police Complaints Commission – in 2016 but the investigation was not completed until last month.

The IOPC was created in January 2018 and given new powers after the IPCC was considered to have lost credibility after a string of controversies.

The IOPC launched 687 investigations in the last year. It also received over 3,000 appeals from those unhappy about the outcome of their complaint.

An IOPC spokesman said last night: 'The investigation into the Metropolitan Police Service application for search warrants was undertaken by a team of experienced investigators.

'A fully qualified lead investigator was supervised by an operation team leader who has worked as an investigator throughout their career.

'The decision on whether to investigate individuals for potential conduct or criminal allegations was overseen and approved at a senior level in the then IPCC.

'The investigation was also supported by our in-house legal team. A comprehensive final report detailing all the evidence we looked at and our decision-making process will be published on the IOPC website in September.'

Explanation: £175,000 a year IOPC boss Lockwood

A guardian not fit for purpose

From Wednesday's Mail

DAILY MAIL 6 August 2019

Something rotten at the heart of the Met

Daily Mail COMMENT

THE inquiry into allegations of a VIP sex abuse ring codenamed Operation Midland ranks as the most disgraceful episode in the recent history of the Metropolitan Police. A scandal suggesting something rotten in the state of our law-enforcement system.

Acting on the flimsiest pretext, Scotland Yard officers invaded the homes of innocent people in lightning raids, employing search warrants obtained after a court was deceived. In an omission described by an eminent former High Court judge as a perversion of justice and potentially criminal, the investigating team failed to disclose evidence that undermined the case for the house searches, carried out in the full glare of national publicity and resulting in enormous distress for those involved.

These were not the misguided acts of a few inexperienced junior officers but the systematic violation of that most basic of rights — the one protecting law-abiding householders from the arbitrary invasion of their homes by agents of the state. This outrage was sanctioned in the highest reaches of the Met and carried out by detectives displaying a cavalier and contemptuous attitude towards due process.

Operation Midland was a rogue investigation fuelled by an insane Met policy demanding that alleged victims of sexual abuse should not only be listened to seriously but automatically believed.

Society bestows upon the police the right to enter private premises if there are reasonable grounds for doing so during a criminal inquiry — and this privilege should be dependent upon officers using this power wisely and proportionately. Otherwise, we will be living in a banana republic.

That the Midland team — backed by then Deputy Assistant Commissioner Steve Rodhouse, now operations chief of the National Crime Agency — abused this power is made abundantly clear in documents obtained by the Mail.

As this scandal — exposed not by politicians or the official police watchdog but by a Mail investigation — emerges, it poses the question: who effectively polices the police?

Our report today reveals investigators had evidence which made it clear allegations by the serial fantasist Carl Beech concerning the supposed torture and murder of boys by Establishment figures were riddled with inconsistencies but these doubts were not placed before the judge granting the search warrants.

This resulted in untold misery for the targets of the search operation — Field Marshal Lord Bramall, one of Britain's most distinguished soldiers, the late Lord Brittan and former MP Harvey Proctor.

There were no less than eight separate factors casting doubt on Beech's version of events. Despite nationwide publicity, no witnesses had come forward to verify his story, and indeed there was no evidence of other victims even existing.

Yet, these failings and other salient facts were not disclosed to the judge who authorised the raids.

This grievous misconduct is there in black and white — in the applications for the search warrants submitted in court. In a declaration by the officer seeking a warrant to search Lord Bramall's home, he agrees that: 'To the best of my knowledge and belief: This application discloses all the information that is material to what the court must decide, including anything that might reasonably be considered capable of undermining any of the grounds of the application.'

Answering the requirement for 'duty of disclosure' in the case of anything that might call into question the credibility of information received by investigators, the officer enters the response 'N/A' — not applicable.

This is utterly false — and it ended in detectives rampaging through the lives of innocent people, living and dead, in a deranged witch-hunt masquerading as a responsible criminal investigation.

All at the behest of Beech, a grandstanding Walter Mitty whose account of devilish sex parties involving Establishment figures torturing and murdering boys would strain the credulity of a sceptical layman, never mind the seasoned detectives of Scotland Yard.

Incompetence on an epic scale is clearly a major ingredient of this fiasco, with common sense flying out of the window. But it is contempt for the law — bordering on criminality — combined with a total disregard for the consequences for individuals that is the mark of this dark farce.

The retired High Court judge who reviewed Midland following its implosion, Sir Richard Henriques, believes some of the police officers involved should face criminal investigation. Amazingly, his full findings are still unavailable to the public — a scandal in itself.

The Met is sticking by its claim that Midland was carried out in good faith. In a weasel-worded statement, it admits that it 'did not get everything right' but reminds us that it was conducted under 'intense scrutiny'. The answer to which is, so what?

The treatment of the Midland victims was appalling. But they were prominent people with access to lawyers. Imagine if this had involved poorer, less prominent families — what chance would they have had of redress? Would these abuses ever have come to light?

And what of the Independent Office for Police Conduct, the supposed police watchdog, which managed to exonerate some of the officers involved without even bothering to interview them? Its credibility as an impartial investigator of alleged malpractice is fatally compromised.

Labour is in the frame, too. Commons home affairs committee chair Yvette Cooper dodges calls for a parliamentary inquiry, while Mayor of London Sadiq Khan is equally mealy-mouthed. Are they afraid of shining too much light on the role in this sordid affair of Labour deputy leader Tom Watson, who stoked the frenzy resulting in Midland?

This imbroglio may not have been the creation of current Commissioner Cressida Dick but it is eating away at the credibility of her force. She must act — and decisively.

Today the Mail demands that the Commissioner publish the Henriques report in full and establish a robust independent inquiry, possibly involving an outside police force. There should also be a thorough review of the workings of the IOPC.

The time has come for people to be called to account, via an independent criminal investigation.

The law is the law — whoever the culprit.

DAILY MAIL 6 August 2019

By Stephen Wright
Associate News Editor

Proctor's fury as Met rejects probe into VIP abuse detectives

A FORMER Tory MP has accused Scotland Yard chiefs of allowing a 'cover-up' of misconduct surrounding the force's disgraced VIP child abuse inquiry.

Harvey Proctor delivered his stinging rebuke after a top officer rejected his criminal allegations against detectives in the case.

Mr Proctor was falsely accused of being a serial child killer by the fantasist previously known as 'Nick' – whose claims the Met once described as 'credible and true'.

Mr Proctor spoke out after Assistant Commissioner Helen Ball's decision to deny his demands for a new, independent investigation into the conduct of five key officers.

He said the force's attitude could best be described as 'a failed authority marking its own homework' and accused senior officers engulfed in the scandal of being part of a 'self-preservation society'.

Miss Ball is a key ally of Scotland Yard Commissioner Dame Cressida Dick, who sanctioned the launch of the disastrous inquiry and is separately under investigation for alleged misconduct in the case.

Mr Proctor revealed he has appealed against Miss Ball's decision and called on the police watchdog to review its previous decision to clear five other officers of wrongdoing.

He said: 'I await with interest to see if the Independent Office for Police Conduct again allows the police to get away with it and continues to participate in the cover-up. Even at this late stage the IOPC can institute a thorough and rigorous inquiry.'

His statement piled pressure on ex-Metropolitan Police deputy assistant commissioner Steve Rodhouse, who oversaw the running of the inquiry, codenamed Operation Midland – and was later promoted to become the £245,000-a-year head of operations at the National Crime Agency.

Rebuke: Harvey Proctor

In November Mr Proctor announced he had reported five former Scotland Yard officers – including Mr Rodhouse – for alleged criminality during Operation Midland. Citing 'fresh and new evidence' of wrongdoing, he revealed he had made allegations of perverting the course of justice and misconduct to an independent force, Northumbria Police, which passed them to the Met.

Mr Proctor, 72, lost his 'home, job and repute' when officers raided his house as part of Operation Midland.

Yet, despite the force paying £100,000 in compensation to both former Armed Forces chief Lord Bramall and the widow of Lord Brittan – and more recently £500,000 to Mr Proctor – not one officer has faced any punishment. Last year a former High Court judge, Sir Richard Henriques, savaged police watchdogs who cleared five 'Nick' scandal detectives. He said justice had been 'perverted'.

'This is not the end of the matter'

In a separate move ex-senior district judge Howard Riddle said in October he was 'misled' by Operation Midland officers seeking permission to raid the homes of Mr Proctor, Lord Bramall and Lord Brittan, all falsely accused of appalling child sex crimes. The Yard's witness known as Nick was in fact former nurse Carl Beech, 51, who was jailed for 18 years last July for his lies about VIP child abuse.

In a letter this month to Miss Ball, head of professionalism at Scotland Yard, Mr Proctor said: 'You have decided, on flimsy pretext, that my complaints are not worthy of formally recording and therefore not to investigate them.'

He said her view was not supported by Sir Richard or Mr Riddle. Mr Proctor, who made the letter public yesterday, said: 'This is not the end of the matter.' He warned Miss Ball's actions and those of the Met would be considered by MPs and a public inquiry.

Miss Ball said in letters to him that seven of his eight allegations had already been investigated or were 'out of time', adding that he had already been apologised to.

DAILY MAIL 31 January 2020

Dutch Newsclips

A few reports now follow from the British Press on affairs in the Netherlands - or Holland if you prefer. Again involving the attitudes of those Norwegianesque clones who hate Islam with vigour. Pym Fortuyn was a homosexual Dutch politician who was murdered in 2002 by a Muslim man who felt sufficiently provoked by the former's outspoken attack on his beloved Prophet Muhammad and his description of Islam as “a backward culture" – the Quran, like the Old Testament, regards homosexuality as an ‘abomination’ and Pym Fortuyn certainly did not like that. His assailant felt as if it was like someone telling him to his face that his mother was “a whore”. The result? The Dutchman was summarily executed with a bullet to the head. The moral of the story being: don't maliciously denigrate one of the world's great faiths and expect nothing to happen. The Dutch liberal elite learnt nothing from this and in 2004 libertine Dutch film-maker Theo van Gogh used methods of critique of Muslim culture that were guaranteed to enrage Dutch Muslims. The result? Theo van Gogh was summarily executed by a bullet to the head. Haters of religion and the Prophet Muhammad in the very irreverent nation of France paid a similar price in the years that followed.

THE EXTREME RIGHT *Although the openly gay Pim Fortuyn was an atypical -nationalist, he had benefited from a pan-European trend*

Brutal end for man tipped to be Dutch leader

BY STEPHEN CASTLE

THE DUTCH newspaper *De Volksrant* said it in banner headlines: one group of political experts had tipped Pim Fortuyn, the maverick right-winger and anti-immigration campaigner, as the man likely to be the next prime minister of the Netherlands.

Yesterday's shooting at a media park in Hilversum was a bloody climax to an extraordinarily political story that had already turned Dutch politics upside down.

Unknown outside the Netherlands only months ago, Mr Fortuyn was becoming one of the most prominent politicians in Europe. His views were not as extreme as those of Jean-Marie Le Pen but Mr Fortuyn derived his political strength from a similar source. Across Europe, voters are worried about crime, immigration and lack of security. Even the Netherlands, which is famous for its economic success and tolerance, is not immune.

Shaven-headed, dapper, openly gay and cultivating an image of high camp, Mr Fortuyn was hardly the typical right-winger. A millionaire former sociology professor, he was a unique figure whose combination of intellect and demagoguery had proved highly effective.

With his chauffeured black Daimler, butler and two small dogs, Mr Fortuyn's undoubted charisma shone brightly in a country where even the bicycling royal family is anxious to stress it is not a cut above the man in the street. To an electorate starved of political drama, here was something new, different and a little dangerous. Consensus seemed to serve the Netherlands well. Its coalition government depended on consultation with all elements of society to deliver steady economic growth.

Mr Kok's coalition resigned last month over a report on how Dutch peace-keepers allowed the 1995 massacre at Srebrenica, staying on in a caretaker role until next week's elections. The three-party coalition had been in power seven years. Before that, Christian Democrats were in office for 70 years, longer than the Communist Party ruled the Soviet Union.

The grip of the Dutch political elite was to prove almost as vulnerable as the Kremlin. At the beginning, the rebellion Mr Fortuyn led was a grassroots one. He was the key figure in *Leefbaar Nederland* (Liveable Netherlands), a leftish umbrella group of local parties that developed into the biggest political movement in the country for 25 years.

But such prominence was not enough for such a populist who sensed a tide of anti-immigration sentiment he could tap. When he called for a reversal of anti-discrimination measures enshrined in the Dutch constitution and for an end to Muslim immigration he was thrown out of the group.

His new springboard to prominence became the Lijst Fortuyn (the Fortuyn list), which naturally, he dominated. He did retain links with Leefbaar, and was able to stand for them in Rotterdam in March, winning a stunning victory with 34.7 per cent of the votes.

Lijst Fortuyn was expected to score about 20 per cent in the 15 May elections, and the Intomart research bureau said this was an underestimate. It based its predictions on the 6 March municipal elections, in which Mr Fortuyn won 17 of the 45 Rotterdam council seats, and on a recent survey that estimated Mr Fortuyn could win between 19 and 25 seats in the national election. That could have made him prime minister.

How could this happen in the tolerant Netherlands? Mr Fortuyn's support is based on a protest vote, part of the mood of disenchantment with established politicians that has been sweeping Europe. In the Netherlands, as in much of Europe, the questioning of immigration was increasingly acceptable. Mainstream politicians highlighted the growing number of asylum-seekers.

After 11 September, the place of Muslims in society became questioned as never before. Mr Fortuyn played his part, trading insults with one Rotterdam imam who said gays were worse than pigs. Mr Fortuyn advocated integration for the 10 per cent of the Dutch population from ethnic minorities. But there was a menacing note of xenophobia behind the call to stop admitting all new immigrants, including close relatives of those already resident.

Mr Fortuyn's latest policy refinement had been to suggest a deal under which there would be residence permits for all illegal immigrants living in the Netherlands for longer than five years, providing they spoke adequate Dutch. In exchange, he said, new asylum-seekers would be allowed to enter the country only in "extremely exceptional" cases, and family reunification in the Netherlands would be discouraged.

Mr Fortuyn dismissed the parallels between himself and Mr Le Pen, whom he openly attacked. Ironically, last week, there were warnings of an assassination attempt against Mr Le Pen, a threat taken seriously in France. Somehow, in the tolerant, reasonable and moderate Netherlands the risk of such an attack on Mr Fortuyn never seemed real. But maybe that country no longer exists.

Top, Pim Fortuyn, the rising man of Dutch politics. Left, Mr Fortuyn, when he was leader of 'Leefbaar Rotterdam', surrounded by opponents; middle, Mr Fortuyn arrives in Rotterdam to his stunning win, and makes a coalition deal with opponents in Rotterdam City Hall last month *EPA/AP/Robert Vos*

IN HIS OWN WORDS FORTUYN'S VIEWS ON IMMIGRATION, ISLAM AND EUROPEAN INTEGRATION

On immigration:
"Full is full and you can't mop the floor while the tap is running."

"I think 16 million Dutchmen are about enough. This is a full country."

"The Netherlands is not an immigration country. The annual stream of tens of thousands of newcomers, who largely end up as illegal aliens, must stop. We're living on a small piece of land here."

"Moroccan boys never steal from Moroccans. Have you noticed that?"

"We have a lot of guests who are trying to take over the house and the owner of the house doesn't like it. I am not racist. I am not xenophobic."

On Islam:
"A backward culture"

"In Holland, homosexuality is treated the same way as heterosexuality. In what Islamic country does that happen?"

"An imam should be able to say about me that homosexuals are worse than pigs. My only demand is that you mustn't incite violence."

(During interview with the BBC's John Simpson)

"Give me a definition of racism. You don't know what a racist (is) because you have negroes who are Muslims, you have white men who are Muslims, you have yellow men who are Muslims, so how can you connect the Muslim religion and culture with a race? Then you are very stupid, Mr Simpson."

On Dutch financial contributions to the EU:
"I will borrow that handbag from Margaret Thatcher, bang on the table and say I want my money back."

On Le Pen
"I am appalled by his anti-Semitic thoughts. A man who describes the Holocaust as a footnote in history is beyond my comprehension."

The Independent 7 May 2002

KILLING OF FORTUYN CAREER ON THE EDGE OF ACCEPTABILITY

Populist politician struck a chord with Dutch voters

By Gordon Cramb in Amsterdam

Pim Fortuyn made in turn an academic, a journalistic and – since only late last year – a political career out of saying things that in the consensus-minded Dutch society were regarded as on the margins of acceptability. Yesterday an opponent went massively further.

The shooting came just as it began to look more than a distant possibility that his List Pim Fortuyn (LPF) could have become the biggest single party at next week's general election. That would have allowed him to claim the premiership, if he could get one or more other parties to enter a coalition with him.

LPF was cobbled together in haste after he was sacked as leader by Liveable Netherlands, another emergent populist grouping, for saying that the country was "full" and that further immigration should be stopped.

"I say what I think, and I do what I say," was the motto he carried into the campaign, in which he debated vigorously with the – initially disdainful – heads of the established parties in numerous televised discussions.

Apart from demanding a curb on migration from developing countries, he struck a chord among voters in his criticism of the cosy deals among parties and other recognised interest groups, which have been a hallmark of the way things are run in The Hague. Public health and education systems could be improved by cutting bureaucracy rather than throwing more money at them, he argued.

Ironically, another plank to his programme was to improve the effectiveness of the police. Conscious of risks to his personal safety, he hired security staff for the LPF headquarters in Rotterdam, and said there were some streets in the city where he would not appear.

Under his leadership, Liveable Rotterdam, a local splinter of the national movement that had just sacked him, became the biggest party at municipal elections in March. Mr Fortuyn claimed his support included a significant proportion of the one-third ethnic minority population of the Netherlands' second city.

To signal his rejection of racism accusations, he put a dark-skinned businessman as second on his party list for the lower house. Yesterday lunchtime, the country's Muslim broadcasting service aired an interview with him in which he again insisted: "I am not a xenophobe. I want to solve things."

While describing Islam as a "backward culture", in the campaign he also drew attention to what he said was the oppressed position of Muslim women in the Netherlands. His call was for integration, not repatriation, of the nearly 10 per cent of the population who come mainly from Turkey, Morocco and former Dutch colonies in the West Indies.

As someone who was openly homosexual, he said he feared that continued growth in the Muslim population was threatening the country's traditional tolerance of diversity and freedom of choice in life.

Pim Fortuyn in his own words

On politics

"It is no joke that I want to be premier. A person needs a purpose – and my purpose has been to lead the country since my youth"

On the upcoming election

"You could say there is stormy weather in the polder"

On immigration

– "If I could arrange it legally, I would simply say: no more Muslims can come in" – "I think 16 million Dutch is enough. The country is full"

On comparisons with other far-right politicians

"I find it intolerable that I am being compared with statesmen such as [Jörg] Haider and [Jean-Marie] Le Pen"

On the European Union

"I am a great supporter of the internal market but I am not a great supporter of striving toward a federal Europe"

POLITICAL IMPACT

Deep shock for one-man movement

By Gordon Cramb in Amsterdam

The assassination of a leading politician comes as the latest and deepest shock in what had already become one of the most extraordinary years in Dutch post-war history.

The initial big development was the rise of Pim Fortuyn himself: a political newcomer who within months built a populist movement strong enough to rival the parties that, in one combination or another, had ruled for decades.

Then came the sudden resignation last month of the centre-left coalition that Wim Kok, prime minister, had headed for nearly eight years. With only four weeks to go before a general election, Mr Kok led the early departure of his cabinet following criticism of the handling by successive Dutch governments of its forces' peacekeeping role in Bosnia.

A report, commissioned by his government from war historians, concluded that the Dutch battalion that failed to prevent the 1995 massacre of Muslims by invading Serbs in Srebrenica had been dispatched on an ill-judged mission. Faced with threats by two of his ministers to quit, the premier decided the whole team should go.

The cabinet remains only in a caretaker capacity. It was the first in modern Dutch history to resign early without either having lost the confidence of parliament or suffering a rift among coalition partners. Mr Kok now faces the task of ensuring an orderly conclusion to the election campaign, in the face of anger among Fortuyn supporters that was already becoming evident last night.

The List Pim Fortuyn had drawn its support largely from voters disaffected with Mr Kok's social democratic PvdA and the free-market VVD, its main coalition partner. The Christian democratic CDA, which they had pushed into opposition in 1994 for the first time since the war, had according to opinion polls been holding on to its support base but failed to make gains.

Pollsters said further backing for the LPF had been coming from among the 27 per cent who did not vote in the last general election.

LPF was a one-man movement. It was last night thought likely to attract a sympathy vote but could no longer expect the 19 to 36 seats in the 150-member lower house that various polling organisations had been forecasting.

Even if the ballot goes ahead as planned on May 15, the electorate and the established parties are both left with the twofold legacy of Mr Fortuyn. First, he brought immigration policy and the need to integrate ethnic minorities to the centre of the political agenda. Second, he pointed tellingly to bureaucratic failings.

Few were last night prepared to predict who would gain politically.

Financial Times 7 May 2002

Srebrenica relatives sue UN and Dutch for £370m

By Harry de Quetteville
Balkans Correspondent

RELATIVES of victims of Europe's bloodiest post-war massacre are to sue the United Nations and the Dutch government for £370 million.

Estimates suggest that more than 7,000 Bosnian Muslim men and boys were rounded up and executed by Bosnian Serb troops during a three-day period in July 1995. The victims had gathered at the eastern Bosnian village of Srebrenica, which had been designated a "safe haven" by the United Nations.

But as Bosnian Serb troops under the command of Gen Ratko Mladic descended on Srebrenica, only a handful of lightly armed Dutch peacekeepers were in place to protect civilians. In the event the peacekeepers left without a shot being fired, opening the way for the biggest act of organised butchery in Europe since the Second World War.

"In the next three or four months we are to file a suit against the UN and the Netherlands before appropriate courts for breaching international laws and the European convention on human rights," said Semir Guzin, who leads a team of lawyers in Bosnia which represents more than 8,000 relatives of victims.

"Survivors demand at least one billion convertible marks in compensation for their loss," he added.

Mr Guzin said Dutch and US legal experts were to join his team to pursue the claim. Both the UN and Dutch authorities have admitted some level of responsibility for the massacre, which prompted the government of the Netherlands to resign in 2002.

Mr Guzin said the compensation claim would be filed in The Hague, where the International War Crimes Tribunal is trying the Serb leader Slobodan Milosevic on charges of genocide over the massacre. Mladic and his wartime leader, Radovan Karadzic, both face similar charges but are on the run.

The Daily Telegraph, 10 November 2003

Film-maker is murdered for his art

A descendant of Vincent van Gogh who championed free speech has been shot dead over his portrayal of Muslim violence to women, writes **Anthony Browne**

A DIRECTOR who outraged Muslims with a film about an abusive arranged marriage was murdered in the street yesterday.

Theo van Gogh, 47, the great-grand nephew of the 19th century painter Vincent van Gogh, was shot and stabbed to death while cycling past Amsterdam's city council offices. Police arrested a 26-year-old man of dual Dutch-Moroccan nationality after a gunfight in a nearby park, which wounded a policeman and the alleged assailant.

The incident sparked immediate comparisons with the assassination two years ago of Pym Fortuyn, the right-wing politician, who campaigned against immigration. Van Gogh had just finished a film on the life of Fortuyn that was due to be broadcast shortly.

But it was his latest film *Submission*, which featured a Muslim woman forced into an abusive arranged marriage and who was raped by her uncle, that caused the most outrage in the Dutch Muslim community.

The 11-minute film, broadcast on national television in August, was narrated and written by Ayaan Hirsi Ali, a refugee who fled Somalia 12 years ago to escape a forced marriage. Describing herself as a former Muslim, Ms Ali has since become a liberal member of the Dutch parliament and high-profile critic of Islam.

After the broadcast, van Gogh and Ms Hirsi Ali, 34, were repeatedly issued with death threats and reluctantly accepted police protection. In a recent radio interview, however, van Gogh was upbeat and dismissed the threats, saying the film was "the best protection I could have. It's not something I worry about."

But at 9am yesterday, he was shot as he cycled past the front door of the city council of Amsterdam. Witnesses said that he managed to get to the other side of the street, where he was again shot and stabbed by the murderer, who pinned a note to his body.

The suspect then ran into a park, where a gunfight broke out with police. Van Gogh's body was left lying in the street under a white sheet as police sealed off the area.

Ms Hirsi Ali, who famously criticised Muhammad as "a pervert" for marrying a six-year-old girl, Aisha, when he was 53, and consummating the marriage when she was nine, was taken to a safe house by police.

The outrage sparked by the murder in 2002 of Fortuyn, a flamboyant homosexual who campaigned against Islamic intolerance, was a watershed in Dutch politics. All political parties were forced to take a tough stance on immigration, with the Government adopting some of the strictest immigration laws in Europe and forcing immigrants to learn more about Dutch culture, language and values.

There are currently one million Muslims in a Dutch population of 18 million.

Tensions are never far from the surface and flared again this year when a teacher was shot dead by a Muslim pupil in a school canteen.

Last night, Jan Peter Balkenende, the Prime Minister, called van Gogh "a champion of the freedom of speech" and appealed for calm.

"It is unacceptable if expressing your opinion would be the cause of this brutal murder," he said. "There is a climate that sees people resorting to violence. That is worrying. On a day like this we are reminded of the murder of Fortuyn. We cannot resign ourselves to such a climate."

The Dutch wing of the European Arab League, one of several organisations to criticise *Submission*, said it was shocked by the murder. Nabil Maruch, its spokesman, said: "It's horrible. We don't know who did it and why, but it's absolutely shocking that someone can be shot dead in a park in Amsterdam. Shots and death threats are not the way to make people think differently."

The Moroccan Municipal Assemby in Amsterdam called for calm, saying: "Escalation is in nobody's best interest."

Van Gogh sparked controversy when he addressed Islamic issues after the September 11 attacks. In a book called *Allah Knows Better*, he attacked Islamic militancy and accused imams of hating women.

Submission criticised the Koran for sanctioning domestic violence and depicted four abused women in see-through robes showing their breasts with Koran text painted on their bodies.

One verse of the Koran states: "And those (wives) you fear may be rebellious admonish, banish them to their couches, and beat them."

AP/THOMAS KIST

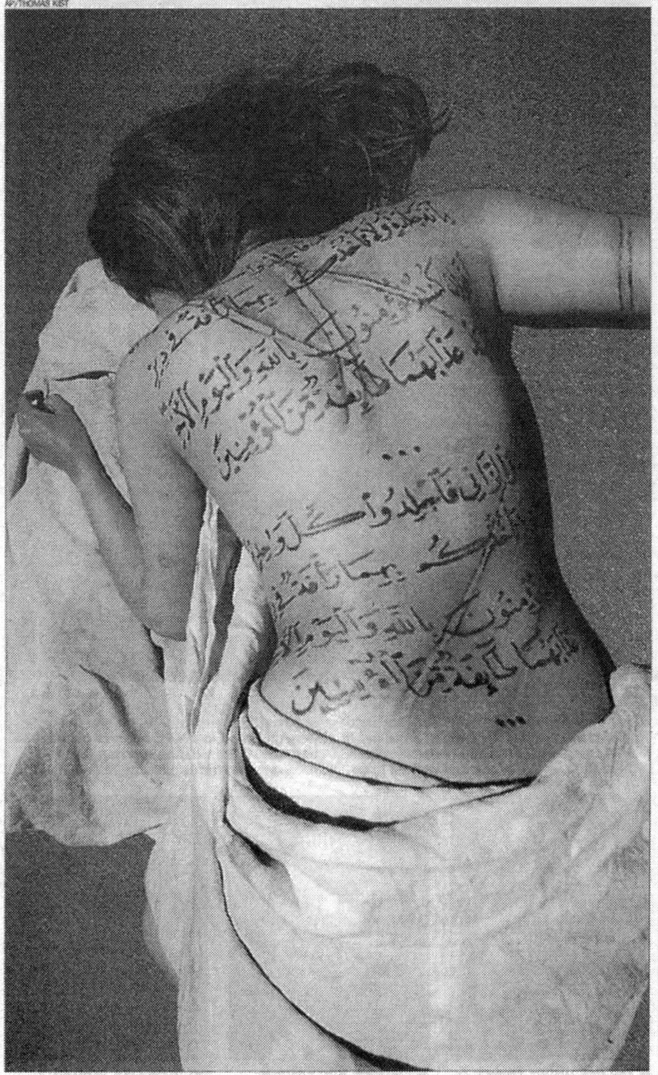

Controversial scene: *Submission* depicts an abused Muslim woman and verses from the Koran

Maverick who spoke out

By Jack Malvern
Arts Reporter

DESPITE a prolific film career in the Netherlands, Theo van Gogh was more famous outside his home country for his artistic ancestor than for his own work.

The great-great nephew of Vincent van Gogh directed 23 films, but only one was released abroad. *1-900, Sex Without Hangups*, about a relationship between a sex-line operator and one of her clients, had a limited release in New York and Los Angeles.

Van Gogh also had a minor role in *The Times* bfi London Film Festival this year. He contributed a five-minute segment to *Visions of Europe*, a collaborative film from 25 European directors. His only other appearance in British cinemas was in a small role in Alex van Warmerdam's 1992 film *The Northerners*. He was also a contestant on the Dutch version of *Celebrity Big Brother*.

REUTERS

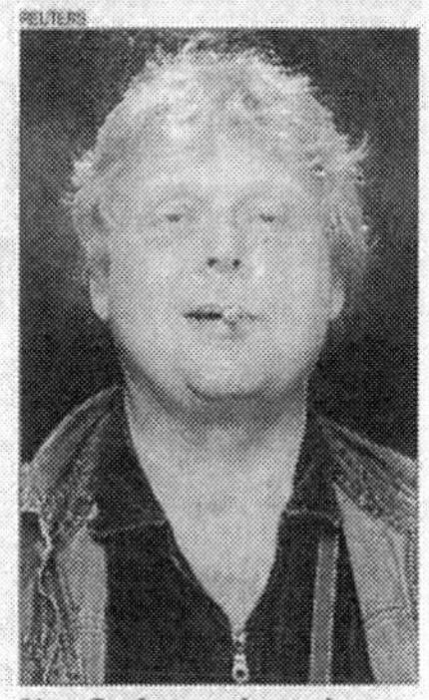

Van Gogh: trenchant views

First night, page 29

Dutch libertine pays with his life for Islamic 'porno' insult

Controversial Dutch film director shot dead in street

Jon Henley

Theo van Gogh, the Dutch artist's great grand-nephew and a provocative filmmaker, was shot dead in a street in Amsterdam yesterday, police said, apparently because of a film he made about Islamic violence against women.

Van Gogh, 47, was stabbed and then shot several times by a man who witnesses said arrived on a bicycle as the filmmaker was getting out of his car outside council offices in the Linnaeusstraat, in the east of the city, at 8.45am, a city police spokeswoman, Elly Florax, said. He was dead by the time ambulances arrived.

The suspected killer, a 26-year-old man with dual Dutch and Moroccan nationality, fled into the nearby Oosterpark and was later arrested after a gunfight with police that left an officer and a bystander wounded. The man was last night under police guard in hospital, being treated for gunshot wounds to the leg.

As the Dutch prime minister, Jan Peter Balkenende, appealed for calm, one witness told Dutch media that the suspect had a long beard and was wearing Islamic or Arabic garb. The Amsterdam public prosecutor said the man had left a letter on Van Gogh's body, but declined to reveal its content until technical and forensic tests had been completed.

Van Gogh had recently drawn fierce criticism and received death threats for his latest fictional drama , Submission, in which a Muslim woman is forced into an arranged marriage, abused by her husband, raped by her uncle and then brutally punished for adultery.

The film, shown on Dutch television, was scripted by Ayaan Hirsi Ali, a Somali refugee given Dutch citizenship after fleeing an arranged marriage 12 years ago. Now a rightwing MP, Ms Hirsi Ali has renounced her faith for its treatment of women and offended many Muslim groups.

In the Netherlands there are around 1 million Muslims in a population of 16 million. Immigration, integration and Islam are all highly emotive issues. According to polls, a majority of the Dutch feel afraid of the rising number of Muslims in Holland and threatened by Islamic militants.

Mr Balkenende said: "Nothing is known about the motive," he said. "The facts must first be carefully weighed. Let's allow the investigators to do their jobs." He praised Van Gogh as a proponent of free speech who had "outspoken opinions", but said it would be "unacceptable if a difference of opinion led to this brutal murder".

Born in Wassenaar, a suburb of The Hague, Van Gogh — who throughout his life courted controversy with ill-concealed joy — arrived in Amsterdam at the age of 17 to attend film school, but the two shorts he submitted were rejected and he was advised to seek psychiatric help.

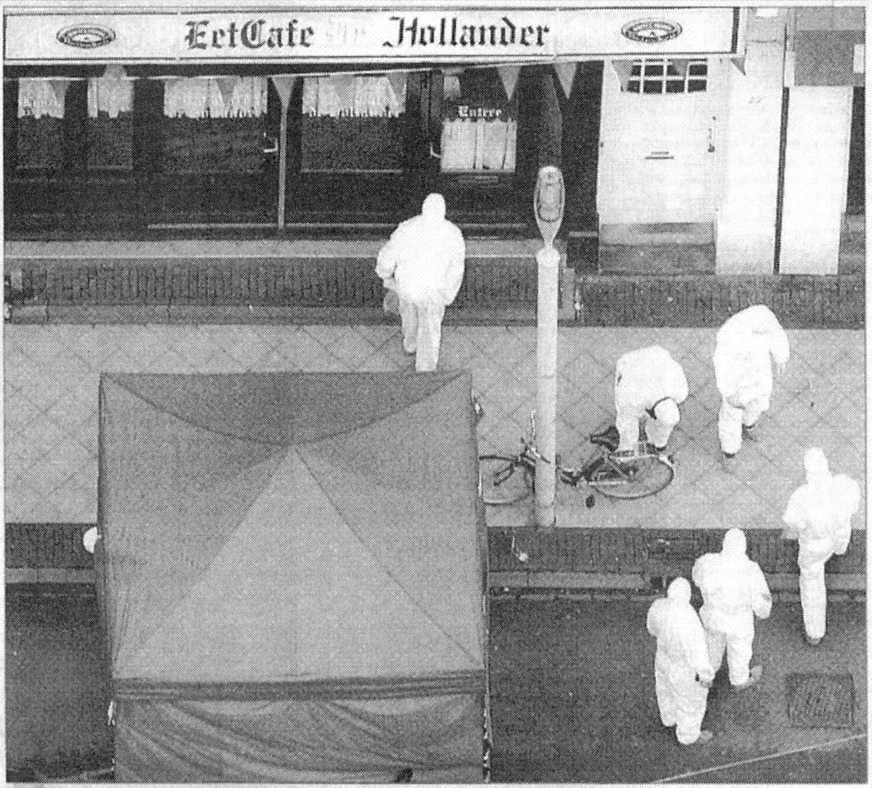

The scene of the shooting of Theo van Gogh, below left, and, right, Ayaan Hirsi Ali Photograph: Robin Utrecht/EPA

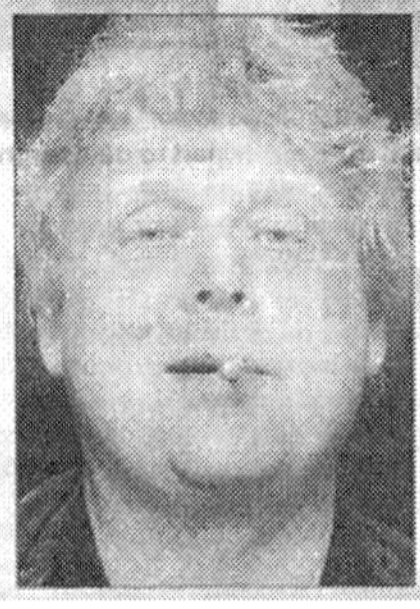

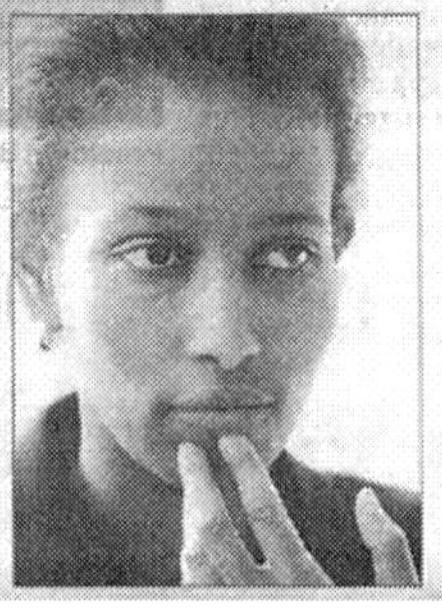

None the less, in a 25-year career, he made 10 original and intelligent feature-length films. Some critics said he never fulfilled the promise of his first film, Luger (1981), mainly because he spread himself too thinly.

Van Gogh was employed at one time or another by every leading Dutch newspaper and magazine; almost all fired him for offending their readers' sensibilities. His latest outlets were the daily freesheet Metro and a popular website, De Gezonde Roker (The Healthy Smoker).

But in the course of several hundred TV shows, Van Gogh also showed himself to be a sensitive and self-effacing interviewer. "Two people inhabited him," his actor friend Cas Enklar said. "A courteous and adorable gentleman, and a devil who liked nothing better than making enemies."

Van Gogh's last film, about the life of the gay anti-immigration populist Pim Fortuyn, assassinated in 2002, was due to be premiered in January.

THE INDEPENDENT
Thursday 4 November 2004

Theo van Gogh

Controversial film-maker

THE FILM-MAKER Theo van Gogh, who was shot dead in Amsterdam on Tuesday, will be remembered as a controversial figure who delighted in provocation and had a penchant for portraying difficult subjects on screen.

Theo van Gogh's name was known around the world. He shared it with his great-great-grandfather, the brother of the artist Vincent van Gogh. But in the Dutch film community he himself was well known: he was regarded as the Netherlands' Michael Moore. He displayed a charming mix of arrogance with skilful argument in the frequent television interviews he gave, wearing his trademark scruffy clothes and chain-smoking his favourite Gauloise cigarettes.

Van Gogh considered himself to be a misunderstood visionary. His website, "*De Gezonde Roker*" ("The Healthy Smoker"), was filled with harsh criticism of multicultural society. He said this was sorely needed as the Netherlands was experiencing a social turmoil that threatened to turn it into a "type of Belfast" in a few years.

An award-winning film-maker, television producer and newspaper columnist, van Gogh could be scathing. He once mocked a prominent Dutch Jew, referred to Jesus as "the rotten fish" of Nazareth and called a radical Muslim politician "Allah's pimp". In his passionate efforts to stir public debate, he branded imams as women-haters and ridiculed the Prophet Mohamed. Many Jewish organisations branded him an anti-Semite. Others called him an extremist and Muslims said they found his work insulting. But he was also hailed as a champion of free speech, as the Prime Minister, Jan Peter Balkenende, pointed out in a statement to the nation following his murder.

Van Gogh probably made more enemies than friends in his patchy film career. His recent English-language film *Submission* was made in conjunction with the Dutch MP Ayaan Hirsi Ali – a Somali refugee who is an outspoken critic of Islam. The film, a protest against domestic violence in Islamic cultures, outraged the Dutch public when it was shown on television in August. It features four women in see-through robes showing their breasts with texts from the Koran painted on their bodies talking about being abused. For that, he received death threats and was placed under police protection, much against his will.

He later rejected the surveillance that could have prevented the shots that killed him as he cycled along an Amsterdam street. In a radio interview only last Friday he said he wasn't concerned about being the victim of an attack. "If it happens, it happens," he said, adding that he didn't believe in the goodness of man, but reckoning that his ego was too big to accept a bullet would be meant for him.

Theo van Gogh was born in 1957 and grew up in The Hague. He studied law in Amsterdam but dropped out to take up acting, directing and writing. He made his début in 1981 with the feature film *Luger*. His films were regularly nominated at the Netherlands Film Festival, where he won five awards. His 1994 film *06*, about a young woman who advertises her services for phone sex, became one of his best-known works. It was renamed *1-900 (Sex Without Hangups)* for the US market. *Blind Date*, two years later, featured a bartender listening to two customers talk, and *Cool!*, which came out this year, was about the rehabilitation of a gang of young criminals.

Van Gogh also found success making television programmes. Among his highlights was *Najib en Julia* (2002), a modern reworking of *Romeo and Juliet* that saw a Dutch girl fall in love with a Moroccan pizza delivery boy. His directing was more successful than his acting but he used his famous name in 2002 when he appeared alongside David Carradine in *Wheatfield with Crows* – which brought Vincent van Gogh into the modern music industry.

His most recent project was *06-05*, a fictionalised version of the events surrounding the assassination of the Dutch populist politician Pim Fortuyn two years ago. Based on a novel by Tomas Ross, the film is due to be released next month.

Theo van Gogh was an anti-monarchist and prominent member of the Republican Society. He admitted he was overweight at 300lb and that he led an unhealthy life style. He said he had intended to change it to set an example to his teenage son: "So I have to stop overdoing the drink and lose 100 pounds."

GERALDINE COUGHLAN

Theo van Gogh, actor and film-maker: born The Hague 23 July 1957; (one son); died Amsterdam 2 November 2004.

Van Gogh: 'If it happens, it happens' *EPA*

MP may be deported over claims she lied to win asylum

It is claimed Ayann Hirsi Ali lived comfortably in Kenya and did not flee a forced marriage and persecution AP

By Isabel Conway
in The Hague

The political career of the Netherlands' most prominent MP was thrown into doubt as an investigation was launched into explosive allegations that she lied about her past in order to gain residence status and Dutch nationality.

Ayann Hirsi Ali, who has won an array of international awards for bravery and free speech, has been accused of making up a story to immigration officers in which she claimed she had fled from a forced, arranged marriage and that she faced persecution in her native Somalia.

A Dutch television documentary, aired last week, featured interviews with Ms Hirsi Ali's family in which her claims of an arranged marriage were denied. The programme also alleged that, contrary to her claims of having fled a war zone in Somalia, the MP had lived in comfortable upper middle-class circumstances safely in Kenya for at least 12 years before she sought refugee status in the Netherlands in 1992. Her family home – which is large and comfortable by Kenyan standards – was shown in the programme.

Rita Verdonk, the Minister for Immigration and a member of Ms Hirsi Ali's own VVD right-wing liberal party, announced a full investigation into the furore last night, insisting that "laws and rules are valid for everyone".

Ms Hirsi Ali, 36, became internationally known when a film she wrote provoked the murder of its controversial director, Theo van Gogh, by an Islamic radical in 2004. With her own life under threat, she went into hiding and still lives under 24-hour protection. She has never, however, strayed far from the international spotlight and has won a string of awards for her battle to raise awareness of the plight of many Muslim women.

When interviewed by the highly-respected *Zembla* TV programme, Ms Hirsi Ali's family members denied she had been forced into marriage against her will to her former husband, a Somalian man who now lives in Canada, or that she had not been present at the wedding ceremony, as she had previously claimed. The couple are said to have parted amicably and her family denied that she had fled a marriage she did not want.

When questioned by the documentary makers, the MP stuck by her denial of being present at her own wedding. Her brother Mahad Hirsi Magan, who first claimed that his sister did attend her own wedding, has since changed his story.

But Kees Driehuis of *Zembla* said: "We stick by the content. We spoke to different members of her family and we know that Hirsi Ali has been in touch with her brother since the programme went out. Perhaps that has something to do with it."

Asked whether she had falsified her asylum application, she told the programme: "I lied", but said this had been public knowledge in 2002 when the VVD chose her as a candidate.

Ms Hirsi Ali, whose real name is Hirsi Magan, pretended she had come to the Netherlands from Somalia, rather than via Kenya and Germany. Refugees are usually required to apply for asylum in the first safe country they reach after fleeing.

Ms Hirsi Ali, who said yesterday that she was "puzzled by the uproar," accused her rivals of a co-ordinated political vendetta against her. "Have they all gone mad?" she asked.

Political opponents want her stripped of her Dutch citizenship and deported. Others say she should be expelled from parliament.

The issue is particularly sensitive for the VVD as the party has taken a hard line on immigration, introducing tough new citizenship tests and leading a drive to expel 26,000 failed asylum-seekers. It has said that any foreigner found to have lied about their circumstances should be prohibited from having Dutch citizenship.

Ms Hirsi Ali rose to fame after the murder of Van Gogh in November 2004. Defiant as ever, Ms Hirsi Ali is working on a sequel to the film she made with Van Gogh on Islam's treatment of homosexuality called *Submission 2*.

Ayann Hirsi Ali - poetic justice for this disturbed woman who led the Dutch up the garden path.

THE UNRAVELLING OF AYAAN HIRSI ALI

The end came quickly for Ayaan Hirsi Ali. Once it looked like allegations that she had lied to enter The Netherlands and fabricated her past were proven true, the same political friends who made her the darling of the Dutch right, speedily retreated from her side. Ali became the thing that she had looked down on in contempt: just another dishonest immigrant. You could almost hear the sniggering amongst Holland's embattled Muslim minority. She's now ditching Europe and taking her secular crusade to the United States.
Mohamed N. Husain reports.

Last year, *Time* hailed Ayaan Hirsi Ali one of the world's "100 most influential people." *The Economist* described her as a "cultural ideologue of the new right". Her first book, *The Caged Virgin* will hit bookshops with much fanfare this month and she is scheduled to tour Britain before she heads off to Washington DC to take up her post at the American Enterprise Institute. Until recently she was the darling of Europe's secular political establishment - a brown face made welcome because of her shrill denunciations of Islam, the Prophet Muhammad and Europe's "backward Muslims". It seemed like the happy days would never end.

Ali arrived in Holland in 1992, falsely claiming to be on the run from an arranged marriage. Having absconded from her well-to-do Somali family (settled in Kenya), she took a job as a cleaner in The Netherlands. Like thousands of other women, she put herself through university and tried to better her economic condition. Unlike many of her generation, however, she accepted all that was taught on her political science course without retaining, or developing, the critical intellect expected of the erudite Muslim intellectual she would soon claim to be.

Instead, she described her time at the University of Leiden as "paradise", admitting to getting drunk regularly, losing her Muslim friends and identity. With a colonised mind, a loss of faith and exposure to excessive secular liberalism, she travelled throughout Europe and China. What she thought she had escaped continued to haunt her.

Now a speaker of several languages, Hirsi Ali worked as a translator in a refugee centre in Rotterdam. She was horrified to learn that immigrant females in Holland, away from Morocco and Turkey, continued to be subjected to one of the most horrid of African and Arab cultural practices, clitoredectomy, or female genital mutilation (FGM). Cases of male domestic violence, rape, and forced marriages were epidemic. That experience, coupled with her unquestioned liberal education and Somali clannish upbringing, moulded her confrontational worldview. Hirsi Ali was rightly alarmed by male brutality: her diagnosis, however, was flawed. She was courageous to speak out against misogynistic practices; her convictions ended up demonising the very people she set out to protect.

A late arrival to Europe (aged 22), she was awestruck by "freedom and lost her equanimity." She moved quickly up the social ladder: from cleaner, to translator to researcher for the social-democratic Labour party. In close contact with the political class in Holland, severed from her Muslim family and faith community, she further developed her ideas about culture, migration, perceived lack of Muslim integration and the role of "ideological Islam" in public life. Hirsi Ali, by her own admission is not well-versed in the Islamic scriptures - she is a critic without the basic tools necessary for criticism. Upon hearing, for example, that Tony Blair had read the Koran 'cover to cover', she mocked him. It was the kind of ignorant, knee jerk edict that she became so good at giving. She recently declared that a report by a Dutch think tank, The Scientific Council for Government Policy, that concluded that their was little conflict between Islam and Dutch values and human rights, undermined free speech. Her utterances, time and again, have confirmed her deep ignorance of Muslim scholarship. This lack of education did not serve her well: she has repeatedly confused Islam with political Islamism, religion with

Sheltering a self-confessed fraudster and awarding her a fellowship is not the best way forward for building bridges between Muslim nations and the United States. In view of Ali's propensity to lie, deceive, and exploit to achieve her own ends and by rearranging her fickle allegiances, US opinion formers would be well advised not to take Hirsi Ali too seriously.

Hirsi Ali was horrified to learn that immigrant females in Holland continued to be subjected to one of the most horrid of African and Arab cultural practices, female genital mutilation (FGM). That, coupled with her unquestioned liberal education and Somali clannish upbringing, moulded her confrontational worldview. Hirsi Ali was courageous to speak out against misogynistic practices but her convictions ended up demonising the very people she set out to protect.

culture. Nevertheless, in a post 9/11 world eager for easily digestible theories and easy answers, much of the Western media continued to promote her as a leading 'critic of Islam'. Hirsi Ali has proven to be a savvy operator.

Habitual Opportunist

Hirsi Ali ran away from Germany to The Netherlands in 1992 and claimed that she had escaped from an arranged marriage in war-torn Somalia. As Professor Jytte Klausen of Brandeis University who knows Ali and has followed her career closely, recently told *The Toronto Star*, this was a fib: "She wasn't forced into a marriage. She had an amicable relationship with her husband, as well as with the rest of her family. It was not true that she had to hide from her family for years." Her estranged husband hadn't spoken up because, "Because Hirsi Ali has asked him not to. They parted company amicably."

There is more to this fabrication than meets the eye: yes, she lied to secure Dutch citizenship but she also demonstrated an acute awareness of Western social and political sensitivities. She played on Dutch liberal vulnerabilities to secure herself a home in Europe, an education and initially joined the Labour party, not the rightwing, crypto-racist VVD party to further her career.

The Dutch Labour party advocated multiculturalism, tolerance, and dialogue. Hirsi Ali was interested in the opposite: assimilation, a marginalisation of faith, zero-tolerance for Muslims who spoke from the religious convictions. She successfully used women's rights as a vehicle to amplify her views, raising her profile within the Labour party. She seized the post-9/11 climate to attack her fellow Muslims and eventually discarded her faith, declaring, "I do not believe in God, angels and the hereafter." Her views on a host of issues were at odds with the Labour party and when her political opponents, the rightwing VVD offered her the lure of a parliamentary seat, she abandoned Labour.

To date, she has exploited and betrayed her family, clan, religion, adopted home, and political party to crusade against what seems like a personal vendetta against the only factor shared by those she opposes: a belief in or respect for Islam.

Secular Extremist Voice

Millions of Muslim women and men are just as concerned as Hirsi Ali, if not more, about the misogynistic practices that pervade many eastern cultures. Forced marriages, domestic violence, child abuse, rape, and female subjugation cut across religions, nations, and cultures. Lebanese Christians and Druze living in Australia have a hideous reputation for these crimes. I have met Christian Armenian women in Lebanon and Syria who were subject to the worst forms of domestic violence. What is more, Amnesty International has repeatedly confirmed that in African countries with large Christian populations such as Eritrea and Ethiopia FGM rates are above 90%. As a cultural practice, it also affects Egypt, Somalia and other predominantly Muslim countries. In contrast, in populous Muslim nations such as Indonesia or Bangladesh, clitoredectomy is unheard of.

Therefore, to blame Islam for male tyranny is wrong. If Hirsi Ali has learnt anything about cultural relativism, then it should be to see the emergence of Islam in its seventh century Arabian context. The Prophet Mohammed uplifted women from being sexual objects to full human beings, on par with men. I concede that many Muslims are at fault, but to blame a religion that liberated women is intellectually untenable. As with so much else in Hirsi Ali's life, she has exploited her own personal tragedy and tarred a billion Muslims with the same broad brush.

Mainstream secularists who argue that religion is a private matter, and desire a neutral, or shared, public place to deter conflict, command following among the Muslim masses. The failure of Islamists in free elections in several Muslim countries underscores this fact. However, extremist secularism seeks to eradicate religion and impose a hollow atheism on society. Hirsi Ali is an avowed advocate of the latter, publicly arguing that "religions should be mocked for fun and entertainment".

An Excellent Neo-Con Adventure

With a proven track record for outgrowing her surroundings and recently offending large sections of the Dutch people by stating that they were appeasing Muslims as they once appeased Hitler, she is said to consider Europe not free enough for her vitriol. Having deceived many along the way her rise to infamy, and ridden many a whirlwind to the fringes of secular extremism, she has now set her eyes on exploiting US concerns about Islam and the Muslim world.

The United States continues to feel and behave like a vulnerable country. Its political leaders have repeatedly stated that they seek to win Muslim hearts and minds. Laudable aims, no doubt. However, in recent years, several leading Muslims, including Yusuf Islam, Tariq Ramadan, and the late Dr Zaki Badawi were all sent back from the US. In comparison, Hirsi Ali has been given a hero's welcome.

The American Enterprise Institute (AEI), the neo-conservative temple where the like of former Bush speechwriter David Frum and Lynne Cheney, cheerlead the war on Iraq, has employed Ali, with the tacit of support of several leading members of the government. The AEI has backed other infamous character like Ahmad Chalabi - who was a favoured Bush Iraqi on the eve of the invasion and who is still feted regularly by the AEI. By befriending Hirsi Ali the AEI is again repeating the same mistake.

Sheltering a self-confessed fraudster and then awarding her a fellowship is not the most productive way forward for building bridges between Muslim nations and the United States. In view of Ali's propensity to lie, deceive, and exploit to achieve her own ends and by rearranging her fickle allegiances, US opinion formers would be well advised not to take Hirsi Ali too seriously. She arrives in the US with a clear intent of what she wants. Her mission statement is clearly laid out in the pages of her book: to subvert Islam by fomenting as much dissent in Muslim ranks as possible. This process, she refers to as "reform". She goes on: "In order to do this we will need the help of the liberal West, whose interest are greatly served by a reform of Islam."

At a time when most responsible, peace-seeking people of all faiths and no faith strive for better understanding and reconciliation, Hirsi Ali and others advocate provocation of Muslims in the name of 'reform', 'entertainment', and pseudo-intellectual 'urgency and necessity'. Ali cunningly claims her argument is only with 'radical Islamism': it is not. Her vilification of the Prophet and the Quran is an attack on all Muslims.

The US has first-rate Islam specialists at home. If it is Islam that US leaders wish to understand, then they must turn to their own sons and daughters- like Hamza Yusuf Hanson, Ingrid Mattson, Zaid Shakir and others. Hirsi Ali does not seek mutual understanding. If a 'clash' is what we want to avoid, then Ayaan Hirsi Ali is, undoubtedly, part of the problem. ■

With contributions from Fareena Alam.

The Unravelling of Ayaan Hirsi Ali - Q News - July 2006

THE TIMES THURSDAY FEBRUARY 3 2005 — EUROPE **WORLD NEWS** 35

Family pictures were 'obscene'

A French appeal court has upheld a painter's conviction over naked portraits of her children, writes **Charles Bremner**

A DUTCH artist was given a suspended prison sentence and fined by a French court yesterday for taking pictures of her naked children that were deemed to be obscene.

Art experts denounced the prosecution of Kiki Lamers, 40, whose work has an international following. She was given an eight-month suspended sentence and fined £3,000 for corrupting minors.

Ghislaine Hussenot, a Paris gallery-owner who has exhibited Ms Lamers's portraits of children, said: "This story is grotesque, idiotic and hysterical. It shows both the climate of puritanism and a profound ignorance of Dutch art."

Ms Lamers, who paints stylised portraits of naked children from photographs, has held shows in Amsterdam and New York and sells paintings for up to £11,000. Last year she published a book of the portraits entitled *Tender Age*.

The appeal court in Riom, in the rural Massif Central, upheld a lower court conviction, but suspended the original jail term. The first court ruled in July that her photographs were of children "in lascivious or obscene positions which could only incite immorality".

Louis Thijssen, 42, Ms Lamers's former partner, received the same sentence and fine on appeal for possessing pornographic photographs of children.

The prosecution began when Ms Lamers handed in for development six rolls of slides picturing her children and those of friends, taken with the parents' permission. The police raided the couple's home in the Massif Central and seized other pictures and Mr Thijssen's computer, which was found to contain internet images of children, the court was told. Mr Thijssen, who has since separated from Ms Lamers, said that he downloaded the pictures, then deleted them while seeking a cover for a thriller that he was writing.

In the retrial last month, the prosecutor said that Ms Lamers's paintings were "troubling" and "suggestive", although he acknowledged that they could be considered to be art.

The artist, who has had thousands of children's pictures developed in the Netherlands, said that she had never imagined that the slides would cause a problem in France.

"I never had any bad intentions and I am deeply shocked by the consequences of this prosecution," Ms Lamers said. Her six-year-old son, who spoke no French, had been interviewed under oath, she said.

Jacoba de Jongh-Dunand, for Ms Lamers, said that the Dutch had "a very different attitude to nude children from the Latin cultures".

Le Monde said that the French authorities were reverting to archaic arguments about obscenity and breaching freedom of expression. Paedophilia was being used as a catch-all excuse for censorship, it said.

Ms Lamers now lives in the Netherlands and is painting only face portraits of children. Her lawyers are expected to challenge the conviction in the French national appeal court.

CHESS

▶ Loek Van Wely versus Nigel Short at the Corus tournament

RAYMOND KEENE PAGE 68

Ten years ago, the world was appalled as 8,000 Muslims were slaughtered under

HIDAJET DELIC / AP

July 2005: Graves have been dug for 570 massacre victims

Massacre memorial clouded by desire for bloody revenge

REVENGE seems an incongruous word among the rose gardens and quiet graves of the Srebrenica memorial in Potocari, where on Monday some 50,000 relatives and dignitaries will gather to commemorate the tenth anniversary of the massacre of up to 8,000 Muslim men.

It is hard to imagine that on July 11, 1995, thousands of desperate refugees swarmed into the Dutch UN base here in the futile hope of finding sanctuary from the pursuing Serbs.

The scene is silent, bucolic even, in the green summer valley, except for the shovel scrapes of labourers digging graves for more than 570 newly identified victims who are to be buried at the service. But in the visitor's book, spiky handwriting brims with vengeful intent.

"It is a beautiful place," one unseen hand had written on Tuesday, "only instead should be buried here those who committed crimes on innocent Muslims, and I hope one day this shall be so."

Peacemakers hoping that eastern Bosnia's divided communities may be prepared to forgive and forget will be disappointed. "We live together again only because we have to," said Hatidza Mustafic, 68, who lost her husband and two sons in the massacre. "But whenever I meet a Serb I feel horrible. I know what they have done. And I am sure one day my children will experience the same thing."

Srebrenica was once a thriving town, rich from its mines, timber industry and health spa. But its prewar population of 37,000 has dwindled to 10,000, and they include some 1,500 Muslims who have returned since the war ended.

Unemployment stands at 50 per cent, the reconstruction of war damage is only nascent and the town's youth is bleeding away beneath economic decline and memories of the past. "I curse those who made me come back here," said Ramiza Jakubovic, 55, who lost her three brothers in the massacre. "I feel a huge emptiness everywhere. We can't live together. We know among ourselves who was involved in the killings, but we say nothing. We have to live through the night."

The air of depression is tangible. The international community, which allowed Srebrenica to experience a ghastly fate with its hollow "safe haven" status, seems to have forgotten the town again.

"Nothing has changed here in ten years," said Dragan, an 18-year-old Bosnian Serb in a café. "Every day is the same and everyone wants to leave. There's no life here at all. Considering how many young are leaving there won't be enough people to fuel the next war. We'll have to fight it in Africa."

Ahmo Begic, a 24-year-old butcher, is one of the few former Muslim soldiers to have returned. He was in the 10,000-strong column of men of military age who tried to flee through the forests in July 1995. Fewer than 4,000 survived.

His return is all the more surprising since his brother-in-law is Naser Oric, Srebrenica's infamous wartime commander who is himself on trial for war

HOW A SAFE HAVEN TURNED INTO HELL

January 7, 1993: Muslim forces from Srebrenica attack village of Kravica, killing 43 Serbs

March 1993: Bosnian Serb Army attacks Srebrenica

April 16: Security Council declares Srebrenica a UN safe area

January 1995: Dutch UN battalion sets up HQ in Potocari

July 5: Shelling of Srebrenica begins

July 6: Bosnian Serb Army begins ground offensive

July 9: 30 Dutch peacekeepers taken hostage by Bosnian Serbs

July 10: Dutch commander requests Nato air support. Request denied by UN

July 11: Dutch told request for air support was written on the wrong form
■ Dutch jets drop two bombs on Serbs
■ The Serb General Ratko Mladic threatens to execute Dutch hostages
■ Dutch air strikes halted Serbs resume attack
■ 5,000 Muslim refugees enter base at Potocari, 20,000 more wait in fields outside. 10,000-15,000 others flee through forest
■ Mladic enters Srebrenica
■ Dutch at Potocari surrender weapons and stand by as Serbs separate Muslim men and women.
■ Killings of the men begin

July 12: Serbs bus 23,000 women and children out of Potocari
■ Escaping column in the forest ambushed

July 13: Dutch expel 5,000 Muslims from base at Serb request. Men are executed

July 13-20: Large-scale executions continue
■ No man of military age handed by Dutch to Serbs is seen alive again

the UN's nose. Today, Srebrenica is still in shock and decay, reports **Anthony Loyd**

July 13 1995: Dutch UN troops survey thousands of refugees who had gone to the base near Srebrenica, believing they were safe. The killings began that day

crimes. "I am more optimistic of the future," Mr Begic said. "Though if once you have been bitten by a snake you are always afraid of lizards."

Mr Begic's skin crawls in front of my eyes when I ask him about his flight through the forest, an eight-day trek under continual attack in which the wounded were abandoned, men lost their minds and turned on one another.

"I don't like to talk about it," he said after a pause. "I'm here because the town needed a butcher, and the Serbs accept me as someone who is not a nationalist. But men here always live in fear. As soon as I get a smell of war I'll go to a third country. And I'd recommend my children not to get too attached to this town."

For their part, the area's Serbs, whose livid hatred of Srebrenica's Muslims was born of a tangled history of killing and counter-killing, appear to exist behind a wall of denial. Publicly they deny the massacre happened, saying that the Muslims were killed in action and that the number of dead was wildly exaggerated.

"I hate Srebrenica," said Ilija Nikolic, 53, a former Bosnian Serb soldier, at his café bar in nearby Bratunac. "It brought me much misery and pain. And they lie. I just want to read somewhere that there wasn't a genocide there, that the genocide happened to the Serbs."

Of the many Serb men to whom I spoke, there was only one who even admitted that something terrible had occurred, a man with most reason for revenge. Mihailo Eric, 31, was a Bosnian Serb soldier badly wounded in fighting at the start of the war. His grandfather was killed in a Muslim ambush in 1992, still fighting aged 80. His great uncle, an 82-year-old warrior, fought off a Muslim attack on their village, Kravica, at the Orthodox Christmas in 1993. Running out of ammunition, he killed himself and his wife.

Kravica was overrun and 48 Serbs were killed. The village had its revenge: after the fall of Srebrenica, up to 1,000 Muslim prisoners were corralled into Kravica's agricultural warehouse before being slaughtered. But when the call for revenge came, Mr Eric did not pick up his gun to join the killings. "My family had given enough in this war," he said. "I had no desire for revenge.

"Now we Serbs and Muslims are supposed to live together until the next hothead decides to pit us against each other once more. It is all crazy."

TOMORROW
IN THE MAGAZINE:
Janine di Giovanni meets the mothers and daughters still fighting for justice ten years on

Karadzic's son seized at home by US troops

From Nick Hawton
in Sarajevo

THE son of Radovan Karadzic, Europe's most wanted war crimes suspect, was arrested by Nato troops in Bosnia yesterday in an apparent attempt to increase pressure on the family before Monday's ceremonies.

Aleksandar Karadzic, known as Sasa, was taken by American soldiers from the apartment he shares with his mother and sister in the Bosnian Serb town of Pale, about ten miles from Sarajevo. Witnesses said that he was handcuffed before being led to a helicopter.

"Aleksandar Karadzic is suspected of rendering support to an indicted war criminal and may have information vital to the goal of locating indicted war criminals or identifying their supporters," a Nato spokesman said. "The arrest went ahead without incident."

The Karadzic family said that the operation was a kidnapping to pressure it into revealing Mr Karadzic's whereabouts. The family has repeatedly denied any knowledge of where he is.

The former Bosnian Serb leader has been on the run for eight years. He has been indicted by the UN war crimes tribunal in The Hague on charges of genocide relating to the Srebrenica massacre.

Nato has stepped up its hunt in recent weeks. Soldiers raided the Karadzics' home in Pale last month, removing documents and other materials.

And Serbian and Montenegrin police raided Karadzic family property in Belgrade and Montenegro after reports that Mr Karadzic was in the north-western area of the country, close to the Bosnian border.

World news

Grief and guilt at graveside in Srebrenica

HEATHCLIFF O'MALLEY

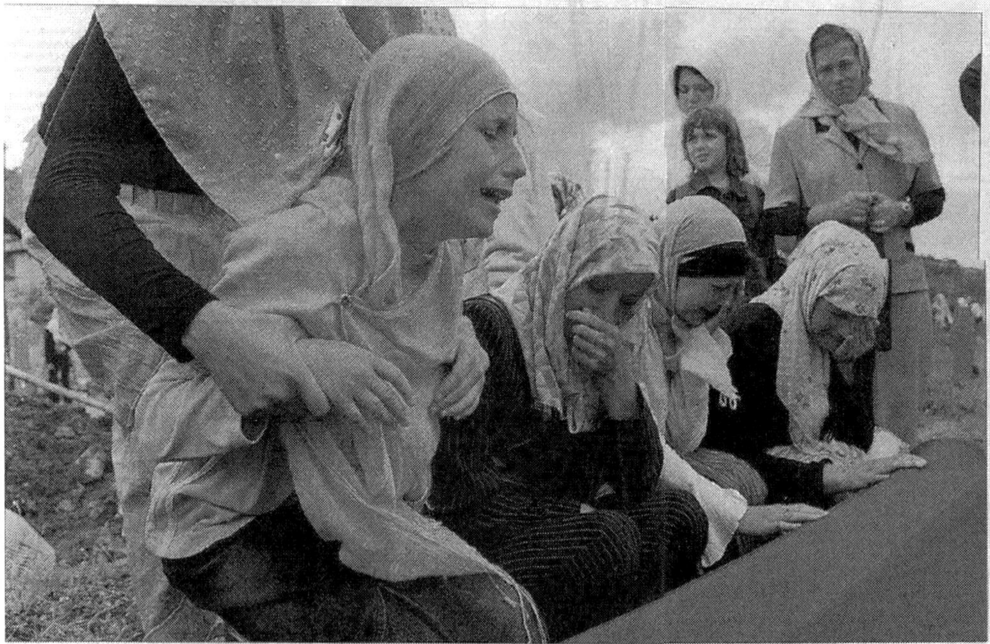

Mothers, wives and daughters watch the reburial of 610 recently identified victims of the Srebrenica massacre whose remains were found in mass graves. Yesterday marked the 10th anniversary of the atrocity when thousands of Muslims were slaughtered

VIPs apologise to Muslim mourners marking 10th anniversary of the massacre of 8,000 of their menfolk in Bosnian war. **Patrick Bishop** reports

THE coffins passed quickly along the long row of mourners. It was easy work. There was nothing too heavy inside the thin wooden boxes, just a few bones and maybe a skull, all that remained of all those Mujos, Husos and Hamids who once lived in these haunted hills and valleys.

Srebrenica's long catharsis continued yesterday as a further 610 of the 8,000 victims were laid to rest on a soggy hillside outside the town.

It was 10 years ago that the great massacre began and the mourners were burning with rekindled grief, the great and good weighed down by guilty consciences.

The VIPs arrived by armoured BMW and Mercedes. The grieving, weather-beaten men and women and fresh-faced boys and girls came by coach, arriving from the many corners of Bosnia to which they were flung by the catastrophe.

Some wore T-shirts emblazoned: "The Dayton Agreement Was Written With The Blood of Srebrenica."

The architect of that agreement, which finally brought an end to the Bosnian war after three years of diplomatic paralysis, was asked if he agreed. "That's true," said Richard Holbrooke.

"Srebrenica should never have happened. It was a failure of Nato, of the West, of the peacekeepers and the United Nations. It is a tragedy that should never be allowed to happen again."

The massacre, during the ethnic war in the former Yugoslavia, was unleashed after Bosnian Serb forces marched on the town, a UN "safe zone".

With only lightly-armed Dutch peacekeepers overseeing the town and the international community disagreeing over air strikes on the Bosnian Serb army, it was taken with ease.

Men and boys were separated from women. Thousands were captured and slaughtered systematically.

Yesterday came the acts of contrition. The UN secretary-general, Kofi Annan, sent a message admitting that the "truth is [a] hard one to face ... we can't evade our own share of responsibility ... the tragedy of Srebrenica will haunt our UN history for ever." The Foreign Secretary, Jack Straw, said: "It's to the shame of the international community that this evil took place under [its] nose ... I bitterly regret this."

He added that it was "sickening" that the men who bore the greatest responsibility for the slaughter, the Bosnian Serb leader, Radovan Karadzic, and his military commander, Ratko Mladic, were still free.

Listening to the condemnations were those providing security. To many of the paramilitary policemen lining the roads, Karadzic and Mladic were heroes. If they were angry or embarrassed, they did not show it, staring with that mixture of menace and contempt familiar to veterans of the war.

The most uncomfortable VIP guest was the Serbian President, Boris Tadic, the first Serb politician to attend the annual memorial.

Surrounded by bodyguards, he paused before the green-draped coffins, then hurried on to join the dignitaries.

Perhaps wisely, he chose not to speak. As he was leaving, he was ambushed by Suada Selimovic who shouted that she lost two brothers in the massacre. He listened patiently before murmuring that he too had lost members of his family in warfare.

That, of course, is not how the Muslims see it. For them, this was a uniquely evil event.

They were the victims, as the crowd was reminded endlessly, of the worst slaughter in post-war Europe. They were dispatched mechanically, often joyfully.

Yet the 20,000 mourners were there to grieve not to demand revenge.

Lord Ashdown, the international community's chief official in Bosnia, was struck by their dignity.

Recalling the London bombs, he said: "It's very important to remember that it was the Muslims who suffered here from terrorism. Terrorism has no ethnic boundaries."

He was standing by a recently excavated mass grave. There are 22 more in the surrounding area yet to be unearthed.

In time the bones buried there will join the rest in the cemetery down the hill. They will be coming to weep at Srebrenica for many years yet.

France Newsclips

One cannot leave the French out when it comes to the art of sexual licence - and how apt that it is the British Press expressing the criticism!

The unlikely rocker
Queen's Brian May rhapsodises about bad hair, stars and his new musical
Interview, page 5

NEWS REVIEW 4

THE SUNDAY TIMES www.sunday-times.co.uk/newsreview MAY 5, 2002

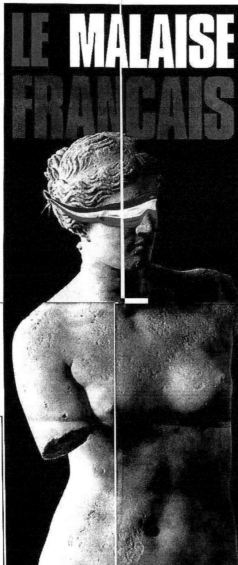

LE MALAISE FRANCAIS

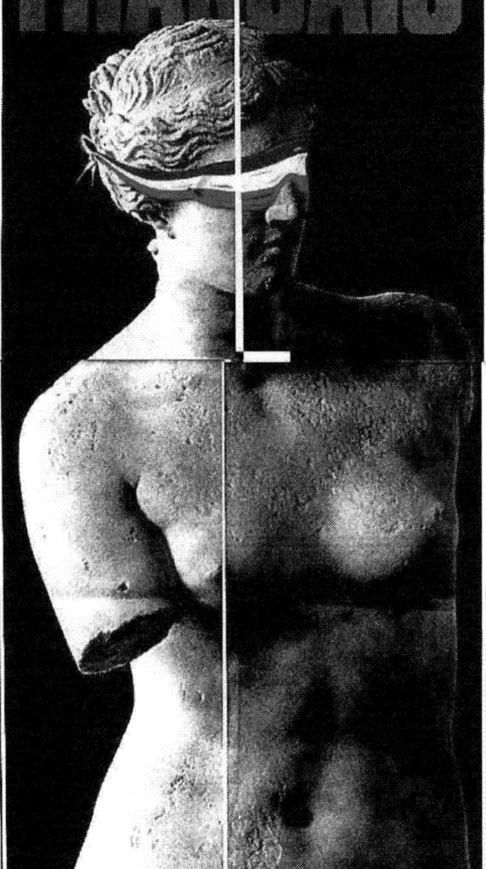

France has a sickness that pervades its politics and corrupts the bourgeoisie, writes Matthew Campbell. Decadence now rules in a morally rudderless society

The number on the wall was barely visible in the dark. We rang the bell. The door opened and a man wrote our first names on a card. We were invited to descend a plush, winding stairway. At the bottom, long red ribbons stretched from the ceiling to the floor, blocking the view beyond. Like explorers parting dense jungle foliage, we passed through.

It was 1am on Wednesday, May Day. France was in the grip of a political crisis. In only a few hours' time the streets would be awash with demonstrators for and against Jean-Marie Le Pen, the right-wing extremist who has shocked the civilised world by winning a place in today's final round of the French presidential election.

At Les Chandelles, however, the party was in full swing. Couples sat chatting politely in a basement bar. Some were dancing.

It could have been a nightclub anywhere but for the man emerging from a doorway putting his shirt back on — and the woman out on the floor wearing only her knickers. Minutes earlier, they had been disporting themselves with friends in a warren of velvet-walled alcoves padded with mattresses, under the gaze of voyeurs.

Les Chandelles is the most exclusive boite *échangiste*, or wife-swapping club, in Paris. Such places have never been so well frequented. Talk around polite dinner tables about which are the best *échangiste* clubs to frequent is one gauge of how widespread the habit of collective heterosexual romping has become.

In Britain, it may go on quietly in the suburbs; America, too, has its "key parties". Yet nothing can compare with France's expanding fascination for the taboo and its transgression.

Last week Time magazine asked on its front cover: "Have the French gone mad?" The article was about the unexpected support for Le Pen in the first round of the election. It could, however, just as easily have summed up the scenes my friend and I witnessed in that nightclub not far from the Louvre.

For years, respectable, middle-of-the-road Frenchmen have insisted enthusiastically that Le Pen puts "spice" into politics. I heard the same defence in Les Chandelles: voyeurism, public troilism and partner-swapping put spice into dull domesticity, too.

From the Marquis de Sade to the Moulin Rouge, France has always been known for its naughty streak. But the *échangiste* trend has taken this to such extremes that even an intelligentsia that prides itself in liberal unshockability is beginning to wonder what is going on.

Jean-François Mattei, a professor of political science at the Institute of Political Studies in Aix-en-Provence, talks of a national *malaise*, a climate of ennui among his increasingly "narcissistic" and "egoistic" countrymen.

"It's a sort of Club Med mentality," he said. "There's been a retreat from political life in favour of personal pleasure. It's a decadent society dedicated to sex and pleasure. We are swimming in hedonism. Nightclubs, wife-swapping, magazines for men, massages for women. It is the pursuit of pleasure all round."

The thesis of a "troubled" society hurling itself into the solace of group sex seems to be born out by numbers: there are not one or two but 50 *échangiste* clubs in Paris — and another 200 in the rest of France.

"This is a big thing here," says Michel Erman, a novelist and professor of literature at Dijon University. "The country is in the grip of a hedonistic, licentious and frivolous mood. People are as confused in their intimate lives as they are in politics."

He added: "There is not the same seriousness as before. There is no political engagement these days. No interest in politics. No ideas. The mad election vote and the high abstentionism is an example of that."

Michel Maffesoli, a sociologist at the Sorbonne, also sees a direct link between French sexual attitudes and the high abstention rate in the first round of the election that handed Le Pen his place in the run-off against Jacques Chirac today.

"Dionysius, the god of orgies, is back," said Maffesoli, "and one manifestation of this hedonistic epoch in France is obviously the fact that there is more and more abstention from voting."

THE unbridled appetite of 21st-century France for the orgy can strike the uninitiated as either sick, charming, sad or bewildering. My niece, who works in a student bar on the left bank, has been propositioned by men who proclaim that their wives find her attractive. Would she like to join them at private suburban "parties"?

Once the preserve of a depraved elite, such events have mushroomed over the past two years into a new lifestyle industry catering to a clientele from all walks of life. They have their own magazines, with titles such as Couples and Swing, and espouse a philosophy known not just as *échangisme* but also as old-fashioned *libertinisme*.

The fad is particularly popular among bourgeois professionals, who leave their children with babysitters so they can frolic away the night with strangers in scenes evocative of Fellini's Satyricon. This is what my companion and I

My evening with Becky, as I shall refer to my friend, had started at the Bastille opera house with a performance of Wagner's The Flying Dutchman.

Before we went into the auditorium, we had looked through the high glass facade at the mighty colonnade rising over the square to commemorate the anti-monarchist rebellion of 1830. Somebody had scrawled on it, in letters 3ft high, the word "F***".

It seemed, albeit bluntly, to reflect the ferment on the streets against the electoral success of Le Pen. Or was it more an example of what Maffesoli, who is head of the Sorbonne's centre for the study of daily life, calls the "rebellion" against conventional totems, be they the sanctity of the couple or the authority of the state?

Regulars at the *échangiste* clubs have no sense of doing anything more unusual than enjoying a night at a restaurant with friends — and this being France, that is in fact how they often start the evening: Les Chandelles has a nautically themed restaurant upstairs where diners get the chance to size each other up before the orgy begins.

Downstairs, initially, Les Chandelles looked normal enough. Then I noticed out of the corner of my eye a woman swaying to the lyrics of I Like to Love. She was tall and tanned and wearing nothing but her expensive-looking lingerie. A lugubrious barman handed us a glass of champagne and a beer. We stood at the bar, snatching furtive glances at the other couples.

Becky told me to turn round. A dark-haired, fortysomething man was rooted to the spot as he observed — with an expression of such intensity it was reminiscent of prayer — a man and two women groping one another 3ft away from him.

Next to us a young man who looked as though he had just left his office began unzipping the black cocktail dress of a woman in her twenties with long dark hair. coquettishly before they headed off towards another doorway strewn with red ribbons. The threesome cavorting behind me had also headed through the same door.

Becky and I followed. We were in a darker room. To one side was a large mattress. Three or four couples lay on it, making love.

Turning a corner, we confronted a woman standing with her back towards us, her arms stretched up above her, her wrists manacled to two bars. A man stood behind her, his thighs moving rhythmically. And so it went on. There was

Continued on page 2

The Sunday Times 5 May 2002

LE MALAISE FRANCAIS

Continued from page 1

nowhere to look without being confronted by a bizarre pornographic tableau. Even with eyes averted, the atmosphere was erotically charged with the sound of primal grunts and sighs. We returned in slack-jawed amazement to the bar.

We approached a respectable looking couple as they rested, fully clothed, in the bar after their alcove exertions. They turned out to be Jean-Paul, a 41-year-old finance company director in a blue shirt, and Françoise, his 38-year-old wife, who was wearing a grey miniskirt with a lacy top.

We explained that our interest was aimed at an article in The Sunday Times rather than a romp on a mattress. Politely, and not put out by the questions, they concurred that spending an evening or two each month at Les Chandelles added a touch of "spice" to their sex life.

"We've been coming here for a long time," said Jean-Paul, cradling a whisky in the palm of his hand. He went on to acknowledge getting a "kick" out of the idea that other people were watching their couplings. "And even if we're just having a drink in the bar, we are excited just by the knowledge of what is going on next door," added Françoise, gesturing at the red ribbons separating the rooms.

"Most couples," said Jean-Paul, "don't really swap partners, but play with other people before making love together." Françoise was nodding vigorously. They might have been discussing the weather.

"You know, it really turns him on to see me playing with other women," she enthused. "It fills him with passion for me — and that cannot be bad."

It is not always such innocent fun, however. Elsewhere in the bar, a man sat with his head in his hands, a picture of despair. "It can provoke outbreaks of terrible jealousy," said Jean-Paul, "particularly among beginners. But they have a rule that couples must leave together and it is very rarely broken."

He explained that until a couple of years ago it used to be "really difficult" to get into Les Chandelles, one of the oldest of the *échangiste* clubs. As the craze for the clubs began to build, however, an original, more secretive circle of "swingers" stopped coming and began attending private "parties" instead. "For those pioneers of *échangisme*, the clubs have become a bit old hat. Everybody is doing it."

Even so, customers are closely scrutinised via video monitor before being granted access. Jeans are not permitted. Trousers of any kind are banned for women. At the same time, a big difference from the old days, when brothels were there to serve only men, is the role of women in the orgiastic revels. It was they who seemed to be initiating most encounters, with the argument that this was preferable to secret, adulterous affairs.

"It is not as if you are cheating on your husband," said Françoise, "because he is standing right there, watching."

LIKE so many other French people on April 21, neither Jean-Paul nor Françoise voted in the first round of the presidential election.

"Now I wish I had," said Jean-Paul, who was considering joining the protest later that May Day morning against Le Pen, which ended up attracting more than 1m people onto the streets of France.

Maffesoli, the Sorbonne sociologist, sees the high abstention rate as an expression of a hedonistic impulse involving the cultural glorification of sex, a fad for body building and an obsession with clothes.

"*Echangisme* is an expression of it, too," he said. "It used to be a question of private debauchery, public morality. Now the wall between them doesn't exist. Look at literature. Look at advertising. There's this atmosphere of eroticism, a generalisation of hedonism of a kind that appeared in other periods such as Renaissance Florence, the Middle Ages and the 18th century during the time of de Sade."

If France's fascination for the erotic is nothing new, it has recently seemed more like obsession. The revered Bibliothèque Nationale has just published Obscénités, a collection of pornographic photographs by Auguste Belloc, and a spate of books and films have also set new standards in sexual explicitness, from confessions of porn stars to the lurid recollections of sex-starved *intellos* of the left bank.

The publishing craze for smut has extended even to Chirac's former chauffeur who, in his memoirs last year, depicted the head of state as a rampant lothario whose appetite for fast sex had led to references to him among female staff as "three minutes — shower included".

Yet this was nothing compared to La Vie Sexuelle de Catherine M. Its author, Catherine Millet, is the founder of a lofty cultural organ called Art Press; but her book is an orgiastic romp through Paris that follows her sexual career from the loss of virginity to her first "gang bang" — a few days later.

Millet describes in a matter-of-fact tone multiple encounters in car parks, including one when the line of men outside her Peugeot became so long that she had to make her excuses and leave.

Then came Michel Houellebecq, whose chronicles of a sick society have made him the most successful contemporary French novelist. One of his most frequent themes is dysfunctional sex. His latest novel, Plateforme, paints a sympathetic portrait of sex tourism.

At the same time advertising campaigns in Paris have pushed to new extremes the promotion of the scantily clad body, while playing with themes from sadomasochism to masturbation. The lingerie company Barbara.Posters depicts a well-endowed woman in only a bra proclaiming: "When somebody says 'no' to me, I take off my sweater."

Here, at least, there has been some reaction from feminists tired of seeing female bodies exploited: the La City clothing chain was forced to withdraw its billboards from the Métro after protests about a poster showing a virtually naked woman on all fours, in a field.

A cultural erotic overload may not be unique to France. Yet imagine the outrage that would accompany the opening of a club such as Les Chandelles in London, which compared with Paris looks as though it is being run by mullahs.

Mattei, the political scientist from Aix, says the pursuit of pleasure is more pronounced in France than anywhere else. He argues that in his country there is even "a hedonistic element to politics itself".

"The vote for Le Pen is an expression of hedonism," he said. "I have spoken to many people who told me they got a sense of pleasure simply from voting for Le Pen. They got pleasure from annoying the parties in power."

Street protests against Le Pen were just as pleasure-oriented, Mattei claimed. "Did you see the young people at the rallies kissing each other in the streets? They were smoking hash and having the time of their lives. It is quite dangerous, actually, because it reduces politics to a game. It turns politics into a sort of Loft Story," he added.

> **❛ The vote for Le Pen is an expression of hedonism. People got a sense of pleasure simply from annoying the parties in power ❜**

Loft Story is the hugely popular Big Brother-like "reality" television series in which young men and women sharing a house are encouraged to couple in front of the cameras.

"I see all this as evidence of what I call a spectacle society, a society in which everything is reduced to a show," said Mattei.

Mental health professionals are just as intrigued by the trend. Boris Cyrulnik, a psychiatrist in Toulon, calls it a "culture of enjoyment" and of "instant gratification", adding that voters for Le Pen had, essentially, been in search of a thrill. "It is the same thing when it comes to *échangiste* adventures."

Does this help to explain the first-round election result? There was widespread boredom with Lionel Jospin, the dourly honest and Protestant prime minister, who was unexpectedly beaten by Le Pen. Chirac, by contrast, retains a level of popularity incommensurate with the crook status conferred on him by socialist enemies.

All the allegations of sleaze, from running slush funds in the Paris town hall when he was mayor, to using public money to buy his fine wines and cigars, have been shrugged off by a public whose pleasure-seeking ways evoke comparisons with the corruption-tinged *climat de fête*, or party atmosphere, noted among the bourgeoisie in the 1920s after the first world war.

Chirac's shenanigans have been the source of more merriment than despair as television audiences revel in his depiction as "super-liar", in a Superman cloak, on Guignols, the French Spitting Image. "Jacques the lad" at least has the virtue of being morally in tune with his time.

Maffesoli points out that *libertinisme* dates back hundreds of years and began essentially as an expression of opposition to authority before taking on any connotation of freewheeling sexuality. The *échangiste* libertines of today are expressing the same sort of dissent as their forefathers in both their sexual and political behaviour.

"It is ultimately to do with

protest, [redacted]

subverting what the state holds most sacred: the family. I ask myself if Jospin's failure was related to the sort of killjoy Protestant morality he represented.

"*Libertinisme* is a sort of rebellion — and the vote for Le Pen is related to that. A lot of people who voted for him don't approve of his policies. They just liked the idea of a big-mouth troublemaker, an outsider belching irreverently at established power."

Ironically, of course, although Le Pen's National Front stands for the family, Le Pen himself has a reputation as an old-fashioned womaniser.

So it is left to ultra-conservative followers of the late, excommunicated Monsignor Marcel Lefèbvre to decry the country's moral drift.

"Our society is very sick," said Christian Bouchacourt, a priest at the schismatic movement's church of St Nicolas du Chardonnet on the left bank. "We regret that the bishops, who have issued a statement condemning Le Pen, are talking politics instead of religious principles."

Bouchacourt called wife-swapping "disgusting" and said the *échangiste* clubs, which he described as drug-infested hotbeds of "every type of iniquity", should be closed immediately.

He went on: "When he opens the floodgates of pleasure, man ceases to think. The government has been doing nothing but encouraging it for years.

"Our youth has become corrupted, we've given up teaching in our schools. More and more of our teachers belong to the libertarian left and families no longer have any influence. It is all very degrading."

AT 4:30am on May Day, many of the satisfied-looking customers were getting ready to leave Les Chandelles.

There was a problem, however. In hushed tones, a young woman was explaining to her man that she did not want to accompany him home and would prefer to stay with Suzanne and George.

The doorman upstairs looked annoyed. "You know the rules," he said. When the boyfriend did not object, however, she was permitted to go back down to rejoin her friends. "It happens sometimes," the doorman explained. "We are all adults here. In the end, it is up to them."

A couple in front of us — she in a minuscule latex skirt and skimpy top — were given back long, dark coats. Concealed in these, they looked as though they could be coming home from the opera.

When it was our turn to pay, we were presented with a bill for €80 (about £50) covering our drinks and entrance fee.

"This could kill off the porn industry," said Becky. "Who needs films when you could just come here and watch?"

With Gallic charm, the doorman presented her with a bouquet of *muguet*, or lily of the valley, the traditional May Day flower.

Outside, as the door clicked shut behind us, the street was deserted. Becky suddenly confessed she had found the spectacle of women kissing one another exciting, although she never would have wanted to join in. I felt a stab of jealousy.

The Sunday Times 5 May 2002

SADDAM

That's what the Press in Washington is calling France for its betrayal of Nato. Here, a legendary British journalist living in America explains why the mood against the French is turning so ugly

HE IS an elegant 56-year-old lawyer, given to impeccably tailored double-breasted suits, not a bouffant hair out of place, but when he walks into a Washington cocktail party he looks as if he has just been dealt a blow to the solar plexus.

And so, in a way, he has.

Jean-David Levitte is just weeks into his new job as France's ambassador to Washington and the atmosphere is Arctic. 'It reminds me of the days of Cold War crisis when the Soviet ambassador came in with his bodyguards and everyone froze,' a member of the diplomatic corps told me.

Ambassador Levitte's predecessor, Francois Bujon de l'Estang, attempted to depart America on a graceful note after seven years mainly spent satisfying his countrymen's curiosity as to why the Americans made such a fuss over the Monica Lewinsky affair. Back home, it was taken for granted that a president would have a mistress.

His farewell address celebrated American vitality and 'renewed understanding' between 'the odd couple'. Despite their knack for irritating one another, the French, he insisted, did not wake up every morning asking themselves how to aggravate the United States.

Tell that to the Marines.

The performance of the new ambassador's close friend, President Jacques Chirac, has aggravated countless ordinary people beyond Bush and the hawks.

It has convinced millions of Americans that the French are bent on appeasing Saddam Hussein as they appeased Hitler— and that they are doing so not out of principle, but for financial gain. Not for glory, but for greed. It is a fair suspicion.

Kenneth Pollack, the CIA analyst who predicted the Iraqi invasion of Kuwait in 1990, recently revealed how France has wheedled its way round the UN ban on commercial flights into Baghdad.

FRANCE, he says, voted for the ban, and it observed it like everyone else for ten years— then it discovered a 'new' interpretation which has let France become one of the largest beneficiaries of Iraq's oil-for-food programme.

They will not, it should be said, be likely to get the same preferential treatment from a new regime in Iraq, should Saddam be toppled. 'Shameless pandering' is how Pollack describes the behaviour of the French.

Not that they are alone in their ignominy. The whole international community solemnly committed itself in 1991 to contain and restrain Saddam in his pursuit of weapons of mass destruction. The majority of nations have failed to honour that promise.

The Russians and the Chinese, as well as the French, have worked actively to undermine what they all agreed. Very few countries have kept their word.

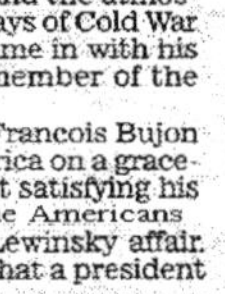

SATURDAY ESSAY

by Harold Evans

AUTHOR OF THE AMERICAN CENTURY

The exceptions are America and Britain, which, with Australia, Holland and Japan, have worked hard and honourably to observe the ban— only to be kicked in the teeth for consistency.

Unsurprisingly, America rather resents being lectured on the same principles of international law, collective security and multilateral diplomacy by those who have betrayed these ideals over Iraq.

Such behaviour might be expected from the Russians and the Chinese, but the perfidy of the French has sickened the public and the ruling classes here in the U.S., inflaming a latent Francophobia.

Chirac has raised bloody-mindedness to an art form. Not only has he lined up with the Russians and the Germans at the UN Security Council, but he has also obstructed Nato's duty to offer emergency military defences to Turkey.

More sickening still, I am told that France and Germany are blocking UN contingency preparations for humanitarian relief in Iraq should war break out.

For the French to do all this with an ineffable air of moral superiority has shattered the coded language of the most prudent of diplomats: nobody in Washington can say 'France' without adding the phrase 'pain in the butt'.

These actions of the French have powerfully reinforced the anti-Atlanticists in the Administration who have been arguing that the U.S. should dispense with the UN, Nato and those old Europeans nitpickers.

And what of the Germans? Their pacifism is understood, but not their unwillingness to reveal the damning intelligence I have been reliably informed they have amassed on Saddam.

Not surprisingly, such behaviour has provoked near-hysterical anger in the U.S. press. The New York Post caught the popular mood with a headline on the French-German link — 'AXIS OF WEASEL'— then by carving another headline, 'SACRIFICE', on its front page above the white-cross tombstones of American dead near Omaha Beach in Normandy, scene of Spielberg's movie Saving Private Ryan.

The paper said many thousands of young Americans had died to save the French from Hitler— 'and now, as more Americans are poised to fight to save the world from an equally vile tyrant, where are the French? Hiding. Chickening out. Proclaiming "*Vive les wimps!*"'

EVEN The Wall Street Journal runs vehement letters of contempt about the French lack of backbone. The Republican commentator George Will screams about French defeatism in 1870 and 1940. No one here is in the mood to remember the 1,300,000 French dead in World War I.

And indeed, to the French, the Great War represents the true parallel with today: a golden period of unequalled peace and prosperity destroyed by overreaction to terrorism.

It was the 1914 murder of the Archduke at Sarajevo which triggered the fatal domino chain of reactions from the great powers. The Europeans fear that America is poised to repeat history.

Le Monde, the newspaper of the French elite which crowned 9/11 with the touching declaration 'We are all Americans', has changed its tune.

In an editorial on Tuesday — noted with regret in America — it mocked what it sees as a caricature of its own country.

'We French are profound cowards, singularly venal, passable anti-semites and dogged anti-Americans.'

It would be in vain to note, wrote Le Monde, that two key elements in the French position 'merit at least debate...1) Iraq does not present such a danger that war is necessary; and 2) a war against an Arab country is exactly what Osama Bin Laden wants.'

Heavy irony does not travel well here. A Gallup opinion poll in the U.S. reports a dramatic collapse in esteem for France among ordinary citizens.

France is now regarded less favourably than Egypt, Russia, Japan and Mexico, down 37 points to 59 per cent (a poll in which the British are top of the pops at 89 per cent approval— a reflection of the admiration for Tony Blair, who is thought to be as bold as Bush but more inspirational). That is the lowest rating for France since the poll began.

The professionals confirm the mood in the American heartlands. Former Secretary of State Madeleine Albright has been on a national speaking tour, and so has Richard Holbrooke, the former UN Ambassador and

'S PIMP

They died to save Europe: The graves of American servicemen in France. Inset: President Jacques Chirac

creator of the Bosnian peace plan.

Both independently reported to me audiences eager to proclaim their disapproval of French politicians, whom they see as the root of anti-Americanism.

'In a speech I gave in California,' said Holbrooke, 'someone asked the question: "What is it about the French?" The place erupted in laughter.'

Albright evokes a more indignant reaction among audiences when she relates how France, having agreed to join a commission on democracy in Europe, was then the only one of 106 countries to refuse to sign it.

SO MUCH of the hostility, she surmises, is culturally rooted. The French resent the charge that they are effete. Americans resent the Gallic implication that America is a coarse, violent, materialistic society.

The author Marie Brenner, who has spent months investigating anti-semitism in France, has returned to New York with a disturbing perception.

'Their bookshop windows are filled with anti-American best-sellers. The working-class understand the potential for terrorism, but the drawing rooms of Paris are parlours of intellectual corruption, filled with anti-semitic chatter that disguises itself as anti-Israel politics.'

To be fair, France has some defenders among sophisticated Americans, who are as critical of 'cowboy' Bush as any Parisian.

Novelist and former French Vogue editor Joan Buck cheers that 'after decades of lily-livered cowering, the French may once again provide a necessary check and balance on our own mad country.'

Elizabeth Sifton, the New York publisher, says that if the French, Germans and Belgians are sensible enough to protest the ethics, feasibility and appropriateness of the war policy, then bless them. 'It has been our own incompetence and arrogance that led to the crisis,' she says.

These handful of apologists argue that France is doing no more than playing its characteristically perverse role of sparking creative friction on the global stage.

On more than one occasion during the height of the Cold War, President Kennedy asked: 'Why is de Gaulle screwing us? What does he want?'

Indeed, Franklin Roosevelt so distrusted the General that when they first met in Casablanca, he had Americans with guns in hand posted outside in case of trouble.

Historically, the French combination of pride and insecurity that nourishes their perversity can be overcome when there are subtle and sensitive negotiators on both sides, as best seen in the days of Henry Kissinger and Giscard d'Estaing.

But now on one side we have an erratic French president who has been granted a position of unexpected power and glory by fluke — the far Right-winger Le Pen's arrival on the ballot papers.

GIVEN an issue on which it is easy to exploit mass opinion, Chirac has done just that. It seems that his influence at the UN over Iraq has so gone to his head that even his own Foreign Minister, Dominique de Villepin, is having a hard time persuading him not to exercise the French veto at the Security Council just for the sake of making his mark in the history books.

On the other side, we have a boisterous American president with a powerful will and no experience at all in the accommodations of big power politics — and a Defence Secretary, Donald Rumsfeld, with a gift for unproductive insult.

So what to conclude? Bush's directness has served America well, in my judgment, in the confrontation with terrorism. But the worry is that we all lose something when the hostility between France and the U.S. is such that both sides ignore reasonable criticism of the other.

The current breach is different from the scowls and upsets that have mostly marked America French relations. In the earli difficulties, there was nothi like the popular emotion today.

One reads in a column in Th Wall Street Journal about 'screaming rat' who has turn 'pimp for Saddam' — and turns out to be the author image of Chirac.

Of course it is more compl cated than that. Personaliti aside, I believe that the Frenc have a serious identity crisis which the anti-America malaise is only a symptor Psychologically, they are no the sick man of Europe.

Simon Schama, the historia suggests that generations French schoolchildren, inclu ing young Chirac, were taug that their empire was create not so much by the exercise power as by the propagation the ideals of the Revolution.

As a nation, they feel more vi tuous when they are making a isolated stand.

Henry Kissinger believes th the French have simply no adjusted from the 18th and 19t centuries, when they were th strongest nation on the Eur pean continent. They are inc pable of ever co-operating with stronger power.

It was said after World War that Britain had lost an empi and had yet to find a role.

Today, the British seem t have discovered their role. It the heart of the current predica ment that the French have not

The Sunday Times 5 May 2002

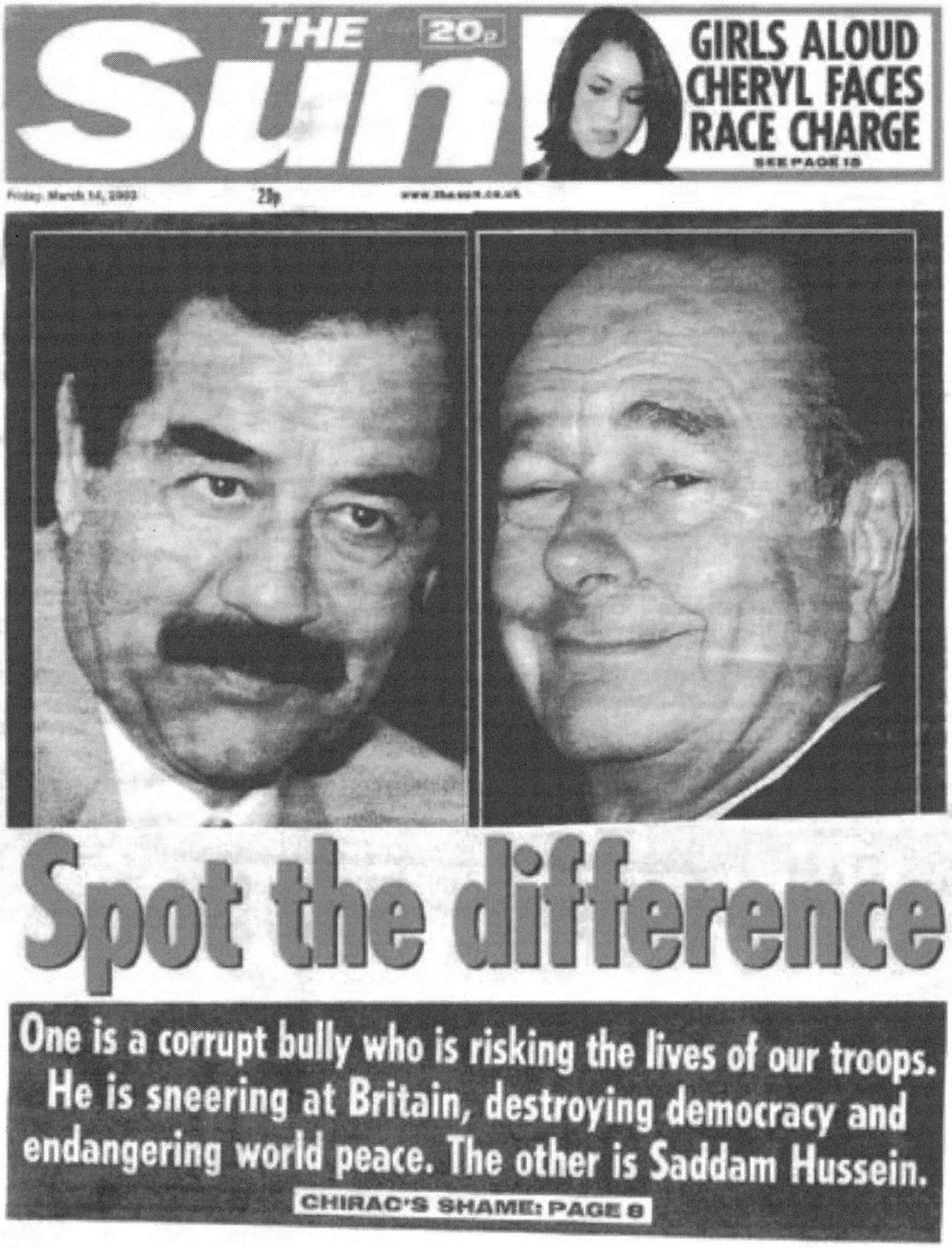

THE Sun 20p

GIRLS ALOUD CHERYL FACES RACE CHARGE

Friday, March 14, 2003

Spot the difference

One is a corrupt bully who is risking the lives of our troops. He is sneering at Britain, destroying democracy and endangering world peace. The other is Saddam Hussein.

CHIRAC'S SHAME: PAGE 8

The Sun 14 March 2003

THE SUN SAYS

Blame Chirac for this war

ONE man has put the lives of 300,000 British and American troops on the line.

Only Jacques Chirac's arrogance, stupidity and personal vanity are to blame for bringing us to the brink of a terrible war with Iraq.

If Allied troops are flown home in bodybags, God forbid, Chirac will have their blood on his grasping hands.

If the French President had acted like an ally, not an enemy, it could all have been so different.

By turning on Britain and America and shattering United Nations unity, Chirac gave Saddam the two things he craved.

Hope and strength.

He threw Saddam a lifeline just as the Iraqi dictator was putting out feelers to other Arab states to grant him exile.

Chirac doesn't give a damn – he had seized the chance to resurrect his tarnished political career at home and protect his dirty oil and trade deals with Iraq.

Now he struts the world stage like a peacock on heat, convincing himself he is a major player. It is the biggest mistake of his life.

Gangster

If Chirac had acted like a statesman instead of a gangster, a second resolution could have been passed in the UN by now.

Waverers like Chile and Mexico and at least two of the three African states had been persuaded to support Blair and Bush's last roll of the diplomatic dice.

Once Chirac said he would use the French veto no matter what, the smaller nations got cold feet.

Why stick their heads above the parapet if the vote was going to be made meaningless?

Single-handedly, Chirac has brought down the UN's fragile house of cards.

Last night he was playing more games, with his Foreign Minister Vile Pin claiming "everything must be done to preserve the unity of the United Nations."

We don't trust a single word that slippery man says.

America and Britain will never forget France's treachery.

Chirac will pay the price in lost trade, lost political clout and lost goodwill when the war is over.

But what price will our young fighting men and women have to pay in the killing fields of the Iraqi desert?

Well done, IDS

IAIN Duncan Smith has made it plain his party will support Tony Blair if he goes to war without a second UN resolution.

We hope Tory MPs back their leader to the hilt.

Britain — and The Sun — will never forgive them if they don't.

Monday April 28th 2003

The Daily Telegraph

Established 1855

France's friends in Iraq

Mocking *la perfide Albion* has been a national pastime in France for centuries, but the documents that are now being disinterred from the smouldering embers of Saddam Hussein's regime suggest that perfidy would be rather a polite word for the conduct of Jacques Chirac and the French government towards their allies. Elsewhere in today's *Telegraph*, Alex Spillius reports that papers found in the Iraqi foreign ministry show how, as recently as three years ago, French diplomats from the Quai d'Orsay were colluding with agents from IRIS (the Iraqi Intelligence Service, better known as the Mukhabarat) to frustrate efforts by the Iraqi opposition and the British-based human rights group Indict to highlight atrocities in Iraq at a conference in Paris. Other documents include a warm thank-you letter from Saddam to M Chirac in response to the French president's campaign to end UN sanctions, a deal between Peugeot and Baghdad, and mysterious payments from IRIS to beneficiaries in France.

The picture that emerges is not a pretty one. Material from the same Iraqi ministry published elsewhere suggests that French diplomats were keeping Baghdad informed about Bush-Chirac summits and other talks between Washington and Paris. This *entente cordiale* with the Ba'athist dictatorship provides a new context in which to consider M Chirac's refusal to countenance a Security Council resolution to authorise military action "under any circumstances". At the time, this was seen as a typically Gaullist "*Non!*", a rhetorical gesture of defiance to the Anglo-American coalition. It appears that M Chirac was also trying to preserve a Franco-Iraqi nexus that now looks quite sinister.

The significance of these intimate links with Saddam will not be lost on America. The Bush Administration's anger with the French was publicly reiterated last week by the Secretary of State, Colin Powell, and in Washington high-level meetings are being held to finalise punitive measures. In Paris, the response so far has vacillated between nervous appeasement and brazen provocation. M Chirac rang the White House to propose a plan, apparently intended to be conciliatory, to establish a role for Nato in Iraq. However, one of the measures being considered in Washington is to downgrade the French role at Nato. Moreover, just as M Chirac was trying to ingratiate himself, his foreign minister, Dominique de Villepin, was making a surprise visit to another member of the "axis of evil", Iran, which had just been warned by Washington not to interfere in Iraq. Tony Blair, who has even more reason than George Bush to feel double-crossed by the French government over Iraq, should be in no hurry to forgive, let alone to forget.

The Daily Telegraph 28 April 2003

Journalist sacked for criticising French

From Charles Bremner
in Paris

A JOURNALIST has been sacked by his newspaper for writing a book accusing the French media of letting anti-American and anti-British bias get the better of truth in their coverage of the Iraq war.

Alain Hertoghe, 44, a Belgian who worked for *La Croix*, a French national daily, lost his job for cataloguing distortions, omissions and fantasy that he said were fed to the public during the three weeks of fighting last spring.

A collective desire to see an Anglo-American defeat, driven by deep-rooted anti-Americanism and a patriotic frenzy, caused the media, and the press in particular, to give a false account of the war, M Hertoghe said. "This [account] was systematically contradicted by the facts.

"Understandably, the outcome of the war left the reader stunned," he wrote in *La Guerre à Outrances — comment la presse nous a désinformés sur L'Irak* (Outrageous War — how the press disinformed us on Iraq).

M Hertoghe, deputy editor of his newspaper's internet site and a former foreign correspondent, was sacked for breaching an employment clause that bars journalists from damaging the interests of their newspaper.

Although his book included criticism of *La Croix*, a Catholic daily, M Hertoghe said yesterday that he had subjected the press to an objective analysis and revealed nothing confidential about his newspaper.

"I thought they would have a thicker skin. I didn't expect the sack. I thought that freedom of opinion would prevail over narrow interests," he said.

La Croix declined to comment.

Since the book's publication in October by Calmann-Levy, a leading firm, the media has subjected it to "a spontaneous collective silence", M Hertoghe said.

News of his sacking has drawn attention to his case, earning him support in a column in *Libération*, the main left-wing daily which, he said, was one of the worst offenders in the war coverage.

Daniel Schneiderman, *Libération's* media critic, said of the book: "This pamphlet will remind journalists cruelly how we can be blinded in the heat of the moment." Schneiderman was sacked from *Le Monde* for criticising it last October.

Most non-French readers would agree with M Hertoghe's analysis, although he ignored the small space that was given to dissenting opinion during the Iraq crisis.

He is the first media insider to blow the whistle on what many foreigners at the time viewed as an extraordinarily unreflective consensus against the US-led war.

M Hertoghe, who has lived in France since 1988, conceded that his Belgian origins gave him a sense of proportion that evaded his colleagues, when France was carried away behind President Chirac's crusade to stop the war.

The media were still in denial, unable to admit to getting it wrong, he told *The Times*. "What I am criticising in this book is that during the war we said they were bogged down right away. It was 'Vietnam', it was 'Stalingrad'. We recounted nonsense but have never explained to readers why we recounted nonsense."

His book examines in detail the war coverage of four main national dailies: *Le Monde, Le Figaro, Libération, La Croix* and the regional *Ouest-France*, which has the biggest circulation. Over three weeks, the five carried 29 headlines that were negative towards the Iraqi regime compared with 135 that were damning for President Bush and Tony Blair.

Reporting from the field was played down when it disagreed with the thesis of American defeat. But M Hertoghe added that the real distortion came from the editors and commentators who continually predicted apocalyse for the coalition until the day that Saddam Hussein's statues were toppled in Baghdad.

Hertoghe said that there was no plot, simply a spontaneous reflex in which "the arrogance of journalists combined with the arrogance of the French".

The Times - Wednesday December 31st 2003

Death of gendarme may reveal France's own 'Dutroux affair'

By John Lichfield
in Paris

FRANCE FACES a judicial scandal comparable to the Dutroux case in Belgium after the revelation that a tenacious gendarme investigating a conspiracy involving sex crimes in Burgundy was almost certainly murdered.

Christian Jambert's death seven years ago was classified as suicide by his colleagues in the gendarmerie and by the local state prosecutor, who had previously blocked his near-single-handed investigations or refused to take them seriously.

A belated autopsy, demanded by the gendarme's family, revealed this week that Adjutant (Sergeant) Jambert had been shot twice in the head, not once as a brief investigation in 1997 had decided. Either wound would have killed him instantly. The revelation threatens to blow open the disturbing case of the unexplained murder, or disappearance, of up to a score of young women, including a 21-year-old British student, in northern Burgundy over 20 years.

"This is a very serious business, a judicial scandal," said Maitre Didier Seban, lawyer for the gendarme's family and the families of some of the dead or missing women.

A pattern of implausible judicial and police bungles in the Auxerre area, 100 miles south of Paris, including the disappearance of scores of prosecution files, has already led to allegations that France is harbouring its own "Dutroux affair". Defence lawyers and a former public prosecutor have suggested that investigations of a string of murders and abductions were prevented by a cover-up of the kind which allegedly protected the Belgian child murderer, Marc Dutroux.

A series of government and judicial investigations into the cases, including the unsolved murder of Joanna Parrish, a 21-year-old Leeds University student in Auxerre in May 1990, have reached no clear conclusions. Three public prosecutors in the Auxerre area, who held office between 1979 and 1999, were punished for incompetence three years ago but they were exonerated on appeal.

Adjutant Jambert began investigating the disappearance of seven young mentally handicapped women between 1977 and 1979. Although the women were dismissed as runaways, the gendarme uncovered evidence that they had been abducted and probably murdered by a bus driver, Emile Louis, the man who drove them to a day centre for the handicapped.

Murdered Joanna Parrish, top; Emile Louis, bottom, and Christian Jambert *Jean-Michel Turpin/Gamma*

Although Adjutant Jambert's evidence was rejected, he continued his investigations single-handed over many years, even when he was transferred to another part of France, and even after he had retired. The gendarme became convinced the case of the handicapped women was linked to a wider pattern of abductions, murders and cover-ups in the Auxerre area. A wealthy local man, Claud Dunand, had been convicted and sentenced to life imprisonment in 1991 for abducting young women and assaulting and torturing them in the cellar of his home in the suburbs of Auxerre. Local newspapers and an investigative book have claimed a list of other local people implicated in the attacks, including several "notables", was drawn up by police but disappeared from the file.

Finally, in late 1997, through pressure from Adjutant Jambert and families of the victims, the case of the seven missing handicapped women was reopened. Emile Louis made confessions to several murders then retracted them.

Louis, 70, will appear in court charged with the killings within months. Last week he was sentenced to 20 years in prison for torturing and sexually assaulting his second wife and stepdaughter. In August 1997, just before the case was reopened, Adjutant Jambert was found dead in his cellar, with a hunting rifle beside him. Apparently, he had made a previous attempt to kill himself and his death was rapidly classified as suicide. A large file of information gathered during his official, and private, investigations, had disappeared.

Last year his son and daughter asked for his death to be reinvestigated. His remains were exhumed on Thursday and a Parisian pathologist examined two bullet-holes in the skull.

The original investigation decided – without a proper post-mortem examination – that these wounds were the entry and exit holes of a single bullet. This week's post mortem decided they were both bullet entry holes and either shot would have killed him instantly. Adjutant Jambert was almost certainly murdered.

The Independent - Saturday April 3rd 2004

Belgium Newsclips

Belgium's darkest hour: Dutroux

Belgium's silent heart of darkness

It is six years since the paedophile scandal in Belgium that sickened the world. Yet the prime suspect has still to stand trial, and 20 potential witnesses have died mysteriously. In this special report, we reveal the lies that are fuelling suspicions of a high-level cover-up

Marc Dutroux, pictured on his arrest, caged young girls in a dungeon he built in the cellar of his home. Photograph by Olivier Matthys

By Olenka Frenkiel

Olenka Frenkiel is an award-winning BBC reporter. Her exposé, Belgium's X Files, is broadcast on BBC2 tonight at 7.15pm

SOMETHING IS ROTTEN in the state of Belgium. Six years after the arrest of Marc Dutroux, the country's notorious paedophile, no date has been set for his trial and the case remains painfully unresolved.

In 1995, when two eight-year-old girls were kidnapped, Dutroux, a convicted sex offender, was a prime suspect from the start, yet he wasn't arrested for 14 months. By that time, four of his captives – including the two girls – were dead. Since his arrest, 20 potential witnesses connected with the case have died in mysterious circumstances, fuelling suspicions of a cover-up reaching the highest levels.

I have spent the last six months making a documentary about the investigation. Early on, I was told by one senior government adviser: 'You must not underestimate the terrible record of our Belgian justice system.'

It's a system which today appears paralysed, unable to prosecute the accused, his wife and an alleged accomplice. With each successive year in jail without trial their case against the Belgian authorities for a breach of human rights grows stronger. The official explanation for the delay is that hysterical conspiracy theories forced investigators to search for paedophile networks which didn't exist. But far from being investigated, leads pointing to a network seem rather to have been ignored or buried.

Dutroux's wife, Michele Martin, a former primary school teacher and the mother of his three children, has admitted that, in 1995, she knew two small girls were incarcerated without food or water in a secret dungeon in the cellar of a house they owned in Charleroi. She told police she visited the house to feed their dogs while her husband was in jail on car-theft charges, but she was 'too frightened' to feed the girls.

Months later Dutroux led police to the emaciated bodies of Julie Lejeune and Melissa Russo, the two eight-year-olds who had been kidnapped more than a year before. They were buried in the garden of another of Dutroux's homes. An accomplice, Michel Lelievre – a drug addict and petty thief – told police soon after his arrest that the girls had been kidnapped to order, for someone else. The chief suspect was Jean Michel Nihoul, a Brussels businessman, pub-owner and familiar face at sex parties. While they had been in prison, Lelievre told police, Dutroux and Nihoul met frequently in the exercise yard, making plans. The judge investigating the case, Jean-Marc Connerotte, believed Nihoul was the brains behind the operation. But, as the network began to unravel, Lelievre suddenly stopped co-operating, saying he had been threatened.

One victim of the paedophile gang described regular 'clients' including judges, one of the country's most powerful politicians and a prominent banker

I met Nihoul in a restaurant in Brussels. 'I am the Monster of Belgium,' he roared at me by way of greeting. He is confident he will never come to trial and that the evidence against him will never be heard by any jury. During the course of our meal he, apparently playfully, grabbed me, tickling, and finally pulled me over on to him in the restaurant booth until I had to appeal to my colleagues for rescue.

He will never come to court, he said, because the information he has about important people in Belgium would bring the government down. The Monster of Belgium denies he's a paedophile but seemed to enjoy his notoriety and demanded £1,000 for his story. We declined his offer. Every documentary likes a monster but we don't pay for interviews and frankly I'd already had enough.

But we did need to offer Nihoul a right to reply to the accusations made by Regina Louf, a woman now aged 33 whose testimony has divided Belgium. Louf came forward after Judge Connerotte made an appeal to victims of paedophiles to tell police what they knew. Connerotte, the man who had arrested Dutroux and saved two teenage girls from his dungeon, was a hero in Belgium. Louf was the first of 10 to come forward.

She told investigators how from the age of 12 she'd been 'given' by her parents to a family friend, Tony Van den Bogaert, who'd had a key to their house. He would collect her from school and take her away for weekends to sex parties where she was 'given' to other men and secretly filmed having sex with them. 'It was highly organised,' she says. 'Big business. Blackmail. There was a lot of money involved.'

In 1996 she related her experiences to a police team under carefully filmed and supervised conditions. She described certain regular clients including judges, one of the country's most powerful politicians (now dead) and a prominent banker. She gave the police the names by which she knew these men, detailed the houses, apartments and districts where she'd been taken with other children to entertain the guests.

This 'entertainment' was not just sex, she told the police. It involved sadism, torture and even murder, and again she described the places, the victims and the ways they were killed. One of the regular organisers of these parties, she claimed, was the man she knew as 'Mich', Jean Michel Nihoul, 'a very cruel man. He abused children in a very sadistic way', she said. Also there, she said, was the young Dutroux.

'Dutroux was a boy who brought drugs, cocaine to these parties – he brought some girls, watched girls. At these events Nihoul was a sort of party beast while Dutroux was more on the side.'

Louf's testimony was vitally important. If true, it placed Dutroux and Nihoul, suspected accomplices in the latest child abductions, together at the scene of similar crimes 10 years before. Police began to check her story. But then something changed.

IN OCTOBER 1996, Connerotte, the only man who has ever advanced the Dutroux investigation, was sacked from the case. He had attended a fund-raising dinner in support of the victims' families and was accused of a conflict of interests.

A crowd of 400,000 marched on the Palace of Justice in Brussels to protest. The father of one of the murdered children, Gino Russo, spoke for the demonstrators. 'It was like spitting on the grave of Julie and Melissa,' he said.

Connerotte was replaced by Judge Jacques Langlois, for whom this case would be his first assignment. Langlois has spent the last five years in constant conflict with the public prosecutor assigned with him to the case, Michel Bourlet. Since Connerotte was sacked, according to the Russos, the Dutroux file has acquired no new evidence.

Next to be dismissed, a few months later, was the special team of police officers who had interviewed Louf and the other witnesses. By now the police believed they had verified key elements of Louf's story. At least one of the murders she described matched an unsolved case. One of the police officers in the team, Rudi Hoskens, had been assigned to re-examine that case and was convinced she had witnessed the murder: 'She gave us some details that made us think it's impossible to give without having been there at that place – the way the body was found at that time, and the way she described the person who was killed.'

What Louf had described was a macabre torture which had eventually killed a 15-year-old girl she knew as Chrissie. 'It was a sort of bondage,' she told me, 'so her legs and her hands and her throat were connected with the same rope, and so when she moved she strangled herself.' Louf insists both Nihoul and Dutroux were there that night. Nihoul, she claims, took part in the murder, a charge he denies. Dutroux, she says, watched.

Christine Van Hees's body had been found in 1984 dumped in the grounds of a disused mushroom farm on the outskirts of Brussels. The farm was later demolished but in 1996 Louf described to the police team its intricate details, the wallpaper, the sinks, hooks on the ceiling, a network of stairs and adjoining rooms unique to that building.

When I put this evidence to Anne Thily, Prosecutor General of Liège, in overall charge of the Dutroux affair, she gave me a shrug and repeated the official line in Belgium, that Louf is a fantasist and has invented everything.

This is not the view of the man who grew up at the farm, the son of the former owner, who showed me photographs of the house and the mushroom factory. He said: 'I have never met Regina Louf. All I know is that she could not have described the house as well as she did unless she'd been there. It was two houses joined together in a strange way. It would be impossible to invent it.'

For 12 years the unsolved murder of Van Hees gathered dust in the Brussels files under the direction of Judge Van Espen. Two years ago a Belgian journalist revealed the close relationship between Judge Van Espen and Nihoul and his then wife.

As a lawyer, Van Espen had represented Nihoul's wife. Van Espen's sister was the godmother of Nihoul's child. Yet, when Louf accused these two of the murder, Judge Van Espen saw no conflict of interest, no reason to resign. Nor was he sacked, as Connerotte had been. Instead he was allowed to order the police officers to stay out of the case. Van Espen only resigned as the judge in charge of the mushroom factory investigation in early 1998 after his relationship with Nihoul was exposed.

IN THE SPRING of 1997 Louf's interrogators had been sent home without explanation and a new team was assigned to 'reread' her testimony. The press was briefed that the previous team had been removed because they had manipulated the evidence of Louf, who was then known by the code name X1. It is a charge which the police team has always vigorously denied and which has never been substantiated.

And then the media campaign began. Louf's name was leaked to the press. The government-owned TV station RTBF began a campaign designed to prove that Dutroux was an 'isolated pervert' kidnapping girls for himself, that there was no network, that Nihoul was innocent and Louf was a liar.

Belgium's flagship current affairs television programme, *Au Nom de La Loi*, floated Louf's face over a backdrop of crows pecking over debris orchestrated by a *Blair Witch*-style soundtrack. Her ageing parents appeared as tragic victims of a deranged fantasist, whose false memories had blighted their last years.

What the programme makers knew but didn't say was that the parents had already admitted to police that a family friend in his forties, Tony Van den Bogaert, had had a key to their home and unlimited access to their 12-year-old daughter. Nor did they tell their viewers that Van den Bogaert had himself admitted his relationship with Louf to police. Van den Bogaert lives freely on the borders of Belgium and Holland unmolested by the law or the press. *Au Nom de La Loi* has never attempted to track him down and expose this self-confessed paedophile. Instead they have devoted hours of air-time to destroying the name of his victim, Louf, whose only offence appears to be that she was prepared to testify about the organised abuse she'd suffered as a child.

Waiting for justice

Regina Louf says she was used as a child prostitute.

Louisa and Jean, the parents of victim Julie Lejeune.

Jean Michel Nihoul, with reporter Olenka Frenkiel. Nihoul is accused of working with Dutroux to kidnap young girls.

This campaign has succeeded. Judges have announced that Louf will not be called as a witness in any future trial of Dutroux or his associates. Her testimony and that of all the 10 witnesses who came forward to Judge Connerotte has been declared worthless.

NO ONE HAS followed the Dutroux investigation more closely than Gino and Carine Russo, the parents of Melissa. What alarms them more than anything is the dearth of evidence or independent witnesses in the whole affair.

The Russos have access to the dossier of evidence which will, eventually, be presented to a jury. What alarms them, they say, is that it contains little more than the highly suspect version of events offered by Dutroux and his wife. This is crucial because while Dutroux admits incarcerating their daughter in his home, he denies her kidnap, rape or murder. Dutroux even claims he tried in vain to save the girls and that Melissa died in his arms.

The Russos have lived this nightmare ever since Melissa disappeared with her friend Julie in June 1995. Although Dutroux was a known paedophile, police didn't search his house for five months, and when they did they failed to find the girls, despite the sound of children in the cellar.

When a parliamentary commission examined the series of failures in the Dutroux investigation the police officer responsible, René Michaux, claimed it was a genuine mistake, that the entrance to the dungeon was well hidden and that the children's voices seemed to come from outside. He found a speculum on the floor which he lifted, handled and returned to Dutroux's wife without forensic analysis.

They found films which went undeveloped and videos which they didn't watch. Had they done so, they would have seen Dutroux building the dungeon. Instead Dutroux continued to abduct girls. In August 1996, four days after his last kidnap, he was arrested. He showed police the dungeon from where two girls were freed and then he led them to where Melissa and Julie were buried.

Carine Russo was not allowed to see her daughter's body. 'I begged and pleaded. I went with my lawyer but they refused. They told me the law did not permit it. "But who will identify my daughter?" I asked them. "Who will confirm that it's her?" "Dutroux has identified her," they told me.' Then Carine looks at me. 'It is stupefying,' she says.

The autopsy report reveals Melissa was raped repeatedly over a prolonged period. But there is nothing, no DNA evidence, no witness sightings, no forensics of any kind to show whether it was Dutroux, or anyone else.

The parents of one murdered girl barely believe a word of the official version: that Dutroux, the lone paedophile, kidnapped girls for his own use

Carine Russo points to a wall of files in her office. 'Where are the results of the swabs taken from Melissa's body for analysis? We know swabs were taken. It says so in the reports. But there are no results. I've asked the prosecutor repeatedly and no one seems to know.'

After their years of grief and their betrayal by the Belgian police and judiciary, the Russos barely believe a word of the official version: that Dutroux, the lone paedophile, kidnapped the girls for his personal use and kept them in the cage in his cellar until their death of starvation the day he returned home after four months in jail. How, they ask, could two children survive alone with virtually no food or water for four months?

The Russos suspect the girls weren't there at all. A number of reported sightings of Melissa, one in an upstairs room of a Charleroi nightclub, which were never followed up, have convinced them that someone else had access to the girls while Dutroux was in jail. Why else, they ask, were the hairs which detectives gathered from the dungeon in Dutroux's cellar never sent for DNA analysis? Why did Judge Langlois, Connerotte's replacement, refuse to have them tested despite pressure from his prosecutor, Michel Bourlet, who believed that a DNA identification of those hairs might reveal who else was involved?

Langlois's boss, the Prosecutor General of Liege, Anne Thily, says: 'There was no need to get the hairs analysed as no one else entered the cage. There was no network so there was no need to look for evidence of one.

'In any case,' she continued, 'the hairs have all now been analysed – all 5,000.' And the results of this analysis? 'Nothing.' Thily flashed me a triumphant smile. 'No evidence of any relevance in the Dutroux affair. Which proves, of course, that Langlois was right all along.'

But this is not true. Sources central to the investigation confirm that to date the hairs have still not been analysed. How can such a senior figure lie so brazenly? Another Belgian mystery.

'Who raped the children?' I asked Thily. 'Dutroux of course.'

'But he denies it. How will you prove it to the jury? There was no DNA test?' Now she was indignant. 'There were DNA tests, Madame.'

'And the results?' 'Inconclusive. The bodies were too decomposed to test for DNA,' she says.

But this too makes no sense. The autopsy states clearly that the bodies were not decomposed. Samples were taken. But no one seems to know what has happened to the results.

BRUNO TAGLIAFERRO was someone who knew, or claimed to know, about the abduction of Julie and Melissa and the car which was used. The Charleroi scrap metal merchant told his wife in 1995 that Dutroux was trying to get him killed. It was something to do with the car in which girls had been taken.

When he was found dead, apparently of a heart attack, his wife Fabienne Jaupart, refused to accept the verdict. Samples of his body sent to the US for analysis showed he'd been poisoned. Jaupart told reporters she was determined to find her husband's killer, but soon she too was found dead in her bed, her mattress smouldering. It was declared suicide. Since 1995, there have been 20 unexplained deaths of potential witnesses connected with Dutroux.

'In Belgium,' says Regina Louf smiling, 'if you're a potential witness you're either dead, or like me, mad.'

Judge Jacques Langlois did not order DNA tests. AP

Public prosecutor Michel Bourlet lacked evidence. AP

The Observer 5th May 2002

Dutroux: the men in the shadows

Matthew Campbell
Arlon, Belgium

Dutroux, who will be sentenced this week, let two of his victims starve to death in this dungeon

THE court spent 3½ months raking over the details but even after Marc Dutroux was finally convicted of kidnap, rape and murder last week in Belgium's trial of the century, the victims were left grasping for answers.

"We still have questions," said Jean-Denis Lejeune, whose eight-year-old daughter Julie was raped and left to die in a dungeon. "We are left with the shadowy areas that continue to surround the circumstances of the death and abduction of our daughter."

If the government had hoped that the trial would help to restore confidence in a badly tarnished judicial system, it will be disappointed. The parents of Melissa Russo, another abducted eight-year-old, did not even bother to attend the trial, so convinced were they that it would never uncover the truth.

Gino and Carine Russo are not alone in the belief that police, politicians and judges were protecting a paedophile network whose tentacles reach into every corner of Belgian society. According to this theory Dutroux is a small cog in a giant wheel of perversion.

The acquittal of Michel Nihoul, the businessman whom Dutroux had described as the linchpin of the ring, may have put paid, in legal terms at least, to the theory but the issue has polarised Belgium.

The existence of a well connected paedophile network has become a religion for conspiracy theorists who are convinced that the offenders include distinguished royals and even a former prime minister.

They question why certain potential witnesses, including Regina Louf, who claims that her parents sold her when she was a child to a paedophile ring linked to Dutroux, were never called to give evidence. For the conspiracy theorists the manner of Nihoul's acquittal on Thursday was further evidence of a cover-up.

It was the magistrates who decided to acquit Nihoul after the jurors failed to reach a verdict — seven had wanted to convict him as a Dutroux accomplice and five had argued that there was not enough evidence.

"Doubts persist and will always persist," said Joël Kotek, a political scientist at Brussels University. "People don't like to admit that it was just one man."

In a country such as Belgium "where nothing much happens", said Kotek, it was not surprising that people clung so desperately to sinister theories.

The more probable reality, however, was as banal as the featureless landscape of the Ardennes: the court concluded that Dutroux was a lone, sadistic pervert who took pleasure in abducting and raping girls.

He was convicted on Thursday of three charges of murder and of kidnapping, raping and imprisoning six girls aged from eight to 19. He, his ex-wife Michelle Martin and his accomplice Michel Lelièvre are to be sentenced this week along with Nihoul, who was convicted separately of drug dealing. Whether or not it will help the Belgian psyche to heal, the country will breathe a sigh of relief that the trial is over.

The jurors were being offered counselling after hearing so much unsettling evidence. With his monotonous nasal voice, Dutroux talked in a chillingly matter-of-fact fashion about burying Julie and Melissa in his garden after storing their corpses in the family freezer.

He admitted to abducting An Marchal, 17, and Eefje Lambrecks, 19, who were also buried in his garden. Forensic scientists believe the girls had been drugged and were conscious but paralysed at the time of their burial. The same fate was reserved for Bernard Weinstein, one of Dutroux's former associates, whose body was recovered from the garden.

The awful truth about sin
Minette Marrin, page 17

Two other victims lived to tell their story, however, and it was the testimony of Sabine Dardenne and Laetitia Delhez that helped to undermine the idea of Dutroux being part of a wider network. During the time they were held prisoner — Sabine was confined for 80 days — Dutroux was the only person who abused them.

He made them believe that he kept them in his cellar to protect them from a "bad boss". When he finally led police to the hiding place after being arrested, the girls clung to their captor for fear that the police were part of the "network".

He had used the same form of psychological manipulation with Julie and Melissa, who starved to death in the cellar while he served three months in jail for car theft.

Martin faces a sentence of up to 35 years as an accomplice in the abduction of the girls. She is accused of torturing Julie and Melissa by not feeding them while her husband was away.

She testified in court that she knew the girls needed food but could not bring herself to enter the cellar because she had an image of them in her mind as "wild beasts" who would attack her.

It is hardly surprising that so many Belgians think that there has been a cover-up. Dutroux had been jailed previously for raping young women and his wife had been jailed for helping him. By the time he kidnapped Sabine and Laetitia, he had

Jasper Juinen

An anti-paedophile march shows photos of Melissa and Julie. Some Belgians fear a cover-up

been under police surveillance. If they were not protecting Dutroux, the police were unwittingly helping him with their cack-handed incompetence.

When police raided his house in 1995, a detective heard children talking — probably Julie and Melissa — but could not determine the origin of the sound. In 1998 Dutroux managed to escape briefly while being transferred between prison cells.

Even if not all their questions are answered, some of the victims' relatives seemed pleased enough with the outcome. In the bustle outside the court on Thursday evening, Louisa Lejeune, the mother of Julie, chatted happily. "Now we can move on to other things," she said, "even if we will still feel, on every occasion, the absence of Julie, right until the end of our lives."

Sabine and Laetitia were seen laughing together on the court steps. "It's been like having a bone stuck in my throat for the past eight years," said Laetitia. Sabine's lawyer said she was satisfied to have the chance of turning the page.

It may take the Russos much longer, however, to get the answers that they are demanding: although Sabine and Laetitia said Dutroux was the only person they saw during their captivity, forensic detectives were reported to have discovered hairs in the cellar from at least 15 individuals.

The trial has ended but the murmuring about men in the shadows goes on.

Printed in Great Britain
by Amazon

50791941R00330